Lecture Notes in Computer Science   8527

Commenced Publication in 1973
Founding and Former Series Editors:
Gerhard Goos, Juris Hartmanis, and Jan van

T0074408

Editorial Board

David Hutchison
Lancaster University, UK

Takeo Kanade
Carnegie Mellon University, Pittsburgh, PA, USA

Josef Kittler
University of Surrey, Guildford, UK

Jon M. Kleinberg
Cornell University, Ithaca, NY, USA

Alfred Kobsa
University of California, Irvine, CA, USA

Friedemann Mattern
ETH Zurich, Switzerland

John C. Mitchell
Stanford University, CA, USA

Moni Naor
Weizmann Institute of Science, Rehovot, Israel

Oscar Nierstrasz
University of Bern, Switzerland

C. Pandu Rangan
Indian Institute of Technology, Madras, India

Bernhard Steffen
TU Dortmund University, Germany

Demetri Terzopoulos
University of California, Los Angeles, CA, USA

Doug Tygar
University of California, Berkeley, CA, USA

Gerhard Weikum
Max Planck Institute for Informatics, Saarbruecken, Germany

Fiona Fui-Hoon Nah (Ed.)

HCI in Business

First International Conference, HCIB 2014
Held as Part of HCI International 2014
Heraklion, Crete, Greece, June 22-27, 2014
Proceedings

 Springer

Volume Editor

Fiona Fui-Hoon Nah
Missouri University of Science and Technology
Department of Business and Information Technology
101 Fulton Hall, 301 West 14th Street
Rolla, MO 65409, USA
E-mail: nahf@mst.edu

ISSN 0302-9743   e-ISSN 1611-3349
ISBN 978-3-319-07292-0   e-ISBN 978-3-319-07293-7
DOI 10.1007/978-3-319-07293-7
Springer Cham Heidelberg New York Dordrecht London

Library of Congress Control Number: 2014939121

LNCS Sublibrary: SL 3 – Information Systems and Application, incl. Internet/Web and HCI

© Springer International Publishing Switzerland 2014
This work is subject to copyright. All rights are reserved by the Publisher, whether the whole or part of the material is concerned, specifically the rights of translation, reprinting, reuse of illustrations, recitation, broadcasting, reproduction on microfilms or in any other physical way, and transmission or information storage and retrieval, electronic adaptation, computer software, or by similar or dissimilar methodology now known or hereafter developed. Exempted from this legal reservation are brief excerpts in connection with reviews or scholarly analysis or material supplied specifically for the purpose of being entered and executed on a computer system, for exclusive use by the purchaser of the work. Duplication of this publication or parts thereof is permitted only under the provisions of the Copyright Law of the Publisher's location, in ist current version, and permission for use must always be obtained from Springer. Permissions for use may be obtained through RightsLink at the Copyright Clearance Center. Violations are liable to prosecution under the respective Copyright Law.
The use of general descriptive names, registered names, trademarks, service marks, etc. in this publication does not imply, even in the absence of a specific statement, that such names are exempt from the relevant protective laws and regulations and therefore free for general use.
While the advice and information in this book are believed to be true and accurate at the date of publication, neither the authors nor the editors nor the publisher can accept any legal responsibility for any errors or omissions that may be made. The publisher makes no warranty, express or implied, with respect to the material contained herein.

Typesetting: Camera-ready by author, data conversion by Scientific Publishing Services, Chennai, India

Printed on acid-free paper

Springer is part of Springer Science+Business Media (www.springer.com)

Foreword

The 16th International Conference on Human–Computer Interaction, HCI International 2014, was held in Heraklion, Crete, Greece, during June 22–27, 2014, incorporating 14 conferences/thematic areas:

Thematic areas:

- Human–Computer Interaction
- Human Interface and the Management of Information

Affiliated conferences:

- 11th International Conference on Engineering Psychology and Cognitive Ergonomics
- 8th International Conference on Universal Access in Human–Computer Interaction
- 6th International Conference on Virtual, Augmented and Mixed Reality
- 6th International Conference on Cross-Cultural Design
- 6th International Conference on Social Computing and Social Media
- 8th International Conference on Augmented Cognition
- 5th International Conference on Digital Human Modeling and Applications in Health, Safety, Ergonomics and Risk Management
- Third International Conference on Design, User Experience and Usability
- Second International Conference on Distributed, Ambient and Pervasive Interactions
- Second International Conference on Human Aspects of Information Security, Privacy and Trust
- First International Conference on HCI in Business
- First International Conference on Learning and Collaboration Technologies

A total of 4,766 individuals from academia, research institutes, industry, and governmental agencies from 78 countries submitted contributions, and 1,476 papers and 225 posters were included in the proceedings. These papers address the latest research and development efforts and highlight the human aspects of design and use of computing systems. The papers thoroughly cover the entire field of human–computer interaction, addressing major advances in knowledge and effective use of computers in a variety of application areas.

This volume, edited by Fiona Fui-Hoon Nah, contains papers focusing on the thematic area of HCI in Business, addressing the following major topics:

- Enterprise systems
- Social media for business
- Mobile and ubiquitous commerce

- Gamification in business
- B2B, B2C, C2C e-commerce
- Supporting collaboration, business and innovation
- User experience in shopping and business

The remaining volumes of the HCI International 2014 proceedings are:

- Volume 1, LNCS 8510, Human–Computer Interaction: HCI Theories, Methods and Tools (Part I), edited by Masaaki Kurosu
- Volume 2, LNCS 8511, Human–Computer Interaction: Advanced Interaction Modalities and Techniques (Part II), edited by Masaaki Kurosu
- Volume 3, LNCS 8512, Human–Computer Interaction: Applications and Services (Part III), edited by Masaaki Kurosu
- Volume 4, LNCS 8513, Universal Access in Human–Computer Interaction: Design and Development Methods for Universal Access (Part I), edited by Constantine Stephanidis and Margherita Antona
- Volume 5, LNCS 8514, Universal Access in Human–Computer Interaction: Universal Access to Information and Knowledge (Part II), edited by Constantine Stephanidis and Margherita Antona
- Volume 6, LNCS 8515, Universal Access in Human–Computer Interaction: Aging and Assistive Environments (Part III), edited by Constantine Stephanidis and Margherita Antona
- Volume 7, LNCS 8516, Universal Access in Human–Computer Interaction: Design for All and Accessibility Practice (Part IV), edited by Constantine Stephanidis and Margherita Antona
- Volume 8, LNCS 8517, Design, User Experience, and Usability: Theories, Methods and Tools for Designing the User Experience (Part I), edited by Aaron Marcus
- Volume 9, LNCS 8518, Design, User Experience, and Usability: User Experience Design for Diverse Interaction Platforms and Environments (Part II), edited by Aaron Marcus
- Volume 10, LNCS 8519, Design, User Experience, and Usability: User Experience Design for Everyday Life Applications and Services (Part III), edited by Aaron Marcus
- Volume 11, LNCS 8520, Design, User Experience, and Usability: User Experience Design Practice (Part IV), edited by Aaron Marcus
- Volume 12, LNCS 8521, Human Interface and the Management of Information: Information and Knowledge Design and Evaluation (Part I), edited by Sakae Yamamoto
- Volume 13, LNCS 8522, Human Interface and the Management of Information: Information and Knowledge in Applications and Services (Part II), edited by Sakae Yamamoto
- Volume 14, LNCS 8523, Learning and Collaboration Technologies: Designing and Developing Novel Learning Experiences (Part I), edited by Panayiotis Zaphiris and Andri Ioannou

- Volume 15, LNCS 8524, Learning and Collaboration Technologies: Technology-rich Environments for Learning and Collaboration (Part II), edited by Panayiotis Zaphiris and Andri Ioannou
- Volume 16, LNCS 8525, Virtual, Augmented and Mixed Reality: Designing and Developing Virtual and Augmented Environments (Part I), edited by Randall Shumaker and Stephanie Lackey
- Volume 17, LNCS 8526, Virtual, Augmented and Mixed Reality: Applications of Virtual and Augmented Reality (Part II), edited by Randall Shumaker and Stephanie Lackey
- Volume 19, LNCS 8528, Cross-Cultural Design, edited by P.L. Patrick Rau
- Volume 20, LNCS 8529, Digital Human Modeling and Applications in Health, Safety, Ergonomics and Risk Management, edited by Vincent G. Duffy
- Volume 21, LNCS 8530, Distributed, Ambient, and Pervasive Interactions, edited by Norbert Streitz and Panos Markopoulos
- Volume 22, LNCS 8531, Social Computing and Social Media, edited by Gabriele Meiselwitz
- Volume 23, LNAI 8532, Engineering Psychology and Cognitive Ergonomics, edited by Don Harris
- Volume 24, LNCS 8533, Human Aspects of Information Security, Privacy and Trust, edited by Theo Tryfonas and Ioannis Askoxylakis
- Volume 25, LNAI 8534, Foundations of Augmented Cognition, edited by Dylan D. Schmorrow and Cali M. Fidopiastis
- Volume 26, CCIS 434, HCI International 2014 Posters Proceedings (Part I), edited by Constantine Stephanidis
- Volume 27, CCIS 435, HCI International 2014 Posters Proceedings (Part II), edited by Constantine Stephanidis

I would like to thank the Program Chairs and the members of the Program Boards of all affiliated conferences and thematic areas, listed below, for their contribution to the highest scientific quality and the overall success of the HCI International 2014 Conference.

This conference could not have been possible without the continuous support and advice of the founding chair and conference scientific advisor, Prof. Gavriel Salvendy, as well as the dedicated work and outstanding efforts of the communications chair and editor of *HCI International News*, Dr. Abbas Moallem.

I would also like to thank for their contribution towards the smooth organization of the HCI International 2014 Conference the members of the Human–Computer Interaction Laboratory of ICS-FORTH, and in particular George Paparoulis, Maria Pitsoulaki, Maria Bouhli, and George Kapnas.

April 2014   Constantine Stephanidis
                                    General Chair, HCI International 2014

Organization

Human–Computer Interaction

Program Chair: Masaaki Kurosu, Japan

Jose Abdelnour-Nocera, UK
Sebastiano Bagnara, Italy
Simone Barbosa, Brazil
Adriana Betiol, Brazil
Simone Borsci, UK
Henry Duh, Australia
Xiaowen Fang, USA
Vicki Hanson, UK
Wonil Hwang, Korea
Minna Isomursu, Finland
Yong Gu Ji, Korea
Anirudha Joshi, India
Esther Jun, USA
Kyungdoh Kim, Korea

Heidi Krömker, Germany
Chen Ling, USA
Chang S. Nam, USA
Naoko Okuizumi, Japan
Philippe Palanque, France
Ling Rothrock, USA
Naoki Sakakibara, Japan
Dominique Scapin, France
Guangfeng Song, USA
Sanjay Tripathi, India
Chui Yin Wong, Malaysia
Toshiki Yamaoka, Japan
Kazuhiko Yamazaki, Japan
Ryoji Yoshitake, Japan

Human Interface and the Management of Information

Program Chair: Sakae Yamamoto, Japan

Alan Chan, Hong Kong
Denis A. Coelho, Portugal
Linda Elliott, USA
Shin'ichi Fukuzumi, Japan
Michitaka Hirose, Japan
Makoto Itoh, Japan
Yen-Yu Kang, Taiwan
Koji Kimita, Japan
Daiji Kobayashi, Japan

Hiroyuki Miki, Japan
Shogo Nishida, Japan
Robert Proctor, USA
Youngho Rhee, Korea
Ryosuke Saga, Japan
Katsunori Shimohara, Japan
Kim-Phuong Vu, USA
Tomio Watanabe, Japan

Engineering Psychology and Cognitive Ergonomics

Program Chair: Don Harris, UK

Guy Andre Boy, USA
Shan Fu, P.R. China
Hung-Sying Jing, Taiwan
Wen-Chin Li, Taiwan
Mark Neerincx, The Netherlands
Jan Noyes, UK
Paul Salmon, Australia

Axel Schulte, Germany
Siraj Shaikh, UK
Sarah Sharples, UK
Anthony Smoker, UK
Neville Stanton, UK
Alex Stedmon, UK
Andrew Thatcher, South Africa

Universal Access in Human–Computer Interaction

Program Chairs: Constantine Stephanidis, Greece, and Margherita Antona, Greece

Julio Abascal, Spain
Gisela Susanne Bahr, USA
João Barroso, Portugal
Margrit Betke, USA
Anthony Brooks, Denmark
Christian Bühler, Germany
Stefan Carmien, Spain
Hua Dong, P.R. China
Carlos Duarte, Portugal
Pier Luigi Emiliani, Italy
Qin Gao, P.R. China
Andrina Granić, Croatia
Andreas Holzinger, Austria
Josette Jones, USA
Simeon Keates, UK

Georgios Kouroupetroglou, Greece
Patrick Langdon, UK
Barbara Leporini, Italy
Eugene Loos, The Netherlands
Ana Isabel Paraguay, Brazil
Helen Petrie, UK
Michael Pieper, Germany
Enrico Pontelli, USA
Jaime Sanchez, Chile
Alberto Sanna, Italy
Anthony Savidis, Greece
Christian Stary, Austria
Hirotada Ueda, Japan
Gerhard Weber, Germany
Harald Weber, Germany

Virtual, Augmented and Mixed Reality

Program Chairs: Randall Shumaker, USA, and Stephanie Lackey, USA

Roland Blach, Germany
Sheryl Brahnam, USA
Juan Cendan, USA
Jessie Chen, USA
Panagiotis D. Kaklis, UK

Hirokazu Kato, Japan
Denis Laurendeau, Canada
Fotis Liarokapis, UK
Michael Macedonia, USA
Gordon Mair, UK

Jose San Martin, Spain
Tabitha Peck, USA
Christian Sandor, Australia

Christopher Stapleton, USA
Gregory Welch, USA

Cross-Cultural Design

Program Chair: P.L. Patrick Rau, P.R. China

Yee-Yin Choong, USA
Paul Fu, USA
Zhiyong Fu, P.R. China
Pin-Chao Liao, P.R. China
Dyi-Yih Michael Lin, Taiwan
Rungtai Lin, Taiwan
Ta-Ping (Robert) Lu, Taiwan
Liang Ma, P.R. China
Alexander Mädche, Germany

Sheau-Farn Max Liang, Taiwan
Katsuhiko Ogawa, Japan
Tom Plocher, USA
Huatong Sun, USA
Emil Tso, P.R. China
Hsiu-Ping Yueh, Taiwan
Liang (Leon) Zeng, USA
Jia Zhou, P.R. China

Online Communities and Social Media

Program Chair: Gabriele Meiselwitz, USA

Leonelo Almeida, Brazil
Chee Siang Ang, UK
Aneesha Bakharia, Australia
Ania Bobrowicz, UK
James Braman, USA
Farzin Deravi, UK
Carsten Kleiner, Germany
Niki Lambropoulos, Greece
Soo Ling Lim, UK

Anthony Norcio, USA
Portia Pusey, USA
Panote Siriaraya, UK
Stefan Stieglitz, Germany
Giovanni Vincenti, USA
Yuanqiong (Kathy) Wang, USA
June Wei, USA
Brian Wentz, USA

Augmented Cognition

Program Chairs: Dylan D. Schmorrow, USA, and Cali M. Fidopiastis, USA

Ahmed Abdelkhalek, USA
Robert Atkinson, USA
Monique Beaudoin, USA
John Blitch, USA
Alenka Brown, USA

Rosario Cannavò, Italy
Joseph Cohn, USA
Andrew J. Cowell, USA
Martha Crosby, USA
Wai-Tat Fu, USA

Rodolphe Gentili, USA
Frederick Gregory, USA
Michael W. Hail, USA
Monte Hancock, USA
Fei Hu, USA
Ion Juvina, USA
Joe Keebler, USA
Philip Mangos, USA
Rao Mannepalli, USA
David Martinez, USA
Yvonne R. Masakowski, USA
Santosh Mathan, USA
Ranjeev Mittu, USA

Keith Niall, USA
Tatana Olson, USA
Debra Patton, USA
June Pilcher, USA
Robinson Pino, USA
Tiffany Poeppelman, USA
Victoria Romero, USA
Amela Sadagic, USA
Anna Skinner, USA
Ann Speed, USA
Robert Sottilare, USA
Peter Walker, USA

Digital Human Modeling and Applications in Health, Safety, Ergonomics and Risk Management

Program Chair: Vincent G. Duffy, USA

Giuseppe Andreoni, Italy
Daniel Carruth, USA
Elsbeth De Korte, The Netherlands
Afzal A. Godil, USA
Ravindra Goonetilleke, Hong Kong
Noriaki Kuwahara, Japan
Kang Li, USA
Zhizhong Li, P.R. China

Tim Marler, USA
Jianwei Niu, P.R. China
Michelle Robertson, USA
Matthias Rötting, Germany
Mao-Jiun Wang, Taiwan
Xuguang Wang, France
James Yang, USA

Design, User Experience, and Usability

Program Chair: Aaron Marcus, USA

Sisira Adikari, Australia
Claire Ancient, USA
Arne Berger, Germany
Jamie Blustein, Canada
Ana Boa-Ventura, USA
Jan Brejcha, Czech Republic
Lorenzo Cantoni, Switzerland
Marc Fabri, UK
Luciane Maria Fadel, Brazil
Tricia Flanagan, Hong Kong
Jorge Frascara, Mexico

Federico Gobbo, Italy
Emilie Gould, USA
Rüdiger Heimgärtner, Germany
Brigitte Herrmann, Germany
Steffen Hess, Germany
Nouf Khashman, Canada
Fabiola Guillermina Noël, Mexico
Francisco Rebelo, Portugal
Kerem Rızvanoğlu, Turkey
Marcelo Soares, Brazil
Carla Spinillo, Brazil

Distributed, Ambient and Pervasive Interactions

Program Chairs: Norbert Streitz, Germany, and Panos Markopoulos, The Netherlands

Juan Carlos Augusto, UK
Jose Bravo, Spain
Adrian Cheok, UK
Boris de Ruyter, The Netherlands
Anind Dey, USA
Dimitris Grammenos, Greece
Nuno Guimaraes, Portugal
Achilles Kameas, Greece
Javed Vassilis Khan, The Netherlands
Shin'ichi Konomi, Japan
Carsten Magerkurth, Switzerland

Ingrid Mulder, The Netherlands
Anton Nijholt, The Netherlands
Fabio Paternó, Italy
Carsten Röcker, Germany
Teresa Romao, Portugal
Albert Ali Salah, Turkey
Manfred Tscheligi, Austria
Reiner Wichert, Germany
Woontack Woo, Korea
Xenophon Zabulis, Greece

Human Aspects of Information Security, Privacy and Trust

Program Chairs: Theo Tryfonas, UK, and Ioannis Askoxylakis, Greece

Claudio Agostino Ardagna, Italy
Zinaida Benenson, Germany
Daniele Catteddu, Italy
Raoul Chiesa, Italy
Bryan Cline, USA
Sadie Creese, UK
Jorge Cuellar, Germany
Marc Dacier, USA
Dieter Gollmann, Germany
Kirstie Hawkey, Canada
Jaap-Henk Hoepman, The Netherlands
Cagatay Karabat, Turkey
Angelos Keromytis, USA
Ayako Komatsu, Japan
Ronald Leenes, The Netherlands
Javier Lopez, Spain
Steve Marsh, Canada

Gregorio Martinez, Spain
Emilio Mordini, Italy
Yuko Murayama, Japan
Masakatsu Nishigaki, Japan
Aljosa Pasic, Spain
Milan Petković, The Netherlands
Joachim Posegga, Germany
Jean-Jacques Quisquater, Belgium
Damien Sauveron, France
George Spanoudakis, UK
Kerry-Lynn Thomson, South Africa
Julien Touzeau, France
Theo Tryfonas, UK
João Vilela, Portugal
Claire Vishik, UK
Melanie Volkamer, Germany

HCI in Business

Program Chair: Fiona Fui-Hoon Nah, USA

Andreas Auinger, Austria
Michel Avital, Denmark
Traci Carte, USA
Hock Chuan Chan, Singapore
Constantinos Coursaris, USA
Soussan Djamasbi, USA
Brenda Eschenbrenner, USA
Nobuyuki Fukawa, USA
Khaled Hassanein, Canada
Milena Head, Canada
Susanna (Shuk Ying) Ho, Australia
Jack Zhenhui Jiang, Singapore
Jinwoo Kim, Korea
Zoonky Lee, Korea
Honglei Li, UK
Nicholas Lockwood, USA
Eleanor T. Loiacono, USA
Mei Lu, USA

Scott McCoy, USA
Brian Mennecke, USA
Robin Poston, USA
Lingyun Qiu, P.R. China
Rene Riedl, Austria
Matti Rossi, Finland
April Savoy, USA
Shu Schiller, USA
Hong Sheng, USA
Choon Ling Sia, Hong Kong
Chee-Wee Tan, Denmark
Chuan Hoo Tan, Hong Kong
Noam Tractinsky, Israel
Horst Treiblmaier, Austria
Virpi Tuunainen, Finland
Dezhi Wu, USA
I-Chin Wu, Taiwan

Learning and Collaboration Technologies

Program Chairs: Panayiotis Zaphiris, Cyprus, and Andri Ioannou, Cyprus

Ruthi Aladjem, Israel
Abdulaziz Aldaej, UK
John M. Carroll, USA
Maka Eradze, Estonia
Mikhail Fominykh, Norway
Denis Gillet, Switzerland
Mustafa Murat Inceoglu, Turkey
Pernilla Josefsson, Sweden
Marie Joubert, UK
Sauli Kiviranta, Finland
Tomaž Klobučar, Slovenia
Elena Kyza, Cyprus
Maarten de Laat, The Netherlands
David Lamas, Estonia

Edmund Laugasson, Estonia
Ana Loureiro, Portugal
Katherine Maillet, France
Nadia Pantidi, UK
Antigoni Parmaxi, Cyprus
Borzoo Pourabdollahian, Italy
Janet C. Read, UK
Christophe Reffay, France
Nicos Souleles, Cyprus
Ana Luísa Torres, Portugal
Stefan Trausan-Matu, Romania
Aimilia Tzanavari, Cyprus
Johnny Yuen, Hong Kong
Carmen Zahn, Switzerland

External Reviewers

Ilia Adami, Greece
Iosif Klironomos, Greece
Maria Korozi, Greece
Vassilis Kouroumalis, Greece

Asterios Leonidis, Greece
George Margetis, Greece
Stavroula Ntoa, Greece
Nikolaos Partarakis, Greece

HCI International 2015

The 15th International Conference on Human–Computer Interaction, HCI International 2015, will be held jointly with the affiliated conferences in Los Angeles, CA, USA, in the Westin Bonaventure Hotel, August 2–7, 2015. It will cover a broad spectrum of themes related to HCI, including theoretical issues, methods, tools, processes, and case studies in HCI design, as well as novel interaction techniques, interfaces, and applications. The proceedings will be published by Springer. More information will be available on the conference website: http://www.hcii2015.org/

General Chair
Professor Constantine Stephanidis
University of Crete and ICS-FORTH
Heraklion, Crete, Greece
Email: cs@ics.forth.gr

Table of Contents

Enterprise Systems

Social Media for Business

Mobile and Ubiquitous Commerce

Gamification in Business

B2B, B2C, C2C e-Commerce

Supporting Collaboration, Business and Innovation

User Experience in Shopping and Business

Enterprise Systems

Exploring Interaction Design for Advanced Analytics and Simulation

Robin Brewer[1] and Cheryl A. Kieliszewski[2]

[1] Northwestern University, 2240 Campus Drive, Evanston, Illinois 60208
[2] IBM Research – Almaden, 650 Harry Road, San Jose, California 95120
rnbrewer@u.northwestern.edu, cher@us.ibm.com

Abstract. Enterprise businesses are increasingly using analytics and simulation for improved decision making with diverse and large quantities of data. However, new challenges arise in understanding how to design and implement a user interaction paradigm that is appropriate for technical experts, business users, and other stakeholders. Technologies developed for sophisticated analyses pose a challenge for interaction and interface design research when the goal is to accommodate users with different types and levels of expertise. In this paper we discuss the results of a multi-phase research effort to explore expectations for interaction and user experience with a complex technology that is meant to provide scientists and business analysts with expert-level capability for advanced analytics and simulation. We find that while there are unique differences in software preferences of scientists and analysts, that a common interface is feasible for universal usability of these two user groups.

Keywords: Simulation, modeling, expert, analysis, interviews, disruption, ideation.

1   Introduction

Federal lawmakers want to propose a coast-to-coast high-speed rail transportation system to the public. Being that this is a large investment of taxpayer dollars, they want to make the first proposal the optimal proposal so as not to upset citizens. They also realize many decisions are often made with good information and insight such as future needs, demand, and geographic location. Such information is spread across different sources. Assistance is needed aggregating appropriate data sources and models for a large-scale benefit analysis. What would you recommend for developing a seamless high-speed rail infrastructure that reduces airplane and automobile emissions while being cost-efficient, improving overall quality of life for customers, and that is accessible to customers quickly?

Above is an example of a complex problem for which modeling and simulation can provide a solution. Technologies for advanced analytics and simulation are often very complex, requiring specialized knowledge to use them, and are created for experts in a particular domain (domain expert). As an 'expert', the expectation is that she has

F.F.-H. Nah (Ed.): HCIB/HCII 2014, LNCS 8527, pp. 3–14, 2014.
© Springer International Publishing Switzerland 2014

mastered a set of tasks and activities that are performed on a regular basis, and these tasks often become automatic. In turn, this automation can make it difficult to elicit detailed information from the expert about a set of tasks because she may unintentionally leave out important details or essential steps when describing the tasks [1,2].

The research presented in this paper was conducted within the context of a modeling and simulation (M&S) tool called SPLASH (Smarter Planet Platform for Analysis and Simulation of Health) [3]. Through SPLASH, end users with varying degrees of expertise in analytics and simulation can design simulation experiments to apply in a variety of fields including finance, urban planning, healthcare, and disaster planning. This range of fields and end users poses challenges for how to accommodate a wide array of expertise in M&S – that is, for people with deep domain knowledge about the construction of models and simulations to people with skill and expertise in running the simulation system and analyzing the output within a particular field. In addition, the domain of modeling and simulation tends to emphasize algorithm design and implementation rather than interface and interaction design. Without a body of evidence of how scientists and analysts use modeling or simulation tools, we had to work with a community of our intended end users to identify expectations and interface design features. This paper describes the method and results of using exploratory interviews, disruptive interviews, and participatory ideation to elicit information from experts in the field of M&S to inform the design of the SPLASH interaction.

2   Background

The goal of SPLASH is to facilitate the creation of complex, interconnected system-of-systems to advise and guide "what-if" analyses for stakeholders and policy makers. In contrast to the tradition of developing isolated models of phenomena, SPLASH takes a slightly different approach to the question, can we use M&S to help policy makers envision the trades-offs of complex policy and planning problems in a more holistic way? Specifically, SPLASH affords being able to examine real-world complex systems by reusing and coupling models and data of individual systems into a more comprehensive simulation [4]. As such, providing a way to consider the effects of change on the complete system rather than through the independent lens of individual systems models. Smarter Planet Platform for Analysis and Simulation of Health is intended to help the stakeholders consider as much about a complex system as possible to avoid negative unintended consequences by using relevant constituent components (i.e., data, models, simulations) for their desired level of system abstraction and analysis [5]. Our role in the development of SPLASH was to initiate the design of the user interface and end user interaction model.

2.1   Composite Modeling Methodology

Modeling and simulation is a complex research area that typically draws from mathematics, statistics, and business [6]. The process to create models and simulations tends to be subjective and dependent on the stakeholders, the model scope, level of detail of model content, and data requirements [6, 7]. A typical approach to examining a complex problem is for the modeler to use the individual components they are familiar with (i.e., as data, statistics, models, or simulations) to model and simulate a system. The modeler then uses output from these components as analysis of the individual pieces of the larger system. This would include working with key stakeholders to make assumptions about the impact of changes on the overall system using the individual pieces, resulting in an informed but fragmented system perspective [8].

Creating complex system simulations by coupling models and data sources is not a brand new area for the M&S community. There are a number of ways to create complex simulations through model integration, and these can be classified into three types: (1) integrated and uniform modeling framework, (2) tightly-coupled modeling framework, and (3) loosely-coupled modeling framework (see [3] for additional detail about each type of modeling framework). However, unless designed to accommodate one of these three frameworks from the beginning, the coupling of component models typically requires systems development work to integrate independent data sources and/or to re-code models and simulations so they can conform to a particular protocol or standard. By contrast, SPLASH enables the creation of composite models by automatically translating data from one component model into the form needed by another model to create a composite system model. In doing so, SPLASH also helps to alleviate the guesswork and assumptions about impact of changes and the potential for unintended consequences [3].

This suffices from a systems engineering perspective, but how is the stakeholder supposed to actually use such a complex technology? What complicated our role of designing an interface and interaction model for composite modeling is that there is not a standard process for building individual models or simulations to help inform expectations through a set of current conventions. This left us with little interaction guidance to begin prototyping an interface design for SPLASH.

2.2 Expert Elicitation

An expert can be defined as "an individual that we can trust to have produced thoughtful, consistent and reliable evaluations of items in a given domain" [9]. Because experts have, in essence, 10,000+ hours of experience [2], they are very familiar with a particular process and pattern to perform a task or activity. Therefore, it may be easy for the expert to recall the process for performing a particular activity or sequence of tasks but difficult to express the process to a novice. To study expert activities, many routine tasks are documented using some form of observation [10,11]. However, the tacit knowledge and reasoning may not be apparent to the observer when experts are performing a routine task [12].

There are two intended user groups of SPLASH, both of which are considered to be experts: scientists and analysts. The descriptions of our population were that *scientists* typically design, build, and run models and simulation experiments. *Analysts* run experiments after a model has been built and/or analyze results of the simulation run to aid in further decision-making. Both scientists and analysts are experts in performing analytical tasks that we needed to better understand. To design an interface for SPLASH, it was fundamental to understand what processes, tools, and techniques our target users employ to build and run simulations to model and understand potential system behavior.

For this study, we decided to use a series of three interview techniques to elicit expert knowledge in a relatively short period of time – being sensitive to work schedules and volunteer participation of our pool of professionals. Interviewing is a common HCI technique for eliciting information from stakeholders for rich qualitative analysis. Interviews can take many different forms including unstructured, semi-structured, and structured [13]. We started our investigation with semi-structured exploratory interviews to gain an understanding of what it is to do M&S work and to further structure the remaining two investigation phases of disruptive interviews and participatory ideation.

Disruptive interviews are derived from semi-structured interviews and can aid in the recall of past steps to complete a process that may have become automatic and taken for granted [12,14]. The interview technique uses a specific scenario that is then constrained over time by placing limitations on the options available to the participant. The constraints of the scenario are iteratively refined so that the participant must reflect on the processes and their reasoning. This technique borrows from condensed ethnographic interviews [12] that transform discussion from broad issues to detailed steps [15]. It is critical that disruptive interviews consider the context of the interviewees' processes. Understanding such context allows the researcher to design interview protocols appropriate to the constraints a person typically encounters in their work.

Participatory ideation (PI) is a mash-up of two existing techniques, participatory design and social ideation. Participatory design is often described as 'design-by-doing' [16] to assist researchers in the design process. This method is often used when researchers and designers want to accurately design a tool for an audience they are not familiar with [17]. Complementary to this, social ideation is the process of developing ideas with others via a web-enabled platform and utilizes brainstorming techniques to generate new ideas [18]. Both participatory design and social ideation are intended for early stage design and to engage with the users of the intended tool.

We interviewed professional scientists and analysts to investigate their expectations for the design of a technology such as SPLASH. The research questions we aimed to address were:

- RQ1: What are people's expectations for a complex cross-disciplinary modeling and simulation tool?
- RQ2: How should usable modeling and simulation interfaces be designed for non-technical audiences?

3   Methods

To address the above research questions we began with exploratory interviews. We then used the findings from the exploratory interview to design business-relevant scenarios, conduct disruptive interviews, and structure a participatory ideation phase.

We worked with 15 unique participants through the three phases of investigation. Of the 15 participants, nine were scientists, four were analysts, and two held both scientist and analyst roles. (Referred to as scientific analysts here on in, this hybrid categorization included participants who have experience with building models and with analyzing simulation results.) The range of modeling, simulation, and/or analytical domain expertise included atmospheric modeling, healthcare, manufacturing, polymer science, physics, statistics, social analytics, supply-chain management, and text analytics. Participants were recruited opportunistically as references and by snowball sampling.

3.1 Exploratory Interviews and Scenario Design

The first stage of this work was to understand our participant's work context, the type of modeling and/or simulation work that they perform, and their process for building a model and/or running a simulation. We began by interviewing five people, of which four were scientists and one was an analyst. The exploratory interviews were semi-structured, lasted approximately 30 minutes, and were conducted both in-person (for local participants) and by telephone (for remote participants). The results were used to help gauge the level of self-reported expertise of each participant and to develop the scenarios and disruptive interview protocol from the perspective of how M&S activities are performed.

After conducting the exploratory interviews, we aggregated scenario examples provided by participants, examples from our previous publications [3,4,5], and areas of interest to IBM's Smarter Cities initiative [19]. This yielded four scenarios for the disruptive interviews in the fields of transportation, healthcare, disaster recovery, and supply chain. The scenarios are hypothetical contexts in which simulations might be used to help examine a complex business challenge. We used the scenarios developed from the exploratory interviews to scope the disruptive interviews and provide context for the participants of the disruptive interview phase.

3.2 Disruption

Disruptive interviews are "disruptive" in nature because of the ever-increasing constraints placed on a solution set that is available to the participant during the interview itself. In our study, the interviewee was presented a scenario and asked to identify component model and data sources he or she would use to address the challenge highlighted in the scenario. In this phase of the investigation, our participant pool included two analysts, three scientists, and two scientific analysts.

The participants began by describing the models and data sources they thought would be useful in addressing the scenario. This was done without constraint to get the participant engaged in the scenario and to gather thoughts and reasoning of how the participant would approach the scenario challenge. Then, to begin triggering additional and more detailed feedback, the participants were only allowed to choose from a pre-determined list of model and data sources to address the scenario. Lastly, access to component sources was narrowed even further, which required the participant to reflect on the trade-off of potentially not having precisely what component sources they desired and expressing what was important to the design and build of a composite model for analysis. Each interview lasted approximately 1 hour, was transcribed, and then coded for emergent themes using Dedoose [20].

3.3   Participatory Ideation

All of the participants were remote for the participatory ideation phase that was conducted to elicit early-stage interface prototype design ideas. Because all of our participants were remote, we used an asynchronous, online collaboration tool called Twiddla [21] as an aid to collect input. The participants were placed into one of two conditions: individual ideation or group ideation. For this phase we recruited two scientists and one analyst for the individual ideation condition, and two scientists and two analysts for the group ideation condition.

We started with individual ideation, where the participants were given a blank canvas and asked to sketch ideas for model and data source selection, composition, and expected visualization(s) of simulation output based on one of the four scenarios that was created from the exploratory phase. Key interface and interaction features from the individual ideation output were then summarized and displayed as a starting point on the Twiddla drawing canvas for the group ideation participants. We hypothesized that the group ideation would produce more robust ideas because participants wouldn't need to create a new concept, but could simply build upon a set of common ideas [22].

4   Results

The three phases of this work each provided insight towards answering our research questions and built upon the findings of the previous phase(s). Here we provide the key results for each.

4.1   Grounding the Investigation: Exploratory Interview Results

To begin the exploratory interviews, we asked our participants to describe or define a model and a simulation. We received a range of responses for "model". However, the descriptions were all disposed towards being a codified representation (computer program) of a physical process. An example response was:

"A model would be a representation of a physical process, but a simplified representation of that process so that a computer can handle the level of detail, computationally, in an efficient manner."

Similarly, we received a range of responses to describe or define "simulation". The tendency was for both scientists and analysts to define a simulation in the context of their work with modeling, making little or no distinction between a simulation and a model. We provided definitions in the subsequent phases of investigation to overcome any issues with ambiguous use of these terms.

Participants, regardless of their area of expertise, expressed that the software tools used in their daily work were a large source of frustration when building models and running simulations. Software constraints included limitations of existing tools to correctly support and manage the model development and simulation run independent of the problem size and the time trade-off to build custom tools.

We found that all of the scientists had experience using third party tools but would eventually develop customized applications, program extensions to an existing tool, and/or couple multiple third party tools. The main reasons for custom-built tools were: (a) to accommodate legacy models and computer systems, (b) to perform additional analysis of the post-simulation run results, (c) to properly implement error handling during the simulation runtime, and/or (d) to add capabilities to visualize the simulation results.

In addition to frustration with tools used to build models and run simulations, we found that the amount of time to run a simulation was also a critical factor. The main challenges for time were a combination of (a) proper model design, (b) data quality, and/or (c) avoidance of unnecessary runtime delays or re-runs/re-starts. Results from the exploratory interviews were used to scope the four scenarios for the remaining investigations and to define some of the constraints used in the disruptive interviews.

4.2   Revelation through Disruption: Disruptive Interview Results

The disruptive interviews provided insight into the selection and prioritization of model and data sources – a key element to composite modeling. We were able to explore steps taken when options are suddenly limited and how one would work through the challenge. In doing so, there were disruption-based triggers that prompted participants to deliberately reflect on and express how they would complete the scenario – as illustrated in the following statement:

> *"When you build a simulation model you can collect everything in the world and build the most perfect model and you ask what are my 1st order effects? What are the ones I think are most critical? If I don't have them in there, my simulation model would be way off. The second ones are secondary effects... Those are the ones if I don't have enough time, I could drop those."*

By narrowing the selection of available model and data sources available to address a scenario, participants expressed their preferences and expectations for being able to find resources such as data, models, and tools. The research focused on prioritization, selection, and preferences for data sources, type of analysis, kinds of tools, and visualization capabilities. The participants also expressed a preference for a navigational browser to help them visualize data and select the model and data sources to address a scenario. Results from the disruptive interviews were used as guide for a low-fidelity interface design that resulted from this series of investigations.

4.3   Early Design: Participatory Ideation Results

This next phase resulted in sketches of interface ideas generated by the participants. Recall that the participatory ideation phase was designed with two conditions of participation: individual ideation and group ideation. The findings show similarities between the user groups, but also ideas unique to scientists and to analysts. In addition, we unexpectedly found that even though our group ideation participants were provided a sketch to start from (based on the individual ideation results), it was ignored by all of them and each decided to start with a blank design canvas. What follows is a summary of the design ideas that were mutual to analysts and scientists and then those that were specific to each participant group.

Once the results of the participatory ideation phase were aggregated, three mutual interaction and interface design ideas stood-out. The first design idea was a feature to support *browsing and exploration* of model and data sources that would afford examination of schemas and/or variables prior to selection for use in a scenario. The second was a feature to *compare the output* of multiple simulation runs for a particular scenario to better understand the trade-offs of selecting one simulation solution compared to another (Fig. 1). The third feature was an *audience-specific dashboard* for making complex decisions that would provide a summary of the model and data sources that were used when running the simulation.

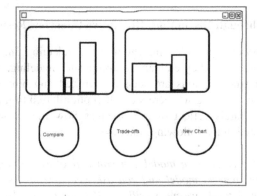

Fig. 1. Example sketch of a simulation output where it would be easy to compare scenarios

Analyst-Specific Design Ideas. Analysts emphasized guidance and recommendation. For example, analysts wanted pre-defined templates for simulation set-up and for analyzing simulation output. They expected the system to provide recommendations for which template to use (similar to the query prediction feature in Google) along with the steps to run a simulation. Also, they did not want technical terms such as "simulation", "model", or "factor" used in the interface. Instead, they preferred words such as "concept" or "category". For visualization, analysts wanted a feature to suggest if one chart style would be better than another style to explain relationships in output data. For example, participants wanted a feature to suggest if a bar chart would be better than a tree map to explain relationships in their data.

Scientist-Specific Design Ideas. Scientists emphasized flow and a rich set of interaction features (Fig. 2). For example, they were consistent in requiring a way to assess the veracity and provenance of model and data sources. This stemmed from past experience with models that did not perform as expected or data that was inconsistent. During this phase, participants were able to query and select curated model and data sources. However, the scientists found the selections to be limiting and wanted to be able to upload their own sources to supplement the existing sources. Lastly, scientists preferred high levels of interaction with the data to examine the source and/or cleanliness of the data, and to determine the appropriateness for their simulation goals when previewing search results *prior* to running the simulation. For example, they wanted to edit parameters of the simulation set-up and interact with the sources before and after they were selected.

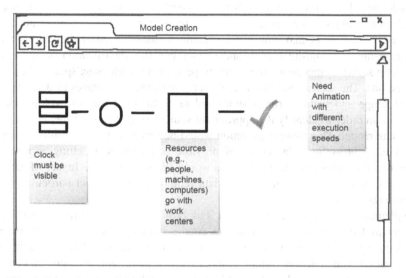

Fig. 2. Example of expected flow and interaction features for composite modeling

5   Discussion

The results of this series of interviews helped us better understand our target users and inform subsequent interface prototype design. Specifically, the use of constraints as disruption in the interviews served as effective triggers, prompting and focusing our experts to provide details about how they would go about designing a composite model. These triggers demonstrated the usefulness of disruptive interviews [12,14,15], and although [9] suggests that experts tend to produce consistent and reliable evaluations of the work that they perform, we found that they are not particularly consistent in the manner that they reflect on their process of doing so. In addition, we were able to efficiently collect interaction expectations and interface design input from the experts we worked with through participatory ideation.

During the initial process of building a composite model, our analyst community expected a tool that would provide recommendations. These recommendations ranged from an automated reference providing which model and data sources to use for a particular scenario to suggestions for how to then couple the data and models in order to run the simulation. This ran counter to what our scientist community expected. Where, they were familiar with building the models and wanted to be able to interrogate the data and model sources to investigate elements such as provenance, robustness, and limitations prior to selection for use. A compromise that may satisfy both participant groups would be to implement an exploratory search and browse feature where users are not recommended models and data sources, but must prioritize the information needed before beginning the information retrieval process.

An exploratory search and browse feature may be useful for interactive navigation of model and data sources to identify the appropriate elements to create a composite model. For example, take two use cases we found for creating a composite model. The first is that users may know the specific scenario or issue that they want to analyze using a composite model; and to facilitate the identification of appropriate and useful source components, they want to perform a search using specific keywords or questions. The second use case is that users are in the early stages of defining their project scope and want to run a simplified or meta-simulation to explore what is important in order to identify the appropriate source components for the design of the composite model. This loose exploration would be equivalent to browsing content on a system, or browsing a larger set of possible scenarios, and getting approximate output based on approximate inputs. This would allow the user the luxury of having a basic understanding of the model and data requirements to target particular source components.

Implementing an exploratory search and browse would require the underlying systems to have information about the source components (most likely through metadata, e.g., [3]) along with a set of composite model templates to enable this manner of recommendation system. Alternatively, a more manual approach could be taken such as prompting the user to identify known factors to be explored prior to building the simulation, or identify the important relationships between source components. This would lead to the system displaying either a dashboard of specific sources or a catalog of different scenarios to consider. Participants agreed this exploration should include a high level of interaction with different tuning knobs and a visualization recommendation interface. In addition, audience-specific dashboards would be useful for making complex decisions, providing a summary of the simulation models and source components used in the simulations.

For the simulation output, our results show that both user groups want a comparison feature that illustrates trade-offs of important scenario factors used in the final simulation. In addition, they would prefer recommended visualizations for the simulation to best understand and interpret the generated output. Overall, we saw a desire to explore model and data sources before and after use in a simulation.

6   Conclusions

This paper describes the results of the first stages of a research effort to explore interaction expectations for a modeling and simulation technology. The study was set within the context of a composite modeling and simulation technology called SPLASH that enables the coupling of independent models (and their respective data sources) to examine what-if trade-offs for complex systems. Our participant pool included scientists and analysts; both considered experts in the areas of modeling, simulation, and analytics. Without the benefit of interaction conventions for modeling and simulation technologies, we used three techniques (exploratory interviews, disruptive interviews, and participatory ideation) to elicit information from experts in the field of modeling and simulation to inform the interaction design of the SPLASH interface.

Our results show that there are differences in interaction expectations between scientists and analysts. Our scientists wanted considerably more explicit features and functionality to enable deep precision for modeling and simulation tasks; whereas our analysts wanted simplified functionality with intelligent features and recommendation functionality. We also found some common ground between our participants, such as both groups wanting a comparison feature to show trade-offs based on simulation output. Our findings point towards a semi-automated interface that provides a recommended starting point and allows for flexibility to explore component sources of models and data prior to selection for use, along with a pre-screening capability to quickly examine potential simulation output based on an early idea for a composite model.

References

1. Chilana, P., Wobbrock, J., Ko, A.: Understanding Usability Practices in Complex Domains. In: Proceedings of the 28th International Conference on Human Factors in Computing Systems, CHI 2010, pp. 2337–2346. ACM Press (2010)
2. Ericsson, K.A., Prietula, M.J., Cokely, E.T.: The Making of an Expert. Harvard Business Review: Managing for the Long Term (July 2007)
3. Tan, W.C., Haas, P.J., Mak, R.L., Kieliszewski, C.A., Selinger, P., Maglio, P.P., Li, Y.: Splash: A Platform for Analysis and Simulation of Health. In: IHI 2012 – Proceedings of the 2nd ACM SIGHIT International Health Informatics Symposium, pp. 543–552 (2012)
4. Maglio, P.P., Cefkin, M., Haas, P., Selinger, P.: Social Factors in Creating an Integrated Capability for Health System Modeling and Simulation. In: Chai, S.-K., Salerno, J.J., Mabry, P.L. (eds.) SBP 2010. LNCS, vol. 6007, pp. 44–51. Springer, Heidelberg (2010)
5. Kieliszewski, C.A., Maglio, P.P., Cefkin, M.: On Modeling Value Constellations to Understand Complex Service System Interactions. European Management Journal 30(5), 438–450 (2012)
6. Robinson, S.: Conceptual Modeling for Simulation Part I: Definition and Requirements. Journal of the Operational Research Society 59(3), 278–290 (2007a)
7. Robinson, S.: Conceptual Modeling for Simulation Part II: A Framework for Conceptual Modeling. Journal of the Operational Research Society 59(3), 291–304 (2007b)

8. Haas, P., Maglio, P., Selinger, P., Tan, W.: Data is Dead... Without What-If Models. PVLDB 4(12), 11–14 (2011)
9. Amatriain, X., Lathia, N., Pujol, J.M., Kwak, H., Oliver, N.: The Wisdom of the Few. In: Proceedings of the 32nd International ACM SIGIR Conference on Research and Development in Information Retrieval - SIGIR 2009, pp. 532–539. ACM Press (2009)
10. Karvonen, H., Aaltonen, I., Wahlström, M., Salo, L., Savioja, P., Norros, L.: Hidden Roles of the Train Driver: A Challenge for Metro Automation. Interacting with Computers 23(4), 289–298 (2011)
11. Lutters, W.G., Ackerman, M.S.: Beyond Boundary Objects: Collaborative Reuse in Aircraft Technical Support. Computer Supported Cooperative Work (CSCW) 16(3), 341–372 (2006)
12. Comber, R., Hoonhout, J., Van Halteran, A., Moynihan, P., Olivier, P.: Food Practices as Situated Action: Exploring and Designing for Everyday Food Practices with Households. In: Computer Human Interaction (CHI), pp. 2457–2466 (2013)
13. Merriam, S.B.: Qualitative Research and Case Study Applications in Education. Jossey-Bass (1998)
14. Hoonhout, J.: Interfering with Routines: Disruptive Probes to Elicit Underlying Desires. In: CHI Workshop: Methods for Studying Technology in the Home (2013)
15. Millen, D.R., Drive, S., Bank, R.: Rapid Ethnography: Time Deepening Strategies for HCI Field Research. In: Proceedings of the 3rd Conference on Designing Interactive Systems: Processes, Practices, Methods, and Techniques, pp. 280–286 (2000)
16. Kristensen, M., Kyng, M., Palen, L.: Participatory Design in Emergency Medical Service: Designing for Future Practice. In: Proceedings of the SIGCHI Conference on Human Factors in Computing Systems, pp. 161–170. ACM Press (2006)
17. Hagen, P., Robertson, T.: Dissolving Boundaries: Social Technologies and Participation in Design. Design, pp. 129–136 (July 2009)
18. Faste, H., Rachmel, N., Essary, R., Sheehan, E.: Brainstorm, Chainstorm, Cheatstorm, Tweetstorm: New Ideation Strategies for Distributed HCI Design. In: Proceedings of the SIGCHI Conference on Human Factors in Computing Systems, pp. 1343–1352 (2013)
19. IBM, http://www.ibm.com/smarterplanet/us/en/smarter_cities/overview/index.html
20. Dedoose, http://www.dedoose.com/
21. Twiddla, http://www.twiddla.com
22. Osborn, A.F.: Applied Imagination, 3rd edn. Oxford (1963)

Decision Support System Based on Distributed Simulation Optimization for Medical Resource Allocation in Emergency Department

Tzu-Li Chen

Department of Information Management, Fu-Jen Catholic University
510 Chung Cheng Rd , Hsinchuang, Taipei County 24205 Taiwan
chentzuli@gmail.com

Abstract. The number of emergency cases or people making emergency room visit has rapidly increased annually, leading to an imbalance in supply and demand, as well as long-term overcrowding of emergency departments (EDs) in hospitals. However, solutions targeting the increase of medical resources and improving patient needs are not practicable or feasible in the environment in Taiwan. Therefore, under the constraint of limited medical resources, EDs must optimize medical resources allocation to minimize the patient average length of stay (LOS) and medical resource wasted costs (MWCs). This study constructs a mathematical model for medical resource allocation of EDs, according to emergency flow or procedures. The proposed mathematical model is highly complex and difficult to solve because its performance value is stochastic and it considers both objectives simultaneously. Thus, this study postulates a multi-objective simulation optimization algorithm by integrating a non-dominated sorting genetic algorithm II (NSGA II) and multi-objective computing budget allocation (MOCBA), and constructs an ED simulation model to address the challenges of multi-objective medical resource allocation. Specifically, the NSGA II entails investigating plausible solutions for medical resource allocation, and the MOCBA involves identifying effective sets of feasible Pareto medical resource allocation solutions and effective allocation of simulation or computation budgets. Additionally, the discrete simulation model of EDs estimates the expected performance value. Furthermore, based on the concept of private cloud, this study presents a distributed simulation optimization framework to reduce simulation time and subsequently obtain simulation outcomes more rapidly. This framework assigns solutions to different virtual machines on separate computers to reduce simulation time, allowing rapid retrieval of simulation results and the collection of effective sets of optimal Pareto medical resource allocation solutions. Finally, this research constructs an ED simulation model based on the ED of a hospital in Taiwan, and determines the optimal ED resource allocation solution by using the simulation model and algorithm. The effectiveness and feasibility of this method are identified by conducting the experiment, and the experimental analysis proves that the proposed distributed simulation optimization framework can effectively reduce simulation time.

Keywords: Simulation optimization, Decision support, Non-dominated sorting genetic algorithm, Multi-objective computing budget allocation, Emergency department.

F.F.-H. Nah (Ed.): HCIB/HCII 2014, LNCS 8527, pp. 15–24, 2014.
© Springer International Publishing Switzerland 2014

1   Introduction

In recent years, Taiwan has gradually become an aging society. The continuous growth of the senior population annually accelerates the increase and growth rate in emergency department (ED) visits. According to statistics from the Department of Health, Executive Yuan, from 2000 to 2010, the overall number of people making emergency visits in 2000 was 6,184,031; the figure had surged rapidly to 7,229,437 in 2010, demonstrating a growth rate of approximately 16%.

People making emergency visits and the growth rate for these visits have risen rapidly in the past 11 years. Such an increase causes an imbalance between supply and demand, and ultimately creates long-term overcrowding in hospital EDs. This phenomenon is primarily caused by the sharp increase in patients (demand side), and the insufficient or non-corresponding increase in medical staffing (supply side). Consequently, medical staff capacity cannot accommodate excessive patient loads, compelling patients to wait long hours for medical procedures, thus contributing to long-term overcrowding in EDs.

The imbalance in supply and demand also prolongs patient length of stay (LOS) in the ED. According to data from the ED at Taiwan National University Hospital, Shin et al. (1999) found that, among 5,810 patients, approximately 3.6% (213 patients) had stayed over 72 hours in the ED. Of these 213 patients, some had waited for physicians or beds, whereas some had waited in the observation room until recovery or to be cleared of problems before being discharged. These issues frequently lead to long-term ED overcrowding. Based on data analysis of the case hospital examined in this research, among 43,748 patients, approximately 9% (3,883 patients) had stayed in the ED for over 12 hours, approximately 3% (1,295) had stayed over 24 hours, and approximately 1% (317 patients) had stayed in the ED for 72 hours.

Hoot and Aronky (2008) postulated three solutions to address the overcrowding of EDs: (1) Increase resources: solve supply deficiency by adding manpower, number of beds, equipment, and space. (2) Effective demand management: address problems of insufficient supply by implementing strategies, such as referrals to other departments, clinics, or hospitals. (3) Operational research: explore solutions to ED overcrowding by exploiting management skills and models developed in operational research. For instance, determining effective resource allocation solutions can improve the existing allocation methods and projects, ultimately enhancing ED efficiency, lowering patient waiting time, and alleviating ED overcrowding.

Among the previously mentioned solutions, the first solution is not attainable in Taiwan, because most hospital EDs have predetermined and fixed manpower, budget, and space; hence, resources cannot be expanded to resolve the problem. The second solution is not legally permitted in Taiwan, and is essentially not applicable. Both of the preceding solutions are seemingly inappropriate and not applicable; therefore, this study adopted the third solution, which entailed constructing an emergency flow simulation model by conducting operational research. Additionally, the simulation optimization algorithm was used to identify the optimal medical resource allocation solution under the constraint of limited medical resources to attain minimal average patient LOS and minimal MWC, subsequently ameliorating ED overcrowding.

The main purpose of this research was to determine a multi-objective simulation optimization algorithm that combines a non-dominated sorting genetic algorithm II

(NSGA II) and a multi-objective optimal computing budget allocation (MOCBA). An additional purpose was to conduct simulations of schemes and solutions by applying an ED discrete event simulation (DES) model produced using simulation software to obtain optimal resource allocation solutions.

In actual solution or scheme simulations, an enormous amount of simulation time is required to perform a large quantity of solution simulations. Therefore, a distributed simulation framework is necessary to save simulation time. This study adopted the concept of "private cloud," and used the distributed simulation optimization framework to implement and solve this multi-objective emergency medical resource optimal allocation problem. The operation of this distributed simulation optimization framework can be categorized into two main areas: a multi-objective simulation optimization algorithm and a simulation model. During implementation and operation, NSGA II is first used to search feasible solutions and schemes. The simulation model is then used to simulate, obtain, and evaluate performance values, whereas MOCBA determines simulation frequency for the solution or scheme during simulation. For the simulation model, this study adopted a distributed framework, in which multiple virtual machines (VMs) are installed on separate computers. For solution or scheme allocation, single control logic is used to assign various resource allocation solutions to simulation models for different VMs to conduct simulation. Performance values are generated and returned after the simulation is complete. This framework is characterized by its use of distributed simulation to rapidly obtain performance values and reduce simulation time.

2   Medical Resource Allocation Model in Emergency Department

2.1   The Interfaces with Associated Tools

This study was based on the ED flow of a certain hospital as a research target. It has been established that patient arrival interval times and service times of each medical service obey specific stochastic distributions; each type of medical resource (such as staff, equipment, and emergency beds), and the presumed resource allocation at any time is deterministic or fixed and does not change dynamically according to time. Under these pre-established conditions, a multi-objective emergency medical resources optimization allocation problem in which the primary goals were minimal average LOS and minimal average MWC was sought. Under restricted medical resources, this study aimed to obtain the most viable solution for emergency medical resource allocation.

Index:

i :Index for staff type ($i = 1,...,I$), such as doctor and nurse etc.

j :Index for working area ($j = 1,...,J$), such as registration area, emergency

and critical care area, treatment area and fever area etc.

k :Index of medical resources type ($k =1,...,K$), such as X-Ray machines, computer tomography (CT) machines, and lab technicians and hospital beds etc.

Parameters:

c_{ij} :Labor cost of staff type i in the working area j

c_k :Cost of medical resource type k

l_{ij} :Minimum number of staff type i in the working area j

l_k :Minimum number of medical resource type k

u_i :Maximum number of staff type i

u_k :Maximum number medical resource type k

Decision Variables:

X_{ij} :Number of staff type i in working area j

$\mathbf{X}$:Matrix of number of all staff types in all working area, $\mathbf{X} = \left(X_{ij} \right)_{I \times J}$

Y_k :Number of medical resource type k

$\mathbf{Y}$ Matrix of number of all medical resource types, $\mathbf{Y} = \left(Y_k \right)_K$

Stochastic medical resource allocation model:

$$\min \ f_1(\mathbf{X},\mathbf{Y}) = E[LOS(\mathbf{X},\mathbf{Y};\omega)] \tag{1}$$

$$\min \ f_2(\mathbf{X},\mathbf{Y}) = E[MWC(\mathbf{X},\mathbf{Y};\omega)] \tag{2}$$

Subject to

$$l_{ij} \le X_{ij} \qquad \forall i, \ j \tag{3}$$

$$l_k \le Y_k \qquad \forall k \tag{4}$$

$$\sum_j X_{ij} \le u_i \quad \forall i \tag{5}$$

$$Y_k \le u_k \qquad \forall k \tag{6}$$

$$X_{ij} \geq 0 \text{ and integer} \qquad \forall i, \ j \qquad (7)$$

$$Y_{k} \geq 0 \text{ and integer} \qquad \forall k \qquad (8)$$

Explanations of these mathematical models are as follows: Equation (1) is minimal expected patient LOS, where ω stands for the stochastic effect; Equation (2) is minimal average MWC, where ω stands for the stochastic effect. There are two levels of significance for minimal average MWC: (a) maximized resource use rate; and (b) minimized medical resource cost; Equation (3) is number of physicians and nurses in each area, which must exceed the lower limit; Equation (4) is the number of X-rays, CTs, laboratory technicians, and beds in the ED, which— must exceed the lower limit; Equation (5) is the sum of the number of physicians and nurses in each area, which must not exceed the upper limit; Equation (6) is the number of X-rays, CTs, and laboratory technicians, beds in the ED, which must not exceed the upper limit; Equation (7) is the number of physicians and nurses in each area, which   must be greater than 0 and expressed as a whole number; and Equation (8) is the number of X-rays, CTs, and laboratory technicians, and beds in the ED, which must be greater than 0 and expressed as whole numbers.

3   Multi-objective Simulation Optimization

Multi-objective medical resource allocation is a stochastic optimization problem, and the ED system shows a stochastic effect. Therefore, to obtain the expected patient LOS and the expected rate of waste of each resource, the ED simulation model and the repetition of simulation are required to obtain the estimation value. However, determining the frequency of simulation repetition during the process of simulation is crucial. Excess simulation repetition improves the accuracy of the objective values, but consumes large amounts of computation resources. Therefore, this research suggests a multi-objective simulation optimization algorithm, incorporating NSGA II and MOCBA, to address the multi-objective ED resource allocation problem. The NSGA II algorithm, multi-objective population-based search algorithm, is used to identify the optimal and efficient Pareto set collected from the non-dominated medical resource allocation solutions through the evolutionary processes. However, to estimate the fitness of each chromosome (medical resource allocation solution) precisely, NSGA II needs a large number of simulation replications within the stochastic ED simulation model to find the non-dominated solution set. Moreover, the simulation replications are identical for all candidate design chromosomes to cause high simulation costs and huge computational resources. Therefore, to improve simulation efficiency, the MOCBA algorithm, new multi-objective R&S method, developed from Lee et al. (2010) is applied to reduce total simulation replications and efficiently allocate simulation replications or computation budgets for evaluating the solution quality of all candidate chromosomes to identify and select the promising non-dominated Pareto set. The algorithmic procedure for integrating NSGA II and MOCBA is demonstrated in Figure 1.

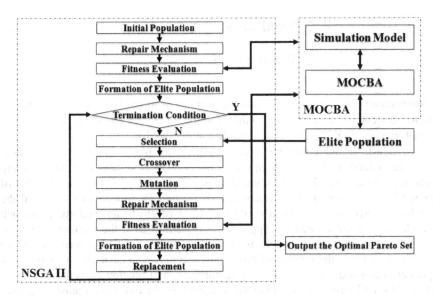

Fig. 1. The flow chart of integrating NSGA II and MOCBA algorithm

4   Distributed Simulation Optimization Framework

This study used eM-Plant 8.1 as a tool for developing the ED flow simulation model.
Figure 2 illustrates the overall ED flow simulation model. In addition, a framework of
distributed simulation optimization is developed to reduce the computation time by
the private cloud technology. In this framework, we initially installed Microsoft

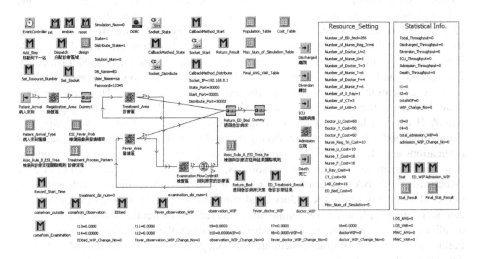

Fig. 2. Simulation model of emergency department flow

Hyper-V, a virtual operating system, on several actual servers to form a computer resource pool concept. We then established numerous virtual machines (VM) in this resource pool and assigned 1 simulation model to each VM. Emergency department procedures were subsequently simulated using these simulation models.

The distributed simulation optimization framework in Figure 3 comprised a client and a server. After the initial client parameters were set, Web services (WS) were employed to obtain the non-dominated sorting genetic algorithm-II (NSGA II) from the server via the Internet. These parameters were subsequently transferred to the NSGA II's WS. Upon receiving the HTTP request and parameter settings, the NSGA II conducts algorithmic procedures, calling WS for the multi-objective optimal budget allocation (MOCBA) algorithm when simulation is required. The MOCBA determines the number of simulation iterations required, calling WS for the simulation coordinator while simultaneously uploading the relevant simulation programs into the database. The SC's WS manages the simulation models, identifies the idle simulation models, and distributes simulation programs to the idle models to perform simulations. After identifying which model to simulate, the SC's WS commands the model to retrieve the simulation program from the database. Consequently, the simulation results are transferred to the SC's WS, which then transfers this data to the MOCBA to determine the simulation iterations required untill achieving the termination conditions. After the MOCBA is terminated, the performance results are transferred to the NSGA II's WS to again achieve the termination conditions. Following the termination of the NSGA II, the optimal program produced is transferred to the client-end.

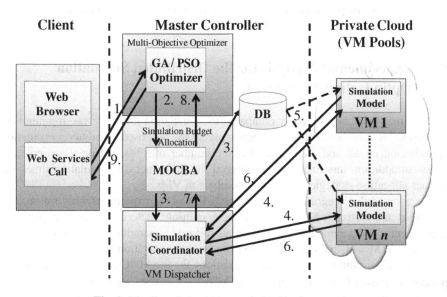

Fig. 3. Distributed simulation optimization framework

This framework was executed in the following process:

Step 1:   The client calls WS for the NSGA II and transfers the parameters set by the user to the NSGA II's WS via the Internet.

Step 2:   When simulation is required, the NSGA II calls WS for the MOCBA and transfers the simulation programs to the MOCBA's WS.

Step 3:   When performance values are required, the MOCBA uploads the required simulation programs to the database via ADO.NET and calls WS for the SC to determine which VM simulation model to simulate.

Step 4:   The SC's WS uses sockets to identify which VM is available and command the simulation model on the VM to perform a simulation.

Step 5:   The simulation model uses open data connectivity to collect the simulation program data from the database after receiving the execution command from the coordinator socket.

Step 6:   After executing the simulation program, the performance values are transferred to the SC's WS via the socket.

Step 7:   The SC's WS transfers the performance results to the MOCBA's WS after receiving them from the simulation model.

Step 8:   After receiving the performance values, the MOCBA's WS executes the MOCBA until the termination conditions are achieved. Subsequently, the performance results for algorithm termination are transferred to the NSFA II's WS.

Step 9:   After receiving the performance values, the NSGA II's WS executes the NSGA II until the termination conditions are achieved. Subsequently, the produced results are transferred to the client via the Internet.

5   Experimental Analysis for the Distributed Simulation Optimization Framework

In this experiment, we primarily compared the simulation times for varying numbers of VMs to identify the differences when applying the proposed distribution simulation optimization model and the effects that the number of VMs had on the simulation times. In addition, this experiment analyzed the differences in simulation times for various allocation strategies with equal numbers of VMs.

We adopted the integrated NSGA II_MOCBA as the experimental algorithm, and employed the optimal NSGA II parameter settings determined in the previous experiments. The parameter settings were as follows: generation = 10, population size = 40, C = .7, M = .3, and the termination condition = generation (10).

The initial number of simulation iterations for the MOCBA was $n_0 = 5$, with a possible increase of $\Delta = 30$, and $P*\{CS\} = 0.95$ for every iteration.

Regarding the number of VMs, we conducted experiments using 1, 6, 12, and 18 VMs. Table1 shows the execution times for the simulation programs with varying numbers of VMs and allocation strategies. Besides 1 VM, two methods can be used for allocating the remaining numbers of VM, specifically, including and excluding allocation of the number of simulation iterations. Excluding the allocation indicates that the simulation program is allocated to 1 VM for execution regardless of the program's number of simulation iterations, that is, the number of iterations for that program is not divided and allocated to separate VMs. Conversely, including the allocation indicates that when the number of iterations for the simulation program exceeds the initial number of iterations n_0 set by the MOCBA, the number of iterations is divided and allocated to numerous VMs for execution.

Table 1. The execution times for the simulation programs with varying numbers of VMs and allocation strategies

Number of VMs	Allocation method	Number of executions	Execution times
1	-	4200 executions	690.5 h (28.77 d)
6	Excluding number of runs allocation	4260 executions	112 h (4.67 d)
	Including number of runs allocation	4260 executions	105.5 h (4.40 d)
12	Excluding number of runs allocation	4290 executions	58 h (2.42 d)
	Including number of runs allocation	4230 executions	52 h (2.17 d)
18	Excluding number of runs allocation	4380 executions	52 h (2.17 d)
	Including number of runs allocation	4350 executions	40 h (1.67 d)

According to the experimental results shown in Table 1, we determined the following insights:

1. The overall execution time for 1 VM approximated a month (28 d). However, the execution time was reduced significantly to approximately 4 and 1.5 days when the number of VMs was increased to 6 and 18, respectively (Table 1). In addition, the curve exhibited a significant decline from 1 VM to 18 VMs. Thus, we can confirm from these results that the proposed distributed simulation optimization framework can effectively reduce simulation times.
2. The overall execution time was reduced from approximately 4 days to 1 day when the number of VMs increased from 6 to 18 (Table 1). In addition, the curve exhibited a decline from 6 VMs to 18 VMs. These results indicate that the simulation times can be reduced by increasing the number of VMs.
3. With a fixed number of VMs, the time required to divide and allocate simulation iterations to numerous VMs is shorter than that for allocating the entire number of iterations to 1 VM (**Error! Reference source not found.**1). Considering 6 VMs as an example, the execution time without dividing and allocating the number of simulation times was 112 h, whereas the execution time with dividing and allocating the number of iterations was 105.5 h. These results indicate that distributing the

number of simulation times among numerous VMs can reduce the overall execution time.

4. According to the experimental results, we infer that a limit exists when the number of VMs is increased to significantly reduce the simulation times. In other words, when a specific number of VMs is added to a low number of available VMs, the simulation time is significantly reduced. However, when the number of VMs increases to a specific amount, the reduction in simulation time becomes less significant, eventually reaching convergence. This indicates that after a certain number of VMs, the simulation time dos not decline with additional VMs.

6   Conclusion

This study investigated the resolution of ED overcrowding through ED medical resource optimal allocation. First, an emergency simulation model for a hospital in Taiwan was designed based on interviews and analysis regarding procedures and flow. A multi-objective simulation optimization algorithm was then designed by integrating the NSGAII algorithm and the MOCBA. To obtain simulation outcomes more rapidly by diminishing simulation time, this study proposes a distributed simulation optimization framework based on the private cloud concept to practice or implement and resolve this multi-objective emergency medical resource optimization allocation problem. In the proposed distributed simulation optimization framework, solutions or schemes are assigned to different VMs on separate computers to conduct simulations and minimize simulation time, as well as obtain simulation results more rapidly.

References

1. Ahmed, M.A., Alkhamis, T.M.: Simulation optimization for an ED healthcare unit in Kuwait. European Journal of Operational Research 198, 936–942 (2009)
2. Chen, C.H., Lee, L.H.: Stochastic simulation optimization: An Optimal Computing Budget Allocation. World Scientific Publishing Co. (2010)
3. Hoot, N.R., Aronsky, D.: Systematic Review of ED Crowding: Causes, Effects, and Solutions. Health Policy and Clinical Practice 52(2), 126–136 (2008)
4. Lee, L.H., Chew, E.P., Teng, S., Goldsman, D.: Finding the non-dominated Pareto set for multi-objective simulation models. IIE Transactions 42(9), 656–674 (2010)
5. Pitombeira Neto, A.R., Gonçalves Filho, E.V.: A simulation-based evolutionary multiobjective approach to manufacturing cell formation. Computers & Industrial Engineering 59, 64–74 (2010)

The Impact of Business-IT Alignment on Information Security Process

Mohamed El Mekawy, Bilal AlSabbagh, and Stewart Kowalski

Department of Computer and Systems Science (DSV), Stockholm University, Sweden
{moel,bilal}@dsv.su.se, stewart@fc.dsv.su.se

Abstract. Business-IT Alignment (BITA) has the potential to link with organizational issues that deal with business-IT relationships at strategic, tactical and operational levels. In such context, information security process (ISP) is one of the issues that can be influenced by BITA. However, the impact has yet not been researched. This paper investigates the BITA impact on ISP. For this investigation, the relationships of elements of the Strategic Alignment Model and the components of Security Values Chain Model are considered. The research process is an in-depth literature survey followed by case study in two organizations located in United States and the Middle East. The results show clear impact of BITA on how organizations would distribute allocated security budget and resources based on the needs and risk exposure. The results should support both practitioners and researchers to gain improved insights of the relationships between BITA and IT security components.

Keywords: Business-IT alignment, BITA, Information Security Process, Security Value Chain, Security Culture.

1 Introduction

The importance of IT as an enabler of business has spawned research on effective and efficient deployment of IT to gain strategic advantage (Sim and Koh, 2001). However, many companies still fail to gain values and advantages from huge IT investments. This failure is partially attributable to a lack of Business-IT alignment (BITA) (Leonard & Seddon, 2012). Strategic alignment refers to applying IT in a way that is timely and appropriate and in line with business needs, goals and strategies (Luftman, 2004). Therefore, in an increasingly competitive, IT-driven and vibrant global business environment, companies can only gain strategic advantages and derive values from IT investments when efforts are made by management to ensure that business objectives are shaped and supported by IT in a continuous fashion (Kearns & Lederer, 2000).

The achievement of such objectives requires strong relationships between business and IT domain not only at strategic level, but at also tactical and operational levels (Tarafdar and Qrunfleh, 2009). This highlights the importance of ensuring internal coherence between organizational requirements and delivery's capability of IT domain. It also highlights the importance of Information Security Process (ISP) as integrated part of IT strategy tactics and operations (Avison et al., 2004). In particular,

F.F.-H. Nah (Ed.): HCIB/HCII 2014, LNCS 8527, pp. 25–36, 2014.
© Springer International Publishing Switzerland 2014

BITA at operational level requires social perspective and aspects like interaction, shared understanding/knowledge across teams and personnel. Even thought BITA is shown to have potential impact on ISP at different organizational levels, little research has been done is this area (Saleh, 2011). Given the fact that the ISP focuses on relationships between business and IT for supporting BITA, the complexity of its nature is increased when considering different views on IT in organizations and how to utilize it in regard of business objectives.

This paper investigates the impact of BITA on ISP. For this investigation, the relationships of elements of the Strategic Alignment maturity Model (SAM) developed by Luftman (2000) and the components of the Security Values Chain Model (SVCM) developed by Kowalski & Boden (2002) are considered. The remainder of the paper is structured as follows: the research approach is discussed in section 2. The implications of BITA and ISP are presented in section 3 and 4 respectively. Potential relationships between BITA components and SVCM are presented in section 5. Results and analyses are presented in section 6 followed by conclusions in section 7.

2   Research Approach

The followed research method and process are namely an in-depth literature survey followed by case study research. The literature survey aimed to study theories behind BITA and ISP and hypothesize the impact of BITA criteria on SVCM's components. Following that, qualitative data was collected from two organizations through semi-structured interviews with four respondents in each organization i.e. selected to represent strategic and senior management at both business and IT in both organizations. The results where codified and compared to the proposed hypotheses.

The first organization (Referred as Company-A) is a midsize insurance company in the Midwest of the United Stated. The second organization (Referred as Company-B) is a governmental entity located in the Middle East and acts as national regulator for communication and technology business.

3   Implications of Business-IT Alignment

In literature, BITA is related to different scopes, and it is therefore defined differently. While some definitions focus more on the outcomes from IT for producing business value, others focus on harmonizing business and IT domains with their objectives, strategies and processes. These two views have affected the way in which BITA is expressed in publications. Publications which studied benefits of IT for business look at leveraging/linking (Henderson and Venkatraman, 1993), enabling (Chan et al., 1997), transforming (Luftman et al., 2000) and optimizing (Sabherwal et al., 2001) business processes. Other studies which focus on relationship between business and IT refer to BITA as fitting (Benbya & McKelvey, 2006), integrating (Lacity et al., 1995), linking (Reich & Benbasat, 2000), matching (Chan et al., 1997), bridging (Van Der Zee and De Jong, 1999), fusion (Smaczny, 2001) and harmonizing (Chan, 2002).

Results from BITA research show that organizations that successfully align their business and IT strategy can increase their business performance (Kearns & Lederer, 2003). BITA can also support analysis of potential role of IT in an organization when it supports to identify emergent IT solutions in the marketplace that can be opportunities for changing business strategy and infrastructure (Henderson & Venkatraman. 1993). Not only researchers, but business and IT practitioners have also emphasized the importance of BITA. In the annual survey of the Society for Information Management, BITA was first on the top management concern from 2003-2009 with the exception of 2007 and 2009 in which it was second (Luftman & Ben-Zvi, 2010). Therefore, practitioners should place special attention on BITA and particularly on how it is achieved, assessed and maintained in organizations.

Fig. 1. Luftman's Strategic Alignment Maturity (SAM) (adapted from Luftman. 2000)

Different efforts have been oriented towards assessing BITA by proposing theoretical models that can be applied as supportive tools for addressing different BITA components. An extensive study by El-Mekawy et al. (2013) collected those models with their components in a comparative framework. Although Henderson and Venkatraman are seen as the founding fathers of BITA modeling (Avison et al., 2004), Luftman's model (SAM) has gained more popularity in practice (Chan & Reich, 2007). This gain is due to the following motivation: a) It follows a bottom-up approach by setting goals, understanding linkage between Business and IT, analyzing and prioritizing gaps, evaluating success criteria, and consequently sustaining alignment, b) It presents strategic alignment as a complete holistic process which encompasses not only establishing alignment but also its maturity by maximizing alignment enablers and minimizing inhibitors (Avison et al., 2004), c) SAM focuses on different BITA areas by modularity in six criteria, and d) Since its inception, SAM has been used by several researchers and in number of industries for assessing BITA and its components. Therefore, SAM is selected to be used in this study for assessing BITA and analyzing the proposed impact on ISP. SAM classifies BITA in six criteria (Table 1) consisting of 38 attributes (Figure 1) in five maturity levels: Ad Hoc, Committed, Established Focused, Managed, and Optimized Process. This classification gives clear view of alignment and helps to spot particular areas of where an organization needs to improve for maximizing values of IT investments.

Table 1. Criteria of SAM

BITA Criterion	Definition and Questions Attached
Communications	Refers to clear understanding between business and IT communities with an effective exchange and sharing of each ideas, processes and needs.
Competency/ Value Measurements	Concerns about demonstrating IT values in compatible figures with the business community understanding. Therefore, both business and IT have usually different metrics of values they add.
Governance	Ensures that business and IT communities formally and periodically discuss and review their plans. Priorities are important for allocating the needed IT resources.
Partnership	Refers to the relationship between business and IT in having shared vision of organisation's processes IT as an enabler/driver for business transformation.
Scope and Architecture	Illustrates IT involvement in organisational processes, and in supporting flexible and transparent infrastructure. This, however, facilitates applying technologies effectively and providing customised solutions responding to customer needs.
Skills	Refers to human resource aspects that influence/(are influenced) by changes and cultural/social environment as components of organizational effectiveness.

4   Information Security Process (ISP)

Information systems (IS) in organizations are implemented to support their business processes that enable to achieve business objectives. With such systems, one should consider information security as a process of answering questions of *'what is needed to protect organization resources'*, *'why do resources need to be protected? from whom and how'* (Schwaninger, 2007). In such context, information security, given its socio-technical nature, requires both social and technical activities. Globalization of Internet has created situations in which security problems are not limited within groups, organizations, or nations. With current trends in IS outsourcing and movement towards open distributed systems, people from different organizational culture are charged to administer security processes that need to meet security requirements and expectations of data owners. International security standards have been made available to address part of the issue by providing standard measures. However, standards are by design attempt to be contextual neutral i.e. do not consider organizational cultures, governance or alignment between business and IT domains.

ISP traditionally has been linked to three main objectives; confidentiality, integrity, and availability. However, achieving information security is unlimited to only achieving these objectives. It is attached to sustaining IS for achieving organizational objectives against security attacks and accidents (Saleh, 2011). One of the main problems in organizations' security is that it is often viewed as an isolated island without established bridges between security requirements and business goals. The rationale for this problem is mainly referred to financial aspects and controls in organizations. This often results in lack of security and financial investments in the organizational core IS. It is therefore important that security to be built as a process with both planning and designing phases of IS. This includes adaptability of security architecture for ensuring that regular and security related tasks are deployed correctly (Amer & Hamilton, 2008). It has been emphasized that security requirements should be linked to business goals and IS through a process-oriented approach (Schwaninger, 2007). This clearly supports for building-up information security as a process dealing with organization's governance, organizational culture, IT architecture and service management (Whitman & Mattord, 2003). In addition to that, best practices in implementing security in organizations is indicated by factors such as complying regulatory equirements and fiduciary responsibility, measuring information security practices and improving efficiency/effectiveness (Saleh, 2011).

Unlimited to researchers, business and IT practitioners also have emphasized the ISP importance. In the annual survey of the Society for Information Management, ISP was among the top 10 management concerns from 2003-2009 and is the only technical issue in 2009 (Luftman & Ben-Zvi, 2010). Therefore, practitioners should place special attention on how information security should be practiced as a process joined with organizational planning, design and performing tasks.

Research in modelling ISP has been going since the introduction of computer systems to business. An early attempt to holistic models in this area is the Security by Consensus (SBC) framework developed by Kowalski (1991) for comparing different national approaches to security. Following that, socio-technical frameworks were developed (e.g. Lee et al., 2005; Al-Hamdani, 2009) for understanding security management as a social process. Other frameworks were developed emphasizing mental models of security (e.g. Adams, 1995; Oltedal et al., 2004; Kowalski & Edwards, 2004; Barabanov & Kowalski, 2010) for linking information security as a cultural process to business objectives. In this study, the Security Value Chain (SVC), developed by Kowalski & Edwards (2004), (Figure 2) is selected to analyze BITA impact on ISP. This is motivated by arguing on its establishment in analyzing different steps of business development process which is clearly influenced by aligning business and IT views. In addition to that, it represents patterns of mental security spending on its steps for visualizing how business and IT inputs intervene.

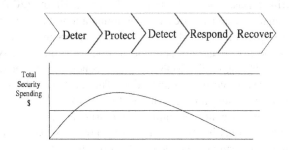

Fig. 2. Security Value Chain

The chain consists of five security access controls: deterrent, protective (preventive), detective, responsive (corrective) and recovery. These controls represent input points to IS (Table 2) in which an action may take place to stop undesired actions on the system. AlSabbagh & Kowalski (2012) operationalized the security value chain as a social metric for modeling the security culture of IT workers individuals at two organizations. Their research showed how IT workers' and individuals' security culture diverse given security problem at personal, at enterprise and national level. The research also studied the influence of available fund on security culture.

Table 2. Definitions of Security Value Chain Control Measures

Control	Definition
Deter	for reducing chances of exploiting existing vulnerability without actually reducing the exposure. E.g. consequences of violating a company security policy.
Protect	for preventing occuring of security incident (e.g. access control implementations).
Detect	for identifying and characterize a security incident (e.g. monitoring system alarm).
Respond	for remediating the damage caused by a security incient (e.g. incidet response plan).
Recover	for compensating for the losses incurred due to a security incident (e.g. security incident insurance).

5   BITA Impact on Information Security Process

Over years, different studies have shown clear impact of business objectives and performance on ISP (e.g. Huang et al., 2005; Johnson & Goetz, 2007). Other studies focused on the impact of IT strategies and how IT is perceived on ISP (e.g. von Solms and von Solms, 2004; Doherty & Fulford, 2005). As the relationship between business and IT is represented by BITA, the impact of BITA on ISP is apparent. However, it is neither analyzed in studies of BITA nor in studies of ISP (Saleh, 2011). In this section, indications of BITA impact on ISP are presented. Each criterion of SAM is described by which it influences the access controls of the security value chain. Hypothetically, we expect to find at least one existing reflection of each SAM criterion on an access control. With the help of SAM's attributes in each criterion, more various interesting relations may be addressed.

- **Communications.** Based on the findings of Herath & Herath (2007), it is indicated that matured channels and metrics for communications between business and IT have a strong impact on how ISP is perceived in an organization. This also influences the way the organization reacts and responses to the security attacks. However, as found by Huang et al. (2006), it can be concluded that achieving complete information security is virtually impossible. This is due to the need for matured communications in an organization to be further extended to include suppliers, partners and customers which potentially increases the risks to attacks. Therefore, matured communications in BITA is found to have less expenditure in *detecting*, *responding* and *recovering* but no clear indications for *deterring* and *protecting*.

- **Competency/ Value Measurements.** Kumar et al. (2007)'s findings indicated the importance of developing IT and business metrics to the expenditure on ISP. They are not only indicating risks through process, but also in incorporating changes in organizational aspects compared to previous results. In addition to that, the findings of Gordon et al. (2005) show that attacks on IS come not only from outside the organization. The loss from 'theft of proprietary information' was, for example, shown to be three times than from virus in 2005 according to the CSI/FBI survey. This indicates that developing matured business and IT metrics will reduce investments in *Detecting* and *Responding* of ISP but increasing expenditure in *Deterring* and *Protecting*. However, there is no clear indication on *Recovering*.
- **Governance.** According to the results of Johnson & Goetz (2007), effective distribution of investment on ISP is influenced by fitting IT security into business goals and processes through its governance structure. In addition to that, Beautement et al. (2008) argue that the misalignment in governance would lead to friction between ISP and business processes into the organizational system. It is then indicated that matured governance can result in reducing the expenditure on *detecting* and *responding*, but increasing the expenditure on *protecting* and *recovering*. No indications can be highlighted for the deterring.
- **Partnership.** According to the findings of Ogut et al. (2005), organizations with high partnership have interconnection between business and technology which supports the organization in better planning and decision making for security. According to Yee (2005), this partnership makes clear goals and trust all over the organization and supports for faster matured ISP. Therefore, it can be indicated that matured partnership would be attached to less expenditure in *detecting*, *responding* and *recovering* but no clear indications for *deterring* and *protecting*.
- **Scope and Architecture.** As found by Huang et al. (2006), complete information security is impossibly achieved. Gordon and Loeb (2002) found that optimal investment in information security is not necessarily increased with vulnerability. Organizations should prioritize to protect the most significant IS. Johnson & Goetz (2007), additionally, found that advancing IT architecture with rigid structure would influence expenditure on ISP. It is then concluded that matured IT architecture would increase its complexity level, and consequently indicates slower *detection* and *responding* to attacks with increasing their expenditure. However, rigid and strong architecture will reduce the cost of *deterring*, *protecting* and *recovering*.
- **Skills.** Huang et al. (2005) found that skills and experiences of decision makers are important players in information security investments. Although, there are strong arguments from different researchers (e.g. Beautement et al., 2008) on reasoning for cost and benefit of ISP to include the impact of individual employees, but it is mainly related to complying security policies. It is then influenced by individual's goals, perceptions and attitudes. However, they influence the development level of systems, platforms and protecting important applications as well. Therefore the impact of matured skills can be indicated on reducing expenditure on *protecting*, *detecting*, *responding* and *recovering*.

6   Results and Analyses

In this section, results and analyses of BITA assessment are presented in subsection 6.1 followed by the analyses of BITA and ISP in subsection 6.2.

6.1   BITA in the Organizations

- **Communications.** In Company-A, the understanding of business by IT is characterized to be higher than understanding of IT by business. Understanding of business by IT is seen focused and established process, but it should be more tied to performance appraisals throughout IT functions. However, the business senior and mid-level managers have limited understanding of IT which results in less Committed process. In overall, communications is assessed at level 2. In Company-B, understanding of business by IT is also more matured than understanding of IT by business. As an IT-related organization, senior and mid-level IT managers have good understanding of business in order to achieve the targeted objects. Knowledge sharing is limited to the strategic level. Such conditions were indicated at matured level 3.
- **Competency/ Value Measurements.** IT metrics and processes in Company-A are perceived primarily technical (e.g. system availability, response time). They do not relate to business goals or functions. However, business metrics are seen far matured than IT metrics and extended as value-based on contributions of customers. The organization has formal feedback processes in place to review and take actions based on results of measures and to assess contributions across organisational functions. In overall, the maturity level is assessed at level 3. In Company-B, IT metrics are more matured. They are extended to formally assess technical, cost efficiency, and cost effectiveness measures (e.g., ROI, ABC). They are also followed by formal feedback processes in place to review and take actions based on results of measures. The business metrics are also matured and customer-based representing an enterprise scope. The overall maturity level is highlighted 2.
- **Governance.** It is indicated in Company-A that both business and IT strategic planning are characterized by formal planning at functional levels. However, it is extended at the business domain. In the IT domain, it is more occasional responsive according to projects or involvement scale in business. The overall maturity level is 2. The governance in Company-B is characterized by strategic business planning at functional units and across the enterprise with IT participation. It is further extended to business partners/alliances. However, the strategic IT planning is less matured without an extended enterprise view to customers/alliances. The federated reporting system further supports for an overall maturity level as 4.
- **Partnership.** Although there is good insights for matured alignment in Company-A, but IT is perceived as a cost to the organization for doing business rather a strategic partner. IT is involved in strategic business planning in limited scope. IT co-adapts with business to enable/drive for some projects and strategic objectives. In overall all, the maturity level is highlighted as 3. In Company-B, IT is perceived having a better role, however, it is still seen as enabler to future business activities.

It is also seen to bring values to the organization and co-adapt with business to enable/drive strategic objectives. These conditions indicate a level of maturity 4.

- **Scope and Architecture.** In both Company-A and Company-B, IT is considered as a catalyst for changes in the business strategy with a matured IT architecture. In addition to that, IT standards are defined and enforced at the functional unit level with emerging coordination across functional units. Although they are integrated across the organisation, but they are not extended to include customer and supplier perspectives which make a matured level of 3.
- **Skills.** In Company-A, the environment is characterized as innovative and encouraging especially at functional units. However, it has initial, technical training and little rewards. The career crossover is limited to only strategic levels, and the environment is dominated by top business managers who have more locus of power than IT managers. The overall matured level is then assessed as 1. In Company-B, innovation is strongly motivated especially at functional units with cross training and limited change readiness. The top business management has domination and locus of power for IT management. Career crossover is extended but to the senior management and functional units. The overall maturity is indicated at level 3.

6.2 BITA Impact on ISP

- **Company-A.** The interviews show potential impact of BITA maturity on ISP. For instance, while business perceives IT as a cost for business, senior and mid-level business managers have limited understanding of IT. Business seems not to care about security spending. The budget is allocated with no questions or awareness on how effectively used. This is also reflected in the fact that IT metrics are primarily technical. BITA maturity level seems to be focused and managed process. There is a formal feedback process for reviewing and improving measurement results. Both business and IT conduct formal strategic planning across the organisation but not extended to partners/alliances. What has also been understood during the interviews is that there is no awareness regarding the need for having the five types of security access controls. One of the interviewees was even supported to get figures providing spending distribution according to the five controls.

Table 3. Ideal and Expected Security Value Chain in Company-A based on Collected Data

Security Access Control	Deter	Protect	Detect	Correct	Recover
Ideal Budget Dsribution (%)	5	40	35	15	5
Expected Current (%)	10	30	25	20	15

- **Company-B.** The interviews revealed potential impact of BITA maturity on ISP. The current SVC distribution almost matches what would be seen ideal. The reason behind this is the optimized levels of BITA *Value Measurements* and *Governance*. The limited business understanding for the importance of implementing deterring controls are apparent. However, there is a potential support and motivation for developing security policies that would state the consequences of misconduct and accountability when security is violated. More than 10% of security budget is allocated to such deterring controls. The same problem is observed regarding recovery controls implementations. As business does not understand why IT needs to have active support licenses for its applications, the business decided not to renew any license. It is known in IT that having such support available is vital for providing means of recovery for potential issues. The business has considered having active support licenses as an extra cost which is not used most of the time. The limited maturity in *Communications* and *Skills* has also resulted in more severe issues related to human resourcing. Business is not allocating enough funds for hiring senior security consultants who can improve the organization's security position. Business perceives IT as an enabler to business objectives and changes, however, with insufficient turnovers. This perception has resulted in having budget constraints for IT and difficulties in approving it.

Table 4. Ideal and Current Security Value Chain in Company-B based on Collected Data

Security Access Control	Deter	Protect	Detect	Correct	Recover
Ideal Budget Dsributon (%)	12	23	23	20	22
Expected Current (%)	10	25	25	18	22

7   Conclusions and Future Work

In this paper, the potential impact of BITA maturity on ISP was explored in two organisations based on SAM and SVCM respectively. The study revealed correlations between BITA maturity level and existing security process. For instance, the lack of *Communications* maturity between business and IT had significant impact on security culture. When business management had limited understanding of IT, it was correlated to difficulties in approving IT security budgets including required human resourcing for hiring security consultants. This lack of communications had also negative impact on implementing *Deterrent* controls desired by IT department. It was also observed that limited business participation in IT strategic planning (i.e. *Governance*) was correlated to limited business understanding while *Recovery* security controls are needed. In turns this had a negative impact on implementing *Recovery* controls.

Immature alignment in *Value Measurement* and *Partnership* was found leading to immature security culture. For instance, when IT uses only technical metrics with no business considerations, it is perceived as a cost for business. This leads to lack of security awareness where business neither has interest to know nor it is aware of security spending or its performance. Optimized levels of BITA *Value Measurement* and *Governance* were correlated with increasing security awareness and its importance in business side and thus have raised interest in requirements related to IT security. This resulted in immediate approval of IT security budgets. Such situation has enabled IT managers to implement the SVC they believe to be ideal.

Suggested future work for this paper would be to conduct more case organisations to confirm whether the findings will lead to the same results we have in this paper.

References

1. Adams, J.: Risk. Taylor & Francis, London (1995)
2. Al-Hamdani, W.A.: Non risk assessment information security assurance model. In: Proceedings of the Information Security Curriculum Development Conference, pp. 84–90. ACM, Kennesaw (2009)
3. AlSabbagh, B., Kowalski, S.: Developing Social Metrics for Security – Modeling the Security Culture of IT Workers Individuals (Case Study). In: Proceedings of the 5th International Conference on Communications, Computers and Applications (2012)
4. Amer, S.H., Hamilton, J.A.: Understanding security architecture. In: Proceedings of the Spring Simulation Multi-conference, Society for Computer Simulation, Canada (2008)
5. Avison, D., Jones, J., Powell, P., Wilson, D.: Using and Validating the Strategic Alignment Model. Journal of Strategic Information Systems 13, 223–246 (2004)
6. Barabanov, R., Kowalski, S.: Group Dynamics in a Security Risk Management Team Context: A Teaching Case Study. In: Rannenberg, K., Varadharajan, V., Weber, C. (eds.) SEC 2010. IFIP AICT, vol. 330, pp. 31–42. Springer, Heidelberg (2010)
7. Beautement, A., Sasse, M.A., Wonham, M.: The compliance budget: managing security behaviour in organisations. In: NSPW 2008, pp. 47–58 (2008)
8. Benbya, H., McKelvey, B.: Using Coevolutionary and Complexity Theories to Improve IS Alignment: A multi-level approach. Journal of Information Tech. 21(4), 284–298 (2006)
9. Chan, Y.E., Huff, S.L., Barclay, D.W., Copeland, D.G.: Business Strategic Orientation, IS Strategic Orientation, and Strategic Alignment. ISR 8(2), 125–150 (1997)
10. Chan, Y.E.: Why haven't we mastered alignment? The Importance of the informal organization structure. MIS Quarterly 1, 97–112 (2002)
11. Chan, Y.E., Reich, B.H.: IT alignment: what have we learned? Journal of Information Technology 22(4), 297–315 (2007b) (advance online publication)
12. Doherty, N.F., Fulford, H.: Do information security policies reduce the incidence of security breaches: an exploratory analysis. IRM Journal 18(4), 21–38 (2005)
13. El-Mekawy, M., Perjons, E., Rusu, L.: A Framework to Support Practitioners in Evaluating Business-IT Alignment Models. AIS Electronic Library (2013)
14. Gordon, L.A., Loeb, M.P.: The Economics of Information Security Investment. ACM Transactions on Information and Systems Security 5(4), 438–457 (2002)
15. Gordon, L.A., Loeb, M.P., Lucyshyn, W., Richardson, R.: CSI/FBI Computer Crime and Security Survey. Computer Security Institute (2005)
16. Henderson, J., Venkatraman, N.: Strategic alignment: leveraging information technology for transforming organizations. IBM Systems Journal 32(1), 472–484 (1993)
17. Herath, H.S.B., Herath, T.C.: Cyber-Insurance: Copula Pricing Framework and Implications for Risk Management. In: Proceedings of the Sixth Workshop on the Economics of Information Security, Carnegie Mellon University, June 7-8 (2007)
18. Huang, C.D., Hu, Q., Behara, R.S.: Investment in information security by a risk-averse firm. In: Proceedings of the 2005 Softwars Conference, Las Vegas, Nevada (2005)
19. Huang, C.D., Hu, Q., Behara, R.S.: Economics of Information Security Investment in the Case of Simultaneous Attacks. In: Proceedings of the Fifth Workshop on the Economics of Information Security, Cambridge University, pp. 26–28 (2006)
20. Johnson, M.E., Goetz, E.: Embedding Information Security into the Organisation. IEEE Security & Privacy 16 – 24 (2007)
21. Kearns, G.S., Lederer, A.L.: The Effect of Strategic Alignment on the use of IS-Based Resources for Competitive Advantage. Journal of Strategic IS 9(4), 265–293 (2000)

22. Kowalski, S.: The SBC Model: Modeling the System for Consensus. In: Proceedings of the 7th IFIP TC11 Conference on Information Security, Brighton, UK (1991)
23. Kowalski, S., Boden, M.: Value Based Risk Analysis: The Key to Successful Commercial Security Target for the Telecom Industry. In: 2nd Annual International Common Criteria CC Conference, Ottawa (2002)
24. Kowalski, S., Edwards, N.: A security and trust framework for a Wireless World: A Cross Issue Approach, Wireless World Research Forum no. 12, Toronto, Canada (2004)
25. Kumar, V., Telang, R., Mukhopahhyay, T.: Optimally securing interconnected information systems and assets. In: 6th Workshop on the Economics of IS, CM University (2007)
26. Lacity, M.C., Willcocks, L., Feeny, D.: IT outsourcing: maximise flexibility and control. Harvard Business (1995)
27. Lee, S.W., Gandhi, R.A., Ahn, G.J.: Establishing trustworthiness in services of the critical infrastructure through certification and accreditation. SIGSOFT Softw. Eng. Notes 30(4), 1–7 (2005)
28. Leonard, J., Seddon, P.: A Meta-model of Alignment. Communications of the Association for Information Systems 31(11), 230–259 (2012)
29. Luftman, J.: Assessing Business-IT Alignment Maturity. Communications of the Association for Information Systems 4, Article 14 (2000)
30. Luftman, J.N.: Managing IT Resources. Prentice Hall, Upper Saddle (2004)
31. Luftman, J., Ben-Zvi, T.: Key Issues for IT Executives: Difficult Economy's Impact on IT. MIS Quarterly Executive 9(1), 49–59 (2010)
32. Oltedal, S., Moen, B., Klempe, H., Rundmo, T.: Explaining Risk Perception. An evaluation of cultural theory. Norwegian University of Science and Technology (2004)
33. Ogut, H., Menon, N., Raghunathan, S.: Cyber Insurance and IT security investment: Impact of interdependent risk. In: Workshop on the Economics of Information Security, WEIS 2005, Kennedy School of Government, Harvard University, Cambridge, Mass. (2005)
34. Reich, B.H., Benbasat, I.: Factors That Influence The Social Dimension of Alignment Between Business And IT Objectives. MIS Quarterly 24(1), 81–113 (2000)
35. Sabherwal, R., Chan, Y.E.: Alignment Between Business and IS Strategies: A Study of Prospectors, Analyzers, and Defenders. IS Research 12(1), 11–33 (2001)
36. Saleh, M.: Information Security Maturity Model. Journal of IJCSS 5(3) (2011)
37. Schwaninger, M.: From dualism to complementarity: a systemic concept for the research process. International Journal of Applied Systemic Studies 1(1), 3–14 (2007)
38. Smaczny, T.: Is an alignment between business and information technology the appropriate paradigm to manage IT in today's organisations? Management Decision 39(10), 797–802 (2001)
39. Tarafdar, M., Qrunfleh, S.: IT-Business Alignment: A Two-Level Analysis. Information Systems Management 26(4), 338–349 (2009)
40. Whitman, M.E., Mattord, H.J.: Principles of Information Security. Thomson Course Tech. (2003)
41. Van Der Zee, J.T.M., De Jong, B.: Alignment is Not Enough: Integrating business and information technology management with the balanced business scoreboard. Journal of Management Information Systems 16(2), 137–156 (1999)
42. von Solms, B., von Solms, R.: The ten deadly sins of information security management. Computers & Security 23(5), 371–376 (2004)
43. Yee, K.P.: User Interaction Design for Secure Systems. In: Faith Cranor, L., Garfinkel, S. (eds.) Security and Usability: Designing Secure Systems that People Can Use, pp. 13–30. O'Reilly Books (2005)

Examing Significant Factors and Risks Affecting the Willingness to Adopt a Cloud–Based CRM

Nga Le Thi Quynh[1], Jon Heales[2], and Dongming Xu[2]

[1] Falcuty of Business Information Systems,
University of Economics HoChiMinh City, Vietnam
[2] UQ Business School, The University of Queensland, Australia
nga.lethiquynh@uq.net.au

Abstract. Given the advantages of and significant impact that Cloud-based CRMs have had on achieving competitive edge, they are becoming the primary choice for many organizations. However, due to the growth of concerns around cloud computing, cloud services might not be adopted with as much alacrity as was expected. A variety of factors may affect the willingness to adopt a cloud-based CRM. The purpose of this study, therefore, is to explore the factors that influence the adoption of a cloud-based CRM in SME's, from the perspectives of the client organizations and users. We then propose a research model, grounded in the Resource Based View Framework (RBV), the Theory of Technology Acceptance Model (TAM2), Risks and Trust Theories. This report recommends a research methodology. It offers recommendations for practitioners and cloud service providers to effectively assist in the adoption of cloud-based CRMs in organizations.

Keywords: cloud computing, CRM, adoption, TAM, risks, trust.

1   Introduction

Although Cloud Computing has been undergoing rapid evolution and advancement, it is still an emerging and complex technology [1], and our understanding of, and regulatory guidance related to cloud computing is still limited [2]. These limitations raise significant concerns about security, privacy, performance, and trustworthiness of cloud-based applications. [3, 4]. While the cloud offers a number of advantages, until some of the risks are better understood and controlled, cloud services might not be adopted with as much alacrity as was expected [5].

Although there are studies investigating the implementation of CRM systems [6, 7], there is a lack of research in adopting cloud-based CRMs. To successfully adopt and implement a cloud-based CRM, client organizations need to have understanding about cloud computing, its characteristics, and need to take into account the risks involved when deciding to migrate their applications to the cloud. Cloud services providers also need to enhance their understanding of client users' behavior such as how they act and what factors affect their choice, in order to increase the rate of adoption.

F.F.-H. Nah (Ed.): HCIB/HCII 2014, LNCS 8527, pp. 37–48, 2014.
© Springer International Publishing Switzerland 2014

Having an understanding of client users' behavior during the examination phase, before a full adoption decision is made, will help cloud service providers better address potential users' concerns.

2 Literature Review

This study explores the roles of Risks relating to Tangible Resources, Intangible Resources, and Human Resources; perceived usefulness, perceived ease of use, subjective norm and Trust in the adoption of Cloud-Based CRMs. The study is informed by the Resource-Based View Framework, Risk and Trust Theories, and the Technology Acceptance Model (TAM2).

2.1 Cloud Computing

We adopt the Efraim, Linda [8] view of Cloud Computing as the general term for infrastructures that use the Internet and private networks to access, share, and deliver computing resources with minimal management effort or service provider interaction. In the cloud context, users pay for the services as an operating expense instead of the upfront capital investment [9].

Cloud computing provides several advantages, including cost reduction [4, 9], organizational agility and often competitive advantage [10, 11]. However, there is a lot of uncertainty and skepticism around the cloud that stakeholders in cloud computing (e.g. providers, consumers and regulators) should take into account, including the gap in cloud capabilities, security, and audit and control risks. The next sections examine these risks more thoroughly.

2.2 Customer Relationship Management (CRM) and Cloud-Based CRMs

Efraim, Linda [8 pg. 324] define CRM as the methodologies and software tools that automate marketing, selling, and customer services functions to manage interaction between an organization with its customers, and to leverage customer insights to acquire new customers, build greater customer loyalty, and increase profit level.

One of the biggest benefits of a cloud-based CRM is that it is easily accessible via mobile devices from any location, at any time [8 pg. 328]. In addition, cloud-based CRM allows enterprises, especially Small and Medium Enterprises (SMEs) not only to achieve cost benefits through pay-per-use, without a large upfront investment, but also to mimic their larger rivals to effectively manage and enhance customer relationship processes.

2.3 Technology Acceptance Model (TAM)

Employing the Theory of Reasoned Action (TRA) [12], TAM [13] has been widely utilized for analyzing and explaining a user's intention to adopt an information system.

The original TAM model does not incorporate the effect of the social environment on behavioral intention. Therefore, we apply TAM2 [14], which hypothesizes perceived usefulness, perceived ease of use, and subjective norm as the determinants of Usage Intention, to our conceptual research model.

We apply TAM2 to our theoretical foundation and define the constructs as follows:

Perceived usefulness, for the purpose of this paper, is defined as the degree to which an individual believes that using a cloud-based CRM would improve his or her job performance. Seven capabilities of cloud computing, namely controlled interfaces, location independence, sourcing independence, ubiquitous access, virtual business environments, addressability and traceability, and rapid elasticity [10], enable users to access the application, internal and external resources over the internet easily and seamlessly. This has made cloud-based CRMs advantageous to client organizations.

Perceived ease of use of cloud-based CRMs refers to the extent to which a user believes that using a cloud-based application would be free of effort.

As one characteristic of cloud-based applications is the ease with which to switch between service providers, the higher degree that the users can use the application and its functions to help them in daily operations without investing a lot of effort on learning how to use during the trial time, the more probability that they will be willing to adopt the application.

Subjective norm, for the purpose of this paper, is the degree to which an individual perceives that others believe he/ she should use a specific cloud-based CRM. The advantage of virtual communities and social networks is that it allows users to share and exchange ideas and opinions within communities. An individual's behavior will be reinforced by the multiple neighbors in the social network who provide positive feedback and ratings [15], especially, when subscribing to a new application or purchasing a product, so users tend to evaluate the product by examining reviews of others [16] . The following propositions follow:

P1: Perceived Usefulness will positively affect the Willingness to Adopt Cloud Based CRMs.

P2a: Perceptions of Cloud-based CRMs Ease of Use will positively affect Perceived Usefulness.

P2b: Perceptions of Cloud-based CRMs Ease of Use will positively affect the Willingness to Adopt Cloud Based CRMs.

P3: Subjective Norm will positively affect the Willingness to Adopt Cloud Based CRMs.

2.4   Trust

Trust has been regarded as the heart of relationships of all kinds [17] and a primary enabler of economic partnerships [18]. Building trust is particularly important when an activity involves uncertainty and risk [19]. In the context of cloud computing, uncertainty and risk are typically high because of the lack of standards, regulations and complexity of technology, etc. [1, 9]. This leads to a significant concern for enterprises about TRUST in cloud-based applications [20].

Antecedents of Trust

Prior research on Trust has proposed a number of trust antecedents: knowledge-based trust, institution-based trust, calculative-based trust, cognition-based trust and personality-based trust [for more details, see 21].

We consider the initial level-of-trust formation, would directly affect the organization's willingness to adopt.

Personality-based trust – Personal perception is formed based on the belief that others are reliable and well-meaning [22], resulting in a general tendency to believe to others and so trust them [23]. This disposition is especially important for new organizational relationships, where the client users are inexperienced with service providers [24].

Cognition-based trust – perception of reputation: is built on first impression rather than experiential personal interactions [23]. In the context of cloud-based CRMs, to access trustworthiness of cloud service providers, client organizations tend to base their evaluation on secondhand information provider's reputation. Reputation of providers is also particularly important when considering cloud adoption and implementation [25].

Institution-based Trust – perception of Structural Assurance: is formed from safety nets such as regulations, guarantees, legal recourse [26].

A Service-level agreement (SLA) is a negotiated contract between a cloud service provider with client organization. Cloud service providers use SLAs to boost the consumer's trust by issuing guarantees on service delivery.

Knowledge-based Trust: is formed and developed over time though the interaction between participants [21, 27]. This type of trust might be absent for the first meet between service provider and client organization. However, during the trial time, interaction and communication between parties will affect to the level of trust in each other, thus improving their behavioral intention to continue adopting the application.

Based on our argument above, and because we are using already validated measures of trust, we make the following complex proposition:

P4: Personal Perception, Perception of Reputation of a cloud-based CRM provider, Perception of Structural Assurances built into a cloud-based CRM, and Knowledge-based Trust will positively affect Trust in a cloud-based CRM provider.

Consequences of Trust

Heightened level of Trust, as a specific belief in a service provider, are associated with heightened willingness to use services supplied by that provider. Cloud computing is still in its infancy [28], and contains a certain level of complexity of technology [29] and immaturity of standards, regulations, and SLAs, thus we propose :

P5: Trust in a Cloud-based CRM Provider will positively affect the Willingness to Adopt a Cloud-based CRM.

Trust in a cloud service provider implies the belief that service provider will deliver accurate and qualified services, as expected. Users are less likely to accept unexpected failure of the system or network, and unqualified performance of service. Therefore, a service provider's subjective guarantee, through SLAs, and other elements such as the provider's reputation or customer services, during the trial time, would bolster user's confidence. Such a guarantee is likely to increase the likelihood that the CRM application will improve users' performance in managing the customer relationship. Conversely, adopting an application from an untrustworthy service provider might result in reduced usefulness. Based on this, we propose that:

P6: Trust in a Cloud-based CRM Provider will positively affect the Perceived Usefulness of Cloud-based CRMs.

2.5   Theory of Resource Based View (RBV) as a Framework Foundation for Risk Assessment

The RBV explains the role of resources in firm performance and competitive advantage [30]. Barney [30] went on to show that to achieve sustained competitive advantage, resources must be "valuable, rare, difficult to imitate, and non-substitutable". When putting the RBV in the context of cloud computing, there are a number of organizational resources that can affect the competitiveness and performance of the firms. First, by accessing current infrastructures and using complementary capabilities from cloud providers, clients can focus on internal capabilities and core competencies to achieve competitive advantage [11]. Second, one characteristic of cloud-based applications is the ease with which to switch between service providers, and the number of options for customers has increased over time. Customers tend to seek qualified products, and if service providers cannot ensure necessary resources and capabilities, they might lose their current and potential customers into their competitors.

Therefore, the more uncertainty that affects the effectiveness of the firm's resources, the less probability that firms might achieve good performance and competitive advantage.

Salient Risks Relating to Tangible Resources in Cloud-Based CRM Adoption

Data – related risks

Migrating to cloud means that the enterprise data would be stored outside the enterprise boundary, at the cloud service provider end, and the client organization entrusts the confidentiality and integrity of its data to the cloud service provider. This raises certain concerns on how adequate a level of security the cloud service provider offers to ensure data security and prevent breaches due to security vulnerabilities in the application, cloud service provider's environment, or through malicious users [29, 31]. Currently many organizations are only willing to place noncritical applications and general data in the cloud [32]. According to an InformationWeek report [33], of those respondents using, planning to use, or considering public cloud services, 39% say they do not / will not allow their sensitive data to reside in the cloud and 31% say they do not /will not run any mission-critical applications in the cloud.

In addition, for CRMs, to provide fast response, and efficient processing services for customers, the data are retrieved from multiple resources via CDIs (Customer Data Integration). Dealing with data changes, data glitches in verification, validation, de-duplication and merging processes also provides significant challenges for service providers [34].

However, trust in a cloud service provider, resulting from the provider's reputation and their structural assurance (e.g. SLAs), to some extent, can lessen the fear of incidents and risks related to data security and privacy. In the cloud context, cloud users face insecure application programming interfaces (APIs), malicious insiders, data breaches, data loss, and account hijacking [4, 31]. In addition, cloud-provider may be perceived to have too much power to view and potentially abuse sensitive customer data. Therefore, a provider with a good reputation and sufficient security mechanisms will provide confidence that customer data will be stored and protected against illegal access, and therefore increase the likelihood of adopting the cloud-based application.

Based on our argument above, we make the following propositions:

P7a: The Data-Related Risks will negatively affect the Willingness to Adopt Cloud Based CRMs.

P7b: Trust moderates the relationship between Data-Related Risks and the Willingness to Adopt Cloud Based CRMs.

Economic Risks

With a cloud-based application, the business risk is decreased by a lower upfront investment in IT infrastructure [3], although there is still the uncertainty of hidden risks during the time customers use the application. For example, to maximize the number of capabilities of an application, customers may have to pay more to get the advanced version [35]. The more reliable and specialized the hardware, software and services offered, the higher the price service providers would set [36].

Furthermore, with the Medium and Large size enterprises migrating their enterprise applications such as CRMs and ERPs to cloud based environments, the cost of transferring organizational data is likely to increase, especially if the organization applies the hybrid cloud deployment model where data would be stored in different distinct cloud infrastructures (e.g. private, community and public) [37]. Thus;

P8: The Economic Risks will negatively affect the Willingness to Adopt Cloud Based CRMs.

IT Infrastructure risks

IT Infrastructure risks are the possibility that the service provider may not deliver the expected level of infrastructure. That is the network infrastructure is not provided with the speed or reliability at the level expected. One positive characteristic of cloud computing is the rapid elasticity, which enables the scaling up or down of service usage, based on virtualization technology [11]. However, risks such as the unpredictable performance of virtual machines, frequent system outages, and connectivity problems, can affect all a provider's customers at once, with significant negative impacts on their business operations. [4].

IT infrastructure risks also include the risk of problems related to the integration between cloud-based applications and internal systems. The perceived IT infrastructure risks mentioned above are likely to influence the user' perception that the CRM might not perform as smoothly and seamlessly as expected. Thus;

P9: The IT Infrastructure Risks will negatively affect the Perceived Cloud-based CRM Usefulness.

Salient Risks Relating to Human Resources in Cloud-Based CRM Adoption

· *Technical skill risks*

Technical skill risks are the possibility that lack of knowledge about cloud computing and CRM, and competence in emerging technologies, will negatively affect the ability to successfully implement cloud-based CRMs.

To effectively deal with the complexities and uncertainties associated with new technologies like cloud computing, and to ensure the smooth adoption and operation of cloud-based applications, organizations require qualified employees. A lack of professional knowledge about cloud computing, as well as information systems from members participating in the cloud based CRM deployment, would create hurdles slowing down the process of adoption [38]. Thus, the client users might need to spend more time and effort to learn how to use the application. Thus;

P10: Lower levels of Technical skill will negatively affect Perceived Ease of Use of the Cloud Based CRMs.

Managerial risks

From the psychosocial view, it is noted that IT executives might be conscious of negative consequences from adopting cloud-based applications [35]. The likelihood of successfully implementing a new system largely depends on good project management and leadership skills [39], and effective coordination and interaction with stakeholders [38]. Because cloud-based CRMs involve business process changes, integration of the new system into an existing IT infrastructure and system, and exploitation new technologies, it is necessary for technological and organization-specific knowledge of how to implement cloud solutions to operate business transactions as well as achieve business objectives [39].

The managerial risk might be reduced if there is a strong belief in the cloud-service providers. Trust can bolster the executive's optimism about the desirable consequences [21, 23], as a result, they might willing to adopt cloud-based application when they trust the service provider. We propose that managerial risk will affect the willingness of adoption of cloud-based CRMs; this proposition is moderated by Trust in a cloud-based CRM provider.

P11a: The Managerial Risks will negatively affect the Willingness to Adopt Cloud Based CRMs.

P11b: Trust moderates the relationship between Managerial Risks and the Willingness to Adopt Cloud Based CRMs.

Salient Risks Relating to Intangible Resources in Cloud-Based CRM Adoption

Strategic risk

Strategic risks include the risks that cloud-based CRM clients might be heavily dependent on the service providers and their applications. The cloud-based CRM applications may not be flexible enough to respond to changes in their business strategies and thus ensure alignment between IT and business strategies [35].

A high degree of dependence on a cloud provider may also cause vendor lock-in and business continuity issues [4, 31].

However, trust in a cloud provider, resulting from the provider's reputation and structural assurance (e.g. SLAs), to some extent, can lessen this fear. When the provider issues guarantees about data ownership, disaster recovery plans, standards, and assurances that regulations are followed, the level of trust is raised. Thus, a provider with a strong reputation can give the impression that it is able to sustain superior profit outcomes. [40].Thus;.

P12a: The Strategic Risks will negatively affect the Willingness to Adopt Cloud Based CRMs.

P12b: Trust moderates the relationship between Strategic Risks and the Willingness to Adopt Cloud Based CRMs.

Audit risk
Audit risk is the probability of there will be material misstatements in the client organization's financial statements. This can result from the lack of internal control and governance, ambiguous agreement on data ownership, and/or immature regulations and standards for cloud computing.

SAS No.107 [41] categorizes audit risk into three components: inherent risk, control risk, and detection risk. Inherent risk is possibility that a material misstatement in the client's financial statements will occur in the absence of appropriate internal control procedures. Control risk is the risk that material misstatement will not be detected and corrected by management's internal control procedures. Detection risk is the risk that the auditor will not detect material misstatement. Cloud computing places an increased burden on the auditor [2], and the lack of understanding of cloud computing in terms of technical and business aspects, as well as the risks associated with cloud computing, might lead to an increase in detection risk.

These risks can affect the Trust in cloud service providers, if they do not issue appropriate SLAs that specify the provider's responsibilities for services, data ownership and regulations and standards they would follow. Thus;

P13: Increasing level of Audit Risk will negatively affect Trust in cloud-based CRM provider.

Performance Functionality Risks
Marketing research suggested the reasons for CRM implementation are to boost the organization's ability to communicate with the customers, to learn about customer preferences in a timely manner, to achieve fast response to customers, and to analyse customer insights [42]. Put these requirements in context of cloud computing, there are the risks that the service provider will not be able to ensure seamless interoperability with home-grown applications [35], as well as with other on-demand applications on the same and different cloud platforms [37].

These risks can result the user's perception that he/she cannot perform his/her job well when he/she uses a cloud-based CRM. Thus;

P14: The Performance - Related Risks will negatively affect the Perceived Usefulness of Cloud Based CRMs.

3   Model of Cloud-Based CRM Adoption

Following from the review presented on the previous section, we propose the research model depicted in Figure 1.

4   Research Method

4.1   Conduct the Research

We seek to gather data from individual users who have commissioned a trial test of a cloud-based CRM and examination phase before deciding to fully adopt the CRM. To test this model we consider a survey-based approach is the most appropriate [see 43]. The following steps need to be taken:

1. We adopt measures from the literature for each of the constructs in the model, and operationalize them so that they can be used to gather the required data.
2. A preliminary web analysis of constructs was performed to validate the measures developed in the model. We collected user comments from 3 cloud-based CRM applications, namely Salesforce.com, Insightly, and Zoho CRM on the Apple Apps store, Google apps Marketplace, Google Play and Blackberry World. 1579 comments were collected by users who were considering trialling, or who were trialling the applications.
3. Based on the analysis of the preliminary data, we ensure all comments can be categorised by our constructs in the final questionnaire.
4. A large-scale survey would then be conducted to test our model of factors and risks involved in the adoption of a cloud-based CRM.

4.2   Questionnaire Development and Measures

The pre-validated questionnaire items were obtained from previous research on CRM, cloud computing, trust, risks, and TAM2. All items specified a seven-level Likert scale, expressed in linguistic terms: strongly disagree, moderately disagree, somewhat disagree, neutral (neither disagree nor agree), somewhat agree, moderately agree, and strongly agree.

5   Analysis of the Findings

This will be presented and discussed at the conference.

6   Implications Drawn from Analysis

This will be presented and discussed at the conference.

7   Conclusions and Limitations

This paper presents the factors and risks involved in the adoption of a cloud-based CRM. These factors and risks were derived from the analysis of research conducted into the adoption of information technology and systems, cloud computing, trust, and audit risk. From this research foundation a model was developed and presented.

This research will help provide more insights about client user behaviour toward the adoption a cloud-based CRM. This study also offers several practical implications. First, perception of risks together may inhibit the cloud-based CRM adoption. It is recommended that cloud service providers develop appropriate strategies to counter these concerns. For example, effective risk-mitigation strategies may include strong guarantees, better transparency and more consumer control of data and processes. Client users may be more willing to overlook the perceived risks if they know what is happening with their application and data, and they are confident that the service provider is trustworthy and can perform efficiently to ensure the system run smoothly.

Second, our study suggests that the cloud-based CRM adoption depends heavily on perceived usefulness, perceived ease of use and a trusting belief in the cloud service provider. By acting in a competent and honest manner, a cloud service provider can maintain high trust, resulting the willingness to adopt and retaining of users of its cloud-based CRM from organization clients.

Future studies may include other aspects that might influence the adoption such as organizational characteristics (e.g. firm size, organizational strategies, maturity of current information systems, etc.), industry characteristics (e.g. competitive intensity) and personals characteristic (e.g. gender, age, experience, etc.)

References

1. Blaskovich, J., Mintchik, N.: Information Technology Outsourcing: A Taxonomy of Prior Studies and Directions for Future Research. Journal of Information Systems 25(1), 1–36 (2011)
2. Alali, F.A., Chia-Lun, Y.: Cloud Computing: Overview and Risk Analysis. Journal of Information Systems 26(2), 13–33 (2012)
3. Pearson, S.: Privacy, Security and Trust in Cloud Computing, in Technical Reports, HP: HP (2012)
4. Armbrust, M., et al.: A View of Cloud Computing. Communications of the ACM 53(4), 50–58 (2010)
5. Youseff, L., Butrico, M., Da Silva, D.: Toward a unified ontology of cloud computing. In: Grid Computing Environments Workshop, GCE 2008. IEEE (2008)
6. Kim, H.-S., Kim, Y.-G., Park, C.-W.: Integration of firm's resource and capability to implement enterprise CRM: A case study of a retail bank in Korea. Decision Support Systems 48(2), 313–322 (2010)
7. Avlonitis, G.J., Panagopoulos, N.G.: Antecedents and consequences of CRM technology acceptance in the sales force. Industrial Marketing Management 34(4), 355–368 (2005)
8. Efraim, T., Linda, V., Gregory, W.: Information Technology for Management, 9th edn. (2013)

9. Marston, S., et al.: Cloud computing — The business perspective. Decision Support Systems 51(1), 176–189 (2011)
10. Iyer, B., Henderson, J.C.: Preparing for the Future: Understanding the Seven Capabilities of Cloud Computing. MIS Quarterly Executive 9(2), 117–131 (2010)
11. Iyer, B., Henderson, J.C.: Business value from Clouds: Learning from Users. MIS Quarterly Executive 11(1), 51–60 (2012)
12. Fishbein, M., Ajzen, I.: Belief, attitude, intention and behavior: An introduction to theory and research (1975)
13. Davis Jr., F.D: A technology acceptance model for empirically testing new end-user information systems: Theory and results. Massachusetts Institute of Technology (1986)
14. Venkatesh, V., Davis, F.D.: A Theoretical Extension of the Technology Acceptance Model: Four Longitudinal Field Studies. Management Science 46(2), 186–204 (2000)
15. Centola, D.: The Spread of Behavior in an Online Social Network Experiment. Science 329(5996), 1194–1197 (2010)
16. Park, D.-H., Lee, J., Han, I.: The Effect of On-Line Consumer Reviews on Consumer Purchasing Intention: The Moderating Role of Involvement. International Journal of Electronic Commerce 11(4), 125–148 (2007)
17. Morgan, R.M., Shelby, D.H.: The Commitment-Trust Theory of Relationship Marketing. Journal of Marketing 58(3), 20–38 (1994)
18. Gefen, D.: What Makes an ERP Implementation Relationship Worthwhile: Linking Trust Mechanisms and ERP Usefulness. Journal of Management Information Systems 21(1), 263–288 (2004)
19. Luhmann, N.: Familiarity, confidence, trust: Problems and alternatives. Trust: Making and Breaking Cooperative Relations 6, 94–107 (2000)
20. Huang, J., Nicol, D.: Trust mechanisms for cloud computing. Journal of Cloud Computing 2(1), 1–14 (2013)
21. Gefen, D., Karahanna, E., Straub, D.W.: Trust and TAM in Online Shopping: An Integrated Model. MIS Quarterly 27(1), 51–90 (2003)
22. Wrightsman, L.S.: Interpersonal trust and attitudes toward human nature. Measures of Personality and Social Psychological Attitudes 1, 373–412 (1991)
23. McKnight, D.H., Cummings, L.L., Chervany, N.L.: Initial Trust Formation in New Organizational Relationships. The Academy of Management Review 23(3), 473–490 (1998)
24. Gefen, D.: E-commerce: the role of familiarity and trust. Omega 28(6), 725–737 (2000)
25. Koehler, P., et al.: Cloud Services from a Consumer Perspective. In: AMCIS. Citeseer (2010)
26. Sitkin, S.B.: On the positive effects of legalization on trust. Research on Negotiation in Organizations 5, 185–218 (1995)
27. Holmes, J.G.: Trust and the appraisal process in close relationships (1991)
28. Misra, S.C., Mondal, A.: Identification of a company's suitability for the adoption of cloud computing and modelling its corresponding Return on Investment. Mathematical and Computer Modelling 53(3-4), 504–521 (2011)
29. Subashini, S., Kavitha, V.: A survey on security issues in service delivery models of cloud computing. Journal of Network and Computer Applications 34(1), 1–11 (2011)
30. Barney, J.: Firm Resources and Sustained Competitive Advantage. Journal of Management 17(1), 99 (1991)
31. Nicolaou, C.A., Nicolaou, A.I., Nicolaou, G.D.: Auditing in the Cloud: Challenges and Opportunities. CPA Journal 82(1), 66–70 (2012)

32. Barwick, H.: Cloud computing still a security concern: CIOs, September 17-20 (2013),
    http://www.cio.com.au/article/526676/
    cloud_computing_still_security_concern_cios/?fp=16&fpid=1
33. Emison, J.M.: 9 vital questions on moving Apps to the Cloud, in InformationWeek Reports
    (2012)
34. Buttle, F.: Customer relationship management. Routledge
35. Benlian, A., Hess, T.: Opportunities and risks of software-as-a-service: Findings from a
    survey of IT executives. Decision Support Systems 52(1), 232–246 (2011)
36. Durkee, D.: Why cloud computing will never be free. Commun. ACM 53(5), 62–69 (2010)
37. Dillon, T., Wu, C., Chang, E.: Cloud computing: Issues and challenges. In: 2010 24th
    IEEE International Conference on Advanced Information Networking and Applications
    (AINA). IEEE (2010)
38. Finnegan, D.J., Currie, W.L.: A multi-layered approach to CRM implementation: An inte-
    gration perspective. European Management Journal 28(2), 153–167 (2010)
39. Garrison, G., Kim, S., Wakefield, R.L.: Success Factors for Deploying Cloud Computing.
    Communications of the ACM 55(9), 62–68 (2012)
40. Roberts, P.W., Dowling, G.R.: Corporate Reputation and Sustained Superior Financial
    Performance. Strategic Management Journal 23(12), 1077–1093 (2002)
41. AICPA, Audit Risk and Materiality in Conducting an Audit. Statement on Auditing Stan-
    dards No.107, AICPA (2006)
42. Sun, B.: Technology Innovation and Implications for Customer Relationship Management.
    Marketing Science 25(6), 594–597 (2006)
43. Yin, R.K.: Case study research: Design and methods, vol. 5. Sage (2003)

Towards Public Health Dashboard Design Guidelines

Bettina Lechner and Ann Fruhling

School of Interdisciplinary Informatics, University of Nebraska at Omaha,
Omaha NE 68182, USA
{blechner,afruhling}@unomaha.edu

Abstract. Ongoing surveillance of disease outbreaks is important for public health officials, who to need consult with laboratory technicians in identifying specimen and coordinate care for affected populations. One way for public health officials to monitor possible outbreaks is through digital dashboards of summarized public health data. This study examines best practices for designing public health dashboards and proposes an optimized interface for an emergency response system for state public health laboratories. The practical nature of this research shows how general dashboard guidelines can be used to design a specialized dashboard for a public health emergency response information system. Through our analysis and design process, we identified two new guidelines for consideration.

Keywords: Medical information system, dashboard interface design, disease surveillance, public health.

1 Introduction

Public health crises such as the recent *Listeria* outbreaks or the 2009 influenza pandemic require the immediate attention of public health directors and practitioners who coordinate diagnosis and care for affected populations. Continual monitoring of the public health environment allows for faster response and may reduce the impact of such emergencies. To address this need, digital dashboards have been shown to be an effective means to quickly assess and communicate the situation. Often these dashboards include computerized interactive tools that are typically used by managers to visually ascertain the status of their organization (in this case, the public health environment) via key performance indicators (Cheng et al., 2011). Dashboards allow users to monitor one or more systems at a glance by integrating them and summarizing key metrics in real time to support decision making (Kintz, 2012; Morgan et al., 2008). In the medical field, dashboards continue to expand and have been used for purposes such as emergency response coordination (Schooley et al., 2011), patient monitoring (Gao et al., 2006), and influenza surveillance (Cheng et al., 2011).

The US states of Nebraska, Kansas, and Oklahoma use a public health emergency response information system (PHERIS) to allow hospital microbiology laboratorians to monitor and report public health episodes across their state. In the case of a potential outbreak the PHERIS is the tool used by the microbiologists at the clinical

F.F.-H. Nah (Ed.): HCIB/HCII 2014, LNCS 8527, pp. 49–59, 2014.
© Springer International Publishing Switzerland 2014

laboratory to consult with epidemiology experts at the State Public Health Laboratory through a secure connection over the Internet. This system provides functionality to send informational text and images of specimens between laboratories and the state public health laboratory. However, to further enhance the functionality and usability of the PHERIS it would be ideal if there were a single display screen (e.g. digital dashboard) where the State Public Health Director could immediately assess if there are any potential outbreaks on the cusp of happening with just a glance.

The first aim of our study is to analyze and apply dashboard specific design guidelines we identified in our literature review through a new dashboard interface optimized for real-time disease outbreak and public health emergency surveillance. Second, we will evaluate if there are any missing guidelines.

In the remainder of this paper, we begin by presenting background information on the public health area, on the PHERIS (the system that is used in this study), and on the various dashboard design guidelines found in the literature. Next, we present our application of the selected medical dashboard guidelines to the new dashboard design. Then we present our analysis of missing dashboard guidelines. We conclude with remarks on the next phases planned for this study.

2   Background

2.1   Public Health

Public health is defined as "all organized measures (whether public or private) to prevent disease, promote health, and prolong life among the population as a whole" (WHO, 2014). The mission of public health is "fulfilling society's interest in assuring conditions in which people can be healthy" (IOM, 1988).

Some of the goals of public health are to prevent epidemics and the spread of disease, protect against environmental hazards, promote and encourage healthy behaviors, respond to disasters and assist communities in recovery, and to assure the quality and accessibility of health services (Turnock, 2009). One of the essential services provided by public health agencies is to monitor the health status and to identify community health problems (Turnock, 2009).

In the USA, the Centers for Disease Control and Prevention (CDC) is the nation's leading public health agency, and is responsible for responding to health threats such as naturally occurring contagious disease outbreaks or deliberate attacks (CDC, 2011). To be able to fulfill this monitoring role, every time a suspected select agent (such as *Bacillus anthracis* ["anthrax"]) is encountered by a state public health organization, it needs to be reported to the CDC. To fulfill this requirement, the state public health laboratories of Nebraska, Kansas, and Oklahoma use a system which allows them to communicate with laboratories in their state electronically and collect photos and metadata of suspected select agents to report to the CDC.

2.2   Public Health Emergency Response Information System

The intent of the PHERIS (STATPack™) system used in this study was to address critical health communication and biosecurity needs in State Public Health Laboratory rural states. The Secure Telecommunications Application Terminal Package (STAT-Pack™) system is a secure, patient-privacy compliant, web-based network system that supports video telemedicine and connectivity among clinical health laboratories. The overarching goal of this public health emergency response system is to establish an electronic infrastructure, largely using web technology, to allow secure communication among state public health hub and spoke laboratory networks in emergency situations.

Specifically, the STATPack™ concept involves taking macroscopic (gross) as well as microscopic digital images of culture samples and sending them electronically for consultation with experts at state public health laboratories. STATPack™ enables microbiology laboratories around the state to send pictures of suspicious organisms to the state public health laboratory, instead of the samples themselves, thus lessening the risk of spreading infectious diseases. The system includes an alert system that is bi-directional and has various levels of priorities (emergency, urgent, routine, and exercise).

STATPack™ is especially useful in states where much of the expertise is located in a hub laboratory, while most triage and decision making regarding specimen processing takes place in smaller spoke hospital laboratories. For some of the spoke laboratories, it is difficult if not impossible for them to describe to experts what they see in a culture sample. STATPack™ allows experts to actually see the sample immediately and assist with the diagnosis in a matter of minutes, eliminating the risks and time delay of shipping the sample by courier.

In the case of an emergency, an expert scientist at a hub laboratory can in real-time, remotely focus the camera on a suspicious organism, analyze the image, and respond to the spoke laboratory. If the organism is deemed a public health threat, the STATPack™ system can be used to send an alert to every laboratory in the network. Prior to STATPack™, the only option was to physically send the sample to the hub laboratory, which could take several hours or even a full day to receive.

State public health experts spend significant time monitoring public health threats such as influenza outbreaks. Monitoring multiple public health laboratories state-wide at a glance is often challenging due to having to search multiple places for information, data overload, continuous changes of statuses, not knowing what information has changed, and a need to evaluate the potential impact. To address some these challenges, we designed a dashboard that would present all the relevant information for a state-wide surveillance system on one screen. We will refer to this new dashboard as STATDash.

2.3   Dashboard Design Guidelines

In this section we present a meta review of existing dashboard design best practices and related guidelines. This includes several studies reporting on the development of different kinds of medical dashboards, ranging from influenza surveillance, patient triage monitoring, to radiology reporting. A list of studies is presented in Table 1. Most of these studies also included guidelines for *medical* dashboard design, not just dashboards in general. The number of guidelines featured in each study is shown in Table 1.

Table 1. Selected relevant research

Study	Subject	# Guidelines
Cheng et al., 2011 *	Influenza surveillance dashboard	5
Dolan et al., 2013	Treatment decision dashboard	0
Few, 2006	Information dashboard design	12
Fruhling, 2004	Public health emergency response system	3
Gao et al., 2006	Patient triage monitoring for emergency response	15
Morgan et al., 2008	Radiology report backlog monitoring dashboard	4
Schooley et al., 2011	Emergency medical response coordination	6
Tufte, 2001	Information visualization	1
Turoff et al., 2004	Medical response information system	8
Zhan et al., 2005 *	Disease surveillance and environmental health	4

As shown in **Error! Reference source not found.**, the number of guidelines specific to public health monitoring dashboards is relatively low -- only two studies providing a total of nine guidelines fall into this field (highlighted with an asterisk). When we widen the criteria to include all medical dashboard guidelines, four more studies presenting 33 guidelines can be included. Furthermore, there are two relevant papers discussing 11 best practices for medical/public health emergency response systems design. Also, two studies in the field of information visualization and general dashboard design have some overlapping relevancy and thus, are included.

The dashboard and data visualization guidelines developed by Few (2006) and Tufte (2001) were reviewed and considered in this study. Even though they are general in nature and not specific to medical dashboards we included them, because they provide important contributions to information visualization and dashboard user interface design.

We also included Turoff et al. (2004)'s eight design principles for emergency response information systems (not necessarily dashboards) in our literature review. We decided to do this because Turoff's principles are concerned with the content required to make emergency response information systems useful.

After identifying the most salient studies, we performed a meta-analysis of all the guidelines for dashboard design. In total, 58 guidelines were identified in the literature. Among these there were several recurring themes as well as guidelines unique to the medical field.

The most common themes were those of designing dashboards as customizable, actionable "launch pads", supporting correct data interpretation, and aggregating and summarizing information. Also frequently mentioned were adherence to conventions, minimalist design, in-line guidance and user training, workload reduction, and using GIS interfaces. 33 of the guidelines were unique to the field of medical dashboards, while 17 were not applicable and 7 were too general.

The other 50 guidelines can be sorted into these eight themes that emerged from their review. **Error! Reference source not found.** shows the number of guidelines in each thematic area and the studies represented within.

Table 2. Categorized guidelines

Theme	# Guidelines	Studies
Customizable, actionable "launch pad"	10	Cheng et al., 2011; Few, 2006; Gao et al., 2006; Morgan et al., 2008; Schooley et al., 2011; Zhan et al., 2005
Support correct data interpretation	8	Few, 2006; Gao et al., 2006; Morgan et al., 2008
Information aggregation	7	Cheng et al., 2011; Few, 2006; Gao et al., 2006; Morgan et al., 2008
Adherence to conventions	6	Few 2006; Gao et al., 2006; Schooley et al, 2011
Minimalist aesthetics	6	Few, 2006; Gao et al., 2006; Tufte, 2001
In-line guidance and training	4	Few, 2006; Gao et al., 2006; Zhan et al., 2005
User workload reduction	3	Gao et al., 2006; Schooley et al., 2011
GIS interface	3	Schooley et al., 2006; Zhan et al., 2005

Designing dashboards as customizable, actionable "launch pads" is the guideline that was mentioned most often. This theme is concerned with allowing users to drill down into different aspects of the dashboard and initiate actions based on the data presented to them. A sample best practice of this theme would be "Design for use as a launch pad" (Few, 2006).

The second most common theme is "support correct data interpretation", which is related to helping the user understand information and perform actions correctly. An example of a best practice would be "Support meaningful comparisons. Discourage meaningless comparisons" (Few, 2006).

Third, the "information aggregation" theme places an emphasis on condensing data to show only a high-level view of the indicators most important to the users. A sample of this theme is "Based on the back-end algorithm, the level and trend of the overall influenza activity are shown in the top left" (Cheng et al., 2011).

Further, the influenza monitoring dashboard in Cheng et al., 2011's study synthesizes five different data types/sources to provide an overview of disease activity from multiple perspectives. It provides drill-down functionality for each individual data stream, a one-sentence summary of the level and trend of influenza activity, and general recommendations to decrease the flu risk.

Similarly, STATDash provides several different data streams that allow for activity monitoring: They are Alerts sent to clients, Alerts received from clients, Images stored by clients, and the Network stability statuses.

3   Applying the Guidelines

We designed a dashboard interface for STATPack™ (STATDash) based on the guidelines we selected in our meta-review discussed above and also we used our own knowledge and expertise where there were gaps (Fruhling, 2006; Lechner et al., 2013; Read et al., 2009). Figures 1 and 2 show the same STATDash, but at different states. **Error! Reference source not found.** shows the overview screen, while **Error! Reference source not found.** shows the location drill-down screen.

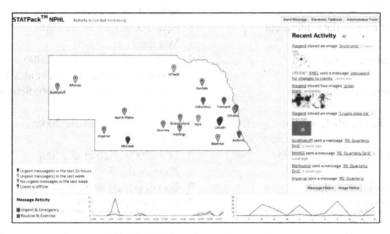

Fig. 1. Dashboard overview screen

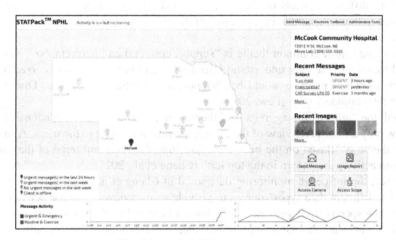

Fig. 2. Location drill-down screen

A discussion on how the selected guidelines were operationalized is presented in the next sections. We begin with the customizable, actionable, "launch pad" guideline.

3.1   Customizable, Actionable "Launch Pad"

The customizable, actionable "launch pad" guidelines (Cheng et al., 2011; Zhan et al., 2005) were implemented by having all surveillance data required by the state public health laboratory experts displayed on a single screen. This was achieved by showing the status of each location with a color code on a map. We also included two charts below the map that show the history of alert activity at various intervals: yearly, monthly or daily.

Activity is organized by routine/exercise and emergency/urgent alerts to allow the user to determine if a state of urgency exists. The right side of the screen shows details of recent activity (recent alerts received, clients becoming unavailable, and images stored). This list can be filtered to show only activity of a certain type. In addition, users can customize the thresholds used to determine the color a location is displayed in.

The dashboard is also actionable (Few, 2006; Morgan et al., 2008). Clicking on a location marker allows the user to view details about that location, such as recent alerts and images, contact information, and access to advanced functionality. In addition, clicking on a point in one of the charts shows the details of that data point.

These dashboard features require few touches/clicks to navigate the system (Schooley et al., 2011). When a user wanted to send an alert to a client in the old user interface, they had to click on the "Send Message" button, then locate the name of the client in a long list, select it, and then type their message.

3.2   Supporting Correct Data Interpretation

As discussed earlier, in the context of dashboard design, this guideline focuses on users correctly and accurately interpreting the data. It also includes that the data is analyzed correctly by the developers and displayed accordingly. By following this guideline, user errors can be reduced (Few, 2006). In our dashboard design, this is instantiated by allowing the user to compare current activity level charts to average activity over the life of the system for the respective time period. Since some disease activity can be seasonal, this allows the specialists to make direct comparisons to historical data.

3.3   Information Aggregation

As mentioned above, aggregated information is data that has been gathered and expressed in a summary form, often for the purposes of statistical analysis. In our example, the STATDash shows information aggregated at different levels. At the top of the screen, a statement informs the user about the overall level and trend of activity. The map allows a user to see activity by location at a glance by implementing a traffic light metaphor and different colors to convey meaning (Cheng et al., 2011; Morgan et al., 2008). The section on the right hand side shows more detailed, actionable information about the most recent -- most urgent -- activity. Finally, the two charts at the bottom give a summary of historical data. These four elements give a non-redundant, condensed, complete picture of disease activity following the guidelines presented by Few (2006) and Gao et al. (2006).

3.4   Adherence to Convention

Adherence to convention can be thought of as systems adhering to the same look and feel across the entire user interface and using familiar, established user interface elements. Convention was observed by retaining the same principles for core functionality as before, including alert meta-data and transmission. The terminology and labels within the system have also remained the same. Familiar symbols such as the map markers and traffic light color coding were employed. As such, it will be easy for users to learn to use the new dashboard, as they will already be accustomed to the functionality and terminology (Gao et al., 2006).

3.5   Minimalist Aesthetics

The design of the dashboard follows a minimalist aesthetic approach by reducing non-data "ink" that does not convey information (such as graphics and "eye candy") (Few, 2006; Tufte, 2001). One example is the map, which has been reduced to only show the outline of the state on a gray background and the locations of the clients as labeled markers.

As a second measure, colors have been used conservatively (Few, 2006). Most of the interface is white, gray, or black. Colors are only used to convey information, such as using colored markers for clients to indicate their status, highlighting urgent/emergency alerts in red, and showing the data lines in the charts as blue (routine and exercise alerts) or red (urgent and emergency alerts).

Advanced functionality such as sending alerts to a specific client is hidden from the initial view of the dashboard, thus reducing clutter and complexity (Gao et al., 2006).

3.6   In-Line Guidance and Training

In-line guidance is provided by choosing easily understandable labels (Few, 2006) that are based on the previous design and already familiar to the users. In cases where this was not possible, labels were chosen with user feedback.

Visual feedback to the user's actions is also important (Gao et al., 2006). This is achieved through a variety of means, such as dimming the other location markers on the map when one location is selected.

3.7   User Workload Reduction

The dashboard by design is intended to reduce the user's workload both cognitively and physically. A lot of this is accomplished through minimalist design and information aggregation.

3.8   GIS Interface

The map in the center of the dashboard provides situational awareness of disease activity and trends. This graphical display is combined with the performance indicators above and below the map for a multi-faceted view of the current status (Schooley et al., 2011). The map allows users to pan and zoom and select clients to view detailed information and interact with them.

3.9   Content

Every alert and image stored within the system is identified by its source and location, time of occurrence, and status (emergency, urgent, routine, or exercise) (Fruhling, 2006; Turoff et al., 2004). This allows users to clearly determine the source and severity of an alert and respond to it accordingly in the case of an emergency.

Up-to-date information that is updated whenever a user loads a screen (Turoff et al., 2004) is of great importance in an emergency response medical system and fully implemented in STATDash, to ensure all users have the most current information available to them for decision making.

3.10   Guidelines

Of the guidelines reviewed for this study, there were two guidelines that were not as salient for PHERIS dashboards; rather they are just best overall practices. "Adherence to conventions" is certainly a useful heuristic for designing dashboards, but it is too general to be included in a set of best practices specific to PHERIS dashboards. In a similar vein, providing "in-line guidance and training" is also too general. This guideline is applicable not only to this specific kind of dashboard, but to all computer systems in general (Nielsen, 1993).

4   Proposed New Dashboard Design Guidelines

The guidelines we found in our literature search were helpful in many ways; however, we identified two gaps. Therefore, we are proposing the following new guidelines.

4.1   Minimize Cognitive Processing

This guideline seeks to reduce the users' cognitive load by including all indicators on a single screen without a need for navigation. In addition, charts and graphs should be used where sensible to show trends visually and for quick interpretation.

4.2   Use Temporal Trend Analysis Techniques

Temporal relationships and comparisons are important in recognizing patterns, trends, and potential issues. Therefore, the dashboard should have temporal capabilities to show trends over time and in relationship to historical data. In addition, information should be presented in a priority order based on recentness, urgency, and impact.

5   Conclusion

In conclusion, our analysis found several of the guidelines cited in the literature to be appropriate and useful for public health surveillance dashboard design, yet, we also discovered there were missing guidelines. Therefore, we propose two new guidelines: minimize cognitive processing, and use of temporal trend analysis techniques. A limitation of this study is that we have not validated the two proposed guidelines nor have we conducted any user usability evaluation on our proposed STATDash design. Therefore, the next phase of our research is to involve users in conducting various usability evaluations on STATDash.

References

1. Centers for Disease Control and Prevention: CDC responds to disease outbreaks 24/7 (2011), http://www.cdc.gov/24-7/cdcfastfacts/diseaseresponse.html
2. Cheng, C.K.Y., Ip, D.K.M., Cowling, B.J., Ho, L.M., Leug, G.M., Lau, E.H.Y.: Digital dashboard design using multiple data streams for disease surveillance with influenza surveillance as an example. Journal of Medical Internet Research 13, e85 (2011)
3. Diaper, D.: Task Analysis for Human-Computer Interaction. Ellis Horwood, Chichester (1989)
4. Dolan, J.G., Veazie, P.J., Russ, A.J.: Development and initial evaluation of a treatment decision dashboard. BMC Medical Informatics and Decision Making 13, 51 (2013)
5. Few, S.: Information Dashboard Design. O'Reilly, Sebastopol (2006)
6. Fruhling, A.: Examining the critical requirements, design approaches and evaluation methods for a public health emergency response system. Communications of the Association for Information Systems 18, 1 (2006)
7. Gao, T., Kim, M.I., White, D., Alm, A.M.: Iterative user-centered design of a next generation patient monitoring system for emergency medical response. In: AMIA Annual Symposium Proceedings, pp. 284–288 (2006)
8. Institute of Medicine: The Future of Public Health. National Academy Press (1988)
9. Kintz, M.: A semantic dashboard language for a process-oriented dashboard design methodology. In: Proceedings of the 2nd International Workshop on Model-Based Interactive Ubiquitous Systems, Copenhagen, Denmark (2012)
10. Lechner, B., Fruhling, A., Petter, S., Siy, H.: The chicken and the pig: User involvement in developing usability heuristics. In: Proceedings of the Nineteenth Americas Conference on Information Systems, Chicago, IL (2013)
11. Morgan, M.B., Brandstetter IV, B.F., Lionetti, D.M., Richardson, J.S., Chang, P.J.: The radiology digital dashboard: effects on report turnaround time. Journal of Digital Imaging 21, 50–58 (2008)
12. Nielsen, J.: Usability Engineering. Academic Press, San Diego (1993)
13. Read, A., Tarrell, A., Fruhling, A.: Exploring user preferences for dashboard menu design. In: Proceedings of the 42nd Hawaii International Conference on System Sciences, pp. 1–10 (2009)
14. Schmidt, K.: Functional analysis instrument. In: Schaefer, G., Hirschheim, R., Harper, M., Hansjee, R., Domke, M., Bjoern-Andersen, N. (eds.) Functional Analysis of Office Requirements: A Multiperspective Approach, pp. 261–289. Wiley, Chichester (1988)

15. Schooley, B., Hilton, N., Abed, Y., Lee, Y., Horan, T.: Process improvement and consumer-oriented design of an inter-organizational information system for emergency medical response. In: Proceedings of the 44th Hawaii International Conference on System Sciences, pp. 1–10 (2011)
16. Tufte, E.R.: The Visual Display of Quantitative Information, 2nd edn. Graphics Press, Cheshire (2001)
17. Turnock, B.J.: Public Health: What It Is and How It Works. Jones and Bartlett Publishers, Sudbury (2009)
18. Turoff, M., Chumer, M., Van de Walle, B., Yao, X.: The design of a dynamic emergency response management information system (DERMIS). Journal of Information Technology Theory and Application 5, 1–35 (2004)
19. World Health Organization: Public health (2014), http://www.who.int/trade/glossary/story076/en/
20. Zhan, B.F., Lu, Y., Giordano, A., Hanford, E.J.: Geographic information system (GIS) as a tool for disease surveillance and environmental health research. In: Proceedings of the 2005 International Conference on Services, Systems and Services Management, pp. 1465–1470 (2005)

Information Technology Service Delivery
to Small Businesses

Mei Lu, Philip Corriveau, Luke Koons, and Donna Boyer

Intel Corporation, United States
{mei.lu,philip.j.corriveau,luke.e.koons,
donna.j.boyer}@intel.com

Abstract. This paper reports findings from a study conducted to evaluate Intel's Service Delivery Platform for small businesses. The Service Delivery Platform adopted a Software-as-a-Service (SaaS) approach, and aimed to deliver information technology (IT) services on a pay-as-you-go subscription model. The majority of small business decision makers found the solution appealing. Nevertheless, wide adoption of the solution will be contingent on quality and breadth of service offerings, cost, reliability of service delivery, and responsiveness of support.

Keywords: Software as Service, information technology.

1 Introduction

Small businesses in all countries are an important part of the economy [2, 4]. In the USA, more than 98% of all firms are small businesses with less than one hundred employees; these businesses employ about 36% of the total work force (USA census data, 2004). They represent a market segment that is eager to explore or grow their business with the help of new information technology. From 2004 to 2008 we visited more than 50 small businesses to understand their technology needs in various areas, including collaboration, information management, and IT manageability. We found that IT landscapes in small businesses were smaller, but just as complex, as those in large organizations. Small business needs included networks, servers, personal computers, phones, printers, and many other hardware equipment. Like larger businesses, they needed software applications for productivity, business process automation, and internal and external collaboration. However, they were much more constrained than larger businesses in terms of resources, knowledge, and expertise regarding information technology. Small business owners consistently told us that they had challenges in understanding and keeping up with the newest developments in technology, and in selecting the best solutions for their businesses. They also had difficulty quickly deploying solutions, maintaining a highly managed computing environment, and providing end-user support. Many small businesses depended on external service providers for IT management. These service providers were looking for solutions that

F.F.-H. Nah (Ed.): HCIB/HCII 2014, LNCS 8527, pp. 60–67, 2014.
© Springer International Publishing Switzerland 2014

could help them to build trusted relationships more effectively with customers, and to manage IT for different businesses more efficiently.

The Service Delivery Platform is designed to address these needs and challenges for business owners and for service providers. The platform adopts a Software-as-a-Service [1] approach. It aggregates services from different vendors, and aims to deliver the services to small businesses with a "pay-as-you-go" subscription model. Services here intend to cover applications that businesses may need for their daily operations, including IT managerial, employee productivity and business processes. The platform provides a web-based portal that is targeted to two types of users – 1) business owners and decision makers, who will use the portal to conduct research on IT solutions, and review recommendations and feedback from other users; 2) Internal or external IT administrators, who manage services and provide support for end users. The portal supports key user tasks such as service subscription, device management, status monitoring, and remote trouble shooting and support. Key portal components include:

- *Service catalog*: Descriptions of platform service offerings, including pricing, screen shots, technical details, user reviews, and user manuals or instructions.
- *Control panel*: A view to allow business owners or IT administrations to remotely add or remove services via a subscription to their clients' end-user computers.
- *"Pay-as-you-go"* subscription service. It allows businesses to pay for services based on the number of users and length of time they use the services. Services can be started or cancelled any time from the web portal.
- *Status monitoring dashboard:*   Allows owners or IT administrators to view all of their devices, and remotely monitor the status of service installations or operations on different devices.

This research was conducted to evaluate an early prototype of the Service Deliver Platform with small business owners and their internal or external IT administrators. In-depth interviews were conducted with twenty businesses in several locations across the United States, including New Jersey, New York, and Oregon. The primary goal was to understand their key perceptions regarding the value of such a solution, intention to adopt, decision factors, and potential adoption hurdles. To support further design and development of the web portal, the research also tried to understand perceived usefulness of its key features, and priorities of potential service offerings on the platform.

2   Method

Several participant recruiting criteria were designed to identify businesses as potential early adopters or early majority on Rogers' innovation adoption curve [3]. The goal was to identify businesses with potential needs for IT services, and at the same time, that could provide objective and balanced views on the values of the Service Delivery Platform. The criteria include:

- *Business verticals*: proprietary market research data suggested different industry verticals had different levels of spending on IT services. Four verticals that had high and middle levels of spending in IT services were selected for the interviews, including 1) professional services; 2) retail; 3) finance, insurance & real estate; and 4) wholesale and distribution.
- *Attitude towards IT*: during the recruiting process, businesses owners were asked about their use and attitudes toward technology. Businesses that were selected for the interview regarded technology as important or somewhat important, and had been using technology enthusiastically or pragmatically.
- *Current IT service models*: the selected businesses represented two types of IT support models whereby IT was mainly 1) self-managed by either part time or full time IT staff; or 2) managed by outsourced service companies.

The two-hour interviews were conducted on the businesses' sites with both the business owners/decision maker and internal or external IT staff.

After general discussions about their business background and current IT practices, the solution of Service Delivery Platform was presented to the interviewees with storyboards and visual paper prototypes or mockups. Afterward, those interviewed were asked to 1) rate usefulness of major features of the platform and describe how the features might be used in their organizations, and 2) review different potential service offerings in the catalog and discuss whether they were interested in subscribe to different IT services from the platform 3) discuss overall appeal of the solution, adoption hurdles and concerns.

3 Results

Out of the twenty businesses we interviewed, fifteen rated the platform solution as appealing or very appealing. The businesses expressed general interest in subscribing to services in areas related to security and protection, employee productivity (e.g., word processing and E-mail), and external service provider support. However, the businesses also pointed out that their adoption would be contingent on a number of factors, including cost, the breadth and quality of service catalog offerings, reliability of service delivery, and responsiveness of support.

3.1   Key Perceived Values

The businesses identified a number of values and benefits in the Service Delivery Platform. Key values include *ease of service deployment, ease of control and management, pay-as-you-go flexibility, and potentials for preventive management.*

Ease of Service Deployment. We frequently heard in previous small business related studies about the difficulty in keeping up with technology development. That sentiment was reiterated in this study. As one business owner said, "*our old technologies worked just fine, but we were often forced to upgrade (because vendors no long provided support to old technologies).*" Or, as other business owners said, "*the most* *challenging is trying to keep up with what's available as far as new equipment and what we can use"*, and *"it is time-consuming (to do research). I have no idea on what is out there."*

The key features of the Service Delivery Platform appear to address this challenge. One key benefit that business owners and IT staff identified was that the platform potentially allowed easy research, and much quicker decision or deployment of IT solutions.

The business owners viewed the service catalog as a place where they could conduct research on new technology, view opinions of other business owners and recommendations from other users. In addition, the platform provided a mechanism for them to easily experiment with different potential solutions. For example, with minimal commitment they could easily install an application on one or several computer and experiment with it. The ability to cancel services at any time gave users more confidence to try out different services.

Ease of Control. Another key perceived benefit is ease of control and management. IT staff liked the remote subscription service. Especially for external IT staff, the ability to remotely install and uninstall services would allow them to more efficiently provide support to customers in different businesses. They were most interested in features allowing them to efficiently manage services for multiple computers. For example:

- Creating an image or configuration with a set of various services, and then applying the image to a computer to install multiple services together.
- Copying the service configuration of one computer to another one: for example, when a user's computer needed to upgrading to a new service configuration. As an IT staff said: *"The hardest thing when upgrading a computer, is to get all that information back over (to the new computer)."*

In addition, the portal provided a centralized location for IT staff to track assets and licenses, allowing businesses to view all their devices and the software installed on each device.

A number of businesses mentioned current challenges in tracking software licenses. As one owner said: *"one of the challenges we run into is trying to keep track of everything we have, all the software versions, all the licenses we have, the latest downloads. That becomes extremely cumbersome."* Another IT staff said: *"it is huge being able to consolidate all your clients into one view."* The businesses pointed out that the visibility also allowed them to more effectively plan for future technology needs.

Flexibility. For the subscription-based payment model, the businesses identified two main potential benefits: flexibility and cost saving. The ability to subscribe to or to terminate service subscription at any time allowed businesses to pay for what they were actually using. It enabled businesses to easily access expensive applications that they did not use frequently, or not all of the time, such as video and image editing applications. The users also identified the benefits of easy decommissioning of services from devices. As one owner said *"That's the hardest thing for a small guy (to decommission devices); Jay leaves the company tomorrow, his laptop is sitting there, no one's using it, I want to be able to turn Jay's office just in a manner that says Jay's not using it."* Another owned pointed out that *"it is a much better approach than the yearly commitment type."*

Preventive Management. Another key perceived benefit was that the Service Delivery Platform would allow businesses to shift from reactive IT management models to *proactive and preventive management models*. It was observed that IT management in these businesses was mostly reactive, in the sense that IT administrators acted when users approached them with problems. The Service Delivery Platform offered features such as asset tracking, device status monitoring, service status monitoring, and service activity support. With these features, businesses would be more aware of what devices were in the environment, how they were used, and how everything was running. As a result, those interviewed said they would be able to *"address issues before catastrophic impact," "more effectively anticipate and plan for user needs," "easily create a budget for IT services,"* and *"do more fire prevention instead of fire-fighting."*

3.2   Usefulness Ratings

The participants were asked to rate usefulness of the main features on the platform, using a five-point scale with 5 being "very useful", and 1 being "not useful at all." Table 1 summarized the highest rated features. These ratings were consistent with participants' discussions on key values of the platform. The most highly rated features were related to ease of service deployment, preventive management, centralized tracking and control.

Both business owners and their IT administrators were interested in ability to quickly deploy services with a "service image or profile", or by "duplicating service configuration from one device to another." The values of these features were abilities to quickly provision or deploy a computer for a user. Similarly, when a computer was no longer used, for example, after a user had left the company, businesses wanted to quickly "decommission" the computer so that they would not pay for the services. The features of "real time service status" and "device status" were found useful because they allowed internal or external IT administrator to closely monitor their computing environments and take proactive actions if needed. Finally, the businesses owners liked the ability to "track all their assets" via the portal, and the ability to receive and review a "service activity report" to understand what services they had received, and how much they had cost; the information would be useful for creating a budget plan for the future.

3.3   Interest in Services

After the discussion of key features on the platform and portal, those interviewed were invited to review potential offerings in the service catalog. The service offerings were related to four categories, including employee productivity, collaboration, security and protection, managed service provider support, backup and restore. The participants were asked to indicate whether they would be interested in purchasing or in subscribing to the services from the Service Delivery Platform. Table 2 summarized their interest in purchasing services.

Table 1. Highest rated platform features (n=20)

Features	Rating
Real time service status	4.4
Device asset tracking on the portal	4.2
Service configuration duplication - Allow quick deployment of PC to replace an old one	4.2
Service image or profile	4.1
Device status information	4.0
Service activity report	4.0
Decommission	4.0

Table 2. Businesses' interest in different services (n=16)

Services	Interested in buying (%)	Services	Interested in buying (%)
Office applications	81	VoIP	44
PC anti-virus	81	Local backup	38
Email anti-virus	81	Database	31
Email anti-spam	75	Remote firewall	31
Intrusion detection	75	BI	19
Remote backup	69	Accounting	19
Email	69	CRM	13
File sharing	50	Project management	13
VPN	44	Content management	13

The businesses were most interested in services related to security and protection, and basic employee productivity including office, email and file sharing applications. High levels of interests in security and protection services were consistent with the participants' discussions on their current challenges. One major challenge pointed out by several different businesses was protection from malware or spam email from the Internet. As one IT staff said *"A big problem is people download some programs that make their PC not working. It (PC) slows down and becomes unusable. It is very time consuming to solve the problem."* As another business pointed out, *"Biggest thing we have to watch is e-mail spam... What the server spends most of its time doing is rejecting spam. .. 5,000 to 8,000 collectively a day we get hit with."*

In contrast, the businesses expressed lower levels of interests (<50%) in more sophisticated applications such as voice over IP (VoIP), database, business intelligence (BI), virtual private network (VPN), remote firewalls, project management, customer relationship management, and content management. The main reasons given for the lower level of interests were: lack of needs, and existence of similar applications that they were not likely to replace in the near term.

3.4   Potential Adoption Hurdles

Even though the businesses demonstrated enthusiasm in the solution of Service Delivery Platform, they pointed out several potential adoption hurdles.

- *Cost*: the interviewees could perceive the cost saving benefits from the subscription-based service model, nevertheless, they mentioned that they would carefully compare its cost to that of more traditional purchase models or shop at multiple places to look for the prices. It was critical for the platform to provide compelling pricing models so that businesses could reduce the total cost of IT operations.
- *Quality and breadth of service offerings*: Even though the businesses expressed more levels of interests in different services, they expected the service catalog to offer a wide collection of high quality of services. The participants mentioned that the best adoption entry points were when businesses were purchasing new computers or a new business was formed. At the time, they expected the service catalog to provide services for all basic computing needs.
- *Reliability*: Businesses expected the platform to deliver and install services in a highly reliable fashion, and that the services would not cause any disruption to PC performance. As one owner said. *"We cannot afford any downtime -- every minute we will be losing money."*
- *Responsiveness of support*: Business owners expected a very quick support response, a response as fast as they currently received from internal staff or local service providers. *"They should be just one phone call or one email away."*

4   Discussions

Small businesses have large and complex demands for information technology, nonetheless lack expertise and resources to stay abreast with the newest developments. From this study, small businesses experience numerous pain points with traditional models of software or service management, including research, purchasing, deployment, license management, maintenance contracts, and expensive upgrades. Software-as-a-service approaches appear to have the advantage of provide the simplicity and flexibility small businesses desire. In this study, business owners demonstrated willingness to trust a reliable external service provider for their computing needs, and adopt a subscription-based model for their software and support. Nevertheless, both service providers and businesses owners will need infrastructure support in order to achieve the required reliability, efficiency and effectiveness for service delivery. The Service Delivery Platform is intended to be such an infrastructure that will connect service vendors, end users, and support providers. The value propositions and key features of the Service Delivery Platform were well received by both businesses owners and internal/external IT staff in the study. Such a platform will need both a compelling business model and user experience to achieve wide adoption.

It is critical that it appropriately addresses needs of both business owners and service/support providers. Key user experience needs for business owners include:

- A service catalog with information tailored to business owners. Typically they are not technology experts and are not interested in technical details.
- Easy communication with external service providers, for example, the ability to receive reports on what services have been provided, proactive and tailored recommendations on what technology might be useful for the businesses.
- Quick deployment, with the ability to easily experiment with different solutions, and then quickly deploy solutions.

For external service providers or internal IT staff, key needs include:

- Technical details in service catalog as they need much more detailed information on different services offered in the catalog.
- Well integrated service management tools, including asset tracking, service subscription management, status monitoring, and device remote control for management or trouble shooting purposes.
- Service bundling and packaging that provides the ability to easily create different service bundling or packages for different business customers or end users.
- Customer management and support tools for external service providers that support customer management, such as billing, support ticket management, and communication with customers.

References

1. Bennett, K., Layzell, P., Budgen, D., Brereton, P., Macaulay, L., Munro, M.: Service-Based Software: The Future for Flexible Software. In: Proceedings of Seventh Asia-Pacific Software Engineering Conference, pp. 214–221 (2000)
2. Berranger, P., Tucker, D., Jones, L.: Internet Diffusion in Creative Micro-business: Identifying Change Agent Characteristics as Critical Success Factors. Journal of Organizational Computing and Electronic Commerce 11(3), 197–214 (2001)
3. Rogers, E.M.: New Product Adoption and Diffusion. Journal of Consumer Research 2, 290–301 (1976)
4. Thong, J.Y.L.: An Integrated Model of Information Systems Adoption in Small Businesses. Journal of Management Information Systems 15(4), 187–214 (1999)

Charting a New Course for the Workplace with an Experience Framework

Faith McCreary, Marla Gómez, Derrick Schloss, and Deidre Ali

Information Technology Group, IT User Experience,
Intel Corporation, Santa Clara, CA USA
{faith.a.mccreary,marla.a.gomez,derrick.j.schloss}@intel.com
deidre.ali@emerson.com

Abstract. Like many, our company had a wealth of data about business users that included both big data by-products of operations (e.g., transactions) and outputs of traditional User Experience (UX) methods (e.g. interviews). To fully leverage the combined intelligence of this rich data, we had to aggregate big data and the outputs of traditional UX together. By connecting user stories to big data, we could test the generalizability of insights of qualitative studies against the larger world of business users and what they actually do. Similarly, big data benefited from the rich contextual insights found in more traditional UX studies. In this paper, we present a hybrid analysis approach that allowed us to leverage the combined intelligence of big data and outputs of UX methods. This approach allowed us to define an over-arching experience framework that provided actionable insights across the enterprise. We will discuss the underlying methodology, key learnings and how the work is revolutionizing experience decision making within the enterprise.

Keywords: UX Strategy, Big Data, Qualitative Data, User Research.

1 Introduction

Today's enterprise experience is often a fragmented one spanning multiple vendors, devices, products, and platforms. Enterprise users shift between very different interfaces which both frustrates them and makes them less efficient. This problem is exacerbated by the number of teams needed to develop and manage the enterprise experience, usually dozens of teams that span the globe who often operate independently of each other with little opportunity to discuss how the pieces fit together to shape the enterprise experience. After years of trying to wrestle the individual components of the enterprise experience into some semblance of a coherent whole, Intel IT took on an audacious goal to define a One IT experience that met employee needs and spanned its many products and services.

Like many businesses, our IT shop had a wealth of data about business users that included both big data by-products of operations (e.g., transactions) and by-products of traditional User Experience (UX) methods (e.g. interviews). This data included over 700 hours of user narratives, 20,000 surveys, and 18 million transactions. In this

F.F.-H. Nah (Ed.): HCIB/HCII 2014, LNCS 8527, pp. 68–79, 2014.
© Springer International Publishing Switzerland 2014

paper, we present a hybrid analysis approach that allowed us to leverage the combined intelligence of big data and outputs of UX methods to define an over-arching experience framework that is being used to frame the One IT experience and seed human-centric transformation within the enterprise. We will discuss the underlying methodology, decompose the framework, and provide examples of how it is being used by the larger IT shop. Lastly, we will map the evolution of this effort over the last two years, share learnings and insights from our journey, and discuss the benefits of having a data-driven, re-usable and over-arching experience vision to guide enterprise decision-making.

2   Background

The data that enterprises collect every day is a storehouse of information about business users. It includes enterprise transactions, social data, support tickets, web logs, internet searches, clickstream data, and much more. Enterprises often manage data related to users in silos around infrastructure or application support. Similarly, analysis efforts focus on identifying problems related to the silo. Despite the rich information contained in this data, it is seldom used to improve the cross-enterprise experience of business users. Similar to how outside corporations examine the customer usage and interactions (e.g. Amazon, Google) to tailor the experience of purchasing or support for customers [1], enterprises could utilize knowledge about employees to enhance their business experience. However, tools to derive insights from big data are immature, especially with respect to UX; and analysis is hampered by the fact that most of this data is incompatible, incomprehensible, and messy to tie together. Further, even when this data is connected, big data is a backwards look at what has been. It cannot help enterprises fully understand what motivates the user behavior that they track or understand the full context in which it occurred. It does not help enterprises spot future looking opportunities for providing new value to their users, design a better solution, or better engage their users; and those places are where user experience has the most potential to add value to the enterprise. Big data lacks the contextual insights necessary for user-centric design and innovation.

Fortunately, where big data falls short, more traditional UX methods excel. Many UX methods rely on user narratives or observations that come from interviews, participatory design sessions, social media, or open-ended comments on surveys. They provide the qualitative color that yields the richer understanding of the holistic experience necessary for experience innovation or improvement. While traditional UX has a wide variety of methods (e.g. affinity diagrams, qualitative coding) to help UX professionals transform qualitative data into insights, they often only talk to small numbers of users which puts their generalizability in question in the corporate environment. In addition, the output of these methods does not lend itself to easy mixing with big data; nor are user narratives usually analyzed to the point where underlying structures are visible [2]. And, much like the transactional data the enterprise collects, data collected by UX professionals often remains siloed and is not re-used or used to form a larger understanding of the enterprise experience.

Leveraging the combined intelligence of big data and traditional UX data can be a daunting task as the data sets lack connections, or a way to pull together the diverse data and connect to specific aspects of the experience. Sociotechnical systems theory and macro ergonomics offer a way of connecting disparate data and provide a theoretical model for understanding the holistic user experience. They have been used successfully to holistically assess how well a technology fits its users and their work environment in relationship to enterprise priorities using diverse data types [3, 4]. They are especially useful for examining the business experience, as success requires IT understand how their "technology" impacts other elements of the user's world.

3   Growing an Experience Framework for the Enterprise

Back in 2011, IT, in partnership with HR, conducted over 200 interviews and 300 participatory design sessions focused on understanding the experience of employees. Since then, IT has increased the data set by 275%. The resulting multi gigabyte data set covers more than 100K employees across Intel and around the world, more than 700 hours of user stories and 18 million user transactions. It provides a high confidence, big data look at the business experience of employees, with the margin of error for the qualitative sample at less than .0495 and less than .0002 for the transactional sample [5]. Growing an experience framework from this massive data set necessitated that we explore and understand hidden relationships within the data sets. This section discusses the various methods that we used to elicit insights and describes the complexity of managing the underlying data.

3.1   Growing Connections in User Transactional Big Data

Enterprises collect large amounts of user data in terms of user demographics (e.g. role, organization) and as by-products of user transactions (e.g., portal usage, support tickets). Aggregated together they provide a holistic picture of the enterprise experience. While some data is considered confidential (e.g., age), other data is more publicly available (e.g., app use). Regardless, all data is typically protected in enterprises which necessitates both legal and privacy negotiation before aggregating the data. Prior to making any attempt to integrate the data sets, the raw data was anonymized by replacing all employee identifiers with an encrypted unique identifier.

When we initially went to gather the user data, we naively expected an enterprise-level data map that would help us locate relevant data. Instead, the process was a treasure hunt for data that could enrich our understanding of employee usage of enterprise products and services. The data was a mix of structured and unstructured data. Data formats were sometimes undocumented, and often inconsistent within and between datasets, with formatting often changing over time resulting in inconsistencies within a single dataset. The management of structured versus unstructured data meant tradeoffs between what was known and what could be feasibly stored or analyzed. We regularly exceeded the limits of our data storage and analysis capabilities and sometimes had to distill raw data into meaningful summary data. For instance, support tickets were reduced to total number of tickets and mean time between tickets. This mountain of data was then distilled into individual employee usage footprints using the coded identifiers. By organizing the data in terms of individual users, we could more easily discern individual patterns, allowing us to more easily integrate new quantitative information as it was discovered.

3.2   Growing Connections in the User Stories

User narratives were captured through interviews, contextual inquiry, participatory design sessions, support tickets, and surveys. Open-ended questions framed discussion of the enterprise experience spanning key sociotechnical elements related to the user's environment, technology, social setting, and organization. The qualitative data provided rich, near verbatim narratives of users' experience. As with earlier work, we took the narratives as a direct representation of experience or critical part of a user's underlying mental model [2]. Each user narrative was associated with an anonymous identifier to connect the narratives to the quantitative data.

We manually coded user narratives using a mix of exploratory and structured coding. For the free-form narratives, we started with the smallest actionable chunks (e.g. low-level requirements) and built the coding structure from the bottom up rather than pre-defining the coding. A single narrative was coded at a time, with the exploratory coding structure iteratively refined as analysis progressed. One coder coded the majority of the narratives, with one other coder doing the exploratory coding for several dozen. Additionally there were several feeder coders who helped build the structured branches of the model (e.g., social networks). Coders regularly met and went thru an affinity diagram type activity [7] to consolidate coding structures. The narratives guided the coding structure but we also coded certain attributes including

- Specifics of user activities (e.g. key steps, triggers, success criteria)
- If the narrative detailed a positive or negative incident from the user perspective
- Environmental factors (e.g., workspace, location)
- Underlying technology (e.g. suite of tools, enterprise system, process, or device)
- Individual user characteristics (e.g., attitudes, motivators)
- Social factors (e.g., social network)
- Organizational factors (e.g. how work was organized)

The final coding tree represented the users' over-arching mental model of the experience [6] and defined the experience users wanted the enterprise to deliver. It mapped patterns of user behavior and needs, with detail to get to requirements. We then looked for meta-patterns, or schemas shared by enterprise users, again using an affinity diagram type exercise [6] as a way of data sense-making. The derived meta-patterns became the foundation of the experience framework.

3.3   Discovering Patterns in the Combined Data

We then connected the narratives with our "big" enterprise data using the coded identifiers. Rather than merge the whole narratives as unstructured data, we defined summary measures based on the coding framework. These summary measures connected the user stories with the larger dataset to help us discover patterns across datasets. For each node in the first few levels, we specified two summary measures: (1) total number of references coded for the node, and (2) number of references coded for the node that were negative (*i.e.*, pain point). Using correlational methods, mathematically best "fit" patterns were identified in the combined dataset based on similarities in how employees used and talked about enterprise products and services. We used non-parametric methods as the data was often non-normal. Cross-references between the datasets allowed us to find connections and validate our findings from other data sets [5]. This process was highly iterative with a continuous cycle of data and user research. By making the combined dataset a living thing, we could add in more as needed and it ensured the enterprise has a constant pulse of user needs, can strategically identify key opportunities, and can respond more quickly when new needs arise. The final best "fit" patterns became the building blocks of the experience framework and will be discussed more in the next section.

4   Bringing the Framework to Life with Stories

The experience framework is a conceptual map of the desired user experience and our intent was for the framework to become the common language and shared framework for designing and evaluating enterprise services for the Intel user. In order to facilitate the ability of product teams to use the framework, we introduced large-scale, layered storytelling to unify the supporting framework collateral. The underlying stories focus on particular elements of the dataset and ignore the rest. Strung together they map the desired enterprise experience but individually only tell a piece. The data set is too large and diverse to be told by a single story. Users of the experience framework take these stories and data to create their own stories relevant to their product; many stories are possible from the same data.

Different framework elements provide different insights. *Themes* define the enterprise experience vision that spans the many products and services provided by Intel IT. *Segments* define the user groups that must be taken into account when creating the enterprise experience, while *influencers* and *activities* help IT understand the role it plays in core enterprise tasks and its impact on the overall experience. Much has been learned about how to most effectively use this information with product teams and the collateral has iteratively evolved to better help teams make sense of the large dataset. Social media is used extensively to socialize the framework; training and workshops were developed to optimize its use by service and portfolio teams.

4.1   Experience Themes

Experience themes describe core user needs that transcend enterprise product or service boundaries. They help service and product teams understand the shared expectations that users have of both the enterprise experience as well as their individual product interactions. To increase the ease of applying a theme to a specific product, each theme was decomposed into *experience qualities* that describe the core theme components and the strategic functionality necessary to bring them to life. They were packaged as quality "trading cards" and are used by teams while setting UX strategy and product roadmaps. Each card details the key use scenarios for that quality and proposed functionality. Experience qualities are further broken down into *experience elements* which document key usage scenarios and requirements users expect in products. This information was packaged in theme vision books and as 8x10 cards to facilitate use during face-to-face design sessions. Three themes, 12 qualities, 59 experience elements and hundreds of requirements detail the desired over-arching experience and are summarized in Table 1.

Table 1. The themes and qualities that framed the envisioned experience [5]

Theme	Qualities
Feed Me I quickly and easily find the information I need to speed my work.	*Seamless* - Transparent. Integrated but flexible. *Simple* - Quick and easy. Language I can understand. *Meaningful* - Points me in the right direction, aids me in sense-making of information, and helps me work smarter. *Proactive* – Push me relevant information, make me aware of changes before they happen, and help me not be surprised.
Connect Me Connect me with the people, resources, and expertise I need to be successful.	*Purposeful* - Together we do work. *Easy* - Easy to work together and connect. *Cooperative* – Larger environment is supportive of me. *Presence* - Always present or at least I feel like you are near.
Know Me My information is known, protected and used to improve provided services.	*Recognized* - Know who I am. *Personalized* - Implicitly know what I need. *Customized* - Give me choices. *Private* - My information is under my control. Always protected and secure.

4.2   Experience Segments

Although themes are based on research with thousands of business users and apply to all enterprise products, how they apply to individual segments may vary. Segments provide target users for product teams to help them design for or tailor the experience for a particular audience. Six segments were identified with some segments further decomposed into sub-segments based on strength of within segment difference. Personas put a face to the experience segments, with each segment having a persona family that represents it. Supporting collateral for the personas summarize their goals and needs, key tasks and behaviors, pain points, usage of enterprise products, and relative priority of different experience qualities. The persona collateral ranges from posters, day-in-the-life, and trading cards.

4.3   Experience Influencers

Experience influencers help product teams assess the relative contribution of core elements of the enterprise world (e.g., IT, HR, physical workspace) on the holistic enterprise experience and detail key pain points associated with a particular element. They also help teams identify potential partners when improving the experience and the potential impact of design changes.

4.4 Core Activities

Core activities provide product teams with specifics in how employees use and interact with enterprise products to accomplish shared tasks common to all employees and provide teams with high-level journey maps for various key activities such as "learn" or "find information." The activity journey maps also describe key segment differences relative to the activity, and provide a jumping off point.

5 Turning Understanding into Experience Transformation

An early adopter of the framework within Intel was the collaboration portfolio, which is comprised of a set of technologies that help Intel employees collaborate and includes social media, meeting tools, meetings spaces, and shared virtual workspaces. The impact of the framework has been wide-ranging, from setting portfolio UX strategy to vendor selection to helping an agile product team move faster. They evolved our original approach by combining use of the experience framework with elements of presumptive design [8]. The experience themes along with what was already known about a particular audience (e.g., field sales) formulated the starting "presumptions" on which designs were based. These starting presumptions were then validated using low cost methods and prototypes. In this section, we provide an overview of how the framework aided their team.

5.1 Providing a Future Vision of Collaboration

The framework provided significant insights about what Intel employees need from the enterprise collaboration experience. We provided teams with experience maps of the employee vision of the future for enterprise collaboration. The key needs included

- Seamless integration of tools, with a single place to access collaborations,
- Consumer grade experiences and increased sense-making across activity streams,
- Easy to find experts thru personalized recommendations and visible connections.
- Increased personal interactions with more in person collaboration, higher fidelity virtual alternatives, and increased access to video.

5.2 Defining Portfolio Strategy

The portfolio team began by identifying intersections between the framework and learnings from deep dive research done by portfolio UX teams. They posted a giant mind map of the experience themes up on the wall and, using sticky notes and highlighters, the team added in data from the deep dive research. The team then used the mindmap and the user needs defined by experience qualities and elements to get the design process started. They isolated the elements relevant to collaboration and completed a heat map to identify how well today's capabilities are meeting target requirements for each collaboration element and how important each of those elements are to enterprise users. Answers to these questions helped the team set their UX roadmap and to prioritize where to focus first. For example, an element critical to initiating collaboration is "Bump into Interesting," which is about helping users serendipitously bump into information or people that are interesting and useful to them. In this case, the team found the portfolio didn't have solutions that were meeting the target requirements.

5.3   Speeding Agile Product Design

Both the framework and deep dive research repeatedly highlighted expert or expertise finding as a key need. The agile-based project team used the experience themes as a starting point for their efforts to rapidly go from concept discussions to prototype. During the initial team kickoff, the team found the strongest affinity with the Connect Me and Feed Me themes which focus on the need to quickly find information and connect employees with expertise. The associated element cards were a starting point for the team's Vision Quest activities and were a catalyst to helping the team form a design hypothesis around core presumptions of what features and capabilities should be included in the solution. Many of the early presumptions the team captured were based on previously gathered user data, and the experience elements.

A series of contextual scenarios were written from the design hypothesis which were then organized to form a high-level "narrative" or persuasive story of the product vision. These were then documented in a storyboard. The experience themes inspired many of the design patterns reflected in the proof-of-concept (POC) prototypes, and the storyboard contained a swim lane the team used to map the experience themes. To validate design presumptions, several intervals of presumptive design tests were conducted with end-users in tandem with design activities. Features not validated as "valuable" by users were removed from the storyboard and product vision. The vision iteratively became more defined and evolved into a 'lightweight' clickable prototype used to engage stakeholders and the technical team in feasibility discussions.

6   Discussion

The experience framework is an innovative way to represent UX research in a way that is consumable within the enterprise. It provides a foundational understanding of the needs of different kinds of employees in spaces that lack the time or resources to invest in more traditional user research. It also mitigates some of the key risks associated with presumptive design [8] by providing a larger holistic look at the experience space and overarching prioritization that helps prevent teams from focusing on the wrong solution to design or ignoring the needs of the larger experience. By taking a "big data" approach to UX and creating an over-arching experience framework that represents core wants and needs employees have of enterprise products and services, we helped those responsible for setting enterprise strategy to incorporate UX more easily in their decision process. By mapping the intersection between experience qualities and elements against portfolio and product roadmaps, teams could identify potential gaps between the planned and desired experience of their products.

Over time, the framework has evolved into a common language and shared understanding of users and design needs that defines the One IT experience vision, spanning the many products and services provided by Intel IT. The supporting collateral helps set enterprise strategy and provides re-usable templates project teams can quickly adapt for their purposes. This shared vision is transforming enterprise products and services resulting in a more cohesive One IT experience and increased velocity of teams. The large-scale, layered storytelling approach made the framework resonate to the larger organization. It allowed framework users to explore the underlying data below the themes to find their own meaning. It also seeds design investigations of features and possible interaction models. This approach to socializing and utilizing the experience framework provides a practical model for the creators of other types of experience themes to more quickly trigger UX transformation in their own spaces.

When working with teams, we discovered creative ways to utilize "big data" past its original role in deriving the framework. By intersecting the over-arching user data with data specific to an enterprise product or service, we discovered new insights about user expectations of their product and how their product needed to align with the over-arching IT experience. The teams gained a much needed understanding of how their users utilized other enterprise products, and their preferences, which helped them more easily make decisions to ensure alignment with the overall user vision.

6.1   Key Learnings

The experience framework is being used across various levels of enterprise products and services to feed UX strategy, technical architecture, and the design of specific products. As a result, new learnings have emerged about how to most effectively integrate into portfolio strategy and design. Key lessons learned include

- Teams should use the qualities to evaluate their own product at the start of using the framework; it is key to learning and provides a baseline for improvement.
- Experience quality cards are paramount for setting vision and strategy. They spark conversation and provide easy functionality checklists to feed UX roadmaps.
- Product teams need experience element cards that provide user requirements, scenarios, and key audience differences once they move from strategy to design.
- Sample designs that embody the experience themes and elements are important to spark new ideas or conversations about how the pattern can be improved.
- Different people have different learning styles and different teams have different ways to work together. If collateral doesn't resonate, iterate, iterate, iterate.
- We have found that generating design ideas is often fastest when you have a hard-copy of element cards and other experience theme collateral so participants can "re-use" collateral elements in discussions and prototyping.

6.2   Key Challenges

There are multiple challenges with an effort of this size. Discovering great experience solutions is as much about collecting and analyzing user data as it is about transforming an organization to actually use it effectively. It's a journey – not a silver bullet. Transforming an organization, a team, or an individual to be 'experience driven' doesn't happen overnight and it doesn't happen just because you have a framework. It's a collaborative process that requires joint partnership and extensive collaboration.

Making the Story Consumable. The size of our dataset made keeping the UX story consumable extremely difficult. How do you turn mountains of user data into a framework that can be digested by a diverse audience? We answered this challenge by developing a multi-layered storytelling approach which included a variety of collateral forms – from vision books to quality cards, element cards, and reference sheets. We also created job aids, including an evaluation spreadsheet that allows teams to grade their solution according to the framework. Even with the wide range of collateral available, teams can still find it unwieldy to work with, especially in the beginning. Newcomers can easily lose their way in the multi-layered story so we work directly with teams to help them understand the framework.

Exponentially Increasing Big Data. In the two years since the introduction of the framework, the underlying data set has grown 275% and the supporting story-telling collateral has grown by 870%. That's a lot of information for anyone to digest and maintain. While the challenges of use are large, the value of incorporating additional data in the framework is immense. Increasing the variety of data allows us to identify correlations of activities, allowing us to refine the enterprise footprint to increase our understanding of user behavior and needs. Lastly, although collateral growth is beginning to stabilize based on active use by Intel IT project teams, the underlying data set is expected to grow even more rapidly in coming years as analysis tools become capable of handling even larger data sets. Only about 30% of available user transactional data has been incorporated in the current framework and the amount of data continues to increase on a daily basis further exacerbating the challenges of re-use and sense-making by project teams.

Enabling Social Storytelling and Knowledge Sharing. The framework and collateral put a face to the big data and provide an approach to defining a unified enterprise experience, but they are merely the tip of the iceberg of potential insights that could be derived from the underlying data set. Today, storytelling is primarily limited to the research team that produced the experience framework or the UX professionals who work directly with them. The rich data available on individuals, specific job roles, different organizations, and geographic areas makes possible a great many more stories than our current collateral. The lack of "self-service" environments to enable utilization of the data limits its broader utilization.

The majority of our collateral resides in flat files or posts in social media forums. The framework has not yet been brought to life online and no easy methods exist for teams to share outside of forum posts. Until the structure is available online and annotatable, widespread sharing and associated efficiencies are unlikely to occur. We need to enable project teams to not only re-use existing knowledge but also to add to it with detailed stories of use and new data.

Experience-Driven Transformation Is a Journey. Even with an experience framework, experience-driven transformation is a journey and what works for one team or individual may not work for another. A corporation's internal culture can also inhibit knowledge sharing if there is internal competitiveness and a reluctance to share information such as datasets and experience artifacts (e.g. personas, scenarios, or design patterns). It takes time, resources, and a willingness to collaborate with the rest of the organization. Every team or individual starts from a different point of faith and understanding of what UX is and how to do it. We have all had to transform our thinking, approach, decisions, and actions – from how we do user research to individual decisions made on enterprise projects all the way up to architectural and overall strategy decisions for IT. We celebrate the small and big wins where we see the framework is used to drive strategy and design. We never expected Intel IT to shift overnight and the journey is still in-progress but there have been big shifts. As researchers, we must maintain agility and flexibility with the teams but make sure they understand the hard work ahead.

7   Conclusion

In a world where businesses are constantly expected to move faster and workers become increasingly sophisticated in their expectations of technology, an experience framework can help speed up the business and become a force for UX transformation. This hybrid approach is a fundamental shift in the management of the business experience from the perspective of UX and enterprise IT. By aggregating big data and the outputs from more traditional UX together, UX teams can more quickly seed UX within businesses. By connecting user stories to big data we can understand if our insights from qualitative studies are generalizable to larger groups of business users. Presenting big data in ways typically used by traditional UX (e.g., personas) can make it more accessible. Together, big data and UX data are more powerful.

The experience framework defines interaction norms across enterprise tools and serves as design guard rails to help developers create better interfaces. A common framework and language understood by all results in more productive team discussions that generate strategy and design ideas faster. However, transformation using the framework is possible only when the findings are communicated in various ways so that it resonates with the broad base of people who work together to define and develop the workplace experience. A developer will look at the framework collateral thru a different lens than a business analyst or a service owner. Furthermore, transformation is a participatory process—it is not something that can be done by merely throwing the framework over the wall to the business. For change to happen, all levels of the organization must participate in the conversation and take ownership of how their own role impacts the enterprise experience. The road to transformation that is paved by an enterprise framework is often hard, uphill, and fraught with challenge, but for those who take this journey, an experience framework can help seed a shared vision and light the way for the action needed to bring the vision to life and significantly improve the business user experience.

Acknowledgements. We would like to thank the collaboration portfolio, especially Anne McEwan, Susan Michalak, and Cindy Pickering. We would like to thank Jayne May for helping evolving the collateral. And lastly, thank you to Linda Wooding who led the Intel IT's UX team; without her support this work would not have been possible.

References

1. Madden, S.: How Companies like Amazon Use Big Data to Make You Love Them, http://www.fastcodesign.com/1669551/how-companies-like-amazon-use-big-data-to-make-you-love-them
2. Tuch, A., Trusell, R., Hornbaek, K.: Analyzing Users' Narratives to Understand Experience with Interactive Products. In: Proc. CHI 2013, pp. 2079–2088. ACM Press (2013)
3. McCreary, F., Raval, K., Fallenstein, M.: A Case Study in Using Macroergonomics as a Framework for Business Transformation. Proceedings of the Human Factors and Ergonomics Society Annual 50(15), 1483–1487 (2006)
4. Kleiner, B.: Macroergonomics as a Large Work-System Transformation Technology. Human Factors and Ergonomics in Manufacturin 14(2), 99–115 (2004)
5. McCreary, F., McEwan, A., Schloss, D., Gómez, M.: Envisioning a New Future for the Enterprise with a Big Data Experience Framework. To appear in the Proceedings of 2014, World Conference on Information Systems and Technologies (2014)
6. Young, I.: Mental Models: Aligning Design Strategy with Human Behavior. Rosenfeld Media (2008)
7. Beyer, H., Holtzblatt, K.: Contextual Design. Interactions 6(1), 32–42 (1999)
8. Frishberg, L.: Presumptive Design: Cutting the Looking Glass Cake. Interactions 13, 18–20 (2006)

The Role of Human Factors in Production Networks and Quality Management

Ralf Philipsen[1], Philipp Brauner[1], Sebastian Stiller[2],
Martina Ziefle[1], and Robert Schmitt[2]

[1] Human-Computer Interaction Center (HCIC)
[2] Laboratory of Machine Tools and Production Engineering (WZL)
RWTH Aachen University, Germany
philipsen@comm.rwth-aachen.de

Abstract. Quality management in production networks is often neglected. To raise awareness for this subject, we developed an educational game in which players are responsible for managing orders and investments in quality assurance of a manufacturing company. To understand individual performance differences and playing strategy, we conducted a web-based study with 127 participants. Individual performance differences were discovered. Players who closely observe the company data and frequently modify order levels and quality investments perform significantly better. Furthermore, we found that the game model works and that the awareness towards quality assurance increases through the interaction with the game. Hence, the game is a suitable educational tool for teaching decision making in quality management.

Keywords: Quality Management, Decision Support, Human Factors, Production Networks, Personality Traits, Game-based Learning.

1 Introduction

Many of today's products are built from a large number of components that are delivered by a number of different suppliers. To enable a company to profitably manufacture its products, an efficient and viable production network is required. However, in today's globalized world these networks have reached a very high complexity [1]. Decision makers in current production networks need to have a comprehensive overview of the interrelationships of their company, the suppliers, and customers of many of different products and components. The arising problems are twofold: Not only do the decision makers have to ensure that enough components are available in the production process, but also a sufficient quality of the components has to be assured.

Modern Enterprise Resource Planning systems support people in their decision making. However, the huge quantity of presented and retrievable information might lead to information overflow and users who might focus on the wrong parameters, leading to inefficiencies, low product quality, or lower profits in the production networks. Human behavior in production networks and quality management is insufficiently explored. In order to study decision making processes in quality management

F.F.-H. Nah (Ed.): HCIB/HCII 2014, LNCS 8527, pp. 80–91, 2014.
© Springer International Publishing Switzerland 2014

and to develop tools that can give suitable support to decision makers, we developed a web based simulation that puts users into the role of decision makers.

This publication serves a dual purpose: First, we present the design and implementation of a simulation game for quality management in production networks. Second, we analyze the effect of human behavior and characteristics in the developed game as well as the consequences for real world companies.

2   Development of a Game for Quality Management

Simulations are experiments within a controlled environment, thereby reducing aspects of the real world in terms of structure and behavior. The behavior of complex systems is neither predictable nor completely understandable. The combination of human intuition and analytical modeling is utilized as a model for decision making in complex systems such as production and supply chain networks [2] [3] [4].

In order to train and support decision making, simulation models and serious games serve as ideal training environments, in which managers are confronted with challenging situations that require fast and important decisions. These games support the awareness of typical problems in production, logistics, or quality management, e.g., the Beer Distribution Game, Goldratt's game [5] [6], KANBAN simulations. However, no games exist that address quality management in production networks.

The Quality Intelligence Game (Q-I Game) is a turn-based game in which players have to fulfill the customer demands by procuring and processing vendor parts into a given product. In contrast to the Beer Distribution Game, players also have to take quality aspects into account. Studies suggest that quality management influences profit in two different ways: First, good quality management increases company profits through higher product quality, resulting in higher customer satisfaction and larger sales volumes. Second, process optimization as a part of quality management leads to lower variable and fixed costs. Therefore, a trade-off between product quality and its costs is required [7].

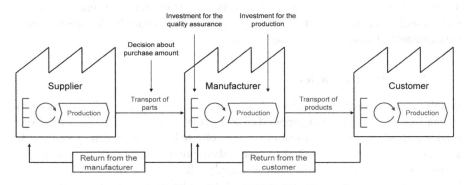

Fig. 1. Principle of the Q-I-Game

The Q-I game model is designed around three pivotal decisions (see Figure 1 for a schematic representation). First, players have to invest in the inspection of incoming goods. Second, players need to control the investments in their company's internal production quality. Third, similar to the Beer Distribution Game, players need to manage the procurement of vendor parts. The players have to find an optimal trade-off between these three dimensions in order to make the highest profit. The influences of these dimensions on the company's profit are explained in the following.

The first dimension contains the inspection planning and control of supplier parts, including complaint management between the manufacturer and his supplier.

Inspections at goods receipt can cause an ambivalent behavior of quality and production managers. While the inspection itself is not a value-adding process and hence a driver of variable and fixed production costs, inspections give the managers the opportunity to protect their production systems from faulty parts and goods. Also, it facilitates the supplier evaluation and development since the quality of supplied parts and goods is measured.

The production quality dimension is taking the production and final product quality of the manufactured goods into account. Investments in production quality will increase costs, but it will decrease the number of customer complaints.

To assure a continuous production, the player has to procure necessary parts from its supplier. Contrary to the Beer Distribution Game, the customer demand is kept constant within the Q-I game, in order to leave the focus on the decisions of quality management. Nevertheless the player has to consider scrapped parts due to low production quality or blocked parts due to poor supplier product quality in their orders.

The Q-I game gains complexity through the introduction of random events. First, the quality of the vendor parts can change drastically. Second, the internal production quality can change. Possible reasons are broken machines, better processes, failures in the measurement instruments, etc. Third, the customer demand may shift.

3   Evaluation of the Q-I-Game

After implementing the Q-I-Game with Java EE 7, it was used in a study to validate the game model and research possible effects of human factors on players' performances within the game. In the following sections, we present the defined variables, the experimental setup, and the sample of the study.

3.1   Independent Variables

In order to understand how decision making in quality management is influenced by human factors, several demographic data and personality traits were gathered. Age, gender and educational qualifications were collected as independent variables. In addition, participants were asked to assess their previous experiences with quality management, production management, supply chain management, logistics and business studies. Furthermore, we measured the technical self-efficacy with Beier's inventory [8], a method already proven to show performance in computer-based supply-chain-management simulations [9]. In order to analyze potential effects of personality, we used a version of the five factor model shortened by Rammstedt [10] to identify the participants' levels of the personality traits openness, conscientiousness, extraversion, agreeableness and neuroticism. Furthermore, previous studies revealed that performance regarding supply chain management was affected by their risk-taking propensity; therefore, we used the "General Risk Aversion" inventory by Mandrik & Bao [11] as well as the "Need for Security" inventory by Satow [12] to measure the participants' willingness to take risks. Xu et al. showed that the personal attitude towards quality contributes to Total Quality Management practices [13]; therefore, we measured the quality attitude with a newly constructed Quality Attitude Inventory, which consists of 8 items. 6-point Likert scales were used for all measurements.

3.2   Experimental Variables

In order to analyze the effects of complexity on players' performances, we implemented two in-game events to vary the degree of difficulty. One was a potential spontaneous drop of the supplier's quality by 30% in the tenth month. The other was a possible drop of the internal production quality in the same month. The occurrence of both events was fully randomized between both the participants and the two rounds played by each player.

The availability of quality signal lights was varied as a within-subject variable; accordingly, all participants played one round with and one without the signal lights. Whether the lights were shown in the first or the second round was randomized.

3.3   Dependent Variables

Detailed logs of investments, incomes, costs and profits of each simulated month were used to analyze the players' behaviors within the game. The achieved profit was used as the central measure for the players' performances. In addition, several information about the players' interactions with the game were recorded: duration of reading the instructions, time to complete a month as well as a round, the number of help accesses and the number of adjustments to investments and orders.

3.4   Ranking Tasks

In addition, the participants were asked to rank factors of data provisioning and corporate strategy according to their importance for a successful performance in the game and for an economical production. They were asked to perform these tasks both before and after the game to discover possible effects on participants' opinions caused by playing the game.

3.5   Experimental Setup

The experimental setting consisted of our web-based quality management simulation, which was embedded between the pre- and post-part of an online survey. Announcements on bulletin boards, social networks, emails and personal invitations were used to recruit participants for the study. Each had to play 2 rounds of 24 month each. 219 people started the online pre-survey, 129 played both rounds of the game and finished the post-survey. The obtained dataset was revised to eliminate players who did not play seriously, i.e. who placed excessive investments or orders or did not change the settings at all. Therefore, two cases had to be removed for not performing any adjustment during both rounds. Accordingly, the final revised dataset contained 127 cases. Although the participants had to play 24 simulated month per round, only the data of up to and including month 20 were used in the analysis to exclude possible changes of players' strategies late in the game like emptying the warehouse completely.

3.6   Participants

97 (76.4%) of the participants were male, 30 (23.6%) were female. They were between 17 and 53 years of age. The mean (M) age was 27.7 years (SD 7.2 years). 58.6% (60) of the participants reported a university degree as their highest achieved level of education. 39.7% (50) participants had a high school diploma and 6.3% (8) had vocational training. The average level of previous experiences regarding the subject matter were rather high. 67.7% (86) had previous knowledge in quality management, 65.9% (83) in business studies and 57.5% (73) in production management.

The participants' average personality traits regarding the five factor model were comparable to the reference sample of Rammstedt [10] with the exception of a slightly lower level of agreeableness. The only significant difference between men and women regarding this model was found at the neuroticism scale ($F(1, 125) = 7.498$, $p = .007 < .05*$): men showed lower average levels ($M = 1.99$, $SD = 0.97$) than women ($M = 2.58$, $SD = 1.22$). In addition, gender related differences were found regarding all three inventories of needs (recognition, power, security) ($p < .05*$ for all needs), technical self-efficacy ($p = .000 < .05*$), willingness to take risks ($p = .002 < .05*$) and performance motivation ($p = .000 < .05*$). With the exception of the need for security men showed higher average levels in all aforementioned scales. In contrast, there was no significant difference found regarding the attitude towards quality.

4   Results

The result section is structured as follows: First, we will present the impact of the game mechanics and instructions on the player's performance. Second, we will have a closer look at the impact of user diversity. Furthermore, we will present the effects of behavior and strategies within the game. Last, we will report the ranking task results.

The data was analyzed by using uni- and multivariate analyses of variance (ANOVA, MANOVA) as well as bivariate correlations. Pillai's trace values (V) were used for significance in multivariate tests, and the Bonferroni method in pair-wise comparisons. The criterion for significance was $p < .05$ in all conducted tests. Median splits were used for groupings unless the factor offered a clear dichotomy.

Unless otherwise described, the effects in the following are valid for both rounds of the game. However, for clarity reasons, only the effect values of the second round will be reported. All profit related values like means and standard deviations will be reported in thousands for similar reasons; for computations the exact values were used.

4.1   Effect of Game Conditions

As expected, the participants made the highest average profit (M = 148.5, SD = 128.0) on the condition that there was no spontaneous drop of supplier's and internal production's qualities during the game. The mean profit in games with a drop of supplier quality was only slightly lower (M = 132.9, SD = 81.2). In contrast, average profits were considerably lower (M = 11.5, SD = 236.8) with drops in either both supplier's and internal production's quality or in internal production's quality only (M = -1.3, SD = 316.4), as shown in Table 1.

Table 1. Achieved average profits under different game conditions

		Drop of supplier's quality	
		no	yes
Drop of internal production's quality	no	148.5	132.9
	yes	-1.3	11.5

A two-way ANOVA revealed that the drop of internal production quality had a significant effect on players' average profits (F(1, 122) = 12.342, p = .001 < .05*); in particular, players averagely performed significantly worse under game conditions containing the aforementioned drop. On the other hand, the spontaneous drop of supplier's quality had no significant influence on average profits.

With both possible quality drops controlled, the presence of signal lights had no significant effect on players' average profits (p = .537, n.s.). Also, the impact of signal light availability within any of the four possible game conditions resulting from quality drop combinations did not reach the criterion of significance. Both the presence of signal lights and the quality drops of supplier and internal production as experimental variables will be controlled in the computations of the following sections.

4.2   Effect of Repetition

There was a strong correlation between players' average profits in the first and in the second round (r=.730, p=.000 < .05*); accordingly, participants who achieved a high/low profit in the first round, on average achieved the same level of profit in the second round. Furthermore, players' mean profit increased significantly between the first (M = -19.0, SD = 258.5) and the second round (M = 76.6, SD = 218.3) with Pillai's trace value (V) = 0.23, F(1, 126) = 36.6, p = .000 < .05*.

4.3   Effect of User Diversity

Several aspects of user diversity have been studied for potential effects on players' performances within the game. First, male participants made a higher average profit (M = 104.9, SD = 187.1) than women (M = -14.7, SD = 282.5). However, the effect is only significant for the second round (F(1, 124) = 7.160, p = .008 < .05*), not the first round (F(1, 124) = 3.235, p = .074, n.s.). Second, there was no correlation between age and the player's profit (r = .057, p = .553, n.s.). Previous experiences did not influence the game performance, e.g., neither knowledge in quality management (p = .087, n.s.) nor business studies (p = .070, n.s.) had a significant effect on performance within the game with game conditions controlled. Although participants with a high level of domain knowledge performed better under game conditions containing the aforementioned drop of internal production's quality (M_{2QM} = 86.8, SD_{2QM} = 150.3) than players with low knowledge (M_{2QM} = -59.5, SD_{2QM} = 333.8), this effect was only significant in the second round of the game (F(1, 58) = 4.928, p = .030 < .05*).

In addition to the customary demographic data several personality traits were analyzed. First, none of the "Big Five personality traits" of Rammstedt et al. [10] impacted the players' performances significantly (p > .05, n.s. for all indexes). Second, and contrary to several previous studies, there was no significant relation between technical self-efficacy and achieved average profit (r = .163, p = .084, n.s.). Third, there was no effect of the willingness to take risks on players' performances. Neither the "General Risk Aversion"-index of Mandrik & Bao [11] (r = -.174, p = .065, n.s.) nor the "Need for Security"-index of Satow [12] (r = .054, p = .573, n.s.) correlated with the achieved profits. Moreover, the personal attitude towards quality did not correlate with participants' average performances within the game (r = .109, p = .248, n.s.).

4.4   Effects of Behavior within the Game

Two main factors were analyzed regarding the players' behaviors within the game. First, the duration of playing correlated with players' average profits in the first round (r = .301, p = .001 < .05*). Therefore, spending a higher amount of time for a game averagely led to significantly higher profits in the first round. However, the effect was no longer significant in the second round (r = .142 p = .112, n.s.).

Second, the number of adjustments correlated with players' performances (r = .303, p = .001 < .05*). Users who adapted their investments and orders frequently achieved higher mean profits. A per-month analysis revealed that the average number of adjustments made by participants who achieved a high profit exceeded the adjustments of low performers in every month, as shown in Figure 2. Moreover, there was a peak in high performers' adjustments in month 11 as a reaction to the spontaneous drops of the supplier's and/or the internal production's quality in month 10. This change in interaction between month 10 and 11 is significant for high performers (V = .164, F(1, 62) = 12.140, p = .001 < .05*). In contrast, there was no significant change in the adaption behavior of low performers at that time (V = .001, F(1, 63) = 0.088, p = .768, n.s.). Also, there is a medium correlation between the averagely performed adjustments in the first and the second round (r = .580, p = .000 < .05*). In particular, players who frequently/rarely adapted their investments and orders in the first round, acted similarly in the second round.

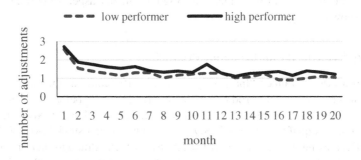

Fig. 2. Average adjustments per month of high and low performers in the second round

4.5   Effects of Strategy

There were several effects on players' performances regarding the used game plans. First, participants who assessed their behavior in the game as highly conscientious made a higher profit (M = 135.0, SD = 111.5) than those with low conscientiousness values (M = 38.4, SD = 261.1). This effect was significant (F(1, 123) = 4.987, p = 0.27 < .05*). Second, the stated level of forward planning in game strategy correlates with average profits (r = .184, p = .040 < .05*): Users who stated their strategy was dominated more by forward planning than by reacting, on average made higher profits. Third, the level of risk taking in the game plan negatively correlated with players' average performances (r = .-.217, p = .015 < .05*), e.g., players who claimed to have taken more risks than they would in real live made significantly lower profits. Also, there was a low correlation between participants' profits and the tendency to keep a small safety buffer of parts readily available (r = .273, p = .002 < .05*).

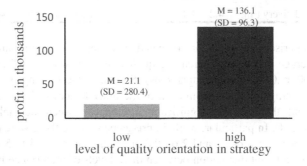

Fig. 3. Means (SD) of profit regarding strategies with different levels of quality orientation

Most of all, the level of quality orientation in players' strategies correlated significantly with the average performances ($r = .370$, $p = .000 < .05^*$); therefore, participants with a quality-oriented strategy averagely performed better ($M = 136.1$, $SD = 96.3$) than participants who were inclined to ignore quality aspects ($M = 21.1$, $SD = 280.4$), as shown in Figure 2.

4.6   Requirements for an Economic Production

Participants averagely ranked "Increasing economic efficiency" as the most important requirement for an economic production ($M = 2.1$, $SD = 1.3$) before they played the game, followed by "Increasing quality of own production" ($M = 2.2$, $SD = 1.1$), "Increasing supplier's quality" ($M = 3.3$, $SD = 1.1$), "Optimizing stock" ($M = 3.7$, $SD = 1.2$) and "Decreasing delivery time" ($M = 3.8$, $SD = 1.2$). Although there is an absolute ranking, which results from comparing the aforementioned means, there is neither a significant difference between the first two ranks ($p = 1.00$, n.s.) nor between the ranks 3 to 5 ($p > .05$, n.s. for all comparisons). The positions of "quality of own production" and "economic efficiency" had been switched in post-game ranking, while there was no difference regarding the absolute ranks 3 to 5, as shown in Table 2.

Table 2. Ranking, means, and standard deviations of requirements for an economical production (left) and data requirements for successful performance (right) (ranked after playing)

Rank	Requirement	M	SD	Rank	Requirement	M	SD
1	Increasing quality of own production	1.8	0.9	1	High quality of data	1.8	0.9
2	Increasing economic efficiency	2.8	1.5	2	Good data visualization	2.3	1.1
3	Increasing supplier's quality	2.9	1.2	3	Decision support	2.8	1.2
4	Optimizing stock	3.3	1.2	4	High data volume	3.8	1.2
5	Decreasing delivery time	4.2	1.1	5	Low data volume	4.3	0.9

Pairwise comparison of all factors revealed that there is a significant difference between the average raking of "Increasing quality of own production" and all other factors ($p = .000 < .05^*$ for all comparisons). Similarly, the ranking of "Decreasing delivery times" averagely differs from each of the other factors with $p = .000 < .05^*$. On the other hand, there was no significant difference between the rankings of the remaining items (2-4). In particular, while in pre-game ranking there were only significant differences between ranks 1 and 2 on the one hand and ranks 3 to 5 on the other hand, there is a significant distinction between three levels of importance in post-game ranking, mainly caused by an averagely higher ranking of one's own quality's importance (Pillai's trace value $(V) = 0.87$, $F(1, 123) = 11.695$, $p = .001 < .05^*$) and a lower ranking of shorter delivery times ($V = 0.81$, $F(1, 123) = 10.848$, $p = .001 < .05^*$) after playing the game.

4.7   Requirements for Data quality

The participants also had to rank different requirements regarding their demands on the provision of data. There was no significant difference in the average rankings of any of the factors before and after playing the game (p > .05, n.s. for all pre-post factor pairs); therefor, the absolute positions were equal in both pre- and post-game ranking. Participants identified the data quality as the most important aspect (M = 1.8, SD = 0.9), followed by the visualization of data (M = 2.3, SD = 1.1), decision support (M = 2.8, SD = 1.2) and the volume of data, as shown in Table 2. Pairwise comparison revealed that there is no significant difference between the average rankings of "Good data visualization" and "Decision support" (p = .059, n.s.). In contrast, for all other comparisons of two factors the criterion of significance (p < .05, n.s. for all comparisons) was reached.

5   Discussion

Regarding the technical factors influencing game complexity we learned the easiest condition is the one without drops in either the supplier's quality or the internal production quality. To our surprise, however, we found that the most difficult condition to play is one with drops only in the internal production quality drops, but the supplier's quality stays constant. Counterintuitively, this condition is even more difficult to play than the condition in which both qualities drop. We suspect that to be the case, because the consequences of the quality drops are easier to notice within the company dashboard, as the number of returned parts increases and the incoming quality decreases (two visible changes), while only one measure changes if only the production quality decreases.

Interestingly, the display of traffic lights indicating the supplier's quality and the internal production quality did not influence the decision quality of the players and the performance within the game. Interviews with players after the game suggest that players had difficulties to understand the correct meaning of the traffic signals.

While the investigation of the game mechanics yielded clear findings, the search for human factors that explain performance was only partially successful in this study. We learned underlying factors exist that explain game performance, as players who did well in the first round of the game also did well in the second round (i.e. high correlation of the performances of the first and second round of the game). However none of the variables assessed prior to the interaction with the game explained game performance with adequate accuracy. Surprisingly, the positive impact of high technical self-efficacy on performance [9] could not be replicated within this study. Nonetheless, players with good performance can be differentiated from players with bad performance when in-game metrics or the post-game survey are considered. First, players who achieved higher profits in the game took more time than players who achieved lower profits. Second, good players not only spent more time on the game, they also perform more changes within the game's decision cockpit. Both findings are in line with previous studies [14] and suggest that intense engagement with the subject leads to a better performance. It is unclear however, what causes this effect:

Are people who perform better in the game just more motivated, and therefore spend more time on the game and on changes within the game, or do better players have an increased overview over the company data and are therefore able to adapt more quickly to changing scenarios.

Using games as a vehicle to mediate learning processes is getting more and more popular in various disciplines [15]. Our findings suggest that our game-based approach for teaching fundamentals of quality management also works very well. First, we found that the game is learnable and that the player's performance increases from the first to the second round of the game, showing that the players gained expertise in making complex decisions for the simulated company. Second, the intention of the game is to raise the awareness about quality management and shift the attention towards quality management techniques within the game. After the game the players' relative weighting of quality management was significantly higher than before the game. Hence we can conclude, that the Q-I game is a suitable tool for teaching quality management within vocational trainings, university courses or advanced trainings.

6   Summary, Limitations, and Outlook

Contrary to previous studies, we could not identify human factors that explain game performance. We suspect that the small number of participants per experimental condition, the large noise and huge spread within the data makes the dataset difficult to evaluate. In a follow-up study we will therefore reduce the number of experimental factors and increase the number of participants per condition, assuming that this will yield clearer results. Furthermore, the questions assessing the game strategy from the post-game survey will be rephrased and used in the pre-game survey, as we then hope to be able to predict game performance according to player strategy. In addition, we assume that information processing ability is also influencing performance within the game; hence we will closely investigate the effect of information processing capacity and speed on the outcome of the game in a follow-up study.

The traffic signs were conceptualized to indicate the results from quality audits of the supplying company and of the internal production quality, not as indicators that represent current quality levels. However, many people misinterpreted these indicators and assumed that they show exactly that. A future version of the decision cockpit will therefore clarify this issue and provide both, a clear indicator of the current supplier quality and the current production quality, as well as clear indicators that represent the results from quality audits.

The overall rating of the game was fairly positive and we found that it increased the awareness of the importance of quality management in supply chain management.

Acknowledgements. The authors thank Hao Ngo and Chantal Lidynia for their support. This research was funded by the German Research Foundation (DFG) as part of the Cluster of Excellence "Integrative Production Technology for High-Wage Countries" [16].

References

1. Forrester, J.W.: Industrial dynamics. MIT Press, Cambridge (1961)
2. Bossel, H.: Systeme Dynamik Simulation – Modellbildung, Analyse und Simulation komplexer Systeme, p. 24. Books on Demand GmbH, Norderstedt (2004)
3. Robinson, S.: Simulation: The Practice of Model Development and Use, pp. 4–11. John Wiley & Sons, West Sussex (2004)
4. Greasley, A.: Simulation Modelling for Business, pp. 1–11. Ashgate Publishing Company, Burlington (2004)
5. Kühl, S., Strodtholz, P., Taffertshofer, A.: Handbuch Methoden der Organisations forschung, pp. 498-578. VS Verlag für Sozialwissenschaften, Wiesbaden (2009)
6. Hardman, D.: Judgement and Decision Making. In: Psychological Perpectives, pp. 120–124. John Wiley & Sons, West Sussex (2009)
7. Kamiske, G., Brauer, J.: ABC des Qualitätsmanagements, p. 24. Carl Hanser Verlag, München (2012)
8. Beier, G.: Kontrollüberzeugungen im Umgang mit Technik [Locus of control when interacting with technology]. Report Psychologie 24(9), 684–693 (1999)
9. Brauner, P., Runge, S., Groten, M., Schuh, G., Ziefle, M.: Human Factors in Supply Chain Management – Decision making in complex logistic scenarios. In: Yamamoto, S. (ed.) HCI 2013, Part III. LNCS, vol. 8018, pp. 423–432. Springer, Heidelberg (2013)
10. Rammstedt, B., Kemper, C.J., Klein, M.C., Beierlein, C., Kovaleva, A.: Eine kurze Skala zur Messung der fünf Dimensionen der Persönlichkeit: Big-Five-Inventory-10 (BFI-10). In: GESIS – Leibniz-Institut für Sozialwissenschaften (eds.) GESIS-Working Papers, vol. 22. Mannheim (2012)
11. Mandrik, C.A., Bao, Y.: Exploring the Concept and Measurement of General Risk Aversion. In: Menon, G., Rao, A.R. (eds.) NA - Advances in Consumer Research, vol. 32, pp. 531–539. Association for Consumer Research, Duluth (2005)
12. Satow, L.: B5T. Psychomeda Big-Five-Persönlichkeitstest. Skalendokumentation und Normen sowie Fragebogen mit Instruktion. In: Leibniz-Zentrum für Psychol. Inf. und Dokumentation (ZPID) (eds.) Elektron. Testarchiv (2011), http://www.zpid.de
13. Xu, Y., Zhu, J., Huang, L., Zheng, Z., Kang, J.: Research on the influences of staff's psychological factors to total quality management practices: An empirical study of Chinese manufacturing industry. In: 2012 IEEE International Conference on Management of Innovation and Technology (ICMIT), pp. 303–308 (2012)
14. Dörner, D.: Die Logik des Mißlingens. Strategisches Denken in komplexen Situationen. rororo, Reinbek (2013)
15. Schäfer, A., Holz, J., Leonhardt, T., Schroeder, U., Brauner, P., Ziefle, M.: From boring to scoring – a collaborative serious game for learning and practicing mathematical logic for computer science education. Computer Science Education 23(2), 87–111 (2013)
16. Brecher, C.: Integrative Production Technology for High-Wage Countries. Springer, Heidelberg (2012)

Managing User Acceptance Testing of Business Applications

Robin Poston[1], Kalyan Sajja[2], and Ashley Calvert[2]

[1] University of Memphis
rposton@memphis.edu
[2] System Testing Excellence Program

Abstract. User acceptance testing (UAT) events gather input from actual system users to determine where potential problems may exist in a new software system or major upgrade. Modern business systems are more complex and decentralized than ever before making UAT more complicated to perform. The collaborative nature of facilitated UAT events requires close interaction between the testers and the facilitation team, even when located in various locations worldwide. This study explores the best approaches for facilitating UAT remotely and globally in order to effectively facilitate geographically-dispersed actual system users in performing UAT exercises. While research suggests user involvement is important, there is a lack of understanding about the specifics of how to best engage users for maximizing the results, and our study addresses this gap. This study examines the following research questions: How should UAT facilitators (1) schedule user participation with a minimum impact to their regular work duties and maximum ability to be present when testing and not be distracted; (2) enable direct interactions with users including face-to-face conversations during the UAT event and access to user computer screens for configuration and validation; and (3) utilize quality management software that can be used seamlessly by all involved in UAT. To examine these questions, we utilize Social Presence Theory (SPT) to establish a conceptual lens for addressing these research questions. SPT supports that the communication environment must enable people to adopt the appropriate level of social presence required for that task. This study proposes a theoretically-derived examination based on SPT of facilitated UAT delineating when and how facilitators should involve actual system users in the UAT activities either through local facilitation or remote hosting of UAT exercises, among other options.

Keywords: User Acceptance Testing, Social Presence Theory, Computer Mediated Conferencing, Quality Management Software.

1 Introduction

The purpose of user acceptance testing (UAT) is to gather input from actual system users, those who have experience with the business processes and will be using the system to complete related tasks (Klein, 2003; Larson, 1995). Actual users bring knowledge of process flows and work systems and are able to test how the system

F.F.-H. Nah (Ed.): HCIB/HCII 2014, LNCS 8527, pp. 92–102, 2014.
© Springer International Publishing Switzerland 2014

meets all that is required of it, including undocumented inherent requirements, and where potential problems may surface. UAT is a critical phase of testing that typically occurs after the system is built and before the software is released. Modern business systems are more complex and decentralized than ever before making UAT more complicated to perform. The global nature of commerce continues to push business systems deployments well beyond traditional geographic boundaries. The global nature of such deployments has created new challenges for the execution of UAT and the effective participation of geographically dispersed actual system users. The collaborative nature of facilitated UAT events requires close interaction between the testers and the facilitation team (Larson, 1995), even when located in various locations worldwide. However current obstacles exist such as, global dispersion of the user base, travel expenses and extended time away from regular work assignments. This study explores the best approaches for facilitating UAT remotely and globally in order to effectively facilitate geographically-dispersed actual system users in performing UAT exercises.

Systems development theory suggests users should be involved throughout the development lifecycle, yet involving the users is often difficult. One study of case organizations found different approaches and strategies for the facilitation of user involvement (Iivari, 2004; Lohmann and Rashid, 2008). An important aspect in human computer interaction is usability evaluation that improves software quality (Butt and Fatimah, 2012). User involvement occurs between industry experts who use the system and the development team suggesting it is imperative to have senior and experienced user representation involved (Majid et al., 2010). One study of the degree of user involvement in the process indicates that user involvement is mainly concentrated in the functional requirements gathering process (Axtell et al., 1997). Software firms spend approximately 50-75% of the total software development cost on debugging, testing, and verification activities, soliciting problem feedback from users to improve product quality (Muthitacharoen and Saeed, 2009).

Today, the distinction between development and adoption are blurring which provides developers with opportunities for increasing user involvement (Hilbert et al., 1997). User involvement is a widely accepted principle in the development of usable systems, yet it is a vague concept covering many approaches. Research studies illustrate how users can be an effective source of requirements generation, as long as role of users is carefully considered along with cost-efficient practices (Kujala, 2003). User's participation is important for successful software program execution (Butt and Fatimah, 2012) and business analyst facilitation and patience in UAT events is critical whether the system is a new installation, major upgrade, or commercial-off-the-shelf package (Beckett, 2005; Klein, 2003; Larson, 1995). In summary, while research suggests user involvement is important, there is a lack of understanding about the specifics of how to best engage users for maximizing the results, and our study addresses this gap.

This study examines the following research questions: How should UAT facilitators (1) schedule user participation with a minimum impact to their regular work duties and maximum ability to be present when testing and not be distracted; (2) enable direct interactions with users including face-to-face conversations during the UAT event and access to user computer screens for configuration and validation; and (3) utilize quality management software that can be used seamlessly by all involved in UAT.

To examine these questions, we recognize the need to resolve the complexity of communication challenges among technology facilitators and business users. We draw on Social Presence Theory (SPT) to establish a conceptual lens for addressing these research questions. Traditionally, SPT classifies different communication media along a continuum of social presence. Social presence (SP) reflects the degree of awareness one person has of another person when interacting (Sallnas et al., 2000). People utilize many communication styles when face-to-face (impression leaving, contentiousness, openness, dramatic existence, domination, precision, relaxed flair, friendly, attentiveness, animation, and image managing (Norton, 1986) or when on-line (affective, interactive, and cohesive (Rourke et al., 2007). SPT supports that the communication environment must enable people to adopt the appropriate level of social presence required for that task. This study proposes a theoretically-derived examination based on SPT of facilitated UAT delineating when and how facilitators should involve actual system users in the UAT activities either through local facilita-tion or remote hosting of UAT exercises, among other options.

2   Theoretical Background

To examine the challenges of facilitating actual system users in UAT events, SPT incorporates a cross-section of concepts from social interdependence and media rich-ness theories. SPT promotes that through discourse, intimacy and immediacy create a degree of salience or being there between the parties involved (Lowenthal, 2010). Researchers have found perception of the other party's presence is more important than the capabilities of the communications medium (Garrison et al., 2000). Thus, UAT events will need to enable the appropriate level of SP for users to learn their role in UAT and execute testing activities.

Facilitating users in remotely-hosted UAT events draws similarities to online teaching activities. The similarities emanate from both activities comprising novice users working with expert facilitators to learn new knowledge, tackle new skills, and express confusion and questions in text-written print. SP has been established as a critical component of online teaching success. Table 1 encapsulates select research in the online teaching domain, illustrating the growing support for designing courses and maintaining a personal presence to influence student satisfaction and learning. This research helps us identify factors needed for user success in an online UAT event context. SP largely reflects the trust-building relationship a facilitator or instructor creates with users or students. SP is more easily developed in face-to-face richer media settings, however SP can be encouraged in computer-mediated learner media settings as well.

Table 1. Select studies of online teaching and social presence

Reference	How Social Presence (SP) was Established	Key Findings
Hostetter and Busch, 2006; Swan and Shih, 2005	Course design by weekly threaded discussion, course credit for discussion participation, provoking discussion questions. Also with instructor and peer presence in online discussions promoting sharing personal experiences and feelings	SP leads to student satisfaction and learning Perceived presence of instructors may be more influential factor than perceived presence of peers for student satisfaction
Richardson and Swan, 2003	Course activities with class discussion, group projects, individual projects, self-tests, written assignments, lectures, readings	SP leads to satisfaction with instructor and perceived learning Women have higher social presence than men No age or experience influence
Russo and Benson, 2005	Course components organized for cognitive learning (student assessment of their learning), affective learning (attitude about the course), perception of presence (peers, instructors, and self)	SP leads to instructor presence and peer presence SP leads to affective learning and student learning satisfaction Important to establish and maintain SP including own SP which leads to higher grades
Tu, 2000	Attention process by drawing interpersonal attractions (inviting public speakers, Good communication style) Retention process by showing images that increase sensory stimulation Motor reproduction process by cognitive organization Motivational process with incentives to learn	SP leads to learner-to-learner interaction SP increases student's performance, proficiency, retention and motivation Student attitudes towards the subject are increased
Picciano, 2002	Course is structured around readings and weekly discussions, students as facilitators Asynchronous and synchronous discussion session with peers and instructors Instructor immediacy	SP leads to student interaction and perceived learning SP has a significant relationship with performance on written assignments which requires discussion with instructor and peers
Aragon, 2003	Course design, instructor, and participant strategies	Creating a platform for SP Instructors can establish and maintain SP encouraging student participation

Research examining UAT activities suggests both facilitator and users need face-to-face communication options when the system under test is newly developed (Larson, 1995). Typical UAT timelines involve: A system almost fully developed, user guides and training materials developed by the technology group, business analytic review and input on these materials then drawing up the test scripts, users performing tests based on the scripts and with open unscripted use, user reporting issues to the business analyst who reviews and logs the appropriate defects for the development team to address. This is repeated until the users sign off that the system works as needed (Larson, 1995). Research illustrates the UAT process can be improved with users having the ability to engage in direct interactions with both the business analyst and development teams when questions arise (Larson, 1995).

Facilitated testing by the real time users can be implemented in 3 ways (Seffah and Habied-Mammar, 2009): 1. Require remote users to travel to a local facility, 2. Send facilitator to remote locations, 3. Facilitator from local facility does computer mediated conferencing (CMC) with users in remote location. Each of these approaches establishes different communication environments. SPT suggests facilitated UAT local facilitation or remote hosting of UAT exercises will require different dimensions of where and how facilitators should involve users in the UAT activities. Table 2 demonstrates researchers' views on facilitated UAT approaches and how SPT attributes are expected to affect three different UAT approaches based on studies of SP in online teaching. Remote users travelling to local facility and facilitator travelling to remote locations are treated as same in Table 2 as both are similar to instructor teaching to students face to face while remote UAT is compared with online teaching. As Table 2 illustrates how attributes of SP tend to be low for remote UAT events because face-to-face communications are highly advantages when establishing high SP. Also, online research on SP for online learning is high if SP is established using various techniques like incentives, course design, etc.

Table 2. Facilitated UAT Approaches

	Remote users travel to local facility	Facilitator travel to remote locations	Computer mediated conferencing between facilitator at local facility & users at remote locations
Facilitator	Local	Remote	Local
User	Local	Remote	Remote
Challenges in approach:			
Type of system[1]	New	New or Upgrade	Upgrade
Costs[2]	$100,000-$150,000 US dollars, excluding cost of deployment, management, training, upgrades, and test analysis software	$15,000-$20,000 US dollars, including test software, per location	More participants form diverse backgrounds, lower budget, and less time

Table 2. (*Continued.*)

Size of group[2]	Limited	Limited	Greater participation
SPT Attributes adopted from online teaching environments[3]:			
Expression of emotions	High	High	Low
Use of humor	High	High	Low
Self-disclosure	High	High	Low
Dialogue	High	High	Low
Asking questions	High	High	Low
Compliment, express appreciation, agreement	High	High	Low
Assertive/ acquiescent	High	High	Low
Informal/formal relationships	High	High	Low
Trust relationship	High	High	Low
Social relationships	High	High	Low
Attitude toward technology	Positive	Positive	Apathetic
Access and location	Easy	Easy	Hard
Timely response	High	High	Low

[1] (Klein, 2003; Larson, 1995; Seffah and Habieb-Mammar, 2009)
[2] (Seffah and Habieb-Mammar, 2009)
[3] (Rourke et al., 2007; Tu and McIsaac, 2002)

Mostly used in research examining online education, SPT informs remote communications environments by examining the way people represent themselves online through the way information is shared (e.g., how messages are posted and interpreted by others) and how people related to each other (Kehrwald, 2008). When face-to-face, people use everyday skills to share information through multiple cues using rich nonverbal communication inherent in tone of voice and facial expression. Richer communications allow individuals to provide and respond to the sight, sound, and smell of others which inherently provides an awareness of the presence of others (Mehrabian, 1969). Online information sharing lacks the cues needed to create an awareness of the presence of others and offers the ability to discuss information but not to connect or bond with others on a more personal level (Sproull and Kiesler, 1986). Research studies of online education have found that the lack of SP impedes interactions and as a result hinders student-learning performance (Wei et al., 2012). One proposed solution is to combine the use of both asynchronous (pre-produced content accessed by users when needed) and synchronous (real-time, concurrent audio and video connections) components, with synchronous efforts providing a much more full social exchange greatly increasing the potential for SP. Thus, SP is an important factor in information exchange when learning and performance are required, as is the case of user participation in UAT events.

3   Case Study Methodology

The research methodology follows a qualitative approach in gathering case study data on UAT practices in order to provide descriptive and explanatory insights into the management activities in software development work. This approach has been used successfully in prior research (Pettigrew, 1990; Sutton, 1997) and allows us to induce a theoretical account of the activities found in empirical observations and analysis of team member's viewpoints. This approach is also known to lead to accurate and useful results by including an understanding of the contextual complexities of the environment in the research analysis and outcomes. Finally, this approach encourages an understanding of the holistic systematic view of the issues and circumstances of the situation being addressed, in this case the issues of managing development projects from team member perspectives about their testing practices (Checkland et al., 2007; Yin, 1989). To identify the practices, we selected a large multinational fortune 500 company known to have successful UAT events. The focus of our study is specific to the UAT practices of large scale complex globally-deployed software development projects.

4   Data Collection

The results reported in the present study are based on interviews with UAT facilitators. Our data gathering began with the creation of semi-structured interview protocols which comprised both closed and open-ended questions. To inform our interview question development, we reviewed documentation about the company, and held background discussions with company personnel. The data collection methods employed focused on interviewees' perspectives on UAT issues, roles played by various stakeholders involved, and the challenges of incorporating actual systems users in the process. Face-to-face interviews of approximately 1 to 1.5 hours were conducted with various project stakeholders. The goal of these interviews was to identify and better understand the issues related to UAT. In total, we interviewed 8 stakeholders. Interviews were conducted between November 2013 and January 2014, with additional follow-up clarification Q&A sessions conducted over e-mail. Job descriptions of those interviewed are shown in Table 3.

Table 3. Job Descriptions of Interviewees

Job Title Description	Years of Experience	Responsibility	Times Interviewed
Business Systems Quality Analysis Analysts	2	UAT test plans, writing UAT test cases, UAT facilitation and defect management	2
Business Systems Quality Analysis Analysts	6	UAT test plans, writing UAT test cases, UAT facilitation and defect management	1
Business Systems Quality Analysis Advisor	6	UAT test plans, writing UAT test cases, leading teams of quality analysts, UAT facilitation, defect management, quality process and standards design, 3rd party contract quality analysis and management	2
Business Systems Quality Analysis Advisor	18	UAT test plans, writing UAT test cases, leading teams of quality analysts, UAT facilitation, defect management, quality process and standards design	2
Business Systems Quality Analysis Manager	16	leading a team of quality analysts and quality advisors responsible for enterprise level activities globally including process and standards, UAT management and execution and third party contracts	2
UAT Tester 1	n/a	testing the "administrative functions" of an app as part of an end user support role	1
UAT Tester 2	n/a	Same	1
UAT Tester 3	n/a	Same	1
		Total Interviews	12

By collecting and triangulating data across a variety of methods, we were able to develop robust results because of the perspectives we gained about UAT issues. This approach provides in-depth information on emerging concepts, and allows cross-checking the information to substantiate the findings (Eisenhardt, 1989; Glaser and Strauss, 1967; Pettigrew, 1990).

5   Findings

In this research, we gathered and analyzed interview data from a large multinational company with multiple stakeholders of UAT events along with best practices from the research literature. From these data sources, we next address the research questions proposed earlier to offer insights about managing UAT events. For completely new complex systems and novice UAT participants, SP will be a critical factor enabling better testing outcomes. In this case, facilitators should schedule user participation locally at the testing location where face-to-face interactions can occur. While cognizant of the need to minimize the impact to users' regular work duties and keep from having work requirements outside of regular working hour, these events can be concentrated into a shorter timeframe and more efficiently administered when everyone is together. Accommodating users locally maximizes users' ability to be present when testing and not be distracted. Complicated tasks and difficult questions can be addressed and more readily communicated. Additionally, peer-to-peer face-to-face learning can be enabled, which has been shown to improve outcomes (Tu, 2000).

Media richness theory has long held that richer media are the key to building trusting relationships (Campbell, 2000). Media richness theory suggests settings should be assessed on how well they support the ability of communicating parties to discern multiple information cues simultaneously, enable rapid feedback, establish a personal message, and use natural language. Richer media tend to run on a continuum from rich face-to-face settings to lean written documents. Thus, consistent with above, for completely new complex systems and novice UAT participants, richer media settings are needed to enable direct interactions with users including face-to-face conversations during the UAT event and access to user computer screens for configuration and validation. Richer settings also enable facilitators to collaborate and train users to improve information sharing. Furthermore, peer-to-peer learning and immediacy of replies for help and answers enables a more productive UAT outcome. When users are located in distant remote locations, time lags between queries and answers impedes productivity and dedication to task.

Quality management software (QMS) enables standard procedures and processes, effective control, maintainability, higher product quality at a reduced cost (Ludmer, 1969). In our interviews with facilitators and user acceptance testers we found that QMS plays a critical role while performing UAT. UAT testers use QMSs to read and execute test scripts, input result of their tests, log defects and verify defects are fixed. Facilitators use QMSs to write test scripts, review the results of test runs, track defects, prioritize defects, and assign defects to developers. In summary, QMS serves as a common platform for facilitators and UAT testers.

Facilitators are tasked with training non-technical business users on how to use QMS technical tools. QMS that are globally available in the market include HP Quality Center, IBM Rational Quality Manager etc. These tools have a plethora of multilingual support with study materials, user guides and social networking communities. The next steps with this research is to determine how to replicate SP created in a face-to-face UAT event within a remote UAT experience.

References

1. Aragon, S.R.: Creating social presence in online environments. New Directions for Adult and Continuing Education (100), 57–68 (2003)
2. Axtell, C.M., Waterson, P.E., Clegg, C.W.: Problems Integrating User Participation into Software Development. International Journal of Human-Computer Studies, 323–345 (1997)

3. Beckett, H.: Going Offshore. Computer Weekly 32–34 (2005)
4. Butt, W., Fatimah, W.: An Overview of Software Models with Regard to the Users Involvement. International Journal of Computer Science 3(1), 107–112 (2012)
5. Butt, W., Fatimah, W.: Overview of Systems Design and Development with Regards to the Involvement of User, HCI and Software Engineers. International Journal of Computer Applications 58(7), 1–4 (2012)
6. Campbell, J.A.: User acceptance of videoconferencing: perceptions of task characteristics and media traits. In: Proceedings of the 33rd Annual Hawaii International Conference on System Sciences, p. 10 (2000)
7. Checkland, K., McDonald, R., Harrison, S.: Ticking boxes and changing the social world: data collection and the new UK general practice contract. Social Policy & Administration 41(7), 693–710 (2007)
8. Eisenhardt, K.M.: Making fast strategic decisions in high-velocity environment. Academy of Management Journal 32(3), 543–576 (1989)
9. Garrison, D.R., Anderson, T., Archer, W.: Critical Inquiry in a Text-Based Environment: Computer Conferencing in Higher Education. The Internet and Higher Education 2(2), 87–105 (2000)
10. Glaser, B., Strauss, A.: The discovery grounded theory: strategies for qualitative inquiry (1967)
11. Hilbert, D.M., Robbins, J.E., Redmiles, D.F.: Supporting Ongoing User Involvement in Development via Expectation-Driven Event Monitoring. Technical Report for Department of Information and Computer Science 97(19), pp. 1–11 (1997)
12. Hostetter, C., Busch, M.: Measuring up online: The relationship between social presence and student learning satisfaction. Journal of Scholarship of Teaching and Learning 6(2), 1–12 (2006)
13. Iivari, N.: Enculturation of User Involvement in Software Development Organizations- An Interpretive Case Study in the Product Development Context. Department of Information Processing Science, pp. 287–296 (2004)
14. Kehrwald, B.: Understanding Social Presence in Text-Based Online Learning Environments. Distance Education 29(1), 89–106 (2008)
15. Klein, Gorbett, S.: Lims User Acceptance Testing. Quality Assurance 10(2), 91–106 (2003)
16. Kujala, S.: User Involvement: A Review of the Benefits and Challenges. Behavior and Information Technology 22(1), 1–16 (2003)
17. Larson, G.B.: The User Acceptance Testing Process. Journal of Systems Management 46(5), 56–62 (1995)
18. Lohmann, S., Rashid, A.: Fostering Remote User Participation and Integration of User Feedback into Software Development, pp. 1–3 (2008)
19. Lowenthal, P.: Social Presence. Journal of Social Computing; Concepts, Methodologies, Tools and Applications, 129–136 (2010)
20. Ludmer, H.: Zero Defects. Industrial Management 11(4) (1969)
21. Majid, R.A., Noor, N.L.M., Adnan, W.A.W., Mansor, S.: A Survey on User Involvement in Software Development Life Cycle from Practitioner's Perspectives. In: Computer Sciences and Convergence Information Technology Conference, pp. 240–243 (2010)
22. Mehrabian, A.: Some referents and measures of nonverbal behavior. Journal of Behavior Research Methods and Instrumentation 1(6), 203–207 (1969)
23. Muthitacharoen, A., Saeed, K.A.: Examining User Involvement in Continuous Software Development. Communications of the ACM 52(9), 113–117 (2009)

24. Norton, R.W.: Communicator Style in Teaching: Giving Good Form to Content. Communicating in College Classrooms (26), 33–40 (1986)
25. Pettigrew, A.M.: Longitudinal Field Research on Change: Theory and Practice. Organization Science 1(3), 267–292 (1990)
26. Picciano, A.: Beyond student perceptions: Issues of interaction, presence, and performance in an online course. Journal of Asynchronous Learning Networks 6(1), 21–40 (2002)
27. Richardson, J.C., Swan, K.: Examining social presence in online courses in relation to students' perceived learning and satisfaction. Journal of Asynchronous Learning Networks 7(1), 68–88 (2003)
28. Rourke, L., Anderson, T., Garrison, D.R., Archer, W.: Assessing social presence in asynchronous text-based computer conferencing. The Journal of Distance Education/Revue de l'Éducation à Distance 14(2), 50–71 (2007)
29. Russo, T., Benson, S.: Learning with invisible others: Perceptions of online presence and their relationship to cognitive and effective learning. Educational Technology and Society 8(1), 54–62 (2005)
30. Sallnas, E.L., Rassmus-Grohn, K., Sjostrom, C.: Supporting presence in collaborative environments by haptic force feedback. ACM Transactions on Computer-Human Interactions 7(4), 461–467 (2000), Science 8(1), 97–106 (2000)
31. Seffah, A., Habieb-Mammar, H.: Usability engineering laboratories: Limitations and challenges toward a unifying tools/practices environment. Behaviour & Information Technology 28(3), 281–291 (2009)
32. Sproull, L., Keisler, S.: Reducing social context cues: Electronic mail in organizational communication. Management Science 32(11), 1492–1513 (1986)
33. Sutton, R.I.: Crossroads-The Virtues of Closet Qualitative Research. Organization Science 8(1), 97–106 (1997)
34. Swan, K., Shih, L.F.: On the nature of development of social presence in online course discussion. Journal of Asynchronous Learning Networks 9(3), 115–136 (2005)
35. Tu, C.H.: Online learning migration: Form social learning theory to social presence theory in a CMC environment. Journal of Network and Computer Applications 2, 27–37 (2000)
36. Tu, C.H., McIsaac, M.: The relationship of social presence and interaction in online classes. The American Journal of Distance Education 16(3), 131–150 (2002)
37. Walther, J.B., Burgoon, J.K.: Relational commination in computer-mediated interaction. Human Communication Research 19(1), 50–88 (1992)
38. Wei, C., Chen, N., Kinshuk: A model for social presence in online classrooms. Educational Technology Research and Development 60(3), 529–545 (2012)
39. Yin, R.K.: Case Study Research: Design and Methods. Sage Publications, Beverly Hills (1984)

How to Improve Customer Relationship Management in Air Transportation Using Case-Based Reasoning

Rawia Sammout[1], Makram Souii[2], and Mansour Elghoul[3]

[1] Higher Institute of Management of Gabes
Street Jilani Habib, Gabes 6002, Tunisia
[2] University of Lille de nord, F-59000 Lille, France
UVHC, LAMIH, F-59313 Valenciennes, France
CNRS, UMR 8201, F-59313 Valenciennes, France
[3] University of Lorraine, Nancy 2, France
Sammout.rawia@gmail.com, Souii_makram@yahoo.fr,
m-elghoul@orange.fr

Abstract. This paper describes research that aims to provide a new strategy for Customer Relationship Management for Air Transportation. It presents our proposed approach based on Knowledge Management processes, Enterprise Risk Management and Case-Based Reasoning. It aims to mitigate risks facing in air transportation process. The principle of this method consists in treating a new risk by counting on previous former experiments (case of reference). This type of reasoning rests on the following hypothesis: if a past risk and the new one are sufficiently similar, then all that can be explained or applied to the past risks or experiments (case bases) remains valid if one applies it to the new risk or for new situation which represents the new risk or problem to be solved. The idea of this approach consists on predicting adapted solution basing on the existing risks in the case base having the same contexts.

Keywords: Customer Relationship Management, Air Transportation, Knowledge Management, Enterprise Risk Management, Case Based Reasoning.

1   Introduction

The aim of knowledge Management (KM) as an organized and crucial process is to protect the organization's intellectual capital (knowledge of employees) for future benefits. In fact, sharing the right knowledge to the right person, at the right time in the right formats are very important steps that lead to max maximize the productive efficiency of the enterprise. In addition, this knowledge will be used and integrated for business needs in many different contexts (such as production, logistics and transport etc.) in order to increase the organization short and long term value to its stakeholders. In this paper, we study how to improve Customer Relationship Management (CRM) in Air Transportation (AT) using Case Based Reasoning (CBR)? A risk is the probability of the occurrence of an external or internal action which may lead to a threat of damage, injury, liability, loss, or any other negative result, and that may be

F.F.-H. Nah (Ed.): HCIB/HCII 2014, LNCS 8527, pp. 103–111, 2014.
© Springer International Publishing Switzerland 2014

avoided and reduced through preemptive action [1] [2]. For example: death, injuries form turbulence and baggage, dissatisfaction, bad provision of information, bad communication , misunderstanding, noise and mobility, bad cleaner staff, bad service quality, bad presentation of safety rules, lack or lost of baggage, uncomfortability of customer, lack of respect etc. Generally, these risks have great impacts on the achieving the origination objectives. In this context, our approach's aim is to mitigate the danger based on the interaction between Enterprise Risk Management (ERM) and KM and using the CBR. The idea is to deal with all the risks that may affect customer during the air transportation process from the registration of the customer to the analytics and feedback post-journey. Furthermore, it also endeavors also to create new opportunities in order to enhance the capacity of building a perceived value to its customers.

2   The Proposed Approach Overview

Based on KM processes [3], our method has four phases (Fig. 1): (1) Knowledge creation and sharing phase, (2) Knowledge analyzing phase, (3) Knowledge storage phase, (4) Knowledge application and transfer phase.

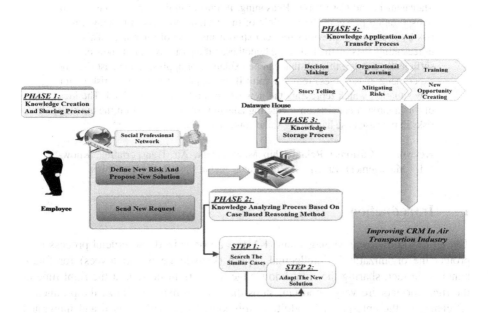

Fig. 1. Our research model design

2.1   Knowledge Creation and Sharing Process

The purpose of this phase is the identification of risk caused customer dissatisfaction. It includes two steps as below:

Identification of Risk and Proposition of Its Appropriate Solution. Each employee adds the risk faced during the air transportation process and that may affect customer satisfaction (such as noise, mobility, bad services, lack of safe, bad communication, lack of baggage, misunderstanding etc). Then he proposes its associate solution in the professional social network in order to, create a Community of Practice (CoP)[1] with other employees, discussing the relative issue and generating a number of solutions (references cases).

Formulate New Request. The employee faces a risk and wants to know how to solve it. He formulates a request to the system specifying the risk. The system treats the request based on the CBR method and answers the employee with the appropriate solution adapted on his/her context based on fuzzy logic.

2.2   Knowledge Analysis Process

The goal of this phase is the optimization of the best adequate solution associated to each risk defined using the CBR. Case-based reasoning is used to solve a new problem by remembering a previous similar situation and by reusing information and knowledge of previous situations. It is based on the following hypothesis: if a past experience and a new situation are sufficiently similar, then everything can be explained or applied to past experience (case base) is still valid when it's applied to the new situation that represents the new problem to solve [5] [6] [7].

The purpose of CBR is to composite a relevant solution in current context by comparing it with other similar contexts of use. CBR is composed by four steps: selecting the similar cases, fuzzy adaptation, revision and learning. The two latest steps (revision and learning) are described in the following phase.

Step1: Selecting the similar cases. This step is based on the contextual filtering. The system uses the characteristics of context in order to compare the new case (NC) with the existing cases (EC) using the following formula:

$$\text{Sim (NC, EC)} = \sum_{a=0}^{A} \frac{NC_{xa} - EC_{xa}}{DM} \tag{1}$$

With NC is the new case, EC is the existing one.

A is the set of the user attributes; NC_{xa} represents the value of the current user attribute and EC_{xa}, the value in the existing contexts.

DM is the difference between the maximum threshold and the minimum threshold.

B_c is the case base filtered by selecting similar cases of the current user request (risk) in the context C.

The contextual filtering aims to measure the similarity between the current context and the existing contexts basing on the Pearson correlation. In this context, the most similar cases are selected from the collection B_c. The context C_i is composed by a finite

---

[1] Communities of Practice (CoP) are techniques used in KM, the purpose is to connect people with specific objective that voluntarily want to share knowledge [4].

set $\{a_{1i}, a_{2i}, ..., a_{ni}\}_{i,n \in IN}$ that differs in number from a risk to another. Two contexts are similar if its attributes are respectively similar. $C_1 = a_{11} \cup a_{21} \cup ... \cup a_{n1}$; $C_2 = a_{12} \cup a_{22} \cup ... \cup a_{n2}$ with $n \in IN$.

$$Sim\ (NC;\ EC) = (Sim_R\ (R_i;\ R_j), Sim_C\ (C_i;\ Cj)) \quad (2)$$

$$Sim_C\ (C_i;\ C_j) = (Sim\ (a_{1i};\ a_{1j}),\ Sim\ (a_{2i};\ a_{2j}),\ ...,\ Sim\ (a_{ni};\ a_n))_{i,j,n \in IN} \quad (3)$$

With a_n represents an attribute that characterises the context C.
And i, j are the coefficients of two different contexts relative to the same risk.

$$Sim(NC;\ EC) = (Sim_R(R_i;\ R_j),\ Sim\ (a_{1i};\ a_{1j}),\ Sim\ (a_{2i};\ a_{2j}),\ ...,\ Sim(a_{ni};\ a_{nj})_{i,j,n \in IN}) \quad (4)$$

Step2: Adapting the new solution. Basing on the selected cases, the idea is to propose an adapted solution to the new context. It is a combination of many parts of the solutions (Si, Sj ...) from the most similar cases. To this end, this step is segmented into three levels fuzzification, fuzzy inference and defuzzification.

Fuzzification. It is the process by which an element is rendered diffuse by the combination of real values and membership functions. It converges an input determined to a fuzzy output. The similarities corresponding to the different dimensions of context calculated in the previous phase are the input variables of fuzzy system.

The fuzzy system is based on n attributes of the context as inputs: $Sim(a_{1i};\ a_{1j})$, Sim $(a_{2i};\ a_{2j})$, ..., $Sim(a_{ni};\ a_{nj})$ with $i, j, n \in IN$. The system output is the relevant solution "S" which is the combination of many parts of the solutions (S_i, S_j ...) from the most similar cases. These input and output variables are the linguistic variables of the fuzzy system.

The linguistic variable is represented by:
Sim is the similarity of the context attribute between two similar contexts i and j with i, j $\in N$.
L is the set of linguistic terms.
U is the universe of discourse.

$$\text{Number of rules} = L^n * S \quad (5)$$

With n is the number of fuzzy system inputs.
S is the number of output

Fuzzy inference. It aims to assess the contributions of all active rules. The fuzzy inference is affected from a rules database. Each fuzzy rule expresses a relationship between the input variables (context attributes similarity Sim) and the output variable (relevance of the solution "S"). The fuzzy rule in our approach is as follows:
If (Sim is A) Then (S is B)
Where Sim is the context attributes similarity correlated (the premises of the rule), S is the relevance of the solution (the conclusion of the rule), and A and B are linguistic terms determined by the fuzzy sets.

In the Mamdani model, the implication and aggregation are two fragments of the fuzzy inference. It is based on the use of the minimum operator "min" for implication and the maximum operator "max" for the aggregation rules.

Defuzzification. It is the process by which fuzzy results of similarities correlated are translated into specific numerical results indicating the relevance of the solution. After combining the rules obtained, we must produce an encryption output. The evaluation of the solution is implemented based on "Mamdani" model.

In our inspired Mamdani model approach, defuzzification is performed by the center of gravity method of rules results.

$$F(r_i, c_i, s_i) = \frac{\int \mu(s) \, s \, d_s}{\int \mu(s) \, d_s} \tag{6}$$

$F(r_i, c_i, s_i)$ is the function associated with the case c_i with $\mu(s)$ is the membership function of the output variable s_i and r_i is the rules.

The fuzzy inference releases a sorted list of relevant solutions L^F.

$$L^F = \{ (s_i, F(r_i, c_i, s_i)) \setminus (r_i, c_i, c_i) \in B_c \}$$

The informational content S^I is an integral part of the relevant solution from the sorted list L^F of relevant solutions, maximizing the similarity Sim correlated to the retrieved case. The solution recommended to the user is a combination of torque solutions (S^I).

2.3   Knowledge Storage Process

To be usable, a base of case must contain a certain number of cases. An empty base of case does not allow any reasoning. Consequently, it is important to initiate the base of case with relevant cases. To this end, the adapted solutions will be revised by the evaluator. Then, the validated solutions will be added to the base of cases $B_c = B_c \cup (R_s, C_s, S)$. In fact, Learning involves the enrichment of the context of use and solutions.

2.4   Knowledge Application Process

This phase represents that the transfer and the use of knowledge can enhance customer value. In this level, decision maker interprets these results (e.g., statistics, classification) and suggests a radical way for a new improvement process through training, storytelling, lesson learned etc [7].

3   Application in Air Transportaation

In order to validate our method, we have implemented a professional network in air transportation described in the following figure (cf.Fig.2). This application provides employees with a relevant solutions responding to the current risk basing on the previous experiences. In an integrated development environment "Netbeans", we developed the application integrating Java API/ Matlab Control.

Fig. 2. Professional network for air transport service

3.1   Phase 1: Knowledge Creation and Sharing Process

When an employee is faced a new risk, he can formulate a new request in order to find an appropriate solution. The figure 3 presents the interface that can be used by an employee.

Fig. 2. Example of an employee request

This request must include the current context. The figure 4 presents an example of a context.

Risk: Cancellation flight

Context: Weather condition

C_2= Hurricane Charley (2004) = Wind 150 mph (240 km/h), pressure 941 mbar (hPa); 27.79 inHg

C_1= Hurricane Katrina (2005) = Wind 175 mph (280 km/h), pressure 902 mbar (hPa); 26.64 inHg

Fig. 3. Example of a context

3.2   Phase 2: Knowledge Analyzing Phase

Step1: Selecting of similar cases. We have to calculate the Sim of the context between the new case C_1 and the existing case C_2 as follow:

$$\text{Sim}_C(C_1, C_2) = (0.545) \tag{7}$$

Step 2: Adapting the new solution. This step is divided into three levels as below:

Fuzzification. The fuzzifier mapes two inputs numbers (Sim(wind) and Sim(pressure)) into fuzzy membership. The universe of discourse represents by U = [0, 1]. We propose Low, Medium and High as the set of linguistic terms. The membership function implemented for Sim(wind) and Sim(pressure) is trapezoid.

The figure 5 describes the partition of fuzzy classes. It aims to divide the universe of discourse of each linguistic variable on fuzzy classes. It is universal for all the linguistic variables as below: Low [-0.36 -0.04 0.04 0.36], Medium [0.14 0.46 0.54 0.86], High [0.64 0.96 1.04 1.36].

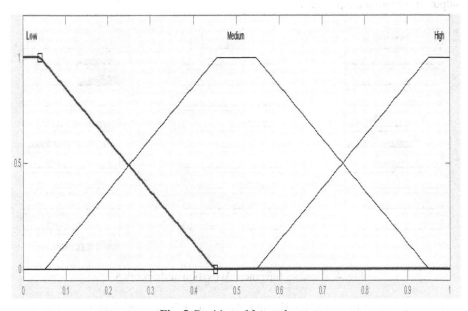

Fig. 5. Partition of fuzzy classes

Fuzzy inference. It defines mapping from input fuzzy sets into output fuzzy sets basing on the active rules (cf. Fig. 6). The number of rules in this case is: $3^2 * 1 = 9$ rules.

R1: If (Sim(pressure) is Low) and (Sim(wind) is Low) Then S is Low
R2: If (Sim(pressure) is Low) and (Sim(wind) is Medium) Then S is Low
R3: If (Sim(pressure) is Low) and (Sim(wind) is High) Then S is Low
R4: If (Sim(pressure) is Medium) and (Sim(wind) is Low) Then S is Low
R5: If (Sim(pressure) is Medium) and (Sim(wind) is Medium) Then S is Medium
R6: If (Sim(pressure) is Medium) and (Sim(wind) is High) Then S is High
R7: If (Sim(pressure) is High) and (Sim(wind) is Low) Then S is Medium
R8: If (Sim(pressure) is High) and (Sim (wind) is Medium) Then S is Medium
R9: If (Sim(pressure) is High) and (Sim (wind) is High) Then S is High

Fig. 6. List of fuzzy rules

Defuzzification. It is based on Mamdani model (cf. Fig.7) which incorporates the center gravity method by the evaluation of the set of rules in the fuzzy inference. It maps output fuzzy into a crisp values.

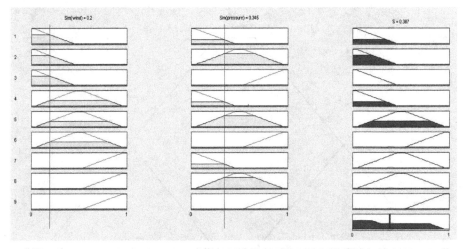

Fig. 4. Mamdani Inference: Activation of the result S

For the example of Hurricane Katrina, the solution is adapted from the solution of Hurricane Charley (wind= 280, pressure= 902) F= 0.387.

3.3   Phase 3: Knowledge Storage Process

At this level of our work, the adapted solution resulted from the previous phase will be evaluated by an expert. Then, the validated solutions will be retain in the case base.

3.4   Phase 4: Knowledge Application Process

Training and lesson learning session will be establishing for the employees basing on the case base retained from the previous phase. The purpose of this process is to exploit the previous experiences in order to improve the intellectual capital and competences of the employees and facilitate the management of risk caused customer dissatisfaction.

4   Conclusion

In this paper, we presented a crucial and generic approach based on the interaction between two disciplines KM and ERM and using CBR and fuzzy logic in order to enhance CRM in AT. First, by identifying risks caused customer dissatisfaction. Second, proposing new solutions responding to risks faced in all touch points of the AT process. Finally, the application of a learning process from the previous experiences (risk and solutions) for the employees will be established. A challenge for future research will be to refine the optimization of the adapted solution based on genetic algorithm.

References

1. Monahan, G.: Enterprise Risk Management: A Methodology for Achieving Strategic Objectives. John Wiley & Sons Inc., New Jersey (2008)
2. International Organization for Standardization, ISO (2009)
3. Alavi, M., Leidner, D.: Review: Knowledge management and knowledge management systems: Conceptual foundations and research issues. MIS Quarterly 25(1), 107–136 (2001)
4. Rodriguez, E., Edwards, J.S.: Before and After Modeling: Risk Knowledge Management is required, Society of Actuaries. Paper presented at the 6th Annual Premier Global Event on ERM, Chicago (2008)
5. Coyle, L., Cunningham, P., Hayes, C.: A Case-Based Personal Travel Assistant for Elaborating User Requirements and Assessing Offers. In: 6th European Conference on Advances in Case-Based Reasoning, ECCBR, Aberdeen Scotland, UK (2002)
6. Lajmi, S., Ghedira, C., Ghedira, K.: CBR Method for Web Service Composition. In: Damiani, E., Yetongnon, K., Chbeir, R., Dipanda, A. (eds.) SITIS 2006. LNCS, vol. 4879, pp. 314–326. Springer, Heidelberg (2009)
7. Aamodt, A.: Towards robust expert systems that learn from experience an architectural framework. In: Boose, J., Gaines, B., Ganascia, J.-G. (eds.) EKAW-89: Third European Knowledge Acquisition for Knowledge-Based Systems Workshop, Paris, pp. 311–326 (July 1989)

Toward a Faithful Bidding
of Web Advertisement

Takumi Uchida, Koken Ozaki, and Kenichi Yoshida

Graduate School of Business Sciences, University of Tsukuba, Japan
{uchida,koken,yoshida}@gssm.otsuka.tsukuba.ac.jp

Abstract. Web marketing is a key activity of e-commerce. Due to the
proliferation of internet technology, available internet marketing data become huge and complex. Efficient use of such large data maximizes the
profit of web marketing. Although there are a variety of studies motivated by these backgrounds, there still remains room for improvement on
data usage. In this paper, we have proposed a method to realize faithful
bidding of web advertisement. The experimental results show: 1) The use
of data by the current operators is unreliable, 2) By using the proposed
method, the advertisement value of bidding becomes clear. For example, the method could find a cluster of advertisements that has clear
cost-effectiveness over other clusters.

Keywords: Internet advertisement, allocation of advertising budget,
decision support.

1 Introduction

Web marketing is a key activity of e-commerce today. Due to the proliferation of
internet technology, available internet marketing data become huge and complex.
Efficient use of such large data maximizes the profit of web marketing. Although
there exist a variety of studies such as [1],[2],[3] motivated by these backgrounds,
actual business scenes still rely on the operators' know-how. There still remains
room for improvement on data usage.

For example, Fig.1 shows how operators who are working for an advertising
agency make their decision on advertisement. They decide the allocation of advertising budget using the Fig.1. X-axis is the number of past actions by the
customers. Here, actions are typically web clicks toward the purchase and the
installation of software. The target of advertising agency is the maximization
of the actions. Y-axis is the budget (costs) used to advertise web pages for the
purchase and the software installation. One another target of advertising agency
is the minimization of this cost. Cost effectiveness which is typically calculated
by X/Y (i.e., actions/costs) is important.

An example of know-how which we interviewed from operators of an advertising agency is: "If the current web advertisement is laid out on the lower right
segment, increase the budget since the past advertisement worked well (having
height cost efficiency)". This know-how is reasonable if the number of data is

F.F.-H. Nah (Ed.): HCIB/HCII 2014, LNCS 8527, pp. 112–118, 2014.
© Springer International Publishing Switzerland 2014

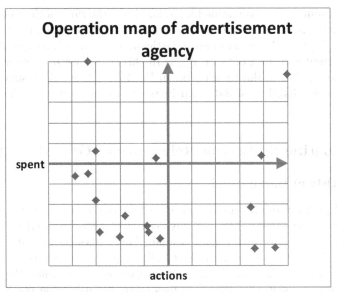

X−axis is number of past actions by the customers such as web clicks toward the purchase and installation of software. Y−axis is the budget used to advertise web pages for the actions.

Fig. 1. Operation Map of an Advertisement Agency

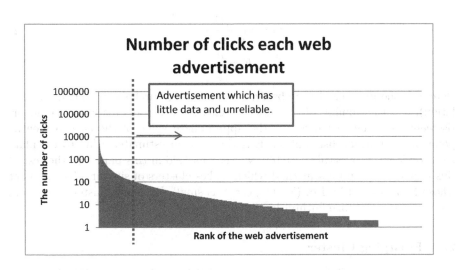

Fig. 2. Number of Clicks for Each Web Advertisements

sufficient and reliable. However, we have found that they don't have enough data in most cases. Fig.2 shows the fact we found. In Fig.2, Y-axis shows the number

of clicks for some web advertisement. X-axis shows the rank of the web advertisement in clicks order. Although the total number of data is large, most of the data
plotted on Fig.1 has little data and statistically unreliable. The operator use too
trifling attributes to plot data on Fig.1. In this study, we propose a method to
enlarge the number of data each plot on Fig.1 has. The enlargement increases
the statistical reliability of data and increases the adequacy of the operators'
judgments.

2   Evaluating Statistical Reliability of Operators Action

2.1   Statistical Background

Statistical problem of current operator's action is the size of data. Since most
of the web advertisement does not have sufficient customer's clicks, the size of
data about each web advertisement is small. This makes the operators judgment
unreliable. Thus, we develop a method to form groups of similar web advertisements. By merging the data for the similar web advertisements, the number of
the data in the resulting cluster becomes large. By using the resulting cluster
as the basic unit of decisions, we can realize faithful bidding for each cluster.
Following equations give us theoretical background [4]:

$$Prob\left(\frac{c}{n} - s\sqrt{\frac{\frac{c}{n}(1 - \frac{c}{n})}{n}} \le p \le \frac{c}{n} + s\sqrt{\frac{\frac{c}{n}(1 - \frac{c}{n})}{n}}\right) \approx 1 - \alpha \qquad (1)$$

$$m = s\sqrt{\frac{\frac{c}{n}(1 - \frac{c}{n})}{n}} \qquad (2)$$

$$E = \frac{m}{\frac{c}{n}} \qquad (3)$$

Here, c is the number of the observed actions (i.e., purchase or software installation). n is the number of the observed clicks which users made on the advertisement. p is the real n/c. s is the approximate value of the each percentile
point of the normal distribution. E is the error of estimated c/n. To calculate
95% confidential interval (α=0.05), we set s as 1.96 in this paper. In the rest of
this paper, we propose a method which makes clusters of similar advertisement
whose E calculated by Eq. (2), i.e., error, is small. By using cluster with small
error, we try to realize faithful bidding.

2.2   Enlarging Cluster

According to the real data, most of actions/clicks are lower than 5%. With such
data, we try to make a model to predict action from clicks. We assume that the
number of actions made by customers follows Poisson distribution [5]. Precisely
speaking, we assume following Poisson regression:

$$f(c_i) = \frac{\mu_i^{c_i} e^{-\mu_i}}{c_i!} \tag{4}$$

$$\mu_i = n_i e^{\beta_0 + \sum_{j=1}^{J} \beta_j x_{ij}} \tag{5}$$

$$log\mu_i = logn_i + \beta_0 + \sum_{j=1}^{J} \beta_j x_{ij} \tag{6}$$

Here, index i is the cluster-id of advertisements. Each cluster is formed by the advertisements whose attributes share common x_{ij}. x_{ij} is the attributes which specify the characteristics of the advertisement and the users who click that advertisement. Table.1 shows example of attributes. Precisely speaking, since all the attributes we found are categorical attributes, we use binary representation of these attributes. In other words, we actually use attributes x_{ij} each corresponds to the attributes values such as "Tokyo" and "Oosaka". If the value of original attribute "Region" is "Tokyo", the corresponding x_{ij} is set to be 1.

Table 1. Example of Attributes

Attribute	Value
Age	Ex) 10-19, 20-29,,,
Region	Ex) Tokyo, Oosaka,,,
Sex	Male, Female
User Interest	Ex) Fashion, Sports,,,
Contents	Ex) Movie, Music,,,

c_i is the number of the observed actions. n_i is the number of the observed clicks which users did on the advertisement. f(c_i) is probability distribution of actions c_i. μ_i is expectation of c_i (actions). β is regression coefficient. Institutions behind above equations are 1) we can use the number of clicks to estimate the number of customers actions, 2) age, region, and other attributes in Table.1 affect the process of user behavior and affect the conversion process from clicks to actions, 3) Poisson process is reasonable way to represent this process. If the number of actions can be modeled by Poisson process based on the number of clicks and attribute x_{ij}, equation (5), i.e., μ_i, estimates the number of actions.

Here some of attributes x_{ij} seems to be non-essential. Thus, we try to eliminate non-essential x_{ij} from the equations. We use Akaike's information criterion to eliminate non-essential attributes. We perfume a greedy elimination process. In each step of elimination process, we select attribute x_{ij} which improves AIC index most. This elimination process terminates when none of remaining x_{ij} improves AIC index.

3 Experimental Results

To shows the advantage of the proposed method, we have applied the proposed method on the data shown in Fig.2. Fig.3 and 4 show results. Fig.3 shows the estimated error for the cluster of advertisements. Here clusters are formed by grouping advertisements with same attributes. All the attributes are used to make clusters for Fig.3. X-axis shows the errors of clusters. It is E calculated by Eq. (3). Y-axis shows the number of actions gained by the advertisement (actions_share). It also shows the total cost for the advertisement (spent_share) and cost-effectiveness (actions_share/spent_share). For example, the height of left most histograms indicates low error rate (E<0.2, i.e. error<0.2). The customer actions won by corresponding advertisements are 62% with error rate less than 0.2. Although the use of budget on this segment seems to be reasonable, the clusters made with all attributes fail in allocating budget on this segment. Actually, budget used on the same advertisements is only 32%. This result shown in Fig.3 shows our start point of improvement.

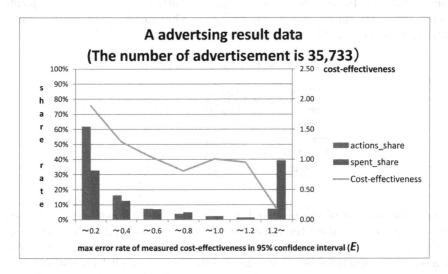

Fig. 3. Reliability of Current Operation

Fig.4 shows the process of improvement by our proposed method. Data shown in Fig.2 is based on 35,733 advertisements of 177 clients. We have applied the method on data of 177 advertisements of one client company to make Fig.4. The reason we have used the data of only one client is that the value of actions/clicks varies according to the industry. For example, the value of actions/clicks for cosmetics is far larger than that of real estimate. Mixing result of such industries makes the figure unclear. In Fig.4, X-axis is the error of estimated cost-effectiveness of operations (E of equation 3). Y-axis is the cost-effectiveness (total actions/total cost for the advertisements). Size of the circle is spent_share (total cost of advertisement / total cost of all advertisements). Fig.4 (a) shows the results of clusters formed with all attributes x_{ij} (i.e., start point). Fig.4 (b) shows results of clusters formed with selected attributes x_{ij} (i.e., the results by the proposed method). Fig.4 (c) shows results of clusters formed with randomly

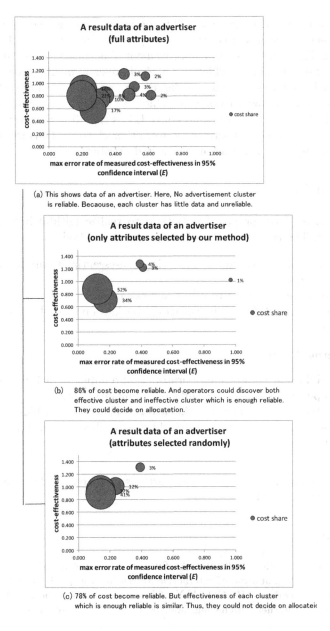

(a) This shows data of an advertiser. Here, No advertisement cluster is reliable. Becaouse, each cluster has little data and unreliable.

(b) 86% of cost become reliable. And operators could discover both effective cluster and ineffective cluster which is enough reliable. They could decide on allocatetion.

(c) 78% of cost become reliable. But effectiveness of each cluster which is enough reliable is similar. Thus, they could not decide on allocatei

Fig. 4. Effect of Enlarged Cluster

selected attributes x_{ij} for the comparison purpose. As shown in figures, using all attributes results too many clusters, and all E of clusters are larger than 0.2 (see Fig.4 (a)). Although, Fig.4 (a) shows the results with slightly larger clusters than that with clusters used in Fig.2, none of cluster has E less than 0.2. In the practical view points, E larger than 0.2 is too large. Thus none of results shown in Fig.2 has enough accuracy. On the contrary, 86% of results in Fig.4 (b) have E less than 0.2. This shows the clear improvement of accuracy. Moreover, it shows the fact the one large cluster which has 52% of advertisements has clear advantage of cost-effectiveness over another large cluster with 34% of advertisements. Note that this improvement cannot be achieved by random attributes selection (Fig.4 (c)). In Fig.4 (c), 78% of results have E less than 0.2. However, the found clusters have no clear cost-effectiveness over other clusters. Thus we cannot use the results of Fig.4 (c), i.e., randomly selected attributes.

4   Conclusion

In this paper, we have proposed a method to realize faithful bidding of web advertisement. The characteristics of the proposed method are:

- Enlargement of data cluster by removing non-essential attributes during the clustering phase.
- A statistical index is used to select non-essential attributes. Poisson regression analysis and AIC are the theatrical background to select non-essential attributes.

The experimental results show:

- The use of data by the current operators is unreliable. In fact, 67% of current bidding operations don't have sufficient number of data.
- By using the proposed method, the advertisement value of bidding becomes clear. For example, the method could find a cluster that has clear cost-effectiveness over other clusters.

Acknowledgments. This work was partly supported by JSPS KAKENHI Grant Number 25280114.

References

1. Schlosser, A.E., Shavitt, S., Kanfer, A.: Survey of Internet users' attitudes toward Internet advertising. Journal of Interactive Marketing 13(3), 34–54 (1999)
2. Manchanda, P., Dube, J.-P., Goh, K.Y., Chintagunta, P.K.: The Effect of Banner Advertising on Internet Purchasing. Journal of Marketing Research 43(1), 98–108 (2006)
3. Shabbir, G., Niazi, K., Siddiqui, J., Shah, B.A., Hunjra, A.I.: Effective advertising and its influence on consumer buying behavior. MPRA Paper No. 40689 (August 2012)
4. Hogg, R.V., McKean, J.W., Craig, A.T.: Introduction to Mathematical Statistics, 6th edn. Person Education, Inc. (June 2004)
5. Dobson, A.J.: An Introduction to Generalized Linear Models, ch. 9, 3rd edn. Chapman and Hall/CRC (November 2001)

Social Media for Business

An Evaluation Scheme for Performance Measurement of Facebook Use

An Example of Social Organizations in Vienna

Claudia Brauer[1], Christine Bauer[2], and Mario Dirlinger[3]

[1] Management Center Innsbruck, Innsbruck,
Austria & Vienna University of Economics and Business,
Department of Information Systems & Operations, Vienna, Austria
[2] Vienna University of Economics and Business,
Department of Information Systems & Operations, Vienna, Austria
[3] WUK Bildung und Beratung, Vienna, Austria
claudia.brauer@mci.edu,
chris.bauer@wu.ac.at,mario.dirlinger@gmail.com

Abstract. Online social networks, and Facebook in particular, have evolved from a niche to a mass phenomenon. Organizations have recognized the importance of using Facebook to achieve their organizational goals. Still, literature lacks a systematic evaluation scheme for measuring the performance of an organization's Facebook use. When investigating how organizations use Facebook, research tends to focus on for-profit organizations, overlooking the way social organizations use Facebook. This article introduces an evaluation scheme that includes nine categories of performance measurement. Applying the scheme to Facebook's use by social organisations in Vienna, we demonstrate the scheme's applicability. Plus, by using various indicators and benchmarks, we evaluate the level of sophistication of each organization's use of Facebook. We investigated all 517 social organizations based in Vienna, including those in all fields of practice, based on publicly available Facebook data from January to June 2012. The analysis reveals that the majority of social organizations are beginners at utilizing Facebook's potential.

Keywords: Facebook, online social networks, performance measurement, social organizations, evaluation scheme.

1   Introduction

Online social networks have evolved from a niche to a mass phenomenon that epitomizes the digital era [1]. With a daily average use of 30 to 60 minutes [2] by one billion users [3], the world's largest social network, Facebook, has become an integral part of everyday life [3]. In recent years, organizations have recognized the importance of using Facebook to achieve their organizational goals. Research on the use of Facebook tends to focus on for-profit companies or end users, and rarely investigates how social organizations use Facebook, especially in German-speaking regions.

F.F.-H. Nah (Ed.): HCIB/HCII 2014, LNCS 8527, pp. 121–132, 2014.
© Springer International Publishing Switzerland 2014

The few existing studies mainly discuss the general importance of social media for social organizations (e.g., [4-6]). Because these studies commonly use qualitative research methods, there are few quantitative results on the use of Facebook in social organizations. For example, Waters [7] investigated the use of social media in non-profit organizations. The analysis of expert interviews and focus groups showed that social organizations use Facebook to build and maintain relationships with their stakeholders. Other studies, in contrast, have revealed that social organizations use Facebook primarily to describe the organization but do not leverage the interaction possibilities and networking opportunities that Facebook offers. Furthermore, research shows that the majority of social organizations start using social media without having an integrated social media strategy or a sophisticated Facebook strategy. Most studies on Facebook use in social organizations comes from the United States (e.g., [8]); in German-speaking regions, empirical research on that topic is scarce. Annually since 2009, Kiefer [5] has investigated the use of online social networks in a cross-sectional study of 60 German non-profit organizations [5, 9, 10]; however, this research only considers organizations in three fields of practice (environmental/nature protection, international affairs, social affairs). While Kiefer's work may identify Facebook as the strongest online social network of non-profit organizations, it has not garnered profound insights about the use and the development potential of online social networks. To date, there is no scientific work based on real data that investigates the use and the development potential of Facebook for social organizations. Against this background, the present article is dedicated to the following research questions: How can the use of Facebook be evaluated in terms of performance measurement? How do social organizations perform with respect to their use of Facebook? To what extent are these organizations utilizing Facebook's potential? This article introduces an evaluation scheme that includes nine categories of performance measurement. Using social organizations in Vienna as our example, we demonstrate the scheme's applicability and, with various indicators and benchmarks, we evaluate the level of sophistication of each organization's use of Facebook. We investigated all social organizations based in Vienna (N=517), including those in all fields of practice, based on publicly available Facebook data from 1 January 2012 to 30 June 2012. We analyzed the organizations' use of the various Facebook functionalities as well as the 2479 publicly available Facebook posts for the respective time period.Due to the topic's relevance and the lack of comparative studies, this research contributes to both science and practice. The next section presents a literature review of Facebook use by non-profit organizations and discusses performance measurement of this use. Subsequently, the data collection is described and the research results and evaluation scheme are presented. Finally, research results are discussed and new fields of research are identified.

2   Related Work

In this section, we present related work concerning online social networks, with a focus on Facebook use by non-profit organizations. Then, we describe performance metrics for measuring the success of a Facebook page for social organizations.

2.1   Facebook Use in Non-profit Organizations

Some studies have already investigated the importance of social media for non-profit organizations [4-6, 9-12]. For example, Waters [7] revealed that non-profit organizations use Facebook to interact with their stakeholders and to build and maintain relationships with relevant stakeholders. Although some studies have investigated the use of online social networks for social organizations in particular, little research has focused on the use of Facebook. For example, Waters, Burnett, Lamm and Lucas [8] studied the importance of Facebook based on a content analysis of 275 randomly selected non-profit organizations in the United States. They found that non-profit organizations do not comprehensively use the information and communication opportunities of Facebook, and that the majority of social organizations have not yet established an integrated Facebook strategy. Other studies have found that non-profit organizations do not comprehensively use the interaction [5, 8] and networking opportunities [10] of Facebook, and that the majority of social organizations have developed neither an online social media strategy nor a specific Facebook strategy [13].

2.2   Performance Metrics for Measuring Facebook Use

Only a few scientific articles are dedicated to the performance measurement of online social networks, or Facebook in particular, which may be due to the novelty of the topic. While some authors refer to performance measurement of any kind of online social networks under the term "social media analytics", other authors focus on Facebook and still use the general term "social media analytics" [14, 15]. In contrast to academic literature, practitioners (e.g., Jim Sterne, Avinash Kaushnik, etc.) and several associations (e.g., Interactive Advertising Bureau, International Association for Measurement and Evaluation of Communication, etc.) have deeply discussed the topic of performance measurement of online social networks, specifically Facebook. They suggested a variety of performance metrics to measure the success of Facebook use (e.g., number of "likes" (fans), number of posts, number of photos uploaded, number of links, number of comments, number of foreign contributions, number and percentage of responses to posts of other users, etc.). In addition, various metrics have been developed to compare different online social networks (e.g., virality, interactivity of posts, use of multiple media in posts). In the present article, we have developed an evaluation scheme based on these metrics.

3   Research Procedure

In order to answer the research questions, we conducted an empirical study of Facebook use among social organizations in Vienna. Our analysis is based on publicly accessible data, from which we calculated the various performance metrics.

3.1   Research Sample

Our first step was to retrieve the names of all social organizations in Vienna that were registered in the online database, "Social Austria", of the Federal Ministry of Labour,

Social Affairs and Consumer Protection; this resulted in a set of 1682 social organizations based in Vienna (retrieved on 12 April 2012). After removing organizations
from the data set that were assigned to multiple fields of practice, we had a list of 517
social organizations. 25 organizations were removed from the list because they were
either not within the scope of the definition of a social organization by Dimmel [16]
or were already closed. Then, for every organization on the list, we investigated
whether it had registered a Facebook page. Only 73 of the 492 (14.8%) social organizations in Vienna had its own Facebook page. For 127 (25.8%) organizations, the
umbrella organization or the carrier of the organization operated the Facebook page.
18 organizations used Facebook via a "Facebook personal profile" and 104 via "Facebook Community". 292 social organizations (59.4%) did not have a Facebook page.

3.2   Coding Schemes for the Analysis of Facebook Pages and Posts

The coding scheme for the analysis of the Facebook pages was developed ex ante
based on Waters, Burnett, Lamm and Lucas [8][1]. Using this coding scheme, the various applications within Facebook (e.g., "information", "views", and "applications")
were analyzed. In addition, the Facebook pages were analyzed to determine which
applications, out of all those offered, were used by the social organizations. Furthermore, for deeper insights into how social organizations use Facebook, we conducted a
content analysis of the posts in the organizations' Facebook timelines (all posts from
1 January 2012 to 30 June 2012). The coding scheme was developed inductively from
raw data and was adapted during the coding phase. For every Facebook post, we captured a formal description and a description of the content. The formal information
included the date of the entry, the number of "likes", the number of comments, and
the sharing frequency of the post within Facebook. Regarding the content of posts, we
recorded whether the posts were manually entered or automatically retrieved (for
instance via other online social networks), and whether they contained links, photos,
videos, or audio files. Finally, we classified all Facebook posts by topic.

4   Research Results

4.1   Fields of Practice

As can be seen from Table 1, social organizations in the "Multicultural / International" (28.6%), "Work / Occupation" (22.9%), and "Migration" (21.8%) fields of
practice use Facebook to a great extent. However, these percentages have a limited
significance, because the number of organizations varies considerably between the
different fields of practice. Looking at the absolute values, the fields of practice of
"Social general" (n=39), "Health / Disease" (n=31), and "Work / Occupation" (n=30)
have the most Facebook pages. The fields of practice of "Delinquency" (22 organizations) and "Administration" (13 organizations) are hardly represented via Facebook.
Although the field of practice of "Family / Partner / Single parents" has a total of 137
organizations, the percentage of those social organizations with a Facebook page is

---

[1] The coding schemes can be requested from the authors.

relatively low (10.9%, n=15). Moreover, there is a significant correlation (Pearson correlation, p<0.01) between the number of organizations per field of practice and the use of a Facebook page.

Table 1. Social organizations ranked by percentage of Facebook pages per field of practice

Field of practice	# of organizations / field of practice	# of organizations with a Facebook page	Share of Facebook pages per field of practice
Multicultural / International	28	8	28.6%
Work / Occupation	131	30	22.9%
Migration	55	12	21.8%
Education	85	18	21.2%
Social general	185	39	21.1%
Health / Disease	161	31	19.3%
Housing / Accommodation	62	11	17.7%
Psyche	121	21	17.4%
Disability	188	28	14.9%
Children / Young adults	178	26	14.6%
Senior	86	12	14.0%
Men / Women	126	17	13.5%
Addiction	60	7	11.7%
Consumer / Legal regulations	44	5	11.4%
Family / Partner / Single parents	137	15	10.9%
Delinquency	22	1	4.5%
Administration	13	0	0.0%
Total	1682	281	-

4.2 Design of Facebook Pages and Use of Applications

On their Facebook pages, the majority of the analyzed social organizations provide a description of the organization (84.9%, n=62), identify their target groups (79.5%, n=58), and provide contact information (80.8%, n=59). Almost all social organizations link their Facebook page to their website (93.2%, n=68). Few organizations link in the notification area of the Facebook page to other online social communication channels (11%, n=8). Of those that do, the organizations have linked their Facebook page to Foursquare (n=3), YouTube (n=2), Twitter (n=2), MySpace (n=1) and Flickr (n=1).The photo application is the most commonly used Facebook application. During the investigation period, 1360 photos were uploaded, with an average of 23 photos uploaded per social organization. The events application is also highly utilized (50.7%, n=37). About a third of the social organizations have integrated the geographic map application, where the location of the organization is automatically shown on a map (34.2%, n=25). In contrast, donation applications (4.1%, n=3), videos (15.1%, n=11), and notes (6.8%, n=5) are hardly integrated into the Facebook pages. Individualized Facebook applications (e.g., netiquette, mission statement, offer, jobs, petitions, invitations, catalogue order, charity event, blog, and newsletter) are used by some organizations (21.9%, n=16). The group application is not used by any social organization.The number of "likes" is a key metric for measuring the success of a Facebook page as well as an organization's Facebook activities. The average number of "likes" per organization is 672 (sd=1.403, max=8.066, min=1). In contrast, Waters, Burnett, Lamm and Lucas [8] found in their study an average number of only 193 (sd=547.71, max=6.062) "likes" per organization. Moreover, in the present study, a significant correlation (Pearson correlation, $p<0.01$) between the number of "likes" and the field of practice was determined. Another key metric is the number of "people talking about this" per post. This metric is an indicator of the interactivity on a Facebook page within the previous seven days. The studied social organizations had an average "talking about" number of 14 (sd=29.74) during the investigation period, with 27 organizations having a "talking about" number of zero. Two social organizations reached a value for "talking about" of more than 100 (171 and 125, respectively). Due to the novelty of this Facebook application, there are currently no benchmarks published. In total, 2479 posts were published by the social organizations on their Facebook pages during the investigation period, which corresponds to an average of 34.43 posts (n=72, sd=45.62) per organization. 13 organizations (18.1%) did not publish any Facebook posts during the investigation period. One social organization published 308 (max. value) posts within that time, which corresponds to a frequency of 1.7 messages per day. Considering that the second-ranked organization published only 154 Facebook posts, the organizations' usage behavior is clearly diverse. The average daily post frequency of the social organizations was 0.19, which illustrates the discrepancy in posting behavior between the leading organization and the other organizations.

4.3   Content of Posts

Most Facebook posts concerned social policy issues (n=402), announcements of an organization's events (n=401), and product / service offers (n=393). Still, only half of the organizations (51.4%, n=37) posted content about social policy issues during the investigation period. Furthermore, the economic importance and impact of social organizations is reflected by their high demand for employees [17]; few social organizations, however, announced job vacancies via Facebook (n=19). In contrast, the messages application was often used by the organizations to provide information about their services and products. More than a tenth of all posts contained information about an organization's own offers (11.3%, n=284). Furthermore, the social organizations often announced internal and external events via Facebook (401 posts; 16.2%). This number only includes posts from 47 (out of 73) social organizations, since 26 organizations never announced an event via Facebook. Still, the rather high frequency of events posting may be due to imitation among competitors or attempts to establish an opinion leadership. The relationship between event announcements and follow-up news of the event (2:1) illustrates that there is room for improvement concerning follow-up on the events. The high number of Facebook posts about opinions on social policy issues reflects the essential goal of social organizations and demonstrates that Facebook is used as an external communication channel rather than as a tool for communicating with internal stakeholders. The relatively low number of posts about issues of organizational structure also indicates that Facebook is used for external rather than internal communication. Fundraising is another of the social organizations' most frequent post topics (190 posts; 7.7%). Fundraising posts were published by 39 of the 73 social organizations. In these posts, the organizations call for donations, report on fundraising activities and fundraising dedications, and express thanks to donors (139 post; 5.6%). During the investigation period, the social organizations published an average of 2.64 posts about fundraising issues. In addition, three social organizations have implemented a specific Facebook application for soliciting donations. Overall, Facebook's potential for fundraising is not being exploited to its full extent; there is room for improvement. Examples of individual success stories were published 30 times out of all the Facebook posts (1.2%). Few posts dealt with volunteer management (2.4%, n = 59). 60 posts (2.4%) included greetings for holidays or seasonal events. Approximately 3% of the posts contained humorous pictures, videos, and recommendations for cultural events.

4.4   Interactivity and Virality

Our analysis of the number of "likes", number of comments, and frequency of shared posts provides information about each organization's level of interaction with Facebook users [18]. In the analyzed period, an average of 287 posts per organization were marked with "like" (sd=723.78), which corresponds to 4.46 "likes" per post. 17 social organizations did not receive any "likes"; however, 13 of those organizations had not published any posts within the investigation period. 23 social organizations did not receive any comments on their posts in their Facebook timelines. The highest number of Facebook comments received by a single organization was 359, a much higher number than all the other social organisations received (m=26.1, sd=59.09). The highest number of "shares" (of comments) and the highest number of responses to posts that were written by users (m=4.88) were achieved by the same social organization. Further analysis shows that a high frequency of self-written posts does not necessarily indicate a high interactivity with users.

4.5   Relation between Self-written Posts and Posts Written by Other Users

The relationship between self-written posts and those written by other users is a key metric of an organization's interaction with Facebook users [18]. During the investigation period, 15.5% of posts were written by users, and 35 social organizations did not receive any posts written by users. In this context, it should be mentioned that 12 organizations deactivated the possibility for users to respond to posts.Overall, posts written by other users resulted in an average of 8.33 "likes" per post and 0.74 comments per post. Posts written by users had reached a total of 391 "likes" and 143 comments. In comparison, the responses to posts written by users had lower interactivity impact and achieved on average only 0.86 "likes" and 0.31 comments.Another indicator of a successful Facebook page is a high number of posts by users that were commented on by the organization [18]. The analysis revealed that 70.4% of posts written by users were marked with "like" or commented on by the respective organizations. Other Facebook users responded significantly more often to user-generated posts with "likes" (69.7%, n=318) or comments (17.8%, n=81) from the organizations, compared to user posts without reactions by the social organizations, where a total of only 16% of user posts had been marked with "like" (n=73) and 13.6% of posts were commented on (n=62).

4.6   Multimediality of Facebook Posts

More than a fifth of the studied Facebook posts contained photos (n=12) or links to photos or to photo-sharing portals (outside of Facebook) (n=4). 79.1% of the posts did not contain any photos or links to photos, although, according to Facebook, posts with attached photos achieve about 120% more interaction with Facebook users [19]. This is also reflected in our data. Posts with photos resulted in 3.07 times more "likes" and 3.02 times more comments than posts without photos. Posts with photos were also more often shared than those without photos.In general, videos were rarely used. 105 of the 2479 posts embedded videos or linked to videos on specialized social media platforms such as YouTube and Vimeo (4.2%). The video application of Facebook was only used in 5 posts. In total, more than half of the posts (53.9%, n=1336) included links to other online services (outside of Facebook). Data suggests that 56.2% of the social organizations linked in at least one post (n=41) to their organization's official website. 308 links (34.2%) referred to external websites containing press releases or press articles. Interestingly, 69.5% of all links to press articles or press releases were published by only three social organizations.

4.7   Links from Facebook to Other Online Social Networks

Various indicators can be used to analyze whether an organization has implemented an integrated social media strategy. Almost all organizations linked to the organization's website (93.2%, n=68) in the notification area. More than half of the organizations linked via posts to the organization's website (56.9%, n=41). Only 8 organizations linked to other social media channels on their "about" pages. 45 of the 73 organizations (61.6%) had implemented a link from their website to their Facebook page and 21 organizations (28.8%) used social plug-ins that provide "like" and "share" buttons on their websites. 40 social organizations implemented such links on a prominent page (e.g., the homepage) of their websites, which indicates that Facebook has a high relevance for these organizations.

5   Evaluation Scheme and Results

Based on the indicators described in Section 4, an evaluation scheme was developed to assess the developmental stage of each organization's Facebook page: "Beginner", "Advanced", "Intermediate", or "Expert". The presented indicators (Section 4) were grouped into nine categories. Category 1 evaluates the existence of an organization description and contact data in the information area of the Facebook page. Category 2 describes whether a social organization uses a profile and a cover photo. Category 3 characterizes the use of photos. Based on the median of uploaded photos within the investigation time period (as a benchmark), at least 23 photos have to be uploaded to Facebook Photo View to achieve the maximum 2 points in this category. Category 4 refers to the number of "likes", taking into account the date of registration of the Facebook page. Therefore, the minimum of "likes" was defined as 0.5 "likes" per day within the first three years (again based on our data set, where the minimum value of 0.5 lies between the median and mean of the "like", taking into account the organization's registration date). Category 5 assesses whether an organization uses applications such as the map, events, or fundraising applications. Category 6 refers to the frequency of self-written posts. The post frequency should be at least one post per week, with a maximum of one post per day; this range corresponds to, during the investigation period, a minimum of 25 posts and a maximum of 181 posts [20]. Higher post frequencies result in lower interaction rates; thus, one post per day is defined as the maximum value. Category 7 analyzes the average number of responses per Facebook post. The minimum values per post were set to at least 3 "likes", 0.3 comments, or 0.3 "shares". These numbers were derived from the means and medians of the responses to the respective posts (as discussed in Section 4). Category 8 evaluates whether a minimum percentage of the posts, as recommended by Facebook, include photos. 20.1% of all analyzed Facebook posts contain photos; thus, the respective organizations are assigned points if at least every fifth post contains a photo. Category 9 analyzes Facebook users' reactions to posts written by users based on the number of "likes" and number of comments. In 7 of the 9 categories, two points are achievable (see Table 2): These categories describe the basic requirements for adequate use of a Facebook page. We consider the use of applications (Category 5) and the integration of photos into posts (Category 8) as advanced Facebook use. Accordingly, we weighted these indicators less than the basic requirements in our evaluation scheme. Therefore, only one point can be achieved in these two categories. Based on this evaluation scheme, four stages can be derived as follows: "Beginner" (0-7 points), "Advanced" (8-10 points), "Intermediate" (11-13 points), and "Expert" (14-16 points).

Table 2. Evaluation Scheme for the Use of Facebook by Social Organizations in Vienna

Category	Description of Category	Points	Dimension
1	Description of the organization and contact information	2	Design of page information, views, and applications
2	Using a profile and cover picture	2	
3	At least 23 uploaded photos in the Photo View	2	
4	Minimum of 0.5 "likes" on the Facebook page per day during the first three years of use	2	
5	Use of applications (e.g., donations, events, map, etc.)	1	
6	Post frequency is at least one post per week and a maximum of one post per day	2	Design of the time-line, reaction to Facebook posts written by other users
7	Minimum requirements of the average responses per post: 3 "likes", 0.3 comments, 0.3 "shares"	2	
8	At least every fifth post contains a photo	1	
9	100% response rate to comments, criticisms, and questions in external posts	2	
Total		16	

Based on the evaluation scheme, 5 of the 73 organizations (6.8%) were assigned the maximum of 16 points. In total (Table 3), 11 organizations (15.1%) can be classified as "Expert", which means that these organizations fulfilled almost all requirements and may be considered as "best practices". About one-fifth of the social organizations (20.5%, n=15) received 11 to 13 points, and therefore these organizations are classified as "Intermediate". The category "Advanced" includes 14 organizations (19.2%). A total of 33 organizations were assigned less than 8 points (45.2%) and therefore are classified as "Beginner".

Table 3. Result overview concerning the evaluation scheme

Category	Organizations (absolute values)	Ratio
Beginner	33	45.2%
Advanced	14	19.2%
Intermediate	15	20.5%
Expert	11	15.1%

6   Discussion and Conclusion

Facebook offers social organizations a range of possibilities to help achieve their organizational goals and build and maintain relationships with stakeholders. So far there have been no empirical studies about the use and development of Facebook by social organizations in the European and German-speaking countries. The present paper contributes to closing this research gap by analyzing all social organizations in Vienna regarding their Facebook pages and posting behavior. Interestingly, a large number of posts were simply holiday greetings and expressions of thanks for donations, which are typical examples of posts by organizations that are less experienced with social media. Also, a rather low number of social organizations link their Facebook pages to other social network platforms, which indicates that the development and implementation of an integrated social media strategy in social organizations in Vienna is the exception; the potential of online social networks is not being fully utilized. Previous studies [5, 7, 8, 13] have demonstrated both the potential and weak use of social media for fundraising and volunteer management. The present study confirms that social organizations in Vienna have not exhausted Facebook's potential for fundraising and volunteer management. The low interactivity rates demonstrate that the majority of social organizations may improve the formal design and content-related aspects of their posts. There are more than twice as many beginner organizations than more experienced ones. The 73 analyzed organizations were classified into four categories by using a self-developed evaluation scheme. Only 11 organizations are classified as "Expert" (15.1%). Most organizations have been classified as "Beginner" (45.2%, n=33). This value has to be considered in relation to the total number of social organizations in Vienna: In the investigation period, only 14.8% of all social organizations in Vienna had registered a Facebook page. Furthermore, on average the evaluated organizations had reached 7.8 out of 16 points, which corresponds to the

"Beginner" category. Thus, overall we conclude that social organizations in Vienna only limitedly use Facebook to achieve their organizational goals. Our evaluation scheme may be adopted for other organizations. While it may be used as is for evaluating the success of Facebook strategies by other social organizations, the reference values (benchmarks) used in the scheme have to be adjusted to reflect the Facebook metrics of the industries to which the organizations belong.The present work also has limitations: Only publicly available data was used, and metrics based on Facebook Insights could not be taken into account. Furthermore, the present study is limited to social organizations in Vienna, resulting in regional limitations of the findings. However, the majority of Austria's social organizations are located in Vienna, which suggests that the results also have value on a national level. Future research may compare Facebook use between social organizations and commercial organizations. Moreover, the development of a comprehensive performance measurement system for measuring activities in various online social networks is a relevant research topic. With respect to this, a study about the importance of social media guidelines for social organizations would be interesting.

References

1. Richter, A., Koch, M.: Funktionen von Social-Networking-Diensten. In: Multikonferenz Wirtschaftsinformatik 2008 (2008)
2. Royal Pingdom: Facebook, YouTube, our collective time sinks (stats) (2011)
3. Facebook, http://newsroom.fb.com/Key-Facts (accessed April 18, 2013)
4. Curtis, L., Edwards, C., Fraser, K.L., Gudelsky, S., Holmquist, J., Thornton, K., Sweetser, K.D.: Adoption of social media for public relations by nonprofit organizations. Public Relations Review 36, 90–92 (2010)
5. Kiefer, K.: Social Media Engagement deutscher NPO. Performance Management in Nonprofit-Organisationen 386 (2012)
6. Lovejoy, K., Saxton, G.D.: Information, Community, and Action: How Nonprofit Organizations Use Social Media. J. of Computer. Mediated Communication 17, 337–353 (2012)
7. Waters, R.D.: The use of social media by nonprofit organizations: An examination from the diffusion of innovations perspective. In: Handbook of Research on Social Interaction Technologies and Collaboration Software: Concepts and Trends. IGI, Hershey (2010)
8. Waters, R.D., Burnett, E., Lamm, A., Lucas, J.: Engaging stakeholders through social networking: How nonprofit organizations are using Facebook. Public Relations Review 35, 102–106 (2009)
9. Kiefer, K.: NGOs im Social Web. Eine inhaltsanalytische Untersuchung zum Einsatz und Potential von Social Media für die Öffentlichkeitsarbeit von gemeinnützigen Organisationen. Institut für Journalistik und Kommunikationsforschung. Universität Hannover, Hanover, Germany (2009)
10. Kiefer, K.: NPOs im Social Web: Status quo und Entwicklungspotenziale. In: Fundraising im Non-Profit-Sektor, pp. 283–296. Springer (2010)
11. Briones, R.L., Kuch, B., Liu, B.F., Jin, Y.: Keeping up with the digital age: How the American Red Cross uses social media to build relationships. Public Relations Review 37, 37–43 (2011)
12. Miller, D.: Nonprofit organizations and the emerging potential of social media and internet resources. SPNHA Review 6, 4 (2010)

13. Reynolds, C.: Friends Who Give: Relationship-Building and Other Uses of Social Networking Tools by Nonprofit Organizations. The Elon Journal of Undergraduate Research in Communications 2, 15–40 (2011)
14. Heidemann, J., Klier, M., Landherr, A., Probst, F.: Soziale Netzwerke im Web–Chancen und Risiken im Customer Relationship Management von Unternehmen. Wirtschaftsinformatik & Management 3, 40–45 (2011)
15. Reisberger, T., Smolnik, S.: Modell zur Erfolgsmessung von Social-Software-Systemen. In: Multikonferenz Wirtschaftsinformatik, pp. 565–577 (2008)
16. Dimmel, N.: Sozialwirtschaft in der Sozialordnung. In: Dimmel, N. (ed.) Das Recht der Sozialwirtschaft, pp. 9–58. Wien/Graz, Austria (2007)
17. Badelt, C., Pennerstorfer, A., Schneider, U.: Der Nonprofit Sektor in Österreich. In: Simsa, R., Meyer, M., Badelt, C. (eds.) Handbuch der Nonprofit-Organisation, pp. 55–75 (2013)
18. Brocke, A., Faust, A.: Berechnung von Erfolgskennzahlen für Facebook Fan-Pages. ICOM 10, 44–48 (2011)
19. Facebook, http://www.facebook.com/business/build (accessed April 18, 2013)
20. Reimerth, G., Wigand, J.: Welche Inhalte in Facebook funktionieren: Facebook Postings von Consumer Brands und Retail Brands unter der Lupe. knallgrau, Vienna, Austria (2012)

Understanding the Factors That Influence the Perceived Severity of Cyber-bullying

Sonia Camacho, Khaled Hassanein, and Milena Head

DeGroote School of Business, McMaster University, Hamilton, ON, Canada
{camachsm,hassank,headm}@mcmaster.ca

Abstract. Cyberbullying is a phenomenon that involves aggressive behaviors performed through Information and Communication Technologies (ICT) with the intention to cause harm or discomfort to victims. Researchers have measured the incidence of cyber-bullying by presenting participants with a list of behaviors and determining whether they have experienced those behaviors or the frequency of their occurrence. However, those measures do not take into account a victim's perspective of those behaviors. This study draws on the Transactional Theory of Stress and Coping and introduces the concept of perceived cyber-bullying severity to measure a victim's appraisal of cyberbullying. This study also proposes a set of antecedents to perceived cyber-bullying severity, which will be validated using a survey-based study and structural equation modeling techniques.

Keywords: cyber-bullying, victim, bully, audience, message.

1 Introduction

Cyberbullying can be defined as hostile or aggressive behaviors performed through information and communication technologies (ICT) (e.g. Internet applications, mobile phones) that are intended to harm or inflict discomfort on others [1]. Although this definition is adopted here, it is important to note that (i) there is a lack of an agreed upon definition of cyberbullying in the literature [2]; and (ii) there is a debate about the elements from the definition of traditional bullying that should be included/excluded in/from the definition of cyberbullying (e.g. power imbalance between bullies and victims) [3]. Cyber-bullying is a phenomenon that can have varied consequences on the victim, such as low academic scores, social anxiety, social isolation, self-harm, low self-confidence, and depressive symptoms [4-6]. In extreme cases, those consequences can lead the victim to commit suicide [7]. Between 2012 and 2013, at least 9 cases of teenage suicides have been linked to cyber-bullying [8].

Studies in cyber-bullying in the area of Information Systems (IS) have focused mainly on the prevalence of this phenomenon [9-10] and the potential motivations and antecedents of online aggression (e.g. gaining social status) [11]. Researchers in other areas (e.g. psychology, healthcare) have also explored (i) the outcomes of cyber-bullying (e.g. psychosomatic problems, depression) [2,12], (ii) the relationship

F.F.-H. Nah (Ed.): HCIB/HCII 2014, LNCS 8527, pp. 133–144, 2014.
© Springer International Publishing Switzerland 2014

between cyber-bullying and traditional bullying [13] and (iii) strategies used by victims to deal with cyber-bullying incidents (e.g. deleting unwanted messages, changing e-mail address) [14-15].

Researchers have used different measures of cyber-bullying, relying mainly on providing specific behavioral examples of what this phenomenon entails and asking a global question as to whether individuals have experienced cyber-bullying [16]. Furthermore, some measures have been developed to specifically measure cyber-victimization [17-18] and those are concerned with the frequency at which certain behaviors (e.g. insulting language in e-mails) occur. In general, cyber-bullying measures used to date are concerned with the incidence of specific behaviors and do not consider that the victims' perception of those behaviors may vary (e.g. the same behavior may be interpreted as harmless by some people and rather hurtful by others) [19]. Moreover, there is a lack of research studying the degree to which victims perceive cyber-bullying as being harmful [20].

This study addresses the above gap by introducing the construct of perceived cyber-bullying severity to measure a victim's evaluation of cyber-bullying. In addition, this study proposes a set of factors that may affect a victim's perception of cyber-bullying severity.

2   Theoretical Background

Lazarus and Folkman (1984) proposed the Transactional Theory of Stress and Coping (TTSC). They defined psychological stress as a relationship between a person and the environment that is seen by the person as taxing her resources or threatening her well-being [21]. Embedded in this definition is the fact that although there may be objective conditions that can be considered as stressors (e.g. natural disasters, having an argument with a loved person), individuals will vary in the degree and type of reaction to these stressors. In order to understand the individuals' varied reactions when facing the same stressful situation, it is necessary to understand the cognitive processes that take place between the stressor and the reaction [21].

TTSC proposes cognitive appraisal as the mediating factor, which reflects the changing relationships between individuals with certain characteristics (e.g. values, thinking style) and an environment that must be predicted and interpreted [21]. Specifically, the theory outlines a primary appraisal of the stressor and a secondary appraisal of the coping mechanisms available to deal with the stressor [22]. In the primary appraisal phase, individuals determine if and how the situation is relevant to their goal attainment or well-being. When the situation affects negatively goal attainment and/or well-being (i.e. it is stressful), individuals determine the extent to which the situation is harming, threatening, or challenging [23]. Harm refers to damage that has already occurred and threat refers to a future potential damage, while challenge produces a positive motivation in individuals to overcome obstacles [24]. After the primary appraisal phase, individuals move to the secondary appraisal phase where they evaluate their options in terms of coping with the stressful situation [24].

The appraisal of a stressful situation is affected by some situational characteristics. In particular, TTSC identifies three factors that can affect individual's assessment of a situation as harming, threatening, or challenging that are relevant in the context of this study. The first factor is novelty, which refers to situations with which the individual has no experience. Completely novel situations are rare since individuals may have information about situations from others. However, if an individual has not experienced a situation yet (i.e. a novel situation), she will consider it as stressful if it is previously associated in her mind with harm or danger (e.g. based on others' experiences). The second factor is uncertainty, which refers to an individual's confusion about the meaning of the situation. Uncertain situations are considered highly stressful. The final factor is duration, which refers to how long a stressful event persists. Enduring or chronic stressful situations may affect an individual psychologically and physically [21].

TTSC offers a suitable framework to study victim's assessment of a cyber-bullying episode. A cyber-bullying episode may constitute one action (e.g. posting a comment on a public forum) or several actions related to the same issue (e.g. sending several threatening text messages over a certain period of time). Cyber-bullying episodes are situations that may be appraised as harmful or threatening to certain extents, depending on the characteristics of the situation (i.e. the message received by the victim, the medium through which the message is sent, the bully's characteristics, and the audience witnessing the episode) and the characteristics of the victim (e.g. neuroticism and self-esteem). The appraisal of these episodes as stressful may affect negatively the victims (e.g. negative emotions, depressive symptoms) and may affect their experience with information and communication technologies through which cyber-bullying occurs (e.g. Facebook).

3   Research Model and Hypotheses

The proposed research model is shown in Figure 1. The constructs and hypotheses included in the model, along with their appropriate support, are described below.

3.1   Perceived Cyber-bullying Severity

Perceived Cyber-bullying Severity (PCS) is a new construct introduced to measure a victim's appraisal of a cyber-bullying episode (a stressful situation), as per TTSC. The assessment of a cyber-bullying episode varies by the context of the situation (i.e. message, bully, medium, and audience) and the victim characteristics [19] as explained below (see section 3.2). The degree of variability of the assessment of a specific episode by a victim is consistent with the primary appraisal involved in TTSC [21], whereby victims evaluate whether the cyber-bullying episode is relevant to their goals or well-being.

Although some studies have explored victims' perceptions of the harshness of cyber-bullying compared to traditional bullying [16], a measure for the victim's perception of the severity of a cyber-bullying episode has not been developed. Studying a victim's appraisal of cyber-bullying is important in pursuing a rigorous understanding of the cyber-bullying phenomenon and its impacts, as the victims' perspective is critical to understand the impacts of the episode on their psychosocial functioning [25].

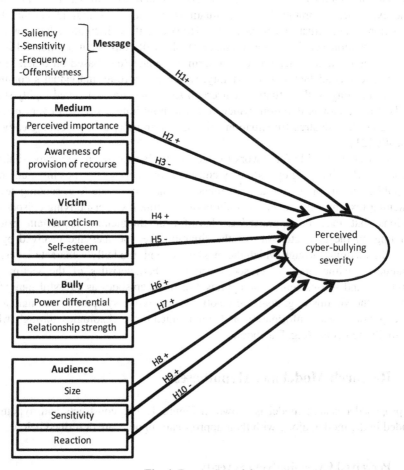

Fig. 1. Research model

3.2   Factors That Influence PCS

According to TTSC, it is the appraisal of a particular situation as harmful or threatening that triggers the need to manage or cope with the situation [21]. This highlights the importance of understanding how variables that are relevant to the cyber-bullying context may affect the appraisal process of the cyber-bullying episode (i.e. perceptions of cyber-bullying severity). Past research on cyber-bullying suggests an initial set of factors that are deemed to be relevant in the appraisal of the severity of a cyber-bullying episode. These sets of factors are explored below, where the most relevant characteristics of each are discussed.

Message Harshness. Four characteristics of the message(s) the cyber-bullying victim receives are explored. The first characteristic is saliency, which refers to "an attribute of a particular stimulus that makes it stand out and be noticed" (p. 1) [26]. The misuse of pictures and videos (i.e. a more salient message) is more stressful for victims than other forms of cyberbullying such as insults using written messages [27]. The second characteristic is the sensitivity of the message. Disclosing secrets (i.e. privacy viola-tion) or embarrassing aspects of the victim's life is more stressful for victims of cy-ber-bullying than messages that do not involve aspects of the victim's real world (e.g. name calling on a chat room) [27]. The third characteristic is frequency, where the occurrence of several acts in a cyber-bullying episode is posited to increase the vic-tim's PCS compared to a single act [28]. The last characteristic is offensiveness, where receiving vulgar, angry messages, or threats of real injuries is more stressful for victims compared to more benign messages [29]. The saliency, sensitivity, frequency, and offensiveness of the message speak of the harshness of the message content and are posited to collectively heighten victims' perceptions of severity in a cyber-bullying episode. Thus, we hypothesize that:

H1: Message harshness is positively related to PCS

Medium Characteristics. Two characteristics of the cyber-bullying medium are explored. The first one is the perceived importance of the cyber-bullying medium for the victim. Individuals prefer to use certain forms of electronic communication in order to maintain their social lives [30] and thus, it is expected that victims will per-ceive a cyber-bullying episode as being more severe if the cyber-bullying medium is among their preferred communication media. The second characteristic is victims' awareness of provision of recourse mechanisms available to them through the cyber-bullying medium. Researchers have found that online buyers rely on institutional mechanisms such as credit card guarantees for reducing their perception of risk [31]. In the same vein, technology providers have mechanisms built into their platforms (i.e. the cyber-bullying medium) that can be used by victims to deal with cyber-bullying episodes (e.g. reporting a bully on Facebook). It is expected that the victim's awareness of such recourse provisions will reduce her/his perception of severity of a cyber-bullying episode. Thus, we hypothesize that:

H2: Perceived importance of the cyber-bullying medium to the victim is positively related to PCS

H3: Awareness of provision of recourse mechanisms is negatively related to PCS

Victim Characteristics. Two individual characteristics deemed relevant in explaining victim's perceptions of bullying [32] are explored. Neuroticism refers to a personality trait characterized by insecurity, anxiousness, and hostility [33]. Individuals high in neuroticism tend to appraise ambiguous situations in a negative manner and perceive threats in situations where others would not [34]. Self-esteem is the subjective percep-tion of one's worth [35]. Individuals with low self-esteem tend to have less confi-dence to overcome any problems they are faced with, leading them to experience higher stress in such situations [36]. In light of these arguments, it is expected that confronted with the same cyber-bullying episode, individuals with low self-esteem or high neuroticism will perceived it as more severe than others. Thus, we hypothesize that:

H4: Neuroticism is positively related to PCS

H5: Self-esteem is negatively related to PCS

Bully Characteristics. Two characteristics of the bully are explored. In terms of power differential, the victim may be afraid of denouncing or taking revenge on a person that holds more power than she/he does (e.g. the bully may be more popular among victim's peers) [3]. The bully may even hold a position of power over the victim and her/his peers (e.g. coach). The second characteristic is relationship strength, which refers to the degree of closeness between the bully and the victim. The perception of severity can be aggravated if the victim is close to the bully, because the bully may have better access to the victim's information and the victim may feel betrayed by someone she/he is close to [27].

H6: Power differential between the victim and bully is positively related to PCS

H7: Relationship strength between the victim and bully is positively related to PCS

Audience Characteristics. Three audience characteristics are explored: size, sensitivity, and reaction. A cyber-bullying episode may be targeted only at the victim (e.g. private e-mail, text message) or may involve posting material that others can see or copy and distribute (e.g. posting a comment on Facebook wall). Past research suggests that the presence of larger audiences makes the victim perceive a cyber-bullying episode as being more serious [37]. A second characteristic to be considered is the type of audience witnessing the cyber-bullying episode (i.e. audience sensitivity). Research on embarrassment suggests that a person will feel a more severe embarrassment when the audience of the embarrassing situation is comprised of individuals whose opinions are important to that person (e.g. high-status individuals, friends) [38]. In light of these arguments, it is expected that the number of individuals witnessing a cyber-bullying episode and their importance to the victim (i.e. audience sensitivity) will affect a victim's perception of cyber-bullying severity. Thus, we hypothesize that:

H8: Audience size is positively related to PCS

H9: Audience sensitivity is positively related to PCS

The third characteristic of the audience is its reaction to the cyber-bullying episode. There are four roles among bystanders involved in a cyber-bullying episode: (1) assistants, who distribute the material in order to bully the victim further; (2) reinforcers, who cheer the bully on; (3) outsiders (the most common role), who watch without distributing the material; and (4) defenders, who try to help the victims [39]. Past research suggests that a supportive audience may help victims reduce their perception of severity of a cyber-bullying episode [3]. Considering audience reaction as varying from assisting the bully to defending the victim, it is proposed that a more supportive audience reaction to the victim will negatively impact a victim's perceived cyber-bullying severity.

H10: A more supportive audience reaction is negatively related to PCS

4   Methodology

The proposed research model will be validated with a survey-based quantitative study. Participants will be university students that experienced a complete cyber-bullying episode on Facebook (i.e. the episode is finished by the time of data collection) within the past twelve months. Facebook is chosen in this study as the cyberbullying medium, because it is one of the most utilized media for cyberbullying [40]. Data will be collected at one point in time using an online survey. This type of survey offers anonymity to participants, which may help them feel safe and increase their willingness to share their experiences given the sensitive nature of the data collected [20]. During the survey, participants will be asked to recall the most recent cyber-bullying episode they experienced on Facebook (if more than one was experienced). Demographic information (i.e. age, gender, and years at school) will also be collected, as well as the period of time that participants have had an active Facebook account and other types of similar social media applications they use. Open ended questions will be used to gather details about the cyber-bullying episode in question: nature of cyber-bullying (e.g. someone posted embarrassing photos of the participant), relationship between the victim and the bully, duration of the episode, previous exposure to cyber-bullying, and exposure to bullying at school at the same time the cyber-bullying episode was occurring. Ethics approval will be sought from the authors' university prior to the beginning of any data collection.

4.1   Measurement Instrument

In order to ensure content validity, and wherever possible, this study will adapt previously validated instruments to measure constructs in the proposed research model. Table 1 summarizes the constructs and items that will be used in this study.

Table 1. Summary of constructs and sources for their scales

Construct	Source	Items
Perceived importance	Ross et al. (2009) [41]	1. Facebook was part of my everyday activity 2. I was proud to tell people 'I'm on Facebook' 3. I dedicated a part of my daily schedule to Facebook 4. I felt out of touch when I haven't logged on to Facebook for a while 5. I felt I was part of the Facebook community

Table 1. (*Continued.*)

Construct	Source	Items
Awareness of provision of recourse	McKnight, Choudhury, and Kacmar (2002) [42]	1. Facebook had enough safeguards to make me feel comfortable using it 2. I felt assured that legal and technological structures adequately protected me from problems on Facebook 3. I felt confident that privacy protection and other technological advances on Facebook made it safe for me to use it 4. In general, Facebook was a safe environment to communicate with others
Neuroticism	McCrae and Costa (2010) [43]	Items not listed for copyright reasons
Self-esteem	Rosenberg (1979) [35]	1. On the whole, I am satisfied with myself 2. At times I think I am no good at all 3. I feel that I have a number of good qualities 4. I am able to do things as well as most other people 5. I feel I do not have much to be proud of 6. I certainly feel useless at times 7. I feel that I'm a person of worth, at least on an equal plane with others 8. I wish I could have more respect for myself 9. All in all, I am inclined to feel that I am a failure 10. I take a positive attitude toward myself
Power differential	Felix et al. (2011) [25]	1. The bully was more popular compared to me 2. The bully was smarter at school work compared to me 3. The bully was emotionally stronger compared to me
Relationship strength	Pierce, Sarason, and Sarason (1991) [44]	1. My relationship with the bully was significant in my life 2. I depended on the bully 3. I expected to have a close long-term relationship with the bully 4. The bully played a positive role in my life 5. I felt responsible for the bully's well-being 6. I would have missed the bully if we could not talk or see each other for a month
Audience reaction	Salmivalli, Voeten, and Poskiparta (2011) [45]	1. The people that received/viewed the cyberbullying message comforted me or encouraged me to tell someone about the cyberbullying episode 2. The people that received/viewed the cyberbullying message told the bully to stop cyberbullying me 3. The people that received/viewed the cyberbullying message tried to make the bully stop cyberbullying me

Table 1. (*Continued.*)

Construct	Source	Items
Perceived cyber-bullying severity	Johnston and Warkentin (2010) [46] Moss-Morris et al. (2002) [47]	1. The cyberbullying episode was a serious situation 2. The cyberbullying episode had major consequences on my life 3. The cyberbullying episode did not have much effect on my life 4. The cyberbullying episode strongly affected the way others see me 5. The cyberbullying episode had serious consequences for me 6. The cyberbullying episode caused difficulties for those who are close to me 7. The cyberbullying episode was severe 8. The cyberbullying episode was significant

For the remaining constructs included in the model (i.e. message harshness - specified as a formative construct, audience size, and audience sensitivity) new scales will be developed and validated by following the methodology outlined by Lewis, Templeton, and Byrd [48]. Briefly, this methodology includes three sequential stages: (i) establishment of constructs' domain, (ii) producing and refining construct scales, and (iii) evaluation of the measurement properties of the scales. A pilot study will be conducted to refine the measurement scales for all the constructs used in the model. All the appropriate validity tests (e.g. convergent validity, divergent validity) will be conducted.

4.2   Model Validation, Sample Size and Post Hoc Analyses

PLS Structural Equation Modeling (SEM) will be used to validate the proposed model, as it is suited for exploratory research like the proposed research under this study [49]. A minimum sample size of 120 participants is required to validate the model in PLS, following Gefen, Straub, and Boudreau's [49] guideline of 10 times the greatest number between (i) the items of the most complex construct (i.e. neuroticism, 12 items) and (ii) the largest number of paths directed at a particular dependent variable (i.e. 10 antecedents of PCS). However, and accounting for possible spoiled surveys, 150 participants will be recruited. Two post hoc analyses will be conducted: (i) ANOVA to explore differences in victim's PCS based on demographics (e.g. gender); and (ii) a qualitative analysis with the information obtained from the open ended questions to strengthen our quantitative findings through triangulation [50].

5   Potential Contributions and Limitations

From an academic standpoint, this paper will contribute to the advancement of the cyber-bullying literature by validating a perceived cyber-bullying severity construct and by understanding the factors that influence victims' perceptions of cyber-bullying severity. This construct and its antecedents can provide a baseline for researchers to use when analyzing the varied responses to cyber-bullying episodes. From a practical perspective, results from this study can help individuals that interact with cyber-bullying victims (e.g. parents, professors, and university staff) understand better the factors that affect victims' assessments of cyber-bullying episodes.

This study has some generalizability limitations. The factors that affect university students' evaluation of a cyber-bullying episode may not be extended to (i) adolescents, who face identity issues and physical changes [1] or (ii) adults, whose appraisal of a cyber-bullying episode may be determined by other variables (e.g. organizational culture, if the cyber-bullying episode occurs at work). Additional factors that may be relevant for these groups should be studied in future research.

References

1. Johnson, C.L.: An examination of the primary and secondary effects of cyber-bullying: development and testing of a cyberbullying moderator/mediator model. Wayne State University Dissertations (2011)
2. Beckman, L., Hagquist, C., Hellström, L.: Does the association with psychosomatic health problems differ between cyberbullying and traditional bullying? EBD 17(3-4), 421–434 (2012)
3. Slonje, R., Smith, P.K., Frisén, A.: The nature of cyberbullying, and strategies for prevention. Comput. Hum. Behav. 29, 26–32 (2013)
4. Tokunaga, R.S.: Following you home from school: A critical review and synthesis of research on cyberbullying victimization. Comput. Hum. Behav. 26, 277–287 (2010)
5. Šleglova, V., Cerna, A.: Cyberbullying in Adolescent Victims: Perception and Coping. Cyberpsychology, 5(2), article 4 (2011)
6. Juvonen, J., Gross, E.F.: Bullying experiences in cyberspace. J. Sch. Health. 78, 496–505 (2008)
7. Hinduja, S., Patchin, J.W.: Bullying, cyberbullying, and suicide. Arch. Suicide Res. 14(3), 206–221 (2010)
8. Broderick, R.: 9 Teenage Suicides in the Last Year Were Linked to Cyber-Bullying on Social Network Ask.fm. In: BuzzFeed (2013),
http://www.buzzfeed.com/ryanhatesthis/
a-ninth-teenager-since-last-september-has-committed-suicide
9. Calvete, E., Orue, I., Estévez, A., Villa, L., Padilla, P.: Cyberbullying in adolescents: Modalities and aggressors' profile. Comput. Hum. Behav. 26, 1128–1135 (2010)
10. Huang, Y.-Y., Chou, C.: An analysis of multiple factors of cyberbullying among junior high school students in Taiwan. Comput. Hum. Behav. 26, 1581–1590 (2010)
11. Law, D., Shapka, J.D., Domene, J.F., Gagné, M.H.: Are cyberbullies really bullies? An investigation of reactive and proactive online aggression. Comput. Hum. Behav. 28, 664–672 (2012)
12. Wang, J., Nansel, T.R., Iannotti, R.J.: Cyber and Traditional Bullying: Differential Association With Depression. J. Adolescent Health. 48, 415–417 (2011)
13. Desmet, A., Bastiaensens, S., Van Cleemput, K., Poels, K., Vandebosch, H., De Bourdeaudhuij, I.: Mobilizing Bystanders of Cyberbullying: an Exploratory Study into Behavioural Determinants of Defending the Victim. Stud. Health Technol. Inform. 181, 58–63 (2012)

14. Aricak, T., Siyahhan, S., Uzunhasanoglu, A., Saribeyoglu, S., Ciplak, S., Yilmaz, N., Memmedov, C.: Cyber-bullying among Turkish adolescents. Cyberpsychol. Behav. 11(3), 253–261 (2008)
15. Parris, L., Varjas, K., Meyers, J., Cutts, H.: High school students' perceptions of coping with cyberbullying. Youth Soc. 1–23 (2011)
16. Campbell, M., Spears, B., Slee, P., Butler, D., Kift, S.: Victims' perceptions of traditional and cyberbullying, and the psychosocial correlates of their victimisation. EBD 17(3-4), 389–401 (2012)
17. Çetin, B., Yaman, E., Peker, A.: Cyber victim and bullying scale: A study of validity and reliability. Comput. Educ. 57, 2261–2271 (2011)
18. Price, M., Chin, M.A., Higa-McMillan, C., Kim, S., Frueh, B.C.: Prevalence and Internalizing Problems of Ethnoracially Diverse Victims of Traditional and Cyber Bullying. School Mental Health, 1–9 (2013)
19. Greif, J.L., Furlong, M.J.: The assessment of school bullying: using theory to inform practice. JSV 5(3), 33–50 (2006)
20. Ševčíková, A., Šmahel, D., Otavová, M.: The perception of cyberbullying in adolescent victims. EBDs 17(3-4), 319–328 (2012)
21. Lazarus, R.S., Folkman, S.: Stress, Appraisal and Coping. Springer, New York (1984)
22. Perrewé, P.L., Zellars, K.L.: An examination of attributions and emotions in the transactional approach to the organizational stress process. J. Organ. Behav. 20(5), 739–752 (1999)
23. Folkman, S.: The case for positive emotions in the stress process. Anxiety Stress Copin 21(1), 3–14 (2008)
24. Lazarus, R.S.: Relational Meaning and Discrete Emotions. In: Schorr, A. (ed.) Appraisal Processes in Emotion: Theory, Methods, Research, pp. 27–67. Oxford University Press, Cary (2001)
25. Felix, E.D., Sharkey, J.D., Greif Green, J., Furlong, M.J., Tanigawa, D.: Getting precise and pragmatic about the assessment of bullying: the development of the California Bullying Victimization Scale. Aggressive Behav. 37, 234–247 (2011)
26. Guido, G.: The Salience of Marketing Stimuli: An Incongruity-Salience Hypothesis on Consumer Awareness. Kluwer Academic Publishers, Norwel (2001)
27. Staude-Müller, F., Hansen, B., Voss, M.: How stressful is online victimization? Effects of victim's personality and properties of the incident. Eur. J. Dev. Psychol. 260–274 (2012)
28. Ortega, R., Elipe, P., Mora-Merchán, J., Calmaestra, J., Vega, E.: The emotional impact on victims of traditional bullying and cyberbullying – A study of Spanish adolescents. Z. Psychol. 217, 197–204 (2009)
29. Welch, J.: Electronic menaces are a flaming liability. People Manag. 3(12), 14 (1997)
30. Fredstrom, B.K., Adams, R.E., Gilman, R.: Electronic and school-based victimization: Unique Contexts for Adjustment Difficulties During Adolescence. J. Youth Adolesc. 40, 405–415 (2011)
31. Pavlou, P.A., Gefen, D.: Building Effective Online Marketplaces with Institution-Based Trust. Inform. Syst. Res. 15(1), 37–59 (2004)
32. Einarsen, S.: Bullying and harassment at work: A review of the Scandinavian approach. Aggress. Violent Beh. 5(4), 379–401 (2000)
33. Devaraj, S., Easly, R., Crant, J.: How does personality matter? Relating the five-factor model to technology acceptance and use. Inform. Syst. Res. 19(1), 93–105 (2008)
34. Boyes, M.E., French, D.J.: Neuroticism, stress, and coping in the context of an anagram-solving task. Pers. Indiv. Differ. 49, 380–385 (2010)
35. Rosenberg, M.: Conceiving the self. Basic Books, Inc., New York (1979)

36. Fleishman, J.A.: Personality characteristics and coping patterns. J. Health Soc. Behav. 25, 229–244 (1984)
37. Dooley, J.J., Pyzalski, J., Cross, D.: Cyberbullying versus face-to-face cyberbullying: A theoretical and conceptual review. Z. Psychol. 217(4), 182–188 (2009)
38. Edelmann, R.J.: The psychology of embarrassment. John Wiley and Sons, Chichester (1987)
39. Slonje, R., Smith, P.K., Frisén, A.: Processes of cyberbullying, and feelings of remorse by bullies: A pilot study. Eur. J. Dev. Psychol. 9(2), 244–259 (2012)
40. Kids Help Phone: Cyberbullying: reality check. Kids Help Phone Research Update (2012), http://org.kidshelpphone.ca/media/ 80712/2012-cir-cyberbullying.pdf
41. Ross, C., Orr, E.S., Sisic, M., Arseneault, J.M., Simmering, M.G., Orr, R.R.: Personality and motivations associated with Facebook use. Comput. Hum. Behav. 25, 578–586 (2009)
42. McKnight, D.H., Choudhury, V., Kacmar, C.: Developing and validating trust measures for e-commerce: an integrative typology. Inform. Syst. Res. 13(3), 334–359 (2002)
43. McCrae, R.R., Costa, P.T.: NEO Inventories for the NEO Personality Inventory-3 (NEO-PI-3), NEO Five-Factor Inventory-3 (NEO-FFI-3), NEO Personality Inventory-Revised (NEO PI-R). PAR, Lutz (2010)
44. Pierce, G.R., Sarason, I.G., Sarason, B.R.: General and relationship-based perceptions of social support: Are two constructs better than one? J. Pers. Soc. Psychol. 61, 1028–1039 (1991)
45. Salmivalli, C., Voeten, M., Poskiparta, E.: Bystanders Matter: Associations Between Reinforcing, Defending, and the Frequency of Bullying Behavior in Classrooms. J. Clin. Child Adolesc. Psychol. 40(5), 668–676 (2011)
46. Johnston, A.C., Warkentin, M.: Fear appeals and information security behaviors: An empirical study. MIS Quart. 34(3), 549–566 (2010)
47. Moss-Morris, R., Weinman, J., Petrie, K.J., Horne, R., Cameron, L.D., Buick, D.: The revised illness perception questionnaire (IPQ-R). Psychol. Healt. 17, 1–16 (2002)
48. Lewis, B.R., Templeton, G.F., Byrd, T.A.: A methodology for construct development in MIS research. Eur. J. Inform. Syst. 14, 388–400 (2005)
49. Gefen, D., Straub, D.W., Boudreau, M.C.: Structural Equation Modeling and Regression: Guidelines for Research and Practice. CAIS 4(7) (2000)
50. Benbasat, I., Goldstein, D.K., Mead, M.: The Case Research Strategy in Studies of Information Systems. MIS Quart. 11(3), 369–386 (1987)

Seeking Consensus: A Content Analysis of Online Medical Consultation

Ming-Hsin Phoebe Chiu

Graduate Institute of Library and Information Studies,
National Taiwan Normal University,
162 He-Ping East Road, Section 1, Taipei (106), Taiwan, R.O.C.
phoebechiu@ntnu.edu.tw

Abstract. Online medical consultation allows patients and caregivers to query, communicate, and interact with medical and health professionals in an online synchronous or asynchronous setting. This study explores the questions and answers (Q&As) posted on an asynchronous online medical consultation website, Taiwan eDoctor. In this paper, preliminary research findings of 720 questions were reported. Analysis of questions was structured around five research themes: (1) length; (2) when to seek consultation; (3) strategies of communicating chief complaints; (4) intent to seek consultation; and (5) types information provided. This study makes implications in designing an interactive online medical consultation system.

Keywords: Online medical consultation, content analysis, medical information retrieval.

1 Introduction

Information asymmetry lays influence on the disclosure of medical information, as it is usually controlled and manipulated by medical and health professionals. The rise of health awareness promotes patients, family and caregivers, and health-aware individuals to actively seek information for their medical information needs. The convergence of the Internet and health and medical practice creates a diversity of medical information communication, and the emergence of online medical consultation substantially changes the mode of physician-patient communication.

Health information seeking takes place in many situations through various approaches. It takes place when people are feeling sick and suffering pain, or when being healthy and wanting to know to stay healthy. People seek health and medical information from friends and relatives; seek medical advice from primary care physicians; and solicit patients' experience from physicians' rating websites or blogs. A special type of health information is online medical consultation. With such service, patients and caregivers interact with health and medical professionals in synchronous chat or asynchronous threaded discussion. Questions can be asked freely and answers are provided by certified health and medical professionals. The communication may

F.F.-H. Nah (Ed.): HCIB/HCII 2014, LNCS 8527, pp. 145–154, 2014.
© Springer International Publishing Switzerland 2014

take form of private email, chatroom or instant message, threaded discussion board, or even video conferencing. The service provides patients and caregivers the ability acquire health and medical knowledge at their convenience, often free of charge. It has also been called teleadvice, telemedicine, teleconsultation, e-consultation, or email consultation if consultation is mediated by email (Umefjord, 2006).

As the rise of IT adoption in healthcare is getting more and more popular, users of health information needs are beginning to see the benefits of online medical consultation. Past research has identified the benefits of online medical consultation as being able to reduce uncertainty and improve medical services (Caiata-Zufferey, Abraham, Sommerhalder, & Schulz, 2010). This study focuses on online medical information seeking in the context of medical consultation. It is designed as two-directional, with the goal to explore the intents demonstrated through the questions and answers (Q&As) in online medical consultation, to analyze the characteristics of physician-patient communication, and to discover the role and function of online medical consultation in the perspective of physician-patient communication.

2　Research Design and Methods

As an exploratory study, it collected and analyzed online medical consultation entries from Taiwan eDoctor (http://sp1.hso.mohw.gov.tw/doctor/Index1.php), a medical consultation website funded and operated by Ministry of Health and Welfare in Taiwan. Taiwan eDoctor is one of the largest and most-used Taiwan-based consultation services. Its' primary communication language is Traditional Chinese. The health and medical related questions are asked by everyday users, while are answered and endorsed by certified health and medical professionals, like physicians, nurses, and nutritionists.

Data collection was conducted by randomly selected and collected 50 resolved consultation entries for each clinical department, resulting a total of 1200 entries as the primary data set. All health consultation entries were classified into 24 clinical departments, predefined by Taiwan eDoctor. These clinical departments are internal medicine, dentistry, surgery, pediatrics, orthopedics, ophthalmology, Chinese medicine, dermatology, urology, family medicine, geriatrics and gerontology, obstetrics & gynecology, physical medicine and rehabilitation, oncology, psychiatry, otolaryngology, neurology, surgical neurology, radiology, pulmonology, plastic surgery, gastroenterology, diving and hyperbaric medicine, cardiology, and breast and thyroid surgery.

Analysis of questions asked by patients and caregivers was structured around five research themes: (1) length of question; (2) when to seek consultation; (3) strategies of communicating chief complaints; (4) intent to seek consultation; and (5) types of consultation. Analysis of health and medical professional's answers were guided by four research themes: (1) length; (2) consultation strategies; (3) intent of seeking consultation; and (4) forms of seeking consultation. Content of the questions were first analyzed qualitatively to construct codes of each of the research theme, and each code can be explained as the properties of the theme. Then the analysis was conducted quantitatively with frequency count to determine the patterns and characteristics of how consultation was sought. Up to date, 600 entries were fully analyzed; questions from askers and answers from medical and health professionals were analyzed and reported separately. This paper will only report on the "Question" part with data of 12 clinical specialties.

3   Preliminary Findings

3.1   Length of Question

The preliminary results presented in Table 1 found that the average length of a question was 153 words, but question length varied between clinical specialties. Questions of psychiatry, cardiology, and oncology with the average length of 303 words, 196 words, and 187 words were among the three longest types. Questions of "diet and nutrition" and "plastic surgery" were among the shortest, with the average length of 102 and 95 words. This finding may reflect differences in behavior among askers facing different medical problems. Medical problems of psychiatry, cardiology, and oncology are often long-term and dramatic, and so are the treatment and recovery. The question length of such problems demonstrates how complicated the nature of medical problems is. In contrast, questions for "diet and nutrition" and "plastic surgery" are mostly fact-based statement. For example, "Does Vitamin C help clear acne?" or "How long does Botox last?" This type of questions are relatively shorter, and often with only one or two statements ending with question marks. Counting the frequency of the actual use of question mark in the question statement is a way to identify the number of explicit concerns addressed during the consultation. The analysis of the average length of questions by clinical specialties allows for understanding of the complexity and ambiguity of different medical concerns.

Table 1. Average length of questions

Clinical Specialties	Average Length (# of words)
Physical medicine and rehabilitation	97
Oncology	110
Psychiatry	219
Otolaryngology	110
Radiology	273
Neurology	114
Surgical neurology	117
Pulmonology	122
Plastic surgery	73
Gastroenterology	84
Cardiovascular surgery	132
Breast and thyroid surgery	117

3.2   When to Seek Consultation

Regarding when to seek consultation, Table 2 shows that over half (53%) of the questions were asked when the user is feeling ill or injured, and starting to thinks s/he might be ill (23%). The "when" factor for about 10% of the questions can't be identified, and these questions are primarily fact-based, for example "How safe is hyaluronic acid?" A sum of the questions occurred at "when feeling ill or injured" and "when thinking might be ill" reaches 75%. It suggests a high utilization of online medical consultation service is for diagnostic purposes. This pattern also indicates an interesting fact that consultation seekers are not only seeking for identification of illness or disorder, but also are concerned about their physicians' medical decision. A closer look at the questions asked "when recovering" and "healthy, but not robust" reveals a "second-opinion" nature of the information that the askers desire.

Table 2. When to seek consultation (#/%)

	When healthy	When feeling ill or injured	When thinking might be ill	Healthy, but not robust	When recovering	Can not identified	Dead (ask by caregivers)
Physical medicine and rehabilitation	1(2%)	25(50%)	4(8%)	5(10%)	14(28%)	1(2%)	0(0%)
Oncology	0(0%)	35(70%)	12(24%)	0(0%)	0(0%)	2(4%)	1(2%)
Psychiatry	5(10%)	26(52%)	16(32%)	0(0%)	0(0%)	3(6%)	0(0%)
Otolaryngology	0(0%)	23(46%)	22(44%)	2(4%)	0(0%)	3(6%)	0(0%)
Radiology	16(32%)	14(28%)	5(10%)	0(0%)	0(0%)	15(30%)	0(0%)
Neurology	0(0%)	44(88%)	2(4%)	0(0%)	0(0%)	4(8%)	0(0%)
Surgical neurology	1(2%)	40(80%)	5(10%)	1(2%)	0(0%)	3(6%)	0(0%)
Pulmonology	1(2%)	31(62%)	12(24%)	0(0%)	0(0%)	6(12%)	0(0%)
Plastic surgery	7(14%)	12(24%)	2(4%)	25(50%)	0(0%)	4(8%)	0(0%)
Gastroenterology	4(8%)	18(36%)	22(44%)	0(0%)	0(0%)	6(12%)	0(0%)
Cardiovascular surgery	1(2%)	30(60%)	14(28%)	1(2%)	0(0%)	4(8%)	0(0%)
Breast and thyroid surgery	2(4%)	18(36%)	19(38%)	5(10%)	0(0%)	6(12%)	0(0%)
Total	6%	53%	23%	7%	2%	10%	0%

To look across clinical specialties, findings show that questions of "plastic surgery" have nothing to do with illness, disease, or disorder, but are raised about enhancing looks to become robust and perfect. High percentage of both neurology and surgical neurology questions are concerned with aspects of signs, symptoms, and worries; consultation and diagnosis service are often requested in these questions.

3.3   Strategies of Communicating Chief Complaints

In disclosing chief complaints, seekers engaged in three types of communication style: contextual, focal, and emotional. Contextual strategy was used to describe background information as well as the information coverage of current illness. Focal strategy, on the contrary, was direct and effective when a question was fact-based. Emotional strategy was often articulated through negative emotional remarks in the question narratives to draw attention to the questions.

Overall, 80% of the questions utilize contextual strategy, followed by emotional strategy (36%) and focal strategy (30%). 92% of oncology questions are contextual in communicating chief complaints. This may explain the lengthy nature of oncology questions presented earlier in the findings, because the cause of cancer is complicated and the treatment and recovery is not a straight-line process. A great detail of information must be provided in the chief complaints in order for medical professionals to make effective and constructive advice. Questions for pulmonology and plastic surgery are highly emotional, with 58% and 54% of the questions are found using emotional strategy. Emotional strategy is mostly employed when negative feelings and thoughts, such as anxiety and worry, arise. Positive feeling is also present in the use of emotional strategy, especially when consultation seekers show gratification to the answerers up front in hope to solicit their contact and help.

Table 3. Strategies of communicating chief complaints (#/%)

	Contextual (#/%)	Emotional (#/%)	Focal (#/%)
Physical medicine and rehabilitation	41(82%)	11(22%)	20(40%)
Oncology	46(92%)	19(38%)	9(18%)
Psychiatry	27(54%)	25(50%)	10(20%)
Otolaryngology	44(88%)	13(26%)	8(16%)
Radiology	24(48%)	19(38%)	29(58%)
Neurology	44(88%)	14(28%)	13(26%)
Surgical neurology	45(90%)	14(28%)	8(16%)
Pulmonology	42(84%)	29(58%)	13(26%)
Plastic surgery	37(74%)	27(54%)	21(42%)
Gastroenterology	44(88%)	13(26%)	15(30%)
Cardiovascular surgery	45(90%)	23(46%)	15(30%)
Breast and thyroid surgery	42(84%)	8(16%)	20(40%)
Total	80%	36%	30%

3.4   Intents of Seeking Consultation

This study identified 23 distinct intents to seek online consultation (See Table 4). Findings indicate that nearly half (47%) of the consultation seekers use the online consultation service for fact-based information. The questions are explicit and obvious, and they require specific answers, but not opinions. 26% of the questions are in need of confirmation regarding health condition and 20% are venting feelings. By cross tabulating clinical specialties and intents, some interesting findings are revealed. 98% of the Radiology questions are seeking fact of knowledge, and questions that demonstrate feelings and emotions most, are Psychology questions. Questions that seek treatment and medication side effect most are Oncology questions.

Table 4. Intent of seeking consultation

	Physical medicine and Rehabilitation	Oncology	Psychiatry	Otolaryngology	Radiology	Neurology	Surgical-neurology	Pulmonology	Plastic surgery	Gastroenterology	Cardiovascular surgery	Breast and thyroid surgery	Total
Seeking fact or knowledge	19(38%)	26(52%)	9(18%)	2(4%)	49(98%)	39(78%)	27(54%)	22(44%)	17(34%)	23(46%)	16(32%)	35(70%)	47%
Seeking explanation	8(16%)	11(22%)	12(24%)	12(24%)	3(6%)	17(34%)	13(26%)	7(14%)	6(12%)	7(14%)	12(24%)	5(10%)	19%
Venting feelings	9(18%)	10(20%)	19(38%)	7(14%)	6(12%)	3(6%)	7(14%)	19(38%)	18(36%)	9(18%)	7(14%)	5(10%)	20%
Helping others to seek help	11(22%)	15(30%)	6(12%)	2(4%)	6(12%)	10(20%)	10(20%)	13(26%)	4(8%)	5(10%)	9(18%)	11(22%)	17%
Seeking advice on improving quality of life	1(2%)	2(4%)	1(2%)	0(0%)	0(0%)	1(2%)	3(6%)	0(0%)	5(10%)	1(2%)	0(0%)	1(2%)	3%
Seeking consultation on operation or surgical procedures	2(4%)	6(12%)	0(0%)	3(6%)	0(0%)	1(2%)	15(30%)	3(6%)	26(52%)	0(0%)	2(4%)	13(26%)	12%

Table 4. (*Continued.*)

Seeking evaluation of inter-hospital transfer	0(0%)	0(0%)	0(0%)	0(0%)	0(0%)	1(2%)	0(0%)	2(4%)	1(2%)	0(0%)	0(0%)	0(0%)	1%
Seeking consultation on medical dispute Consulting	0(0%)	2(4%)	0(0%)	0(0%)	0(0%)	0(0%)	1(2%)	0(0%)	0(0%)	1(2%)	1(2%)	0(0%)	1%
Seeking consultation on diet and nutrition	0(0%)	1(2%)	1(2%)	0(0%)	2(4%)	0(0%)	1(2%)	0(0%)	0(0%)	1(2%)	3(6%)	1(2%)	2%
Seeking consultation on medical supplies and equipment	0(0%)	0(0%)	0(0%)	1(2%)	0(0%)	0(0%)	0(0%)	0(0%)	3(6%)	0(0%)	6(12%)	0(0%)	2%
Seeking clinic and hospital information	15(30%)	4(8%)	0(0%)	8(16%)	1(2%)	5(10%)	9(18%)	10(20%)	7(14%)	1(2%)	2(4%)	4(8%)	11%
Seeking consultation on rehabilitation	11(22%)	0(0%)	0(0%)	0(0%)	0(0%)	0(0%)	4(8%)	1(2%)	0(0%)	0(0%)	0(0%)	1(2%)	3%
Seeking information on medical instruments	1(2%)	0(0%)	0(0%)	2(4%)	1(2%)	0(0%)	0(0%)	0(0%)	0(0%)	0(0%)	0(0%)	0(0%)	1%

Table 4. (*Continued.*)

Seeking consultation on treatment	4(8%)	16(32%)	2(4%)	7(14%)	1(2%)	5(10%)	6(12%)	6(12%)	8(16%)	0(0%)	0(0%)	0(0%)	9%
Seeking consultation on operation	0(0%)	0(0%)	0(0%)	0(0%)	0(0%)	0(0%)	8(16%)	0(0%)	0(0%)	0(0%)	0(0%)	0(0%)	1%
Confirming health condition	0(0%)	10(20%)	8(16%)	19(38%)	13(26%)	7(14%)	12(24%)	16(32%)	7(14%)	20(40%)	19(38%)	23(46%)	26%
Evaluating need for diagnosis	5(10%)	4(8%)	3(6%)	7(14%)	2(4%)	4(8%)	14(28%)	10(20%)	13(26%)	12(24%)	8(16%)	20(40%)	17%
Seeking information on medical after-effect	0(0%)	8(16%)	0(0%)	0(0%)	0(0%)	0(0%)	3(6%)	0(0%)	0(0%)	0(0%)	0(0%)	0(0%)	2%
Seeking support	0(0%)	0(0%)	1(2%)	0(0%)	0(0%)	0(0%)	0(0%)	0(0%)	0(0%)	0(0%)	0(0%)	0(0%)	0%
Seeking consultation on health and medical insurance	0(0%)	0(0%)	0(0%)	0(0%)	0(0%)	1(2%)	3(6%)	0(0%)	2(4%)	0(0%)	0(0%)	0(0%)	1%
Seeking consultation on drugs and medical products	1(2%)	0(0%)	3(6%)	1(2%)	0(0%)	7(14%)	4(8%)	6(12%)	6(12%)	3(6%)	2(4%)	1(2%)	5%
Seeking advice on healthy living	0(0%)	0(0%)	0(0%)	0(0%)	0(0%)	0(0%)	0(0%)	2(4%)	0(0%)	1(2%)	0(0%)	0(0%)	1%

Table 5. Types of information provided

	Physical medicine and rehabilitation	Oncology	Psychiatry	Otolaryngology	Radiology	Neurology	Surgical neurology	Pulmonology	Plastic surgery	Gastroenterology	Cardiovascular surgery	Breast and thyroid surgery	Total
Past medical examination results	0(0%)	2(4%)	3(6%)	5(10%)	5(10%)	7(14%)	0(0%)	4(8%)	0(0%)	6(12%)	8(16%)	11(22%)	9%
Current mental state	0(0%)	0(0%)	29(58%)	0(0%)	1(2%)	5(10%)	0(0%)	0(0%)	0(0%)	0(0%)	1(2%)	0(0%)	6%
Present health and medical concerns	8(16%)	0(0%)	20(40%)	1(2%)	36(72%)	10(20%)	9(18%)	6(12%)	3(6%)	24(48%)	8(16%)	10(20%)	23%
Medical history	29(58%)	29(58%)	9(18%)	16(32%)	5(10%)	17(34%)	31(62%)	16(32%)	4(8%)	7(14%)	7(14%)	10(20%)	30%
Symptom description	23(46%)	33(66%)	5(10%)	30(60%)	2(4%)	39(78%)	35(70%)	34(68%)	17(34%)	37(74%)	12(24%)	47(94%)	52%
Drug history	1(2%)	5(10%)	3(6%)	2(4%)	0(0%)	12(24%)	4(8%)	4(8%)	1(2%)	4(8%)	6(12%)	5(10%)	8%
Possible causes or reasons for medical encounter	17(34%)	1(2%)	0(0%)	0(0%)	2(4%)	1(2%)	1(2%)	1(2%)	6(12%)	0(0%)	1(2%)	0(0%)	5%
Medical signs	1(2%)	6(12%)	0(0%)	10(20%)	0(0%)	1(2%)	0(0%)	0(0%)	21(42%)	4(8%)	0(0%)	22(44%)	11%
Nutrition supplements	0(0%)	0(0%)	0(0%)	0(0%)	0(0%)	0(0%)	0(0%)	0(0%)	0(0%)	0(0%)	1(2%)	1(2%)	0%
Recovery process	0(0%)	0(0%)	0(0%)	0(0%)	0(0%)	0(0%)	1(2%)	0(0%)	0(0%)	0(0%)	0(0%)	0(0%)	0%
Health condition	12(24%)	6(12%)	10(20%)	7(14%)	12(24%)	14(28%)	3(6%)	3(6%)	0(0%)	20(40%)	6(12%)	15(30%)	16%
Not specified	2(4%)	1(2%)	4(8%)	4(8%)	11(22%)	1(2%)	4(8%)	6(12%)	10(20%)	2(4%)	2(4%)	8(16%)	9%
Life story and experience	0(0%)	0(0%)	3(6%)	0(0%)	0(0%)	0(0%)	0(0%)	0(0%)	0(0%)	0(0%)	0(0%)	0(0%)	1%

3.5   Types of Information Provided

This study identifies 13 types information included in the questions. In face-to-face medical consultation in the hospital or clinic, description of symptoms and briefing on medical history and are critical sources for physicians to make diagnosis decision and to determine treatment and prognosis. However, in online medical consultation, only about half (52%) of the questions describe symptoms and medical history (30%). It reflects the intent that not all questions are medical diagnosis related (See Table 5) and require instant medical attention. This pattern shows that medical consultation seekers are not necessarily people who are ill; healthy or health-aware people are more responsible in seeking to cultivate their health knowledge. Questions that intend to seek fact or medical knowledge can be clearly answered without detailing chief complaints.

4   Implications of the Study

The content analysis of the online medical consultation questions uncovers a series of undergoing activities during the search formulation stage. For example, soliciting second opinion on diagnosis and seeking alternative treatment at the same time, suggests the multi-tasking nature of medical information seeking and retrieval. This study makes implications in designing an interactive online medical consultation system. For example, social tagging may be one aspect that allows consultation seekers to identify their intent and define the problems, considering the fact that online consultation seekers don't necessarily come to the service for medical information needs. In addition, providing a drop-down menu for a selection of current health status and intent, and allowing users to choose from the list may improve the clarity of question, increase the answering rate, and improve the quality of the answers .An analysis coexistence of health conditions, intents, consultation types, and strategies of communicating chief complaints may provide insight into effective physician-patient communication.

References

1. Caiata-Zufferey, M., Abraham, A., Sommerhalder, K., Schulz, P.: Online Health Information Seeking in the Context of Medical Consultation in Switzerland. Qualitative Health Research 20(8), 1050–1061 (2010)
2. Umefjord, G.: Internet Consultation in Medicine: Studies of a Text-based Ask the Doctor Service. Umeå, Sweden: University of Umeå (2006)

Social Media Marketing on Twitter:

An Investigation of the Involvement-Messaging-Engagement Link

Constantinos K. Coursaris, Wietske van Osch, and Brandon Brooks

Michigan State University East Lansing, MI, USA
{coursari,vanosch,brook205}@msu.edu

Abstract. With the rise of social media marketing as an important domain of practice and research, a growing number of scholarly and practitioner articles have emerged highlighting best practices in social media marketing. Despite this proliferation of articles exploring the topic of social media marketing, no comprehensive frameworks exist that offer insight into the underlying components of effective social media marketing messages and the relations between them. Amalgamating constructs from a variety of disciplinary backgrounds—including marketing, advertising, communication, and information systems—this paper offers a theoretical framework and empirical investigation of the relations between four message components, namely purchase involvement, messaging strategy, message content, and media types. Using longitudinal data from ten Fortune 500 companies, we validate our comprehensive framework and find support for all hypotheses, thereby validating the importance of using an integrated approach to social media message design. Implications for research and practice are outlined.

Keywords: social media marketing, purchase involvement, media richness, content categories typology, Twitter.

1   Introduction

Recent studies have revealed that companies have grown their social media marketing spending and are expected to continue to increase social media budgets in the next five years (Moorman, 2013), making social media one of the fastest growing marketing platforms in the world. The popularity of social media for marketing purposes can be attributed to a number of advantages associated with social media when compared to traditional marketing channels. First, the scope of consumer markets that can be reached and served through social media platforms are nearly unlimited. Second, social media offer businesses significant cost advantages compared to traditional channels given its relatively free or low-cost nature. Third, social media enable personalized marketing strategies and allow the targeting of small niche markets (Carpenter and Shankar, 2012). Finally, due to the social nature of these platforms, companies can benefit from accruing earned media exposures and referral markets in unprecedented ways (Carpenter and Shankar, 2012).

F.F.-H. Nah (Ed.): HCIB/HCII 2014, LNCS 8527, pp. 155–165, 2014.
© Springer International Publishing Switzerland 2014

Simply browsing the social media feeds of Fortune 500 companies reveals a plethora of marketing strategies and executions with some companies posting huge amounts of content with little to no impact, while others have immense followings or fan bases allowing for greater consumer engagement and enhanced branding. Although the lack of strategy may come as an initial surprise given the huge investments companies are making into the social space, the lack of research offering a comprehensive assessment, classification, and analysis of social media marketing techniques and strategies poses a major challenge to the design of effective social media marketing practices.

To fill this gap, this study draws upon and amalgamates three distinct and interdisciplinary theoretical perspectives for analyzing three dimensions of a business' social media marketing strategy, namely purchase involvement, message appeal, and message richness, in the context of Twitter. Additionally, we analyze and classify message content using the typology of social media messages as developed Coursaris, van Osch and Balogh (2013) in which the authors use a Multi-Grounded Theory approach to develop a coding scheme for message content within the context of Facebook. Given the extension of their approach to Twitter and the integration of an analysis of message content with purchase involvement, strategy, and media richness, we can offer a multi-dimensional framework for understanding and informing social media marketing as well as potential differences between the two social media platforms.

Consequently, the research questions underpinning this study are as follows:

1. What is the effect of purchase involvement of a brand's product or service on the adopted messaging strategy?
2. What is the interplay between message content and message richness? I.e., are certain content categories more likely to be combined with particular media types?
3. What is the effect of message richness on consumer engagement?

To answer these questions, this paper reports on the findings from a longitudinal multiple case study of the messaging practices from nine fortune 500 brands—Delta Airlines, JetBlue, KLM, Wal-Mart, Meijer, Target, McDonalds, Starbucks, and Pepsi—of six weeks of Twitter messaging data (n=1169 posts). The focus of this study is on Twitter and the unit of analysis is the tweet. The nine brands were selected because they represent a range of consumer purchase involvement across three industry categories, namely airlines, big box retailers, and fast-moving consumer goods (FMCGs).

The testing of our proposed multi-dimensional framework and the underlying hypotheses allows for the exploration of differences in the relative frequency and effectiveness of the messaging appeal and messaging content through ANOVA and regression analyses of the relationships between brand characteristics, messaging strategy (i.e., appeal, content, and richness), and consumer engagement.

The findings from our analyses reveal that purchase involvement of the brand significantly predicts the messaging strategy employed by a brand. Additionally, our findings show the importance of establishing a "fit" between the level of abstraction and complexity of the content category and the level of richness of the media type that is included in a tweet, and that this "fit" may be more important in increasing consumer engagement than increasing levels of media richness alone.

2   Theoretical Underpinnings

In order to provide a holistic assessment of brand marketing messages on social media, we integrate a set of interdisciplinary theoretical constructs with their origins in marketing, advertising, communication science, and information systems, on purchase involvement, messaging strategy, messaging type, and media type, as follows.

2.1   Purchase Involvement

Purchase involvement represents the extent of interest and concern that a consumer brings to bear upon a purchase-decision task (Mittal, 1989; Beatty et al., 1988). As such, it refers to the amount of time, effort, and costs invested when making a purchase. In general, higher levels of purchase involvement are present when purchases involve high uncertainty as well as high levels of economic and time concerns (Houston and Rothschild, 1978).

Thus, purchase involvement relates to risk reduction and price comparison. While involvement inherently refers to a consumer's behavior during the purchase process, certain product categories have been identified as being either high or low in purchase involvement. For instance, high involvement products are generally expensive and are associated with high potential risk, such as buying a home, financial investments, and/or airline tickets (primarily business travel). In making purchase decision regarding any of these high involvement goods, consumers seek extensive information in order to reduce risk and uncertainty. Consequently, messages from brands selling high purchase involvement goods tend to focus on informing the consumer—with the aim of assisting their problem-solving process and reducing associated risk—rather than entertaining (Lally, 2007).

On the other hand, low involvement products are perceived neither as risky nor fascinating (Lally, 2007), and include such products as food, beverages, and office supplies. In these instances, consumers are unlikely to make a significant time investment to explore and evaluate product information extensively. As a result, low involvement brands center their messaging content on providing rapid hedonic appeals (Hawkins et al., 1983). Thus, in the case of low involvement commodities, brands entertain rather than inform in order to get consumers to purchase their brand over any other.

2.2   Messaging Strategies: Informational versus Transformational

Within the traditional advertising literature, various schemes have been developed for the classification of messaging strategies. However, both practically and theoretically, the consistent application of these schemes—the majority of which are too complex or too simplistic—has proven challenging (see, e.g., Simon 1971, Frazer 1983, Aaker 1982). One exception has been the dichotomous messaging strategy framework developed by Laskey, Day and Crask (1989), which has proven to be valuable for both practitioners and researchers alike.

Laskey et al.'s (1989) classification scheme of brand messaging strategies is grounded in the typology proposed by Puto and Wells (1984), who distinguish between informational and transformational messages. While informational advertising focuses on the transmission of factual, verifiable data about the brand, transformational advertising emphasizes the consumer's affective experience with the brand. Described differently, informational advertising is often directed at problem-solving—providing the consumer with insights into how the particular brand or service can help solve a particular problem at hand—transformational messages rather aim to endow the use of the advertised brand with a particular experience that is different from that of using any similar brand.

Given that the informational/transformational dichotomy has broad applicability and generalizability, we adopt Laskey et al.'s (1989) classification scheme to analyze social media marketing messages.

When integrating the former theory on purchase decision involvement with the informational-transformational dichotomy, the following two hypotheses can be inferred:

H1a: The higher the brand involvement, the more informational the messaging strategy on Twitter
H1b: The lower the brand involvement, the more transformational the messaging strategy on Twitter

2.3   Messaging Typologies

Coursaris et al. (2013) present a review of existing typologies for analyzing the content of social media marketing messages. Based on their review the authors conclude only a limited number of existing typologies exist, none of which adopt a strategic lens as evident from their lack of analysis of engagement metrics and the isolated analysis of a single message dimension (e.g., media type, content, or brand).

Given the lack of existing typologies, Coursaris et al. (2013) use a grounded theory strategy to inductively develop a holistic typology of content categories based on the analysis of 256 Facebook posts. Their typology revealed seven overarching messaging categories of Brand Awareness, Corporate Social Responsibility, Customer Service, Engagement, Product Awareness, Promotional, and Seasonal, which in turn encompass a total of 23 subcategories.

Although a single message could be categorized under more than one umbrella category—e.g., a post that fosters both Brand Awareness and Product Awareness simultaneously—the underlying subcategories are designed to be mutually exclusive. Although it is beyond the scope of this paper to provide detailed definitions and examples for all categories and subcategories, Table 1 below offers definitions for the seven umbrella categories. For a more extensive overview of conceptualizations and illustrations we refer to Coursaris et al. (2013). Furthermore, Appendix 1 offers an overview of the frequency of occurrence of each of the messaging categories and subcategories for the three purchase decision involvement categories analyzed.

Table 1. Social Media Marketing Typology

Categories	Definitions
Brand Awareness	Posts that build company presence and attentiveness in digital consumer market
Corporate Social Responsibility (CSR)	Posts that build brand image of supporting, strengthening community
Customer Service	Posts that aim to build consumer knowledge about product, industry, and brand changes.
Engagement	Posts that build consumer connections/communities through brand interaction
Product Awareness	All posts which build product knowledge/understanding, and existence.
Promotional	Posts that are designed to stimulate immediate or near future purchases through monetary incentives.
Seasonal	Posts that remind, inform consumers of seasonal, annual events and related products by the brand

2.4 Media Richness Theory

One of the earlier and most widely used theories in communication and information science is Media Richness Theory (MRT) as proposed by Daft and Lengel in 1986. MRT asserts that each communication medium can be described by its ability to reproduce any associated contextual cues (e.g., visual ones such as gestures) during a message's transmission. This ability is referred to as the medium's "richness." Thus, the richness of a video message would be considered higher than that of a text-based message.

Twitter allows brands to employ different media types in a message (i.e., tweet). Hence, tweets can employ media types ranging from very lean media—i.e., text-only tweets—to media associated with an increasing level of richness, such as URL, photo, and video. Here, we treat URLs as rich media since their inclusion in a tweet is associated with a thumbnail image and these URLs frequently link to external, rather than embedded, videos.

One obvious observation about the content categories described in the previous paragraph is their varying levels of abstraction and complexity. Whereas some of the content categories are highly abstract—e.g., brand awareness, CSR, and customer service—other categories are concrete—e.g., promotional and seasonal messages. Using MRT, we anticipate that for tweets (i.e., messages) to be effective, abstract content categories need to be associated with richer media, in order to make the message more informative and appealing to consumers. Hence, the following hypothesis emerges:

H2a: More abstract content categories—i.e., brand awareness, CSR, and customer service—are associated with richer media (i.e., video, photo, or URL) on Twitter

Furthermore, for concrete content categories we anticipate no significant relationship to exist with media richness as they can be effectively associated with any media type. Finally, for product awareness, we anticipate increased use of photos—for enhanced product recognition—or direct links (i.e., URLs) to the product. Thus:

H2b: Product awareness messages on Twitter are associated with posts containing a photo or URL.

Ultimately, however, richer, more personal communication is more effective than leaner, less rich media (Newberry, 2001). Therefore, we propose that:

H3: The inclusion of richer media types—photo, video, or URL—on Twitter is associated with higher consumer engagement

3   Research Design

We use a multiple case-study approach rather than a single case-study design in order to avoid apparent challenges to generalizability. The multiple case-study design allows for the collection of data from two or more sources, which can then be compared (Yin, 1994). Cross-case comparisons augment within-case analysis (Eisenhardt, 1989) strengthening results though pattern-matching increasing confidence in the robustness of theoretical results (Yin, 1994).

3.1   Multiple-Case Study Design and Case Selection

All ten brands selected for this study are leaders in their respective domains for social media marketing. The brands rank among the top Fortune 500 companies by gross revenue, enjoy strong brand equity, and maintain a considerable social media presence. Three different levels of purchase-decision involvement can be represented from the brands: low-involvement among fast-moving consumer goods (FMCGs) including McDonalds, Coca Cola, Pepsi Cola, and Starbucks, mixed levels of involvement are found within Wal-Mart, Meijer, and Target representing Big Box Retailers (BBR), and high purchase-decision involvement for expensive and more risk-bearing goods and services represented by the airlines Delta, KLM, and JetBlue.

3.2   Data Collection

Data collection occurred over a six-week period during late Summer 2012. This provided a longitudinal aspect to our data giving us the ability to mitigate generalizability concerns. One brand, Walmart, was collected in late Winter 2013 due to complications with rate limiting on Twitter. Data were collected using a web crawler program that automatically went to each brand's Twitter account to collect the Tweets. Table 2 summarizes the number of brand posts analyzed for each purchase-decision involvement category—low, medium, and high. The unit of analysis is the brand tweet.

Table 2. Data Collection Details

	High Involvement (Airlines)	Mixed Involvement (Big Box Retailers)	Low Involvement (FMCGs)
Observations (N)	192 tweets	592 tweets	430 tweets

3.3   Coding Process

A pair of independent coders analyzed all tweets from a single brand, i.e., a total of ten pairs of independent coders analyzed the tweets from all ten brands. The final coding scheme encompassed the typology of brand messaging content categories as well as codes for messaging strategy (transformational versus informational), media types (text only, includes URL, photo, and/or video), timing (date/time of post; date/time of first and last comment), and consumer engagement (favorites, retweets, replies-to, and hashtags).

The overall interrater agreement across the 10 brands was .73 Cohen's kappa (computed as the average from the Cohen's kappa scores of each pair of independent coders), which is considered substantial agreement, noting that all 10 dyads' interrater agreement was well above the 0.60 threshold for substantial agreement. Following the completion of the data coding process, face-to-face meetings were organized to discuss and reconcile any disagreements. After the entire dataset had been coded and reconciled, summary tables and graphs were constructed for each category of the coding scheme.

3.4   Data Analysis

In order to test our hypotheses, we used SPSS ANOVA—for pairwise comparisons between purchase involvement categories—and SPSS Regression—for analyzing the effects of media richness on consumer engagement.

Due to the large differences in the number of tweets per category of purchase-decision involvement and the high sensitivity of ANOVA to unequal sample sizes (Howell, 2009), we used SPSS Select Cases to randomly select an equal amount of tweets across all three categories of purchase-decision involvement as determined by the group of brands with the least posts, namely the high involvement brands (i.e., airlines; including Delta, KLM, and JetBlue) (N = 192). For SPSS regression, we used the full data set, i.e., without randomly selecting an equal subset of tweets per purchase-decision involvement category. Since the aim of the regression analysis was not to compare across brands but rather to assess the effect of media richness on consumer engagement, unequal sample sizes do not pose a problem.

For the regression of the different messaging components—strategy, content category, and media type—we used the raw counts for likes, comments, and shares associated with each tweet, as well as computed an additional weighted dependent variable, social media engagement index on Twitter, which we define and calculate as follows:

Social Media Engagement Index on Twitter = $.5*\Sigma(F) + 1*\Sigma(R) + 1.5*\Sigma(Rt)$

Where F refers to Favorites, R refers to Replies, and Rt refers to Retweets.

The weighing of favorites, replies, and retweets, is based on the increasing level of cognitive involvement, exposure, and vulnerability (in terms of visibility in one's own personal network) associated with each of these activities for the consumer.

For the analysis of media richness, we additionally computed a compound media richness variable that encompasses the combined values for photos, videos, and/or URLs; i.e., a text-only post will have a media richness value of 0, a post that includes only one of these media types will have a value of 1, and a post that includes two or all three of these media types would have a value of 2 or 3 respectively.

4   Findings

In what follows, we will discuss the findings of our hypotheses testing as summarized in Table 3.

With respect to messaging strategy—i.e., informational versus transformational messages—we analyzed the link between brand purchase-decision involvement and strategy and between strategy and engagement.

First, a one-way ANOVA for brand purchase involvement on strategy reveals that there are significant differences between Airlines (M = .30, SD = .46), Big Box Retailers (M = .27, SD = .45), and Fast-Moving Consumer Goods (M = .64, SD = .48) with Airlines and Big Box Retailers using significantly more informational messages (Welch test; p = .00).

With respect to the content categories from our messaging typology, we analyzed the link between the level of abstraction of the messaging category and the richness vis-à-vis the set of media types used in a tweet. The results of the regression analysis showed that abstract messages are indeed significantly correlated with richer media (p = .00) supporting H3a. Interestingly, CSR (p = .03), Engagement (p = .006), and Product Awareness (p = .00) were significantly associated with richer media. On the other hand, Seasonal messages (p = .008), which tend to be quite specific in terms of the ideas being communicated to the consumers, were associated with less rich media.

In partial support of H2b, we found that product awareness tweets are indeed more likely to include photos (p = .00), but not URLs (p = .54), in order to support enhanced product recognition and recall.

With respect to the effect of media richness on engagement—Hypothesis 3—we found a marginally significant effect of the former on weighted engagement (p = .089).

Table 3. Hypotheses Testing

Hyp.	Specification	P-Value	Result
H1a:	Higher purchase involvement → Informational Strategy	.00	Supported
H1b:	Lower purchase involvement → Transformational Strategy	.00	Supported
H2a:	Abstract Content Categories → Richer Media	.00	Supported
H2b:	Product Awareness Messages → Photo/URL	.00/.54	Partial
H3:	Richer Media → Higher Engagement	.089	Marginal

5   Discussion

In this paper, we drew upon interdisciplinary theories from marketing, advertising, communication, and information systems to build a comprehensive framework. Amalgamating four constructs representing various components of a brand message, namely purchase involvement, messaging strategy, messaging content, and media richness, we aim to understand the effects of (i) purchase involvement on messaging strategy, (ii) messaging content on media richness, and (iii) media richness on consumer engagement. Combining the various theoretical domains, we proposed and tested three sets of hypotheses, pertaining to each of these relations, using Twitter data from ten Fortune 500 companies across three industries, airlines, big box retailers, and consumer packaged goods (CPGs).

First, hypotheses testing—using both SPSS ANOVA and SPSS Regression—revealed that brand purchase involvement significantly predicts the messaging strategy employed by brands in their tweets, with high involvement brands using mostly informational messaging strategies and low involvement brands using mostly transformational strategies. Second, our analysis of content categories showed that significant relationships exist between the content of a brand tweet and the richness of the media type—text only, photo, video, or URL—included in the post. Specifically, abstract content categories are best combined with rich media in order to more effectively communicate a brand's message to the consumer. Also, product awareness messages are best combined with photos in order to reinforce product recall. Finally, we found marginal support for the hypothesis that the use of richer media result in higher engagement, thereby potentially underlining that creating a "fit" between content category and media type is more important than the media type per se.

In sum, this study offers two main contributions. First by proposing and testing a multi-dimensional messaging framework, we aim to offer valuable and comprehensive insights to both researchers and practitioners interested in social media marketing. We hope this framework will be useful for researchers in exploring additional social media platforms, also in exploring other relationships between the four components—purchase involvement, strategy, content, and media type—of social media marketing, as well as in the importance of strategic fit among the components in order to establish high consumer engagement. Second, we hope that the proposed framework can help managers better understand the diversity of messaging components and the potential for a very large number of variations available between these components, as well as offer an analytical tool for assessing the nature of engagement associated with each strategy and category.

References

1. Aaker, D.A., Norris, D.: Characteristics of TV Commercials Perceived as Informative. Journal of Advertising Research (22), 22–34 (1982)
2. Carpenter, G.S., Shankar, V.: Handbook of marketing strategy. Edward Elgar Publishing (2012)

3. Coursaris, C.K., Van Osch, W., Balogh, B.A.: A social media marketing typology: classifying brand facebook page messages for strategic consumer engagement. In: European Conference on Information Systems (ECIS), Utrecht, Netherlands, June 6-8 (2013)

4. Daft, R.L., Lengel, R.H.: Organizational Information Requirements, Media Richness and Structural Design. Management Science 32(5), 554–571 (1986)

5. Day, G.S.: Buyer Attitudes and Brand Choice. Free Press, New York (1970)

6. Eisenhardt, K.: Building theories from case study research. Academy of Management Review 14(4), 532–550 (1989)

7. Frazer, C.F.: Creative Strategy: A Management Perspective. Journal of Advertising 12(4), 36–41 (1983)

8. Glaser, B.G., Strauss, A.L.: The Discovery of Grounded Theory: Strategies for Qualitative Research. Aldine Publishing Company, Chicago (1967)

9. Goldkuhl, G., Cronholm, S.: Adding Theoretical Grounding to Grounded Theory - Towards Multi-Grounded Theory. International Journal of Qualitative Methods 9(2), 187–205 (2010)

10. Hawkins, D.I., Best, R.J., Coney, K.A.: Consumer Behavior: Implications for Marketing Strategy. Business Publications Inc., Plano (1983)

11. Hoffman, D.L., Fodor, M.: Can you measure the ROI of your social media marketing? MIT Sloan Management Review 52(1), 41–49 (2010)

12. Houston, M.J., Rothschild, M.L.: Conceptual and Methodological Perspectives on Involvement. In: Jain, S.C. (ed.) 1978 Educators' Proceedings, pp. 184–187. American Marketing Association, Chicago (1978)

13. Howell, D.C.: Unequal Cell Sizes Do Matter (2009), http://www.uvm.edu/~dhowell/StatPages/More_Stuff/Unequal-ns/unequal-ns.html (retrieved on April 19, 2013)

14. Jenkins, B.: Consumer Sharing of Viral Video Advertisements: A Look into Message and Creative Strategy Typologies and Emotional Content, Capstone Project. (2011), http://www.american.edu/soc/communication/upload/blaise-jenkins.pdf (retrieved on December 3, 2012)

15. Jensen, M.B., Jepsen, A.L.: Online Marketing Communications: Need for a New Typology for IMC? Journal of Website Promotion 2(1/2), 19–35 (2006)

16. Kwok, L., Yu, B.: Spreading Social Media Messages on Facebook: An Analysis of Restaurant Business-to-Consumer Communications. Cornell Hospitality Quarterly 20(10), 1–11 (2012)

17. Lally, L.: Degrees of Delight: A Model of Consumer Value Generated by E-Commerce. In: IRMA International Conference, pp. 1006–1007 (2007)

18. Landis, J.R., Koch, G.G.: The measurement of observer agreement for categorical data. Biometrics 33(1), 159–174 (1977)

19. Laskey, H., Day, E., Crask, M.R.: Typology of Main Message Strategies for Television Commercials. Journal of Advertising 18(1), 36–41 (1989)

20. Mittal, B.: Measuring Purchase-decision involvement. Psychology & Marketing (6), 147–162 (1989)

21. Newberry, B.: Media Richness, Social Presence and Technology Supported Communication Activities in Education (2001), http://learngen.org/resources/module/lgend101_norm1/200/210/211_3.html (retrieved on April 20, 2013)

22. Puto, C.P., Wells, W.D.: Informational and Transformational Advertising: The Differential Effects of Time. In: Kinnear, T.C. (ed.) Advances in Consumer Research XI, pp. 638–643. Association for Consumer Research, Provo (1984)

23. Rossiter, J.R., Bellman, S.: Marketing Communications: Theory and Applications. Pearson, Prentice Hall, New York (2005)
24. Simon, J.L.: The Management of Advertising. Prentice Hall, Englewood Cliffs, NJ (1971)
25. Sullivan, A., Sheffrin, S.M.: Economics: Principles in action. Pearson Prentice Hall, Upper Saddle River (2003)
26. Waters, R.D., Burnett, E., Lamm, A., Lucas, J.: Engaging stakeholders through social networking: How nonprofit organizations are using Facebook. Public Relations Review (35), 102–106 (2009)
27. Yin, R.K.: Case study research: Design and methods, 2nd edn. Applied Social Research Methods Series, vol. 5. Sage, Thousand Oaks (1994)

The Internet, Happiness, and Social Interaction: A Review of Literature

Richard H. Hall[1] and Ashley Banaszek[2]

[1] Department of Business and Information Technology,
Missouri University of Science and Technology, Rolla, Missouri
rhall@mst.edu
[2] Union Pacific Railroad, Information Technology, Omaha, Nebraska
abanasz@up.com

Abstract. This paper is a review of literature relevant to the Internet, happiness, and social interaction. The definition of happiness is discussed, emphasizing its subjective quality, followed by a review of studies that have examined the correlates of happiness. This is followed by a review of studies on internet use, happiness, and social interaction, which yields the conclusion that the internet can facilitate social communication and interpersonal connections, which is, in turn, associated with higher levels of happiness and well being.

Keywords: Happiness, Internet.

1 Why Study Happiness and the Internet?

Following the dawn of the new millennium, research on happiness increased dramatically, largely spurred on by the fact that people increasingly rate happiness as a major life goal. For example, recent surveys have indicated that the strong majority of people across many countries rate happiness as more important than income [1]. Lyubomirsky [2] sums this research up, "…in almost every culture examined by researchers, people rank the pursuit of happiness as one of their most cherished goals in life" (p. 239).

In addition, there is a large body of evidence that suggests situational factors, in particular wealth, play a surprisingly small role in determining happiness. Some suggest that this may be the result of society moving into a post-materialistic phase, where basic needs have been largely met for many in industrialized countries, so pursuit of self fulfillment becomes more important [3].

Finally, there are number of studies that indicate that happy people, in general, have a positive effect on society. For example, there is evidence that happier people are more successful and socially engaged [4].

2 What Is Happiness?

For the most part, researchers agree that happiness is inherently subjective, In fact, the term is often used interchangeably with "subjective well-being" (SWB) [5]. David

F.F.-H. Nah (Ed.): HCIB/HCII 2014, LNCS 8527, pp. 166–174, 2014.
© Springer International Publishing Switzerland 2014

Myers [6], one of the leading researchers in the area, stated that happiness is "…whatever people mean when describing their lives as happy." (p. 57). Despite the potential for ambiguity with such a definition, there is considerable agreement, at least across Western culture as to what happiness means [7]. Most people equate happiness with experiences of joy, contentment, and positive well being; as well as a feeling that life is good, meaningful, and worthwhile [8].

As a consequence, self-report measures have served as the primary measure of happiness in most of the research we review. Examples include the Satisfaction with Life Scale (SLS), the Subjective Happiness Scale (SHS), and the Steen Happiness Index (SHI). Psychometric studies of these self-report measures indicate that they are, by and large, reliable over time, despite changing circumstances; they correlate strongly with friends and family ratings of happiness; and they are statistically reliable. Sonja Lyubomirsky [8] sums this up, "A great deal of research has shown that the majority of these measures have adequate to excellent psychometric properties and that the association between happiness and other variables usually cannot be accounted for by transient mood" (p. 239). These psychometric studies further illustrate the general agreement among people as to what constitutes happiness.

One other interesting point regarding the definition of happiness and its measurement is that mean happiness is consistently above a mid-line point in most populations sampled [5]. For example, three in ten Americans say they are "very happy", only 1 in ten report that they are "not too happy", and 6 in 10 say they are "pretty happy" [6]. Therefore, there appears to be a positive set-point, where most people appear to be moderately happy, and this is independent of age and gender [6].

3   What Predicts Happiness?

Over the years, particularly during the last two decades, there have been a number of studies that set out to determine the correlates of happiness in an effort to determine what makes some people happier than others. We will review the variables that have been examined most frequently, and discuss their relationship to happiness.

3.1   Individual Differences and Happiness

Happiness is surprisingly stable over time [9] even with major changes in life circumstances [10], and there appears to be no time in life that is most satisfying [11]. These findings are consistent with research that indicates some individual difference traits are predictive of happiness. Further, happiness may also be strongly tied to genetic predisposition. We now turn to a discussion of this research.

Twin studies indicate that there is a strong genetic component in happiness [12, 13]. For example, Lykken and Tellegen [12] assessed the well being of twins at ages 20 and 30. They correlated the happiness scores between monozygotic twins at stage 1 with the score for their twin at stage 2 (cross time/cross twin) and found a correlation of .4, while the test-retest correlation where each twin's score was correlated with himself/herself was only .5. Further the cross twin/cross time correlation for dizygotic twins was only .07. Therefore, heritability appears to account for a large part of the stability in happiness.

As mentioned, some other individual difference measures have been found to consistently correlate with happiness, in particular extroversion. For example, in a cross-cultural study Lucas and colleagues found that extraversion correlated with positive affect in virtually all 40 nations they examined [14]. Extroversion, as a predictor of happiness, is strongly related to the literature to be discussed, which relates social interaction with happiness, in that there is a clear relationship between the number and quality of social relationships and happiness. One would expect that an extrovert would be more likely to seek out and form these types of relationships.

Religiosity is another variable that has been found to consistently predict happiness [6]. In addition, those who report higher levels of religiosity tend to recover greater happiness after suffering from negative life events [15]. This finding has been found for peoples' self reports of their degree of religiosity, and for behavioral measures such as Church attendance [6]. As with extroversion, the impact of religiosity may be, at least partly, explained by the importance of social interaction in determining happiness, in that those who attend Church regularly, and interact with others in a positive social environment, are more likely to be happy [16]. Further, people often derive meaning and purpose from religious practices, which is another important correlate of happiness [6].

In addition to behavioral tendencies, with respect to individual differences, the research of Lyubomirsky and colleagues provides substantial evidence that there are consistent differences between happy and unhappy people in the ways they process ("construe") information. For example, studies from Lyubomirsky's laboratory have found that happy people are less sensitive to social comparisons [17], tended to feel more positive about decisions after they were made [18], construed events more positively [19], and are less inclined to self-reflect and dwell on themselves [18]. This difference in information processing dispositions in happy vs. unhappy people is presumably one reason why the effects of circumstantial factors are relatively minimal.

Another individual difference factor, which has been identified as important in predicting happiness, is the autotelic personality, which refers to people who tend to regularly experience "flow" [20]. Flow refers to a kind of experience that is engrossing and enjoyable to such a degree that it becomes "autotelic" – worth doing for its own sake [20]. The autotelic personality and the flow concept are consistent with the views of happiness researchers who have suggested that engagement is a fundamental component of a happy life [21].

3.2   Wealth and Happiness

Common sense tells us that environmental variables, such as wealth, should have a strong influence on happiness. In fact, wealth has been examined in a number of studies as a potential correlate with happiness, both in comparisons of the wealthy with the non-wealthy, and in examination of the effect of changes in wealth on happiness. As we will see, wealth, in general, plays a surprisingly small role.

Many of these studies have found a small, but significant, relationship between wealth and happiness. However, the relationship appears to disappear once there is enough income to provide for basic needs.

For example, Suh and colleagues found that those living in wealthier countries (where basic needs were met) were significantly happier than those in non-wealthy countries. However, within the wealthy and non-wealthy clusters there was virtually no relationship between the wealth of average individuals in a country and their reported happiness [1]. In the United States, the wealthiest are barely above those with average income in reported happiness [22]. Further, changes in wealth appear to have virtually no impact on long-term happiness. One study, which compared Lottery winners with those struck with traumatic events, found no differences in reported happiness a short period of time after the event [23]. Finally, though the average income in the United States more than doubled between 1960 and 1990, the percentage of people describing themselves as "very happy" remained the same [24].

3.3   Social Interaction and Happiness

The number and quality of social interactions and acquaintances has been found consistently to have a strong and positive impact on happiness. For example, people report feeling happier when they are with others [25]. Further, a study conducted by the National Opinion Research Center found that 26% of those who reported having five or less friends reported being very happy, but the number jumped to 38% for those who reported having more than 5 friends [6]. Those who enjoy close relationships also cope more effectively with various stressors [26].

Myers reports on a "mountain of data" (p. 62) that indicates that those who are married are, on average, happier and more satisfied with life. It appears this is particularly true in comparison to those who are separated or divorced [6]. Studies on the relationship between marriage and happiness provide yet more support for the importance of social interactions on happiness.

3.4   Volitional and Non-volitional Activities

Before we consider the relationship between Internet activities and happiness we will consider one other interesting issue involving activities that are associated with happiness, by considering the role of volition.

Lyubomirsky and colleagues propose a model of happiness, which poses that happiness is the result of three primary sources: a) personal set point (genetic predisposition); b) circumstances; and c) intentional activities [4].

We have discussed the importance of genetic pre-disposition but have made no distinction between circumstances (e.g., life events) and intentional activities (e.g. exercising). According to Lyubomirsky and colleagues [4] "…circumstances happen to people, and activities are ways that people act on their circumstances." p. 118.

Although it is very difficult to operationalize given activities as volitional or not [4], we mention this distinction because it has important practical implications. Specifically, if volitional activities can impact long term happiness then presumably, happiness can be changed. That is, people can have some control in affecting their own happiness.

In fact, Lyubomirsky and colleagues have some initial support for their model, in that they have found that relatively short-term happiness "interventions" can have a positive effect on well being. In one case they asked students to carry out acts of kindness and, in the other case they asked students to consider what they were grateful for [4].

Interestingly, this leads to our discussion of the Internet and happiness, in that there was a similar study, which examined the effect of relatively simple happiness interventions. This study was conducted completely over the Internet. Participants were recruited, given the materials describing the activity, and asked to complete a survey that used ratings to measure happiness, completely online. Despite the relatively simple and short-term nature of the intervention, participants who were asked to identify their "signature strengths" and then carry out activities associated with these strengths, and those who were encouraged to daily recall things for which they were thankful, had increased levels of happiness and decreased levels of depression, compared to a control group six months later [21].

4   Happiness and the Internet

Studies that have examined the relationship between the Internet and happiness have been conducted at least since the relatively early days of the World Wide Web. Most of these have focused on communication/collaborative activities and the internet. As we mentioned, these types of activities have been found in non-internet studies to be strongly related to happiness. Consequently, our discussion will focus on the internet as a tool for communication and collaboration as this relates to happiness.

4.1   The Internet Paradox

In 1998 Kraut and colleagues reported the results of a reasonably extensive study of early World Wide Web users where they followed the activity of mostly first time Internet users over a period of years. Researchers administered periodic questionnaires and server logs indicating participant activity on the web were analyzed. (Participants were provided with free computers and internet connections) [27].

Over all, the results showed that the Internet had a largely negative impact on social activity in that those who used the Internet more communicated with family and friends less. They also reported higher levels of loneliness. Interestingly, they also found that email, a communication activity, constituted the participants main use of the Internet. The researchers coined the term "internet paradox" to describe this situation in which a social technology reduced social involvement.

These researchers speculated that this negative social effect was due to a type of displacement, in which their time spent online displaced face-to-face social involvement. Although they note that users spent a great deal of time using email, they suggest that this constitutes a low quality social activity and this is why they did not see positive effects on well being [27]. They find further support for this supposition in a study reported in 2002, where they found that business professionals who used email found it less effective than face-to-face communication or the telephone in sustaining close social relationships [28].

Since the time that this Internet paradox was identified, a number of studies over the next twelve years have found, fairly consistently, results that contradict the Kraut et al. results. More recent studies have indicated the potential positive social effects of the Internet and their relationship to well being. Further, the effect appears to be getting stronger as the internet and the users mature.

In fact, one of the first challenges to this Internet paradox was provided by Kraut himself when he published follow up results for participants in the original Internet-paradox study, including data for additional participants. In this paper, "Internet Paradox Revisited," researchers report that the negative social impact on the original sample had dissipated over time and, for those in their new sample, the Internet had positive effects on communication, social involvement, and well being [29]. Therefore, it appears that the results of the original Kraut et al. study were largely due to the participants' inexperience with the Internet. Within just a few years, American society's experience with the Internet had increased exponentially. Further, the Kraut studies concentrated on email, whereas there are many other social communication tools available on the modern web.

4.2   Displacement versus Stimulation Hypothesis

More recently, researchers have examined the relationship between on-line communication and users' over all social networks, explicitly addressing the question of whether or not on-line communication "displaces" higher quality communication, or "stimulates" it. Presumably, the former would negatively effect well being, while the latter would enhance it [30].

In this large scale study, over 1000 Dutch teenagers were surveyed regarding the nature of their on line communication activities, the number and quality of friendships, and their well being.

They found strong support for the stimulation hypothesis. More specifically, these researchers developed a causal model, which indicated that instant messaging lead to more contact with friends, which lead to more meaningful social relationships, which, in turn, predicted well being. Interestingly, they did not find this same effect for chat in a public chat room. They attributed this finding to the fact that participants reported that they interacted more with strangers in the chat room as compared to their interaction with friends in with instant messaging [30].

4.3   The Internet and Social Connectedness

Despite studies, such as the one just mentioned, which have found a relationship between internet use and positive outcomes, there is still a great deal of press suggesting that the internet can effect users negatively, causing social isolation, and shrinking of social networks. This is purported to be especially true for adolescents [31].

Researchers with the Pew Internet and Daily Life Project set out to examine this concern directly in one of the most comprehensive studies of the effect of the Internet on social interaction, reported in 2009 [31]. Contrary to fears, they found that:

- A variety of internet activities were associated with larger and more diverse core discussion networks.
- Those who participated most actively with social media were more likely to interact with those from diverse backgrounds, including race and political view.
- Internet users are just as likely as others to visit a neighbor in person, and they are more likely to belong to a local voluntary organization.
- Internet use is often associated with local activity in community spaces such as parks and restaurants, and Internet connections are more and more common in such venues.

Although these outcomes did not explicitly include happiness, they do support the contention that Internet activities can enhance the amount and quality of social relationships, which has been implicated in a number of studies as a strong and consistent predictor of happiness.

5   Conclusions

Though happiness is an inherently subjective construct, our review indicates that there is agreement among people as to what constitutes happiness and relatively simple and straightforward self-report measures of happiness are psychometrically sound. Research using these measures has identified important predictors of happiness; including predisposition and temperament measures that appear to be relatively fixed; and behavioral and processing variables that appear to be more amenable to change. Among these are social interaction variables, which have been found to be strongly and consistently predictive of happiness. A review of literature on the Internet, social communication, and happiness; indicates that the Internet can be a powerful tool for promoting numerous and high quality social interactions, which can positively impact well being. This effect appears to be growing stronger as Internet users and Internet culture matures.

References

1. Suh, E., et al.: The Shifting Basis of Life Satisfaction Judgements Across Cultures: Emotions versus norms. Journal of Personality and Social Psychology 74, 482–493 (1998)
2. Lyuborirsky, S.: Why are Some People Happier Than Others? The Role of Cognitive and Motivational Processes in Well-Being. American Psychologist 56(3), 239–249 (2001)
3. Inglehart, R.: Cultural Shift in Advanced Industrial Society. Princeton University Press, Princeton (1990)
4. Lyubomirsky, S., King, L., Diener, E.: The Benifits of Frequent Positive Affect: Does Happiness Lead to Success. Psychological Bulletin 6, 803–855 (2005)

5. Diener, E.: Subjective Well-Being: The Science of Happiness and a Poposal for a National Index. American Psychologist 55(1), 34–43 (2000)
6. Myers, D.G.: The Funds, Friends, and Faith of Happy People. American Psychologist 55, 56–67 (2000)
7. Freedman, J.: Happy People: What Happiness IS, Who Has it, and Why? Harcourt Brace Jovanovich, New York (1978)
8. Lyubomirsky, S.: Why are Some People Happier Than Others? The Role of Cognitive and Motivational Processes in Well-Being. American Psychologist 56(3), 239–249 (2001)
9. Magnus, K., Diener, E.: A Longitudinal Analysis of Personality, Life Events, and Subjective Well-Being. In: Annual Meeting of the Midwestern Psychological Association, Chicago, IL (1991)
10. Costa, P.T., McCrae, R.R., Zonderman, A.B.: Environmental and Dsipositional Influences on Well-Being: Logitudinal Follow-Up of an American National Sample. British Journal of Psychology 78, 299–306 (1987)
11. Myers, D.G., Diener, E.: Who is Happy? Psychological Science 6, 10–19 (1995)
12. Lykken, D.T., Tellegen, A.: Happiness is a Stochastic Phenomenon. Psychological Science 7, 186–189 (1996)
13. Tellegen, A., et al.: Personality Similarity in Twins Reared Apart and Together. Journal of Personality and Social Psychology 54, 1031–1039 (1988)
14. Lucas, R.E., et al.: Cross-Cultural Evidence for the Fundamental Features of Extraversion. Journal of Personality and Social Psychology 79, 452–468 (2000)
15. McIntosh, D.N., Silver, R.C., Wortman, C.B.: Religion's Role in Adjustment to a Negative Life Event: Coping with the Loss of a Child. Journal of Personality and Social Psychology 65, 812–821 (1993)
16. Ellison, C.G., Gay, D.A., Glass, T.A.: Does Religious Commitment Contribute to Individual Life Satisfaction. Social Forces 68, 100–123 (1989)
17. Lyubomirsky, S., Ross, L.: Hedonic Consequences of Social Comparison: A Contrast of Happy and Unhappy People. Journal of Personality and Social Psychology 73, 1141–1157 (1997)
18. Lyubomirsky, S., Ross, L.: Changes in Atractiveness of Elected, Rejected, and Precluded Alternatives: A Comparison of Happy and Unhappy Individuals. Journal of Personality and Social Psychology 76, 988–1007 (1999)
19. Lyubomirsky, S., Tucker, K.L.: Implications of Individual Differences in Subjective Happiness for Perceiving Interpreting and Thinking about Life Events. Motivation and Emotion 22, 155–186 (1998)
20. Csikszentmihalyi, M.: If We Are So Rich, Why Aren't We Happy? American Psychologist 54(10), 821–827 (1999)
21. Seligman, E.P., et al.: Positive Psychology Progress: Empirical Validation of Interventions. American Psychologist 60(5), 410–421 (2005)
22. Diener, E., Horwitz, J., Emmons, R.A.: Happiness of the Very Wealthy. Social Indicators 16, 263–274 (1985)
23. Brickman, P., Coates, D., Janoff-Bulman, R.: Lottery Winners and Accident Victims: Is Happiness Relative? Journal of Personality and Social Psychology 36, 917–927 (1978)
24. Myers, D.G.: The Pursuit of Happiness. Avon, New York (1993)
25. Pavot, W., Diener, E., Fujita, F.: Extraversion and Happiness. Personality and Individual Differences 11, 1299–1306 (1990)

26. Abbey, A., Andrews, F.M.: Modeling the Psychological Determinants of Life Quality. Social Indicators Research 16, 1–34 (1985)
27. Kraut, R., et al.: Internet Paradox: A Social Technology that Reduces Social Involvement and Psychological Well-Being? American Psychologist 53(9), 1017–1031 (1998)
28. Cummings, J., Butler, B., Kraut, R.: The Quality of Online Social Relationships. Communications of the ACM 45, 103–108 (2002)
29. Kraut, R., et al.: Internet Paradox Revisited. Journal of Social Issues 58(1), 49–74 (2002)
30. Valkenburg, P.M., Peter, J.: Online Communication and Adolescent Well-Being: Testing the Stimulation Versus the Displacement Hypothesis. Journal of Computer-Mediated Communication, 12(4), Article 2 (2007)
31. Hampton, K.N., et al.: How the Internet and Mobile Phones Impact Americans' Social Networks. Report of the Pew Internet and American Life Project (2009)

Small and Medium Enterprises 2.0:
Are We There Yet?

Pedro Isaias[1] and Diogo Antunes[2]

[1] Universidade Aberta (Portuguese Open University) and ADVANCE – ISEG,
Rua Fernão Lopes, 9, 1º Esq.,
100-132 Lisboa – Portugal
pisaias@uab.pt
[2] ISEG - Lisboa School of Economics and Management – University of Lisbon
Rua do Quelhas, 6,
1200-781 Lisboa – Portugal
diogotavaresantunes@gmail.com

Abstract. The concept of Enterprise 2.0 relates to the use of Web 2.0 technologies such as blogs, social networks or wikis, in enterprises and it has been at the centre of several debates among the business community. Controversy aside, many enterprises have already openly adopted and supported the implementation of Web 2.0 technologies. This growing interest in the Social Web as a business resource has captured the attention of Small and Medium Enterprises (SMEs). This paper focuses on the adoption of Enterprise 2.0's practices inside SMEs and uses the Portuguese case as an illustration of the current scenario. It examines the implementation of Web 2.0 tools inside Portuguese elite SMEs and provides guiding principles for the general proficiency of SME 2.0.

Keywords: SMEs, Web 2.0, Enterprise 2.0.

1 Introduction

The term Enterprise 2.0 (E2.0), coined by McAfee [1], refers to the "use of social software platforms within organizations or between organizations, their business partners and customers".E2.0 stands, thus, for the utilization of Web 2.0 tools within enterprises. There is a plethora of Web 2.0 technologies that can be used for business purposes such as wikis, blogs, Really Simple Syndication (RSS), social bookmarking, podcasts, and social networks. The advantages of incorporating Web 2.0 applications in business are manifested in four core levels: innovation, growth, transformation of customer relationship and cost reduction [2].

SMEs; account for 90% of all companies in the United States of America and 99% of enterprises in Europe [3]. Hence, the examining of the proliferation of E2.0 demands the analysis of SMEs and their own practices of Web 2.0 adoption. There is a significant parcel of SMEs that are investing in a proactive attitude toward Web 2.0 technologies' adoption as a manner of addressing their existing knowledge scarcity [4]

F.F.-H. Nah (Ed.): HCIB/HCII 2014, LNCS 8527, pp. 175–182, 2014.
© Springer International Publishing Switzerland 2014

SMEs present a relatively low survival rate. Despite the large number of SMEs that emerge every year, only 40% of them survive 10 years [5]. These companies operate in an increasingly complex and competitive market which makes their survival challenging [6]. Thus, given the lack of resources and limited innovation capacities of SMEs, E2.0 may be a way to overcome the current difficulties, as it promotes knowledge sharing, internal and external communication [7], collaboration, and productivity, as well as a greater proximity to the market [5]. Web 2.0 technologies are not only free or cheap, but also simple and comfortable to use, which enables their adoption [7].

This paper begins by briefly examining the concept of E2.0 and its extension to SMEs. In order to ignite the outline of a global depiction of the adoption of Enterprise 2.0 inside SMEs peculiar settings, this study presents an empirical research concentrating on the particular case of Portuguese elite SMEs. To conclude, this paper imports the results of this research and outlines a set of guidelines aimed at the successful development of SME 2.0.

2   Enterprise 2.0

According to Frappaolo and Keldsen [8] there are three essential elements in the definition of E2.0: collectivity, in the sense that the harnessing of Web- based technology warrants the existence of a system to succeed; Swiftness and agility, that account for E 2.0's flexible nature and user-friendliness; and the notion of extended enterprise, which encompasses enterprises themselves, and their relation with other companies, their costumers or partners. Hence the definition that they provide states that E2.0 is " a system of Web-based technologies that provide rapid and agile collaboration, information sharing, emergence, and integration capabilities in the extended enterprise." [8].. The development of a business strategy that includes Web 2.0, demands the engagement of several stakeholders: the enterprise, its customers, partners and also competitor companies. The participation of all these parties enables the creation of network of information sharing and social knowledge [9].

3   SMEs and Web 2.0

As Levy and Powell [6] argue , SMEs' strategies tend to be emergent, informal, and based on reactive decisions. Their strategies are, above all, focused on surviving. On the other hand, these companies are characterized by a high level of flexibility and innovation that can mitigate the weaknesses that have been highlighted. The fact that Web 2.0 tools are mainly free of charge and easy to use, makes them an important ally for SMEs. The technical accessibility of Web 2.0 and employees' familiarity with tools in their private lives are some of the forces driving E2.0's deployment [7].

3.1   The Benefits of Using Web 2.0 in SMEs

Gagliardi [9] conducted a study on SMEs from France, Italy, Poland and Spain from several activity sectors that amounted to 85 questionnaires in total. The author reports that the adoption of Web 2.0 technologies inside SMEs remains timid and as a complement to other innovative tools. "SMEs see this technology with particular interest concerning the potential offered but they are also concerned about making the firm's boundaries more porous." [9].

SMEs face challenges at several levels, namely in terms of knowledge management, reduced degree of knowledge transfer, insufficient information on communication and cooperation practices. Additionally, SMEs still employ more traditional methods of information sharing and communication. Hence, it is important to invest in new methods of corporate learning to guarantee that SMEs are empowered to address these issues. [10]. One of the resources derived from E-Learning 2.0, are communities of practice. Communities of practice have the potential to support innovation and enable the development of new skills inside SMEs. These communities are ideal instruments for corporate learning because they overcome space and time obstacles, two of the biggest impediments for training professionals [10]. Web 2.0 is also suggested as a valuable solution for the isolation of SMEs, which are mainly faced with the need to solve their issues alone, namely in terms of training. Social networks and communities of practice have been often indicated as a viable answer [11].

Collaborative technology enhances intra and inter-enterprises' communication practices [12]. Software can pose a challenge to SMEs budget and IT capacity of response. The notion of software as service benefits smaller companies which lack the capital and human resources to employ expensive and intricate softwares that were mainly designed for enterprises of significant size [7]. Social networks have proved their preponderance over traditional marketing in terms of word-of-mouth generation. Also social network sites have been demonstrating their value in creating revenue and platforms for online shopping [13]. Social network sites play an important role in the direct connection between customers and businesses, they enable the creation of communities and they are a important asset in information distribution and feedback collection [13]. The use of online social networks for business purposes obeys to a set of rules of its own that adapts the social nature of these sites with the intention of promoting sales and attract clients. Overall, it is important to encourage participation, to listen to what is being said about specific products and brands, to address negative feedback, to ensure a presence in mainstream websites and to use a professional, but informal tone [14].

3.2   Web 2.0 Challenges for SMEs

There is a general tendency for SMEs to be significantly less prone to deploy pioneering technology than larger enterprises [15].

The consideration of Web 2.0 technology as a valuable business asset requires SMEs to be aware of the challenges that this union poses. The absence of control over the content that is created, edited and shared in Web 2.0 platforms constitutes one of the most significant issues in the full adoption of E2.0. SMEs are often concerned with matters related to Intellectual Property Rights that emerge from the use of Web 2.0 instruments. Alongside with these issues of control, the ubiquitous character of Social Web's technology is often indicated as a heavy hurdle [4]. SMEs' reduced human capital is sometimes seen as an impediment for the proliferation of E2.0, in the sense that it restrains internal networking [4]. Moreover the allocation of personnel for the management of social technology is challenging. The fact that the ratio of digital natives in management teams remains low is a deterrent for E2.0's growth [4].

The absence of relevant methods of assessment of Web 2.0's effectiveness constitutes an important downside of its deployment in business settings. It is important to underline that in terms of marketing efficacy, for example, the conventional evaluation methodologies of success are inadequate to measure E2.0's outcomes [13].

The benefits of E2.0 are not felt uniformly through the different economical sectors. Certain businesses, such as construction or house maintenance services, have a more limited use for Web 2.0 technology than SMEs that specialize in IT consultancy or Web design, for example [7].

4   Methods

The empirical evidence of Web 2.0 implementation inside SMEs is paramount both for researchers and practitioners. Hence to add to the current body of research on this subject, this study isolated a specific group of Portuguese SMES and questioned their employees as to the dissemination of Web 2.0 practices inside their enterprises. This group was composed of a sample of 438 companies which were selected from a total population of 1481 "excellence" companies. The "SME excellence" is an annual award which prizes the best SMEs in Portugal. The sample was obtained via a simple stratified sampling method to guarantee the representativeness of the selected SMEs. The participants were asked to respond to an online questionnaire focused on collecting demographic data, information on each company's specific features and records on the corporate and personal usage of Web 2.0.

5   Results

The data, from the online questionnaire that was administered to 438 SMEs in Portugal, purported that technologies such as blogs, wikis, RSS and podcasts have reasonable levels of initial adoption.

The survey was completed by 99 participants aged 31 to 54 years old. Around 70% of the respondents were male. In terms of their role inside their companies, about one third of all participants were CEOs and around 20% were part of management. The participants reported that privately, their use of Web 2.0 remains overshadowed by their use of email. Additionally, wikis and podcasts are in their initial stages of adoption, while blogs and instant messaging are assuming a growing part in the private sphere of the respondents lives. The preponderance of conventional communication methods was equally evident, when the respondents were questioned about corporate communication: e-mail (circa 67%), telephone/mobile phone (circa 47%) and personal contact (circa 50%). This result is supported by De Saulles [7] conclusion that SMEs remain greatly dependent on electronic mail as their basic communication instrument.

With regard to the concept of E2.0 there was a significant division among the participants, which became apparent in the different levels of knowledge about and implementation of E2.0 (Figure 1).

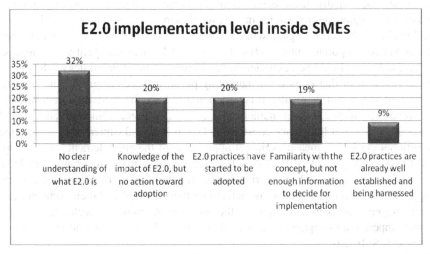

Fig. 1. Different levels of E2.0 adoption inside SMEs

A relevant number (32%) of SMEs' employees remains confused as to the definition of E2.0, what it entails exactly and the extent of its business value. Moreover, around 19% of the participants stated that despite having an elementary notion of what E2.0 amounts to, that knowledge is still insufficient cause for deciding to use it. Among those who declared that they were familiar with the term, there was still a significant part of them (20%) that does not use it in practice. Those on an initial phase of adoption account for 20% of the total respondents. The pioneers of E2.0 implementation constitute 9% of the sample and state that E2.0 is well rooted inside their SMEs and its potential is being maximised.

Furthermore, around 29% of survey participants confirmed that E2.0 implementation in their companies is integrated in their business strategy and takes advantage of the efforts of employees and top management. E2.0 shows a high level of dissemination in organizations' departments. Also, 29% of respondents said their company had spread E2.0 practices while 79% of survey participants confirmed that their organizations have recently been focusing on these technologies. More than 92% were sure that the impact was positive. Finally, the data showed that 83% of study participants were satisfied or very satisfied with E2.0. This percentage rises to 100% in companies that have established E2.0 practices.

6   Guidelines for SME 2.0 Effectiveness

As stated in the AT&T and Consulting [16] study, there is no "Holy Grail" of E2.0 implementation, but there are certain measures that can be put in place to potentiate the successful implementation of E2.0 in SMEs. These technologies present advantages in terms of costs as they are mainly free or demand a low cost [7]. There is an outsourcing of innovation among customers, which may increase revenues and decrease cost. Additionally, there is sufficient motivation and a correct combination of incentives and organizational values involving all employees' voluntary use [17].

Culturally, SMEs must engage with flexible organizational structures and an open and innovative corporate culture [16]. In order to harness competitive advantage, these technologies should be integrated in the company's business strategy [18].

Every instrument that is used for marketing purposes needs to provide a clear and unequivocal account of its results. It is paramount to have the capacity to measure the effectiveness of Web 2.0 tools, namely in a context of fierce competitiveness, need for accountability and budgetary constraints. Given Web 2.0's interactive nature, the conventional marketing measures do not apply. One of the core elements of developing a thriving concept of SME 2.0 is the creation of suitable measurements [13]. Management represents a decisive role in the implementation of Information Technology (IT). The managers' impact is dictated by their mindset and their competences. Since managers play such a vital part in the adoption of innovative technology [15] it becomes imperative to engage them with Web 2.0, so that they can lead their companies towards SME 2.0.

Employees must also be considered in this Web 2.0 adoption equation. Their routine problem-solving skills can benefit significantly from the information flow and sharing that Web 2.0 allows, improving their ability to address day to day issues [3]. The "generational turnover of entrepreneurs" [4] is expected to favor Web 2.0 technologies which will impact the future of E2.0. The generation commonly known as digital natives is likely to invest in the development of interactive and collaborative technologies [4]. SMEs' reduced human capital is sometimes seen as an impediment for the proliferation of E2.0, in the sense that it restrains internal networking. Moreover the allocation of personnel for the management of social technology is challenging [4]. Web 2.0 is people-centered, its improvement is dependent on the activity and engagement of its users. Similarly, SME 2.0 requires the employees of SMEs to actively interact with the Web 2.0 applications that their companies have chosen to implement [19].

User participation is a underlying driver of Web 2.0 presence, according to the Web 2.0 reference framework proposed by Isaias, Miranda and Pifano [20], which consists of the following critical success factors: Users' inputs; Users' critical mass figures; Ease of use of component; Component feedback; Availability of content to justify users' access; User content addition features; User content development tools; and Revenue models. Since participation is greatly dependent on trust, SMEs should make an effort to develop acceptable levels of trust among their partners. A strategy that can be followed to create such trust is the exchange of information, the sharing of mutually beneficial knowledge [19].

Stocker and Tochtermann [21] concluded in their study on the use of blogs among SMEs, that the employees were less inclined to read their enterprise blog, if its content was perceived as being significantly less important than their day to day work responsibilities. This raises an important issue in terms of real value for individual productivity. It is paramount to ensure that whatever Web 2.0 tools might be used, their benefits must be clear to the employees.

Albeit the nearly ubiquitous use of the internet in SMEs, there are certain Web-based resources that remain untapped by enterprises of reduced size due to budget limitations and lack of skills. The technological innovation of SMEs must be derived from an in-depth knowledge of their needs, so that collaborative platforms can be created to assist organizational success [12]. Moreover, in order to fruitfully deploy Web 2.0 technologies, SMEs must undergo a transformation process that relies greatly on a mental model shift. Web 2.0 requires openness to the exterior to potentiate innovation. Hence SMEs must learn to look outside their own wall and people to search for more relevant resources [19].

7   Conclusion

Fierce competition, budgetary constrictions and demand for IT innovation are conducing SMEs toward a path of Web 2.0 adoption. Similarly to what has been happening to larger companies and renowned brands, SMEs seem to be progressing in the direction of E2.0 precepts.

The affordances of E2.0 have reshaped internal and external working relationships and practices. The benefits of E2.0 are manifested mainly in a closer relationship with customers, a more personalized product delivery, viral marketing and the collaborative working routines. "Enterprise 2.0 is much more about businesses' adoption of "2.0 mindsets" than with the consumer-facing side of the coin." [8]. As Web 2.0 technologies become increasingly popular in the business sector it is paramount to examine how SMEs are dealing with the changes it warrants and the benefits it allows.

The assessment of Portuguese SMEs' fluency in E2.0 depicts an initial concern with innovation and intent to employ Web 2.0 tools and projects the need for a broader diagnose of Web 2.0's level of incursion into small and medium businesses.

Acknowledgements. Authors wish to thank ADVANCE research center and ISEG - Lisboa School of Economics and Management – University of Lisbon.

References

1. McAfee, A.P.: Enterprise 2.0: The dawn of emergent collaboration. Management of Technology and Innovation 47(3) (2006)
2. Hinchcliffe, D.: Why all the fuss about Web 2.0. Infonomics 24(1), 26–31 (2010)
3. Peris, M., et al.: Acceptance of Professional Web 2.0 Platforms in Regional SME Networks: An Evaluation Based on the Unified Theory of Acceptance and Use of Technology. In: 2013 46th Hawaii International Conference on System Sciences (HICSS). IEEE (2013)
4. Gagliardi, D.: Next generation entrepreneur: innovation strategy through Web 2.0 technologies in SMEs. Technology Analysis & Strategic Management 25(8), 891–904 (2013)

5. Blinn, N., Lindermann, N., Fäcks, K., Nüttgens, M.: Web 2.0 in SME networks - A design science approach considering multi-perspective requirements. In: Nelson, M.L., Shaw, M.J., Strader, T.J. (eds.) AMCIS 2009. LNBIP, vol. 36, pp. 271–283. Springer, Heidelberg (2009)
6. Levy, M., Powell, P.: Strategies for Growth in SMEs: The Role of Information and Information Sytems. Butterworth-Heinemann (2004)
7. De Saulles, M.: Never too small to join the party. Information World Review, 10–12 (2008)
8. Frappaolo, C., Keldsen, D.: Enterprise 2.0: Agile, Emergent & Integrated. AIIM Intelligence Quarterly, AIIM: Silver Spring, MD (2008)
9. Gagliardi, D.: Next Generation Entrepreneur: How Web 2.0 Technologies Creep into SMEs (2011)
10. Hamburg, I., Engert, S., Anke, P.: Communities of Practice and Web 2.0 to support learning in SMEs, Online PDF (2007)
11. Hamburg, I., Hall, T.: Social Networks, Web and Mentoring Approaches in SME Continuing Vocational Education and Training. Journal of Information Technology and Application in Education 2(2) (2013)
12. Robertson, A., et al.: The search for innovators and early adopters of e-collaborative technologies within small and medium sized enterprises in the UK (2007)
13. Michaelidou, N., Siamagka, N.T., Christodoulides, G.: Usage, barriers and measurement of social media marketing: An exploratory investigation of small and medium B2B brands. Industrial Marketing Management 40(7), 1153–1159 (2011)
14. Isaías, P., Pífano, S., Miranda, P.: Social Network Sites: Modeling the New Business-Customer Relationship. In: Social Networking and Community Behavior Modeling: Qualitative and Quantitative Measures, pp. 248–265. IGI Global (2012)
15. Wamba, S.F., Carter, L.: Twitter adoption and use by SMEs: An empirical study. In: 2013 46th Hawaii International Conference on System Sciences (HICSS). IEEE (2013)
16. AT&T and E.S. Consulting Speeding the Adoption of Enterprise 2.0. (2009)
17. Manyika, J.M., Roberts, R.P., Sprague, K.L.: Eight business technology trends to watch. McKinsey Quarterly 1, 60 (2008)
18. Levy, M., Powell, P., Yetton, P.: SMEs: aligning IS and the strategic context. Journal of Information Technology 16(3), 133–144 (2001)
19. Lindermann, N., Valcárcel, S., Schaarschmidt, M., von Kortzfleisch, H.: SME 2.0: Roadmap towards Web 2.0-Based Open Innovation in SME-Networks – A Case Study Based Research Framework. In: Dhillon, G., Stahl, B.C., Baskerville, R. (eds.) CreativeSME 2009. IFIPAICT, vol. 301, pp. 28–41. Springer, Heidelberg (2009)
20. Isaías, P., Miranda, P., Pífano, S.: Critical success factors for web 2.0 – A reference framework. In: Ozok, A.A., Zaphiris, P. (eds.) OCSC 2009. LNCS, vol. 5621, pp. 354–363. Springer, Heidelberg (2009)
21. Stocker, A., Tochtermann, K.: Investigating Weblogs in Small and Medium Enterprises: An Exploratory Case Study. In: BIS, Workshops (2008)

Finding Keyphrases of Readers' Interest
Utilizing Writers' Interest in Social Media

Lun-Wei Ku, Andy Lee, and Yan-Hua Chen

Institute of Information Science, Academia Sinica, Taipei, Taiwan
lwku@iis.sinica.edu.tw, {andycyrus,dorayhc}@gmail.com

Abstract. Suggesting further reading materials is an application of recommendation. Considering context, current systems usually rely on topic information and related materials to propose options for users, while users behavior is also commonly used if log information is involved. However, the users interests, which are aroused by the content of the current article they read instead of what they have had, are seldom detected from the context, and they are usually the motive that readers want to read more. This paper presents an approach to detect readers' interest from the current article they read and the users feedback of it. TED talks are utilized as the experimental materials. InterestFinder proposes interest keywords/keyphrases for each talk, where different kind of words and phrases are provided to it to find suitable candidate terms. Experiments show that the best setting proposed achieves a NDCG@50 0.6392, and the detail results are discussed. Results conclude that considering both words and phrases in a proper selection criteria benifits, and finding conceptual keyphrases as interest terms is necessary to further improve the system performance.

Keywords: interest analysis, reading recommendation, TED talk, keyword and keyphrase extraction.

1   Introduction

The Internet is a modern source for getting information. Because of the information explosion, how to satisfy users' information need efficiently is very important. Good search engines or information retrieval systems can find related articles by queries, but users might need a sequence of querying operations just to fulfill their information need brought up by the current article. To save time and effort and to automatically provide reading materials for readers, we propose a research topic named "readers' interest analysis" which aims to find possible further interest of readers after reading the current article. When browsing an article within a site, it is common for the site to suggest related articles that the reader might be interested in. For example, a reader of a movie review article is interested in where and when he could see this movie, and unless the review is from a professional movie website, it is often that the reader needs to search for the theater site and look up the time table manually as it may not be provided by the review article. Knowing the readers' interest, i.e., the time table

F.F.-H. Nah (Ed.): HCIB/HCII 2014, LNCS 8527, pp. 183–193, 2014.
© Springer International Publishing Switzerland 2014

and the theater of the movie (and there may be more interests) in the previous example, help to create a satisfying reading process dynamically.

Researchers have developed some content recommendation techniques. For example, when browsing a video on YouTube, suggestions for related videos are on the side [1]. Sometimes suggestions are generated by extracting topical keywords from the current article [2]. However, this research is different from the previous ones from four aspects:

1. Detecting interest terms instead of topical keywords.
2. Finding users' interest from the content of articles instead of the user behavior.
3. Detected interest does not need to be internal (in the current article).
4. The proposed method is not domain specific.

Previously we developed InterestFinder, a prototype system, based on PageRank, tfidf score of words, and social interaction content to extract keywords that reflect the reader's interest of the current article [3]. In this paper, we improve InterestFinder by also extracting keyphrases instead of only keywords to capture more complete concepts. For example, in the article introducing apple computers the keyphrase "apple computer" is extracted instead of the keyword "apple" or "computer". The quality of the extracting terms is also improved by considering coverage and coherence [4]. We further try to search interests from social media by the keyphrases proposed by InterestFinder from the current article and its user feedback (internal keyphrases). The resulting articles will be sent to InterestFinder to find more interest keyphrases (external keyphrases). These keyphrases can be utilized as the input to an article recommendation system. The system flow is shown in Figure 1.

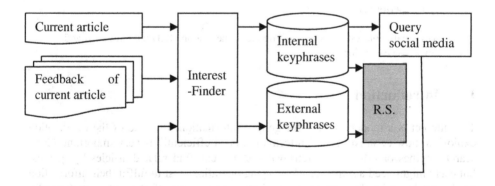

Fig. 1. System flow. R.S. is a recommendation system, which is not included in this research

2   Related Work

Keyword extraction has been a popular research area. Natural language processing tasks including document categorization and summarization [5], indexing [6], information retrieval, and text mining on social networking or micro-blogging services [7][8][9] have utilized keyword extraction techniques as a tool widely and explored them intensively. Like these researches but more specifically, this paper focuses on extracting those keywords that are reader interests, and further, not only keywords but also keyphrases. Extracting interest keyphrases is the first step toward article recommendation, i.e., reader interest prediction after article reading.

The core of keyword extraction systems mainly depends on automatically learning word statistics in a document collection. Traditional approaches such as term frequency and inverse document frequency (tfidf) poses a strong baseline. Other interesting approaches such as the word graph presented by Mihalcea and Tarau [10], which uses connectivity of words in local document to extract keywords, and word graph by Liu's research group [11], which extracts keyphrases by graph-based ranking methods, all remind us that relations between words are useful clues for keyword extraction. Therefore in our core algorithm (InterestFinder), a semantic aware PageRank is designed to gives partial scores to the candidate terms when selecting interest keyphrases.

Recently, collaborative tagging or social tagging has grown in popularity among Web services and received much attention [12][13]. In their research, user (tagging) activity or tag frequencies were analyzed. In our research, we viewed the social interaction content as a kind of social tagging which points out terms in the main article that are more likely to be interests.

HEADY proposed by Alfonseca and his team [14], which generated the headline of news articles, is another concept to find keywords/keyphrases. It is an abstraction process for the original article. It considered the people, events, time, location, objects. Though HEADY focused on the generation process, the concept that parts of speeches are utilized to select useful terms is also adopted in this paper.

3   Approach, Materials and Settings

We utilized the materials from TED talks (http://www.ted.com) for experiments. The title, English transcript and user responses of each talk were extracted. These materials were then parsed by the Stanford parser and stemmed by the Porter stemmer. Experiments were performed with two sets of talks: one set includes all talks from TED (ALL), and the other set includes 500 talks of TED topic "technology" (TECH).

By experimenting by the above different sets of terms, we expected to filter out noises and find more proper terms for extracting representative interest keywords/keyphrases. As mentioned, these candidate interest keyword/keyphrases and their ranks were given by InterestFinder [3].

Interest Finder is a system which proposes terms to indicate readers' interest by exploiting social interaction content (e.g., reader responses) and words' semantic features (e.g., content sources and parts of speech). The approach adopted by Interest Finder involves estimating topical interest preferences and determining the informativity between articles and their social content. Interst Finder considers quality responses which represent readers' opinions to balance authors' statements. The topical interest preferences were estimated by TFIDF, a traditional yet powerful measure shown in formula (1). Then semantic aware PageRank in formula (2) is used on candidates to find reader interest with the help of their interestingness scores. We construct a word graph for both the article and social content. The word graph is

represented by a v-by-v matrix **EW** where v is the vocabulary size. **EW** stores normalized edge weights for word w_i and w_j (Step (4) and (5) in Fig. 2). Note that the graph
is directional (pointing from w_i to w_j) and that edge weights are the words' co-
occurrence counts satisfying window size limit *WS*. We set the one-by-v matrix **IP** of
interest preference model using interest preferences for words in Step (6) and initial-
ize the matrix **IN** of PageRank scores or, in our case, word interestingness scores in
Step (7). Previous experiments has showed that the social interaction content and its
proposed selection process help to accurately cover more span of reader interest [3].
InterestFinder works on words. However, compared to words, phrases usually
represent more complete concepts. Therefore, in our experiments, we aim to find a

```
procedure PredictInterest(ART,FB,IntPrefs,λ,α,N)
(1) qualityFB=selectInformativeFB(ART,FB,IntPrefs)
(2) Concatenate ART with qualityFB into Content
//Construct word graph for PageRank
(3) EW_{vxv}=0_{vxv}
for each sentence st in Content
        for each word w_i in st
            for each word w_j in st where i<j and j-i≤WS
        if not IsContWord(w_i) and IsContWord(w_j)
(4a)          EW[i,j]+=1×m×srcWeight
              elif not IsContWord(w_i) and not IsCont-
Word(w_j)
(4b)          EW[i,j]+=1×(1/m)×srcWeight
              elif IsContWord(w_i) and not IsContWord(w_j)
(4c)          EW[i,j]+=1×(1/m)×srcWeight
              elif IsContWord(w_i) and IsContWord(w_j)
(4d)          EW[i,j]+=1×m×srcWeight
(5) normalize each row of EW to sum to 1
//Iterate for PageRank
(6) set IP_{1×v} to
[IntPrefs(w_1), IntPrefs(w_2), ..., IntPrefs(w_v)]
(7) initialize IN_{1×v} to [1/v,1/v, ...,1/v]
        repeat
(8a)   IN'=λ×IN×EW+(1-λ)×IP
(8b)   normalize IN' to sum to 1
(8c)   update IN with IN' after the check of IN and IN'
until maxIter or avgDifference(IN,IN')≤smallDiff
(9) rankedInterests=Sort words in decreasing order of
IN
return the N rankedInterests with highest scores
```

Fig. 2. Determining readers' words of interest by semantic aware PageRank

```
procedure selectInformativeFB(ART,FB,IntPrefs)
(1) ngrams_art=generateNgram(ART)
(2) Focused=findFocused(IntPrefs)
(3) selectedSt=NULL
for each sentence st in FB
(4a)    ngrams_st=generateNgram(st)
(4b)    informativity_co=Coverage-
evaluate(ngrams_st,ngrams_art)
(4c)    informativity_fo=Focus-evaluate(ngrams_st,Focused)
(4d)    append st into selectedSt if conditions hold
     return selectedSt
```

Fig. 3. Identifying quality reader responses

proper way to include phrases into the candidates for InterestFinder in order to propose better keywords/keyphrases which indicate readers' interest.

$$\text{tfidf}\,(art,w) = \text{freq}\,(art,w)\,/\,\text{artFreq}\,(w) \tag{1}$$

$$\mathbf{IN}'[1,j]=\lambda\times\left(\begin{array}{l}\alpha\times\sum_{i\in v}\mathbf{IN}[1,i]\times\mathbf{EW}[i,j]+\\ (1-\alpha)\times\sum_{k\in v}\mathbf{IN}[1,k]\times\mathbf{EW}[k,j]\end{array}\right)+(1-\lambda)\times\mathbf{IP}[1,j] \tag{2}$$

We tried not to limit the source of interest words to the current talk and its responses. (i.e., internal keyphrases in Fig.1) To find other keywords/keyphrases (i.e., external keyphrases shown in Fig.1) to indicate possible readers' interest not mentioned in the talk and responses, we searched from blogs and social media. Posts from blogs and social media serve as an bridge to link other possible related interests to the current article. It is common when people are interested in something new but not familiar with it, they may consult their friends who has been long time paying attention to it and try to know what they should start with. The idea is like that. We find people of the same interest group in social media from their posts which contain internal interest terms. Then we try to extract other interests mentioned by them. This is a process to find what "people who are interested in the internal interest terms are also interested in." In this paper Engaget serves as the external source. These extracted interests are then treated as external interest keyphrases and will be proposed as the interest keyphrases together with the internal ones.

In transcripts of talks, seven different sets of terms were considered as candidates of interest keywords and the performance of using these seven sets were compared in our experiments. These seven sets were composite of terms which are:

1. noun phrases and verb phrases: $(NP+VP)_{tech}$
2. noun phrases and verb phrases (NP+VP) which contain words of parts of speech NN, NN, NNP, NNS, NNPS: $(PN)_{tech}$

3. noun phrases and verb phrases (NP+VP) which contain words of parts of speech NN, NN, NNP, NNS, NNPS and other words (which are not phrases) of parts of speech NN, NN, NNP, NNS, NNPS: (PN+WN) $_{tech}$
4. words: (W) $_{tech}$
5. interest terms from (3) which contains words from (4), ranked by (3) first then (4): (PN+WN+W) $_{tech}$
6. using top 10 terms from (3) as the queries to Engaget, and find relevant posts, including post titles, post bodies and readers' feedback. For each post, calculate tf-idf scores of terms in these posts. Merge all posts and calculate the pagerank scores of composite terms. Select interest terms according to their pagerank scores and then tf-idf scores. Terms from Engaget are external keyphrases in Fig. 1: (EXT) $_{tech}$

Scores of terms for the above (a) to (f) are calculated from the talk set TECH, and those for the following

7. noun phrases and verb phrases (NP+VP) which contain words of parts of speech NN, NN, NNP, NNS, NNPS and other words (which are not phrases) of parts of speech NN, NN, NNP, NNS, NNPS: (PN+WN) $_{all}$

are from the talk set ALL.

To evaluate, three annotators annotates the interest keywords/keyphrases from the list proposed by InterestFinder. We treat these annotations as gold standard and calculate the number of interest terms and NDCG (normalized discounted cumulative gain) to know the characteristics of this research problem and the ability of the proposed approach to rank the interest keywords/keyphrases.

4   Experiment Results and Discussions

We randomly select 10 TED talks for evaluation, shown in Table 1. After extracting all interet keyphrases from these talks, we ask annotators to label their interest from top 50 keyphrases. Sample top 10 keyphrases of one of these talks, "Shyam Sankar: The rise of human-computer cooperation", are shown in Table 2. (Talk 1, http://www.ted.com/talks/shyam_sankar_the_rise_of_human_computer_cooperation. html)

Table 1. Ten talks for evaluation

Talk	Title
1	The Rise of Human-Computer Cooperation
2	The Case for Anonymity Online
3	One Laptop per Child, Two Years on
4	Reach into the Computer and Grab a Pixel
5	The Astounding Athletic Power of Quadcopters
6	One Very Dry Demo
7	My Radical Plan for Small Nuclear Fission
8	10 Top Time-saving Tech Tips
9	Why Google Glass?
10	Hack a Banana, Make a Keyboard!

Table 2. Sample interest keyphrases of Talk 1

Rank	Keyphrase	Rank	Keyphrase
1	man and machine	6	Tim Huang
2	machine	7	human-computer symbiosis
3	foreign fighter	8	A computer science titan
4	computer	9	Licklid
5	Human	10	Cooper

The numbers of the interest keyphrases labeled by the annotators from the top 50 candidates proposed by the setting (PN+WN) all are listed in Table 3. We found that the number of interest keyphrases varies among annotators and also among talks. The former conforms to our expectation as people have different interessts, and the latter tells us words and phrases in some topics are especially not proper to represent related interests.

Table 3. Number of labeled interest keyphrases@50

Annotator/Talk	1	2	3	4	5	6	7	8	9	10	AVG
A	5	6	5	10	10	5	10	7	6	5	6.9
B	11	3	4	5	5	11	9	3	4	2	5.7
C	12	12	13	14	13	4	8	3	6	3	8.8
AVG	9.3	7.0	7.3	9.7	9.3	6.7	9.0	4.3	5.3	3.3	

Table 4, 5, and 6 show the NDCG@10, 20, 50 of 10 talks from 3 annotators, respectively. The performances of 7 settings in three tables show the same tendency. From experiment results of (W)tech, we find that some words do serve as good interest terms. However, we also find that sometimes words cannot express a complete interest concept. (NP+VP)tech and (PN)tech attempt to find interest terms from phrases. (PN)tech uses a subset of candidates from (NP+VP)tech by applying a more strict selection criteria to noun and verb phrases. Experiments show that (PN)tech performs better than (NP+VP)tech as (PN)tech filters out phrases including pronouns, which are less possible to be interests.

As words and phrases may serve as good candidates of interest keywords/keyphrases, selecting interest terms from both of them is our next move. $(PN+WN)_{tech}$ takes both words and phrases which satisfy some part of speech requirements into consideration. However, compared to $(PN)_{tech}$, the performance of $(PN+WN)_{tech}$ decreases a bit, which tells that WN is not a good candidate word set for selection, at least, not good enough. Therefore, we additionally add W into $(PN+WN)_{tech}$, i.e., $(PN+WN+W)_{tech}$, to keep the candidate phrase set but enlarge the candidate word set. Experiments show that $(PN+WN+W)_{tech}$ outperforms $(PN+WN)_{tech}$ but only comparable to $(W)_{tech}$. From results of annotator A, B, and C, we further find that though performances of $(PN+WN+W)_{tech}$ and $(W)_{tech}$ are comparable, obviously annotator A prefers terms proposed from $(W)_{tech}$ while annotator C prefers that from $(PN+WN+W)_{tech}$, both of which tell us using pure phrases will not bring us the best results.

$(EXT)_{tech}$ includes candidate terms from the external source: Engadget. We have expected that involving the collaborative filtering would find us better interest terms that are not include in the original talk or its users' feedback. However, topics of retrieved articles and their comments are too diverse by querying with top 10 internal interest terms. The annotators have problems to link interest terms extracted from these articles to the original talk so that they can only select some general interest terms. Moreover, the proposed terms from Engadget include some commonly seen irrelevant terms in technology related social media or blog posts, such as display, iphone, and screen. Experiments show that the performance of $(EXT)_{tech}$ drops a lot. We will need to solve the mentioned issues to well utilize external resources.

The tfidf scores are important for InterestFinder. They calculate the topical interest preference and involve in the semantic aware PageRank as described in section 3. The postulation that enlarging the corpus for the tfidf calculation may help to detect topics more accurately is confirmed by the performance of $(PN+WN)_{all}$. Using the ALL set, $(PN+WN)_{all}$ performs betther than other settings using the TECH set, which shows discriminative terms are also more likely to be interest terms.

Figure 4 shows the NDCG@50 of each talk at the setting $(PN+WN)_{all}$. The performances vary and the individual difference among talks exists. For some talks, even performances among annotators vary a lot. This is because finding interests is a subjective task. We may only expect the system to find interests which fit most people's need. However, there are some talks whose performances are comparably low for labels from all annotators, like talk 8 and talk 10. We further analyze the proposed terms of these two talks and find some interesting phenomena. For talk 8, whose topic is about "tips", it is difficult to find words or phrases to represent related interests. Words and phrases are too short to properly express tips or procedures and even they do, tips or procedures are usually not interests. In addition, talks like this could arouse more conceptual interests, such as "useful" and "helpful" that we may not find in talks. Terms for Talk 10 are of similar problem. Talk 10 describes an interesting idea and an interesting stuff, while the name of this stuff is not well written in the article. Instead, its components, functions, and usages are described in paragraphs. Therefore, the concrete interest keywords/keyphrases should be the name of this stuff but we cannot find a proper name of it from the talk; the conceptual interest terms could be "interesting", "creative" sort of words which cannot be found either like in talk 8. Table 3 also shows that the proposed interest terms of talk 8 and talk 10 are less annotated as readers' interest in average. In fact, possible conceptual interest terms like "inspiring", "amazing" are also commonly searched by TED users and they are tagged to some talks. Therefore, we will have to provide an approach which proposes the adjectives describing the overall comment, maybe sentiment, of the talk to enlarge the candidate interest term set.

Table 4. NDCG@10 of 10 talks from 3 annotators

Setting	A	B	C	AVG
$(NP+VP)_{tech}$	0.1324	0.1485	0.0927	0.1246
$(PN)_{tech}$	0.3350	0.2930	0.2574	0.2951
$(PN+WN)_{tech}$	0.3073	0.3336	0.2236	0.2882
$(W)_{tech}$	0.4904	0.4591	0.2018	0.3838
$(PN+WN+W)_{tech}$	0.3827	0.4269	0.3034	0.3710
$(EXT)_{tech}$	0.1921	0.3746	0.2348	0.2672
$(PN+WN)_{all}$	0.5260	0.3927	0.3411	**0.4199**

Table 5. NDCG@20 of 10 talks from 3 annotators

Setting	A	B	C	AVG
$(NP+VP)_{tech}$	0.2532	0.2884	0.2103	0.2506
$(PN)_{tech}$	0.4442	0.3992	0.3143	0.3859
$(PN+WN)_{tech}$	0.3915	0.3810	0.3025	0.3583
$(W)_{tech}$	0.5715	0.4853	0.2582	0.4383
$(PN+WN+W)_{tech}$	0.5084	0.4954	0.3936	0.4658
$(EXT)_{tech}$	0.2526	0.4199	0.3229	0.3318
$(PN+WN)_{all}$	0.6239	0.4629	0.4037	**0.4968**

Table 6. NDCG@50 of 10 talks from 3 annotators

Setting	A	B	C	AVG
$(NP+VP)_{tech}$	0.4558	0.4496	0.4365	0.4473
$(PN)_{tech}$	0.5860	0.5581	0.5562	0.5667
$(PN+WN)_{tech}$	0.5652	0.5374	0.5329	0.5452
$(W)_{tech}$	0.6401	0.5940	0.4966	0.5769
$(PN+WN+W)_{tech}$	0.6257	0.6017	0.5591	0.5955
$(EXT)_{tech}$	0.3828	0.5229	0.5294	0.4784
$(PN+WN)_{all}$	0.7298	0.5856	0.6021	**0.6392**

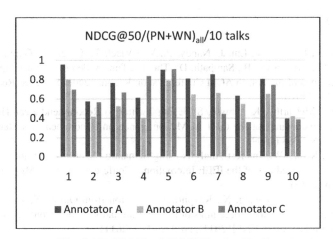

Fig. 4. NDCG@50 of $(PN+WN)_{all}$ for 10 talks

5   Conclusion and Future Work

Through the work we aimed to detect readers' interest aroused from the current article they were reading. Keywords/keyphrases were used to represent the interests for further reading materials recommendation. TED talks which usually contained novel topics were selected for experiments. We prepared several different sets of candidates for InterestFinder to extract interest terms. Experiments conclude that words and phrases could both be good terms to describe interests. However, specific words are necessary for representing a concept, while precision or relativeness is the requirement when selecting interest phrases. The proposed approach achieves an NDCG@50 of 0.6392.

We found that this research problem can actually be divided into three problems. The first is "where can we find candidate interest terms?" External sources should be considered in a suitable way. Then the second is "what kind of words/phrases can represent an interest?" After we found terms which may represent interests, we further need to solve the problem "which interest terms among them have some kind of relations with the current article?" Focusing on these three problems and solving them will be our next step to propose better interest keywords and keyphrases.

From results we know that characteristics of the articles may determine their related interest terms. Considering article types when selecting interest terms could be useful. In addition, conceptual terms which tell the overall feelings after reading articles such as "inspiring" and "funny" could also be interest terms. Integrating sentiment analysis technique and searching from the tagxonomy of talks to provide this kind of interest terms is our next goal.

Ackowledgements. Research of this paper was partially supported by National Science Council, Taiwan, under the contract NSC101-2628-E-224-001-MY3.

References

1. Davidson, J., Liebald, B., Liu, J., Nandy, P., Van Vleet, T., Gargi, U., Gupta, S., He, Y., Lambert, M., Livingston, B., Sampath, D.: The YouTube Video Recommendation System. In: Proceedings of the Fourth ACM Conference on Recommender Systems (RecSys 2010), pp. 293–296 (2010)
2. Phelan, O., McCarthy, K., Smyth, S.: Using Twitter to Recommend Real-Time Topical News. In: Proceedings of the third ACM Conference on Recommender systems (RecSys 2009), pp. 385–388 (2009)
3. Huang, C., Ku, L.-W.: Interest Analysis using Semantic PageRank and Social Interaction Content. In: Proceedings of the IEEE International Conference on Data Mining, SENTIRE Workshop (2013)
4. Ding, Z., Zhang, Q., Huang, X.: Keyphrase Extraction from Online News Using Binary Integer Programming. In: Proceedings of the 5th International Joint Conference on Natural Language Processing (IJCNLP 2011), pp. 165–173 (2011)
5. Manning, C.D., Schutze, H.: Foundations of statistical natural language processing. MIT Press (2000)
6. Li, Q., Wu, Y.-F., Bot, R., Chen, X.: Incorporating Document Keyphrases in Search Results. In: Proceedings of the Americas Conference on Information Systems (2004)
7. Li, Z., Zhou, G., Juan, Y.-F., Han, J.: Keyword Extraction for Social Snippets. In: Proceedings of the WWW (WWW 2010), pp. 1143–1144 (2010)
8. Zhao, W.X., Jiang, J., He, J., Song, Y., Achananuparp, P., Lim, E.-P., Li, X.: Topical Keyword Extraction from Twitter. In: Proceedings of the ACL (ACL 2011), pp. 379–388 (2011)

9. Wu, W., Zhang, B., Ostendorf, M.: Automatic Generation of Personalized Annotation Tags for Twitter Users. In: Proceedings of the NAACL, pp. 689–692 (2010)

10. Mihalcea, R., Tarau, P.: TextRank: Bringing Orders into Texts. In: Proceedings of the EMNLP, pp. 404–411 (2004)

11. Liu, Z., Huang, W., Zheng, Y., Sun, M.: Automatic Keyphrase Extraction via Topic Decomposition. In: Proceedings of the EMNLP, pp. 366–376 (2010)

12. Golder, S.A., Huberman, B.A.: Usage Patterns of Collaborative Tagging Systems. Information Science 32(2), 198–208 (2006)

13. Halpin, H., Robu, V., Shepherd, H.: The Complex Dynamics of Collaborative Tagging. In: Proceedings of the WWW, pp. 211–220 (2007)

14. Alfonseca, E., Pighin, D., Garrido, G.: HEADY: News Headline Abstraction Through Event Pattern Clustering. In: Proceedings of the 51st Annual Meeting of the Association for Computational Linguistics (ACL 2013), pp. 1243–1253 (2013)

The Role of Interactivity in Information Search on ACG Portal Site

Juihsiang Lee[1,2] and Manlai You[3]

[1] Department of Digital Multimedia Design, China University of Technology, China
[2] Graduate School of Design, National Yunlin University of Science and Technology, China
[3] Department of Industrial Design,
National Yunlin University of Science and Technology, China
Juihsiang Lee, leockmail@gmail.com

Abstract. The purpose of this study is to examine the relationships between three dimensions of interactivity (user control, responsiveness and connectedness) and consumers' perceived value composed of utilitarian and hedonic values on ACG resources searching, finally determining the level of overall satisfaction on using interactivity features in ACG portable site service. A total of 430 respondents participated and the usable sample size was 136 of goal-directed users and 180 of experiential users, after the screening process. The results indicate that both perceived utilitarian and hedonic values have a positive effect on satisfaction in the ACG portal site. But goal-directed users more concern about utilitarian than hedonic value, and experiential users more concern about hedonic value than utilitarian.

Keywords: ACG, Perceived interactivity, Goal-directed, Experiential.

1   Introductory

Effective communication with customers is the key to successful business. One of the most important factors for effective communication is known as interactivity (Yoo, Lee, & Park, 2010). In the real world shopping, consumers no longer interact with salespeople or have a direct physical experience of a store and its products. Instead, their experience is mediated through the web, using a graphical display without any face-to-face interaction with the e-vendor. Interactivity is therefore the central to these emerging computer mediated environments.

Novel applications of website interactivity are important to attract and retain online users. High accessibility to Internet technology and popularization of focus media has given rise to various emerging subcultures among the younger generation who constantly seek novelty.

Japanese manga, anime, games, and related consumer electronic devices which target the younger generation not only attract much more Japanese young male enthusiasts (Sangani, 2008) but are also popular in the overseas markets (Niu, Chiang, & Tsai, 2012), especially the ACG (animation, comic, game) users from Asia, whom would searching information to Japanese platform to get first hand resources aggressively.

F.F.-H. Nah (Ed.): HCIB/HCII 2014, LNCS 8527, pp. 194–205, 2014.
© Springer International Publishing Switzerland 2014

As Niu et al. (2012) portrayed, in Taiwan, in addition to Japanese culture and life-style have being partly preserved from the time of Japanese colonization, the young peoples' behavior is greatly influenced by Japanese culture due to the powerful marketing strategies and the communication of the Internet and mass media.

In the current investigation we aim to test user perceived interactivity using a Japanese ACG products sharing platform design. ACG products sharing platform is meant to solicit quick input/opinions and trial/demo reels from a web user, which is typically displayed for viewing by other visitors to the site.

Acquire from Wolfinbarger and Gilly's report (2000), a majority of Internet buyers are goal-oriented rather than the being experiential. And in the contrast, they also pointed out, ongoing hobby-type that's why buyers online search engage in experiential browsing.

When pre-purchasing ACG products, dose the information search more hedonic than information search for manufactured goods of utilitarian? Dose choices of ACG products involve considerable emotional significance or instrumental benefits?

The purpose of this study is to examine the relationships between three dimensions of consumers perceived interactivity and perceived value composed of utilitarian and hedonic, finally determining the level of overall satisfaction with ACG portal site service. And find out if there have differences between goal-directed and experiential users in the information search experience.

Based on the prior literature, a model was proposed and structural equation modeling was conducted using Amos to evaluate the fit of the research model. Structural equation modeling is appropriate for this study, because the proposed relationships can be analyzed simultaneously for their associations.

2   Literature Review

2.1   Internet Users' Searching Behavior

Product information seeking often is portrayed as a critical early stage in the consumer buying process (Shim et al. 2001; Hodkinson et al. 2000; Haubl and Trifts 2000). For marketing departments, it is crucial to understand the determinants of information search behavior for designing effective marketing communication.

Obtain from Rowley's research (2000) in online shopping environments, consumers looking for pre-purchase information can be engaged in two modes of seeking activity: browsing and directed search.

After reviewed 5 offline and 4 online focus groups, Wolfinbarger & Gilly (2000) pointed out consumers shop with utilitarian, goal driven motives as well as for experiential motives, such as fun and entertainment; in sum, they shop to acquire products or they shop to shop (Babin, Darden and Griffen 1994; Bloch and Richens 1983; Hirschman 1984; Hoffman and Novak 1996; Schlosser and Kanfer 1999).

Sánchez-Franco & Roldán (2005) suggested that a user is influenced not only by utilitarian motives, but also by a feeling occurring while active on a medium in itself (i.e. flow). Although the influences of flow on attitudes and intentions are higher among experiential users than among goal-directed users, our results suggest that flow might play an influential role in determining the attitude and intention towards usage within the web-based context.

Drawing these distinctions between goal-directed and experiential behavior is particularly important in online environments, because the experiential process is, for many individuals, as or even more important than the final instrumental result (Hoffman & Novak, 2003).

Table 1. Distinctions Between Goal-Directed and Experiential Behavior

Goal-Directed	Experiential
Extrinsic motivation	Intrinsic motivation
Instrumental orientation	Ritualized orientation
Situational involvement	Enduring involvement
Utilitarian benefits/value	Hedonic benefits/value
Directed (pre-purchase) search	Non-directed (ongoing) search; browsing
Goal-directed choice	Navigational choice
Cognitive	Affective
Work	Fun
Planned purchases; repurchasing	Compulsive shopping; impulse buys

Source: (Hoffman & Novak, 2003)

Hypothesis 1. Goal-directed and experiential users have different online searching experience on the same ACG portal site.

2.2 Interactivity

The Internet is by definition an interactive medium (Rust & Varki, 1996). An essential part of this interactive ability is the hyperlinks technique (namely, the ability to move from one place to another with a click on the mouse and so reach a new layer of information by a simple movement).

Effective communication with customers is the key to successful business. One of the most important factors for effective communication is known as interactivity (Yoo, Lee, & Park, 2010).

Although there have been many studies on interactivity under various contexts and disciplines, researchers still have mixed views on the concept of interactivity (Yadav and Varadarajan, 2005).

Srinivasan et al. (2002, p. 42) operationalize interactivity as the availability and effectiveness of customer support tools on a website, and the degree to which two-way communication with customers is facilitated.

Interactivity is central to Internet marketing communication. On the Internet, consumers no longer interact with salespeople or have a direct physical experience of a store and its products. Instead, their experience is mediated through the web, using a graphical display without any face-to-face interaction with the e-vendor. Therefore, understanding users' communication behavior in these emerging Computer Mediated Environments is important.

Online interactivity can supplement online decision-making with added product information. Huang's research (2003) showed that interactivity increases control, curiosity, and interest.

Among the diverse online communication mechanisms, interactivity has played a noticeable role in constructing online users' perceptions of Web interfaces (Jiang, Chan, Tan, & Chua, 2010). Perceived interactivity is measured by user evaluations of the interactivity of the evaluated website using the Measures of Perceived Interactivity (MPI) based on previous researches.

McMillan (2005) define interactivity more broadly as the perceived direction of communication, control, and time. Yadav and Varadarajan (2005) define interactivity in the electronic marketplace as "the degree to which computer-mediated communication is perceived by each of the communicating entities to be (a) bi-directional, (b) timely, (c) mutually controllable, and (d) responsive."

Previous research by Lee (2005) has particular relevance to the current work. Lee identified (1) user control, (2) responsiveness, (3) personalization, and (4) connectedness as important components to interactivity in a mobile commerce setting. User control refers to the user's ability to control the information display and content. Responsiveness refers to the site as being able to respond to user queries. Personalization concerns the mobile Internet site that enables the purchase of products and services that are tailored to the user and unique desires. Finally, perceived connectedness refers to whether customers share experiences regarding products or services offered with other visitors to the mobile site. We adopt these three components: user control, responsiveness, connectedness, to fit on the website environment.

Although they call them in different ways, the three key elements are common across the researchers. Therefore, we propose that the three key elements of website interactivity will have a positive effect on user perceived interactivity of online ACG portal site.

Hypothesis 2. Higher levels of user control in the ACG websites will have a positive effect on perceived interactivity.

Hypothesis 3. Higher levels of responsiveness in the ACG websites will have a positive effect on perceived interactivity.

Hypothesis 4. Higher levels of connectedness in the ACG websites will have a positive effect on perceived interactivity.

2.3   Consequence of Perceived Interactivity

The different ways of searching information arguably lead a consumer to browse different kinds of online contents in different kinds of ways, which is expected to have a number of behavioral outcomes, including purchasing (Hoffman & Novak, 2009).

Users visit websites not only for information, but also for entertainment. We identify utilitarian and hedonic two aspects of Web performance from the definition by Huang (2003, p. 429-430): "The utilitarian aspect of Web performance is the evaluation of a website based on the assessment by users regarding the instrumental benefits they derive from its non-sensory attributes. It is related to the performance perception of usefulness, value, and wisdom (Batra & Ahtola, 1990). Utilitarian performance results from user visiting a site out of necessity rather than for recreation; therefore, this aspect of performance is judged according to whether the particular purpose is accomplished (Davis, Bagozzi, & Warshaw, 1992; Venkatesh, 2000).

The hedonic aspect of Web performance is the evaluation of a website based on the assessment by users regarding the amount of fun, playfulness, and pleasure they experience or anticipate from the site. It reflects a website's entertainment value derived from its sensory attributes, from which users obtain consummatory affective gratification (Batra & Ahtola, 1990, Crowley, Spangenberg, & Hughes, 1992). A website performs well in the hedonic aspect when users perceive the site to be enjoyable in its own right, apart from any performance consequences that maybe anticipated (Davis et al., 1992; Igbaria, Schian, & Wieckowski, 1994; Venkatesh, 2000)".

Hypothesis 5. Perceived interactivity of ACG websites will have a positive effect on utilitarian value.

Hypothesis 6. Perceived interactivity of ACG websites will have a positive effect on hedonic value.

2.4   Website Satisfaction

Satisfaction is a post-consumption evaluation based on the comparison between the expected value in the pre-consumption stage and the perceived post-consumption value after the purchase or after the use of services or products (Oliver, 1981; Ravald and Gröroos, 1996). This is especially true for companies selling goods and services on their websites. Customers must be satisfied with their experience with the website or they will not return. A qualitative study of online pharmacy patrons found that website quality attributes of customer service, product cost/availability, and online information systems were associated with customer satisfaction (Yang et al., 2001).

In this study, specific online experiences were significant predictors of e-satisfaction in the following order of strength: interactivity, utilitarian, hedonic, and product information.

Hypothesis 7. Perceived higher levels of utilitarian value in the ACG websites will have a positive satisfaction.

Hypothesis 8. Perceived higher levels of hedonic value in the ACG websites will have a positive satisfaction.

Therefore we propose the research model as fig 1, to examine the relationships between the constructs.

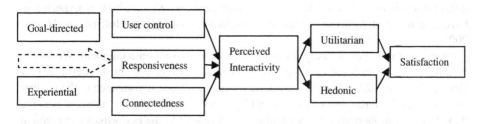

Fig. 1. Proposed model

3   Methodology

3.1   Sample and Data Collection

As the literature points out that online ACG users tend to be younger and to have a higher level of education than conventional consumers (McKnight et al., 2002), the data were collected from a sample of digital multimedia design department students who are currently enrolled at a vocational universities of two sites in north Taiwan.

NICONICO (www.niconico.jp) is a Japanese ACG portal site populated in Asia, This ACG portal website offer users the latest news of Japanese ACG related publishing, sharing their artificial works with VAT (Video Annotation Tool) functions. A fair and open ranking system was trustworthy for users.

A total of 430 volunteered respondents to take part in the study (303 female and 127 male) two groups of goal-directed (score ≤ 21) and experiential (score ≥ 27) were differentiated with their reports score of six questions, the sample size of goal-directed one is 136 the other one is 180. They were all familiar with the Internet and all have ACG portal site visited experience before.

3.2   Measures

The questionnaire consisted of the following five sections: (1) online ACG information searching experience, (2) perceived interactivity, (3) perceived consumption value, (4) satisfaction. Since the population was limited to users who had at least one online ACG searching experience, the first part of the questionnaire was designed to screen out the participants into two different groups.

The evaluation of the information searching experience was measured using a 6-item (Q1_1~Q6_1) two-factor 7-point semantic differential self-report scale to distinct goal-directed or experiential approach the user is (see table 2).

To analyze the relationship among these variables and examine the fitness of the conceptualized framework, this study conducts online ACG portal websites, niconico, as the sharing platform. The operational definition of each variable is tailored to fit the characteristics of online ACG portal sites and shown in the table 2.

The questionnaire is designed in Likert 7 point scale and adjusted according to researches on e-commerce. Participants are asked to fill in the questionnaire and indicate their current situation for each variable item (1 = strong disagreement and 7= strong agreement). The higher score the respondents indicated, the more they agree with these questions. 1 means that the subject disagrees highly with the questions while 7 signifies high agreement.

Table 2. Questionnaire for survey

---

(1) Online searching experience Items Based on (Novak, Hoffman, & Duhachek, 2003)

Q1_1. I visit an ACG portal site, most of the reason by my extrinsic motivation or intrinsic motivation
Extrinsic or Intrinsic

Q2_1. I visit an ACG portal site, cause of the reason by its instrumental orientation or my ritualized orientation
Instrumental or Ritualized

Q3_1. I visit an ACG portal site, cause of the reason by its situational involvement design or my enduring involvement
Situational or Enduring

Q4_1. I visit an ACG portal site, cause of the reason by its utilitarian benefits/value or hedonic benefits/value?
Utilitarian or Hedonic

Q5_1. I visit an ACG portal site, cause of the reason by my directed search or non-directed browsing?
Directed (pre-purchase) or Non-directed (ongoing) search

Q6_1. I visit an ACG portal site, cause of the reason by its cognitive reason or emotional affect?
Goal-directed choice or Navigational choice

	Construct	Question
(2)	**User Control** (Based on Lee, 2005)	UCL1. I was in control over the content of this website that I wanted to see UCL2. I was in control over the information display format, condition when using this website UCL3. I was in control over the order of this web pages that I wanted to browse UCL4. I was in control over the personal homepage of this web site for my revisit next time UCL5. I was in control over the clips sharing what I want
(2)	**Responsiveness** (Based on Lee, 2005; Johnson et al., 2006)	RES1. The information shown when I interacted with the site was relevant RES2. The information shown when I interacted with the site was appropriate RES3. The information shown when I interacted with the site met my expectations RES4. The information shown when I interacted with the site was useful RES5. The information feedback instantly when I interacted with the site
(2)	**Connectedness** (Based on Lee, 2005)	CON1. Customers share experiences about the product or service with other customers of this website CON2. Customers of this website benefit from the community visiting the website CON3. Customers share a common bond with other members of the customer community visiting the website CON4. Customers share opinions from the video annotation tool of this website CON5. Customers affect wider searching from the online discuss of this website
(3)	**Utilitarian** (Based on Yoo et al., 2010)	UTI1. I accomplished just what I wanted to do on this searching trip UTI2. While searching, I found just the item(s) I was looking for UTI3. While searching, I found the information update instantly UTI4. The rankings I found has significant influence
(3)	**Hedonic** (Based on Yoo et al., 2010)	HED1. I continued to search online, not because I had to, but because I wanted to HED2. During online searching, I felt the excitement of the hunt HED3. During online searching, I was able to forget my problems HED4. The community discussions I found were interesting
(4)	**Satisfaction** (Based on Yoo et al., 2010)	SAT1. Overall of this website searching was good decision SAT2. Overall of this website searching was satisfying SAT3. Overall of this website searching was enjoyable SAT4. Overall of this website searching was easy to find informations SAT5. Overall of this website service was satisfying

3.3   Model Evaluation and Modification

Structural equation modeling was conducted using Amos 21.0 to evaluate the fit of the research model (Fig. 1). Structural equation modeling is appropriate for this study, because the proposed relationships can be analyzed simultaneously for their associations.

When conducting SEM, researchers often first evaluate the measurement model (whether the measured variables accurately reflect the desired constructs or factors) before assessing the structural model. As noted by Thompson (2004), it makes little sense to relate constructs within an SEM model if the factors specified as part of the model are not worthy of further attention? (p.110). In many cases, problems with SEM models are due to measurement model issues.

Confirmatory factor analysis provided satisfactory support for the six-construct model. The factor loadings associated with each of the six constructs all exceeded 0.50 and were significant at the 0.01 level. And all the value of C.R. in the range of 0.8~1. All the AVE value in the range 0.538~0.902. Only one item of the 'connectedness' construct with large standardized residuals were removed, resulting in the retention of 4 items, with four to five items per construct (see Table 3). Discriminant validity among the six constructs was assessed by comparing the fit with Hair, et al (2009), Fornell and Larcker (1981) suggested value (factor loadings > 0.5, C.R > 0.6, AVE > 0.5, SMC > 0.5) all are passed.

Table 3. The valid analysis of constructs

Construct	Item	Unstandardized Factor Loadings	S.E.	C.R. (t-value)	P	Standardized Factor Loadings	SMC	C.R.	AVE
User control	UCL1	1.000				0.812	0.659		
	UCL2	0.873	0.050	17.501	***	0.813	0.661		
	UCL3	0.784	0.054	14.640	***	0.693	0.480	0.851	0.538
	UCL4	0.672	0.059	11.411	***	0.557	0.310		
	UCL5	0.856	0.052	16.314	***	0.761	0.579		
Responsiveness	RES1	1.103	0.047	23.244	***	0.872	0.760		
	RES2	1.000				0.853	0.728		
	RES3	1.066	0.050	21.474	***	0.831	0.691	0.924	0.709
	RES4	1.012	0.047	21.325	***	0.828	0.686		
	RES5	1.023	0.048	21.255	***	0.826	0.682		
Connectedness	CON1	1.000				0.853	0.728		
	CON2	0.945	0.045	21.161	***	0.845	0.714	0.902	0.697
	CON3	0.891	0.047	19.077	***	0.787	0.619		
	CON5	0.994	0.046	21.400	***	0.852	0.726		
Utilitarian	UTI1	1.000				0.820	0.672		
	UTI2	1.002	0.052	19.178	***	0.848	0.719	0.875	0.638
	UTI3	1.038	0.056	18.627	***	0.824	0.679		
	UTI4	0.822	0.054	15.110	***	0.695	0.483		
Hedonic	HED1	1.000				0.837	0.701		
	HED2	1.007	0.056	17.932	***	0.847	0.717	0.842	0.575
	HED3	0.900	0.069	12.994	***	0.620	0.384		
	HED4	0.820	0.054	15.089	***	0.704	0.496		

Table 3. (*Continued.*)

Satisfaction	SAT1	1.000				0.819	0.671		
	SAT2	0.986	0.055	17.802	***	0.781	0.610		
	SAT3	0.960	0.052	18.357	***	0.800	0.640	0.893	0.625
	SAT4	0.910	0.056	16.239	***	0.727	0.529		
	SAT5	1.014	0.053	19.033	***	0.823	0.677		
Interactivity	User control	1.000				0.986	0.972		
	Respon-siveness	0.873	0.050	17.377	***	0.930	0.865	0.965	0.902
	Connec-tedness	0.895	0.050	17.810	***	0.933	0.870		

The construct of perceived interactivity examined in the second order factor confirmatory analysis is good to fit than examined in first order CFA, see Table 4.

Table 4. The Indicators of Model Fit

Second order CFA Model	X^2	DF	X2/DF	GFI	AGFI	CFI	RMSEA
1. Null Model	4630.909	91	50.889	0.177	0.050	0.000	0.341
2. First Order Single Factor Analysis	351.656	77	4.567	0.871	0.824	0.8853	0.091
3. First Order Three Factor Analysis uncorrelated	1158.472	77	15.045	0.758	0.670	0.762	0.181
4. First Order Three Factor correlated	147.803	74	1.997	0.952	0.932	0.980	0.063
5. Second order Factor Confirmatory Analysis	147.803	74	1.997	0.952	0.932	0.984	0.048
suggest value	The smaller the better	The bigger the better	< 5	> 0.8	> 0.8	> 0.9	< 0.08

As researchers try to estimate the value of path coefficients in SEM, Hancock & Nevitt (1999) suggested bootstrapping more than 250 times at least. In this study, we implement bootstrapping 1000 times. In AMOS bootstrap, it offers two methods for estimate, one is Bias-corrected Percentile Method, and other is Percentile Method. Table 5 shows the value that no one exceed 1 from lower to upper level. Thus, discriminant validity was assessed to ensure that a construct differed from others (see table 5).

Table 5. Discriminant Validity of reflective constructs

Parameter			Estimate	Bias-corrected		Percentile method	
				Lower	Upper	Lower	Upper
Satisfaction	<-->	Interactivity	0.857	0.786	0.919	0.784	0.919
Utilitarian	<-->	Interactivity	0.935	0.888	0.974	0.884	0.973
Utilitarian	<-->	Hedonic	0.914	0.849	0.980	0.838	0.974
Utilitarian	<-->	Satisfaction	0.900	0.821	0.958	0.824	0.961
Hedonic	<-->	Satisfaction	0.922	0.866	0.980	0.857	0.971
Hedonic	<-->	Interactivity	0.916	0.857	0.970	0.848	0.961

Finally the model fit provided satisfactory support for the fixed proposed model ($\chi 2$ = 714.577; df = 317***, Normed Chi-sqr ($\chi 2$/DF) = 2.254, GFI = 0.087, AGFI = 0.886, RMSEA = 0.054, SRMR = 0.032) .

4   Results

The results of the structural equation modeling reveal the following three findings. First, user control, responsiveness, connectedness, the three dimensions of interactivity are positive affect users perceived in online ACG interactive environments, and almost no difference between goal-directed and experiential users (factor loadings of G group 0.984:0.971:0.964, see table 6; E group 0.988:0.789:0.808, see table 7).

Second, this study confirms that perceived interactivity has a significantly positive effect on utilitarian and hedonic value creation in online ACG information searching environments. Almost no difference between goal-directed and experiential users (factor loadings of G group 0.957:0.986, see table 7; E group 0.87:0.71, see table 7).

Finally, both perceived utilitarian and hedonic values have a positive effect on satisfaction in the ACG portal site. But goal-directed users more concern about utilitarian than hedonic value (factor loadings 0.74:0.25, see table 6), and experiential users more concern about hedonic value than utilitarian (factor loadings 0.55:0.38, see table 7).

Table 6. Results of hypotheses tests within goal-directed group

Construct			Standardized Estimate	Unstandardized Estimate	S.E.	C.R.	P
Utilitarian	<--	Interactivity	0.957	0.946	0.088	10.714	***
Hedonic	<--	Interactivity	0.986	1.013	0.093	10.948	***
User control	<--	Interactivity	0.984	1			
Responsiveness	<--	Interactivity	0.971	1.084	0.092	11.772	***
Connectedness	<--	Interactivity	0.964	1.004	0.09	11.106	***
Satisfaction	<--	Utilitarian	0.741	0.772	0.194	3.981	***
Satisfaction	--	Hedonic	0.246	0.246	0.18	1.37	0.171

Table 7. Results of hypotheses tests within experiential group

Construct			Standardized Estimate	Unstandardized Estimate	S.E.	C.R.	P
Utilitarian	<--	Interactivity	0.87	0.914	0.127	7.208	***
Hedonic	<--	Interactivity	0.71	0.673	0.101	6.691	***
User control	<--	Interactivity	0.988	1			
Responsiveness	<--	Interactivity	0.789	0.749	0.106	7.053	***
Connectedness	<--	Interactivity	0.808	0.717	0.105	6.859	***
Satisfaction	<--	Utilitarian	0.378	0.444	0.12	3.685	***
Satisfaction	<--	Hedonic	0.548	0.713	0.142	5.027	***

5   Discussion

As Wolfinbarger and Gilly (2000) pointed out, website design and strategy issues should be based on motivations and satisfiers for online buyers. Companies anxious to build experiential features and encourage customers to spend longer times at their site (or increasing "stickiness" as widely encouraged in industry publications) may be overlooking the fact that transaction-oriented customers can build ties to an online business even when they do not spend much time at a site.

Because the Web mixes goal-directed and experiential behavior, our results can be used to develop and evaluate websites in terms of the extent to which they satisfy these two needs.

This research has some limitations that need to be considered. First, the sample has not been proved representative of the general population. Thus, the results must be interpreted with considerable caution. Second, although the goodness-of-indices suggest a good of the model to the data, future research is encouraged to test our instrument across different settings. To do so, researchers are suggested to add more new items to the scale or to delete some of the existing ones, and to use alternate factors applicable to the research setting.

References

1. Babin, B.J., Darden, W.R., Griffen, M.: Work and/or Fun: Measuring Hedonic and Utilitarian Shopping Value. Journal of Consumer Behavior (20), 644–656 (1994)
2. Bloch, P.H., Richens, M.L.: Shopping without Purchase: An Investigation of Consumer Browsing Behavior. In: Bagozzi, R.P., Tybout, A.M. (eds.) Advances in Consumer Research, vol. (10), pp. 389–393. Association for Consumer Research, Ann Arbor (1993)
3. Novak, T.P., Hoffman, D.L., Duhachek, A.: The Influence of Goal-Directed and Experiential Activities on Online Flow Experiences. Journal of Consumer Psychology 13(1 & 2) (2003)
4. Fornell, Larcker: Evaluating Structural Equation Models with Unobservable Variables and Measurement Error. Journal of Marketing Research 18, 39–50 (1981)
5. Haubl, G., Trifts, V.: Consumer Decision Making in Online Shopping Environments: The Effects of Interactive Decision Aids. Marketing Science 19(1), 1:4–1:21 (2000)
6. Hancock, G.R., Nevitt, J.: Bootstrapping and the identification of exogenous latent variables within structural equation models. Structural Equation Modeling 6, 394–399 (1999)
7. Hirschman, E.: Experience Seeking: A Subjectivist Perspective of Consumption. Journal of Business Research (12), 115-136 (March 1984)
8. Hodkinson, C., Kiel, G., McColl-Kennedy, J.R.: Consumer Web Search Behaviour: Diagrammatic Illustration of Wayfinding on the Web. International Journal of Human-Computer Studies 52, 805–830 (2000)
9. Hoffman, D.L., Novak, T.P.: Marketing in Hypermedia Computer-Mediated Environments: Conceptual Foundations. Journal of Marketing 60(3), 50–68 (1996)
10. Huang, M.H.: Designing website attributes to induce experiential encounters. Computers in Human Behavior 19 (2003)

11. Lee, T.: The impact of perceptions of interactivity on customer trust and transaction intentions in mobile commerce. Journal of Electronic Commerce Research 6(3), 165–180 (2005)
12. McMillan, S.J.: The researchers and the concept: moving beyond a blind examination of interactivity. Journal of Interactive Advertising 5 (1) (2005), http://jiad.org
13. Oliver, R.L.: Measurement and evaluation of satisfaction process in retail settings. Journal of Retailing 57(3), 25–48 (1981)
14. Niu, H.J., Chiang, Y.S., Tsai, H.T.: An Exploratory Study of the Otaku Adolescent Consumer. Psychology and Marketing 29(10) (2012), doi:10.1002/mar.20558
15. Novak, T.P., Hoffman, D.L., Duhachek, A.: The Influence of Goal-Directed and Experiential Activities on Online Flow Experiences. Journal of Consumer Psychology 13(1 & 2) (2003)
16. Ravald, A., Gröroos, C.: The value concept and relationship marketing. European Journal of Marketing 30(2), 1990 (1996)
17. Rowley, J.: Product Search in e-Shopping: A Review and Research Propositions, Journal of Consumer Marketing 17(1), 1:20–1:35 (2000)
18. Sangani, K.: Otaku world. Engineering & Technology 3, 94–95 (2008)
19. Sánchez-Franco, M.J., Roldán, J.L.: Web acceptance and usage model: A comparison between goal-directed and experiential web users. Internet Research 15(1) (2005)
20. Schlosser, A.E., Kanfer, A.: Interactivity in Commercial Web Sites: Implications for Web Site Effectiveness, Working Paper, Vanderbilt University (1999)
21. Shim, S., Eastlick, M.A., Lotz, S.L., Washington, P.: An Online Pre -purchase Intentions Model: The Role of Intention to Search. Journal of Retailing 77, 397–416 (2001)
22. Thompson, B.: Exploratory and Confirmatory Factor Analysis: Understanding Concepts and Applications. American Psychological Association, Washington, DC (2004)
23. Torkzadeh, Koufteros, Pflughoeft: Confirmatory analysis of computer self-efficacy. Structural Equation Modeling 10(2), 263–275 (2003)
24. Wolfinbarger, M., Gilly, M.: Consumer Motivations for Online Shopping. Paper presented at the AMCIS 2000 (December 31, 2013) (2000)
25. Yang, Z., Peterson, R.T., Huang, L.: Taking the pulse of Internet pharmacies. Marketing Health Services 21(2), 5–10 (2001)
26. Yadav, M.S., Varadarajan, P.R.: Interactivity in the electronic marketplace: an exposition of the concept and implications for research. Journal of the Academy of Marketing Science 33(4), 585–603 (2005)
27. Yoo, W.S., Lee, Y., Park, J.: The role of interactivity in e-tailing: Creating value and increasing satisfaction. Journal of Retailing and Consumer Services 17 (2010)

Factors Affecting Continued Use of Social Media

Eleanor T. Loiacono[1] and Scott McCoy[2]

[1] Worcester Polytechnic Institute
Worcester, USA
eloiacon@wpi.edu
[2] Mason School of Business, College of William and Mary, 23187
Williamsburg, USA
Scott.mccoy@mason.wm.edu

Abstract. This research paper focuses on factors which affect the continued use of social media technology. Using the Technology Acceptance Model, the Theory of Reasoned Action and the Theory of Planned Behavior, a research model was constructed which focused on a set of core constructs, including Perceived Usefulness, Social Norms, Self-Efficacy, and Attitudes and their overall impact on users Continuous Intent to Use social media technologies. Results will be shared with conference participants.

Keywords: Theory of planned behavior, Social media technologies.

1   Introduction

Much research in the last three decades has investigated the acceptance and use of information technology (IT). However, only a limited number of studies have focused on the acceptance of social media technology.

With the advent of the Internet and the proliferation of social media, users now have a choice of technologies that not only can increase productivity at work but can also impact their social lives. SMTs, like Facebook, Twitter, Instagram, LinkedIn and others, have transformed the way users communicate with each other on both a personal and professional level.

2   Literature Review

Since research on the acceptance of technology is central to the field of IS, it is unfortunate that most of the work in the area has focused on productivity-based IS. Most research has neglected the entertaining (van der Heijden 2004) and social technologies that have grown dramatically since the Internet was first privately operated.

Because this research focuses on a unique set of factors and their impact on continued use of SMTs, we determined that the Theory of Reasoned Action and the Theory of Planned Behavior were more appropriate theoretical frameworks from which to base our work.

F.F.-H. Nah (Ed.): HCIB/HCII 2014, LNCS 8527, pp. 206–213, 2014.
© Springer International Publishing Switzerland 2014

2.1   Theory of Reasoned Action

The original Theory of Reasoned Action (TRA) is a social psychology model concerned with the determinants of consciously intended behaviors (Fishbein et al. 1975a).

According to the TRA (Figure 1), a person's actual behavior is influenced by his or her behavioral intentions (BI), and BI is jointly determined by the person's attitude and subjective norm (SN). Attitude is, in turn, determined by the person's beliefs and evaluations, while SN is determined by normative beliefs and motivations to comply.

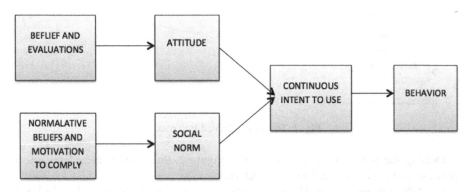

Fig. 1. Theory of Reasoned Action

Attitude is concerned with a person's feelings about performing a behavior. According to Fishbein and Ajzen (1975a), "an attitude represents a person's general feeling of favorableness or unfavorableness toward some stimulus object" (p. 216). Further, "as a person forms beliefs about an object, he automatically and simultaneously acquires an attitude toward that object" (Fishbein et al. 1975a, p. 216). Positive attitudes lead to intentions to perform the behavior, while negative attitudes lead to intentions not to perform the behavior.

Subjective norm refers to a "person's perception that most people who are important to him think he should or should not perform the behavior in question" (Fishbein et al. 1975a, p. 302). One can think of SN as peer pressure.

2.2   Theory of Planned Behavior

The Theory of Planned Behavior (Ajzen 1991; Ajzen 2002; Ajzen et al. 1980) is an extension of the Theory of Reasoned Action (Fishbein et al. 1975a) with the central factor in both models being the individual's intention to perform a behavior. TPB adds a third antecedent, which refers to the "degree of perceived behavioral control" (Ajzen et al. 1986, p. 132). This antecedent refers to the perceived ease or difficulty of

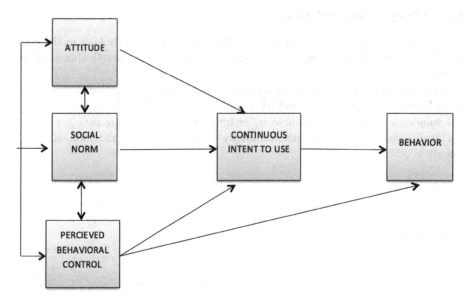

Fig. 2. Theory of Planned Behavior

performing the behavior. As can be seen in Figure 2, these three antecedents affect intentions, which in turn lead to actual behavior.

The TPB assumes that PBC has "motivational implications for intentions" (Ajzen et al. 1986, p. 134). There is then an "association between perceived behavioral control and intention that is not mediated by attitude and subjective norm" (Ajzen et al. 1986, p. 134). The arrow linking perceived behavioral control to intention represents this expectation.

3   Model Development and Hypotheses.

Based on the literature review above, we now turn to building our research model. Figure 3 details this model.

3.1   Continued Intentions

An important indicator of behavior is intention. However, intentions is more appropriate to focus on if the technology is already in use. If the technology use is a pleasant experience then continued use is expected, but if it is unpleasant, continued use is not expected.

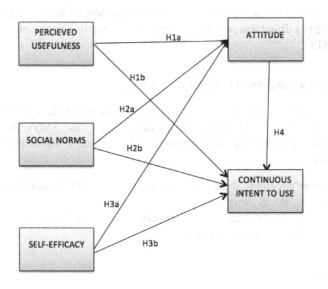

Fig. 3. Research Model

3.2   Beliefs (Perceived Usefulness)

According to the TRA and TPB, key influencers of attitudes are beliefs. Their significance is quite applicable to the IS literature as well (Davis 1989). Perceived usefulness (PU), in particular, is one belief that has been shown to have a significant impact
on intention (Davis 1989). It has been defined as "the prospective user's subjective
probability that using a specific application system will increase his or her job performance within an organizational context" (Davis et al. 1989, p. 985). As detailed in
the model, the beliefs about the usefulness of the SMT are thought to affect attitudes.
More formally stated,

— H1a. The more useful a user finds a SMT the more positive their attitudes towards
  the SMT will be.
— H1b. The more useful a user finds a SMT the more positive their intention to continue using the SMT will be.

3.3   Subjective Norm

Similarly, SNs are thought to impact attitudes and intention. In the context of SMT,
SN reference groups would be both on- and off-line friends who use or plan to use the
technology. As the reference group pressures the user to use the SMTs, the user's
attitudes toward the technology become more positive and he or she is more likely to
continue to use the technology. More formally stated:

— H2a: There is a direct and positive link between subjective norm and attitudes.
— H2b: There is a direct and positive link between subjective norm and continued use of the SMTs.

3.4   Perceived Behavioral Control (Self-Efficacy)

In the context of our research, PBC manifests itself as Self-Efficacy (SE) (Compeau et al. 1995). If a person feels he or she has the ability to use SMTs, then his or her attitudes toward the technology and overall intentions to use it will be affected. . More formally stated:

— H3a: As a user's feelings about his or her ability to use SMTs increases so does his or her attitude towards using it.
— H3b: As a user's feelings about his or her ability to use SMTs increases so does his or her intentions to continue to use it.

3.5   Attitude

In terms of attitudes towards a behavior, they have a direct impact on one's intentions to behave in a certain way. A positive attitude towards a behavior is likely to result in a person performing that behavior. Thus,

— H4. The higher a user's attitude towards an SMT, the more likely he or she will be to intend to continue to use it.

4   Research Methodology

In order to understand the impact of the model factors, a research model and corresponding survey were developed based on a comprehensive literature review (Moore et al. 1991; Straub 1989) and data collected from actual SMT users.

4.1   Data Collection and Current Status

Survey items, adopted from existing measures, were collected and pre-tested with a small set of subjects. The survey was adjusted and is currently being administered to a larger set of SMT users.

5   Planned Analysis and Expected Results

The data will be analyzed in two stages. First, the data will be used to evaluate the measurement model. Next, the structural model will be evaluated. Using PLS we will be able to test the significance of each hypothesis. We expect to find a significant result in each of our predicted relationships, and those results will be shared with conference participants.

References

1. Ajzen, I.: The Theory of Planned Behavior. Organizational Behavior and Human Decision Processes 50(2), 179–211 (1991)
2. Ajzen, I.: Perceived behavioral control, self-efficacy, locus of control, and the theory of planned behavior. Journal of Applied Social Psychology (32), 665–683 (2002)
3. Ajzen, I., Fishbein, M.: Understanding Attitudes and Predicting Social Behavior, Englewood Cliffs (1980)
4. Ajzen, I., Madden, T.J.: Prediction of goal directed behavior: Attitudes, intentions, and perceived behavioral control. Journal of Experimental Social Psychology (22), 453–474 (1986)
5. Compeau, D., Higgins, C.: Computer Self-Efficacy: Development of a Measure and Initial Test. MIS Quarterly 19(2), 189–211 (1995)
6. Davis, F., Bagozzi, R.P., Warshaw, P.R.: User Acceptance of Computer Technology: A Comparison of Two Theoretical Models. Management Science 35(8), 982–1003 (1989)
7. Davis, F.D.: Perceived Usefulness, Perceived Ease of Use, and User Acceptance of Information Technology. MIS Quarterly 13(3), 319–339 (1989)
8. Fishbein, M., Ajzen, I.: Belief, Attitude, Intention and Behavior: An Introduction to Theory and Research. Addison-Wesley, Reading (1975)
9. Moore, G.C., Benbasat, I.: Development of an instrument to measure the perceptions of adopting an information technology innovation. Information Systems Research 2(3), 173–191 (1991)
10. Straub, D.W.: Validating Instruments in MIS Research. MIS Quarterly 13(2), 147–169 (1989)
11. van der Heijden, H.: User Acceptance of Hedonic Information Systems. MIS Quarterly 28(4), 695–704 (2004)

Appendix 1: Table of Hypotheses

H1: Usefulness Hypotheses
- H1a. The more useful a user finds a SMT the more positive their attitudes towards the SMT will be.
- H1b. The more useful a user finds a SMT the more positive their intention to continue using the SMT will be.

H2: Subjective Norm Hypotheses
- H2a: There is a direct and positive link between subjective norm and attitudes.
- H2b: There is a direct and positive link between subjective norm and continued use of the SMTs.

H3: Self-Efficacy Hypotheses
- H3a: As a user's feelings about his or her ability to use SMTs increases so does his or her attitude towards using it.
- H3b: As a user's feelings about his or her ability to use SMTs increases so does his or her intentions to continue to use it.

H4: Attitude Hypothesis
- H4. The higher a user's attitude towards an SMT, the more likely he or she will be to intend to continue to use it.

Appendix 2: Survey Items

Self-Efficacy:
I could use this social network:
- If there was no one around to tell me what to do as I go.
- If I could call someone for help if I got stuck.
- If I had a lot of time to complete my task for which I am using this social network.
- If I had just this social network's built-in help features for assistance.

Social Norms:
- People who influence my behavior think that I should use this social network.
- People who are important to me think that I should use this social network.

Intention to Continue Usage:
- My intentions are to continue using this social networking site rather than using an alternative social networking site.
- If I could, I would like to discontinue my use of this social networking site.
- I intend to continue using this social networking site.

Attitude towards Using:
- Using this social networking site is a good idea.
- This social networking site makes my life more interesting.
- Using this social networking site is fun.
- I like using this social networking site.

Perceived Usefulness:
- Using this online social network improves my ability to manage my social connections.
- Using this online social network increases my productivity in managing my social connections.
- Using this online social network enhances my effectiveness in managing my social connections.
- Overall, this online social network is useful in managing my social connections.

Image-Blogs: Consumer Adoption and Usage

(Research-in-Progress)

Eleanor T. Loiacono and Purvi Shah

Worcester Polytechnic Institute
Worcester, MA USA
{eloiacon,pshah}@wpi.edu

Abstract. Bloggers are now turning to more creative ways to share their knowledge, thoughts, ideas, and opinions (information) while making it an easier experience for them and their viewers. image-blogging has become a tool for those looking to share information through multimedia with their viewers. This paper is part of a larger project looking into a broader investigation of image-blog usage. Understanding what encourages adoption and use of a image blog by its audience is of interest to companies looking to utilize such technologies to their benefit.

Keywords: Image-blog, Technology Acceptance Model, Consumer Behavior.

1 Introduction

Many have taken to blogging as a means of sharing with others. In a broad perspective, blogs refer to "a website that contains an online personal journal with reflections, comments, and often hyperlinks provided by the writer" (Merriam-Webster.com November 1, 2013). Almost seven million (6.7) people blog on websites, while approximately 12 million do so over other social media, such as Twitter. A large portion (77%) of Internet users read blogs during their time online (McGrail 2013).

The idea of "blogs" started slowly in the late 1990's, but grew fast (Blood 2000). Blogs are now a regular occurrence on the Web. In today's hectic and data-rich world, however, people can easily get overwhelmed with an abundance of textual-based blogs. Bloggers are now turning to more creative ways to share their knowledge, thoughts, ideas, and opinions (information) while making it an easier experience for them and their audiences. Image-blogs are blogs that focus on images (e.g., pictures, photographs, drawings, paintings) to convey thoughts and meaning. They have become a tool for those looking to share information through multimedia with their viewers (see Figure 1). It allows them to get their ideas and opinions across to others with greater efficiency. There is less to write, thus less to read, but more visual data to help convey information to the observer.

This research will serve as the initial study into a broader investigation of image-blog usage. Understanding what encourages adoption and use of an image blog is of interest to companies looking to utilize such technologies to their benefit. Specifically, this study looks at what makes people willing to adopt and continue to use an image blog. The technology acceptance model (TAM) will serve as the theoretical foundations of this research.

F.F.-H. Nah (Ed.): HCIB/HCII 2014, LNCS 8527, pp. 214–220, 2014.
© Springer International Publishing Switzerland 2014

Planning for the future

September 20, 2013

Updated Oct. 9: Starting to test promoting pins

We wanted to let you know that we are starting our first test with promoting pins today, so you may spot a few in your search results or category feeds on the web or in mobile apps. Here's what they look like:

They work just like regular pins, only they have a special "promoted" label, along with a link to learn more about what that means. Remember we're still just testing things out right now, so we'd really like to hear what you think. We'll be listening closely to what you have to say and will continue to keep you posted about how things go.

Fig. 1. Samples of Image-blogs

2 Literature Review

The technology acceptance model (TAM) (Figure 2) consists of two factors: Perceived usefulness and perceived ease of use. Perceived usefulness refers to the "the degree to which a person believes that using a particular system would enhance his or her job performance". Perceived ease of use is the "the degree to which a person believes that using a particular system would be free from effort" (Davis, Bagozzi et al. 1989). Both factors impact a person's intention to adopt a particular website.

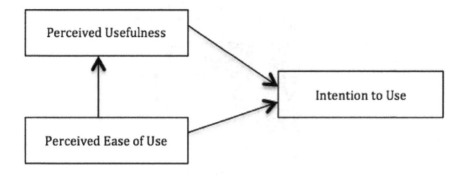

Fig. 2. Technology Acceptance Model

Because image-blogs are online and thus possess similar characteristics to websites, two relevant website quality factors (Loiacono, Watson et al. 2007) are also relevant to this research. They are perceived response time and perceived trust.

TAM and WebQual are well-established frameworks which have been utilized to study the adoption and usage of various information technologies (Venkatesh 2000, Caber, Albayrak et al. 2013). In this research we use a modified TAM, including relevant WebQual factors, to predict adoption and continued usage of an image-blog by users (Figure 3).

At the core of TAM is a person's intention to use a system. If a person does not intend to use a system, then it is of little value. Thus, the factors that impact intention to

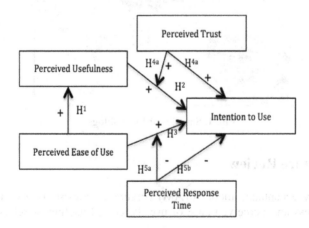

Fig. 3. Research Model

use are critical to ensure its usage, since there is a high correlation between intention to use and actual usage (Davis, 1989). According to TAM, the two factors that have the greatest impact in a person's intention to use a system are perceived usefulness and and perceived ease of use. Perceived usefulness is defined as "the degree to which a person believes that using a particular system would enhance his or her job performance" (Davis, 1989). Perceived ease of use is "the degree to which a person believes that using a particular system would be free from effort" (Davis, 1989). Additionally, perceived ease of use is has been shown to impact perceived usefulness.

Thus, in terms of image-blog intention to use, it is hypothesized that:

— H1: The perceived ease of use of an image-blog will positively influence perceived usefulness.
— H2: The perceived usefulness of an image-blog will positively influence a person's intention to use it.
— H3: The perceived ease of use of an image-blog will positively influence a person's intention to use it.

Image-blogs are online and viewed using the open Internet. For these reasons the speed and trust in the image-blog are thought to impact the relationship between the two TAM factors and intention to use (Loiacono, Watson et al. 2007). Specifically, the greater the trust in a website, the more likely a person is to use it. Similarly, the faster the response time of the website to a user's request, the more likely a user is to continue use.

Additionally, the trust an individual feels in a website may impact the relationship between perceived usefulness and intention to use. Concurrently, the level of response time may also mediate the relationship between perceived ease of use and intention to use.

Applying this to image-blogs, it is hypothesized that:

— H4a: Trust in the image-blog will positively influence a person's intention to use it.
— H4b: Trust in the image-blog will moderate the relationship between perceived usefulness and intention to use.
— H4a: Response time of the image-blog will negatively influence a person's intention to use it.
— H4b: Response time of the image-blog will moderate the relationship between perceived ease of use and intention to use.

3   Methodology

In order to understand the factors that impact image-blog adoption and usage, a survey methodology will be employed. A total of 100 subjects will be solicited to participate. They will be recruited from a northeastern university. They will all be adult online Web users, over the age of 18. Additional demographic information, such as gender, level of education, experience using the Internet, and Web usage will be collected. Prior to beginning the study, subjects will be asked to review and, if they agree, sign a consent form, approved by the university's Internal Review Board. The incentive to participate will be a $3 gift card to a local coffee shop.

3.1 Measures

TAM. The technology acceptance model (Figure 3) consists of two independent factors, perceived usefulness and perceived ease of use, and the dependent factor, behavioral intention to use. The measures will be adapted from previous research (Davis, Bagozzi et al. 1989) where they have shown high internal reliability as well as discriminant and convergent validity.

WebQual. In addition to gathering TAM factors, three questions for both of the adapted WebQual factors, perceived trust and perceived response time, will be collected as well. The measures will be adopted from Loiacono et al. (2007) (See Appendix 1). Each factor has shown high internal reliability and convergent and discriminant validity in past research. Appendix 2 contains the survey items.

Task. Upon accessing the survey site, subjects will be briefed about the study and asked to read and agree to the terms in the consent form before proceeding. Those who are unwilling to participate will be thanked and directed away from the survey site. Those who agree to participate will begin the study by providing some demographic information, such as gender, age, education level, and Web usage. They will then move on to the actual viewing of the image-blog. Next, the subjects will be asked to respond using a 7-point Likert scale as to their agreement with the TAM and WebQual items. Once they finish responding to the survey items, they will be directed to a page thanking them for their participation. The total survey time is not expected to last more than 20 minutes.

4   Expected Results

Previous research has shown stronger intention to adoption a system based on its perceived usefulness and ease of use. We would expect that the level of perceived trust would positively enhance the impact perceived usefulness has on adoption. Similarly, increased levels of perceived response time would have a negative effect on perceived ease of use.

5   Discussion and Future Research

The results from this research will be interesting to both researchers and practitioners. Researchers would benefit from understanding the potential mediating effects perceived trust has on perceived usefulness and perceived response time has on perceived ease of use. These findings would provide practitioners a greater understanding of how perceived trust and response time could enhance or reduce image-blog adoption.

References

1. Blood, R.: Weblogs: A History and Perspective. Rebecca's PocketRebecca's Pocket (2000)
2. Caber, M., et al.: The Classification of Extranet Attributes in Terms of Their Asymmetric Influences on Overall User Satisfaction: An Introduction to Asymmetric Impact-Performance Analysis. Journal of Travel Research 52(1), 106–116 (2013)
3. Davis, F., et al.: User Acceptance of Computer Technology: A Comparison of Two Theoretical Models. Management Science 35(8), 982–1003 (1989)
4. Loiacono, E., et al.: The Effect of Web Site Quality on Intention to Revisit and Purchase. International Journal of Electronic Commerce 11(3), 51–87 (2007)
5. McGrail, M.: The Blogconomy: Blogging Stats (2013)
6. (November 1, 2013), http://Merriam-Webster.com
7. Venkatesh, V.: Determinants of Perceived Ease of Use: Integrating Perceived Behavioral Control, Computer Anxiety and Enjoy into the Technology Acceptance Model. Information System Research 11(4), 342–365 (2000)

Appendix 1: WebQual Items

Usefulness
1. Information Fit-to-Task
2. Tailored Communications
3. Online Completeness
4. Relative Advantage
Ease of Use
5. Ease of Understanding
6. Intuitive Operation
7. Trust
8. Response Time
Entertainment
9. Visual Appeal
10. Innovativeness
11. Emotional Appeal
12. Consistent Image

Appendix 2: Survey Items

Trust:
- This social networking site is trustworthy.
- This social networking site vendor gives the impression that it keeps promises and commitments.
- I believe that this social networking site vendor has my best interests in mind.

Response Time:
- When I use the image-blog there is very little waiting time between my actions and the image-blog's response.
- The image-blog loads quickly.
- The image-blog takes long to load.

Intention to Use:
- I am likely to disclose personal information on this social networking site.
- I am likely to recommend this social networking site to my friends.
- I am likely to disclose personal information on this social networking site in the future.

Perceived Usefulness:
- Using the T/P/V enabled me to carry out product information search more quickly.
- Using the T/P/V improved my performance in product information search.
- Using the T/P/V increased my productivity in product information search.
- Using the T/P/V enhanced my effectiveness in product information search.
- Using the T/P/V made it easier to search for product information.
- I found the T/P/V useful in product information search.

Perceived Ease of Use:
- It was easy for me to make use of the T/P/V.
- I found it easy to get the T/P/V to do what I want it to do.
- My interaction with the T/P/V was clear and understandable.
- I found the T/P/V flexible to interact with.
- I was easy for me to become skilful at using the T/P/V.
- I found the T/P/V easy to use.

Main Factors for Joining New Social Networking Sites

Carlos Osorio and Savvas Papagiannidis

Newcastle University Business School, Newcastle University, UK
{c.osorio,savvas.papagiannidis}@newcastle.ac.uk

Abstract. The popularity of Social Networking Sites (SNS) such as Facebook or Twitter, along with their potential as marketing tools, is drawing the attention of entrepreneurs and developers to create their own SNS. Research about SNS users' behaviour is focused on users' participation, leaving a gap in relation to users' reasons for joining a new SNS. Thus, our work aims to contribute to the literature by investigating the main motivations that a SNS user has for joining a new SNS. Following the framework of the decomposed theory of planned behaviour (DTPB), a two-step structural equation model was implemented in order to answer the research question. Findings made it possible to explain 55% of the intention to join a new SNS. In order to explain the intention, the attitude towards the new network plays a key role, which in turn is directly influenced by perceived usefulness. Our findings invite SNS practitioners working on creating new social media websites or services to pay special attention to how to portray the new SNS in order to be appealing for the users. On the theoretical implications, the proposed model confirmed the need to include additional variables to the TPB in order to gain a better understanding of the phenomena studied.

Keywords: SNS, decomposed theory of planned behaviour, DTPB, joining, SEM.

1 Introduction

SNS popularity has motivated the creation of new SNSs aspiring to be the 'next Facebook' or 'the Facebook of a specific niche target'. However, whatever innovative, creative or solid structure features these networks may offer, many of them have struggled for the same reason: an active critical mass of users. A popular example is the case of Google+, which, despite having the technological and financial support of Google, has not managed to overtake Facebook's first place in the SNS market. In order to understand SNS user behavior, an initial review of the existing literature on this topic showed a strong focus on user participation and SNS applications, both of them assuming that users are already registered with the SNS. Our work aims to contribute to the literature by investigating the main motivations that a SNS user has for joining a new SNS. Thus, being interested in finding out what the main factors in joining a new SNS are, a two-step structural equation model was implemented following the framework of the DTPB in order to answer this question

F.F.-H. Nah (Ed.): HCIB/HCII 2014, LNCS 8527, pp. 221–232, 2014.
© Springer International Publishing Switzerland 2014

2   Theoretical Framework

Previous research has approached the reasons for joining an SNS tangentially as part of their studies. Some authors have studied the differences between users and non-users [1-3], and others have studied continuance of use [4-7]. From this research authors like Coursaris et al. [1] and Hsu et al.[5] have obtained good results using models related to the theory of planned behaviour (TPB), which has been widely used in information systems (IS) research [8]. Despite the broad and successful use of TPB, this theory has been criticised for the unidimensionality of the factors involved in the model in order to explain the attitude antecedents [9, 10]. This issue is reflected in the limited predictive ability, as presented in the meta-analysis performed by Armitage and Conner [11], who found that TPB explained 27% and 39% of the variation in behaviour and intention constructs respectively [11], encouraging researchers to complement TPB in order to improve this issue. For this reason, our research chose the decomposed theory of planned behaviour (DTPB) as a framework to find the main motivations to join a new SNS

2.1   Decomposed Theory of Planned Behaviour

The decomposed theory of planned behaviour (DTPB) was proposed by Taylor and Todd [10], looking to improve the results obtained with TPB by extending the model to the constructs' antecedents [10]. As a result, a second order model was proposed deconstructing attitude, subjective norms and perceived behavioural control. Based on previous research comparing DTPB with related models such as TRA and TPB, the DTPB provides a better explanation of intentions (55.36%) and behaviour (39.80%), improving the results obtained by Armitage and Conner [11] by 16% and 12% respectively [10, 12-14] . Based on the improvement in the explanatory power of the DTPB, this theory was adopted as the main framework of this research in order to gain a better understanding of the main factors influencing the registration with a new social networking site (SNS).

Based on previous research done using DTPB, the variables listed in Table 1 are included in the model used for this research.

Table 1. DTPB variables considered for the research

Construct	Definition	Reference
Intention	"How hard people are willing to try, or how much of an effort they are planning to exert, in order to perform the behaviour"	[15]
Attitude	"The degree to which a person has a favourable or unfavourable evaluation or appraisal of the behaviour in question"	[15]
Perceived useful-ness	"The degree to which a person believes that using a particular system would enhance his or her job performance"	[16], [17]

Table 1. (*Continued.*)

Perceived ease of use	"The degree to which a person believes that using a particular system would be free of effort"	[18], [17]
Compatibility	"The degree to which an innovation is perceived as being consistent with existing values, needs"	[10]
Subjective Norms	"The perceived social pressure to perform or not to perform the behaviour"	[15]
Peer influence	Perceived expectation from peers for an individual to perform the behaviour of interest	[10, 19]
Superior influence	Perceived expectation from peers for an individual to perform the behaviour of interest	[17]
External Influence	"Influence exerted by external sources" (e.g. mass media)	[20]
Perceived Behavioural Control (PBC)	"The perceived ease or difficulty of performing the behaviour"	[15]

Based on these variables, the following hypotheses are proposed:

1. Attitude towards joining a new SNS has a significant influence on the intention to join a new SNSs
2. The perceived usefulness of new SNSs has a significant influence on the attitude towards joining them.
3. The perceived ease of use of new SNSs has a significant influence on the attitude towards joining them.
4. The perceived compatibility of new social networks with the existing SNSs has a significant influence on the attitude towards joining them.
5. Social norms have a significant influence on the intention to join a new SNS
6. Peer influence about joining new SNSs has a significant influence on the social norms connected with joining these sites
7. Superior influence about joining new SNSs has a significant influence on the social norms connected with joining these sites
8. External influence about joining new SNSs has a significant influence on the social norms connected with joining these sites
9. Perceived behavioural control has a significant influence on the intentions of joining new SNSs
10. Self-efficacy has a significant influence on the perceived behavioural control towards joining new SNSs.
11. Facilitating condition has a significant influence on the perceived behavioural control when it comes to joining new SNSs.

2.2   Extending the DTPB Model

A common practice among DTPB researchers is to include additional variables to the original model in order to improve its explanatory power. One of the most commonly used constructs is trust, considered by Nor and Pearson [21] as well as by Merikivi and Mantymaki [22] as an external factor. As Bart [23] suggested, there are differences between offline and online trust, with the trust subject in the online case being the website. For this reason, our study adopted the trust definition proposed by Dinev and Hart. They conceive online trust as "the confidence that personal information submitted to internet websites will be handled competently, reliably, and safely." [24, P. 64].

In order test the influence of trust in the model, the following hypotheses are proposed:

12. Trust towards new SNSs has a significant influence on the attitude toward joining these sites.
13. Trust towards new SNSs has a significant influence on the social norms connected with joining these sites.
14. Trust towards new SNSs has a significant influence on the perceived behavioural control when it comes to joining these sites.

The model proposed is presented in Fig. 1

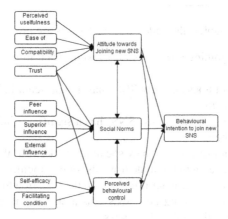

Fig. 1. Research model

3   Methodology

Following the guidelines proposed for TPB and DTPB [10, 15], a quantitative methodology was adopted using online questionnaires for data collection. As the research question is aimed at finding the main reason for joining a new SNS, the sample framework considered current SNS users who have been living in the UK for at least six months. This framework was selected in order to take advantage of users' existing experience and knowledge of SNS, which can provide better insight than first time users, in addition to easier access to this population.

The data analysis strategy followed a common practice among DTPB researchers, using structural equation modelling based on the two step analysis proposed initially by Anderson and Gerbing [25] for the TPB. Our analysis included conducting a confirmatory factor analysis to test the measurement model, followed by a path analysis to test the structural model in order to test the model proposed in Fig. 1.

3.1   Measurements

The items included in the survey were adapted and operationalized from previous research. The questions are based on a 5 points Likert scale (1:strongly disagree to 5:strongly agree.) with exception of external influence, self-efficacy and facilitating which follows a 7 point scale, keeping the scale range as the original authors proposed them. Intention questions were adapted from Ajzen, (26), Attitude from Peslack et al. [28], perceived usefulness and ease of use from Davis [16], ease of use from Lorenzo-Romero and Chiappa [29], compatibility, social norm, peer influence, superior influence and PBC from Taylor and Todd [10], trust from Dinev et al. [24], external influence from Hsu [5] and self-efficacy and facilitating from Lin [27]

4   Data Analysis

The questionnaire was available online from July to August 2013. 464 people started the questionnaire and 282 managed to complete it. Of the sample, 44% are male with an average age of 29.01 years (S.D =7.6 years) and 56% female with an age of 31.81 years on average (S.D=9 years). A majority of the respondents are students (52.1%), followed by full time workers (31.9%), leaving 16% for other options (part-time jobs, self-employment, voluntary work and unemployed). As far as their nationality is concerned, 53% of the respondents are European (of which 35% of the total are from the UK), 32.27% Asian and 8.87% from Latin-American countries.

When it comes to use, Facebook is the most used SNS with 92%, followed by Twitter and LinkedIn with 39.3% and 38.3% respectively. Regarding the number of networks with which the respondents are registered, 30.8% of the respondents have a profile in only one SNS, leaving 70.2% for a range between two and six SNSs. From this range, users with presence in two networks represent 32.2% of the total, with Facebook and LinkedIn being equally popular to Facebook and Twitter with 11% each (other combinations account for the rest). Likewise, 24.4% of the total have a profile in three SNSs, with Facebook-Twitter-LinkedIn the most popular combination (12.4% of the total).

4.1   Descriptive Statistics

Table 3 presents the constructs applied in the questionnaire with their respective mean, standard deviation and reliability measures. Most of the items present means around the midpoint values of the scale and a standard deviation of one point showing a moderate opinion on the part of the respondents. The intention to join new social networks has the lowest mean (mean=2.33, S.D=0.92), which can be explained by the fact that users are already in the most popular SNSs such as Facebook and Twitter, making them feel that they do not need to join additional networks. In contrasting, the variables related to the PBC, self-efficacy and facilitating present the higher values of the mean, evidencing how users feel in control of their interaction with SNSs. The reliability of the variables will be discussed in the following section.

Table 2. Proposed influential factors in joining an SNS

Factor	Mean	Std. Deviation	Reliability (Cronbach's Alpha)	CR	AVE	MSV	ASV
Intention	2.33	0.92	0.956	0.950	0.864	0.331	0.118
Attitude	2.94	0.84	0.959	0.952	0.833	0.686	0.183
Usefulness	3.20	0.85	0.911	0.911	0.719	0.686	0.204
Ease of use	3.57	0.77	0.928	0.929	0.685	0.284	0.112
Compatibility	3.20	0.89	0.832	0.847	0.653	0.403	0.164
Trust	2.82	0.89	0.87	0.871	0.693	0.230	0.100
Social norm	3.21	0.97	0.857	0.860	0.755	0.506	0.108
Peer influence	3.09	0.93	0.904	0.904	0.825	0.506	0.132
Superior influence	2.95	1.00	0.79	0.816	0.694	0.383	0.116
External influence	3.97	1.29	0.899	0.901	0.696	0.339	0.179
Perceived behavioural control	3.94	0.81	0.896	0.896	0.742	0.413	0.105
Self-efficacy	4.97	1.10	0.9	0.900	0.644	0.413	0.115
Facilitating	6.07	1.19	0.969	0.969	0.939	0.297	0.053

4.2   Measurement Model

Table 3 shows the measurements related to reliability obtained by using this model. The indices presented in the table are: Cronbach's alpha, Composite Reliability (CR), Average Variance Extracted (AVE), Maximum Shared Variance (MSV), and Average Shared Variance (ASV). All the alpha coefficients and CR are greater than 0.7, as recommended in the literature [30, 31], showing good reliability. Likewise, all the AVE are greater than 0.5 and the CR is greater than the AVE, which is a good sign regarding the convergent validity. Regarding discriminant validity, all the MSV and ASV are less than AVE, following the standards recommended by Hair and Anderson [31]. The Cronbach's alpha was obtained using SPSS v.19 and the AVE and CR, MSV and ASV were calculated using the Excel macros developed by Gaskin [32].

As the reliability and validity test were successful, a confirmatory factor analysis (CFA) was implemented in Amos V19. The fitness indices ($\chi2/df=1.524$, RMSEA=0.043; GFI=0.833; AGFI=0.798; CFI=0.959 and NFI=0.891) meet the standards based on Hair and Anderson [31] or are close enough to the threshold, showing a good model overall.

4.3   Structural Model

In order to find the main motivations to join a new SNS, the structural model proposed in Fig. 1 was implemented in AMOS v 19, covariating the exogenous variables of attitude, social norms and perceived behavioral control. Likewise, trust was linked to attitude, social norms and PBC in order to test the direction and strength of the relationships, with these factors following the model proposed by Wu, Chen and Chung [33]. Due to the large number of combinations from covariating variables, a specific search was performed in order to find better results based on the initial model [34]. However, as the results obtained were very similar ($\chi2/df=1.686$, RMSEA=0.049; GFI=0.818; AGFI=0.788; CFI=0.945 and NFI=0.875 for the DTPB + Trust model and $\chi2/df=1.686$, RMSEA=0.049; GFI=0.818; AGFI=0.789; CFI=0.945 and NFI=0.875 for the specific search), the initial model will be used for the data analysis. Table 7 presents a summary of the estimators for the standardized weight and the p-value. The test is based on the Critical ratio and the p-value [34].

5   Discussion

Considering that the SNS market is already competitive in terms of people already registered with at least one SNS. Finding the most influential variables that can help to improve the likelihood to join a new SNS becomes a critical task. Based on the results obtained from the structural model proposed, most of the hypotheses stated are significant. The results related to attention, social norms and PBC are supported, showing the suitability of TPB as a framework for working with IS topics. Furthermore, hypotheses extending TPB to DTPB evidenced the utility of using a second order model to improve the explanation of the intention to join a new SNS. As far as trust is concerned, the model showed a significant relationship with attitude and PBC.

Research into SNS has been approached from different fields, with a common characteristic being the assumption of the presence of registered users in the network. This research went one step back, studying the reasons that would make a person join a new SNS. Findings show that our proposed model makes it possible to explain 55% of the intention, 71.2% of the attitude, 59% of the social norms and 60% of the perceived behavioral control. These values are consistent with previous research implementing DTPB [10, 35-37], and confirming the need to extend the TPB framework in order to gain a better understanding of the phenomena studied.

Examining the variables directly related with intention (see Table 7), the dominant role of attitude ($\beta=1$) was found, followed by PBC ($\beta=-0.15$) and social norms ($\beta=0.13$). The order in which variables are sorted regarding their weight is concordant with the original DTPB model and other researchers using this theory [35-37]. This finding indicates how important the perception that potential users have about what the new SNS could do for them is. Going one step deeper in the attitude, it was found that perceived usefulness has a bigger impact, revealing the following chain: Perceived usefulness --> attitude --> intention. This finding is especially interesting considering that the sample is composed of current SNS users, because in a highly competitive market such as SNS with an established leader such as Facebook or twitter, if people have the impression that new SNSs could be useful for their interest, then they are more likely to become a member of that new network.

Table 3. Summary of the Model's Hypotheses and Results

Hypotheses	Direct effect	Standardised weight estimate	p-value	Results
h1	1	0.71	0	Supported
h2	1	0.768	0	Supported
h3	-0.029	-0.028	0.535	Not supported
h4	0.048	0.055	0.346	Not supported
h5	0.138	0.126	0.005	Supported
h6	1	0.802	0	Supported
h7	-0.08	-0.074	0.22	Not supported
h8	0.028	0.034	0.603	Not supported
h9	-0.155	-0.117	0.008	Supported
h10	1	0.758	0	Supported
h11	0.085	0.114	0.028	Supported
h12	0.119	0.118	0.008	Supported
h13	-0.029	-0.022	0.702	Not supported
h14	-0.188	-0.176	0	Supported

Regarding PBC, the sign of the coefficient is rather unexpected when compared with previous research. However, the inverse relationship with intention means that the more in control the user of the network feels, the lower the intention of joining. Analyzing the PBC from users' familiarity with other SNS, the negative sign starts to make sense. Thus, if the user feels too familiar with the network it would feel like something he is already using or has used. Therefore, if the SNS has nothing new to offer, the user will not join the new SNS. The results associated with social norms are as expected, confirming the relevance of peers influencing the intention to join new SNSs [10, 38-41]. Consequently, the word of mouth coming from the acquaintances of the potential network's new member is more influential than the influence that people might receive from external media such as TV, newspapers or any other way of advertising.

The role of trust in the model shows its influence on attitude ($\beta=0.118$) and PBC ($\beta=-0.186$). The direct relationship between trust and attitude suggests that a trusted perception of the network benefits the perceived attitude towards the new SNS and consequently the intention to join it. In contrast, trust is negatively related with PBC, which in turn has an inverse relationship with intention, as a result producing a positive influence of trust on intention. These findings identify trust as an important variable in order to improve the chance of making people join a new SNS. From the attitude side, users have to perceive that the network will help them to meet their expectations regarding the purpose of the network. At the same time, the new SNS has to give a sense of trust in the users regarding how the network will perform in terms of the tasks or functions it is supposed to do. From the PBC side, the trust is linked to that sense that the new network is offering something that current or previous networks are not using, a feeling about the way in which the new SNS is doing things differently to what users have tried before.

6   Conclusion

The present study was aimed at finding the main factors that influence the decision to join a new SNS. Previous research on SNS user behaviour showed the utility of DTPB as a framework to develop the research, finding that behaviour and intention compromises a combination of different variables. This theory turns out to work adequately for understanding users' motivations to join new a SNS, explaining 55% of the intentions. Likewise, the model identified attitude as the most influential factor, followed by PBC and social norms. Interestingly, PBC presents a negative influence on the intention, suggesting that if the potential user feels that he knows all he needs to know about the networks, it means that there is nothing new to offer, reducing the odds of joining the new SNS. A third important factor is the trust perception, which is related to attitude and PBC. Therefore, a combination of highly useful SNS carrying on the tasks in a way that has not been done before and complemented with the feeling of trust in the network will increase the odds of joining a new SNS.

PBC, although important, has to be handled carefully, due to the inverse relationship with the intention. This can be interpreted as people needing a challenge in operating the network, otherwise it would feel like more of the same, and in that case they will stay with the networks they are already registered with.

6.1   Theoretical Implications

SNS user behaviour is growing along with the interest in SNS research. However, as most of the research focuses on user participation, there is a need to understand the reasons why a potential user will join. This research has shed some light on this question based on the DTPB. The model proposed included trust as an additional variable, showing satisfactory results to explain user motivations. The results obtained with the model are consistent with previous research implementing this theory regarding the order of importance of the variables. Although the negative relationship between PBC and intention was unexpected, it makes sense in view of how familiar the new SNS seems to the users when compared with their current or past SNS experiences. Thus the more familiar the new SNS is perceived to be, the lower the intention to join it.

6.2   Implications for Practitioners

Results show the SNS market to be a highly competitive field in which people tend to be registered with several networks, making the entrance of new SNS initiatives a hard job. Therefore, having a good SNS service/idea, combined with good advertising and word of mouth is not enough to move a person to join a new SNS. Based on our research, SNS developers /entrepreneurs have to pay extra attention to offering a new SNS, emphasising how useful it is related to the purpose of the network, performing its task/functions as has not been done before, giving that sense of novelty that will make users generate word of mouth and curiosity to join the new SNS.

6.3   Limitations and Further Research

The DTPB model was developed to study the factors influencing the user behaviour based on the intention. As this research is framed in the hypothetical scenario of receiving an invitation to join a new SNS, it is not possible to measure the behaviour. Having intention as the main dependent variable is common practice in DTPB research ([8], [27], [42], [21], [38]). However, for future research it is recommended to include behaviour in order to complete the model. This research considered all SNSs without differentiating between categories. For future research the study could be narrowed towards specific types of network, either general purpose or niche SNS, in order to test whether there are differences in the factors. Likewise, future research could consider a broader research framework in order to study whether there is cultural impact on the variables influencing the decision to join a new SNS.

References

1. Coursaris, C.K., Van Osch, W., Sung, J., Yun, Y.: Disentangling Twitter's Adoption and Use (Dis) Continuance: A Theoretical and Empirical Amalgamation of Uses and Gratifications and Diffusion of Innovations. AIS Transactions on Human-Computer Interaction 5, 57–83 (2013)
2. Coursaris, C.K., Yun, Y., Sung, J.: Twitter Users vs. Quitters: A Uses and Gratifications and Diffusion of Innovations approach in understanding the role of mobility in microblogging. In: 2010 Ninth International Conference on Mobile Business and 2010 Ninth Global Mobility Roundtable (ICMB-GMR), pp. 481–486. IEEE (Year)
3. Hargittai, E.: Whose space? Differences among users and non‐users of social network sites. Journal of Computer-Mediated Communication 13, 276–297 (2007)
4. Bhattacherjee, A.: Understanding information systems continuance: An expectation-confirmation model. MIS Quarterly: Management Information Systems 25, 351–370 (2001)
5. Hsu, C.W.: Frame misalignment: Interpreting the implementation of information systems security certification in an organization. European Journal of Information Systems 18, 140–150 (2009)
6. Al-Debei, M.M., Al-Lozi, E., Papazafeiropoulou, A.: Why people keep coming back to Facebook: Explaining and predicting continuance participation from an extended theory of planned behaviour perspective. Decision Support Systems (2013)
7. Cheung, C.M.K., Lee, M.K.O.: Understanding the sustainability of a virtual community: model development and empirical test. Journal of Information Science 35, 279–298 (2009)
8. Hsu, M.H., Chiu, C.M.: Predicting electronic service continuance with a decomposed theory of planned behaviour. Behav. Inform. Technol. 23, 359–373 (2004)
9. Hsu, T.-H., Wang, Y.-S., Wen, S.-C.: Using the decomposed theory of planning behavioural to analyse consumer behavioural intention towards mobile text message coupons. Journal of Targeting, Measurement and analysis for Marketing 14, 309–324 (2006)
10. Taylor, S., Todd, P.A.: Understanding Information Technology Usage - a Test of Competing Models. Information Systems Research 6, 144–176 (1995)
11. Armitage, C.J., Conner, M.: Efficacy of the theory of planned behaviour: A meta‐analytic review. British Journal of Social Psychology 40, 471–499 (2001)

12. Hung, S.Y., Chang, C.M.: User acceptance of WAP services: test of competing theories. Comput. Stand. Inter. 27, 359–370 (2005)
13. Huh, H.J., Kim, T., Law, R.: A comparison of competing theoretical models for understanding acceptance behavior of information systems in upscale hotels. Int. J. Hosp. Manag. 28, 121–134 (2009)
14. Lee, J.H., Kim, J.H., Hong, J.H.: A comparison of adoption models for new mobile media services between high-and low-motive groups. Int. J. Mob. Commun. 8, 487–506 (2010)
15. Ajzen, I.: The Theory of Planned Behavior. Organ. Behav. Hum. Dec. 50,179–211 (1991)
16. Davis, F.D.: Perceived usefulness, perceived ease of use, and user acceptance of information technology. MIS Quarterly: Management Information Systems 13, 319–339 (1989)
17. Taylor, S., Todd, P.: Assessing IT usage: The role of prior experience. MIS Quarterly: Management Information Systems 19, 561–568 (1995)
18. Davis, F.D.: Perceived usefulness, perceived ease of use, and user acceptance of information technology. MIS quarterly 319–340 (1989)
19. Hsieh, J.J.P.A., Rai, A., Keil, M.: Understanding digital inequality: Comparing continued use behavioral models of the socio-economically advantaged and disadvantaged. Mis. Quart. 32, 97–126 (2008)
20. Bhattacherjee, A.: Acceptance of e-commerce services: The case of electronic brokerages. IEEE T. Syst. Man. Cy.A 30, 411–420 (2000)
21. Nor, K.M., Pearson, J.M.: An exploratory study into the adoption of internet banking in a developing country: Malaysia. Journal of Internet Commerce 7, 29–73 (2008)
22. Merikivi, J., Mantymaki, M.: Explaining the continuous use of social virtual worlds: An applied theory of planned behavior approach. In: 42nd Hawaii International Conference on System Sciences, HICSS 2009, pp. 1–10. IEEE (2009)
23. Bart, Y., Shankar, V., Sultan, F., Urban, G.L.: Are the drivers and role of online trust the same for all web sites and consumers? A large-scale exploratory empirical study. Journal of Marketing 133–152 (2005)
24. Dinev, T., Bellotto, M., Hart, P., Russo, V., Serra, I., Colautti, C.: Privacy calculus model in e-commerce–a study of Italy and the United States. European Journal of Information Systems 15, 389–402 (2006)
25. Anderson, J.C., Gerbing, D.W.: Structural equation modeling in practice: A review and recommended two-step approach. Psychol Bull. 103, 411 (1988)
26. Ajzen, I.: Constructing a TPB questionnaire: Conceptual and methodological considerations (2002)
27. Lin, H.F.: Understanding behavioral intention to participate in virtual communities. CyberPsychology & Behavior 9, 540–547 (2006)
28. Peslak, A., Ceccucci, W., Sendall, P.: An empirical study of social networking behavior using theory of reasoned action. In: Proc. of CONISAR, vol. 11 (2011)
29. Lorenzo-Romero, C., Del Chiappa, G.: Adoption of social networking sites by Italian. Information Systems and e-Business Management, 1–23 (2013)
30. Field, A.P.: Discovering statistics using SPSS: (and sex and drugs and rock 'n' roll). SAGE (2009)
31. Hair, J.F., Anderson, R.E.: Multivariate data analysis. Prentice Hall (2010)
32. Gaskin, J.: Stat tools package - Validiy master (2012), http://statwiki.kolobkreations.com
33. Wu, J.-J., Chen, Y.-H., Chung, Y.-S.: Trust factors influencing virtual community members: A study of transaction communities. Journal of Business Research 63, 1025–1032 (2010)

34. Byrne, B.M.: Structural Equation Modeling With AMOS: Basic Concepts, Applications, and Programming, 2nd edn. Taylor & Francis (2009)
35. Ajjan, H., Hartshorne, R.: Investigating faculty decisions to adopt Web 2.0 technologies: Theory and empirical tests. Internet High Educ. 11, 71–80 (2008)
36. Zhang, W., Gutierrez, O.: Information technology acceptance in the social services sector context: An exploration. Soc.Work 52, 221–231 (2007)
37. Lin, H.-F.: Predicting consumer intentions to shop online: An empirical test of competing theories. Electronic Commerce Research and Applications 6, 433–442 (2008)
38. To, P.-L., Liao, C., Chiang, J.C., Shih, M.-L., Chang, C.-Y.: An empirical investigation of the factors affecting the adoption of Instant Messaging in organizations. Comput. Stand. Inter. 30, 148–156 (2008)
39. Mantymaki, M., Merikivi, J.: Uncovering the motives for the continuous use of social virtual worlds (2010)
40. Lee, Y.C., Hsieh, Y.F., Guo, Y.B.: Construct DTPB model by using DEMATEL: a study of a university library website. Program-Electron Lib. 47, 155–169 (2013)
41. Lee, J.H., Kim, J.H., Hong, J.H.: A comparison of adoption models for new mobile media services between high- and low-motive groups. Int. J. Mob. Commun. 8, 487–506 (2010)
42. Hong, S.J., Thong, J.Y.L., Moon, J.Y., Tam, K.Y.: Understanding the behavior of mobile data services consumers. Inform. Syst. Front. 10, 431–445 (2008)

"There's No Way I Would Ever Buy Any Mp3 Player with a Measly 4gb of Storage": Mining Intention Insights about Future Actions

Maria Pontiki and Haris Papageorgiou

Institute for Language and Speech Processing, Athena Research Center
Artemidos 6 & Epidavrou, GR-151 25 Maroussi, Athens, Greece
{mpontiki,xaris}@ilsp.gr

Abstract. In this paper we present a method for the automatic detection of user-stated intentions in terms of desires, purposes and commitments as specific insights deriving from the semantics of the intention expressions. The method is based on a linguistic data-driven and domain-independent framework for textual intention analysis and achieves substantial levels of accuracy in detecting future intention expressions and their structural components. Furthermore, we demonstrate several usage scenarios in the business intelligence context showing that the introduced insights can be interpreted from various perspectives and serve as variables in predictive or decision making models in any domain of interest.

Keywords: Social Media, Text Analytics, Intention Analysis, Future Intention, Desire, Purpose, Commitment.

1 Introduction

In this paper we focus on linguistically instantiated intentions about future actions expressed by an author of a text (e.g. Twitterer, blogger, Facebook user) and present a method for the automatic detection of desires, purposes and commitments as intention insights. Intention as *"the cognitive representation of a person's readiness to perform a given behavior"* is considered the immediate antecedent of human behavior [1]. Since intentions are intimately linked to behaviors, the ability to recognize and understand them is of critical importance for their correlation with KPIs, prediction and decision making in domains like business intelligence and national or cyber security, among others. Understanding users' intentions can provide business advantages like indicating potential customers, personalizing contents or displaying targeted commercials [9].

Intention Recognition (IR) -as the task of inferring an agent's intention by analyzing his/hers actions and their effects on the environment [13]- focuses on actions and given behaviors of an observed agent using logic-based formalisms and reasoning mechanisms [20]. Major application areas include assisted living, ambient intelligence, terrorism and computer system intrusion detection. Within the last decade

F.F.-H. Nah (Ed.): HCIB/HCII 2014, LNCS 8527, pp. 233–244, 2014.
© Springer International Publishing Switzerland 2014

considerable work has been done also in the domain of understanding users' intentions based on their web browsing and/or searching activity, i.e. a user's intention to purchase or participate in commercial services [9]. Another way to obtain such insights is to directly ask individuals to state their intentions; intentions data, that are in this case available through questionnaires or interviews, are being used as a prediction and decision making tool in several domains (e.g. prediction of election outcomes). In the business intelligence context purchase intentions are widely used as a measure for sales forecasting or evaluating promotions' effectiveness [24], among others. With the advent of Social Media (SM) and online fora people publicly voice their needs and plans without being asked to do so; stated intentions data are freely available in massive amounts providing new paths for intention research. However, the user-generated content has been scarcely explored from the IR standpoint. The palpable advantages of exploiting the availability of massive amounts of SM data for mining user-stated intentions are derived through a) the ability for low-cost and almost real-time monitoring of different kinds of intentions stated by multiple users (agents/survey participants) in any domain of interest, and b) the nature of the stated intentions: the Intention Holders (IH) are acting as users of a particular medium by freely expressing their thoughts and plans and not reacting as subjects of a particular survey. Thus user-stated intentions are not affected by the "systematic intention bias" [24] that underlies survey-stated intentions because the respondents may try to guess the correct answer or misunderstand the question. Furthermore, textual IR can be efficient in multiple ways, if combined with other types of information contained in the user-generated content (e.g., information about when or how the IHs are planning to achieve their goals) and/or extra-linguistic information available through SM analytics i.e. spotting users/agents of interest based on users' profile information (age, gender, location, education) and/or their influence (network statistics, communities).

The contribution of this paper is twofold: the first is a linguistically driven framework for textual intention analysis (section 3). The second is a precision-oriented method for the automatic detection of user-stated intentions and their structural components according to the proposed framework (section 4). The experimental evaluation of the proposed method has shown significant levels of accuracy in all types of the extracted information (section 5). This paper concludes with a demonstration of some usage scenarios of the intention insights in the business intelligence domain (section 6) and a discussion about future directions (section 7).

2   Relation to Prior Work

2.1   Theoretical Background

The mental content of intentions has been a subject of philosophical debate due to the different renditions it involves: intention as practical attitude marked by its pivotal role in planning for the future [5]; intention-with-which an action is done in terms of a primary reason in doing something [10]; intentional action in terms of acting for a reason [2]. In our work the notion of intention coincides with the first interpretation. Within the scope of language philosophy the notion of intention has been deployed in a multitude of ways in explaining speaker meaning [12] and speech acts [21, 22], among others. A speech act is the basic functional unit of language used to express meaning. The Speech Act Theory [3, 21, 22] attempts to explain how speakers use language to accomplish intended actions and how hearers infer the intended meaning based on the assumption that each speech act expresses the speaker's intention to communicate certain content (e.g. ask questions, give directions, make statements) to some audience/addressee. Based on their content, speech acts are classified in a variety of types [6, 8, 17, 22]. In the present work, we focus on speech acts communicating future intentions, namely acts through which a writer of a text/message intends to communicate what he/she intends (thinks, plans or wants) to do in the future. In this regard, intention expressions as speech acts are only partially linked to the commissive speech acts of Searle's taxonomy [22], since they do not necessarily entail the commitment of the writer to some future action.

2.2   Computational Approaches

Future intentions have been studied within the scope of commissives in the broader context of speech acts classification of different kinds of text genres such as emails [8, 17], message boards [18] and chat rooms [25]. For example, authors in [18] treat plan expressions found in message boards as implicit commitments and create a feature for recognizing plan expressions such as *"I am going/planning/plan to"*, excluding however decisions. In the work of [8], email messages are classified based on an ontology of verbs and nouns, which jointly describe the "email speech act" intended by the email sender; the "commit" class refers to messages committing the sender to some future course of action or confirming the sender's intent to comply with some previously described course of action, whilst the commitment aspect is included in "propose" messages e.g. emails suggesting a joint meeting. Desires about something to happen have been studied in terms of "wishes" in the work of [11], in the context of building wish detectors applied on datasets of product reviews and political comments, whilst finer-grained approaches like [19, 27] focus on purchase and suggest wishes in the product reviews domain. In the recent work of [6], SM users' intentions as speech acts are classified according to a novel ten-way classification schema (e.g. intention to criticize, wish or purchase) linking the intention analysis output with specific benefits in business functions (sales, marketing and customer service). The very idea of Intent Analysis in natural language text was introduced in [16], a work presenting a prototypical implementation of generating intent profiles of natural language text documents based on the social-psychological theoretical framework of [7] that organizes high-level intentions of people into 135 categories (e.g. Charities, Helping Others). Our task differs from approaches like [8, 17, 18, 25] in that our interest in limited to speech acts communicating future intentions yet not restricted to the content of commissives; focusing on user-generated content in SM and online fora, we present a novel fine-grained intention classification schema based on the semantics of the stated intentions rather than the type of the intended activity like in [6, 16]. From a methodological perspective, our work is closer to the rule-based method of [19].

3   Identifying User-Stated Future Intentions

Intention is examined in terms of linguistic expressions transmitting a writer's future intention (FI) as regards a plan, an aim or a desire about the future. Hopes and wishes are out of the scope of the present study. In this section we describe a linguistic data-driven framework for Textual Intention Analysis as the task of the automatic extraction of stated intentions from user-generated content using NLP (Natural Language Processing) techniques.

3.1   Datasets

To build the intention analysis framework presented in this section and the computational method described in section 4 we used the following datasets:

- SemEval 2014 ABSA[1] Task datasets consisting of 6092 sentences from the restaurant (3044 sentences) and the laptops (3048 sentences) reviews domains;
- WISH corpus [11] consisting of 7614 sentences from political discussions (6379 sentences with Web postings at politics.com) and product reviews (1235 sentences from Amazon.com and cnet.com);
- A corpus of 3000 tweets compiled using as keywords words used to express FIs (e.g. plan, want, purpose, aim).

We observed that FIs are highly domain dependent, i.e. purchase intentions (e.g. *"We'll return many times for this oasis in mid-town"*) are common in the product and restaurant reviews domain, but unlikely to occur in the politics domain, and vice versa; vote intentions (e.g. *If she's the nominee however I will probably vote for her"*) are frequent in the politics domain but not found in reviews. This coincides with the findings of [11] for wishes. As concerns the frequency of FI expressions, they are rare in the politics and reviews corpora. In the case of the product and restaurant reviews, negated FIs (e.g. *"I will never visit this restaurant again"*, *"It was a total Dell experience that I will never repeat"*) are more frequent than positive ones (e.g. *"My next computer will be a MAC"*) serving as means to express negative sentiment. On the other hand, the domain-independent Twitter corpus contains plenty of FIs ranging from plans, thoughts and desires having to do with daily routine (e.g. *"I wanna buy a shovel #snowproblems*, *"Going to watch hangover 3 tonight"*), to life decisions (e.g. *"I'm seriously about to quit my job"*, *"I'm thinking of going back to London"*) or (repressed) emotions   (e.g. *"I wanna buy Real Madrid"*, *"One day I'm going to bang Ian"*), among others.

3.2   Further Observations and Analysis

FIs as Intended Meaning. Assuming that a user's x intended meaning is a purchase-FI z about a specific product P, here are some frequent types of examples expressing

---

[1] http://alt.qcri.org/semeval2014/task4/index.php?id=
data-and-tools

z: a) *"I' m thinking of buying P"*, b)*"Tomorrow I'm going to P-stores"*, c) *"Do you know how much a P costs"?*, d)*"I want to buy P"*, e)*"I want P"*. In (a) *x* states *z* for *P* in an explicit manner, whilst in (b-c) *z* may be inferred making the abduction: *x* wants P/ *x* intends to visit *P*-store/ *x* is interested for the price of *P*, hence *x* probably has a *z* for *P*. In (b) the explicitly communicated message is *x*'s intention to visit *P*-store, whilst in (c) is an inquiry about the price of *P*. Apparently *x* intends to visit *P*-store and asks for the price of *P* for a reason, which may be the actual intended message communicated indirectly through the specific utterances. Recovering *z* as the implied/indirect message involves, among others, knowing the (conversational) context i.e. (b-c) replying to questions/tweets like *"Have u bought/seen the new P yet"*. However, depending on the context, (b) may as well entail other indirect messages i.e. going to *P*-stores in order to return/fix an already purchased *P*, whilst *x* may be uttering (c) with the implicit intend of discouraging someone else from buying *P* by implying that it is very expensive. In these cases *z* as the communicated meaning can be considered to be what is known as conventional implicatures [12], namely (acts of) meaning implying one thing by saying something else. In the present study we focus on utterances like (a), whereby a FI meaning is a product of deduction based on the logical consequence of what is being explicitly stated: *"x states that x is thinking of buying P → x intends to purchase P"*. In this respect explicitly stated future intentions can be defined in terms of "intended explicatures", namely assumptions developed from the "logical form" encoded by an utterance [23], where "logical form" is a semantically complete structured set of constituents. In the case of desires like (d-e), also included in the present work, depending on the utterance type, the FI meaning may be inferred deductively e.g. (d) or abductively e.g. (e).

FIs Expressions Structure. Explicit FIs utterances as "semantically complete structured sets of constituents" appear to follow a typical recurrent pattern irrespectively of the domain and the type of the FI (e.g. purchase or vote):

        \<Subject> + \<Intention Lexical Unit(s) (ILU)> + \<Object of FI>

Where

    \<Subject> belongs to {I, we, my, our}

    \< ILU> may be a verb, participle, adjective or noun instantiating the FI (e.g. thinking of, plan, promise, unavailable, willing, ...)

    \<FI Object> may be a verb instantiating the intended activity (e.g. buy, sell, change, vote, watch, ...} and/or a noun or nominal phrase instantiating the object of the activity (e.g. phone, car, house, Hangover 3, her,...)

An important aspect of FIs is their polarity: the subject may express his/her intention to perform (positive polarity) or not (negative polarity) a given activity; in other words, the object of the FI may be intended or not. A second important aspect of FIs is their probability to be realized as it can be derived from the semantics of their linguistic instantiations.

Probability as an Aspect of FIs and Intention Insights. Focusing on the semantics of the FI utterances we classify them into three semantic categories –i.e. intention insights– with regards to the confidence in which they are stated. Confidence is examined in terms of user's commitment to the communicated FI. Based again on user-generated content observations, we adopt a binary classification: a writer may simply state a purpose, aim or plan about a future activity e.g. (*"I'm thinking of buying a mp3 player"*) or commit himself/herself to this future activity, e.g. (*"There is no way I would ever buy any mp3 player with a measly 4gb of storage"*). Finally, a third category stands for utterances expressing desires e.g. (*"I would like to have an mp3 player"*). Respectively, we use the terms PURPOSE, COMMITMENT and DESIRE to name the designated insights.

DESIRE does not involve a commitment to act [5] and is considered as a separate semantic class in that the FI meaning may be a product of abduction as opposed to explicitly stated plans and purposes. An important aspect of desires is that they may motivate a future plan or purpose [26]. Desires may range from simple needs and volitions to intense appetites. The PURPOSE category stands for expressions of plans, purposes or thoughts for future actions not providing any information about how likely it is that the user will actually perform the intended activity. Finally, COMMITMENT refers to expressions emitting the user's determination (promise or decision e.g. *"Of course I'll sell my iPhone"*) or obligations (e.g. *I have to go to the doctor tomorrow*) for a specific activity. The commitment aspect is usually instantiated through the semantics of the ILU (e.g. promise, swear) or through additional elements, such as high probability-strong confidence adverbs (e.g. definitely, of course), negation (e.g. there is no way, never) or temporal expressions referencing a specific time (e.g. *tomorrow, by the end of the week*).

The three-degree probability incorporated in the insights is qualitative rather than quantitative and results from the semantics of the intention predicates; it can be analyzed from various perspectives in correlation with different types of factors (behavioral, social, economic etc.) and thus have different interpretations depending on the domain and the intended activity. In section 6 we demonstrate several usage scenarios in the business intelligence context focusing on purchase intentions.

3.3   Intention Analysis Framework

The outcome of the above described types of analysis is the representation of FIs expressions as instantiations of a framework for textual intention analysis. The proposed framework can be formulated as follows:

"An agent x expresses her/his intention i at a specific time t with some degree or confidence y to perform or not a future action z".
Where

   x is the user/writer of the text;
   i is a desire, purpose or commitment;
   y is the confidence of i;
   t is the time of the statement expressing i;
   z is the object of i.

The object values vary depending on the activity's nature and the domain (e.g. purchase, sell, suicide, attack, vote, support or participate intentions). Further analysis of the potential objects is out of the scope of this paper. Based on this formula, we built a rule-based method for the automatic detection of user-stated FIs described in the following section.

4   Methodology

The method for the automatic detection of FIs consists of (a) a data-driven lexicon (Intention Lexicon) of lexical items conveying intentionality (e.g. aim, attempt, inclined, choice, decision), and (b) a set of linguistic rules designed to detect intention expressions and their structural components (Intention Grammar - IG). Furthermore, the system integrates a Negators lexicon (e.g. no, any). For the preprocessing phase we use the resources of ANNIE[2]. The overall workflow is depicted in Figure 1.

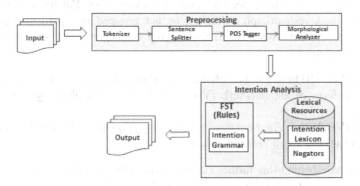

Fig. 1. NLP pipeline for Intention Analysis

Given an input text or text span, the illustrated NLP pipeline performs tokenization, sentence splitting, POS tagging and morphological analysis. The pipeline then detects and annotates in the input text the words or phrases that are contained as entries in the integrated lexical resources. Each detected lexicon entry is being assigned with the relevant metadata provided by the lexicon (see 4.1). Finally, the rules exploit the lexico-syntactic information incorporated in the metadata of IL in combination with contextual information by modelling shallow syntactic relations (see 4.2) in order to determine which spotted IL's entries are used by the author of the text (agent) to express FIs. IG returns as output the type and the object of each identified intention expression. The polarity of the intention is considered by default positive, unless it has been assigned the value "negated".

---

[2] http://gate.ac.uk/sale/tao/splitch6.html#chap:annie

4.1   Intention Lexicon

Intention Lexicon (IL) is a data-driven lexicon designed as the core component of IG in order to enable it to detect explicitly stated intention expressions in text. The lexicon was built upon a primary set of ILUs, namely terms conveying intentionality (e.g. want, will, plan, purpose, intend, goal, eager) and was then expanded manually using semantically related terms (e.g. synonyms, antonyms, troponyms) from Wordnet[3] and Wordnik[4]. Each entry is classified according to its syntactic category as VB (verb), MD[5] (modal verb), JJ (adjective or participle) or NN (noun) and assigned with a prior "desire", "purpose" or "commitment" semantic label. For the semantic classification of each entry we used information about its potential meaning from dictionaries and Framenet[6] [4] focusing, however, on the semantic content of the three insights. For example, in Framenet the lexical units "promise" and "will" are tied to the meanings of "commitment" and "desiring" semantic frames respectively. In our case "promise" is also classified in the "commitment" class but "will" is considered a "purpose" predicate. Entries conveying a negated polarity in their semantics (e.g. unavailable for, refuse) have been assigned a relevant label. Finally, intention verbs (VBi) and adjectives/participles (JJi) are further grouped into particular categories based on their syntactic behavior. Each category corresponds to a specific type of a syntactic complement:

1. Noun (VBi1, JJi1) e.g. I want a phone. I' m unavailable for the meeting on Friday.
2. Infinitive form of another verb (VBi2, JJi2) e.g.   I am about/ willing to get a divorce.
3. Gerund (VBi3, JJi3) e.g. *I am thinking of/ intent upon going back to London.*
4. Verb (VBi4) e.g. I will visit this restaurant again.

The rationale behind this further classification is that a VBi or a JJi are likely to express a FI when followed by one or more of the above types of complements. A sample of the structure of IL is provided below in Table 1:

Table 1. Example of Intention Lexicon

Entry	POS	Insight	Syntactic group	Polarity
thinking of	VB	purpose	VBi3	-
plan	NN	purpose	-	-
want	MD	desire	VBi1, VBi2	-
unwilling	JJ	desire	JJi2	Negated
intent upon	JJ	commitment	JJi1, JJi3	-

---

[3] http://wordnetweb.princeton.edu/perl/webwn
[4] https://www.wordnik.com/
[5] We classify as Modal verbs (MD) also expressions like "have (got) to", which are closely related to modals in meaning and are often interchanged with them-, as well as informal types like "wanna" (want to), "gonna" (going to), "gotta" (have got to).
[6] https://framenet.icsi.berkeley.edu/fndrupal/framenet_search

4.2   Intention Grammar

Intention Grammar (IG) is a precision-oriented FST grammar aiming to detect FIs in text. It relies on IL and a manually built Negators lexicon. Given an input text, IG determines which spotted IL's entries express FIs -in terms of desires, purposes and commitments- based on sets of linguistic rules of shallow syntactic relations patterns that exploit the lexico-syntactic information incorporated in the metadata of IL and impose specific restrictions in the context around a candidate FI expression. In particular, IG contains three sets of rules: rules based on intention verbs, adjectives/participles and nouns respectively. Here are two examples of rules based on VBi:

Rule 1: << PP$_1$>> << Negator?>> << VBi4>> << Negator?>> <<VB>>   <RB?> <to?> <DT?> <JJ?> <<NN>>

Rule 2: << PP$_1$>> <be?> <MD?> <<Negator?>> << VBi3>> << Negator?>> <<VBG>> <RB?> <to?> <<NN?>>

Where

PP$_1$ belongs to {I, we};
Negator belongs to Negators Lexicon;
VBi4 belongs to Intention Lexicon;
DT is a determiner {the, a, this,…};
JJ is any adjective;
NN is any noun;
VBG is any gerund;
RB is any adverb.

These rules match sentences containing the described patterns (The "?" is used for non-core elements, double "< >" stand for the core elements). For example, Rule 1 matches sentences like (a) and (b), whilst Rule 2 sentences like (c) and (d).

a)   I (don't) have to buy a new phone.
b)   I will go back to this (amazing) restaurant one day.
c)   I am (not) thinking of switching to Mac.
d)   I (may) consider moving back to London.

Rules 1 & 2 return as output the following information types for the specific examples:

- Insight type: "purpose" in all cases (a-d) as derived from the semantic labels of *"have to"*, *"will"*, *"thinking of"* and *"consider"* in IL.
- Polarity: if *"not"* or *"don't"* are activated in sentences (a) and (c), then they are assigned a negative polarity.
- Object of intention: *"buy"* and *"phone"* in (a), *"go back"*, *"restaurant"* in (b), *"switching"* and *"Mac"* in (c), *"moving"* and *"London"* in (d).

5   Experimental Evaluation

To evaluate our method we ran a specific case study in the Customer Product Reviews domain using the dataset of [14, 15]; the dataset consists of approx. 4250 sentences - customer reviews of five products. We annotated it with intention-related labels according to the intention analysis framework using the GATE[7] platform. The evaluation results for each information type are illustrated in Table 2:

Table 2. Evaluation Results on Customer Reviews Dataset

	Recall	Precision	F-Measure
Intention	62%	80%	70%
Insight type	57%	74%	61%
Object_of_Intention	48%	82%	61%
Negated Polarity	55%	100%	71%

The results confirmed our expectations favoring a precision-orientated method, since IG achieves substantial precision in all types of the extracted information. The false positives that affect the precision of our results are mainly due to factors that the method is not yet designed to address, as for example the semantic content of the object of the intention i.e. in sentences like *"I will just say this: I will never go back to my archos again"* the rules correctly identify *"will just say this"* and *"will never go back..."* as intention expressions; however, in the first case the semantics of the object *"say"* cancel the FI meaning since in this context the particular expression is a prefatory statement. The low recall results are mainly due to the limitations of the shallow syntactic relations modelling, since long distance dependencies cannot be captured through a window of a limited number of Tokens i.e. for the sentence *"I have but plan on selling my rebel ti and all of the equipment with it"* IG returns as objects of the intention *"selling"* and *"rebel ti"*, but cannot detect the object *"all of the equipment"*. In the negated polarity class, the low recall is also due to negation expressions that are not included in our Negators lexicon yet i.e. *saved me from* (e.g. *"saved me from having to buy an expensive optical cable"*).

6   Usage Scenarios

Assuming placing "purchase" as a value for the object of the intention, a company having access to the information contained in the above described framework automatically extracted from Twitter could benefit by a) getting a first-hand view of a new product launch or sale campaign i.e. measure impact in terms of how many people tweeted that they are thinking or have already decided to buy it, and b) reputation monitoring, i.e. negated intentions like *"I will never buy an x product again"*, where x is the name of a particular brand, (re)tweeted by highly influential users (e.g. celebrities) can spread within a few only minutes and cause significant damage. Focusing on

---

[7] https://gate.ac.uk/

the three insights per se, here are some possible interpretations: a) Stating a purchase desire about something ('want it') instead of a purpose ('planning to buy it') may indicate that perhaps the potential customer cannot afford it. Subsequently, a large amount of purchase desires about a specific product correlated with low sales rates may indicate that a company may have to do something about the price. b) Purchase purpose instead of commitment may indicate that the potential customer is just shopping around i.e. a frequent type of purchase purposes is *"I'm thinking of buying x, any ideas/ opinions/ suggestions /alternatives/...?*. Depending on the value of "x" (own or competitive product) a company can customize accordingly its SM strategy. c) Purchase commitments can be correlated with sales rates.

7   Conclusions and Future Work

We presented a novel study of intentions from an NLP perspective involving a linguistic data-driven framework and method for textual intention analysis. Our notion of intention refers only to future actions and to the best of our knowledge our work is the first to introduce desires, plans and commitments as insights deriving from the semantics of intention expressions. The introduced insights can be interpreted from various perspectives and serve as variables in predictive or decision making models in any domain of interest, since the proposed framework is domain-independent. Future work includes evaluating our method on SM datasets, enhancing it with deep linguistic processing like dependency parsing and analyzing specific types of intended activities (i.e. purchase intentions).

Acknowledgements. The authors would like to acknowledge the contribution of Thanasis Kalogeropoulos, MSc student in Language Technology, University of Athens, during building the linguistic resources. We are also grateful to the two anonymous reviewers for their constructive comments on the abstract version of the manuscript. Research presented in this paper was supported by the IS-HELLEANA project 09ΣYN-72-922.

References

1. Ajzen, I.: The theory of planned behavior. Organizational Behavior and Human Decision Processes 50, 179–211 (1991)
2. Anscombe, G.E.M.: Intention, 2nd edn. Blackwell, Oxford (1963)
3. Austin, L.J.: How to Do Things With Words, Oxford (1962)
4. Baker, C., Fillmore, C., Lowe, J.B.: The Berkeley Framenet Project. In: Proceedings of ACL/COLING 1998, Montreal, Canada (1998)
5. Bratman, M.: Intention, Plans, and Practical Reason. Harvard University Press, Cambridge (1987)
6. Carlos, C.S., Yalamanchi, M.: Intention Analysis for Sales, Marketing and Customer Service. In: Proceedings of COLING (2012)
7. Chulef, A.S., Read, S.J., Walsh, D.A.: A hierarchical taxonomy of human goals. Motivation and Emotion 25(3), 191–232 (2001)

244   M. Pontiki and H. Papageorgiou

8. Cohen, W., Carvalho, V.R., Mitchell, T.M.: Learning to classify email into"speech acts". In: EMNLP, pp. 309–316. ACL (2004)
9. Dai, H.K., Zhao, L., Nie, Z., Wen, J.-R., Wang, L., Li, Y. (2006). Detecting online commercial intention (OCI). In: WWW 2006, pp. 829–837 (2006)
10. Davidson, D.: 'Actions, Reasons, and Causes. Reprinted in Essays on Actions and Events, pp. 3–20. Oxford University Press, Oxford (1963)
11. Goldberg, A.B., Fillmore, N., Andrzejewski, D., Xu, Z., Gibson, B., Zhu, X.: May all your wishes come true: a study of wishes and how to recognize them. In: NAACL 2009 Proceedings of Human Language Technologies, pp. 263–271. Association for Consumer Research, Stroudsburg (2009)
12. Grice, H.P.: Meaning. Philosophical Review 66, 377–388 (1957)
13. Han, T.: A and Pereira, L.M, State-of-the-art of intention recognition and its use in decision-making-a research summary. AI Communication Jourbal (2013c)
14. Hu, M., Liu, B.: Mining and summarizing customer reviews. In: Proceedings of the ACM SIGKDD International Conference on Knowledge Discovery & Data Mining, KDD-2004 (2004)
15. Hu, M., Liu, B.: Mining Opinion Features in Customer Reviews. In: Proceedings of Nineteenth National Conference on Artificial Intelligence, AAAI-2004 (2004)
16. Kröll, M., Strohmaier, M.: Analyzing Human Intentions in Natural Language Text. In: Gil, Y., FridmanNoy, N. (eds.) Proceedings of the 5th International Conference on Knowledge Capture (pp, pp. 197–198. ACM, New York (2009)
17. Mildinhall, J., Noyes, J.: Toward a stochastic speech act model of email behavior. In: CEAS (2008)
18. Qadir, A., Riloff, E.: Classifying Sentences as Speech Acts in Message Board Posts. In: Proceedings of the 2011 Conference on Empirical Methods in Natural Language Processing, EMNLP 2011 (2011)
19. Ramanand, J., Bhavsar, K., Pedanekar, N.: Wishful thinking: finding suggestions and 'buy' wishes from product reviews. In: CAAGET 2010 Proceedings of the NAACL HLT 2010 Workshop on Computational Approaches to Analysis and Generation of Emotion in Text, Stroudsburg, PA (2010)
20. Sadri, F.: Logic-Based Approaches to Intention Recognition. In: Handbook of Research on Ambient Intelligence: Trends and Perspectives (2010)
21. Searle, J.R.: Speech Acts. Cambridge University Press, Cambridge (1969)
22. Searle, J.R.: A taxonomy of illocutionary acts. Language, Mind and Knowledge (1975)
23. Sperber, D., Wilson, D.: Relevance: Communication and cognition. Blackwell, Oxford and Harvard UP, Cambridge (1986)
24. Sun, B., Morwitz, V.G.: Predicting Purchase Behavior from Stated Intentions: A Unified Model. International Journal of Research in Marketin 27(4), 356–366 (2005)
25. Twitchell, D.P., Adkins, M., Nunamaker Jr., J., Burgoon, J.K.: Using speech act theory to model conversations for automated classification and retrieval. In: Proceedings of the International Working Conference Language Action Perspective Communication Modelling (LAP 2004) (2004)
26. Velleman, J.D.: Practical Reflection. Princeton University Press, Princeton (1989)
27. Wu, X., He, Z.: Identifying wish sentence in product reviews. Journal of Computational Information Systems 7(5), 1607–1613 (2011)

Experts versus Friends: To Whom Do I Listen More? The Factors That Affect Credibility of Online Information

DongBack Seo[1] and Jung Lee[2]

[1] Hansung University, Seoul, Republic of Korea
[2] Bang College of Business, KIMEP University, Almaty, Kazakhstan
dongbackseo@gmail.com, junglee@kimep.kz

Abstract. This study aims to examine how the relationship with an information source affects the perceived credibility of online information. We develop a general framework that explains how people perceive information credibility when they are familiar with the information source and/or when the information source seems credible. We then compare the associations of the model in two contexts, namely, online review and social media sites, to examine the difference. The result confirms that credibility of information is strongly mediated by credibility of information source than familiarity with information source in online review sites and vice versa in social media sites.

Keywords: Information Credibility, Information Source, Goal Similarity, Personal Similarity, Social Media Site, Review Site.

1 Introduction

In 2012, Facebook announced that it has reached one billion subscribers, which is equivalent to one out of seven persons in the world [40]. Moreover, the Social Media Report by Nielsen [29] stated that the total amount of time spent on social media in the United States has increased to 121 billion minutes in July 2012 compared with 88 billion minutes in the previous year. The rapid emergence of social media has resulted in the natural extension of its use as a marketing vehicle for businesses. The social media not only allows businesses to interact with their customers but also provides a platform in which customers gather. Customers form a community and behave as a tribe with shared interests [19]. With the founding of such strong, specified online communities, businesses can build a stronger brand power, collect additional ideas from their customers, and even support knowledge creation for organizations [6].

One of the advantages of social media as a marketing tool is that it delivers information with enhanced personal closeness [24]. It can be viewed as another form of electronic word of mouth (eWOM) but is more advanced because it lessens the level of anonymity incorporated in online world. eWOM has benefitted customers with its extensive product information with less bias; however, its credibility is sometimes questioned because of its anonymity. Nevertheless, users of social media can now enjoy the power of eWOM with less anonymity. Considering the level of anonymity

F.F.-H. Nah (Ed.): HCIB/HCII 2014, LNCS 8527, pp. 245–256, 2014.
© Springer International Publishing Switzerland 2014

depending on websites (review versus social media websites), which information source (i.e., a renowned source vs. a person with whom the user has personal interaction, such as a social media friend) is more credible to the use of posted information is not clear. People usually perceive that information from the people they know is credible. However, numerous renowned bloggers and reviewers produce more influential information compared to the majority of a user's friends. Thus, it is doubtable that information from a social media friend is more influential than that from renowned bloggers because of a user's personal interaction with his or her friend.

Therefore, this study aims to examine how the relationship with an information source affects the perceived credibility of online information. We develop a general framework that explains how people perceive information credibility when they are familiar with the information source and/or when the information source seems credible. We then compare the associations of the model in two contexts, namely, online review and social media sites, to examine the difference. The result confirms that credibility of information is strongly mediated by credibility of information source than familiarity with information source in online review sites and vice versa in social media sites.

2   Theoretical Development

2.1   How People Believe the Words of Others

One of the challenges in Internet shopping is that all transactions are conducted without face-to-face interaction. Customers experience a level of ambiguity due to the impersonal online transaction, that customers are unable to see or touch the products, but should make a decision mostly based on the information on the web [23]. Although rich product information is now widely available in online, such as video simulation and consumer reviews, the credibility of the information on the web is not always easily assured [10].

To assist such customers with ambiguity and anxiety, leading online malls have devised various methods, especially to assure the credibility of the information source. For example, Amazon.com grants special labels to reviewers with high reputations, such as *Top 1000 Reviewer*, to verify the credibility of the information source. For another example, customers can browse all the reviews written by the same reviewer, to confirm the consistency in his information credibility.

These efforts to verify the credibility of information source have effectively benefitted online consumers mainly based on the belief that people with experience and reputation would provide accurate and factual information [22]. Credibility refers to the accuracy, depth, and factuality of the information as well as the intention and knowledge of the information providers [34]. Information that is provided by a knowledgeable person is often perceived as factual. Therefore, the following hypothesis is proposed:

H1: The credibility of the information provider has a positive influence on the perceived credibility of the online information.

The credibility of the information is also influenced by the familiarity of the information seeker with the information provider. Familiarity refers to the acquaintance of an individual with a particular entity that is formed via previous and direct transactions between both parties [21]. Familiarity improves the understanding of a person toward particular information as well as the reasoning behind such knowledge, which reduces inaccuracies or misinterpretations. Additional knowledge or information is transferred between people who are familiar with each other than between people who are unfamiliar with each other [13]. The familiarity of the information seeker with the information provider reduces their uncertainty toward the provided knowledge and the perceived risks in the transaction [14]. Therefore, the following hypothesis is proposed:

H2: The familiarity of the information seeker with the information provider has a positive influence on the perceived credibility of the online information.

2.2   Similarities between the Readers and the Reviewers

Numerous studies have identified credibility and familiarity as important building blocks of interpersonal relationships [15]. Credibility implies the present belief about the other party, whereas familiarity implies previous behaviors and experiences [13]. Given the existence of trust between familiar parties, these parties tend to choose each other when they are presented with a wide selection of potential partners [15]. Although certain studies have simultaneously discussed familiarity and credibility, these two concepts are distinguished from each other.

The similarity–attraction theory is proposed for drawing out the antecedents of these two factors. This theory suggests that people tend to engage in highly positive social interactions with people who are similar to them in various aspects [4]. Such similarities, from demographics to self-esteem, have been extensively studied to investigate their effects on teamwork [11, 39]. The similarity–attraction theory emphasizes the vital role of the perceived similarity in the transfer of knowledge and affect from one stimulus to another [9]. An increase in the similarity between two people increases the tendency for knowledge, affect, and intention to be transferred between both parties [25]. Similar people tend to communicate often and understand each other easily, which produces better outcomes [35].

The present study focuses on the similarity between two people in terms of their goals and personalities. On the one hand, goal similarity highlights the differences between the review and social media sites in terms of the information perceiving and processing objectives of the information seekers. Customers who visit review sites aim to search for information on a specific product, whereas customers who visit social media sites aim to search for information on other aspects. On the other hand, personality similarity highlights the differences between the review and social media sites in terms of the relationship types between the information provider and the information seeker. No relationships are observed between information providers and information seekers on review sites, whereas these two parties regularly connect and communicate with each other on social media sites. Based on these concepts the following hypotheses are developed further.

Goal Similarity. Goal refers to the abstract benefit that is sought by people [17], which determines the salient pieces of information that are readily accessible to the information seeker in a particular situation [9]. People without definitive goals tend to utilize any information that they find without considering their importance [25]. Goal similarity refers to the degree to which two people are perceived to share a common goal. People who are highly similar in terms of their goals tend to seek for the same pieces of information.

The roles of the information provider (i.e., the reviewer) and the information seeker (i.e., the reader) in the online shopping context are clarified when they share a common goal [5], which improves their understanding of each other. For example, the reader perceives the comments of the reviewer as very useful and agreeable when they share the same goals, hence developing an affinity between the two parties. Goal similarity develops a mutual understanding between the reviewer and reader by facilitating an information exchange [18]. The following hypothesis is proposed:

H3: The goal similarity between the information provider and the information seeker enhances the perceived familiarity of the latter with the former.

Similar goals facilitate the transfer of information among people and strengthens the foundation of relationships [36]. Goal similarity results in an affinity and mutual understanding that can improve the quality of the relationship [18]. The customer obtains the information that they seek by reading the comments of a reviewer who shares the same goal. Therefore, the information that is shared by the reviewer becomes highly credible. The following hypothesis is proposed:

H4: The goal similarity between the information provider and the information seeker enhances the perceived credibility of the former.

Personality Similarity. Personality similarity is an important factor in online transactions given its association with various business factors, such as leader–member exchange, organizational commitment, and job satisfaction [3, 27]. People with similar personalities easily and effectively communicate with each other [28]. Such similarity also increases the number of members in an organization [31] and reduces conflict and ambiguity in the roles of individuals [37]. Therefore, personality similarity improves the relationships among people.

In the online shopping context, the personalities of the reviewer and the reader are mostly reflected by their perspectives on a product that they have bought or are thinking of buying. Reviewers and readers with similar personalities can comfortably interact with each other by facilitating an open information exchange. Many studies have found that people from the same generation and with the same interests can easily communicate with one another. Thus, the following hypothesis is proposed:

H5: The personality similarity between the information provider and the information seeker enhances the perceived familiarity of the latter with the former.

This similarity allows both parties to evaluate each other positively [1] by enabling an individual to predict the behavior of other people, hence interpreting various behaviors and environmental events in a highly predictive manner [7]. Such predictability reduces conflict and ambiguity between the involved parties [37], which eventually promotes trust. In the online shopping context, the reviewer and the reader share the same perception toward a product when their personalities are also similar, which greatly improves the perceived credibility of the reviewer. The following hypothesis is proposed:

H6: The personality similarity between the information provider and the information seeker enhances the perceived credibility of the former.

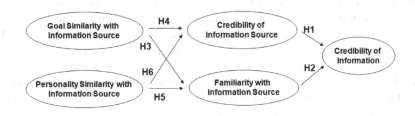

Fig. 1. Research Model

2.3   Comparison between Review and Social Media Sites

Review and social media sites mainly differ in terms of the objectives of their users. On the one hand, people visit review sites to shop, and they search for relevant information on a specific product before making the purchase. On the other hand, people visit social media sites to share information, such as their educational background, family, work, and origins, with their close friends [20].

Such differences in the objectives of review and social media site users also generate differences in the attitudes of reviewers and readers. In review sites, the reviewers are responsible for publishing quality reviews of a particular product [12]. These reviewers are often treated as professionals by their readers who find their reviews useful. These reviewers rely on the quality and credibility of their reviews to protect their reputation. Readers in review sites place more emphasis on the credibility of reviewers. To verify if the credibility of the reviewer is more pronounced in review sites rather than in social media sites, the following hypothesis is proposed:

H7: The credibility of the information provider produces a much stronger mediating effect in review sites rather than in social media sites.

The reviews in social media sites are often written in conversational or casual tones. However, readers continue to take these reviews seriously, and their purchasing decisions are influenced by their familiarity with the reviewer rather than by the quality of the reviews that they are reading. People tend to believe information that comes from someone whom they are closely affiliated with [14]. Given that social media sites connect people that are personally affiliated, the reviews that are published in these sites, whether positive or negative, are perceived as friendly conversations. The following hypothesis is proposed:

H8: The familiarity of the information seeker with the information provider produces a stronger mediating effect in social media sites rather than in review sites.

3   Data Collection

3.1   Item Development

Studies on information accuracy and objectivity are reviewed to collect data on information credibility. These studies explain the key concepts that are used in this study [34, 38]. Studies on business trust are reviewed to collect data on information provider credibility given that such credibility reflects the sincerity of the information provider in helping the information seeker [10, 26]. Studies that measure the depth and frequency of the information seeker–provider interactions are reviewed to collect data on the familiarity of information seekers with the information providers [13, 21]. Major business studies are reviewed to collect data on goal and personality similarities. Most of these studies describe the similarities between supervisors and their subordinates or the similarities among the peers within a firm. Such information is modified to fit in the electronic commerce context [8, 25, 35, 36].

3.2   Data Collection Process

The data was electronically collected. The online questionnaire was built and 400 potential subjects were invited through emails, social networking sites, and review sites. The questionnaire described what review sites and social media sites were with examples (Tweakers.net and Facebook.com, respectively) to provide a clear idea of two different types of websites. The questionnaire clearly asks subjects to consider the reviews of reviewers on the review sites and the comments of their friends on social media websites they often visit.

A mobile phone was selected as an experimental product for a subject to collect and evaluate information to purchase one. A mobile phone is considered a personal product that most people need and use, at least, in developing and developed countries. Although there are different kinds of mobile phones, people tend to personalize and use them for a couple of years, especially for smart phones. For these reasons, people are likely to seek information about potential mobile phones they will purchase.

To measure *credibility of information*, questions, for example, "The consumer reviews information on review sites (or social media site) do not contain any false information about mobile phone." were asked. To measure *credibility of information source*, questions, for example, "I trust reviewers at review sites (or my friends at social media sites) when they post something on the review sites (or the social media sites)," were asked. To measure *familiarity with information source*, questions, for instance, "I do often exchange information with reviewers at review sites (or my friends at social media websites)," were asked. To measure *goal similarity with information source*, questions, for instance, "to me, the information about a mobile phone provided by reviewers at review sites (or my friends at social media websites) is important," were asked. To measure *personality similarity with information source*, questions, for instance, "I feel similarity with people on review sites (or my friends on social media sites)," were asked.

4   Data Analysis

The sample comprised 70 subjects, in which 50% were male and 50% were female, 92.9% were aged between 12 and 25 years, 95.8% were from Netherlands, and 100% managed social media accounts, such as Facebook, Myspace, and Twitter (Table 1).

Table 1. Respondents Demographics

Gender	Freq. (%)	Age	Freq. (%)	Nationality	Freq. (%)
Male	35 (50)	12-19	31	Netherlands	67
Female	35 (50)	20-25	34	Belgium	1
Total	**70 (100)**	26-35	2	Germany	1
		36 and older	3	USA	1
		Total	**70 (100)**	**Total**	**70 (100)**

4.1   Measurement Model

Exploratory factor analysis was conducted on the four data sets, and the SPSS 17.0 software was used to test the convergent and discriminant validities of the items. The items within a set are divided into five major components (Table 2) with factor loading values ranging from 0.6 to 0.9. The convergent and discriminant validities of the items are justified given that they satisfy the baseline factor loading value [16]. A Cronbach's alpha test was conducted to verify the internal consistency of the items. The Cronbach's alpha values of all items range from 0.72 to 0.86 (Table 2), which satisfies the minimum prescribed value for social science studies (alpha = 0.7) [30]. The correlations among most constructs in Table 3 are below 0.7, which indicates that multicollinearity is not a potentially serious problem in the model [2].

Table 2. Exploratory Factor Analysis

Items	Review Site					Social Media Site				
	C1	C2	C3	C4	C5	C1	C2	C3	C4	C5
GoS1	.139	.032	**.873**	-.001	-.131	.146	-.071	**.884**	.073	.022
GoS2	-.071	-.001	**.905**	.053	-.050	.185	.087	**.847**	.178	-.135
GoS3	.132	.098	**.839**	.047	.159	.136	.179	**.827**	.107	.109
CtS1	.035	.081	.123	**.785**	.250	-.204	**.780**	-.018	.074	.143
CtS2	.015	.077	.046	**.865**	.233	.007	**.827**	.102	.109	.188
CtS3	.050	.101	-.059	**.897**	-.119	-.064	**.789**	.089	.056	.137
Fam1	.010	**.704**	.005	.127	.071	.071	-.270	.193	**.552**	.327
Fam2	.023	**.893**	.053	-.047	.031	.173	.116	.167	**.729**	.180
Fam3	.021	**.871**	-.070	.015	.108	.094	.273	.181	**.796**	.004
Fam4	.172	**.615**	.170	.176	.076	.133	.051	-.051	**.806**	-.194
Cre1	.387	.036	-.077	.176	**.602**	-.041	.367	.013	.091	**.757**
Cre2	.218	.020	.015	.129	**.776**	.180	.212	.066	.011	**.705**
Cre3	.028	.239	-.020	.076	**.798**	.002	.026	-.074	.008	**.801**
CrI1	**.899**	.116	.088	-.014	.063	**.842**	-.159	.158	.162	.003
CrI2	**.893**	.094	-.004	.040	.033	**.762**	-.214	.151	.111	-.026
CrI3	**.628**	.056	.177	-.032	.409	**.824**	-.072	.169	.053	.200
CrI4	**.846**	-.037	.042	.096	.248	**.844**	.130	.049	.137	.009
Cronbach's Alpha	0.851	0.730	0.833	0.715	0.872	0.851	0.725	0.801	0.714	0.860

Table 3. Exploratory Factor Analysis

	Review Site					Social Media Site				
	GoS	CtS	Fam	Cre	CrI	GoS	CtS	Fam	Cre	CrI
GoS	1					1				
CtS	0.09	1				0.13	1			
Fam	0.12	0.22	1			0.32**	0.17	1		
Cre	0.02	0.29*	0.25*	1		0.06	0.38**	0.17	1	
CrI	0.16	0.12	0.17	0.43**	1	0.33**	-0.15	0.31**	0.08	1
Mean	4.04	3.23	1.92	4.06	4.48	4.04	4.8	4.05	4.30	2.45
(SD)	(0.97)	(1.21)	(1.32)	(1.42)	(1.61)	(0.97)	(1.45)	(1.51)	(1.19)	(1.47)

*. Correlation is significant at the 0.05 level (2-tailed).
**. Correlation is significant at the 0.01 level (2-tailed).

4.2   Structural Model

LISREL 8.71 was used to test the structural model fit. Most statistics in the model indicated a marginally adequate fit (Table 4). The AGFIs and RMRs were lower and higher than the recommended level, respectively. Such gap was deemed acceptable for the analysis given the small sample size of the study. The other indexes, such as GFI and RMSEA, all showed an acceptable fit. The results of the hypotheses testing are presented in Fig. 2 and Fig. 3 as well as in Table 5. The credibility of the information provider has a significant effect on the credibility of information in review sites ($b = 0.51$, $t = 3.30$, $p < 0.01$) but shows an insignificant effect on the credibility of information in social media sites ($b = -0.10$, $t = -0.69$, $p > 0.10$), which partially supports H1.   The familiarity of the information seeker with the information provider has a significant effect on the credibility of information in social media sites ($b = 0.36$, $t = 2.07$, $p < 0.10$) but shows an insignificant effect on the credibility of information in review sites ($b = 0.05$, $t = 0.42$, $p > 0.10$), which partially supports H2.

Table 4. Exploratory Factor Analysis

Fit Index	Recommended Level	Structural Model	
		Review Site	Social Media
Absolute Fit Measures			
Chi-square test statistic (χ^2); df		155.65: 112	123.64: 112
p-value	> 0.10	0.00403	0.21292
Goodness-of fit index (GFI)	> 0.80	0.79	0.83
Root mean square error of app. (RMSEA)	< 0.08	0.075	0.039
Root mean squared residual (RMR)	< 0.05	0.093	0.10
Incremental Fit Measures			
Adjusted goodness-of-fit index (AGFI)	> 0.80	0.71	0.76
Normed fit index (NFI)	> 0.80	0.78	0.80
Parsimonious Fit Measure			
Normed chi-square	1.00 ~ 3.00	1.39	1.10

Goal similarity shows a significant effect on the familiarity of the information seeker with the information provider in social media sites ($b = 0.37$, $t = 2.14$, $p < 0.10$) but shows an insignificant effect on such familiarity in review sites ($b = 0.06$, $t = 0.40$, $p > 0.10$), which partially supports H3. Goal similarity shows an insignificant effect on the credibility of the information provider in both review ($b = -0.13$, $t = -0.62$, $p > 0.10$) and social media sites ($b = -0.05$, $t = -0.36$, $p < 0.01$), which does not support H4.

Personality similarity shows a significant effect on the familiarity of the information seeker with the information provider in social media sites (b = 0.25, t = 1.60, p < 0.10) but shows an insignificant effect on such familiarity in review sites (b = 0.15, t = 1.11, p > 0.1), which partially supports H5. Personality similarity shows a significant effect on the credibility of the information provider in both review (b = 0.39, t = 2.63, p < 0.01) and social media sites (b = 0.57, t = 4.03, p < 0.01), which supports H6.

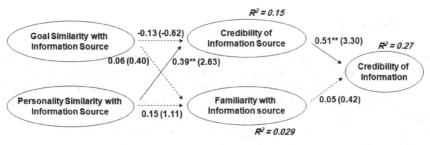

Fig. 2. Professional Review Site

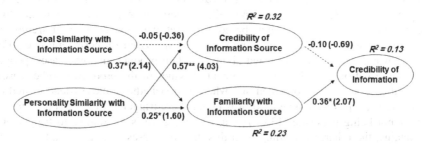

Fig. 2. Social Media Site

Table 5. Hypotheses Test Summary

	Hypotheses	Review Site	Social Media
H1	Info. Source Credibility → Info. Credibility	S	NS
H2	Info. Source Familiarity → Info. Credibility	NS	S
H3	Goal Similarity → Info. Source Familiarity	NS	S
H4	Goal Similarity → Info. Source Credibility	NS	NS
H5	Personality Similarity → Info. Source Familiarity	NS	S
H6	Personality Similarity → Info. Source Credibility	S	S
H7	Mediating effect of Info. Source Credibility is stronger in Review site than in social media.	S	
H8	Mediating effect of Info. Source Familiarity is stronger in Social media than in review site.	S	

S: supported; NS: not supported.

H7 was tested by comparing the mediating effects of information provider credibility in review and social media sites. Given that the path from information source credibility to information credibility is insignificant, the former does not produce a mediating effect on the latter in social media sites. The opposite is observed in review sites, in which the information source credibility produces a mediating effect from personality similarity to information credibility. Therefore, H7 is supported.

The mediating effects of the familiarity of the information seeker with the information provider in review and social media sites are also compared. No mediating effect is observed in review sites given that all paths to and from the variable are insignificant. However, information source familiarity produces a mediating effect from goal and personality similarity to information credibility in social media sites. Therefore, H8 is supported.

5   Discussion

The result indicates that the credibility of information between review sites and social media sites are mediated by different constructs that are also affected by different antecedents. The credibility of information on review sites is mediated by the credibility of information source, while the credibility of information on social media sites is mediated by the familiarity with information source. It means that people tend to rationally evaluate information by whether they can trust information source on review sites. Meanwhile, they tend to rely on their relational familiarity with information source to evaluate information on social media sites. This result confirms the idea of dual processes by Petty and Cacioppo [32]. In persuasion literature, there are two distinct routes – one is *central route* based of the rational consideration of arguments central to the issue and the other is *peripheral route* based on peripheral cues. For example, when information is posted about a certain product, in some cases, people analyze information directly relevant to central issues of the product, in other cases, peripheral cues such as who posted and when read (whether a close friend posted or whether a reader just have nice food or is hungry) are triggered to reach a decision of being or not being persuaded [33]. It implies that there is a stimulus to trigger one route against the other. Coinciding with this dual processes idea, the result confirms that people tend to use the central route to evaluate information when they read information posted by anonymous reviewers on review sites. Meanwhile, they use the peripheral route to evaluate information on social media sites.

As hypothesized Goal Similarity and Personality Similarity with Information Source positively influence on Familiarity with Information Source at social media websites. Although Familiarity with Information Source is related to peripheral route, Goal Similarity (b=0.37) plays more significant role on building Familiarity with Information Source than Personality Similarity (b=0.25). It implies that posters can increase the familiarity of readers by posting important and relevant information to the readers. However, for review sites, only Personality Similarity with Information Source positively influences on Credibility of Information Source, which is a surprising result. It suggests that posters can increase Credibility of Information Source by revealing their personal lives. One explanation of this surprising result can be derived from the sample size (n=70) and the composition of the respondents within the sample. The sample size can be considered small and the composition of the sample implies a need for caution in interpreting the result, because more than 90 percent of respondents are from the age group between 12 and 25. Yet, this study opens different perspectives and factors influencing on the credibility of information between online review and social media sites.

Acknowledgment. This research was financially supported by Hansung University.

References

1. Antonioni, D., Park, H.: The Effects of Personality Similarity on Peer Ratings of Contextual Work Behaviors. J. Appl Psychol. 54, 331–360 (2001)
2. Bagozzi, R.P., Yi, Y., Phillips, L.W.: Assessing Construct Validity in Organizational Research. Admin. Sci. Quart. 36(3), 421–458 (1991)
3. Bauer, T.N., Green, S.G.: Development of Leader-member Exchange: A Longitudinal Test. Acad. of Manage. J. 39, 1538–1567 (1996)
4. Byrne, D.: The Attraction Paradigm. Academic Press, New York (1971)
5. Chen, Z.X., Aryee, S., Lee, C., Hui, C.: Processes Linking Perceived Leader-subordinate Goal Similarity to Subordinate Performance. Acad. of Manage Best Paper (2005)
6. Dutta, S.: What's Your Personal Social Media Strategy? Harvard Business Rev. 88(11), 127–130 (2010)
7. Engle, E.M., Lord, R.G.: Implicit Theories, Self-schemas, and Leader-member Exchange. Acad. of Manage. J. 40, 988–1010 (1997)
8. Ensher, E.A., Murphy, S.E.: Effects of Race, Gender, Perceived Similarity, and Contact on Mentor Relationships. J. Vocat. Behav. 50, 460–481 (1997)
9. Fazio, R.: On the Power and Functionality of Attitudes: The Role of Attitude Accessibility. In: Pratkanis, A. (ed.) Attitude Structure and Function, pp. 153–180. Lawrence Erlbaum Associates, Mahwah (1989)
10. Flavián, C., Guinalíu, M., Gurrea, R.: The Role Played by Perceived Usability, Satisfaction and Consumer Trust on Website Loyalty. Inform. Manage. 43(1), 1–14 (2006)
11. Flynn, F.: How Much Should I Give and How Often? The Effects of Generosity and Frequency or Favor Exchange on Social Status and Productivity. Acad. of Manage. J. 46, 539–553 (2003)
12. Forman, C., Ghose, A., Wiesenfeld, B.: Examining the Relationship Between Reviews and Sales: The Role of Reviewer Identity Disclosure in Electronic Markets. Info. Sys. Res. 19(3), 291–313 (2008)
13. Gefen, D., Wyss, S., Lichtenstein, Y.: Business Familiarity as Risk Mitigation in Software Development Outsourcing Contracts. MIS Quart. 32(3), 531–551 (2008)
14. Gulati, R.: Does Familiarity Breed Trust? The Implications of Repeated Ties for Contractual Choice in Alliances. Acad. Manage. J. 38(1), 85–112 (1995)
15. Gulati, R., Singh, H.: The Architecture of Cooperation: Managing Coordination Costs and Appropriation Concerns in Strategic Alliances. Admin. Sci. Quart. 43(4), 781–814 (1998)
16. Hair, J.F., Black, W.C., Babin, B.J., Anderson, R.E., Tatham, R.L.: Multivariate Data Analysis. Prentice-Hall, Englewood Cliffs (2006)
17. Huffman, C., Houston, M.J.: Goal-Oriented Experiences and the Development of Knowledge. J. Consum. Res. 20(2), 190–207 (1993)
18. Johnson, J., Cullen, J., Takenouchi, M.: Setting the Stage for Trust and Strategic Integration in Japanese-US Cooperative Alliances. J. Int. Bus. Stud. 27, 981–1004 (1996)
19. Kane, G.C., Fichman, R.G.: Community Relations 2.0. Harvard Business Rev. 87, 45–50 (2009)
20. Kaplan, A.M., Haenlein, M.: Users of the World, Unite! The Challenges and Opportunities of Social Media. Bus. Horizons 53(1), 59–68 (2010)
21. Komiak, S.Y.X., Benbasat, I.: The Effects of Personalization and Familiarity on Trust and Adoption of Recommendation Agents. MIS Quart. 30(4), 941–960 (2006)

22. Lee, J.: What Makes People Read An Online Review? The Relative Effects of Early Posting and Helpfulness on Review Readership. Cyberpsychol., Behav., and Social Networking 16(7), 529–535 (2013)
23. Lee, J., Lee, J.-N.: Understanding Product Information Inference Process in Electronic Word-of-Mouth: an Objectivity-Subjectivity Perspective. Inform. Manage. 46(5), 302–311 (2009)
24. Mangold, W.G., Faulds, D.J.: Social Media: The New Hybrid Element of the Promotion Mix. Business Horizons 52(4), 357–365 (2009)
25. Martin, I.M., Stewart, D.W.: The Differential Impact of Goal Congruency on Attitudes, Intentions, and the Transfer of Brand Equity. J. Marketing Res. 38(4), 471–484 (2001)
26. McKnight, D.H., Choudhury, V., Kacmar, C.: Developing and Validating Trust Measures for e-Commerce: An Integrative Typology. Info. Sys. Res. 13(3), 334–359 (2002)
27. Meglino, B.M., Ravlin, E.C., Adkins, C.L.: A Work Values Approach to Corporate Culture: A Field Test of the Value Congruence Process and its Relationship to Individual Outcomes. J. Appl. Psychol. 74, 424–432 (1989)
28. Meglino, B.M., Ravlin, E.C., Adkins, C.L.: Value Congruence and Satisfaction with a Leader: An Examination of the Role of Interaction. Hum. Relat. 44, 481–495 (1991)
29. Nielsen report (2012), http://www.nielsen.com/us/en/reports/2012/state-of-the-media-the-social-media-report-2012.html
30. Nunnally, J.C., Bernstein, I.H.: Psychometric theory, 3rd edn. McGraw-Hill, NY (1994)
31. O'Reilly, C.A., Caldwell, D.F., Barnett, W.P.: Work Group Demography, Social Integration, and Turnover. Admin. Sci. Quart. 34, 21–27 (1989)
32. Petty, R.E., Cacioppo, J.T.: Personal Involvement as a Determinant of Argument-Based Persuasion. J. of Pers. and Soc. Psy. 41(5), 847–855 (1981)
33. Ray, S., Seo, D.: The Interplay of Conscious and Automatic Mechanisms in the Context of Routine Use: An Integrative and Comparative Study of Contrasting Mechanisms. Infor. and Manage. 50, 523–539 (2013)
34. Radoilska, L.: Truthfulness and Business. J. Bus. Ethics 79(1), 21–28 (2008)
35. Schaubroeck, J., Lam, S.K.: How Similarity to Peers and Supervisor Influences Organizational Advancement in Different Cultures. Acad. Manage. J. 45(6), 1120–1136 (2002)
36. Si, S.X., Bruton, G.D.: Knowledge Acquisition, Cost Savings, and Strategic Positioning: Effects on Sino-American IJV Performance. J. Bus. Res. 58(11), 1465–1473 (2005)
37. Tsui, A.S., O'Reilly, C.A.: Beyond Simple Demographic Effects: The Importance of Relational Demography in Supervisor-Subordinate Dyads. Acad. Manage. J. 32, 402–423 (1989)
38. Underwood, R.L., Ozanne, J.: Is Your Package an Effective Communicator? A Normative Framework for Increasing the Communicative Competence of Packaging. J. Marketing Comm. 4(4), 207–220 (1998)
39. Zenger, T.R., Lawrence, B.S.: Organizational Demography: The Differential Effects of Age and Tenure Distributions on Technical Communication. Acad. Manage. J. 32, 353–376 (1989)
40. Vance: Facebook: The Making of 1 Billion Users (2012), http://www.businessweek.com/articles/2012-10-04/facebook-the-making-of-1-billion-users

To Shave or Not to Shave?

How Beardedness in a Linkedin Profile Picture Influences Perceived Expertise and Job Interview Prospects

Sarah van der Land[1] and Daan G. Muntinga[2]

[1] Erasmus University Rotterdam, The Netherlands
[2] University of Amsterdam, The Netherlands
vanderland@eshcc.eur.nl

Abstract. This study explores whether wearing a beard in a LinkedIn profile picture affects a candidate's prospects of being invited for a job interview and whether this is contingent on the type of job vacancy. Based on Ohanian's (1990) three sub dimensions of *credibility*, three different job vacancies were constructed: (1) architect for an expertise-job, (2) back cashier officer for a trustworthiness-job, and (3) sales representative for an attractiveness-job. Results of a 2 (candidate: beard versus no beard) x 3 (job type: expertise, trustworthiness, attractiveness) experiment conducted among 216 participants show that bearded candidates are perceived as having more expertise than clean-shaven candidates. Moreover, a candidate's perceived expertise is a significant predictor of the intention to invite the candidate for a job interview. Theoretical and practical implications of these findings are discussed.

Keywords: Personal Branding, Strategic Social Media, recruitment, beards, credibility, job interview success, LinkedIN.

1 Introduction

As a sign of fashionable masculinity, the male facial beard has risen and fallen regularly throughout history. Quite consistently, however, it has been associated with divine and political authority [11]. Hence, many kings grew beards and often had themselves portrayed wearing one, in order to emphasize their power and reigning expertise.

As evidenced by the many European monarchs currently growing a beard, kings are among the many professionals that are well aware of the fact that visual cues are essential in forming impressions of others [7]. A strong first impression, in particular, is vital in the context of job recruitment [3]. Today's employers are increasingly using Social Network Sites (SNSs; e.g., Facebook and LinkedIn) to screen potential job applicants before inviting them to a job interview [13]. Based on minimal visual cues for online self-presentation (e.g., a candidate's profile picture or affiliations), employers judge a candidate's personality and intelligence without ever meeting him/her [13]. Thus, the cues a potential job candidate displays on their online profile may determine interpersonal impression formation and, evidently, job interview success.

F.F.-H. Nah (Ed.): HCIB/HCII 2014, LNCS 8527, pp. 257–265, 2014.
© Springer International Publishing Switzerland 2014

This study therefore explores whether one specifically salient visual cue in a LinkedIn profile picture, namely wearing a beard, affects a candidate's prospects of being invited for a job interview, and whether this is contingent on the type of job vacancy. This study builds on prior work by Guido, Peluso, and Moffa (2011) on the effects of bearded endorsers in advertising, and extends their research design to the context of job recruitment. In the next section, the theoretical rationale for our hypotheses is provided. Subsequently, the methodology used to empirically test our hypotheses is described. In the fourth section, the results are presented. Finally, we discuss the theoretical and practical implications of this study.

2   Theoretical Framework

Because recruiters have limited time and information processing capabilities to search among the online pool of potential job candidates on LinkedIN [13], they must resort to heuristic inferential strategies to economize their judgments [19]. Therefore, their judgments are likely to be guided by peripheral cues displayed on a profile picture such as gender, ethnicity, glasses, and facial hair. Online, such simple cues may magnify the effects of impression formation [24]. According to research in the field of impression formation, one specifically relevant cue is facial hair [20]. Colloquial evidence suggests that there is a negative correlation between professional success and facial hair [24]. Therefore, this study focuses on the role of beardedness as a cue, which refers to the presence (or absence) of a well-groomed beard on a job candidate's face.

Throughout history studies have shown that beards have been associated with positive personality traits such as maturity [3], intelligence, courage, sincerity, composure, and competence [20, 23, 4]. However, in terms of attractiveness, some research suggests that bearded men are perceived to be less attractive than those who are clean-shaven [17, 5], while other studies, have indicated differently. Barber (2001) for instance, from a biological standpoint suggests that wearing a beard makes men more attractive because they "are seen as having the biological and social qualities that would enhance their value as husbands" (p. 262).

Based on Guido et al.'s (2011) research on the effects of bearded endorsers in advertising, Johnston's (2011) exploration of beards' socio-cultural meaning, Dixson and Brooks' (2013) recent study of the evolutionary function of beardedness, and Reed and Blunk's (1990) finding that bearded men are more competent than clean-shaven men, we hypothesize the following:

H1: A candidate who is displayed wearing a beard in his LinkedIn profile picture is perceived more as an expert than a candidate who is displayed without a beard.

In the context of persuasive communication, higher levels of perceived expertise have been linked to attitude change and consumer purchase behavior [18, 26]. For example, Woodside and Davenport (1974) found that salesmen who were perceived as an expert were able to gain a significantly higher number of customer purchases for their product than salesmen who were not perceived as such. In a similar vein, we therefore argue that the perceived expertise of job candidate will affect the intentions to invite him for a job interview and offer the following hypothesis:

H2: The more a candidate is perceived as an expert, the more likely he is to be invited for a job interview.

Beardedness increases a candidate's perceived credibility, and could prompt the likeliness of recruiters to invite the candidate for an interview, especially when the attributes of the candidate's personality are congruent with the available job. Based on the match-up hypothesis [12, 16] and Guido et al.'s (2011) prior work, we argue that for jobs associated with expertise (e.g., an architect), men with beards elicit a higher level expertise which could positively influence a recruiter's perception of a bearded candidate's suitability for the job than a clean-shaven candidate. This effect would not occur for attractiveness-jobs or trustworthiness-jobs, as the incongruence between the image of the bearded candidate with the attributes related to the job could inhibit job interview success. Therefore the following hypothesis is presented:

H3: Wearing a beard on a LinkedIn profile picture positively affects expertise perceptions, which in turn increases the likeliness to be invited for a job interview, but only for expertise-jobs.

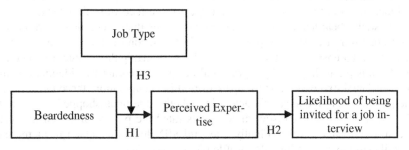

Fig. 1. Conceptual model of this study

3 Method

To test these hypotheses graphically displayed in Figure 1, a 2 (candidate: beard versus no beard) x 3 (job type: attractiveness, trustworthiness, expertise) between subject factorial design was conducted.

3.1 Sample

This study was carried out among a convenience sample of 216 adults between 18 and 69 years old (53.2% female, Mage = 29.01, SD = 10.81). Participants were recruited via the social networks of the students who participated in a Master's level Communication Science course at a high-ranked University in the Netherlands. Of these participants, 27.6% indicated using LinkedIN at least once a week.

3.2 Research Design

Three job vacancies were established to represent Ohanian's (1990) three sub-dimensions of credibility: attractiveness, trustworthiness, and expertise. The corresponding types of job vacancies were determined by a focus group of fifteen university students consisting of thirteen women and two men. It was determined that the attractiveness job vacancy should be represented by a sales person at a fashion store, the trustworthiness job vacancy by a back office bank cashier, and the expertise job vacancy by an architect. The job vacancy descriptions were based on existing online job postings for similar vacancies. A manipulation check was performed to check whether each job represented the correct sub-dimension of credibility. For the manipulation check, eleven participants were asked to give the three most important qualities needed in a candidate for each of the three job categories. Their answers verified that each job vacancy was a valid representation of the intended sub-dimension. Appendix A shows the final job vacancies.

In terms of facial stimuli, *beardedness* in this study constitutes of a well-groomed beard, since research has shown that employers consider grooming one of the most important physical factors of candidates' suitability for the job [21]. A relatively young male (30 years of age) was chosen as a model, because candidates in this age category are rewarded more positive replies to their job application by recruiters than older candidates [10]. The model wore a black shirt because employers prefer candidates to wear dark, conservative clothing during job interviews [21]. The model expressed a neutral face, in order to avoid unwanted interpersonal effects of smiling [15].

In this study, beardedness is a dichotomous rather than a continuous variable: in the first condition a beard was present, and in the second condition the model was clean-shaven. To ensure that the beard was the only manipulation cue, the picture of the model was photoshopped by a graphical designer, creating two identical pictures in terms of facial expression. Thus, apart from this manipulation, these two LinkedIn profile pictures were identical. To determine whether the photoshopped facial stimuli for the experiment were realistic, three judges rated the picture of which the results were confirmed satisfactorily. Finally, the LinkedIN logo was added to increase the photo's likeness to a real LinkedIN profile picture (see Figure 2).

Fig. 2. Facial Stimuli

3.3   Procedure

Respondents were led to a Qualtrics survey website after having clicked on the online link. The first page of the survey presented a short overview of the purpose of the study and background of the researchers. Subsequently, the respondents were randomly assigned to one of the six experimental conditions (e.g. with beard versus without beard in combination with one of the three designed jobs). Respondents were forced to look at the job description for at least 20 seconds first (a timer only activated the "next" button after 20 seconds) and at least ten seconds at the LinkedIn profile picture, after which the post experiment questionnaire was activated.

3.4   Measures

The post experiment questionnaire used Ohanian's (1990) seven-point semantic differential scale to measure the perceived credibility of the candidate. The scale consisted of fifteen items, five for each of the three sub-dimensions. The scales for attractiveness, trustworthiness, and expertise were all shown to be sufficiently reliable (Cronbach's alpha = .81, = .91, and = .90 respectively). To measure the intention to invite the candidate for a job interview, a two-item rating scale was adopted from Fishbein and Ajzen (1975). One item measured the strength of the likeliness to invite the job candidate ("If you were a recruiter, how likely is it that you would invite this person to a job interview?"); the second item measured the subjective probability that the inviting behavior would be effectively performed within the next three months ("If a vacancy opens in your office in the next three months, would you invite this candidate for a job interview?"). Both questions were answered using a seven-point Likert scale ranging from 1 (not very likely) to 7 (very likely).

4   Results

Results show that wearing a beard (M = 4.38, SD = .99) versus no beard (M = 4.13, SD = .86) significantly increases a candidate's perceived expertise, $F(1, 215) = 4.01$, $p < .05$. Using Hayes' (2013) method for assessing mediation and moderated mediation effects, this perceived increase in expertise is in turn shown to be significantly related to the likeliness to be invited for a job interview, such that perceived expertise mediates the relationship between beardedness and job interview invitation intentions ($b^* = .133$, 95% CI = .016 - .290). Moreover, findings suggest that this effect is particularly conducive for jobs that are associated with expertise ($b^* = .130$, 95% CI = .015 - .288). For jobs that are related to attractiveness and trust, beardedness did not significantly improve perceived expertise and invitation prospects.

5   Discussion

Our study contributes to research and practice in the following ways. First, although prior research shows that SNSs are increasingly popular recruitment tools, there has been very little empirical research into effective personal branding of job candidates on SNSs [14]. Second, in stark contrast to the attention that Facebook has received from marketing and computer-mediated communication scholars, very little research has been dedicated to professional SNSs such as LinkedIn (cf. 1). Third, from a practical perspective, for jobs seekers today, it is important to know which visual cues in an online profile picture can help create positive impressions on employers, and how these self presentation mechanisms work in relation to different job categories. For instance, depending on the type of job one aims for, it may be wise or unwise to wear a colorful shirt, put on a bow tie – or grow a beard.

A limitation of this study with respect to its external validity relates to the cultural context. For instance, studies in the United States have found that in terms of attractiveness, females preferred men to be clean shaven [5], while studies conducted in Europe indicated that bearded men are perceived as more masculine and attractive [2]. Although Barber (2001) suggests that the biological message that wearing a beard is not bound by history and traverses cultural boundaries, especially in the Western hemisphere, future research should take a more formative approach and investigate whether the results also hold in different cultural contexts, and with different types of beards. Wearing a long beard in, for instance, India, unquestionably conveys a different meaning than wearing a long beard in this study's focal country, the Netherlands. Furthermore, as the implications of this research are restricted to the male gender, we encourage future research to focus on the female equivalent of beardedness. According Terry and Krantz (1993), glasses may have a similar effect on the perceived expertise of females, as do beards for males.

In conclusion, based on this research's findings, we advise those who pursue an academic career to question whether it is wise to shave. Getting rid of your Gillettes may open the door to the job of your dreams!

References

1. Arnold, T.C., Rynes, S.L.: Recruitment and job choice research: Same as it ever was? In: Schmitt, N.W., Highhouse, S., Weiner, I.B. (eds.) Handbook of Psychology, 2nd edn., pp. 104–142. John Wiley & Sons, Hoboken (2013)
2. Barber, N.: Mustache fashion covaries with a good marriage market for women. Journal of Nonverbal Behavior 25(4), 261–272 (2001)
3. De Souza, A.A.L., Baumgasten, V., Baiao, U., Otta, E.: Perception of men's personal qualities and prospect of employment as a function of facial hair. Psychological Reports 92(1), 201–208 (2003)
4. Dixson, B.J., Brooks, R.C.: The role of facial hair in women's perceptions of men's attractiveness, health, masculinity and parenting abilities. Evolution and Human Behavior 34(3), 236–241 (2013)
5. Feinman, S., Gill, G.W.: Females' response to males' beardedness. Perceptual and Motor Skills 44(2), 533–534 (1977)
6. Fishbein, M., Ajzen, I.: Belief, attitude, intention, and behavior: An introduction to theory and research. Addison-Wesley, Reading (1975)
7. Goffman, E.: The presentation of self in everyday life. Garden City, New York (1959)

8. Guido, G., Peluso, A.M., Moffa, V.: Beardedness in advertising: Effects on endorsers' credibility and purchase intention. Journal of Marketing Communication 17(1), 37–49 (2011)
9. Hayes, A.F.: Introduction to Mediation, Moderation, and Conditional Process Analysis: A Regression-Based Approach. The Guilford Press, New York (2013)
10. Jackson, W.C., Bendick, M., Romero, H.J.: Employment discrimination against older workers. Journal of Aging & Social Policy 8(4), 25–46 (1997)
11. Johnston, M.A.: Beard fetish in early modern England. Ashgate Publishing Limited, Farnham (2011)
12. Kamins, M.A.: An investigation into the match-up hypothesis in celebrity advertising:When beauty be only skin deep. Journal of Advertising 19(1), 4–13 (1990)
13. Kluemper, D.H., Rosen, P.A.: Future employment selection methods: evaluating social networking web sites. Journal of Managerial Psychology 24(6), 567–580 (2009)
14. Labrecque, L.I., Markos, E., Milne, G.R.: Online personal branding: Processes, challenges, and implications. Journal of Interactive Marketing 25, 27–50 (2011)
15. Martin, W.W., Gardner, S.N.: The relative effects of eye-gaze and smiling on arousal in asocial situations. The Journal of Psychology 102(2), 253–259 (1979)
16. Misra, S., Beatty, S.E.: Celebrity spokesperson and brand congruence: An assessment of recall and effect. Journal of Business Research 21(2), 159–173 (1990)
17. Muscarella, F., Cunningham, M.R.: The evolutionary significance and social perception of male pattern baldness and facial hair. Ethology and Sociobiology 17(2), 99–117 (1996)
18. Ohanian, R.: Construction and validation of a scale to measure celebrity endorsers' perceived expertise, trustworthiness, and attractiveness. Journal of Advertising 19(3), 39–52 (1990)
19. Petty, R.E., Cacioppo, J.T.: Communication and Persuasion: Central and Peripheral Routes to Attitude Change. Springer, New York (1986)
20. Reed, J., Blunk, E.M.: The influence of facial hair on impression formation. Social Behavior and Personality 18(1), 169–175 (1990)
21. Ruetzler, T., Taylor, J., Reynolds, D., Baker, W.: Understanding perceptions of professional attributes using conjoint analysis. International Journal of Hospitality Management 30(3), 551–557 (2011)
22. Terry, R.L., Krantz, J.H.: Dimensions of trait attributions associated with eyeglasses, men's facial hair, and women's hair length. Journal of Applied Social Psychology 23(21), 1757–1769 (1993)
23. Tobak, S.: Want a great job? Then shave! (September 12, 2012), http://www.cbsnews.com/news/want-a-great-job-then-shave/ (accessed February 7, 2014)
24. Walther, J.B.: Computer-mediated communication: Impersonal, interpersonal and hyperpersonal interaction. Communication Research 23(1), 3–43 (1996)
25. Willemsen, L.M., Neijens, P.C., Bronner, F.: The ironic effect of source identification on the perceived credibility of online product reviewers. Journal of Computer-Mediated Communication 18(1), 16–31 (2012)
26. Woodside, A.G., Davenport, J.W.: The effect of salesman similarity and expertise on consumer purchasing behavior. Journal of Marketing Research 11(2), 198–202 (1974)

Appendix A: Job Vacancies

Job vacancy: attractiveness

Imagine you are a recruiter. As a recruiter, you are searching for a suitable job candidate for the following open vacancy:

<u>Sales Person Fashion Store:</u>

For an international male fashion brand, we are looking for males to promote our fashion clothes at the entrance of our store in Amsterdam. As a Sales Person, your duty will be to welcome and establish the first contact with our customers.

Requirements:

- Representative appearance
- Camera and photo friendly
- Aged between 25-35
- Prior experiences in promotion
- Preferably around 1,80 – 1,90 meters tall

Job vacancy: expertise

Imagine you are a recruiter. As a recruiter, you are searching for a suitable job candidate for the following open vacancy:

<u>Architect at an Architectural Firm</u>

An established architectural firm currently holds a vacant position for an Architect designing new apartment buildings in the North side of Amsterdam. These buildings will rise at the side of the IJ River as a prestigious project where the very upper class of the city is expected to be housed. Candidates will be requested to submit their resume including portfolio to apply for this position.

Requirements:

- a Master's (or equivalent) degree in Architecture
- 7-10 years of experience with architectural design; conceptual thinker
- Expertise in leading residential property development projects from initial design process to property transfer
- Comprehensive technical knowledge of residential building codes
- Computer skills: experience required in 3ds Max and AutoCAD

Job vacancy: trustworthiness

Imagine you are a recruiter. As a recruiter, you are searching for a suitable job candidate for the following open vacancy:

Back Office Cashier at a Bank

For a banking company we are looking for a cashier to work in the back office. As a Back Office Cashier you are responsible for the daily operations and financial security procedures of this bank.

Requirements:

- You must be self-disciplined and reliable
- You will possess two or more years of back office cashier experience at a bank or comparable environment
- You will count money in cash drawers at the beginning of shifts to ensure that amounts are correct and that there is
- adequate change
- You will ensure safe keeping records are all up to date
- You will be trusted with confidential client information

Empowering Users to Explore Subject Knowledge by Aggregating Search Interfaces

I-Chin Wu, Cheng Kao, and Shao-Syuan Chiou

Department of Information Management, Fu-Jen Catholic University
510 Chung Cheng Rd , Hsinchuang, Taipei County 24205 Taiwan
icwu.fju@gmail.com

Abstract. Due to the popularity of link-based applications, one of the most important issues in web searching is how to retrieve information effectively from multiple sources. Consider Wikipedia as an example; users browse content by following hyperlinks from one page to another. A regular hyperlink states that there are some relationships between the two pages. Search engines like Google successfully use this type of information to rank pages in keyword search scenarios. Wikipedia can go even beyond that as a link is interpreted as the semantic relations between two concepts described within articles. Search engines and web-based, free-content encyclopedias have become key tools for finding and extracting useful information from the tremendous amounts of data that are available online. We extended our previous application, *WNavi^s*, by integrating the search function with the term and semantic path suggestion techniques for aggregated searches. Note that research into aggregated searches (integrated searches) addresses the issues of presenting to users a result list with information from various websites and media types. Accordingly, the *WikiMap^#* application, extended from our previous application, *WNavi^s*, was developed. Finally, we proposed our preliminary research design and extended evaluation measures in this study.

Keywords: Aggregated Search, Interactive Information Retrieval, Information Visualization, Semantic Paths.

1   Introduction

Search engines and web-based, free-content encyclopedias have become key tools for finding and extracting useful information from the tremendous amounts of data that are available online. Recently, the interfaces of IR systems (IRs) with various types of information visualization (IV) tools have been designed to help users search and explore information from the Web, digital libraries, etc. more effectively [7]. Research into aggregated searches (integrated searches) addresses the issue of presenting users with a result list with information from various websites and media types [14].

In this study, the *WikiMap^#* application, extended from our previous application, *WNavi^s*, was developed by integrating the search function for aggregated search results from multiple information sources. The *WikiMap^#* application consists of two

F.F.-H. Nah (Ed.): HCIB/HCII 2014, LNCS 8527, pp. 266–276, 2014.
© Springer International Publishing Switzerland 2014

IV tools: a topic network (TN) and a topic-based hierarchy tree (HT). In addition, it has a search tool with term suggestions. Generally, the interactions between the user and the different IV tools in the provided interfaces depend on the user's knowledge and the tasks and goals. Additional recent studies regarding the evaluation of HCIR systems have shifted focus to the perspective of the search process, which includes user engagement [11], time-based gain [1], and learning as a function of exploration time [13]. Marchionini (2006) [10] points out that there is an emerging demand for designing interactive user interfaces with the lessons from human information behavior to create the new types of search systems. He calls the new field human-computer information retrieval (HCIR). That is, information retrieval (IR) and human-computer interaction (HCI) are related fields that aim to help users explore the large scale of Web data and continuously control the search process. In recent years, the interactive IR (IIR), which focuses on users' behaviors and their interactions with systems and information, has become an important issue in IR [9].

Actually, establishing a set of reliable metrics is an emerging topic in interactive studies that could be critical to the development of effective HCIR [16][18]. However, there are only a few existing studies that examine the extent to how the use of each IV support tool and multiple information sources has contributed to successful exploration of subject knowledge from aggregated search results. Vakkari et al. (2010) [16] point out that the goals of the IIR or HCIR system should be identified initially so that the measurement for evaluating system-provided features can then be inferred from those goals. Based on the introduction of research backgrounds, we will define the goal and the outputs and outcomes of the tools and design search tasks for measurement of whether the proposed tools can guide users toward attaining the goals during the search process [16][21]. The outputs are the products delivered by the search tool, and the outcomes are the benefits the search tool provides to the user [15]. Evaluating only the outputs is insufficient to reflect the aims of the search tools and explain the search behaviors of the users [6] [16]. We will also consider the outcomes provided by the tools of the system, or conceptualizing differently, the benefits searchers derive by using the tools observed.

2   WikiMap#: The Aggregated Search Interface

2.1   The Interfaces with Associated Tools

We developed two interfaces: *WNavi*^{s}, and *WikiMap*$^#$. The *WNavi*^{s} application consists of three IV tools: a topic network (TN), a topic-based hierarchy tree (HT), and topic summaries [20]. The *WikiMap*$^#$ application consists of two IV tools: a TN, and a topic-based HT. In addition, it has an integrated search function with term and semantic path suggestions. The tools and the information sources for each interface are shown in Table I.

IV Tools in Both Interfaces: We propose a link strength-based (LS-based) hybrid measure, i.e., an internal link-based semantic topic network analysis measure for con structing a topic network with stronger semantic relationships. We utilized the

Table 1. IV Tools and Information Sources for Each Interface

	Wikipedia.com	WNavi[s]	WikiMap[#]
Tools	None	Topic Map (TM), Hierarchy Tree (HT)	Topic Map (TM), Hierarchy Tree (HT), Google Search with Term Suggestion, Semantic Path Suggestion
Information Sources	Articles on Wikipedia	Articles on Wikipedia	Articles on Wikipedia, Web pages

Normalized Google Distance algorithm [4] to quantify the strength of the semantic relationships between articles in the topic network via key terms. The goal of the topic map (TM) tool is to help users find the major concepts of a topic and identify relationships between these major concepts easily. Furthermore, we aim to group articles in order to generate a hierarchy tree (HT) based on the structure of the topic network. Technically, we employed the *k-clique* technique of the cohesive measure, i.e., in the social network analysis (SNA) to cluster the articles of the topic network. To help users search for information, the interface applies centrality-based and cohesive measures in the SNA to highlight the important nodes of the TM. Accordingly, two IV tools—a TM, and a topic-based HT—are developed in the proposed applications.

The Search Tool with Additional Suggestion Functions in the *WikiMap*[#] Interface: To support users in searching for needed information, the interface will give the suggested terms, suggested semantic paths, and then revise the queries based on the users' feedback behaviors. To integrate the *WikiMap*[#] with the search function, we use Google AJAX Search API to implement the search function. It first obtains users' initial queries, sends them to the search API, and in turn receives more search results from web pages to present to the user. In addition, the system will offer the term suggestion function to help users revise queries. To take advantage of the relevance feedback (RF) technique for better term suggestion, we will adopt the RF algorithm to calculate the weights of terms for iterative query reformulation. With regard to the semantic paths mining and suggestions, we will utilize the constrained-based spreading activation (CSA) process to mine and infer upon the semantic paths of the network. We will measure the strength of the explicit and implicit relationships between two objects on Wikipedia by considering three factors: distance, degree, and topic. We will explore how the interactive search technique with the aid of the terms and semantic path suggestion process might help users search for subject knowledge precisely and efficiently. We will evaluate the effects of aggregating search results for helping users to search subject knowledge. For example, we may determine specifically-whether some of the information sources are suitable at a particular information-seeking stage, e.g., Wikipedia as an introductory source in the early stages of information seeking.

2.2   The WikiMap[#] Interface

The *WikiMap*[#] interface provides the topic map (TM), which is generated from articles of Wikipedia, as shown in Figure 1(a). The TM uses the yellow node as the center to the outside, although the links and nodes can extend to a variety of subthemes.

Searchers can drag the TM by using the mouse to zoom in or zoom out of the map and can click the related nodes to open the articles. In addition, there is a topic hierarchy tree (HT) in the second tab which is constructed based on the topology analysis of the TM, as shown in Figure 1(b). We use the tabs to change the two IV tools, i.e., TM and HT. In the third tab, we embed a browser for showing the Wikipedia website. In the *WikiMap#* interface, we integrate the search tool. For the search function, the system will automatically send the query to the Google search API and retrieve sixteen promoted search results, including the title and abstract, back to users, as shown in the right part of Figures 1(a) or 1(b). Moreover, we have term and path suggestions based on the search results in the presented interface. We introduce the techniques in the following sections.

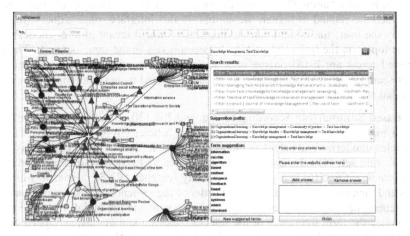

Fig. 1. (a): A snapshot of the interface with a topic map and the search function

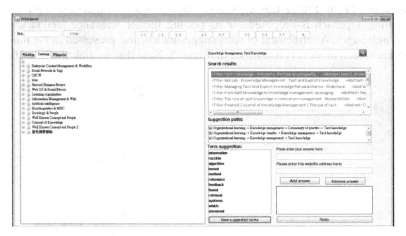

Fig. 2. (b): A snapshot of the interface with a hierarchy tree and the search function

3   Empowering the Search Process: Term and Path Suggestions

3.1   The Social Network Analysis-Based Term Suggestion Process

Users usually use simple and short queries in their search tasks. Generally, they could not completely express their information needs by queries or by selecting the options provided from the systems. Thus, we ought to provide term suggestion service for assisting users engaged in the search tasks. Term suggestion could help users refine queries and find the needed information via a series of relevance feedback processes. For example, if users want to search for "Jaguar animal," but they use only "Jaguar" as their initial query, the system lists a series of results about "Jaguar cars." However, according to the system with the function of term suggestions, users would be prompted to enter "animal" to revise the original query; then they could have the results which are related to Jaguar, the animal. In this interface, once a query (topic) is given by the user, the system can automatically infer relevant articles (nodes) for a specific topic via the link relationships between nodes in the topic network. Then the suggested terms are listed on the interface for assisting the user in conducting the further search process. Note that the terms are extracted from summaries of important nodes that are relevant to the specific topic.

SNA-Based Summaries: According to Wu, and Lin (2012) [20], the steps for generating a summary are: (1) pre-process the source articles (from Wikipedia); (2) parse the articles into terms and calculate the weight of each term; (3) select the terms based on the feature set; (4) calculate the sentence scores; (5) generate summaries from the top-N sentences; and (6) apply relevant novelty sentence (RNS) metrics to filter sentences and then resort them based on the order of the sentences in the original articles. After generating the summaries, we used them to generate the initial suggested terms. We counted the term frequency of the selected relevant summaries, and listed out the top ten terms as initial suggested terms. The details of an SNA-based article summarization technique can be found in [20].

SNA-Based Term Suggestions: Accordingly, a query expansion with a term reweighting approach is proposed for supporting further relevance feedback on retrieved web pages. A refinement of term suggestions is also presented in the interface. The entire search process is illustrated in Figure 2. Note that we link the *WikiMap*[#] -

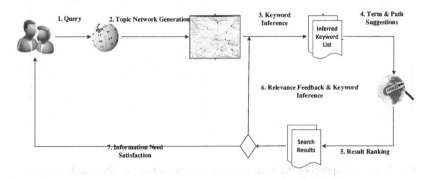

Fig. 3. Search process with the aid of SNA-based term suggestions

application with the Terrie information retrieval platform. Terrie is a robust open source software for large scale IR projecta as well as a state-of-the-art test-bed for research and experimentation in the IR area [12]. We will utilize the Language Model and query expansion classes offered by the Terrier IR system to do the index and retrieve tasks. Figure 2 shows the overview of the search process with RF function. Operationally, the users give the initial query in Wikipedia, and the system generates a topic network for the specified topic and then utilizes the summaries to infer a list of keywords. These keywords are used for term suggestions to help users revise queries. The system would take the keyword that users have chosen to the search module, and the module would take advantage of the Google search engine and return more information back to the users iteratively. We utilized the query expansion (QE) class supported by the Terrier IR platform to suggest terms, i.e., the terms with high weights for each run of query expansion. By doing so, the user would find needed information by interaction with the system.

3.2   The CSA-Based Path Suggestions

Identifying user information needs is a challenge and critical task for an interactive search. Term suggestion is one of the IR techniques to help users refine queries and may provide comprehensive aids for users if the suggested terms are well organized. In this study, we further propose the idea of path suggestions to help users understand the relationship between terms via articles. Thus, we propose a subject knowledge inference approach for identifying nodes with strong semantic relationships in subject-oriented, encyclopedia-based semantic networks. We utilize the constrained-based spreading activation (CSA) process to infer from the semantic paths of the network [5]. Accordingly, a CSA-based framework will be constructed for finding semantic paths from the topic network. We will focus on measuring relationships between pairs of objects (i.e., article pages) on the topic network constructed from page articles on Wikipedia. Both the direct and implicit relationships between articles on Wikipedia are identified. The explicit relationship means there is a direct link between the two articles. The implicit relationship is represented by a link structure containing two objects [22]. An implicit relationship may consist of many strong explicit relationships. We will measure the strength of explicit and implicit relationships between two objects on Wikipedia by three factors: distance, degree, and topic, based on the operations of a CSA process. That is, we will explore if these three factors can improve the quality of the inference results when compared to the baseline (SA) approach.

Wikipedia consists of a set of articles and hyperlinks among which can be expressed as a topic network (V, E). That is, we define the Wikipedia topic network as that whose vertices are articles of Wikipedia and whose edges are links between articles. Basically, V is a set of objects (articles) and an edge $(v, v) \in E$ exists if and only if object $v \in$ V. Furthermore, if the topic network with path flow TP=$\{$ V,E, s, ω, $\delta\}$ is the topic network (V, E) with the starting point $s \in$ V, the weight ω between articles that are derived from the link strength (LS) value. After the cycles of activation process, each node will be updated its own activation value, δ. We focus on the concepts of the proposed CSA-based approach to infer from the semantic paths of the network but skip the detail of the operation process of the approach due to the limitation of pages. As we stated previously, we consider three factors, which are distance, degree, and topics, in this preliminary study. We introduce the rationale for having the three factors briefly below.

- **Distance Factor:** The longer the distance between two objects, the weaker the relationship between the source and the destination nodes. Thus, we design a distance decay function to degrade the importance of the nodes which are far away from the starting node of the path.
- **Degree Factor:** The path will become small if a popular object exists in a path. We consider the outlink of the object. If an article has too many outlinks, it could be an index article. Thus, we design a decay function to degrade its importance within the path.
- **Topic Factor:** We consider that if the two nodes are within the same topic, they will have a higher level of relationship. Thus, we design the "topic grow" parameter to increase the relationship between nodes.

By considering the three factors, we believe that mining elucidatory objects and representing the results in paths will help users explore relationships between concepts. The extended experiments for evaluating the methods will be conducted in our future works.

4   The Research Design and the Extended Evaluation Measures

4.1   The Research Design

We want to evaluate whether the two proposed interfaces, *WNavi^s*, and *WikiMap$^#$*, help participants to find more precise answers compared to the traditional Wikipedia interface. In the task design, all the search tasks are related to Knowledge Management (KM) and Information Retrieval (IR). There are four kinds of tasks designed to reflect the aims of the constructed navigation tools for Wikipedia. We could not lean on standardized search tasks; therefore, we inferred the tasks from the goals of the tools designed. Thus, we follow our recent research to do research design [21].

Tasks 1 and 2 are designed to measure if the users can (1) identify the relationship between concepts correctly and in a timely manner (Tasks 1 and 2). We examine both direct (explicit) and indirect (implicit) relationships between the concepts. The explicit relationship means that the users can find the answers via the main page or the links on the main page. The implicit relationship means that the users cannot find the answers directly from the main page or that the users can find the answers via the main page or the links of the main page. Tasks 3 and 4 are designed to investigate whether the proposed tool (2) supports users in finding correct answers (Tasks 3 and 4). The visual organization tool with additional content information in the developed interface aims to help users gain topical knowledge via the links. Our optimal goal is to help searchers to learn more about the topic with the aid of these tools.

Identifying user information needs is a challenge and critical task for an interactive search. In this study, we aim to find out to what extent the use of the navigation support tools contribute to successful exploration of topics. That is, the outputs and outcomes of the proposed tools in *WNavi*[s] and *WikiMap*[#] will be evaluated [15]. We suppose that the outcome of the developed tools is the users' increased ability to identify more relationships between important concepts in a shorter amount of time and an increase in their topical knowledge. The output will be improved correctness of answers. In summary, the expected outcomes of *WNavi*[s] and *WikiMap*[#] compared to the traditional Wikipedia interface are:

Less Time for Identifying Relationships between Important Concepts Correctly (Outcome 1): If the participants use less time to find the answers via the developed tools, this time period indicates that the tool helps them identify more efficiently the relationship between concepts.

Higher Gain for Identifying Relationships between Important Concepts (Outcome 2): We define the metric gain as Eq. (1). That is, we measure how much cost will receive the benefits via the interface to identify relationships between important concepts. If the participants achieve higher gain via the interface, it indicates that the IV tools or the search tool can help them to identify relationships between important concepts to get more correct answers in an efficient way.

$$\text{Gain} = Score \ / \ Time \ cost \tag{1}$$

Fewer Traversal Articles (Shorter Path, Outcome 3): The shorter the path to find the answers, the more effective it is to find the relationship between important concepts with the help of the tools.

Less Time for Finding Topical Knowledge Correctly (Outcome 4): If the participants use less time to find the answers to the set of questions that are related to a topic by using the developed tools, the time indicates that the tools help in finding topical knowledge more rapidly. In addition, the participants have an overview of the subtopics for a KM or IR topic, which supports faster growth of topical knowledge and, therefore, faster arrival at correct answers.

Higher Gain for Finding Topical Knowledge (Outcome 5): Similar to outcome 2, we measure how much cost will receive the benefits via the interfaces to find topical knowledge. If the participants achieve higher gain via the interfaces, it indicates that the IV tools or search tool help them to find topical knowledge more efficiently and gain it in more effective ways.

Time Use and the Scores of Correct Answers Are Indicators of the Learning of topical Knowledge and, Therefore, the Construing of a Correct Answer (Outcome 6): Since we provide visual organizations of the articles for topical knowledge, we expect that they help users to learn the topic during exploration and, therefore, construe a correct answer.

4.2   The Evaluation Process

The evaluation process included a pretest, selection of subjects, task execution on interfaces, a post–questionnaire, and the tagging and coding of usage behavior. It is introduced as below.

Pretest and Selecting Subjects: Each subject's English proficiency should be above average. The English abilities were measured according to the scores of TOEIC, TOEFL, or entry examination of a university in Taiwan. We asked them about their experiences using Wikipedia and their confidence level in searching for information. In addition, all of the subjects should have taken or are taking KM or IR courses.

Task Execution for Interface Evaluations: Thirty participants at the Department of Information Management at Fu-Jen Catholic University (Taipei) perform the search tasks during the evaluation. To make sure participants understand how to use the new interface with multi-functions, we set a "Practice" button for them so that they could use the interface during the tutorial process. The whole evaluation process, including the tutorial, took about one hour to complete. We assigned the interface randomly to each participant for accomplishing the assigned tasks (topics). Note that we monitored the users' on-screen behaviors and keyboard/mouse inputs during the search process through Morae software. It facilitates the observation of usage behaviors in each tool of the interface. Moreover, We will adopt zero-order state transition matrices and maximal repeating patterns (MRP) to analyze users' sequences of moves made by searchers [19].

Search Behaviors Tagging and Analyzing: At the end of the evaluation, subjects were asked to fill out a questionnaire. Finally, we tag every subject's behaviors during the task performance according to the event coding sheet, as shown in Table 2. We analyzed the frequencies of using each tool in the interface and record the search time. The progress of their search behaviors were recorded as video files. We will analyze how the users adopt the IV tools and the search tool to find the answers and how these actions connect to their task performance.

Table 2. The coding sheet

10 subjects for each interface	Interfaces: *Wikipedia* / *WNavi^s* / *WikiMap$^#$*	
Events	**Frequency**	**Time (Sec.)**
Wikipedia, *WNavi^s* ,*WikiMap$^+$*		
Use Internal Links		
Web Page Opening		
WNavi^s ,WikiMap$^+$		
Use Topic Map (Zoom in and Zoom out the network)		
Click the Topic Node to Open an Article		
Click the Class Tree to Open an Article		
WikiMap$^+$		
Use the Search Tool		
Click Search Result		
Browse Search Result		
Use Blue-Node Topic to Generate Suggested Terms		
Use Suggested Terms		
Use Suggested Paths		
Average Keywords		

Post-questionnaires: We asked the particintpas to describe their experiences after having used the three interfaces to perform the assigned tasks. Basically, we designed the questions to reflect our expected outcome of the developed interfaces compared to the traditional Wikipedia. We designed the questions to measure the effectiveness and usefulness of the systems. We utilized Kelly et al.'s (2008)[9] and Wu and Vakkari's (2014) [21] studies to design the questionnaire from the three aspects of ease of use, effectiveness, and satisfaction. Then we adopted Bron et al.'s (2013) [3] work to evaluate the search effectiveness of the $WikiMap^{\#}$ interface.

5   Conclusions and Future Works

In this study, we extended our previous application, $WNavi^s$, by integrating the search function for aggregated search results from multiple information sources. Accordingly, the $WikiMap^{\#}$ application, extended from our previous application, was developed. We aimed to design the interactive, task-based evaluation method to discover to what extent the use of navigation support tools contributed to successful exploration of topics. To evaluate the effectiveness of the proposed interface, we designed a series of user-oriented search tasks and proposed the extended evaluation measures to examine how the developed tools support exploratory searching. A series of evaluations were conducted based on the user-oriented search tasks and the extended evaluation measures. In the future, we will analyze the evaluation results. Furthermore, we will explore how the level of the learner's subject knowledge influences the search process and task outcome and how this is connected to the developed information visualization (IV) tools and the search tool, and then we will aggregate the search results for successful searches.

References

1. Baskaya, F., Keskustalo, H., Järvelin, K.: Time Drives Interaction: Simulating Sessions in Diverse Searching Environments. In: Proceeding 35th International ACM SIGIR Conference on Research and Development in Information Retrieval, pp. 105–114 (2012)
2. Borlund, P.: Experimental Components for the Evaluation of Interactive Information Retrieval Systems. Journal of Documentation 56(1), 71–90 (2000)
3. Bron, M., Gorp, J., Nack, F., Baltussen, L.-B., Rijke, M.: Aggregated Search Interface Preferences in Multi-session Search Tasks. In: Proceeding 36th International ACM SIGIR Conference on Research and Development in Information Retrieval, pp. 123–132 (2013)
4. Cilibrasi, R.L., Vitányi, P.M.B.: The Google Similarity Distance. IEEE Transactions on Knowledge and Data Engineering 19(3), 370–383 (2007)
5. Crestani, F.: Application of Spreading Activation Techniques in Information Retrieval. Artificial Intelligence Review 11, 453–482 (1997)
6. Järvelin, K.: Explaining user performance in information retrieval: Challenges to IR evaluation. In: Azzopardi, L., Kazai, G., Robertson, S., Rüger, S., Shokouhi, M., Song, D., Yilmaz, E. (eds.) ICTIR 2009. LNCS, vol. 5766, pp. 289–296. Springer, Heidelberg (2009)

7. Julien, C.-A., Leide, J.E., Bouthillier, F.: Controlled User Evaluations of Information Visualization Interfaces for Text Retrieval: Literature Review and Meta-Analysis. Journal of the American Society for Information Science and Technology 59(6), 1012–1024 (2008)
8. Kelly, D., Harper, D.J., Landau, B.: Questionnaire Mode Effects in Interactive Information Retrieval Experiments. Information Processing & Management 44(1), 122–141 (2008)
9. Marchionini, G.: Toward Human–Computer Information Retrieval. Bulletin of the American Society for Information Science 32(5), 20–22 (2006)
10. O'Brien, H.L., Toms, E.G.: The Development and Evaluation of a Survey to Measure User Engagement. Journal of the American Society for Information Science and Technology 61(1), 50–69 (2009)
11. Ounis, I., Amati, G., Plachouras, V., He, B., Macdonald, C., Lioma, C.: Terrier: A High Performance and Scalable Information Retrieval Platform. In: Proceedings of ACM SIGIR 2006 Workshop on Open Source Information Retrieval OSIR, Washington, USA (2006)
12. Rao, R., Card, S.K.: The Table Lens: Merging Graphical and Symbolic Representations in an Interactive Focus + Context Visualization for Tabular Information. In: Proceedings of ACM SIGCHI, pp. 318–322 (1994)
13. Sushmita, S., Lalmas, M., Tombros, A.: Using Digest Pages to Increase User Result Space: Preliminary Designs. In: SIGIR 2008 Workshop on Aggregated Search, Singapore
14. Vakkari, P.: Exploratory Searching as Conceptual Exploration. In: Proceedings of the 4th Workshop on Human-Computer Interaction and Information Retrieval (HCIR 2010), New Brunswick, N.J, pp. 24–27 (2010)
15. Vakkari, P., Kekäläinen, J.: An Evaluation Methodology Reflecting the Aims of Search Tools. In: Proceedings of the TPDL 2011 Workshop on User Oriented Evaluation of Digital Library Interfaces, Berlin, pp. 1-9 (2011)
16. White, R.W., Jose, J.M., Ruthven, I.G.: A Task-oriented Study on the Influencing Effects of Query-biased Summarization in Web Searching. Information Processing & Management 39(5), 707–733 (2003)
17. White, R.W., Capra, R.G., Golovchinsky, G., Kules, B., Smith, C.L., Tunkelang, D.: Introduction to Special Issue on Human-Computer Information Retrieval. Information Processing and Management 49(5), 1053–1057 (2013)
18. Wildemuth, B.-M.: The Effects of Domain Knowledge on Search Tactic Formulation. Journal of the American Society for Information Science and Technology 55, 246–258 (2004)
19. Wu, I.-C., Lin, Y.-S.: WNavi^s: Navigating Wikipedia Semantically with an SNA-based Summarization Technique. Decision Support Systems 54(1), 46–62 (2012)
20. Wu, I.-C., Vakkari, P.: Supporting Navigation in Wikipedia by Information Visualization: Extended Evaluation Measures. Journal of Documentation 70(3) (2014)
21. Zhang, X., Asano, Y., Yoshikawa, M.: A Generalized Flow-Based Method for Analysis of Implicit Relationships on Wikipedia. IEEE Transactions on Knowledge and Data Engineering 25(2), 246–259 (2013)

Mobile and Ubiquitous Commerce

Follow-Me: Smartwatch Assistance
on the Shop Floor

Mario Aehnelt and Bodo Urban

Fraunhofer IGD, Joachim-Jungius-Str. 11, 18059 Rostock, Germany
{mario.aehnelt,bodo.urban}@igd-r.fraunhofer.de

Abstract. The growing complexity of manufacturing calls for new approaches to support the human workforce with situation-aware information and tools which in consequence ease the process of understanding and applying work related knowledge. With this paper we introduce a theoretical model for a systematic information transfer between assistance system and worker. It defines assistance objectives and reviews the role of artifacts during the assistance process focusing on the cognitive aspects of work. Our approach was implemented using smartwatches for application in industrial assembly environments extending the Plant@Hand manufacturing performance support system.

1 Introduction

In manufacturing we are facing a dynamic work environment and continuously changing work conditions. Streamlining production processes means here to streamline information processes in order to increase not only efficiency but also manufacturing flexibility. Novel interaction and information devices, for example *smartwatches* or similar wearable technologies, allow us the design of completely new assistance systems for a manufacturing environment, specifically for the shop floor.

The paper introduces our concept of *follow-me assistance* which uses a combination of smartwatches and mobile as well as stationary computer displays to guide the worker situation-aware through his work day and through single assembly work tasks. Follow-me uses smartwatches as a means for providing awareness displays, information assistance, interaction opportunities and activity recognition.

With our approach we focus on assisting by improving information processes which finally influence the workers awareness and understanding, and thus work performance.

2 Related Work

With a continuously growing complexity of manufacturing data we witness new challenges in order to work efficiently with this data on all operational levels.

F.F.-H. Nah (Ed.): HCIB/HCII 2014, LNCS 8527, pp. 279–287, 2014.
© Springer International Publishing Switzerland 2014

Emerging assistance technologies address specific scopes. With a semantic enrichment of data and manufacturing information systems [1] propose smarter data logistics which are required to improve the management of manufacturing data. In addition, novel approaches, such as the *cognitive factory*, combine a high degree of self-organization and automation with the individual strengths and flexibility of the human workforce [2]. Although manufacturing efficiency and intelligence grows, it still requires information assistance which integrates manual work into the automated smart factory. Here we can found our work on long-term research which focuses on assisting workers with information and tools helping to understand work tasks and improving work performance and quality. Studies show a direct influence of systematic information assistance and the outcome of work processes. For example, Kokkalis et al. [3] could demonstrate that people provided with generated work instructions completed their tasks more quickly than people without it. Known assistance solutions bring together work related data and documents (e.g. construction plans, assembly manuals or videos) from the product design phase with production work plans, or they analyze work results in order to find quality issues.

3   Approach

Follow-me is founded on a theoretical model which describes the information transfer between assistance system and worker through the use of artifacts. This model helps us to understand the implications and limits of assistance technologies. It consists of:

- hierarchical *information objectives* which define the degree of required information and tool assistance,
- *assistance artifacts* which mediate both information and tool between assistance system and worker, and
- a formal *process model* which describes the dependency of information, knowledge and work process as well as the transitions of data, information, knowledge and the work product.

The next sections introduce basic concepts of our theoretical model followed by describing our approach in more detail.

3.1   Objectives

Similar to formal education processes, information assistance can be understood as an informal way of learning facts (*what*), procedures (*how*) and concepts (*why*) required for a specific task. Here we can apply Bloom's taxonomy of educational objectives [4] and their revision by Anderson and Krathwohl [5] which lead us to more general knowledge objectives with respect to the cognitive processing of information: *remember*, *understand*, *apply*, *analyze*, *evaluate* and *create*. At least the first four objectives are hierarchical. Thus, the objective *apply* includes both objectives *remember* and *understand* for example. They describe basic competences to be achieved by systematic information assistance. In table 1 we show how educational objectives can be applied to the manufacturing work domain for structuring the information process, defining assistance goals and deriving assisting information and tools.

Table 1. Application of educational objectives for supporting assembly tasks

Objective	Description	Example
Remember	memorize and repeat the information	remember a work instruction and tools as well as material to be used
Understand	summarize, re-structure and reproduce the information	understand the sequence of assemble steps of an instruction
Apply	use the information in a new situation	execute the work instruction to assemble in described order using correct tools and material
Analyze	deconstruct and compare the information e.g. for problem solving	adjust the assembly order in case of a modified construction part
Evaluate	review and judge the information	examine the practicability of a new assembly sequence
Create	produce new information from information	define a practical assembly sequence for a new construction design

Depending on specific work situations and the work tasks to be carried out the assistance system needs to vary information objectives in order to provide the worker with required information and tool assistance. Both can be based on assistance artifacts which are introduced with the next section.

3.2   Assistance Artifacts

Each technological system which provides assistance to a user works through the mediation of support by using physical or virtual tools and representations - *artifacts*. In literature, there can be found a wide range of research addressing the nature and role of artifacts in human computer interaction. Bødker and Klokmose [6] give us here a very detailed overview on the lifecycle, dynamics and ecologies of artifacts while focusing on the relationship with human activities. Following their definition, we understand assistance artifacts as any tool or representation which is used as a *mediator* for the purpose of assisting the user. In manufacturing such assistance artifacts can be work orders describing the tasks to be done, additional documents (e.g. construction plans, assembly guides), annotations on material to be used, the work tools themselves, or machine displays with progress details. Even a component to be built mediates information about its' current configuration and assembly state. It depends on the abilities of a worker to perceive, understand and interpret the given information correctly.

Each artifact is used to provide awareness about required information pieces or to support the operational execution of single work tasks. The more artifacts are designed to fulfill a specific assistance purpose within the context of work, the better they integrate with existing work processes and the easier they can be applied by the worker. Thus, it is important to know work context and situation in detail in order to provide suitable tools and representations, especially in dynamic work environments with changing conditions.

3.3   Process Model

We must understand that an effective work process requires first the successful acquisition, interpretation and application of work related information including organizational collection, filtering and provision of data sources [7]. Each physical work activity implies cognitive activities in order to consume and apply available information to the work task.

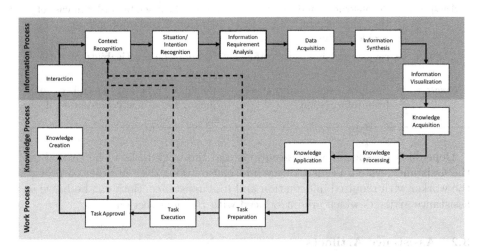

Fig. 1. Simplified assistance process model combining information, knowledge and work processes

We use the relationship between physical and cognitive work in order to design an *assistance process* (see Fig. 1) which provides the worker with required information and influences both his knowledge and work processes and subsequently his work performance. The process model focuses on the information transfer between assistance system and worker. Within the information process *data* from heterogeneous sources is collected, filtered and processed in order to create a situation adequate representation. Then, this *information* is transfered from assistance system to the worker using suitable artifacts. Once it is perceived by the worker, the knowledge process starts, beginning with acquiring and processing *knowledge* from the given information. It ends when the worker is able to apply the knowledge to a work task. The work process consists of preparing the work task, executing it and approving the *work product*. New findings or conclusions from the work process lead to new knowledge which is finally feed back to the information process through an interaction with the assistance system. In parallel, a context recognition acquires data from the interaction or from the ongoing work process for a following situation and intention recognition which is the basis for the information requirement analysis.

The assistance model in Fig. 1 shows a simplified circular sequence of process steps which reproduce the technological and cognitive information transfer between assistance system and worker. There are also direct connections between work steps and information process steps. They illustrate the continuous analysis of work situations by the assistance system.

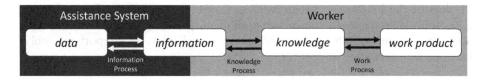

Fig. 2. Transition process of data, information and knowledge between information, knowledge and work processes

The assistance process causes transitions between data, information, knowledge and the work product (see Fig. 2). While an assistance system can only support transitions between data and information, the worker's cognitive processing transfers information into knowledge and through the application of knowledge into a work product. This shows in consequence the need for efficient and effective information processes which finally influence the quality of knowledge and work processes. Here, it is our intention to enrich the information process and assistance artifacts with *contextual information* in order to ease the workers' perception, cognitive processing and application of information and thus to improve his work performance. The next section introduces the assistance design which is derived from our theoretical approach.

4 Assistance Design

In manufacturing we find similar conditions on the shop floor in comparison to ambient assisted living homes. Although the work environment is normally more dirty and noisy, the worker is in continuous movement and not restricted to a single workplace. This leads to situations in which assistance artifacts need to be allocated close to the worker in order to allow an interaction or visualization. Computer terminals can already be found in each assembly group or line. They are used to provide access to work related documents (e.g. work plans, construction details, machine programs). However, with *follow-me* we aim to be much closer to the worker and his surrounding work environment, close enough to assist him while he assembles a complex machine. For this reason, we concentrate on an accompanying form of information assistance at the workplace which:

- *keeps aware* of the changing physical and virtual work environment including information updates,
- *filters and visualizes* required information for current and upcoming work tasks,
- *balances* the information amount and level of detail to avoid cognitive overload situations, and
- *recognizes* work situations in order to improve the quality of the information demand analysis.

Novel developments in general and wearable devices in particular allow us the design of assistance artifacts which stimulate the information transfer and can be worn even at the workplace. We use *smartwatches* in combination with additional displays at the interface between assistance system and worker. They allow us a non-obtrusive work assistance using familiar technologies. Fig. 3 shows the abstract sequence of information and interaction displays to support assembly tasks on a smartwatch.

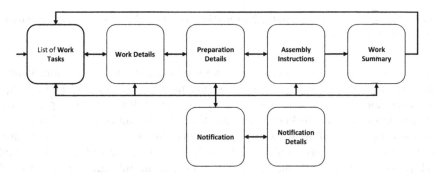

Fig. 3. Information design for smartwatch based assembly assistance

The assistance user interface is designed to provide following assisting functions:

- *awareness display:* emerging occurrences (e.g. new work tasks, incidents) in the work environment which have an impact on the worker or his current and upcoming work tasks are brought to attention by the smartwatch allowing him to align his own activities accordingly.
- *information assistance:* for each work task related manufacturing data, required information and work instructions are collected as well as presented adapted to the given work situation on the smartwatch and an alternative display.
- *interaction:* the smartwatch is used as the main interaction device for working with the assistance system reducing the distraction from work tasks. Hand gestures control the visualization of information (e.g. construction models) or allow simple commands and feedback.

- *activity recognition:* the worker's progress and activities are monitored by collecting and interpreting data from his interaction with the assistance system and acceleration data from the smartwatch (bodily movements).

With *follow-me* we propose an *interaction design* using the metaphor of step-by-step guidance. Work tasks and instructions are generated by the assistance system in advance. It then transfers the information to the worker on two different levels. On *macro-level* the worker is made aware of planned work tasks and occurrences in his work environment which influence his own planning, on *micro-level* he finds step-by-step instructions and related information on how to carry out a single assembly step. Depending on the *work situation* (e.g. task, urgency, impact), *information* to be provided (e.g. instruction, construction plan, how-to media) and the available work *environment* (e.g. tools, displays), we automate the virtual information preparation and physical information distribution at the workplace. Thus, the information follows from one workplace to another not only through the smartwatch, but also by delivering it on additional available displays there.

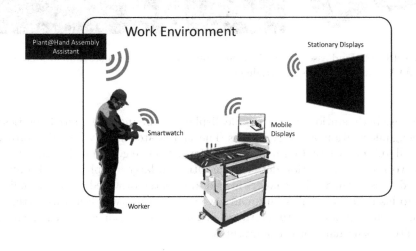

Fig. 4. Schematic setting of industrial application scenario

5   Industrial Application

Our proposed follow-me assistance approach was implemented using different smartwatches (Metawatch STRATA, Sony Smartwatch) as an functional addition to the *Plant@Hand* manufacturing performance support system [8]. The *Plant@Hand Assembly Assistant* collects information from the work environment and distributes required visualizations to the smartwatch an available displays (see Fig. 4).

From analyzing sensory input we make estimations on current activities of the worker and a forecast on his next intended work step. This is the basis for displaying helpful assembly information (construction details, assembly instructions, etc.) in his physical environment. In [9] we describe the formal models and our technological approach for this situation aware information provision in more detail.

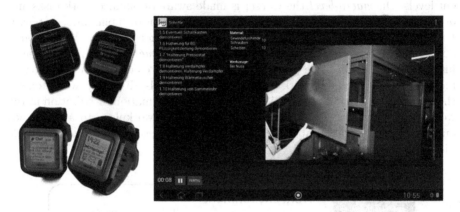

Fig. 5. Plant@Hand assembly assistance application on Sony Smartwatch, Metawatch STRATA (left) and on display (right)

We use both, stationary and mobile displays to enhance the limited abilities of showing information on smartwatches. The smartwatch display is used to provide a small subset of situation-dependent information (e.g. planned start time of next work task, instruction detail) in addition to larger displays which provide more details. If the worker changes his workplace, the provided assistance follows him to his next location. Additionally, we use the smartwatch in this setting as main interaction device with information. Thus, information can be changed and submitted using hand or touch gestures.

6   Conclusions and Future Work

The Plant@Hand Assembly Assistant was designed to support all assistance objectives as described in section 3.1. It supports the step-by-step instruction of single assembly steps as well as the creation of new assembly sequences. Both smartwatch and additional display can be understood as maim assistance artifact used for the information transfer between assistance system and worker which follows our introduced process model (section 3.3). Further work is required to evaluate the influence of our proposed assistance methodology on the overall work performance in comparison to alternative approaches.

References

1. Li, S., Qiao, L. (eds.): Ontology-based modeling of manufacturing information and its semantic retrieval. In: 2012 IEEE 16th International Conference on Computer Supported Cooperative Work in Design, CSCWD (2012)
2. Zaeh, M.F., Ostgathe, M., Geiger, F., Reinhart, G.: Adaptive job control in the cognitive factory. In: ElMaraghy, H.A. (ed.) Enabling Manufacturing Competitiveness and Economic Sustainability, pp. 10–17. Springer, Heidelberg (2012)
3. Kokkalis, N., Köhn, T., Huebner, J., Lee, M., Schulze, F., Klemmer, S.R.: Taskgenies: Automatically providing action plans helps people complete tasks. ACM Transactions on Computer-Human Interaction 20(5), 1–25 (2013)
4. Bloom, B.S., Englehart, M., Furst, E., Hill, W., Krathwohl, D.: Taxonomy of educational objectives: The classification of education goals. In: Handbook I: Cognitive Domain. Longmans, New York (1956)
5. Anderson, L.W., Krathwohl, D.R.: A taxonomy for learning, teaching, and assessing: A revision of Bloom's taxonomy of educational objectives. Complete ed edn. Longman, New York (2001)
6. Bødker, S., Klokmose, C.N.: The human–artifact model: An activity theoretical approach to artifact ecologies. Human–Computer Interaction 26(4), 315–371 (2011)
7. Kelloway, E.K., Barling, J.: Knowledge work as organizational behavior. International Journal of Management Reviews 2(3), 287–304 (2000)
8. Aehnelt, M., Bader, S., Ruscher, G., Krüger, F., Urban, B., Kirste, T.: Situation aware interaction with multi-modal business applications in smart environments. In: Yamamoto, S. (ed.) HCI 2013, Part III. LNCS, vol. 8018, pp. 413–422. Springer, Heidelberg (2013)
9. Bader, S., Aehnelt, M.: Tracking assembly processes and providing assistance in smart factories. In: Proceedings of the 6th International Conference on Agents and Artificial Intelligence, ICAART (2014)

A Qualitative Investigation of 'Context', 'Enterprise Mobile Services' and the Influence of Context on User Experiences and Acceptance of Enterprise Mobile Services

Karen Carey and Markus Helfert

Dublin City University (DCU),
Glasnevin, Dublin 9, Ireland
Karen.carey6@mail.dcu.ie,
Markus.helfert@computing.dcu.ie

Abstract. Within this paper an account of a qualitative investigation into Enterprise Mobile Services and their 'Context' is recorded. Employing Qualitative Content Analysis, two taxonomies are derived; An Enterprise Mobile Service Taxonomy and a 'Context' Taxonomy. The researcher also investigates current Context factors which have been proven to influence users' experiences and the acceptance of Enterprise Mobile Services. These are highlighted in the 'Context' taxonomy. The researcher intends to further investigate the influence of Context on users' acceptance of Enterprise Mobile Services subsequently it is necessary to select appropriate Context criteria for inclusion. This paper describes this selection process; a focus group with Industry experts was conducted following the KJ method. The Context criteria to be further investigated were selected. The criteria which describe enterprise mobile services were also selected. The results of the qualitative investigation reveal Context items which may potentially influence the acceptance of Enterprise Mobile Services. The HCI and IS domains could benefit from further investigations into the influence of these Context items on users experiences and acceptance to allow for an even deeper understanding of the influence of Context.

Keywords: Enterprise Mobile Services, Context, User Experience, User Perceptions, User Acceptance.

1 Introduction

User acceptance is defined as the demonstrable willingness within a user group to employ information technology for the tasks it is designed to support, [1]. This is usually measured based on user's perceptions of the IT. According to [2] user experience is defined as a person perceptions and responses that result for use and or anticipated use of a product system or service, consequently users experiences are important to consider when investigating user acceptance. Research concerning potential factors which would

F.F.-H. Nah (Ed.): HCIB/HCII 2014, LNCS 8527, pp. 288–298, 2014.
© Springer International Publishing Switzerland 2014

affect user experiences and consequently user acceptance of Enterprise Mobile Services is scarce, [3]. [3] argues that Context is an important factor to consider when measuring the acceptance of mobile services. Nevertheless, scholars have suggested that the concept of "Context" is complex and there is a tendency to overlook characteristics of the Context in which a product is being used [4].

This paper is part of a larger PhD study which aims to further investigate the influence of Context on the acceptance of Enterprise Mobile Services. Within this paper an account of a qualitative investigation into Enterprise Mobile Services and their 'Context' is recorded. Employing Qualitative Content Analysis, two taxonomies are derived; An Enterprise Mobile Service Taxonomy and a 'Context' Taxonomy. The researcher also investigates current Context factors which have been proven to influence users' experiences and the acceptance of Enterprise Mobile Services. These are highlighted in the Context taxonomy. As the researcher intends to further investigate the influence of Context on users experience and consequently the acceptance of Enterprise Mobile Service, it is necessary to select appropriate criteria for inclusion. To select these criteria a focus group with Industry experts was conducted following the KJ method, an account of this approach and the results are detailed within this paper.

This qualitative investigation emphasizes key Context items which require further investigation; this study will hopefully stimulate further research in these domains, the results of which will expand both the scholarly body of knowledge, but also have direct and tangible benefits for everyday users of Enterprise Mobile Services.

2   Related Work

The Technology Acceptance Model (TAM), [5-6] is one of the most widely accepted acceptance models in Information Systems literature. TAM has been tested in some domains of e-business and proved to be quite reliable to predict user acceptance of some new information technologies such as the intranet [7], World Wide Web [8] electronic commerce [9] and online shopping [10]. There are two primary factors in TAM: perceived usefulness (PU) and perceived ease of use (PEOU) that are of particular importance to determine user intention of adopting a new technology or information system. PU is defined as the degree to which a person believes that using a particular system would enhance his or her job performance [6]. PEOU is defined as the extent to which a person believes that using a particular system would be free from effort [6]. While acceptance of IT services has been one of the most prevailing IS research topics (e.g. [6;11;12]) the pervasiveness of mobile business raises new questions in exploring the adoption of Enterprise Mobile Services, such as what are the key factors determining the adoption of enterprise mobile services and how context factors affect user adoption of mobile services. [3], extended the TAM and constructed a mobile services acceptance model [13]. In addition to perceived ease of use and perceived usefulness, the mobile services acceptance model includes Trust, Context and Personal Initiatives and Characteristics Factors to study user acceptance of mobile services.

Within their model, Context is described as; any information that can be used to characterize the situation of entities (i.e. a person, place or object) that are considered relevant to the interaction between a user and an application, including the application and the user themselves, [14]. Based on their definition, Context can be viewed as a composite construct.

Scholars have argued that the concept of "Context" is complex and there is a tendency to overlook characteristics of the Context in which a product is being used, [4]. Consequently there is a need to further investigate the Context of Enterprise Mobile Services and its influence on user acceptance. To describe how the Context of Enterprise Mobile Services is scoped within this research, the researcher qualitatively codes (using content analysis) the literature and selects criteria that comprise Context. Along with this the researcher qualitatively codes the literature to scope Enterprise Mobile Services within this research. Two taxonomies are developed; a description of this procedure is outlined in section 3. Although impossible to derive a complete list of factors that would represent the context with which enterprise mobile services are operated this research provides comprehensive Taxonomy. The researcher also reviews relevant literature to highlight Context items which have been included and measured in existing instruments which measure the influence of context on the acceptance of mobile services, these items are discussed further in section 4.

3   Investigating 'Context', 'Enterprise Mobile Services' and the Influence of Context on the Acceptance of Enterprise Mobile Services

This paper qualitatively investigates 'Enterprise Mobile Services' and their 'Context'. The researcher also investigates current Context factors which have been proven to influence users' experiences and consequently the acceptance of Enterprise Mobile Services. As a result this paper addresses the following questions;

- What criteria scope the Enterprise Mobile Services?
- What criteria scope the Context of Enterprise Mobile Services?
- How is the influence of Context on the acceptance of mobile services currently measured?
- What additional Context measurement items are selected for further investigation?

To address the first three questions "Qualitative Content Analysis" is employed. Qualitative content analysis is one of the numerous research methods used to analyze text data. In this research, qualitative content analysis is defined as a research method for the subjective interpretation of the content of text data through systematic classification process of coding and identifying the themes or patterns, [15]. Two taxonomies are constructed; An Enterprise Mobile Service taxonomy comprising of the factors relating to Enterprise Mobile Services and A Context taxonomy; comprising of the factors relating to Context. Following this, a review of the literature was conducted to highlight those context factors which have been included in existing instruments which measure the acceptance of mobile services. To answer the final question a focus group with Industry Experts was conducted and the KJ method implemented to select the Context criteria that will be further investigated, [16]. The KJ method allows groups to quickly reach a consensus on priorities of subjective qualitative data.

3.1   Qualitative Content Analysis

Initially the research objectives of the qualitative content analysis process were highlighted. Once these objectives were set, the researcher selected a sample of data sources to be analyzed. To avoid omission of key considerations, we conducted a comprehensive literature review and identified three domains (Information Systems, Human Computer Interaction, Human Factors and Ergonomics) that offer data sources that can contribute to the construction of the two taxonomies. By extensively analyzing a selection of significant contributions from the three overlapping domains, we mitigate the risk of overlooking key considerations. Providing a broad spectrum of sources enabled the researcher to construct the taxonomies which are reasonably comprehensive. Here we discuss the related research domains, explaining their relevance to the exercise of constructing the two taxonomies and identifying existing context items (that influence acceptance of mobile services) investigated.

3.2   Data Sources

Information Systems (IS) within the enterprise context capture and manage data to produce useful information that supports an organization and its employees, customer's suppliers, and partners, [17]. The term socio-technical systems was originally coined by [18] to describe systems that involve complex interaction between humans, machines and environmental aspects of the work system – nowadays this interaction is true of most enterprise systems. In recent years the term mobile service, mobile-commerce or enterprise mobile services have become a central topic in the Information Systems (IS) research community, [19]. Consequently, several contributions in the IS domain have committed to defining essential factors such as – people, machines and context – which need to be considered when developing such systems, ([20]. Therefore sources within this domain are included in the data analysis. Additionally the IS field is committed to studding the factors which influence user intention to adopt new technologies. Over the years several models have been developed to test user attitude and intention to adopt new technologies. These models include; the Technology Acceptance Model [5-6]), Theory of Planned behavior (TPB) [21], Innovation Diffusion Theory, (IDT) [22] and the Unified Theory of Acceptance and Use of Technology (UTAUT), [23]. Subsequently sources within this domain are also included in the data analysis.

Human Computer Interaction (HCI) is concerned with the design, evaluation and implementation of interactive computing systems for human use and with the study of major phenomena surrounding them, [24]. Hence, HCI is concerned with enhancing the quality of interaction between humans and computer systems within the physical, organizational and social aspects of the users' environment to produce systems that are usable, safe and functional [25]. With the intention of providing further insight to design several contributions within this domain have also investigated people, machine and context characteristics which may restrict the interaction between humans and computer systems. Consequently sources within this domain are included in the data analysis.

Human Factors and Ergonomics is the multidisciplinary study of human biological, physical, psychological, and social characteristics in relation to environments, objects and services. The practice of human factors applies to the design, operation, and evaluation of "Systems" to ensure that that they are safe, efficient, comfortable and aesthetically pleasing to humans, [26]. Evidently overlap exists among the domains however, the main difference between Human Factors and Ergonomics and HCI is that HCI focuses more on users working specifically with computers, rather than other kinds of machines or design artifacts. There is also a focus in HCI on how to implement the computer software and hardware mechanisms to support human-computer interaction, thus Human Factors is a broader term. However contributions in this domain are relevant when describe the context of mobile services and also context factors which may influence these services. Therefore sources within this domain are included in the data analysis.

A keyword search was conducted using the following; Mobile Services, Enterprise Mobile Services, Context of Use, Perceptions of Mobile Services, Acceptance of Mobile Services, those articles deemed relevant by the researcher were included based on the following criteria;

- Must be related to mobile services.
- Must be related to Context of Mobile services.
- Must be related to users' perceptions of mobile services.
- Must be related to users' perceptions of mobile services in varying contexts.
- Must be related to users' acceptance/adoption of mobile services.
- Must be related to users' acceptance/adoption of mobile services in varying contexts.

From the three related domains, a total of (39) individual works are selected for inclusion in the analysis process. Out of the 39 individual works (13) will render the initial taxonomy for Enterprise Mobile Services and (26) individual works will render the initial taxonomy for Context. Whist examining the literature to identify contributions to highlight context characteristics that have been included in existing measurement instruments, the researcher could find only one data contribution which has focused on a thorough examination of an instrument (which includes context items) to measure the adoption of mobile services, and thus this source is included.

3.3   Qualitative Coding Process

Once the data sources were selected, the coding process commenced, the researcher followed the coding process described in [15], which involved four main steps; Open coding, Categorization of Codes, Coding on and Data reduction. An account of this process is recorded here.

3.3.1   Open Coding
Each line of the contributions was read by the researcher, and when a characteristic of an enterprise mobile service or the context of the service was apparent the researcher highlighted this part of the text and allocated a code. For example, Context has been previously defined as "The users, tasks, equipment (Hardware-software and materials) and the physical and social environments in which a product is used, [2]" consequently user's 'motion' was allocated a coded as it is a Context characteristic. During this stage each code was allocated a definition to ensure consistency of coding. This process continued until all studies were coded and a long list of initial codes existed.

3.3.2   Categorization of Codes

This step involved renaming, merging, distilling and clustering related codes into broader categories of codes, consequently all codes related to mobile services were categorized under mobile services for example communication, Transaction etc. All codes related to Context were characterized under User, Task, Technology and Environment characteristics, for example for example, age, gender, skills were categorized under user. Also during this stage similar codes were clustered and renamed, for example codes such as display size and screen size were merged and renamed screen size. This continued until an initial taxonomy for both Enterprise Mobile Services and Context began to emerge and all related codes were structured under these taxonomies.

3.3.3   Coding on

This step involved breaking down the reorganized codes from step two into sub-codes so as to better understand the meanings embedded therein. For example under user categorization the user experience code was divided into the sub categories, novice intermittent and expert and under the task characteristics, task complexity was subdivided into low medium and high with a definition provided for each sub category. This step was continued until meanings were allocated to the each sub codes and the taxonomy began to represent taxonomy of Enterprise Mobile Services and taxonomy of Context.

3.4   Data Reduction

This step involved collapsing the coding tree/taxonomy into more abstract and generalized set of codes which represent enterprise mobile services and the Context of these services. This was done in conjunction with industry experts from an enterprise partner. The researcher arranged a focus group with industry experts, in doing so the KJ method was followed [16]. This includes six steps; an account of this process is summarized here.

3.4.1   Determine a Focus Question

It is necessary to outline the focus question as this drives the results. The researcher set the objective - to derive a list of criteria that would appropriately represent Enterprise mobile services and the Context of these services from an enterprise perspective. For a successful outcome it was important to the researcher that the participants would understand these objectives. The participants selected were industry experts in Small Form Factors and Human Factor Design. To ensure participants had a consistent understanding of the focus group objectives a presentation was given prior to the commencement of the focus group, 15 minutes covered the overall research aim and another 15 minutes for the aim of the focus group and the agenda.

3.4.2   Organize the Group

To organize the group members the two main sources in the industry partner were contacted and the intentions of the focus group were outlined. The researcher suggested that a diverse group of members would be beneficial to get different perspectives. A total of 5 participants were organized, these included small form factor and human factor specialists, a business analyst and a project manager, all who were familiar with enterprise mobile services. The time required was outlined and a date was set for 3hours over 3 days (every Tuesday for 3weeks).

3.4.3   Put Data Onto Sticky Notes and Put Sticky Notes on the Wall
After the presentation and the objectives of the focus group was outlined to members, the taxonomies of derived criteria were put onto yellow sticky notes and put on the walls in a large room. At the very top of the wall the focus group objectives were posted on orange paper, this was to ensure that members could keep focus. Participants were given pink sticky notes and told to read all sticky notes on the wall, if at any time they felt that something else should be added, something should be renamed or something should be removed they were asked to write this down on the pink sticky notes beside the criteria they felts should be revised.

3.4.4   Group Similar Items and Name Each Group
Once all opinions and contributions had been posted on pink sticky notes, participants were asked to group the criteria which they felt belonged in the same category. This involved moving all the criteria under the following five main criteria, Mobile Service, Context (Task, Technology, User, and Environment). Each of these main groups had a number of sub criteria, the naming and grouping of these sub-criteria were very important to the researcher as these would detail the mobile service and the context. The participants were asked to then read each group and review everything on the wall and consider its position. The results of this are illustrated in Appendix A and B. During this stage the literature was reviewed to highlight those context items that have been included in existing measurement instruments, these items are the shaded in criteria in Appendix B. It is evident in Appendix B that, user experience, attitude, safety, enjoyment, accessibility, compatibility, social factors and location have been included in existing measurement instruments, which measure the acceptance of mobile services.

The Context criteria in the Context taxonomy which are not highlighted include items which need further investigation. Consequently, this qualitative investigation emphasizes key Context items which require further examination; hopefully this will stimulate further research in these domains. As the researcher intends to further investigate a selection of these Context criteria, the selection process is detailed the next section. The researcher was also interested in scoping Enterprise Mobile Services from an Enterprise Perspective. This is also discussed in the next section.

3.4.5   Voting for the Most Important Group
After the participants had reviewed the revised and categorized criteria they were asked select the three most important criteria to them that represent Enterprise Mobile Services and then for Context. Each of the participants votes were recorded by the researcher.

3.4.6   Ranking the Most Important Group
Once all participants' votes were recorded, the researcher ordered each criterion selected by the number of votes they received, with the highest at the top. The participants were asked to review the selected criteria and discuss. At this stage conflicting selection was discussed and participants continued to move the sub categories around. After discussing and moving the sub-categories around to reach a unanimous agreement a final count of the votes allocated to each subcategories under the five main categories were counted, i.e. there are sub- criteria under each of the five main categories that are ranked much higher than the rest. At this point the process stopped as any further combinations are unlikely to change the top priorities voted by the participants. The focus group was

declared finished and the researcher reviewed the final selection of criteria along with the continuous opinionated data recorded throughout the focus group process. The results of the final list of criteria to classify Enterprise Mobile Services and the Context criteria for inclusion are recorded in table 1.

Table 1. Selected Criteria from Focus group

Enterprise Mobile Services		Context Criteria							
		User		Task		Technology		Environment	
Criteria	%	Criteria	%	Criteria	%	Criteria	%	Criteria	%
Communication	48	Cognitive load	52	Criticality	8	Portability	8	Ambient Conditions	32
Transaction	25	Motion	20						
Information	24								
Web 2.0	20								
Learning	16								

It is evident in table 1 that to scope Enterprise Mobile Services the criteria, Communication (48%), Transaction (24%), Information (24%), Web 2.0 (20%) and Learning (16%) have been selected. Consequently Enterprise Mobile Services can be categorized under these. It also evident from table 1 that the selected criteria that describe the Context of these services and will be further investigated by the researcher include, User Cognitive load (52%), Environmental Ambient conditions (32%), User Motion (20%), Task criticality (8%) and Portability (8%). Future work involves testing for convergent and discriminant validity of these criteria, testing the reliability of these criteria and to demonstrate the influence of these criteria on the acceptance of Enterprise Mobile Service Acceptance.

4   Conclusions, Limitations and Future Work

Within this paper an account of a qualitative investigation into Enterprise Mobile Services and their 'Context' is recorded. Employing Qualitative Content Analysis, two taxonomies are derived; An Enterprise Mobile Service Taxonomy and a Context Taxonomy. The researcher also investigates current Context factors which have been proven to influence users' experiences and the acceptance of Enterprise Mobile Services. These are highlighted in the Context taxonomy. As the researcher intends to further investigate (as part of a larger PhD project) the influence of Context on users experience and consequently the acceptance of Enterprise Mobile Service, it is necessary to select appropriate criteria for inclusion. To select these criteria a focus group with Industry experts was conducted following the KJ method, an account of the selection approach and the results are detailed within this paper. Future work involves testing the validity and reliability of these constructs while also investigating the influence of these Context criteria on the acceptance of Enterprise Mobile Service. Currently the researcher is planning a field study within an Enterprise partner. In conclusion this qualitative investigation has emphasized key Context items which require further investigation; these will hopefully stimulate further research in the IS and HCI domains, the results of which will expand both the scholarly body of knowledge, but also have direct and tangible benefits for everyday users of Enterprise Mobile Services.

References

1. Dillon, A., Morris, M.G.: User acceptance of information technology: theories and models. Journal of the American Society for Information Science 31, 3–32 (1996)
2. ISO 9241-210. Ergonomics of human system interaction Part 2 Human centred design for interactive systems (2010)
3. Gao, S., Krogstie, J., Siau, K.: Developing an Instrument to measure the adoption of Mobile Services. Mobile Information Systems 7, 1 (2011)
4. Alonso-Rios, D.: Usability a critical analysis and taxonomy. International Journal of Human-computer Interaction 26(1), 53–74 (2009)
5. Davis, F.: Perceived usefulness, perceived ease of use, and user acceptance of information technology. MIS Quarterly, 139–140 (1989)
6. Davis, F.D., Bagozzi, R.P., Warshaw, P.R.: User acceptance of computer technology: a comparison of two theoretical models. Management Science 35, 982–1003 (1989)
7. Horton, R.P.: Explaining Internet use with the technology acceptance model. Journal of Information Technology 16, 281–298 (2001)
8. Lederer, A.L.: The technology acceptance model and the World Wide Web. Decision Support Systems 29, 269–282 (2000)
9. Pavlou, P.A.: Consumer Acceptance of Electronic Commerce: Integrating Trust and Risk with the Technology Acceptance Model. International Journal of Electronic Commerce 7, 101–134 (2003)
10. Gefen, D.: TAM or Just Plain Habit: A Look at Experienced Online Shoppers. Journal of End User Computing 15, 1–13 (2003)
11. Taylor, S., Todd, P.: Understanding Information Technology Ugase: A Test of Competing Models. Information Systems Research 6, 144–176 (1995)
12. Ven, K., Verelst, J.: The Impact of Ideology on the Organizational Adoption of Open Source Software. Journal of Database Managemnet 19, 58–72 (2008)
13. Gao, S., Krogstie, J., Gransaether, P.A.: Mobile Service Acceptance Model. In: Proceedings of the 2008 International Conference on Convergence and Hybrid Information Technology. IEEE Computer Society (2008)
14. Dey, A.K.: Understanding and Using Context. Personal Ubiquitous Computing 5, 4–7 (2001)
15. Krippendorff, K.: Content Analysis: An Introduction to its Methodology. Sage, Thousand Oaks (2004)
16. Spool, J.: The KJ-Technique: A Group Process for Esablishing Priorities, http://www.uie.com/articles/kj_technique/
17. Whitten, J.L., Barlow, V.M., Bentley, L.: Systems analysis and design methods. McGraw-Hill Professional (1997)
18. Emery, F.E., Trist, E.: LSocio-Technical systems. In: Chruchman, C.W. (ed.) Management Science Models and Techniques, Oxford, UK, vol. 2, pp. 83–97 (1960)
19. Wang, F.Y.: Social computing: from social informatics to social intelligence. IEEE Intelligent Systems 22(2), 79–83 (2007)

20. Baxter, G., Sommerville, I.: Socio-tecnical system: From design methods to system engineering. Interacting with Computers 23(1), 4–17 (2011)
21. Ajzen, I.: The thepry of planed behavior. Organisational Behaviour and Human Decision Processes 50, 179–211 (1991)
22. Rogers, E.M.: The Diffusion of Innovations. Free Press, New York (1995)
23. Venkatesh, V.: User Acceptance of Information Technology: Toward a Unified View. MIS Quarterly, 425–478 (2003)
24. Zhang, P., Li, N.: An assessment of human-computer interaction research in management infomation systems: topics and methods. Computers in Human Behavior 20(2) (2004)
25. Preece, J.: Human Computer Interaction. Addison-Wesley, Harlow (1994)
26. Usability Body of Knowledge. Usability Body of Knowledge, http://www.usabilitybok.org/glossary

Appendix A

Classification	Factors	Bouwman et al, 2012	Kargin et.al, 2006	Niekerson et.al, 2009	Lehmann & Lehner, 2002	Zhang et.al 2011	Gebauer & Shaw, 2002	Nikou & Mezei, 2013	Basoglu et. al 2013	Anderson et. al 2010	Yu et. al 2012	Emmanauilidis et.al 2013	Giaglis, 2003	Ngai & Gunasekaran, 2005
	Communication			●	●		●	●				●	●	
	Entertainment		●					●				●		●
	Information			●	●	●	●	●				●	●	●
	Web 2.0					●		●				●		
	Transaction			●	●	●		●			●	●	●	●
	Innovativeness	●	●						●					
	Usage Context	●												
	Temporal		●											
	Location Based			●		●				●	●		●	●
Mobile Services	Identity			●									●	
	Multiplicity			●										
	Public			●										
	Interaction				●	●						●		
	Data Processing						●							
	Credibility								●					
	Adaptivity								●					
	Cost								●					
	Flexibility								●			●		
	Personalisation								●					
	Mobility										●			
	Learning											●	●	
	Messaging							●				●		

Appendix B

Context of Use Classification	Factors	Kros et al 2010	Kargin et al., 2006	Staale & Bahli, 2005	Xu & Yuan, 2009	Maguire, 2001	Hassenzahl &	Lommela, et al 2008	Cadenas et al, 2009	Byrd & Caldwell 201	Courains et al, 2012	Zhang et al 2011	Yuan & Zhong, 2006	Yuan et al, 2010	Venkatesh, Thong, Xu	Ryan & Gonsalves,	ISO 20282-1-2006	ISO 9241-210:2010	Courainss & Kim, 201	Kuo & Troshani, 2007	Wang, et al 2006	Mallat et al 2009	Villalon, et al 2010	Liu & Li, 2011	Bevan & Macleod,	Emmanouilidis et al	Guo et al 2013
User	Role	●						●										●						●		●	
	Experience	●	●		●	●			●		●					●		●	●	●	●				●	●	●
	Edcuation	●			●												●	●	●	●	●				●		
	Attitude	●	●		●												●	●	●				●				●
	Culture				●						●						●	●	●				●				
	Aural Characteristics						●										●										
	Visual Charteristics						●										●										
	Physical Characteristics	●					●										●	●									
	Cognitive characteristics	●					●										●										
	Satisfaction		●														●										
	Innovativeness		●														●		●								
	Cognitive Absorption			●													●		●					●			
	Motion				●								●														
	Personal Attributes					●										●		●	●	●				●			
	Hedonic							●								●											
	Emotion & Effect						●												●							●	
	Habbit															●			●								
	Image																				●						
	Self Efficacy																			●							
	Cognitive Load										●	●															
Task	Complexity	●									●								●								
	Temporal Characteristics	●																						●	●		
	Demands	●																									
	Workflow Controllability	●																									
	Safety	●			●														●							●	
	Criticality	●			●								●	●	●												
	Enjoyment		●																●			●		●			●
	Duration				●			●										●				●					
	Task Goal/Output					●											●	●	●			●					
	Steps/Interaction					●						●				●											
	Frequency					●							●						●				●				
	Flexibilities					●																	●				
	Physical and Mental					●																	●				
	Task Difficulty												●														
	Task Interdependence												●					●									
	Mobility												●	●								●					
Technology	Compatability	●																		●	●						●
	Portability		●								●	●					●	●									
	Personalization		●																								
	Interface								●		●						●	●			●						
	Accessability																										●
	Conectivity								●		●										●			●			
	Aesthetics						●																				
	Screen Size									●											●						
	Device																				●			●		●	
Environment	Ambient Conditions -	●						●		●	●					●	●	●	●		●			●	●		
	Ambient Condition -	●		●				●		●	●					●	●	●	●		●			●	●		
	Ambient Conditions -	●			●					●	●					●	●	●	●		●			●	●		
	Safety	●			●														●					●	●	●	
	Social Factors		●														●	●	●	●		●			●	●	
	Location				●				●				●	●	●			●			●	●			●	●	

Designing for Success: Creating Business Value with Mobile User Experience (UX)

Soussan Djamasbi[1,*], Dan McAuliffe[2], Wilmann Gomez[1], Georgi Kardzhaliyski[1], Wan Liu[1], and Frank Oglesby[1]

[1] User Experience & Decision Making Research Laboratory,
Worcester Polytechnic Institute, USA
[2] User Experience, Dyn Inc., USA
{djamasbi,w.gomez.r,gkardzhaliyski,
Tammy_Liu,foglesby721}@wpi.edu, dmcauliffe@dyn.com

Abstract. The popularity of mobile devices, such as smart phones and tablets, provides both new opportunities and challenges for companies. Mobile devices allow companies to reach users anywhere, anytime; however, these devices present the challenge of designing websites that can adapt to smaller screen sizes. Because competition is shifting more and more toward user experience, creating a positive mobile experience is becoming increasingly important in maintaining a competitive edge in the market place. To address this issue, we measured the user experience of an actual e-commerce website before and after it was optimized for mobile devices and used Google Analytics to follow user behavior. The results suggested that optimized websites are likely to have a major positive impact on the ROI for a company.

Keywords: User Experience Design, Mobile Websites, Mobile Optimization, Mobile User Experience, Return on Investment (ROI), Business Value, Google Analytics.

1 Introduction

Online browsing via mobile devices is becoming increasingly popular [7]. Last year alone in the US, there were more than 100 million smart phones users and more than 60 million tablet users. The population of mobile device users is expected to grow substantially in the future [4, 5]. People use mobile devices because they can provide a quick and easy way to access the Internet [7]. This fast and convenient access to information, in turn, is likely to have a major impact on consumer behavior. For example, using a smart phone can not only make it convenient to search for a product anywhere, anytime but can also make it quite easy to compare products at various stores and/or arrange follow up activities such as visiting the store or calling for additional information.

Consumers' fast and convenient access to information via mobile devices provides new business opportunities for companies. It allows companies to reach a broader

---

* Corresponding author.

F.F.-H. Nah (Ed.): HCIB/HCII 2014, LNCS 8527, pp. 299–306, 2014.
© Springer International Publishing Switzerland 2014

consumer base. The opportunity to reach consumers via mobile devices, however, presents companies with some serious challenges as well. In order to reach customers anywhere, anytime companies need to develop websites that can be accessed effectively via various devices. Lessons learned from research shows that staying competitive in the market place requires companies to provide superior user experience for their websites [2, 3, 10]. While designing websites for various screen sizes has been one of the major topics in web development circles [8], little work has been done to look at mobile user experience with a business lens.

The objective of this research is to take a basic step toward examining the value of mobile user experience from a business point of view. In order to achieve this goal, we conducted two user studies to track changes in mobile experience and utilized web analytics to track changes in behavior after the website was optimized for mobile devices.

As customary in industry research, first we assessed the current state of mobile experience via an initial study to identify whether there were any opportunities for improvement, and if so, identify changes that would be most impactful [11]. This approach is crucial in practice for two important reasons: 1) it allows companies to benchmark experience before implementing changes, and 2) it facilitates data driven experience design should the process identify opportunities for improvement.

Next, we optimized the website based on the results obtained from the initial user experience study. Then, we conducted a second user experience experiment centered around the same task and settings. This arrangement allowed us to directly assess the impact of optimization on users' subjective experience of the mobile website.

Companies often use web analytics to estimate the business value of their user research and to plan their future research efforts [6, 11]. Because we were interested in the business value of user experience, we used Google Analytics to see whether there were any improvements in mobile traffic and sales after the website was optimized for mobile devices.

The results of the user studies as well as the results of Google Analytics are discussed in the following sections.

2   Background

Mobile optimization supports the "One Web" recommendation of the World Wide Web Consortium (W3C), which advocates that users should be able to receive the same service and information regardless of the type of device they are using. While W3C's One Web concept emphasizes the accessibility of information irrespective of the medium used, it does not require the provided information to have the same representation across various devices. This is both helpful and necessary for mobile optimization. To explain this better, Figure 1 shows amazon.com's website accessed via a desktop computer and a mobile phone. As shown in Figure 1, while both devices provide access to the same content they differ in how they represent information. Due to the smaller screen size, the mobile website has to adjust its content to fit the smaller screen of a mobile phone. The visual attributes of the content on the mobile screen are also modified to create an appropriate visual balance for the smaller screen. The original visual structure is adjusted so that the page can convey the same hierarchy of information on a smaller display [3]. The navigation bar, links, and menu on the mobile site are also modified to occupy less visual space.

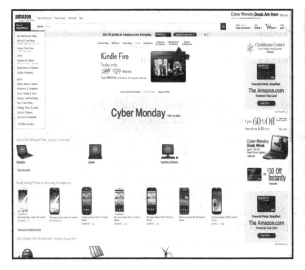

1a: Amazon.com
displayed on a desktop

1b: Amazon.com displayed
on a smart phone

Fig. 1. Example of an optimized mobile website

3   Measuring the Mobile UX

3.1   Study I: Benchmarking the Mobile Experience

The objective of this study was to assess the experience of a mobile website and to identify possible opportunities for improvement. In order to do so, we used an actual e-commerce website. We conducted our investigations in a laboratory setting to facilitate a controlled environment for observing and measuring user experience.

Task
To avoid user fatigue, we focused on testing the mobile experience of the purchasing process on the website. The task required users to look for a specific product on the e-commerce website and complete the checkout process for that specific product.

Measurements
We used the System Usability Scale (SUS) [1] to measure a user's subjective experience of the website. SUS captures a person's evaluation of interaction with a product via a 10-item questionnaire. This instrument is widely used in industry research to assess website experience [9]. Compared to other frequently used instruments in industry research, such as Questionnaire for User Interaction Satisfaction (QUIS), Computer System Usability Questionnaire (CSUQ), and Microsoft's Product Reaction Cards, SUS is more senestive in detecting diffrences in smaller sample sizes [12]. SUS provides a simple method for converting the results of the questionnaire into a single value, which can be used to compare webpages [9]. These SUS values can

range between 0 to 100, with 0 indicating the worst and 100 indicating the best attainable score. To achieve an above average user experience, a minimum SUS score of 68 is recommended [9]. In addition to SUS scores, we also used observation and post task interviews to assess user experience of the mobile website.

Participants and Design

Seventeen graduate and undergraduate students (10 male, 7 female) participated in the study. All participants were expert web users who accessed the Internet via mobile devices on a regular basis. Participants were asked to look up and complete the purchasing process for a specific service offered on the e-commerce website. For the purpose of the experiment, a test account was created (username and password) to be used by all the participants. All participants used the same fictitious information (e.g., credit card number and expiration date) to make the purchase with the test account. The study was conducted on a Samsung Galaxy S3 smartphone running Android 4.0.4, and an Apple iPhone 4S running iOS 5.1.1.

Results

Our analysis did not show any significant quantitative differences in scores between the two mobile devices, therefore we used the pooled data to assess the user experience of the website.

The results of surveys, observations, and interviews all indicated an opportunity for improvement. For example, the survey results showed an average SUS score of 57, which is below the recommended threshold for an above average user experience [9]. The interviews and observations confirmed the SUS results indicating an opportunity for improving the user experience of the mobile e-commerce website. In particular, the observation and interview data showed that the following changes would have the most impact on the user experience of the mobile website: 1) minimizing "pinch and zoom" interactions, 2) minimizing horizontal scrolling in a way that the content fits the screen appropriately, 3) minimizing redundancies so that the content fits the screen without creating clutter, and 4) using an optimized menu to minimize the visual space required for navigating the website and to facilitate an easy way to move between webpages.

3.2   Study II: Assessing the Impact of Modifications on Mobile Experience

The objective of this study was to examine the impact of mobile optimization on user experience. Thus, before conducting this second experiment, we implemented the improvement opportunities that were identified in the first study. We used the Cascading Style Sheets specification (CSS), a web styling computer language to format the content of the webpages. In addition to formatting the content, we also changed the structure of the content to minimize "pinch and zoom" interactions. This also ensured that the content would fit appropriately on the screen of a mobile device, thereby eliminating the need for horizontal scrolling. We also removed redundancy in the content to minimize clutter and/or the amount of scrolling needed to see below the fold of the page, and modified the structure of links and menus to optimize the use of available visual space.

Task
We used the same task (purchasing of a specified product) that was tested in the first laboratory experiment.

Measurements
As in the first study, we used SUS to measure the subjective experiences of the participants in our study. We also used observation as well as interview data to examine user reactions to the website.

Participants and Design
As in the first experiment, participants were recruited from a pool of graduate and undergraduate students (27 participants, 19 male and 8 female). As in the first experiment, the study was conducted on a Samsung Galaxy S3 smartphone running Android 4.0.4, and an Apple iPhone 4S running iOS 5.1.1.

Results
Again, our analysis did not show any significant differences between the two mobile devices and therefore we pooled the data to evaluate the user experience of the website. Our analysis showed a major improvement in SUS scores (SUS=73), a score well above the recommended threshold for an above average positive experience (SUS=68). We ran a t-test to see whether the observed SUS scores in the two studies were significantly different. The results of the t-test showed that the user experience captured via the SUS score was significantly improved after the website was optimized for mobile devices (Table 1). The observations and interviews also confirmed this improvement in experience.

Table 1. SUS scores before and after mobile optimization

	Mean	SD
Before optimization	57	23.34
After optimization	73	21.28
	$t=2.25, df=40, p=0.03$	

4   Google Analytics

Companies often look at web and sales analytics before and after they change their websites to estimate the business value of their usability improvements [6, 11]. Similarly, we looked at the website traffic and transaction volume of the e-commerce site before and after it was optimized to see if there were any changes in consumer behavior. In order to measure web traffic, we looked at Unique Page Views and Bounce Rate. The former represents the aggregated page views of a single user during the same session. The latter refers to the percentage of visits in which the user views only one page on the website before exiting the site. Lower levels of Unique Page Views and/or higher levels of Bounce Rate could indicate a lack of engagement with the site. We also looked at Quantity Sold, which refers to the total number of items sold for a product.

We tracked mobile traffic for the same pages that were used in Studies 1 and 2. Additionally, we compared user behavior 12 months before and 12 months after the e-commerce website was optimized for mobile devices. While, we noticed improvements for shorter periods (e.g., three months before and after the launch of the new website), we used a 12-month period to account for seasonal differences that may have an impact on consumer behavior.

Table 2 shows the percentage of change over a period of 24 months, comparing user behavior 12 months before and 12 months after the e-commerce website was optimized for mobile devices. As shown in Table 2, after pages were optimized for mobile devices, the number of times these pages were viewed by visitors increased by 40% and number of visitors who did not leave the site after viewing the first page doubled as evidenced by a 50% decrease in the Bounce Rate. The results displayed in Table 2 also show a 31% increase in the sales quantity of the specific product that was the focus of examination in our user experience studies. These statistics are consistent with the results of our user studies, which showed significant improvement in SUS scores, from 57 before optimization to 73 after optimization for mobile devices.

Table 2. Changes in user behavior before and after mobile optimization

Unique Page Views	41.31%	increase
Bounce Rate	50.00%	decrease
Quantity Sold (the product examined in Study 1 and 2)	31.10%	increase

5   Discussion

A growing body of research acknowledges that paying attention to user experience plays a major role in business competition. However, little work has been done to look at mobile user experience from a business point of view. A major objective of this study was to look at user experience through a business lens.

Our results show that optimization can have a significant impact on how users experience a mobile website. Study 1 and Study 2 provide evidence that mobile optimization facilitated a statistically significant improvement in experience (from SUS=57 to SUS=73). The improvement in user experience was supported by Google Analytics comparing consumer behavior a year before and a year after the website was optimized for mobile devices. While improvements in user behavior were evident shortly after the implementation was completed, we used a 12-month time period to control for possible seasonal differences. These results showed about 40% increase in Unique Page Views and 50% decrease in Bounce Rate. Because both of these metrics could be associated with user engagement, an impressive increase in Unique Page Views along with a substantial decrease in Bounce Rate could indicate increased engagement, which in turn could indicate that optimization had a major positive impact on how users viewed the pages.

The results also showed over 30% increase in sales of the product that was under investigation in this study. While assessing the impact of optimization on the entire product line was outside the scope of this project, it is important to note that Google Analytics showed an impressive improvement (over 70% increase) in quantity of all products sold over the mobile optimized site.

While the results of our laboratory study cannot be directly linked to the results of web analytics, the fact that both user studies and Google Analytics showed significant improvements after the website was optimized make a compelling case for the business value of mobile user experience.

6   Limitations and Future Research

As with any investigation, the results reported in this study are limited to the setting and the task. For example, the investigation in Study 1 and 2 were conducted in a laboratory setting and the task used in the study was limited to a specific website and a specific product. However, to minimize threats to external validity, we used an actual live website and an actual product to conduct our investigations. Our laboratory experiments had also a relatively small sample size, which can affect the chances of finding statistically significant differences. However, our results showed significant differences in user experience before and after the website was modified. While these results suggest the possibility of a large effect size, future studies using different tasks and settings are needed to increase confidence in the generalizability of the findings.

We used web analytics to look at the value of our mobile optimization through a practical business lens. While user experience is an important factor in website traffic and/or product sales [2, 11], factors other than user experience (e.g., promotions) can also influence traffic and sales. To minimize the impact of such effects we compared traffic and sales statistics for a longer period of time (12 months) before and after the changes were made to the websites. Nevertheless, care must be taken when generalizing the results.

7   Contribution

While additional research is needed to increases the generalizability of the findings in this study, the results of the laboratory experiments in our study show that mobile optimization can have a significant impact on the user experience of a website. The results of Google Analytics suggest that mobile optimization is likley to help increase traffic and sales volume of mobile e-commerce websites. Thus, this study contributes to the HCI literature in three ways: 1) it establishes the importance of mobile optimization in improving the user experience of a mobile website, 2) it looks at user experience from a business point of view, and 3) by doing so, it highlights the value and significance of user experience research in theory and practice.

References

1. Brooke, J.: SUS: a "quick and dirty" usability scale. In: Jordan, P.W., Thomas, B., Weerdmeester, B.A., Mcclelland, I.L. (eds.) Usability Evaluation in Industry, pp. 189–194. Taylor & Francis, London (1996)
2. Djamasbi, S., Siegel, M., Skorinko, J., Tullis, T.: Online viewing and aesthetic preferences of generation y and the baby boom generation: Testing user web site experience through eye tracking. International Journal of Electronic Commerce 15(4), 121–158 (2011)
3. Djamasbi, S., Siegel, M., Tullis, T.: Generation y, web design, and eye tracking. International Journal of Human-Computer Studies 68(5), 307–323 (2010)
4. eMarketer. Smartphone users as percentage of all mobile users in the u.S. From 2010 to 2016 (2013 a) (Statista retrieved May 6, 2013)
5. eMarketer. Tablet users in the united states from 2010 to 2015 (in millions) (2013b) (Statista retrieved May 6, 2013)

6. Foraker 2010, Usability ROI, Case Study: Breastcancer.org Discussion Forums, `http://www.usabilityfirst.com/documents/` `Ulst_BCO_CaseStudy.pdf` (retrieved)

7. Google/Nielsen, Life 360 mobile search moments (2013), `http://ssl.gstatic.com/think/docs/` `creating-moments-that-matter_research-studies.pdf` (retrieved)

8. Northington, D.: Why Mobile Site Optimization Matters- 6 Best Practices for Mobile Design (2011), `http://www.thesearchagents.com/2011/11/` `why-mobile-site-optimization-matters-6-best-practices-for-` `mobile-design/` (retrieved)

9. Sauro, J.: Measuring Usability With The System Usability Scale (SUS). From Measuring Usability (2011), `http://www.measuringusability.com/sus.php` (retrieved August 24, 2013)

10. Tractinsky, N.: Does Aesthetics Matter in Human-Computer Interaction. In: Stary, C. (ed.) Mensch & Computer, pp. 29–42. Oldenbourg Verlag, München (2005)

11. Tullis, T.: Conducting Large scale online User Research Studies, The User Experience Professionals Association (UXPA), Shanghi, China (2013)

12. Tullis, T.S., Stetson, J.N.: A Comparison of Questionnaires for Assessing Website Usability, Usability Professionals Association (UPA) 2004 Conference, Minneapolis, USA, June 7-11 (2004)

The Performance of Self in the Context of Shopping in a Virtual Dressing Room System

Yi Gao, Eva Petersson Brooks, and Anthony Lewis Brooks

Centre for Design, Learning and Innovation,
Department of Architecture and Media Technology,
Aalborg University, Niels Bohrs Vej 8, 6700 Esbjerg, Denmark
gao@create.aau.dk

Abstract. This paper investigates the performance of self in a virtual dressing room based on a camera-based system reflecting a full body mirrored image of the self. The study was based on a qualitative research approach and a user-centered design methodology. 22 participants participated in design sessions, semi-structured interviews and a questionnaire investigation. The results showed that the system facilitated self-recognition, self-perception, and shared experience, which afforded an enriched experience of the performing self.

Keywords: Virtual dressing room, mirroring, self-perception, self-recognition, shared experience, hedonic shopping experience.

1   Introduction

In this paper, we investigate how a virtual dressing room facilitated the performance of self in terms of self-recognition and self-perception to identify how potential shoppers organize such interactions and experiences. In line with [1] online shopping is considered as a creative and social activity incorporating diverse meanings where both shopping and commodities invoke personal as well as collective interests and motivations. The study illustrates in different ways that the virtual dressing room system user interface invoked certain interactions that are afforded by the technique of mirroring in line with [2].

This on-going research is financed by the Danish National Advanced Technology Foundation to realize a turnkey solution of a Virtual Dressing Room (VDR), which should reduce customer purchase returns. In this regard, the practice of shopping clothes online is considered as framed by shoppers through the influence of affordances and personal agency. This is in line with [3], who states that:

> "When the behavior of the computer is coherent and the application is designed so that a human interactor knows what to do and receives clear and immediate feedback on the results of their actions, the interactor experiences the pleasure of agency, of making something happen in a dynamically responsive world." [3, p. 100].

F.F.-H. Nah (Ed.): HCIB/HCII 2014, LNCS 8527, pp. 307–315, 2014.
© Springer International Publishing Switzerland 2014

2   Background

A virtual dressing room, in which shoppers cannot only view apparel commodities but also view as an overlay on their bodies, addresses many of the concerns that shoppers have about purchasing apparel online. The Forrester report [4] states how customers prefer shopping in stores as this offers possibilities to touch and feel the items and, also, avoiding issues related to returns. 56% of shoppers considered lack of touch and feel as a primary concern when it comes to online shopping. Currently, online garment purchases are subject of approximately 30% returns [5]. Forrester research [6] and [7] claims that approximately 35% of online garment clothes are returned. This is costly for the e-commerce retail outlet and creates logistical problems in re-selling returned stock. We contribute to this field by introducing a turnkey solution that allows e-commerce clothing retailers to create digital clothing by scanning real clothes using a RGB-D sensor. Creating digital clothing using specialized programs such as Marvelous Designer 2 is a time consuming process, whereas the 3D scanning process is relatively fast [8]. With this kind of virtual dressing room solution, shoppers will view accurate models of the self, wearing clothing in different colors and sizes and receive information about how the garments fit [9]. [10] identified constraints and affordances related to a previous prototype of the virtual dressing room system involved in this paper, focusing on ludic activities, where access, movement based interaction, social activity, self-image recognition, and authority constituted core factors to be enhanced in order to provide a more hedonic shopping experience. The freedom to freely move was a required affordance, which enabled expressions of self and fostered ludic engagement.

Another body of work that intends to address the problem of returns on purchased-online apparel is Fits.me, a company that utilizes a robotic mannequin created by a consortium involving roboticists from the University of Tartu in Estonia, who enlisted the help of Human Solutions, a German firm specializing in body dimensions and ergonomic simulation. The mannequin has 50 actuators embedded, which push panels in and out to form different shapes. It is covered in Pedilin, a material used on prosthetic limbs, so fabrics will drape like they would on real skin. Fits.me collects user's data to compile a database of customers, which each individual can use to view clothed in chosen apparel. However, the company also plans to sell retailers garnered information on shoppers, which could help outfitters design clothing and target sales.

The VDR system included in this study shows promising results of creating digital clothing of high quality by scanning real clothes. The paper discusses the major affordances and constraints originating from apparel online shopping in a virtual dressing room and addresses how shoppers experiences derives from the concept of mirroring [2]. However, before the discussion, it is necessary to detail the system and the design concepts.

3   Analysis of Design Concepts: Mirroring for the Virtual Dressing Room

The catalyst of the Virtual Dressing Room (VDR) is unencumbered interaction with a computer-based system. Unencumbered interaction relates to the field of Natural User Interfaces (NUIs) in that a participant interacts with a system via gesture without wearing, holding or otherwise operating a tangible device. The latest gesture-control peripherals for games are based on such interactions that are a direct result from the advent of camera-based software and related advances in computer-vision and hardware such as computer graphic cards.

In our VDR project, two systems were initially explored to establish the required tracking of gesture matched to affordability as the work targets a commercially viable product for the general public. The two systems that were explored spanned a wide cost range in order to determine if a more costly solution would be justified in the final product. These systems are (1) the Microsoft Kinect, and (2) the OpenStage® V2.0 Markerless Motion Capture System by Organic Motion.

3.1   The Microsoft Kinect

The Kinect is a well-known affordable video game camera-based peripheral operating at 30 frames per second that enables gesture control of software via predictive algorithm mapping in a scan area 1.2–3.5 m and with a latency of 250 milliseconds. The device uses a "time-of-flight camera" for its range imaging. Such technology enables the tracking of humans through providing distance images in real time. The cost of the stand-alone device is approximately 150 UK pounds.

Fig. 1. 1st generation Kinect device sold with Microsoft X-Box (*source: Microsoft*)

The second-generation of the Kinect can be plugged into a standard PC (so the need for the X-Box gaming platform module is redundant) where a SDK is used to program the interactions. The system is mobile for indoors and outdoors use (but a power supply is needed). It also operates through clear glass, thus, allowing shop-frontage use 24/7.

The most-recent Kinect is a self-contained platform that can also accept spoken commands via a microphone array. It uses a motion-sensing camera that tracks the whole body, thus, when one interacts it is about more than solely a hand or wrist gesticulation as arms, legs, knees, hips, and torso are all also involved.

When one interacts, a digital skeleton is created that is based upon the depth data received, which enables the player's integration into the specific software, be it a game or a system such as the VDR. The Kinect ID has an in-built memory that has the capability to 'remember' each player from the physical information stored in the game console or VDR system. Thus, after an initial set-up and profile calibration, each session can begin straight away through an ID configuration recall. Voice recognition is via four in-built microphones that can determine room noise or player verbal commands. 24/7. The Kinect sold 18 million units in 2011. The built in biofeedback for the player advances this field.

In summary, find below an overview of the Kinect technology:

- Relies on interpretation and predictive algorithms to determine the most probably upcoming pose.
- Uses a library containing a large number of preloaded poses.
- Each detected area in the scan space is matched with a potential body part and assigned the probability that it actually matches such body part.

Based on the above probabilities, Kinect comes up with the most probably skeleton building on its experience and pre-programmed kinematics models. This skeleton is then outfitted as a 3D avatar. In context of the VDR, the avatar may be clothed with selected apparel, cf. [11].

3.2   The Organic Motion OpenStage®

The OpenStage® V2.0 Markerless Motion Capture System by Organic Motion is a multiple-camera (optimal 18 color cameras) full 3D real-time data tracking system (i.e. 360 degrees) that captures movement at an adjustable rate of 60 to 120 frames per second in a scalable scan area of up to 5m by 5m with a maximum latency of 50 to 100 milliseconds. Human bones (21 points) are tracked accurately with each having 5 to 6 degrees of freedom each. Objects can also be tracked in 360 degrees. The OpenStage® is only for indoors use, cf. [11].

Fig. 2. OpenStage® V2.0 Markerless Motion Capture System (*source: Organic Motion*)

OpenStage harnesses Organic Motion's core computer vision technology, enabling computers to cognitively "see" people's complex movements and generate accurate 3D tracking data in real-time: A video sub-system acquires lens and space calibrated video from 8 - 18 cameras and delivers these synchronized streams to the 3D reconstruction processor. The 3D reconstruction system turns the 2D video streams into 3D point and surface clouds by triangulating the various 2D viewpoints. In this way the 3D reconstruction system acts much like a 3D scanner. The final step involves "recognizing" the human figure in this 3D data cloud. Here Organic Motion uses a complex rules based approach that maps a 3D humanoid skeleton into the data.

The output data OpenStage delivers is the X, Y and Z positions and orientation of 21 segments of this skeleton. This information is then ready to be loaded directly via plug-ins or SDK into any form of animation software, game engine, biomechanical or other processing software, all in real-time. Tracking customized objects, non-typical humans, or non-human shapes requires the modelling of new character fitting systems, which OpenStage offers as part of its new software architecture.

Organic Motion sold systems in over 20 countries worldwide, and is used in both commercial and academic settings for multiple applications in various markets including:

- Digital media & arts (animation, game development, VFX).
- Life sciences (bioengineering, physical therapy and rehabilitation, neuroscience, sport).
- Training and simulation (military and defence).
- Public Installations (theme parks, museums).

OpenStage interfaces with various 3D animation systems, 3D game engines and Virtual World systems and 3D immersive visuals, biofeedback and other applications. For therapeutic applications, movement 'rules' may be incorporated to encourage people to be more actively engaged in the recovery regime. This improves outcome and reduces recovery times.

The high accuracy of OpenStage allows clinicians and researchers to identify multi-level movement disorders, develop predictive models of pathology and gather statistical relevant data for long-term improvements, see also [11].

Summary. The Kinect was selected for the VDR system included in this study. This meant a more affordable system that enabled mirroring of the participant, however, problems were apparent with different sized participants – e.g. adults vs. children; and with gesture interactions with the interface (resolution/efficiency). This was apparent through the evaluation with various participants, see [12] and [10]. The next section presents the methodology and methods used in this study.

4   Method

The study applied a qualitative research approach and was based on a user-centered design methodology, including video observations, questionnaires and interviews. In line with a user-centered approach, participants also took part in a design session followed by an interview. The task for the participants was to provide suggestions on improvements for the VDR system prototype, particularly addressing reflections on self-performance in terms of the perception and recognition of the projected self-image.

A total of 22 people were involved in the study. The data was analyzed using an interpretative approach [13], in which the researchers draw on the understanding, and shared perspective of the users, as well as the domain of their actions, to determine the reality of the prototype (VDR system).

The procedure of the study started with that the participants were introduced to the VDR system and the evaluation procedure. They were instructed to freely interact with the system and to try on different pieces of clothes until they experienced they were done. After this, the participants were requested to fill out a questionnaire, to take part in a semi-structured interview, and, finally, to participate in a design session directed towards possible design improvements.

The questionnaires focused on general participant background information as well as preferences when it comes to the 'projected self'. The interviews and the design session were directed towards different aspects of the user interface in terms of usability and user experience; however, the focus of this paper is on the affordances and constraints when it comes to the performance of self. The video observations focused on the user's interaction with the VDR system (the prototype); facial expressions and actions indicating self-recognition and perceptions of self.

The next section discusses the results of the study and concludes with an outlook indicating potential directions of development for a sufficient virtual dressing room system.

5   Analysis and Discussion

It was deemed optimal to use such a sensing device to achieve the desired state-of-the-art capturing of a customer's torso image for further system processing. Using a camera-based device means that the system is non-invasive to enable data-generation from unencumbered motion, i.e. no need to wear, hold or touch any input device. In this way unencumbered gesture controls responsive feedback that is pleasing, direct and immediate so as to digitally mirror input to stimulate the user to further react intuitively in such a way as to become immersed in the interaction. The mirroring technique reinforces a participant's awareness of movement and proprioception and is developed from observations of traditional silver mirroring use in research.

The participants experienced the VDR system as a goal-oriented solution [14] where the navigation was defined and the selection and purchasing of clothes were efficient and convenient, for example by following certain steps and browsing the collection of clothes. However, the selection of clothes was limited, which constrained the performance and, furthermore, the sensorial adventure of exploring different kinds of clothes in terms of textiles, shape, size, and colors. This was in many cases described as closely related to an optimal clothes-shopping event. This addresses an issue concerned with a mismatch of the correlation between the participants' expectations and the computational expectations of the VDR system.

The system provided the participants with a quick access time due to that it simply required them to stand in front of the Kinect (camera) and the clothes were then auto-scaled and applied to the image of the user. Again, this experience was constrained due to the limited access to a variety of clothes, but on the other hand the freedom to move back and forth to judge the fitting of the clothes afforded a sense of exploration value. These results also show that the participants considered that their body could be used to manipulate the system in an interactive mode.

Due to the camera-based system, the participants clearly could recognize themselves via the mirrored image presented on the screen. The fact that it was a full body image seemed to facilitate the performance of self, for example in terms of more movements by the participants in order to express themselves with different clothes and different postures, gestures, and facial expressions. This kind of performance of self refers to a direct self-recognition [cf. 15], which is related to performing actions such as pointing at oneself, or rearranging clothes as a reaction to the captured self-image.

The system user interface provides tracking of multiple participants, which opened up for the participants to try out clothes together with others. For example, a mother brought her son (3 years of age) to try out the system. While doing so, she tried to pick up the virtual clothes placed on her body and pass them on to her son. This action was, then, repeated by the son, who moved the clothes placed on his body back to the mother's body. Two male participants acted in a similar way when they tried on different clothes. If we relate this to the concept of mirroring, which can be defined as a personal experience, but in this paper it relates more to the instances of seeing a projection of the self in a virtual world designed for the motion sensing input device; the Microsoft Kinect. Mirroring in this sense, influenced the self-perception where the self was capable of taking the role of another or, like in the mother-son example, being influenced by someone 'like me' [15, p. 235]. Furthermore, the interaction between the mother and the son as well as between the two males mentioned in the above text, shows that a system providing opportunities for multiple participants to interact when trying out clothes afford shared experiences. This includes a joint performance fostering a hedonic [16] shopping experience.

5.1   Conclusions

This study investigated how a virtual dressing room can facilitate the performance of self in terms of self-recognition and self-perception. The performance of self was fostered by a camera-based system, which efficiently reflected a full body mirrored image of the self. This, in turn, facilitated a range of movements and expressions (postures, gestures, facial expressions) where the participants, for example, rearranged their projected clothes in a direct self-recognition manner. Furthermore, the performance of self was afforded by the mirroring experience, which influenced the self-perception where the self was capable of acting together with another person, who was considered as 'someone like me'. Finally, social aspects such as joint performance, which was not only fostering a hedonic shopping experience, but also afforded an enriched experience of the performing self.

The constraints related to the performance of self in a virtual dressing room were merely related to the technical accuracy of the system, for example the fit between the mirrored body and the tried on clothes. Also, exploring different kinds of clothes in terms of textiles, shapes, sizes and colors constrained the performance of self. These constraints address technical challenges related to the further development of the system, which will be elaborated upon in the following section.

Outlook. Because of the lacking of feel of apparel it is important to make an effort to enhance another sense of the clothing that a person is considering to purchase. Advancing the VDR display could be a glasses-free 3D-Multi-View Portrait format auto stereoscopic display (Fig. 3). In line with the argument presented in the previous section related to the lack of feel of cloth, is that the SKOPOS Institute for market and communication research conducted a study on advertising in 3D in October 2010. In the study, 312 people were divided into two equal groups, each of whom was presented a commercial either in 3D or in 2D. The differences between the test groups were clear: the 3D viewers found the commercial to be modern, original and unique. After the test, 82% of the 3D viewers were convinced of the product. In the 2D group, only 64% were convinced. After the 3D broadcast, viewers also felt more of a desire to try the advertised product; in other words, the purchase probability was significantly greater.

Fig. 3. A 65" glasses-free 3D-Multi-View Portrait format autostereoscopic display[1]

In addition, in both test groups, 43% said they would also like to watch 3D at home. These test results show that there is generally a strong willingness to view 3D content, which can thus be exploited very advantageously for the advertising industry.

In the recent past, 3D technology has experienced a boom, especially in the consumer market. Early in 2010, the Korean display market research company DisplayBank added glasses-free 3D solutions to their list of the most important display innovations for the next ten years. And it's only a matter of time until

---

[1] http://www.tridelity.com/fileadmin/user_upload/Produkte/
MP5700_3.jpg

companies in all industries adapt to the market changes. Latest advances are 3D glasses-free display solutions in portrait mode – the question is whether this can be a real-time solution for a VDR in boutique or online, to enhance the shopping experience.

Acknowledgements. The Danish National Advanced Technology Foundation who funds the Virtual Dressing Room project. The authors would also like to thank Virtual Lab ApS and Commentor ApS for the VDR prototype.

References

1. Miller, D.: A Theory of Shopping. Cornell University Press, Ithaca (1998)
2. Brooks, A., Petersson, E.: Play Therapy Utilizing the Sony EyeToy®. In: The Proceedings of Presence 2005, London, UK, pp. 303–314 (2005)
3. Murray, J.H.: Inventing the Medium. Principles of Interaction Design as a Cultural Practice. The MIT Press, Cambridge (2012)
4. Mulpuru, S.: U.S. E-commerce Forecast: 2008 to 2012. Forrester Research Report, January 18 (2008)
5. Beck, B.: Key Strategic Issues in Online Apparel Retailing. The Need for an Online Fitting Solution (2000), http://www.yourfit.com (retrieved October 31, 2013)
6. Evans, P.F.: Retail Executive Survey, 2008: Using Maslow To Set Site Investment Priorities. Forrester Report, April 1 (2009)
7. Grimaldi, P.: Day of Rejects: Store Clerks Gear Up for Gift Exchanges. Tribune Business News, Washington, December 26 (2008)
8. Holte, M.: 3D Scanning of Clothing using a RGB-D Sensor with Application in a Virtual Dressing Room (under review, 2014)
9. Valente, A., Marchetti, E.: The Elusive Phenomenon of Returns in Online Apparel Shopping. The International Journal of Technology, Knowledge, and Society 10 (2014)
10. Gao, Y., Petersson Brooks, E.: Designing Ludic Engagement in an Interactive Virtual Dressing Room System – A Comparative Study. In: Marcus, A. (ed.) DUXU 2013, Part III. LNCS, vol. 8014, pp. 504–512. Springer, Heidelberg (2013)
11. Brooks, A.L., Czarowicz, A.: Markerless Motion Tracking: MS Kinect and Organic Motion OpenStage. In: Sharkey, P., Klinger, E. (eds.) Proceedings of the 9th International Conference on Disability, Virtual Reality and Associated Technologies, pp. 435–437 (2012)
12. Kristensen, K., Borum, N., Christensen, L.G., Jepsen, H.W., Lam, J., Brooks, A.L., Brooks, E.P.: Towards a Next Generation Universally Accessible 'Online Shopping-for-Apparel' System. In: Kurosu, M. (ed.) HCII/HCI 2013, Part III. LNCS, vol. 8006, pp. 418–427. Springer, Heidelberg (2013)
13. Walsham, G.: Interpreting Information Systems in Organizations. Wiley, Chichester (1993)
14. Parsons, A.G.: Non-Functional Motives for Online Shoppers: Why we Click. The Journal of Consumer Marketing 19(5), 380–392 (2002)
15. Brooks-Gunn, J., Lewis, M.: The development of early visual self-recognition. Developmental Review 4(3), 215–239 (1984)
16. To, P.-L., C. L.-H.: Shopping Motivations on Internet: A Study Based on Utilitarian and Hedonic Value. Technovation, 774–787 (2007)

Understanding Dynamic Pricing for Parking
in Los Angeles: Survey and Ethnographic Results

James Glasnapp[1], Honglu Du[1], Christopher Dance[2], Stephane Clinchant[2],
Alex Pudlin[3], Daniel Mitchell[4], and Onno Zoeter[2]

[1] Palo Alto Research Center (PARC)
{glasnapp,hdu}@parc.com
[2] Xerox Research Centre Europe
{chris.dance,stephane.clinchant,onno.zoeter}@xrce.xerox.com
[3] Xerox, Los Angeles, CA
alex.pudlin@xerox.com
[4] Department of Transportation, City of Los Angeles
dan.mitchell@lacity.org

Abstract. The field of parking is going through a period of extreme innovation. Cities in the United States are now exploring new technology to improve on-street parking. One such innovation is dynamic pricing based on sensors and smart meters. This paper presents the results of two surveys and an ethnographic study in the context of LA Express Park™ to understand users' behaviors, knowledge and perceptions around parking. Survey results demonstrated that a high number of users misunderstood one of three tested stickers that convey time of day pricing. Furthermore, after discovering the availability of cheaper parking spots nearby, people expressed willingness to change their future behavior to park in those places. Ethnographic field studies found that it is common for many parkers to use handicapped placards for over eight hours in one parking session. A percentage of these parkers may be using placards illegally. We propose that increasing some parking restrictions during the day may curb placard use by making it more difficult to park for long periods.

Keywords: Parking technology, dynamic pricing, ethnography.

1   Introduction

In many urban centers traffic is becoming an issue because of congestion and its associated effect on air quality. Technology related to parking has evolved relatively slowly since the first parking meter was installed in 1935 [14]. Recently, however, cities around the world have begun to experiment with the use of technology to improve the parking experience. One way technology is being used is the use of dynamic pricing as a means to reduce congestion. With the support from the United States Department of Transportation, cities like San Francisco (SFPark, 2013) and Los Angeles (LA Express ParkTM, 2013) have installed sensors that report the occupancy of each street parking space and new parking meters that charge variable rates depending on time of the day. [6, 11, 16]. Moscow, Barcelona, Toulouse, Auckland,

F.F.-H. Nah (Ed.): HCIB/HCII 2014, LNCS 8527, pp. 316–327, 2014.
© Springer International Publishing Switzerland 2014

and Indianapolis [3, 4, 12, 19, 23] are just a few of the other cities around the world who are experimenting with sensors and technologies to help drivers find and pay for parking. Washington DC has also piloted sensors in a four block area and has plans to expand that pilot to 1000 spaces [15]. Likewise, New York City has incorporated 177 magnetic sensors in a pilot program, ParkSmart [8].

In this paper, we address these emerging questions in the context of LA Express Park[TM]. We first review related work in the field of dynamic pricing for parking. Then the results from two surveys and an ethnographic study conducted in Los Angeles are presented. We conclude with recommendations about how to improve the dynamic pricing for parking from a user's perspective.

2   Related Work

In this part, we give a brief review of the sensor based parking management system which supports dynamic pricing for parking. We then review related work in the literature on the effectiveness of dynamic pricing for parking.

2.1   Sensor Based Parking Management System

The technology that allows demand based pricing is wireless parking sensors that are typically embedded in the center pavement within the parking spot. The sensors detect the change in parked vehicles' occupancy and these data are then used to determine parking availability. In turn, motorists have real-time information about available parking through websites and applications while enforcement officers, with the combination of meter payment data, are able to see potential violations. A variety of parking sensors are available including solar and battery-powered sensors based on a variety of magnetic, optical, ultrasonic and radar techniques [20]. Although sensors have been used in off-street parking for some time, it has not been widely adopted in on-street parking management because of the higher cost of on-street sensor installation due to the need for wireless communication. Generally, sensors need demarcated spaces in order to accurately assess parked vehicles, and may not always work if people parking don't park in expected ways. [17]

2.2   Dynamic Pricing

Cruising the streets to find an open space for parking is common and greatly increases traffic congestion. It is estimated that an average of 34% of cars in congested downtown traffic are cruising for parking [18]. Economists have advocated matching prices to demand as an effective way to solve parking problems. Nobel prize winning economist William Vickery recommended that street parking prices should be set "at a level so determined as to keep the amount of parking down sufficiently so that there will almost always be space available for those willing to pay the fee" [22]. However, the primitive metering technology in 1954 made the proposal of dynamic pricing appear outlandish [13]. Following Vickrey, several theoretical economic analyses of parking demonstrated that cruising could be eliminated by an adequate pricing policy [1, 2, 7].

Recent developments in sensor and payment technologies have made dynamic demand based pricing of parking a reality. It has also afforded the possibility of time of day pricing meaning that times/days when demand for parking is low, rates are low and visa versa. Pierce and Shoup's research on SFpark showed that time of day pricing is effective in reducing on-street parking occupancy rates and that the average price elasticity for parking is -0.4 (every 10% increase in parking price leads to a 4% fall in occupancy).

The above-mentioned studies focused on using mathematical methods to model driver's driving and parking behavior and showed some positive potential of using dynamic pricing for parking, yet there are still many unanswered questions in this area. For example, it is not clear what drivers' reactions are to the concept of dynamic pricing for parking. Drivers may not know that the price of parking is dynamic and thus the question of how to communicate the concept of dynamic pricing to drivers is essential to its success [13].

Further, dynamic pricing of parking works in some places, but not in others and it is not always clear what attributes to its success or demise. There are several noted obstacles to achieving the desired results from congestion pricing that include infrequent enforcement, meter failures, government vehicles (that are exempt from payment) and those drivers with handicapped placards (also exempt from payments in certain U.S states and cities). The California vehicle code allows handicapped parkers to park for as long as they want at no cost [5].

In this study, we took a user-centered approach to explore dynamic pricing and to gain deeper understanding about people's reactions and behavior with regard to dynamic pricing of parking in the context of LA Express ParkTM.

3   LA Express Park^{TM}

In 2010, the Los Angeles Department of Transportation began a process of installing new parking meters in downtown Los Angeles that accepted credit and debit card payments. A network of wireless payment sensors keep track of parked vehicles and help officials determine what meters are currently in use. The key goal of the program is to increase availability of parking spaces and decrease traffic congestion and pollution.

Stakeholders wanted to develop communication strategies to inform parkers of cheaper parking nearby, test current communication strategies and develop new ways to convey the complexity of time of day pricing. The implementation of time of day pricing in August 2012 further highlighted the need for a clear communication strategy and required new ways to convey the complexity of variable pricing.

3.1   Dynamic Pricing Stickers

A sticker design solution was implemented to convey pricing information for two conditions. One sticker design was developed for meters in blocks where a range of rates were available in a small geographic area but where time of day pricing had not yet been implemented. The goal of this sticker was to easily convey to the parker where they were, the price of parking where they parked and the relative price of parking on nearby block faces (Figure 2). The sticker was designed to fit on the front facing side of the meter. We created many iterations of the sticker to find the optimal design for driver comprehension.

The second scenario for which stickers were designed was time of day pricing (AKA variable rate pricing). Previously, the city of Los Angeles conveyed time of day pricing information using a sticker known as the Max Rate sticker (Fig. 3, left part of figure). This sticker conveyed the maximum rate a user would pay, but did not answer the question: "What is the price of parking right now?" A new sticker was developed to be more descriptive about the range of hourly rates throughout the week (Fig. 3, right portion).

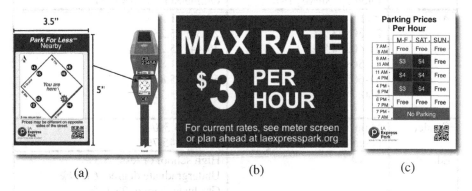

Fig. 1. a: Flat rate sticker; **b:** Maximum rate sticker; **c:** time of day sticker

The key research questions related to these stickers on which data collection was targeted were: How well did parkers comprehend the stickers? What were parkers' intentions around future parking behavior because of TOD pricing? What were people's knowledge of parking fees? What were people's knowledge of recent parking price increases?

4   Methods

On-street Intercept Survey. We developed an intercept survey and conducted open-ended interviews with individuals parking in four pilot areas. Each of the four areas included one block face with a relatively higher hourly parking rate and neighboring block faces with less expensive rates. Individual water resistant stickers were developed and placed on meters (see Fig.2). Anyone parking within the pilot block area qualified to participate. Respondents received twenty dollars if they agreed to answer the survey questions and talk with us for a few minutes after the survey was complete.

During the week of February 11 and the week of March 19, 2013, ethnographic observations and intercept surveys were conducted on those four downtown Los Angeles streets. Seventy-three (73) people of different ages (from 20s to 60s) were interviewed in intercept surveys.

Online Targeted Survey. To reach a larger population and understand the general acceptance of the concept of dynamic pricing of parking, we worked with a third party survey firm and launched an online survey targeted at people in the Los Angeles area. As a result, responses from 158 participants were collected. See Table 1. below for detailed demographic information about the participants in each survey.

In both surveys, we asked questions about people's awareness of dynamic pricing for parking and their comprehension of different dynamic pricing stickers.

Table 1. Demographic information of survey respondents

	Intercept Survey *(N=73)*	Online Survey *(N=158)*
Age	<=20: 4.3% 21-30: 23.2% 31-40: 34.8% 41-50: 26.1% 51-60: 10.1% >60: 1.4%	18-24: 11.26% 25-34: 15.23% 35-44: 15.23% 45-54: 21.85% 55-64: 25.83% 65-74: 7.95% >75: 2.65%
Gender	Male: 63.2% Female: 36.8%	Male: 54.3% Female: 45.7%
Education	NA	High school or less: 5.3% Undergraduate degree: 61.59% Graduate degree: 23.18% Professional: 9.9%
Annual Income	NA	<$25k: 25.4% $25k-$50k: 13.3% $50k-$100k: 21% $100k-$150k: 14.7% >$150k: 26.6%

Ethnographic Observations. In addition to the surveys, ethnographic observations were conducted to understand any social and physical aspects related to parking in the four pilot areas. Observations were targeted to identify any routinized patterns of behavior among parkers; who is parking and why; the physical environmental elements present that might affect parking in the pilot areas; and to understand the human need fulfillment that is attempted to be met (vis a vis parking) within the pilot settings. Information on Handicapped Placard parking was a result of these observations and became a primary finding of the study.

5   Results

In this section we first report on results from the intercept and online surveys which include: factors influencing parking decisions, awareness of parking prices, distance parked from intended location, comprehension of dynamic pricing stickers, possible changes in behavior, and feelings about dynamic pricing. Second, we will report the findings on handicapped placard observations.

5.1   Factors Influencing Parking Decisions

Proximity is the most important factor that people consider when selecting a parking space while time is the least important factor. In the online survey, participants were asked to rank how the following factors influenced their decision when selecting a parking space (1 as least important, and 4 as most important): availability of parking spots; cost of parking; proximity of the parking spot; and, time (whether in a rush or not). Proximity is rated as the most important factor people would consider when deciding where to park, with a weighted average score of 2.99. Cost is the second most important factor with a weighted average score of 2.50 and availability the third most important factor (weighted average score of 2.46). Time is the least important factor (weighted average score of 2.03).

In the intercept survey, similar questions were asked and similar results were obtained. Instead of asking participants to rank the importance of factors, we ask participants to choose all the factors that they think are important. Proximity was considered by 63.8% of the respondents   as an important factor that influences their parking decisions, followed by 33.3% of the respondents who thought availability was an important factor. Cost was regarded by 18.8% of the participants as an important factor while only 7.2% of the respondents regarded time as a factor to consider when selecting a parking spot.

In the intercept survey, respondents also mentioned other factors to consider when choosing a parking space. Included as other factors were fear of being towed and safety concerns.

5.2   Awareness of Parking Prices

In both the online and on-street intercept surveys, participants' awareness of dynamic pricing was studied. More specifically, participants' awareness of recent parking price changes (Price Change), awareness of time of day dynamic pricing for parking in downtown Los Angeles (TOD Pricing) and awareness of the availability of mobile parking apps were assessed. If the participant indicated that they were aware of some mobile parking applications, they were asked to identify the names of those mobile parking applications.

In general, participants' awareness of recent parking price changes; time of day dynamic pricing for parking and the availability of mobile parking apps was low (Fig. 4). In the online survey, 31 (20%) participants were aware of price changes, while in the intercept survey, 22 (31%) participants said that they were aware that parking prices changed in downtown Los Angeles.

About 20% of the participants in the online survey indicated that they were aware of TOD pricing in downtown Los Angeles, and this is consistent with the results from the intercept survey where 17 participants (24%) indicated that they were aware of TOD pricing.

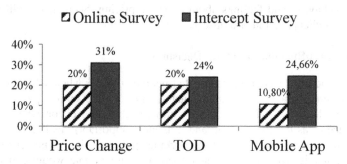

Fig. 2. Awareness of price change, TOD and mobile parking apps

People's awareness of the mobile parking application were particularly low. Only 17 (10.8%) of the participants in the online survey indicated that they were aware of mobile parking apps, and only 5 of them could name a mobile parking app. In the intercept survey, a higher percentage of the participants claimed that they were aware of some mobile parking apps (18 or 24.66%), but only 4 of them could name a mobile parking app.

It is noted that participants' awareness of price changes, TOD and mobile parking applications is always lower in the online survey group than in the intercept survey group. This may be due to differences in the characteristics of the two samples participating in each survey. The online survey respondents tended to be older and more females were respondents. Further, based on our experience, we felt that it was because in the intercept survey participants had the opportunity to interact with the researchers and the researcher can briefly clarify or explain things that participants did not quite understand at the beginning. For example, some of the participants did not quite understand the concept of TOD in the beginning, but after explaining it to them, they confirmed that they were aware of it. However, the combination of results from both surveys should provide sufficient representativeness to offer reasonable generalization of results as responses tended to be in the same direction in both groups.

5.3   Distance Parked from Intended Location

In the on-street intercept survey we asked respondents how many blocks from their intended location they actually had to park. Over half (54.79%) parked within one block of their intended location.

We then asked survey respondents "What is the maximum number of blocks you would be willing to park from your intended location. The mean number of blocks that respondents were willing to walk was 3.07 (SD = 1.54).

5.4   Comprehension of Dynamic Pricing Stickers

We tested comprehension of three types of stickers. For the flat-rate sticker (Fig. 2), overall comprehension of the sticker was quite high with over 80% of respondents from both samples answering the questions correctly. We asked respondents three questions.

First, "From looking at the sticker above, what is your current location?" Eighty-three percent (83%) of intercept survey respondents and 91% of online survey respondents answered this question correctly. Next we asked, "From looking at the sticker above, what is the price of parking where you are right now? Similarly, 92% and 85% answered this question correctly. Finally we asked, "From looking at the sticker above can you identify which of the following streets has the least expensive parking? Eighty-nine percent (89%) and 86% answered this question correctly.

For the intercept survey we approached comprehension of the Max Rate sticker (Fig.3, left) with an open-ended question to respondents: "What does this sticker mean to you? Not surprisingly, we found that only 20.9% of those we spoke with accurately understood the intended message of the sticker. In contrast, for the online survey we asked respondents to select among multiple choices that included the following: 1) "The price of this spot can change, but won't go over $3/hour;" 2) "Parking is $3/hour; and 3) The parking limit is one hour. Roughly 7 in 10 respondents (69.1%) correctly identified the answer: "The price of this spot can change, but won't go over $3/hour." We believe that the disparate findings are due to the open ended versus multiple choice response formats and the time online respondents had to consider the question as well as the setting. Upon careful consideration the Max Rate sticker would appear to be sufficiently clear in its meaning. However, in a test environment, more participants are able to identify the correct answer when they have the ability to select that answer among three choices. In contrast, when on the street and directly asked, people's first impression was that it is $3/hour.

5.5   Behavioral Change Intentions

In the online survey, we asked respondents "Now that you know there is cheaper parking nearby, would you be inclined to park where there is cheaper parking on your next visit?" Roughly 84% of the respondents expressed willingness to change their parking based on flat rating pricing. This finding is consistent with results from the intercept survey (76.4%), across genders (Chi square (1, N=151)=.47, p=.49) and groups with different levels of income (Chi square (1, N=113)=.07, p=.78).

In the online survey, we also asked, "How likely is Time of Day pricing to affect your parking behavior?" Approximately 48.4% of the respondents were somewhat or extremely likely to change their parking based on TOD, however about another 32.5% of the respondents were unlikely to change their parking behavior. This result is consistent with the result from the on-street intercept survey (49.3% of them were likely to change their parking based on TOC).

5.6   Feelings about Dynamic Pricing

We asked participants to provide reasons when they indicated that they were unlikely to change parking behavior based on TOD pricing in both the online and the intercept surveys. The following themes emerged:

- People with inflexible schedules (business, employment, etc.) are unlikely to change their parking based on TOD.
- People who don't park frequently in downtown LA or don't park long hours were also unlikely to adjust their parking based on TOD pricing.

- Convenience of parking and availability of parking spaces are other factors that influence people's parking decisions. Some people care more about parking convenience than cost.
- The fact that parking price would increase during peak hours intensifies the competition between public on-street parking and private garage parking.

To summarize, it is interesting to observe that the discussion of parking choices correspond quite nicely with what theory predicts. The valuation for a close on-street space is different for different types of users. In particular, short stay parkers will be less influenced by a rate change. Longer stayers, who are less inconvenienced by walking to a nearby off-street lot will be the first to change their parking location. And by doing so, they will open up spaces for users that have a higher benefit to park close and for short stay parkers (shoppers, etc.).

5.7   Ethnographic Observations: Handicapped Parking Placards

Our ethnographic observations revealed that many streets were full of cars parked with handicapped placards. In this section we discuss these observations in more detail and propose a potential solution.

The First Encounter. South Oliver Street (at 7th) has 21 on-street parking spots. However, this location was virtually full of vehicles with handicapped placards. As a result, there was no turnover and we were unable to conduct interviews. We were intrigued with the number of placards and noted that as the observation days progressed we observed the same vehicles parking on or near this particularly block. As by Manville [21], one of the significant roadblocks to achieving the desired behavior change via economic interventions to pricing is handicapped parking. Drivers for whom price doesn't matter affect overall pricing and demand because one can't affect behavior change with this subset of parkers because price doesn't matter.

We observed this particular block systematically for two days, on March 20th and 21st, 2013. We counted the number of handicap placards in vehicles parked in legal spaces 4 times during the day over the two days and observed the following. On average, 75% of cars parked had handicap placards. We observed many people who parked with handicap placards walking presumably to their place of employment nearby without any detectable physical handicapping condition. The percentage of occupied spots with handicapped placards peaked at midday (Fig.3). When spots opened up, paying customers filled them.

Handicapped Parking Placards in Downtown LA. We also identified nine blocks that were known to have high handicap placard usage (learned from city parking enforcement officers) and we observed these blocks on at least one occasion. Four out of the nine blocks have different parking restrictions on two sides of the street. We found that occupancy rates of handicapped placards were higher on sides of the streets that had fewer parking restrictions. For example, on the block of 700 & 701 S Flower St, on the side of the block where there is parking available between 8 AM and 8 PM, 60% of the occupied spots had vehicles with handicap placards. On the opposite side of the street with tighter restrictions (9AM - 3 PM), there were no placard users.

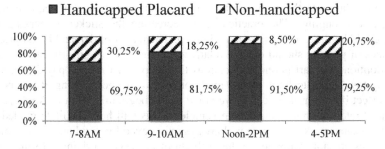

Fig. 3. Handicapped placard occupancy rate on South Oliver Street (at 7th)

We combined all the data that were collected on those four blocks, and found that handicapped placard usages was much lower on the side of the street where there are more parking restrictions (chi-square $(1,N=103)=13.97$, p=.0002).

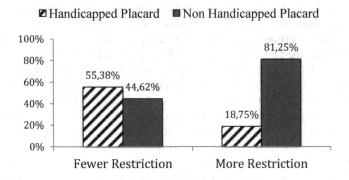

Fig. 4. Handicapped placard rate comparison

6   Discussion and Conclusion

In this paper, the results of two surveys and an ethnographic study on users' beha-viors, knowledge and perceptions about dynamic pricing for parking are presented. While most of the previous work on dynamic pricing for parking heavily focused on using mathematical models to demonstrate the efficacy of dynamic pricing for park-ing to reduce traffic congestion and make more parking spots available, our study contributes to the literature by taking a human centered approach to understand the dynamics around parking.

As presented, we found that overall comprehension of the stickers were quite high. However, it appeared that those individuals who had more difficulty were those for whom English is a second language, or for those who may appear to have low literacy levels. This is an important point to consider in any public design consideration.

While as a pilot, the flat rate sticker was an interesting way to alert people that there was cheaper parking nearby. The time of day sticker also demonstrated a feasi-ble way to communicate pricing. The actual implementation of these stickers as a permanent solution to the problem of promoting behavior change and communicating pricing is challenging. The practicality of recreating the sticker as parking prices change could be time consuming and a burden. The tenant of demand based pricing is that prices of parking should change relative to demand. It is unfortunate that at this time, adoption of smart phone applications that help you find and pay for parking is relatively low. Until technology can guide people to cheaper parking, it will be difficult to affect behavior change. As we noted in the beginning section, Apple recently announced integration of their IOS in vehicles. This will help facilitate guided navigation to cheaper parking. There will always exist several individuals for whom these technologies are not available, so the problem of conveying pricing information in a low-tech way will likely continue in one form or another.

In this study it was found that there was high incidence of handicap placard usage in downtown Los Angeles. We observed many people who parked with handicap placards easily walking presumably to their place of employment nearby. Further it was found that in places where there were more parking restrictions (9AM - 4PM vs. 8AM-8PM), the incidence of handicap placard was much lower. This is a promising result because in the short term, policy makers can potentially solve some of the handicap parking issues by adjusting the parking restrictions. However, it is suggested that larger scale experiments are needed to verify the aforementioned hypothesis and it is feasible given the fact that this data could be gathered from sensors.

In the longer term, technologies that can help parking enforcement officers easily identify illegal handicap placards are in great need. We noticed that another important reason that contributes to the high incidence of handicap placard in LA is that it is hard to verify a legitimate placard for a legitimate user. Someone could simply get a handicap placard from his or her grandparents. It is also easy to get a fake placard from the black market. Thus, it is suggested that there are three main technologies to be tackled. The first challenge is how to verify the validity of a given placard and the second is how to verify that the current user of a given placard is a valid user. The third challenge is how to design a technology that is user friendly and efficient. The ultimate goal is to design technologies that can protect legitimate handicap placard users' benefits while at the same time making sure that on-street parking, a public and social resource, is properly utilized in the interests of the whole society.

References

1. Anderson, S.P., de Palma, A.: The economics of pricing parking. Journal of Urban Economics 55(1), 1–20 (2004)
2. Arnott, R., Inci, E.: An integrated model of downtown parking and traffic congestion. Journal of Urban Economics 60(3), 418–442 (2006)
3. Beardsley, E.: French city implements new public parking spot sensors, http://www.dw.de/french-city-implements-new-public-parking-spot-sensors/a-14731361 (accessed September 13, 2013)
4. Berishvili, N., Novosti, M.: November parking revolution. The Moscow New (2013)
5. California vehicle code V C Section 22511.5 Disabled Parking Authorized Parking Zones, http://www.dmv.ca.gov/pubs/vctop/d11/vc22511_5.htm (accessed September 13, 2013)

6. Glasnapp, J., Isaacs, E.: No More Circling Around the Block: Evolving a Rapid Ethnography and Podcasting Method to Guide Innovation in Parking Systems. EPIC (2010)
7. Glazer, A., Niskanen, E.: Parking fees and congestion. Regional Science and Urban Economics 22(1), 123–132 (1992)
8. Kazis, N.: City Tests Out Parking Sensors, But So Far Just For Space-Finding App. (2013), http://Streetsblog.org
9. LA Express Park™ (2013), http://www.laexpresspark.org/
10. Muller, T., Kerris, N.: Apple Unveils iOS 7, http://Apple.com
11. Newcomb, D.: Audi adds parking-spot finder to new and existing models. MSN Autos (2013)
12. ParkIndy, http://www.parkindy.net (accessed September 13, 2013)
13. Pierce, G., Shoup, D.: Getting the Prices Right: An Evaluation of Pricing Parking by Demand in San Francisco. Journal of the American Planning Association 79(1), 67–81 (2013)
14. POM. Park-O-Meter (July 16, 1935) http://Pom.com (retrieved September 16, 2013)
15. Ross, V.: Smart Parking Systems Steer Drivers to Open Spaces. Popular Mechanics (2013)
16. SFpark (2013), http://sfpark.org/
17. SFpark. Parking sensor performance standards and measurement (2011)
18. Shoup, D.: The High Cost of Free Parking. Planners Press, Chicago (2011)
19. Smith, B.C.: Parking sensor trial launched on busy Akl road. The New Zealand Herald (2013)
20. Tewolde, G.S.: Sensor and network technology for intelligent transportation systems. In: Proc. IEEE Electro/Information Technology (EIT), pp. 1–7 (2012)
21. Manville, M., Williams, J.: The Price Doesn't Matter if You Don't Have to Pay: Legal Exemption as an Obstacle to Congestion Pricing. Journal of Planning Education and Research 32(3), 289–304 (2012)
22. Vickrey, W.: The economizing of curb parking space. Traffic Engineering, 62–67 (1954)
23. WoldSensing. World Sensing- Fast Prk, http://anima.es/en/technology/world-sensing-fast-prk (accessed September 16, 2013)

Full-Body Interaction for the Elderly
in Trade Fair Environments

Mandy Korzetz[1], Christine Keller[1], Frank Lamack[2], and Thomas Schlegel[1]

[1] Software Engineering of Ubiquitous Systems,
Institute of Software and Multimedia Technology,
Technische Universität Dresden,
Dresden, D-01062, Germany
[2] E-Business Solutions, T-Systems Multimedia Solutions GmbH,
Dresden, D-01129, Germany
{Mandy.Korzetz,Christine.Keller,Thomas.Schlegel}@tu-dresden.de,
Frank.Lamack@t-systems.com

Abstract. In the near future, more and more personalized products will
be offered. Presenting physical, customizable products to the customer
in all possible variations can be very complicated and space-consuming.
Virtual life-size representations of these kinds of products are common
and offer an attractive product experience. An interactive product configuration allows customers to explore several variations on their own.
The combination with natural interaction technologies, such as gesture
input, also allows users, which are mostly unfamiliar with technology, to
explore product variety efficiently. The research presented in this paper
focuses on motion-based interaction in public spaces. The application
field are trade fair environments and the target group are elderly people
with specific needs. We present a design methodology for the development of full-body gestures adapted to our application field of configuring
large-sized products (specifically caravans) on large displays in trade fair
environments using full-body interaction.

Keywords: Gesture, elderly, interaction design, large display, customizable products, public interactive installation.

1 Introduction

Gesture-based interaction technologies are an effective method to interact with
information on large displays [4]. Interaction concepts for such innovative technologies should be developed bearing the target group in mind to optimally take
into account the users' needs. Furthermore, it is important to consider the field
of application where the users will interact.

Our application field is the configuration and presentation of products in
trade fair environments. In the near future, more and more highly configurable
products will be offered, which can be personalized by customers. Presenting
physical, customizable products is a huge challenge for exhibitors. Even if the
product comprises only a few parameters, the possibilities of configuration are

F.F.-H. Nah (Ed.): HCIB/HCII 2014, LNCS 8527, pp. 328–338, 2014.
© Springer International Publishing Switzerland 2014

enormous. Furthermore, if the product has large dimensions, e.g. vehicles or caravans, a large physical space is required to present several variations. Therefore, virtual life-size representations are used to visualize the product options. Many companies address older people with special products, e.g. caravans, that are considered in our work. They are highly configurable and can be easily presented at fairs in life-size on large displays. We present a configuration system for large-sized customizable products on large displays providing full-body interaction, especially for elderly people. Gesture interfaces can be attractive and make applications more accessible to older users, because they are perceived more natural than interacting via mouse and keyboard [7,3]. Generally, applications and the used gestures should be easy to handle and easy to learn.

In this paper, we present a design approach for an application which can be used by elderly people by utilizing gestural interaction to customize products on large displays. To develop intuitive gestures we employed an user-centered design approach. In the following chapters, we discuss existing research and analyze the requirements of the target group and the application scenario. Moreover, we present an early interaction concept including an early interactive prototype as well as an adapted procedure for full-body gesture development. Finally, we discuss our results and show starting points for future work.

2   Background and Related Work

Full-body interaction that does not use explicit input devices is successfully established in the entertainment industry. Primarily, this technology is used for games, e.g. exergames that support your personal fitness at home [10,16]. The best-known device is the Kinect sensor by Microsoft, which is also used in applications for elderly people [7]. It is low-cost and easy to handle, which is why it is used more and more by designers and developers for elderly people, among many other purposes. But not only in private but also in public spaces, full-body interaction is getting increasingly attractive. There are a number of public installations with the main purpose to advertise, e.g. *Paximadaki*, an advergame installation for promoting the brand and products of a food company at exhibitions [8]. But only a few projects use touchless interaction for productive use, e.g. the touchless user interface by Ruppert et al. for interactive image visualization in urological surgery [18].

In full-body interaction you use your whole body. Most research projects about gesture interaction have focused on hand gestures which may be due to technological progress. Humans naturally use gestures to communicate [15]. By using gestures they do not use exclusively hands [12]. In certain interaction scenarios, it is conceivable that gesture interaction with other body parts or the whole body is more intuitive than hand gestures. A human-based approach is needed to identify those gestures for interacting as intuitively as possible with a system [17].

In current research, gestures are characterized by different properties depending on the viewpoint. McNeill distinguishes gestures from a linguistic view: deictic (pointing), iconic, metaphorical and beats [15]. Wobbrock et al. classified surface gestures to form (static, dynamic), nature (symbolic, physical, metaphorical, abstract), binding (object-/world-dependent, mixed) and flow (discrete, continuous) [21]. Depending on the users, different gesture types are preferred. Stößel and Blessing investigated touch-based gestures on mobile devices for older users and compared their preferred gestures to those of younger users. They found out that preferred gestures differ significantly on characteristics such as basic gesture type, fingers involved, or gesture complexity [19]. Thus, we include especially older users, our target group, in the development process.

Our work focuses on the development of a full-body interaction concept for productive use (configuring products) in public space (trade fairs). We include users (older people) in the design process pursuant to Nielsen et al. and Wobbrock et al. and adapted their method to full-body interaction using a generic, technology-independent definition of gestures.

3 Methodology

General ergonomic findings of Nielsen et al. and Wobbrock et al. suggest an user-centered approach for the development of highly intuitive and ergonomic gestures for tabletop interactions [17,21]. The approach includes four stages: analyzing the using context and finding functions, collecting gestures by involving the potential users, extracting gesture vocabulary and testing resulting vocabulary. The approach is transferable to various fields of interaction, e.g. multitouch and pen gestures [5], mobile phone gestures via integrated sensors [13] and free-hand gestures without explicit input devices [20]. We adapted the user-centered approach for hand gestures to support the development of full-body gestures.

The underlying gesture definition is a decisive factor in the development procedure. Regardless of the used gesture recognition technology, for a highly generic development approach, it is necessary to use a generic gesture definition. Kurtenbach and Hulteen define gestures as a *motion of the body that contains information*, which focuses on a dynamic aspect [14]. Harling and Edwards distinguish between static and dynamic hand gestures [11]. These definitions can be combined to a general definition of full-body gestures: *Gestures are a motion (dynamic) or a position (static) of the body or parts of it that contains information.*

If we use the general approach of the gesture definition, we can develop technology-independent natural gestures. A second benefit is that gestures are probably more natural because there are no restrictions in users' body movements and body parts. For the development of the gesture interface of our configuration system we started with a small survey, which we present in section 5. We followed the user-centered approach according to Nielsen et al. and Wobbrock et al. to design an appropriate gesture vocabulary, but adapted the procedure to technology-independent gestural full-body interaction.

4   Towards Developing an Interaction Concept

A gesture-based interaction concept used by elderly people in the context of public spaces has to meet certain criteria. Therefore we have to answer the following questions: Who are the users? And which parameters of the fair environment influence interacting? After analyzing the requirements, we suggest how to meet these requirements in the system adopted to the application field of configuring large-sized products.

4.1   Requirement Analysis: Target Group and Application Scenario

At first, we analyzed the user group and the context of fairs. The special user group, the elderlies, who are mostly unfamiliar with technology, are subjected to changes due to age in the field of physical, perceptual and cognitive abilities [6]. There are many older people who can use applications designed for younger users, but it is clear that learning those applications is very difficult because of normal aging process [3]. The lack of computer experience requires a user-centered approach for interaction development because elderly users do not have the knowledge of typical gestures.

In addition, trade fairs enhance the probability that the interacting user is a so-called first time user. There is hardly any learning effect because these trade fair visitors use these gestures for the first time and only for a short period of time. Due to the fact that trade fairs are usually noisy, users can be easily distracted from interacting. Therefore the cognitive demand should remain low. That is why we suggest a configuration wizard to customize the product step-by-step in a linear way concerning application navigation. Along with a short interaction time the application should provide just a limited configuring functionality. On the other hand, the physical demand needs to remain low.

All these facts lead to the necessity of an interaction concept, which is easy to use and easy to learn [1]. Embodied interaction with gestures which are as intuitive as possible supports learnability. Thus, a user-centered approach should be applied, e.g. by involving the target group in the development process. Furthermore, the application needs to be easy to handle with a small range of functions. The following sections describe in detail how we meet the requirements as outlined above. Our interaction concept for elderly people using full-body interaction includes simplicity at three levels: *navigation, functions* and *gestures*.

4.2   Navigation: Preprocessing the Product Data

We developed a generic approach for preprocessing the product information to configure them step-by-step in a configuration wizard. Product data are typically structured in hierarchies with any level of detail. There are product parts which can be organized in groups (e.g. *bed* and *bedside table* to a *bed arrangement*). Consequently, the result is a product tree. This product structure can be

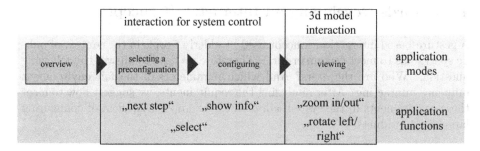

Fig. 1. Structure of interaction sequence within the application

used to sequence the different options for each customizable product part. After sequencing customizable product options there is a simple sequential structure. This structure can be used for implementing a configuration wizard. Complex product structures should be divided into simple constructs. The sequencing forms the basis for a clear and consistent navigation. The total interaction sequence should be kept to a minimum by organizing customizable parts in whole customizable groups (e.g. a *table* and *chairs* can be grouped to a *seat set*). A resulting linear navigation facilitates the interaction in each configuration step because of its reduced range of functions.

4.3   Functions: Configuration Functionality

In order to simplify the customizing of products for the user, it is necessary to provide just a basic but adequate configuration functionality. Therefore, we divided the application into three main stages (see figure 1): preconfiguring, configuring and viewing mode. The first step to simplify interaction sequences in the field of functions is to offer different preconfigurations of the product which can then be customized in a further stage. In general, these stages can be separated by their interaction focus (system control and 3d model interaction). During the configuring stage we mapped the functionality to basic functions for system control, including menu interactions (*next step, show info, select*). To support the imagination of the customer it is useful to present tangible products as 3d model in real time. While configuring different parts of the product, the application should help to navigate through the 3d scene by focusing relevant scene parts automatically (see figure 4). In the final stage, the viewing mode, the customer can explore their customized product on their own (*zoom in/zoom out* and *rotate left/rotate right*).

4.4   Gestures: Development Procedure

In a next step, we wanted to find those gestures that may trigger the functions. Because of the compact set of functions, the resulting set will comprise only a few number of gestures. The gesture vocabulary is kept at a minimum, so that it

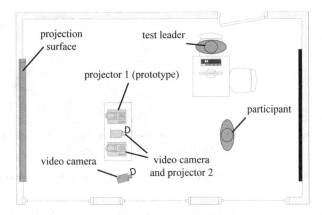

Fig. 2. The setting of the laboratory where the study had been conducted

is easy-to-understand and users do not have to learn much. There is a wide gap between the young designer's personal experience and the experiences of older users. To bridge this gap we adopted the user-centered approach and based the development process on a general gesture definition as we presented in section 3.

5   User Study for Developing Gesture Interaction

Participants and Technical Setup. In a first iteration, we conducted a user study with five participants (2 male, 3 female; average age of about 60) to identify first full-body gestures for the configuration system of caravan products. None of the participants had much experience with computer systems or prior experience with gesture interaction.

The technical setup of the user study can be seen in figure 2. The system was simulated by a low-fidelity prototype (slide show) which was displayed with a projector. We implemented two passes: without and with visual feedback. Visual feedback was given by installing a second projector, which overlayed the prototype picture and showed the reflection of the participant. The test leader described a typical interaction scenario step-by-step which the participant should turn into body movements. They were asked to move freely with their whole body to interact with the prototype.

Results. Movements of hands and arms were often performed by participants. One of the participants tended to take a few steps forward to enlarge the presented caravan. All in all, gestures of different categories were shown: physical related to the caravan transformations (e.g. beckoning to enlarge as you see in figure 3(b)), metaphorical (e.g. a sleeping gesture in order to switch to the sleeping area of the caravan by putting both hands beside the head) and deictic to interact with menu options. There was no essential difference between the two passes, but the pass with visual feedback shows interactions with a stronger

 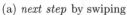 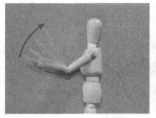 

(a) *next step* by swiping   (b) *zoom in* by beckoning   (c) *rotate left* by moving
                               with both arms   clock-wise

Fig. 3. Extracted dynamic gestures for interacting with the configuration application

object-dependency. One participant complemented some of his gestures with voice-commands.

The results showed an initial, compact set of five full-body gestures of different categories. In the next step, we sorted out those body movements and gestures, which would not to be used at fairs (e.g. clapping). It was interesting to observe that the participants without any technological background performed very similar movements spontaneously. They differed from the designer's expected gestures, but are well-known from everyday life (e.g. beckoning to zoom in) and are therefore applicable in the specific context of trade fairs.

A standard concept for interacting with systems is point-and-click [2,9]. Besides the gestures showed in figure 3, we could observe this central concept in our study. Participants pointed to something and tried to confirm their selection by tipping in the air. Furthermore, the test persons preferred discrete gestures, which means they repeated e.g. their rotation movement up to the desired position of the caravan.

Interactive Prototype. Based on the interaction concept and study results we implemented a first interactive prototype by using Microsoft's Kinect (figure 4). For the development of the basic functionality we used the Unity3D-Engine[1]. For rapid gesture development we used the Omek Beckon Development Suite[2]. Technology restrictions for gesture recognition imply in this development stage. For a better recognition rate, some of the gestures had to be performed with exaggerated movements, e.g. rotating in a more vertical plane in relation to the Kinect sensor. Thus, the resulting prototype includes the configuration stages and functionality as shown in figure 1.

6   Discussion

Our study has been conducted with a small number of five participants composed by representatives of the user group. On this account, the results are

---

[1] http://www.unity3d.com/

[2] http://www.omekinteractive.com/

Fig. 4. Screenshot of an early interactive prototype

only a set of initial thoughts of a final gesture vocabulary and interaction concept. Nevertheless, it has been demonstrated that older users with less computer and gesture experience prefer other gestures than the young designers expected (e.g. zooming - our designers expected a movement similar to the multitouch pinch/spread). Our findings indicates that elderly users prefer certain gesture types (deictic, metaphorical). Stößel and Blessing showed similar results in the field of preferences concerning multitouch gesture types [19]. They also identified that most of preferred gestures were discrete. A comparison of discrete and continuous gestures for shown dynamic gestures with an interactive prototype could show to what extent this results can be transferred to full-body interactions.

Further improvements will focus on refining the extracted gestures using the interactive prototype like presented in section 5 as well as evaluating the interaction concept itself. Resultant gestures have to be tested reverse according to distinctness, memorability and ergonomics as stated in Nielsen et al. and Wobbrock et al. [17,21]. In addition, future work will include refinement and evaluation of the application navigation. For example, an extension, which includes orientation metaphors would be useful for an understandable linear structure. The limited configuration functionality, as a second simplicity factor, is only applicable to products which are less complex. In case of highly configurable products, it might be necessary to adjust configurations in a last step by the seller. It is essential to determine under which conditions a product is too complex for customization with the developed interaction concept.

We have presented an adapted methodology of developing intuitive gestures for full-body interaction originally proposed by Nielsen et al. and Wobbrock et al. for tabletop interaction. Participants were introduced to the general gesture definition with no restrictions concerning their body movements and body parts.

Most participants used mainly specific body parts like arms and hands, but there were also hints that they actually would use their whole body to interact naturally with systems, e.g. take a few steps forward to zoom in. To refine extended methodology we should conduct a user study with more people and of different target groups.

7   Conclusions and Future Work

In this work, we presented a design approach for an interaction concept to customize large-sized products by using full-body interaction especially for elderly people. Beside the requirements of older people, our application field of trade fair environments needs special attention. We concluded based on the requirements to an interaction concept which includes simplicity at navigation, functions and gestures. We implemented a linear navigation, a basic configuration functionality and developed gestures by involving elderly users.

For designing full-body gestures, we adapted the methodology of Nielsen et al. and Wobbrock et al.: on the one hand to the development of full-body interaction, and on the other hand to our application field of configuring products using large-sized products in context of trade fairs. The extracted gesture set might be transferred to other domains, where older people want to interact.

Due to our application field of the public space, collaboration and multi-user interaction scenarios have to be investigated. People rarely visit a trade fair alone, so that there will be scenarios where you could use the configuration system by customizing a product in collaboration with a friend or a partner. In the long run, we have to investigate how the user group of older people accept full-body interaction in a productive interaction scenario like customizing products. The participants of our study were at least excited about the possibilities. Full-body interaction on large displays has a high potential to experience products in a very special way and provides access to computer systems to elderly people.

Acknowledgments. This research has been partially funded within the VICCI project under the grant number 100098171 by the European Social Fund (ESF) and the German Federal State of Saxony. We also thank the Senior Academy of the TU Dresden for the support and constructive criticism during the user study.

References

1. Ball, R., DellaNoce, M., Ni, T., Quek, F., North, C.: Applying embodied interaction and usability engineering to visualization on large displays. In: ACM British HCI - Workshop on Visualization & Interaction (2006)
2. Bolt, R.A.: Put-that-there: Voice and gesture at the graphics interface. In: Proceedings of the 7th Annual Conference on Computer Graphics and Interactive Techniques, SIGGRAPH 1980, pp. 262–270. ACM, New York (1980)

3. Chen, W.: Gesture-based applications for elderly people. In: Kurosu, M. (ed.) HCII/HCI 2013, Part IV. LNCS, vol. 8007, pp. 186–195. Springer, Heidelberg (2013)

4. Fikkert, W., van der Vet, P., van der Veer, G., Nijholt, A.: Gestures for Large Display Control. In: Kopp, S., Wachsmuth, I. (eds.) GW 2009. LNCS, vol. 5934, pp. 245–256. Springer, Heidelberg (2010)

5. Frisch, M., Heydekorn, J., Dachselt, R.: Diagram Editing on Interactive Displays Using Multi-touch and Pen Gestures. In: Goel, A.K., Jamnik, M., Narayanan, N.H. (eds.) Diagrams 2010. LNCS, vol. 6170, pp. 182–196. Springer, Heidelberg (2010)

6. Gamberini, L., Alcaniz, M., Barresi, G., Fabregat, M., Ibanez, F., Prontu, L.: Cognition, technology and games for the elderly: An introduction to eldergames project. PsychNology Journal 4(3), 285–308 (2006)

7. Gerling, K., Livingston, I., Nacke, L., Mandryk, R.: Full-body motion-based game interaction for older adults. In: Proceedings of the 2012 ACM Annual Conference on Human Factors in Computing Systems - CHI 2012, pp. 1873–1882 (2012)

8. Grammenos, D., Margetis, G., Koutlemanis, P., Zabulis, X.: Paximadaki, the game: Creating an advergame for promoting traditional food products. In: Proceeding of the 16th International Academic MindTrek Conference, MindTrek 2012,, pp. 287–290. ACM, New York (2012)

9. Hansen, J.P., Johansen, A.S., Hansen, D.W., Itoh, K.: Command without a click: Dwell time typing by mouse and gaze selections. In: Rauterberg, M. (ed.) Proceedings of Human-Computer Interaction, INTERACT 2003, pp. 121–128. IOS Press (2003)

10. Harley, D., Fitzpatrick, G., Axelrod, L., White, G., McAllister, G.: Making the Wii at Home: Game Play by Older People in Sheltered Housing. In: Leitner, G., Hitz, M., Holzinger, A. (eds.) USAB 2010. LNCS, vol. 6389, pp. 156–176. Springer, Heidelberg (2010)

11. Harling, P.A., Edwards, A.D.N.: Hand tension as a gesture segmentation cue. In: IProceedings of the Progress in Gestural Interaction, pp. 75–88. MIT mimeo (1997)

12. Kendon, A.: Current issues in the study of gesture. In: The Biological Foundations of Gestures: Motor and Semiotic Aspects, pp. 23–47 (1986)

13. Kühnel, C., Westermann, T., Hemmert, F., Kratz, S., Müller, A., Möller, S.: I'm home: Defining and evaluating a gesture set for smart-home control. International Journal of Human-Computer Studies 69, 693–704 (2011)

14. Kurtenbach, G., Hulteen, E.: Gestures in Human-Computer Communication. In: Laurel, B. (ed.) The Art and Science of Interface Design, pp. 309–317. Addison-Wesley Publishing Co. (1990)

15. McNeill, D.: Hand and Mind: What Gestures Reveal about Thought. University of Chicago Press, Chicago (1992)

16. Mueller, F., Agamanolis, S., Picard, R.: Exertion interfaces: Sports over a distance for social bonding and fun. In: Proceedings of the SIGCHI Conference on Human Factors in Computing Systems, CHI 2003, pp. 561–568. ACM, New York (2003)

17. Nielsen, M., Störring, M., Moeslund, T.B., Granum, E.: A procedure for developing intuitive and ergonomic gesture interfaces for HCI. In: Camurri, A., Volpe, G. (eds.) GW 2003. LNCS (LNAI), vol. 2915, pp. 409–420. Springer, Heidelberg (2004)

18. Ruppert, G.C.S., Reis, L.O., Amorim, P.H.J., Moraes, T.F., Silva, J.V.L.: Touchless gesture user interface for interactive image visualization in urological surgery. World Journal of Urology 30(5), 687–691 (2012)

19. Stößel, C., Blessing, L.: Mobile device interaction gestures for older users. In: Proceedings of the 6th Nordic Conference on Human-Computer Interaction: Extending Boundaries, pp. 793–796. ACM, New York (2010)
20. Vatavu, R.-D.: User-defined gestures for free-hand TV control. In: Proceedings of the 10th European Conference on Interactive tv and Video, EuroiTV 2012. ACM, New York (2012)
21. Wobbrock, J.O., Morris, M.R., Wilson, A.D.: User-defined gestures for surface computing. In: Proceedings of the SIGCHI Conference on Human Factors in Computing Systems, CHI 2009, pp. 1083–1092. ACM, New York (2009)

Human-Computer vs. Consumer-Store Interaction in a Multichannel Retail Environment: Some Multidisciplinary Research Directions

Chris Lazaris and Adam Vrechopoulos

ELTRUN – The E-Business Research Center,
Department of Management Science & Technology,
Athens University of Economics & Business, Greece
{lazaris,avrehop}@aueb.gr

Abstract. The increasing availability of electronic applications in physical retail stores has created a series of interesting research opportunities with challenging managerial implications for practitioners. Since the graphical user interface design constitutes a critical user-consumer influencing factor in the context of a multichannel retailing environment, there are several multidisciplinary research initiatives that could add value towards an integrated investigation of this topic. To this end, the paper discusses the promising role of combining Information Systems and Marketing disciplines for conducting behavioural studies in the context of multichannel/omnichannel retailing, approaching humans both as users of information systems and consumers of retail stores. Similarly, the paper treats the screen of the electronic applications available in online and offline retail stores both as a graphical user interface of an information system and as the atmosphere/servicescape of a retail store. The paper provides several future research directions and practical implications for this fast evolving topic.

Keywords: HCI, Consumer Behaviour, Multichannel Retailing, Omnichannel Retailing, Multidisciplinary Research.

1   Introduction

Since the emergence of the WWW, the Graphical User Interface (GUI) design of a web site also serves as the retail storefront for selling products and services. Humans interacting with web-based retail stores are both users of information systems and consumers visiting online stores.

Nowadays, consumers interact with multiple channels (touchpoints) throughout their shopping journey. In some cases, they even interact with multiple channels simultaneously. This type of multichannel retailing has been characterized as omnichannel ("omni" means all, universal in Latin) (Brynjolfsson & Rahman, 2013, Rosenblum & Kilcourse, 2013). According to Ortis (2010), omnichannel retailing refers to the simultaneous use of all the available business-to-consumer channels, while multichannel retailing refers to the use of each of these channels in parallel (i.e. not at the same time). Similarly, Ortis and Casoli (2009) report that omnishoppers use

F.F.-H. Nah (Ed.): HCIB/HCII 2014, LNCS 8527, pp. 339–349, 2014.
© Springer International Publishing Switzerland 2014

available retail channels (e.g. offline and online) at the same time (e.g. use of smart phones in the physical store for price comparison in order to negotiate prices with the physical store's sellers).

The evolution of multichannel in the form of "omnichannel" retailing along with the employment of Information and Communication Technologies (ICT) applications with innovative user interfaces (e.g. ubiquitous mobile devices, new technologies in physical stores (Pinel 2005), etc.) create several corresponding research challenges in the alternative retail channels (e.g. call centers, physical stores, mobile ecosystems, social media, etc.). As a result, HCI in an omnichannel retailing environment translates to Mobile Commerce and Pervasive Computing HCI concepts. Omnichannel concepts are not new (Roussos et al. 2003, Kourouthanassis et al. 2007), but now it is the first time they appear so often in practice, since enabling technologies are widely available and consumers are familiar with them. Indicatively, in a recent report (Wurmser, 2014) it was found that 80% of US mobile Wi-Fi users use their mobile devices while shopping in-store.

Furthermore, as presented by Dijk, Laing, & Minocha (2005), multichannel interaction is found to be complex and dynamic: consumers switch between channels in order to achieve the best deals and support, throughout the shopping process. For example, users-consumers could visit the GUI design of a web-based retail store to search and evaluate alternative products and services (decide online) and then they could visit the physical store to buy the desired products or services by using (or not) the available interfaces of the information systems applications that are available in the store. Conversely, users-consumers could visit the physical store to inspect products (i.e. decide offline) and then they could conduct their purchases online through a web site that offers their desired product at the lowest price. However, it should be noted that with the use of mobile phones, this activity can take place while in-store and/or in physical commercial environments (e.g. while walking in a commercial street) and, thus, another GUI plays an important part in the process. In the second of the aforementioned scenarios (i.e. decide offline and buy online), the physical store operates as a "showroom" and, thus, retailers should consider how to face this emerging consumer behavioural practice, also called "free-riding behaviour" (Van Baal, S., & Dach, C., 2005, Chiu et al. 2011).

Moreover, retailers have to deal with multichannel integration and coordination, both at the frontend (e.g. responsive design) and at the backend (e.g. online and offline data integration) of their operations. In other words, their physical and electronic touchpoints must be aligned with their multichannel strategies, in order to provide consumers with a unified shopping experience at all times.

Thus, while on the one hand the rapid diffusion and adoption of multichannel/omnichannel user-consumer practices increases the complexity of relevant research initiatives, it creates several attractive research and business opportunities that deal with several aspects of this emerging user-consumer behavioural pattern (e.g. interface design, integrated marketing communications, decision-making, etc.) on the other.

Elaborating on these evolutions, the present paper aims at documenting the need to adopt multidisciplinary research approaches when investigating humans' behaviour in the context of multichannel/omnichannel retailing and provide a series of corresponding calls for further research in this area. In other words, the objective of the paper is to justify the research needs and challenges in this fast evolving landscape as well encourage and guide corresponding further research initiatives.

The paper is structured as follows. After the Introductory section, section 2 briefly presents some indicative business dynamics and available research insights in this topic. Then, section 3 includes the research calls and propositions derived through the present research attempt as well as some practical implications.

2   Business Dynamics and Indicative Research Insights

The importance of today's multichannel research initiatives is emphasized by several recent calls for papers in the academic community (Verhoef, P., et al. (2013), Palmatier, et al. (2013), Grewal D., et al. (2013), Yang K (2013)).

On the other hand, several multichannel business and IT initiatives have recently emerged, such as:

Launch of the Universal Analytics platform by Google, which merges both online and offline data, providing valuable feedback for research in this field.

Mobile apps that support the in-store purchase process (e.g. Apple Store App[1], Shopbeacon[2]).

In-store technologies supporting the purchase process (e.g. iBeacon, camera face-recognition[3]).

New software platforms that aim to merge online & offline operations (e.g. Index[4], Euclidanalytics[5], Retailnext[6]).

Existing research, however, has not adequately investigated this topic by employing multidisciplinary and multichannel research approaches. Usually, customer interfaces are examined separately and not in parallel or simultaneously (Burke, 2002).

Indicatively, in mobile HCI literature it has been found that visual design aesthetics significantly impact perceived usefulness, ease of use, enjoyment and ultimately users' loyalty intentions towards a mobile service (Cyr, D. et al. 2006). Nevertheless, this study was solely single-channel.

In another study close to the omnichannel concept, Jan-Willem et al. (2010) examined the role of mobile recommendation agents in the shopping process. They found that the perceived usefulness variable was much more important than the ease of use one, as it influenced product purchases and predicted usage intentions and store preferences of consumers. However, it should be noted that the mobile devices and interfaces employed by the study were used only for experimental purposes instead of real shopping situations.

---

[1] http://news.yahoo.com/apple-guides-shoppers-inside-stores-ibeacon-082910193--finance.html
[2] http://www.shopkick.com/shopbeacon
[3] http://www.brickstream.com/products/brickstream-devices/
[4] http://www.index.com/technology
[5] http://euclidanalytics.com/product/technology/
[6] http://www.retailnext.net/analytics-technology

Also, Xu et al. (2008, p.401) explored the emerging patterns of how users switch their attention between the physical and the digital world. They revealed that "mobile interface design needs to allow the flexibility of interaction process" and that "connecting the mobile tasks with real world intentions need to be considered in the design".

Another important aspect of mobile HCI is presented by Bellman et al. (2011) study, the one of mobile apps. They found that apps with an informational/user-centered style were more effective at shifting purchase intention and creating brand awareness. Nevertheless, since omnichannel mobile apps have been only recently launched, their role (as part of the multichannel/omnichannel experience) through a mobile HCI research perspective remains unexplored.

Moreover, Yang & Kim (2012, p.786) found out that "mobile shopping services/applications need to be designed and positioned with various consumer motivations in using a new shopping channel". Finally, responsive design as a means of implementing universal HCI across multiple devices draws significant attention in research studies (e.g. Mohorovicic 2013).

On the other hand, in pervasive retailing IS literature there is evidence that in-store shopping experience can be greatly enhanced by utilizing supportive HCI interfaces in the form of tablets that assist shopping carts (Kourouthanassis et al. 2007). Longo et al. (2013) recently introduced an approach of innovative in-store experience applications leveraging the Internet of Things, HTML5 and Pervasive Display Networks. Lastly, Pantano (2013) reports that research has focused on the identification and development of new applications for pervasive retailing and that its concepts will significantly affect searching for goods, payment modalities and shopping atmosphere.

Table 1 presents some indicative Omnichannel HCI touchpoints that the User/Consumer interacts with, both physically and electronically, according to the location he/she is situated in a retail setting.

Table 1. Indicative Omnichannel HCI Touchpoints

Location	Physical Touchpoint	Electronic Touchpoint
Mobile	Phone Call	Mobile Channels (Web, Apps, Social)
Wearable	Physical Senses	Wearable Computing (e.g. Google Glass)
Product	Packaging	RFID, QR Code, etc.
Store Environment	Catalogs	Info Kiosks, Pervasive Displays
	Cashier	Electronic Checkout (e.g. NFC, iBeacon)
	Dressing Room	Virtual Dressing Room
	Physical Entry	Visibility Login (e.g. camera monitoring)
	Shopping Cart	Electronic Cart (e.g. featuring RFID readers, electronic displays)

Indicatively, the diffusion of digital interfaces in physical retail settings like info kiosks, QR codes, barcode/RFID readers, iBeacon/BLE, NFC, augmented reality (e.g. Google Glass), etc. calls for the combined use of the Marketing (e.g. Retailing, Consumer Behaviour) and the Information Systems disciplines (e.g. Human Computer

Interaction, User Behaviour) towards investigating humans' behaviour in these business settings through an integrated and robust manner. Along these lines, Benou et al. (2012) underline the need to adopt multidisciplinary research approaches in user-consumer behavioural studies in the context of mobile commerce. Specifically, they call for a combined use of Information Systems and Marketing disciplines when studying humans' behaviour in this context.

In this manner, the GUI of a web store constitutes at the same time the virtual retail store Atmosphere of this store (Vrechopoulos, 2010). Therefore, while the GUI approach is positioned in the Information Systems domain, the Store Atmosphere approach is positioned in the Marketing one, since it is related with one of the 7Ps of the services marketing mix (physical evidence) called servicescape for services' retail contexts (see Bitner 1992, Zeithaml et al. 2006). It is evident than an Omnichannel Retail Store Atmosphere (ORSA) includes both similarities and differences when compared to the atmosphere of a conventional retail store. Therefore, an interesting insight would be to identify these differences and investigate how consumer behaviour is affected by them.

Also, research could be conducted in order to clarify how consumers handle the complexity of the increased number of retail channels and how they interact across multiple touchpoints and GUIs in relation to the conventional consumer purchase decision model (Peter et al., 1996).

In parallel, moving towards the Information Systems backend, several research attempts investigated the relationship of Customer Relationship Management Information Systems and multichannel environments (Görsch 2002, Payne & Frow 2004, Sinisalo 2011, Verhoef et al. 2010 and Atapattu & Sedera 2012). CRM integration with E-Commerce platforms and technologies is crucial for merging online & offline data towards providing a seamless unified experience to consumers, as well as multichannel analytics to retailers. Indicatively, a key concept of omnichannel retailing is the electronic customer login in the physical store, which requires deep Information Systems integration of all platforms and the appropriate HCI interfaces to accompany them (Ganesh, 2004, Ganesh, Padmabhun, & Moitra, 2004).

In sum, Human Computer Interaction, Mobile & Pervasive Computing, Customer Relationship Management Information Systems, are some indicative topics under the umbrella of the Information Systems domain that could add value to such research initiatives. Similarly, the Marketing discipline could contribute towards the execution of such research attempts through the active involvement of the Consumer Behaviour, Retail Management, Marketing Research, Services Management, Relationship Marketing, etc. topics.

Figure 1 diagrammatically depicts the roles and options in humans-retail store interaction process in the context of multichannel and omnichannel retailing. It should be clarified that non-store retailing refers to both traditional retail channels (e.g. door-to-door selling, vending machine retailing, catalogue retailing, telephone selling, etc.) and new ones (e.g. e-mail, CRM-enabled call centers, etc.). However, also the traditional non-store retailing category could potentially include several Information and Communication Technologies (ICT) features (e.g. QR codes-enabled interactive printed catalogues, advanced ICT options in vending machine retailing, ICT supported door-to-door personal selling through smart personal devices with Internet access carried by salesman, etc.).

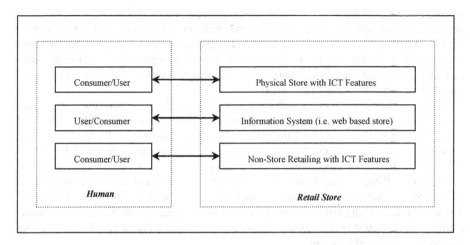

Fig. 1. Roles and Options in Humans-Retail Stores Interaction Process

3   Research Calls, Propositions and Practical Implications

While user and consumer behavioural studies have thoroughly investigated humans' behaviour in the context of online and offline retailing until today, it is clear that there is still room for research designs that will investigate human behaviour in the context of multichannel and omnichannel retailing through a multidisciplinary approach (i.e. Marketing and Information Systems).

In other words, the research gap is reflected on the existence of few empirical words that have fully exploited the interdisciplinary nature and dynamics of humans' behavioural studies in the context of the fast evolving business-to-consumer "mixed" offline and online retail environment.

Thus, future research positioned in the intersection of these disciplines, could focus on measuring cause-and-effect relationships through causal research designs (e.g. experiments) in order to test whether and how the features of electronic applications (e.g. GUI, IS integration, network connectivity, responsive design, location-based services) affect user-consumer behaviour.

In other words the new directions suggested in terms of this point in order to further improve the knowledge in this field, refer to the fact that such research designs will not neglect the multidisciplinary nature of the topic and, thus, will treat the manipulated variables (i.e. treatments) as both store's and information system's features. Similarly, as far as the dependent variables of such experimental research designs are concerned, these will also follow the aforementioned logic in the sense that humans interacting with these features are at the same time users of information systems and customers of a store. Finally, a series of moderating factors that determine the effects of the manipulated variables to the dependent ones will be also approached and measured through a multidisciplinary approach (e.g. mood effects from the Marketing literature vs. telepresence effects from the Information Systems one).

Thus, the research propositions #1 and #2 are formulated as follows:

- **Research Proposition #1:** There are statistical significant differences among alternative omnichannel retail settings in terms of a series of users'-consumers' behavioural variables (e.g. perceived ease of use, perceived service quality, etc.).
- **Research Proposition #2:** The effects of omnichannel retail settings on users'-consumers' behaviour is determined by a series of moderating factors that refer to users'-consumers' demographic, behavioural and psychographic data as well as to situational ones.

Furthermore, a promising future research direction is to focus on the combination of the alternative retails channels in the context of multichannel/omnichannel retailing (see Rigby, 2011). To that end, researchers could investigate the predicting and influencing role of shopping interfaces to user-consumer behaviour by examining potential differences among various retail settings in terms of the importance users attach to the features of the employed applications' interfaces. For example, users/consumers may attach significantly more importance to the graphical user interface of a web site than the corresponding one of a smart phone device that they use within the store to compare prices, in the sense that in the second scenario they may attach more emphasis to the specific information they are seeking for (i.e. the best price) instead of the interface. Similarly, they may attach more importance to security related graphical user interface design features when they are navigating online from their home, compared to the corresponding importance they attach to this feature when they use a device offered to them by a retailer in order to effectively navigate within a physical store.

Thus, the Research Proposition #3 could be formulated as follows:

- **Research Proposition #3:** There are statistical significant differences among various retail channels in terms of the importance users/consumers attach to the graphical user interface features of the corresponding electronic applications.

Finally, another research proposition lies in the area of "showrooming" and "free-riding" behaviour (as earlier discussed in the paper) regarding the relationship of these emerging consumer behavioural patterns to the HCI touchpoints. Specifically, the open question is whether and how omnichannel HCI touchpoints in the physical stores affect such kind of behaviour. Therefore, Research Proposition #4 could be formulated as:

- **Research Proposition #4:** The integration of additional in-store HCI touchpoints that support omnichannel retailing user-consumer practices, affects free-riding behaviour and store loyalty.

Following the aforementioned discussion, researchers should focus on employing to their research designs variables that come from various disciplines and topics in a combined manner. For example, while "ease of use", "usability", "perceived usefulness", etc. are some important Human Computer Interaction variables, the "shopping motivation/orientation", "perceived service quality", "patronage intention", etc. are some important ones for the Marketing discipline. To this end, Pantano & Di Pietro (2012), after thoroughly analyzing existing TAM variables and constructs in the literature, acknowledge the development of deeper measurement scales in order to make more detailed predictions on future consumer's behaviours regarding advanced technologies and innovation management for retailing.

Furthermore, some other interesting research topics positioned in the context of the present study could deal with the following issues:

- User-consumer co-creation of GUI (control, flow): how should the omnichannel retailing atmosphere be controlled (Vrechopoulos, 2010)?
- 3D GUI design both online and in physical retail stores (e.g. displays, infokiosks). This design could be expanded to virtual worlds & virtual reality (e.g. Second Life) as part of a multichannel strategy. An interesting aspect would be to combine virtual and physical worlds simultaneously (e.g. virtual dressing rooms in physical stores).
- Use of the online environment (due to low cost and applicability) to conduct online experiments for offline implications. However, it should be clarified that the generalizability of the results provided through such type of research designs may be limited mainly due to the important differences that exist between the offline and the online environment. Nevertheless, both practitioners and researchers have already started employing 3D technologies to execute such type of online experimental designs to test online design ideas in order to provide implications for the offline stores (e.g. store layout effects on consumer behaviour).
- "Create once, publish everywhere" approaches that are proposed by the media industry (Chorianopoulos & Lekakos, 2007). Similar to responsive design, it would be interesting to explore ways where content is seamlessly distributed across all available touchpoints, maintaining its usability while enhancing the shopping experience.

It should be also noted that since it is applicable to customize graphical user interfaces at the individual level, future research should consider whether providing "generic" (i.e. one for all) user interface design guidelines would add value. In other words, since each consumer/user is different (i.e. "segments of one" in the context of the segmentation-targeting-positioning process followed by Marketing practitioners in their Strategic Marketing Planning) retailers (ICT-enabled) could provide a personalized shopping experience also in terms of the graphical user interface design they offer to their customers (Vrechopoulos, 2010). For example, in the traditional personal selling process, experienced salesmen treat their customers through a one-to-one manner. Similarly, a graphical user interface as a "sales tool" could be potentially designed for each customer separately. However, since the issue of customization requires advanced technical skills and experience, such decisions should be taken with caution as well as should be aligned with the strategic marketing planning of the firm.

In addition to this, Ahearne & Rapp (2010, p.119) state that "the technologies that include both the salesperson and the customer offer the most intriguing areas of discovery". In omnichannel environments it would be crucial for salesmen in physical stores to use consumer-monitor interfaces that identify each customer that enters the physical store in order to assist him/her in a personalized manner. Such interfaces should provide salesmen with the full customer profile, history and needs, as well as valuable information to assist them in the selling process. Nowadays it is critical to "know what the customers want before they do" (Davenport et al. 2011). Similarly, access to multichannel universal analytics could even prevent "showrooming" and "free-riding" behaviour, since the salesman would negotiate more efficiently.

An important managerial implication derived through this discussion refers to whether and how retailers should employ additional touchpoints within their physical stores. Obviously, with the diffusion of e-commerce, maintaining a physical store would be a huge liability if it doesn't provide a competitive advantage. Thus, traditional retailers should concentrate on providing the "best of the two worlds", focusing on enhancing the shopping experience and ensuring the provision of a superior customer support. These business objectives could be potentially met by employing supportive in-store technologies and interfaces, as already encountered in this paper.

Furthermore, as also discussed in the previous sections, the GUI (either the online one or the one employed by the electronic applications available in the physical stores) could be potentially treated as one of the 7Ps of the services marketing mix. Thus, it could be accordingly adjusted within the positioning process in the context of the implementation of the strategic Marketing planning of the firm in order to build its image. Similarly, as also discussed above, personalizing or not the GUI could be a matter of strategic marketing planning in the sense that any type of such strategic and/or tactic decisions could be included in the marketing plan of the firm and could be taken having always in mind the marketing objectives that the firm has. In other words, the GUI along with the other 6 elements of the services marketing mix (i.e. price, promotion, etc.) could be manipulated in order for the company to achieve the desired positioning in the market as this is perceived by customers (perceptual positioning maps). Finally, it must be underlined that the collection, processing and exploitation of user-consumer data must always follow permission marketing guidelines and, of course, laws.

To sum up, the future research agenda for such research initiatives should not neglect the key concept of omnichannel retailing: an integrated shopping experience that melds the advantages of physical stores with the information-rich experience of online shopping (as defined by Rigby, 2011). Therefore, future multichannel HCI research should concentrate on the right blending of physical and electronic interactions, exploiting the unique characteristics of each, in order to achieve a unified shopping experience, beneficial to all participants.

References

1. Ahearne, M., Rapp, A.: The role of technology at the interface between salespeople and consumers. Journal of Personal Selling & Sales Management 30(2), 111–120 (2010)
2. Atapattu, M., Sedera, D.: Ubiquitous customer relationship management: unforeseen issues and benefits. In: Proceedings of the Pacific Asia Conference on Information Systems, PACIS (2012)
3. Bellman, S., Potter, R.F., Treleaven-Hassard, S., Robinson, J.A., Varan, D.: The Effectiveness of Branded Mobile Phone Apps. Journal of Interactive Marketing 25(4), 191–200 (2011)
4. Benou, P., Vassilakis, C., Vrechopoulos, A.: Context management for m-commerce applications: determinants, methodology and the role of marketing. Information Technology and Management 13(2), 91–111 (2012)
5. Bitner, M.J.: Servicescapes - the Impact of Physical Surroundings on Customers and Employees. Journal of Marketing 56(2), 57–71 (1992)

6. Brynjolfsson, E., Rahman, J.: Competing in the Age of Omnichannel Retailing. MIT Sloan Management Review 54(4), 23–29 (2013)
7. Burke, R.R.: Technology and the Customer Interface: What Consumers Want in the Physical and Virtual Store. Journal of the Academy of Marketing Science 30(4), 411–432 (2002)
8. Chiu, H.-C., Hsieh, Y.-C., Roan, J., Tseng, K.-J., Hsieh, J.-K.: The challenge for multichannel services: Cross-channel free-riding behavior. Electronic Commerce Research and Applications 10(2), 268–277 (2011)
9. Chorianopoulos, K., Lekakos, G.: Methods and Applications in Interactive Broadcasting. Journal of Virtual Reality and Broadcasting, 4(19) (2007)
10. Cyr, D., Head, M., Ivanov, A.: Design aesthetics leading to m-loyalty in mobile commerce. Information & Management 43(8), 950–963 (2006)
11. Davenport, T.H., Mule, L.D., Lucker, J.: Know What Your Customers Want Before They Do. Harvard Business Review, 89(12) (2011)
12. van Dijk, G., Laing, A., Minocha, S.: Consumer Behaviour in MultiChannel Retail Environments: Consumer movement between online and offline channels. In: 5th American Marketing Association Academy of Marketing Joint Biennial Conference (2005)
13. Ganesh, J., Padmabhun, S., Moitra, D.: Web services and multi-channel integration: a proposed framework. In: Proceedings of IEEE International Conference on Web Services, pp. 70–77 (2004)
14. Ganesh, J.: Managing customer preferences in a multi-channel environment using Web services. International Journal of Retail & Distribution Management 32(3), 140–146 (2004)
15. Görsch, D.: Multi-Channel Integration and Its Implications for Retail Web Sites. In ECIS 2002 Proceedings, p. Paper 11 (2002)
16. Grewal, D., Roggeveen, A.L., Nordfält, J.: Call for Papers for the Special Issue on Special Issue on Shopper Marketing: In-store, On-line, Social, and Mobile. Journal of Business Research (2013)
17. Jan-Willem, S., Armin, W., Kowatsch, T., Maass, W.: In-store consumer behavior: How mobile recommendation agents influence usage intentions, product purchases, and store preferences. Computers in Human Behavior 26(4), 697–704 (2010)
18. Kourouthanassis, P.E., Giaglis, G.M., Vrechopoulos, A.P.: Enhancing user experience through pervasive information systems: The case of pervasive retailing. International Journal of Information Management 27(5), 319–335 (2007)
19. Longo, S., Kovacs, E., Franke, J., Martin, M.: Enriching shopping experiences with pervasive displays and smart things. In: Proceedings of the 2013 ACM Conference on Pervasive and Ubiquitous Computing Adjunct Publication - UbiComp 2013 Adjunct, New York, USA, p. 991 (2013)
20. Mohorovicic, S.: Implementing responsive web design for enhanced web presence. In: 36th International Convention on Information & Communication Technology Electronics & Microelectronics (MIPRO), pp. 1206–1210. IEEE (2013)
21. Ortis, I., Casoli, A.: Technology Selection: IDC Retail Insights Guide to Enabling Immersive Shopping Experiences. IDC Retail Insights Report (2009)
22. Ortis, I.: Unified Retailing - Breaking Multichannel Barriers. IDC Retail Insights Report (2010)
23. Palmatier, R.W., Krafft, M., Coughlan, A.T.: Call for Papers for the Special Issue on The Past, Present, and Future of Marketing Channels. Journal of Retailing (2013)

24. Pantano, E., Di Pietro, L.: Understanding Consumer's Acceptance of Technology-Based Innovations in Retailing. Journal of Technology Management & Innovation 7(4), 1–19 (2012)
25. Pantano, E.: Ubiquitous Retailing Innovative Scenario: From the Fixed Point of Sale to the Flexible Ubiquitous Store. Journal of Technology Management & Innovation 8(2), 13–14 (2013)
26. Payne, A., Frow, P.: The role of multichannel integration in customer relationship management. Industrial Marketing Management 33(6), 527–538 (2004)
27. Peter, P.J., Olson, J.C., Rosenblatt, J.A.: Understanding Consumer Behaviour. First Canadian ed. McGrawHill Ryerson, Toronto (1996)
28. Pinel, F.: Pervasive computing technologies for retail in-store shopping. In: Proceedings of International Conference on Pervasive Services, ICPS 2005, pp. 111–116. IEEE (2005)
29. Rigby, D.: The Future of Shopping. Harvard Business Review 89(12), 64–75 (2011)
30. Rosenblum, P., Kilcourse, B.: Omni-Channel 2013 - The Long Road To Adoption. Retail Systems Research Report (2013)
31. Roussos, G., Kourouthanasis, P., Moussouri, T.: Designing appliances for mobile commerce and retailtainment. Personal and Ubiquitous Computing 7(3-4), 203–209 (2003)
32. Sinisalo, J.: The role of the mobile medium in multichannel CRM communication. Int. J. of Electronic Customer Relationship Management 5(1), 23–45 (2011)
33. Van Baal, S., Dach, C.: Free riding and customer retention across retailers' channels. Journal of Interactive Marketing 19(2), 75–85 (2005)
34. Verhoef, P., Kannan, P.K., Inman, J.: Call for Papers for the Special Issue on Multi-Channel Retailing and Customer Touch Points. Journal of Retailing (2013)
35. Verhoef, P., Venkatesan, R., McAlister, L., Malthouse, E.C., Krafft, M., Ganesan, S.: CRM in Data-Rich Multichannel Retailing Environments: A Review and Future Research Directions. Journal of Interactive Marketing 24(2), 121–137 (2010)
36. Vrechopoulos, A.: Who controls store atmosphere customization in electronic retailing? International Journal of Retail & Distribution Management 38(7), 518–537 (2010)
37. Wurmser, Y.: Retailers Playing Catch-Up with Consumers. eMarketer Report (2014), http://www.emarketer.com/public_media/docs/ state_of_omnichannel_retail.pdf (retrieved)
38. Xu, Y., Spasojevic, M., Gao, J., Jacob, M.: Designing a vision-based mobile interface for in-store shopping. In: Proceedings of the 5th Nordic Conference on Human-computer Interaction Building Bridges, NordiCHI 2008, p. 393. ACM Press, New York (2008)
39. Yang, K.: Call for Papers for the Special Issue on The Impact of Digital Shopping Channels on Multi-channel Marketing and Attribution in the Changing Retail Landscape. Journal of Research in Interactive Marketing (2013)
40. Yang, K., Kim, H.-Y.: Mobile shopping motivation: an application of multiple discriminant analysis. International Journal of Retail & Distribution Management 40(10), 778–789 (2012)
41. Zeithaml, V.A., Bitner, M.J., Gremler, D.D.: Services Marketing – Integrating Customer Focus Across the Firm, 4th edn. McGraw – Hill International Edition (2006)

Market Intelligence in Hypercompetitive Mobile Platform Ecosystems: A Pricing Strategy

Hoang D. Nguyen, Kajanan Sangaralingam, and Danny Chiang Choon Poo

Department of Information Systems, National University of Singapore, Singapore
{hoangnguyen,skajanan,dpoo}@comp.nus.edu.sg

Abstract. The recent years have seen a spurt of mobile developers in hyper-competitive mobile platform ecosystems. Yet, this is an unfair game where platform owners such as Apple, Google or Microsoft fence the information of their app store as top secrets. Our study, therefore, takes an important step in investigating the structure of rankings and sales revenue through 2,761 paid applications with weekly aggregated 32,109 observations to unveil a new indicator of market intelligence, *earning per download*. With the consideration of category effects, time effects and endogenity issues, our empirical results show that top-ranked paid apps can earn up to $7.80 per download. Our findings generate a number of insights for app developers to take actions in designing highly-ranked apps as well as manipulating prices, promotions or in-app purchases in order to unlock the full potential of their app sales.

Keywords: mobile apps, big data, ranking, pricing, power law, earning per download.

1 Introduction

With the increasing ubiquity of mobile devices, the world has been witnessing the boom of a new era of mobile applications ("apps"). On average, there are over 15,000 new apps launched weekly; and over 1.5 million apps are currently available on various mobile app stores such as Apple AppStore, Google Android Market, and Microsoft Phone Store [1–3]. In 2011, Apple Inc. announced their payment of $2.5 billion to app developers; and Gartner [4] forecasted a tenfold growth of mobile revenue between 2010 and 2014. These tremendous figures present the spectacular market of mobile apps with multifarious opportunities; however, it is a hypercompetitive and unfair mobile platform ecosystem where market information of million apps such as sales revenue and app demands remain the top secrets by platform owners [5].

The stiff competition requires app developers to adopt an appropriate pricing strategy in order to penetrate the app stores. There are four typical revenue models for mobile apps: paid, in-app purchases, in-app subscriptions or advertisement-based [6]. Each of them has unique advantages in promoting app sales; however, developers always face the trade-off between the demands and their pricing. Moreover, identifying market niches such as categories for publishing is daunting since it is extremely difficult for an app to get noticed in shoals of million apps. For instance, in Apple

F.F.-H. Nah (Ed.): HCIB/HCII 2014, LNCS 8527, pp. 350–359, 2014.
© Springer International Publishing Switzerland 2014

AppStore, there are only 240 mobile apps which win the laurels and become prominent to smartphone owners in short times [7]. Therefore, our study aims to reveal decisive factors which led to the success of a mobile app in these challenging markets.

In recent years, developing insights of market intelligence in mobile app stores has been drawing a number of research venues. Previous studies [5, 8] addressed competitive strategies in these markets by examining the takeoff and continued survival of apps. Motivated by their results, we investigated not only the various effects of dynamic attributes related to app positioning, developer actions and user engagement on app rankings, but also proposed a structural model of sales revenue and app rankings which accounted for numerous endogenity and heterogeneity issues. In this study, we conceptualized a new indicator of marketing intelligence, Earning Per Download (EPD). This brings us one step closer to the reality in mobile analytics and unlocks new directions for existing studies on estimating app downloads or sales revenue [9, 10]. Furthermore, our study provides useful visions for app developers to decide on their pricing strategy. We found that a top-ranked app yielded a gross up to $7.80 per download in the Apple AppStore during 2011.

The structure of the paper is as follows. In the immediately following section, we explain the data collection and our empirical models to investigate sales revenue and app rankings. After presenting our empirical results, we discuss our findings and conclude with a recommendation for future work.

2   Empirical Context, Conceptualization, and Data Collection

2.1   Background on Apple AppStore

In this paper, we primarily studied the Apple AppStore which is the foremost marketplace for mobile apps on iOS operating systems. With about half the market share of worldwide mobile app markets [11], Apple AppStore offers a convenient channel for developers to reach out to mobile users easily. It is a highly potential market; however, Apple does not publicly disclose the market information such the number of downloads, sales revenue or even their concealed formula for ranking apps.

According to Venturedata [12], Apple's ranking mechanism were shaped based on a number of criteria. This study focuses on two important criteria: the amount of downloads and the grossing revenue. First, in each category, Apple published a top list of mobile apps where there exists high correlation between the ranking and the number of downloads of an app, conventionally named as "App ranking based on downloads". Second, the list of "App ranking based on grossing" was built based on the total sales revenue of apps.

The data of our study were collected using a crawler from MobileWalla [1]. The dataset has been utilized and audited independently in previous research [2, 13], thus its reliability and accuracy are very high.

There are two dominant types of data available: (i) Time-Invariant data, such as name, descriptions, and features of apps and developer, etc., and (ii) Time-Variant data, such as user ratings, ranks, and reviews that change continuously. We organized our variables according to the conceptualization of key factors impacting rankings and sales revenue: 1) app positioning-related variables, 2) developer actions-related variables, 3) user engagement-related variables, 4) app features-related variables, 5) other control variables, and 6) ranking data.

Table 1. Data Collected and Derived from iTunes App Store

Variable	Description	Type
App Positioning		
Category popularity	Total number of apps released in a given category till a current week.	Time-Variant
Competition	Number of similar apps from different developers till the current week during the study period. The similarity is calculated using TF-IDF distance.	Time-Variant
Developer Actions		
Price	Market price in USD.	Time-Variant
Frequency of updates	Number of versions released for an app till the current week.	Time-Variant
Price reduction	Flag indicates whether price was reduced, for example due to the marketing promotions.	Time-Variant
User Engagement		
Review score	Average user review score for current version.	Time-Variant
App Features		
Size	Application footprint in Mega Bytes (MB).	Time-Variant
Design for iPad	Is the app designed only for iPad? Yes = 1.	Time-Invariant
3G/4G connectivity	Flag indicates whether the app supports 3G/4G Connectivity. It is extracted from the platform compatibility list.	Time-Invariant
Controls		
Age	Age of an app (weeks since launch).	Time-Variant
Developer's experience	Number of apps developed by the app developer.	Time-Variant
Dependent Variables		
App rank based on downloads	Average download-based rank of an app in its popular category during the current week. The value ranged from 1 (highest) to 240 (lowest).	Time-Variant
App rank based on grossing revenue	Average gross revenue-based rank of the app in its popular category during a current week. The value ranged from 1 (highest) to 240 (lowest).	Time-Variant

2.2 Data Collection

During the study period of 9 months from 1st May 2011 to 31st Jan 2012, we tracked 2,761 mobile apps with 32,109 weekly aggregated observations. App ranks are maintained in various top charts: i) top download for free apps (with and without in-app purchases), ii) top download for paid apps (with and without in-app purchases), iii) top grossing for both free apps and paid apps (with and without in-app purchases). Our analysis focuses on ii) and iii).

The summary statistics of the mobile app data we collected and derived are presented in Table 2 and the correlation matrix is shown in Table 3.

Table 2. Descriptive Statistics (N = 32109)

Variable	Mean	Std. Dev.	Min	Max
Price	4.5133	7.2750	0.14	299.99
Review score	1.4671	1.9218	0	5
Popular category	755.5918	69.0068	329	1006
Age	10.4075	7.9928	0	34.14
Size	47.5099	179.2242	0.0049	1863.6797
Competition	5.0401	4.1749	0	10
Developer experience	6.0228	8.3509	1	95
Frequent updates	2.3515	1.8323	1	17
Price Reduction	0.3797	0.4853	0	1
Design for iPad	0.2910	0.4542	0	1
3G/4G connectivity	0.0164	0.1271	0	1

Table 3. Correlation Matrix

Variable		1	2	3	4	5	6	7	8	9	10	11
ln(Price)	1	1.00										
Review score	2	-0.05	1.00									
Popular category	3	-0.01	-0.16	1.00								
Age	4	0.03	0.12	0.06	1.00							
Size	5	0.26	0.06	-0.03	0.01	1.00						
Competition	6	-0.11	-0.04	0.09	-0.02	-0.07	1.00					
Developer experience	7	-0.06	-0.07	0.03	0.01	0.07	0.00	1.00				
Frequent updates	8	-0.03	0.22	0.05	0.46	-0.04	0.06	-0.05	1.00			
Price reduction	9	0.10	0.20	-0.07	0.06	0.13	-0.06	-0.03	0.14	1.00		
Design for iPad	10	0.23	-0.05	-0.02	-0.04	0.03	-0.04	0.00	-0.03	0.06	1.00	
3G/4G connectivity	11	-0.06	0.06	-0.02	0.01	-0.03	-0.03	-0.04	-0.01	0.04	-0.03	1.00

As reported in Table 3, we can observe that the correlations between attributes are in the acceptable range. The highest correlation is 0.458 between Age and Frequent Updates. As we controlled for time effects in our subsequent model, there is no serious issue for modelling in our dataset.

2.3 Empirical Modeling

The download-based ranks can be influenced by the process of App Store Optimization (ASO) through app features, app positioning, developer actions and keywords; thus, we derive the below model, given app i and week t. The ranks and prices have been log-transformed rather than actual values to model the non-linear relationships amongst them and other attributes.

$\ln(Download\ Rank_{it})$
$$= \beta_3 \times \ln(Price_{it}) + \beta_4 \times (Price\ Reduction_{it})$$
$$+ \beta_5 \times (Review\ Score_{it}) + \beta_6 \times (Frequency\ Updates_{it})$$
$$+ \beta_7 \times (Category\ Popularity_{it}) + \beta_8 \times (Competition_{it})$$
$$+ \beta_9 \times (Size_{it}) + \beta_{10} \times (Age_{it})$$
$$+ \beta_{11} \times (Developer's\ Experience_{it})$$
$$+ \beta_{12} \times (Design\ for\ iPad_i)$$
$$+ \beta_{13} \times (3G/4G\ Connectivity_i) \tag{1}$$
$$+ (Category\ Dummies_{it}) + \propto_i + cons$$

On the other hand, *Sales Revenue* can be computed based on Power Laws and log-log distribution [14] using the following equation:

$$\ln(Sales\ Revenue_{it}) = b_{01} + b_{02} \times \ln(Grossing\ Rank_{it}) \tag{2}$$

We similarly posit an equation which depicts the relationship between downloads and download-based ranks:

$$\ln(Download_{it}) = b_{11} + b_{12} \times \ln(Download\ Rank_{it}) \tag{3}$$

In this study, we conceptualize a key variable, *Earning per Download (EPD)*, which plays a crucial role in measuring the effectiveness of pricing strategies for app developers. *EPD* is calculated as follows:

i.   In paid model:

$$EPD_{it} = Price_{it} \tag{4}$$

ii. In paid model with in-app purchases:

$$EPD_{it} = Price_{it} + InApp_{it}\ ,\ where\ InApp_{it} = (InApp\ Sales)_{it}/ \atop Download_{it} \tag{5}$$

iii. In free model with ad-supports

$$EPD_{it} = Ads_{it}\ ,\ where\ Ads_{it} = (Ads\ Revenue)_{it}/Download_{it} \tag{6}$$

iv. In free model with in-app purchases

$$EPD_{it} = InApp_{it}\ ,\ where\ InApp_{it} = (InApp\ Sales)_{it}/Download_{it} \tag{7}$$

We argue that *EPD* is computable as a function of prices and in-app purchases. The following equation was developed based on the definition of *EPD*:

$$Sales\ Revenue_{it} = Download_{it} \times EPD_{it} \tag{8}$$

Based on equations (2), (3), and (8), we posit that the grossing-based ranks are the result of pricing strategies which are reflected in the configuration of *EPD*:

$$\ln(Grossing\ Rank_{it})$$
$$= \beta_0 + \beta_1 \times \ln(Download\ Rank_{it}) + \beta_2 \times \ln(EPD_{it}) \qquad (9)$$

$$\text{where: } \beta_0 = \frac{(b_{11}-b_{01})}{b_{02}}, \quad \beta_1 = \frac{b_{12}}{b_{02}}, \quad \beta_2 = \frac{1}{b_{02}}$$

Knowing the prices of paid-only apps, top-download ranks for paid apps, and top-grossing ranks for all apps, EPD for paid apps with in-app purchases can be inferred using the following formula:

$$EPD_{it} = e^{\left(\frac{1}{\beta_2}\ln(Grossing\ Rank_{it})-\frac{\beta_1}{\beta_2}\ln(Download\ Rank_{it})-\frac{\beta_0}{\beta_2}\right)} \qquad (10)$$

where: $EPD_{it} = Price_{it} + InApp_{it}$ for paid apps with in-app purchases

3   Data Analysis and Results

We analyze our structural model using two-stage regressions on the panel data in order to account for both endogenous variables: download-based ranks and grossing-based ranks.

In the first stage, we estimate the app ranking based on downloads using the Hausman-Taylor model as the hybrid model of both Fixed Effects (FE) and Random Effects (RE). The estimator allows us to capture unobserved individual heterogeneity and estimate the effects of both time-variant and time-invariant attributes. We also checked for panel-level autocorrelation, heteroskedasticity, Hausman's test and the effect of outliers to ensure robust and unbiased results. Table 4 summarizes the results of the app ranking model estimation.

The following are our findings from the first stage regression:

- **Developer actions:** As observed in Table 4, the effects of Price and Price Reduction are highly significant. When the Price is high, the app rank or the amount of download tends to be worst; however, Price Reduction such as having a short-term promotion can be a strategic factor to improve the app rank. Besides, releasing frequent updates of the app would also lead to a superior ranking.
- **User engagement:** The effect of good ratings on the app demand where highly-rated apps would probably draw more attentions from mobile users; thus they achieve better rankings in our model.
- **App features:** Mobile apps which are solely designed for iPad tend to be ranked better in terms of downloads. This suggests app developers to take advantages of the larger screen of the tablet rather than blowing up smartphone screens. Furthermore, as mobile devices are getting improved considerably on storage size and connectivity; these features are no longer the concerns for app users.
- **App positioning:** The effect of category popularity is significant where a category with a larger number of apps shows stiffer competition. For example, news, reference or sports categories are highly potential for publishing new apps; while, games, photo & video, or utilities are hypercompetitive to achieve better rankings. Table 5 reports the effects of categories on download-based app rankings.

Table 4. Estimation of App Ranking based on downloads

ln(Download Rank)		Coefficient	z	P>z
ln(Price)	β_3	0.3340190	26.12	0.000
Price Reduction	β_4	-2.5275620	-5.36	0.000
Review Score	β_5	-0.0234028	-10.15	0.000
Frequency Updates	β_6	-0.0048836	-1.48	0.139
Category Popularity	β_7	0.0001563	3.44	0.001
Competition	β_8	0.0074840	1.56	0.119
Size	β_9	0.0000002	1.02	0.309
Age	β_{10}	0.0213924	38.01	0.000
Developer's Experience	β_{11}	0.0119192	8.62	0.000
Design for iPad	β_{12}	-0.1288068	-2.25	0.025
3G/4G Connectivity	β_{13}	0.3072291	1.47	0.141
Category Dummies		(shown in table 6)		
_cons		5.2987120	22.49	0.000

Number of observations: 32,109, number of apps: 2,761, R^2 = .7123

Table 5. Effects of categories on App Download Rankings

Category	Coefficient	P>z	Category	Coefficient	P>z
Books	-0.5595051	0.008	News	-1.011974	0.000
Business	-0.3238371	0.137	Photo & Video	-0.1083963	0.637
Education	-0.1993899	0.381	Productivity	-0.2158032	0.318
Entertainment	-0.4565721	0.024	Reference	-1.026778	0.000
Finance	-0.5922686	0.003	Social Networking	-0.9275086	0.000
Games	-0.1427003	0.584	Sports	-0.9738315	0.000
Lifestyle	-0.93245	0.000	Travel	-0.7910265	0.000
Medical	-0.9302471	0.000	Utilities	-0.3871226	0.060
Music	-0.7792271	0.000	Weather	-0.8063683	0.000
Navigation	-0.8063852	0.000			

In the second stage, we estimate the equation (9) where download-based ranks are computed as the residuals of the first stage regression and *EPD* is equivalent to Price for paid-only apps as in the equation (4). We performed various models such as Pooled OLS, Random Effect, or Fixed Effect; and Hausman Test to justify the effectiveness and unbiasness of our ultimate Fixed Effect estimator. Moreover, we corrected the variance–covariance by applying the accurate mean squared error.

The below table reports partial elasticity of download ranks and *EPD* on the grossing ranks.

Table 6. Estimation of App Ranking based on grossing revenue

ln(Grossing Rank)		Coefficient	t	P>z
ln(Est. Download Rank)	β_1	0.9478962	5.16	0.000
ln(EPD)	β_2	-0.4327684	-2.91	0.004
_cons	β_0	0.8889208	1.18	0.237
Number of observations: 32,109, number of apps: 2,761, R^2 = .7341				

There is the significant effect of earning per download in which a one percent increase in *EPD* results in 0.43% better in the grossing-based rank. On the other hand, an increment in the download-based rank is associated with an increment of 0.95 in the grossing-based rank; thus, the lower number of download leads to the decline in sales revenue, however, at a diminishing rate. These effects demonstrate the trade-off between the demand and the *EPD* for an app; nevertheless, there is an appropriate value of earning per download where the app unseals the full potential of its position.

Based on the equation (10), we depict the estimated *EPD* as follows:

$$EPD = 7.7992964x \frac{Grossing\ Rank^{-2.3107048}}{Download\ Rank^{-2.1903083}}$$

Table 7 lists several estimated values of *EPD*.

Table 7. Estimation of Earning Per Download

No.	Ranking based on downloads	Ranking based on sales revenue	Estimated Earning Per Download
1.	1	1	7.80
2.	10	10	5.91
3.	20	25	3.25
4.	30	40	2.66
5.	50	70	2.24
6.	70	100	2.05
7.	100	150	1.76
8.	100	180	1.15

The above numbers provide a guideline for developers to infer an appropriate revenue model and price settings given the known demand. According to the results, a paid app can earn up to $7.80 per download when it ranked no. 1 in both download-based and grossing-based lists.

For illustration, the estimated app no. 4 in Table 7 (ranked 30th in the download-based list and 40th in the grossing-based list) should be profited up to $2.66 per download in which the price should be set at $1.99 and $0.67 should be earned from in-app purchases.

Similarly, in order to crack into top 10 in the top grossing list, an app which is ranked at 10th in the top paid list should earn at least $5.91 per download. Thus, the app developer should consider to fix the app price at $5.99 or to set a lower price, along with introducing in-app purchases to draw more impressions.

Figure 1 shows the average prices and earning per download of apps at ranks between 1 and 50 during the study period.

In comparison to app prices, earnings per download for high-demanded apps are higher which rootle out the effects of in-app purchases in the light of converting new users into sales revenue.

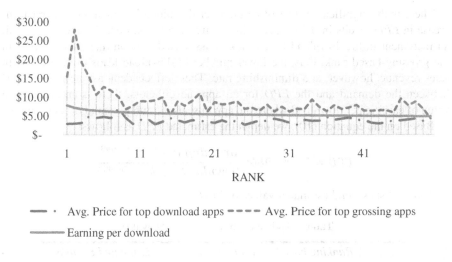

Fig. 1. Comparison of app prices and earning per download

4   Conclusion

Our study takes one step further in advancing mobile analytics on pricing strategies in the fast-growing environment of mobile apps. We proposed a structural model which is capable of generating reliable insights for market intelligence with publicly available data. Time and category effects, along with endogenity and heterogeneity issues are also considered in the model. Most importantly, we conceptualized a new indicator of market intelligence, Earning Per Download, which is useful for both app developers and researchers in the mobile industry.

There are several implications for app developers and publishers. First, we provided directive numbers for them to design effective pricing strategies and to unlock the full potential of their app positioning. Second, app developers should target their market niches based on our findings of category effects. Third, in AppStore, most of potential customers are forgiving and paying attentions on the latest review score; thus, releasing frequent updates is a perfect solution to gain customers' confidence and downloads. Last, designing apps for larger screen devices such as iPad would be strategic to capture shares in the app store.

This paper is not an end, but rather a beginning of forthcoming research. We note that app ranks are extremely volatile and being varied in the matter of hours; thus, crawling and matching of the data on a finer time scale rather than weekly basis are necessary. Furthermore, we are in the process of fetching additional in-app purchase data which would shed new lights on market intelligence of free apps with in-app purchases. By extending our model with them, app market best-kept secrets such as sales revenue or ranking mechanism would be publicly exposed.

References

1. Datta, A., Dutta, K., Kajanan, S., Pervin, N.: Mobilewalla: A mobile application search engine. In: Proc. 3rd Int. Conf. Mob. Comput. Appl. Serv. (2011)
2. Murphy, D.: Mobilewalla: The Market is Inches Away from One Million Mobile Apps, http://www.pcmag.com/article2/0,2817,2397200,00.asp
3. Shevchik, L.: Mobile App Industry to Reach Record Revenue in 2013 (2013), http://blog.newrelic.com/2013/04/01/mobile-apps-industry-to-reach-record-revenue-in-2013/
4. Inc., G.: Gartner Says Worldwide Mobile Application Store Revenue Forecast to Surpass $15 Billion in 2011, http://www.gartner.com/newsroom/id/1529214
5. Ramasubbu, N., Sangaralingam, K., Pervin, N., Dutta, K., Datta, A.: Surviving Hyper-Competitive, Unforgiving Platform Ecosystems: Examining Developer Strategies in iOS and Android Marketplaces. In: The 22nd Annual Workshop on Information Technologies and Systems, Orlando, Florida, USA (2012)
6. Kanada, P.: Which Can Be Best Mobile App Revenue Models?, http://theappentrepreneur.com/mobile-app-revenue-models
7. Apple: App Store Downloads on iTunes, http://itunes.apple.com/us/genre/ios-games/id6014?mt=8
8. Sangaralingam, K., Pervin, N., Ramasubbu, N.: Takeoff and Sustained Success of Apps in Hypercompetitive Mobile Platform Ecosystems: An Empirical Analysis. In: Proceedings of 2012 International Conference on Information Systems (ICIS)., Orlando, Florida, USA (2012)
9. Fang, F.: A method for mobile app download estimation (2013)
10. Garg, R., Telang, R.: Inferring App Demand from Publicly Available Data. MIS Q. (2012)
11. NPD Group Consumer Tracking Service, M.P.: OS Share of Smart phone sales (2011)
12. Venturedata: Apple Updates App Store Application Ranking Algorithm: Downloads a Greater Impact (2012)
13. Freierman, S.: One million mobile apps, and counting at a fast pace. New York Times (2011)
14. Goolsbee, A., Chevalier, J.: Measuring prices and price competition online: Amazon and Barnes and Noble. Quant. Mark. Econ. 1, 203–222 (2003)

A User-Centered Approach in Designing NFC Couponing Platform: The Case Study of CMM Applications

Antonio Opromolla[1], Andrea Ingrosso[2], Valentina Volpi[1],
Mariarosaria Pazzola[2], and Carlo Maria Medaglia[3]

[1] ISIA Roma Design, Piazza della Maddalena 53,
00196 Rome, Italy
[2] CORIS, Sapienza Università di Roma, Via Salaria 113,
00198 Rome, Italy
[3] DIAG, Sapienza Università di Roma, Piazzale Aldo Moro 5,
00185 Rome, Italy
{anto.opro,valentina.volpi84,m.pazzola14}@gmail.com,
{andrea.ingrosso,carlomaria.medaglia}@uniroma1.it

Abstract. In this paper, we will introduce CMM, a mobile couponing platform that allows retailers to create virtual coupons, and consumers to download and redeem them through NFC technology. In developing the system, we followed a user-centered design approach, adopting an iterative design process. Moreover, we studied the way consumers interact through NFC technology in mobile couponing applications. For this purpose, we arranged an analysis on user needs, a usability evaluation performed by experts, and a survey involving final users. The paper will show the most important findings from these studies.

Keywords: User-Centered Design Process, Marketing and HCI, New technology and its usefulness, NFC Couponing Applications.

1 Introduction

The enterprise marketing strategies are conferring to final consumers an increasingly central role. In such a context, the "conversation" between businesses and consumers is fundamental [1], since it allows companies to know their customers' attitudes, and customers to have new products and services meeting their own needs [2-3].

The personalization of the offer is strictly related to the main goal of businesses and retailers, i.e. retaining the loyal customer base [4]. According to [5], 94% of marketers declared that personalization is a key factor to "current and future success" and that it caused an increase in sales of 19%.

Among marketing strategies used for this aim, couponing is one of the most effective in building up a relationship with the customer [6]. Coupons are tickets that allow a purchase discount for a good or service. They can be categorized on the basis of: business goals (e.g. to make customers familiar with a new good or service, to sell out residual products, to reserve offers to loyal customers), distribution channels (e.g. print media, Internet, mobile), players that enable their emission (e.g. store coupons, manufacturer coupons).

F.F.-H. Nah (Ed.): HCIB/HCII 2014, LNCS 8527, pp. 360–370, 2014.
© Springer International Publishing Switzerland 2014

Mobile phones are increasingly employed in marketing strategies. New ICTs, especially those integrated in mobile devices, provide new opportunities to create a direct contact between businesses and consumers. According to Nielsen, LBS (Location Based Services), QR Code, and NFC (Near Field Communication) are the main technologies that consumers use in mobile shopping. Moreover, according to [6] these technologies can enable delivery and redemption of coupons.

As consumers become users of these services, enterprises and retailers should consider and analyze the relative user experience and interaction modes occurring with these new technologies. At the same time, enterprises need to be more ready and reactive at the requests that emerged from the "conversations" with the customers. So, using efficient and quick tools to easily create marketing campaigns is a clear advantage for businesses.

In this paper we will introduce CMM (Custom Mobile Marketing), a mobile couponing platform that allows, on the one hand, enterprises and retailers to create virtual coupons, on the other hand, consumers to download and redeem them through NFC technology. In details: in the next section we will introduce NFC technology; in the third one we will pay attention to related work focused on usability and user experience in NFC and mobile couponing applications; in the fourth section we will focus on the features of the CMM platform. The fifth section will illustrate the design process followed in order to develop the web and mobile applications, from the analysis of the user needs to the usability evaluation. The last section will focus on the main findings of our research and future work.

2   Technological Characteristics and Operating Modes of NFC

NFC (Near Field Communication) is a short range and wireless technology that enables two-way interactions between electronic devices [8]. It has been jointly developed by Sony and Philips, and later standardized by ISO (ISO/IEC 18092) [9]. As an evolution of RFId technology, it operates at the frequency of 13.56 MHz. NFC technology can be integrated into mobile devices and can be used in a lot of application scenarios.

The typical elements of an NFC-enabled mobile device are: the *antenna*, which allows a mobile device to communicate via radio waves with another device, e.g. a contactless reader, an NFC-enabled mobile device, an unpowered NFC chip (tag); the *NFC Controller*, which processes the data carried by the antenna; the *Secure Element*, which is a *tamper-resistant* chip containing sensitive data (it can reside on the handset, within the SIM Card, the CPU, or an external plug-in, e.g. sticker, micro SD, etc.).

There are three operating modes [10] for NFC technology: *reader/writer mode* (i.e. mobile phone can read or write the information stored in a RFId/NFC tag, e.g. product information, geographic information, etc.); *peer-to-peer mode* (i.e. two NFC-enabled devices can be placed closer to each other to share data); *card emulation mode* (i.e. mobile phone can be used as a contactless card. Some application scenarios are: ticketing, access control, payment, loyalty, etc.).

3   Related Work

According to [11], in the academic literature about NFC technology, technical infrastructure and security issues are the main research fields. Moreover, in the last few years, the focus on user experience and usability of NFC applications has widened. In particular, the work of [12-13-14] shows that in using an NFC application or service it is not necessary for the user to have a technical knowledge; on the contrary, this technology is generally considered *ease to use* and *intuitive*. In fact, NFC technology can support a user-friendly interaction and allows the access to technologically advanced services, too [15]. In [16], the authors demonstrate that the use of NFC technology enables simple and fast "micro-interactions" in our daily life. The research on usability and user experience about NFC technology led the authors of [17], to define the human-system interaction patterns, in order to classify NFC services and to design appropriate NFC interfaces in mobile applications.

However, in the research about usability of NFC technology, the focus is on measuring the usability of specific mobile applications through the most popular evaluation methods (i.e. heuristic evaluation, test with potential users, questionnaires of satisfaction). In details, the most part of the research concerns the main application areas of NFC technology, such as ticketing for transportation [18] and events [19], payment [18], heritage enjoyment and use [20], security in information management [21]. The most studied dimensions regarding NFC technology are: *ease* and *speed of use, usefulness, reliability* and *security, performance, satisfaction in use*.

In the academic literature about the NFC prototypes, a large emphasis is given to the shopping experience via mobile applications. The main services developed in this field are: obtaining additional product information [22], payment [23], loyalty [24], social networking [25]. Mobile couponing is a mobile shopping service exploitable via NFC technology, too. In fact, although today the available mobile couponing services use the most diverse technologies, according to [26-27], NFC simplifies distribution and redemption of coupons. These services are not only studied from an academic point of view, where the focus is also on the security of the system [28-29], but they are also marketable solutions [30]. In this regard, according to [31], mobile couponing via NFC can also be considered as a service that increases the demand of advanced services, such as mobile proximity payments.

4   CMM Platform

The CMM platform consists of a web application and two mobile applications for Android OS. Following, the description of the interaction process with the CMM platform:

1. The enterprise or the retailer starts a new marketing campaign via web application (*CMM website*) by creating new coupons relating to a specific product or service. He/She can also modify the related information, or deleting, disabling, and renewing the created coupons (Fig. 1).
2. The consumer uses his/her mobile application (*CMM consumer application*) to search and download the coupons he/she wants, if necessary the user can filter them by different product categories (Fig. 2). Then he/she visualizes on the map the stores where he/she can use them.

3. Inside the store, the consumer chooses among the downloaded coupons the one he/she wants to redeem (Fig. 3).
4. By placing the customer's NFC-enabled smartphone close to the retailer's one, the latter checks the validity of the coupons that the consumer decided to use via his/her mobile application (*CMM retailer application*). If the coupon is valid, the price of the good or service that the customer wants to buy is automatically discounted.
5. By using NFC technology the consumer can also directly exchange coupons with friends who have both an NFC-enabled smartphone and the CMM consumer mobile application.

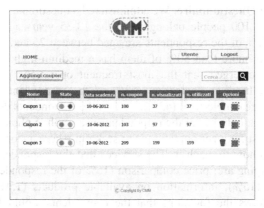

Fig. 1. The enterprise or the retailer can create new coupons relating to a specific product or service

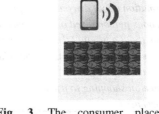

Fig. 2. The consumer searches and downloads the coupons he/she wants

Fig. 3. The consumer places his/her smartphone close to the retailer's one in order to use the selected coupon

5   Design and Evaluation Process

In order to develop the CMM platform, as described in the previous section, we followed a *user-centered design approach*, adopting an *iterative design process* [32].

In the next sections, we will describe the steps of the process that led to the production of the first mobile applications and website prototypes. We will focus on user needs analysis, usability evaluation performed by experts, and survey involving final consumers. Below, we will show the main findings from our research.

5.1   User Needs Analysis and Definition of the Functional Requirements

Firstly, we made an analysis concerning the habits and characteristics of potential users of CMM, in order to provide a couponing service that satisfies their needs. The main topics of the survey were mobile technologies use and shopping experience. This analysis was based on an *online structured questionnaire* and two *focus groups*. We involved only final consumers (not merchants) since we believe that the solution to be adopted mainly depends on the disposition of the user toward it.

Online Structured Questionnaire. We administered a questionnaire with 10 *multiple choice questions* to 100 people belonging to the 18-35 years age range (the main target of CMM). 57% of the respondents are aged between 26 and 30 years old; 70% of them are women; more than 50% of them has a medium-high qualification level. From the analysis emerged that the most frequent operations performed through mobile phone are: browser navigation (53% of the respondents), use of mobile applications (44%), reading e-mail (43%). 48% of the respondents declared to be avid shopper. Despite that, only 8% of the respondents uses mobile phone during shopping experience. The most frequent operation is to seek out where a store is located and to visualize on a map how to reach it. The services that the respondents need the most when they go shopping are: price comparison (16% of the respondents), information about promotions (15%), information on available products (15%), store location (14%). Table 1 shows the functions that the respondents would find in a mobile shopping application.

Table 1. Online structured questionnaire. Question: *"Which functions would you like to find in a mobile shopping application?"* (More than one answer was allowed). Total: 100 respondents.

Answers	Percentage of respondents
"Share information about discounts and promotions"	81%
"Collect coupons personalized on your purchases"	65%
"Tell a friend about a product that could interest him"	65%
"Ask for advice on what you want or would like to purchase"	57%
"Exchange coupons with friends"	42%
"Giving advice on shopping to friends"	38%
"Post the purchases"	25%

As shown in Table 2, the respondents are moderately familiar with NFC technology.

Table 2. Online structured questionnaire. Question: *"Are you familiar with NFC technology?"* (Only one answer was allowed). Total: 100 respondents.

Answers	Percentage of respondents
"Yes, I am"	18%
"Yes, I am but I never used it"	35%
"No, I am not"	47%

Focus Groups. We conducted two *focus groups*, involving a sample of 16 participants belonging to the 18-35 years age range. During these sessions, we focused on the use of NFC technology in shopping experience. We showed the participants different mobile applications using NFC as an enabling technology in different shopping contexts. First of all, the results of the focus groups show that consumers would establish a loyal relationship with a merchant or a brand, in order both to obtain personalized services and to reduce the cost of a product or service. Considering the use of NFC technology in shopping, the reactions of the participants are generally positive. Above all, they appreciate that this technology allows an automatic identification, enabling a variety of customizable services.

Defining Functional Requirements and Information Architecture. *Functional requirements* identify what a system should do [33] for the different users. On the basis of the user needs emerged from the surveys, we defined the main functional requirements of the CMM platform. In details, the system has to allow: the retailer and the final consumer to register their account; the retailer to create and manage a couponing campaign; the consumer to choose and download the coupon he/she wants; the redemption of coupons; the consumer to exchange coupons with friends; the consumer to visualize where he/she can redeem coupons.

Following these functional requirements, we designed the architecture of the CMM platform, as defined in section 4. Since the retailer has to perform different functions, he/she needs two tools to interact with CMM: on one hand, through the *CMM website* he/she can create and manage the mobile coupons; on the other hand, through the *CMM retailer application* he/she can confirm them.

After defining the components of the system (*CMM website, CMM consumer application,* and *CMM retailer application*), we designed the relative *information architectures*. A *use case diagram* [33] was useful to define to which applications and related functions the two typologies of users can access, and the individual actions that they have to perform in order to reach the related goals.

5.2   Usability Evaluation Performed by Experts

The analysis described in the previous section led us to the realization of the first *high-fidelity prototype* of the website and the mobile applications. The *usability evaluation* of these prototypes was performed by usability experts using two *predictive evaluation methods: heuristic evaluation technique* [7], that consists in observing the software compliance with given principles, and *cognitive walkthroughs* [34], that consists in simulating the behavior of the users while interacting with the software. The experts used their experience in usability field, in order to identify potential problems from the point of view of the *efficiency* and *effectiveness* dimensions [32].

Heuristics Evaluation Technique. During a preliminary briefing session, two evaluators decided the heuristics and the specific elements to analyze for each one. In particular, they focused on: *visibility of system status* (e.g. "Are users kept informed about what is going on?", "Are the feedbacks appropriate?"); *match between system* *and real world* (e.g. "Is language simple and familiar?"); *consistency of the system* (e.g. "Is there a consistency in graphic, information architecture, and contents among the different sections?"; *error prevention* (e.g. "Is it easy to make errors?"); *help users recover from errors* (e.g. "Are error messages clear and helpful?"); *design* (e.g. "Are icons, colors, and layout appropriate?").

Cognitive Walkthroughs Method. We involved two evaluators, to which we give a description of users and tasks related to each function. They walked through the action sequence for each task, evaluating the following elements: *availability of correct sequence* (e.g. "Will users know what to do?"); *evidence of correct sequence* (e.g. "Will users see how to do it?"); *interpretation of response of the action* (e.g. "Will users understand if the action is correct or not?").

Problems and Solutions. At a second stage of the usability evaluation, the evaluators individually inspected products by interacting with them and pointing out the occurred problems. Later, they discussed them during the final sessions of the debriefing, from which a set of solutions emerged. The most pressing usability problems concerned the CMM website and the CMM consumer application. Table 3 and Table 4 show the findings of the analysis, as evaluators organized them.

Table 3. CMM website. Some problems and solutions emerged from the usability evaluation.

Function	Problem	Solution
Login	No feedback for the login operation	Addition of feedback after the login
Registration	Use of the Italian language mixed to the English one	Use of only one language
	No details about the standards required to complete the registration form	Addition of an "hint" to fields requiring standards of compilation (e.g. password requirements)
Renewal coupon	No suitable icons	Icons replacement

Table 4. CMM consumer application. Some problems and solutions emerged from the usability evaluation.

Function	Problem	Solution
Registration	No details about the standards required to complete the registration form	Addition of an "hint" for the fields requiring standards of compilation (e.g. password requirements)
Download coupon	No automatic update of the number of the available coupons after the download	Automatic update of the number of the available coupons after the download
Exchange coupon	Message visualized by the user who receives the coupon via NFC: "Place your phone close to the other one and tap the screen to *transfer* the coupon"	Replacement with the message: "Place your phone close to the other one and tap the screen to *obtain* the coupon"

5.3   Survey Involving Final Consumers

After the usability evaluation, a new version of the CMM system was delivered and shown to potential end users. We administered two *semi-structured questionnaires*: the first to final consumers and the second to retailers. Here, we focus on the first.

Methodology and Aims. We administered the questionnaire to 30 potential consumers, belonging to the 18-35 years age range, 18 men and 12 women, with a medium-high qualification level. It consists of: 5 *multiple choice questions*; 7 *open-ended questions*; *5-point Likert scale* with 7 items. Each item was represented by an adjective describing CMM, with which the respondents had to express their level of agreement or disagreement (1: strongly disagree; 5: strongly agree). The adjectives could have a positive position (describing positively CMM) or a negative one (describing negatively CMM). So, a high appreciation for the product would record values close to "5" in case of adjectives with positive position and values close to "1" in case of adjectives with negative position. Our aim was to observe the *satisfaction* level towards the CMM solution, with a focus on perceived *usefulness* and *convenience*, *ease of use* and perceived *speed* of NFC technology in mobile couponing services, and *willingness to use* CMM.

The Findings. In General, the Evaluation of CMM System Is Positive. According to the results of the multiple choice questions and the open-ended ones, all respondents agreed that CMM would be *easy to use*. The main reasons are: *intuitive functions* (in the respondents' opinion, all functions are addressed to a single and clear task. Also the labeling is considered clear and the information architecture of CMM applications suitable for its goal); *intuitive technologies* (the respondents consider NFC technology easy to use and quick in downloading and using coupons); *look and feel* (it is considered minimal and captivating).

All respondents stated to be *willing to use* the CMM system. Mostly because of: *convenience* (users can perform all the process via mobile phone); *customization* (users can access the coupons they are most interested in); *innovation of the solution* (compared with other couponing services).

Table 5 shows the positive evaluation inferred from Likert scale method.

Table 5. Evaluation through Likert scale. Question: "Express your level of agreement or disagreement (1: strongly disagree; 5: strongly agree) in relation to the following adjectives describing the CMM platform". Total: 30 respondents.

Adjective	Position of the adjective	Average level
Interesting	Positive	4.53
Useful	Positive	4.43
Inconvenient	Negative	1.43
Complex	Negative	1.43
Pleasant	Positive	3.7
Unusual	Positive	4.03
Lacking	Negative	1.43

Table 6 shows the stores where the respondents are willing to use CMM at the most. Almost all the respondents indicated "clothing and accessories stores".

Table 6. Question: *"In which type of stores are you willing to use CMM?"* (More than one answer was allowed). Total: 30 respondents.

Store	Number of respondents (/30)
"Clothing and accessories stores"	26
"Shoe stores"	20
"Restaurants"	20
"Technology products stores"	18
"Bookstores"	18
"Food and beverage stores"	16
"Perfume shops"	11
"Supermarkets"	11
"Gyms"	11
"Appliance stores"	7
"Furniture stores"	5
"Jewelers"	3

Focusing on NFC technology, 28 respondents of 30 consider it *easy to use*, and 29 *quick*. They define it as an intuitive and practical technology, allowing almost no interaction and little time for data exchange. The respondents who have not found NFC technology easy to use, say that they are not familiar with it and they never used it before. The *lack of familiarity* with NFC technology is one of the main disadvantages perceived in using CMM; other disadvantages are about the security of personal data and the high competition from other similar services.

Finally, we asked the respondents to indicate some needed functions to add to the CMM platform. Among the main ones, they indicated: *social interactions; push notifications* (expiry of a coupon, new coupons availability)*; history of coupons; mobile payment; information about stores; loyalty programs; alerts geo-located; social ranking of coupons; indication of the coupons consumers may be interested in.*

6   Conclusion and Future Works

Our research shows that NFC technology is considered by end users not only ease to use and intuitive, but also useful and convenient. In fact, it can automate even the most complex processes, requiring a basic user interaction. The case study here discussed shows that a user-friendly technology, like NFC, can give new impetus to successful applications, implementing new useful and pleasant services. However, to do that, it is fundamental to get the end users familiar with NFC technology, currently little-know. In order to accomplish this goal, we planned a specific event for the market launch of CMM, i.e. the organization of an urban marketing game, based on social networks and actively involving consumers and retailers in the use of technologies and in the specific interaction modes expected for CMM. According to

[35], social influence is a key factor in accepting new technologies; so, all the occasions to get the user in contact with others should be fostered. In the future work we will analyze the findings from the survey involving the retailers. Since we followed an iterative design process, we intend to research about the additional functions indicated by the end users, in order to possibly implement them in the system. Then, we will perform a usability test with end users (final consumers and retailers), in order to study the interaction via NFC in an actual context of use.

References

1. Levine, R., Locke, C., Searls, D., Weinberger, D.: The Cluetrain Manifesto: The End of Business as Usual. Perseus Publishing (2000)
2. Kwak, R., Lee, H., Park, Y.: On the construction of a service map: How to match the service features and the customer needs. In: International Conference on Networking and Information Technology, pp. 298–302 (2010)
3. Schuurman, D., Mahr, D., De Marez, L.: User characteristics for customer involvement in innovation processes: deconstructing the Lead User-concept. In: 22th International Society for Professional Innovation Management (2011)
4. The International Customer Service Institute: The International Customer Service Standard (2009)
5. Econsultancy: The realities of online personalization (2013)
6. Mobile Marketing Association: Introduction to mobile coupons (2007)
7. Nielsen, J., Molich, R.: Heuristic evaluation of user interfaces. ACM Computer Human Interaction, 249–256 (1990)
8. NFC Forum: What is NFC, http://nfc-forum.org/what-is-nfc
9. ISO/IEC 18092:2013: Information technology - Telecommunications and information exchange between systems - Near Field Communication - Interface and Protocol (NFCIP-1)
10. NFC Forum: What it does,
http://nfc-forum.org/what-is-nfc/what-it-does/
11. Aydin, M.N., Ozdenizci, B.: Design Science Perspective on NFC Research: Review and Research Agenda. Informatica 37(2), 203–218 (2013)
12. NFC Forum: Near Field Communication and the NFC forum: The keys to truly interoperable communications. White paper (2007)
13. Ok, K., Coskun, V., Aydin, M., Ozdenizci, B.: Current benefits and future directions of NFC services. In: International Conference on Education and Management Technology, pp. 334–338 (2010)
14. Csapodi, M., Nagy, A.: New applications for NFC devices. In: 16th IST Mobile and Wireless Communications, Budapest, Hungary, pp. 245–249 (2007)
15. Andersen, A., Karlsen, R., Munch-Ellingsen, A.: NFC provided user friendliness for technologically advanced services. In: Yamamoto, S. (ed.) HCI 2013, Part II. LNCS, vol. 8017, pp. 337–346. Springer, Heidelberg (2013)
16. Dodson, B., Lam, M.S.: Micro-interactions with NFC-Enabled Mobile Phones. In: Zhang, J.Y., Wilkiewicz, J., Nahapetian, A. (eds.) MobiCASE 2011. LNICST, vol. 95, pp. 118–136. Springer, Heidelberg (2012)
17. Volpentesta, A.P., Frega, N., Filice, G.: Interactions Patterns in NFC Interfaces for Applications and Services. In: Camarinha-Matos, L.M., Scherer, R.J. (eds.) PRO-VE 2013. IFIP AICT, vol. 408, pp. 324–334. Springer, Heidelberg (2013)

18. Ferreira, M.C., Nóvoa, M.H., Dias, T.G.: A proposal for a mobile ticketing solution for metropolitan area of oporto public transport. In: Falcão e Cunha, J., Snene, M., Nóvoa, H. (eds.) IESS 2013. LNBIP, vol. 143, pp. 263–278. Springer, Heidelberg (2013)
19. Chaumette, S., Dubernet, D., Ouoba, J., Siira, E., Tuikka, T.: Architecture and comparison of two different user-centric NFC-enabled event ticketing approaches. In: Balandin, S., Koucheryavy, Y., Hu, H. (eds.) NEW2AN 2011/ruSMART 2011. LNCS, vol. 6869, pp. 165–177. Springer, Heidelberg (2011)
20. Biader Ceipidor, U., Medaglia, C.M., Volpi, V., Moroni, A., Sposato, S., Carboni, M., Caridi, A.: NFC technology applied to touristic-cultural field: A case study on an Italian museum. In: 5th International Workshop on Near Field Communication (NFC), pp. 1–6 (2013)
21. Franssila, H.: User Experiences and Acceptance Scenarios of NFC Applications in Security Service Field Work. In: Second International Workshop on Near Field Communication, pp. 39–44 (2010)
22. Seifert, J., Schneider, D., Rukzio, E.: MoCoShoP: Supporting Mobile and Collaborative Shopping and Planning of Interiors. In: Kotzé, P., Marsden, G., Lindgaard, G., Wesson, J., Winckler, M. (eds.) INTERACT 2013, Part II. LNCS, vol. 8118, pp. 756–763. Springer, Heidelberg (2013)
23. Alpár, G., Batina, L., Verdult, R.: Using NFC Phones for Proving Credentials. In: Schmitt, J.B. (ed.) MMB & DFT 2012. LNCS, vol. 7201, pp. 317–330. Springer, Heidelberg (2012)
24. Ozdenizci, B., Ok, K., Coskun, V.: NFC Loyal for Enhancing Loyalty Services Through Near Field Communication. Wireless Personal Communications 68(4), 1923–1942 (2013)
25. Biader Ceipidor, U., Medaglia, C.M., Volpi, V., Moroni, A., Sposato, S., Tamburrano, M.: Design and development of a social shopping experience in the IoT domain: The ShopLovers solution. In: 19th International Conference on Software, Telecommunications and Computer Networks (SoftCOM), pp. 1–5 (2011)
26. Mobile Marketing Association, Mobile Couponing Guidelines (2011)
27. Smart Card Alliance: Chip-Enabled Mobile Marketing (2010)
28. Dominikus, S., Aigner, M.: mCoupons: An Application for Near Field Communication (NFC). In: 21st International Conference on Advanced Information Networking and Applications Workshops (AINAW 2007), vol. 2, pp. 421–428 (2007)
29. Borrego-Jaraba, F.M., Garrido, P.C., García, G.C., Ruiz, I.L., Gómez-Nieto, M.Á.: Discount Vouchers and Loyalty Cards Using NFC. In: Bravo, J., López-de-Ipiña, D., Moya, F. (eds.) UCAmI 2012. LNCS, vol. 7656, pp. 101–108. Springer, Heidelberg (2012)
30. Cityzi: Loyalty Avenue, fidélité et coupons, http://nice.cityzi.fr/ actualites/fidelite/loyalty-avenue-fidelite-et-coupons
31. Mobey Forum: Mobile Wallet – Definition and Vision Part 1 (2011)
32. ISO 9241-210:2010 - Ergonomics of human-system interaction - Part 210: Human-centred design for interactive systems
33. Polillo, R.: Plasmare il web, Apogeo (2006)
34. Blackmon, M.H., Polson, P.G., Muneo, K., Lewis, C.: Cognitive Walkthrough for the Web. In: CHI 2002, vol. 4(1), pp. 463–470 (2002)
35. Venkatesh, V., Morris, M.G., Davis, G.B., Davis, F.D.: User acceptance of information technology: Toward a unified view. MIS Quarterly 27(3), 425–478 (2003)

Mobile Design Usability Guidelines
for Outdoor Recreation and Tourism

Sarah J. Swierenga[1], Dennis B. Propst[1], Jennifer Ismirle[1],
Chelsea Figlan[1], and Constantinos K. Coursaris[2]

[1] Usability/Accessibility Research and Consulting
Michigan State University, East Lansing, MI, USA
[2] Department of Telecommunication, Information Studies and Media
Michigan State University, East Lansing, MI, USA
{sswieren,propst,ismirlej,figlanc,coursari}@msu.edu

Abstract. Information-intensive websites such as those for outdoor recreation and tourism present complex design considerations and issues that need to be researched for mobile access. To gain a better understanding of the expectations and desires of users regarding a mobile application for outdoor recreation, researchers created a mobile application prototype for the US Army Corps of Engineers, which was subsequently tested for usability at two recreation sites in Kentucky with local participants. We provide an overview of our methods and results, and best practices we have gleaned from our findings. Our research is especially applicable for mobile applications that require access to a large amount of information and for a broad audience, and we also hope our study encourages more research in these areas.

Keywords: Mobile applications, mobile interfaces, usability, outdoor recreation, tourism, public websites.

1 Introduction

The popularity of mobile devices and applications has continued to explode, and the number of US adults who own smartphones has increased from 35% in May of 2011 to 56% in May of 2013 [1]. Outdoor recreation participation has been increasing steadily since The Outdoor Foundation began documenting participation in 2006, with 141.9 million participants in the United States getting outdoors in 2012 and "an average of 87.4 outings per participant for a total of 12.4 billion outings overall" [2]. The most popular activities included running, bicycling, fishing, camping, and hiking.

With the ever-climbing popularity of mobile devices and applications and the widespread and steady interest in outdoor recreation, comes the need to provide recreation and tourism information via mobile devices. However, currently there is a lack of mobile guidelines or standards based on research, especially for applications or websites that need to provide a large amount of information to a broad audience.

The Corps Lakes Gateway (CLG) website provides an enormous amount of information about US Army Corps of Engineers outdoor recreation resources for visitors. The CLG website (Fig. 1) received over 47 million hits in 2011, showing the

F.F.-H. Nah (Ed.): HCIB/HCII 2014, LNCS 8527, pp. 371–378, 2014.
© Springer International Publishing Switzerland 2014

desirability of this information. The Corps' 422 lakes in 43 states receive 370 million visits a year. To enhance the experiences of visitors and increase public interaction with the Corps, our aim was to create a mobile application to meet the growing expectation and need of the public for interactivity at their fingertips at all times.

Fig. 1. US Army Corps of Engineers, Corps Lakes Gateway website homepage

To learn what types of features and information users expected for this mobile recreation application, we first conducted the following studies, with each subsequent study using and building on the findings of the previous:

1. Meta-review of existing parks and recreation mobile applications to analyze the content and common features of over 50 applications, and to select representative interfaces.
2. Usability-based focus group in which participants rated the importance of potential features and discussed several alternative designs.
3. Survey of mobile mock-up designs asking participants to rank designs by choosing among three different designs for each type of page.

The results of these studies were then used to create a CLG mobile application prototype, which was usability tested at two US Army Corps of Engineers (USACE) projects: Green River Lake and Nolin River Lake, Kentucky, in June of 2013. The goal of this study was to identify user interface issues with the CLG mobile prototype in order to improve the user experience and generate research-based mobile interaction design best practices.

1.1   Related Work

Given the growth of mobile devices and application use, there is a critical need for a set of standards specifically for mobile interaction design based on research. Guidelines have been provided for iOS and Android for developers using these platforms to employ consistent design, yet these often "do not make recommendations for mobile websites, which run on different kinds of operating systems" [3]. Other guidelines have begun to emerge with practitioners and researchers working to bridge the gap between established web standards and standards for mobile. For example, Shneiderman's "Golden Rules of Interface Design" have been applied to mobile usability [4], and Nielsen's five attributes of usability [5]. Additionally, Wroblewski's mobile design strategies are based on real-world projects [6]. However, these efforts demonstrate the need for mobile's own set of standards for usability.

Research on the usability of mobile devices, websites, and applications has and is being conducted, but the majority of this testing has involved controlled experiments [5], most in a lab setting. This type of testing can be problematic, as it can limit the research by not capturing contextual cues and issues that could be found in a field study [7]. Therefore, in our study we moved outside of the lab and conducted usability testing at two outdoor recreation locations (campgrounds and boat launches) with a variety of recreation users to increase the ecological validity of our findings and preserve the context in which this mobile application would be used.

Nielsen and Budiu have recently offered strategies and guidelines for mobile usability, such as the need to focus the attention of users only on the essential content [9]. However, the amount of information that needs to be represented on a recreation or tourism mobile application leads to the issue of what is essential content for these types of users. Research for information-intensive mobile websites and applications is needed, and therefore to increase the validity and accuracy of the results of our studies for this issue, we used multiple methods throughout our design process [10].

2   Evaluation Scope

The goal of this research was to identify usability issues with the CLG mobile prototype and develop best practices for designing mobile user interfaces based on these findings. Usability refers to how easily a specific task can be accomplished with a specific tool. More verbosely, the International Organization for Standardization (ISO) defined usability as the "extent to which a product can be used by specified users to achieve specified goals with effectiveness, efficiency and satisfaction in a specified context of use" [11]. Effectiveness is defined as "accuracy and completeness with which users achieve specified goals," efficiency is defined as "resources expended in relation to the accuracy and completeness with which users achieve goals," and satisfaction as "freedom from discomfort, and positive attitudes towards the use of the product." While other conceptualizations of usability have been proposed [12-14], the ISO definition is the most widely accepted and was used by the research team.

2.1   Evaluation Metrics

Usability was evaluated in terms of its three constituent components: effectiveness, efficiency, and satisfaction. Effectiveness was measured as the percentage of tasks completed successfully. Efficiency was measured as the average time to perform a task and assessed based on issues observed during performance of the tasks. Satisfaction was measured by post-task questionnaires, post-study questionnaire, written feedback, and verbal comments during the session. While effectiveness and efficiency measures were quantitative, satisfaction was measured qualitatively.

2.2   Evaluation Strategy

Testing was designed to answer the following questions:

- What do users like and dislike about the flow of the CLG mobile prototype, e.g., navigation, organization of task flows, and grouping of content?
- What aspects of the user interface are hard to understand?
- What aspects of the process need to be enhanced?

Tasks designed to address these questions were developed by the project team, which consisted of researchers with experience conducting visitor studies in park and outdoor recreation settings and performing user-focused evaluations. The tasks pertained to three phases of a typical recreation trip: pre-trip planning, on-site activities, and post-trip reflection and feedback. The mobile application tested was not "live," since these rural locations have little or no internet connectivity. However, its basic functionality and several levels of screens tied to actual project data were made available to Corps recreation visitors for evaluation.

Participants consisted of a convenience sample of visitors who were recruited at two Corps of Engineers lakes in Kentucky: Green River Lake and Nolin River Lake, with the permission of the park managers. To maximize diversity in the sample, the Corps managers advised the research team of two campgrounds (one at each lake) where the team was likely to encounter a fairly large number of visitors who would be participating in a variety of outdoor recreation activities.

2.3   Procedure

The research team occupied a campground site and set up the data gathering station (Fig. 2) consisting of a table, tablet computer with mobile app mock-up and recording

Fig. 2. Data gathering station with participant, research team member, tablet with mobile application, and recording devices

software, video camera for recording tablet usage, and umbrella to darken the screen for ease of viewing in a bright, outdoor setting. Visitors were recruited by walking around the campground and asking for volunteers, who would receive $25 compensation for the 30-minute sessions. After reviewing and signing the consent forms and filling out a demographic questionnaire, participants performed up to nine tasks and filled out a post-study survey on-site about their experience with the mobile application prototype. Both audio and video recordings of the interviews were made using TechSmith's Morae® (v3.2.1) software.

In the Usability/Accessibility Research and Consulting research lab at Michigan State University, two independent reviewers, working with written observation notes, reviewed the Morae recordings to transcribe relevant user quotes, compute task completion times, and record difficulties and successes in completing the tasks. This analysis was verified by the principal investigators and discussions with the independent reviewers took place to resolve any differences in interpretation of the data.

2.4   Participants

Twelve participants, six females and six males, took part in the usability testing of the prototype at Green River and Nolin River Lakes (with 6 users participating at each site). Participants' ages ranged from 19 to 72; five participants were between 18 and 30 years old, two were between 31 and 40 years old, and four were between 51 and 80.

3   Usability Results

Participants attempted up to nine task scenarios using the CLG mobile prototype (Fig. 3). The tasks focused on finding information using the application, such as directions to the park, weather forecast, activities at the lake, and where to leave feedback. Participants were also asked whether they would use the mobile application and for what purposes to determine what additional information users would like.

Participants were mostly or entirely successful on 4 of the tasks, somewhat successful for 2 of the tasks, and encountered difficulties with 3 of the tasks. In general, participants were able to find the lake and lake area pages (e.g., Nolin River Lake is divided into 9 recreation areas), but they often had trouble finding more specific information in the lower layers of the application, such as the status of boat ramps at a lake (i.e., closed/open) and information about special events at the different recreation areas.

Even though several participants encountered difficulties finding some of the information and completing tasks successfully, the majority of participants provided positive feedback and expressed interest in using the application in the future. They also gave a variety of suggestions for enhancements and information they would like to be added to the application, which are being used for revisions to the prototype.

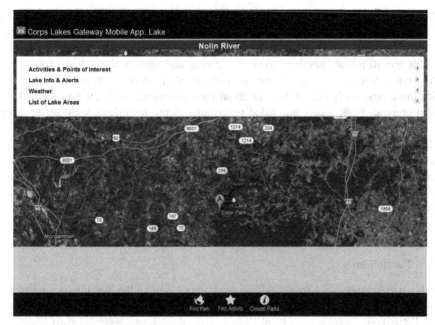

Fig. 3. Corps Lakes Gateway mobile prototype, Nolin River Lake page

4   Best Practices Based on Observations and Results

Usability testing of the mobile application prototype, with our observations and feedback from outdoor recreation users in the field, provided results consistent with other mobile studies, such as:

- Clear navigation is needed at the bottom of the screen
- Minimal scrolling should be needed; pages should be visually easy to scan
- Clickable features should have large clickable areas
- Fewest number of clicks needed to reach information
- Accurate and expected titles for pages, buttons, etc. should be used
- Links, buttons, etc. should be spaced to allow for easy clickability

Our usability testing also provided unique findings, specific for an outdoor recreation or tourism application for a broad range of users:

- Many outdoor recreation locations have weak or no wireless signals, and therefore users need the ability to download a static or cached version of the application.
- Options to access weather and a general search feature do not necessarily need to be custom made or contained within this type of application, as users often already have a preferred resource for this type of information.
- Environmental conditions, particularly sunlight, need to be considered. Font size and contrast should most likely go beyond typical standards to increase readability in the environment and also serve a diverse audience.
- Separate applications should be developed for smartphones and tablet devices in order to meet differences in size and user expectations.

5   Conclusion

Researchers created and evaluated a mobile application prototype for the US Army Corps of Engineers at two recreation sites in Kentucky with local participants. Research-based mobile field testing revealed best practice user interface design guidelines especially applicable for mobile recreation applications that require access to a large amount of information and diverse audience in outdoor settings.

The use of multiple methods in usability research, while not unique, is infrequent but highly recommended. Particularly, the combination of qualitative and quantitative procedures applied to participants in situ enhances the validity of results in contrast to single-method evaluations.

Acknowledgements. This research was funded through a grant to Michigan State University via an Interagency Agreement between the US Department of Agriculture National Institute of Food & Agriculture and the US Army Engineer Research and Development Center, entitled, "Role Of Internet and Mobile Technologies in Knowledge Transfer, Knowledge Management and Public Participation In Outdoor Recreation." (USDA/CSREES, Grant # 2012-39573-20165, Swierenga (PI), 9/1/12-8/31/13).

Special thanks go to Corps of Engineers Project Managers, Chris Boggs (Nolin River Lake) and Lori Brewster (Green River Lake), for facilitating the research team's data gathering efforts.

References

1. Smith, A.: Smartphone Ownership – 2013 Update (2013), http://www.pewinternet.org/Reports/2013/Smartphone-Ownership-2013.aspx (retrieved September 9, 2013)
2. Outdoor Foundation: Outdoor Recreation Participation Report Topline 2013 (2013), http://www.outdoorfoundation.org/research.participation.2013topline.html (retrieved September 9, 2013)
3. Dundar, B., Yumusak, N., Arsoy, S.: Guided-Based Usability Evaluation on Mobile Websites. In: Proc. ICIW 2013, IARIA, pp. 212–217 (2013)
4. Gong, J., Tarasewich, P.: Guidelines for Handheld Mobile Device Interface Design. In: Proc. DSI Annual Meeting, pp. 3751–3756 (2004)
5. Harrison, R., Flood, D., Duce, D.: Usability of Mobile Applications: Literature Review and Rationale for a New Usability Model. Journal of Interaction Science (2013)
6. Wroblewski, L.: Mobile First. New York: A Book Apart (2011)
7. Coursaris, C.K., Kim, D.J.: A Meta-Analytical Review of Empirical Mobile Usability Studies. Journal of Usability Studies 6(3), 117–171 (2011)
8. Po, S., Howard, S., Vetere, F., Skov, M.B.: Heuristic evaluation and mobile usability: Bridging the realism gap. In: Brewster, S., Dunlop, M.D. (eds.) Mobile HCI 2004. LNCS, vol. 3160, pp. 49–60. Springer, Heidelberg (2004)

9. Nielsen, J., Budiu, R.: Mobile Usability. New Riders, Berkeley (2013)
10. Rosenbaum, S.: Not Just a Hammer: When and How to Employ Multiple Methods in Usability Programs. In: Proc. UPA (2000)
11. International Organization for Standardization: Ergonomic Requirements for Office Work with Visual Display Terminals (VDTs) – Part 11: Guidance on Usability. (ISO Reference No. 9241-11:1998[E]) (1998)
12. Nielsen, J.: Usability Engineering. Academic Press/AP Professional, Cambridge (1993)
13. Quesenbery, W.: Dimensions of Usability. In: Albers, M., Mazur, B. (eds.) Content and Complexity: Information Design in Technical Communication. Lawrence Erlbaum Associates, Mahwah (2003)
14. Rubin, J., Chisnell, D.: Handbook of Usability Testing, 2nd edn. Wiley Publishing, Indianapolis (2008)

Gamification in Business

Gamification in Business

A Framework for Evaluating the Effectiveness of Gamification Techniques by Personality Type

Charles Butler

The Norwegian School of Information Technology, Oslo, Norway
charlesabutler@gmail.com

Abstract. This paper first examines the theoretical underpinnings of a number of popular gamification mechanics. Next, it examines the motivational and behavioral tendencies displayed by various personality types (based on the Myers-Briggs Type Indicator assessment) before attempting to pair them with the gamification techniques that most closely map to these tendencies. The specific gamification techniques were chosen due to their popularity and effectiveness in commonly used tools and applications, such as productivity tools and social games. The Myers-Briggs Type Indicator was chosen because of its relative popularity within corporate environments (as compared to other potential options, such as the Five Factor Model). This is seen as beneficial in order to facilitate the acceptance and utilization of the research within business-oriented settings, such as training programs or consumer applications.

Keywords: gamification, personality type, MBTI, Meyers-Briggs Type Indicator, motivations.

1 Introduction

Despite the increasing popularity of the concept of gamification, it seems to be quite a polarizing topic. Anyone with an interest in increasing their own performance (or the performance of others) may well fall into the pro-gamification side of the argument (as is shown by the quantified-self movement or the increasing interest in gamifying education). It may be a bit difficult to find fault with those reasons, at least conceptually (though a specific implementation is easy to criticize, of course). However, we also find huge companies, such as Zynga, building their products (which in Zynga's case, also happen to be games) entirely around various gamification techniques in order to elicit the desired behavior from their users. A negative outlook is very understandable when people feel like they are the target of someone else's attempts to manipulate them, and gamification has the potential to do that as well.

One of the more problematic areas of gamification actually lies in the difficulty in designing a gamification mechanic to encourage an appropriate outcome. While some people may decry the use of manipulative mechanics by massive commercial enterprises as unethical, a problem that has the potential to be even more serious is that of unintended consequences. Game mechanics can have a very powerful effect on our behavior, and even a legitimately well-intentioned gamification attempt can have very serious adverse consequences if it incentivizes the wrong behaviors. Consider a fitness application that seeks to encourage more exercise among its users. In theory,

F.F.-H. Nah (Ed.): HCIB/HCII 2014, LNCS 8527, pp. 381–389, 2014.
© Springer International Publishing Switzerland 2014

that sounds like a productive use of gamification, but consider the implications if a specific implementation actually encouraged users to race their bicycles at unsafe speeds, potentially resulting in tragic consequences.

The objective of this paper is to present a framework intended to improve the gamification efforts of both researchers and practitioners by aligning various gamification techniques with the user segments that respond most readily to each. In order to accomplish this, the paper will discuss the theoretical underpinnings behind the effectiveness of a number of categories of gamification mechanics. Additionally, similar factors must be detailed for each of the personality types. By making more carefully considered choices of the specific mechanics to pursue, hopefully it is possible to achieve both a greater effectiveness at eliciting the intended behavior and a reduced chance of producing unforeseen negative consequences.

2   Background

2.1   Gamification

In short, gamification is the application of game mechanics to a non-game context (though the same techniques are arguably applicable to game-based contexts as well). This is typically done in order to encourage (or discourage) certain behavior in a user. A simple example might be tracking post counts on an online forum, thus turning post counts into a type of pseudo-score, providing more prolific posters with some degree of reputation and credibility within the community. Another example is the increasingly common addition of badges, or symbols of progression, to various services. (While some online services have popularized the notion of *badgification*, note that similar techniques are commonly used in many military organizations, which alone should illustrate the power that progression and symbols can have in our lives.)

Gamification is becoming an essential part of human-computer interaction in any area where performance is a concern, and thus, enabling the designers of gamified products or tools to improve the performance of their designs could be of great value to the field. Despite the best efforts of their respective designers, many current implementations of gamification techniques fail to consider the innate tendencies of the specific user segments involved. This can cause the efforts to fall short of their potential and can even be counter-productive in certain situations. This paper intends to provide a framework that can aid in the selection and implementation of various gamification mechanics in order to elicit the best possible results based on the personality types of the users.

2.2   User Segmentation

If one were to examine the most popular video games from a variety of different gaming platforms and genres, one would be certain to find games that, while each individually very popular, have very different audiences. For example, there is likely a minimal overlap between a hardcore, competitive game such as Valve's *Counter-Strike* and the target audience for casual, social games, such as those made by the previously mentioned Zynga. Both types of games use mechanics that have very powerful effects on their respective users, but the mechanics and their effects are often as different as they are powerful. The point is essentially that if you wanted to create a game that caters to a hardcore, competitive audience, you would make a very different game than you would make for a casual, social audience. While this seems to be well understood in the game industry, it also seems like this distinction often gets overlooked by many of the gamification attempts present in today's products and services. Products that are meant to serve a diverse set of users often have a limited offering of gamified mechanics which may be effective (and even pleasing) to some percentage of the potential users at the expense of being distracting or even actively disruptive to others. If anyone attempting a gamified design and implementation could segment their users into various categories based on the types of game mechanics that would be most effective (and desirable) by each group, then both the users and the product owner would be in a better position. Additionally, if, due to limited resources or the desire for a simple solution, only a single mechanic (or some suboptimally limited number) were to be used, then it would be reasonable to choose the mechanic that would be most effective based on your target group of users. Of course, the next issue would be how you could most effectively segment your users.

2.3   Personality Types

For many games, an initial jump to the typical demographic breakdowns can be fairly effective. However, for products or services that hope to have a broader demographic reach than a typical video game, a demographic breakdown may not be sufficient. In addition, even among similar demographics, there can obviously be any number of preferences exhibited among its members. Even though a great many video games end up being targeted at the 18-35 year old male demographic, there can still be some amount of diverging interest within that group. The method considered here is to segment the users by personality type. Though the various personality types may not be fully uniform in their distribution, they are likely to be largely independent of factors such as age or gender, which may physically describe a person but tell us little about how that person may think or act. In contrast, personality types specifically seek to categorize people based on such things as their thoughts, motivations, behaviors, and tendencies. While the myriad of various testing methods all have their own specific categorizations, they are all at least attempting to sort people into usefully differentiated groups.

3   Developing a Framework

3.1   Meyers-Briggs Type Indicator

As mentioned above, there are many different personality type categorizations that this paper could have used. The Meyers-Briggs Type Indicator (MBTI) was chosen for this paper largely because of its popularity as a corporate training and development tool. While other methods may have a stronger foundation in research, it is expected that the MBTI's extensive user-base (more than 10,000 companies and 2,500 colleges and universities [1]) would enable practitioners to more readily apply the suggestions made here in the field, both in industry and in research applications.

The MBTI, initially developed by Katherine Briggs and Isabel Briggs Meyers, built on the earlier work of Carl Jung [2]. The tool has participants rate themselves by answering a number of questions which are then evaluated in order to score the participant along a continuum in four dimensions.

Table 1. The four dimensions of MBTI and their poles [2]

(E)	Extroversion	**Energy**	Introversion	(I)
(S)	Sensing	**Perception**	Intuitive	(N)
(T)	Thinking	**Judgment**	Feeling	(F)
(J)	Judging	**Orientation**	Perceiving	(P)

Participants are associated with the poles in which they rank highest, giving them a four-letter indicator of their personality type. For example, someone who ranked highest in each of the leftmost poles from the table above would be an ESTJ. It should be mentioned that it is possible to score extremely high on one pole or just slightly, but that isn't clear from simply looking at the letter indicator. Even though there are sixteen different indicator rankings, there are multitudes of different potential outcomes when the specific points on the dimensions are considered. This is but one of the many reasons that it should never be assumed that all people of a certain type exhibit identical thought or behavior patterns. It is certainly possible to behave in a different manner than the indicator would predict, and people can potentially score differently based on the context (for example, answering the questions as your "work-self" instead of your "home-self"). The indicator is simply a starting point for examining the potential tendencies of a participant or group of participants. For any individual, the results may be considerably less than predictive, but the usefulness in user segmentation exists so long as we can make some assumptions about user behavior that, on average, tend to be true for the particular segments.

3.2   Examining the Motivations

There are a number of ways to interpret the results of the MBTI as applied to an individual or group. Participants typically receive information relevant to their specific type, and one option is to take each of the sixteen types individually and create motivational profiles for each. However, depending on the application, that level of complexity may be unwarranted. In a research or employer/employee setting, it may be possible to administer the assessment to each user individually to ascertain the exact makeup of the group, but that is likely unfeasible in many settings, especially when the application in question is a product or service. Also, even where individual testing may be a possibility, it may be more resource-intensive than would be preferred.

There are a number of ways to narrow the field of choices to a more manageable level. It could be possible that the potential user-base has a higher than typical concentration of a specific type or group of types. For example, one study [3] found that, among software engineers, certain types, dimensions, and pairs of dimensions were significantly over or underrepresented compared to the distribution for all US adults. For specific types, INTJ was the most over-represented type, at 3.4 times the frequency of the general population, though still only making up 7% of the sample. For the pairs of dimensions, it found that Intuitive Thinkers (NT) was the most over-represented, making up 26% of the sample but only about 10% of the general population, and for individual dimensions, Thinkers (T) made up 81% of the sample while only constituting about 40% of the general population. To keep things quite simple, focusing on techniques that would be most effective for Thinkers would seem to be a sound strategy in the software engineering field, while looking at the data for the general population might lead to the opposite conclusion.

Table 2. Selected dimensional tendencies [4]

Extroverts:	Introverts:
• Talk more than listen	• Listen more than talk
• Think out loud	• Think inside their head
• Act, then think	• Think, then act
• Like to be around others	• Feel comfortable being alone
• Prefer to do many things simultaneously	• Prefer to focus on one thing at a time
	• Not take action
• Be attuned to their external environment	• Be attuned to their inner world
• Learn best through doing or discussing	• Prefer to communicate in writing
Sensors:	**Intuitives:**
• Focus on details and specifics	• Focus on the big picture and possibilities
• Admire practical solutions	
• Notice details and remember facts	• Admire creative ideas
• Live in the here-and-now	• Notice things that are new or different
• Trust actual experiences	• Trust their instincts
• Like step-by-step instructions	• Prefer to learn new skills
• Work at a steady pace	• Like to figure things out for themselves
	• Work in bursts of energy
Thinkers:	**Feelers:**
• Make decisions based on logic and evidence	• Make decisions based on their values and feelings
• Be direct	• Appear to be friendly
• Appear to be reserved	• Be convinced by how they feel
• Be convinced by rational arguments	• Be tactful
• Value honesty and fairness	• Value harmony and compassion
• Take few things personally	• Take things personally
• Be motivated by achievement	• Compliment others
Judgers:	**Perceivers:**
• Make decisions easily	• Have difficulty making decisions
• Pay attention to time	• Be less aware of time
• Finish projects	• Start projects
• Work first and play later	• Play first, work later
• See the need for rules	• Keep their options open
• Make a plan and stick to it	• Question the need for many rules
• Find comfort in schedules	• Keep plans flexible
	• Be spontaneous

Another way to segment MBTI users is in quadrants based on certain pairings of the dimensions. One common pairing consists of the 2nd and 3rd dimensions, what Pearman and Albritton call the Cognitive Core [2]. The combinations of these pairings, makes up the four quadrants, ST, NT, SF, and NF.

Table 3. Cognitive Core tendencies [2]

Sensing with Thinking (ST):	Intuition with Thinking (NT):
• Tough-minded	• Psychologically minded
• Reasonable	• Ingenious
• Matter-of-fact	• Analytical
• Practical	• Focuses on theoretical relationships
• Verifies facts – weighs, measures	• Likes autonomy
• Orderly	• Has defined interests
• Self-controlled	• Pride of objectivity
• Internally consistent	• Methodically attentive to theory
Sensing with Feeling (SF):	**Intuition with Feeling (NF):**
• Factually oriented	• Tender minded
• Gentle and modest	• Enthusiastic
• Seeks to meet needs	• Insightful
• Expresses personal warmth	• Seeks new projects, complexity
• Seen as compassionate	• Identifies symbolic and theoretical relationships
• Responsible	• Aesthetic
• Conscientious	• Inventive, non-conforming
• Focuses on things concretely affecting others	• Unconventional thought process

3.3   Choosing the Mechanics

Once a specific user segment is chosen, an attempt to design a gamification implementation catered specifically to that segment's tendencies and preferences could be engineered. This can be done by considering the motivations behind the effects that each game mechanic has on its users. These mechanics often have, at their root, some aspect that triggers the effect because of a cognitive bias or behavioral quirk, such as intermittent reinforcement schedules, commitment/consistency, and intrinsic focus maintenance. We can also look to a number of topics in behavioral economics to build an understanding of the motivations behind certain game mechanics, such as loss aversion and sunk costs. Historically, the designers creating these mechanics likely weren't formally considering these theories when using the mechanics (though they may have had an instinctive notion of the effects), but they have evolved over time, with designers keeping the mechanics that proved effective, regardless of the reasons. Included here are the results at an attempt to translate the tendencies listed above for each of the MBTI dimension poles into motivations or preferences relevant to game mechanics, and then, based on this translation, a number of game mechanics are suggested that could be especially appealing to the users associated with that dimension pole.

Table 4. Suggested game-related tendencies and corresponding mechanics

Extroverts:	Extrovert Mechanics:
• Robust communication channels • Social play • Multiple objectives • Identity • Quickly accessible	• Voice or face-to-face interaction • Multiplayer (competitive or cooperative) • Opportunities to multitask (arcade-style engagement) • Avatar customization • Quick/intuitive play
Introverts:	**Introvert Mechanics:**
• Limited communication channels • Solo play • Focused objectives • Things to ponder or consider • Deep, complex content	• Text chat, or no interaction • Single-player • Clearly identified goal to pursue • Story arcs/lore • Deep rule sets with optimization opportunities
Sensors:	**Sensor Mechanics:**
• Limited choices • Managing data • Dealing with immediate issues • Specific processes • Linear progression toward objectives	• Few but meaningful choices • Resource management • Real-time challenges • Repeatable sequences of events • Gradually "grindable" progression
Intuitives:	**Intuitive Mechanics:**
• Variety of choices • Mystery, discovery • Conceptual coherence • Customization of progression • Irregular play sessions	• Open-ended or branching decisions • Plot-twists, exploration • The context must make sense • Enable progression along multiple paths, and horizontal progression • Infrequent but long sessions should be rewarding
Thinkers:	**Thinker Mechanics:**
• Mental challenges • Open to competition, if fair • Status building • Progression	• Puzzles to solve • Sports, contests, etc. • Awards/badges, public ranks/titles • Leveling up, objective chains
Feelers:	**Feeler Mechanics:**
• Social challenges • Cooperative activities • Diplomacy	• Situations to deal with/figure out • Caretaking/support roles • Negotiation, political activities

Table 4. (*Continued.*)

Judgers:	Judger Mechanics:
• Exercising control	• Numerous decisions to make
• Urgency	• Timers and deadlines
• Completionists	• Collections, progress tracking
• Complexity	• Deep, unintuitive rule sets
• Planning	• Min/maxing opportunities
• Work towards a reward	• Long, difficult progression
Perceivers:	**Perceiver Mechanics:**
• Freedom	• Sandbox style play
• Unbounded play	• No restrictions/penalties
• Try a bit of many things	• Variety of activities
• Simplicity	• Simple rules (if any)
• Surprise/delight	• Unexpected events, "Easter eggs"
• The game is the reward	• The mechanics themselves should create enjoyment, not as a means to an end

4   Conclusion

4.1   Implications

The end result of this paper is a simple framework, made up of a number of tendencies and accompanying mechanic suggestions that any researcher or practitioner can use to potentially improve their gamification attempts by selecting the mechanics that most closely match the motivational and behavioral tendencies of their specific users. To achieve the greatest improvement possible, the gamification designers would likely need to specifically test their users for personality types, which should be possible in a research setting though admittedly more difficult in a commercial endeavor. However, if the target market of a commercial gamification attempt is focused enough, it should be possible to make reasonable assumptions about the users within that market.

4.2   Future Work

Future work would likely benefit from expanding the research with different methods of user segmentation to allow for more focused targeting options. Additionally, conducting experiments to measure the effect of various gamification techniques on user segments based on personality types could be incredibly valuable in order to help quantify the theoretical differences asserted by this paper. A first step in this direction could be to test a single game mechanic on a population of known personality types, attempting to verify if it has more of an effect on some types than others. This could eventually be expanded to include most major game mechanics, providing what would essentially be a codification of game mechanic effectiveness.

References

1. Cunningham, L.: Does it pay to know your type? The Washington Post,
   http://www.washingtonpost.com/business/on-leadership/
   myers-briggs-does-it-pay-to-know-your-type/2012/12/14/
   eaed51ae-3fcc-11e2-bca3-aadc9b7e29c5_story.html
   (accessed February 6, 2014)
2. Pearman, R.P., Albritton, S.C.: I'm Not Crazy I'm Just Not You. Davies-Black, Mountain View (1997)
3. Capretz, L.F.: Personality types in software engineering. International Journal of Human-Computer Studies 58, 207–214 (2003)
4. Truschel, J.: Using the Meyers-Briggs in Tutoring: Understanding Type. Association for the Tutoring Profession, http://www.myatp.org/wp-content/uploads/2012/06/Synergy-Vol-2-Truschel.pdf (accessed February 6, 2014)

The Global Leadership of Virtual Teams in Avatar-Based Virtual Environments

Paul Hayes Jr.

Indiana Institute of Technology
hayepj01@gmail.com

Abstract. This research is part of an ongoing study of the usefulness of avatar-based collaborative environments in comparison to software platforms that mostly utilize audio and video in two dimensional settings like those used in GoToMeeting/Traning. Second Life is explored as a viable option for avatar-based collaborative teams and other telework. This research investigated a potential relationship between engagement, in terms of leader-member exchange and team interaction in software platforms that utilized an avatar-based collaborative environment in relation to one that did not. This initial pilot study examining feedback gathered from user experience of engagement and leader-member exchanges is used to develop insight into the proper instrument selection that will be utilized to conduct a larger quantitative study. A mixed methods approach consisting of inquiry from past instruments that measure engagement (Gajendra et al., 2012), satisfaction (Camman et al., 1998), social presence within a virtual environment (Witmer & Singer, 1998) and the technology acceptance model (TAM)(Shroff, Deneen, & Ng, 2011) is used. The findings suggest that avatar-based environments may impact leader-member exchange through increased engagement.

Keywords: 3D web and virtual worlds, Computer-supported collaboration, Gamification in business, Ubiquitous commerce.

1 Introduction

There is research that suggests there is a large population of Chinese citizens that are very fond of (information technology) IT and SNSs and are seeking to maximize integration potential for business collaboration. Clark, Nooruddin, and Zhang (2012) write that No-one loves social media like the Chinese. In fact, research firm Forrester has dubbed them "hypersocial".

China controls close to a tenth of the online/virtual game global market, which makes China the third largest market in the world, and second only to South Korea in Asia (South Korea has 32%): the United States has about 21% and all of Europe combined only represents 23% of the market (Yue & Stuart, 2009). The growth implication are huge not only for game designers and social networking applications, but also for any business that can successful bridge their business experience with this "hypersocial" love for gaming. There is no doubt China will be the strongest consumer of innovative use of avatar-based game-like collaborative products for the foreseeable

F.F.-H. Nah (Ed.): HCIB/HCII 2014, LNCS 8527, pp. 390–400, 2014.
© Springer International Publishing Switzerland 2014

future. It is strategic for businesses looking to conduct business in China to create customer interactions that include social media and engaging avatar mediums that cater to the sense of play consistent with a video game.

Schackman (2010) discusses the implications for India and the engaged use of avatars in Second Life (Linden Lab, 2011). His discourse includes that India is the second most populated country in the world, and also has one of the top five GDP's in the world as well.

1.1   The Virtual Landscape

In order to maximize organizations ability to quickly become the next globally integrated enterprise (GIE), leaders need to understand how these evolving environments work in order to maximize their resources and stay competitive in a world where organizations are beginning with becoming "global" in mind (Cateora, Gilley, & Graham, 2011; White & Rosimilia, 2010). Research by top Stanford communication professor and virtual reality researcher, Dr. Jeremy Bailenson explains that "The brain often fails to differentiate between virtual experiences and real ones. The patterns of neurons that fire when one watches a three-dimensional re-creation of a supermodel, such as Giselle or Fabio, are very similar-if not identical- to those that fire in the actual presence of the models" (Bailenson & Blascovich, 2011, p. 1). That suggests that there is a blur between things that are virtually there and those things that are real. This blurred distinction between the "real" and the virtual explains the expansion of the study of virtual environments into the disciplines of leadership and business due to the increased frequency. Computer-mediated collaborative work environments, telework, geographically dispersed teams, and computer-mediated communication among workers that are geographically collocated is prominent in global business practice, and understanding what keeps these virtual workers engaged is critical (Richardson, 2013).

Leaders must remain flexible while planning for the integrations of technological advances that innovative software and mobile applications are demanding in the globalized world. Global leaders must utilize strategy in combination with research, development, knowledge management and information management to ensure they are moving at the speed of technology to adjust for a rapidly shrinking global market. Critical concerns in maximizing the impact of global leaders' efforts in managing geographically dispersed teams are managing the intersection of digital technology, and culture with globalization.

1.2   Technology Advancing

Digitally-based technologies are the most important driving force behind the continued interconnectedness of people as they transition into a true global village (Bartlett & Beamish, 2011). Digital-based technologies are leading businesses to operate and explore the virtual global market that is quickly becoming the hideaway of choice for consumers disenchanted with the typical shopping experience that involves travel, lines and time that could be dedicated to other home-based responsibilities resulting in nothing less than a "virtual Diaspora" (Schackman, 2010). The consequences of this Diaspora, is the evolution of a new way of communicating and connecting.

2   Team Member Interaction

Communication scholars have compartmentalized NVC into nine distinct categories; i.e. kinesics, more commonly referred to as body language; physical appearance; chronemics, or communication through time; proxemics, or communication using space; paralanguage, communication through tone of voice; artifacts, communication by physical objects; haptics, communication through touch; facial expressions; olfactics, communication by means of smells; and oculesics, more commonly referred to as eye contact (Richmond, McCroskey, & Hickson, 2008). An informed understanding of virtuality and an effective use of computer-mediated communication through the use of avatar-based platforms will allow leaders to maximize confidence, control of virtual outcomes and decision-making (Nardon & Aten, 2012).

Virtual teams are not traditional face-to-face teams over technology (Nicholson, Sarker, Sarker, & Valacich, 2007). Many of the same problems that affect face-to-face teams persist on virtual ones; specifically poor communication and trouble with decision-making. The newer avatar based software systems could allow for more specific interpersonal communication, but without solutions to some of the other leadership and planning problems they could be easier to criticize (Cash-Baskett, 2011). Bad agenda and planning problems, as a result of poor leadership execution, could just expedite and magnify the recognition of frustration and disapproval by team members and create more conflict within the group. Thorough research conducted on current business oriented systems could provide more insight into whether or not problems are more a result of poor virtual leadership or lack of understanding of the use of progressive medium (Bosch-Sijtsema & Sivunen, 2013). Also, seeking face-to-face solutions to virtual problems could prove challenging and ineffective. The use of avatars should be researched

2.1   Effective Communication

There is something intrinsic about the way that the human experience facilitates the development of trust and closeness (Lohle, 2012). Communication theorists believe that closeness is developed through interpersonal communication, which covers theories based around the reduction of uncertainty, social construction, social information processing and shared contexts based around narrative (Griffin, 2009; Mehrabian, 2008; Poole & Hollingshead, 2005). Also, Mehrabian (2008) has researched that between 65 and 93 percent, of communicative depth comes from nonverbal richness. Avatars provide one of the easiest ways to increase communicative effectiveness and develop human interaction skills that will take virtual participants to higher levels of meaningful interaction (Gillath, McCall, Shaver, & Blascovich, 2008). These trends collectively suggest that there is merit in studying the effective use of avatars in developing strategies pertinent to the future of global leadership and management.

2.2   Virtual Worlds Enhance Nonverbal Communication

The patterns of neurons that fire when one watches a three-dimensional re-creation of a supermodel, such as Giselle or Fabio, are very similar-if not identical- to those that fire in the actual presence of the models" (Blascovich & Bailenson, 2011, p. 1). This implies that there is a blur between that which is virtually there and that which is real. Increases of virtual work and the distribution of work load to virtual team members geographically separated, of increasing amounts of distance, leaves team members feeling disassociated and unhappy due to stress, time management and a missing component of attachment (Bosch-Sijtsema, Fruchter, Vartiainen, & Ruohomäki, 2011). The focus behind using virtual world environments for virtual team workplaces is that the simulation of the actual world may allow virtual workers to identify with the shared context and themselves in the form of a three dimensional (3D) graphical representation or human simulation of an actual person; often referred to as avatars (Yee & Bailenson, 2009). This mixed methods research study proposal is primarily concerned with how individual members of global virtual teams experience different degrees of engagement when interacting in 3D virtual collaborative environments versus when they interact in audio and video meeting software/programs through the understanding of a shared context within a social constructivist's understanding of semiotic and symbolic interaction (Johansen & Larsen, 2002)

2.3   Global Leadership

Global leaders are often found in working in groups over large divides of geography with virtual workers in environments dominated by audio and email (Cash-Baskett, 2011; Meyer, 2010). Those teams speak of virtuality as if it were all or nothing. Research explains that organizations have varying levels of virtuality (Mihhailova, Oun, & Turk, 2009), but there is a need for additional research that can support whether more money should be invested in the development and continued use of virtual worlds as vehicles for distributed work. "According to KZERO, a consulting company focusing on virtual worlds and virtual goods, the total market for virtual items created and exchanged between users was worth around 5 billion USD in June 2010 and the value is expected to more than double within the next two years. The Asian market is the largest with around USD 3.8 billion being generated in 2009 (OECD, 2011, p. 14) Global business leaders should recognize that Asian markets are not the only global regions interested in the continued development and investment of virtual worlds. European countries are conducting business research and information gathering in virtual environments (Atlas & Putterman, 2011).   According to one of the leading providers of business information on technology information gathering, the French market research firm Repères, the cost for a qualitative focus group within a virtual setting is about 33% lower, and quantitative surveys can be conducted at half the cost of a comparable real life project (Kaplan & Haenlein, 2009). The investment of large sums of money could be indicative of the type of returns foreign countries plan to receive, which would make these very expensive "games."

2.4   Global Leaders and Technology

Clark Aldrich (2009) makes his call to action clear. The Complete Guide to Simulations and Serious Games is "nothing less than a manifesto intended to overthrow the intellectual legacy of civilization to date" (p.iv). Aldrich is signaling the end of the age of Gutenberg, a time of great learning, no doubt, but of linear learning—learning "how to know" rather than "how to do" or "how to be" in a complex, interactive world. Why should you care? If you are an education reformer, Aldrich's revolution could transform the way we learn. If you are a CEO, this is the way the next generation will want to be addressed. And if you are an entrepreneur, the intersection of serious games and simulations may signal one of the greatest investment opportunities in a generation" (Aldrich, 2009, p. xxi).

2.5   Leadership and Technology

The existing research on virtual teams focuses on the roles of leaders, and the emergence of leadership as an important factor to the success of virtual teams. Leadership has traditionally been conceptualized as an individual-level skill. Review of global leadership theory covers individual traits, behaviors, opinions and self-efficacy (Jex & Britt, 2008; Osland, 2008; Yukl, 2010). However, recent research speaks to the shared aspects of leadership and how they are more playful and innovative than traditional interpretations of leadership phenomenon (Hoch, 2013; Kark, 2011). There is a call for action to investigate technologies that advance social context within groups using innovative technologies.

There are many businesses that have worked or are currently in avatar-based collaborative environments like Second Life or other similar virtual worlds, like Learning Immersive Virtual Environments (LIVE), that are exploring the usefulness of avatar-based collaborative environments. Research suggests that there are significant advantages and increased engagement from the teams that use avatar-based virtual collaborative environments for innovative work and prototype creation (OECD, 2011). A mixed methods study of how present education, business, IT professional experts and future employees would give new direction to research and development sections of new technologies interested in using virtual worlds for virtual/dislocated teams, while simultaneously providing them strategic environments that gives them every opportunity to succeed, save money, stay engaged and communicate as clearly as possible (Boughzala, de Vreede, & Limayem, 2012; OECD, 2011).

3   Research Rationale

The research for this study explores the viability of theories that support in-creased interest and engagement of workers in these worlds are true or not. If they are found to be unsupported, then researchers can spend more time developing other methods of virtual team interaction that is not focused around the graphic heavy conception of a virtual environment. If the theories are supported then that would provide research and development a vector towards improving these environments for more effective use. The next step of research could be to provide insight into useful strategies for global leaders of virtual teams to employ when working with foreign nationals in foreign countries. The business, professional and educational institutions would be able to create a more uniform program with true unilateral continuity and uniformity and more intuitive controls for computer users not so skilled with the virtual world technologies that presently exist. The research would be used by industry and businesses that could produce software that could be purchased by university officials and then use it to provide better education for the evolving job market and future employees. There are over 150 universities with a presence in Second Life and over 80 with their own island in Second Life (OECD, 2011). The proposed research will prove invaluable to the planning and development of those institutions. It is in the best interest of continued education and instructional design that universities and business build more solidarity on the most effective ways to use the virtual world and cyberspace for the purpose of advancing global cooperation and intercultural understanding.

3.1   Leadership Constructs to Be Evaluated

This mixed methods research study proposal is primarily concerned with how individual members of global virtual teams experience different degrees of engagement when interacting in 3D virtual collaborative environments versus when they interact in audio and video meeting software/programs through the understanding of a shared context within a social constructivist's understanding of semiotic and symbolic interaction (Griffin, 2009). Other interests include the manifestation of shared leadership within avatar-based virtual environments, leader/team member cross-cultural communicative exchange, if individual member engagement is altered through the use of avatar-based virtual environments used for virtual team collaboration in the pursuit of achieving team goals, and if using these environments bring significant value to the efforts of the leaders of global/virtual teams with distributed workloads? Ultimately, this research will provide much needed insight into the possibility of using avatar-based collaborative environments to understand individual engagement and contribution to global virtual teams.

3.2   Research Questions

The specific Research questions for this research are:

1. Do individual members of global virtual teams experience different levels of engagement when interacting in 3D virtual collaborative environments versus when they interact in audio and video meeting software?
2. Can global leaders use avatar-based simulations in professional virtual worlds as a leadership tool for knowledge workers?
3. How do simulations within virtual worlds support global and professional communication in a virtual/geographically distributed context?
4. How does the environment that knowledge work takes place in, both physically and virtually, affect distributed work?

This research could lead to measures that could be validated in terms of effectiveness through the use tools that are created from past instruments that measure engagement (Gajendra et al., 2012), satisfaction (Camman et al., 1998), and social presence within a virtual environment (Witmer & Singer, 1998). The lack of validated instruments that properly measure the virtual team and leadership experience exclusively would limit the effects of the groups experience as it would only be described in relating terms that did not capture the effect of the specific experiences of the participants as it is capture in time and dynamic occurrence. However, current research (Shroff,

Deneen, & Ng, 2011) has focused on "the technology acceptance model (TAM) because the research seeks to understand the relationship between perceptions (such as perceived usefulness and perceived ease of use of technologies) and usage behavior" (p. 601).

4   Pilot Study

A pilot study was conducted with undergraduate college freshman students randomly selected to participate in either the control (GoToMeeting) or the avatar-based (Second Life) environment first before they switch to the other. The participants had no experience with either Second Life or GoToMeeting. Instructors recommended students to the study that did not have experience in either platform. A list of participants was determined and then randomly arranged. A randomly selected student was assigned the role of the group leader. There were 8 teams of four to six individuals on each team. Four of the teams started with Second Life and four started with GoToMeeting/Training. Then when both groups completed the experiment, they were interviewed. For the purposes of the experiment the GoToMeeting groups represented more traditional teleconferencing software because it has audio, video and screen-sharing capabilities as well as text and private text. The participants were from several different countries and background and brought a substantial amount of credibility to the weight of the results as there wer(Van Pelt, 2009)e cross-cultural implications with the findings. The participants were separated before they have a chance to interact with each other in group work or with one another in any other virtual setting. The participants were diverse with nationalities ranging from China, USA, Cameroon, Venezuela, Bermuda, Singapore, Colombia and Russia. The teams simulated virtual work in these environments by being separated and then completing assigned tasks that represented the type of work typical in virtual team settings like collaboration, negotiation and problem solving (Davis, Murphy, Owens, Khazanchi, & Zigurs, 2009; Van Pelt, 2009).

5   Findings

The feelings were mixed and the order did not change the fact that members of both of the groups felt more engaged when they were in Second Life than they reported when they were in GoToMeeting/Training. The groups that felt stronger affinity and connection with the leader of the group also reported higher levels of engagement.

5.1   The Second Life Starters

The teams that started with Second Life first and then switched to GoToMeeting/Training Second reported higher levels of affinity towards the leader of the groups in both environments. The groups who started with Second Life first seemed to describe GoToMeeting/Training with less enthusiasm. The participants explained that the initial experience was overwhelming and that feeling made it difficult to focus on the tasks. The group also explained that it became easier to focus on the tasks as the time went on. The group that started with Second Life first explained that they had a better sense of where the other team members were located and that made it easier to associate names with voices than when they later interacted in GoToMeeting/Training.

5.2   The GoToMeeting/Training Starters

The teams that started with GoToMeeting/Training reported that it was much easier to get started on tasks and process with team communication because they were not overwhelmed with heavy technological skill requirements that became instantly apparent after they switched to Second Life. These teams also reported that the members would often disconnect from each other to work on separate computing endeavors even though they were all in the same virtual place. The teams that started with Go-ToMeeting/Training also reported that it was not as disrupting to not have a headset and microphone in GoToMeeting/Training unlike Second Life where it was very challenging to prevent audio overlap and redundancy of communicative efforts.

5.3   Miscellaneous Findings

A strong majority of the participants, regardless of which medium they started with, expressed that it was difficult for them to think of GoToMeeting/Training as an actual environment. The two-dimensional nature of if seemed more like an accessory, but operating in Second Life seemed more like an interaction.

6   Discussion

These introductory findings have fashioned an underpinning for the completion of additional, and significantly larger quantitative research study that is being conducted to investigate the relationship between leader-member exchange, engagement and computer-mediated platforms that serve as virtual environments for virtual teams. The projected route for this research includes the different levels of engagement experienced by leaders and team members as experienced in different virtual circumstances and different reported levels of leader-member exchange. There are indications made buy this preliminary work that would suggest some answers to the research questions.

Do reported levels of engagement differ between teams interacting in 3D virtual collaborative environments compared to audio and video meeting software?
The interviews of the participants are indicative of individuals who are more involved with sharing the Second Life experience. Those participants have longer and more detailed responses to questions. There was a broad array of engagement levels reported, but they were mostly more supportive of continued use and exploration of the use of Second Life as a place for meaningful collaboration. Comments like: *The interaction that I had with one of the members in my group was very engaging. It definitely broke some communication boundaries between us even though we were in an online environment* and *I liked the use of second life because you have a visual indicator of the guys on your team.*

Can global leaders use avatar-based simulations in professional virtual worlds as a leadership tool for knowledge workers?

The leadership qualities of the participants were not readily available. The emergence of leaders in many situations is not always scripted and leaders with many different levels of knowledge, experience and formal training can emerge as leaders. These findings suggest that leaders of engaged virtual teams can use an avatar-based simulated worlds, like Second Life, to keep workers engaged and inclined to communicate more effectively with the leadership.

How do simulations within virtual worlds support global and professional communication in a virtual/geographically distributed context?

The participants of this research reported higher levels of exchange, engagement and leader-member exchanged. The participants did not put as much pressure on the leader when they were operating inside of Second Life as compared to when they were operating in GoToMeeting/Training. The research would suggest that the heightened sense of the individual's awareness of both themselves and the other team members made for more meaningful communication engagement and interaction.

How does the environment that knowledge work takes place in, both physically and virtually, affect distributed work?

The research addressed an interesting aspect to what exactly an environment is and what it means to team members to be in an "environment" or not. Some of the participants did not recognize GoToMeeting/Training as an environment and discussed it as if it were like using a telephone. The findings could support that maybe environments are places were meaningful rapport is built and tools are more processing information and solving problems.

7   Future Research Implications

The research conducted here suggests that there are many different components to understanding team communication and nonverbal interaction. The findings suggest that a study with more teams provide quantitative data that can provide clarity about the qualitative results. Would instruments that gage the relationships and levels of engagement experiences by virtual team members support what was observed with this pilot? More research should be conducted on the effects of avatars on team collaboration not only in terms of engagement, but in relation to the appearance of the avatars used. In Second Life the users have the option to not only be humanoid in appearance, but they can also be animals and fictitious characters like vampires and vehicles.

8   Conclusions

The results of this study and the continued research being conducted can be joined to question the practicability and maximization of the utilization of avatar-based collaborative environments for the purposes of meaningful virtual team building and telework

(Boughzala et al., 2012; Lohle, 2012) The next phase of the research into the differences between avatar-based collaborative environments and audio/video environments like GoToMeeting/Training is a larger scaled study that will include more small teams of international participants across the globe. The researcher will limit the use of having both groups of teams switch mediums and only have users report on experiencing the first medium. The quantitative measures will include the Pearson correlation to determine relationships between engagement and leader-member exchange.

References

1. Aldrich, C.: The Complete Guide to Simulations and Serious Games: How the Most Valuable Content Will be Created in the Age Beyond Gutenberg to Google, p. xxi. Wiley, San Francisco (2009)
2. Bailenson, J.N., Blascovich, J.: Infinite Reality. Hape Collins, New York (2011)
3. Bartlett, C.A., Beamish, P.W.: Transnational management: text, cases, and readings in cross-border management, 6th edn. McGraw-Hill/Irwin, New York (2011)
4. Bosch-Sijtsema, P.M., Fruchter, R., Vartiainen, M., Ruohomäki, V.: A Framework to Analyze Knowledge Work in Distributed Teams. Group & Organization Management 36(3), 275–307 (2011), doi:10.1177/1059601111403625
5. Boughzala, I., de Vreede, G.-J., Limayem, M.: Team Collaboration in Virtual Worlds: Editorial to the Special Issue. Journal of the Association for Information Systems 13(10), 714–734 (2012)
6. Callen, D.: How intercultural teams drive success in global virtual teams. Graziadio Business Review 1(4) (2008)
7. Cash-Baskett, L.J.: Global virtual team members' perceptions of leader practices. Argosy University/Sarasota Ed.D., Argosy University/Sarasota, United States – Florida. ProQuest database (2011)
8. Cateora, P., Gilley, M., Graham, J.: International Marketing, 15th edn. McGraw-Hill, New York (2011)
9. Gillath, O., McCall, C., Shaver, P.R., Blascovich, J.: What can virtual reality teach us about prosocial tendencies in real and virtual environments? Media Psychology 11(2), 259–282 (2008), doi:10.1080/15213260801906489
10. Griffin, E.A. (ed.): Communication in our lives, 5th edn. Wadsworth/Cengage Learning, Boston (2009)
11. Hoch, J.: Shared Leadership and Innovation: The Role of Vertical Leader ship and Employee Integrity. Journal of Business & Psychology 28(2), 159–174 (2013), doi:10.1007/s10869-012-9273-6
12. Jex, S.M., Britt, T.W.: Organizational psychology: a scientist-practitioner approach, 2nd edn. John Wiley & Sons, INC., Hoboken (2008)
13. Kaplan, A.M., Haenlein, M.: The fairyland of Second Life: Virtual social worlds and how to use them. Business Horizons 52, 563–572 (2009), doi: 10.1016/j.bushor,07.002
14. Kark, R.: Games Managers Play: Play as a Form of Leadership Develoment. Academy of Management Learning & Education 10(3), 507–527 (2011)
15. Lohle, M.F.: Implications for Real Project Management Success: A Study of Avatar Identity as an Antecedent of Virtual Team Trust. Ph.D., Nova Southeastern University, United States – Florida (2012)
16. Mehrabian, A.: Communication without words. In: Mortensen, C.D. (ed.) Communication Theory, 2nd edn., pp. 193–200. Transaction Publishers, Piscataway (2008)

17. Meyer, E.: The four keys to success with virtual teams (2010),
    http://www.forbes.com/2010/08/19/
    virtual-teams-meetings-leadership-managing-cooperation.html
    (retrieved May 20, 2011)
18. OECD. Virtual Worlds: Immersive online platforms for collaboration, creativity and learning. OECD Economy Papers, 49 (2011)
19. Osland, J.S.: Leading global change. Routledge, London (2008)
20. Poole, M.S., Hollingshead, A.B. (eds.): Theories of small groups: interdisciplinary perspectives. Sage Inc., Thousand Oaks (2005)
21. Richardson, R.A.: The relationship between perceived social presence and development of interpersonal trust in a virtual environment. 3555180 Ph.D., Capella University, United States – Minnesota. ProQuest Dissertations & Theses A&I; ProQuest Dissertations & Theses Full Text database (2013)
22. Schackman, D.: Avatars in a virtual Diaspora: Developing a theory of cultural ties and identityin Second Life. Ph.D. 3459385, Syracuse University, United States – New York. ProQuest Dissertations & Theses A&I database (2010)
23. Shekhar, S.: Understanding the virtuality of virtual organizations. Leadership & Organization Development Journal 27(6), 456–483 (2006), doi:10.1108/01437730610687755
24. Shroff, R.H., Deneen, C.C., Ng, E.M.W.: Analysis of the Technology Acceptance Model in Examining Students' Behavioural Intention to Use an e-Portfolio System. Australasian Journal of Educational Technology 27(4), 600–618 (2011)
25. White, K., Rosimilia, T.: Developing global leadership: How IBM engages the workforce of a globally integrated enterprise (I. G. Business, Trans.) (2010)
26. Witmer, B., Singer, M.: Measuring Presence in Virtual Environments: A Presence Questionnaire. Presence, 7, 225–240 (1998), doi: citeulike-article-id:4444937
27. Yee, N., Bailenson, J.N.: The Difference Between Being and Seeing: The Relative Contribution of Self-Perception and Priming to Behavioral Changes via Digital Self-Representation. Media Psychology 12(2), 195–209 (2009), doi:10.1080/15213260902849943
28. Yukl, G.: Leadership in organizations, 7th edn. Prentice Hall, Upper Saddle River (2010)

Gamification of Education: A Review of Literature

Fiona Fui-Hoon Nah[1,*], Qing Zeng[1], Venkata Rajasekhar Telaprolu[1],
Abhishek Padmanabhuni Ayyappa[1], and Brenda Eschenbrenner[2]

[1] Department of Business and Information Technology,
Missouri University of Science and Technology, Rolla, Missouri, United States
{nahf,qzdg9,vtfnd,apt59}@mst.edu
[2] College of Business and Technology, University of Nebraska at Kearney, Kearney, Nebraska,
United States
eschenbrenbl@unk.edu

Abstract. We synthesized the literature on gamification of education by
conducting a review of the literature on gamification in the educational and
learning context. Based on our review, we identified several game design elements that are used in education. These game design elements include points,
levels/stages, badges, leaderboards, prizes, progress bars, storyline, and feedback. We provided examples from the literature to illustrate the application of
gamification in the educational context.

Keywords: Gamification, Game design elements, Education, Learning.

1   Introduction

Gamification refers to the application of game design elements to non-game activities
and has been applied to a variety of contexts including education [1]. Various elements have been used in gamification to increase user engagement. Examples of these
elements include points, badges, leaderboards, and storyline [2]. Educational institutions are interested in gamification of education, where educators create gamified
learning environments to enhance learner engagement and improve learning outcomes
[3-5]. Given the potential of gamification of education, we are interested in identifying game design elements that have been used to gamify education as well as the
impact on learner outcomes. Hence, in this paper, we review the literature on gamification of education and report our synthesis of the findings from the literature.

2   Review of Literature

We carried out a review of the literature on gamification in the educational and learning contexts. Various design elements for gamification of education are discussed in
these papers along with their impact on the learners, which we referred to as learner
outcomes. Table 1 provides a summary of the review.

---

* Corresponding author.

F.F.-H. Nah (Ed.): HCIB/HCII 2014, LNCS 8527, pp. 401–409, 2014.
© Springer International Publishing Switzerland 2014

Table 1. Summary of Literature Review

Reference	Design Elements for Gamification	Learner Outcome(s)
Barata et al. (2013)	Experience points, Levels, Leaderboards, Challenges, Badges	Engagement, Participation
Berkling & Thomas (2013)	Levels, Progress bars, Points, Immediate feedback, Leaderboards, Peer interaction and collaboration	
Betts et al. (2013)	Experience points, Levels, Freedom to choose difficulty level	
Brewer et al. (2013)	Points, Prizes	Motivation
de Freitas & de Freitas (2013)	Experience points, Levels, In-game rewards	Engagement, Enjoyment
Eleftheria et al. (2013)	Onboarding, Points, Levels, Badges, Challenges, Replay or do over, Unlockable content, Customization	Engagement, Enjoyment, Productive learning experience
Gibson et al. (2013)	Badges	Motivation, Engagement, Sense of achievement, Status
Goehle (2013)	Levels, Experience points, Achievement	Engagement, Sense of accomplishment
Kapp (2012)	Storytelling, Feedback	Engagement
Kumar & Khurana (2012)	Levels, Stages, Points, Badges	Engagement
O'Donovan et al. (2013)	Storyline, Visual elements, Goals, Rewards - Points, Progress bars, Badges, Leaderboard	Engagement, Performance

Table 1. (*Continued.*)

Raymer (2013)	Frequent feedback, Progress bars, Rewards, Character upgrades, Peer motivation	Engagement
Santos et al. (2013)	Badges	Achievement, Engagement, Motivation, Recognition
Todor & Pitic (2013)	Avatar, Feedback, Points, Badges, Rewards	Interest in course
Villagrasa & Duran (2013)	Storyline, Scoreboard	Engagement, Motivation

Barata et al. [6] gamified a course in Information Systems and Computer Engineering by introducing multiple game design elements into the course design, including experience points, levels, leaderboards, challenges, and badges. The results suggest that the gamified course led to greater student engagement and participation in online course activities based on the number of downloads of the lecture slides and number of online posts (e.g., online discussions of class materials and online queries related to course content). The gamified approach also had a positive influence on lecture attendance. However, gamification did not significantly improve student grades.

Berkling and Thomas [7] introduced a gamification platform that was used to teach a course in Software Engineering. A web-based learning platform that contained game dynamics, such as status, achievements, competition, altruism, and game elements, such as points, levels, progress, immediate feedback and leaderboards, were introduced to students to learn the course. A survey was administered to the students to understand the effectiveness of the new teaching method. The results revealed that students were generally not interested in such a gamified environment because they did not find it helpful. Berkling and Thomas [7] noted that students who underwent a traditional classroom style of education for more than 12 years did not automatically get enticed to the new ways of learning.

Betts et al. [8] described a gamified web-based collaborative learning tool called Curatr (www.curatr.co.uk) that was used in an online course. Game design elements such as experience points, levels, and freedom to choose difficulty level were used. The results show that the number of experience points earned was correlated with assignment scores. There was also a correlation between the level of participation and the overall scores. However, those who received the highest overall scores did not have the most experience points, whereas those who received the lowest overall scores had the lowest experience points. Hence, the authors suggest that quality or performance may not be reflected by experience points. Instead, educators may use a minimum participation threshold for assessment of effort that can be integrated into the final grades.

Brewer et al. [9] conducted a lab experiment to assess the effect of gamification on children. To address the problem of lack of motivation among children, the authors introduced the scoring system and the prize system into the experimental tasks. The result indicates that the task completion rate increased from 73% to 97% with the gamified systems. Hence, gamification helped to increase the motivation of children in task completion.

de Freitas and de Freitas [10] applied the concept of gamification into a system called "Classroom Live" which was used in a computer science class for undergraduate students. The authors took into account various game design elements including experience points, levels, and in-game rewards. The learning experience of the students was more enjoyable while students' engagement was also enhanced.

Eleftheria et al. [11] proposed using augmented reality and gamification techniques to design a gamified augmented reality book for learning science. By using augmented reality, a book can provide 3D simulations of science experiments to increase student understanding of the concepts. To enhance motivation and engagement of the students, game design elements such as onboarding, points, levels, badges, challenges, replay or do over, unlockable content, and customization were applied. The objective of gamification was to create an alternative method to make the learning experience more engaging, enjoyable and productive.

Gibson et al. [12] explained that badges, when used with points and leaderboards, can be a powerful means of creating competitions and signaling goal attainment, achievement, and status. Badges can also motivate learners to improve their performance through higher engagement, greater skill acquisition, and time spent on learning.

Goehle [13] implemented two video game mechanics, i.e., leveling/experience points system and achievement system, into a web-based homework program called WebWork. By comparing the final levels and achievements of the students, it was found that most students with high scores on their homework also received high achievement scores, indicating that their high engagement levels could be attributed to the achievement system. The results also suggest that the implementation of the leveling/experience points system and achievement system heightened the sense of accomplishment of the students.

Kapp [14] indicated that gamification can increase learner engagement in the learning process. Game design elements such as storytelling and feedback were discussed. Storytelling refers to the narrative of the game which can be used to sustain learners' interest and engagement. The frequency, intensity, and immediacy of feedback are also important for sustaining engagement throughout the learning process. Kapp [14] also noted that the balance between learning and gameplay is a key success factor for a gamified educational project.

Kumar and Khurana [15] found that students did not show much interest in learning programming languages, such as C and C++, in the traditional method of classroom teaching. Students were, however, interested in a gamified approach to learning programming languages. Utilizing the gamification approach, a game design was proposed that incorporated elements such as levels, stages, points, and badges to motivate students to learn. In addition, students were assigned different levels of expertise, such as "Beginner", "Intermediate", "Advanced", and "Expert", as they progressed through the gamified learning process. Kumar and Khurana [15] indicated that the goal of gamifying an educational scenario or a pedagogical approach is not fulfilled unless the objective of "learning with fun" is incorporated into the game.

O'Donovan et al. [16] utilized storyline, vivid elements, goals and subgoals, points, progress bars, badges, and leaderboard to gamify a game development course and assessed the effectiveness of gamification using a questionnaire administered to students. The results indicate that student engagement (e.g., lecture attendance) and performance (e.g., course grade) improved as a result of gamification.

Raymer [17] suggested that providing frequent feedback, measuring progress, offering character upgrades, rewarding effort, and utilizing peers as a source of motivation can help to increase learner engagement.

Santos et al. [18] conducted a case study that explored students' experiences while earning badges in a learning process. More than 90% of the students agreed that the badge system in education made them more focused, motivated, and engaged. The results suggest that badges are considered as "symbols of recognition" and they offer a sense of achievement during classroom activities.

Todor and Pitic [19] incorporated game elements such as avatar, feedback, points, badges, and rewards into an e-learning platform for a course in electronics. The results indicate that after applying the gamified platform, the students' interest in the course increased.

Villagrasa and Duran [20] introduced gaming components, such as storyline and scoreboard, in gamifying a 3D art class for university students. The goal of gamification is to increase engagement and motivation of students as compared to traditional teaching methods.

3   Game Design Elements for Education

Based on our review of the literature, we identified eight game design elements that are used extensively in the educational and learning contexts.

1. Points

   The point system functions as a measure of success or achievement. These points may be used as rewards, as a form of investment for further progression towards the goals, or to indicate one's standing. There are different types of points and they vary across games. For example, Experience Points (XP) (i.e., points earned by completing tasks) and Steam Points (i.e., points that correspond to in-game currency) were used for some of the role-playing games in education [16]. Points can also be considered as credits in an academic environment [15].

2. Levels/Stages

   The level system is used in various game designs to give players a sense of progression in the game. Initial levels tend to require less effort and are quicker to achieve, whereas the advanced levels require more effort and skills. Even though levels/stages are a widespread and popular gamification concept and they serve as a form of rewards for task or assignment completion, students' learning abilities may not progress or improve as a result of leveling [13].

3. Badges

   Badges are recognized as a mark of appreciation or task accomplishment during the process of goal achievement. In order to maintain learners' motivation, the use of badges is helpful for engaging the learners in subsequent learning tasks. Badges are effective in inspiring learners to work towards future goals [16]. The majority of the student respondents in Santos et al.'s [18] survey also felt that badges helped to keep them engaged, especially in the classroom context, and motivate them to carry out future learning tasks.

4. Leaderboards

The objective of a leaderboard is to keep the learners motivated and create a sense of eagerness to advance their names for the achievements they have accomplished. Leaderboards are used to create a competitive environment among students. A leaderboard is used to display the current levels of high scorers and the overall scores. In order to avoid demotivation for those who are lower ranked, leaderboards usually display the top 5 or 10 scorers only. The survey findings by O'Donovon et al. [16] suggest that leaderboards rank highest in motivating learners.

5. Prizes and Rewards

The use of prizes has been found to be effective in motivating learners [9]. The timing and scale of rewards can also affect learner motivation [17]. In general, it is better to give multiple small rewards than one big reward. Also, the schedule for giving out rewards should be evenly distributed throughout the learning process. An example of in-game rewards is character upgrades [17]. A character upgrade is a way to motivate learners by displaying their progress in the form of characters. It allows others to recognize the amount of effort a learner has spent to reach his or her current level. In order to use character upgrades as a game design element, one must be given a virtual character which allows him or her to upgrade from time-to-time by means of the points or rewards earned [17].

6. Progress bars

Several researchers [7], [16], [17] have utilized progress bars to gamify education. While badges demonstrate achievements towards a particular level/goal, progress bars are used to track and display the overall goal progression. In an educational game, progress bars are used as a display mechanism to motivate people who are close to achieving their educational goal or sub-goals. Progress bars can also encourage them if they are falling behind in their progress.

7. Storyline

Storyline refers to the narrative or story in the game. Kapp [14] suggests that a good storyline can help learners to achieve an ideal interest curve, where interest peaks around the beginning and end of the learning process, and to stay motivated throughout the learning process. A storyline also provides a context for learning and problem solving as well as helps to illustrate the applicability of concepts to real-life [16].

8. Feedback

The frequency, intensity, and immediacy of feedback are helpful for learner engagement [7], [14], [17]. The more frequent and immediate the feedback is, the greater the learning effectiveness and learner engagement. Clear and immediate feedback has been shown to be important for attaining the flow state, which is a state of engagement and immersion in an activity [2], [21], [22]. Hence, feedback is an important criterion for performance and engagement.

4   Examples of Other Gamified Educational Applications

A variety of applications have been developed based on the gamification concept. In order to engage and motivate learners, companies and educational institutions are investing time and money into gamification. An example of such applications is a website development tool provided by DevHub (www.devhub.com) [23]. In this particular website, users can develop and launch their own websites. An interesting component of this website is that as users progress towards their goals, online rewards, such as points and badges, will be awarded. The use of progress bars also keeps users motivated. Another example is Stack Overflow (www.stackoverflow.com) where computer programmers interact with one another in a community-like environment [24]. Those who answer questions posted by their fellow website users will earn rewards such as reputation points and badges. After collecting a certain number of points, they will be provided with special privileges, such as moderator, which enhance the user's reputation.

The gamification concept is also being implemented in a library by an application development company, RunningInTheHalls [24]. In order to reward those who use the libraries frequently and to make academic studies or search tasks in a library more interesting, a library game (www.rith.co.uk/#librarygame) was developed. Using the game, some of the activities, such as borrowing a book, spending time in the library, and visiting the library frequently, will be rewarded. There is another variant of this library game called 'Lemontree,' where the focus is on libraries in academic institutions. A trial of this game was conducted at the University of Huddersfield where positive feedback and outcomes of the game were received. Based on observations, it was found that students utilized library resources more effectively and the game facilitated friendly competition among students and between departments.

There are many gamified systems in the market to help increase user engagement when learning new techniques. Games, such as "QuizeRo", that are based on geolocations have been shown to be of interest to users by motivating them to explore places and learn about new locations [25]. Microsoft Ribbon Hero (http://www.ribbonhero.com/) offers an example of gamification in learning Microsoft Office tools. Adobe LevelUp (http://success.adobe.com/microsites/levelup) is a gamified system to help users explore Photoshop through puzzle games. Online services, such as Khan Academy (http://www.khanacademy.org), are available for users to learn about various subjects while experiencing gamefulness [6].

5   Conclusions

In this paper, we carried out a review of the literature on gamification of education and identified several game design elements that have been used to gamify education. Gamification of education has increased in popularity but systematic studies to assess and evaluate its impact on learning are in the infancy stage. We encourage practitioners and researchers to use a design science approach [26] to evaluate the impact of gamification in education. Specifically, they can develop gamified educational applications and carry out systematic evaluations of them using scientific approaches and methodologies such as experiments and surveys.

References

1. Nah, F., Telaprolu, V., Rallapalli, S., Venkata, P.: Gamification of Education using Computer Games. In: Yamamoto, S. (ed.) HCI 2013, Part III. LNCS, vol. 8018, pp. 99–107. Springer, Heidelberg (2013)
2. Nah, F., Eschenbrenner, B., Zeng, Q., Telaprolu, V., Sepehr, S.: Flow in Gaming: Literature Synthesis and Framework Development. International Journal of Information Systems and Management 1(1) (forthcoming, 2014)
3. Eschenbrenner, B., Nah, F., Siau, K.: 3-D Virtual Worlds in Education: Applications, Benefits, Issues, and Opportunities. Journal of Database Management 19(4), 91–110 (2008)
4. Chen, X., Siau, K., Nah, F.: Empirical Comparison of 3-D Virtual World and Face-to-face Classroom for Higher Education. Journal of Database Management 23(3), 30–49 (2012)
5. Siau, K., Nah, F., Mennecke, B., Schiller, S.: Co-creation and Collaboration in a Virtual World: A 3D Visualization Design Project in Second Life. Journal of Database Management 21(4), 1–13 (2010)
6. Barata, G., Gama, S., Jorge, J., Goncalves, D.: Engaging Engineering Students with Gamification. In: 5th International Conference on Games and Virtual Worlds for Serious Applications, pp. 1–8 (2013)
7. Berkling, K., Thomas, C.: Gamification of a Software Engineering Course. In: International Conference on Interactive Collaborative Learning, pp. 525–530 (2013)
8. Betts, B.W., Bal, J., Betts, A.W.: Gamification as a Tool for Increasing the Depth of Student Understanding using a Collaborative E-learning Environment. International Journal of Continuing Engineering Education and Life-Long Learning 23(3-4), 213–228 (2013)
9. Brewer, R., Anthony, L., Brown, Q., Irwin, G., Nias, J., Tate, B.: Using Gamification to Motivate Children to Complete Empirical Studies in Lab Environments. In: 12th International Conference on Interaction Design and Children, pp. 388–391 (2013)
10. de Freitas, A.A., de Freitas, M.M.: Classroom Live: A Software-assisted Gamification Tool. Computer Science Education 23(2), 186–206 (2013)
11. Eleftheria, C.A., Charikleia, P., Iason, C.G., Athanasios, T., Dimitrios, T.: An Innovative Augmented Reality Educational Platform using Gamification to Enhance Lifelong Learning and Cultural Education. In: 4th International Conference on Information, Intelligence, Systems and Applications, pp. 1–5 (2013)
12. Gibson, D., Ostashewski, N., Flintoff, K., Grant, S., Knight, E.: Digital Badges in Education. Education and Information Technology. Springer, New York (2013)
13. Goehle, G.: Gamification and Web-based Homework. Problems, Resources, and Issues in Mathematics Undergraduate Studies 23(3), 234–246 (2013)
14. Kapp, K.M.: Games, Gamification, and the Quest for Learner Engagement. Training and Development 66(6), 64–68 (2012)
15. Kumar, B., Khurana, P.: Gamification in Education – Learn Computer Programming with Fun. International Journal of Computers and Distributed Systems 2(1), 46–53 (2012)
16. O'Donovan, S., Gain, J., Marais, P.: A Case Study in the Gamification of a University-level Games Development Course. In: Proceedings of the South African Institute for Computer Scientists and Information Technologists Conference, pp. 242–251 (2013)

17. Raymer, R.: Gamification - Using Game Mechanics to Enhance eLearning. eLearn Magazine (2011), http://elearnmag.acm.org/featured.cfm?aid=2031772
18. Santos, C., Almeida, S., Pedro, L., Aresta, M., Koch-Grunberg, T.: Students' Perspectives on Badges in Educational Social Media Platforms: The Case of SAPO Campus Tutorial Badges. In: IEEE 13th International Conference on Advanced Learning Technologies, pp. 351–353 (2013)
19. Todor, V., Pitică, D.: The Gamification of the Study of Electronics in Dedicated E-learning Platforms. In: 36th International Spring Seminar on Electronics Technology, pp. 428–431 (2013)
20. Villagrasa, S., Duran, J.: Gamification for Learning 3D Computer Graphics Arts. In: First International Conference on Technological Ecosystem for Enhancing Multiculturality, pp. 429–433 (2013)
21. Csikszentmihalyi, M.: Flow - The Psychology of Optimal Experience. Harper & Row, New York (1990)
22. Csikszentmihalyi, M.: Finding Flow - The Psychology of Engagement with Everyday Life. HarperCollins, New York (1997)
23. Takahashi, D.: Website Builder DevHub Gets Users Hooked by 'Gamifying' its Service. VentureBeat (August 25, 2010), http://venturebeat.com/2010/08/25/devhub-scores-engagement-increase-by-gamifying-its-web-site-creation-tools/
24. Armstrong, D.: The New Engagement Game: The Role of Gamification in Scholarly Publishing. Learned Publishing 26(4), 253–256 (2013)
25. Erenli, K.: Gamify Your Teaching - Using Location-Based Games for Educational Purposes. International Journal of Advanced Corporate Learning 6(2), 22–27 (2013)
26. Hevner, A.R., March, S.T., Park, J., Ram, S.: Design Science in Information Systems Research. MIS Quarterly 28(1), 75–105 (2004)

An Investigation of User Interface Features of Crowdsourcing Applications

Robbie Nakatsu[1] and Charalambos Iacovou[2]

[1] Loyola Marymount University, Los Angeles, CA
rnakatsu@lmu.edu
[2] Wake Forest University, Winston-Salem, NC
iacovou@wfu.edu

Abstract. We investigated the user interface features of seven different types of crowdsourcing applications, which were classified along three dimensions of task type: (1) Task Structure: does the task have a well-defined solution? (2) Task Interdependence: can the task be solved by an individual or does it require a community of problem solvers? (3) Task Commitment: what level of resources is required to perform the task? Our initial investigation revealed a number of differences in the seven categories including: site searchability, on-line credentialing, community building features, gamification, mobility, and the use of wiki software.

Keywords: crowdsourcing, user interface, task complexity.

1   Introduction

Howe [1] defines crowdsourcing as, "the act of taking a job traditionally performed by a designated agent (usually an employee) and outsourcing it to an undefined, generally large group of people in the form of an open call." In recent years, this trend has taken several different forms and meanings, including, but not limited to: distributed labor marketplaces, online contests, customer-driven innovation and other forms of open innovation, distributed data collection, crowdfunding, crowdsharing, open-content projects like Wikipeda, among a host of other applications. Due to the breadth and variety of the crowdsourcing approaches, we created a taxonomy that characterizes the crowdsourcing applications by degree of task complexity [2]. Our view is that a primary reason for using crowdsourcing is that a company or individual wants to use the crowd to perform some kind of task on its behalf; hence a taxonomy based on task type is a natural way to classify crowdsourcing approaches.

There has been much confusion and disagreement in the literature as to what crowdsourcing is and what it is not. Some definitions of crowdsourcing have been very inclusive and have included everything from social media sites (Facebook, Twitter, and Vine) to Google flu epidemic prediction using Google search results [3]. Others have been more restrictive in limiting what constitutes crowdsourcing, like Brabham [4] who defines crowdsourced initiatives as those that are "managed from the top-down by a sponsoring organization issuing the task" (p. 121). (This definition

F.F.-H. Nah (Ed.): HCIB/HCII 2014, LNCS 8527, pp. 410–418, 2014.
© Springer International Publishing Switzerland 2014

excludes from consideration requestors who are individuals). We define crowdsourcing, broadly, as a four-step process in which:

1. A requestor (either an individual or organization) identifies a specific task to be performed or problem to be solved.
2. The requestor broadcasts the task or problem online.
3. The crowd performs the task or solves the problem.
4. Depending on the nature of the task, the requestor either
   (4a) sifts through the solutions and selects the best solution (Selective Crowdsourcing), OR
   (4b) aggregates/synthesizes the crowd's submissions in a meaningful way (Integrative Crowdsourcing).

Notably, while our definition of crowdsourcing is broad enough to include a wide range of activities and applications, it does not include all activities involving a crowd. For example, we exclude from consideration problem-solving that is not broadcast online (for example, a contest that is held within an organization). Furthermore, according to Step1, we require that a specific task is requested.   By this restriction we do not include social media sites, or content sharing sites like YouTube.

2   Classifying Crowdsourcing Approaches by Task Complexity

We report in [2] on how we arrived at our taxonomy on crowdsourcing approaches based on task complexity. Review of the prior literature on task types and task complexity suggests highly complex tasks can be classified along a number of dimensions: (1) unknown or uncertain alternatives [5], (2) non-prescribed processes, in which there exist several ways to complete a task [6,7], and (3) multiple performance dimensions [8], among others. Campbell [9] provides a good overview of the literature on task complexity. We created a dimension, task structure, that represents in an aggregated way the degree of structure in terms of alternatives, process, and outcome measures.

To capture the nature of the group dynamics involved in the crowdsourcing approach, we drew from the literature on virtual teams. Bell and Kozlowski [10] distinguish between team processes that are low in complexity versus those that are highly complex. Low complexity team dynamics have weak linkages: "they require minimal collaboration and information sharing among members" (p. 19). Many of these team tasks are structured such that activities are performed separately by individuals and then combined into a finished product. In contrast, high complexity team dynamics are more challenging, involving "greater levels of synchronous collaboration and information sharing among team members" (p. 19). Because of this, such tasks require collaborative and intensive workflow arrangements. Again, to keep our model simple, we created a binary dimension to represent task interdependence: independent tasks vs. interdependent tasks.

	Independent Tasks (Individuals)	**Interdependent Task** (Virtual Communities)
Well-Structured Tasks (The solution to the problem is well-defined.)	**I. Contractual Hiring** *Low Commitment*: Human intelligence tasks Crowdsharing marketplaces *High Commitment*: Online employment platforms	**II. Distributed Problem-Solving (Coordinated Interdependence)** *Low Commitment* Geo-located data collection Distributed knowledge gathering Crowdfunding
Unstructured Tasks (There is no known or well-defined solution to the problem.)	**III. New Idea Generation – Solo** *Low Commitment*: Consumer-driven innovation *High Commitment:* Online problem-solving platforms Contests	**IV. Collaboration (Conflicting Interdependence)** *Low Commitment:* Real-time idea jams *High Commitment:* Open source software development Open source design of hardware Open content projects

Fig. 1. A Task-Fit Model of Crowdsourcing (Source: See [2])

Finally, we added a third dimension, task commitment (or task difficulty) to our final taxonomy. The literature suggests that task difficulty is related to, but not synonymous with task complexity. Some tasks, without necessarily being complex, are difficult because they require a high effort to perform [9]. Other tasks are difficult because they are complex.

In the end, our final taxonomy is based on three dimensions of task complexity (see Fig. 1):

(1) Task Structure: Is the task well-defined or does it require a more open-ended solution? (well-structured vs. unstructured)

(2) Task Interdependence: Can the task be solved by an individual or does it require a group of problem solvers? (independent vs. interdependent)

(3) Task Commitment: What level of effort and resources are required to perform a task? (low vs. high)

Although the three dimensions, taken together would result in eight (2X2X2) categories, we discovered that well-structured and interdependent tasks were, by nature, low commitment. Hence our final taxonomy contains seven categories.

3   User Interface Features of Each Category of Crowdsourcing

In this section, we explore one representative example in each crowdsourcing task type, and investigate user interface features associated with each. Some of the user interface characteristics that we explore in this section include the following: searchability of information, stickiness of website (i.e., the use of gamification and other techniques to create an addictive user experience), online credentialing, community building, features of a mobile phone user interface, the ability to learn from crowd reports, and other features.

3.1   Contractual Hiring, Low Commitment

Tasks that fall in Quadrant I (see Fig. 1) are well-structured and solved independently. For example, Amazon Mechanical Turk is a marketplace in which anyone can post tasks to be completed and specify a price to be paid for the successful completion of them [11, 12]. The motivation behind this system is to allow human users to complete simple tasks (known as human intelligence tasks or HITs) that would be difficult for computers to complete—e.g., tagging video images, judging the relevance of search results, transcribing podcasts.   In general, the type of tasks publicized in Mechanical Turk require little time and effort to perform.

With 265,965 HITs posted (as of 2/5/2014), an important and necessary user interface feature is to have extensive searching capabilities.   Mechanical Turk allows you to search and filter by a number of criteria, including reward amount, date created, expiration date, time allotted,   and title (of task).   An interesting feature is that the user interface allows for online credentialing: some HITs are available only to users with certain qualifications.   You can earn qualifications by taking online tests to demonstrate your ability to give high quality answers.   In terms of site stickiness, a dashboard enables you to display a list of daily activities and earnings, along with the number of HITs that were submitted, approved, rejected, or pending that day.   This ability to monitor and track your progress, can keep some users "hooked" to the site.

3.2   Contractual Hiring, High Commitment

Elance bills itself as the world's leading online employment agency. The Elance website allows businesses to post jobs and search for freelance professionals. Through the web user interface, you can evaluate contractors applying for jobs.   Unlike Mechanical Turk, Elance specializes in tasks requiring more skillsets to complete and more effort to perform—e.g. design a web site, write an article, or write a program.

Because of the large database of online jobs available, Elance allows you to easily search for information.   For instance you can search by job categories (IT, Web, & Mobile, Data Science, Writing, Translation, Design & Multimedia, and so on). The site has several features that promote stickiness and community building. For example, you can track job progress, set milestones, view works-in-progress, and video-conference with other freelancers.   In addition you can rate jobs and post comments about freelancers you have used in the past. Job seekers can post a "portfolio" of work—e.g. if you are a graphic design artist, the user interface enables you to upload samples of your work. Elance skill tests are offered in a variety of areas including IT and Programming, Writing and Translation, Design & Mulitimedia. For example, in Design & Multimedia, you can take tests in 3D Modeling, Adobe Photoshop, Pagemaker, and a host of other topics.

3.3   Distributed Problem-Solving (Coordinated Interdependence)

In this quadrant, crowd individuals perform a well-structured task, and still act independently, but the outputs of the individual's activities are combined and aggregated (i.e., coordinated) in some meaningful way. We have found that tasks that fall in this category tend to be low commitment by nature [2]. We discuss two types of crowdsourcing applications: (1) geo-located data collection and (2) distributed knowledge gathering.

Geo-located Data Collection. Waze is a GPS app that enables a community of drivers to share real-time traffic and road information. Because it involves the reporting of geo-located data, it is most effective on a GPS-enabled mobile device such as a smartphone or tablet computer. In fact, almost all crowdsourcing applications that require geo-located data collection are primarily used on mobile devices (another good example is ATT's Mark the Spot, an app that lets you report wireless coverage problems). All this real-time information is aggregated so that the GPS knows how to re-route you to a different route based on traffic reports and other road alerts reported by the crowd. The ability to learn from crowd reports is a key user interface feature of Waze.

The user interface enables you to very easily report events with one or two mouse-clicks (the driver—in some cases the passenger—of the vehicle must be able to do this very quickly while driving). A Report icon on the main screen quickly takes you to a Report screen, which contains a number of icons, representing the different types events you can report: traffic jam, police, accident, and hazard. An interesting feature is the Map Issue icon, which lets you report maps errors, and other driving errors as a result of receiving wrong driving instructions—hence Waze, unlike a traditional and more static GPS system, is able to correct errors in real time.

In terms of building community, Waze offers a number of features: Because of the immediacy of the app, and its ability to detect real-time events, Wazers feel a part of a community of drivers united by their mutual hatred of traffic. You can also connect to Facebook to arrange meet-ups with your friends. Other features promote stickiness: map chat lets you chat with other Wazers; a gas option shows the prices of gas around your area; and a points system allows you to earn a higher status, the more you use Waze .

Distributed Knowledge Gathering. Like Waze, CureTogether involves distributed data gathering, except that it does not collected geo-located data. CureTogether is a web site where patients around the world can share quantitative information on their medical conditions. By gaining access to millions of ratings reported to the web site, patients can learn from the experiences of other patients suffering from similar medical conditions.

The user interface enables you to browse from over 500 conditions organized topically—e.g., mental health, digestive system, eyes and ears, cardiovascular, and men's health. By clicking on a particular condition, you can get statistics on symptoms, treatments, side effects, and causes. For example, by clicking on treatments you can retrieve statistics on average effectiveness, popularity, and % reporting major improvement (rank-ordered from top to bottom). One information graphic—a 2D plot—helps you visualize the effectiveness versus the popularity of treatments. In terms of building community, members of CureTogether can connect with other members suffering from a similar condition.

3.4   New Idea Generation – Solo, Low Commitment

These crowdsourcing approaches, which fall in Quadrant III, involve unstructured tasks in which individuals in the crowd, working solo, generate new ideas. Low commitment task examples include companies that use the Internet to listen to customer input on new product ideas and offerings, what is often referred to as customer-driven innovation. A good example is Dell's IdeaStorm, which was launched in 2007 to allow Dell to understand and gauge which ideas are most important by their customers.

The user interface allows visitors to easily search for ideas by different categories, for instance: Product Ideas (Accessories, Desktops and Laptops, Mobile Devices, Operating Systems, etc.) as well as Topic Ideas (Education, Enterprise, Gaming, Small Business, and so on). Visitors can comment on other's ideas, as well as vote on them. Gamification techniques are employed so that contributors can earn points for their ideas, with the top recent contributors displayed on the home page.

3.5   New Idea Generation – Solo, High Commitment

High commitment tasks typically follow one of two approaches: (1) direct compensation for online problem-solving or (2) contests.

Direct Compensation. One of the most well-known online problem-solving platforms is Innocentive. InnoCentive is an open innovation and crowdsourcing platform that enables organizations to solve their R&D problems by connecting them to diverse sources of problem-solvers throughout the world. When a company internal R&D department is stumped by a problem, it can post the problem on Innocentive for thousands of professional or amateur scientists around the world to solve it. The company then pays the problem-solver in exchange for the intellectual property. Successful solvers have earned awards of $5,000 to $1 million [13]. (They also allow for simple ideation challenges, so the commitment level can be low or high).

The user interface (i.e., the Challenge Center) is organized around searching for problem-solving challenges. A visitor can search by area of expertise, award amount, company, and submission type (individual solver vs team). The system is gamified in that winning solutions are posted and featured on the site (this enables winning solvers to promote themselves in the community). Community building is promoted in that you can join discussion groups and meet like-minded problem-solvers.

Contests. A well-known example of an online contest is Cisco's quest to find a new billion-dollar business. The business idea had to fit into the company's strategy and take advantage of the company's lead in Internet technology. More than 2,500 innovators from 104 countries submitted 1,200 ideas in pursuit of a prize of $250,000 for the best business idea [14].

A technology platform enabled allowed people to sign up, contribute ideas, and comment and vote on everyone else's submissions. Although this platform assisted Cisco in selecting a winning submission, the winnowing process turned out to be time-consuming and laborious: "The evaluation process was far more labor-intensive than we'd anticipated; significant investments of time, energy, patience, and imagination are required to discern the gems hidden within the rough stones" [14, p. 1]. For many unstructured, high commitment tasks, it is very difficult to automate the process of selecting the best solution with a computer alone; human leadership and intervention is usually necessary.

3.6   Collaboration (Conflicting Interdependence), Low Commitment

While Quadrant III (see Fig. 1) can be solved by individuals working independently, Quadrant IV collaboration problems require crowd members to cooperate at some level and set aside their individual differences and competitive impulses. We refer to these problems as "conflicting" interdependence because diverse individuals working together may sometimes disagree with one another. In crowdsourcing initiatives, mechanisms must be in place—be they technological or otherwise—to resolve these differences.

An example of a low commitment, collaboration task is IBM's Innovation Jam. In 2006, IBM which brought together more than 150,000 participants from 104 countries and 67 companies, to promote innovation at IBM. Over two 72-hour jam sessions, participants posted their ideas on how IBM's research technologies could be used to solve real-world problems, and find new business opportunities [15].

To conduct the jam sessions, IBM used a technology platform that enabled participants to easily post ideas, and see what others were saying in real time. (Interestingly, IBM neglected to include an option that allowed participants to vote on and view what the most popular ideas were; their belief was that there was a danger of good ideas being lost, if participants focused on only the most popular ideas). A few problems about conducting the jam sessions are noted by Bjelland and Wood [15]. One was that it was very difficult to guide conversations—the freedom of the jam made it difficult for a human moderator to exert influence on the online posts. A second problem is that it was rare to find participants who built on, and refined previously posted suggestions—there was a tendency to add a new post without much reflection on what was said previously. Future work might look at how a technology platform can better support a jam session, and facilitate the difficult task of synthesizing and choosing from thousands of separate ideas. (As it turned out, some 50 senior executives spent a week reviewing the output of the brainstorming session, in order to synthesize it into 31 "Big Ideas.")

3.7   Collaboration (Conflicting Interdependence), High Commitment

Open source software development, and open content projects fall in this category of crowdsourcing approaches. Here we focus on the mechanisms that Wikipedia uses to keep its online encyclopedia up-to-date.

Wikipedia, the largest and most popular wiki and encyclopedia in the world, is a good illustration of how a large crowdsourced project can be managed by the crowd. At the top of any Wikipedia page is a tab that says, "Edit this page." Using this tab, any visitor at all can edit any page. How does Wikipedia, then, prevent errors and vandalism from occurring on its thousands of pages if it is possible for anyone at all to edit content? The crowdsourcing effort is largely managed by a team of editors, and administrators who work together to fix errors and resolve any conflicts that might arise [16,17]. When you enter a change, a community of editors monitor and watch out for the change. If they are OK with what you wrote, then the change will remain there unaltered. On the other hand, if what you wrote is vandalistic or incorrect in some way (e.g., full of grammatical errors), it is likely that someone will quickly fix the change. In this way, Wikipedia is a self-monitoring, self-correcting, and self-governing system that requires very little top-down management.

An important point to underscore about a high commitment collaborative project like Wikipedia is that the Wiki software and user interface features allow for easy editing and updating of the content, but the process of managing the potential conflicts must still be performed by human editors and administrators.

4   Discussion and Conclusions

Our initial investigation on the seven types of crowdsourcing revealed several differences and similarities in terms of user interface features. Among the more important findings of our investigation were the following:

Searchability for Information. In all seven types of crowdsourcing, the user interface allowed for easy searching of information. The ability to quickly locate information generated from the crowd is a key feature of all types of user interfaces.

Community-Building Features. We found community building features important in almost all forms of crowdsourcing. One exception was well-structured, low commitment tasks that involved some form of direct compensation. This type of crowdsourcing appears not to require community building features as much as the others.

Site Stickiness and Gamification. Gamification techniques were used extensively throughout the different types of crowdsourcing. One exception was the Quadrant IV (Collaboration) examples.

Online Credentialing. Not surprisingly, the ability to test for skillsets was especially important in the Quadrant I (Contractual Hiring) forms of crowdsourcing in which companies and individuals are hiring individuals online.

Mobility. A mobile user interface was most important for Quadrant II (Distributed Problem-Solving) especially for tasks requiring geo-located data collection.

Wikis and the Ability to Share and Update Information. The Quadrant IV (Collaboration) crowdsourcing examples required a technology platform that supported the use of wikis to update and share information among the crowd.

Future work will involve the collection and analysis on more crowdsourcing examples. We hope to detect trends in the crowdsourcing examples, and report further on the similarities and differences among the seven approaches.

References

1. Howe, J.: Crowdsourcing: Why the power of the crowd is driving the future of business. Three Rivers Press, New York (2009)
2. Nakatsu, R.T., Grossman, E.B., Iacovou, C. L.: A Task-Fit Model of Crowdsourcing: Finding the Right Crowdsourcing Approach to Fit the Task. Under Review in Journal of Information Science
3. Doan, A., Ramakrishnan, R., Halevy, A.Y.: Crowdsourcing systems on the world-wide web. Communications of the ACM 54(4), 86–96 (2011)
4. Brabham, D.C.: A Model for Leveraging Online Communities. In: Delwiche, A., Henderson, J.J. (eds.) The Participatory Cultures Handbook, pp. 120–129. Routledge, New York (2012)
5. March, J.G., Simon, H.A.: Organizations. Wiley, Oxford (1958)
6. Frost, P.J., Mahoney, T.A.: Goal setting and the task process: An interactive influence on individual performance. Organizational Behavior and Human Performance 17(2), 328–350 (1976)
7. Terborg, J.R., Miller, H.E.: Motivation, behavior, and performance: A closer examination of goal setting and monetary incentives. Journal of Applied Psychology 63(1), 29–38 (1978)
8. Latham, G.P., Yukl, G.A.: A review of research on the application of goal setting in organizations. . Academy of Management Journal 18(4), 824–845 (1975)
9. Campbell, D.J.: Task complexity: A review and analysis. . Academy of Management Review 13(1), 40–52 (1988)
10. Bell, B.S., Kozlowski, S.W.: A typology of virtual teams implications for effective leadership. Group & Organization Management 27(1), 14–49 (2002)
11. Kittur, A., Chi, E.H., Suh, B.: Crowdsourcing user studies with Mechanical Turk. In: Proceedings of the SIGCHI Conference on Human Factors in Computing Systems, pp. 453–456. ACM (2008)
12. Kittur, A., Smus, B., Khamkar, S., Kraut, R.E.: Crowdforge: Crowdsourcing complex work. In: Proceedings of the 24th Annual ACM Symposium on User Interface Software and Technology, pp. 43–52. ACM (2011)
13. Spradlin, D.: Are you solving the right problem? Harvard Business Review 90(9), 84–93 (2012)
14. Jouret, G.: Inside cisco's search for the next big idea. . Harvard Business Review 87(9), 43–45 (2009)
15. Bjelland, O.M., Wood, R.C.: An Inside View of IBM's 'Innovation Jam'. MIT Sloan Management Review 50(1), 32–40 (2008)
16. Pink, D.H.: The book stops here. Wired Magazine 13(3) (2005)
17. Forte, A., Larco, V., Bruckman, A.: Decentralization in Wikipedia governance. Journal of Management Information System 26(1), 49–72 (2009)

Co-design of Neighbourhood Services Using Gamification Cards

Manuel Oliveira and Sobah Petersen

Sintef, Technology and Society, S.P. Andersensv. 5, NO-7465 Trondheim, Norway
manuel.oliveira@sintef.no, sobah.petersen@sintef.no

Abstract. Gamification is the design process that applies the principles of digital games along with behavior economics and psychology to enhance existing processes that facilitate user behavior transformation. The application of gamification remains very much a craft, difficult to understand and harder to master without the benefit of experience. Consequently, there is a lack of comprehensible tools that lower the barrier to use and leverage the benefits of gamification by non-experts. This paper presents the gamification cards created within the context of the European MyNeighbourhood project to support co-design activities by the citizens. The paper also shares the lessons learnt from one of the gamification workshops involving stakeholders from neighbourhoods from four European cities (Aalborg, Birmingham, Lisbon and Milan).

Keywords: Co-design, gamification.

1 Introduction

It is undeniable the power of user engagement that digital entertainment games have, which with careful game design manage to place a user in a state of flow, being sufficiently challenging whilst avoiding both boredom (too easy) and frustration (too difficult). It is not unheard of users getting lost in time, as they spend time completing level after level of a game. Consequently, many have tried to harness the power of digital entertainment for other purposes other than enjoyment, thus the emergence of serious games across a wide range of fields including management science, economics, psychology, interpersonal skill development [1]. However, the potential of achieving user engagement by leveraging careful game design was attractive, and the approach was to reduce the scope to focus on a process. As a result the term gamification [2] was coined and its potential success is based on the use of game mechanics such as points, badges and leaderboards, supported by careful game design driven by behavioral economics and psychology. However, this success may not continue as people can get tired of counting their points and following their loyalty programs. Designers are challenged in gamifying processes in creative ways that are also meaningful for people and their work [3] and most of all, engage and keep them engaged. It is not surprising that Gartner group estimated that 70% of the Forbes Global 2000 will be using gamified apps by 2015 [4]. However, the same report also states that 80% of the gamified processes will fail due to bad design. This corroborates that

F.F.-H. Nah (Ed.): HCIB/HCII 2014, LNCS 8527, pp. 419–428, 2014.
© Springer International Publishing Switzerland 2014

gamification, similar to the game design of serious games, remaining a craft that only a few experts are capable of producing results consistently.

2   MyNeighbourhood Project

Our society has evolved over the millennia, with people congregating together in urban cities. However, along the way, the social cohesiveness has been lost and addressing this challenge is the aim of the MyNeighbourhood project. The project aims at using 'smart' ICT services and citizen/neighbourhood generated data to help recreate the social mechanisms which, in the past, ensured that urban neighbourhoods coincided with a social system of connected and trusted communities, where the quality of life was very high and people felt safe and happy with a true sense of belonging.

MyNeighbourhood builds upon three key components: Urban Living Labs (ULL), Neighbourhood and Sustainability. ULL are considered in MyNeighbourhood as creative environments where diverse stakeholders (non-governmental organisations (NGOs), municipalities, business partners, and citizens) collaborate to explore new services for tackling their urban issues. Here, creativity has the opportunity to gain a market perspective: in such environments, in fact, it is possible to start from considering daily life problems and the way they are locally experienced; then, citizens' experiences are transformed into resources for innovation. The neighbourhood is the appropriate urban scale at which creativity for community innovation can be effectively activated and cultivated. This conviction is also driven by a firm belief in the urban studies domain, which locates at this urban scale some of the biggest environmental and economic challenges that cities are currently facing. Moreover, it is at this scale the project believes in "community power", or a sense of community igniting citizens' capacity to become drivers of change. The MyNeighbourhood project does not necessarily look for conventional market solutions, i.e. products and services situated and profiled in the market and having a price determined in coherence with the traditional "cost based, profit oriented" economic model. Instead, the project assumes that an alternative economy is possible, in coherence with the idea that citizens are not only service users, but primarily human beings. Therefore, it considers the opportunity to rely on non-conventional, non-marketable "micro" solutions: small, practical ideas developed ad hoc, to solve problems right where the problems are experienced, at the scale they are experienced; frugal services that can be envisioned in urban co-design environments, while working with and for the citizens; and that are used to push the citizens themselves in the direction towards systemic change.

At the heart of the MyNeighbourhood is the use of an ICT platform that embodies all the concepts in the form of social services. The challenge lies in attracting citizens to start using the platform and to interact with their neighbours through the platform as well as in the real world. Ideas from playful interactions can be used to support this and the gamification process by creating opportunities for people to start interacting either with the platform or with one another.

To evaluate and pilot MyNeighbourhood models, methodologies and tools, the project will be piloted in four neighbourhoods distributed across Europe (Aalborg in Denmark, Birmingham in the United Kingdom, Lisbon in Portugal and Milan in Italy).

3   The MyNeighbourhood Gamification Methodology

The gamification of a process implies a more narrow scope than building a serious game, but the ability of achieving user engagement and behaviour transformation through the artful application of game design remains very much a craft. Although various elements that support gamification are known, such as points, leaderboards, awards, badges, amongst many others, it is not sufficient to combine elements together to achieve an effective gamified solution. In fact, on the contrary, poor designed solutions may achieve the opposite results, disenchanting the audience and causing aversion to desired process. As an example, one can consider the case of leaderboards, which consist of the ranking of users according to some measure, traditionally points attributed or earned by users. In the case of a leaderboard with a large number of users, it may discourage a new user to be confronted with the required threshold to enter the leaderboard. An improved approach is to always place the user in the middle of a leaderboard, indicating two or three other users both above and below the user. This will give the encouragement that the user is already on the leaderboard and is given hints to what they need to do for progressing further in the leaderboard. However, when the user is located in the top of the leaderboard, then the traditional approach to ranking a leaderboard is adopted.

Within the context of MyNeighbourhood, from the onset of the project it was recognized the challenge of applying gamification successfully to either the MyNeighbourhood software platform or its localized services. The abundant tottering of gamification as the silver bullet for improving any solution did little to ameliorate the challenge and consequently, the overselling from the hype did little to improve the limited understanding amongst the MyNeighbourhood consortium. This made it difficult to enhance any of the existing co-design methodologies to incorporate gamification. In addition, emerging approaches for gamification do not provide sufficient support for non-experts to carry out gamification of existing processes, as in the case of Francisco et al.'s method that is based on four steps without much detail beyond the selection of an objective and initial scoping [5]. There exists gamification methodologies based on the use of cards, such as playgen's and SCVNGR's, but these solutions require significant gamification experience from the facilitators, which makes it inappropriate for the use in the MyNeighbourhood pilots where the expertise of gamification is close to non-existent. In addition, the cards of these decks are tailored for more general application domains and do not address the particularities of user engagement of communities. Consequently the MyG(ame) methodology was created, which consists of a workshop that is divided into three main parts:

- **Setting the context.** The MyG methodology makes the assumption that the workshop participants know little or nothing about gamification. Consequently, it is necessary to provide some context with regards to what gamification is along with some examples of gamified solutions. This provides the foundation for describing the MyG process.
- **MyG Process.** The MyG process is an iterative process that supports gamestorming of ideas and concepts towards a gamified solution. Depending on the time constraints of the workshop, the MyG process can be executed one or more times.

When considering groups over 4 participants, it is recommended that these groups are facilitated, preferably by someone with experience in playing games.

- **Crowning of best gamified solution.** The workshop participants are organized into teams of users that compete with each other for the best gamified solution, thus giving them incentive to excel at their gamestorming. The participants themselves vote and rank for the best gamified solution

3.1   MyNeighbourhood Gamification Card Deck

At the heart of the MyG methodology is the MyG process based on the use of a deck with 52 cards. An example of a card is illustrated in Fig. 1.

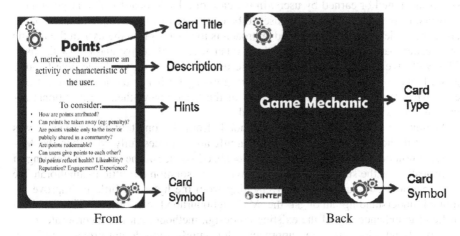

Front   Back

Fig. 1. Sample of gamification card

The deck of cards includes six different types of cards:

- **User Archetype.** These are the yellow cards in the deck and they identify the user archetype based on what their personality and how it affects their behaviour and decision making. These cards are best used to scope the solution space.
- **User Experience.** These are the black cards in the deck and they characterize the level of experience of the user. Similar to the User Archetype, these cards help scope the solution space.
- **Goal.** These are green cards in the deck and they indicate the type of goal(s) to be achieved and that will shape the gamification process.
- **Motivation.** These are the red cards in the deck and they represent the intrinsic motivation of a user that will influence and shape their decisions.
- **Social Mechanic.** These are the orange cards in the deck and they capture the social drivers that influence the behaviour of an individual user.
- **Game Mechanic.** These are the dark blue cards in the deck and they capture a component of gamification.

- **Game Pattern.** These are the light blue cards in the deck and they represent complex game mechanics that may depend on 2 or more game mechanics.

Each of the card types are distinctive from each other based on the colour and symbol used. This makes it easier to identify the cards without the need of visualizing them.

3.2 MyG Process

The MyG process consists of an iterative process that supports gamestorming of ideas and concepts towards a gamified solution as co-designed by the citizens. Depending on any time constraints, the MyG process can be executed one or more times within a workshop setting. Participants work in groups of 4-6, people with one facilitator. The job of the facilitator is to support the group as necessary and to ensure that the group remains focused and keep their task well scoped. The facilitator will also take the responsibility to either document or ensure that the gamified idea is documented by the group.

The first step in the MyG process is to set up the MyG cards. This is done by selecting a card for the goal, the player type and the player experience. The latter two cards are for scoping purposes and should be gradually introduced by the facilitator when deemed appropriate.

Then the cards for the mechanics, the social mechanics, drivers and game patterns are selected: 3 cards for mechanics, 2 cards for the social mechanics, 4 cards for the drivers and 2 cards for the drivers for the game patterns. All the cards may be selected at the same time or the cards for the goal, the player type and the player experience can be selected first and the others later once the goals and the player nature has been determined.

Once the MyG cards have been selected, the context for gamification must be identified. Once a context has been decided and agreed upon by the group, the scope of the gamification should be determined. This involves identifying a specific goal within the context which can be realised through gamification. This step is encouraged to ensure that the group can remain focussed on their context and a specific goal.

4 Gamified Neighbourhood Services

The MyNeighbourhood gamification methodology described above has been tried out in the project by all the pilots. Gamification workshops consisting of group work among the pilots were conducted, where each pilot considered how they could design gamified services. Group work was conducted for the phases in the methodology referred to as scope definition, scope refinement and gamification mechanics and they lasted about one and a half hours, during which time the groups used around 10-15 minutes to prepare the presentation of their gamified ideas to the project participants. Each group was provided a stack of gamification cards, a large sheet of paper and coloured pens. Blackboards were available in the area for the groups to use as they desired.

In the rest of this section we will describe the gamified services that were designed by stakeholders belonging to three of the MyNeighbourhood pilots. The descriptions are based on the input provided by the groups and the presentation material created by them during the group work sessions.

4.1   Engaging Volunteers

One of the pilots is based on supporting services for mentally handicapped citizens by engaging volunteers. The context for this group was to get a volunteer (user type A) to pay a visit to a mentally handicapped person living in a care home (user type B). The specific goal was to "build" relations between user types A and B. The final gamified idea was presented as a poster as shown in Fig. 2, which also included the gamification cards that were used. The gamified process was organising social visits for the handicapped citizen and organising and arranging volunteers to support the services. The organisation of the services was done my mediators; mediators were considered necessary in this context due to the nature of the citizens. The service was focussed on engaging volunteers to arrange outings for the handicapped citizens such as taking them out shopping or to an event in the city. This requires arranging a bus that the volunteers could use when they went on a trip with the handicapped citizens.

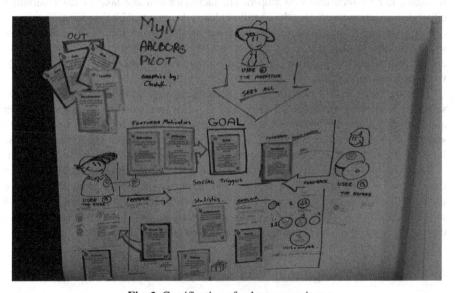

Fig. 2. Gamification of volunteer services

The goal for the service was identified using the card goal or driver "Build". The motivations for the service were identified using the Motivator cards "Affiliation" and "Belonging", recognizing that the handicapped citizens were motivated to establish connections and their need to belong to a community or a place. Considering that the focus was on designing neighbourhood services, the choice of these motivators high-lighted the social context of the service. The game mechanics that were used include "Points", "Awards" and "Power up". The volunteers received badges based on points indicating a tier, e.g. a super care taker. The different types of badges that could be earned were identified, e.g. a wheelchair badge or a bus trip badge, depending on the activity that the volunteer took part in. The recognition through the badges was an indicator to the mediators how well a volunteer was progressing and this influenced the assignments that were given to the volunteers. Social game mechanics were used to encourage and motivate the volunteers to continue contributing to the service. The card "Leaderboards" was used to provide the means for volunteers to compare among themselves and "Gifting" was used to reward volunteers for their activities. The feedback provided by both the volunteers and the handicapped citizens were considered very important.

4.2 Overcoming Digital Divide

Another example of a service that was designed was on the challenge of overcoming the digital divide of elderly people by matching them with young ICT students. The service was aimed at reciprocity between generations through a synergetic approach: some basic needs of the elderly could become opportunities for young people to do work experience; e.g. a young student bringing fresh products from the supermarket or the market to an elderly citizen and in return gaining a small salary or course credits from the educational institution. The actors involved in this service could include elderly people, young ICT students, an educational institution and the local shopping mall.

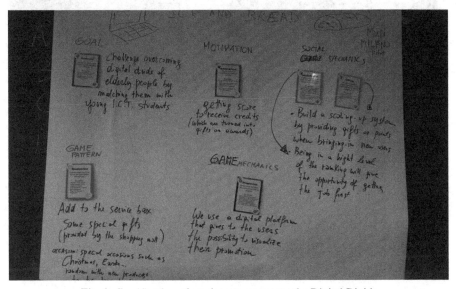

Fig. 3. Gamification of services to overcome the Digital Divide

The goal for the service was identified as overcoming the digital divide for the elderly citizens and the goal card "Overcome" was used. The aim is to engage young ICT students to help elderly people overcome their digital divide by providing the elderly some help with technology. In exchange, the students would receive some credits which can be turned into gifts that are offered from the local shopping mall. The poster that was used to present the gamified idea is shown in Fig. 3. It was assumed that the students will be motivated to achieve credits which can be credits on their course or redeemed for gifts from the shopping mall. Thus, the motivator card "Achievement" was used. The social mechanics cards "Leaderboard" and "Gifting" were used to scale up the service by offering gifts to students who bring new students onboard and the high achievers (from the leaderboards) could have the first choice in selecting jobs. The "Randomness" card was used to give special gifts on special occasions such as Christmas or Easter as an incentive to sustain the engagement of the students. The game mechanic "Progression" card was used to provide the users the possibility to visualize their progress.

4.3   Engaging Women to Cycle

Another pilot is based on a project called Women on Wheels aiming to encourage women to cycle. The specific goal was to build confidence among groups of women and develop a sense of belonging whilst mastering a skill: cycling. The project provides a course which lasts for 6 weeks and they would like to encourage the women to continue cycling after the end of the 6 week course. Thus, ideas of gamification were explored to identify how the women could be encouraged to continue, enroll new women and become active cyclists as well as trainers for new beginners.

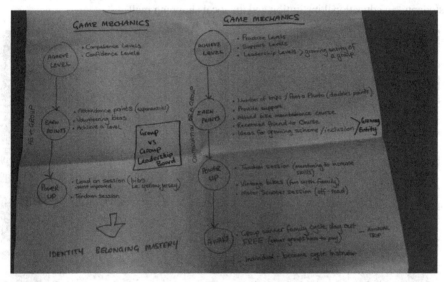

Fig. 4. Gamification of services for social re-engagement and while mastering cycling

Unlike the first two examples, this one focused on describing the type of user or player using cards of the types Player type and Experience. The poster in Figure 4 shows the ideas for the gamification of the services. The cards were not included in the poster. However, the terminology used to describe the gamified service indicates the cards that were used. The card for the goal was "Social Re-engagement". The cards that were used to indicate the player type were "Socializer" and "Explorer" and the user experience was "Novice" as most of the people enrolled in the project were novice cyclists. However, it was clear that achieving the goal of the service would lead to users of the type "Master", who belong to the community and identify them-selves with the community; thus using the –Motivator cards "Belonging" and "Identity". The game mechanic "Power up" was used to recognise cyclists that have achieved a certain level, which may be based on a number of different things such as their attendance, improvements in skills and contribution of ideas.

5   Feedback from Workshop Participants

The MyNeighbourhood gamification workshop had 23 participants in total. Feed-back from the participants was gathered using a questionnaire; 21 of the participants responded. All the participants in the workshop had played games during their lives; 23.81% had played games only recently, 28.57% played games as a child and 47.62 had played games all their lives. The participants play different genres of games; board games and card games were the most popular. The participants were also asked to rate their proficiency as gamers using a likert scale of 1-7, where 1 is "not at all" and 7 is "very much so". There was a big variation in the responses where none responded with the score 7 and the mean value was 2.

While the main aim of the workshops was for the pilots to design their neighbourhood services, some of which are described in the earlier section, the questionnaire aimed to establish the value of the workshop. Thus, one of the interesting feedback is summarized in Figure 5 (vertical scale shows the no. of responses and the horizontal scale shows the likert scale), where the participants reported that their knowledge about Gamification increased as a result of the MyNeighbourhood gamification workshop. Some comments provided by the participants as responses to the open questions about the usefulness of the methodology are: "It is a good tool to promote thinking about the process", "A great way of creating focus on the "motivators" in the system" and "*The workshop is a good way of defining the context conditions for the service. E.g. we got more info on pre- and post conditions for the service and the actors to be involved*"

When asked how useful the participants found the MyNeighbourhood gamification cards, the mean value was 6, with a standard deviation of 0.9. None of the participants responded with a value of 1 or 2 on the likert scale. When asked if the participants would use the cards again, the mean value of the responses was 6 from the likert scale of 1-7.

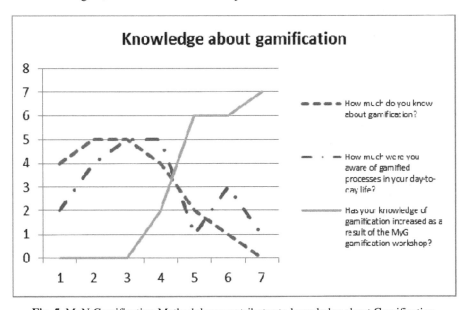

Fig. 5. MyN Gamification Methodology contributes to knowledge about Gamification

Some comments provided by the participants as responses to the open questions in the questionnaire are: "*Very productive! Shaping ... thoughts, common concept and aiding the process overall*", and "*Good way of taking an idea and thinking about how it could work in detail - focus on demand from users*".

Acknowledgements. This work was partially funded by MyNeighbourhood European project (FP7-IST-231717).

References

1. Raybourn, E., Bos, N.: CHI 2005, Extended Abstracts on Human Factors in Computing Systems. Paper presented at the Conference on Human Factors in Computing Systems, Portland, OR, USA (2005)
2. Zichermann, G., Cunningham, C.: Gamification by Design. O'Reilly Media Inc. CA (2011)
3. Gopaladesikan, S.: Following Gamification Through Gartner's Hype Cycle (2012), http://www.gamification.co/2012/12/11/following-gamification-through-gartners-hype-cycle/ (retrieved June 10, 2013)
4. http://www.gartner.com/newsroom/id/1629214
5. Francisco, A., Luis, F., Gonzalez, J., Isla, J.: Analysis and Application of Gamification. Paper presented at the Interaccion 2012, Spain (2012)

Applications of a Roleplaying Game for Qualitative Simulation and Cooperative Situations Related to Supply Chain Management

Thiago Schaedler Uhlmann and André Luiz Battaiola

UFPR – Universidade Federal do Paraná, Curitiba, PR, Brazil
{tsumkt,ufpr.design.profe.albattaiola}@gmail.com

Abstract. This article presents the current stage in the development of a serious game. The main goal of this game is to provide an environment where students and professionals can train Supply Chain Management (SCM) accordingly to a qualitative point-of-view. The Serious Game consists of a Roleplaying Game system for SCM training and simulation, where players simulate, as characters, organizations placed into a Supply Chain with mutual interdependence relationships. During the play session, players respond to situations faced in a simulated organizational setting (a market, a producer or consumer of goods and services) and experience the challenges of an organizational environment. The research method consisted of four consecutive phases: research, development, application and evaluation of this game. The article concludes pointing future possibilities to use the game system in purposes related to SCM area, such as Quality and Environmental Management, Health and Safety, development of new products and services, among other.

Keywords: Gamification in business, Supply chain management, Serious Games.

1   Introduction

One of the possible tools for building knowledge in organizations is the use of games and simulations, particularly the use of Serious Games (games developed for purposes beyond simple entertainment, such as games that simulate behavioral situations, processes, among other themes in the management of organizations).

This paper describes a survey done as part of T. S. Uhlmann Master's thesis at the Post-Graduate Program in Design in UFPR – Universidade Federal do Paraná (Federal University of Paraná), in Brazil. The main objective of this research is to develop and apply a Roleplaying Game that simulates Supply Chain Management (SCM), in order to verify the usefulness of this game system as training and simulation tool. The name of the game is SCMDesign (Supply Chain Management Design). The target public are business courses students and business and management professionals.

During a game session, players respond to possible situations occurring in a simulated organizational setting (a market, a producer or consumer of goods and services) and experience the challenges of an organizational environment, under the mediation

F.F.-H. Nah (Ed.): HCIB/HCII 2014, LNCS 8527, pp. 429–439, 2014.
© Springer International Publishing Switzerland 2014

of another player, called Game Moderator. The Game Moderator presents a narrative that contains situations and proposed challenges to be solved by the players using the resources provided by the game.

The research described in this paper is mainly justified based on three arguments. First, the need for further research on possible applications of Design concepts and tools in areas related to SCM, in particular 3PL activities (Third-Party Logistics Service Providers) [11]. Second, the authors noticed the lack of games, in particular, Roleplaying Games, addressing qualitative issues related to Strategic Management, Quality Management or SCM [10]. The SCMDesign game intends to fill this gap. Finally, the authors detected the existence of board games for entertainment available in the market that discuss various issues related to SCM, as well as academic papers that address the development of games with these themes. But these board games, as well as the games developed in these academic papers, use a quantitative approach in SCM (players essentially manages quantities such as, for example, numeric demands, currency values, among others). SCMDesign, however, simulates behavioral, social and relationship elements between people involved in organizations, which are part of a supply chain structure.

2 Methodology

This research was divided in 4 phases described below.

Phase 1. The first phase was a literature review. At this phase, academic and commercial games related to SCM and Collaboration/Professional Training (especially Management Training) were evaluated. [12]

Phase 2. The second phase was about the development process. Based on the information collected in phase 1, the first prototype of the game was developed. The development process considered three main parts: Roleplaying Game system, game elements and game narratives (stories to be played using the developed game system). The game elements were created considering Järvinen's approach [6] (figure 1). The narratives were developed based on literature evaluated in phase 1, and based on information collected in interviews conducted with two SCM professionals. However, only one of the narratives has been used so far.

Phase 3. The third phase comprehended the tests. Game play sessions were conducted, with several groups of students and professionals whose interests include SCM. In all, five game sessions were conducted, three of them in an academic environment (under-graduate and graduate business courses) and two of them in a business environment (SCM professionals, both in a multinational electrical appliances industry, and in a national logistic provider company). The play sessions were moderated by one of the authors and thoroughly monitored in order to ascertain the effectiveness of the game.

Phase 4. The fourth phase was the evaluation of the results. At the end of each game section, the group was invited to evaluate the game and suggest improvements. After that, both the group's and the authors' findings about the game were reevaluated, and the resulting recommendations were incorporated in the game. Now, after the fifth playtest session, the game is substantially evolved, but it is not finished yet. The authors consider that more tests will be necessary to further improve the game in order to reach a final version.

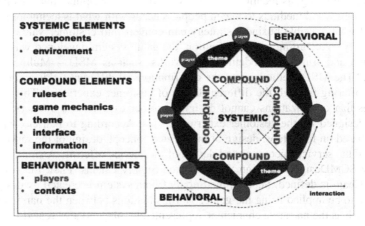

Fig. 1. Game elements overview [6]

3   Theoretical Elements Used in the Game Development

SCM, Design Thinking and Game Design concepts support the SCMDesign development. The main aspects of these concepts are described below.

3.1   Supply Chain Management and Design Thinking

This research considered many definitions of SCM in order to develop the game system, and especially the narrative applied in the game tests [12].

However, the principal definition of SCM used in the game development is a systemic approach. According to Slack and Johnson [9], SCM is the "management of the interconnection of organizations that relate to each other through upstream and downstream linkages between the different processes that produce value in the form of products and services for the end consumer." This definition is important because the game, as a qualitative solution for SCM simulation, emphasizes the relationship between companies and people through collaborative and interconnected actions.

Mehrjerdi [7] defends interconnected and collaborative actions between organizations in a Collaborative Supply Chain due to the fact that "the basic idea behind the collaboration is that it is not possible for a company to compete in this competitive market successfully by itself." So, in a Collaborative Supply Chain, "to ensure optimum performance, companies must work to reduce costs, accelerate operation, and improve quality both in their own processes and in their partner organizations.

By gaining cross-company visibility and control, companies can identify and pursue opportunities for SC improvements. Both buyers and suppliers can benefit by collaborating on critical SC issues." [7]

Collaboration and interconnection are principles used also in Design Thinking processes. Thus the developed game system intends to stimulate, among other factors, creative thinking in solving organizational problems according to the mentioned Design Thinking principles.

Design Thinking, as mentioned by Brown [3], "is a discipline that uses the designer's sensibility and methods to match people's needs with what is technologically feasible and what a viable business strategy can convert into customer value and market opportunity." According to this definition, the game system developed was based also in Design and Business Modeling frameworks, such as MSD – Multilevel Service Design. "The MSD method unites the contributions of different fields and designs the service offering through the different levels of customer experience. This method recognizes that organizations cannot design customer experiences, but service systems can be designed for the customer experience." [8]. According to Patricio [8], this method is based on four steps: design of the service concept, design of the service system, design of the service encounter and design of the service offering. A similar method is used by SCMDesign to design the simulated Supply Chains. First, the concept of a Supply Chain is defined. Second, the Supply Chain system is created by designing the narrative to be applied using the game. Third, situations between the narrative components (such as the narrative characters, represented by players) are created.

3.2   Game Design

Also, this research considered Game Design concepts, such as Roleplaying Games and Serious Games, as described below.

A Roleplaying Game "is one in which the player controls one or more characters, typically designed by the player, and guides them through a series of quests." [1] By completing these quests, players become winners. There is a narrative presented by a Game Moderator, and, according to the situations presented, the players make decisions using their characters, which are present in the applied narrative.

A Serious Game, according to Iuppa and Borst [5], consists of a game that, in addition to providing entertainment to the players, enables learning, persuasion and behavior transformations. The SCMDesign game intends to be a Serious Game because its main goal is to simulate situations in a Supply Chain, emphasizing learning, persuasion, and relationships between the participants, among other elements. In order to achieve this goal, the game development was also based on other educational and commercial board games, as described below.

4   Board Games and Academic Games

The game system development was also based on existing games.

One of the academic games considered is the classical Beer Game, developed in the 1960s by Jay Forrester at MIT - Massachusetts Institute of Technology, and also commercially available in different versions.

The Beer Game "is a replica of a system for producing and distributing a single brand of beer. There are four positions at each game board: Factory, Distributor, Wholesaler and Retailer. Two people are typically assigned to each position, one to actually play the game and another to keep score. The number of participants at each position is flexible and can vary depending on the number of people in the class." [4] Different from SCMDesign, the Beer Game adopts a quantitative view of SCM (players manages time, demand, monetary values, among other quantitative values). SCMDesign adopts a qualitative view, emphasizing behaviors and relationships in the management of the simulated supply chain.

Another game considered was Brass [14]. The game scenario is England in the Industrial Revolution era. The board is composed of places like Liverpool, Ellesmere Port, Southport, among others. Each place has its own vocation (some have ports, other are iron or coal producers, among other characteristics). The objective of the game is to manage a Supply Chain and evolve in terms of score. Figure 2 illustrates this game.

Fig. 2. Brass game (Source: photo taken by the researcher)

5   Game Development (First Version)

The first version of SCMDesign game was developed using the theoretical elements described previously and concepts found in available academic and commercial board games.

The game board, a major component of the game, represents the Supply Chain where organizations, stakeholders and characters controlled by players are role-played. Figure 3 illustrates the first version game board. The square black chips represent units (production, storage or contact) controlled by the players. The colored chips represent the different stakeholders of the organization controlled by players. The characters role-played by the players were described in cards.

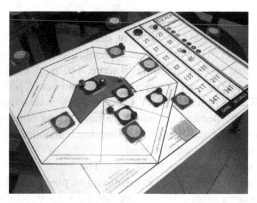

Fig. 3. The first version of SCMDesign game system (Source: [12])

In order to test the game, two narratives were developed. One narrative's theme was activities performed by 3PL Logistics Service Providers [13]. The other narrative was based on the case discussed in Integrated Logistics for DEP/GARD [2].

6   Test Applications of the Game

The following subsections describe the game tests, three in academic environments and two in commercial organizations.

6.1   Tests in Academic Environment

The first, second and third tests of the SCMDesign game system occurred as part of under-graduated classes taught in private colleges located in Curitiba, Parana State, Brazil.

First Test. Local: classroom of a Business Under-Graduate course. Audience: 5 under-graduate students. Period: September 2013. Narrative: Integrated Logistics for DEP/GARD [2]. Game session time: around 1 hour.

An agreement between the game authors and the professor responsible for the discipline established the narrative case. The game session emphasized dialogues between players-to-players and players-to-Game_Moderator. Each player (a student) represents a specific game character. The Game Moderator drives the story actions and represents other auxiliary characters. Players were allocated around a table (figure 4), but they had freedom to move to other places to talk in private with other players.

Fig. 4. Players around a table in the first game test (Source: authors´ video file)

In general, during the debriefing, the participants recommended a better introductory presentation of the game and narrative characteristics. The players' recommendations resulted in several improvements in the game system.

The textual introductory presentation of the narrative was remodeled in a comic story style with the use of photographs, drawings and text. The narrative was also modified, in order to describe, in more detail, each character involved in the narrative. Modifications were also made in Organizational Worksheet; its content and layout were restructured by use of a new spreadsheet format. The game board, which represented a Supply Chain, was also enlarged. The rules of the game were modified to incorporate more dynamism in the game play.

Second Test. Local: classroom of a Business Under-Graduate course. Audience: 6 under-graduate students. Period: November 2013. Narrative: Integrated Logistics for DEP/GARD [2]. Game session time: around 1 hour.

The test began with a slide show, in a comic book style, describing the main research objective, the game system, the narrative, and the characters. After this presentation, the cards of the characters controlled by players were distributed. Also, the researcher presented the representation of the simulated supply chain on the board, involving the transformation of raw materials into finished products, and the distribution of the products to the client organization represented in the narrative.

The narrative was organized in turns, each player representing his character in their respective turn, making individual decisions from the situations presented by the Game Moderator. After each character/player made their decision, the supply chain was simulated: raw material was transformed in products that were distributed to clients of the company represented on the board). The various challenges in the presented narrative (conflicts between sectors, a quality audit, variations in the amount of goods in the warehouses of the organization, conflicts between the organization and its customers, differences of opinion regarding outsourcing processes, among others) were played in this game session. Figure 5 illustrates the second test event.

Fig. 5. Players around a table in the second game test. The man at the extreme left side of this picture is the Game Moderator (Source: authors´ video file).

The players noticed some positive points in the game: its general purpose, the experience provided by the game, allowing for the training of negotiation skills. On the other hand, players related difficulties to understand some elements in the characters' cards. They considered the time of the test (about one hour) insufficient to fully experience the game. More time for the game session, in their opinion, would be more appropriate. Finally, players suggested emphasizing some specific topics in the narrative, especially the topics related to Production and Logistics in a SCM.

The third test was applied just a few days after the second one, and thus the improvements resulting from the second test were made after the third test.

Third Test. Local: classroom of a Business Under-Graduate course. Audience: 7 under-graduate students. Period: November 2013. Narrative: Integrated Logistics for DEP/GARD [2]. Game session time: around 1 hour.

This test was conducted like the previous one. Figure 6 illustrates the third test event. As occurred in the previous test, the players complained about the duration of the game session. They argued that the introductory presentation of the narrative and game system was too complex and would require more time to be fully understood. They also observed that the game board and other game components were little used.

Based on the comments from the players in the second and third tests, the board was simplified. Other game components were also modified.

Fig. 6. Players around a table in the third game test (Source: authors´ video file)

6.2   Tests in a Commercial Environment

The audience of the fourth and fifth game tests included personnel from two private companies located in Curitiba, Parana state, Brazil. The players were planning analysts and team coordinators, among others.

Fourth Test. Local: training room of a Third-Party Logistics service providing company located in São José dos Pinhais, a city of Paraná State. Audience: 7 workers. Period: December 2013. Narrative: Integrated Logistics for DEP/GARD [2]. Game session time: around 1 hour.

The participants of this test were selected by the company among planning analysts, area coordinators, and Personnel Management professionals. The game system presentation process followed the schema of the previous tests. Figure 7 illustrates the fourth test event.

Fig. 7. Players around a table in the fourth game test (Source: authors´ video file)

After an unfinished game session, the players analyzed the game ability to produce immersion (the game allows high involvement of players with the game elements and narrative). Also, this version of the game, according to some players, allowed systemic view regarding aspects of SCM but, again, the time available for the test prejudiced the performance of the players (it is to be noted that office personnel, just like students, do not have much available time). The participants suggested that the game could encourage players to adopt faster responses in a specific pre-defined time.

Regarding the theme, one participant suggested possibilities for practical application of that game, for example, in Personnel Management applications, such as selection processes, coaching and professional development.

After the test, another improvement was made to the game system. To control the time of each participant during the play session, as well as limiting the response time of each character (in order to make the game a more dynamic system in terms of performance), one more component was adopted: an hourglass, which limits the time allowed to each player in each game turn.

Fifth Test. Local: meeting room of a multinational company located in Curitiba, a city of Paraná State. Audience: 6 players. Period: December 2013. Narrative: Integrated Logistics for DEP/GARD [2]. Game session time: around 1 hour.

The audience of the fifth test was composed of SCM analysts, an assistant and a SCM area coordinator. Figure 8 shows the fifth test event.

Fig. 8. Players around a table in the fifth test of the game (Source: authors´ video file)

The game session started as the previous one, with the game system presentation. After the game session, participants recommended a production of an instruction manual to be distributed to the players before the game session. In this case, players could read and understand the game system before they started to play.

Once again, according to one participant, the time available for the game session was insufficient to fully understand the game system and play.

Participants also recommended a more balanced distribution of players around the table; for example, participants that represent characters that will have conflicts could sit in a face to face position.

In addition, there were suggestions regarding the introduction of badges identifying the characters, as well as the department to which they belong in the simulated organization.

Based on this feedback, the authors decided to stimulate the use of the game board. They incorporated to the game ten-sided dice to represent materials and product quantities in the supply chain simulated in the game (quantities of raw material, finished products, and stored products, among others). Also, houses were included in the game board, which are in turn covered by pieces representing the characters; in every house covered, the player must make a decision related to that house. The movement of pieces on the board is the players' responsibility. Besides, nameplates were developed, to be positioned on the table in front of each player. This new component can help the identification and positioning of each character.

The improvements made after these two tests resulted in the current game version, described in Figure 9. Further tests will result in new improvements to the game.

Fig. 9. The final version of SCMDesign game system (Source: author photo)

7   Final Considerations

The game evolved with respect to its board shape (from the format described in Figure 3 to the current hexagonal format presented in Figure 9), to the characters used in the narrative (who acquired personality traits, as suggested by some players), to the counters used (the format of the counters was also modified according to the suggestions collected in the tests), and to the rules (they were more adapted to SCM concepts in accord to each test results).

The research, as described above, faced several limitations, especially in the time available for play sessions in colleges and organizations. However, it was possible to reach the current version, which will be used in a future work – an electronic version of the game.

References

1. Adams, E.: Fundamentals of Game Design, 2nd edn. (2008)
2. Bowersox, D.J., Closs, D.J., Cooper, M.B.: Gestão Logística de Cadeias de Suprimentos. Bookman, Brazil (2007)
3. Brown, T.: Design thinking. Harvard Business Review (June 2008)
4. Goodwin, J.S., Franklin, S.G.: The Beer Distribution Game: Using Simulation to Teach Systems Thinking. Journal of Management Development 13(8), 7–15 (1994)
5. Iuppa, N., Borst, T.: End-to-end game development: creating independent serious games and simulations from start to finish. Kindle Version. Elsevier (2010)
6. Järvinen, A.: Games without Frontiers. Theories and Methods for Game Studies and Design. Doctoral dissertation study for Media Culture. University of Tampere, Finland (2008)
7. Mehjerdi, Y.Z.: The collaborative supply chain. Assembly Automation 29, 127–136 (2009)
8. Patricio, L., Fisk, R.P., Cunha, J.F., Constantine, L.: Multilevel Service Design: From Customer Value Constellation to Service Experience Blueprinting. Journal of Service Research 14, 180 (2011)
9. Slack, N., Chambers, S., Johnston, R.: Administração da produção, Atlas, Brazil (2009)
10. Uhlmann, T., Battaiola, A.L.: Aplicações possíveis dos RPGs na tomada de decisões em Administração Estratégica. In: Anais do 4° Congresso Internacional de Design de Interação. São Paulo - SP, Brazil. Blücher (2012)
11. Uhlmann, T., Heemann, A., Battaiola, A.L.: Serviços logísticos e design de serviços: relações colaborativas. In: II International Conference on Design, Engineering, Management for Innovation (2012)
12. Uhlmann, T., Battaiola, A.L.: Desenvolvimento de um Serious Game para a simulação de atividades de Gestão da Cadeia de Suprimentos. In: Brazilian Symposium on Computer Games and Digital Entertainment, pp. 152–161 (2013)
13. Uhlmann, T., Battaiola, A.L.: Desenvolvimento de Narrativa para Serious Game com o uso da notação BPMN – Business process Model Notation. In: Interaction South America 2013, Recife, Brazil (2013)
14. Wallace, M.: Brass. Board game. Warfrog games (2007)

Gamification Design for Increasing Customer Purchase Intention in a Mobile Marketing Campaign App

Don Ming-Hui Wen[1], Dick Jen-Wei Chang[2,*], Ying-Tzu Lin[3],
Che-Wei Liang[3], and Shin-Yi Yang[4]

[1] Department of Digital Multimedia Design, China University of Technology, Taipei, Taiwan
donwen@cute.edu.tw
[2] Department of Electrical Engineering, National Taiwan University, Taipei, Taiwan
jenweichang@ntu.edu.tw
[3] Service System Technology Center, Industrial Technology Research Institute, Taiwan
{yingtzl,jared}@itri.org.tw
[4] Department of Business Administration, National Central University, Chungli, Taiwan
shiny119@ncu.edu.tw

Abstract. Mobile apps have been developed for marketing purposes and for creating new opportunities for firms to communicate with and satisfy their target audience. However, numerous mobile apps are added daily to the Google Play and Apple App Store. This study developed a mobile application to encourage customers to participate and engage in a marketing campaign in order to increase their potential opportunity for making purchases in an internationally branded apparel store. In this study, we applied a systematic framework of Internet marketing with four strategic stages: attract, engage, retain, and monetize, for guiding and ensuring the success of the marketing campaign. Two human factor researchers were planned, and we administered a focus group interview with six computer game designers for retrieving persuasive game mechanics from existing games. Afterward, we classified the collected gamification mechanics into the four stages, according to their Internet marketing functionality. By referring to the generated gamification mechanics, we then developed a mobile application for supporting a apparel store marketing campaign. Customers' engagement behavior and purchase results were measured. This paper discussed the implications of this study on both research and practice.

Keywords: mobile app, gamification, augmented reality, social network.

1 Introduction

Gamification design is a new HCI approach that involves using the application of computer game design elements to solve nongame problems, which is a new HCI research area involving several real cases, particularly for applications in sales and marketing [1-2], management and administration [3-4], and educating young people [5-7]. Gamification technologies have been proven to be able to manipulate either

F.F.-H. Nah (Ed.): HCIB/HCII 2014, LNCS 8527, pp. 440–448, 2014.
© Springer International Publishing Switzerland 2014

individual or social factors for motivating customers' intentions and changing customers' behavior [8-10]. For example, a Starbucks mobile app, called My Starbucks Rewards, provides customers with an incentive system that promotes repeat visits. The Starbucks app rewards customers with a gold star every time they use it to pay for a transaction. As the customer reaches the first 5-star milestone, that customer is immediately rewarded with a "Green Level" status and is granted free refills of coffee purchased that day.

In this study, we applied gamification technologies to develop a mobile application for encouraging customers to engage in a marketing campaign and increasing the potential opportunity for making purchases in an internationally branded apparel store. Specifically, we first developed a gamification framework with four strategic stages: attract, engage, retain, and monetize, by adopting an online marketing framework [11]. Based on the proposed framework, the related gamification design feature, which we expected to achieve the Internet marketing goal of each stage in general, was generated and introduced in session two. Session three involved identifying the appropriate gamification feature from the results of session two, and we realized those features as a mobile application regarding iOS and an Android version in session four. Finally, we analyzed the campaign marketing results by collecting data from both the mobile application database and the brand's Facebook page insights.

2 The Internet Marketing Framework and Related Gamification Technologies

In this study, we developed a framework with four stages: attract, engage, retain, and monetize, for general online marketing and Internet business operation purposes. Using gamification technologies, the framework was expected to reinforce the participants' motivation to engage in a marketing campaign and to retain the mobile application of the marketing campaign. The ultimate goal of the gamification framework was to increase the purchase intention of the campaign participants and to monetize the apparel store.

Specifically, "attract" refers to enticing customers, so that they become aware of, understand, and ultimately accept and adopt the services or products; for example, free for a limited time gamification mechanics cross-site quests, and dynamic social feeds. "Engage" represents satisfying customers through positive experiences in interacting with the provided services or applications; for example, by using gamification mechanics such as the progress bar, item collection, and leaderboards. "Retain" involves the customers' loyalty to reuse or revisit the services or products, as well as related gamification mechanics such as daily visit rewards, virtual characters, and community systems. "Monetize" means to increase customers' intentions to purchase and, in turn, to create revenue or cash flow for the Internet service; for example, by using gamification mechanics such as sale packages, group buying, and transition feeds.

Based on the proposed framework, the related gamification design feature achieved the goal of each stage of Internet marketing, as expected. Two human factor researchers and six junior multimedia designers were invited to gather, classify, and evaluate each gamification mechanic by reviewing and identifying possible gamification mechanics based on existing online services, including gamification platforms (e.g., Badgeville and Bigdoor), web services, mobile apps, and online game-user experience research [12]. Each of the mechanics are associated with one of the four stages of the proposed framework by using the card sorting technique. The following sections explain the four stages and the 30 gamification mechanics.

2.1 Attract—Make Users Aware of the Available E-marketing Events

The purpose of the *attract* stage is to encourage increasingly greater numbers of Internet users to become aware of, understand and ultimately use the service. There are thirteen gamification mechanics to attract users:

- voting contests: organize public voting contests using a social network plug-in (e.g., Facebook's "Like" feature); each vote will generate viral promotion for the service.
- referral rewards: allow users to share the service with their social networks for a reward (e.g., Dropbox users invite others to earn extra space).
- O2O (online to offline) rewards: cross-promote with physical brands. Users can obtain coupons from inside physical products and use them online.
- high visibility interaction: design mobile online services to include a high visibility gesture (e.g., some puzzle games require a special gesture to play) that will catch other people's attention when someone uses the service in a public space.
- require a team: require users to join or form a team before using the service (e.g., before playing table games or chess games, which require multiple users).

2.2 Engage—Encourage Users to Remain on the Site for Longer

The *engage* stage involves satisfying users and encouraging them to continue using the service. thirteen gamification mechanics to engage users:

- virtual try-on: providing users an on-line in-store changing room – that is, it enables users to try on clothes to check one or more of size, fit or style, but virtually rather than physically. The virtual try -on engage users by providing them more immersive experience.
- progress bars: simplify user tutorials into a few steps that are easy to follow. Additionally, provide rewards (e.g., points or applause) and offer clear hints to encourage users to move to the next step.
- avatar tutorials: help new users to quickly develop an understanding of the service by using a character-based tutorial (e.g., Microsoft Clippy).

- leveling systems: a common way to encourage use by allowing users to master each level at the appropriate speed. Each user's level must be visible to other members so that they can gain recognition from fellow users.
- effort-based rewards: reward users according to their contributions to the service or community; for example, reward them for sharing useful information or inviting friends to sign up for the service.
- item collection: provide item collection systems that encourage users to collect cards, badges or resource collections. Users will make an effort to complete the collections and will be satisfied with their achievement when they do so.
- group quests: create group-level goals. This will encourage the user to exert more effort on the site, not only for himself or herself but also for the team.
- virtual currency: use a virtual currency system (usually with points as the currency) to create an economic system within the service. Users will participate in a system of supply and demand and will make an effort to earn points.
- points for time spent on the site: provide virtual rewards (e.g., Experience point, virtual currency, or gifts) to users based on how long they stay on the site.

2.3   Retain—Make Sure That Users Revisit the Service and Event Frequently

The purpose of the *retain* stage is to ensure that users revisit the site or use the service frequently. To ensure that users will return, one must consider both personal and social user motivations.

- leaderboards: leaderboards are an effective way to motivate people to compete for high rankings.
- daily visit rewards: each user can receive a default or random gift on his or her first site visit per day.
- real world events: give special gifts to celebrate real world holidays and events online.
- continuous login rewards: encourage users by offering daily login rewards: those who use the site on more days will receive higher-value rewards.
- locked stages: motivate user quests using locked stages: users must pass through one stage before they can progress to the next. Offer high-value rewards in high-level stages.
- time-declining items: depreciate the value or function of virtual items over time. Users will return to the service to prevent the depreciation of virtual goods.
- subscription fee: charge users a monthly or annual subscription fee. Users will tend to return to the service frequently once they have pre-paid the fee.
- time-interval rewards: make attractive rewards available within a quest at a certain time of day (e.g., 3:00 pm). Users will tend to revisit the service at that time.
- one-week marathons: use a weekly ranking leaderboard to encourage high-ranked users to return for daily competitions and to encourage laggards to return the next week.

2.4   Monetize—Motivate the User to Pay for the Service

The purpose of the *monetize* stage is to create business revenue. This study has identified gamification mechanics that support two consumption methods—top-up and direct payment.

- sales package: sell points in packages. Users can obtain more points (or other rewards) when they purchase a large number of points at one time.
- accumulate rewards: provide rewards to users when their top-up quotas reach a certain level.
- highlight VIP users: make user levels visible on their profiles. This can help encourage users to top-up to gain recognition and benefits (ex: sales promotion code or prize) from others.
- group buying: allow users to top-up their accounts together with a certain number of friends to obtain special discounts or extra rewards.
- special talents: sell items that allow users obtain superpowers that they can use in the online service. The superiority of an item can encourage users to purchase their first top-up points.
- earned coupons: Provide coupons after user purchases that may help them to secure a win. The coupon should be able to stimulate consumption, but issuing the coupon should not cost the service anything.
- crowdfunding: Make collective action possible for users, allowing them to pool their money to do good things such as disaster relief or scientific research.

3   Applying Gamification Mechanics to Design the Mobile App for the Marketing Campaign

The mobile marketing campaign application was designed by following the proposed four Internet marketing stages, and was realized by applying both gamification mechanisms and informative technologies for achieving customer satisfaction. The mobile application was developed by the Service Systems Technology Center of the Industrial Technology Research Institute (ITRI) in Taiwan, and the application was uploaded to both Google Play and Apple's App Store by December 1, 2013.

3.1   Attract

As illustrated in Figure 1, we used O2O (online to offline) rewards as the gamification mechanism to appear in in-store posters, street flyers, and staff t-shirts for improving the marketing campaign's visibility. Users were motivated to participate in the campaign because of the appealing rewards that appeared on the posters and flyers. Based on the results of this study, we can ensure that customers will be willing to download and access the marketing campaign's mobile application.

3.2 Engage

At the engage stage, we converted the seasonal clothing and accessories of the branded apparel store from physical objects to 3D virtual objects. We used the character customization system as a gamification metaphor in the study and imported the generated objects into the system to allow users to conduct a virtual appraisal (see Figure 2). Thus, the customers can collect the 3D seasonal products by obtaining pictures from the photographs on the brochure or from the tags on the in-store goods. The app system also provided a feature allowing customers to appraise seasonal products with the augmented reality (AR) feature in the app. The customers can therefore generate photomontages by combining their own photo and the 3D objects. This feature was expected to bring a fantastic interactive experience to the customers and, in turn, encourage them to spend time in either the physical store collecting 3D objects or using the app for appraising seasonal products.

3.3 Retain

At the retain stage of the study, we applied redeemable points to reward the customers for their personal achievements and a leaderboard to encourage interpersonal competition among the customers. The two gamification features were designed by referring to the customer interface style of popular SNS games (e.g., Candy Crush Saga, and Farmville). These two features provided a reinforcing loop to satisfy the personal and social motivation of the customers. The two types of motivation were expected to encourage customers to revisit the app frequently. As shown in Figure 3, the marketing campaign leaderboard can be used to enhance and retain the user's interpersonal competition.

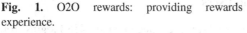

Fig. 1. O2O rewards: providing rewards experience.

Fig. 2. Virtual try-on: engage users through providing O2O rewards a highly immersive and interactive to attract users.

Fig. 3. Leaderboard: enhance campaign

Fig. 4. Highlight VIP users: encourage users to participant's interpersonal competition top-up to gain recognition and benefits from others.motivation to retain them

3.4   Monetize

Finally, the mobile app allows customers to display their user levels on their profiles, thereby highlighting VIP users, as illustrated in Figure 4. This can motivate users to accumulate points to gain recognition and benefits from others. The social influence from the customers' social network is the gamification feature allowing customers to receive praise and recognition from their online families and friends. This feature was expected to increase customers' intentions to purchase and to lead customers' impulsive buying.

3.5   The Evaluation of the Promotion Effect of a Gamification App on a Marketing Campaign

We evaluated the promotion effect of the proposed app after developing the four-step function in this study. We collected users' engaging and purchasing behavior data from December 25, 2013 to January 29, 2014. The engaging behavior data were collected from the app background system and the Facebook fan page. The purchasing behavior data were collected from users' in-store purchasing data and feedback.

4   Result

4.1   The Engaging Behavior of App Users

The marketing campaign attracted a total of 1456 users and created 14188 logins from December 25, 2013 to January 29, 2014. The app maintained 200 to 400 users/hour online in session. As shown in Figure 5, all app users created 13205 "likes" for the Facebook fan page, and the gender distribution was predominantly female (92% vs. 8%), which is consistent with the general gender distribution of the branded apparel store. Regarding age distribution, 37% of the users were 25–34 years old, 29% were 18–24 years old, and 21% were 35–44 years old.

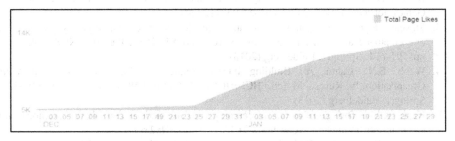

Fig. 5. The engaging behavior of marketing campaign participant on Facebook Fan Page

4.2   The Purchasing Behavior of App Users

An additional 637 purchasing behaviors were created in the app campaign. All app users uploaded 458 pictures, and 42% of the users revisited the store to purchase in session. Therefore, the users' purchasing behaviors were substantially influenced by using the proposed app.

5   Conclusion

The main goal of this study was to develop a mobile application to encourage customers to engage in a marketing campaign and increase the potential opportunity for affecting purchases in an internationally branded apparel store. Specifically, we deconstructed the processes involved in online service operations by using a model involving four stages: attract, engage, retain, and monetize. Moreover, we identified 52 gamification mechanics to determine the design implications of the mobile app. The promotion effect of the proposed app was also evaluated in this study. The limitations of this study will be addressed in our future research. The proposed gamification mechanics were not explained in detail in this study; more examples or cases of each identified mechanic will be provided in the future. Future studies will focus on explaining how these mechanics motivate people and, in turn, trigger their online shopping behavior.

Acknowledgments. We thank all the volunteers and students who helped with this study. We also thank the National Science Council (NSC) in Taiwan for providing financial support under grant NSC 102-2218-E-163 -002.

References

1. Huotari, K., Hamari, J.: "Gamification" from the perspective of service marketing. In: Proc. CHI 2011 Workshop Gamification (May 2011)
2. Terlutter, R., Capella, M.L.: The Gamification of Advertising: Analysis and Research Directions of In-Game Advertising, Advergames, and Advertising in Social Network Games. Journal of Advertising 42(2-3), 95–112 (2013)
3. Stevens, S.H.: How gamification and behavior science can drive social change one employee at a time. In: Marcus, A. (ed.) DUXU 2013, Part II. LNCS, vol. 8013, pp. 597–601. Springer, Heidelberg (2013)
4. Webb, E.N., Cantú, A.: Building Internal Enthusiasm for Gamification in Your Organization. In: Kurosu, M. (ed.) HCII/HCI 2013, Part II. LNCS, vol. 8005, pp. 316–322. Springer, Heidelberg (2013)
5. Kapp, K.M.: The gamification of learning and instruction: game-based methods and strategies for training and education (2012), http://Wiley.com
6. Landers, R.N., Callan, R.C.: Casual social games as serious games: The psychology of gamification in undergraduate education and employee training. In: Serious Games and Edutainment Applications, pp. 399–423. Springer, London (2011)
7. Raymer, R., Design, E.L.: Gamification: Using Game Mechanics to Enhance eLearning. Elearn Magazine 2011(9), 3 (2011)
8. Shang, S.S., Lin, K.Y.: An Understanding of the Impact of Gamification on Purchase Intentions (2013)
9. Deterding, S.: Gamification: designing for motivation. Interactions 19(4), 14–17 (2012)
10. Jackson, S.: Cult of Analytics: Driving Online Marketing Strategies Using. Routledge (2009)
11. Hsu, S.H., Chang, J.W., Lee, C.C.: Designing Attractive Gamification Features for Collaborative Storytelling Websites. Cyberpsychology, Behavior, and Social Networking 16(6), 428–435 (2013)
12. Hsu, S.H., Wen, M.H., Wu, M.C.: Exploring user experiences as predictors of MMORPG addiction. Computers & Education 53(3), 990–999 (2009)

B2B, B2C, C2C e-commerce

An Individual Differences Approach in Adaptive Waving of User Checkout Process in Retail eCommerce

Marios Belk[1], Panagiotis Germanakos[1,4], Stavros Asimakopoulos[3],
Panayiotis Andreou[1], Constantinos Mourlas[3], George Spanoudis[2],
and George Samaras[1]

[1] Department of Computer Science, University of Cyprus, CY-1678 Nicosia, Cyprus
{belk,pgerman,panic,cssamara}@cs.ucy.ac.cy
[2] Department of Psychology, University of Cyprus, CY-1678 Nicosia, Cyprus
spanoud@ucy.ac.cy
[3] Faculty of Communication and Media Studies, National & Kapodistrian University of Athens,
5 Stadiou Str, GR 105-62, Athens, Hellas
{sasimako,mourlas}@media.uoa.gr
[4] SAP AG, Dietmar-Hopp-Allee 16, 69190 Walldorf, Germany

Abstract. Developing a usable checkout process is pivotal for e-business success. However, recent research has shown that users frequently abandon their shopping carts and lacking a clear direction through the process. In this context, aiming to improve the usability and overall user experience of checkout processes in ecommerce Web-sites, this paper reports on a study, primarily inspired by concepts driven from theories of individual differences in cognitive processing, and considers content presentation and navigability as a measure of checkout usability and task quality. Concurrent think-aloud, short interviews and questionnaires were conducted with a convenient sample of 15 users to understand the preference of a particular type of checkout process, and users' task completion time while interacting with ecommerce Web-sites for a set of different checkout scenarios. Preliminary results revealed that cognitive styles have an effect on users' task completion and checkout process preference.

Keywords: Ecommerce, Checkout Process, Individual Differences, Cognitive Styles, User Study.

1   Introduction

Ensuring that *checkout process* design in an ecommerce retail environment is in alignment with the task at hand and providing satisfactory user experience (UX) is critical to business success. Meanwhile, user behaviours are changing profoundly; particularly due to the ways that technology is now being used as part of the shopping process. Researchers have devoted effort to develop metrics, guidelines and theories of Web-site and ecommerce usability, yet there still is a lack of consensus on the multi-faceted dimensions of checkout process as well as the relationships among user cognitive styles and their influence on checkout designs. The checkout process has

F.F.-H. Nah (Ed.): HCIB/HCII 2014, LNCS 8527, pp. 451–460, 2014.
© Springer International Publishing Switzerland 2014

become widely known over the years on the World Wide Web and making purchases online is a fairly standard process, with clear steps and expected outcomes [1]. Despite its popularity, research reveals that astonishingly between 60-70% of online users abandon shopping carts [2, 3], while a recent study by [4], investigating the top 100 ecommerce checkout processes showed that 82% have usability issues. The authors in [2] argue that despite placing items in virtual shopping carts, online shoppers frequently abandon them; an issue that perplexes online retailers and has yet to be explained by scholars. Shopping cart abandonment occurs when a potential customer initiates an order by starting the checkout process, but exits the Web-site before the purchase is made. The most important reason for shopping cart abandonment appears to be that users are not given a clear direction through the process [4].

Studies on shopping cart abandonment mainly focused on the influence of psychological factors on this phenomenon [2, 5, 6, 7]. Moreover, several studies examined the relationship between navigational decisions and online purchase behavior [8, 9, 10]. In this realm, taking into consideration that human-computer interactions during a checkout process are in principal cognitive tasks, we suggest that these interactions should be examined in more detail based on cognitive styles. Among numerous dimensions of individual differences in cognitive processing proposed in the literature [11], the work presented in this paper focuses on cognitive styles of the human mind as prior research has shown that cognitive styles of individuals affect user preference and performance in hypermedia systems [12]. Accordingly, the main research question is as follows: *Do cognitive styles affect user preference and performance in different checkout process designs?*

The remainder of the paper proceeds as follows: Section 2 briefly describes the relevant work on checkout process and theories of individual differences in cognitive styles. Section 3 describes the study methodology and results. Finally Section 4 concludes the paper.

2   Related Work

The World Wide Web has dramatically changed the way consumers purchase goods and services, collect information to compare products, and companies conduct their business. Recent statistics indicate that although there is a growing number of people that use the World Wide Web to search for product information, to do price comparisons, and to collect useful information in order to make their purchasing decision, the number of actual online purchases remains still relatively small [8, 13]. Although in the last years many scholars have provided frameworks and a number of methods to evaluate ecommerce Web-sites [14, 15], there is generally a lack of theoretical justifications of the frameworks and evaluation criteria they adopt. Moreover, these approaches do not effectively model the cognitive process of online users that determines how they perceive the quality of the Web-sites that are experiencing. Indeed, information processing and cognition are central activities when consumers interact with Web-sites [16].

2.1   Checkout Processes

Recent findings by industry analysts revealed that online consumers are impatient, easily dissatisfied and are likely to abandon their shopping carts and move to a different retailer if a Web-site's features fail to meet their expectations [17]. The work in [17] reports that attributes such as fast loading of pages, ease of navigation, efficient search and detailed product content are some of the features that online consumers expect from retail Web-sites and decrease the likelihood that consumers will leave sites without making purchases. The study in [6] found that besides immediate purchase intention, online shopping carts are also used for hedonic purposes such as securing price promotions, organizing items and as a 'wish list' for future purchases. This can be explained by the fact that, similarly to traditional retail shoppers, consumers shop online with utilitarian (e.g., goal-directed, task based) and/or hedonic (e.g., enjoyment gained by the shopping experience) motivations [18, 19]. Perceived risk related to privacy issues (e.g., sharing personal information with third parties), security aspects (e.g., non-delivery of products, transaction), and perceived waiting time (loading time), were found to influence shopping cart abandonment [2, 7]. The study in [5] also found contextual factors (e.g., time pressure, uncertain need) and consumer characteristics (e.g., attitude toward online shopping) as factors influencing this phenomenon. The authors in [20] investigated the customization of the online purchase process of 422 electronic retailers relevant to the two constituent sub-processes in the online purchase process: i) decision customization; the customization of the information content delivered to users to help them in the decision-making sub-process; and ii) transaction customization; the customization of the purchase transaction sub-process for each user. The results indicated that decision customization that provides choice assistance by way of personalized product recommendations is positively associated with user satisfaction; and transaction customization, oriented towards making the transaction sub-process personal, convenient, and interactive is positively associated with user satisfaction with the purchase transaction sub-process. Additionally, the results indicate that both decision customization and transaction customization are associated with overall customer satisfaction with the online purchase process of electronic retailers. Recent research by [21] compared static displays with two rich media presentation formats (product videos and virtual product experience) and their impact on purchase intentions and willingness to pay in online stores. The results confirmed that the rich media displays enhanced the feeling of informedness about the examined products and increased excitement regarding the shopping experience. Virtual product experience had a direct positive effect on consumer purchase intentions, suggesting that virtual product experience-focused tools have the potential to outperform passive videos. Moreover, consumers showed higher willingness to pay values for experience products than for search products when interaction was possible.

2.2   Individual Differences in Cognitive Styles

Among numerous dimensions of individual differences proposed in the literature [22, 23, 24], the work presented in this paper focuses on cognitive styles. Research on cognitive styles is an area of human sciences that explains empirically observed differences in information mental representation and processing. Different theories have been proposed over time suggesting that individuals have differences in the way they process, remember, and recall information.

A widely accepted and accredited cognitive style dimension is considered the Wholist/Analyst cognitive style [11, 24] that refers to how individuals organize information and indicates a preference of structuring information as a whole to get the big picture (Wholists) or structuring the information in detail (Analysts). The main characteristics of each cognitive style are as follows:

Wholists: Users that belong to the Wholist type view a situation and organize information as a whole, proceed from analyzing the whole to its parts and organize information in loosely clustered wholes. Wholists have higher levels of assertiveness, and especially in extreme types, they are decisive in different situations.

Analysts: Users that belong to the Analyst type view a situation as a collection of parts, stress one or two aspects at a time, proceed form the parts to the whole and organize information in clear-cut groupings (chunking down). Analysts have low assertiveness and especially in extreme types, they are indecisive.

Several studies revealed that the Wholist/Analyst dimension has an effect on users' learning patterns and navigation behaviour within hypermedia systems [12, 26, 27]. A recent work in [12], which investigated the effect of cognitive styles on users' learning patterns within Web-instruction programs, revealed implications of cognitive style on users' preferred ways of using different navigation tools and display options. In particular, analyst users tended to actively group relevant concepts utilizing an alphabetical index tool of the hypermedia system, while Wholist users tended to be passive and relied on hierarchical maps to build relationships among different concepts [12]. A more recent study in [26] revealed a relationship between the Wholist/Analyst dimension and the users' navigation behaviour in terms of linearity/non-linearity. In particular, results revealed that Wholists tended to follow linear hyperlink sequences within online encyclopaedia articles, in contrast to Analysts who did not reveal any significant differences in navigation behaviour.

3   Checkout Designs

Based on the theoretical analysis, given that the Wholist/Analyst dimension is particularly related to the way hypermedia content is structured [12, 26], this paper aims to investigate the effect of the Wholist/Analyst dimension on user performance and preference of different content representation and navigation designs of checkout processes. We utilized different checkout designs of three existing ecommerce Web-sites: nordstrom.com (Nordstrom), discovery.com (Discovery), amazon.com (Amazon). The selection of the Web-sites was based on their different content presentation designs (i.e., textual or diagrammatical representation of content), and different navigation techniques (i.e., top-down checkout process or horizontal step-by-step checkout process). Figure 1 illustrates screenshots of each of the Web-sites. Table 1 presents the features of each Web-site based on the content presentation and navigation techniques used in the checkout process.

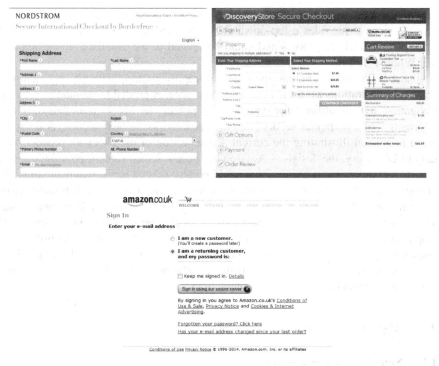

Fig. 1. Checkout process designs

Nordstrom illustrates content in a diagrammatical representation and follows a simple top-down navigation style in which users can freely enter the required information for performing the checkout process. All required information (shipping information, payment information, etc.) is visible in one single Web-page. This design has been selected since it freely enables users to access all steps of the checkout process in a single Web-page and could be related to the analytical approach that Analysts follow.

Table 1. Content presentation and navigation styles of each Web-site used in the study

	Content Presentation	**Navigation Technique**
Nordstrom	Graphical	Top-down with all steps visible
Discovery	Graphical	Top-down step-by-step with only one step active a time
Amazon	Textual	Horizontal step-by-step with only one step active at a time

Discovery similarly illustrates content in a diagrammatical representation and follows a guided top-down navigation style, with a single section being only active for entering the required information. In particular, users can only view and enter the required information for a single section (e.g., shipping information), and then need to submit the entered data in order to proceed to the next section. This design has been selected since it provides a top-down approach, guiding the user throughout all the steps of the checkout process and could be related to the wholistic, linear approach that Wholists follow.

Amazon illustrates content in a textual representation, without any additional graphical illustrations as in the other two Web-sites. A guided horizontal step-by-step navigation style is utilized for the checkout process in which users can only enter information of a particular section, and then proceed to the next section. A horizontal menu is utilized illustrating the current active section of the checkout process. Similarly to Discovery, the design of Amazon has been selected since it provides guidance throughout the checkout process that could be also related to the wholistic dimension of cognitive styles since it once more presents content through a constrained, guided environment. The main difference is that Amazon provides a horizontal guided approach and illustrates content in a clear textual representation, in contrast to the graphical representation of content in Discovery. It is important to mention that we intentionally selected two different content representations (textual vs. graphical) since we subsequently aimed to investigate whether the different type of content representation would affect the user interactions.

4   Method of Study

4.1   Sampling and Procedure

A total of 15 individuals (10 female and 5 male) participated voluntarily in a user study carried out during the first week of December 2013. All participants were undergraduate students and their age varied from 20 to 25. The participants first completed a series of questions using a Web-based psychometric test based on Riding's CSA [25] that measured the response time on two types of cognitive tasks and computed the ratio between the response times for each task type in order to highlight differences in cognitive styles. Participants were required to compare whether two figures are identical, and whether one simple figure is part of another complex figure.

A within-subjects design was followed in which all participants navigated in three different ecommerce Web-sites; Nordstrom, Discovery and Amazon, for a set of different checkout scenarios. In each scenario, users were provided with a virtual credit card and assigned to select a product of their choice by adding it in their shopping basket and then execute the checkout process until buying the product. Given that users were interacting in a hypothetical, and not a real scenario of purchasing products, the think aloud protocol was conducted to investigate whether participants would complete or abandon the checkout process. In order to elicit users' subjective preference and perception of each Web-site checkout process, short interviews were conducted and questionnaires were provided at the end of each navigation scenario. Finally, the total time to complete the checkout process was measured to compare the usability of each checkout process in terms of efficiency.

4.2   Hypotheses

The main hypothesis of this research is that cognitive styles affect task efficiency and user preference of checkout processes with different navigation styles. In particular, the following hypotheses were formulated for the purpose of our research.

H_1. Wholists are more efficient when interacting with designs that provide a step by step guided approach throughout the checkout process.

H_2. Analysts are more efficient when interacting with non-constrained designs that enable full controllability of users during the checkout process.

H_3. Cognitive styles affect user preference towards different design types of checkout process.

4.3   Analysis and Results

Results of the psychometric tests classified users as follows regarding their cognitive styles: 7 Wholists and 8 Analysts. The analysis investigates whether differences exist in task completion time and user preference toward a particular checkout design among users having different cognitive styles.

Task Efficiency. The total time to complete the checkout process for each design was recorded with the aim to investigate effects of cognitive styles on task efficiency of the different checkout designs. Table 2 illustrates the mean of time to complete the checkout process in each Web-site per cognitive style group. Results indicate that on average, Nordstrom had the most efficient checkout process. Based on the cognitive style groups, Analysts were more efficient in Nordstrom, whereas Wholists were more efficient in Amazon. Also, a comparison between the two cognitive style groups revealed that Analysts were more efficient in Nordstrom than Wholists, and Wholists were more efficient than Analysts in Amazon. Given that Wholists need more guidance in a hypermedia environment, the guided navigation style provided in Amazon has improved task efficiency of the checkout process. On the other hand, given that Analysts follow a more analytical approach during navigation and proceed from the parts to the whole, the fully-controllable and non-constrained checkout process of Nordstrom has positively affected task efficiency of that particular user group.

Table 2. Means of performances (in sec) for each checkout process and cognitive style group

	Wholists	Analysts	Overall
Nordstrom	117.07	99.88	107.9
Discovery	134.71	170.38	153.73
Amazon	116	130.88	123.93

The results are very promising and indicate a tendency of verifying Hypothesis 1 and Hypothesis 2, however further studies need to be conducted with a larger sample to investigate main effects of cognitive styles on task efficiency in different designs of checkout processes.

User Preference. In order to assess users' perceived preference and perception toward the different checkout processes, a five-item Likert-scale (1 Strongly Disagree - 5 Strongly Agree) was designed that focused around perceived checkout preference, efficiency and effectiveness. Example questions were: *"I completed the checkout process quickly"*, *"I liked the design of the checkout process"*.

A tendency of Analysts preferring Nordstrom and Wholists preferring Amazon has been revealed (Figure 2). Based on the comments provided by the participants, the main reason of their preference was based on the particular navigation style followed in each checkout process. In particular, some Analysts that preferred Nordstrom reported that *"I could access all information at once, without requiring navigating back and forth"*. On the other hand, Wholists that preferred Amazon reported that *"I felt safe navigating through the steps with all the necessary information at hand"*. Another reason for the users' preference was based on the fact that users were already familiar and experienced using Amazon. Given that Analysts follow a scattered approach during navigation and need freedom of operation, the design of Nordstrom has positively affected their preference, compared to Wholists who preferred Amazon since this user group needs more guidance during navigation.

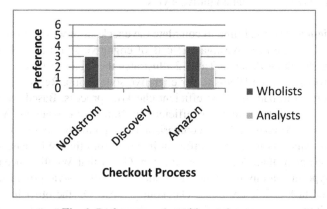

Fig. 2. Preference per cognitive style group

Finally, when asked with which checkout process they felt more secure, and whether users would abandon the checkout process in a real-life scenario, the majority of Wholist users reported that they would most probably abandon the Nordstrom checkout process compared to the other Web-sites. The main reason was that they didn't like the overall "look-and-feel" of the checkout process, and mainly because no guidance or any status about the process was provided by the Web-site during interaction. Regarding the Discovery checkout process, the majority of users across all user groups would abandon the checkout process. As participants responded, the main reason is that *"I didn't like the design"* (Analyst), *"I didn't know what the next step was"* (Wholist), *"There was too much content illustrated"* (Wholist). In contrast, in the case of Amazon, the majority felt secure during interaction and would not abandon the checkout process. Based on responses, this might be based on the familiarity factor of Amazon being a popular and accredited ecommerce Web-site.

5   Conclusions

Checkout is an important stage of online purchasing; thus allowing users more efficient decision-making and supporting their information processing and cognitive ability is of critical importance. In this realm, aiming to understand users during inter-actions within checkout processes, a user study was conducted that explored the im-pact of the Wholist-Analyst cognitive style to evaluate checkout process from the user viewpoint in a retail ecommerce setting. Preliminary results based on quantitative and qualitative measures revealed that cognitive styles affect users' task completion and checkout process preference. In particular, Wholist users have shown a preference toward checkout processes following a more guided approach, as in the case of Ama-zon. Quantitative measures obtained have shown that Wholist users were also more efficient during interaction in Amazon. Similarly, Analyst users were more efficient and preferred Nordstrom which did not follow a guided approach and provided more freedom to users for entering their information. Such a result suggests that designers and developers should bear in mind individual differences in cognitive styles when designing checkout processes. A practical implication of this result would be based on a personalization engine for providing the "best-fit" navigation style (non-constrained or guided) in a checkout process, considering the users' cognitive styles.

Findings of this study are expected to provide useful insights for practitioners to develop more usable checkout processes and for researchers to better assess the effect of user cognitive styles on online checkout process behavior. In future work we plan to further extend our study with a larger sample and different checkout process de-signs as well as utilize different cognitive styles such as the Verbal/Imager dimension [11], and more basic cognitive processes such as Working Memory.

Acknowledgements. The work is co-funded by the PersonaWeb project under the Cyprus Research Promotion Foundation (ΤΠΕ/ΠΛΗΡΟ/0311(BIE)/10), and the EU project SocialRobot (285870).

References

1. Nielsen, J.: Ecommerce Usability, http://www.nngroup.com/articles/e-commerce-usability (retrieved October 12, 2013)
2. Kukar-Kinney, M., Close, A.G.: The Determinants of Consumers' Online Shopping Cart Abandonment. Journal of the Academy of Marketing Science 38(2), 240–250 (2010)
3. Close, G.A., Kukar-Kinney, M.: Beyond Buying: Motivations Behind Consumers' Online Shopping Cart Use. Journal of Business Research 63, 986–992 (2010)
4. Appleseed, J., Holst, C.: E-Commerce Checkout Usability: Exploring the Customer's Checkout Experience. Baymard Institute, Copenhagen (2013)
5. Cho, C.H., Kang, J., Cheon, H.J.: Online shopping hesitation. Cyber Psychology and Behavior 9(3), 261–274 (2006)
6. Moore, S., Matthews, S.: An exploration of the online shopping cart abandonment syndrome: A matter of risk and reputation. Journal of Website Promotion 2, 71–88 (2006)

7. Rajamma, R.K., Paswan, A.K., Hossain, M.M.: Why do shoppers abandon shopping cart? Perceived waiting time, risk, and transaction inconvenience. Journal of Product and Brand Management 18, 188–197 (2009)
8. Moe, W.W., Fader, P.S.: Capturing evolving visit behavior in clickstream data. Journal of Interactive Marketing 18(1), 5e–19e (2004)
9. Sismeiro, C., Bucklin, R.E.: Modeling purchase behavior at an E-commerce web site: A task-completion approach. Journal of Marketing Research 41, 306–323 (2004)
10. Van den Poel, D., Buckinx, W.: Predicting Online Purchasing Behaviour. European Journal of Operational Research 166(2), 557–575 (2005)
11. Riding, R., Cheema, I.: Cognitive Styles – An Overview and Integration. Journal of Educational Psychology 11(3-4), 193–215 (1991)
12. Chen, S., Liu, X.: An Integrated Approach for Modeling Learning Patterns of Students in Web-Based Instruction: A Cognitive Style Perspective. ACM Transactions on Computer-Human Interaction 15(1), 1–28 (2008)
13. Storto, C.: Evaluating ecommerce websites cognitive efficiency: An integrative framework based on data envelopment analysis, Applied Ergonomics 44, 1004e–1014e (2013)
14. Boyd, A.: The goals, questions, indicators, measures (GQIM) approach to the measurement of customer satisfaction with e-commerce web sites. Aslib 54(3), 177e–187e (2002)
15. Merwe, R., Bekker, J.: A framework and methodology for evaluating e-commerce web sites. Internet Research: Electronic Networking Applications and Policy 13(5), 330–341 (2003)
16. Zhang, P., von Dran, G.M.: Satisfactor and dissatisfactors: a two-factor model for website design and evaluation. Journal of the American Society for Information Science 51(4), 1253e–1268e (2000)
17. Forrester Consulting: eCommerce Web Site Performance Today: An Updated Look At Consumer Reaction To A Poor Online Shopping Experience (2009)
18. Arnold, M., Reynolds, K.: Hedonic shopping motivations. Journal of Retailing 79(2), 77–95 (2003)
19. Bridges, E., Florsheim, R.: Hedonic and utilitarian shopping goals: the online experience. Journal of Business Research 61(4), 309–314 (2008)
20. Thirumalai, S., Sinha, K.K.: Customization of the online purchase process in electronic retailing and customer satisfaction: An online field study. Journal of Operations Management 29, 477–487 (2011)
21. Li, T., Meshkova, Z.: Examining the impact of rich media on consumer willingness to pay in online stores. Electronic Commerce Research and Applications 12(6), 449–461 (2013)
22. Sternberg, R.J.: Thinking Styles. Cambridge University Press, New York (1997)
23. Witkin, H.A., Moore, C.A., Goodenough, D.R., Cox, P.W.: Field-dependent and Dield-independent Cognitive Styles and their Educational Implications. J. Review of Educational Research 47(1), 1–64 (1977)
24. Peterson, E., Deary, I., Austin, E.: A New Reliable Measure of Verbal-Imagery Cognitive Style. Personality and Individual Differences 38, 1269–1281 (2005)
25. Riding, R.: Cognitive Styles Analysis. Learning and Training Technology, Birmingham, U.K (2001)
26. Belk, M., Papatheocharous, E., Germanakos, P., Samaras, G.: Modeling Users on the World Wide Web based on Cognitive Factors, Navigation Behaviour and Clustering Techniques. J. Systems and Software 86(12), 2995–3012 (2013)
27. Germanakos, P., Tsianos, N., Lekkas, Z., Mourlas, C., Samaras, G.: Realizing Comprehensive User Profile as the Core Element of Adaptive and Personalized Communication Environments and Systems. J. The Computer Journal 52(7), 749–770 (2008)

Do You Trust My Avatar? Effects of Photo-Realistic Seller Avatars and Reputation Scores on Trust in Online Transactions

Gary Bente, Thomas Dratsch, Simon Rehbach, Matthias Reyl, and Blerta Lushaj

University of Cologne, Cologne, Germany
bente@uni-koeln.de

Abstract. We investigated the influence of photo-realistic avatars and reputation scores on trust building in online transactions. In Experiment 1, 126 participants played a computer-mediated trust game with three avatar conditions (trustworthy, untrustworthy, and no seller avatar) and three reputation conditions (positive, negative, and no seller reputation). Both trustworthy avatars and positive reputation scores led to higher purchase rates. We also found a significant interaction between avatars and reputation scores, suggesting that the effect of avatars was stronger when the reputation score induced uncertainty. To further support this effect, we systematically varied uncertainty levels in Experiment 2, in which 147 participants played another trust game. Results again confirmed that participants relied more on avatars in their decisions under high uncertainty. Taken together, the results show that avatars can help to reduce uncertainty and to improve trust building in e-commerce settings.

Keywords: Trust, Avatars, Reputation, E-commerce.

1 Introduction

Disembodiment has been identified as a major threat to trust in online transactions. However, virtual avatars can help to re-embody social interactions and to increase trust in online encounters [1]. Future e-commerce platforms can be expected to provide virtual market places, in which trading partners are reunited in time and space, thus allowing for embodied encounters between actors. Avatars as representatives of real persons will play a crucial role in these environments, and it is important to explore whether real life principles of social interaction and perception apply to such settings [2]. Even though seller photos have been shown to have a considerable impact on online trust [3-5], empirical evidence for a comparable influence of avatars is still missing. Thus, we analyzed the influence of photo-realistic avatars on purchase decisions in a standard trust-game.

2 Experiment 1

2.1 Background and Hypotheses

The Influence of Seller Reputation on Online Purchase Decisions. One central feedback in e-commerce is the reputation system [6,7]. Previous findings have shown

F.F.-H. Nah (Ed.): HCIB/HCII 2014, LNCS 8527, pp. 461–470, 2014.
© Springer International Publishing Switzerland 2014

that reputation and trust are closely related phenomena and that reputation scores constitute a very influential factor in online transactions [8-10]. Also, Bente et al. [11], on which our study builds, found a significant effect of reputation scores on trust. Positive reputation contributed toward buyers' trust and higher purchase rates while missing reputation performed worse than negative reputation [11]. In line with this empirical evidence, we formulate the following hypothesis:

Hypothesis 1: Reputation scores affect purchase behavior in online transactions. Positive reputation leads to higher purchase rates than negative and missing reputation (H1a.) Negative reputation leads to higher purchase rates than missing reputation (H1b).

The Influence of Seller Avatars on Online Purchase Decisions. Photos are another central feedback for trust in e-commerce. The effects of photos on trust in CMC and C2C transactions are more equivocal than the effects of reputation [3-5]. With regard to impression formation, it has been shown that the human face, even if only visible in the form of a photo, can serve as evidence for the disposition of honesty [12] and trustworthiness [13]. Furthermore, it has been shown that impressions based on faces are largely automatic and extremely fast [14-16]. Bente et al. [11] found that trustworthy photos contributed toward buyers' trust and higher purchase rates. There was no significant difference between missing and untrustworthy photos [11]. A reason for this result might be the act of self-disclosure by putting a photo on an e-commerce website. It holds the potential to foster trust and cooperative behavior in online transactions by reducing interpersonal uncertainty and potentially making the discloser recognizable and "appear vulnerable" [17]. With regard to the impact of avatars as a signal of trustworthiness [18], we follow the assumptions of Bente et al. [11], using avatars instead of photos, and hypothesize:

Hypothesis 2: Seller avatars affect purchase behavior in online transactions. Trustworthy seller avatars lead to higher purchase rates than untrustworthy or missing avatars (H2a). There is no difference in purchase rates between avatars with an untrustworthy appearing seller or missing avatars (H2b).

The Effect of Involvement on the Influence of Reputation and Seller Avatars. According to the Elaboration Likelihood Model [19], decisions can be influenced by two different pathways or routes of information processing: the peripheral and the central route. The peripheral route relies on a quick but shallow processing of tacit cues, whereas the central route uses elaborative cognitive processing of factual information. The central route should prevail when involvement is high and cognitive capacity is sufficient to process the available information. Bente et al. [11] found equal effect sizes for reputation ($\eta^2_p = .27$) and seller photos ($\eta^2_p = .20$), indicating that participants were equally influenced in their decisions by tacit cues (seller photos) and factual information (reputation scores). One possible explanation for this might be the low cognitive involvement of the participants, which caused them to use a shallow mode of processing. In order to vary the involvement of the participants in this study, we varied the amount of virtual units at stake in the trust game. In our high involvement game (high amount at stake), we expected that a central processing mode based on factual information (reputation scores) should prevail. In our low involvement game (low amount at stake), we expected participants to use a peripheral mode based on tacit cues (seller avatars). Therefore, we hypothesize:

Hypothesis 3: Seller avatar and involvement show an interaction effect. High involvement leads to a weaker influence of seller avatars on purchase decisions (H3).

2.2   Methods

Design and Experimental Setup. To analyze the influence of avatars, reputation scores, and involvement on purchase decisions, we used a 3 (avatar: trustworthy vs. untrustworthy vs. no avatar) × 3 (reputation: positive vs. negative vs. no reputation) × 2 (involvement: high vs. low) design, with avatar and reputation as within-subjects factors and involvement as a between-subjects factor.

Seller avatars and reputation scores were presented in a standard trust game [20], which models a trust situation framed as a sales transaction between a buyer (trustor) and a seller (trustee). Instead of real products only monetary equivalents are exchanged in the game. Figure 1 depicts the payoff matrix for the trust game.

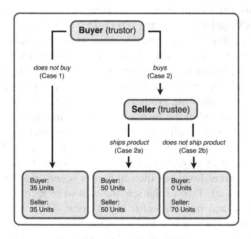

Fig. 1. Payoff-matrix for the trustgame

If the buyer decides not to buy (Case 1), both buyer and seller keep their 35 units. If the buyer decides to buy and the seller ships the product (Case 2a), both buyer and seller receive 50 units for the successful trade. If the buyer decides to buy and the seller does not ship the product (Case 2b), the buyer loses his/her 35 units to the seller, who receives 70 units.

The trust game was conducted as a web survey, allowing for the full experimental control over the pay-off matrix, fictitious sellers, and reputation scores (see Figure 2).

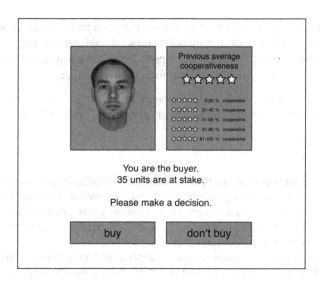

Fig. 2. Screenshot of the trust game user interface with avatar and reputation score

Stimulus Materials. 30 virtual avatars (15 male; 15 female) were created using the software FaceGen (Singular Inversions, 2011). In a prestudy, 35 participants (8 male; 27 female; M_{age} = 27.00) rated the trustworthiness of the avatars on a 7-point scale (1 = *high distrust* to 7 = *high trust*). Based on the trustratings in the prestudy, six trustworthy and six untrustworthy avatars were selected. The trustworthy avatars were rated to be significantly more trustworthy than the untrustworthy avatars, $t(34)$ = 8.69, $p < .001$, d = 1.48. The remaining avatars were used in filler trials.

Reputation was presented in the form of a five-star-index, indicating the percentage of previous trades in which a seller had shipped the product after payment (one star: 0–20%; two stars: 21–40%; three stars: 41–60%; four stars: 61–80%; five stars: 81–100%). In another prestudy, 30 participants (16 male, 14 female) rated the trustworthiness of the different levels of the reputation score on a 7-point scale (1 = *high distrust* to 7 = *high trust*). Two of the star-indexes were identified as adequate representations of negative and positive seller reputations: Three stars (the seller shipped 41–60% of past trades) led to a low average trust rating representing a negative reputation, whereas four stars (the seller shipped 61–80% of past trades) led to a high trust rating indicating a positive reputation. The positive reputation received significantly higher trust ratings than the low reputation, $t(29)$ = 8.95, $p < .001$, d = 1.7.

Participants' involvement in the trust game was modified through the amount of units at stake in the game. In the low involvement condition, both buyer and seller received a basic amount of 35 units. In the high involvement condition, the amount was raised to 3500 units.

Participants. Overall, 126 students (66 male, 60 female, M_{age} = 24.15, SD_{age} = 5.66) participated in the online trust game. Participants were recruited by the use of email invitations sent via several mailing lists of a large University in Western Germany where the study was conducted. Participants were invited to play an online trust game in which they could earn between 7 and 10 Euros.

Procedure. All participants completed the study online using their own computers. First of all, participants were randomly assigned to the high or low involvement condition. Regardless of this assignment, all participants were subsequently assigned to the role of the buyer and were informed that they would play online with several other participants, who had been randomly assigned to the role of the seller. Participants were further informed that the sellers were represented by virtual avatars that had been generated out of their real photographs. After that, participants were introduced to the five-star reputation score indicating the percentage of previous trades in which the seller had decided to ship the product. The buyers were told that there would be no immediate information about the shipping decision of the seller but that the money they earned would be added up depending on the seller's decisions. After that, participants were presented with the individual profiles of the sellers that included the sellers' avatar and reputation and decided for each profile whether they would buy from that particular seller.

2.3   Results and Discussion

Effect of Involvement. Buying decisions were analyzed in a $3 \times 3 \times 2$ mixed ANOVA (avatar $\times$ reputation $\times$ involvement). There was neither a significant main effect of involvement nor any significant interactions between involvement and the other variables, $F < 1$. Thus, hypothesis H3 could not be supported. The degree of involvement did not influence participants' buying decisions.

Effect of Avatar and Reputation. Because there was no significant main effect of involvement, we collapsed the data of both conditions into one single group and performed another mixed ANOVA. The results are shown in Figure 3.

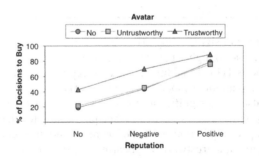

Fig. 3. Effects of reputation and avatar on purchase decisions

There was a significant main effect of avatar, $F(2, 250) = 39.57$, $p < .001$, $\eta^2_p = .240$, a significant main effect of reputation, $F(2, 250) = 124.58$, $p < .001$, $\eta^2_p = .499$, and a significant interaction effect between avatar and reputation, $F(4, 500) = 3.66$, $p = .006$, $\eta^2_p = .028$.

To test the specific hypotheses regarding the effects of information valence within both factors (avatar, reputation), pairwise comparisons for the three levels of each factor were conducted separately (see Table 1 and Table 2).

Table 1. Results of post-hoc comparisons for reputation across the levels of each factor

Avatar	Reputation	$t(125)$	p	d
No	Negative vs. No	5.35	< .001	0.48
	Positive vs. No	12.39	< .001	1.10
	Positive vs. Negative	7.45	< .001	0.67
Untrustworthy	Negative vs. No	5.52	< .001	0.50
	Positive vs. No	13.51	< .001	1.21
	Positive vs. Negative	7.19	< .001	0.64
Trustworthy	Negative vs. No	6.15	< .001	0.55
	Positive vs. No	10.63	< .001	0.98
	Positive vs. Negative	5.25	< .001	0.49

Table 2. Results of post-hoc comparisons for avatar across the levels of each factor

Reputation	Avatar	$t(125)$	p	d
No	Untrustw. vs. No	0.75	.455	0.07
	Trustw. vs. No	5.71	< .001	0.51
	Trustw. vs. Untrustw.	5.77	< .001	0.52
Negative	Untrustw. vs. No	0.37	.714	0.03
	Trustw. vs. No	6.07	< .001	0.55
	Trustw. vs. Untrustw.	6.32	< .001	0.56
Positive	Untrustw. vs. No	0.82	.415	0.07
	Trustw. vs. No	2.75	.007	0.26
	Trustw. vs. Untrustw.	4.43	< .001	0.41

Reputation scores did significantly affect purchase behavior in online transactions. Positive reputation lead to higher purchase rates than negative and missing reputation, supporting hypothesis H1a. In addition, negative reputation lead to higher purchase rates than missing reputation, supporting hypothesis H1b.

Seller avatars also had a significant effect on purchase behavior in online transactions. Trustworthy seller avatars lead to higher purchase rates than untrustworthy or missing avatars, supporting hypothesis H2a. There was no difference in purchase rates between avatars with an untrustworthy appearing seller or missing avatars, supporting H2b.

As for the combined effect of reputation and seller avatars, there was a significant interaction between reputation and seller avatars. In their original study, Bente et al. [11] did not find a significant interaction between reputation and seller photographs, which they interpreted as evidence for the independent influence of both cues on purchase decisions. Our results, however, hint at an important difference in the effect of seller photographs as opposed to seller avatars: In the study by Bente [11], the effect of the seller photographs was independent of the effect of reputation. In our study, the effect of the seller avatars differed with the levels of reputation. In the negative reputation condition, where there was high uncertainty whether the seller would ship the product (only 41–60% of the time), participants were more susceptible to the influence of the seller avatars. In the positive reputation condition, where there was high certainty that the seller would ship the product (61–80% of the time), the influence of the seller avatars was weaker. This suggests that even though participants do use seller avatars in their decision process, they give less weight to this cue as opposed to reputation scores. This is also supported by the larger effect size for reputation ($\eta^2_p =$ .499) as opposed to seller avatars ($\eta^2_p = .240$). However, if the reputation is negative, participants rely more strongly on seller avatars in their decisions. Because we did not predict this interaction effect, we conducted Experiment 2 to replicate the interaction between reputation and seller avatars.

3   Experiment 2

3.1   Background and Hypotheses

As the results of Experiment 1 have shown, there was a significant interaction effect between reputation and trustworthiness of the seller avatar. More precisely, the effect of avatar was stronger if there was high uncertainty that the seller would ship the product. If the uncertainty that the seller would ship the product was low, the effect of the trustworthiness of the avatar was weaker. However, Experiment 1 suffered from one major limitation: Reputation score number 3 was both more negative and represented a higher uncertainty than reputation score number 4 —thus confounding negativity and uncertainty. To rule out this possibility, we replicated Experiment 1 using all five reputation scores. Especially reputation scores 1 (seller shipped 0–20% of the time) and 2 (seller shipped 21–40% of the time) are important in this context because they are more negative than reputation score number 3 but represent less uncertainty—it is certain that the seller will not ship the product. Therefore, to replicate the effect and to rule out other explanations, we performed Experiment 2. Based on the results of Experiment 1, we hypothesize:

Hypothesis 4: The effect of seller avatars is strongest in the condition with the highest uncertainty that the seller will ship the product compared to all other conditions.

3.2   Methods

Design and Experimental Setup. To analyze the interaction between reputation scores and trustworthiness of the seller avatars, we used a 2 (avatar: trustworthy vs. untrustworthy) × 5 (reputation: 1 vs. 2 vs. 3 vs. 4 vs. 5 stars) design, with both avatar and reputation as within-subjects factors.

Stimulus Materials. Based on the pretest of Experiment 1, ten trustworthy and ten untrustworthy avatars were selected. The trustworthy avatars were rated to be significantly more trustworthy than the untrustworthy avatars, $t(34) = 8.45$, $p < .001$, $d = 1.43$.

To vary the reputation of the sellers, we used the same five-star-index as in Experiment 1.

Participants. Overall, 147 students (21 male, 126 female, M_{age} = 23.88, SD_{age} = 4.56) participated in the online trust game. Participants were recruited through email invitations sent via mailing lists of several universities in Germany. Participants were invited to play an online trust game in which they could earn between 7 and 14 Euros.

Procedure. The procedure for the study was the same as in Experiment 1.

3.3   Results and Discussion

Effect of Avatar and Reputation. To analyze the effect of reputation and avatar on purchase decisions, we performed a 2 × 5 repeated measures ANOVA (avatar × reputation). There was a significant main effect of avatar on purchase decisions, $F(1, 146)$ = 28.5, $p < .001$, η^2_p = .163. There was a significant main effect of reputation on purchase decisions, $F(4, 584)$ = 517.6, $p < .001$, η^2_p = .780. There was a significant interaction effect between avatar and reputation, $F(4, 584)$ = 3.7, $p = .006$, η^2_p = .024.

To break down this significant interaction effect, we subtracted the mean purchase decisions for the untrustworthy avatars from the mean purchase decisions for the trustworthy avatars for each of the five levels of reputation (see Figure 4).

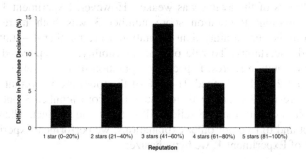

Fig. 4. Difference in purchase decisions between trustworthy and untrustworthy avatars for all five levels of reputation

To test our specific hypothesis that the difference in purchase decisions between trustworthy and untrustworthy avatars should be largest for the reputation score with the highest uncertainty that the seller would ship the product, we used a Helmert contrast. The difference in purchase decisions between trustworthy and untrustworthy avatars for the reputation score with the highest uncertainty (3 stars: 41–60 %) was compared to the mean difference in purchase decisions between trustworthy and untrustworthy avatars of all other reputation scores (1, 2, 4, and 5 stars). As predicted, this contrast was significant, $F(1, 146)$ = 6.26, $p = .013$, η^2_p = .041, supporting hypothesis H4, which states that the effect of the seller avatar should be strongest in the condition with highest uncertainty that the seller would ship the product.

4   General Discussion

Using a standard trust game, the current study aimed to identify differential contributions of seller reputations and seller avatars on purchase decisions (trust related behavior) in online trading. Overall, we found significant main effects of seller reputation and seller avatar. Positive reputation as well as trustworthy avatars led to significantly higher purchase rates than negative or missing information. Missing reputation led to significantly lower purchase rates than negative reputation, whereas missing avatars did not lead to lower purchase rates than negative avatars, supporting hypotheses H1 and H2. In order to extend the results of Bente et al. [11], we also varied the involvement of the participants by varying the stake size for each transaction. However, our results do not show an interaction between seller avatars and involvement (H3). A high involvement did not mediate the influence of the seller avatars. The absence of this anchoring effect may be due to the fact that participants knew that they could earn a reward of up to 11 Euro. Therefore, it is possible that participants did not pay attention to the amount of units displayed during each transaction. A future study should vary the involvement of participants by varying the actual amount of money at stake.

In contrast to the results by Bente et al. [11], we did find an interaction effect between seller avatar and reputation score. When the reputation score was high, the avatar had a weaker influence on buying decisions, suggesting that the reputation score functions as the primary information source in this trust related e-commerce setting. Supporting this notion, we also observed a larger effect size for reputation ($\eta^2_p = .499$) compared to avatar ($\eta^2_p = .240$), indicating that the effect of seller avatars was generally weaker than the effect of reputation. Hinting at an important difference in the effect of seller avatars as opposed to seller photographs, this result is in contrast to the findings by Bente et al. [11], who found similar effect sizes for reputation ($\eta^2 = .27$) and seller photographs ($\eta^2 = .20$). However, as evidenced by the significant interaction between reputation and seller avatars in both Experiment 1 and 2, participants' responses to seller avatars were influenced by the uncertainty inherent in the reputation scores. When the uncertainty that the seller would ship the product was high, participants were more susceptible to the influence of the seller avatars. As our results show, there are subtle differences in the effects of virtual avatars as opposed to photographs.

In sum, our study shows that in online transactions we are influenced by both reputation scores and seller avatars in our decisions. However, the effect of seller avatars can be moderated by reputation scores. Our findings support the notion that seller avatars can serve as cues to build trust in online transactions, but that reputation scores have a greater impact on purchase decisions than avatars.

References

1. Nowak, K.L., Rauh, C.: The influence of the avatar on online perceptions of anthropomorphism, androgyny, credibility, homophily, and attraction. Journal of Computer-Mediated Communication 11, 153–178 (2005)
2. Yee, N., Bailenson, J.N., Urbanek, M., Chang, F., Merget, D.: The unbearable likeness of being digital: the persistence of nonverbal social norms in online virtual environments. CyberPsychology & Behavior 10, 115–121 (2007)

3. Steinbrück, U., Schaumburg, H., Duda, S., Krüger, T.: A picture says more than a thousand words: photographs as trust builders in e-commerce websites. In: Proceedings of CHI 2002, pp. 748–749 (2002)
4. Riegelsberger, J., Sasse, M.A., McCarthy, J.D.: Shiny happy people building trust?: photos on e-commerce websites and consumer trust. In: Proceedings of CHI 2003, vol. 5, pp. 121–128 (2003)
5. Golbeck, J., Fleischmann, K.R.: Trust in social Q&A: the impact of text and photo cues of expertise. Proceedings of the American Society for Information Science and Technology 47, 1–10 (2010)
6. Resnick, P., Kuwabara, K., Zeckhauser, R., Friedman, E.: Reputation systems. Communications of the ACM 43, 45–48 (2000)
7. Resnick, P., Zeckhauser, R.: Trust among strangers in Internet transactions: Empirical analysis of eBay's reputation system. In: Baye, M.R. (ed.) The Economics of the Internet and E-Commerce, Advances in Applied Microeconomics, pp. 127–157. Elsevier, Amsterdam (2002)
8. Corritore, C.L., Kracher, B., Wiedenbeck, S.: On-line trust: concepts, evolving themes, a model. International Journal of Human-Computer Studies 58, 737–758 (2003)
9. Jøsang, A., Ismail, R., Boyd, C.: A survey of trust and reputation systems for online service provision. Decision Support Systems 43, 618–644 (2007)
10. Melnik, M.I., Alm, J.: Does a seller's ecommerce reputation matter? Evidence from ebay auctions. The Journal of Industrial Economics 50, 337–349 (2002)
11. Bente, G., Baptist, O., Leuschner, H.: To buy or not to buy: Influence of seller photos and reputation on buyer trust and purchase behavior. International Journal of Human-Computer Studies 70, 1–13 (2012)
12. Dion, K., Berscheid, E., Walster, E.: What is beautiful is good. Journal of Personality and Social Psychology 24, 285–290 (1972)
13. Todorov, A.: Evaluating faces on trustworthiness: an extension of systems for recognition of emotions signaling approach/avoidance behaviors. In: Kingstone, A. (ed.) Ann. N Y Acad. Sci., United States, pp. 208–224 (2008)
14. Todorov, A., Pakrashi, M., Oosterhof, N.N.: Evaluating faces on trustworthiness after minimal time exposure. Social Cognition 27, 813–833 (2009)
15. Todorov, A., Duchaine, B.: Reading trustworthiness in faces without recognizing faces. Cognitive Neuropsychology 25, 395–410 (2008)
16. Willis, J., Todorov, A.: First impressions. Psychological Science 17, 592–598 (2006)
17. Zheng, J., Veinott, E., Bos, N., Olson, J.S., Olson, G.M.: Trust without touch: jumpstarting long-distance trust with initial social activities. In: Proceedings of CHI 2002, vol. 4, pp. 141–146 (2002)
18. Oosterhof, N.N., Todorov, A.: Shared perceptual basis of emotional expressions and trustworthiness impressions from faces. Emotion 9, 128–133 (2009)
19. Petty, R.E., Cacioppo, J.: The elaboration likelihood model of persuasion. In: Berkowitz, L. (ed.) Advances in Experimental Social Psychology, pp. 123–205. Academic Press, New York (1986)
20. Bolton, G.E., Katok, E., Ockenfels, A.: Trust among Internet traders: A behavioral economics approach. Analyse Und Kritik 26, 185–202 (2004)

What Web Analysts Can Do for Human-Computer Interaction?

Claudia Brauer[1,2], David Reischer[3], and Felix Mödritscher[2,4]

[1] MCI, Innsbruck, Austria
claudia.brauer@mci.edu
[2] Vienna University of Economics and Business, Vienna, Austria
{claudia.brauer,felix.moedritscher}@wu.ac.at
[3] University College London
david.reischer@gmail.com
[4] University of Applied Sciences Technikum Wien, Vienna, Austria
felix.moedritscher@technikum-wien.at

Abstract. Fostered by the emergence of web technologies and of new streams like ubiquitous computing, social media or mobile technologies, a lot of attention has been directed to the field of Web Analytics in order to learn about technology usage behavior of end-users, such as customers or employees of enterprises. Going beyond the scope of online marketing and business intelligence, Web Analysts can be of relevance for typical Human-Computer Interaction (HCI) activities, i.e. designing user interfaces for new business software or evaluating the usability of an existing solution. Thus, this paper aims at elaborating the usefulness of Web Analytics for the HCI domain. Therefore, we conducted an empirical study in order to gather working tasks and professional competencies of Web Analysts by analyzing international job advertisements. Consequently, we draw conclusions on how Web Analysts can support HCI activities with regard to this task and competence profile. It shows that Web Analysts can be of use in HCI practice, i.e. within the usability engineering life-cycle, in HCI research, e.g. for typical design science approaches, and whenever users interact with web-based software applications.

Keywords: E-Commerce, Web Analytics, Job Advertisement Analysis, Working Tasks, Professional Competencies, Regional Variation, Quantitative Content Analysis, Benefits for HCI.

1 Introduction

In recent years, Web Analytics has gained attention due to the necessity to measure the success of web-based business models as well as the integration of internet applications in business processes and functions (e.g., online marketing, social media marketing). Although Web Analytics is, especially in companies of German-speaking countries, still in infancy, its importance will increasing due to the growing amount of web data in the next years [1], [2]. Some authors have already concluded that Web

F.F.-H. Nah (Ed.): HCIB/HCII 2014, LNCS 8527, pp. 471–481, 2014.
© Springer International Publishing Switzerland 2014

Analytics has risen to being a strategic tool for the management of organizations [3]. Besides, it can be also considered a valuable instrument for supporting user interface designers and improving the usability of software systems [4].

Against this background, this paper examines the occupational field of Web Analytics experts – in further consequence referred as 'Web Analysts' – in order to draw conclusions on its benefits for Human-Computer Interaction (HCI) research and practice. It seems that this profession is not accurately defined and accompanied by a lot of uncertainties about working tasks, required professional competencies, and the organizational assignment [5]. Consequently, we conducted an empirical study in order to characterize this profession adequately and on the basis of topical data, precisely of international job advertisements. Hereby, we address the following research questions: How is the profession of a Web Analyst characterized? To which departments are Web Analysts normally assigned to? What are their working tasks and professional competencies in companies? After drafting a task and competence profile of this profession we explain how Web Analysts could be supportive for HCI.

The rest of the paper is structured as follows. The next section gives a brief overview of Web Analytics and HCI, including possible overlaps between these two fields and possible strategies to analyze a professional field. Then, the following two sections report about an empirical study which was necessary to create an authentic profile of working tasks and professional competencies of Web Analysts. In Section 5 we depict possible scenarios in which Web Analysts could be supportive for HCI practice and research. Finally, the paper is concluded, and an outlook on future work is given.

2   Web Analytics and Its Application for HCI Practice

2.1   Web Analytics

Web Analytics can be understood as the "*measurement, collection, analysis and reporting of internet data for the purposes of understanding and optimizing Web usage*", i.e. to optimize websites and web-based marketing initiatives [6]. Going beyond this definition it consists of two parts. On the one hand, Analytics is defined as the "*practice of supporting decision-making through number crunching*", i.e. by applying Business Intelligence techniques and tools (e.g., scorecards or dashboards) in order to support specific stakeholders in their decision-making process [7]. On the other hand, the focus of this discipline is set to web technologies and applications, thus restricting the stakeholder groups that interact with web applications and, additionally, have decision-making power.

Technically, Web Analytics use different techniques to collect, store and analyze data. The most common data collecting methods are log-file analysis that exploits log-files of web servers and page tagging which is based on pixel that sends user interaction data to a tracking server. Typical activities of Web Analytics comprise tracking and measurement of users' online activities, data analysis, statistical evaluation, or analysis of web traffic and click-streams. The application areas comprise the evaluation and improvement of the usability of websites, analysis of usage behavior and characteristics of web users, analysis of online and offline marketing activities or analysis of web-based business processes etc. Amongst others, indicators include (but are not limited to) number of hits, page views, events, visits, (unique) visitors and page impressions or measures like the visit duration, click paths, and so on. However, and with respect to HCI, the original objective of Web Analytics was to improve the usability of websites [8].

2.2 Human-Computer Interaction

HCI deals with the design and study of interactions between people (i.e., users) and computers and can be considered as the intersection between computer science, behavioral science (psychology), user interface design and any field of study in which computer software is developed [9]. Accordingly, HCI addresses human-related aspects of user interfaces (UI), like information processing of human brains, language and communication or ergonomics of hardware, as well as computer-related issues of software, like dialogue techniques, interface metaphors, input/output devices and graphic designs. The overall goal is to provide a UI design that fits the needs of humans. Therefore, the development includes different design approaches, implementation techniques and tools but also methods to evaluate user interfaces.

Consequently, HCI focuses on two important application areas. On the one hand, it addresses the design and implementation of user interfaces for software applications. Hereby, literature suggests following certain mantras, applying well-established methodologies or methods, and making use of professional tools and UI elements [10]. On the other hand, HCI also deals with the evaluation of user interfaces and interactions in order to learn about the usage behavior of end-users and to improve the usability of a software application. While the traditional Usability Engineering Process builds upon methods for exploratory, formative and summative evaluation of user interfaces [10], predictive evaluation aims at estimating how good the usability of an application will be. In all of these areas Web Analytics is considered to be useful, as it provides indicators and graphics generated from real-world data on technology usage. Selected experiences from literature are summarized in the following.

2.3 The Application of Web Analytics in the Context of HCI

Interactions between Web Analytics and HCI research can be observed in both directions. On the one hand, HCI techniques are often applied to design and improve user interfaces of Web Analytics software or support analysts in their everyday tasks, e.g. through contemporary information visualization techniques [11]. The more interesting approaches reported in literature comprise the application of Web Analytics techniques to examine or enhance the usability of web applications.

Amongst others, Hasan et al. [12] report about making use of Google Analytics to evaluate the usability of e-commerce sites and identify UI problems, i.e. even for specific stakeholder groups. This research suggests that specific web metrics, like the percentage of time spent, visits of the percentage of click depth visits, allow a quick evaluation of features such as the navigation, the internal search, the information architecture, the content and design of the site, the customer service and even the efficiency of the purchasing process. Similar experiences on the usefulness of Web Analytics for analyzing and improving user interactions with websites are documented in other areas, like library services [13].

All in all, we consider Web Analytics as an important tool to analyze the usability, the content, the layout and design, the navigation, as well as the availability and system quality of websites. Yet, given the range of tasks and required competencies of Web Analysts, this discipline can even have more benefits for HCI, as we will explain later. However, in the first place, we have to characterize the profession of Web Analysts, which is being achieved through the empirical study summarized in the upcoming sections.

3   Research Design and Dataset

In order to get a topical, close-to-market picture of Web Analysts, we decided to conduct an occupational analysis [14], i.e. a specialized type of job analysis that aims at focusing on how a specific profession is employed across multiple organizations or even across a whole industry. Precisely we collected data on the profession and analyzed it according to different characteristics. Similar experiences have been reported over the last decades. For instance, Grob and Lange [15] describe an approach to analyze printed job advertisements (job ads) in order to characterize the occupational field of Business Informatics.

Table 1. Distribution of job ads by online job portal

Online job portal	Number of job ads	Percentage
Monster.co.uk	57	25,56%
LinkedIn.com	38	17,04%
Stepstone.de	28	12,55%
Monster.de	23	10,31%
Monster.com	22	9,86%
totaljobs.co.uk	12	5,38%
LinkedIn.co.uk	9	3,98%
xing.de	9	3,98%
Jobsearch.co.uk	7	3,13%
LinkedIn.de	5	2,42%
Karriere.at	4	1,79%
derStandard.at	2	0,9%
Stellenanzeigen.de	2	0,9%
indeed.com	2	0,9%
backinjob.de	1	0,45%
careesma.at	1	0,45%
xing.com	1	0,45%
Overall	**223**	**100%**

For this research study we collected international 223 online job advertisements between July 2012 and November 2012 and applied the method of Quantitative Content Analysis[1] along 130 variables (28.990 characteristics) to describe Web Analysts and develop a comprehensive task and professional competency profile of this profession. Moreover we conducted multivariate analysis method, e.g. regression analysis to identify correlations between different variables by using SPSS and Excel. In order to get a holistic view on this profession we consider job advertisements in the German-speaking countries (i.e., Germany, Austria and the Switzerland) and compared them to the characteristics and job requirements of Web Analysts in the UK and the US. During the data collection it has been turned out that job advertisements in printed magazines and printed newspapers are hardly verifiably. Therefore, the present research study focuses on country-specific and user-highest online job portals and online social network portals (Xing; LinkedIn). Table 1 shows the distribution of job ads for Web Analysts depending on the different online portals.

We used the following search words to retrieve the job ads: 'Internet Analyst', 'e-Business Analyst', 'eBusiness Analyst', 'e-Commerce Analyst', 'eCommerce Analyst', 'Web Analyst', 'Webanalyst', 'Web Analyse', 'Webanalyse', 'Web Analytics', 'Web Controller', 'Web Controlling' and 'Web Insights'. In order to obtain meaningful research results and to get deeper insight into the profession of Web Analysts, the present research study includes job advertisements from Austria, Germany, Great Britain, United States and Switzerland. We analyzed 84 (37.67%) job ads from Great Britain, 67 (30.04%) from the United States, 64 (28.07%) from Germany, 6 (2.69%) from Austria and 2 (0.9%) from Switzerland. We sorted out identical job advertisements, which were published in different online portals to ensure the accuracy of the research results. About two-thirds (65.47%) of the job advertisements were directly published by the company and about a third (34.53%) of the job ads were published by recruitment agencies.

4   Job Profile of Web Analysts

In the following the profession of Web Analysts is characterized through the results of the empirical study we conducted on the basis of the job ads.

4.1   General Description

The job title 'Web Analyst' is widely used in German-speaking (47.83%) and English-speaking countries (49.09%); almost the half of all analyzed job ads was found under this term. Moreover, the title 'Web Analytics Manager' is also common in German-speaking countries (28.43%) and English-speaking countries (26.09%). Besides, job titles such as 'Online Insight Analyst' (3.18%) or 'E-Commerce Analyst' (2.27%) are hardly used in both language areas. In Germany, Austria and Switzerland this profession is sometimes called 'Web Controller' (8.70%).

---

[1] Raw data and results of the analysis can be requested by the authors.

The non-food consumer goods industry has the highest demand for Web Analysts (23.94% in German-speaking countries and 20.59% in English-speaking countries). Furthermore the industry sectors 'IT/Software/Telecommunication', 'Media/Internet' and 'Advertising/Marketing/PR' have a rather high demand for this profession, while the healthcare industry, 'Electrical/Electronics', social economy organizations, the 'Printing/Paper' industry and the educational sector have started to recognize the importance of Web Analytics but have a lower demand for dedicated specialists.

Especially the industries 'New Media/Internet', 'Telecommunications and Consulting' if in German-speaking countries sought Web Analysts. 13.97% of the English-speaking companies and 2.82% German-speaking companies which are looking for Web Analysts can be associated with the 'Advertising/Marketing/PR' industry. Respectively 11.76% of English-speaking companies are working in the field of IT, software or media (film/radio/publishing).

By comparing the job ads of English-and German-speaking countries we identified intercultural differences concerning the operational assignment of Web Analytics in companies. The majority of English-speaking companies (38.46%) have already established a Web Analytics department in the company, while in German-speaking countries only 14.29% companies have such a department and it is more common to integrate this business function into the e-Business department. In addition, it is verifiable, that in English-speaking countries Web Analytics is still a part of the marketing department (34.42%). Finally, 2 out of 54 German-speaking companies have assigned Web Analytics to the controlling department while no English-speaking company considers Web Analytics as part of controlling.

A research study by Zumstein et al. [5] has revealed different research results related to organizational assignment of Web Analytics within enterprises in German-speaking countries. Only a few companies (1%) in the Germany, Austria and Switzerland have established an independent Web Analytics department within the company. The majority of German-speaking companies (48%) have integrated Web Analytics in the marketing department, another 17% of them in the Business Intelligence department and 15% in the IT department.

Salary is an essential part of a job. Only 56 of 223 job ads contained information about salary of a Web Analyst. The salary band shows a wide range in Austria, Germany, Great Britain, the United States and Switzerland. The mean value of the salary is EUR 3,222.09 per month. Hereby the lower boundary was EUR 1,655 per month while the upper boundary for a management position was 7,179 EUR per month. In the German-speaking countries the average salary was 2,346.67 EUR ($n = 3$) and in the English-speaking countries 3,377.30 EUR ($n = 53$). A multiple correlation analysis showed a high correlation between the salary and the required working experience (Pearson correlation coefficient $r = 0.81$ with only $n = 5$ samples and the significance value $p = 0.0931$) and a good albeit not significant correlation between the salary and the required university degree ($r=0.36$, $n=19$, $p = 0.1334$).

4.2   Professional Competencies

The majority of companies (62.33%) expect working experience in the field of Web Analytics. The required working experience lies between of 2.5 to 5 years and corresponds with a mean of 3.17 years. We identified no significant correlations between the language region and work experience. 61.88% of companies require a university degree in technical, economic or scientific numerical studies. In English-speaking countries (60%) and in the German-speaking countries (46.67%) technical or numerical studies are preferred by companies. Overall the required university degree indicates high requirements for working as a Web Analyst.

Profound knowledge about web technologies is required by 29.15% of the companies. This comparatively low percentage indicates that companies do not necessarily expect that Web Analysts make technical changes, while the majority of the companies a basic understanding of the structure and design of websites. About one fifth of the analyzed job ads in both language areas explicitly mention knowledge about HTML (19.73%) and JavaScript (18.39%). Knowledge about CSS, XML, jQuery and PHP is only sporadically requested in both language regions.

Experience with dedicated Web Analytics software is a basic requirement for Web Analysts. Currently there exists a variety of Web Analytics software products [7]. About three quarters (76.23%) of the companies expect experience with at least one Web Analytics software solution. There exist intercultural differences between German- and English speaking countries. 54.26% of English-speaking companies and 30.56% of German-speaking companies expect expertise in using Adobe Omniture. Google Analytic is free of charge and is regarded as important Web Analytics software for companies, especially for novices. Therefore 53.64% English-speaking companies and 29.17% of German-speaking companies expect experiences with Google Analytics. Hence we assumed that in the English-speaking countries experiences with Google Analytics is a fundamental prerequisite for Web Analysts.

The research studies by Zumstein et al. [5] gives evidence for a dominance of Google Analytics in German-speaking countries. This finding can be interpreted differently. On the one hand, Google Analytics is a free of charge and user-friendly Web Analytics software solution. On the other hand, it can be assumed that many companies still have little experience with Web Analytics, and thus Google Analytics regarded as a good software solution for novices. Furthermore, Coremetrics (US/UK: 24.50%; Austria/Germany/Switzerland: 4.17%) and Webtrends (UK/US: 21.19%; Austria/Germany/Switzerland: 5.56%) are used occasionally in companies. Other software solutions, e.g. Webtrekk, etracker, econda are preferably used in the German-speaking companies only.

We did not identify a dependency between the experience with Web Analytics software solutions and salary. Nevertheless conclusions can be drawn concerning correlations between the following variables: Experience with Web Analytics software is well correlated with Omniture ($r = 0.48$, $n = 223$, $p < 0.001$) and Google Analytics ($r = 0.43$, $n = 223$, $p < 0.001$) - there are hardly any differences in the both two language areas. Moreover, good correlations can be identified for the combined mentioning of econda and etracker ($r = 0.5$, $n = 223$, $p < 0.001$), Omniture and Google Analytics ($r = 0.32$, $n = 223$, $p < 0.001$), Omniture and Coremetrics ($r = 0.27$ $n = 223$, $p < 0.001$) as well as Omniture and Webtrends ($r=0.26$, $n = 223$, $p < 0.001$). Omniture and Google Analytics seem to be the state-of-the-art in the everyday practice of Web Analysts.

4.3   Working Tasks

The Web Analytics process is the basis for the analysis of working tasks [7]. The working tasks can be categorized according to the four process steps, namely (a) planning, (b) analysis, (c) reporting and (d) optimization of web sites.

Hereby, analysis (84.30%) and reporting (85.20%) activities are the most frequently listed working tasks of Web Analysts in both language areas. About half of the companies listed planning (54.26%) and optimization (56.95%) activities as important tasks of Web Analysts. Especially German-speaking companies (75%), in comparison to the English-speaking companies (44.37%), consider planning as an important responsibility of Web Analysts. The optimization activities (56.95%) are, compared to the other categories, of less relevance. Moreover, the working tasks in the four categories differ in terms of the importance which we measured through their occurrences in the job ads. We identified a strong correlation between analysis and reporting tasks ($r = 0.42$, $n = 223$, $p < 0.001$), while correlations between analysis and optimization tasks ($r = 0.31$, $n = 223$, $p < 0.001$) as well as planning and 'other' activities ($r = 0.31$, $n = 223$, $p <= 0.001$) are moderate.

The development of analysis concepts (53.52% in German-speaking countries vs. 31.13% in English-speaking countries) and the definition of key performance indicators (22.54% vs. 25.17%) are the most frequently mentioned **planning activities of Web Analysts**. In German-speaking countries the development of reporting concepts is listed significantly more often than in English-speaking countries (38.03% vs. 8.61%). Therefore, it can be indicated that Web Analytics is in German-speaking countries still in infancy, as this activity is specific for novices of Analytics. Only 5.83% of all companies explicitly mentioned the development of conversation rates as a working task of Web Analysts.

Analysis activities are the second-most frequently listed working tasks of Web Analysts (84.30%). Especially, analysis of visitor behaviour is considered to be very important in the job ads (50.70% in German-speaking countries vs. 65.56% in English-speaking countries). Furthermore, analysis of conversation rates (32.39% vs. 35.10%) and statistical testing (33.80% vs. 32.45%) are of relevance for job applicants. Monitoring of key performance indicators (26.76% vs. 34.44%) and analysis of marketing activities (23.94% vs. 30.46%) are also required in this task category.

Reporting activities are the working tasks that appear frequently in the job ads (85.2%). Hereby, the preparation of reports (70.85%) and the deduction of recommendations to act (58.74%) are mentioned very often compared to other activities. The preparation of dashboards seems to be more important in the English-speaking countries than in German-speaking countries (32.45% vs. 15.49%). This difference, as already explained, can be considered as an indicator for development stage of Web Analytics in German-speaking countries.

Optimization activities are less demanded compared to other categories (56.95%) although this category includes various important tasks of Web Analysts. This indicates the efficient use of financial resources and the increased need of coordination between the different online marketing channels. The optimization of conversation rates (23.94% in German-speaking countries vs. 35.76% in English-speaking countries) is the most notable optimization activity in this category. The optimization of the online marketing activities (21.97%) and the optimization of the website (18.83%) are less important, while search engine optimization (12.56%) and the control of the online budget (5.83%) are hardly mentioned in the job ads in both language areas.

Besides, there were also **other activities** listed in job ads which cannot be assigned to one of the Web Analytics process steps. In German and English-speaking countries the Web Analyst has a central communication role (48.83%) within the company, which indicates that companies are aware of interdisciplinary role and importance of Web Analysts. Moreover, data quality assurance plays a crucial role. Almost 30% of analyzed job ads listed data quality assurance (29.60%) as an important working task of Web Analysts. The implementation of Web Analytics software is also mentioned in many job ads (26.91%). Customer support and customer service (16.14%) as well as management activities (16.14%) are less expected tasks of Web Analysts.

5 Relevance and Implications for Human-Computer Interaction

Based on this job profile of Web Analysts the benefits of such experts for Human-Computer Interaction are elaborated along two dimensions. From a **practical perspective**, the usefulness of Web Analytics for usability engineers is examined according to their typically field of activities. With respect to literature [16] Web Analysts can be useful within the scope of formative and summative evaluation, i.e. if a user interface mock-up, a web-based prototype or a full-featured web application is available. Here, the expertise of Web Analysts for planning evaluation studies, analyzing results and creating reports seems to be particular benefits.

An analysis concept in combination with performance indicators might exhibit usability problems that cannot be identified through traditional usability engineering methods, like a heuristic evaluation of thinking aloud tests. According to the authors' opinion an Analytics approach should be even more sustainable for designing and evaluating user interfaces of software solutions, as they provide a framework and (domain-specific) indicators for HCI-relevant factors and enable repeated measurement of the performance. Concerning optimization concepts the qualifications of Web Analysts seems to be not that relevant – thus HCI has to rely on methods provided by software engineering and usability engineering.

From the **scientific perspective**, Web Analytics can be applied multi-disciplinary fields that include Human-Computer Interaction as a method to develop software systems or examine interactions of humans with computers. In this context, Web Analysts can be also useful due to their competencies concerning reporting and their social competencies. Amongst others, possible research areas in which Web Analysts can be supportive for HCI comprise e-commerce [17], online and social media marketing [18] and any other applied discipline that involves interactions between humans and computers. Similarly to HCI practice, Web Analysts can support scientists through different activities of the four process steps, e.g. in designing a research initiative, determining and measuring performance indicators, evaluating (web-based) prototypes and proposing improvements for both the research methodology and proto-typic software solution.

In both application areas Web Analytics is useful concerning **technology and hand-on skills** if HCI research includes user interactions with web-based tools and platforms. Hereby, scientists would benefit from various competencies of Web Analysts, like handling and analyzing data-sets, calculating (performance) indicators from data, planning data-driven research and design science activities [19].

6   Conclusions and Future Work

Taking into consideration the increasing importance of technology and digitalization in our society, this paper argues for the necessity of Web Analytics and professionals who fulfill the job requirements for this field. We have conducted a preliminary empirical study in order to characterize the profession of a Web Analyst on the basis of a data-set of international job advertisements. Hereby we identified various problematic issues, such as the unclear definition of the job title, the non-uniform integration of Web Analysts in companies or regional differences in the competency and task profiles of this profession.

On the other hand, we see clear advantages for companies and HCI-related activities if Web Analysts can be involved. Most notably, the job profile we elaborated on the basis of our job advertisement analysis indicates that professional Web Analysts can be beneficial in planning HCI activities and measuring their performance. Moreover, they can be supportive within initiatives that deal with or aim at developing web-based software tools, in particular in design science approaches which are very common in applied science. Overall, Web Analytics is considered to be relevant for HCI, as it aims at understanding usage behavior of web users and, thus, can lead to valuable results for HCI designers, evaluators and researchers.

In order to validate our findings, it would be necessary to note down the improvements of HCI activities suggested by Web Analysts or to compare the performance of HCI procedures that involve a dedicated Web Analytics expert to those that are conducted by regular HCI experts (i.e., single and double specialists [10]). It is worth mentioning that for the latter case – comparative studies about Analytics-enhanced HCI – Web Analysts can be beneficial for defining and measuring performance indicators of activities and processes. Moreover, we would like to argue for the involvement of Web Analysts in the context of (web-based) digital ecosystems due to the data-driven and dynamic nature of such systems. Finally, and as part of future work, we see a clear need for developing methods and metrics for Analytics-enhanced HCI.

References

1. Kumar, L., Singh, H., Kaur, R.: Web Analytics and Metrics: A Survey. In: ICACCI 2012, pp. 966–971 (2012)
2. Nakatani, K., Chuang, T.T.: A web analytics tool selection method: an analytical hierarchy process approach. Internet Research 21(2), 171–186 (2010)

3. Delone, W., McLean, E.: Measuring e-commerce success: applying the Delone & McLean information systems success model. International Journal of Electronic Commerce 9(1), 31–47 (2004)

4. Pakkala, H., Presser, K., Christensen, T.: Using Google Analytics to measure visitor statistics: The case of food composition websites. International Journal of Information Management 32(6), 504–512 (2012)

5. Zumstein, D., Züger, D., Meier, A.: Web Analytics im Unternehmen – Empirische Untersuchung über den Einsatz, Nutzen und die Probleme im deutschsprachigen Raum, Université de Fribourg, Fribourg (2011),
http://diuf.unifr.ch/main/is/sites/diuf.unifr.ch.main.is/
files/documents/research/resultate_web_analytics_umfrage.pdf
(last access: February 05, 2014)

6. Digital Analytics Association: The Official DAA Definition of Web Analytics (2006),
http://www.digitalanalyticsassociation.org/?page=aboutus
(last access: May 22, 2013)

7. Park, J., Kim, J.J., Koh, J.: Determinants of continuous usage intention in web analytics services. Electronic Commerce Research and Application 9(1), 61–72 (2010)

8. Weischedel, B., Huizingh, E.: Website optimization with web metrics: a case study. In: Proceedings of the 8th International Conference on Electronic Commerce, pp. 463–470 (2006)

9. Hewett, T.T., Baecker, R., Card, S., Carey, T., Mantei, M., Perlmann, G., Strong, G., Verplank, W.: ACM SIGCHI Curricula for Human-Computer Interaction. ACM, New York (2009), http://old.sigchi.org/cdg/ (last access: February 05, 2014)

10. Andrews, K.: Human-Computer Interaction. Lecturer Notes, Graz University of Technology, Graz (2013), http://courses.iicm.tugraz.at/hci/ (last access: February 05, 2014)

11. Chi, E.H.: Improving Website usability through visualization. Internet Computing 6(2), 64–71 (2002)

12. Hasan, L., Morris, A., Probets, S.: Using Google Analytics to Evaluate the Usability of E-Commerce Sites. In: Kurosu, M. (ed.) HCD 2009. LNCS, vol. 5619, pp. 697–706. Springer, Heidelberg (2009)

13. Black, L.: Web Analytics: A Picture of Academic Library Web Site User. Journal of Journal of Web Librarianship 3(1), 3–14 (2009)

14. Blackmore, P.: A categorisation of approaches to occupational analysis. Journal of Vocational Education & Training 51(1), 61–78 (1999)

15. Grob, H.L., Lange, W.: Zum Wandel des Berufsbildes bei Wirtschaftsinformatikern: Eine empirische Analyse auf Basis von Stellenanzeigen. Arbeitsberichte des Institutes für Wirtschaftsinformatik, Westfälische Wilhelms-Universität Münster, Münster (1995)

16. Andrews, K.: Evaluation Comes in Many Guises. In: Proceedings of the CHI 2008 Workshop: Beyond Time and Errors: Novel Evaluation Methods for Information Visualization (2008)

17. Schefels, C., Eschenberg, S., Schoneberger, C.: Behavioral Analysis of Registered Web Site Visitors with Help of Mouse Tracking. In: Proceedings of the 14th International Conference on Commerce and Enterprise Computing, pp. 33–40 (2012)

18. Leskovec, J.: Social media analytics: tracking, modeling and predicting the flow of information through networks. In: Proceedings of the 20th International Conference Companion on World Wide Web, pp. 277–278 (2011)

19. Hevner, A., March, S., Park, J., Ram, S.: Design science in information systems research. MIS Quarterly 28(1), 75–105 (2004)

Persuasive Web Design in e-Commerce

Hsi-Liang Chu[1,2], Yi-Shin Deng[3], and Ming-Chuen Chuang[4]

[1] Department of Marketing and Logistics Management,
Minghsin University of Science and Technology, Xinfeng Hsinchu, Taiwan
[2] Institute of Applied Arts, National Chiao Tung University, Hsinchu, Taiwan
[3] Center of Innovation and Synergy for Intelligent Home and Living Technology,
National Taiwan University, Taipei City 100, Taiwan
[4] Institute of Applied Arts, National Chiao Tung University, Hsinchu, Taiwan
chu@must.edu.tw, yishin.deng@gmail.com,
cming@faculty.nctu.edu.tw

Abstract. This research is to investigate what persuasive tactics are utilized by current e-commerce Web sites, how consumers react to the persuasive triggers on e-commerce Web sites, and what about the relative importance of the salient persuasive factors that are salient to online consumers. A total of 15 persuasive tactics and 9 salient factors were identified from the data of Web site reviews and user interviews. The AHP analysis revealed that the persuasive factors appealing to a site's credibility and logic are more important than appealing to users' emotions.

Keywords: persuasive design, e-commerce, Web design.

1   Introduction

Web sites is an important medium that facilitates online transactions. The design of an e-commerce Web site plays an important role in its success [6]. Researchers have suggested that while usability is still important for effective Web site design, it is no longer the key differentiator. A successful e-commerce Web site should be able to inspire their customers' trust, engage them, and persuade them to buy products or services. [1, 5, 9, 10]

This research is to investigate what persuasive tactics are utilized on current e-commerce Web sites, how consumers react to the persuasive triggers on e-commerce Web sites, and what about the relative importance of the persuasive factors that are salient to online consumers.

2   Related Research

A broad range of persuasion principles have been identified. Cialdini [2] argued that many tendencies to comply with another's request can be explained in terms of six principles of influence: reciprocity, commitment and consistency, social proof,

F.F.-H. Nah (Ed.): HCIB/HCII 2014, LNCS 8527, pp. 482–491, 2014.
© Springer International Publishing Switzerland 2014

scarcity, liking, and authority. These principles serve as rules of thumb that assist in decision making. Fogg [3] focused on human-computer interaction and describes more than forty principles. His framework, the functional triad, shows that interactive technologies can operate in three ways: as tools, as media, and as social actors. Oinas-Kukkonen and Harjumaa [7] adopted and modified Fogg's framework in their Persuasive System Design (PSD) model and listed twenty-eight principles for persuasive system content and functionality. Their principles are grouped into four categories: primary task support, dialogue support, system credibility support, and social support. Winn and Beck [11] argued that e-commerce sites and the design elements from which they are built serve a classic rhetorical function: they are means of persuading potential customers to explore, to interact, and ultimately to reach the act of purchasing. They examined how design elements on an e-commerce Web site carry out the rhetorical function of persuasion, and suggested that the way design elements are presented on a site affects their persuasive power. Besides, the visual manifestations of price, variety, product information, effort, playfulness, tangibility, empathy, recognizability, compatibility, assurance, and reliability are among those persuasive triggers in e-commerce Web design. Weinschenk [10] applied the research on motivation, decision-making, and neuroscience to the Web design and presented the concept of Neuro Web Design. She argued that several principles, such as invoking scarcity, using pictures and stories, and speaking to the unconscious mind, can be applied to make Web sites more persuasive and take users from 'can do' to 'will do' and 'still do'. Jones [5] highlighted the importance of content and argued that content should not be excluded from the discussion of persuasive design and must have a central role in planning, executing, and evaluating a persuasive experience. Chak [1] described that 'persuasive web sites guide users by providing good navigational usability, they educate users on how to make an informed choice, they allow users to be motivated by eliminating any qualms about trust and security…In short, persuasive web sites remove barriers and motivate users toward transaction.'

3   Study 1: E-Commerce Web Sites Review

3.1   Method

Study 1 was to explore what important persuasive tactics are leveraged by current e-commerce Web sites. We selected six most popular shopping Web sites in Taiwan and 10 most frequently browsed product categories from the data provided by a convenience sample of 32 online shoppers. For each selected Web site, we chose 10 Web pages for investigation, including the home page, two category pages, three product pages that promote products of the most frequently browsed categories, one registration page, one instruction page, and two checkout pages. Therefore, a total of 60 Web pages were reviewed. Based on the literature, we identified 33 persuasive tactics for Web investigation. The selected Web pages were then reviewed feature-by-feature with the list of the 33 persuasive tactics.

3.2   Results

The six popular shopping Web sites selected in this study were:

- `http://buy.yahoo.com.tw`
- `http://www.pcstore.com.tw`
- `http://www.momoshop.com.tw`
- `http://books.com.tw`
- `http://www.7net.com.tw`
- `http://www.lativ.com.tw`

The most frequently browsed product categories were clothing, bags, shoes, mobile phones, digital cameras, foods, skin care, stationery, tour packages, and articles for babies.

From our results, a total of 15 prominent and often seen persuasive triggers were identified. They were *reduction, tailoring, personalization, rewards, reminder, suggestion, similarity, attractiveness, trustworthiness, surface credibility, third-party endorsements, social proof, scarcity, real-world feel,* and *tunneling.* The followings describe how these tactics were utilized and manifested:

- *Reduction* was used to reduce users' efforts and enable them to navigate easily and search successfully. Example manifestations were product categorization, search boxes, winnowing tools, and sorting tools.
- *Tailoring* was used to provide particular information for different users groups. Example implementation was categorizing the products based on users' characteristics, rather than product attributes, and presenting product information for particular user groups such as office girls, electronics hobbyist, and housewives.
- *Personalization* was used to provide information or services for specific individual. Example implementations were elements of 'Recently Viewed Items', shopping cart, member preference, and the setting of 'Security Stamp.'
- *Rewards* were used to motivate users to register or to buy by offering gifts or price preference. Marketing programs that offer welcome gifts for new members, discounts for those who buy in bulk, reward point accumulation for frequent buyers, benefits for higher grades of membership, were commonplace. Somewhat surprisingly, *reciprocity* was not found on the pages investigated.
- *Reminder* was used to remind user of or call user's attention to certain target behavior. For example, when a user login, the system will display how much the user should spend more to get a membership upgrade. Another example was to repeatedly display certain information, such as a new service announcement or the information about a marketing campaign, on the screen to catch users' attention.
- *Suggestion* was used to present message to guide the thoughts or behaviors of the users. For example, on the registration page, system would suggest re-setting a stronger password when an account was created with a less secure password. The 'People Who Bought This Item Also Bought' feature on the checkout pages was another example of implementing *suggestion.*

- *Similarity* was used to remind users of themselves in some meaningful ways so as to establish rapport and create likability. Example implementations were to embed the fashionable topics, popular expressions, or emoticons in the titles, copies, or content of product information.
- *Attractiveness* was used to draw users' attention and create favorable impressions. Example implementations were to present a professional Web design look, an eye-catching title, large and high quality photos, and a beautiful model or famous spokesperson.
- *Trustworthiness* is to capture the perceived goodness or morality of the vender or Web site. Example implementations were to highlight the security and privacy policies and present logos of reputed brands on the Web site.
- *Surface credibility* relied on a site's overall look and feel and surface features for giving the impression that the site is believable and competent. Most of the sites under investigation were clear, uncluttered, and looked professionally designed. It was observable that none of the selected sites had remarkable problems with surface credibility.
- *Third-party endorsements* means to solicit recommendation or testimonial from an entity other than the manufacturer and seller of a product. Example implementations were to display seals of certificate secured transaction on the Web site or place seals of product certification on the product pages.
- *Social proof* means to persuade by showing the user what other people are doing on their Web sites. The 'Number of items sold' indicator and customer feedback on the product pages were examples of implementing *social proof.*
- *Scarcity* was used to create shopper urgency. 'Limited quantities' and 'expiration date' indicators were the most common implementations.
- *Real-world feel* means to increase the site's credibility by showing the people or organization behind the site. Most of our selected shopping Web site have detailed company profiles and contact information on the pages of 'About us.'
- *Tunneling* means guiding the user by leading him/her through a predefined sequence of actions. Prominent examples can be found at the pages of registration, checkout, and user's guide.

The results of the Web site review revealed that a persuasive trigger can be as simple as a single icon, a button, a label, or a line of text; it can be as complex as a combination of multiple interactive elements (such as incorporating pull-down menu within the breadcrumbs trail) or even a mechanism crossing several pages. In addition, same design element can be used to implement different persuasive tactics at the same time.

From the perspective of persuasive tactics implementation, *tailoring, rewards, similarity, third-party endorsements, social proof, scarcity,* and *real-world feel* are mainly related to content design; *attractiveness* and *surface credibility* are mainly related to appearance design; *tunneling* is mainly related to functionality design; *personalization, reminder,* and *suggestion* are mainly related to content and functionality design; *reduction* is mainly related to functionality and usability design; and *trustworthiness* is mainly related to appearance and content design.

4   Study 2: User Research

4.1   Method

Study 2 was to understand online shoppers' reactions and experiences in response to the persuasive triggers on the Web sites when shopping online. We conducted a series of semi-structured field interviews with 12 experienced online shoppers (7 females and 5 males ranging in age from 21 to 33). The interviews mainly addressed, but not limited to, the persuasive tactics identified in the Study 1. The interview questions included "How do you assess the persuasiveness of a shopping Web site?", "What is your favorite shopping Web site? Why?", "Do you think the tactics (on our list) can persuade you to take such actions as registering, browsing, buying, or revisiting? Why or why not?", "How do you assess the persuasiveness of the tactics (on our list)?", and "Please describe your online experiences of being persuaded to make unplanned purchases?" The data obtained from the interviews were recorded, transcribed, and then interpreted.

4.2   Results

The followings are a number of important findings from the results of our interviews:

- While most of the participants felt alright with the site look, site organization, product categorization, and customer services of current shopping Web sites, several participants indicated need for better winnowing and more intelligent search tools. How to successfully locate a desired product and make purchase decisions seemed to be their most important concerns.
- When participants had no specific product to look for, they relied on site brand, site look, navigation design, and photos quality to assess a shopping site's overall persuasiveness. When they had something to look for, product variety, product price, product information, and search functions became dominant persuasive factors. If a Web site is not easy to use or cannot guide them through the processes of registration or checkout, they were more likely to abandon the shopping process or even discard the site. Usability seems to be a hygiene factor and is not enough to motivate users to make a purchase.
- Most of the participants did not make good use of the personalized services that required users to login for identification. They preferred entering personal data at the stage of checkout.
- Though tailored content was recognized to be able to make product search faster and give the impression of benevolence and respect, users treated the tailored content as merely another ordinary product categorization and were not sure that the content was tailored to their needs and interests.
- Though we did not find examples of using *reciprocity* on the selected sites, most of the participants indicated that they did not feel obligated to return favors performed for them, meaning that the principle of *Reciprocity* was not so compelling in the B2C context. However, when shoppers were interested in or considering buying a

specific product, messages indicating that there are some rewards offered or the product is running out would become the last push to motivate them to take buying actions. About half of our participants inclined to buy or buy more due to vendors' rewards programs or the scarcity of the products.

- For some participants, showing them an unavailable but interesting product can decrease their trust in the vender as well as the Web site. Nevertheless, for other participants, "Sold Out" or "Coming Soon" indicators add credibility to the other scarcity warnings and add a sense of urgency to the shopping process.
- *Reminders* were found helpful when used to notify shoppers of something important or personally related. However, they would be considered annoying when used as tools of product promotion.
- Participants were interested in viewing the product information suggested by 'People Who Bought (or Viewed) This Item Also Bought (or Viewed)…' The information of 'Best Sellers Ranking' also worked well in raising users' interests. However, the product groups labeled as 'Hot Sales' or 'Recommended by the shop-owner' appeared to fail in attracting users to browse the detailed information. Knowing what products are really popular seemed to be important for users to make purchase decisions.
- Younger participants appeared to be more susceptible to the title or product descriptions that contain fashionable topics or popular expressions. Female participants tended to pay more attention to the product photos of beautiful models or spokespersons. Salient texts and big photos that deliver nice and beautiful visuals can attract users' attention. However, the labels with vaunted writing and the advertisement with exaggerated copy were loathsome to all of the participants.
- Most of the participants indicated that using multiple persuasive tactics, such as *scarcity*, *social proof*, and *rewards* at the same time would be more likely to affect their attitudes or behaviors than using any of them individually.
- The page layout with clean and minimal design was positively related to a site's surface credibility. Though error information may affect a site's credibility, participants seemed not too care about the typos or small mistakes in the product descriptions as long as they were not made at prices and did not occur very often.
- *Third party endorsements* appeared to be effective to build consumers' initial trust towards unfamiliar Web sites, products, or vendors. The expert endorsements were useful in promoting health-related products while celebrity endorsements worked well with the clothing and accessories. Moreover, participants who though themselves as rational buyers would emphasize the celebrities' credibility rather than their attractiveness.
- There is a mismatch between what people say is important and what they actually do. For example, though users claimed that security and privacy protection are vital elements in evaluating a site's trustworthiness, they almost never referred to the site's policies about security or privacy. In addition, many of them were not able to recognize the seals of secured transaction.
- *Social proof* was a powerful tool in promoting 3C products such as mobile phones and digital cameras because it is an implied testimonial. However, for products that manifest individuality, using the tactic of *social proof* may result in opposite of the

intended effect. For example, the shoppers who don't like to wear the same kind of clothes as others may consult the *social proof* information and avoid buying the hot selling clothes.

- When users considered buying high-priced, experience-type, or unfamiliar products, they would spend more time to scrutinize the product descriptions and other customers' comments/ratings about the products of similar categories. We also found that free riding, i.e. buying from a shopping Web site other than the primary source of product information, occurs more often for high-priced products.
- As experienced online shoppers, our participants were confident in purchasing online. Though they were unaware that there are so many persuasive tactics embedded in the interface when interacting with the Web site, they did not feel themselves to be gullible and easily persuaded. Showing people or organization behind the content or service to create a *real-world feel* about the venders seemed not to be so important. An e-mail address and a phone number would be fine for them.
- By and large, the participants felt that the current shopping Web sites were more like online brochures or catalogues of the company's products rather than instruments of persuasion.

According to [11], knowing factors that are salient to users as they form attitudes and intentions to online shopping can help demystify the process of how a persuasive tactic can affect the users. Based on the findings of this study, we identified *usability, product information, premium, scarcity, social conformity, visual appeal, tailoring/personalization, reassurance,* and *reliability* as the salient persuasive factors that may influence the persuasive power of a shopping Web site. While some of these factors, such as premium determination and reassurance policy making, are beyond the scope of design, we believe that their perceptions are shaped by how they are presented on the Web site.

5   Study 3: Importance Ranking for the Persuasive Factors

5.1   Method

Study 3 aimed at assessing the level of importance of the salient persuasive factors that may influence online shoppers' attitudes as well as behaviors. Previous research suggested that dividing elements into categories allows for a better assessment of their importance [12]. According to [11], the persuasive means of *logos* (appeal to logic), *pathos* (appeal to the emotions), and *ethos* (appeal to credibility) in classical rhetoric are suitable for categorizing the persuasive factors. Therefore, in measuring the relative importance of the persuasive factors using Analytic Hierarchy Process (AHP) method [8], the hierarchy was established by categorizing the persuasive factors within those three means of persuasion.

Five judges participated in a pretest to group the persuasive factors by assigning each of the nine factors into one of the three categories of *logos, pathos,* and *ethos.* The judges consisted of five experts in e-commerce, business planning, marketing, Web design, and advertising.

The pair-wise comparisons for the elements in the hierarchy were conducted with 13 participants (7 females and 6 males with 4-6 years of experiences in online shopping). The comparisons were based on a nine-point relational scale of importance. After checking for inconsistencies, two respondents were excluded, giving a response rate of 0.846.

5.2   Results

The reliability of agreement in the pretest was calculated using the measure of Fleiss' Kappa [13]. The resulting estimate of $k = 0.651$ indicated that there was a substantial agreement among the judges. According to the results of the pretest, we can attribute the persuasive power of an online shopping Web site to the persuasive means of *logos*, *pathos*, and *ethos*. The *logos* dimension is dependent on the factors of premium, usability, and product information; the *pathos* dimension is dependent on the factors of attractiveness, scarcity, personalization, and social conformity; and the *ethos* dimension is dependent on the factors of reassurance and reliability. Fig. 1 depicts the hierarchy for the persuasive factors.

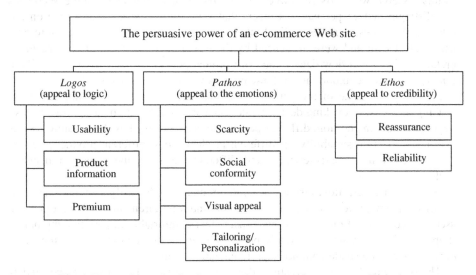

Fig. 1. Factors hierarchy for the persuasive power of e-commerce Web sites

Table 2 illustrates the AHP results of the importance weighting as well as ranking for the persuasive factors. The aggregated weights were obtained by calculating the geometric means of the individual pair-wise comparisons. All of the consistency indices (*C.I.*) and consistency ratios (*C.R.*) were below 0.1, indicating that the judgments were acceptable. As shown in Table 2, the weights of importance for the salient persuasive factors in sequence were: reassurance (22.9%), reliability (22.5%), premium (17.2%), usability (11.7%), product information (7.9%), visual appeal (6.2%), scarcity (5.0%), tailoring/personalization (4.6%), and social conformity (2.0%). The results also revealed that appealing to credibility (45.3%) and logic (36.7%) are more important than appealing to the emotions (17.9%).

Table 1. The weights and ranking of the importance of salient persuasive factors

Dimension	Weights	Persuasive factors	Weights (global)	Ranking (global)	Consistency test	
Appeal to logic	0.367	Usability	0.117	4	$\lambda_{max} = 3.002$	
		Product information	0.079	5	$C.I. = 0.001$	
		Premium	0.172	3	$C.R. = 0.002$	$\lambda_{max} = 3.001$
Appeal to emotions	0.179	Scarcity	0.050	7		
		Social conformity	0.020	9	$\lambda_{max} = 4.016$	$C.I. = 0.000$
		Visual appeal	0.062	6	$C.I. = 0.005$ $C.R. = 0.006$	
		Personalization	0.046	8		$C.R. = 0.001$
Appeal to credibility	0.453	Reassurance	0.229	1	$\lambda_{max} = 2$	
		Reliability	0.225	2	$C.I. = 0$ $C.R. = 0$	

6   Discussion

In this research we firstly reviewed 60 Web pages of 6 popular shopping Web sites and distinguished 15 persuasive triggers that were prominent and often seen on our selected Web sites. A series of field interviews were then conducted to explore how users coped with and were influenced by these persuasion attempts. From the interpretation of the interview data, a total of 9 salient persuasive factors were identified. Finally, the relative importance of these persuasive factors was assessed.

As indicated, some of the persuasive tactics are effective in grabbing attention, peaking interests, or evoking desire, while some are useful in motivating users to take buying actions. In addition, different persuasive tactics as well as their manifestations may have different suitability for different product types, different product price levels, different user characteristics, and different stages in the consumer decision cycle.

Wide product selection, fast and accurate product search, easily used interface, and security/privacy protection appeared to be minimum requirements to form a positive users attitude toward the site and make users feel comfortable in participating online shopping. However, what can really persuade users to buy and revisit the sites is to provide more value added but not superficial enticements.

The shopping Web sites investigated in our study should have more deeper understanding of their users, reach those who are interested in the products or services of the sites, remove their barriers, accommodate them with better tailored content and personalized services, and help them make informed choice so as to motivate them toward transaction.

7   Conclusion

Every Web site has its purpose. Persuasive design pushes designers to clearly define a Web site's purpose and its persuasion objectives. Armed with insights from our study, designers of e-commerce Web sites can be able to make more informed choices to enhance their sites' appeal and attain their persuasion objectives. Future researches may include: (1) addressing the best practices of implementing persuasive tactics, (2) quantitatively examining the persuasive power of the persuasive tactics, (3) investigating the persuasiveness of combining multiple persuasive tactics, (4) exploring the implementations of other persuasive tactics, and (5) investigating how persuasive techniques are applied to other types of Web sites.

References

1. Chak, A.: Submit now: Designing persuasive Web sites. New Riders, Indianapolis (2002)
2. Cialdini, R.B.: Influence: Science and practice, 4th edn. HarperCollins, New York (2001)
3. Fogg, B.J.: Persuasive technology: Using computers to change what we think and do. Morgan Kaufmann Publishers, San Francisco (2003)
4. Horvath, J.: Persuasive Design: It's Not Just about Selling Stuff. In: Marcus, A. (ed.) HCII 2011 and DUXU 2011, Part II. LNCS, vol. 6770, pp. 567–574. Springer, Heidelberg (2011)
5. Jones, C.: Clout: The Role of Content in Persuasive Experience. In: Marcus, A. (ed.) HCII 2011 and DUXU 2011, Part II. LNCS, vol. 6770, pp. 582–587. Springer, Heidelberg (2011)
6. Nathan, J.N.: Crucial web usability factors of 36 industries for students: a large-scale empirical study. Electron Commerce Research 11(2), 151–180 (2010)
7. Oinas-Kukkonen, H., Harjumaa, M.: Persuasive Systems Design: Key Issues, Process Model, and System Features. Communications of the Association for Information Systems 24(1), 28, 485–500 (2009)
8. Saaty, T.L.: The Analytic Hierarchy Process. McGraw-Hill, New York (1980)
9. Schaffer, E.: Beyond Usability: Designing Web Sites for Persuasion, Emotion, and Trust, http://www.uxmatters.com/mt/archives/2009/01/beyond-usability-designing-web-sites-for-persuasion-emotion-and-trust.php
10. Weinschenk, S.M.: Neuro web design: what makes them click?. New Riders, Berkeley (2009)
11. Winn, W., Beck, K.: The persuasive power of design elements on an e-commerce web site. Technical Communication 49(1), 17–35 (2002)
12. Lepkowska-White, E., Eifler, A.: Spinning the Web: The Interplay of Web Design Features and Product Types. Journal of Website Promotion 3(3/4), 196–212 (2008)
13. Fleiss, J.L.: Measuring nominal scale agreement among many raters. Psychological Bulletin 76(5), 378 (1971)

Creating Competitive Advantage in IT-Intensive Organizations: A Design Thinking Perspective

Alma L. Culén[1] and Mark Kriger[2]

[1] Department of Informatics, University of Oslo, Oslo, Norway
almira@ifi.uio.no
[2] Department of Strategy and Logistics, Norwegian Business School, Oslo, Norway
mark.kriger@bi.no

Abstract. In this paper, we consider the role of design thinking and human computer interaction design (HCID) in shaping conditions for a long-term health of technology intensive organizations. Design thinking is gaining acceptance in management, strategy and leadership and is increasingly seen as a way towards finding solutions to complex problems of today's economy. We present our view on relationships between HCID and design thinking on one hand, and creative leadership, vision, values, knowledge and organizational culture on the other, as factors in shaping the competitive advantage for IT-intensive organizations. We find that, while HCID is systematically contributing to design of innovative technological solutions, it does so at a micro level, while design thinking holds a central position in our competitive advantage framework. Through a small case of innovation in the academic library, we provide insight in how design thinking and HCID facilitated changes in how the library sees its users, products, services and how it, subsequently, started changing its organizational vision, values, culture and knowledge.

Keywords: design thinking, strategy, HCI design, innovation, academic library, competitive advantage.

1 Introduction

The academic discourse around design thinking has started more than twenty years ago [35]. However, during the last few years the discourse has turned into a multidisciplinary discussion focusing first on design thinking in innovation [6], and then broadening to the field of economy, touching in particular management [30], strategy [19], and leadership [28].

Information technology (IT) is an essential element of the infrastructure of competitive economies and a key enabler of sustainable economic growth. However, IT no longer evokes images of computers or supercomputers, but of all the computational power they had at a fingertip of some mobile device. Computational ability and bandwidths are something few think of these days. Business value of technology is now more bound to capability of the leadership to invent new processes, procedures and organizational structures that utilize potential of these new technologies [7].

F.F.-H. Nah (Ed.): HCIB/HCII 2014, LNCS 8527, pp. 492–503, 2014.
© Springer International Publishing Switzerland 2014

Researchers in economics investigated the relation between economic growth of a nation and how close the nation is to the technological frontier. In, for example, [1], the authors analyzed a range of issues related to technological progress and economic growth. They conclude that economies that are far from the technological frontier, favor investment-based growth strategies, while closer to the frontier, the value of innovation based strategies increases. On the other hand, Cairncross [10] claims that technology may accomplish one thing globally: it may reduce distances and enable truly global businesses, and ultimately, a true global economy. Technologies are, and will, continually evolve and improve, but they, according to Cairncross, were already at the beginning of this century good enough to enable speculations around their potential to influence whole economies and societies.

Design thinking and technological advancement are thus moving economies towards innovation-based strategies. There are various ways to define innovation. Oslo Manual [27] defines it as: *"the implementation of a new or significantly improved product (good, or service) or process, a new marketing method, or a new organizational method in business practices, workplace organization, or external relations."*

In line with [6, 26, 28, 30], we consider design thinking as a paradigm changer in innovation.

In this paper, we discuss just how design thinking introduces the change and affects long-term innovation. It is known that, while easy to understand the need for innovation and the benefits it brings, innovation is hard to achieve in practice [31]. Does and how design thinking changes this? The paper presents the case of innovation at the university library, and the role of design thinking in that process. This process has, at its start, applied design thinking through design practice and development of new products and services by human-computer interaction design (HCID) students [12], then evolved to engage also employees [11], and finally, leadership, enabling organizational changes that foster long-term focus on innovation. The change was very much bottom-up, powered up by design thinking and designerly practices as understood by HCI designers, and not design thinkers from design disciplines. Our case differs from, for example, that of Procter & Gamble [25, 30] that became a flagship for arguing in favor of design thinking, where a visionary leader introduced and enforced design thinking in the company, with remarkable results. However, we hope that discussion of the case will help provide an empirical study which, together with other similar ones, would lead towards increasing academic understanding of how design thinking is used in practice and how it facilitates innovation, and creation of competitive advantage.

In line with [26], we believe that involving collaborative, multidisciplinary teams in innovation processes is a great way to create new opportunities for organizations. Collaboration in science, across disciplines, has its challenges, and results may not be repeatable [41]. Including design thinkers in collaborative efforts, might change this situation. Our experience from the library case indicates that it just might be so. The power of design thinking comes, in part, from its ability to synthesize different views, and activities in related processes are often experienced as positive and valuable.

In other words, it builds teams that are capable of overcoming differences, both individual and disciplinary.

The paper is structured as follows: in Section 2, we discuss design thinking and design thinkers and draw some parallels and differences from HCI and HCI designers. In Section 3, we set up the stage leading towards our framework for gain of competitive advantage for technologically intensive organizations based on creative leadership, vision, values, knowledge and development of exploration based organizational culture as factors. In Section 4, we present our framework, where both HCID and design thinking are factors. Section 5 presents the case of user driven innovation in the academic library and Section 6 short discussion and conclusion.

2   Design Thinking and HCI

In [6], Brown defined design thinking as *"a discipline that uses the designer's sensibility and methods to match people's needs with what is technologically feasible and what a viable business strategy can convert into customer value and market opportunity."* Thus, design thinking emerged as a multidisciplinary, human-centered approach to innovation. So what does it takes to become a design thinker?

Martin [30] explicates that everyone can work on becoming a design thinker. In order to become a design thinker one needs a stance, tools and experience that facilitate design thinking. The stance is related to one's worldview and the role one has in it, tools are the mental models used to understand the world and organize thinking, while experience is needed for building of skills and sensitivities. This implies that one becomes a keen observer and finder of opportunities for design that could help reduce complexities of large, global problems such as poverty, health care, energy, education etc. [42].

Kolko, [21], provides an explicit relationship between design thinking and wicked problems:

> *"A wicked problem is a social or cultural problem that is difficult or impossible to solve for as many as four reasons: incomplete or contradictory knowledge, the number of people and opinions involved, the large economic burden, and the interconnected nature of these problems with other problems. Poverty is linked with education, nutrition with poverty, the economy with nutrition, and so on. ... These problems can be mitigated through the process of design, which is an intellectual approach that emphasizes empathy, abductive reasoning, and rapid prototyping."*

Even this minimal selection of two definitions shows how the work of a design thinker may require different set of skills, yet both Martin and Kolko agree that these skills are suitable for tackling complex 'real world problems', such as the ones listed above. Faced with enormity of this task, we then asked ourselves the question: what is it that design thinking can actually do? A lot of scholarly work on design thinking in managerial realm was already reviewed and presented in [20]. The authors sort through what design thinking can be used for, instead of focusing on what it is:

"As social constructionists we regard an approach that begins with the question, 'What is design thinking?' as an essentialist trap. We do not believe that there is a unique meaning of 'design thinking', and accordingly we should not look for one. Instead, we look for where and how the concept is used in different situations, both theoretical and practical, and what meaning is given to the concept", [20, p. 12].

The authors also include an important discussion on the role of design research and designerly practices with core concepts which include reflexive practice [36], meaning making and designerly ways of knowing [8].

The discourse involving the above concepts can also be seen as central for many HCID practitioners and researchers. HCI is no longer a field whose main concern is the interaction between a human and a computer, with a goal of making a better fit between the two [37]. The focus has broadened to include shaping diverse technologies for the use by people, focusing on a much broader aspects of interaction, including user experience design, design of services, environments, ecologies and systems. As a discipline, HCI is relevant for all IT-facilitated organizations, although they may differ in their use of HCI methods and tools. For example, how Apple Inc. and Microsoft design their operating systems is in a stark contrast: while Microsoft makes good use of users' feedback and users' experience, Apple is secretive about how their products are tested and improved [18].

There is a general trend in HCI to include more design-oriented practices and design thinking, see, for example, [16]. One of the authors of this paper, has explored introducing design thinking and designerly practices in project oriented teaching of HCI [13, 14], mainly in order to enable students to bridge the gap between 'finding' and 'making' [33], e.g., understanding intellectually and using making (prototyping) to explore possible solutions by visualizing them. Most people, depending on their sensory-motor makeup, environment and, in particular, education, develop preference for either finding or making. Engaging both makers and finders in collaborative innovation may indeed open some new possibilites.

Winograd and Klemmer, discussing now famous d.school at Stanford, an innovation hub with a core in innovation through design and HCID, say:

"The basic premise of the d.school is that students need two complementary kinds of training. The disciplinary training provided by conventional departments provides them with depth in the concepts and experience of a specific field. This gives them intellectual tools, but often misses the larger context of relevance and integration with other kinds of knowledge, which are required to innovate effectively in the 'real world'", [7, p. 1].

The school's basic model of collaboration is centered in design thinking, but includes fields of business, technology and human values.

In our view, design thinking and HCID are complementary when it comes to the new product development. Many HCID practitioners are also moving into the area of service design, thus bringing HCI as a field closer to business and innovation. HCI designers still retain their finding paradigm as the dominant one, which makes them valued members of collaborative teams when designing technology, or discussing its feasibility. In addition, many of the tools used in HCID trade are very similar to those of design thinkers, such as rapid prototyping. In addition, HCI designers have a very rich specter of user involvement tools and techniques in research and design. As we see it, the most important distinction between a design thinker and an HCI designer is how they view their work domain. While for a design thinker, the complexities of the 'real world' are the focus, the HCI designer have a lot more modest domain of developing innovative technological products and services.

3   Design Thinking and Competitive Advantage for IT-Intensive Organizations

The information-technology intensive organizations in industries that were previously quite separate are now rapidly converging on the same competitive spaces [22]. This is resulting in a 'dance of the elephants' – firms such as Amazon, Facebook, Google, eBay, Apple, Microsoft and Samsung that did not even exist 30 years ago or were a small start-ups and quite agile, have become large and increasingly hobbled in their agility by the sheer size and scope of their products and/or services [22]. As Porter notes, advanced technology or innovations are not by themselves enough to make these industries attractive or unattractive: *"Mundane, low technology industries with price-intensive buyers, ..., are often far more profitable then sexy industries, such as software and internet technologies, that attract competitors"*, [34, p. 22].

These IT-intensive organizations have in the past used traditional ways to expand, by either exploiting known technology on new markets, or by developing new technology for established markets. However, when one grows to the size of these global giants, there are scarcely new markets to win. One way of remaining innovative for these firms is to develop innovative services and other offerings, as well as providing ways of creating other values in addition to profit [23], for either the organization, or its customers. As competition, and thus competitive advantage, is still a central concept in economy, we look into factors that lead to gaining competitive advantage over rivals.

According to Porter, competitive advantage arises from leadership:

> "[Organizations] *must recognize the central role of innovation – and the uncomfortable truth that innovation grows out of pressure and challenge. It takes leadership to create a dynamic, challenging environment. And it takes leadership to recognize the all-too-easy escape routes that appear to offer a path to competitive advantage..."* [34, p. 207].

In the process of becoming 'elephants', Apple, Microsoft, Facebook and other afore-mentioned companies had some rather exceptional leaders (e.g., Jobs, Gates, Zuckerberg), who also had a strong organizational vision.

In [24], Larwood et al. have conclusion their study proposing that vision is multidimensional, with factors for vision being formulation, implementation and innovative realism. Vision may start with "I have a dream", where one clearly sees the goal in the future, and that is important. Being capable of implementing the vision often requires innovation. Pointing back to Cairncross [10], in IT facilitated organizations, technology has been more than powerful these last years, for further growth of the organization and gaining the competitive advantage one needs innovative processes. A good example [17, p. 12] is how Apple created a new concept in the consumer's mind, and new relationships between its products, e.g., iPhone and iTunes or Apps Store.

Competitive advantage also grows from the particular, hard to duplicate organization-specific knowledge and resource orchestration, discussed, for example, by Sermon et al. in [39]. Since this knowledge is hard to duplicate, the companies do not compete with others, but are depending on their own capacity for using this knowledge towards innovation.

Yet another concept, that of a knowledge funnel, is proposed by Martin in [29] as a driver of competitive advantage:

> "Neither analysis nor intuition alone is enough. In the future, the most successful businesses will balance analytical mastery and intuitive originality in a dynamic interplay that I call "design thinking." Design thinking enables leaders to innovate along the path of the knowledge funnel, and the firms that master it can gain long-term business advantage."

This is in line with basis for grounding d-school and Owen's makers and finders categories, as described above. Abductive reasoning, or the inference to the best explanation, balances analytic and intuitive thinking and guides one through the knowledge funnel with greater reliability than the intuition alone.

This brings in yet another discussion, that of organizational culture, and how it views innovation. A leader might be visionary and creative, but if all initiatives were stopped by rules and regulations, lack of enthusiasm among employees etc., not much innovation would happen. A culture, which supports exploration long enough to see at least two intuitive breakthroughs, has a much better chance to create truly innovative products. As above cited case of Procter & Gamble shows, even exploitation oriented organizations, can change and develop skills needed to generate value from exploration insights.

4   Design Thinking and Competitive Advantage Framework

From the above discussion, we view leadership, vision, knowledge and resource orchestration, values and culture of an organization, to be leading factors in creating competitive advantage for organizations facilitated by information technology. For these organizations, which are already either global or getting there, traditional factors such as clustering and geography become less influential.

Below, we offer the framework for gaining long term competitive advantage for IT-facilitated organizations, Fig. 1.

Long-term health and effectiveness of these organizations, as mentioned previously, has been described in terms of values, visions, knowledge work and creative leadership [5, 9, 23, 24]. Originally, design thinking was placed as the fifth instrumental factor in promoting this long-term health in Fig. 1, but design thinking is infusing all those factors, and has come to play a central role in them, thus the positioning.

Fig. 1. Framework for gaining long term competitive advantage for IT players. Exhibit: Culén & Kriger.

The interesting part of Fig. 1, from the point of view of HCID, is that HCI certainly has a role in the development of new technology, through HCID and designerly practices. However, this role is more on a micro-economic level.

To increase the influence of HCID, the HCID practitioners also need to think bigger, as they have started doing within sustainable technology design.

The sustainable technology design has become one of larger issues in the field of HCID [15]. Design thinkers have perhaps paved the road, as they have been instrumental in successfully bringing forward and addressing issues of sustainability, see for example, [4, 15, 40]. HCID practitioners, on one hand, strive to design technology that supports us in our everyday lives, to make technology easier to use, more useful, cooler, to support aging and so on. Blevis [3] suggests explicit coupling of invention and disposal, as well as renewal and reuse when designing new products. Other researchers within interaction design and HCID are trying to understand why we keep some things and discard others [32], can we make green solutions, as well as asking questions such as: do we need all this technology [2]? And finally, there are those opting for structural change:

> *"Technology creates possibilities for structural change mainly by amplifying efforts to achieve existing, institutionally recognized goals. In the context of the transition to sustainability, such goals may include the reconfiguration of institutions and infrastructures themselves. HCI can contribute significantly to the transition to sustainability by exploring how information tools can support such efforts", [38, p. 1].*

Thus, participation in global changes would position also HCI as a more central factor in strategic innovation.

5   HCID and Design Thinking: The Future of the Library

We conclude this discussion on innovation, competitive advantage and the role of design thinking and HCI in innovative processes with a small case from practice.

The case is based on a public sector organization, with long and well established tradition, and until recently little urge to innovate: an academic library. For the past decade, the Internet has been a game changer for academic libraries. Appearance of disruptive technologies, such as eBooks first, and tablets later, posed further challenges. The libraries, and in particular academic libraries, are practically forced to re-think their role in academic life, their use of technology and their willingness to innovate.

One of the authors of this paper started cooperation with the academic library approximately three years ago. At the time, the main issues the library had were around transfer of web-services to mobile devices. Since the author teaches project-based course in interaction design, several student projects for the past three years were dedicated to developing innovative information technology solutions for the library. The way the students work is very similar to Kolko's description of what design thinkers do: they make a series of rapid prototypes, evaluate them with users, brainstorm, role play, etc. until they find a concept that they want to develop further. Within a 3-month time-framework, they develop a high fidelity prototype, which is also evaluated in real use context, with actual users. Since students themselves are users of the library, the ideas they came up with were many and varied. Already after the first semester of students' projects, the library recognized the value of user-driven innovation and made resources available to support it. After the second year, some of the solutions were implemented, and found to be working well, both for students, librarians and library leadership. The "new" concept was taken in use, the concept of the living lab [12]. Now design students could work in the science library, engage other students and use design thinking to come up with more creative solutions. After the third year, a seminar about design thinking, as well as a series of workshops with focus on service design innovation were organized and carried out with library employees, including leadership, digital services, librarians and others [11]. The effect of these workshops was that library employees could experience, first hand, design thinking. They used service design cards, made and re-made customer journeys, past, present and future. The consequence of this work, summative over three years, is that we could witness emergence of creative leadership, change of culture towards exploration, change in vision, now dedicated to creating a large user experience center and changing the library status to that of a research library, change in knowledge and willingness to build competence in user experience and innovation.

6   Discussion and Conclusion

Considering the case presented above, as well as the attendant discussion, we find that, although HCID and design thinking both have their roles in innovation processes, in particular for IT-facilitated organizations, HCID could position itself more centrally in relation to explaining the long-term health of IT-intensive organizations.

Several future avenues are possible. HCID, for example, may focus more on sustainability issues and take a more central role as regards sustainable global development. Thus, at a minimum the position as shown in Fig. 2 should be achieved, moving the field from incremental innovations towards actively helping to shape future technology policies.

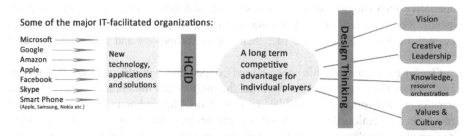

Fig. 2. Possible positioning of HCI in the framework. Exhibit: Culén & Kriger.

The future is obviously hard to predict. Distribution of wealth is at present highly uneven in the world, in both the developed and still developing countries, and as a result is not sustainable. Below is a visual summary of the above discussion, some-what simplified, but nonetheless thought-provoking (see Figure 3).

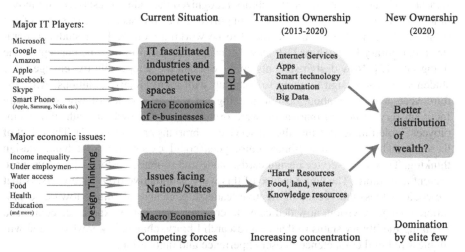

Fig. 3. How HCI and design thinking potentially influence global change Exhibit: Culén & Kriger.

6.1   Conclusion

This paper has explored the future role of design thinking and HCID in shaping the conditions for long-term competitive advantage for IT-intensive organizations. From a case of innovation in an academic library, where HCID and design thinking were instrumental in starting not only product and service innovation processes but also subsequent organizational changes, we find that both HCID and design thinking can be important simultaneous facilitators of change. HCID can open doors to innovation of products and services, wherein design thinking is a salient element of HCID processes and an important initiator of organizational change. However, innovation driven through HCID will not be lasting without the presence of supportive, and larger, top-down changes. In our case, design thinking helped to change the vision and culture of a library organization. A limitation of the current study is that it uses a single case to provide empirical justification. Future research is called for using a larger and more diverse sample of organizations. Such future research might aim to provide answers the following: (1) a detailed understanding of the processes by which such changes happen, (2) what sets these changes in motion in the first place, and (3) what causes the results of the change process to endure over longer periods of time.

References

1. Acemoglu, D., Aghion, P., Zilibotti, F.: Vertical integration and distance to frontier. Journal of the European Economic Association 1(2-3), 630–638 (2003)
2. Baumer, E.P., Silberman, M.: When the implication is not to design (technology). In: Proceedings of the SIGCHI Conference on Human Factors in Computing Systems, pp. 2271–2274 (2011)
3. Blevis, E.: Sustainable Interaction Design: Invention & Disposal, Renewal & Reuse. In: Proceedings of the SIGCHI Conference on Human Factors in Computing Systems, pp. 503–512. ACM (2007)
4. Bonn, I., Fisher, J.: Sustainability: the missing ingredient in strategy. Journal of Business Strategy 32(1), 5–14 (2011)
5. Brown, S.L., Eisenhardt, K.M.: The Art of Continuous Change: Linking Complexity Theory and Time-Paced Evolution in Relentlessly Shifting Organi-zations. Administrative Science Quarterly 42(1), 1 (1997)
6. Brown, T.: Change by design: how design thinking can transform organizations and inspire innovation. HarperCollins Publishers, New York (2009)
7. Brynjolfsson, E., Hitt, L.M.: Beyond Computation: Information Technology, Organizational Transformation and Business Performance. Journal of Economic Perspectives 14(4), 23–48 (2000)
8. Buchanan, R.: Wicked Problems in Design Thinking. Design Issues 8(2), 5–21 (1992)
9. Burgelman, R.A.: Strategy is destiny: how strategy-making shapes a company's future. Free Press, New York (2002)
10. Cairncross, F.: The death of distance: how the communications revolution is changing our lives. Harvard Business School Press, Boston (2001)
11. Culén, A.L., Gasparini, A.: Find a Book! Unpacking Customer Journeys at Academic Library. In: The Seventh International Conference on Advances in Computer-Human Interactions, pp. 89–95. ThinkMind (2014)
12. Culén, A.L., Gasparini, A.A.: Student Driven Innovation: Designing University Library Services Centric. In: The Sixth International Conference on Advances in Human Oriented and Personalized Mechanisms, Technologies, and Services, pp. 12–17 (2013)
13. Culén, A.L., Joshi, S., Atif, A.: HCID: Who is an interaction designer? In: Proceedings of the 2nd International Conference for Design Education Researchers, pp. 1924–1937. ABM Media (2013)
14. Culén, A.L., Mainsah, H.N., Finken, S.: Design Practice in Human Computer Interaction Design Education. In: The Seventh International Conference on Advances in Computer-Human Interactions, pp. 300–306. ThinkMind (2014)
15. Dourish, P.: HCI and environmental sustainability: the politics of design and the design of politics. In: Proceedings of the 8th ACM Conference on Designing Interactive Systems, pp. 1–10 (2010)

16. Fallman, D.: Design-oriented human-computer interaction. In: Proceedings of the SIGCHI Conference on Human Factors in Computing Systems, pp. 225–232 (2003)
17. Hitt, M.A., Ireland, R.D., Hoskisson, R.E.: Strategic Management Cases: Competitiveness and Globalization. CengageBrain.com (2012)
18. Jobs, Q. by S., Press, C.S.V., and Press, S. by E. of C.S.V. Steve Jobs: His Own Words and Wisdom (Steve Jobs Biography). Cupertino Silicon Valley Press (2011)
19. Johansson, U., Woodilla, J.: Towards an epistemological merger of design thinking, strategy and innovation. In: 8th European Academy of Design Conference, pp. 1–5 (2009)
20. Johansson-Sköldberg, U., Woodilla, J., Çetinkaya, M.: Design Thinking: Past, Present and Possible Futures. Creativity and Innovation Management 22(2), 121–146 (2013)
21. Kolko, J.: Austin Center for Design. Wicked problems problems worth solving. Ac4d, Austin, Texas (2012)
22. Kriger, M., Culén, A.L.: IT-Facilitated Industries and Competetive Spaces: the Dance of the Elephants. In: The Second International M-sphere Conference on Multidisciplinarity in Science and Business, pp. 302-307. Accent (2013)
23. Kriger, M.P., Hanson, B.J.: A value-based paradigm for creating truly healthy organizations. Journal of Organizational Change Management 12(4), 302–317 (1999)
24. Larwood, L., Falbe, C.M., Kriger, M.P., Miesing, P.: Structure And Meaning Of Organizational Vision. Academy of Management Journal 38(3), 740–769 (1995)
25. Leavy, B.: Design thinking – a new mental model of value innovation. Strategy & Leadership 38(3), 5–14 (2010)
26. Leavy, B.: Collaborative innovation as the new imperative – design thinking, value co-creation and the power of "pull". Strategy & Leadership 40(2), 25–34 (2012)
27. Luxembourg. The Measurement of Scientific and Technological Activities Oslo Manual: Guidelines for Collecting and Interpreting Innovation Data. OECD Publishing (2005)
28. Maeda, J., Bermont, B.: Redesigning leadership. MIT Press, Cambridge (2011)
29. Martin, R.: Design thinking: achieving insights via the "knowledge funnel". Strategy & Leadership 38(2), 37–41 (2010)
30. Martin, R.L.: The Design of Business: Why Design Thinking is the Next Competitive Advantage. Harvard Business Press (2009)
31. O'Connor, G.C.: Major Innovation as a Dynamic Capability: A Systems Approach. Journal of Product Innovation Management 25(4), 313–330 (2008)
32. Odom, W., Pierce, J., Stolterman, E., Blevis, E.: Understanding why we pre-serve some things and discard others in the context of interaction design. In: Proceedings of the SIGCHI Conference on Human Factors in Computing Systems, pp. 1053–1062. ACM (2009)
33. Owen, C.: Design thinking: Notes on its nature and use. Design Research Quarterly 2(1), 16–27 (2007)
34. Porter, M.E.: On Competition (Harvard Business Review Book). Harvard Business Review Press (2008)
35. Rowe, P.G.: Design Thinking. The MIT Press (1991)
36. Schön, D.A.: The reflective practitioner: How professionals think in action. Basic Books (1983)
37. Sharp, H., Rogers, Y., Preece, J.: Interaction Design: Beyond Human-Computer Interaction. Wiley (2007)
38. Silberman, M.S., Interpreter, F.: Sustainability and structural change: the role of HCI (2013), http://systemsinterpretation.org/note/002.pdf

39. Sirmon, D.G., Hitt, M.A., Ireland, R.D., Gilbert, B.A.: Resource orchestration to create competitive advantage breadth, depth, and life cycle effects. Journal of Management 37(5), 1390–1412 (2011)
40. Spangenberg, J.H., Fuad-Luke, A., Blincoe, K.: Design for Sustainability (DfS): the interface of sustainable production and consumption. Journal of Cleaner Production 18(15), 1485–1493 (2010)
41. Wagner, C.S., Roessner, J.D., Bobb, K., et al.: Approaches to understanding and measuring interdisciplinary scientific research (IDR): A review of the literature. Journal of Informetrics 5(1), 14–26 (2011)
42. Wagner, T., Compton, R.A.: Creating innovators: the making of young people who will change the world. Scribner, New York (2012)

Understanding the Antecedents and Consequences of Live-Chat Use in E-Commerce Context

Lele Kang[1], Xiang Wang[2,*], Chuan-Hoo Tan[1], and J. Leon Zhao[1]

[1] Department of Information Systems, City University of Hong Kong, Hong Kong
Lele.Kang@my.cityu.edu.hk, {ch.tan,jlzhao}@cityu.edu.hk
[2] Department of Electronic Business, Nanjing University,
No. 22, Hankou Road, Nanjing, China
wxiang@nju.edu.cn

Abstract. Online shopping has progressed from having consumers passively browse through web pages of products to having them proactively engage in communication dialogs with product sellers via Live-Chat. Through Live-Chat, consumers can directly contact the sellers and inquire about their products of interest. This study extends the conceptual framework of motivation, opportunity, and ability (MOA) to understand the antecedents and consequences of Live-Chat usage in consumers' online shopping process. Our survey involving 222 online consumers validated the proposed conceptual model and confirmed most of our assumptions. For antecedents, we found that MOA factors generally influence the Live-Chat usage of consumers in their shopping process. Specifically, perceived information asymmetry, fears of seller opportunism and perceived personal expertise have strong positive effects on Live-Chat usage. For consequences, Live-Chat usage positively affects consumers' perceived interactivity, thereby reducing their uncertainty in transaction. Our findings contribute to the understanding of real-time communication technology in specific and digital service for e-commerce in general.

Keywords: Motivation-Opportunity-Ability Framework, Live-Chat, E-Commerce.

1 Introduction

Present-day consumers expect more from sellers, particularly in the electronic commerce (e-commerce) context. The mere act of passively browsing through the web pages of products is no longer deemed adequate. Furthermore, the lack of engagement or interaction with sellers, a typically offline marketplace feature, has dampened consumers' purchase inclinations (Jiang et al. 2010; Qiu and Benbasat 2005). Empirical evidence has shown that engaging in communication dialogues with consumers is important in establishing product brand loyalty and sustaining positive customer relationships (Guo et al. 2010). A more recent effort among many website operators is to embed the Live-Chat feature on the shopping platform, which could

---

* Corresponding author.

F.F.-H. Nah (Ed.): HCIB/HCII 2014, LNCS 8527, pp. 504–515, 2014.
© Springer International Publishing Switzerland 2014

provide one-to-one instant responses to consumer questions (Andrews et al. 2002). These website operators include large online retailers such as Amazon (United States) and "Taobao" (Mainland China).

Despite the increasingly prevalent Live-Chat medium, which is embedded on shopping websites, research on Live-Chat usage by consumers is limited. Our primary knowledge on computer-mediated communication (CMC) has predominately focused on supporting asynchronous communication among consumers (Adjei et al. 2010), or allowing sellers to post additional product information through social platforms such as forums (Flanagin 2007). The investigation on synchronous communication, such as the Live-Chat medium, is limited. Thus, the current research aims to identify the antecedents and consequences of consumers' usage of the Live-Chat medium, a form of synchronous communication tool with sales representatives in online shopping.

We adopted the conceptual framework of motivation, opportunity, and ability (MOA) (MacInnis and Jaworski 1989; MacInnis et al. 1991) to identify and model the MOA factors influence consumer's Live-Chat usage. The framework argues that individuals' engagement in medium usage is influenced by their motivation, opportunity, and ability, which enable them to undertake preferred behavior. After understanding the key antecedents of Live-Chat usage, this study also aims to explore how Live-Chat usage impacts consumer's online purchase. Consistent with prior CMC literature, we propose that Live-Chat use contributes to improving consumer perception of interactivity because of its bidirectional and synchronized characteristics (Jiang et al., 2010; Merrilees, 2002). With the increased perception of interactivity, consumers feel the helpfulness of e-commerce websites, and thus reduce their uncertainty in e-commerce transactions (Pavlou et al. 2007). A survey was subsequently conducted to examine the relationships among the MOA factors, Live-Chat use, and the consequences.

2 Theoretical Foundation

2.1 Live-Chat Medium in E-Commerce Websites

Live-Chat is a shopping website-embedded communication tool that facilitates a consumer to engage in synchronous text-based one-to-one communication with a designated seller to obtain product and service information that may not be readily available on a product description web page (Ou and Davison 2009). The Live-Chat medium is typically placed on the product-listing page, which can be clicked by consumers when they need more information about a product.

From a seller's perspective, the use of Live-Chat extends traditional customer service channels by providing personalized service for consumers through formulating one-to-one relationships between sellers and consumers. Having the tool allows e-commerce websites to mimic a physical store shopping experience (Goes et al. 2011). Consumers have a channel to communicate with the sales representatives and express their product expectations. Compared to telephone and traditional email services, communication through the Live-Chat medium is immediate, interactive, and efficient (Tezcan 2011).

From the consumer's perspective, he/she can obtain real-time help from sellers, and facilitate his/her information gathering process (Jiang et al. 2010). Such synchronized communication faciliates consumers' information gathering and therefore reduces their concerns about the transaction before making the purchase decision. More importantly, consumers actively engage in the generation of the seller's information disclosure. Ou, Davison, Pavlou, & Li (2008) examined the role of Live-Chat in consumers' purchase processes using survey methodology, and found that the medium enhanced consumer perception of interactivity and presence, thus leading to improvements in trust, relationship between buyer and seller, and repeated transaction intentions. In the following section, we review the MOA framework, which serves as the theoretical foundation for our research, focusing on the consumer's perspective.

2.2   Motivation, Opportunity, and Ability (MOA) Framework

The MOA framework is adopted in this study to identify consumers' antecedents of the Live-Chat medium use. The essential thesis of the theory is that individuals' behavior is determined by three main sets of factors, namely motivation, opportunity, and ability. Traditionally originating from the social marketing literature (MacInnis and Jaworski 1989; MacInnis et al. 1991), the MOA framework proposes that the behavior of consumers is determined by their motivation, opportunity, and ability (Gruen et al. 2007). This theoretical framework has been applied to examine the antecedents of consumer's advertisement information processing (MacInnis et al. 1991), knowledge-sharing behavior among employees (Siemsen et al. 2008), and customer-to-customer information exchange (Gruen et al. 2007; Tseng et al. 2012). In information systems (IS) research, Strader and Hendrickson (1999) adapted this theory to guide the electronic market research.

The usefulness of MOA is evaluated as a theoretical approach by linking individuals' attitudes toward Live-Chat usage. An understanding of individuals' MOA factors may help e-commerce researchers to better understand how consumers use customer service (e.g., Live-Chat) to facilitate their online purchase. Moreover, we further broaden the boundary of the MOA theory by extending this theory to observe the antecedent of Live-Chat usage in e-commerce websites.

3   Research Model and Hypotheses

3.1   Motivation Factors

We define motivation as a consumer's desire or willingness to use the Live-Chat. Motivation represents a force that leads individuals toward the target (MacInnis and Jaworski 1989). Extending to the Live-Chat use, motivation factors address the uncertainty resulting from online shopping, which refers to the degree to which consumers fail to accurately predict the outcomes of a transaction due to seller-, product-, and process-related issues (Chatterjee and Datta 2008; Pavlou et al. 2007).

Two factors are identified as the motivational factors of Live-Chat medium usage, namely perceived information asymmetry and fears of seller opportunism.

Perceived information asymmetry is defined as the extent to which consumers perceive sellers to have more information about a product and the transaction process (Pavlou et al. 2007). Physical separation renders consumers unable to assess the quality of a product through touching and observing it directly on e-commerce websites. The provision of information on websites, such as images, descriptions, product reviews, and the purchasing process, is limited, and thus may not convey the information desired by consumers (Chiu et al. 2005). Dimoka et al. (2012) extended information asymmetry literature by proposing that buyers have difficulty in predicting the outcomes of online transactions due to information asymmetry, which was also confirmed by Pavlou et al. (2007). Two-way communication via the Live-Chat medium enables consumers to control the form and content of information exchanged and accelerates the economic negotiation (Chiu et al. 2005; Peterson et al. 1997). Thus, perceived information asymmetry, which dampens consumer confidence in a product's quality as well as the order fulfillment quality, encourages consumers to use the Live-Chat medium. We thus posit:

H1: Perceived information asymmetry (PIA) has a positive effect on Live-Chat medium usage (LCMU).

Fears of seller opportunism refer to buyers' concern about that sellers try to exploit the situation to maximize their profits (Pavlou et al. 2007). Because of the isolation between purchase and delivery process, online buyers have no opportunity to physically check the products when they make the purchase decision. In this situation, sellers could maximize their profit by providing low quality or fake products (i.e., lemons). Buyers seek for different methods to control and avoid seller opportunism. For instance, buyers use the online reviews to gain enough information of the products for their purchase decision. Live-Chat medium contributes for buyers to reduce their perceived fears of seller opportunism by recording the buyer-to-seller communication. Live-Chat medium enables buyers to easily confirm the product features and related selling policies by asking the relevant questions to seller. For instance, many buyers confirm the delivery policy with the sellers through Live-Chat medium. Seller's response is recorded by the Live-Chat functions. If sellers violate the agreements, the record of Live-Chat could serve as the evidence for the arbitration. Thus, we posit:

H2: Fears of Seller Opportunism (FSO) have a positive effect on Live-Chat medium usage (LCMU).

3.2   Ability and Opportunity Factors

Given that consumers have the motivation to conduct Live-Chat communication, the next issue is whether they have the ability to do so. Ability refers to consumers' related skills or knowledge that supports the technology usage. Ability, such as personal expertise and proficiency, influences consumer utilization of a given tool (Thompson et al. 1994). Personal technological expertise has been recognized as a major ability factor of technology usage, which refers to how individuals perceive themselves to be knowledgeable, competent, trained, and experienced in a particular domain (Adjei et al., 2010). Fulk (1993) included expertise variables in his model of communication technology usage, and stated that individuals' experience should facilitate their technology assessments, which influence their utilization. Users' perceived personal expertise affects individuals' assessments and mastery of the Live-Chat medium as a form of technology (Schmitz and Fulk 1991). Consumers equipped with such expertise are likely to perceive the advantages of using the medium, including gaining access to needed information without the need to exert significant effort in learning about the medium. Therefore, perceived personal expertise is expected to have a significant impact on consumers' Live-Chat medium usage. Thus, we hypothesize:

H3: Perceived personal expertise (PPE) has a positive effect on Live-Chat medium usage (LCMU).

Opportunity is defined as the extent to which an environment or situation is conducive to achieving a goal. From a positive view, opportunity could be manifested in the form of a conductive context, or the low costs required for the action (Gruen et al. 2005). As a necessary condition for technology usage, the Live-Chat medium provided by e-commerce websites offers consumers the opportunity to directly interact with the sellers. As an exogenous factor, technology support (i.e., opportunity) is considered as a contextual and situational constraint relevant to Live-Chat usage in this research (Hughes 2007; MacInnis and Jaworski 1989). "Taobao," the largest e-commerce website in China, provides an embedded communication tool, called "WangWang," on every seller's web page. Such provision allows consumers to directly interact with the sellers before making the purchase decision. Consistent with the suggestion of Strader and Hendrickson (1999), we propose that the existence of the Live-Chat support, as an opportunity factor, influences consumers' Live-Chat medium usage.

3.3   Consequences of Live-Chat Usage

As a CMC tool, Live-Chat medium usage contributes to the improvement of consumers' perceived interactivity in their online shopping process. Perceived interactivity refers to the degree to which a communicator considers the dialogue with another person to be bi-directional and occurring in real-time. Compared to other customer service technologies (e.g., email), Live-Chat more closely resembles face-to-face communication because of its real-time, on-demand availability, and short waiting time (Zhu, Benbasat, & Jiang, 2010). To understand how interactivity can impact consumers' online shopping, Jiang et al. (2010) controlled the reciprocal communication function (i.e., Live-Chat feature) of websites and regarded communication as an important factor of website interactivity design. The results suggested that consumer perception of interactivity was determined by whether a Live-Chat feature was available on websites. Such synchronized interactions improve consumer ability to obtain the desired information in real-time and create a sense of closeness with the sellers. Perceived interactivity is reflected in terms of several aspects, such as bi-directional communication, personalization ability, control ability, and total website shopping experience (Merrilees, 2002; Ou et al., 2008). Live-Chat, as a synchronous communication tool, allows consumers to control the information seeking process and change their information seeking method from passively reading product descriptions to actively addressing related questions concerning the relevant products. Thus, we posit:

H4: Live-Chat medium usage (LCMU) has a positive effect on consumers' perceived interactivity (INT).

Consumers experience uncertainty during their online shopping experiences, and this could be the result of the lack of information about the seller (i.e., seller identity anonymity), inadequate product information, and insufficient knowledge about the purchase process (Chatterjee and Datta 2008; Dimoka, Benbasat, et al. 2012). In other words, uncertainty generally often arises due to the lack of information, which makes it difficult for consumers to make decisions (Achrol and Stern 1988). An interactive website design (e.g. the Live-Chat medium) alleviates consumers' uncertainty perceptions by enhancing their ability to get information (Weathers et al. 2007).

Customer support denotes the interactivity aspect most frequently used by consumers. As we mentioned previously, a consumer's perception of interactivity refers to the degree in which consumers can communicate directly with sellers at anytime and anywhere. The perception of interactivity makes customers feel that they are enabled to receive help from sellers during an online shopping process. In the research context, it is built upon Live-Chat medium usage and reduces consumers' uncertainty through enhancing their ability to obtain the desired information. A high degree of perceived interactivity implies that consumers can get their desired information in real-time, and this perception reduces their purchase uncertainty (Adjei et al. 2010, Weiss et al. 2008, Berger and Calabrese 1975). Hence, Live-Chat medium usage enhances consumers' sense of interactivity, which leads to uncertainty reduction. Thus we posit:

H5: Perceived interactivity (INT) is positively related to perceived uncertainty reduction (UR).

H6: Live-Chat medium usage (LCMU) has a positive effect on consumers' uncertainty reduction (UR).

4   Research Methodology

4.1   Sample and Data Collection

Our research focuses on the Live-Chat medium. We developed a questionnaire to test the theoretically driven hypotheses in "Taobao" website, which captures 79.2% of the entire online shopping market in China (You et al. 2011). Existing validated scales were adopted where possible. Based on our research context and prior measurements of technology usage, we developed three items to assess consumers' Live-Chat usage based on the following scale: "frequently used it to communicate with sellers," "frequently used it to communicate with the sellers before I made a purchase decision," and "frequently used it to communicate with a seller after the transaction."

We adapted items from Pavlou et al. (2007) to measure perceived information asymmetry and fears of seller opportunism. To measure perceived personal expertise, we adapted scales from Adjei et al. (2010) in consideration of our online communication context. Interactivity was adapted to our research context from Ou et al. (2008) and Liu (2003). To assess uncertainty reduction, we adapted items from Achrol and Stern (1988). Respondents were asked to respond to a questionnaire based on a seven-point Likert scale (1=strongly disagree; to 7=strongly agree). Finally, 222 complete and valid responses were collected. Conducting the t-tests of demographics in early and late responders enabled us to determine that non-response bias was not a serious problem in our research. Thus, we can argue that the survey process is adequately designed.

4.2   Measurement Model and Preliminary Analyses

The measurement model was tested by assessing the reliability, convergent validity, and discriminant validity. We calculated Cronbach's alpha (from 0.868 to 0.925) and composite reliability (from 0.920 to 0.944) to confirm the reliability of measurements.

Table 1. Correlations between Constructs

	Mean	S.D	LCMU	PPE	PIA	FSO	INT	UR
LCMU	4.856	1.749	**0.892**					
PPE	4.078	1.586	0.328	**0.904**				
PIA	5.725	1.395	0.223	0.111	**0.908**			
FSO	4.707	1.257	0.238	0.100	0.357	**0.869**		
INT	5.122	1.368	0.584	0.353	0.329	0.255	**0.843**	
UR	4.225	1.372	0.322	0.524	0.234	0.018	0.440	**0.921**

Note: The diagonal elements are the square roots of the AVEs; off-diagonal elements are the correlations between constructs.

Table 1 displays the means and standard deviations of all variables in the research model, along with the correlations among the variables. To assess the convergent and discriminant validity of the constructs, the AVEs of the constructs were also computed. The AVEs of all constructs were larger than 0.5. Thus, we deemed that the convergent validity for the variables was supported by the analysis. In addition, the convergent validity is also confirmed by the high level of item loading. The discriminant validity of the measurement model was further confirmed as the results showed the square root of the AVEs of all the constructs was greater than the correlations between constructs. In addition, the correlations among all variables were well below 0.6, suggesting that all the constructs were distinct from each other.

The single survey method of collecting data may cause common method variance (CMV) in our research. We used the method suggested by Liang, Saraf, Hu, & Xue (2007) to examine CMV. The substantive factors explained approximately 78% of the variance, whereas the method factor only explained approximately 0.5% of the variance. The results suggested that our data did not suffer from high CMV.

4.3   Hypothesis Testing Using PLS

The PLS results for the structural model are illustrated in Figure 1, in which the relationships between perceived information asymmetry and Live-Chat medium usage (β=0.135, p<0.05) and fears of seller opportunism and Live-Chat medium usage (β=0.163, p<0.05) are significant, thus supporting the hypotheses regarding the motivation factors. The results also indicate that ability factor (i.e., perceived personal expertise) significantly influences Live-Chat medium usage (β=0.17, p<0.001); thus, the positive impact of ability on usage is supported. The results from the inclusion of control variables and MOA factors as predictors explain 23.0% of the variance in Live-Chat medium usage.

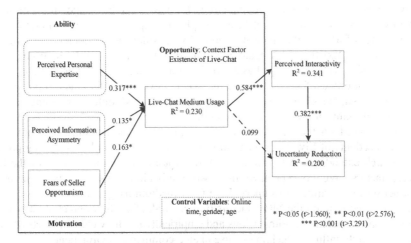

Fig. 1. PLS Results of the Proposed Research Model

For consequences, the results also suggest that Live-Chat medium usage has a positive effect on consumers' perceived interactivity (R2=0.341, β=0.584, p<0.001), which in turn significantly increases their uncertainty reduction (R2=0.200, β=0.382, p<0.001). The results of mediation effect test also confirm that the impact of Live-Chat media usage on uncertainty reduction is mediated by users' perceived interactivity. Thus, all proposed conceptual hypotheses are proposed.

5   Discussion

5.1   Limitations and Directions for Future Research

Before discussing the contributions of this study, we first state several limitations in this research, which are considered as opportunities for future research. First, this research only focuses on a subset of MOA antecedents of the Live-Chat medium in the model. Second, the interaction effects among MOA factors are not examined in our research. Inconsistent with prior MOA literature, we propose the sub-dimension constructs to present the MOA factors. Therefore, we could not simply evaluate their interdependent relationships in our study. Third, our research is based on "Taobao" website. Customers may exhibit different behaviors when the Live-Chat medium is used on other websites (i.e., Amazon), which may cause bias in the analysis of the gratification factors. Therefore, extending this study to other cultures, such as the Western websites, will be interesting.

5.2   Theoretical Contributions and Implications

Our study contributes to the research in technology use, with a focus on the Live-Chat medium, a relatively new customer support technology that is gaining popularity on current online shopping websites. The theoretical implications of this study are as follows. First, it offers a new explanation for CMC media usage in e-commerce websites, a topic that has not yet been completely explored in the IS literature. Our research sheds further light on CMC studies by considering the interactive Live-Chat medium usage. Existing Live-Chat medium literature has mainly focused on the interface design (Qiu and Benbasat 2005) rather than on the perspective of the underlying rationale of consumer usage. We believe that this study represents an effort to investigate CMC medium usage in consumers' online shopping process, which is important for e-commerce research.

Second, based on the MOA theory, we explore the motivation, opportunity, and ability antecedents of Live-Chat medium usage in consumers' online shopping process. Our research extends the MOA framework to explore the sub-dimensions of the three general factors. We conceptualize that two motivation constructs and one ability construct positively affect consumers' Live-Chat medium usage. Although prior studies have shed some light on the MOA factors (Gruen et al. 2007; Siemsen et al. 2008), they did not propose specific sub-dimensions and empirically test how the constructs of MOA factors separately influence technology use in an e-commerce environment.

Third, the research results contribute in presenting the impacts of Live-Chat usage in the e-commerce context. Consumers' perceived interactivity is enhanced through Live-Chat. This premise suggests that the synchronized nature of Live-Chat is seen to benefit users by providing immediate information, which may also improve consumers' intention to transact on e-commerce websites. Although prior literature provides a rich understanding of how perceived interactivity influences consumers' online purchase, limited research has explained how interactivity influences consumers' uncertainty reduction in e-commerce websites. Our research suggests that the impact of Live-Chat medium usage on uncertainty reduction is mediated by their perceived interactivity.

5.3   Practical Contributions and Implications

This study also has practical implications for website designers and sellers to improve their service quality through CMC media in the e-commerce context. In view of the need for e-commerce websites to facilitate online shopping, this study offers practical implications by identifying the antecedents and consequences for consumers' usage of the Live-Chat medium. This medium is widely adopted by e-commerce websites in which consumers experience a high level of uncertainty when they conduct business transactions with strangers. Human-to-human interaction enhances purchasing and renders the purchase process similar to a physical store encounter. Our empirical findings can provide insights for Live-Chat medium implementation. Furthermore, our findings suggest that motivation, opportunity, and ability factors are the key determinants of consumer Live-Chat medium usage. If consumers perceive a high level of information asymmetry and fears of seller opportunism in the shopping process, the Live-Chat medium can be adopted to facilitate purchase decision making. Website designers should also provide the necessary training for their consumers to improve their skills on using the related tools, such as Live-Chat. Furthermore, website designers should promote the use of the medium by consumers. Understanding what consumers want from Live-Chat use is vital for sellers. Sellers can serve their customers better only if they understand their goals and needs. For instance, this study indicates that consumers use Live-Chat to perceive interactivity. This finding cautions sellers to quickly answer consumers' questions and provide them with the feeling of companionship with other customers. In addition, improving consumers' perceived interactivity could significantly reduce their uncertainty in online transaction.

6   Conclusions

Building on the MOA framework, this study investigates consumers' antecedents and the consequences of Live-Chat usage in e-commerce websites. Our empirical findings suggest that motivation factors (e.g., information asymmetry and fears of seller opportunism), opportunity factors (e.g., existence of Live-Chat support), and ability factors (e.g., personal expertise) influence the Live-Chat usage of consumers in their online shopping process. The findings also imply that Live-Chat use improves consumers' perception of interactivity, which in turn reduces their uncertainty in online shopping. This research reinforces the understanding of the utility of computer-mediated communication in the e-commerce environment, and motivates website designers to offer better support of consumer behavior in information seeking.

Acknowledgement. The work was partially supported by a grant from City University of Hong Kong (Project No. 6980108) and a grant from NSFC (Project No. 71110107027).

References

1. Achrol, R.S., Stern, L.W.: Environmental Determinants of Decision-Making Uncertainty Marketing Channels. Journal of Marketing Research 25(1), 36–50 (1988)
2. Adjei, M.T., Noble, S.M., Noble, C.H.: The Influence of C2C Communications in Online Brand Communities on Customer Purchase Behavior. Journal of the Academy of Marketing Science 38(5), 634–653 (2010)
3. Andrews, C.C., Haworth, K.: Online Customer Service Chat: Usability and Sociability Issues. Journal of Internet Marketing 2(1), 1–20 (2002)

4. Chatterjee, S., Datta, P.: Examining Inefficiencies and Consumer Uncertainty in E-Commerce. Communications of the Association for Information Systems 22(29), 525–546 (2008)
5. Chiu, H.C., Hsieh, Y.C., Kao, C.Y.: Website Quality and Customer's Behavioural Intention: An Exploratory Study of the Role of Information Asymmetry. Total Quality Management 16(2), 185–197 (2005)
6. Dellaert, B.G.C., Stremersch, S.: Marketing Mass-Customized Products: Striking a Balance Between Utility and Complexity. Journal of Marketing Research 42(2), 219–227 (2005)
7. Dimoka, A., Benbasat, I., Davis, F.D., Dennis, A.R., Gefen, D., Weber, B.: On the Use of Neurophysiological Tools in IS Research: Developing a Research Agenda for NeuroIS. MIS Quarterly 36(3), 679–702 (2012)
8. Dimoka, A., Hong, Y., Pavlou, P.A.: On Product Uncertainty in Online Markets: Theory and Evidence. MIS Quarterly 36(2), 395–426 (2012)
9. Flanagin, A.J.: Commercial Markets as Communication Markets: Uncertainty Reduction through Mediated Information Exchange in Online Auctions. New Media & Society 9(3), 401–423 (2007)
10. Fulk, J.: Social Construction of Communication Technology. The Academy of Management Journal 36(5), 921–950 (1993)
11. Goes, P., Ilk, N., Yue, W.T., Zhao, J.L.: Live-Chat Agent Assignments to Heterogeneous E-Customers under Imperfect Classification. ACM Transactions on Management Information Systems 2(4), 24:1–24:15 (2011)
12. Gruen, T.W., Osmonbekov, T., Czaplewski, A.J.: How E-communities Extend the Concept of Exchange in Marketing: An Application of the Motivation, Opportunity, Ability (MOA) Theory. Marketing Theory 5(1), 33–49 (2005)
13. Gruen, T.W., Osmonbekov, T., Czaplewski, A.J.: Customer-to-customer Exchange: Its MOA Antecedents and Its Impact on Value Creation and Loyalty. Journal of the Academy of Marketing Science 35(4), 537–549 (2007)
14. Guo, Z., Tan, F.B., Cheung, K.: Students ' Uses and Gratifications for Using Computer-Mediated Communication Media in Learning Contexts. Communications of the Association for Information Systems 27, Article 20 (2010)
15. Hughes, J.: The Ability-Motivation-Opportunity Framework for Behavior Research in IS. In: Proceedings of the 40th Annual Hawaii International Conference on System Sciences, pp. 1–10 (2007)
16. Jiang, Z., Chan, J., Tan, B.C.Y., Chua, W.S.: Effects of Interactivity on Website Involvement and Purchase Intention. Journal of the Association for Information Systems 11(1), 34–59 (2010)
17. Liang, H., Saraf, N., Hu, Q., Xue, Y.: Assimilation of Enterprise Systems: the Effect of Institutional Pressures and the Mediating Role of Top Management. MIS Quarterly 31(1), 59–87 (2007)
18. Liu, Y.P.: Developing a Scale to Measure the Interactivity of Websites. Journal of Advertising Research 43(2), 207–216 (2003)
19. Lowry, P.B., Romano, N.C., Jenkins, J.L., Guthrie, R.W.: The CMC Interactivity Model: How Interactivity Enhances Communication Quality and Process Satisfaction in Lean-Media Groups. Journal of Management Information Systems 26(1), 155–196 (2009)
20. MacInnis, D.J., Jaworski, B.J.: Information Processing from Advertisements: Toward an Integrative Framework. The Journal of Marketing JSTOR 53(4), 1–23 (1989)

21. MacInnis, D.J., Moorman, C.M., Jaworski, B.J.: Enhancing and Measuring Consumers' Motivation, Opportunity, and Ability to Process Brand Information From Ads. The Journal of Marketing 55(4), 32–53 (1991)
22. Merrilees, B.: Interactivity Design as the Key to Managing Customer Relations in E-Commerce. Journal of Relationship Marketing 1(3-4), 111–126 (2002)
23. Ou, C.X.J., Davison, R.M.: Why eBay Lost to TaoBao in China: The Global Advantage. Communications of the ACM 52(1), 145–148 (2009)
24. Ou, C.X.J., Davison, R.M., Pavlou, P.A., Li, M.Y.: Leveraging Rich Communication Tools: Evidence of Online Trust and Guanxi in China. In: ICIS 2008 Proceedings (2008)
25. Pavlou, P.A., Liang, H., Xue, Y.: Understanding and Mitigating Uncertainty in Online Exchange Relationships: A Principal-Agent Perspective. MIS Quarterly 31(1), 105–136 (2007)
26. Peterson, R.A., Balasubramanian, S., Bronnenberg, B.J.: Exploring the implications of the Internet for consumer marketing. Journal of the Academy of Marketing Science 25(4), 329–346 (1997)
27. Qiu, L., Benbasat, I.: Online Consumer Trust and Live Help Interfaces: The Effects of Text-to-Speech Voice and Three-Dimensional Avatars. International Journal of Human-Computer Interaction 19(1), 75–94 (2005)
28. Schmitz, J., Fulk, J.: Organizational Colleagues, Media Richness, and Electronic Mail: A Test of the Social Influence Model of Technology Use. Communication Research 18(4), 487–523 (1991)
29. Siemsen, E., Roth, A., Balasubramanian, S.: How motivation, opportunity, and ability drive knowledge sharing: The constraining-factor model. Journal of Operations Management 26(3), 426–445 (2008)
30. Teo, H.-H., Oh, L.-B., Liu, C., Wei, K.-K.: An Empirical Study of the Effects of Interactivity on Web User Attitude. International Journal of Human-Computer Studies 58(3), 281–305 (2003)
31. Tezcan, T.: Design and Control of Customer Service Chat Systems. Working Paper (2011)
32. Thompson, R.L., Higgins, C.A., Howell, J.M.: Influence of Experience on Personal Computer Utilization: Testing a Conceptual Model. Journal of Management Information Systems 11(1), 167–187 (1994)
33. Tseng, C., Chang, M., Chen, C.: Human Factors of Knowledge Sharing Intention among Taiwanese Enterprises: A Preliminary Study 22(4), 328–339 (2012)
34. Weathers, D., Sharma, S., Wood, S.L.: Effects of online communication practices on consumer perceptions of performance uncertainty for search and experience goods. Journal of Retailing 83(4), 393–401 (2007)
35. You, W., Liu, L., Xia, M., Lv, C.: Reputation Inflation Detection in a Chinese C2C Market. Electronic Commerce Research and Applications 10(5), 510–519 (2011)

Productivity of Services – An Empirical View on the German Market

Stephan Klingner, Michael Becker, and Klaus-Peter Fähnrich

Institut for Informatik Abteilung Betriebliche Informationssysteme,
Universität Leipzig, Germany
{klingner,mbecker,faehnrich}@informatik.uni-leipzig.de

Abstract. The growingly important role of services in economies leads to an increasing competition. Thus, services have to be provided as efficient as possible. Corresponding to the industrial domain, the management of productivity is an important factor of success. Since productivity management of services is relatively new compared to the industrial domain, only few scientific studies exist. The paper adds to this topic by conducting an extensive survey of the current status of productivity management of service companies in Germany. The findings could support both business and science by giving a reference of service productivity management in practice and identifying gaps regarding the development of tools and methods.

Keywords: Service Productivity, Service Performance.

1 Introduction

Corresponding to the growing economic relevance of the service sector, methodical approaches concerned with the increasing competition become more and more relevant. Offering customer-individual service configurations is one option to set a company's portfolio apart from a competitor's portfolio. A price-related differentiation is another option. Thus, the management of productivity is an important, competition-relevant factor. In order to achieve both of the somewhat conflicting aims of customer-individuality and high efficiency, powerful tools and methods are required.

In the industrial domain, the management of productivity has a long tradition. A widespread practical use and an extensive scientific discussion have led to a range of established and well-developed tools and methods. Since the economic transformation from the secondary (manufacturing) to the tertiary sector (services) has only recently been realized it can be assumed, that the maturity level of methods and tools used in the service sector is lower compared to the domain of manufacturing. Therefore, it is worthwhile to analyze the state of the art for managing the productivity of services. The results can be used to identify methodical gaps, leading to both practical and scientific challenges as well as future trends.

The paper presents the results of a quantitative empirical study conducted in the service sector in Germany. The aim was to capture and analyze the state of the art of

F.F.-H. Nah (Ed.): HCIB/HCII 2014, LNCS 8527, pp. 516–525, 2014.
© Springer International Publishing Switzerland 2014

service productivity. The paper is structured as follows. First, the empirical approach is described in the next chapter to allow for a sensible evaluation of the statistical relevance of the survey. Since the term "service" subsumes various forms of services, the third chapter describes the profiles of the companies for a better characterization of the offered services. Chapter four presents various tools and methods and their frequency of application as well as potential obstacles. The economical relevance of productivity management is deduced in chapter five. Finally the paper is concluded outlining future trends and emphasizing the importance of service productivity management.

2   Empirical Approach

In order to develop a basic understanding of productivity management in the domain of services, two qualitative pre-studies were conducted. The first study analyzed service productivity from the viewpoint of the structured description and modularization of service portfolios as the basis for productivity management. Semi-structured interviews with various companies were conducted. Key findings include difficulties of companies regarding the description and modularization of service portfolios, both required for an effective productivity management [1]. The second study was based on the results of a working group consisting of various participants from business and science. The result of the working group comprises the collection of currently used methods and tools as well as the delineation of future scenarios [2].

Both studies showed the relevance of productivity management of services but lacked statistical significance due to the chosen methodical approach. Therefore, a consecutive quantitative study was devised. Capturing the current status and future trends of productivity management in the German service sector was the aim of the study. Furthermore, the identification of current challenges and demands of business practice regarding tools and methods could support the alignment of the scientific focus and practical needs.

The population of the study consisted of almost 55.000 German companies of different service industries. These included ICT, EDP, telecommunications, architecture, advertising, metal working, machine building industry, tax and business consultancy, accounting as well as research and development. The companies' addresses were extracted from the database "Hoppenstedt". A stratified sample of 1990 companies was selected randomly. The questionnaire was sent to all participants by regular mail, with 88 letters being undeliverable. To offer various, convenient ways of response, the participants could use an included, reply-paid envelope, send the questionnaire by fax or complete it online. After removing incomplete and unusable questionnaires, a number of 120 responses could be used for further statistical analyses. This corresponds to a response rate of 6.44%.

Due to the limited sample size and the chosen population, the results are only meaningful for certain German service companies. Nevertheless, the insights provided might be valuable for a wider range of corporations as well. Furthermore, the identified gaps between business needs and scientific results indicate general topics for further scientific research.

The questionnaire contained three different chapters focusing on the company's service profile, the use of methods and tools as well as expected trends. Basically, the subsequent chapters are following this structure.

3   Characteristics of Services

Due to the growing importance of services in today's economy, services are not solely provided by pure service companies. Instead, more and more product companies tend to provide services to distinguish themselves from their competitors. To get an insight into the prevalence of service providers, companies were asked to define their main industry domain. Due to the wide variance of possible answers, Table 1 gives a consolidated overview of the responses.

Table 1. Domain distribution of surveyed companies

Industry domain	Number of companies
Metal working and machine building	21
EDP, ICT, telecommunications	30
Tax consultancy, accounting, business consulting, research and development	37
Architecture	19
Advertising	13

As a second characterization concerning the surveyed companies, the amount of service revenue compared to the overall revenue is used. Based on the results of the survey, the companies were divided in five classes as shown in Table 2. Almost half of the participating companies are pure service providers, i.e. their service revenue is 100% of the overall revenue. The high ratio of pure service providers needs to be connected to the industry domains in Table 1. More than 60% of all responding companies represent domains that usually do not sell any products.

Table 2. Amount of service revenue of surveyed companies

Share of service revenue of total revenue	Relative frequency
0 – 24%	12.5%
25 – 49%	8.3%
50 – 74%	15.8%
75 – 99%	15.0%
100%	48.3%

The surveyed companies were asked to characterize their service portfolio according to the following criteria: degree of standardization, degree of customer-individualization, product relatedness, person relatedness, degree of customer interaction (Fig 1). According to the survey, a high degree of standardization is defined as a highly homogeneous service portfolio. Commonly, standardized services require less information about customers and are provided in higher production volumes [3].

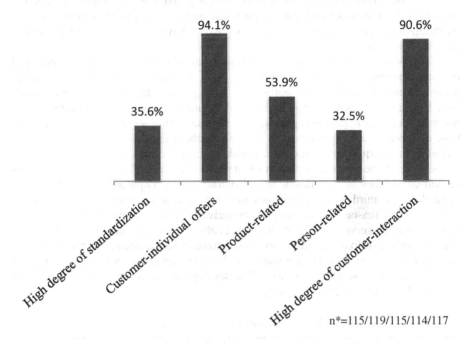

n*=115/119/115/114/117

Fig. 1. Service characteristics

Services that are customized according to customer requirements are characterized as having a high degree of customer-individualization. Customizing services usually leads to higher quality as perceived by customers because the service is tailored to specific requirements. However, there often exists a trade-off between customization and service profitability, particularly in situations where customization is not structured according to a predefined process. Although customization and standardization seem to be contrary and incompatible approaches, standardization may help to foster customization in a cost efficient way. Using modularization, the definition of standardized service components that can be combined according to customer requirements is possible [4].

Product relatedness and person relatedness are two characteristics focusing on the service object. Product-related services are provided in association with or for a specific product, e.g. maintenance. On the contrary, person-related services directly address humans as the service object, e.g. consulting.

The degree of standardization and customization is of special importance during service definition. The degree of customer interaction is assessed based on the time that the customer is involved during service provision. It can be assumed that person-related services have a higher degree of customer interaction than product-related services. It is necessary to note that this is a solely quantitative measure, i.e. it does not allow for statements about the customer influence on service provision. For example, services rendered to the customers generally have a higher degree of customer interaction than services that can be provided without the customer being present. Furthermore, single decisions of customers possibly have a high impact on the ways a service is provided.

As can be seen in Table 3, an overwhelming majority of 95 percent of the surveyed companies provides customer-individual services. In addition, 90 percent of the companies characterize their service portfolio as having a high degree of customer interaction. This has an immense impact on research regarding human service interfaces. It is not only necessary to provide appropriate interfaces during service provision. In addition, companies need methods and tools for gathering customer requirements and mapping these requirements to customer-individual service offers.

As stated above, standardization is often seen as an enable for providing customer-individual services in an efficient way. Contrary to this popular belief, only a little more than one third of the companies use standardization. Though not part of the survey, several reasons for this fact are conceivable. For example, companies with a highly complex service portfolio that has evolved over time might not be able to structure their portfolio according to standardization requirements. Furthermore, the customers of a service provider might have different requirements that cannot be met using standardized service portfolios. The development of appropriate methods and tools for these companies is necessary.

Table 3. Influence factors on service development

During service development...	Acknowledgment	Absolute values
... services of competitors are a valuable source of inspiration.	43.9%	114
... customer integration is a valuable source of approaches regarding effective service provision.	88.4%	112
... customer requirements and complaints provide important suggestions for service improvement.	82.8%	116
... employees with customer contact provide valuable ideas.	75.2%	113

As presented in Table 3, customer feedback is seen by a vast majority of companies as a valuable source for service evaluation. This feedback can be gathered in two different ways. First, customer complaints can be evaluated according to weaknesses in service design. Second, customers can be integrated in the service development process by imposing requirements on the service provider. Both ways of gathering feedback need to be supported by companies.

Several approaches exist for enabling customer feedback. First, the service processes need to be designed with flexibility in mind. Therefore, it is possible to react according to changing customer requirements. If processes are fixedly defined, front-end employees might not be able to take changing requirements into account. However, this approach is limited by possible legal parameters. Various approaches and requirements for service customization during provision have been proposed so far by, e.g. [5,6].

Another enabler for allowing customer feedback during service provision includes the implementation of customer feedback software systems. Using these systems, the gathering of customer complaints and suggestions for improvements is possible. This feedback can be integrated during service redesign and optimization. In doing so, the next generation of a provided service can be tailored more specifically to customer requirements.

4   Usage of Tools and Methods

Although the measurement of productivity is a precondition for analyzing and evaluating the efficiency of the provided services, around a third of the questioned companies do not conduct any productivity management. The reasons for this situation vary with lack of suitable methods and tools as well as an unfavorable cost-value ratio as the dominating explanations.

Productivity management is a process mainly consisting of three steps. The first step encompasses the measurement of productivity, including the sometimes challenging quantification. The second step is the analysis of the measurement results and the deduction of corresponding actions. The third and last step covers the introduction of different tools and methods for improving productivity. The structure of the questionnaire reflects this three-fold classification. Since the deduction of adequate actions is an individual process, which can hardly be supported by tools or methods, the study focused on surveying tools and methods related to the steps of measurement and improvement only. The selection of the presented tools and methods was based on the findings gathered in the pre-studies described above.

The dominating approaches for the *measurement* of service productivity are the direct quantification of key performance indicators (KPI) and the calculation of such indicators based on the relation of input and output factors (see Fig. 2). These methods are originating from the industrial domain. Service specific approaches such as Balanced Scorecards (BSC) or Data Envelopment Analysis (DEA) are hardly used. Furthermore, the pre-studies showed that the identification of appropriate key performance indicators is another challenge. On possible solution is the provision of a structured library of common KPI [7].

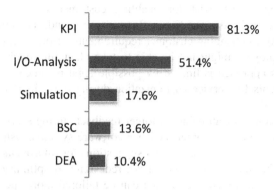

Fig. 2. Approaches for measuring service productivity

The reasons why the methods are not applied in business practice vary. Whereas BSC, Simulation and Input/Output-Analysis are mainly assessed as inappropriate for specific services, DEA is mainly unknown.

Looking at the methods supporting the improvement of productivity of services, standardization and modularization are among the most common approaches (see Fig. 3). Together, these two methods form the conceptual core of mass customization, an approach to allow for the use of economies of scale and customer individual configurable offers at the same time. Although originating from the domain of industrial engineering, this concept can also be applied on services [8]. A more service specific approach for improving productivity is the integration of customers in the service provision process, which use almost two thirds of the questioned companies. Due to an increasingly specific scope, further methods such as outsourcing, automation and Six Sigma are used only by a minority of the companies.

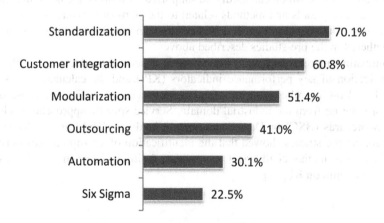

Fig. 3. Approaches for improving service productivity

5   Relevance of Productivity Management

Besides the question *what* is done for productivity management of services, a more important point is whether it is *economically sensible* to conduct productivity management. Based on the results of the survey, the intuitively obvious relationship between productivity and success could be statistically substantiated.

Since the direct surveying of financial key performance indicators is not feasible the survey used the abstract concept of 'success' to model and analyze the potential connection between productivity and economic success. First, the companies were asked to describe their relative performance of the three operational figures: profit, total revenue and number of employees over the last three years. The performance indicators were captured using a scale of five possible categories (highly decreased, decreased, unchanged, increased, highly increased). Then a number between 1 and 5 was assigned to each category. Finally, the average of the three scales was calculated, representing the overall success of a company. Thus, a numeric value of "3" represents a constant success, whereas higher values indicate a growing success. Based on this model, two thirds of the questioned companies are successful companies.

Based on this approach of identifying successful companies, advanced analyses can be conducted. Correspondingly, a regression model was created, evaluating the influence of

- conducting productivity management,
- the companies' location and
- the companies' industry affiliation

on the companies' success. The analysis shows an index value of 2.854 for West German advertising companies not managing productivity. This indicates a slightly declining success during the last three years. As Table 4 shows, conducting productivity management leads to an index value increased by 0.451. This coefficient is highly significant, which leads to the conclusion that conducting productivity management is a decisive factor for a company's success. Another factor is the location of the company.

Table 4. OLS-Regression

Variable	Coefficient	Standard error	p-Value
Constant (success index)	2.854	0.237	0.000
Conducting productivity management	0.451	0.156	0.005
East-German company location	-0.473	0.170	0.006
Metal working/machine building industry	0.520	0.257	0.046
$R^2 = 0.176$			

East German companies are less successful than companies from West Germany by an averaged index value of 0.473. The last statistically significant factor is industry affiliation. Although the effects are statistically not as strong as the factors of productivity management or location, companies active in the metal working or machine building industry have an index value increased by 0.52, thus tend to be more successful than the index. The model also included other industries, which are not listed due to a high p-Value.

Accordingly, the relevance of productivity management is recognized by the companies. 78% of the questioned companies expect a growing relevance of this topic and 21% assume at least a constant relevance. This implies that almost every participant (99%) expects a constant or growing relevance of service productivity. If these numbers are put into connection with the third of the companies not conducting any productivity management at the moment, a high potential and demand for suitable methods emerges.

6   Conclusion

The paper presented a quantitative survey among German service companies studying the current status of service productivity in business practice. Besides the depiction of the current usage of various tools and methods, the survey also provided evidence for the relevance of service productivity management as an essential factor of company success.

Although showing a broad consensus of the importance of service productivity management, around a third of the companies did not conduct any productivity management. A closer look at the applied tools and methods can provide potential reasons hindering a further application of service productivity. Predominantly, tools and methods originating from the manufacturing industry are used. Tools and methods specifically developed for service are hardly applied. Since the lack of suitable methods and tools is a major obstacle for productivity management, approaches adapted to the specifics of services might lead to a higher penetration rate of tools and methods for service productivity. Therefore, corresponding research actions support a broader application of service productivity management.

There are some limitations regarding the study. Due to the low response rate and small numbers of cases, it is not possible to make generalizable statements for German service companies or to analyze single industries. Since only German companies participated in the study, the study presents a view on the German service sector only.

The findings of the survey can be the basis for additional research. Subsequent studies may be conducted for answering several specific questions. For example, an in-depth analysis of challenges using existing approaches for measuring and improving productivity for businesses might seem relevant. In addition, the findings show a clear mission for academic research to establish appropriate methods and tools for productivity management of services.

References

1. Böttcher, M., Meiren, T. (eds.): Anforderungen an die Produktivität und Komponentisierung von Dienstleistungen. Fraunhofer Verlag, Stuttgart (2012)
2. Böttcher, M., Klingner, S., Becker, M., Schumann, K.: Produktivität von Dienstleistungssystemen. LIV, Leipzig (2012)
3. Tether, B.S., Hipp, C., Miles, I.: Standardisation and particularisation in services: evidence from Germany. Research Policy 30(7), 1115–1138 (2001)
4. Böttcher, M., Klingner, S.: Providing a Method for Composing Modular B2B-Services. Journal of Business and Industrial Marketing 26(5), 320–331 (2011)
5. Gwinner, K.P., Bitner, M.J., Brown, S.W., Kumar, A.: Service Customization Through Employee Adaptiveness. Journal of Service Research 8(2), 131–148 (2005)
6. McCarthy, I.P., Pitt, L., Berthon, P.: Service Customization Through Dramaturgy. In: Fogliatto, F.S., da Silveira, G.J.C. (eds.) Mass Customization. Springer London, London (2011)
7. Freitag, M., Lamberth, S., Klingner, S., Böttcher, M.: Method of collecting and categorising performance indicators to measure the productivity of modular services using an IT tool. In: Freitag, L., et al. (eds.) 2011 – Method of Collecting and Categorising (2011)
8. Heiskala, M., Paloheimo, K.-S., Tiihonen, J.: Mass Customisation of Services: Benefits and Challenges of Configurable Services. In: Heiskala, P., et al. (eds.) 2005 – Mass Customisation of Services (2005)

Consumer Preferences for the Interface of E-Commerce Product Recommendation System

Yi-Cheng Ku[1], Chih-Hung Peng[2], and Ya-Chi Yang[1]

[1] Dept. of Computer Science and Information Management, Providence University, Taiwan
ycku@pu.edu.tw
[2] Department of Information Systems, City University of Hong Kong, China
chpeng@cityu.edu.hk

Abstract. A recommendation system (RS) in a website is increasingly significant for consumer's decision making. A RS includes several important benefits, such as increasing user satisfaction and building user trust. Despite the growing literature that examined the usefulness of a specific attribute of a RS, less is known about which combination of attributes of a RS is preferable and how the combination influences consumer decision making. By using a conjoint analysis, we can further explore the impacts of combination attributes. In a lab experiment, we find that the importance ranking of attributes of a RS for the participants is quite different. Specifically, all the participants consider the attribute, "Explanation for Recommendation", is important. In addition, "Rating" is important for the specific participants. Furthermore, "Comment" seems to be less important to all the participants. Our results have important implications for the design of a RS.

Keywords: recommendation system, user interface preferences, adaptive interface, conjoint analysis.

1 Introduction

A recommendation system (RS) has played an increasingly important role in the success of e-commerce websites. A RS helps online customers facilitate their product searching and improve decision quality. In addition, through explicit or implicit learning, a RS can predict consumers' product preferences and provide customized recommendations. These benefits of a RS increase customers' satisfaction and trust toward the RS [1]. A RS is beneficial for not only consumers but also an e-commerce website. According to the report from Experian Marketing Services, the total revenue at Amazon.com in 2012 was $61.1 billion, and around 30% of its total revenue came from product recommendations. Therefore, how to increase RS performance is a critical issue for practitioners and researchers.

Most previous studies have measured RS performance by either objective prediction accuracy (e.g. mean absolute error) or users' subjective perception (e.g. user satisfaction) [2]. However, these two measures pay less attention to the utility of interaction between users and a RS (i.e., user experience). Considering user experience is

F.F.-H. Nah (Ed.): HCIB/HCII 2014, LNCS 8527, pp. 526–537, 2014.
© Springer International Publishing Switzerland 2014

necessary because accuracy is not the only one criterion to evaluate an information system. Memorable experience will enhance users' continuous usage intention [3]. Hence, researchers have proposed a novel measure of RS performance by including the concept of user experience [3-5].

Our study focuses on designing a user interface of a RS. Although previous studies have proposed several guidelines for designing a user interface of a RS, most of the studies have focused on one recommendation mechanism at a time rather a combination of recommendation mechanisms (e.g., average ratings, associate products, expert review, and other related recommendations). However, when users are browsing a RS, the interface of a RS is composed of multiple mechanisms instead of a single mechanism. Therefore, investigating a combination of recommendation mechanisms in an RS interface is reasonable and needed. The purposes of our research are twofold: First, we conduct a conjoint analysis to explore how users prefer different RS interfaces. Second, we explore the importance ranking of RS mechanisms for different user populations.

The rest of this study was organized as follows. First, we review related literature and Amazon.com to understand the principles of user interface design pertaining to RSs in section 2. Then, the research methods are described in section 3. In section 4, the results of conjoint analysis and research findings are discussed. We make a brief conclusion in final section.

2   Literature Review

Prior studies have proposed several principles to design a user interface. A user interface is defined as a platform which allows users to interact with a system. The first principle is to keep a user interface simple. Specifically, a user interface should only include necessary information, and information included should be concise. The second principle is related to an interface representation. Users spend less cognitive effort interacting with an interface when they use a visual representation interface than a text representation interface. To reduce user's cognition burden, interface designers can replace texts with simple icons on an interface. For instance, a thumb up emoticon means "recommended", while a thumb down one means "not recommended".

These principles have suggested that interface designers can design a better interface for users when they understand how users interact with an interface by minimum cognitive effort. Based on cognitive load theory, humans keep minimum load on working memory to seek optimum learning [6]. That is, optimum interface which provides easily recognized, sufficiently and necessarily detailed interface can reduce RS users' cognitive load [7]. Previous studies have explored how interface contents should be presented. For instance, Lee and Benbasat [8] have shown that the size and clarity of product pictures on the interface affect users' memory of products. Cai and Xu [9] have proposed that different arrangements have different impacts on users. They found that users tend to buy higher quality products when products are sorted by a quality criterion in a descending order than in an ascending order.

2.1   RS Interface Design

A user interface of a RS is the key to affecting whether users are willing to use the system continuously. An adaptive RS interface can increase such willingness because users can find products interested efficiently and effectively. Previous studies have proposed several important mechanisms which are used in designing an interface of a RS. Wang and Benbasat [1] found that users have a higher level of initial trust in a RS with an explanation mechanism than a RS without it. If a RS offers explanation why a product was recommended, users' understanding and acceptance of the system will increase [10]. They will find that the process of recommendation is useful, and different degrees of transparency will provide them with different experiences. In addition, Jones and Pu [11] have suggested that a successful design of a RS should focus on a simple and clear interface that can reduce users' decision effort (e.g. the time spent on acquiring recommendation) and maximize the quality of recommendation (e.g. precision, satisfaction and novelty). In this study, we focus on how to design an adaptive interface of a RS by considering a set of mechanisms together.

We used Amazon.com to identify which general mechanisms are used often in a RS. Since Amazon.com is a global and large-scale e-retailer and many previous studies investigated the effects of RS by using Amazon.com [12], mechanisms provided by the RS of Amazon.com are typical and applicable. Based on recommendation page at Amazon.com, as shown in Fig. 1, our study identified six general attributes, including *rating, explanation, associate products, the number of recommended products, customer review,* and *review comment.*

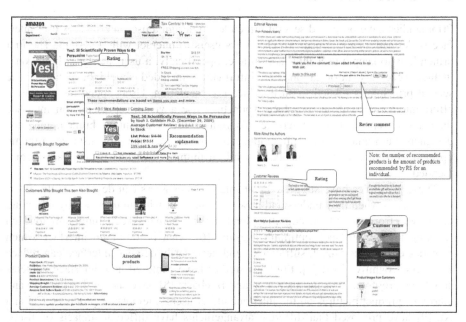

Fig. 1. Attributes in RS interface (An example of Amazon.com)

When a user has limited knowledge of a field or in a field with a variety of goods, visual representation can effectively increase recommendation effectiveness and user's satisfaction. It can also attract users to use the comments more often without increasing their cognitive load [13]. Since the area of a web page is limited, it's important to adaptively present recommendation message. In particular, RS has been applied to mobile device which has smaller screen than monitor, it's necessary to understand RS users' priority in interface attributes and format. Since there are six attributes with different levels, this study adopted the conjoint analysis to evaluate users' preferences for the interface design of a RS.

2.2   Conjoint Analysis

When consumers are facing with a variety of products including goods and services, they would evaluate every attribute of products to make the final decision, and consumers will also establish a preference for a certain product in the process. Conjoint analysis is a multivariate method that uses the final decision and goes through the decomposition process to evaluate customers' preference structure. For example, conjoint analysis was used to explore shopping attribute combinations of website's characteristics preferred by consumers in order to offer reference basis for constructing websites [14]. Hence, conjoint analysis can be applied to understand how products with multiple attributes affect consumers' preferences. It contains all tangible and intangible functions of products, and it is able to pre-determine consumers' reaction and evaluation of potential product attribute combination.

Researchers often use a conjoint analysis to evaluate consumers' preferences of a certain product attribute combination. Subjects evaluate different product attribute combinations and their preference structure will then be decomposed, adding the part-worth of each attribute under different levels to obtain an overall utilities. The product with the highest overall utilities is favored by consumers, and it has higher opportunity of being chosen. Besides obtaining the overall utilities, we can also calculate the relative importance of each attribute, which can explain each attribute's importance to the overall preferences. Hence, conjoint analysis was applied to design an adaptive IS interface. For example, Seneler et al. [15] adopted conjoint analysis to explore the interface feature prioritization for web services. Based on an experiment study, they found that interfaces that have high-speed, minimal memory load, adaptive behavior, low content density, and customization features are more preferable than those that do not. Therefore, this study used a conjoint analysis to explore users' preference for RS interface combination and prioritization of attributes.

3   Research Method

3.1   Prototypes of RS Interface

In this study, we selected six attributes of a RS and each attribute has different levels to investigate RS users' attitudes and preferences toward a RS interface.

Combinations of the attributes with different levels allow us to have several proto-types of a RS interface. We briefly describe these attributes and their levels.

Rating. RS rating scales influence the level of cognitive effort users exert when using a RS. A delicate scale requires users to increase their cognitive effort to process in-formation. In contrast, a coarse scale reduces their cognitive effort, but discourages them from making a precise evaluation. Therefore, we propose three types of a rating scale: 2-point, 5-point, and 10-point.

Explanation. Previous studies have suggested that, when a RS explains why a prod-uct is recommended, users are more satisfied with the recommend product and have a higher level of trust toward the system [1]. Therefore, we propose two levels of an explanation mechanism. That is, a RS is with an explanation and without it.

Associate Products. Associate products are the products that are relevant to a rec-ommended product. For example, associate products of a mobile phone could be its screen protectors. Consumers may be interested in associate products when browsing recommended products. However, what kind of associate products should be recom-mended is not clear. Thus, we propose three kinds of associate products, including related goods, goods of the same type, and other items customers bought after view-ing the item.

The Number of Recommended Products. The number of recommended products which were generated by a RS influences users' shopping decisions. If there are too many recommendations, it will cause users information overload. If there are too few recommendations, the products which users like may not be in the recommendation list. Hence we propose three levels of the number of recommended products: 14 items, 21 items, and 28 items.

Customer's Review. Customer review is one of the main information sources for consumers to understand the quality of goods [16]. We argue that information rich-ness of a review affects how a user judges a product. For example, it's difficult to describe the effects of cosmetic goods by text. It would be useful to present "before" and "after" pictures for cosmetic goods experiences, so that consumers can easily evaluate the goods. As a result, customer's review may be revealed by multi-media content. Since users' preference on the format of customer review may vary, there are two levels of customer's review attribute, including "literary description" and "lite-rary description with pictures".

Review Comment. A review comment is an evaluation of a specific review. Users can judge whether a review is helpful based on its feedback [17]. Review comment can be presented in a simple way (e.g., agreed or not) or with rich contents (e.g., criti-cisms with voting), and it can also describe a user's viewpoint on a certain review. Therefore, our study investigates what kind of comments is attractive to users and proposes two levels of comment, i.e., "literary description" and dichotomous "helpful or not".

3.2   Conjoint Analysis Design and Survey

According to the observation of Amazon.com and previous relevant studies, this study proposes 216 (3 x 2 x 3 x 3 x 2 x 2) interface combinations of RS interface types to explore the relationships between RS interface attributes and users' preference for RS interface design. Following Green et al. [18], we conducted the mixed model of conjoint analysis. First, we establish the prototypes (i.e., stimuli in conjoint analysis) based on the combination of each level of each attribute. Our research adopts the orthogonal design in SPSS software package. We reduce the number of stimuli in the overall outline from 216 to 20, 4 of which are reserved observations that are mainly used to check the effectiveness of the models. Even though we've reduced the number of stimuli to 20, it will still lead to subjects' information overload if we give them all 20 stimuli for evaluation at a time, and this will reduce the accuracy of the information we collect. In order to solve this problem, our research uses 20 stimuli as a unit. Each unit will be randomly divided into four groups with five stimuli in each group, where one of the stimuli becomes the reserved stimulus and the other four are experimental stimuli. A snapshot of an example of stimuli is shown in Appendix 1. Every subject only needs to evaluate one group; that is, each subject evaluates no more than five stimuli, giving them 1-9 points, where 1 point means that their preference for the specific stimulus is the lowest and 9 points the highest. Since the purpose of our research is to explore users' preferences for interface design of RS, we adopt narrative and graphical presentation to describe stimuli. Narrative is used to explain the function of each attribute, while graphical presentation allows subjects to truly feel the presentation of the interface. In particular, we adopted a full-profile to present stimuli, which allows subjects to do preference evaluation based on the stimulus with the overall profile of recommendation message (Appendix 1).

Then we adopted a mixed model combining self-explicated preference model and traditional conjoint analysis model to conduct conjoint analysis. We collect the relative weights of attributes and the ideal rating of every level under all the attributes, and then establish the questionnaires with limited overall profile and demographic variables. All subjects were asked to arrange the order of the six attributes, including rating, explanation, associate products, the number of recommended products, customer review, and review comment. The order of the attributes represents their importance. Then we listed all the levels of each attribute, and then ask subjects to arrange the order based on their preferences. The order of the levels represents their importance. We adopted cellphones as the recommended products in the stimuli. There are two main reasons: One is that almost people have one or more cellphones, and they use cellphones frequently and thus are familiar with them. The other reason is that cellphones are unisex goods. Hence, it would be easy to recruit voluntary subjects.

A pretest was conduct to validate the questionnaire. 14 graduate students and 14 college students were recruited from a medium university in Taiwan to evaluate the prototype and the questionnaire. The modification of the questionnaire was to increase the design type combination of the stimulus versions, and the purpose of this modification is to mark the features of each stimulus, which allows subjects to quickly grasp the difference and makes it easier for them to answer the questions. All 236 volunteers were recruited from a university and a government department in central Taiwan to participate in our survey. All subjects were asked to evaluate self-explicated preference and a randomly assigned group of stimuli. Finally, 193 questionnaires were effectively completed. The valid ratio of our questionnaire is 81.78%. Most subjects' age falls between 21 to 30 years old (58.55 %) and females take up 63.21% of sample. As for Internet using experience, only 8.29 % of the sample had less than 5-year Internet usage. Furthermore, 94.82% of the sample had online shopping experience. In particular, most subjects (79.79 %) had the experience of browsing the e-stores with RSs.

4   Data Analysis

4.1   Market Segment

In order to understand similar consumers' preference for the interface factors of a RS more precisely, we adopted the componential segmentation model to segment subjects. The componential segmentation model uses the self-explicated preference data of subjects to conduct cluster analysis. The value of self-explicated preference was calculated by relative weights of attributes x the ideal rating of every level under all the attributes. And then, we use ANOVA and discriminant analysis to identify the validity of clustering and to distinguish the capacity of the discriminant function. First, we use Ward's method of hierarchical clustering approach to do cluster analysis and find that the ideal number of cluster is three. Then, we use the K-means method of non-hierarchical cluster approach to divide subjects into three clusters, and the number of subjects in cluster A, B, C is 52(26.94%), 79(40.93%), and 62(32.13%), respectively. Finally, we apply ANOVA analysis to test whether there are significant differences among these three clusters. The analysis results show that, based on the linear relationships of the 15 levels, the value of Pillai's Trace is 1.321 (F=24.728, p<0.05) and the value of Wilks' Lambda is 0.101 (F=27.213, p<0.05). It means that the average values of the three clusters in each attribute level are not equal. As Table 1 shown, we also conducted Duncan's post-hoc analysis to compare the mean difference between the three clusters in each attribute level. If there is no comma between two cluster codes, the mean difference is non-significant.

Discriminant analysis is used to identify the validity of clustering and the identification ability of the discriminant function after the grouping of samples. We used the segmentation results of the three clusters as the dependent variables and the 15 self-explicated values of subjects as discriminant variables to do discriminant analysis. In this way, we would be able to identify the validity of clustering and the identification ability of the discriminant function. Both hit ratio and Press Q were used to test whether the result of the predicted clustering has discriminant ability. The hit ratio is 97.93%, and Press Q is 362.37 > 6.63, which means that the discriminant function has high discriminant ability. Therefore, we can infer that the consumers from different clusters have significant difference in their preference for the interface design combination of a RS.

Table 1. The analysis of the difference in average value of each cluster

Attribute	Level	Cluster 1 (n=52)	Cluster 2 (n=79)	Cluster 3 (n=62)	F	p-value	Duncan
Rating (x_1)	2-point	0.0447	0.0513	0.0910	44.555	.000	(12, 3)
	5-point	0.0603	0.0727	0.1155	47.830	.000	(1, 2, 3)
	10-point	0.0424	0.0463	0.0562	3.342	.037	(12, 23)
Explanation (x_2)	No	0.0635	0.0843	0.0678	9.664	.000	(13, 2)
	Yes	0.1160	0.1546	0.1157	15.822	.000	(31, 2)
Associate Products (x_3)	Related goods	0.0391	0.0661	0.0349	22.211	.000	(31, 2)
	Goods of the same type	0.0505	0.0906	0.0421	41.457	.000	(31, 2)
	Other items customers bought after viewing the item	0.0322	0.0528	0.0328	12.646	.000	(13, 2)
The number of recommended products (x_4)	14 items	0.0304	0.0595	0.0410	14.843	.000	(13, 2)
	21 items	0.0259	0.0571	0.0330	26.889	.000	(13, 2)
	28 items	0.0179	0.0412	0.0197	18.215	.000	(13, 2)
Customer review (x_5)	Literary description	0.0855	0.0491	0.0765	47.858	.000	(2, 3, 1)
	Literary description with pictures	0.1709	0.0867	0.1416	121.187	.000	(2, 3, 1)
Review comment (x_6)	Literary description of comment	0.1264	0.0462	0.0714	87.743	.000	(2, 3, 1)
	Helpful or Not Helpful	0.0943	0.0415	0.0607	35.953	.000	(2, 3, 1)

4.2   Results of Conjoint Analysis

We estimate the part-worth utilities of each segment on the basis of the mixed model of the conjoint analysis and the market segmentation model. As formula 1 shown, ordinary Least Square Regression (OSL) was adopted to estimate the parameters in order to obtain the regression coefficient, i.e., the estimation of part-worth.

$$y_{ih} = a + b\hat{y}_{ih} + B_{11}x_{i11} + B_{12}x_{i12} + B_{21}x_{i21} + B_{31}x_{i31} + B_{32}x_{i32} + B_{41}x_{i41} + B_{42}x_{i42} + B_{51}x_{i51} + B_{61}x_{i61} \tag{1}$$

y_{ih} : The hth subject's overall preference value for the ith stimulus

$\hat{y}_{ih}$: The hth subject's self-explicated preference value for the ith stimulus

B_{al} : Subject's estimated part-worth of attribute a with level l

    ($a = 1, 2, ..., n$, $l = 1, 2, ..., m$)

x_{ial} : A dummy variable which presents attribute a with level l in the ith stimulus
(For instance: $X_{11}=1$ and $X_{12}=0$ was defined as 2-point (1,0), while $X_{11}=0$ and $X_{12}=1$ was defined as 5-point (0,1))

Each subject has to evaluate one of the four groups pertaining to the stimulus unit and there are five stimuli in each group, but one of them is reserved observation value that won't be included in the regression equation. Therefore, each subject has five evaluation data of the overall profile and each level was coded by dummy variable.

As a result, there are 52 subjects in the cluster 1 with 208 observation values, 79 in cluster 2 with 316 observation values, and 62 in cluster 3 with 248 observation values. The regression results of cluster 1 to cluster 3 are shown in Table 2.

Table 2. The linear regression models in each segment

Model	Standardized coefficient of $\hat{y}_{th}$	Standardized Coefficient of Dummy variables $X_{11} \sim X_{61}$								
		X_{11}	X_{12}	X_{21}	X_{31}	X_{32}	X_{41}	X_{42}	X_{51}	X_{61}
Cluster 1	0.092	0.136^{φ}	0.129	0.161*	-0.162*	-0.106	0.015	0.156*	-0.203*	-0.046
Cluster 2	0.14	-0.033	0.126^{φ}	0.105	0.08	0.017	-0.04	0.057	-0.134*	0.071
Cluster 3	0.161	0.048	0.158^{φ}	0.081	-0.08	-0.078	-0.054	0.062	0.002	-0.034

* $p<0.05$; φ $p<0.1$

All three regression models are reasonable because there is no autocorrelation between error terms (D-W value is between 1.5 and 2.5). The R^2 of regression model for cluster 1 is 0.177 (F=4.235, $p<0.001$). The result of our analysis shows that the subjects in cluster 1 have preference for the shopping websites that offer explanations for recommendation, 21 items at a time for the number of recommended products, and the 2-point rating. However, they have less preference for the websites that offer the recommendation of related goods and the review with only literary description. The R^2 of regression model for cluster 2 is 0.118 (F=4.091, $p<0.001$). The subjects in cluster 2 have preference for the 5-point rating. However, they have less preference for the websites that offer the review with only literary description. The R^2 of regression model for cluster 3 is 0.079 (F=2.044, $p <0.05$). The subjects in cluster 3 have preference for the 5-point rating. These three regression models were used to predict the subjects' preferences of reserved stimuli in each segment respectively. The results show that the explanation powers are acceptable.

4.3   The Analysis of Part-Worth Utilities

Based on the results of the discussions in the previous sub-section and the part-worth utilities of each attribute's base level being 0, we can obtain a complete set of part-worth utilities, which can represent the common preference structure of all subjects in a specific segment. In this sub-section, we are going to use the part-worth utilities of each segment to further explore the attribute's weight of each segment and the preference combination. According to Wind et al. [19], we use the differences between the part-worth utilities of levels within an attribute to estimate the relative importance of the attributes. The formula is as follows,

$$RIA_k = \frac{A_k}{\sum_{p=1}^{p} A_k} \times 100\% \tag{2}$$

RIA_k : the relative weight of the attribute k

A_k : the highest part-worth minus lowest part-worth within attribute k

We can infer from the formula above that the greater difference between levels within an attribute is, the higher the relative weight of the attribute becomes. Thus, we can find out which changes in attribute levels can cause greater consumer preference variation. The top three most preferred attributes of the RS interface in each cluster was summarized in Table 3.

Table 3. Preferred attributes with preferred level

Cluster	Preferred attributes	Preferred level
Cluster 1	Review (22.42%)	literary description with pictures
	The number of recommended goods (20.00%)	21 items
	Explanation (17.94%)	Giving explanations
Cluster 2	Rating (24.26%)	5-point
	Review (22.11%)	literary description with pictures
	Explanation1 (7.39%)	Giving explanations
Cluster 3	Rating (39.17%)	5-point
	Associate products (19.97%)	customers' final purchase item
	Explanation (17.39%)	Giving explanations

5   Discussions and Conclusions

A RS has been used as a tool that helps consumers make shopping decisions in e-commerce, and it has three advantages: turning Internet surfers into buyers, increasing product cross-selling opportunities, and securing customers' loyalty to the website. Most of the previous studies focused on the accuracy of RS. However, there are few studies investigating the effects of adaptive RS interface on users' usage behaviors. The results of this study not only have important practical insights but also provide researchers theoretical implications. Our research adopts a conjoint analysis to explore the difference in the consumers' preference for the attribute combination of a RS interface. Three clusters segmented by customer's self-explicated value were grouped and the ordinary least square regression which estimates part-worth utility of each attribute level was also proposed for each segment. In addition, we also examine the importance ranking of RS's attributes in different segments when RS users are browsing recommended messages. As for the rating, its importance in cluster 2 and cluster 3 is relatively high, and it's ranked No.1 in both. However, for the consumers in cluster 1, it's not an important attribute, and it's ranked No.5. Most subjects prefer the 5-point scale. About the customer review, the consumers in cluster 1 and cluster 2 put much emphasis on it, and its importance rank is No.1 and No.2 relatively. However, consumers in cluster 3 don't consider it to be an important attribute, and it is ranked No.6. Most consumers prefer the format of review to be presented in literary description with pictures.

About explanation, its attribute importance percentages in each segment are close, and the importance rank is 3 in all the segments. Providing explanation will enhance consumers' utilities in all segments. This result is consistent with the findings of previous studies which indicated that a RS with transparency can also affect users' perceived usefulness during the recommendation process and increase their acceptance and understanding of RS. Regarding to associate products and the number of recommended products, the consumers' preferences for these two attributes are inconsistent among the three segments. The rank of associate products is No. 4 in cluster 1 and cluster 2, and No. 2 in cluster 3. The rank of the number of recommended products is No. 2 in cluster 1, No. 6 in cluster 2, and No. 4 in cluster 3. In addition, most consumers prefer the interface to show 21 recommended items at a time. Our findings indicate that RS users' preferences for RS interface are different. Website designer can enhance RS users' experience by providing adaptive interface. As for the comment function, its importance percentage and rank are relatively low in all the segments, and it's ranked No.6 in cluster 1, No.5 in cluster 2 and cluster 3. These results indicate that consumers may consult customer reviews when they are evaluating the recommended products, but they may skip the comments which criticize the customer reviews.

Acknowledgements. This work was partially supported by the National Science Council of the Republic of China under the grant NSC 101-2410-H-126-005-MY2 and a grant from the City University of Hong Kong [Project No. 7200328].

References

1. Wang, W., Benbasat, I.: Recommendation Agents for Electronic Commerce: Effects of Explanation Facilities on Trusting Beliefs. Journal of Management Information Systems 23, 217–246 (2007)
2. Cremonesi, P., Garzotto, F., Turrin, R.: Investigating the Persuasion Potential of Recommender Systems from a Quality Perspective: An Empirical Study. ACM Transactions on Interactive Intelligent Systems 2, 1–41 (2012)
3. Knijnenburg, B.P., Willemsen, M.C., Gantner, Z., Soncu, H., Newell, C.: Explaining the User Experience of Recommender Systems. User Modeling and User-Adapted Interaction 22, 441–504 (2012)
4. Zins, A.H., Bauernfeind, U.: Explaining Online Purchase Planning Experiences with Recommender Websites. In: Frew, A.J. (ed.) Information and Communication Technologies in Tourism 2005, pp. 137–148. Springer Vienna (2005)
5. McNee, S.M., Riedl, J., Konstan, J.A.: Making Recommendations Better: An Analytic Model for Human-Recommender Interaction. In: CHI 2006 Extended Abstracts on Human Factors in Computing Systems, Montreal, Canada, pp. 1103–1108 (2006)
6. Sweller, J.: Cognitive Load during Problem Solving: Effects on Learning. Cognitive Science 12, 257–285 (1988)
7. Ozen, C., Basoglu, N.: Impact of Man–Machine Interaction Factors on Enterprise Resource Planning (ERP) Software Design. In: Proceedings of Portland International Conference for Management of Engineering and Technology 2006, Istanbul, Turkey, pp. 2335–2341 (2006)
8. Lee, Y.E., Benbasat, I.: Interface Design for Mobile Commerce. Communications of the ACM 46, 48–52 (2003)
9. Cai, S., Xu, Y.: Designing Product Lists for E-Commerce: the Effects of Sorting on Consumer Decision Making. Intl. Journal of Human–Computer Interaction 24, 700–721 (2008)
10. Gretzel, U., Fesenmaier, D.R.: Persuasion in Recommender Systems. International Journal of Electronic Commerce 11, 81–100 (2006)

11. Jones, N., Pu, P.: User Technology Adoption Issues in Recommender Systems. In: Proceedings of the NAEC 2007, Riva del Garda, Italy, pp. 379–394 (2007)
12. Pathak, B., Garfinkel, R., Gopal, R.D., Venkatesan, R., Yin, F.: Empirical Analysis of the Impact of Recommender Systems on Sales. Journal of Management Information Systems 27, 159–188 (2010)
13. Hu, P.J.-H., Ma, P.-C., Chau, P.Y.K.: Evaluation of User Interface Designs for Information Retrieval Systems: A Computer-Based Experiment. Decision Support Systems 27, 125–143 (1999)
14. Chen, Y.H., Hsu, I.C., Lin, C.C.: Website Attributes That Increase Consumer Purchase Intention: a Conjoint Analysis. Journal of Business Research 63, 1007–1014 (2010)
15. Seneler, C.O., Basoglu, N., Daim, T.: Interface Feature Prioritization for Web Services: Case of Online Flight Reservations. Computers in Human Behavior 25, 862–877 (2009)
16. Hu, N., Liu, L., Zhang, J.J.: Do Online Reviews Affect Product Sales? The Role of Reviewer Characteristics and Temporal Effects. Information Technology and Management 9, 201–214 (2008)
17. Ku, Y.C., Wei, C.P., Hsiao, H.W.: To Whom Should I Listen? Finding Reputable Reviewers in Opinion-Sharing Communities. Decision Support Systems 53, 534–542 (2012)
18. Green, P.E., Goldberg, S.M., Montemayor, M.: A Hybrid Utility Estimation Model for Conjoint Analysis. Journal of Marketing 45, 33–41 (1981)
19. Wind, Y., Grashof, J.F., Goldhar, J.D.: Market-Based Guidelines for Design of Industrial Products. Journal of Marketing 42, 27–37 (1978)

Appendix 1: A Sample Screen of Stimuli

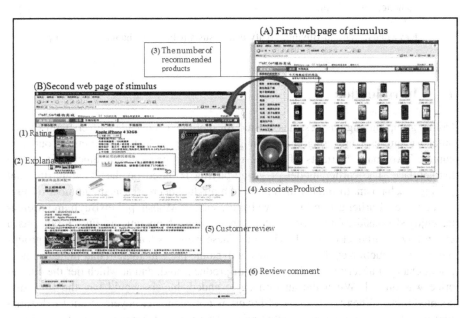

Critical Examination of Online Group-Buying Mechanisms

Yi Liu[1], Chuan Hoo Tan[2], Juliana Sutanto[1], Choon Ling Sia[2], and Kwok-Kee Wei[2]

[1] Chair of Management Information Systems, D-MTEC, ETH Zurich, Switzerland
{yiliu,jsutanto}@ethz.ch
[2] Department of Information Systems, City University of Hong Kong, Hong Kong
{ch.tan,iscl,isweikk}@cityu.edu.hk

Abstract. Online group-buying mechanism evolves from earlier variant with dynamic discount pricing mechanism to daily-deal variant with fixed discount pricing mechanism. Both mechanisms still face the challenge of attracting customers, either merchants or buyers. In this paper, we examine online group-buying mechanisms by conducting an exhaustive review of online group-buying literature. Through identifying key design features for group-buying business models, we aim to propose a more sustainable group-buying mechanism. Based on the review of 46 articles, we propose that sustainable group-buying mechanism need to balance the benefits of both merchants and buyers. The nature of group-buying needs to be emphasized, but the mechanism should not be too complicated or simple.

Keywords: Group-Buying, daily-deal, sustainable mechanism, literature review.

1   Introduction

Online group-buying business has existed for more than a decade. Buyers with similar purchase interests are congregated on group-buying websites to obtain group discounts. Two major variants of online group-buying mechanisms emerge in online marketplace. The earlier model of group-buying is based on the dynamic discount pricing mechanism, through which price of a product decreases as the number of buyers increases. Earlier group-buying websites, such as Mobshop, LetsBuyIt and Mercata, enjoyed considerable success at the beginning of operations. Fig. 1 presents a group-buying product on LetsBuyIt.com. These websites featured products for group-buying in an auction cycle and provided a dynamic price histogram that indicated how prices changed according to the number of products sold, and at which tier the current price was on [1]. When the auction cycle ended, buyers would pay the final discounted price. When the number of buyers is not adequate, buyers might be dissatisfied with the not-so-deep discounted price. These websites ceased operations after a few years by facing the critical challenge of a lack of buyers. The complicated group-buying mechanism and long waiting time for buyers are considered as key contributing factors for the failure [2] [3] [4]. A later group-buying model, coined in 2010,

F.F.-H. Nah (Ed.): HCIB/HCII 2014, LNCS 8527, pp. 538–548, 2014.
© Springer International Publishing Switzerland 2014

terms as daily-deal variant that adopts fixed discount pricing mechanism has taken over the market globally. These websites feature interesting deals, such as dining, fitness or spa, with a high discount rate (typically more than 50%). If the minimum required number of consumers is met at the end of the day, consumers will receive redeemable coupons. Merchants need to pay service fees, which could be as high as 50% of the coupon sales, to the websites. Groupon, the leading daily-deal website in the world, has operated in 48 countries and each featured deal can drive 350 sales and $8,750 in revenue [5]. Fig. 2 shows a featured deal on Groupon.com. Although daily-deal variant of online group-buying attracts buyers' attentions, this model brings about a refresh set of challenges including the lack of merchant participation. The deep discount offered by the website prompts the majority of buyers who are bargain hunters to not purchase again at normal prices [6]. In China, the survival rate of daily-deal group-buying website is just 18.6%, which indicates that a large number of on-line group-buying businesses have bankrupted [7]. There is an urgent need for a more sustainable group-buying mechanism.

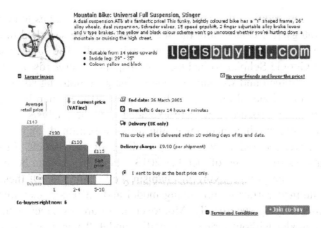

Fig. 1. Earlier group-buying website LetsBuyIt.com (Source: [1])

In this paper, we examine online group-buying mechanisms by conducting an exhaustive review of online group-buying literature. Through the review, we aim to discover the problems emerged from previous online group-buying mechanisms, figure out the research gaps of online group-buying and identify key design features for future group-buying mechanism. This study contributes to researchers and practitioners in several ways. First, although online group-buying has been popular for years, there are still few group-buying studies in academia. This study presents a comprehensive overview of the existing knowledge in this research field. Second, future research areas are identified through extant literature review, which could inspire new group-buying studies. Third, our review and could help group-buying practitioners improve their businesses by adopting more sustainable group-buying mechanism.

Fig. 2. Daily-deal website Groupon (Source: Groupon.com)

2   Literature Review

A literature review requires the development of criteria for studies to be included and the search strategy [8]. Concerning the search strategy, we searched in Scopus database with the keywords "group buying" and "daily deal". The same search was also conducted on Google Scholar to include more papers. Afterwards, abstracts of these articles were examined and we only include online group-buying studies and the studies which target individual buyers. Studies of pure offline group-buying and group-buying for company procurement were excluded. For the analysis scheme, we first identified the group-buying mechanism the articles examined, and then obtain the research objective, methodology, and key findings of each article. In total, we reviewed 46 articles till the end of October 2013. These articles can be split into three streams based on the group-buying mechanism they examined. Of these 46 articles, 15 papers examined earlier group-buying model and 13 papers examined daily-deal variant of group-buying specifically. Moreover, there are 18 papers which examined group-buying model without targeting specific model. Table 1 indicates the number of studies in each stream, categorized by the employed methodologies, whereas Table 2 shows the details of group-buying literatures. In the following three subsections, we discuss the literatures in details.

Table 1. Methodologies employed in the literatures

Methodology	Business model/Group-buying mechanism examined		
	Earlier	Daily-deal	General
Case study	1		
Ethnography		2	
Lab experiment	4	3	2
Survey		4	1
Secondary data	1	4	
Modeling analysis/ simulation	9		15

Table 2. Online group-buying literatures

Author(s)	Methodology	Objective
Earlier mechanism		
Anand and Aron (2003)	Modeling analysis	Compared the dynamic discount group-buying mechanism with the traditional fixed pricing mechanism
Chen et al. (2002)	Modeling analysis	Investigated buyers' bidding strategy
Chen et al. (2004, 2007, 2010)	Modeling analysis/simulation	Compared the dynamic discount group-buying mechanism with the traditional fixed pricing mechanism
Chen et al. (2006, 2009)	Modeling analysis	Explored the benefits of buyer co-operation
Chen et al. (2012)	Modeling analysis	Explored the benefits of buyer co-operation
Lai and Zhuang (2004, 2006)	Lab experiment	Compared the performance of incentive mechanisms
Kauffman and Wang (2001)	Secondary data	Explored buyer purchasing behavior
Kauffman and Wang (2002)	Case study	Discussed the online group-buying mechanism and analyzed the business model
Kauffman et al. (2010a)	Lab experiment	Investigated the effect of incentive mechanisms
Sharif-Paghaleh (2009)	Modeling analysis/simulation	Investigated the purchase intention of buyers
Tan et al. (2007)	Lab experiment	Investigated the purchase intention of buyers
Daily-deal mechanism		
Boon (2013)	Ethnography	Explored buyer purchasing behavior
Chen (2012a)	Ethnography	Investigated the adoption of buyers
Cheng and Huang (2013)	Survey	Investigated the adoption of buyers
Coulter and Roggeveen (2012)	Secondary data/Lab experiment	Investigated the purchase intention of buyers
Krasnova et al. (2013)	Focus group and survey	Investigated buyer loyalty to daily deal websites
Ku (2012)	Survey	Investigated the purchase intention of buyers
Li and Wu (2013)	Secondary data	Investigated the effect of word-of-mouth communication
Liu and Sutanto (2012)	Secondary data	Explored buyer purchasing behavior
Parsons et al. (2013)	Lab experiment	Investigated the purchase intention of buyers
Pentina and Taylor (2013)	Lab experiment	Investigated the purchase intention of buyers

Table 2. (*Continued.*)

Shiau and Luo (2012)	Survey	Investigated the continuous use of daily-deal buyers
Zhang et al. (2013)	Secondary data	Investigated the continuous use of daily-deal buyers
Zhou et al. (2013)	Secondary data	Explored buyer purchasing behavior

General/no specific

Breban and Vassileva (2001, 2002a, 2002b)	Modeling analysis/ simulation	Proposed group formation mechanism based on the trust relationships
Chen (2012b)	Modeling analysis	Proposed group formation mechanism by facilitating buyers to find group-buying products
Hyodo et al. (2003)	Modeling analysis/ simulation	Proposed group formation mechanism by allocating buyers into different into websites
Ito et al. (2002a, 2002b)	Modeling analysis	Proposed cooperative mechanisms for merchants
Kauffman et al. (2010b)	Lab experiment	Investigated the purchase intention of buyers
Lai and Su (2007)	Lab experiment	Investigated the effect of word-of-mouth communication
Lee and Lin (2013)	Modeling analysis	Proposed a new mechanism to secure and monitor the group-buying transaction
Li et al. (2004, 2010)	Modeling analysis/ simulation	Proposed group formation mechanism
Mastuo and Ito (2002, 2004)	Modeling analysis/ simulation	Proposed a decision support system based on buyer preferences to help buyers join the most suitable group.
Mastuo (2009)	Modeling analysis	Proposed a volume discount mechanism
Sheu et al. (2008)	Survey	Investigated the effects of the characteristics of buyers on participation
Yamamoto and Sycara (2001)	Modeling analysis/ simulation	Proposed group formation mechanism based on the category of products
Yuan and Lin (2004)	Modeling analysis/ simulation	Proposed group formation mechanism based on the concept of credit-based group negotiation

2.1   Stream 1: Earlier Mechanism

In the first stream, studies have compared the dynamic discount pricing mechanism with the non group-buying fixed pricing mechanism. It has been found that the optimal dynamic discount pricing mechanism is equivalent to the optimal fixed pricing mechanism [9] [10]. Dynamic discount group-buying pricing mechanism outperforms fixed pricing mechanism when the demand regime is uncertain [9] [11], production postponement combines with economies of scale [9] [10], the merchant is a risk-seeker wishing to expand into a market with new products [10], or there is a greater low-valuation demand than a high-valuation demand [12]. Although dynamic discount group-buying pricing mechanism may be a better choice for merchants, congregation of enough number of buyers before the end of the auction to reach a lower price is difficult which motivates researchers to study the buyer behavior of group-buying. On group-buying website, Kauffman and Wang [2] observe the positive participation effect, the price drop effect, and the cycle-ending effect. In order to take advantage of the positive participation effect, incentive mechanisms which are time-based incentive mechanism, quantity-based incentive mechanism, and sequence-based incentive mechanism, are proposed to motivate buyers to place their orders earlier [13] [14] [15]. Buyers are also more likely to place their orders when they are provided with conditional purchase options (purchase only with reserved price) rather than dynamic price histogram [16]. Buyers can also cooperate for the group-buying bid if the number of buyers with higher valuations to a product is large [17]. Buyer collusion could reduce the bidding prices and market expansion, which were beneficial to both merchants and buyers [18] [19]. Chen et al. [20] reveal a weakly dominant strategy for buyers which is the highest permitted bidding price that is no greater than the buyer value to the product is always the optimal bid price. In summary, dynamic discount pricing mechanism is complicated for buyers to understand and they may even do not know the price they should pay [1]. Moreover, the group-buying auctions cost too much time for buyers to wait and get the products they bought. The long waiting time diminished buyers' willingness to obtain slight discounts [3].

2.2   Stream 2: Daily-Deal Mechanism

As the invention of daily-deal group-buying model, the second stream of group-buying literatures emerges. Daily-deal variant overcomes some problems from earlier group-buying mechanism and adopts fixed discount pricing mechanism and short auction time (i.e. one or a few days). Merchants who feature their deals on group-buying websites are mostly not well known to the buyers and buyers worry about the service quality and their image [21]. Thus, the adoption of daily-deal websites and purchase intention of deals are studied. Profit, value, emotion, and achievement are identified as four types of motivations for adopting daily-deal group-buying [22]. Consumer satisfaction, trust, and merchant creativity also contribute to this adoption behavior [23]. The purchasing intention of buyers is positively affected by the previous number of buyers, the purchase limit of deals [24], service quality [25] [26], and online WOM communication [27] [25]. Social media are also integrated in daily-deal websites and sharing the deals via Facebook "Like" could generate more sales of coupons [28]. Since the minimum required number of buyers for deals is low and the discount is deep, positive starting effect exists during the auction [29] and observational learning effect is also observed [28] [30] [31]. In addition, matching the framing of daily-deal promotional message with the regulatory focus of buyers could strengthen the persuasion effect [32]. Although buyers who are mainly deal seekers prefer deep-discounted deals, merchants shows little interest and loyalty to daily-deal website for future collaboration which results in the lack of deals on daily-deal website [33]. Regardless of the required minimum number of buyers, daily deal variant simplifies group-buying mechanism and exists in the form of time-limited sales, where the nature of group-buying is weakened.

2.3   Stream 3: General

Besides the above studies, there are 18 studies which do not target specific group-buying mechanism. Among these studies, a significant number of them investigate coalition formation for group-buying activities. Buying group can be formed based on the category of products [34], trust relationships [35] [36] [37], various website allocation [38], credit negotiation [39], reservation prices for a combination of items from buyer [40] [41], reservation prices and payment adjustment values from merchants [42], buyer preferences [43] [44], and the web browsing history of buyers [45]. Merchants can also cooperate to exchange goods in an agent-mediated electronic market system [46] [47]. In addition, a group-buying agent which secures and monitors the transactions could mitigate the risk for consumers and merchants [48]. Other studies offer general understandings of group-buying models. For instance, people with higher incomes, and more online shopping experience and time more actively participate in online group-buying [49]. Textual comments positively affect buyers' perceived trust of group-buying [14], whereas the source of group-buying information (friends vs. merchants) affected the attitudes and purchase intentions of buyers [50].

3   Discussions

Online group-buying business faces enduringly critical challenges as earlier online group-buying model ceased operations and the latest daily-deal online group-buying model confronts survival crisis. The sustainability of the online group-buying mechanism becomes an important research topic. Through the extant review of group-buying literature, we find that the sustainable group-buying mechanism should first consider the benefits of both merchants and buyers. Earlier group-buying model, which adopts dynamic pricing mechanism, focuses on merchants' benefits and the first stream of studies mainly investigates whether merchants can gain from this pricing mechanism. However, the complicated mechanism and long auction time diminish buyers' willingness to participate in [1][3]. Subsequent daily-deal model that adopts a simple pricing mechanism with deep discount and short auction time attracts buyer interests. However, since merchants can hardly attain profits via daily-deal promotions, merchants shows little interest and loyalty to daily-deal website which results in the lack of merchant participation [33]. Future research can study group-buying businesses from both merchant and buyer sides. The mechanism should not be too complicated which ignore buyers' benefits or too simple which ignore merchants' benefits.

Second, daily-deal mechanism weakens the nature of group-buying by converting group-buying into a form of time limited sales. The first stream of group-buying studies emphasizes the importance of buyer collusion, which could lower down the prices and be beneficial to both merchants and buyers [18] [19]. Buyers are encouraged to form a large group actively. However, daily-deal discount does not depend on a large group any more. Buyers do not need to worry about the depth of discounts if size of the buyer group is small. Although the second stream of literatures notices the importance of WOM and social media on sales, the mechanisms to encourage buyers to form groups via WOM still lack. Thus, the nature of group-buying needs to be emphasized in the future sustainable group-buying mechanism.

4   Conclusion

Online group-buying mechanism needs to be improved given the crisis faced by online group-buying businesses. The extant literatures of online group-buying facilitate us the knowledge on how to design more sustainable group-buying mechanisms. By reviewing 46 articles, we propose that sustainable group-buying mechanism could generate benefits for both merchants and buyers. In addition, group-buying mechanism needs to take advantage of social media to congregate bargaining power from buyers and get deep discounts reasonably from merchants. Buyers can be encouraged to actively interact with others and seek buyers with similar purchasing interests on social media, in order to form large groups for group-buying deals.

Acknowledgement. The work described in this paper was supported by a grant from the Research Grants Council of the Hong Kong Special Administrative Region, China (CityU 150511).

References

1. Kauffman, R.J., Wang, B.: Bid together, buy together: On the efficacy of group-buying business models in Internet-based selling. In: Handbook of Electronic Commerce in Business Society, pp. 1–44. CRC Press, Boca Raton (2002)
2. Kauffman, R.J., Wang, B.: New buyers' arrival uder dynamic pricing market microstructure: The case of group-buying discounts of the Internet. Journal of Management Information Systems 18(2), 157–188 (2001)
3. Sharif-Paghaleh, H.: Analysis of the waiting time effects on the financial return and the order fulfillment in web-based group buying mechanisms. In: IEEE/WIC/ACM International Conference on Web Intelligence and Intelligent Agent Technology Workshops (2009)

4. Kauffman, R.J., Lai, H., Ho, C.T.: Incentive mechanism, fairness and participation in online group-buying auctions. Electronic Commerce Research and Applications 9(3), 249–262 (2010)
5. Spoon, R.: 10 Fun Groupon Statistics, from Geography to Sushi to NBA. In: Business Insider, http://www.businessinsider.com/10-fun-groupon-statistics-from-geography-to-sushi-to-nba-2011-3#ixzz2sNNlAWGB
6. Sutherland, B.: It's a half-price kind of world: Millions of bargain hunters flock to online coupon sites. McClatchy-Tribune Business News, Washington (2010)
7. Group-buying websites in China face funding crisis. In: Want China Times, http://www.wantchinatimes.com/news-subclass-cnt.aspx?id=20130813000019&cid=1102
8. Leidner, D., Kayworth, T.: A Review of Culture in Information Systems Research: Toward a Theory of Information Technology Culture Conflict. MIS Quarterly 30(2), 357–399 (2006)
9. Anand, K.S., Aron, R.: Group buying on the Web: A comparison of price-discovery mechanism. Manegement Science 49, 1546–1562 (2003)
10. Chen, J., Chen, X., Song, X.: Comparison of the group-buying auction and the fixed-pricing mechanism. Decision Support System 43(2), 445–459 (2007)
11. Chen, J., Liu, Y., Song, X.: Group-buying online auction and optimal inventory policy in uncertain market. Journal of Systems Science and Systems Engineering 13(2), 202–218 (2004)
12. Chen, J., Kauffman, R.J., Liu, Y., Song, X.: Segmenting uncertain demand in group-buying auction. Electronic Commerce Research Application 9(2), 126–147 (2010)
13. Lai, H., Zhuang, Y.-T.: Comparing the Performance of Group Buying Models with Different Incentive Mechanism. In: Proceedings of the Third Workshop on e-Business, pp. 1–12 (2004)
14. Kauffman, R.J., Lai, H., Lin, H.C.: Consumer adoption of group-buying auctions: An experimental study. Information Technology and Management 11(4), 191–211 (2010)
15. Lai, H., Zhuang, Y.-T.: Comparing the Performance of Group-Buying Models-Time Based vs. Quantity Based Extra Incentives. In: Proceedings of the Fourth Workshop on Knowledge Economy and Electronic Commerce, pp. 81–90 (2006)
16. Tan, C.-H., Goh, K.-Y., Teo, H.-H.: An investigation of online group-buying institution and buyer behavior. In: Jacko, J.A. (ed.) HCI 2007. LNCS, vol. 4553, pp. 124–131. Springer, Heidelberg (2007)
17. Analysis on buyers' cooperative strategy under group-buying price mechanism. Journal of Industrial and management Optimization 9(2), 291-304 (2012)
18. Chen, J., Chen, X., Kauffman, R.J., Song, X.: Cooperation in Group-Buying Auctions. In: Proceedings of the 39th Annual Hawaii International Conference on System Sciences, HICSS (2006)
19. Chen, J., Chen, X., Kauffman, R.J., Song, X.: Should We Collude? Analyzing the Benefits of Bidder Cooperation in Online Group-buying Auctions. Electronic Commerce Research and Applications 8(4), 191–202 (2009)
20. Chen, J., Chen, X., Song, X.: Bidder's Strategy under Group-buying Auctions on the Internet. IEEE Transaction on Systems, Man and Cybernetics: Part A 32(6), 680–690 (2002)
21. Boon, E.: A Qualitative Study of Consumer-Generated Videos about Daily Deal Web sites. Psychology & Marketing 30(10), 843–849 (2013)
22. Chen, C.P.: Online Group Buying Behavior in CC2B e-Commerce: Understanding Consumer Motivations. Journal of Internet Commerce 11(3), 254–270 (2012)

23. Shiau, W.-L., Luo, M.M.: Factors affecting online group buying intention and satisfaction: A social exchange theory perspective. Computers in Human Behavior 28(6), 2431–2444 (2012)
24. Coulter, K.S., Roggeveen, A.: Deal or no deal?: How number of buyers, purchase limit, and time-to-expiration impact purchase decisions on group buying websites. Journal of Research in Interactive Marketing 6(2), 78–95 (2012)
25. Ku, E.C.S.: Beyond price: How does trust encourage online group's buying intention. Internet Research 22(5), 569–590 (2012)
26. Zhang, Z., Zhang, Z., Wang, F., Law, R., Li, D.: Factors influencing the effectiveness of online group buying in the restaurant industry. International Journal of Hospitality Management 35, 237–245 (2013)
27. Cheng, H.H., Huang, S.W.: Exploring antecedents and consequence of online group-buying intention: An extended perspective on theory of planned behavior. International Journal of Information Management 33(1), 185–198 (2013)
28. Li, X., Wu, L.: Measuring effects of observational learning and social-network word-of-mouth (WOM) on the sales of daily-deal vouchers. In: Proceedings of 46th Hawaii International Conference on System Sciences, Wailea, HI, USA, pp. 2908–2917 (2013)
29. Zhou, G., Xu, K., Liao, S.: Do starting and ending effects in fixed-price group-buying differ. Electronic Commerce Research and Applications 12(2), 78–89 (2013)
30. Liu, Y., Sutanto, J.: Buyers' purchasing time and herd behavior on deal-of-the-day group-buying websites. Electronic Markets 22(2), 83–93 (2012)
31. Parsons, A.G., Ballantine, P.W., Ali, A., Grey, H.: Deal is on! Why people buy from daily deal websites. Journal of Retailing and Consumer Services (2013) (in press)
32. Pentina, I., Taylor, D.G.: Regulatory Focus and Daily-Deal Message Framing: Are We Saving or Gaining With Groupon? Journal of Interactive Advertising 13(2), 67–75 (2013)
33. Krasnova, H., Veltri, N.F., Spengler, K., Gunther, O.: "Deal of the day" platforms: What drives consumer loyalty? Business & Information Systems Engineering 5(3), 165–177 (2013)
34. Yamamoto, S.T., Sycara, K.: A Stable and Efficient Buyer Coalition Formation Scheme for E-Marketplaces. In: Proceedings of the Fifth International Conference on Autonomous Agents, Montréal, pp. 1–8 (2001)
35. Breban, S., Vassileva, J.: Long-Term Coalitions for the Electronic Marketplace. In: Spencer, B. (ed.) Proceedings of the E-Commerce Applications Workshop, Canadian AI Conference, Ottawa, pp. 6–12 (2001)
36. Breban, S., Vassileva, J.: Using Inter-Agent Trust Relationships for Efficient Coalition Formation. In: Cohen, R., Spencer, B. (eds.) Proceedings of the 13th Canadian Conference on AI, Calgary, pp. 28–30 (2002)
37. Breban, S., Vassileva, J.: A Coalition Formation Mechanism Based on Inter-Agent Trust Relationships. In: Johnson, L., Castelfranchi, C. (eds.) Proceedings of the First Conference on Autonomous Agents and Multi-Agent Systems, Bologna, pp. 17–19 (2002)
38. Hyodo, M., Mastuo, T., Ito, T.: An Optimal Coalition Formation among Buyer Agents Based on a Genetic Algorithm. In: Chung, P.W.H., Hinde, C., Ali, M. (eds.) IEA/AIE 2003. LNCS, vol. 2718, pp. 759–767. Springer, Heidelberg (2003)
39. Yuan, S.T., Lin, Y.H.: Credit Based Group Negotiation for Aggregate Sell/Buy in E-markets. Electronic Commerce Research and Applications 3(1), 74–94 (2004)
40. Li, C., Chawla, S., Rajan, U., Sycara, K.: Mechanism Design for Coalition Formation and Cost Sharing in Group-buying Markets. Electronic Commerce Research and Applications 3(4), 341–354 (2004)

41. Li, C., Sycara, K., Scheller-Wolf, A.: Combinatorial Coalition Formation for Multi-item Group-buying with Heterogeneous Customers. Decision Support Systems 49(1), 1–13 (2010)
42. Mastuo, T.: A Reassuring Mechanism Design for Traders in Electronic Group Buying. Applied Artificial Intelligence 23(1), 1–15 (2009)
43. Mastuo, T., Ito, T.: A Decision Support System for Group Buying based on Buyers' Preferences in Electronic Commerce. In: Eleventh World Wide Web International Conference (WWW 2002), pp. 84–89 (2002)
44. Mastuo, T., Ito, T.: A Group Formation Support System Based on Substitute Goods in Group Buying, pp. 23–31 (2004)
45. Chen, T.: Towards convenient customer-driven group-buying: an intelligent centralised P2P system. International Journal of Technology Intelligence and Planning 8(1), 16–31 (2012)
46. Ito, T., Ochi, H., Shintani, T.: A Cooperative Exchanging Mechanism among Seller Agents for Group-based Sales. Electronic Commerce Research and Applications 1(2), 138–149 (2002)
47. Ito, T., Ochi, H., Shintani, T.: A Group Buy Protocol Based on Coalition Formation for Agent-mediated E-Commence. International Journal of Computer & Information Science (2002)
48. Lee, J.S., Lin, K.S.: An innovative electronic group-buying system for mobile commerce. Electronic Commerce Research and Applications 12(1), 1–13 (2013)
49. Sheu, J.J., Chang, Y.W., Chu, K.T.: Applying decision tree data mining for online group buying consumers' behavior. International Journal of Electronic Customer Relationship Management 2(2), 140–157 (2008)
50. Lai, M., Su, C.C.: An Empirical Test of the Effectiveness of Communication Source: A Case of Group. In: Proceedings of the 13th Asia Pacific Management Conference, Melbourne, pp. 1263–1269 (2007)

A Case Study of the Application of Cores
and Paths in Financial Web Design

Dongyuan Liu, Tian Lei, and Shuaili Wei

Department of Industrial Design,
Huazhong University of Science and Technology, Wuhan, China
{murmurldy,andrew.tianlei,yibianxue}@gmail.com

Abstract. This paper illustrates how Cores and Paths work together with the user inter-views in web design by a real case of the design for a fund web. The Cores and Paths method which lays more emphasis on the core demand was first put for-ward by Are Halland. The framework of the website is decided by both the user goals and business goals. Through the analysis of inward paths and outward paths, the redundant information is reduced. Cores and Paths is a method of high efficiency and effectiveness for information construction. In this design project, we go through the process of the desk study, the user interviews, the information construction, the interactive prototyping, the usability test and the final improvement. We know that the user interviews serve as a crucial part throughout the whole process by giving an effective and direct guidance to the following design.

Keywords: B2C e-commerce, Cores and Paths, Information Architecture, Findability.

1 Introduction

1.1 Cores and Paths

The Cores and Paths method was put forward by Are Halland in the 2007 Euro IA Conference. He pointed that users would never care about navigation or structure but content and functions of websites. So, content findability of websites is important. Peter Morville thought the same and he said, "Findability is more important than usability whatever in the alphabet or in the web, because it can't be used until it's found.[1]"

But traditional websites are designed from homepages and content is organized from top to bottom, which will truly endow websites with a clear structure.[2] However, not all users have access to detail pages through navigations; instead, Google search results, ad links in third-party websites or other pages on the websites are all possible ways. Then the problem is whether the detail pages can deliver clear and correct content to users. For e-commerce websites, it has a direct effect on conversion rates. The Cores and Paths method can be a solution, which emphasizes that

F.F.-H. Nah (Ed.): HCIB/HCII 2014, LNCS 8527, pp. 549–558, 2014.
© Springer International Publishing Switzerland 2014

website designs should start from the core content because that is what users care. The method is used as an attempt in redesigning a fund website.

1.2   Fund Websites

On most fund websites, fund information is more authoritative. It is listed on pages (Fig.1) and usually classified, using tab to shift among different types. But information under each tab is presented in lines with no difference in priority. So, key points are hard to be found and users need to carefully seek for them. If you're a green hand without much fund knowledge, you'll lose patience very soon.

Compared to stock, trust, bank wealth management or other financial products, however, fund is featured with a low threshold and less energy input. You may have access to one fund without much money and manage it without much energy. These features make fund acceptable to more ordinary people, and thus buying funds is just like shopping on a B2C e-commerce website.

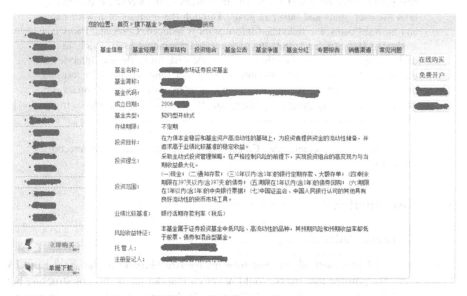

Fig. 1. A typical fund product page

1.3   E-Commerce Websites

What are the features of B2C e-commerce websites? Popular e-commerce websites in China, such as Amazon.com.cn, tmall.com, and jingdong.com, mainly sell physical products. Their product pages contain abundant information: detailed parameters, instructions, detail pictures, comments and comments from former customers. The information is presented in different ways according to its priority. Because according to Mooers' Law, "users tend not to use an information retrieval system when it is more painful and troublesome for them to have information than not to have it,[3]" and individuals will choose the way with least overall consumption to achieve their goals . Therefore, various ways of information presentation contribute to users' quickly focusing on key points which act as a direct reference for purchase decision making.

2 Research Process

2.1 User Interviews

Before designing, we need some information of users:

- What type of people are they? What features do they have?
- How much experience do they have in buying funds?
- How do they use fund websites?
- What do they pay attention to on fund websites?
- How do they make decisions on buying funds?
- What problems do they have when using fund websites and how do they deal with them?
- What's their expectation of fund websites?
- What's their attitude towards e-commerce websites?
- Is there any other point worth paying attention to?

These questions will help us find out users' demands and thoughts, which are of vital significance to the following design. We can have some conclusions through user interviews. User interview is an "ideal tool that can collect abundant and exact information in an effective manner"[4]. In this case, the method of user interviews is adopted to understand fund users.

Users
In order to understand fund users, those who have experience in fund need to be recruited for the interviews. Because users without experience may not provide anything valuable during the interviews for lack of understanding of the fund and enough using experience; on the contrary, users with experience can express their experience, feelings and problems, which are exactly what we care. In this case, we recruit 12 real fund users (Table 1). Among them, users of the redesigned fund website are called "existing users" while users of other fund websites are called "potential users".
Users to be recruited should meet the following requirements:

- With experience in buying funds of 3 years or more
- With experience in buying funds online of 1 year
- With experience in shopping on B2C e-commerce websites of over 2 years, including but not limited to www.jingdong.com, www.tmall.com, and www.amazon.com.cn, etc.
- Sex ratio: male: female= 1:1

552   D. Liu, T. Lei, and S. Wei

- Age: 25-55
- User type ratio: existing users: potential users= 1:1

Table 1. Basic information of fund users in the interview

User No.	Gender	Age	Existing users	Years of buying
P1	M	40	Yes	6 years
P2	F	42	Yes	11 years
P3	F	28	No	7 years
P4	M	28	No	6 years
P5	F	30	No	6 years
P6	M	27	Yes	3 years
P7	M	32	Yes	5 years
P8	F	37	Yes	6 years
P9	F	30	No	6 years
P10	M	37	Yes	8 years
P11	F	30	No	6 years
P12	M	31	No	5 years

Interview Results and Analysis

After the interview, according to the interview results and interviewer's feelings to users, users' overall features are summarized and it is found that all the 12 users have shown their rational and cautious character.

Table 2. Overall features of fund users

User No.	Keywords
P1	Relatively rational and veteran
P2	Veteran, rational and strongly independent
P3	Careful and rational
P4	Strongly independent
P5	Professional, rational, careful and considerate
P6	Cautious and less professional
P7	Relatively emotional, easy to be satisfied and patient
P8	Relatively rational and "so-so"
P9	Conservative, with a strong sense of wealth management
P10	Good at analyzing statistics, down-to-earth, independent and rational
P11	Conservative, not independent, with clear goals and logic, safety-oriented
P12	Willing to try new things, efficient, professional, with clear goals

Then some key points are analyzed. As for users' wealth management conditions, it is found that most of them started buying financial products such as stocks and funds from the year 2007, and they usually held funds of several fund companies. It shows that they care more about fund products than fund companies.

When it comes to users' experience of buying funds, 2 of them started from friends' introduction and turned to fund websites, 5 of them started from banks' introduction and turned to fund websites or third-party platforms, and 3 of them started from e-banks and turned to fund websites. These changes in purchase channels show that most users start purchase under the influence of others and move towards rational judgments. The main reason is that funds are easy to operate and the rate is low.

Over 2 users' points of focus on funds are shown in Table 3. We can see that users pay attention to more than 2 key statistics points when they buy funds. Of all the points, rate of return, net value, investment portfolio, risk and fund manager attract most attention.

Table 3. Users' points of focus on funds

Points of focus	Number of people	Points of focus	Number of people
Rate of return	7	Fund manager	4
Net value	5	Scale	3
Investment portfolio	4	Comprehensive rank	2
Stability and risk	4	Historical performance	2

Problems that users usually come across on fund websites include:

- Users are uncertain about time of redemption to account for lack of obvious instructions.
- Mature products are automatically renewed, without users' validation.
- Few similar products are recommended.
- Primary wealth management consultants are not available for green hands.
- It's not convenient to check historical returns.
- Users can't make decisions on buying funds with outdated information.
- Users prefer to call customer services in case of problems.
- Customer services are not available when support staff gets off work.
- The hotline is hard to get through and online customer services don't respond in time.

It can be seen that green hands need more instructions and assistance in basic information and operations of funds, which should be easy to understand, avoid too many professional words or give detailed explanations and instructions. Besides customer services, there should be more service channels such as offering contact information and listing FAQ online, etc.

2.2   Page Design

Based on the interview results, it is seen that users mainly demand that fund websites should be efficient, convenient, safe, reliable, clear and easy to understand.

Meanwhile, through the inter-views we confirm further that fund products are the core content of fund websites. So our design will center on fund products.

Determining the Core Page

The core page of fund websites is fund product page. Fund users examine fund information, make purchase decisions and buy funds on this page; companies expect to sell more funds and publicize themselves on this page.

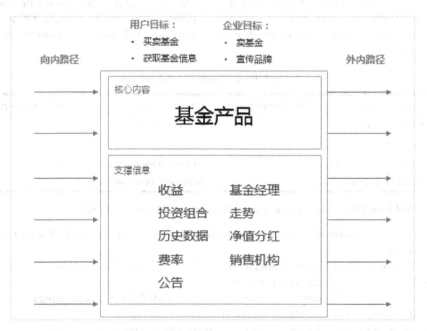

Fig. 2. Core content

Determining the core content

So what detailed information will the core content be composed of?

In the user interviews, it is known that for fund products, it is composed of the following content (Table 4):

Such information may be obtained from current fund websites and rivals' fund websites or from users during the interviews. The next problem is that such information, as the core content, also has different priorities. So, which is important and needs to be presented first? Which is less important and may be hidden moderately?

Table 4. Components of fund products

Content	Description
Basic information	Basic description information, including fund name, fund code, date of establishment, fund type, trustee, etc.
Returns	Rate of return, including that of the last week, the last year or since its establishment
Fund manager	Current and former fund managers and their relevant information
Investment portfolio	Fields and ratios of fund investment
Trend	Trends of rate of return, net value and other key data
Historical data	Historical data of funds, such as IOPV and cumulative returns
Net value	The latest net value statistics and historical net value statistics or trends
Dividend	Ways and records of dividend payment
Rate	Rate of subscription and redemption and its calculation method
Sales organization	Sale channels and organizations
Announcement	Relevant announcements, messages and information disclosure, etc.

Through user interviews it is known that users care most about fund returns, net value, invest-ment portfolio, risk and fund manager (Table 3), especially fund returns and net value. So, this part will be placed with top priority in design. In addition, fund companies expect to sell more funds, so a quick entrance should be placed at a strategic place. Therefore, a program has been designed and the basic framework has been determined (Fig.3).

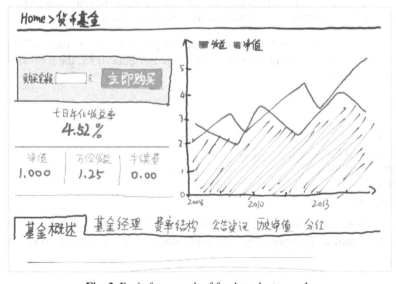

Fig. 3. Basic framework of fund product page 1

Determining inward paths

Next, the inward path will be determined. Brainstorming will be used to locate possible entries to fund product pages. What methods will be used to enter into the fund product page? There may be several ways, stated as follows:

Site navigation, internal accounts, newsletters, SMS, SNS, other fund products, e-mail, search engines, third-party information sites, sales organizations, event marketing page, IM, traditional media, favorites and so on.

For these inward paths, each entry has provided reminders that can be optimized and assisted in thinking about more user scenarios. Descriptions of user scenarios have a vital role in design. For example, "for visitors from Google and other search engines, it is necessary to optimize search engines and entry pages "[5]. Similarly, for visitors from SNS, it is also necessary for fund product pages to be able to be shared to SNS.

Determining outward paths.

Finally, outward paths need to be determined. That's, after the fund product pages, where will users go and what will they do? These will directly decide what is put on our core page. Ac-cording to user interviews, the following situations are listed:

- Purchase: users have understood some fund through other channels previously, and decide to purchase after reading relevant information on the fund product page.
- Share: they think highly of the fund and share to friends via SNS.
- Information: learn more information related to the fund.
- Calculate: perform revenue trails according to historical data of the fund.
- Download: download documents related to the fund.
- Customer service: they turn to customer service staff for help in case of any problem.
- Account: they decide the purchase amount according to account conditions.
- Collect: they add this page to the favorites through a browser.

Then, the key points will be sorted and their positions on the page will be determined according to different priorities. Based on user interviews, the following priorities are identified:

1. Purchase
2. calculate
3. information
4. customer service
5. share- account
6. collect
7. download

The content is supplemented and content and structure of the core page can be basically deter-mined. Therefore, the page framework is improved further (Fig. 4):

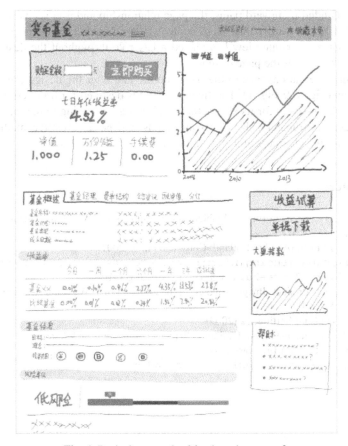

Fig. 4. Basic framework of fund product page 2

2.3   Follow-Up Process

The core page is designed through the Cores and Paths method. During the follow-up process, navigation design is carried out through the card method, and visual design is performed through the emotional version. After key process pages of the entire website are designed, low-fidelity prototype fast usability testing is conducted for these key processes, so as to discover some serious usability problems prior to the devel-opment. These contents are not detailed here.

3   Discussions

It is seen from the aforesaid case that when performing page design using the Cores and Paths method, navigation and homepage of the entire website can be ignored; instead, the core content should be located directly, which acts as a starting point in the design. The whole process revolves around the core content and thinks about user scenarios. Guided by inward paths, the page relationship and user scenarios are sorted out; guided by outward paths, page content is structured. During the process, it is made clear that user interview has played a key role throughout the design process, which directly guides the page design.

In addition, great changes to the pages before and after the design are obvious by comparison (Fig. 4 & Fig. 1). The financial field is destined for transaction; however, it has been exclusively for its abstractness and rationality owing to the intangibility of the products. Fortunately, the Cores and Paths will be an effective method in web designing for the clearness and convenience.

References

1. Morville, P.: Product Image Ambient Findability: What We Find Changes Who We Become, 144 (2007)
2. Kalbach, J.: Euro IA – Are Halland: Cores and Paths (2007),
   http://experiencinginformation.wordpress.com/2007/09/25/
   euro-ia-2007-are-halland-cores-and-paths/
3. Morville, P.: Product Image Ambient Findability: What We Find Changes Who We Become, 56 (2007)
4. Spencer, D.: Card Sorting, 12 (2009)
5. Kalbach., J., Lindemann, K.: Designing Screens Using Cores and Paths,
   http://boxesandarrows.com/
   designing-screens-using-cores-and-paths/

WebQual and Its Relevance to Users
with Visual Disabilities

Eleanor T. Loiacono and Shweta Deshpande

Worcester Polytechnic Institute
School of Business
Worcester, MA USA
{eloiacon,pdeshpande}@@wpi.edu

Abstract. The number of people with vision-related disabilities is on the rise. Since a significant portion of the population is "Web-reliant" already, understanding how visual impairments effect website usage and evaluation is important from both a business and societal perspective. This research tests the relevance of the website quality measure, WebQual, in low vision populations. Specifically, the website evaluation, using WebQual, of "sighted" users is compared to those with low to no vision. Preliminary results show that WebQual remains a highly valuable website quality measure in both populations.

Keywords: WebQual, Website Quality, Visual Disabilities.

1 Background

Due to various reasons, including the aging of the baby boomer generation, the population of people with visually impairments is on the rise (Martin et al. 2013)(see Figure 1). A concern of many companies is how to ensure that their websites meet the needs of this growing population, since a poor website can cause bad press, customer dissatisfaction, and even customer loss.

There are current measures that evaluate website quality, such as WebQual, but one concern is how adaptable they are to people with visual impairments given that the Web is such a visual medium. Thus, the main question of this research is: Is WebQual an appropriate measure of website quality for consumers who have vision disabilities? Can it be used to evaluate websites quality for consumers with low to no vision?

2 Literature Review

WebQual is a highly validated and reliable measure of website quality (Kesharwani et al. 2011; Kim et al. 2004; Loiacono et al. 2002; Loiacono et al. 2007). As such, it offers practitioners and researchers a proven instrument for evaluating the quality of websites through its consumers. WebQual provides both broad and fine-grained measures to evaluate websites.

F.F.-H. Nah (Ed.): HCIB/HCII 2014, LNCS 8527, pp. 559–565, 2014.
© Springer International Publishing Switzerland 2014

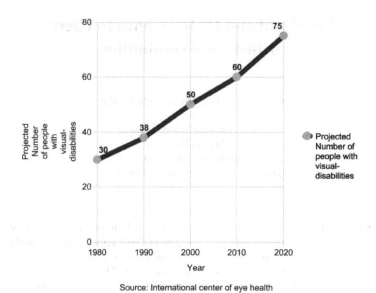

Source: International center of eye health

Fig. 1. Increasing population of visually impaired people over period of time

The evaluation is based on 12 constructs, which vary independent of each other. The first is informational fit-to-task. This construct checks if the information on a website meets the expectations of the user. Second is tailored information, which checks if the information of the website is tailored to the user's needs. Next is trust and response time. Trust refers to the user's trust in the website to keep his or her information safe. Response time relates to how quickly the website responds to user requests. Ease of understanding refers to how easy the website is to understand. Next, intuitive operations pertains to how easy to maneuver (without training) the user finds the website operations. Visual appeal highlights how visually appealing the website is to the user. Innovativeness refers to how innovative and creative the website is. The emotional appeal of the website reflects the positive feelings the website generates in the user. Consistent image refers to how well the website fits the user's image of the company website. Next, online completeness measures the extent to which the transactions on the website can be completed online. Finally, relative advantage determines the relative advantage of using the website over alternative interactions with the company, such as telephone communications or an in-store visit.

The overall structure of a website evaluation is conceptualized as bottom up, meaning that the 12 constructs are not treated as "reflections" of some single underlying overall construct, but instead the overall evaluation is seen as "produced by" the combination of the 12 underlying constructs.

One of the values of WebQual is that it provides a fine-grained analysis of a site's shortcomings. Companies conceivably could attempt to address inadequacies in any one of the 12 constructs independently of the others. Organizations using WebQual gain from knowing how well they rate on the basic Web site evaluation constructs, such as intuitive operations and informational fit to task.

In addition, WebQual also serves as a means of benchmarking against competitors. Barnes and Noble may determine, given its business strategy that it is willing to score lower on certain components of WebQual, such as relative advantage, but not on online completeness or consistent image.

3 Hypothesis

The overall hypothesis of interest in this research is the null hypothesis, which states that there will be no difference between those who are sighted and those who are visually impaired (with visual appeal excluded). The sub-hypotheses for each first-order category (not including visual appeal) are highlighted below.

H0: There will be no difference in the WebQual evaluation of a website between those who are sighted and those who are visually impaired.

H1: There will be no difference in the informational fit-to-task evaluation of a website between those who are sighted and those who are visually impaired.

H2: There will be no difference in the tailored information evaluation of a website between those who are sighted and those who are visually impaired.

H3: There will be no difference in the trust evaluation of a website between those who are sighted and those who are visually impaired.

H4: There will be no difference in the response time evaluation of a website between those who are sighted and those who are visually impaired.

H5: There will be no difference in the *ease of understanding* evaluation of a website between those who are sighted and those who are visually impaired.

H6: There will be no difference in the *intuitive operations* evaluation of a website between those who are sighted and those who are visually impaired.

H7: There will be no difference in the *innovativeness* evaluation of a website between those who are sighted and those who are visually impaired.

H8: There will be no difference in the *emotional appeal* evaluation of a website between those who are sighted and those who are visually impaired.

H9: There will be no difference in the *Consistent image* evaluation of a website between those who are sighted and those who are visually impaired.

H10: There will be no difference in the online completeness evaluation of a website between those who are sighted and those who are visually impaired.

H11: There will be no difference in the relative advantage evaluation of a website between those who are sighted and those who are visually impaired.

4   Methodology

Participants with and without visual impairments were included in the study. Participants were divided into two groups, based on their level of vision. Group 1 consisted of users without visual impairments. Group 2 contained users with complete blindness, partial blindness and low vision. They are asked to visit a website (Amazon.com). Questions are asked about site relating site's convenience, ease of use and reliability and other 12 factors of Webqual.

While conducting the survey to evaluate the website, multiple questions for the same construct are included randomly, so as to provide accurate and unbiased evaluation. Additionally, there were some validity-checking questions included, in order to check if the user is paying attention to the survey or just clicking some random questions.

4.1   WebQual

Each first-order WebQual construct consisted of three items. Additional data was collected on intention to reuse the website as well. The measures were adopted from Loiacono et al. (2007). Each factor showed high internal reliability and convergent and discriminant validity in past research.

4.2   Task

Each participant received an email invitation to participate. Those who accessed the survey site were briefed on the study and asked to read and agree to the terms in the consent form before proceeding. Those who were unwilling to participate were thanked and directed away from the survey site. Those who agree to participate began the study by providing some demographic information, such as gender, age, education level, Web usage, and vision acuity. They then moved on to the actual viewing of a website (in this case Amazon.com). Next, the subjects were asked to respond to each of the WebQual items using a 7-point Likert scale (1 being strongly disagree and 7

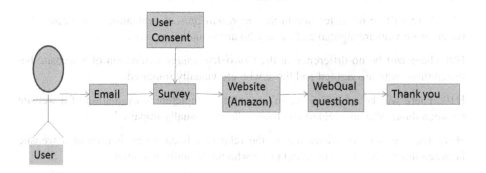

Fig. 2. Data Collection Procedure

being strongly agree) (see Appendix for items). Once subjects finished responding to the survey items, they were directed to a page thanking them for their participation. The total survey time was approximately 20 minutes.

5   Methodology

In order to understand the factors that impact image-blog adoption and usage, a survey methodology will be employed. A total of 100 subjects will be solicited to participate. They will be recruited from a northeastern university. They will all be adult online Web users, over the age of 18. Additional demographic information, such as gender, level of education, experience using the Internet, and Web usage will be collected.

Prior to beginning the study, subjects will be asked to review and, if they agree, sign a consent form, approved by the university's Internal Review Board. The incentive to participate will be a $3 gift card to a local coffee shop.

6   Results

We use a series one-way ANOVA to examine the response of website users depending on their level of vision.

Table 1. Results

Items by Construct	Mean for sighted users	Mean for Visually-impared users	P-Value
Response Time	4.94	5.76	0.00
Emotional Appeal	5.06	5.6	0.19
Innovativeness	5.4	5.79	0.27
Intuitive Operations	6.32	6.06	0.34
Consistent Image	5.49	5.75	0.38
Ease of Understanding	6.09	5.8	0.38
Informational Fit-to-Task	5.68	5.93	0.43
Tailored information	5.68	5.51	0.62
On-Line Completeness	6.26	6.34	0.76
Relative Advantage	6.18	6.11	0.76
Trust	6.14	6.2	0.78

7   Conclusions and Recommendations

There do not appear to be significant differences between the WebQual measures for those who are sighted versus those who have visual impairments. This suggests that WebQual is an appropriate measure of Website quality for users with and without visual impairments. Though visual appeal could not be evaluated for obvious reasons, the other measures seem to be consistent across groups.

There is, however, a significant difference in response time between the sighted group and those with visual impairments website. This means that, those with visual impairments do not mind if the website is a little slower, compared to those who are fully sighted. This may indicate that consumers with visual impairments are used to waiting longer for things in general and thus may have a longer tolerance for delays.

References

1. Kesharwani, A., Tiwari, R.: Exploration of Internet Banking Website Quality in India: a WebQual Approach Introduction. Great Lakes Herald 5(1) (2011)
2. Kim, S., Stoel, L.: Apparel Retailers: Website Quality Dimensions and Satisfaction. Journal of Retailing and Consumer Services 11(2), 109–117 (2004)
3. Loiacono, E., Chen, D.Q., Goodhue, D.L.: WebQual Revisited: Predicting the Intent to Reuse a Website (2002)
4. Loiacono, E., Watson, R., Goodhue, D.: The Effect of Web Site Quality on Intention to Revisit and Purchase. International Journal of Electronic Commerce 11(3), 51–87 (2007)
5. Martin, L.G., Schoeni, R.F.: Trends in disability and related chronic conditions among the forty-and-over population: 1997–2010. Disability and Health Journal (August 12, 2013) (forthcoming)

Appendix

Survey Items (Loiacono, et al. 2007)

Informational Fit-to-Task

— The information on the Web site is pretty much what I need to carry out my tasks.
— The Web site adequately meets my information needs.
— The information on the Web site is effective.

Tailored Communications

— The Web site allows me to interact with it to receive tailored information.
— The Web site has interactive features, which help me accomplish my task.
— I can interact with the Web site in order to get information tailored to my specific needs.

Trust

— I feel safe in my transactions with the Web site.
— I trust the Web site to keep my personal information safe.
— I trust the Web site administrators will not misuse my personal information.

Response Time

— When I use the Web site there is very little waiting time between my actions and the Web site's response.
— The Web site loads quickly.
— The Web site takes long to load.

Ease of Understanding

— The display pages within the Web site are easy to read.
— The text on the Web site is easy to read.
— The Web site labels are easy to understand.

Intuitive Operations

— Learning to operate the Web site is easy for me.
— It would be easy for me to become skillful at using the Web site.
— I find the Web site easy to use.

Visual Appeal

— The Web site is visually pleasing.
— The Web site displays visually pleasing design.
— The Web site is visually appealing.

Innovativeness

— The Web site is innovative.
— The Web site design is innovative.
— The Web site is creative.

Emotional Appeal

— I feel happy when I use the Web site.
— I feel cheerful when I use the Web site.
— I feel sociable when I use the Web site.

Consistent Image

— The Web site projects an image consistent with the company's image.
— The Web site fits with my image of the company.
— The Web site's image matches that of the company.

On-Line Completeness

— The Web site allows transactions on-line.
— All my business with the company can be completed via the Web site.
— Most all business processes can be completed via the Web site.

Relative Advantage

— It is easier to use the Web site to complete my business with the company than it is to telephone, fax, or mail a representative.
— The Web site is easier to use than calling an organizational representative agent on the phone.
— The Web site is an alternative to calling customer service or sales.

First in Search – How to Optimize Search Results in E-Commerce Web Shops

Gerald Petz and Andreas Greiner

University of Applied Sciences Upper Austria, Campus Steyr, Austria
{gerald.petz,andreas.greiner}@fh-steyr.at

Abstract. Customers of e-commerce web sites frequently use the full text search to find the desired products. The ranking of the search result page depends on various criteria such as the matching of search terms or popularity of the product. E-commerce vendors usually use additional ranking criteria and may want to increase conversion rates by varying the rankings of the search hits. This paper proposes a method to measure the impact of changing the ranking of the search result page. The method is applied to a b2b e-commerce shop with office products.

Keywords: ranking, search result page, web shop, e-commerce, measurement, A/B-testing, conversion.

1 Introduction and Motivation for Research

Although the estimates about global e-commerce trends vary, it is certainly true that e-commerce is growing fast; developed economies dominate the market, but emerging economies are expected to catch up soon. [1–5] According to the "e-commerce-guideline"-study e-commerce revenues in Germany rose from 18.3 billion Euros in 2010 to an estimated 25 billion Euros in 2012.[6] About 86% of Germany's online retailers run their own web shop; of course other channels such as online auction platforms are used as well.[6]

Whenever a user wants to buy products from a specific web shop he can use various alternatives to find the desired product: rummage in product lists, browse products by category, use faceted search or use full text search. The full text search plays an essential role in an e-commerce system: up to 80% of the visitors use only the full text search to find the desired products – a phenomenon that seems to be learned from usage of the Google search engine. One third of the visitors leave a web shop because they cannot find the desired products – even if the products are offered. The search engine has to deliver search hits accurately and quickly and has to be tolerant of typing mistakes and synonyms, and the search has to understand industry jargon.[6] If the customer uses the full text search it leads to the question as to how the search hits in the search result page can be ordered. Several sort criteria can be identified and of course combined together such as matching of search text to product title and / or product description and / or product category, average customer review, popularity, price, and many others. However, the ranking that is desired by the customer will be different to the desired ranking of

F.F.-H. Nah (Ed.): HCIB/HCII 2014, LNCS 8527, pp. 566–574, 2014.
© Springer International Publishing Switzerland 2014

the company that runs the web shop. A company may want to rank products according to different criteria. It may, for example, rank those with the highest contribution margins highest or those which are discontinued items or fast moving consumer goods. Alternatively, it may be important for a company to rank goods which are on stock highest or which should be sold as quickly as possible for various other reasons. As a result of this, web shop operators try to combine and weigh several ranking criteria and assume that products that are displayed at the top of the page have better conversion rates and are thus ordered more often. A number of software products (like Factfinder, exorbyte, celebros, and many others) support these considerations. However, two questions remain: What is the impact on the conversion when a product is better ranked? And how can we measure this impact in an environment that does not support a simple parallel A/B test setting due to technical restrictions?

The *objective* of this paper is to develop a method to measure the impact of variations of the search result page of a web shop, to apply this method and to evaluate the factual impact. In order to attain this objective, we set up a methodology as follows:

1. Development of the measurement method.
   The quite technical complex infrastructures of larger web shops (web shop software, combined with an ERP-system, a system that enables rankings according to specific product attributes, load balancers) and the complex environment (b2c- as well as b2b-customers with different price structures, product portfolios, etc.) prohibit the application of a simple A/B-test setting. Hence a method to measure the impact of different rankings has to be developed. Due to these technical restrictions, the method is a trade-off between a scientifically sound measurement and a technically realizable measurement method.
2. Implementation of the method.
   The method will be implemented with several tools, e.g. Google Analytics.
3. Application of the method.
   The method will be used in one specific case (web shop with office materials).

2   Related Work, Background

A/B testing and multivariate testing are commonly used in web development; these methods allow website operators to run experiments on website users. A/B testing is an experiment that compares two versions (A and B) of a webpage; the versions are identical except for one variation. The versions are randomly displayed to the visitors; the version that contributes most to the goal conversions is the one which is preferred by the visitors. Multivariate testing is similar to A/B testing, but enables us to test more than two different versions at the same time. [7, 8]

Several studies and publications focus on "success-factors" for e-commerce websites. A number of researchers investigate the connection between usability and the success of e-commerce sites: [9] evaluated commercial websites in order to find usability problems; [10] emphasize the importance of user-friendly interface of electronic shops; they applied heuristic evaluation to examine the usability of several e-commerce sites. As a result the authors provided a set of usability guidelines. Some researchers broadened the evaluations and also took related attributes into consideration (e.g. design attributes [11], aesthetic design and complexity [12]). Some researchers discuss convenience as an important factor for online shopping; convenience in e-commerce is defined as the range to which customers feel that a website is simple, sensory and user-friendly. [13, 14] Additionally, sometimes the cultural context in multilingual websites is considered as well (e.g. [15]).

An important factor for the success of e-commerce sites is trust. Users often hesitate to place orders on web shops because of uncertainty about the vendor, vendor behavior or perceived risks. A variety of research work focusses on this topic, e.g. [16] developed a typology and trust measures for e-commerce, [17] investigate the impact of trust on purchase decisions in the context of e-products and e-services.

The impact of online reviews and electronic word-of-mouth offers a broad range of research activities: e.g. [18] investigate the impact of online reviews on revenues of consumer electronics and video games. The authors show that reviews have significant impacts on revenues, but that the effect decreases over time. [19] determine the impact of online travel reviews, [20] test the impact of hotel reviews.

Interestingly, to our best knowledge we could not find scientific papers that research the impact of the ranking of search results in e-commerce shops. One can find many blogs and more or less reliable "studies" about this topic (e.g. [21]); especially in the area of search engine optimization we can find many hints, blog posts and "studies". We can summarize the discussions simply as: the better the ranking of a search hit, the better the conversion rate is. Unfortunately, there are no publicly available reliable investigations about the impact of search rank on the conversion rate of a product in e-commerce systems.

3   Measurement Method

The setup of the measurement method is proposed as follows:

- Experimental setup.
  We define a control group and an experimental group of products in three different product categories. The control groups have the "usual" ranking factors; the experimental groups are based on other ranking factors. Since it is technically not possible to measure the effects (comparable to an A/B test setting) temporally parallel, the measurements are carried out alternately in time sequence (see figure below). In order to avoid biases, we use product categories that have no seasonal fluctuations and chose weeks that contain no bank holidays.

Table 1. Setup of timing

		Week							
		1	2	3	4	5	6	7	8
Category 1	control group 1	X		X		X		X	
	experimental group 1		X		X		X		X
Category 2	control group 2	X				X		X	
	experimental group 2		X		X		X		X
Category 3	control group 3	X				X		X	
	experimental group 3		X		X		X		X

- Tracking.
  In order to track the effects, we set up a web analytics tool (Google Analytics). Several settings and prerequisites have to be undertaken: event tracking and e-commerce tracking have to be configured and the tracking code has to be implemented in the web shop. The event tracking should detect that (i) the full text search was used, (ii) a product of one of the monitored categories was put into the basket from the search engine result page or from the subsequently loaded product page, (iii) a product of one of the monitored categories was put on the watch list. The e-commerce tracking logs the transaction data.
- Export and data analysis.
  The gathered data have to be exported from the analytics tool and merged with the exported product data from the ERP-system that contains the detailed configuration ranking settings.

Discussion of the setup and remaining challenges:

- Trade-off
  As mentioned above, the proposed measurement method is a trade-off between a scientifically sound measurement and a technically and economically possible measurement.
- Deleted cookies, different browsers
  Most web analytic tools rely on cookie tracking which means there is already an inaccuracy resulting from the use of different browsers or deleting existing cookies.
- No transfer of the referrer
  Our javascript event tracking needs for the tracking of "add to basket" clicks from the product page (after the use of the full text search) the referrer. Some company's firewalls don't transfer it, so this may lead to fuzziness of the tracking.
- Impact of situation in b2b-webshops
  Since the measurement takes place in a b2b-environment, we were able to find find an order scenario as follows: user A puts products in basket, user B approves the basket and places the order. Thus, the question as to how this scenario could be measured (or excluded) arises.
- Effects of users' behavior
  The web shop offers the users a watch list to collect products for later ordering; the impact on the usage is not easy to measure.
- Inaccuracies due to different browsers
  Most of the common web analytics tools use cookie tracking. Therefore inaccuracies can arise if different browsers are used or if existing cookies are deleted.
- Temporal connections
  We have to face order scenarios where a user searches a product und puts it in the basket, but orders the basket a couple of days later. In this scenario the question remains concerning how the temporal connection between the search event and the order event can be established.

4   Application of Measurement Method, Results

4.1   Application of Measurement Method

We applied the suggested measurement method to a specific web shop: the web shop is a b2b-web shop and contains office products. The b2b-scenario implies that different customers are offered a different product spectrum and that customers may have different prices, terms and conditions.

As described in the section above, we defined three different product categories: file folder (108 products), text highlighter (116 products) and correction products and correction fluids (30 products). These product categories were chosen because there are no seasonal fluctuations. The next step was to implement the tracking functions; we decided to use Google Analytics. In order to track the interesting measures, we had to implement the following functions:

- E-Commerce tracking
  The first step was to activate the e-commerce tracking option. After activation one can use the Javascript-functions "_addTrans()", "_addItem()" and "_trackTrans()" to track transactional data.
- Tracking site search
  This option is an elective one, but it is useful to record search terms.
- Event tracking
  Subsequently, the event tracking has to be implemented. Google Analytics offers the Javascript-function "_trackEvent(category, action, opt_label, opt_value, opt_noninteraction)" to track events. The following events have to be taken into consideration: (i) search leads to products in the defined categories, (ii) product is put into the basket (directly from the search engine result page or indirectly from the product-detail page), and (iii) product is put on the watch list. The function "_gaq.push" fires the tracking events to Google Analytics.

As described in chapter 3, the measurement took place during 8 weeks between mid-September and mid-November. Both the control group the experimental group contained the same product categories and products. The only difference was that different ranking weights ("spread configuration") were applied to the experimental group. The meaning of the spread is as follows:

- Spread 0: no devaluation
- Spread 1: devaluation of 0.33%
- Spread 2: devaluation of 0.66%
- Spread 3: devaluation of 0.99%

We hypothesize that products that are devaluated with a spread-configuration (i) are put into the basket less often and (ii) are less often ordered. The comparison takes place by using the control group (no spread configuration applied) and the experimental group (spread configuration is active).

4.2   General Results

As a first step some general statistics were examined. Fig. 1 exhibits the number of search terms used in full text search. 64% of the searches contain only 1 search term, 22% contain two terms; the remaining 14% contain more than two terms. The searches with one term can be distinguished in searches with a keyword (78%) and searches with a specific product ID (22%). These numbers lead to the assumption that the users do not have one specific product in mind when using the full text search.

Fig. 2 exhibits, how many users visit the second, third, etc. page of the search result pages. 80% of the visitors examine only the first search result page and about 9% click on the second page as well.

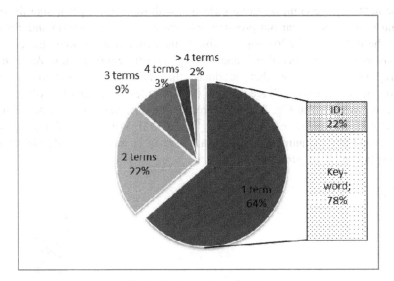

Fig. 1. Number of search terms

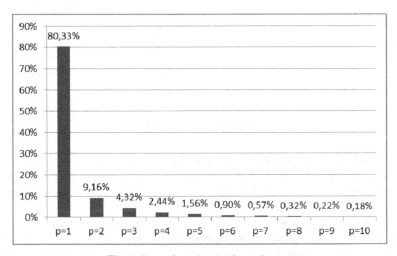

Fig. 2. Page views in search result page

The shop offers a "gallery" at the top of the search result page, where featured products are displayed and highlighted. This gallery contains 5 products, the rest of the page contains as the default setting 15 products (all following search result pages contain 20 products). The gallery (which contains 25% of the displayed products) generates 28% of the clicks, where products are put into the basket (resp. 33% unique clicks). Hence we can summarize that products displayed in a "featured area" are put in the basket more often than products from a list.

4.3   Specific Results

In the next step we compared two measures with the control group and the experimental group: clicks that put products into the basket (n = 13,981) and clicks that place the order (n = 8,876). Fig. 3 exhibits the differences between the clicks into the basket with the "spread on" and the "spread off" configuration. As mentioned before, we hypothesize that products that are devaluated with a spread-configuration ("spread on") are put into the basket less often and less often ordered. However, as shown in Fig. 3, the differences are only marginal and not significant (tested with chi-square, e.g. spread 3: $\chi^2 = 0.0792$). With spread 0,1 and 2 we actually found that the number of clicks into the basket was marginally higher than in the "spread on" configuration.

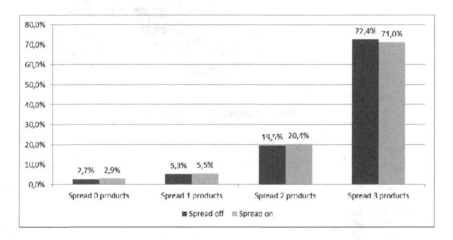

Fig. 3. Clicks into basket

As shown in Fig. 4 one can observe a similar situation; the differences are not very high, but with the exception of the "spread 0"-configuration - they are significant ($\chi^2 < 0,05$). Again, with spread 0, 1 and 2 configuration we observe the opposite of our expectations.

In order to be able to go into more detail we split these data into the defined categories (file folder, text highlighter and correction products) and carried out the same evaluations. The detailed analyses show the same characteristics as in Figure 3 and 4.

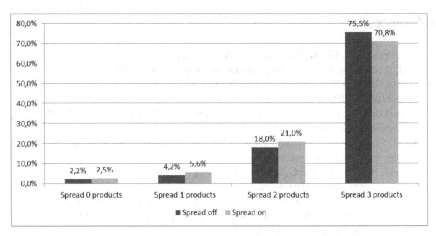

Fig. 4. Transactions

4.4 Discussion

The measurement setting still has some weaknesses. Unfortunately, we are not able to measure, estimate or exclude the possible biases, but the evaluation of random samples leads to the assumption that the impact of these biases is small. The measurement has a drawback: because of the b2b-environment (each customer has his own product selection) there is no technical possibility to determine by how many positions a product that has a spread configuration is ranked poorer.

The results indicate that higher devaluations (spread 3) have an impact on the number of clicks into the basket and the number of orders. The reason why products with a smaller devaluation (spread 0, 1 and 2) are ordered more often could be because the "unwanted" products (spread 3-configuration) are ordered less often and customers want or need to order alternative products.

These results were measured in a b2b-e-commerce-environment consisting of office materials and therefore certainly cannot be generalized to other scenarios.

5   Conclusion and Further Research

This paper discusses a method to measure the impact of variations of the rankings of the search result page of a web shop. The measurement method was applied to an e-commerce shop containing office products in the b2b-area. The results show that small variations of the positions of the research result page have no significant impact on clicks-to-basket or placed orders; more extensive variations of the positions have an impact on clicks-to-basket or placed orders – at least in the case of office materials and a b2b-e-commerce environment.

Further research work should be conducted on: (i) application of the measurement method in a b2c-scenario, which is less complex, (ii) in order to gain a deeper understanding of customers' behavior the measurement could be supplemented with usability-studies.

References

1. Goldman Sachs, Global Ecommerce to Accelerate (2013)
2. Wei, D.: Nothing But Net - Asia, Internet Investment Guide (2013)
3. Oracle (2013) B2C E-Commerce Trends for 2013
4. Oracle (2013) 2013 B2B Commerce Trends
5. Fredriksson, T.: E-commerce and Development. Key Trends and Issues. In: Workshop on E-Commerce, Development and SMEs (2013)
6. Stahl, E., Wittmann, G., Krabichler, T., et al.: E-Commerce-Leitfaden, 3rd edn. Noch erfolgreicher im elektronischen Handel.
7. Chopra, P.: The Ultimate Guide To A/B Testing (2010),
   `http://www.smashingmagazine.com/2010/06/24/`
   `the-ultimate-guide-to-a-b-testing/` (accessed January 29, 2014)
8. Clifton, B.: Advanced Web metrics with Google Analytics, 3rd edn. Sybex serious skills. John Wiley & Sons, Indianapolis (2012)
9. Benbunan-Fich, R.: Using protocol analysis to evaluate the usability of a commercial web site. Information & Management 39(2), 151–163 (2001)
10. Chen, S.Y., Macredie, R.D.: The assessment of usability of electronic shopping: A heuristic evaluation. International Journal of Information Management 25(6), 516–532 (2005)
11. Lee, S., Koubek, R.J.: The effects of usability and web design attributes on user preference for e-commerce web sites. Computers in Industry 61(4), 329–341 (2010)
12. Deng, L., Poole, M.S.: Aesthetic design of e-commerce web pages – Webpage Complexity, Order and preference. Electronic Commerce Research and Applications 11(4), 420–440 (2012)
13. Salehi, F., Abdollahbeigi, B., Langroudi, A.C., et al.: The Impact of Website Information Convenience on E-commerce Success of Companies. Procedia - Social and Behavioral Sciences 57, 381–387 (2012)
14. Srinivasan, S.S., Anderson, R., Ponnavolu, K.: Customer loyalty in e-commerce: an exploration of its antecedents and consequences. Journal of Retailing 78(1), 41–50 (2002)
15. Hillier, M.: The role of cultural context in multilingual website usability. Electronic Commerce Research and Applications 2(1), 2–14 (2003)
16. McKnight, H.D., Choudhury, V., Kacmar, C.: Developing and Validating Trust Measures for e-Commerce: An Integrative Typology. Information Systems Research 13(3), 334–359 (2002)
17. Gefen, D., Straub, D.W.: Consumer trust in B2C e-Commerce and the importance of social presence: experiments in e-Products and e-Services. Omega 32(6), 407–424 (2004)
18. Cui, G., Lui, H., Guo, X.: The Effect of Online Consumer Reviews on New Product Sales. International Journal of Electronic Commerce 17(1), 39–58 (2012)
19. Gretzel, U., Yoo, K.: Use and Impact of Online Travel Reviews. In: O'Connor, P., Höpken, W., Gretzel, U. (eds.) Information and Communication Technologies in Tourism, pp. 35–46. Springer, Vienna (2008)
20. Vermeulen, I.E., Seegers, D.: Tried and tested: The impact of online hotel reviews on consumer consideration. Tourism Management 30(1), 123–127 (2009)
21. Chitika, Inc., The Value of Google Result Positioning (2013),
    `http://chitika.com/google-positioning-value`
    (accessed January 28, 2014)

The Value of User Centered Design in Product Marketing: A Simulated Manufacturing Company Product Offering Market Strategy

April Savoy[1] and Alister McLeod[2]

[1] Indiana University East, Informatics, Richmond, IN, USA
asavoy@iue.edu
[2] Indiana State University, Applied Engineering and Technology Management,
Terre Haute, IN, USA
Alister.McLeod@indstate.edu

Abstract. The field of manufacturing is mainly concern with the creation of products for consumers who demand these items. At Indiana State University's Advance Manufacturing Management (AMM) Program, phases of the entire value chain are emphasized to students in a senior level undergraduate course structured as a simulated industrial manufacturing company (SIMCO). The course entails design, prototyping, manufacturing and finally marketing of a product. While the first three phases are easily emphasized the final phase, marketing, lacks a holistic strategy that embodies the previous activity. Marketing activities are therefore disjointed, in turn, affecting the potential revenue of the product. This research project originated as a demonstration and proof of concept- human-computer interaction and marketing strategies become equally valuable as the product in the later stages of the value chain, where ecommerce is integrated.

The objective of this study is to determine the most effective marketing strategy for university-related products manufactured by students for ISU students, alumni and families. The uniqueness of the processes involved in the products manufactured and their target population affords a distinct comparative evaluation between two marketing strategies, where one promotes the product through emphasis on university pride/association and the other emphasizes general product characteristics. The analysis and results support the use of a customized marketing strategy with emphasis on ISU school spirit to increase customer information satisfaction and gain a competitive edge.

Keywords: Customer Information Satisfaction, Information Utility, Usability, Marketing Strategies, Psychographic Characteristics, Ecommerce.

1 Introduction

In academic settings, the replication of manufacturing environments can be a daunting task. Facilitating such an environment requires a diverse group of faculty that span the areas of product design through to product marketing and sales. Indiana State University's (ISU) Advanced Manufacturing Management (AMM) program is one such

F.F.-H. Nah (Ed.): HCIB/HCII 2014, LNCS 8527, pp. 575–582, 2014.
© Springer International Publishing Switzerland 2014

academic environment in which a manufacturing operation is replicated. This replication occurs in a senior level capstone class that employs students who are tasked with the operation of a company that designs, manufactures and then sell products. Typically, these senior level students have been exposed to product design methodologies, such as 2D and 3D solid modeling, in addition to tool and material processing technologies. Students organize themselves into groups that are typically responsible for the creation of new products or modification of existing products. The groups that they form are all part of a company known as the Simulated Industrial Manufacturing Company (SIMCO).

The skill set that these students possess resides mainly in the building and designing of products, creating a big disadvantage when products are to be marketed and sold. This disadvantage creates two interrelated problems, a lack of product exposure which in turn significantly affects cash-flow. An ad hoc marketing strategy is used and it involves the use of a website that acts as a platform for potential customers to view the products. Customers are solicited by word of mouth to view products on a webpage, which may or may not contain descriptions. Marketing tends to be very problematic because once the few customers that have been solicited enter the SIMCO webpage they are immediately turned off by the lack of cohesion and clarity. In an effort to make their products more attractive, its presentation becomes paramount. Simply redesigning their products from semester to semester, without gaining any new customers, has had a profound impact on SIMCO's profitability. The root cause effect is poor customer experience and satisfaction.

2   Background and Related Work

The need for a competitive edge has motivated website designers and marketing professionals alike to study factors impacting usability, customer experience, and customer satisfaction. One of the most impacting factors relates to information content (i.e. information utility, customer information satisfaction, value-added information) [1-4]. Determining *what* information is important and useful to customers is vital to the design process. The success of user-centered approaches that commence with methods to better understand the customer information needs are most effective. User-centered design and usability tools -focus groups, questionnaires, surveys, and task analysis- have all been used to identify *what* information is important for customer-based decisions[1,2,4,5]. Studies have shown that informations needs are influenced by product/service type sold and customer segments in the target audience [6].

Researchers have investigated the information needs of ecommerce customers for various products and services [1,2,4]. Results have indicated that the type of product serviced or sold has significant impact on customer information needs. Wang et. al. (2001) measured factors of customer information satisfaction for websites selling digital products/services. Wang's model for measuring included 7 factors highlighting that customers want information related to Customer Support, Security, Digital Products/Services, Transaction and Payment, and Innovation. The remaining two factors were related to the Ease of Use of the website and the accuracy of the Information Content. Buys and Brown (2004) demonstrated the shift of value placed on information items when customers used banking websites, where importance was concentrated on information related to transactions and their accurate reporting. Savoy (2008) conducted a literature review of studies focused on customer information needs to develop a conceptual model of fundamental information requirements for all product/services and identified 7 factors: Price, Customer Service, Member Transaction, Shipping, Durability, Company, and Production Description. Product and/or service description is one of the most important information items on ecommerce websites. This gives users short on time, indispensable information about products and facilitates goal directed purchases [7,8].

Feedback from customer segments in target audiences provides great insight on information value. These segments can be formed using demographic characteristics. Past studies have found differences among customers based on gender, age, education, and culture [9,5,10]. Liao et al (2009) investigated the difference of information needs among US and Chinese online customers. For example, Chinese online customers value information describing cost-effectiveness, weight, warranties, and post-sales assistance more than US online consumers. In addition, US online consumers value information describing convenience features and new technologies used in the product more than Chinese online customers. Lingyu and Ying (2010) studied impacts of product picture information on online shopping impulses. The results indicated that products pictured with real humans had a significantly higher influence on female shopping impulse than male shopping impulse. Furthermore, Seock and Bailey (2007) published gender difference on online information searches and purchase behavior using 1277 college students. Results reported that female customers conduct a greater number of online information searches than males.

For consumers within each market segment or target audience, in addition to demographics the value of different type of information can vary based on customer attitudes, interests, and activities [3,11,12]. Seock and Bailey (2007) study also included 7 psychographic characteristics and their relationship with online information searches and purchase behaviors. It was reported that college students who were brand/fashion conscious and enjoy shopping were significantly and positively related to information searches and online purchases. In particular, customers who were brand/fashion conscious were interested in information describing new products and trends. Dutta-Bergman (2006) demonstrated that demographic and lifestyle factors contribute to the attitude toward advertising, which impacted both the information value of advertising and the support for its censorship. Fourteen lifestyle factors impact were evaluated and guidelines for advertisement strategies based on psychographic impacts, such as brand consciousness and innovativeness, on perceived information value. Brand consciousness customers rated advertisement information valuable for consumer purchase decisions. Arguably, advertisements could be viewed as an effective mechanism for reinforcing the consumption choices of the brand conscious shopper. Innovativeness was also positively associated with high ratings of advertisement information value. Innovative customers, who like to buy new and different products, were more likely to use advertising information. Thus, advertising is an effective channel for the communication of information about new products.

Accordingly, product/service descriptions and details are important to customer-based decisions. Furthermore, ecommerce websites could offer more information that would appeal to psychographic characteristics to increase customers' satisfaction with information and provide a competitive edge [13].

3   Methodology

The SIMCO course web designers are trying to find the feature, function, or information that will provide an edge. They believe that a design approach appealing to their target populations' psychographic characteristic is the key. As mentioned above the target populations are ISU students, ISU alumni, and ISU families. For this study, school spirit is the essential psychographic characteristic. It is hypothesized that the implementation of a website design that appeals to the customer's school spirit will increase customer satisfaction, purchases, and traffic.

For this study, we are focused on the early stages of the design process and concentrating on the information design and content. Thus, lower level hypotheses were derived - 1) Additional information describing how products were manufactured by ISU students and on ISU campus would appeal to ISU students as potential customers; 2) ISU students would prefer a website that provided additional information describing ISU student involvement and/or association. This study's evaluation plan included two websites demonstrating two marketing strategies. The first website was designed with only product-based information. This site included only standard product description information -Product Name, Product Cost, Product Availability, Product Material, and Product Styles. The second website was ISU-centric including the standard product description and additional information appealing to the customers' school pride, psychographic characteristic. This information provided the users with more detail of the related to the products' ISU student manufacturers and SIMCO course facility, which served as the manufacturing environment. To ensure the focus would be on the information content presented, both websites had the same page layout, colors, and limited functionality.

Participants were asked to browse both websites (Website 1 - Product-only Information; Website 2 – Product and ISU Student Work Information) and then complete a questionnaire. The average amount of time spent browsing each website was two minutes. The questionnaire included eleven questions related to the websites (2 – Minutes to browse website; 2 – Cross measures for website preference; 7- Individual website measures). The individual website measures used a 5-point Likert scale, with anchors of 1= Strongly Agree and 5=Strongly Disagree. In addition, there were four questions to collect demographic information, which is discussed below.

This survey was conducted online and the link was emailed to 174 students in the College of Technology at ISU. All participants were solicited over a six day period to view and answer a questionnaire based on the two websites. A total of 105 responses were received; however, only 67 responses were retained for analysis due to missing data. Calculated after the removal of 38 responses with missing data, the response rate (39%) was reasonable [14]. The participant group was reflective student population in the college, which tends to be male dominant. The majority of the participants were male (61%), and over 56% of the participants were between the ages of 18 and 23. Demographic data also revealed that 52% of the participants reported that they had been a student for at least three years. Psychographic data collected revealed that 68% of the participants reported an average level of ISU school spirit (See Table 1).

Table 1. Demographic Information

Gender	Frequency	Percentage
Male	41	61%
Female	26	39%
Age		
18-24	41	61%
25-32	15	22%
> 32	9	13%
No Response	2	3%
Years as ISU STUDENT		
less than a year	20	30%
1-2 years	10	15%
3-4 years	30	45%
5 years or longer	3	4%
No Response	4	6%
ISU school spirit or pride		
Below Average	9	13%
Average	45	67%
Above Average	12	18%
No Response	1	1%

4   Results and Discussion

Two questions directly asked participants about their website preference. The first question asked participants which website would you prefer to use. Responses demonstrated a preference for Website 2 (82%) over Website 1(18%). The other question was posed last in the questionnaire and asked if the website that presented ISU student work details better than the website with only product information. The results recorded counts - Yes: 52 (78%) and No: 15 (22%).

There was one inquiry about the appeal of the ISU Student Work information included on Website 2. The responses to this question were recorded using the 5-point Likert scale, and the mean was 1.82 with a standard deviation of 0.95. Thus, the participants did find the ISU Student Work information appealing.

In addition, there were three questions repeated for each website using the Likert scale (see Table 2).

1. How useful was the product information provided on the website to you?
2. How satisfied are you with the information provided?
3. Was there any missing information that would prevent you from making a decision to buy a product?

The means reported for Website 1 ranged from 2.19 to 3.02 with standard deviations ranging from 0.92 to 1.05. The means reported for Website 2 ranged from 1.86 to 1.95 with standard deviations ranging from 0.80 to 1.04. Lower mean values indicate stronger agreement with the statements presented in Table 2.

Table 2. Statistical Analysis Results of Likert Scale Responses

	Website 1		Website 2		alpha < 0.05		
Questionnaire Item	**Mean**	**Std**	**Mean**	**Std**	**Diff**	**t-value**	**p-value**
Product Information Useful	2.19	0.92	1.86	0.80	0.32	3.16	0.0024
Satisfaction with All Information	2.36	0.99	1.95	0.96	0.40	2.82	0.0064
Information was Missing	3.02	1.05	3.23	1.04	-0.21	-1.97	0.0533

Based on the results of Paired T-tests for each item as illustrated in Table 2, there were statistically significant differences between the ratings of Product Information Usefulness and Satisfaction with All Information for Website 1 and Website 2. The ratings of both measures were higher for Website 2. Thus, participants found the product information presented on Website 2 more useful than the product information presented on Website 1. In addition, participants found the information presented on Website 2 more satisfying than the information presented on Website 1. There was no significant difference in the responses related to the perception that some information was missing on the websites.

Further, associations among the Likert measures for each website were inspected using a Pearson Correlation matrix. For both websites the highest correlations were among the Product Information Usefulness and Information Satisfaction ratings (Website 1 = .73; Website 2 = .67). Therefore, higher perceived usefulness of the product information was associated with higher perceived satisfaction with the information displayed on the website. For Website 2, there were strong correlations between ISU Student Work Appeal and Product Information Usefulness (.67) ISU Student Work Appeal and Information Satisfaction (.69). Therefore, high rates of appeal were associated with high rates for usefulness of the product information and perceived satisfaction with the information displayed on Website 2. Moreover, correlations among the measures aforementioned and the perception that Information was Missing were negative and low (less than .45).

The results support the tested hypotheses- 1) Additional information describing how products were manufactured by ISU students and on ISU campus would appeal to ISU students as potential customers; 2) ISU students would prefer a website that provided additional information describing ISU student involvement and/or association. Website 1 presented standard product information, which is what students are familiar with viewing when visiting other websites that sell similar products – ISU paraphernalia. Thus, the ratings were average and the students did not have a strong opinion on whether the website was missing any information. Website 2 presented the standard information plus additional information describing how the products were made by their peers. This information was included to invoke a response from students that appeal to a sense of school spirit or pride, which was reflected in the results[3,9,10]. The opinions about missing information were similar for Website 2, mainly neutral. It could be the case that product information that is normally used for purchases is the most important as supported by literature [1,2,4]. Then, additional information appealing to other characteristics has an additive effect. Notice, that ratings for Product Information Usefulness were higher on Website 2 despite the fact that the Product Information was exactly the same as displayed on Website 1.

It is vital for companies to try and understand the nature of heterogeneity of customer preferences and information needs [6]. Smaller market segments formed based on demographic and psychographic characteristics, such as education level and school spirit, provide a deeper level of understanding the impact those characteristics have on customer information satisfaction, information utility, or value-added information. Devising marketing strategies and website design based on customer information needs is the first step to gaining a competitive edge.

5   Limitations and Future Work

The survey analysis and results supported the objective of this study and produced statistically significant results. However, this effort did have limitations and there are goals for future work.

ISU Student-Only Population. All of the participants in this study were ISU students and as the results depict the levels of school spirit did not vary greatly. In a future study, the authors would like to include a more diverse group of participants with different levels of affiliation/ association with ISU and a wider range in levels of school spirit/pride. Then, an experiment can be devised to investigate how levels of school spirit/pride affect website preference and customer information satisfaction ratings.

Non-randomized Ordering. Due to some technical limitations with the experimental software, the order in which the students visited the two websites was not randomized. The ordering could have had an impact on the ratings recorded by students, especially related to perceived missing information. It would be advised to randomize the order in future studies to reduce order effect.

Limited Website Functionality. For this study, the websites functionality was limited to focus the participants' attention on the information presented. In the next study, the websites will have more functionality to allow the participants to evaluate a higher order of usability.

References

1. Wang, Y.-S., Tang, T.-I., Tang, J.-t.E.: An Instrument for Measuring Customer Satisfaction Toward Web Sites That Market Digital Products and Services. J. Electron Commerce Res. 2(3), 89–102 (2001)
2. Buys, M., Brown, I.: Customer satisfaction with internet banking web sites: an empirical test and validation of a measuring instrument. Paper presented at the Proceedings of the 2004 Annual Research Conference of the South African institute of Computer Scientists and Information Technologists on IT Research in Developing Countries, Stellenbosch, Western Cape, South Africa (2004)

3. Dutta-Bergman, M.J.: The Demographic and Psychographic Antecedents of Attitude toward Advertising. Journal of Advertising Research 46(1), 102–112 (2006)
4. Savoy, A., Salvendy, G.: Foundations of content preparation for the web. Theoretical Issues in Ergonomics Science 9(6), 501–521 (2008)
5. Liao, H., Proctor, R.W., Salvendy, G.: Content Preparation for E-Commerce Involving Chinese and U.S. Online Consumers. International Journal of Human-Computer Interaction 25(8), 729–761 (2009), doi:10.1080/10447310903025503
6. Bhatnagar, A., Ghose, S.: A latent class segmentation analysis of e-shoppers. Journal of Business Research 57(7), 758–767 (2004), doi:http://dx.doi.org/10.1016/S0148-2963(02)00357-0
7. Bellman, S., Lohse, G.L., Johnson, E.J.: Predictors of online buying behavior. Commun. ACM 42(12), 32–38 (1999), doi:10.1145/322796.322805
8. Zhang, P., von Dran, G.M.: User Expectations and Rankings of Quality Factors in Different Web Site Domains. International Journal of Electronic Commerce 6(2), 9–33 (2001)
9. Seock, Y.-K., Bailey, L.R.: The influence of college students' shopping orientations and gender differences on online information searches and purchase behaviours. International Journal of Consumer Studies 32(2), 113–121 (2008), doi:10.1111/j.1470-6431.2007.00647.x
10. Lingyu, R., Ying, Z.: Empirical Study on Gender Differences in Merchandise Picture Information Influencing Online Shopping Impulse. In: 2010 International Conference on Management and Service Science (MASS), August 24-26, pp. 1–4 (2010), doi:10.1109/icmss.2010.5576834
11. Germanakos, P., Tsianos, N., Lekkas, Z., Mourlas, C., Samaras, G.: Capturing essential intrinsic user behaviour values for the design of comprehensive web-based personalized environments. Computers in Human Behavior 24(4), 1434–1451 (2008), doi: http://dx.doi.org/10.1016/j.chb.2007.07.010
12. Massey, A.P., Khatri, V., Minas, R.K.: The Influence of Psychographic Beliefs on Website Usability Requirements. AIS Transactions on Human-Computer Interaction 5(4), 157–174 (2013)
13. Keeker K.: Improving Web Site Usability and Appeal (1997) http://Microsoft.com, http://msdn.microsoft.com/en-us/library/office/cc889361%28v=office.11%29.aspx (accessed January 25, 2014)
14. Dillman, D.A.: Mail and internet surveys, 2nd edn. John Wiley & Sons, Inc., New Jersey (2007)

Supporting Collaboration, Business and Innovation

Principles of Human Computer Interaction in Crowdsourcing to Foster Motivation in the Context of Open Innovation

Patrick Brandtner[1], Andreas Auinger[1], and Markus Helfert[2]

[1] Department for Digital Business,
University of Applied Sciences Upper Austria Campus Steyr, Austria
{patrick.brandtner,andreas.auinger}@fh-steyr.at
[2] School of Computing, Dublin City University, Ireland
markus.helfert@computing.dcu.ie

Abstract. In order to use external knowledge sources for innovation activities in organizations, recently Crowdsourcing platforms have been increasingly suggested and used. Critical success factors for such platforms include user motivation and participation, however the effect of those factors is still little understood. The aim of this paper is to analyze the extent to which selected Crowdsourcing platforms consider motivating and incentive factors from a human computer interaction perspective. Motivated by Malone's principles for designing enjoyable user interfaces we employed this framework as reference to conduct a participatory heuristic evaluation. The results of this paper demonstrate that there are several areas of improvement. At present intrinsically motivating factors in regard to the user interface are only addressed to a limited extent.

Keywords: crowdsourcing, open innovation, motivation, human computer interaction, gamification.

1   Introduction

Shorter product lifecycles as well as increasing competition and cost pressure paired with rising quality requirements, product individualization and mass customization challenge enterprises in global markets. Advanced industrial nations are no longer able to compete solely by cost-leadership. The capability to innovate has become a vital core competency in developing a sustainable competitive advantage [1]. At the same time the process of managing innovation is one of the most sophisticated and complex challenges an enterprise faces [2, 3].

An interesting concept in this regard is "open innovation" which describes a change in an organization's innovation process and the integration of external stakeholders and knowledge sources in a company's innovation activities. This not only increases the efficiency, but also the effectiveness of the activities and tasks along the innovation process [4, 5]. Hence, it is important to define appropriate process-support. Recently the concept of Crowdsourcing has been suggested for this phase.

F.F.-H. Nah (Ed.): HCIB/HCII 2014, LNCS 8527, pp. 585–596, 2014.
© Springer International Publishing Switzerland 2014

The integration of the crowd to find solutions to current problems and to address urgent issues in organizations is known as "Crowdsourcing" [6, 7]. This approach allows organizations to employ large numbers of dispersed works (users) over the internet through open calls for contributions with the goal of finding solutions to problems by outsourcing tasks to the general internet public [8, 9]. In the context of the Open Innovation approach, Crowdsourcing can be considered as an opening of the innovation process by sourcing out the phase of idea generation to integrate numerous outside competencies in a potentially large and unknown population by using web facilities and Web 2.0 tools and concepts [10]. According to authors like Sloane, Crowdsourcing is even *"one particular manifestation of Open Innovation"* [11].

There is a large number of existing web-based Crowdsourcing solutions to support innovation management, which differ from each other in terms of functionality, main purpose and the underlying processes. An important, but often overlooked aspect of these platforms is the human computer interaction, and in particular the motivation and willingness of individuals to contribute to those platforms. Several researchers have suggested that platforms should consider motivating principles to foster and maintain user engagement [7, 12], however these factors are often neglected. Several studies have already investigated factors that influence participation in Crowdsourcing [13, 14]. Most of these studies focused on extrinsic motivation, only some of them addressed the role of intrinsic motivation or the importance of the user interface to foster and maintain user motivation [13–16].

The aim of the current paper is to analyze the design of user interfaces of existing Crowdsourcing solutions from a human-computer interaction perspective. We examine how selected Crowdsourcing platforms address intrinsic user motivation in conjunction to the user interface and implement motivating principles to foster human computer interaction in the context of Open Innovation. In a first step, we analyze based on literature, the principles and processes of Crowdsourcing in the context of Open Innovation (section two). In a second phase, relevant types of motivating and incentive factors in the course of Crowdsourcing are dealt with (section three). Thirdly, existing Crowdsourcing platforms are selected and the most relevant ones are analyzed and evaluated in regard to motivational factors meant to create, increase and maintain user involvement and motivation in conjunction to user interface design (section four). Finally, the results of the heuristic evaluation (section five) and the conclusion of the current research paper (section six) are presented.

2   Crowdsourcing in the Open Innovation Process

2.1   The Open Innovation Process

For this research we selected an appropriate open innovation process in a first step to serve as a reference framework for the particular research. Many process models do not specifically focus on open innovation or do not cover corresponding aspects and factors. One of the most seminal researchers in this context is Henry Chesbrough. First mentioning the term Open Innovation in 2003 [19], he is often referred to as the "father of Open Innovation" [20, 21].

Based on Chesbrough's principles and concept of Open Innovation, many open innovation process models have been developed so far, e.g. the Model by Docherty [22], which was employed by Robert Cooper to adapt his popular and widely used Stage-Gate-model [23–25] to become an Innovation process model, which specifically addresses open innovation aspects [26]. It consists of a front-end process, a development and a commercialization stage. Companies should use information across the stages as well as from external sources. This makes open innovation challenging and extremely complex. Especially the activities at the front end process do not only create internal but also need to consider externally generated ideas from multiple sources [26].

2.2   Crowdsourcing

The term Crowdsourcing was first used by Jeff Howe in 2006 [6] and refers to as "the act of taking a task traditionally performed by a designated agent (such as an employee or a contractor) and outsourcing it by making an open call to an undefined but large group of people." [9]. According to Gassmann, Crowdsourcing can be seen as an interactive strategy of outsourcing knowledge generation and problem solving to external actors through a public or semi-public call for inputs. Such calls typically adress creative tasks and topics and are usually realized through a website or platform [27]. Crowdsourcing typically involves three categories of actors: the crowd, companies or organizations who benefit from inputs of the crowd and an intermediate platform which links the crowd and the companies and serves as a Crowdsourcing enabler [28]. In this paper an emphasis was laid on Crowdsourcing platforms as well as on the crowd respectively the individual users it consists of. More precisely, user interfaces of most successful platforms were analyzed in regard to motivating and incentive factors.

2.3   The Principles of Crowdsourcing in the Open Innovation Process

As mentioned before, Crowdsourcing can be considered as an opening of an organization's innovation process by sourcing out some of the activities at the front end of innovation, especially of the idea generation phase [10, 11]. Crowdsourcing shares several principles and similarities with the concept of Open Innovation. Chesbrough postulates that an organization is not only depending on internal but also increasingly on external sources of knowledge and that there are inside-out and outside-in flows of knowledge [5, 3, 19]. Crowdsourcing follows the same principle: by distributing knowledge and by opening an organization's R&D process to the crowd, competitive advantages can be reached [29]. The main difference between these two concepts is that Open Innovation focusses on the innovation process while Crowdsourcing can be applied in many different application domains [27]. Furthermore, Crowdsourcing does on the one hand provide access to a large number of dispersed, anonymous individuals and their knowledge for organizations, but one the other hand only concentrates on outside-in flows of knowledge in the sense of Open Innovation [28]. In our research we view Open Innovation and Crowdsourcing complementary, by seeing Crowdsourcing as an opportunity to provide inbound flows of knowledge.

3   Motivational Factors in Conjunction to the User Interface

There are basically two categories of motivating factors in Crowdsourcing: intrinsic and extrinsic [30]. Extrinsic motivations are "the motivation to work for something apart from and external to the work itself" [16] and include e.g. financial rewards respectively free products [31] or new career opportunities [32]. As the current research project laid an emphasis on intrinsic motivations only, extrinsic motivations are not part of this research paper. Intrinsic motivation can be defined as "the motivation to engage in work for its own sake because the work itself is interesting or satisfying" [16]. Intrinsic motivations are e.g. exchange of information [33] social identity and influence [32], an entrepreneurial mindset [31], a sense of membership and attachment to a group [34] and also fun, enjoyment or entertainment [35-36].

The aim of the current research project is to analyze motivating and incentive factors in conjunction to the user interface of Crowdsourcing platforms. Motivated by the work of Malone, who developed a framework for designing enjoyable and intrinsically motivating user interfaces [18, 17], we aim to examine Crowdsourcing platforms through the lense of this prominent framework. The framework seems suitable as it emphasizes the intrinsic motivational factors of HCI. More specifically, Malone suggests that factors that make computer games enjoyable and fun to use may also be applicable in a none-gaming context [18]. This approach of using game design elements in a different context dates back to Malone himself and is known as gamification [37]. According to Fitz-Walter et al. Gamification is a growing trend to motivate users and enhance user experience [38], which are both important prerequisites for Crowdsourcing too.

Malone's seminal work dates back to the 1980ies, when he conducted several studies about what makes computer games so captivating and exactly which design elements motivate people to interact with computer games [17, 39]. The primary purpose of these studies was to derive recommendations for highly motivating instructional systems, but Malone's findings and gamification in general are also of great relevance for designing other user interfaces, e.g. Crowdsourcing, Idea Competition or Open Innovation platforms [38, 37]. In his paper [18] Malone developed a questionnaire to analyze the appeal of computer systems based on three categories: challenge, fantasy and curiosity [18]. Those categories and the corresponding subcategories and questions are explained in more detail in section 4.3 of the current paper. According to Malone, those categories include the major features of computer games that can be incorporated into other user interfaces [18]. In the course of the current research, this list is taken as a reference framework and will be adopted for the application of analyzing Crowdsourcing platforms (cf. section 4.3).

4   Selection of Platforms and Evaluation Methodology

For our research, relevant Crowdsourcing solutions had to be selected in regard to specific criteria. Subsequent we selected solutions and examined those regarding motivational and incentive factors from a human-computer-interaction perspective based on appropriate measures and Malone's criteria for designing enjoyable user interfaces.

4.1 Definition of Selection Criteria

Following from the discussion in section 2.2, criteria were defined to specifically discover and select only those Crowdsourcing platforms which meet the requirements to support the activities and tasks along the innovation process. Applied to the definition of selection criteria for the current project, this means that only Crowdsourcing-solutions with an emphasis on supporting organizations in accessing and effectively integrating the knowledge of the crowd are considered relevant. According to Gassmann, Crowdsourcing activities can be divided into five different application domains: user initiated Crowdsourcing, Crowdsourcing intermediaries, public Crowdsourcing initiatives, idea market places and company initiated platforms [27].

Based on this categorization of Crowdsourcing activities and our understanding of Crowdsourcing in the context of Open Innovation (cf. section 2.3), only intermediary and company initiated platforms are relevant for the current research project. Only these two categories include platforms which support organizations in their innovation activities by providing inbound knowledge flows. Gassmann further subdivides those two categories in R&D platforms, marketing & design platforms, freelancer, idea platforms, product ideas and problem solution platforms and branding and design platforms [27].

In order to reduce the large amount of intermediary and company initiated Crowdsourcing platforms, we focused on three subcategories in an initial phase: R&D platforms, idea platforms, and product idea and problem solution platforms. For each of those we selected one exemplary Crowdsourcing platform in a next step. As an exemplary Crowdsourcing intermediary platform in the R&D area we chose InnoCentive (http://www.innocentive.com/), which is often mentioned in scientific publications to be a quite popular and successful Crowdsourcing platform for utilizing the crowd as one particular knowledge source to support an organization's R&D activities [40, 41, 29]. As an example for a Crowdsourcing intermediary idea platform, we selected Atizo.com (https://www.atizo.com/) because of the high scientific attention this platform received within specific literature [42, 43, 27]. As a typical company initiated product idea and problem solution platform, we took the example of Dell's IdeaStorm platform (http://www.ideastorm.com/), which received much scientific attention recently and is considered quite popular and successful [44–46].

Those solutions were subjected to an in-depth analysis regarding motivational and incentive factors according to a specifically developed evaluation scheme (cf. section 4.2 and 4.3)

4.2 Evaluation Methodology

In order to evaluate the selected Crowdsourcing solutions we adopeted a participatory heuristic evaluation [47] using Malone's motivating principles. This allows combining the domain expertise of a user with a usability-expert's know-how. By that, not only the necessary usability knowledge but also the required process-expertise can be integrated in the evaluation [48, 47]. Applied to the current research, this means that the evaluation of selected Crowdsourcing platforms is conducted pair-wise, whereby the usability expert gets an overview of the specific platform and its target process before the actual evaluation starts.

During evaluation, the usability expert has to fulfill specific tasks addressing Malone's motivating principles for human computer interaction in presence of the domain expert, who comments on the usability expert's actions and answers process-related questions when necessary. Hence, the participatory heuristic evaluation was structured by the following methodological steps [47]:

- Preparation:
  - An independent examiner develops realistic application scenarios.
  - To be able to perform various, meaningful scenarios, the usability experts get an overview of the solution and its underlying processes. Hereby the challenge of learning the system is taken away from the user.
- Evaluation:
  - During evaluation, the usability expert works through the defined application scenarios in presence of the user (domain expert). The user is asked to comment on the usability expert's actions on the one hand, one the other hand he is also available for comprehension questions regarding the particular sequences of tasks and actions. By commenting and answering questions, the user supports the usability expert in taking a standard user's role and the corresponding domain expertise.

Due to the fact, that Malone's criteria could not be evaluated on a standard heuristic evaluation scale, we decided to adapt Nielsen's acknowledged usability evaluation scale, which was designed specifically for usability problems [49], to a simple 3-level rating scale (0=no support, 1=weak support, 2=good support). Following the methodological steps mentioned above, we developed three scenarios which are core elements respectively standard processes in Open Innovation Crowdsourcing platforms:

- Scenario 1: Use the provided profile and adjust it according to your preferences, include personal information to position yourself and to present your knowledge.
- Scenario 2: Select an existing challenge or problem on the platform and post your own idea or contribution to it.
- Scenario 3: Take a look at existing ideas / possible solutions for the challenge and interact with other users respectively respond to existing content elements.

4.3   Definition of Evaluation Criteria

Based on Malone's criteria for designing an enjoyable user interface (cf. section 3), we developed a set of criteria respectively a questionnaire to analyze the selected Open Innovation Crowdsourcing solutions (cf. section 4.1) in regard to intrinsically motivating factors (cf. section 3). Table 1 provides a juxtaposition of Malone's criteria and our project specific ones, which were adapted to be applicable in the course of the participatory heuristic evaluation (cf. section 4.2).

Table 1. Derivation of project specific evaluation criteria based on Malone [18]

Malone's evaluation criteria (cf. section 3)			Adopted evaluation criteria
1. Challenge	(a) Goal	• Clear goal definition? • Provision of performance feedback?	1.1 Is a clear goal visible for the user? 1.2. Does the platform provide performance feedback for the user in regard to the level of goal attainment ?
	(b) uncertain outcome	• Variable difficulty level?	1.3. Are difficulty levels defined? 1.4. Can the user adjust / select the difficulty level?
		• Multiple level goals?	1.5. Is the goal outcome uncertain? 1.6. Do goals offer multiple levels of target attainment?
2. Fantasy	(a) Does the interface embody emotionally appealing fantasies?		2.1. Does the platform embody emotionally appealing fantasies? 2.2. Does the interface adress the user's desire for social connection? 2.3. Does the interface embody a feeling of respect and social status?
	(b) Does the interface embody metaphors with physical or other systems that the user understands?		2.4. Does the platform utilize metaphors with recognised and understood physical or other systems?
3. Curiosity	(a) Level of infor- mational complexity	• Use of audio & visual effects as decoration / to enhance fantasy / as representation system?	3.1. Does the platform provide an optimal level of complexity? 3.2. Are audio and visual effect used as decoration or to enhance fantasy? 3.3.Does the platform use audio or visual effect as representation system?
		• Use of randomness to add variety without unreliability?	3.4. Is randomness used to add variety to the platform without making it unreliable?
		• Appropriate use of humor?	3.5. Does the platform utilize humor to increase the enjoyment of using it in an appropriate way?
	(b) Knowledge structure	• Capitalization on the user's desire for clear knowledge structures?	3.6. Does the platform evoke user curiosity by making them think their knowledge structures are incomplete, inconsistent or unparsimonious?
		• Introduction of new information when existing knowledge is unsatisfactory?	3.7. Does the platform support users in making their knowledge structures complete, consistent and parsimonious?

5   Results of Heuristic Evaluation

In this paper we present a summary of our evaluation results and focus on the most significant observations, the overall and general results are visualized in figure 1.

Amongst the selected Crowdsourcing platforms, Innocentive met most of the evaluation criteria. Compared to Atizo and IdeaStorm, it e.g. includes functionality to evoke user curiosity by making user-specific suggestions of relevant challenges according to personal interests and knowledge fields. To encourage user cooperation, Innocentive tries to foster team forming by suggesting forming or joining a group of users when stuck. Furthermore, InnoCentive was the only platform which had different levels of difficulty for challenges (e.g. premium challenge, grand challenge). Overall, the level complexity was perceived as "just right" in comparison to Atizo (simple but functional) or IdeaStorm (too complex).

Our analyses revealed the following most important areas for improving motivating and incentive factors:

- 1.2. – Performance feedback: None of the tools offered feedback on the level of goal attainment in a systematic way.
- 1.4. – Adjustable difficulty levels: Although Innocentive offered different difficulty levels, adjusting it was not possible in any of the platforms.
- 1.6. – Multiple Level targets: In all of the three analyzed platforms, only top- and no sub-level targets were defined.
- 2.1. - Appealing fantasies: Emotionally appealing fantasies were only embodied in a very limited way and mainly addressed the user's need for self-achievement by awarding badges or titles (e.g. "Dell Community Rockstar").
- 2.4. – Use of metaphors: Metaphors were used only to a very limited extent by using terms like "innovation pavilion" or "project room" (Innocentive), symbols like a trophy (Atizo) or titles like "Rockstar" (IdeaStorm).
- 3.2. – Audio and visual effects to enhance fantasy: Such effects were mainly used as representational systems and not to enhance creativity and fantasy systematically. When used to enhance fantasy, it was only in a few challenges and thus depending on the challenge creator.
- 3.4. – Use of randomness and 3.5. – Use of humor: Neither could any variety-adding randomness be observed, nor was humor systematically used in any of the analyzed platforms.
- 3.7. - Knowledge structures: Only Innocentive supported the user in completing his knowledge structures by providing the suggestions to form or join a team when stuck. However, additional, more effective features couldn't be found neither in Innocentive nor in Atizo or IdeaStorm.

Criteria that are already implemented very well across all three platforms are:

- 1.1. - Clear goal: Each platform provided clear goal description.
- 1.5. - Uncertainty of outcome: Goal outcome was unclear in all platforms.
- 2.2. - Social connection: Internal (groups, teams, community) as well as external (e.g. Facebook, LinkedIn, Twitter) networking was a core element of the analyzed platforms.

- 2.3. – Respect and social status: Each platform provided top solver rankings, awards or expert search.
- 3.3. - Audio and visual effects as representation systems: Network maps, symbols or activity diagrams were used for representational purposes, Innocentive even offers a mobile app for download.

The following figure 1 summarize the results of the conducted heuristic evaluation. On a scale from 0 to 2 (0=no support, 1=limited support, 2=good support) the result of each evaluation criterion (cf. section 4.3) is visualized for each platform:

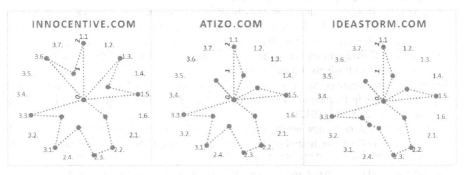

Fig. 1. Results of the heuristic evaluation

6   Conclusion

The results of the heuristic usability evaluation demonstrate the importance of motivational factors and the areas for improvement for Crowdsourcing platforms from a human computer interaction perspective. The study reiterates the lack of research in this area. Using participatory heuristic evaluation together with Malone's framework for designing enjoyable user interfaces, we have analyzed several Crowdsourcing platforms. The paper also demonstrated the usefulness of our evaluation approach, which will be expanded in further research. Especially the use of fantasy and creativity enhancing features and effects, the utilization of metaphors or the systematical use of randomness and humor could be applied to make Crowdsourcing user interfaces more enjoyable and fun to use. Again we observed that gamification is of great relevance and offers great potential in the context of Open Innovation Crowdsourcing platforms. To further analyze the connection between intrinsically motivating factors in games and to refine the recommendations of the current paper, additional studies have to be conducted in the future.

References

1. Wagner, K.: With Innovation Management to organic growth and performance excellence. In: Spitzley, A., Rogowski, T., Garibaldo, F. (eds.) Open Innovation for Small and Medium Sized Enterprises. Ways to Develop Excellence, pp. 7–18. Fraunhofer-Institute for Industrial Engineering, Stuttgart (2007)
2. Maital, S., Seshadri, D.V.R.: Innovation management. Strategies, concepts and tools for growth and profit. Sage, New Delhi (2012)

3. Chesbrough, H.W., Vanhaverbeke, W., West, J.: Open innovation. Researching a new paradigm. Oxford University Press, Oxford (2006)
4. Reichwald, R., Piller, F.: Interaktive Wertschöpfung. Open Innovation, Individualisierung und neue Formen der Arbeitsteilung. Gabler, Wiesbaden (2006)
5. Chesbrough, H.: Open business models. How to thrive in the new innovation landscape. Harvard Business School Press, Boston (2006)
6. Howe, J.: The Rise of Crowdsourcing. Wired Magazine 14(6), 1–4 (2006)
7. La Vecchia, G., Cisternino, A.: Collaborative workforce, business process crowdsourcing as an alternative of BPO. In: Daniel, F., Facca, F.M. (eds.) ICWE 2010. LNCS, vol. 6385, pp. 425–430. Springer, Heidelberg (2010)
8. Kazai, G.: In search of quality in crowdsourcing for search engine evaluation. In: Clough, P., Foley, C., Gurrin, C., Jones, G.J.F., Kraaij, W., Lee, H., Mudoch, V. (eds.) ECIR 2011. LNCS, vol. 6611, pp. 165–176. Springer, Heidelberg (2011)
9. Howe, J.: Crowdsourcing. How the power of the crowd is driving the future of business. Random House Business, London (2008)
10. Poetz, M.K., Schreier, M.: The Value of Crowdsourcing: Can Users Really Compete with Professionals in Generating New Product Ideas? Journal of Product Innovation Management 29(2), 245–256 (2012)
11. Sloane, P.: The brave new world of open innovation. Strategic Direction 27(5), 3–4 (2011)
12. Brabham, D.C.: Crowdsourcing the Public Participation Process for Planning Projects. Planning Theory 8(3), 242–262 (2009)
13. Brabham, D.C.: Moving the Crowd at Threadless. Motivations for participation in a crowdsourcing application. Information, Communication & Society 13(8), 1122–1145 (2010)
14. Leimeister, J.M., Huber, M., Bretschneider, U.: Leveraging Crowdsourcing: Activation-Supporting Components for IT-Based Ideas Competition. Journal of Management Information Systems 26(1), 197–224 (2009)
15. Lakhani, K.R., Jeppesen, L.B., Lohse, P.A.: The Value of Openness in Scientific Problem Solving. Working Paper 07-050. Harvard Business School (2007)
16. Zheng, H., Li, D., Hou, W.: Task Design, Motivation, and Participation in Crowdsourcing Contests. International Journal of Electronic Commerce 15(4), 57–88 (2011)
17. Malone, T.W.: Toward a theory of intrinsically motivating instruction. Cognitive Science 5(4), 333–369 (1981)
18. Malone, T.W.: Heuristics for designing enjoyable user interfaces: Lessons from computer games. In: Proceedings of the 1982 Conference on Human Factors in Computing Systems, pp. 63–68. ACM, New York (1982)
19. Chesbrough, H.W.: Open innovation. The new imperative for creating and profiting from technology. Harvard Business School Press, Boston (2003)
20. Munkongsujarit, S., Srivannaboon, S.: An integration of broadcast search in innovation intermediary for SMEs: A preliminary study of iTAP in Thailand. In: 2012 Proceedings of Technology Management for Emerging Technologies, PICMET 2012, pp. 2117–2124 (2012)
21. Lindgren, P., Rasmussen, O.H.: Poulsen. H.: Open Business Model Innovation in Healthcare Sector. Journal of Multi Business Model Innovation and Technology 1(1), 23–52 (2012)
22. Docherty, M.: Primer on open innovation: Principles and practice. PDMA Visions Magazine 30(2), 13–17 (2006)

23. Ahn, J., Skudlark, A.: Managing risk in a new telecommunications service development process through a scenario planning approach. Journal of Information Technology 17(3), 103–118 (2002)
24. Valeri, S.G., Rozenfeld, H.: Improving The Flexibility Of New Product Development (Npd) Through A New Quality Gate Approach. Journal of Integrated Design and Process Science 8(3), 17–36 (2004)
25. Van Oorschot, K., Sengupta, K., Akkermans, H.: Get Fat Fast: Surviving Stage-Gate in NPD. Journal of Product Innovation Management 27(6), 828–839 (2010)
26. Cooper, R.G.: Perspective: The Stage-Gate Idea-to-Launch Process - Update, What's New, and NexGen Systems. Journal of Product Innovation Management 25(3), 213–232 (2008)
27. Gassmann, O.: Crowdsourcing. Hanser Verlag, München (2012)
28. Schenk, E., Guittard, C.: Towards a characterization of crowdsourcing practices. Journal of Innovation Economics 7(1), 93–107 (2011)
29. Albors, J., Ramos, J.C., Hervas, J.L.: New learning network paradigms: Communities of objectives, crowdsourcing, wikis and open source. International Journal of Information Management 28(3), 194–202 (2008)
30. Pan, Y., Blevis, E.: A survey of crowdsourcing as a means of collaboration and the implications of crowdsourcing for interaction design. In: 2011 International Conference on Collaboration Technologies and Systems (CTS), pp. 397–403 (2011)
31. Tapscott, D., Williams, A.D.: Wikinomics. How mass collaboration changes everything. Portfolio, New York (2006)
32. Bagozzi, R.P., Dholakia, U.M.: Intentional social action in virtual communities. Journal of Interactive Marketing 16(2), 2–21 (2002)
33. Ridings, C.M., Gefen, D.: Virtual Community Attraction: Why People Hang Out Online. Journal of Computer-Mediated Communication 10(1) (2004)
34. Hertel, G., Niedner, S., Herrmann, S.: Motivation of software developers in Open Source projects: an Internet-based survey of contributors to the Linux kernel. Research Policy 32(7), 1159–1177 (2003)
35. Hars, A., Shaosong, O.: Working for free? Motivations of participating in open source projects. In: Proceedings of the 34th Annual Hawaii International Conference on System Sciences, p. 9 (2001)
36. Lakhani, K., Wolf, R.G.: Why Hackers Do What They Do: Understanding Motivation and Effort in Free/Open Source Software Projects. In: Feller, J., Fitzgerald, B., Hissam, S., Lakhani, K. (eds.) Perspectives on Free and Open Source Software, MIT Press, Cambridge (2005)
37. Deterding, S., Sicart, M., Nacke, L.: Gamification. Using game-design elements in non-gaming contexts. In: Proceedings of the 2011 Annual Conference Extended Abstracts on Human Factors in Computing Systems (CHI EA 2011), Vancouver, BC, Canada, pp. 2425–2428 (2011)
38. Fitz-Walter, Z., Tjondronegoro, D., Wyeth, P.: Orientation Passport. Using gamification to engage university students. In: Proceedings of the 23rd Australian Computer-Human Interaction Conference, pp. 122–125 (2011)
39. Malone, T.W.: What Makes Computer Games Fun. Xerox Palo Alto research center (1981)
40. Saxton, G.D., Oh, O., Kishore, R.: Rules of Crowdsourcing: Models, Issues, and Systems of Control. Information Systems Management 30(1), 2–20 (2013)
41. Brabham, D.C.: Crowdsourcing as a Model for Problem Solving: An Introduction and Cases. Convergence: The International Journal of Research into New Media Technologies 14(1), 75–90 (2008)

42. Muhdi, L., Daiber, M., Friesike, S.: The crowdsourcing process: an intermediary mediated idea generation approach in the early phase of innovation. International Journal of Entrepreneurship and Innovation Management 14(4), 315–332 (2011)

43. Mladenow, A., Kryvinska, N., Strauss, C.: Towards cloud-centric service environments. Journal of Service Science Research 4(2), 213–234 (2012)

44. Schildhauer, T., Voss, H.: Open Innovation and Crowdsourcing in the Sciences. In: Bartling, S., Friesike, S. (eds.) Opening Science, pp. 255–269. Springer International Publishing, Cham (2014)

45. Kimmel, A.J., Kitchen, P.J.: WOM and social media: Presaging future directions for research and practice. Journal of Marketing Communications 20(1-2), 5–20 (2014)

46. Dahlander, L., Piezunka, H.: Open to suggestions: How organizations elicit suggestions through proactive and reactive attention. In: Research Policy (2013)

47. Sarodnick, F., Brau, H.: Methoden der Usability Evaluation. Wissenschaftliche Grundlagen und praktische Anwendung. Verlag Hans Huber, Bern (2010)

48. Brau, H., Schulze, H.: Kooperative Evaluation - Usability Inspektion in komplexen und verteilten Anwendungsdomänen. In: Hassenzahl, M (ed): Usability Professionals 2004. Berichtband des zweiten Workshops des German Chapters der Usability Professionals Association e. V., German Chapter der Usability Professionals Association, Stuttgart (2004)

49. Nielsen, J.: Reliability of severity estimates for usability problems found by heuristic evaluation. In: Posters and Short Talks of the 1992 SIGCHI Conference, pp. 129–130 (1992)

Search in Open Innovation: How Does It Evolve with the Facilitation of Information Technology?

Tingru Cui[1], Yu Tong[2], and Hock Hai Teo[3]

[1] University of Wollongong, Australia
tingru@uow.edu.au
[2] City University of Hong Kong, Hong Kong
yutong@cityu.edu.hk
[3] National University of Singapore, Singapore
teohh@comp.nus.edu.sg

Abstract. As a cornerstone of open innovations' success, the work of external search has been altered by the advancement in information technologies (ITs). This study depicts the IT-induced evolution of open search patterns in two case firms. While three patterns were observed in both firms, they took different trajectories of open search pattern change due to the different enabling roles of ITs. ITs were found to serve as an amplifier and a catalyst to induce different trajectories. This study contributes to the literature by unveiling the process of open search evolution including identifying different open search patterns and the roles of ITs. The managerial lessons learned from the two case firms can be applied by other firms.

Keywords: IT-induced Evolution, Open search, Case studies, Open innovation.

1   Open Innovation and IT-Induced Open Search

External search has played a very critical role in a firm's innovation process (e.g., Berchicci 2012). Past studies have shown that firms must acquire and exploit new scientific knowledge and technological developments from the external environment in order to innovate and remain competitive (Cohen and Levinthal 1990; Escribano et al. 2009). This external environment includes sources such as customers, suppliers, universities, research institutions, industry consortia, and even rival firms (Chesbrough 2003). It is noteworthy that conventional external search work is characterized by the use of a small number of individuals taking managerial positions in the R&D department to act as the firm's boundary spanners to scan the outside world through personal networks for knowledge, and process and disseminate them to the R&D employees (e.g., Allen 1984; Katz and Tushman 1981). However, as a cornerstone of open innovations' success, the work of external search has been altered by the advancement in information technologies (ITs). Employees at different organizational levels can now source and share external knowledge with other employees with consummate ease and speed.

F.F.-H. Nah (Ed.): HCIB/HCII 2014, LNCS 8527, pp. 597–608, 2014.
© Springer International Publishing Switzerland 2014

However, extant literature has paid scant attention to capture such a change. While prior literature provides valuable insights on conventional work of external search, there are some gaps limiting our understanding on how external search can be evolved from conventional pattern with the support of advanced ITs. Furthermore, despite IT tools serve as the key boundary objects to sustain the intense interaction and knowledge sharing across organizational boundaries for open innovations, there remains a paucity of research on how IT can facilitate the external search activities in open innovations.

Therefore, we employed two case studies to unveil the changing work process of "open search", which consists of sourcing external knowledge (i.e., technology or collaborator) and assimilating acquired knowledge into internal R&D employees' work. Two firms leading in open innovation were selected. Based on detailed field observations, documents and interviews with key stakeholders, we observed three different patterns of open search strategies: centralized, differentiated, and decentralized and explored the evolutionary processes of how ITs change the patterns of open search (e.g., ITs as an amplifier and a catalyst). As evident in two cases, the search work became more complex and dynamic with the inclusion of more and different boundary spanners and broadened search domains compared to the work identified in the literature.

More specifically, advances in ITs induced the evolution of open search pattern in two case firms, their impacts were different. In one case firm, ITs (e.g., data mining tools, data analytics, and open innovation platforms) served as the amplifier to enhance the speed and intensity of external sourcing and selection capabilities. When more powerful ITs were employed, managers have limited ability and time to employ them, which required the technological experts in sourcing, and led to the differentiated open search pattern. In contrast, for another case firm, intra- and inter-firm ITs (e.g., enterprise resources planning systems, supply chain management systems) served as the catalyst to accelerate knowledge access and sharing among R&D employees with value network partners (e.g., suppliers, customers). It stimulated R&D employees to discover innovation opportunities in the interconnected networks and resulted in the new decentralized open search pattern. IT indeed induced the work pattern change of open search in firms.

Through this study, we contribute to extant open innovation literature by providing a theoretically grounded exposition of different open search patterns and their evolution process. Additionally, this study explicates the differentiated roles of ITs in open search. ITs are found to serve as an amplifier and a catalyst to induce different trajectories of open search evolution. Our findings can also provide useful insights to firms' managers to design their innovation units and effectively use ITs to facilitate the evolution.

2   IT-Induced Evolution of Open Search Patterns

Two firms leading in open innovation were selected at this stage (see Table 1 for firms' details). Such a selection makes our findings more robust and generalizable than selecting single case (Eisenhardt and Graebner 2007). The qualitative data were collected through four sources: (1) interviews with key stakeholders, (2) onsite observations of innovation products and work places, (3) follow-up emails and phone calls to track the innovation processes and clarify details, (4) archives including media and corporate materials. Such triangulation bolsters confidence in the accuracy of the findings. In total, 11 onsite interviews were conducted from two leading firms in open innovation (see Table 1). Each interview last 45-60 minutes, and was taped and transcribed. The interview questions largely focused on the evolution of work in conducting open search. Sample interview questions included "How does your firm conduct open search? Who and how to source external knowledge? How can the sourced knowledge be assimilated internally? Is there any change in terms of how your firm conducts open search? What factors drive the changes of open search work? What's the role of ITs in open search?"

Table 1. Details of firms and interviews

Firm*	Business description	Number of employees	Number of interviews	Interviewees' position
Pluto	A global top American multinational consumer goods company. Its products include pet foods, cleaning agents and personal care products.	7000 (China branch)	6	Senior technology manager, R&D director, R&D employee
Neptune	The largest and leading solar energy company in China. Its products range from solar water heaters, solar collectors to solar lights and PV lighting products.	4000	5	Chief executive officer, senior technology manager, R&D employee

* To protect the confidentiality of participants' data, names of both firm have been replaced with pseudonyms.

We addressed potential informant bias in several ways. First, we triangulated data from multiple sources and informants for a firm. At least two evidences were used to support each finding (Klein and Myers 1999; Myers 1997). Second, we used "courtroom question" that focused on factual accounts of what informants knew (e.g., dates, meetings, participants) and avoided speculation (Huber and Power 1985). Third, we gave anonymity to our informants and their firms, which encourages candor. The transcribed field notes and interviews were coded by three researchers, who then met to discuss the codes to ensure the interpretation consistency. An initial set of coding themes was derived based on our objective to understand the open search work and its evolution. The findings were moved back and forth between empirical data and conceptual themes. This process ended when "theoretical saturation" was reached, where the incremental improvement on the research findings became minimum (Eisenhardt 1989).

2.1   Case Pluto

Episode 1: Centralized Open Search. Operating in a competitive market, Pluto envisioned new ideas and new products as its lifeblood and continuously searched for innovative ideas. As a leading firm in the consumer goods market, R&D managers in Pluto paid huge attention to assimilating state-of-the-art technologies into its product lines. Similar to the conventional external search pattern identified in Figure 1, the responsibility of open search fall upon the managers, who selected appropriate external knowledge (technologies or collaborators) from personal networks or reach potential ones through mutual acquaintances in personal networks. These technologies and collaborators were used for achieving long-term goals and gaining competitive advantage. However, ITs played prominent roles along the two stages of the open search process (i.e., external sourcing and internal assimilation). Since decision making is also a critical work responsibility and the stakeholders to perform it have changed, we include the discussion of it in the open search process. For managers, ITs had facilitated roles of broadening their networks, facilitated the decision making, and eased the internal knowledge assimilation process.

External sourcing: The work of external sourcing in Pluto was conducted by R&D managers. Besides existing network, managers also employed IT tools such as Internet to source potential external knowledge. After identifying potential targets, the possibility of collaboration was first negotiated mainly in the offline setting such as site visits and conference attendance. For example, the senior technology manager stated the following strategy to establish the network:

> *"Some top researchers at Chinese Academy of Sciences were invited to seminars and visits at our company a long time ago before our collaborative innovation projects started."*

Once the network was initiated, communication technologies such as emails, video conferencing and chat applications were used by managers to strengthen the relationships with external parties and build shared structures of interactions, cognition, and trust.

Decision making: We learnt from our informants that electronic reports available on the Internet were used by Pluto's managers to evaluate the potential collaborators. To ensure that the chosen external knowledge fit the firm, they also used executive information systems to monitor customer demands and competitors' movements before making the final selection.

Internal assimilation: After selecting the external collaborator, decision and the collaborator' information were passed downward from managers to lower level R&D employees, mainly through emails. This is referred to as top-down assimilation. R&D employees then planned the collaboration details with external partner together. Besides face-to-face meetings, communication ITs (e.g., emails, electronic noticeboards, newsletters, phone, fax) were used to facilitate interactions between the cooperating parties.

During this episode, Pluto had twelve innovation projects collaborating with two universities and one research institution. By sharing resources, leveraging ideas, and tapping the expertise, Pluto was able to create vibrant innovation ecosystems, multiply its efforts, and derive more strategic value for the firm.

Episode 2: Differentiated Open Search. To mark the completion of the first innovation episode, a specialized sourcing unit focusing on sourcing external knowledge was established in Pluto. We understood that the establishment of this unit was mainly due to two reasons. First, IT tools such as data mining applications, analytic techniques, and open innovation platforms significantly amplified the speed and intensity of external sourcing and selection capabilities. Under such circumstances, managers had limited ability and time to employ these IT tools. Second, the open mindset toward innovation had taken root in Pluto. Managers and R&D employees viewed external search not merely as a task but also as a way of building useful knowledge sources for future innovation projects.

External sourcing: The sourcing unit initially consisted of 11 employees, who were both IT experts and PhD holders in the areas relevant to Pluto's products. These employees in the sourcing unit not only handled requests for searching external knowledge from R&D unit, but also proactively probed cutting-edge external knowledge, mapping these emerging technologies to products and monitoring the technological capabilities of competitors. Employees in the sourcing unit were good at filtering, interpreting and synthesizing information from vast amount of web pages, scientific literature and patent databases using data mining and retrieval technologies.

In addition, employees in the sourcing unit also utilized open innovation portals to identify innovative external knowledge. First, they built a portal to post their needs and look for solutions from people all over the world. Second, they also utilized existing portals such as InnoCentive, NineSigma, and Alibaba to source for potential technologies, partners and monitor the development of new technologies. For instance, the R&D director mentioned that,

> "Alibaba, [note: an online China manufacturer portal],linked our company to various manufacturers, suppliers, exporters, importers and buyers. For one innovation project, we searched for an important technology for two years, but did not find any satisfactory technology provider. With Alibaba, our sourcing unit managed to find one small company in China that met our requirements."

Decision making and internal assimilation: After the new idea was identified by the employees in the sourcing unit, the knowledge was then assimilated throughout the R&D department. A down-top-down communication was used for knowledge assimilation. Managers of R&D department served as boundary spanners between the employees in the sourcing unit and R&D employees. As a supporting unit of the R&D department, the sourcing unit sourced external innovation solutions or potential technology or collaborators for the R&D department during their innovation projects. As we learnt from Pluto, R&D employees sent open search requests through managers of the R&D department to the employees in the sourcing unit. The acquired external knowledge was also transmitted through managers. Although R&D employees participated in the decision making process, R&D managers still possessed more decision making power of deciding whether and which of the sourced external knowledge would be assimilated among R&D employees. For sourcing unit's proactive open search, they also disseminated new and innovative technologies they thought useful for R&D employees through managers to R&D employees. As illustrated by the R&D director,

"We had a structured and organized communication way between the sourcing unit and the rest of the R&D employees. The communication was bridged by the managers."

Episode 3: Decentralized Open Search. As the benefits of external knowledge spread, more and more open search requests were requested by R&D employees. Only a small number of open search requests were handled by employees in the sourcing unit due to their limited capacities. Besides that, the communication and coordination costs involved in discussing open search requests and sourced knowledge with the sourcing unit were high. The R&D employees at Pluto started to search externally for their own innovation problems. They engaged in both external open search and traditional R&D work.

External sourcing: As the technology sourced by the sourcing unit benefits the entire R&D department, the objective of open search by R&D employees was to find solution to solve more specific innovation problems they encountered during their work. One R&D employee in Pluto indicated,

"Once during our innovation process, our bottle sealing technology failed to develop the new product. Since this needed technology may only be applied in this particular innovation project. Rather than sending request to the sourcing unit, we took the responsibility of open search. Finally my colleagues and I found the satisfactory technology in an exhibition in Hong Kong."

Since open search was only a part of and not the focus of R&D employees' work, the search was not conducted systematically, but focused on finding a feasible solution for immediate practical use. They tapped closed proprietary networks (e.g., suppliers, retailers, competitors, and development and trade partners) and prior collaborative networks of firms available to the firm. They also looked for ideas and solutions in exhibitions, industrial associations, and organizational yellow pages. Various IT tools were also implemented by R&D employees to source external knowledge. We learnt through interviews that RSS technologies helped R&D employees in Pluto synthesize and share information from multiple sources; wikis and blogs had opened up new opportunities to integrate knowledge and ideas, accelerating knowledge discovery and innovation. R&D employees also actively participated in external communities of practice and Internet-based technology forums, which facilitated interactive and timely tacit knowledge acquisition. Therefore, ITs provided the means by which R&D employees engaged in their sourcing tasks with flexibility and agility.

Decision making and internal assimilation: If the sourcing R&D employees were also users of the acquired external knowledge, they would then made decisions about whether and which of the acquired external knowledge will be used in the innovation projects. If the sourced external knowledge would be used by all of the innovation project team members, the R&D managers also participated in the decision making process to select the right external knowledge. Since R&D employees knew very well who required the sourced external knowledge, they also took on the role of internal assimilator to disseminate the sourced the sourced external knowledge among the innovation project team members. Face-to-face meetings and discussions were used for internal assimilation. However, as a very large R&D department with around 550 R&D employees, the project team involved a large number of members, with some members who were distributed around the world. IT significantly enhanced interactions among individuals for knowledge assimilation in Pluto. A senior technology manager of Pluto said,

"When some R&D employees identified the potential external knowledge, they uploaded it to a knowledge management system, called InnovationNet, and provided access to other innovation project team members to it. In addition, intranet and online communities also connect our R&D employees to facilitate their communication."

Today, open innovation has permeated into each and every corner of Pluto's firm. All of its R&D employees actively search externally during the innovation process.

2.2   Case Neptune

Episode 1: Centralized Open Search. Neptune is the largest and leading solar energy firm in China. Its products range from solar water heaters, solar collectors to solar lights and PV lighting products. Neptune started its collaborative innovation journey as early as 2000. Similar to Pluto, in the early stage, the senior and R&D managers of Neptune undertook the work of open search through their personal networks.

External sourcing: Managers of Neptune, a Chinese firm, adopted a different approach from their Pluto counterparts by paying more attention to cultivate government ties in their social networks. Through attendance of association meetings and industrial development events, managers took opportunities to interact with government officers, which in turn brought them valuable connections to managers from other firms. The chief executive officer of Neptune recounted:

"I know some government officers who are in charge of the technological development park. Our collaborative innovation project with the Institute of Electrical Engineering was brokered and supported by the municipal Science & Technology Commission."

In addition, as illustrated by our informants, managers of Neptune sourced in areas of the United States, Japan, and Europe for breakthrough research and many more for state-of-the-art development capabilities. Managers of Neptune purposefully attended international fairs, exhibitions and visited foreign firms, with the deliberate aim of expanding the pool of potential partners. During their interactions with managers from foreign countries, they identified technologies and collaborators of great potential value to their own firm.

Decision making and internal assimilation: The sourcing managers played the same role of decision makers as managers in Pluto did in deciding on their collaboration partners. However, unlike the case of Pluto that applied the top-down assimilation of collaborative intentions with external partners, Neptune managers relied more on face-to-face meetings than on electronic communication. We learnt from our informants that they were various face-to-face communications among executive managers, middle level managers and R&D employees to create awareness and foster consensus on the innovation collaboration projects. Team briefings were also used to enable project managers to communicate and consult with R&D employees. Team briefings took place on a weekly basis or more frequently.

"Our CEO regularly delivered inspiring speeches to employees about the organizational strategic development. Senior managers also meet R&D employees regularly to communicate about the collaborative innovation projects."

Episode 2: Decentralized Open Search. In this later stage, Neptune took a different trajectory of open search pattern change from Pluto. The change was due to two reasons. First, during this stage, Neptune hired some new engineers in the R&D department with new work practice and external knowledge. Second, the implementation of office automation systems, and supply chain management system in Neptune provided these new R&D employees access to external knowledge sources and consequently stimulated them to discover innovation opportunities in the interconnected networks.

External sourcing: The organizational informatization of intra-organizational and inter-organizational systems provided R&D employees access to codified knowledge in Neptune's knowledge base and enhanced interactions among individuals for knowledge transfer and sharing. It created a collaborative workplace, provided interconnected networks and systems for enhancing interactions for knowledge access and sharing externally across geographical regions, and value network partners (e.g., suppliers, customers). These technologies provided a window into the engine room of the innovation, where new innovative ideas may emerge.

Through the interconnected networks with external firms, these new employees in the R&D department discovered some innovation opportunities associated with external knowledge. This triggered an open search culture among R&D employees, a trend that was also encouraged by the R&D director in Neptune. For any innovation project, R&D employees first seek to find out if an external source already had a solution. Neptune also created a secure IT platform that allowed R&D employees to share technology briefs with its suppliers.

"If we are trying to find ways to improve our current technology or product, one of our suppliers may well have the solution. Since the creation of our supplier network system, we have had some innovation projects that are jointly staffed with Neptune and suppliers' researchers. In some cases, suppliers' researchers came to work in our labs, and in others, we worked in theirs."

Decision making and internal assimilation: Similar to Pluto, we also learnt from our informants that during the open search process, R&D employees were given more decision making power for selecting external knowledge. But unlike Pluto, Neptune had a R&D department with approximately 60 R&D professionals. To disseminate externally acquired knowledge, they relied more on regular face-to-face meetings and discussions. Meanwhile, ITs such as groupware systems were also instrumental in cultivating social interactions and connectedness among R&D employees. Electronic message software helped with communication and coordination.

Episode 3: Differentiated Open Search. Through the collaborative innovations with external partners, Neptune had accelerated innovation processes and improved products. However, in the meantime, they realized that there were significant overlaps in sourcing outcomes in their R&D employees' open search and their sourcing also tended to only focus on the current innovation projects. To achieve better innovation outcomes, it required early identification of innovative ideas and technological trends for the entire R&D department. Thus, to overcome these handicaps and to attain greater benefits through external knowledge, a specialized sourcing unit that focused on open sourcing and accumulating external knowledge to support the innovation development of Neptune was formed.

External sourcing: The major tasks of this sourcing unit were the same as Pluto's. But unlike Pluto, the employees in the sourcing unit did not have PhD degrees. They were assigned to the sourcing unit because they were good at using ITs compared to other R&D employees. Their sourcing activities were done mainly through the Internet and the sourced external knowledge was stored in custom-made knowledge management systems.

Decision making and internal assimilation: After a new idea was identified by the employees in the sourcing unit, the knowledge was assimilated throughout the R&D department. R&D managers were the key decision makers of selecting the sourced external knowledge. To disseminate the sourced external knowledge, the communication between the sourcing unit and R&D unit did not take a top-down knowledge assimilation path. In contrast, the two units directly communicated. As suggested by our informants, the sourcing employees were treated as just other R&D employees with different work.

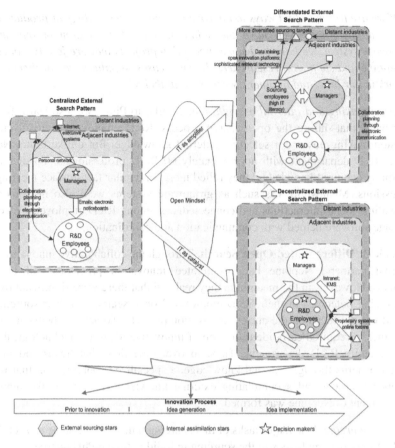

Fig. 1. Evolution of Three Emerging Open Search Patterns

3   A Cross-Case Discussion

3.1   Changing Work of Key Stakeholders

Three new work patterns in open search and their evolution in two firms are depicted in Fig.1. As evident in two cases, the search work became more complex and dynamic with the inclusion of more and different boundary spanners and broadened search domains compared to the work identified in the literature (see Fig.1). First, instead of occurring only at the idea generation stage of innovation process, open search could occur along the open innovation process due to different open search objectives. Second, not only managers, but R&D employees took roles of boundary spanners. Specifically, in centralized open search pattern, managers delegated part of the internal assimilation work to R&D employees. Compared to the external search patterns in prior literature that oral communication was the primary way to communicate with external partners, with communication ITs, R&D employees could work with distributed external partners together on collaborative innovation plan.

In differentiated open search pattern, external sourcing work supported by advanced ITs was assigned to employees in the sourcing unit. Managers took a new coordinating role between the employees in the sourcing unit and R&D employees. Managers and employees in the sourcing unit decided the selection of the sourced external knowledge together. In the decentralized open search pattern, the roles and work nature of R&D employees changed from being executor of the sourced external knowledge and conducting routine R&D work to being empowered to have work of external sourcing, decision making and internal assimilation of the sourced external knowledge. They also had more decision making power and autonomy on external sourcing work.

Table 2. Open search work of key stakeholders

Work pattern	R&D/senior managers	Employees in sourcing unit	R&D employees
Centralized open search	External sourcing; decision making; internal assimilation	N.A.	Internal assimilation (work with external partners on collaborative innovation plan)
Differentiated open search	Decision making (participative); internal assimilation	Decision making (participative); external sourcing	Internal assimilation (work with external partners)
Decentralized open search	Decision making (participative)	N.A.	External sourcing; decision making (participative); internal assimilation

3.2   Role of ITs

While advances in ITs induced the evolution of open search pattern in two case firms, their impacts were different. In Pluto, ITs (e.g., data mining tools, data analytics, and open innovation platforms) served as the amplifier to enhance the speed and intensity of external sourcing and selection capabilities. When IT became more powerful, managers had limited ability and time to employ them, which required the IT and technological experts in sourcing, and led to the differentiated open search pattern. In contrast, for Neptune, intra- and inter-firm ITs (e.g., enterprise resources planning systems, supply chain management systems) served as the catalyst to accelerate knowledge access and sharing among R&D employees with value network partners (e.g., suppliers, customers). It stimulated R&D employees to discover innovation opportunities in the interconnected networks and resulted in the new decentralized open search pattern. IT indeed induced the work pattern change of open search in firms.

4   Conclusion

While three patterns of open search were observed in both firms, they took different trajectories of open search pattern evolution, largely due to the different enabling roles of ITs. Firms' managers need to be mindful of the different roles that ITs can serve (e.g., as an amplifier and a catalyst). Appropriate ITs can then be employed to induce the suitable trajectory of open search evolution for the firm.

References

1. Allen, T.J.: Managing the Flow of Technology: Technology Transfer and the Dissemination of Technological Information within the R&D Organization. MIT Press Books (1984)
2. Berchicci, L.: Towards an Open R&D System: Internal R&D Investment, External Knowledge Acquisition and Innovative Performance. Research Policy 42(1), 1–11 (2012)
3. Chesbrough, H.W.: Open Innovation: The New Imperative for Creating and Profiting from Technology. Harvard Business Press (2003)
4. Cohen, W.M., Levinthal, D.A.: Absorptive Capacity: A New Perspective on Learning and Innovation. Administrative Science Quarterly 35(1), 128–152 (1990)
5. Eisenhardt, K.M.: Building Theories from Case Study Research. Academy of Management Review 14(4), 532–550 (1989)
6. Eisenhardt, K.M., Graebner, M.E.: Theory Building from Cases: Opportunities and Challenges. Academy of Management Journal 50(1), 25–32 (2007)
7. Escribano, A., Fosfuri, A., Tribó, J.A.: Managing External Knowledge Flows: The Moderating Role of Absorptive Capacity. Research Policy 38(1), 96–105 (2009)
8. Huber, G.P., Power, D.J.: Retrospective Reports of Strategic-Level Managers: Guidelines for Increasing Their Accuracy. Strategic Management Journal 6(2), 171–180 (1985)
9. Katz, R., Tushman, M.: An Investigation into the Managerial Roles and Career Paths of Gatekeepers and Project Supervisors in a Major R & D Facility. R&D Management 11(3), 103–110 (1981)
10. Klein, H.K., Myers, M.D.: A Set of Principles for Conducting and Evaluating Interpretive Field Studies in Information Systems. MIS Quarterly 23(1), 67–93 (1999)
11. Myers, M.D.: Qualitative Research in Information Systems. MIS Quarterly (21), 241–242 (1997)

Technology Acceptance Model:
Worried about the Cultural Influence?

Cristóbal Fernández Robin[1], Scott McCoy[2],
Luis Yáñez Sandivari[1], and Diego Yáñez Martínez[1]

[1] Universidad Técnica Federico Santa María,
Departamento de Industrias, Valparaíso, Chile
{cristobal.fernandez,luis.yanez,diego.yanez}@usm.cl
[2] Mason School of Business, Williamsburg, Virginia
scott.mccoy@mason.wm.edu

Abstract. The Technology Acceptance Model (TAM) has shown in the USA that the Perceived Usefulness (PU) and the Perceived ease-of-use (PEU) determine the intention to use (IU) a specific technology or information system. In this research, the TAM model is validated in Chile, considering the cultural factors of this country, through an application of the model to university students. The results show that the TAM model works in Chile, regardless of the studied technology or the cultural aspects of the country. Finally, new questions arise related to this topic such as the influence of the intensity of use, familiarity with the technology and the individual's reference group for the technologies aimed to encourage communication among people.

Keywords: Technology Acceptance Model (TAM), Intention to Use, Information and Communication Technologies, Cultural Dimensions.

1   Introduction

In a globalized and highly competitive world, innovation and continuous improvement of processes in organizations is a key factor. That is the reason why the communication and information systems are so important. However, an organization is, basically, a group of people working together to achieve a specific objective. After that, it is not always possible to implement or to adopt technologies inmediately, or at least, it is difficult to guarantee the success of such measures without considering the human nature of the people composing the organization.

Some studies have concentrated its efforts to predict the intention to use a specific system based on the Perceived Usefulness (PU) and the Perceived Ease-of-Use (PEU) as the causal factors. This is known as the Technology Acceptance Model (TAM) (Davis, F., 1989). More recently, it has been proposed to validate this model in various countries considering the influence of cultural factors. (McCoy et al., 2007).

This research focuses on validating de TAM model in Chile considering the influence of the cultural dimensions (Hofstede, G. 2001) found in the country.

F.F.-H. Nah (Ed.): HCIB/HCII 2014, LNCS 8527, pp. 609–619, 2014.
© Springer International Publishing Switzerland 2014

2   Literature Review

2.1   Technology Acceptance Model, TAM

The Techonology Acceptance Model (Davis, F., 1989) is an adaptation of the Theory of Reasoned Action (TRA) (Ajzen & Fishbein, 1980) specially developed for the technology adoption case, in which two of the factors, known as PU and PEU, are presented as indicators of the intention to use the system or technology in question. Additionally there is a causal relationship, rather than a parallel, direct determinant of usage (Davis, F., 1989).

Through the last decades, researches have focused their attention to improve the predictive ability of the model. That is when the TAM2 model appeared, introducing the external or social influence to the model (subjective norm, voluntariness and image) and the cognitive process (job relevance, output quality, result demonstrability, perceived ease-of-use) as influential factors of the perceived usefulness and then the intention to use. The results showed a 60% effectiveness, but subject to a mandatory usage context to validate the external or social influence to the model (Venkatesh el al., 2000).

In the same way, several investigations have been carried out that try to validate or refute the TAM model in various environments and with different research subjects, such as students because they represent well the values and beliefs of individuals employed in a wide variety of occupations (Voich, D., 1995), obtaining results that converge and validate the model typically explaining 40% of the variance in usage intentions and behaviour (Venkatesh et al., 2000).

Naturally, the next step was to validate this model outside their country of origin, United States, and to evaluate the influence of certain factors typical of each country (McCoy et al., 2007).

2.2   Cultural Dimensions Theory

The Cultural Dimensions Theory (Hofstede, G., 2001) suggests identifying the culture of a specific country according to the following dimensions: Power Distance (PDI), Individualism vs Collectivism (IDV), Masculinity vs Femininity (MAS) and Uncertainty Avoidance (UAI).

2.3   Technology Acceptance Model, TAM, Outside USA.

To validate the TAM model outside the country of origin, the results obtained of the application of the TAM model were combined with the indicators of the cultural dimensions theory for each of the countries. In fact, for each of Hofstede's cultural dimension, two groups were created (high and low) leaving out the main 80%. The results showed that countries scoring low UA, high PDI, high MAS (high masculinity) and low IC (high collectivism), the relationships in the TAM model didn't work (McCoy et al., 2007).

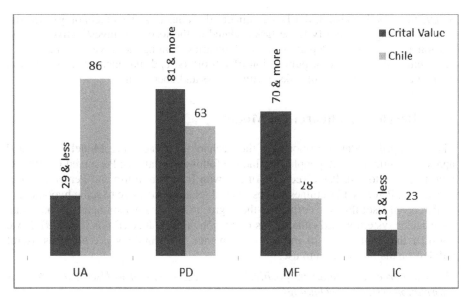

Fig. 1. Chile's Cultural Dimensions versus Critical Values for TAM (Source: Self made)

In Chile, people rely on moderate rates in all cultural dimensions. In fact, we have Power Distance (63), Individualism vs Collectivism (23), Masculinity vs Femininity (28) and Uncertainty Avoidance (86) (Hofstede, G., 2001).

When this is evaluated in Chile, the attention must be concentrated especially on the behaviour of the model according to the Power Distance Index (63) that represents a slightly high value and the Individualism vs Collectivism (23) that represents a slightly low value.

2.4   Used Technologies

The following technologies were used in our research:

SMS: Short text Messaging Service, is a text messaging services that can be used as a means of communication between mobile phones.

IM: Instant Messaging is a real time communication technology based on text, between two or more people. Both people must be connected to the same network or protocol and use a specific client of instant messaging.

Email: Electronic Mail is an online service that allows people to send and receive messages from different people through the Internet.

SIGA: Sistema de Información de Gestión Académica, is a technology developed in Universidad Técnica Federico Santa Maria, which main goal is to provide a platform that allows managing the academic information of the entire University community. Among the services available can be mentioned the registration of courses, personal schedule, teacher survey, career plans, student's personal record.

SGDI: Sistema de Gestión del Departamento de Industrias. This technology was developed aiming to simplify those tasks related to the teaching, investigative and extension activities of the Departamento de Industrias. Among the services available, we have, enrollment practices, publication of job offers, and management of courses in areas such as: calendar, mail tasks, forums, news and documents.

3   Developed Theoretical Model

The developed model corresponds to the Technology Acceptance Model (TAM) and applied in Chile in which people can find the following relations: Perceived Usefulness with Intention to use, Perceived ease-of-use with Intention to use and Perceived ease-of-use with Perceived Usefulness. These causal relations give rise to some hypotheses.

Perceived Usefulness is defined as the degree to which a person believes that using a particular system would enhance his or her job performance (Davis. F, 1989). If we consider the significance of the job performance, a technology perceived as useful will have a major intention to use.

H1: The Perceived Usefulness positively influences Intention to Use of a particular information system or technology.

Perceived ease-of-use is defined as the degree to which a person believes that using a particular system would be free of effort (Davis, F., 1989). If we consider effort as a limited resource that must be assigned to multiple tasks, a technology that does not require efforts when it is used is going to have a major intention to use.

H2: The Perceived Ease of Use positively influences Intention to Use of a particular information system or technology.

To the extend that a system or technology requires less effort in being used, and understanding that the effort is a limited resource, more effort can be assigned to other tasks. That way, the productivity or job performance will grow.

H3: The Perceived Ease of Use positively influences Perceived Usefulness of a particular information system or technology.

Chile presents moderated values for the cultural dimensions of Hofstede and only two of the cases are important for observations: Power Distance Index (63) considering that when an authority figure recommends or requests the use of a system in a high PD culture, users will not need the added attraction of usefulness and ease of use to make use of the system. (McCoy et al., 2007).

The other case is Individualism vs Collectivism (23), considering that people who focus on Collectivism are more willing to suffer with lower usability to accomplish the goals valued by others. They would focus less on their own effort and more on what seems to be valued or needed by others (McCoy et al., 2007).

H4: The values that cultural dimension takes in Chile do not affect the performance of the TAM model.

The TAM Model has been extensively applied in several areas by predicting typically 40% of the use of a system (Legris et al., 2003). Consequently, it is expected that the model is going to give values close to the typical trend for the five cases studied in this research.

H5: The technology acceptance model operates independently of the technologies used for study.

User evaluations such as PU and PEU are updated sequentially with target system experience. (Kim and Malhotra, 2005). After that, it is expected that the TAM model will explain a large number of the changes in the results of intensive users.

H6: The Intensity of use of a technology affects relationships within the technology acceptance model.

4   Methodology

The study considered a sample of 427 students from different courses of the Universidad Técnica Federico Santa María where they participated in exchange for a grade to the course they were taking. At first, an exploratory research was carried out to analyze knowledge around the TAM model in depth, and the validity of this model outside USA. On the same path, researches were carried out to investigate more about Hofstede cultural dimensions and the clasification of Chile according to these rates. A concluding investigation was carried out, that focused on a univariate analysis aiming to know the profile of the survey respondent to determine the representation of this model regarding the students of the university. This stage also intends to establish some a priori links of the variables of the TAM model. After that, an exploratory factor analysis was conducted to see how the variables were grouped around the exogenous factors of the TAM model. Subsequently, a structural equations analysis, a confirmatory factor type, was carried out, analysing the results in relation to Hofstede cultural dimensions of Chile. Finally, an analysis was conducted according to the intensity of use of the different evaluated technologies (SMS, IM, Email, SIGA, SGDI) with the aim to establish differences in the results of the model according to the associated segments of the intensity of use.

5   Analysis and Results

From the first analysis, a consistent survey respondent profile was obtained, in which 69% were male, 61.6% of the survey respondents have an average age of 23 years old, a 70.5% have no work experience in a full time job and 23.4% have only one year of work experience. Regarding the regions of residence of the family group, 47.1% of them live in the Región Metropolitana (Santiago) and a 23.2% live in the fifth region (Valparaíso). In terms of socioeconomic level, 47% of the survey respondents were classified on the ABC1 segment and 41% of them on the C2 segment. This confirms the representativeness of the sample for the students of the university, considering that the respondents were from the Campus Santiago and the Casa Central (Valparaíso), also that they were from the second year of study onwards, so that respondents have a degree of knowledge of information systems, as the SIGA and SGDI.

Therefore, an analysis of the intensity of use measured in hours and amount of times during a week where a determined technology is used was carried out. Also an analysis of the perceived complexity of system information for each treatment was conducted. From this, a direct relation between the perceived easy of use and the intensity of use in four of the five technologies was obtained. In fact, the technologies used most and the ones felt as the easiest to use were IM and Email. In the same way, the least used technologies and the ones people considered as the more complex were SIGA and SGDI. From these results, it was suggested that the SMS were mainly regulated by the other construct: Perceived usefulness.

Table 1. Indicators of the exploratory factor analysis

Variable	Factor 1	Factor 2
P1: I find (technology) easy to use.	[0,885 – 0,937]	-
P2: Learning to operate (technology) is easy for me.	[0,861 – 0,918]	-
P3: It is easy for me to become skillful at using (technology).	[0,722 – 0,880]	-
P4: I find it easy to get (technology) to do what I want them to do	[0,563 – 0,784]	-
P5: (Technology) are simple technologies to use.	[0,866 – 0,912]	-
P6: Using (technology) improves my performance.	-	[0,853 – 0,910]
P7: Using (technology) improves my effectiveness.	-	[0,885 – 0,908]
P8: Using (technology) improves my productivity.	-	[0,866 – 0,912]
P9: I find (technology) useful.	[0,535 – 0,843]	-

Source: Self-made with information from the rotated factor matrix of each used technology.

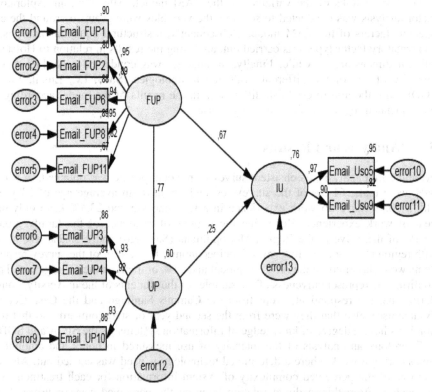

Fig. 2. TAM model applied to email (Source: Self-made with IBM SPSS Amos 20)

Subsequently, an exploratory factor analysis was conducted, in which it was possible to validate the existence of two factors compound by observable variables, that according to the theoretical base, were measured on one hand by the perceived usefulness and on the other hand by the perceived ease-of-use. The results were consistent in all the five evaluated technologies.

The previous table shows the variation of the correlation of each variable regarding the factor that relates better with it. This corroborates the independence of technology acceptance model with respect to the information or technology system studied.

In addition, the study gave satisfactory and coherent results for the composition of the two proposed dimensions. The exception to the rule was the question *I find (technology) useful,* that showed a major correlation with the Perceived Ease of Use factor considering that it was created to measure Perceived Usefulness. It should be noted that this variable also presented a low communality in all five conducted studies.

After that, a confirmatory analysis was carried out, a structural equations modelling, SEM. The results of the proposed model showed an unsatisfactory fit; as a consequence, it was decided to modify the model by eliminating the variable associated to the question *I find (technology) useful,* considering that in the previous analysis it showed low communality and a better correlation with the wrong factor, all together with the problem of goodness of fit in the proposed model and considering that the existent theory explains the TAM model inside USA. Thus, a proper fit was achieved for the model TAM justifying the validity and reliability of the model according to the results exhibited by the SEM method.

Finally, an analysis was conducted establishing segments regarding the intensity of use of the survey respondent. From this, it was obtained that there are differences depending the intensity of use, mainly in technologies aimed to communicate.

Table 2. Standardized Coefficients of the Confirmatory Analysis

Relation	SMS	IM	Email	SIGA	SGDI
UP←FUP	0,055	0,499	0,774	0,218	0,651
IU←FUP	0,146	0,668	0,667	0,034	0,291
IU←UP	0,647	0,161	0,246	0,599	0,520
P1←FUP	0,923	0,959	0,936	0,918	0,925
P2←FUP	0,800	0,919	0,946	0,833	0,899
P3←FUP	0,623	0,900	0,893	0,667	0,806
P4←FUP	0,461	0,790	0,817	0,582	0,771
P5←FUP	0,891	0,927	0,949	0,877	0,890
P6←UP	0,859	0,936	0,916	0,815	0,923
P7←UP	0,860	0,913	0,928	0,870	0,910
P8←UP	0,868	0,897	0,927	0,869	0,921
P10←IU	0,881	0,963	0,974	0,919	0,958
P11←IU	0,901	0,922	0,904	0,856	0,936

Source: own production with data from the SEM analysis

6   Discussion

The proposed model showed to be valid and reliable regarding the validity and reliability tests to which it was subjected based on the structural equation modelling. In both, a measure model level (relation between observable variables and latent variables) and the structural model (relation between proposed factors or latent variables). In fact, the results show the existance of the proposed connections between the Perceived Ease of Use, Perceived Usefulness and Intention to use (H1, H2, H3).

The TAM model proved to be applicable in Chile because, according to Hofstede's multidimensional model, this country has moderated indicators for each of the dimensions: Uncertainty avoidance (86), Femininity (28), Individualism (23) and Power Distance (63). The last one was the only dimension that requires more attention considering that a high rate of Power Distance implies that some connections of the TAM model do not work. However, the results prove that this dimension was not influential (H4).

The TAM model works independent of the studied technology (H5) since it showed similar results in terms of the R2, or the variance explained by the model, for SMS (0.45), IM (0.58), Email (0.76), SIGA (0.37) and SGDI (0.55) that additionally go in the same line, and better, than the historical results (40%).

The TAM model is an excellent tool to predict and explain the behaviour or the Intention to use of a technology. However, it is not solid enough when a comparison between different systems is required. This becomes evident when you see that SGDI shows better indicators of adjust, reliability, estimators and coefficients of determination than the SIGA. Both technologies were mainly created to be mandatory used by the students of the university and designed with similar objectives and functioning. The biggest difference between SGDI and SIGA lies on the intensity of use with each system. SGDI was created to be used daily and that is why it is not strange to think that there is a higher level of familiarity regarding the SIGA of which seasonal use presents peaks during the student's courses registration periods. In this way, it can be seen that the results of the TAM model vary according to the degree of use or the familiarity regarding the system (H6).

Also, it was shown that when the Perceived Ease of Use has a large importance in the model, there is a causal connection between PEU and PU. That was the case of the IM (0.5), Email (0.77) and SGDI (0.65). Therefore, and understanding that the effort is a limited resource that must be dessignated to multiple tasks, an easy to use technology requires less effort which must be allocated to other tasks increasing the productivity of an individual. As productivity is important in the job, this will increase the intention to use of the technology in question.

In case of the SMS, the intention to use mainly comes from the Perceived Usefulness. That makes sense when considering technologies that have replaced the SMS nowadays. In fact, applications like Whatsapp displays possibilities such as group conversations, sending and receiving pictures and videos, an organized history of each conversation, while they keep as an inherited characteristic the functioning over mobile phones. This results in a greater use of this application in comparison to SMS in the sense of the amount of things that allow increasing the productivity of an individual.

In case of the IM, the Intention to use mainly comes from PEU. This makes sense when considering the characteristics of the most popular application in 2013 (Facebook Chat) compared with the leader a few years ago (Windows Live Messenger).

In fact, Facebook chat does not required to be installed, it has a clean and simple interface and to communicate with someone else, people just need to know the name of the person they want to communicate. This results in a higher PEU. In contrast, a possible problem was discovered in the formulation of the questions that intended to measure PU when measuring in a communication technology like IM or SMS, considering that the survey respondent can be answering that the use of IM decreases his productivity, effectiveness and performance, due to the fact that it represents a distraction source to their tasks or pending works. This information was confirmed by making a comparison of the results according to the intensity of use: the more intensity of use, the less weight of the Perceived Usefulness for the technologies aimed to communication (H6).

Based on these conclusions, some recommendations arise for future studies related to the same topic. It is suggested to evaluate the impact of the next variables regarding the functioning of the TAM model.

Intention to use explains the difference exhibited when analizing the same technology based on how intensive is the use of the surveys respondents. The level of familiarity with the studied technology, as a consequence of the intensity of use, can also be used to explain the differences between similar technologies under the same contexts but that differ in the intensity of use.

Unfortunately, we cannot compare mandatory versus voluntary use pattersns, as technologies cannot be compared if the contexts of use are different. However, technologies for information purpose compared to technologies used for communication purpose can be evaluated. In this case, there seems to be a greater weight of PEU in the case of technologies for communication purposes (SMS, IM), while a greater weight of PU when it is about technologies for information purposes (SIGA, SGDI).

In terms of subjective norms, reference groups are influential mainly for technologies aimed at communication. It is reasonable to think that a technology can have a high level of PEU and PU, and a low Intention to use if the family and friends of the respondents do not use that technology.

References

1. Byrne, B.M.: Structural equation modeling with AMOS: Basic concepts, applications, and programming. CRC Press (2009)
2. Canessa, E., Maldifassi, J., Quezada, A.: Características sociodemográficas y su influencia en el uso de Tecnologías de Información en Chile. Polis (Santiago) 10(30), 365–390 (2011)
3. Cook, J., Finlayson, M.: The impact of cultural diversity on web site design. SAM (2005)
4. Davis, F.D.: Perceived usefulness, perceived ease of use, and user acceptance of information technology. MIS Quarterly, 319–340 (1989)
5. Fishbein, M., Ajzen, I.: Belief, attitude, intention and behavior: An introduction to theory and research (1975)
6. Hwang, Y.: Investigating enterprise systems adoption: uncertainty avoidance, intrinsic motivation, and the technology acceptance model. European Journal of Information Systems 14(2), 150–161 (2005)

7. Hofstede, G.: Culture's consequences: International differences in work-related values, vol. 5. Sage (1984)
8. Hofstede, G., Hofstede, G.J., Minkov, M.: Cultures and organizations: Software of the mind, vol. 2. McGraw-Hill, London (1991)
9. Hofstede, G.H.: Culture's consequences: Comparing values, behaviors, institutions and organizations across nations. Sage (2001)
10. Hofstede, G.: The Hofstede Centre en Cultural Insights – Geert Hofstede (2013), http://geert-hofstede.com/
11. Jan, A.U., Contreras, V.: Technology acceptance model for the use of information technology in universities. Computers in Human Behavior 27(2), 845–851 (2011)
12. Kassim, N., Abdullah, N.A.: The effect of perceived service quality dimensions on customer satisfaction, trust, and loyalty in e-commerce settings: a cross-cultural analysis. Asia Pacific Journal of Marketing and Logistics 22(3), 351–371 (2010)
13. Kim, S.S., Malhotra, N.K.: A longitudinal model of continued IS use: An integrative view of four mechanisms underlying postadoption phenomena. Management Science 51(5), 741–755 (2005)
14. King, W.R., He, J.: A meta-analysis of the technology acceptance model. Information & Management 43(6), 740–755 (2006)
15. Lee, Y., Kozar, K.A., Larsen, K.R.: The technology acceptance model: past, present, and future. Communications of the Association for Information Systems 12(1), 50 (2003)
16. Legris, P., Ingham, J., Collerette, P.: Why do people use information technology? A critical review of the technology acceptance model. Information & Management 40(3), 191–204 (2003)
17. Lonner, W.J., Berry, J.W., Hofstede, G.H.: Culture's Consequences: International Differences in Work-Related Values. University of Illinois at Urbana-Champaign's Academy for Entrepreneurial Leadership Historical Research Reference in Entrepreneurship (1980)
18. Marcus, A., Gould, E.W.: Crosscurrents: cultural dimensions and global Web user-interface design. Interactions 7(4), 32–46 (2000)
19. McCoy, S., Everard, A., Jones, B.M.: An examination of the technology acceptance model in Uruguay and the US: a focus on culture. Journal of Global Information Technology Management 8(2), 27 (2005)
20. McCoy, S.: Integrating national culture into individual IS adoption research: The need for individual level measures (2003)
21. McCoy, S., Galletta, D.F., King, W.R.: Applying TAM across cultures: the need for caution. European Journal of Information Systems 16(1), 81–90 (2007)
22. Rouibah, K.: Social usage of instant messaging by individuals outside the workplace in Kuwait: a structural equation model. Information Technology & People 21(1), 34–68 (2008)
23. Srite, M., Karahanna, E.: The role of espoused national cultural values in technology acceptance. MIS Quarterly 30(3), 679–704 (2006)
24. Teo, T.: Modelling technology acceptance in education: A study of pre-service teachers. Computers & Education 52(2), 302–312 (2009)
25. Teo, T., Noyes, J.: An assessment of the influence of perceived enjoyment and attitude on the intention to use technology among pre-service teachers: A structural equation modeling approach. Computers & Education 57(2), 1645–1653 (2011)
26. Turner, M., Kitchenham, B., Brereton, P., Charters, S., Budgen, D.: Does the technology acceptance model predict actual use? A systematic literature review. Information and Software Technology 52(5), 463–479 (2010)

27. Venkatesh, V., Davis, F.D.: A theoretical extension of the technology acceptance model: four longitudinal field studies. Management Science 46(2), 186–204 (2000)
28. Venkatesh, V., Morris, M.G.: Why don't men ever stop to ask for directions? Gender, social influence, and their role in technology acceptance and usage behavior. MIS Quarterly, 115–139 (2000)
29. Venkatesh, V., Morris, M.G., Davis, G.B., Davis, F.D.: User acceptance of information technology: Toward a unified view. MIS Quarterly, 425–478 (2003)
30. Voich, D., Macesich, G.: Comparative empirical analysis of cultural values and perceptions of political economy issues. Praeger, Westport (1995)
31. Wixom, B.H., Todd, P.A.: A theoretical integration of user satisfaction and technology acceptance. Information Systems Research 16(1), 85–102 (2005)

Towards the Development of a 'User-Experience' Technology Adoption Model for the Interactive Mobile Technology

Jenson Chong-Leng Goh[1] and Faezeh Karimi[2]

[1] SIM University, 461 Clementi Road Singapore 599491, Singapore
[2] The University of Sydney, Center for Complex Systems,
Faculty of Engineering & IT, NSW 2006, Australia
jensongohcl@unisim.edu.sg, faezeh.karimi@sydney.edu.au

Abstract. Traditional Human-Computer Interaction (HCI) studies on interactive products are mostly instrumental in nature, focusing on usability issues when performing tasks in a work environment. This stream of research is frequently criticized for its narrow focus. More recently, the field of HCI is embracing a new concept called 'user experience' (UX) which consists of 3 facets: (1) beyond instrumental; (2) emotion and affect; and (3) the experiential to address its criticism. UX is acclaimed to be the 'thing' that can capture the full variety and the emerging aspects of technology use. In similar situation like traditional HCI studies, traditional technology adoption studies are also criticized as being overly cognitive-oriented with little consideration for affective factors and emotional experiences of the individuals. Applying the concept of UX to traditional technology adoption model, this paper synthesizes these two streams of research to propose a 'user experience'-based technology adoption model for the interactive mobile technology.

Keywords: User experience, Technology acceptance model.

1 Introduction

Since the birth of the first iPhone in 2007, we have seen a sudden explosive growth in the use of interactive mobile technology (e.g. smartphones and tablets). Most of us can agree that these interactive mobile technologies have fundamentally changed the way we work and play. Today, we spend a significant amount of time on using these interactive mobile technologies. Yet, our understanding of what draws us towards them remains unclear. Over the last decade, the research field of Human-Computer Interaction (HCI) has been attempting to use the concept of 'User-experience' (UX) to help enhance our understanding on the use of any interactive product by an individual (Park et al., 2013). One of the key drivers behind the increase in the research activities on UX is the UX researchers' belief that the success of an interactive product is largely influenced by the extent to which it could *"promote a high quality experience"* for its users (Editorial, 2010, pp. 313). Such high quality 'User-experience' will influence not just a user's intention to adopt that product (Hassenzahl and Tractinsky, 2006), but also his/her 'loyalty' towards it (Editorial, 2010). It is believed, by both practitioners

F.F.-H. Nah (Ed.): HCIB/HCII 2014, LNCS 8527, pp. 620–630, 2014.
© Springer International Publishing Switzerland 2014

and researchers, that the UX of an interactive mobile technology is likely going to become the main factor that differentiates one technology from another in the near future (Editorial, 2010, Nielsen, 2008). The recent launch of the iPhone 5C is one good example. Despite the widespread perceptions of the general public that it is 'poorer' in quality, compared to its competing products (e.g. Samsung S4), loyal consumers queued for hours to get their hands on them (Swift, 2013). This seems to suggest that Apple has built a high quality User-experience of the iPhone for its consumers which moves them beyond just the adoption of its technologies.

Unfortunately, despite the last decade of researches done on UX, most HCI researches are still predominately focused on the usability of a technology, such as the: (1) time to learn; (2) error rate; and (3)time to complete a task (Bulter, 1996). This approach, however, neglects other relevant UX aspects, such as the: (1) emotions; (2) aesthetics; and (3) symbolism (Hassenzahl and Tractinsky, 2006). A quote from an extant HCI research - "If it is pretty, it won't work", summarizes the prejudices in general (Hassenzahl, 2004, pp. 320) and sometimes a pretty technology is 'accused of hiding harm behind its beauty' (Russo and De Moraes, 2003, pp. 146), the HCI community sees it. In spite of the many attempts to incorporate UX into the contemporary HCI researches, Hassenzahl & Tractinsky (2006) notice that research on UX rarely enters into the relevant academic journals and they elucidate that much of this is due to the lack of empirical support to substantiate its significance in the field of HCI. This is unfortunate. As highlighted above, understanding UX is going to become increasingly essential in the design of an interactive mobile technology.

Similarly, the over-emphasis on the usability of a technology is also challenging the researchers contributing to the Technology Acceptance literature. Technology acceptance models (TAM) have been predominately based on cognitive-oriented constructs to help explain the technology adoption behavior of an individual (Bagozzi, 2007). Some past TAM researches did attempt to include 'UX-like' factors, such as 'enjoyment' (e.g. Davis et al., 1992, Thong et al., 2006, Venkatesh, 2000) and 'computer-anxiety' (Compeau et al., 1999, Hackbarth et al., 2003) into the TAM model. Nonetheless, the number of such studies is relatively small compared to those that focus primarily on cognitive-constructs. By and by, this type of research quickly becomes unfavorable among researchers who become more aware of its limitation (e.g. Bagozzi, 2007, Hirschheim, 2007). Furthermore, UX factors such as 'aesthetics' and 'symbolism', which are equally important to the adoption of an interactive mobile technology, have rarely been considered (Cyr et al., 2006) in TAM researches. This has prompted several TAM researchers to call for the incorporation of 'UX-like' factors into the TAM model (e.g. Kim et al., 2007). This paper attempts to synthesize the HCI and TAM researches to propose a 'User- experience' technology acceptance model for the interactive mobile technology. We believe that this model will fill the identified gaps in both literatures, and it will also provide a basis to help us understand better the synergy between UX factors, such as 'emotions', 'aesthetics' and 'symbolism' and the cognitive-oriented constructs in TAM, that influences an individual's intent to adopt any interactive mobile technology. Like several researchers and practitioners, we believe this proposal is timely because we are approaching a 'user-loyalty decade' when the user-experience is a key factor for the interactive mobile technology (Editorial, 2010, Nielsen, 2008). This is especially vital when we consider how the interactive mobile technologies have permeated into every aspect of our daily lives.

2   Literature Review on UX

Looking down the history of the Human-computer interaction (HCI) research on any interactive product, the focus has always been on the instrumental qualities (e.g. functionalities, usefulness and etc.) of it. Traditional research emphasizes on the instrumental quality of an interactive product by analyzing and improving the effectiveness and efficiency of the task performance in a typical work environment. This emphasis has several shortcomings when it is applied onto the area of interactive mobile technology. For instance, it is rational for an individual who is contemplating on the purchase of an interactive mobile technology to consider both the instrumental qualities (e.g. functionalities, usefulness, etc.) and the non-instrumental qualities (aesthetics, hedonic, etc.) with equal measures. While the instrumental qualities of a product are significant influences on a consumer's adoption intent, non-instrumental qualities also play important roles as deciding factors. Unfortunately, the latter qualities have been neglected by traditional HCI researches (Hassenzahl and Tractinsky, 2006). In order to create a more holistic conceptual foundation that can capture the variety and emerging aspects of technology use in today's world, researchers in Human-Computer Interaction (HCI) have relooked at an old concept called 'user-experience' (UX) (Hassenzahl and Tractinsky, 2006). In summarizing the current state of UX researches, Hassenzahl and Tractinsky (2006) identify 3 perspectives of UX and they are: (1) beyond the instrumental; (2) emotion and affect; and (3) the experiential.

Non-instrumental quality of product. The 'beyond the instrumental' perspective moves away from the concentration on solely the task and pragmatic aspects of an interactive product (i.e. its fit to behavioral goals) that used to be the pivotal focus of Human-Computer Interaction (HCI) studies. It also considers the hedonic aspects of an interactive product (Hassenzahl, 2004). In his study, Hassenzahl (2004) conducted two experiments to investigate the interplay among; (1) user-perceived usability (i.e. pragmatic attributes); (2) hedonic attributes (e.g. stimulation, identification); (3) goodness (i.e. satisfaction); (4) and beauty (i.e. aesthetics) using four different MP3-play skins. His result concluded that beauty (i.e. aesthetics) appears to be rather related to the self-oriented, hedonic attributes, more specifically identification of a product than its goal-oriented, pragmatic attributes. In similar vein, Rafaeli and Vilani-Yavetz (2004) and Crilly et al. (2004) all posit that the appreciation of the quality of a product can be divided into three conceptually distinct aspects, namely the: (1) product's pragmatic attribute; (2) asethetics attribute; and (3) hedonic attribute. This view supports our assertion that we need to take non-instrumental qualities of a product into consideration when investigating into an interactive product.

Emotion and affect. Emotion plays a critical role in the shaping of the interaction between the user and the product. It is also a factor for the evaluation and communication about the product's User-experience (Forlizzi and Battarbee, 2004). It is arguable that the emotion and experience resulted from the use of a product cannot be separated and should be investigated together when conducting a research on the effectiveness of an interactive product (McCarthy and Wright, 2004, Hassenzahl and Tractinsky, 2006).

The extant literature in HCI documented numerous researches that emphasize on the elements and relationships between usability and affect stemming from the use of a product (e.g. Cho et al., 2011, De Angeli et al., 2003, Han et al., 2000, Han et al., 2001, Hassenzahl, 2001). To better document and grasp the subjective feeling of the user of a product, Russell(1980)'s Circumplex Model of Affect has been widely used in both the literature of UX and the Technology Acceptance Model. Thuring and Mahlke (2007) have studied three carefully designed experiments to illustrate the importance of the aesthetic qualities; emotional experiences; and instrumental qualities as influential factors that affect the overall judgment of an interactive product. Outside of the Human-Computer Interaction (HCI) research, Kim et al. (2007) propose a balanced 'thinking-feeling' model of information systems continuance. They divide an experience into two distinct components: (1) thinking; and (2) feeling. Using Russell (1980)'s Circumplex Model of Affect, they classified emotions into two states: (1) pleasure; and (2) arousal. Hence, we concur with both studies on the appropriateness of the use of Russell's Circumplex Model of Affect for the measurement of the emotions and advocate it to be used as well for our proposed research model.

Experiential. On the 'experiential' perspective of 'User-experience' (UX), Hassenzahl and Tractinsky (2006) elaborate that there are two aspects of the use of technology, namely: (1) 'situatedness'; and (2) 'temporality'. A user's experience can be defined as a unique combination of various elements, such as the physical product and the internal states of the user (e.g. mood, expectation, active goal). The user's experience extends over time, with a definitive beginning and end, and these elements are interrelated and their interactions define the actual experience. The comprehensive review presented in Hassenzahl & Tractinsky (2006) not only provides us with a strong foundation defining 'User-experience' (UX), it also helps us to understand and appreciate the way it can be applied in the Human-Computer Interaction (HCI) study. Furthermore, it convinces us of the practical applicability and theoretical applicability of UX that can be incorporated into the traditional technology adoption model.

3   Literature Review on Technology Acceptance

Cognition (i.e. thinking) denotes the mental process of knowing and it includes aspects such as perception; reasoning; and judgment (Kim et al., 2007). Belief is defined as an individual's subjective probability (which involves cognitive processing) that performing the target behavior will result in a specified outcome (Fishbein and Ajzen, 1975). Under these two definitions, most traditional technology adoption models can be classified as cognitive-centric models. They illustrate that the formation of perception within an individual that eventually influences his/her attitude towards the use and/or the behavioral intent to use a new technology. For instance, the technology acceptance model (TAM) contains cognitive-centric constructs, such as: (1) 'perceived ease of use'; and (2) 'perceived usefulness', employed to predict the user behavioral intent of a new technology. Like TAM, constructs in many other popular technology adoption models are predominately cognitive-centric and this trait is summarized in Table 1.

Table 1. Models and Theories of Technology Acceptance

Models and Theories of Technology Acceptance	Cognitive Constructs
Theory of Reasoned Action (TRA) (Sheppard et al., 1988)	Attitude Toward Behavior & Subjective Norm
Technology Acceptance Model (TAM) (Venkatesh and Davis, 2000)	Perceived Usefulness, Perceived Ease of Use & Subjective Norm
Motivational Model (Vallerand, 1997)	Extrinsic Motivation & Intrinsic Motivation
Theory of Planned Behavior (TPB) (Ajzen, 1991)	Attitude Toward Behavior, Subjective Norm & Perceived Behavioral Control
Combined TAM and TPB (C-TAM-TPB) (Taylor and Todd, 1995)	Attitude Toward Behavior, Subjective Norm, Perceived Behavioral Control and Perceived Usefulness
Innovation Diffusion Theory (IDT) (Rogers, 1995)	Relative Advantage, Ease of use, Image, Compatibility, Results Demonstrability & Voluntariness of Use

Although these models and theories have received overwhelming success in helping us to understand an individual's cognitive decision making process in the context of technology adoption, other important factors that can equally influence technology adoption, such as; emotional experience; affective factors of an individual; aesthetics; and symbolism of the technology, are relatively under-explored. For instance, Kim et al. (2007) reviewed the literature of technology acceptance and continuance studies and conclude that only a limited set of affective factors are used in prior studies. Among these are: (1) 'enjoyment'; and (2) 'anxiety'. We believe it is not coincidental that 'affective factor' and 'emotional experience' are left out of the technology adoption researches. Technology was mainly intended for task improvement in work settings in the past. In this context, the definition of a task was specific and typically well-defined. Any individual was assumed to be highly motivated in task accomplishment. Hence, the focus on purely cognitive processes to analyze an individual's adoption intention of a new technology, leaving out other factors, seemed appropriate and adequate then. The inclusion of the aesthetics as a form of hedonic quality for the explanation of an individual's technology adoption intent was also rarely seen in the extant technology acceptance literature, until more recent time. Some instances quoted include a study done by Cyr et al. (2006). They combined the design aesthetics and the extended technology acceptance model (TAM), which included a hedonic component of enjoyment, and applied them in a mobile commerce context. Similarly, the study done by van der Heijden (2004) attempts to differentiate between the systems that are 'productivity-oriented' (utilitarian) and 'pleasure-oriented' (hedonic). It indicates that the latter intends to provide self-fulfilling value and prolonged use, rather than the instrumental value and the productive use. When van der Heijden (2004) was examining the determinants of hedonic systems acceptance, he added a forth construct, namely "perceived pleasure" to the TAM. His results indicate that perceived enjoyment and perceived ease of use have more influence on the intention to use hedonic systems than perceived usefulness.

As technology rapidly proliferates out of work into our lifestyles, the nature of task evolves from structured to less-structured. That increases the complexity of the scope of technology use from work-related demands to personal fulfillment of an individual. This fundamental shift in the context of technology use weakens the explanation and prediction power of the current technology adoption models. It is most apparent when they are applied to the interactive mobile technology, such as smartphones and tablets. One of the main explanations for such 'weakness' in the traditional technology adoption models is best put forth by Kim et al. (2007). They note that unlike traditional users, a user in the emerging form of information technology has to bear the cost of 'voluntary adoption and usage' and typically has to play the dual roles of both the technology user and the service consumer. When being a technology user, the instrumental (economic/cognitive view of consumption) benefit is clearly more important. But when assessing as a service consumer, the emotional (hedonic view of the situation) benefit may also become important for consideration. Kim et al. (2007) conclude that both types of benefit may affect the decision making. We share similar viewpoint as theirs. As a consequence of their observation on the dual roles of an individual, we believe that the cognition; the emotion of a user; the asethetics; and the symbolism of an interactive product are expected to be featured more frequently and prominently in the future IS adoption studies.

4   Proposed Research Model

By combining the cognitive, emotion, aesthetics and symbolism constructs from the UX and TAM literature, we have developed our proposed research model that can be applied to the investigation of the adoption of the 'interactive mobile technology'. The definitions of the constructs used within our model are outlined in Table 2. Figure 1 illustrates our proposed research model.

Russell (1980)'s Circumplex Model of Affect is particularly suitable to be applied to our research model, to model the emotion and the affect of the user of an interactive mobile technology, because it provides an overarching framework that adequately captures almost all of the existing emotional and affective factors documented in the IS adoption literature (Kim et al., 2007). For instance, the model can be broken down into two continuous, bipolar and orthogonal dimensions: (1) the pleasantness-unpleasantness dimension, representing pleasure; and (2) the arousal-quietness dimension, representing arousal. Using these two dimensions, almost all the extant constructs on emotion used in previous IS adoption literature can be mapped onto them. According to Romer (2000), the decision making process of an individual, when choosing an action to be undertaken, can follow two mechanisms: (1) thinking-based; and (2) feeling-based. In a thinking-based mechanism, a decision maker chooses an action to be undertaken by selecting the action that gives the highest value after computing the outcome function for each action using its realization probability. In contrast, he/she becomes conscious of the hedonic state generated by each action and chooses the action that offers the higher hedonic state, in a feeling-based mechanism.

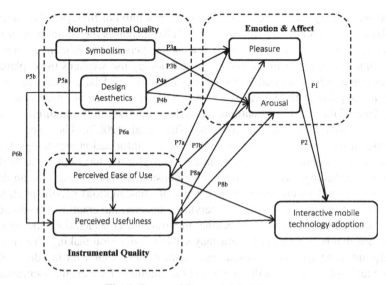

Fig. 1. Proposed Research Model

Table 2. Definitions of the constructs used in the Research Model

Construct	Definition
Pleasure (Holbrook et al., 1984, Kim et al., 2007)	The degree to which a person feels good or happy when using interactive mobile technology.
Arousal (Holbrook et al., 1984, Kim et al., 2007)	The degree to which a person feels excited, stimulated or active when using interactive mobile technology.
Perceived ease of use (Davis, 1989)	The degree to which a user believes that using interactive mobile technology would enhance his or her task performance
Perceived usefulness (Davis, 1989)	The degree to which a user believes that using interactive mobile technology would be free of effort.
Design aesthetics (Lavie and Tractinsky, 2004)	The degree to which design of interactive mobile technology looks orderly and clear.
Symbolism (Tractinsky and Zmiri, 2006, Rafaeli and Vilani-Yavetz, 2004)	The degree to which the association of using interactive mobile technology communicates favorable messages about the user and his/her personality to relevant others.

Following the same line of argument as the feeling-based mechanism, we advocate the following propositions:

> **Proposition 1:** Pleasure generated from the use of the 'interactive mobile technology' has a *positive* influence on the behavioral intent to adopt it.
> **Proposition 2:** Arousal generated by the use of the 'interactive mobile technology' has a *positive* influence on the behavioral intent to adopt it.

Another perspective of the User-experience model deals with the non-instrumental qualities of an interactive mobile technology. Non-instrumental qualities refer to the quality aspects of a product that go beyond tasks and goals to meet the needs of the users (Mahlke, 2007). Two distinctive categories of these non-instrumental qualities are the 'design aesthetics' and the 'symbolism' aspect of an interactive mobile technology. They are known to influence the 'emotion' and 'affect' (Thuring and Mahlke, 2007) positively. Rafaeli and Vilani-Yavetz (2004) and Tractinsky and Zmiri (2006) also provide empirical support to demonstrate the positive effect of the 'symbolism' quality of an artifact on the emotion. Hence, we advocate that:

Proposition 3a: Symbolism of the 'interactive mobile technology' has a *positive* influence on pleasure.

Proposition 3b: Symbolism of the 'interactive mobile technology' has a *positive* influence on arousal.

In addition to the justification provided by Thuring and Mahlke (2007)'s study, the study conducted by Cyr et al. (2006) demonstrates that 'design asethetics' will also positively influence the perceived enjoyment of a web site. Since enjoyment is expressed as pleasure and arousal under Russell (1980)'s Circumplex Model of Affect, we propose that:

Proposition 4a: Design Aesthetics of the 'interactive mobile technology' has a *positive* influence on pleasure.

Proposition 4b: Design Aesthetics of the 'interactive mobile technology' has a *positive* influence on arousal.

Cyr et al. (2006)'s study also shows that the design aesthetics of a web site positively influence the technology acceptance model (TAM) variables and perceived enjoyment; and consequently they influence the user's loyalty intent for a particular mobile service. Other similar studies also confirmed similar positive effects of design aesthetics on TAM variables and perceived enjoyment (e.g. van der Heijden, 2004, Schultz, 2013, Zhang and Li, 2004). Based on all these empirical studies, we predict that the same effect of the design aesthetics of an 'interactive mobile technology' will also influence the 'perceived ease of use' and 'usefulness'. For 'symbolism', we found several studies that demonstrate empirical support for the positive effect of 'symbolism' on the overall judgment about 'goodness', which encompass 'perceived ease of use' and 'perceived usefulness' of products (Hassenzahl, 2004, Mahlke, 2007). Hence, we propose that:

Proposition 5a: Symbolism of the 'interactive mobile technology' has a *positive* influence on 'perceived ease of use'.

Proposition 5b: Symbolism of the 'interactive mobile technology' has a *positive* influence on 'perceived usefulness'.

Proposition 6a: Design Aesthetics of the 'interactive mobile technology' has a *positive* influence on 'perceived ease of use'.

Proposition 6b: Design Aesthetics of the 'interactive mobile technology' has a *positive* influence on 'perceived usefulness'.

Empirical studies on 'User-experience' (UX) in Human-Computer Interaction provide evidence for the influence of instrumental qualities of the interactive systems on the user's emotional response. The first experiment in Thuring and Mahlke (2007)'s study shows that a manipulation to the usability properties affects the user's emotional reaction. Rafaeli and Vilani-Yavetz (2004) have also conducted a qualitative study on the artifacts to explore the influence of 'instrumentality'; 'aesthetics'; and 'symbolism' on the emotional response and conclude that all three categories significantly affect the emotion. Applying Rafaeli and Vilani-Yavetz (2004)'s idea on the interactive domain of the websites, similar results are also obtained by Tractinsky and Zmiri (2006). Thus, we posit that cognitive-centric constructs will affect a user's emotional reaction and propose that:

Proposition 7a: Perceived ease of use of the 'interactive mobile technology' has a *positive* influence on pleasure.
Proposition 7b: Perceived ease of use of the 'interactive mobile technology' has a *positive* influence on arousal.
Proposition 8a: Perceived usefulness of the 'interactive mobile technology' has a *positive* influence on pleasure.
Proposition 8b: Perceived usefulness of the 'interactive mobile technology' has a *positive* influence on arousal.

5 Contribution and Conclusion

The contribution of our research proposal is in introducing the 'beyond the instrumental' and 'emotion & affect' perspectives of the 'User-experience' (UX) from the Human-Computer Interaction (HCI) researches to the world of the technology acceptance literature. With this research proposal, we hope to help both researchers and practitioners to better understand the importance of the influence of these factors on the technology adoption intent of an individual in the context of the interactive mobile technology. As highlighted in earlier sections, the focus on these UX factors in this study is especially relevant in today's context, because: (1) technology is proliferating rapidly into every facet of our lives; (2) an individual is becoming both a technology user, as well as, a service consumer; and (3) the cost of the voluntary adoption and usage of the emerging mobile technology, such as smartphone and tablets, is being borne by the individual (Kim et al., 2007). The more inclusive the conceptual model of our proposed research model, in comparison to traditional HCI studies, the more it is current and relevant for the modeling of today's interactive mobile technology. Through our research model, we are firm in our belief that empirical evidence will be discovered to justify our position.

References

1. Ajzen, I.: The Theory of Planned Behavior. Organizational Behavior and Human Decision Processes 50, 179–211 (1991)
2. Bagozzi, R.P.: The Legacy of the Technology Acceptance Model and a Proposal for a Paradigm Shift. Journal of the Association for Information Systems 8, 244–254 (2007)
3. Bulter, K.A.: Usability engineering turns 10. Interactions 3, 59–75 (1996)
4. Cho, Y., Oark, J., Han, S.H., Kang, S.: Development of a web-based survey system for evaluating affective satisfaction. International Journal of Industrial Ergonomics 41, 247–254 (2011)
5. Compeau, D., Higgins, C.A., Huff, S.: Social cognitive theory and individual reactions to computer technology: a longitudinal study. MIS Quarterly 23, 145–158 (1999)

6. Crilly, N., Moultrie, J., Clarkson, P.: Seeing things: Consumer response to the product design. Design Studies 25, 547–577 (2004)
7. Cyr, D., Head, M., Ivanov, A.: Design aesthetics leading to m-loyalty in mobile commerce. Information & Management 43, 950–963 (2006)
8. Davis, F.D.: Perceived Usefulness, Perceived Ease of Use and User Acceptance of Information Technology. MIS Quarterly 13, 319–339 (1989)
9. Davis, F.D., Bagozzi, R.P., Warshaw, P.R.: Extrinsic and intrinsic motivation to use computers in the workplace. Journal of Applied Social Psychology 22, 1111–1132 (1992)
10. de Angeli, A., Matera, M., Costabile, M.F., Garzotto, F., Paolini, P.: On the advantages of a systematic inspection of evaluating hypermedia usability. International Journal of Human-Computer Interaction 15, 315–335 (2003)
11. Editorial, Modelling user experience - An agenda for research and practice. Interacting with Computers 22, 313–322 (2010)
12. Fishbein, M., Ajzen, I.: Belief, Attitude, Intention and Behavior: An Introduction to Theory and Research. Addison-Wesley, Reading (1975)
13. Forlizzi, J., Battarbee, K.: Understanding experience in interactive systems. In: Proceedings of the 2004 Conference on Designing Interactive Systems (DIS 2004): Processes, Practices, Methods, and Techniques, pp. 261–268. ACM, New York (2004)
14. Hackbarth, G., Grover, V., Yi, M.: Computer playfulness and anxiety: positive and negative mediators of the system experience effect on perceived ease of use. Information & Use 40, 221–232 (2003)
15. Han, S.H., Yun, M.H., Kim, K.K., Kwahk, J.: Evaluation of product usability: Development and validation of usability dimensions and design elements based on empirical models. International Journal of Industrial Ergonomics 26, 477–488 (2000)
16. Han, S.H., Yun, M.H., Kwahk, J., Hong, S.W.: Usability of consumer electronic products. International Journal of Industrial Ergonomics 28, 143–151 (2001)
17. Hassenzahl, M.: The effect of perceived hedonic quality on product appealingness. International Journal of Human-Computer Interaction 13, 481–499 (2001)
18. Hassenzahl, M.: The interplay of beauty, goodness, and usability in interactive products. Human-Computer Interaction 19, 319–349 (2004)
19. Hassenzahl, M., Tractinsky, N.: User experience - a research agenda. Behaviour & Information Technology 25, 319–349 (2006)
20. Hirschheim, R.: Introduction to the Special Issue on "Quo Vadis TAM – Issues and Reflections on Technology Acceptance Research". Journal of the Association for Information Systems 8, 204–205 (2007)
21. Holbrook, M.B., Chestnut, R.W., Oliva, T.A., Greenleaf, E.A.: Play as a consumption experience: the roles of emotions, performance and personality in the enjoyment of games. Journal of Consumer Research 11, 728–739 (1984)
22. Kim, H.-W., Chan, H.C., Chan, Y.P.: A balanced thinking-feelings model of information systems continuance. Journal of Human-Computer Studies 65, 511–525 (2007)
23. Lavie, T., Tractinsky, N.: Assessing dimensions of perceived visual aesthetics of web sites. Journal of Human-Computer Studies 60, 269–298 (2004)
24. Mahlke, S.: Aesthetic and Symbolic Qualities as Antecedents of Overall Judgements of Interactive Products. In: People and Computers XX — Engage Proceedings of HCI. Springer, London (2007)
25. Mccarthy, J., Wright, P.C.: Technology as experience. MIT Press, Cambridge (2004)
26. Nielsen, J.: Usability ROI declining, but still strong (2008),
   http://www.nngroup.com/articles/
   usability-roi-declining-but-still-strong/ (accessed October 30, 2013)

27. Park, J., Han, S.H., Kim, H.K., Oh, S., Moon, H.: Modeling user experience: A case study on a mobile device. International Journal of Industrial Ergonomics 43, 187–196 (2013)
28. Rafaeli, A., Vilani-Yavetz, I.: Instrumentality, aesthetics and symbolism of physical artifacts as triggers of emotion. Theoretical Issues in Ergonomics Science, 91–112 (2004)
29. Rogers, E.M.: Diffusion of Innovations. Free Press, New York (1995)
30. Romer, P.M.: Thinking and feeling. The American Economic 90, 439–443 (2000)
31. Russell, J.A.: A circumplex model of affect. Journal of Personality and Social Psychology 39, 1160–1178 (1980)
32. Russo, B., De Moraes, A.: The lack of usability in design icons: An affective case study about Juicy Salif. In: Proceedings of the, International Conference on Designing Pleasurable Products and Interfaces. ACM, New York (2003)
33. Schultz, L.: Effects of graphical elements on perceived usefulness of a library web page (2013), http://www.tarleton.edu/faculty/schultz/ finalprojectinternetsvcs.htm (accessed February 4, 2014)
34. Sheppard, B.H., Hartwick, J., Warshaw, P.R.: The Theory of Reasoned Action: A Meta-Analysis of Past Research with Recommendations for Modifications and Future Research. Journal of Consumer Research 15, 325–343 (1988)
35. SWIFT, E.: Die-hard Apple fans queue for new iPhones (2013), http://www.newstalkzb.co.nz/auckland/news/nbnat/ 1465631846-die-hard-apple-fans-queue-for-new-iphones (accessed October 30, 2013)
36. Taylor, S., Todd, P.A.: Assessing IT Usage: The Role of Prior Experience. MIS Quarterly 19, 561–570 (1995)
37. Thong, J.Y.L., Hong, S.-J., Tam, K.Y.: The effects of post-adoption beliefs on the expectation-confirmation model for information technology continuance. International Journal of Human-Computer Studies 64, 799–810 (2006)
38. Thuring, M., Mahlke, S.: Usability, aesthetics and emotions in human-technology interaction. International Journal of Psychology 42, 253–264 (2007)
39. Tractinsky, N., Zmiri, D.: Exploring Attributes of Skins as Potential Antecedents of Emotion in HCI. In: Aesthetic Computing, MIT Press, Cambridge (2006)
40. Vallerand, R.J.: Toward a Hierarchical Model of Intrinsic and Extrinsic Motivation. Advances in Experimental Social Psychology 29, 271–360 (1997)
41. van der Heijden, H.: User acceptance of hedonic information systems. MIS Quarterly 28, 695–704 (2004)
42. Venkatesh, V.: Determinants of perceived ease of use: integrating control, intrinic motivation and emotion into the technology acceptance model. Information Systems Research 11, 342–365 (2000)
43. Venkatesh, V., Davis, F.D.: A Theoretical Extension of the Technology Acceptance Model: Four Longitudinal Field Studies. Management Science 45, 186–204 (2000)
44. Zhang, P., Li, N.: Love at first sight or sustained effect? The role of perceived affective quality on user's cognitive reactions to information technology. In: Proceedings of the Twenty-fifth International Conference on Information Systems (ICIS), Washington DC, USA, pp. 283–295 (2004)

Using Participatory Design and Card Sorting to Create a Community of Practice

Delia Grenville

Intel Corporation, Hillsboro, Oregon, USA
delia.grenville@intel.com

Abstract. In this case study, we developed a scenario-based card sorting lmethod to assist in the co-design of a community of practice in user experience. Card sorting is typically used for the development of a computer interface. In this work, we modified and extended the use of card sorting to the participatory design of an organizational interface: a community of practice. The data we gathered informed the design of the both the real-world community and the virtual/digital artifacts that supported our community.

Keywords: Community, Card Sort, Participatory Design, Engagement.

1 Introduction

In 2011, we completed an investigation of communities within in our company. We talked to leaders and participants of thriving and defunct communities, to understand what it might take to design a self-sustaining, connected community of practice [1].

Using what we learned, in 2012, we took a focused approach to co-designing a community for our target discipline, user experience, based on three ideas we thought would be most successful. At the time, our user experience community was decentralized. Business groups managed and funded their own user experience resources. User experience initiatives were broadly categorized as "research" or "practice" or "metrics" or "design". The community of practice was envisioned to ensure continued success of a shared user experience philosophy with practitioners, key stakeholders, and all employees who were interested in the domain. The three ideas we thought would be most successful were: 1) to include experts, stakeholders, co-travelers, and employees at large; 2) to foster shared ownership, leadership, and vision; and, 3) to integrate the community into the product development life-cycle as a mechanism for information sharing and collaboration.

One additional challenge with business users is actively engaging them in participation since there are so many competing requests for their time [2]. Our fourth idea was 4) to design a study that also facilitated learning and discussion on a relevant topic while we were collecting data for our design initiative. It was important to design the study in a way that it complemented work objectives at an individual or team level.

Each of the ideas we identified aligned with known principles and guidelines for Participatory Design projects [3], [4]. As a discipline, participatory design focuses on co-design technology with the people who use them and over the years has

F.F.-H. Nah (Ed.): HCIB/HCII 2014, LNCS 8527, pp. 631–637, 2014.
© Springer International Publishing Switzerland 2014

extended to the design of different types of communities [5]. We believe our methodology can be applied to other organizations or disciplines that have the goal of broadening the targeted discipline or community beyond specialized experts.

2   Methodology

Our approach was developed to reflect critical design decisions of our community:

What would people in a community value so that they would continue participating? What topics would be considered an enhancement to their job responsibilities? What would work as a community experience and what wouldn't? We followed six steps, listed below, to help us design a study that fit with our goals.

1. **Create a Value Proposition:** Since we were not developing for physical interaction with a device, with menus or a tangible interface, we developed a metaphor to represent an interface. Our rationale was that the value proposition was a primary reason employees would interact with the community and in some way, the value proposition was analogous to a "main menu" of the organizational interface. This was the rationale we used to support the use of a modified card sorting technique. We developed a value proposition through refining insights from a series of strategic and tactical activities with partners and key stakeholders. For example, we created a strategic roadmap with end goals that provided insight into what participants would value. The value proposition of our community was "shared ownership, leadership, and vision while further integrating the targeted discipline into the product development life cycle."

2. **Understand Wants and Needs:** The design requirements gathering process [6] for the community began by categorizing what participants thought would make the community a valuable service. We collected this data by conducting interviews within our company with past and current community of practice facilitators and members. The insights from these interviews helped to create the scenarios for card sorting and questions for group discussion.

3. **Recruit participants and Conduct Focus Groups:** The participant pool reflected the population of the proposed community. We invited subject matter experts in the target discipline, people were invited via word-of-mouth, and we posted on internal social media sites to attract people from all areas of the company who had interest in the topic. We held 11 sessions at Intel campuses in Arizona, California, and Oregon. Our recruiting efforts attracted more than 300 people and 112 people (44 women, 68 men) participated in the focus groups. We met our goal to have a representative set of participants that would reflect the community we wanted to foster. Twelve participants were domain experts (human factors engineers, designers, or scientists). The remaining participants were from various disciplines through the company (Figure 1). In order for the community to flourish, we believed that every part of the product development process should be represented during the design of the community.

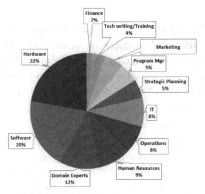

Fig. 1. Breakdown of Participant Expertise

4. Scenario-Based Card Sort: From our research in Step 2, the value proposition in Step 1, and our understanding of the goals of the target discipline, we picked six events that would define the community over the next year. Each event was listed on a scenario card with boxes labeled "me" and "community". Each participant independently rank ordered each scenario from 1-6 as shown in Figure 2. First, from the perspective of what was most important/relevant to him or her as an individual contributor and, then what was most important/relevant to him/her as a community member.

Fig. 2. One participant's ranked cards. In column 1, by what is relevant to "me" and in column 2, by what is relevant to the community.

5. Moderator Discussion and Data Analysis: With some help from the moderators, all of the cards were laid on one table as in Figure 2. The visual grouping formed by color coding allowed for easy probing by the moderators. The visual grouping also allowed participants to see patterns and easily make suggestions about why certain scenarios were prioritized over others. Each session was also recorded and the conversations analyzed for themes and insight. Below are examples of sample discussion and card sort responses at two different sites.

Sample Discussion

Moderator 1: Let's look at the most important cards: What jumps out at you?
Participant 1: People work in different modes; the whole lifecycle involves plan-ning, development, execution and some of the later details also and people are in different responsibilities, not everyone is creating, and some people are manag-ing processes also so such kind of decisions would take place...
Moderator 2: Yeah that's a really good point!
Moderator 1: What do you see?
Participant 2: I see olive greens: more emphasis on methods and practices across And the other one, biz group sharing, maybe groups that have very similar charters
Participant 3: I am not surprised that the orange, for the community I thought of it was of highest value. It's cross-org sharing, so it impacts large number of people so I would have expected it to be high priority but doesn't seem like that...."

Fig. 3. Real-time visualization of group card sort responses

3   Analysis and Findings

We aggregated the data from all of the sessions to understand trends that we could use to design our community. We looked at the frequency distribution as prioritized most important to least important; and created a cut-off of 22 cards or more for high rank-ing scenarios.

The data collected showed that Community ranking (Figure 3) tended to be more direction-focused and strategy-driven, and Individual ("Me") ranking (Figure 4) tended to focus more on learning that is driven by applied knowledge. We understood more about the differences in the rankings from the participant discussions as they reviewed the findings as a group. We heard a variety of comments:

"Events, announcements and compelling speakers are not the 'real' work. Real work would be cross-org sharing, learning methods and practices." HR, Program Manager
"It's the learning that takes place before the implementation that is more critical than the actual implementation." Sales and Marketing, Strategic Planner

"High profile speakers are my preference. I like to see the new way of thinking, a thought-leader" Chipset, Strategic Planner.

"If I want to be motivated, I can just go on YouTube and find videos or maybe have it on my iPod. I don't need to be there if I have another competing priority. And I think that's why listening to a high profile speaker is in lower bin for me." Investor Relations Manager

"I want the internal practices and seamless flow of people working on almost the same things across business units." Interaction Designer

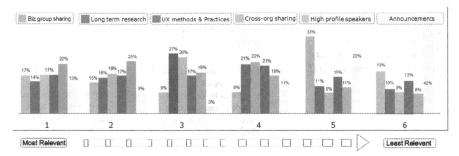

Fig. 4. Community rankings and discussion were direction-focused

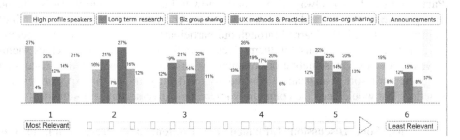

Fig. 5. Individual rankings and discussion were application-focused

4   Implications for Design

Social Media Continues to Redefine Collaboration. We learned quickly that our distributed community was highly dependent on many technologies to support it. In an ideal world, our community required an interactive webcast, split-screen environment where moderator, presenter, and presentation could be on a shared screen. Not all corporate environments have unlimited access to this type of technology, but, the technological advances are leading us there quickly.

Interactive Collaborative Technology Balances Individual vs. Community. The ability to post ideas and questions real-time during the speaker series helped the interaction with the speaker to be at both the individual and the community level. We learned quickly that one-way communication would constrain the community and we required a technology solution that was interactive and allowed people to have two-way communication with the presenter.

The Community Should be Designed with the Available Internal Social Media tools in Mind. The community design cannot be disjointed from the available technology. We experienced bottlenecks when the community began to grow and the technology at hand could not sustain a growing population. We learned that in our case, people will come but we had to ensure the technology solution available could accommodate the community.

Table 1. Example of data summary and ideation for top ranking scenarios

Top Rank Scenarios	Interpretation	Solution
E X A M P L E • High profile speakers (I) • Cross-org (I) • Announcements (I) • Biz group sharing (I, C)	• Find ways to let individuals know about events directly. • Select speakers that could address topics that generalized within their business group, across the company, and impacted the target discipline.	• Speaker Series open to all interested • Global access • Teleconference • Video enhanced when possible. • Instant Message used for comments, questions, and "tweet-like" interaction.

The Community We Designed Reflected the Wants and Needs of the Participants. There is always debate about how to build a community that is a blend of experts, co-travelers, and partners and how to achieve the right balance of depth of information shared. We learned through our participatory design approach that people have different expectations for themselves as individual contributors versus themselves as a team representative or community member. The feedback and discussion from the card sort visualization allowed us to identify important expectations and practices that would keep the community interesting, diverse, and well-attended.

The Card Sort Discussion Informed the Content and Presentation of our Communication and Events. We learned how to tailor the voice of our speaker series presentation, our newsletter articles, and our community announcement so that we were speaking simultaneously to the individual and the community. Without the design input from the community, we would have more than likely tailored our communication and events using more traditional approaches e.g. creating speaker series for specific groups with similar job functions. Instead what we learned (Table 1) was that every element of the community was an opportunity for cross-organizational sharing, if designed effectively.

5   Conclusion

The participatory card sorting technique for ranking scenarios when designing an organizational interface was successful for our design and implementation purposes. In total, 112 employees volunteered their time to participate in our study. We received positive feedback on the process. People enjoyed the opportunity to engage in the community's design, to network with other participants and to have their opinions heard.

Color-coding the scenario cards and laying them out on the table was an effective and rapid technique for creating a visualization of the card ranking data. Everyone in the room had the opportunity to move cards around while reflecting on them and could easily point out patterns that they identified in the data to support or refute discussion points.

The feedback from the card sort was used to design our speaker series and the training preparation we conducted with every speaker who presented in our speaker series. Every single speaker from an individual contributor who was a researcher to high profile speaker, changed and/or enhanced his or her presentation based on our finding from the card sort and discussion. The enhancements made always tuned the presentation more effectively to the individual and community perspectives that each listener expects.

Speaker series events were well attended. We hosted on average 5 speakers per quarter, with an average attendance rate of 125 people per call, and a range from 95-200 participants. At the onset our expectation was about 40 people per call which would be an acceptable turnout. The feedback from the participatory design card sort helped us to understand the tricky balance between individual versus community expectations in order to create a thriving community experience.

Acknowledgements. I would like to thank Rachna Tiwary for her work as an intern on this project and her participation in the execution of the research process. Debra Lavell for moderating and providing input during the data collection phase. Our team members who helped out by participating in pilots of our card sorting method. I would also like to thank Ralph Brooks for his management sponsorship, support and funding.

References

1. Communities of Practice (February 12, 2014),
   http://www.kstoolkit.org/Communities+of+Practice
2. Konrad, A.M.: Engaging Employees Through High-Involvement Work Practices (March/April 2006), http://iveybusinessjournal.com/topics/the-workplace/engaging-employees-through-high-involvement-work-practices#
3. Kensing, F., Blomberg, J.: Participatory Design: Issues and Concerns. In: Computer Supported Cooperative Work, pp. 167–185 (1998)
4. Bratteteig, T., Bodker, K., Dittrich, Y., Mogensen, P.H., Simonsen, J.: Methods: organising principles and general guidelines for Participatory Design projects. In: Simsonsen, J., Robertson, T. (eds.) Routledge International Handbook of Participatory Design, pp. 117–144. Routledge (2013)
5. Wikipedia, Card Sorting (October 3 2013),
   http://en.wikipedia.org/wiki/Card_sorting
6. Baxter, K., Courage, C.: Understanding Your Users, 1st edn. A Practical Guide to User Requirements Methods, Tools, and Techniques. Morgan Kaufmann (2004)

"Crowdsense" – Initiating New Communications and Collaborations between People in a Large Organization

Sue Hessey, Catherine White, and Simon Thompson

BT Plc Research and Innovation, Adastral Park, Ipswich, UK
{sue.hessey,catherine.white,simon.thompson}@bt.com

Abstract. Crowdsense is a novel information and communication system, intended to promote and enable exploration and collaboration within large organizations. The system is designed with the aim of solving several of these organizations' requirements. The first is to provide employees with information which is relevant to them dynamically, without requiring them to spend time logging onto intranet and internet sites. The second is stimulating communication between people with relevant expertise who may not know about each other. The third requirement is to provide a knowledge centre within the organization which people can both search and contribute to. The system provides an accessible layer which enables easy exploration, addition and correction of data by users. The contributions of this paper are the background to the project, system and trial description, feedback from user testing and discusses a central success factor – that of engagement.

Keywords: Collaboration, Social Media, Prototype, Concept testing, Engagement.

1 Introduction – Origins of Crowdsense

Crowdsense was inspired by Glass Infrastructure [1], a MIT Media Lab knowledge system provided via large touch screen kiosks designed to aid visitors and members to explore the relationships between projects, people and groups in the Media Lab. Sophisticated similarity analysis based on text analysis using Luminoso [2] is used to back up the recommender system for related projects. The original Glass Infrastructure has evolved since its initial implementation with the introduction of a series of "apps", e.g. a map and route finding app that provides visitors with directions to an office, and a "lunch date" system that recommends a suitable colleague to accompany a user to lunch. Based on demonstrations of the Glass Infrastructure system and an evaluation of the system using the client source code and infrastructure designs a number of observations were made on the potential for implementation of a similar system in a corporate environment.

F.F.-H. Nah (Ed.): HCIB/HCII 2014, LNCS 8527, pp. 638–648, 2014.
© Springer International Publishing Switzerland 2014

These observations are:

- The original system was underpinned by various databases in the MIT information architecture.
- The component parts of the system (displays, recognition/authentication components, operating system and implementation language) were enabled by their origin in an academic environment. For example the displays in the system were best in class and as such presented an obstacle to creating a viable business case for delivering a similar system.
- The underpinning purpose/objective of the Glass Infrastructure was to enable visitors to make links with an academic community.

The first two observations could be dealt with by re-engineering with cheaper components and a decoupled data back end. The final observation was more significant. The business issues that we believed could be potentially addressed with a system like the Glass Infrastructure in the workplace are the support of knowledge sharing and collaboration within and between working groups. These issues are elucidated and expanded upon in the next section.

1.1   The Business Rationale for Crowdsense

Previous studies [3] have highlighted the significant benefits of improving col-laboration and communication in the workplace in terms of both increased efficiency and employee morale. The existence of information "silos" within and between departments of large organisations cause problems such as duplication of project effort, loss of innovation, oversight of employees' valuable skills and knowledge and time wasted searching for people and information. McKinsey Global Institute [4] estimates that use of social technologies which enable collaboration could result in a 20-25% potential improvement in knowledge worker productivity and that between $900 billion to $1.3 trillion could be unlocked by social technologies. We believe that the Crowdsense system or systems like it has the potential to be one of these social technologies.

Unfortunately, mass engagement within businesses is still problematic [5]. There have been previous studies related to micro-blogging in enterprises [6] [7] highlighting the particular issue of "attention economy break down" (in other words, the saturation of human attention by information from different sources) which can form a barrier for organisations to adopt new social medias. The Crowdsense project aims to solve this problem by presenting the most relevant content to individual employees in a form that is easily consumable and with minimum effort and barriers to access.

Crowdsense is differentiated from other communication systems designed for the workplace, such as Trello [8] and Yammer [9] - the system provides a surface for the exchange of information without proactive access by users. Some information is available without authentication or a registered device. More information is available to authenticated users and users that contribute content are rewarded by improved recommendation based on their contribution and activity.

Crowdsense offers fully open communication, together with personalisation/recommendation and integration of social and chain-of-command messages. Existing tools focus on collaboration on individual projects, and are designed for access via personal devices such as mobile phones and PCs. Crowdsense is designed to filter messages and other content using dynamic recommendation that operates on many factors, therefore it is able to provide a single layer of communication that can in principle go across projects and span very large organisations. In addition, the primary point of access to Crowdsense is via large, touchscreen kiosks which also mark its differentiation from these existing personal-device centric systems.

2   What Is Crowdsense? An Overview of the Concept

Crowdsense is a platform designed to increase transparency and collaboration across an organization. It enables users to create and share knowledge about people, activities and projects and provides a system for sending information and requests across an organization to the right people. Messages and other new content are forwarded openly on the basis of relevancy creating open lines of communication. The primary mode of access is via physical touch-screen kiosks distributed in shared areas of the workplace. The kiosks are designed for rapid, ad hoc use and are placed in locations which encourage spontaneous interactions and viewing.

Access is also available via a web browser app (accessible to authenticated intranet users) to accommodate users with different accessibility needs, such as screen readers, as well as those who are based off site.

Both registered individuals and anonymous visitors can actively search all assets including messages, user profiles and project pages; and explore relationships in the knowledge graph. The results of a search are a set of matching interactive nodes, each of which can be explored by touch and browse. The underlying graph layer (see below) provides connections between assets, so that users also can browse to related assets (for example from projects to related people, and vice versa).

The initial requirements for the trial system were distilled from desk research into Interactive Kiosks, a user requirements workshop with other members of the Human Factors discipline in our research department, interviews with employees and evidence from surveys which monitor organizational "health". The requirements were then prioritized according to technical and logistical practicality and usability.

Technical Implementation

The client user interface is browser based, and written in HTML5/JQuery. The server is a distributed system of Java servlets backed by PostgreSQL DB that communicate with the client and each other via a REST interface. Each kiosk has a local servlet to cache data and handle data processing with low latency. This provides a scalable architecture. The servlets contain the graph layer which manages the connections and metadata between different knowledge entities (such as user profiles, messages, projects and other general entities.) The system supports the definition of new types of entity on the fly, so that it is not necessary to anticipate every future node that could be added to the data structure.

Identification of Users to the System

For the current trial, users identify themselves by either presentation of an ID card with unique QR code to the kiosk camera or by typing their existing corporate ID in combination with a new 4 digit pin. (Preferably, the method of identification should be passive to reduce effort by the user, and we are experimenting with facial recognition for this purpose).

User Interface – Controls and Content
Each logged-in user is represented on the kiosk's touchscreen by an icon/avatar which also functions as a cursor for the user's interaction with the system. We call these avatars "Personicons". They are both draggable icons with droppable targets and also have an associated context dependent menu [10]. The assets of the Crowdsense system are presented on the user interface as discrete components, which are also draggable and droppable. Logged-in users can perform actions such as bookmarking an asset, adding a connection (for example the logged-in user can link to a project), initiating a reply or sending a message of interest or introduction to an asset owner. These actions involve minimal, simple touch gestures. An onscreen popup touch keyboard allows text entry where required (such as search strings and message reply text.) We are also working on providing in air gesture control as an alternative to touch control [10].

The current kiosks provide a personalised interface to an identified audience of one (or more) users. When users are registered by the kiosk, the displayed messages and content are personalized using information about them extracted from their self-completed profile such as keywords and biographies. This provides the users with useful information, and the opportunity to become engaged with relevant discussions. Users can view passively, or can interact by posting further messages and responses.

When the system is dormant, i.e. there is no user logged into the system by the kiosk, the screen displays recent and general "floating questions" – open questions and requests for help posed by researchers to their colleagues which dynamically move and are presented in a rolling fashion appearing and disappearing at intervals of 30 seconds. The "floating questions" concept was identified in one of the early requirements workshops, as a way of engaging the research community, who we anticipated to be motivated to display their knowledge to a wider community for the reward of reputation and satisfaction – following the understood motivation of users for contribution to other knowledge systems such as Wikipedia [11]. (The "floating questions" interface has been broadened during the course of the trial to include any succinct message of interest to the research community, for example interesting news and events).

Multi-user Capability
When an audience of greater than one is detected by the kiosk, the possibilities of interaction with the system become more complex. Users can exchange details with each other, or perform interactions which specifically relate to just one of the logged- in users. An example is that one user may show another user their list of stored contacts, and the second user may choose to send an introduction to one of the people in the contact list. This is done by dragging and dropping their Personicons to relevant action boxes on-screen.

Anonymous Use
In addition to personalized use (involving user registration) we allow anonymous access to enable visitors to use the kiosks to learn about the organization. Unrestricted access to view the content is secure due to the kiosks being physically based within an access-controlled site, and being isolated on a firewalled intranet. This has meant that

the kiosks are never used for sharing data which might be sensitive or confidential. Also, we recognize that even basic information such as employee skills or the topics of discussions could have some commercial sensitivity in the wrong hands. We are now making decisions about restricting some data from anonymous users as the trial proceeds; particularly if kiosks are placed in areas outside our secure area. Our planned approach is to provide only a subset of search and browse capabilities to anonymous users, and to provide certain visitors with login accounts for increased functionality.

Fig. 1. Small kiosk in use browsing a user profile

3   Engagement

For the current trial, we are promoting the use of the touchscreen kiosks as smart message boards presenting messages and other new/interesting content – (ie the "floating questions" mentioned in the previous section) in a constantly updating cycle, to raise awareness in the office where they are located. In the initial phases we seeded the system with messages to stimulate interaction from the rest of the community. As well as posting messages at the kiosks, users emailed messages directly to the system, which automatically identifies and authenticates them from the email headers.

To further stimulate engagement with the collaborative aspects of the system, we sent a welcome e-mail to all 300+ members of the research community, inviting them to complete a profile for the system, which populates the database with their photo, skills, interests and keywords. Because each individual was sent a unique PIN code, the e-mail was sent from the Crowdsense system, using a third party domain which was not familiar to the participants. Despite using the department name in the email subject, and white-listing the e-mail address on the company servers, many recipients dismissed this e-mail as spam. As a result we re-sent the e-mail, after a preliminary e-mail from the director of the research group explaining and endorsing the trial.

19 people originally completed a profile in response to the first e-mail invitation. After the director's intervention and the incentive of a raffle prize this number had grown to 56. One month later a second invitation was sent out to people who had not completed a profile. Within a few days 110 people had completed a profile, roughly a 1 in 3 response, including those who work off-site.

We then analyzed those who had filled in a profile to discern levels of engagement against certain parameters - those being a) location and b) level of seniority within the department - which may affect a user's willingness to take part. We did this to identify the users most likely to engage with the system and for those who do not, to develop strategies to "nudge"[12] them towards participating. These analyses are covered in the section below.

3.1 Position in Company

First, we analyzed numbers of profiles completed by each level of management within the department, and the percentage of these against total numbers per level. Level 1 is the most senior position of management, descending to the non-managerial grades which are support staff, graduates and contractors. (see Fig. 2.):

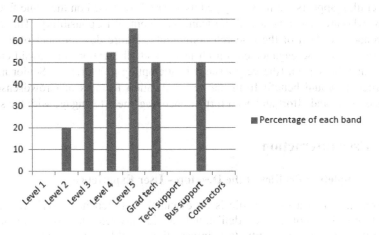

Fig. 2. Distribution of engagement with Employee grade. Level 1 is most senior band, top level management, Level 5 is most junior band (with no staff management duties).

There is a gradual increase in engagement lower down the hierarchy with the most engaged being Level 5 (researchers with no team management responsibilities). This group constitutes the largest group within the research department. Researchers of this group have similar objectives and may be showing a willingness to take part in an exercise which enables collaboration and therefore contributes to the greater good. The highest levels of seniority are the least engaged, even though location is not an issue as these individuals are primarily office-based near to the kiosks (see next section). We can surmise that the nature of work at these levels are more strategy-focussed and less concerned with core research projects to be able to prioritize their busy workload to engage with the system, even for short periods of time, coupled with a resistance to opening themselves to another deluge of information[13]. Even with a prototype system such as Crowdsense within the vicinity, there is still reluctance from some these users to participate. In free-form conversations and from analyzing behavior within the office, lack of time is often cited as the most significant barrier to engagement among senior managers.

3.2   Location

Equal numbers of employees based nearest to the kiosks were deemed to be engaged and disengaged with the system (44 engaged, 44 disengaged), but surprisingly, a higher proportion of those on the same floor, but further away from the kiosks were engaged than disengaged. There were a reasonable number of profiles completed by people located in different buildings to the kiosks and a high level of willingness to engage from researchers in the most remote locations such as London, Bath and the USA – suggesting that the system could play an important role in providing interaction between colleagues based at remote sites, for which full availability of the browser based version of the platform will be needed.

Overall, it appears the most engaged users are those based on the same floor as the kiosks, who are researchers with no team management responsibility. This accounts for around one third of the research community. Future development of the system must try to increase engagement on all levels and all locations and avoid creating a silo around the system (the very issue it is attempting to address). Senior managers in particular would benefit from the personalization features of Crowdsense which minimize time and effort and need further encouragement to engage with the system.

4   User Interaction

4.1   Completing Profiles at the Desktop – User Experience

The completion of a user profile is an essential first step in a user's journey with Crowdsense. The profile editor deliberately avoids any reference to hierarchical position in the company or job title (this information is held elsewhere in static directory services). Crowdsense consolidates this data from the business directory, and does not need the user to re-enter data that is obtainable from other sources. Indeed the Crowdsense profile does not require the user to specify even which department they belong to. The UI of the profile editor is deliberately simple to complete and very basic at this stage. The elements required of users in the profile were to upload a photo, add interests, bio, "working on" and keywords.

A survey was conducted to assess the subjective experience of the profile completion, using Survey Monkey™. This was sent to the 110 people who had completed a profile. There were 24 respondents (representing 1 in 4.5 of the total). Of these the vast majority of respondents found the profile completion process "easy" (on a scale of – "Very Easy", "Easy", "Not Easy", "Unusable"), which we considered to be a positive result.

In addition we conducted 4 in-depth user journey analyses of the profile completion exercise which highlighted behavioral details which need considering in future iterations – e.g. many employees do not have photos of themselves on secure work-provided computers, meaning sometimes the image they used to represent them was random (4 penguins, a lab coat, cartoon characters etc). Security features also need development – the current system of 4-digit PINS can add to the cognitive load for people who already need to remember PINs for credit cards and network and building access etc.

4.2   Operating the Prototype Kiosk – User Experience

Subjective user testing of the kiosks has been, and continues to be conducted in two steps. First, we captured user experience of the participants carrying out simple tasks[1]. Second, we conducted interviews with the participants to understand their motivation, or lack thereof, to use Crowdsense. For both, semi-structured questioning was used. The simple tasks evaluated in the first step included reading messages, sending messages, and searching for people and projects. The questions covered in the interview included deeper questions such as how the participant feels about using Crowdsense in a public space.

All concept tests were video recorded for purposes of analysis. The 27 inch touch screen was set up in a closed meeting room so as to a) not disturb colleagues in the vicinity and b) to allow participants to speak freely about their opinions. This created an environment slightly dissimilar to that intended for the system ultimately, in that the participants were sitting and were not "just passing", but allowed us to ask more probing questions.

Participants

For the overall trial, the participant group entirely comprises of employees within BT's Research department. This participant group was selected as a) many are physically located near to the test kiosks, b) this represented a diverse community of small groups who could benefit from greater collaboration and communication across projects and c) participants in user tests were presumed to be easier to engage and willing to help as fellow researchers. We acknowledge that participants within the research domain have a technical, well-educated bias and are "knowledge workers"[14], but in other respects are diverse in age, gender and specific skills (which range from network analysis to optics to business-modelling), with very few of the researchers involved in any aspect of usability.

From this participant base, we recruited 9 participants to take part in the user experience tests. All were employees but not all were from technical backgrounds. The age range was between 24 and 52, with 7 male and 2 female which broadly reflects the gender difference of the department. One had a physical impairment in the form of a tremor of the right hand. All participants were familiar with touch-screen technology.

Key Findings

On the whole, the participants found completion of the tasks simple to carry out. Logging on, either using QR code or Employee number and PIN was easily achieved by all. All experienced the system logging out after a short while which was welcomed as a security feature, considering our intention to have the system operating in a public space.

Sending messages, replying and searching were all achievable with little intervention from the researchers. UI features such as dragging and dropping were intuitively handled by all participants.

---

[1] This is not a full usability test involving the timing of set tasks, but more of an exploration of the user journey and the users' overall opinion of the concept.

The consensus was drawn that the on-screen keyboard involving touch interaction was too wide, with the keys too far apart to be completely usable. This infers that the public kiosk is more suited to discovering, tagging and bookmarking. System data indicates that trial participants are using their desktops to e-mail messages to the large screen as a workaround.

Many participants requested the ability to "send" details about messages (such as events, papers or items of interest) to their own e-mail accounts. A web (desktop accessible) version of the system was considered by all to be an important complementary feature to the kiosks.

A common point of view was that the system had the potential to address prob-lems experienced in everyday life within the organisation, those being the lack of sharing of knowledge and understanding more about what each others do (a new graduate commented that he did not even know who the people on the next "island" of desks in the office were).

The number of messages displayed at any one time (6) was considered appropriate for the size of screen itself. This is broadly in line with previous research conducted on the presentation of recommendations for TV recommendations which showed this number was between 5 and 7 [15].

Size and Position of Screens

The size and position of the Crowdsense kiosks was also discussed in the interviews in the context of how users feel about operating the kiosk in a public space. One kiosk (a 52 inch touch screen, right, Fig. 3.) is located in the middle of a small seating area where people tend to sit for informal meetings and to eat lunch or drink coffee. The other (a 27 inch touch screen, left, Fig. 3.) stands on a raised surface at a kitchen area where there are no seats but where people informally chat while making drinks.

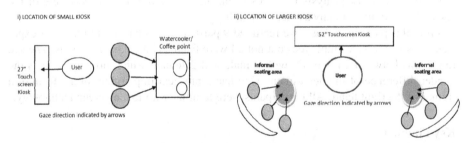

Fig. 3. Locations of large and small kiosk

According to user input, for the small screen in the kitchen area, people making coffee are facing the other way, so it feels slightly more private. One user felt as if their shoulders "block" the view – it is *"open and secluded at the same time"*. The larger screen was seen as most useful for the display of important messages, or for multi-touch (multi-user) function, whereas the smaller one was seen as one a single person could use while waiting for tea to brew. We will need to test these ideas further in subsequent iterations.

Suggestions for Improvements to the Prototype
The participants were encouraged to give their ideas for improving the system. These included methods for differentiating different kinds of messages in terms or the message's age or genre, constraining the message field to be similar to Twitter in length, implement complementary "ticker"-style news feeds for the desktop or Smartphone, and ensure the UI consistent with other touchscreens allowing "swipe" as well as drag and drop. A "network" view which connects nodes (projects) to other projects and people was particularly mentioned as being useful for navigation.

5   Next steps

The authors are implementing the refinements and improvements revealed during user testing with a view to trialing the prototype in other contexts and with other user groups such as field engineers and call centre operatives for whom the sharing of information within the peer network is important.

We are continuing to analyze data on the overall level of interactions with the system to infer patterns of behaviors based on day, time of day, location, level of seniority in the company to make suggestions for enhancing engagement.

6   Conclusions

Our testing indicates a growing awareness of the possibilities offered by Crowdsense, i.e. the breaking down of internal barriers and the opening up of new collaborations. We extended our research into domains such as behavioural analyses (realised by engagement analysis), prototype testing and exploring novel UI features (such as in-air gesture control in related experiments [10]). This we believe gives a more rounded view of the issues and opportunities presented by Crowdsense not covered by usability testing alone, especially with a view to eventual implementation more widely across the organization and beyond.

During the trial of the prototype, we have found high levels of interest and engagement among working researchers, who have persisted with the system despite some technical teething issues in the prototype implementation. There has been great interest from some remotely-based researchers, who see the personal device version in particular as a way of becoming less isolated from the team. The most senior members of the department were less engaged and this is a critical issue to address. We will do this by further exploration of their requirements which will be used to increase "stickiness" of the system and remove barriers to adoption.

Ultimately, with development, we envisage Crowdsense to offer a method for breaking down internal barriers to maximize the power of knowledge and therefore commercial success of organizations, by engaging all its members – which remains one of its most significant challenges.

648   S. Hessey, C. White, and S. Thompson

References

1. Havasi, C., Borovoy, R., Kizelshteyn, B., Ypodimatopoulos, P., Ferguson, J., Holtzman, H., Lippman, A., Schultz, D., Blackshaw, M., Elliott, G.: The Glass Infrastructure: Using Common Sense to Create a Dynamic, Place-Based Social Information System. AI Magazine 33, 91 (2012)
2. http://www.luminoso.com/
3. Hardy, B.: Morale: Definitions, Dimensions and Measurement. PhD Thesis, Judge Business School, University of Cambridge (2010),
http://www.repository.cam.ac.uk/handle/1810/229514
4. Chiu, M., et al.: The Social Economy: Unlocking Value and Productivity through Social Technologies. McKinsey & Company (2012),
http://www.mckinsey.com/insights/
high_tech_telecoms_internet/the_social_economy
5. Preece, J., Shneiderman, B.: The Reader-to-Leader Framework: Motivating Technology-Mediated Social Participation. AIS Transactions on Human-Computer Interaction 1(1), 13–32 (2009)
6. Yardi, S., Golder, S.A., Brzozowski, M.J.: Blogging at Work and the Corporate Attention Economy. In: Proceedings of the SIGCHI Conference on Human Factors in Computing Systems, pp. 2071–2080. ACM, New York (2009)
7. Zhang, J., Qu, Y., Cody, J., Wu, Y.: A Case Study of Micro-blogging in the Enterprise: Use, Value, and Related Issues. In: Proceedings of the SIGCHI Conference on Human Factors in Computing Systems, pp. 123–132. ACM, New York (2010)
8. Trello, https://trello.com/
9. Yammer: Enterprise Social Network, https://www.yammer.com/
10. Hessey, S., Chen, S.H., White, C.: Beyond Fingers and Thumbs – a Graceful Touch UI - Elegant Multitouch and Gesture UI with Context Dependent Prompting. In: Marcus, A. (ed.) DUXU 2014, Part II. LNCS, vol. 8518, pp. 562–573. Springer, Heidelberg (2014)
11. Nov, O.: What Motivates Wikipedians? Communications of the ACM 50(11) (2007)
12. Thaler, R.H.: Sunstein: Nudge: Improving Decisions about Health, Wealth and Happiness. Penguin Books, London (2009)
13. Deiser, R., Newton, S.: Six Social-Media Skills Every Leader Needs. McKinsey Quarterly (2013)
14. Drucker, P.F.: Landmarks of Tomorrow: A Report on the New "Post-Modern" World. Transaction Publishers, New Brunswick (1996)
15. Hessey, S., Matthews, I.: How Can Recommendations be Presented to TV Viewers? In: 2010 14th International Conference on Intelligence in Next Generation Networks (ICIN), pp. 1–6 (2010)

Accelerating Individual Innovation: Evidence from a Multinational Corporation

Qiqi Jiang[1], Yani Shi[2], Chuan-Hoo Tan[2], and Choon Ling Sia[2]

[1] Tongji University, China
jiangqq@tongji.edu.cn
[2] City University of Hong Kong, Hong Kong
{yanishi2,ch.tan,iscl}@cityu.edu.hk

Abstract. With the understanding that individual innovativeness plays an important role in organizations, both practitioners and researchers are interested in finding ways to promote individual innovation. Based on the theoretical lens of Structural Holes Theory and Social Cognitive Theory, we examined the impact of network positions, degree of participation and social interaction on individual innovativeness based on the archival data of an organization's online system. The results reveal that individuals who have more structural holes contribute more innovative ideas in the online community, and more responding from peers encourages more future innovation contribution. Implications for research and practice are discussed.

Keywords: individual innovation, structural holes, social interaction, network position.

1 Introduction

The organizational innovation capability is viewed as the key tacit resource for organizational competence [1]. To unveil which factors can drive such capability and to what extent by each factor, increasing number of studies covering different topics can be found in current literatures. Such works can be broadly summarized into two approaches by the characteristics of the driving factors. One side, the organizational innovation capability was assessed via examining the interplays with other organizations, such as inter-organizational collaborations [2, 3] or the pressure from the competing firms[4, 5]. Such literatures attempted to explicate the question, "How do the extrinsic factors affect the innovation process of an organization?" Differing from such approaches concentrating on the extrinsic forces accelerating innovation, another perspective elucidated how the intrinsic factors like organizational capability, influence the innovation capability. For instances, Eisenhardt and Tabrizi [6] investigated the role of organizational structure and team composition affected the innovation paces in computer industry; the organizational learning capability was also found to be conductive to the organizational innovation capability [7]. In sum, most previous works accentuated the impact of the determinants in the institutional level, such as organizational structure or inter-organizational relationships, on driving the organizational innovation

F.F.-H. Nah (Ed.): HCIB/HCII 2014, LNCS 8527, pp. 649–658, 2014.
© Springer International Publishing Switzerland 2014

capability, but ignored the power of talents [8], namely the managerial employees. However, the innovation process has been studied as an active combination of diverse resources, such as people and their possessed knowledge [9-12]. Thus, as the basic component of any organization, the consequence of inspiring each individual's innovation ability is conductive to the overall organizational innovation.

After surveying the existing literatures, several studies delving into individual innovation ability in a scope of organization and business research have been found. For instances, Rao and Drazin [9] used the resource-based approach for arguing that constant metabolism of talents from outside organizations or rivals could result in increasing organizational competitiveness on product innovation. Another article by Kickul and Gundry[13] found organizational innovation could be reinforced in terms of improving the talent management like recruitment or rewarding mechanism for e-commerce firms. Although such works have accentuated the importance of individual ability for the organizational innovation, however, the individual innovative capability was somewhat viewed as whole, like a type of resource, rather than articulating how organization leverages individual ability on innovation to achieve the firm's innovative competitiveness. Such insufficiency was improved with the emergence of SNA (Social Network Analysis), where increasing amounts of researchers attempted to shed light upon facilitation of individual innovation from the network approaches, like weak ties or structural holes theories [11, 12, 14, 15].

Although the individual innovation ability can be facilitated in terms of their network position from the structural holes approach, we do not think it is substantial to interpret individual innovation mechanism by purely deploying network theory with two reasons. First, the structural holes theory depicts a fatalistic tone somewhat, where the individual innovation capability is determined by his/her superior position in the whole network. Nevertheless, people may not be easily aware whether they are positioned in superior or inferior network positions in the reality. Second, the network analysis deployed in structural holes theory can only depict the role of positions in leveraging individual innovation ability, but the extent or strength of interaction between individuals is not well elucidated. However, previous literatures have indicated individual's behavior is constantly evolving in terms of social interactions and experiences with others [16, 17], which is called social influence. In this regard, social cognitive theory can serve as an appropriate supplementary basis to consolidate our understanding of the factors influencing individual innovativeness, which is also confirmed in the subsequent empirical analysis.

The rest of this article is organized as follows. First, a comprehensive extent of literature reviews on theoretical basis is presented with the proposed hypotheses in Section 2. In Section 3, we will elaborate the research design, methodology, and data analysis. The overall discussion and conclusion are discussed in Section 4.

2   Theoretical Basis and Hypotheses Development

In current literature, innovativeness associated with network structural positions have been widely discussed. For instances, Perry-Smith[18] studied the network constructed by research scientists and found individual creativity was significant influenced by structural positions in the networks, and such relationship was patricianly mediated by their background heterogeneity; Cattani and Ferriani [19] verified the network positions affected individual creativity and innovativeness in the Hollywood actor networks, but such positions are cohered at the interstices in lieu of prominent holes in the network; After empirically investigating a network constituted by R&D scientists from one multinational corporate, Tortoriello and Krackhardt [20] found the bridging ties affecting individual innovativeness is contingent upon the nature of the ties, and the significant influence only works across the Simmelian ties[1]. In general, such works found the individual innovativeness was achieved from their network positions providing superior access to the unique information. These findings echo the argument of structural holes theory, where the innovativeness is driven by the accessible information from the structural holes. In this regard, we adopted structural holes theory as the key theoretical basis for this study.

Consistent with Burt [21], we used constraint measure to depict the degree of structural holes. Such constraint measure depicted the extent to which individual depends upon others in his/her network and his/her access to the unique and non-redundant information, and the higher access to novel information confers the greater opportunity for innovation [21]. In the ego-network, the extent to which a vertex j has direct ties with another vertext i and vertex j has other ties q which is located in i's network. The mathematical expression of constraint measure is presented below.

$$c_{ij} = \left(p_{ij} + \sum_{i \neq j \neq Q}^{Q} p_{iq}p_{qj} \right)^2 \qquad (1)$$

where p_{ij} is the proportion of i's relations invested in vertex j, and $\sum_{i \neq j \neq Q}^{Q} p_{iq}p_{qj}$ is the extent of triadic closure among i, j, and third parties q. The value of constraint measure is in inverse proportion to the number of structural holes. In line with the argument of structural holes theory, we can reach that the individual with lower value of constraint measure indicates the higher innovational ability. Thus, we propose our hypotheses as that:

Hypothesis 1: The degree of structural holes in an individual's social network positively influences his/her innovativeness.

As depicted previously, individual innovativeness is not only facilitated by the located network positions, but the extent of social interactions and experiences between each other as well. Previous literatures solely elaborated the effectiveness of structural positions, but understated the role of social interactions. To bridge such gap in the existing literatures, we refer to Social Cognitive Theory (SCT) to understand how the consequence of individual innovativeness could be promoted by the social interactions.

According to SCT, a person's behavior is shaped by the influences of social systems and the person's cognition [16]. A lot of prior studies emphasize the role of a person's cognition, specifically, the importance of self-efficacy and outcome expectations [22]. This view has been adopted in the IS studies to improve computer usage or Internet behaviors [17]. However, the other perspective, the influences of social systems, should not be neglected. SCT suggests that an individual's behavior is related to

---

[1] The basic element of a clique (with three connected vertexes).

observing others within the context of social interactions and experiences [16]. The social interactions serve as the environmental factors that influence an individual's behavior. Virtual community is treated as a place to meet others, to seek support and belongingness [23]. Research in knowledge sharing and participation in virtual communities has shown the importance of the social supports provided by the interaction environment. In understanding knowledge sharing in virtual communities, social influences, such as community ties, social interactions in the network, are suggested to play an important role. For example, satisfaction with member-member interactions and organizer-member interactions positively impact member's participation [24]. The sense of community could also enhance members' contribution and participation in a virtual community [25]. Thus, we proposed the following hypothesis:

Hypothesis 2: The degree of participation in online commutative platform positively influences individual innovativeness.

In the online community of our context, social influences mainly come from the interactions among members, the commenting behaviors. If an individual shares a new idea for product innovation, others can provide comments to the ideas shared. The more social interactions undertaken by each other, the greater the intensity, frequency, and breadth of knowledge exchanged. We propose that the social influences from the interactions would promote an individual's sharing of new ideas. To measure the extent of interaction, number of words is used in this study. This measurement has been traditionally used in studies of social influence in computer-mediated communication [26]. The more words responding to an individual's idea, the stronger the tie and social influence is. Such social interactions builds more connected social network, which encourages more sharing of new ideas. Therefore, we propose:

Hypothesis 3: Amount of responding to an individual contribution has positively influence individual innovativeness.

3   Research Methodology and Data Analysis

This work was collaborated with a leading consumer electronic company headquartered in Western Europe, and we name this firm as Blue in the subsequent paragraphs. In order to improve the product design and innovation, Blue attempted to encourage their own staff to contribute innovative knowledge to operate the business. Thus, a new internal online system was implemented on April 2009. After a trial round for six months by several key firm members, the system was officially launched. All managerial employees of Blue distributed in different countries have access to it. This system was designed for helping the decision-makers to read and select the innovative ideas and suggestions generated by the staff in terms of their posting and commenting content, and the adopted knowledge like ideas or suggestions might be applied to the different sectors of Blue's business and operations. In this regard, users' participation, namely posting innovative knowledge and commenting others' knowledge, plays a key role in the whole innovation process.

3.1   Data Description and Model Specification

The longitudinal sectional data was collected from October 2009 to April 2010. As depicted previously, only the managerial staffs were offered the access to the system. In the end, 63 people have been observed in the system logs during that period. To longitudinally observe the social interactions among the users, we constructed the social network by each month. Eventually, there were five[2] social networks constructed for further analysis. Thus, the dependent variable (DV) and independent variables (IVs) were measured with time lags. In particular, the DV, the extent of innovation contributed by individual, was measured by the amounts of suggestions or ideas at time t+1 along with the values of three IVs at time t for each observation. As mentioned previously, we used the constraint proposed by Burt [21] to depict the structural holes. For measuring the extent to which individuals were involved in this system, we used the frequency of visits to systems, as an indirect measurement rather than a relatively direct measurement as most of the self-reported studies adopted. To elucidate the extent of such interactions, we counted the words of each comment under the posted content to represent the extent of responses to each piece of contribution. In addition, we controlled for numbers of factors that might be associated with the social interactions and individual performances, including in/out-Closeness centrality, amounts of suggestions or ideas at time t, and individual gender. The descriptive statistics are shown in Table 1. Referring to the suggestion by Gelman [27], we normalized the abnormally distributed variables in terms of logarithmical and inversed transformation. From Table 1, we can find the DV, number of ideas/suggestions contributed by individual, is a counting variable.

Table 1. Descriptive Statistics (130 observations)

Variable	Description	Mean	Std.Dev.	Min.	Max.	VIF
$N\_o\_I_{i(t+1)}$	Number of ideas/ suggestions contributed by individual i at time $t+1$	0.362	1.251	0	10	
$constraint_{it}$	Index of structural hole for individual i at time t	0.949	0.368	0.292	1.837	1.18
$involvement_{it}$*	Number of visits to the platform for individual i at time t	0.767	0.385	0.004	1	1.13
$S\_o\_W_{it}$**	Number of words responding to individual i	0.649	1.768	0	6.616	1.09
$gender_i$	Gender of individual i	0.915	0.279	0	1	1.06
$inclose_{it}$	Indegree of closeness centrality of individual i at time t	4.284	1.862	2.439	7.722	1.19
$outclose_{it}$	outdegree of closeness centrality of individual i at time t	4.262	1.872	2.439	8.386	1.15
$N\_o\_IT_{it}$*	Number of ideas/suggestions contributed by individual i at time t	0.827	0.297	0.033	1	1.07

*Inversed transformed; ** Logarithmically transformed

---

[2] The network on March 2010 was dropped because we attempted to use the social metrics at time t to predict their behaviors at time t+1, thus including the social metrics of last month makes nonsense.

From the descriptive statistics, the mean of N_o_Ii(t+1) is not equal to its variance, thus the Poisson regression is not proper to be used here. Thus, we applied the negative binomial regression (NBR) model to test our proposed hypotheses and estimate the coefficients of the formula presented below. To control the heterogeneity of individual observation and time lag, we used the pooled, random effect, rather than simple linear NBR model. Notably, the μi and εit is the individual specific unobserved effect and panel error term respectively.

$$N\_o\_I_{i(t+1)} = \beta_0 + \beta_1 constraint_{it} + \beta_2 engagement_{it} + \beta_3 S\_o\_W_{it} + \beta_4 gender_i$$
$$+ \beta_5 inclose_{it} + \beta_6 outclose_{it} + \beta_7 N\_o\_IT_{it} + \mu_i + \varepsilon_{it} \qquad (2)$$

We present the correlation matrix in Table 2, where we can find all the values between each pair of inputting variables are less than 0.6. Besides the correlation matrix, we diagnosed the multicollinearity by computing the VIF values (in Table 1). Suggested by Greene (2003), if the VIF exceeds10, it is often thought the existence of multicollinearity. It is obvious that the VIF values of the inputting variables are low enough to avoid the concern of multicollinearity.

Table 2. Correlation Table

	constraint	involvement	gender	S o W	inclose	outclose	N o IT
constraint	1.000						
involvement	0.197	1.000					
gender	-0.022	-0.114	1.000				
S_o_W	-0.236	-0.074	0.008	1.000			
inclose	0.083	-0.230	-0.089	0.073	1.000		
outclose	-0.178	-0.106	-0.050	0.089	0.272	1.000	
N_o_IT	0.098	-0.001	-0.164	0.102	0.041	-0.110	1.000

3.2   Results

The results of the estimated coefficients are presented in Table 3. We have tested all models, from the baseline model including all control variables to the full model. Model 1 is the baseline model, where none of the control variables influences on individual innovation contribution. Although previous literatures on both information systems and organizational management [28-30] have indicated the gender differences in using the IT artifact in the organization and innovation, such difference was yet unfound in our empirical results. It is not that the current findings are contradicting to the previous works, but our research context restrained to highlight the gender difference. As a consumer electronics company, it is intuitive to be understood that the males predominate the whole employee population. Based on the descriptive statistics, our speculation can be affirmed, where most of the users are males (mean value is 0.915). The (in/out) closeness centrality is not significant across all models, which indicate the network position does not affect the results. In addition, the amounts of innovative ideas/suggestions contributed by individuals are not affected by that in pre round, which indicates the inexistence of unobserved heterogeneity due to the time lags.

Model 2 presents the results after the involvement, indicating the frequency of visits, was entered. The coefficient is not significant, indicating the extent of individual involvement does not influence them to subsequently contribute their knowledge to the system for innovation. Such insignificant results could be resulted from the characteristics of the system that we are studying. Differing from conventional IT-artifact, the system implemented by Blue is a kind of knowledge aggregator. Thus, there are at least two purposes for employees to use such system, namely contributing knowledge (posting and commenting) and seeking knowledge, from previous literatures [31]. In this research context, how individuals seek knowledge in terms of using this system is unknown due to the limitation of our dataset. Thus, we are only able to empirically investigate the relationship between the extent of involvement and one dimension of system usage, namely knowledge contribution, which could be an alternative explanation why the involvement of system usage did not conduce to the dependent variable.

We entered the variable S_o_W, representing the extent to which each individual received the responses from others, into Model 3. The coefficient of S_o_W is significant and in the expected direction in our proposed hypothesis, indicating the stronger extent of social interaction to individual who have posted content can motivate him/her to subsequently contribute more. Model 4 is the full model with all independent focal variables and the control variables. The coefficient of constraint has significantly negative impact, which implies more structural holes in the communication network are conductive to the individual innovation. Remarkably, the estimated coefficients of other inputting variables in full model are consistent with those presented in previous models, which suggests the results from our empirical investigation are solid and convincing.

Table 3. Results of Negative Binomial Regression Models

Variables	Base model	Model 1	Model 2	Full Model
	Coef. *(Std. Err.)*	*Coef.* *(Std. Err.)*	*Coef.* *(Std. Err.)*	*Coef.* *(Std. Err.)*
$constraint_{it}$	--	--	--	-1.815**
				(0.894)
$S\_o\_W_{it}$	--	--	0.321***	0.282***
			(0.106)	(0.091)
$involvement_{it}$	--	-0.582	-0.231	-0.349
		(0.673)	(0.581)	(0.651)
$gender_i$	-0.015	-0.141	-0.455	-0.852
	(0.625)	(0.634)	(0.666)	(0.637)
$inclose_{it}$	-0.025	-0.037	-0.036	0.033
	(0.147)	(0.151)	(0.132)	(0.173)
$outclose_{it}$	-0.084	-0.088	-0.093	-0.102
	(0.153)	(0.156)	(0.137)	(0.180)
$N\_o\_IT_{it}$	0.604	0.529	0.562	2.215
	(0.860)	(0.876)	(0.795)	(1.673)
Log Likelihood	-109.599	-109.224	-107.287	-69.035
df	4	5	6	7

*p<0.1; **p<0.05; ***p<0.01

4   Discussion and Conclusion

In this article, we empirically investigated how the network positions and external factors, i.e. degree of participation and social interaction, influence the individual innovativeness. In particular, our results echoed the argument of structural holes theory that the individuals having more structural holes show the stronger involvement of innovations, i.e. contributing more novel ideas or suggestions in the online platform. Different from previous studies, the higher extent of participation in the platform does not affect individual subsequent innovation activities. Interestingly, consistent with social cognitive theory, the higher extent to which the individuals obtained the responding from his/her peers will encourage his/her future innovation contribution. This work serves as the first study jointly adopting the notions of structural network positions and extent of social interactions to articulate the individual innovativeness. In the IS literatures, previous works studying social cognitive theory only unveiled the social interactions do influence on the adoption or usage of online community. We extended such findings, and initially applied such theoretical framework in the organizational context. Besides the theoretical contribution, the findings from this work are conductive to the practitioners. We provided two solutions for managers to leverage their employees' intelligence for future innovation, namely 1) manually regulating the position of the individuals in communicative, and 2) encouraging staffs to increase their social interactions to maximize their individual innovativeness. Furthermore, the individual employee can also attempt to locate him/herself in the brokerage positions achieve higher extent of innovation ability, which may benefit for his/her future career development.

Like all studies, our paper has several limitations, which serves as suggestions for future research. First, we only used the archival data to empirically investigate our proposed hypotheses. Future studies may adopt multiple sources like self-reported or interviewed data to have a holistic understanding. Second, although the panelists in our dataset come from different nations, the proportion of Asians are not high. One alternative explanation could be that the oriental people are relatively restrained comparing with the western people. Thus, they may not be used to share their ideas in terms of such open environment. Last but not least, future studies are encouraged to continue to investigate the survivability of the contributed ideas. Although numerous ideas covering from product innovation to corporate governance can be found in the idea pool, this study is not able to foresee the consequence of such contributed ideas. Understanding how decision-makers refined such ideas for future usage will be very imperative.

References

1. Danneels, E.: The Dynamics of Product Innovation and Firm Competences. Strategic Management Journal 23, 1095 (2002)
2. Powell, W.W., Koput, K.W., Smith-Doerr, L.: Interorganizational Collaboration and the Locus of Innovation: Networks of Learning in Biotechnology. Administrative Science Quarterly 41, 116–145 (1996)

3. Faems, D., Van Looy, B., Debackere, K.: Interorganizational Collaboration and Innovation: Toward a Portfolio Approach. J. Prod. Innovat. Manag. 22, 238–250 (2005)
4. Calantone, R., Garcia, R., Dröge, C.: The Effects of Environmental Turbulence on New Product Development Strategy Planning. J. Prod. Innovat. Manag. 20, 90–103 (2003)
5. Olavarrieta, S., Friedmann, R.: Market Orientation, Knowledge-Related Resources and Firm Performance. J. Bus. Res. 61, 623–630 (2008)
6. Eisenhardt, K.M., Tabrizi, B.N.: Accelerating Adaptive Processes: Product Innovation in the Global Computer Industry. Administrative Science Quarterly 40, 84–110 (1995)
7. Jiménez-Jiménez, D., Sanz-Valle, R.: Innovation, Organizational Learning, and Performance. J. Bus. Res. 64, 408–417 (2011)
8. Cheese, P.: The Talent Powered Organization: Strategies for Globalization, Talent Management and High Performance. Kogan Page (2007)
9. Rao, H., Drazin, R.: Overcoming Resource Constrains on Product Innovation by Recruiting Talent From Rivals: a Study of the Mutual Fund Industry, 1986-1994. Academy of Management Journal 45, 491-507 (2002)
10. Hargadon, A.: How Breakthroughs Happen: The Surprising Truth about How Companies Innovate. Harvard Business Review Press (2003)
11. Obstfeld, D.: Social Networks, the Tertius Iungens Orientation, and Involvement in Innovation. Administrative Science Quarterly 50, 100–130 (2005)
12. Zhixing, X., Tsui, A.S.: When Brokers Not Work: The Cultural Contingency of Social Capital in Chinese High-tech Firms. Administrative Science Quarterly 52, 1–31 (2007)
13. Kickul, J., Gundry, L.K.: Breaking Through Boundaries for Organizational Innovation: New Managerial Roles and Practices in E-Commerce Firms. Journal of Management 27, 347–361 (2001)
14. Granovetter, M.S.: The Strength of Weak Ties. American Journal of Sociology 78, 1360–1380 (1973)
15. Burt, R.S.: Structural Holes and Good Ideas. American Journal of Sociology 110, 349–399 (2004)
16. Bandura, A.: Human Agency in Social Cognitive Theory. Am. Psychol. 44, 1175–1184 (1989)
17. Chiu, C.-M., Hsu, M.-H., Wang, E.T.G.: Understanding Knowledge Sharing in Virtual Communities: An Integration of Social Capital and Social Cognitive Theories. Decis. Support Syst. 42, 1872–1888 (2006)
18. Perry-Smith, J.E.: Social Yet Creative: the Role of Social Relationships in Facilitating Individual Creativity. Academy of Management Journal 49, 85–101 (2006)
19. Cattani, G., Ferriani, S.: A Core/Periphery Perspective on Individual Creative Performance: Social Networks and Cinematic Achievements in the Hollywood Film Industry. Organ Sci. 19, 824–844 (2008)
20. Tortoriello, M., Krackhardt, D.: Activating Cross-Boundary Knowledge: The Role of Simmelian Ties in the Generation of Innovations. Academy of Management Journal 53, 167–181 (2010)
21. Burt, R.S.: Structural Holes. Harvard University Press, Cambridge (1992)
22. Compeau, D., Higgins, C.A., Huff, S.: Social Cognitive Theory and Individual Reactions to Computing Technology: A Longitudinal Study. Mis. Quart. 145–158 (1999)
23. Andrews, D.C.: Audience-Specific Online Community Design. Communications of the ACM 45, 64–68 (2002)
24. de Valck, K., Langerak, F., Verhoef, P.C., Verlegh, P.: The Effect of Members' Satisfaction with a Virtual Community on Member Participation. Advances in Consumer Research 31 (2004)

25. Yoo, W.-S., Suh, K.-S., Lee, M.-B.: Exploring the Factors Enhancing Member Participation in Virtual Communities. J. Glob. Inf. Manag. 10, 55–71 (2002)
26. Postmes, T., Spears, R., Sakhel, K., De Groot, D.: Social Influence in Computer-Mediated Communication: The Effects of Anonymity on Group Behavior. Personality and Social Psychology Bulletin 27, 1243–1254 (2001)
27. Gelman, A.: Data Analysis Using Regression and Multilevel/Hierarchical Models. Cambridge University Press (2007)
28. Ahuja, M.K., Thatcher, J.B.: Moving Beyond Intentions and Toward the Theory of Trying: Effects of Work Environment and Gender on Post-Adoption Information Technology Use. Mis. Quart. 29, 427–459 (2005)
29. Gefen, D., Straub, D.W.: Gender Differences in the Perception and Use of E-mail: An Extension to the Technology Acceptance Model. Mis. Quart. 389–400 (1997)
30. Ilie, V., Van Slyke, C., Green, G., Lou, H.: Gender Differences in Perceptions and Use of Communication Technologies: A Diffusion of Innovation Approach. Information Resources Management Journal (IRMJ) 18, 13–31 (2005)
31. Sutanto, J., Jiang, Q.: Knowledge Seekers' and Contributors' Reactions to Recommendation Mechanisms in Knowledge Management Systems. Inform. Manage-Amster 50, 258–263 (2013)

Determinants of Continued Participation in Web-Based Co-creation Platforms

Sangyong Jung[1], JiHyea Hwang[2], and Da Young Ju[3]

[1] School of Integrated Technology, Yonsei University, South Korea
sangyong.jung@gmail.com
[2] Department of English Language and Literature, Yonsei University, South Korea
jihyeahwang@yonsei.ac.kr
[3] Yonsei Institute of Convergence Technology, Yonsei University, South Korea
dyju@yonsei.ac.kr

Abstract. Co-creation is gaining popularity as a means to collect creativity from the crowd. With web-based co-creation platforms, the general public can participate in the product design process and also gain rewards. In this paper, the demands of users to participate in co-creation was explored through the implementation of a co-creation competition, and the motivations of users were verified through an empirical research using a web-based experiment with a theoretical framework built on the Technology Acceptance Model (TAM). The result of the co-creation competition confirmed the existence of demands to co-create and the analysis of the experiment verified the explanatory power of TAM under the context of co-creation, verifying only a part of the TAM3 constructs.

Keywords: co-creation, creativity, crowdsourcing, TAM, TAM3.

1 Introduction

Co-creation is gradually and effectively changing user involvement in all levels of industry. Most digital content platforms handling image scraps, video clips, or writings are already dependent on user participation as a main source of contents, and even some manufacturers of tangible products ranging from tee shirts to automobiles are already trying to extract unique values by including customers in the process of product design. Especially in manufacturing tangible products, the advancement of 3D printing technology is accelerating the increase of the depth of user participation. Now users hold significance not only as consumers but also as producers of the products. Consequently, there is an increase of needs for manufacturers to understand the motivation of users participating in co-creation in order to promote co-creation. Through the implementation of a co-creation competition and web-based experimentation, this research will explore the demands of users and the determinants of continued participation in co-creation.

In terms of contents co-creation, two important factors made it possible to motivate people to create and share digital contents. The first is the advancement of digital

F.F.-H. Nah (Ed.): HCIB/HCII 2014, LNCS 8527, pp. 659–669, 2014.
© Springer International Publishing Switzerland 2014

imaging technology that led to the development of the digital camera and cameras embedded in mobile phones. Since digital cameras are convenient and did not require additional costs following the purchase of the device, people started to create a tremendous amount of contents. The other factor is the emergence of web 2.0, online platforms such as blog services, YouTube, and social media such as Facebook and Twitter that allow for users' sharing of contents. Moreover, the two factors become all the more interconnected with the emergence of smart phones, allowing for even larger amounts of contents to be created and shared. Some platforms even enable users to create profit by creating contents. Through blogs and YouTube, contents creators are gaining profit by advertisement profit sharing; moreover, in platforms for advanced contents creators such as App Store and Play Store, developers are given more chances to monetize their skills than they were given in the past.

While research on web 2.0 websites such as user-created contents (UCC) based on technology acceptance model or other behavioral models [7], [8], [9] can be regarded as empirical research on co-creation in a broader sense, this paper solely focuses on co-creation platforms for tangible products. Through empirical analysis of motivation in web-based co-creation for tangible products based on Technology Acceptance Model (TAM), this study will suggest how to design the platform and procedure for the creation for increased participation of users. In this paper, TAM is applied as the base theory to analyze the motivation for co-creation.

2   Background

The increased convenience of creation and the marketability of created product are also important factors that enabled co-creation of tangible products. Manufacturers that apply co-creation provide both tools for creation and platforms for actual production and sales. Threadless (http://www.threadless.com/), one popular co-creation platform for tangible products, gathers designs from the community and also receives evaluations of those designs from the community. Then, Threadless introduces top rated designs as actual products every week, and rewards the winner monetarily. As of October 6th, 2013, 4,735 designs among 522,033 designs submitted are printed and sold. Over 1,200 artists are made profit of 8,774,411 as a reward. The total number of the members is over 2.5 million (threadless website, http://www.threadless.com/). Such records of Threadless display the feasibility of the co-creation of tangible products.

Local Motors (http://localmotors.com/), a micro automobile manufacturer introduced by Chris Anderson [5], is another popular example of co-creation. Local Motors produces and sells a vehicle named Rally Fighter. To design Rally Fighter, Local Motors organized a competition for vehicle design to avoid similarities with vehicles manufactured by big companies. The components of the vehicle were also selected by community members, and the entire design of the vehicle was then open sourced under Creative Commons License. Local Motors shows that co-creation can be applied to even in industries of sophisticated products as automobiles.

The advancement of 3D printing technology has opened another dimension of co-creation possibilities. In Shapeways (http://www.shapeways.com/), designers who can create 3D models of products can upload and sell their products immediately.

Shapeways use industrial-grade 3D printers rather than low-cost printers that designers can offer, enabling the production of high quality outputs that are apt for selling [6]. The products are printed after the purchase and designers do not have to worry about actual production, delivery, or inventory. The service offered by Shapeways can make a huge impact to the industries of simple products such as bath supplies and desk utilities because the designers can commercialize their ideas without any support of organizations. As Local Motors' Rally Fighter aims for the niche market of consumers who want unique vehicles [5], Shapeways can trigger the emergence of market of unique and customized home supplies.

There are many advantages of co-creation that make it an important trend in industry. For the platforms and companies utilizing co-creation, various ideas or designs can be sourced by user participation. These new concepts are usually closely related to the users' actual needs; thus, it signals the possibility of the demand for them. Creation processes involving other users allow enhanced ideas to be produced and filter insignificant ideas at an early stage. Furthermore, the fact that the creation went through the filtering of the social community further guarantees the interests in the products.

Regarding the participants, co-creation platforms can provide opportunities to actualize the development of self-made designs and ideas. It usually takes much effort to produce tangible products out of a design model or ideas of their own. But with co-creation platforms, designs or even very crude ideas can become seeds for great products. Quirky (http://www.quirky.com/) is a company that sources ideas from the community and convert the ideas to real products. Unlike Shapeways, which requires participants to submit a 3D model of the ideas, Quirky collects crude ideas from community members. The ideas collected then receive feedback and get votes also from community members. In other words, co-creation platforms publicize the means of commercialization and production to ordinary people.

Despite the industry's interest in co-creation platforms and the need for promoting user participation, there is only limited research on the motivation of users' participation in co-creation platforms. Vladimir Zwass suggested taxonomy of co-creation and listed possible motivators of participation in co-creation [4]. Zwass listed further research on those motivators and other factors that affect continued motivation to participate in co-creation platforms.

Furthermore, Zwass divided co-creation into two categories by the co-created values: autonomous co-creation and sponsored co-creation. According to Zwass, autonomous co-creation can be found in the forms of production of procedural content (open source software), production of declarative content, hardware co-creation, development of social capital, reputation system, word-of-mouth promotion, collective sense-making, appropriable collective ranking for importance, collective sentiment expression, and task redistribution. Meanwhile, sponsored co-creation can be found in the forms of ideation, idea evaluation, product co-design, product testing, consumer resource contribution, product promotion, consumer self-revelation, and consumer-side customer service. Among those listed forms of co-creation, sponsored co-creation as a form of product co-design is closest to the web based co-creation platform defined and analyzed in this paper.

3   Research Model and Hypotheses

In this paper, a research model named Co-Creation Participation Model was developed by modifying the TAM3 suggested by Venkatesh and Bala [3] to confirm the validity of TAM and TAM3 as proper models for explaining the motivational factors of co-creation participants.

3.1   TAM and Co-creation

TAM was first developed by Fred D. Davis, who integrated diverse perspectives from expectancy theory, self-efficacy theory, and behavioral decision theory, diffusion of innovations, marketing, and human-computer interactions to explain the two primary factors that affect the behavioral intention to use the information system in organizations [2]. Davis suggested Perceived Usefulness and Perceived Ease of Use as two factors affecting the attitude for usage. Then with series of empirical studies that followed, he confirmed that Perceived Usefulness is significantly related to attitude toward usage and Perceived Ease of Use is indirectly affects attitude toward usage through Perceived Usefulness as mediator [2], [10].

A number of confirmatory researches on TAM is followed and supported by the validity of Perceived Usefulness and Perceived Ease of Use as a determinant of intention to use the new technology [11]. However, despite solid validations of the model and popularity as a base theory of empirical analyses in the field of information systems, TAM has limited explanatory power due to the parsimonious model.

Therefore, as an effort to elaborate TAM, Viswanath Venkatesh and Davis suggested Technology Acceptance Model 2 (TAM2), which includes Computer Self-Efficacy, Perception of External Control, Computer Anxiety, Computer Playfulness, Perceived Enjoyment and Objective Usability as factors affecting Ease of Use in 2000 [12]. In 2008, Venkatesh and Hillol Bala added Subjective Norm, Image, Job Relevance, Output Quality and Result Demonstrability as determinants of Perceived Usefulness and suggested technology acceptance model 3 (TAM3) [3].TAM has already been used in previous research on various information systems including contents co-creation research, even without organizational settings [7], [8], [9]. Since the main mediator of the TAM is Behavioral Intention to Use and Actual System Use is measured with the frequency and continuity of the system usage, technology acceptance can be also defined as development of intention to continued use of the technology. Therefore, TAM is generally applicable to the various contexts regarding introduction of new IT based service including co-creation platforms.

3.2   TAM3 and Co-creation

Among those validated by Venkatesh, the constructs of Experience, Voluntariness, Image, Job Relevance, Computer Anxiety, Objective Usability, and Actual System Use were excluded due to the incompatibility caused by the setting of the experiment.

In case of Experience, because there is no popular co-creation platform with tangible output in Korea, no participants had significant experience in platforms of interest. Moreover, because participants were not recruited within organizational context,

Voluntariness, Image, and Job Relevance were not able to be measured. And since the experiment was carried out with a dummy web platform with one time visit, Objective Usability and Actual System Use were also unable to be measured properly.

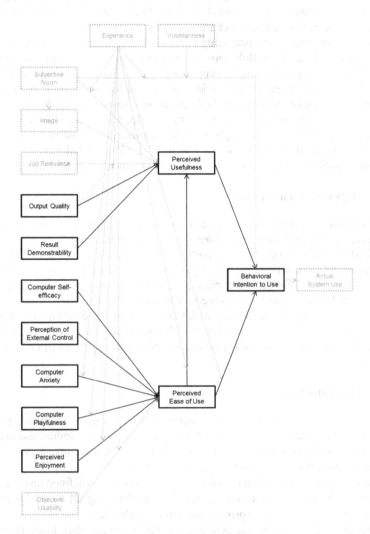

Fig. 1. Co-Creation Participation Model Derived from Technology Acceptance Model 3

4   Experimental Procedure

4.1   Measures

Survey questionnaires to measure the constructs were prepared by translating the questionnaires provided by Venkatesh and Bala [3] into Korean.

4.2   Stimulus Preparation

The stimulus was designed based on the structure of threadless, one popular co-creation platform. Threadless was chosen as the service model because although uploading an illustration of tee shirt design is relatively easy, the illustration is one of the main features that define the characteristic of the product.

The stimulus was developed using Ruby on Rails (Rails), a popular web development framework based on Ruby programming language. Rails was chosen because it is suitable for fast prototyping by supporting scaffolding functionality which provides basic structure for create, update, delete, show, and list the records. A big number of plug-ins called Gems are also available as an open source, which make it easy to add functionalities including authentication, image upload and image handling.

After development of web application, the application at first was hosted using heroku (Sic.). Heroku (https://www.heroku.com/) is a PaaS (Platform as a Service) that provides a package of virtual machine, web server, and PostgreSQL database.

4.3   Data Collection Method

The stimulus was composed of a fully functional web platform for uploading and rating tee shirt designs and task guides floating on the bottom right corner of the website. Tasks were designed to guide participants to use all the basic functionalities including signing up, editing profile, uploading, and rating designs. Since evaluating other designs is as important as uploading designs for the community to operate, the task required participants to rate more than 5 designs to proceed.

After conducting the tasks requested, participants were redirected to an online survey composed of measures from TAM3. The questionnaires were translated into Korean and the answers were measured using 7 point likert scale as in Davis research in 1986 [2].

4.4   Pilot Interview

Before actual data collection, a pilot interview was conducted to check the existence of bugs or errors and to confirm that participants could fully understand and perform tasks as guided. The interviewee was a college student majoring in visual design to assure the interest in co-creation services on designs.

The interviewee was asked questions while following predefined tasks and changes on-screen. The conversation was recorded. After finishing all the tasks defined, the interviewee was requested to provide additional feedbacks.

After the pilot interview, the acquired feedbacks were applied to the stimulus website, modifying the design for better understandability and correcting vague expressions in the questionnaire.

4.5   Participant Recruiting

The roles of users in co-creation platforms can be classified into three categories: creators, evaluators, and consumers. However, the users of co-creation platforms tend to not to choose a single role. Both creators and consumers actively participate in evaluating creations and according to Vladimir Zwass, the roles of users become fluid that even formerly consumers easily become creators. [4] Nonetheless, users initially can be divided into two big groups of creator-evaluators and consumer-evaluators.

In this paper, creator-evaluators were targeted participants of research, since consumer-evaluators are not recruitable until the platform has enough of creations to offer, and the primary interest of the research was to promote the creation rather than purchase in co-creation platforms.

Participants of the experiment were recruited from acquaintances and members of another web-based co-creation platform called byillust (http://www.byillust.com/) by email, without any reward being provided. Surveys by 30 participants composed of 15 male and 15 female were collected. The range of participants' age was from 19 to 31.

5   Results and Discussion

Data collected by the survey were coded and analyzed using the structural equation model to check the reliability and validity of measurement models and to verify the relationship suggested by TAM and TAM3 in the co-creation context. Statistical analysis was processed using Partial Least Square (PLS). PLS is a widely used method for factor analysis and regression analysis in the field of information systems, where TAM is developed and mostly used [20]. SmartPLS (http://smartpls.de/) software was used for PLS analysis.

5.1   Reliability and Validity of Variables

Reliability Analysis. For verification of reliability, Cronbach Alpha and Composite Reliability were used. Cronbach Alpha above 0.5 and Composite Reliability above 0.7 verify the reliability of the construct. According to the Table 1, for all of constructs, Cronbach Alpha is bigger than 0.5 and Composite Reliability is bigger than 0.7, verifying that the measures of the constructs are reliable.

Table 1. Composite Reliability and Cronbachs Alpha

	Composite Reliability	Cronbachs Alpha
BI	0.875094	0.781075
CANX	0.822352	0.763494
CPLAY	0.765451	0.664613
CSE	0.862399	0.792430
ENJ	0.938365	0.902142
OUT	0.947172	0.915867
PEC	0.827082	0.687272
PEOU	0.916040	0.878002
PU	0.960404	0.944989
RES	0.819293	0.617145

Construct Validity Analysis. For verification of construct validity, convergent validity and discriminant validity were examined. For convergent validity, loading between constructs and corresponding measures, and cross loading between constructs and unrelated measures were used. According to the analysis, loading between constructs and corresponding measures are bigger than 0.5 except measure CANX1 and RES4, verifying convergent validity. Measure CANX1 and RES4 were excluded in the research model verification.

In the case of discriminant validity, square root of AVE (average variance extracted) should be above 0.5 and bigger than latent variable correlation with other constructs to confirm discriminant validity [21]. However, according to the Table 2, correlation between Perceived Enjoyment and Behavioral Intention to Use is bigger than square root of AVE of Behavioral Intention to Use. Since Behavioral Intention to Use is more important than Perceived Enjoyment, Perceived Enjoyment was also excluded in the research model verification.

Table 2. Square root of AVE (average variance extracted) and Latent Variable Correlations

	$\sqrt{AVE}$	BI	CANX	CPLAY	CSE	ENJ	OUT	PEC	PEOU	PU
$\sqrt{AVE}$		0.845	0.767	0.672	0.784	0.914	0.926	0.784	0.856	0.927
BI	0.845									
CANX	0.767	0.212								
CPLAY	0.672	0.160	0.099							
CSE	0.784	0.322	0.113	0.369						
ENJ	0.914	0.856	0.176	0.444	0.488					
OUT	0.926	0.542	0.097	0.460	0.254	0.553				
PEC	0.784	0.385	−0.064	0.404	0.404	0.635	0.404	0.627		
PEOU	0.856	0.718	0.256	0.165	0.331	0.565	0.548	0.609		
PU	0.927	0.825	0.252	0.084	0.278	0.692	0.406	0.242	0.729	
RES	0.769	0.638	0.101	0.545	0.527	0.685	0.692	0.647	0.616	0.520

5.2   Research Model Verification

Verification of the research model was processed through bootstrapping and the result is depicted in Figure 2 and Table 3. Generally, t-value bigger than 1.96 accepts the relation with significance level of 0.05 and t-value bigger than 2.58 accepts relation with significance level of 0.01.

According to Table 3, path from Perceived Usefulness to Behavioral Intention and Perceived path from Perceived Ease of Use to Perceived Usefulness were accepted, confirming that TAM is verified under the context of web-based co-creation platform. Furthermore, among constructs listed in TAM3, only Computer Anxiety and Perception of External Control are confirmed to affect Perceived Ease of Use.

In conclusion, it is more proper to extend basic TAM with confirmed constructs from TAM3 and other contextual constructs that can be derived from possible motivators in co-creation rather than to use TAM3 fully as the base model for co-creation platform research.

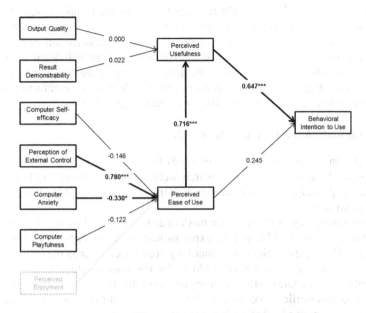

Fig. 2. Final Model

Table 3. Composite Reliability and Cronbachs Alpha

Path	T Statistics	Verification
CANX ->PEOU	2.093593	Accepted
CPLAY ->PEOU	0.57136	Rejected
CSE ->PEOU	0.746272	Rejected
ENJ ->PEOU	-	Excluded
OUT ->PU	0.000975	Rejected
PEC ->PEOU	4.315112	Accepted
PEOU ->BI	1.340673	Rejected
PEOU ->PU	3.257242	Accepted
PU ->BI	3.806427	Accepted
RES ->PU	0.127541	Rejected

6   Conclusion

6.1   Research Summary

The existence of demand to participate in co-creation was verified through co-creation competition. The co-creation participation model based on TAM and TAM3 was suggested and analyzed through the experiment with web-based co-creation platform.

As a result of the analysis, TAM turned out to be applicable to the acceptance of co-creation platforms, while constructs in TAM3 are not verified except Perception of External Control. In TAM3, Perception of External Control is defined as "the degree to which an individual believes that organizational and technical resources exist to support the use of the system"[18], [3] which means that providing technical support and giving high level of freedom while using the co-creation platform can positively affect the perceived ease of use, eventually promoting continued participation in co-creation. In addition, Computer Anxiety is defined as "The degree of 'an individual's apprehension, or even fear, when she/he is faced with the possibility of using computers'"[18, 3] in TAM3 which suggests setting target users with people who are comfortable with using computers may decrease negative effect on continued participation.

6.2   Limitations and Further Research

Although confirming the existence of needs for co-creation platforms and validating TAM as the base of co-creation research were successful, providing the direction to promote the participation of co-creation was unsuccessful due to the limited confirmation of constructs.

The inconsistency of the research model can be explained by the difference of context between TAM, TAM3, and the experimentation in this paper. TAM was originally developed for explanations of technology acceptance in organizational setting, and TAM3 was for the expansion of TAM under the same context. Even though TAM was applicable in context other than organization due to its parsimoniousness, TAM3 is too context-specific to be used under non-organizational context. Therefore, it is more proper to expand TAM under the context of co-creation than to apply TAM3 as a research model.

Besides the suitability of the research model, another limitation results from the short duration of service usage. For example, the assessment of Output Quality and Result Demonstrability can be affected over persistent use of the service. The Output Quality can especially be dependent on the score rated by community members but participants were not able to receive proper social feedback because they visited the website only once before answering survey questions. Regarding the specificity of the context, different methodology such as field research surveying the actual users of existing service or longitudinal research with development and execution of real service is suggested for future research.

Acknowledgements. This research was supported by the MSIP (Ministry of Science, ICT and Future Planning), Korea, under the "IT Consilience Creative Program" (NIPA-2014-H0201-14-1001) supervised by the NIPA (National IT Industry Promotion Agency).

References

1. Lim, J.: Quirky.com, Turning Your Ideas into Products That Sell! TechNode (2011)
2. Davis, F.D.: A technology acceptance model for empirically testing new end-user information systems: Theory and results. PhD thesis, Massachusetts Institute of Technology (1986)
3. Venkatesh, V., Bala, H.: Technology Acceptance Model 3 and a Research Agenda on Interventions. Decision Sciences 39, 273–315 (2008)
4. Zwass, V.: Co-Creation: Toward a Taxonomy and an Integrated Research Perspective. International Journal of Electronic Commerce 15, 11–48 (2010)

5. Anderson, C. In: the next industrial revolution, atoms are the new bits. Wired, 59–67, 105–106 (2010)
6. Copeland, M.V.: The $30M Bet That Shapeways Becomes a Factory for Everyone. Wired (2013)
7. Oum, S., Han, D.: An empirical study of the determinants of the intention to participate in user-created contents (UCC) services. Expert Systems with Applications 38, 15110–15121 (2011)
8. Ryu, M.-H., Kim, S., Lee, E.: Understanding the factors affecting online elderly user's participation in video UCC services. Computers in Human Behavior 25, 619–632 (2009)
9. Wu, M.-Y., Chou, H.-P., Weng, Y.-C.: and Y.-H.Huang: A Study of Web2.0 Website Usage Behavior Using TAM 2. In: 2008 IEEE Asia-Pacific Services Computing Conference, pp. 1477–1482. IEEE (2008)
10. Davis, F.D.: Perceived usefulness, perceived ease of use, and user acceptance of information technology. MIS Quarterly 13(3), 319–340 (1989)
11. You, J., Park, C.: A Comprehensive Review of Technology Acceptance Model Researches. Entrue Journal of Information Technology 9(2), 31–50 (2010)
12. Venkatesh, V.: Determinants of Perceived Ease of Use- Integrating Control, Intrinsic Motivation, and Emotion into the Technology Acceptance Model. Information Systems Research 11(4), 342–365 (2000)
13. Fishbein, M.: i ajzen, i.(1975). belief, attitude, intention, and behaviour: An introduction to theory and research (1975)
14. Venkatesh, V., Davis, F.D.: A Theoretical Extension of the Technology Acceptance Model: Four Longitudinal Field Studies. Management Science 46, 186–204 (2000)
15. Moore, G., Benbasat, I.: Development of an instrument to measure the perceptions of adopting an information technology innovation. Information Systems Research 2, 192–222 (1991)
16. Compeau, D.R., Higgins, C.A.: Application of social cognitive theory to training for computer skills. Information Systems Research 6(2), 118–143 (1995)
17. Compeau, D.R., Higgins, C.A.: Computer self-efficacy: Development of a measure and initial test. MIS Quarterly, 189–211 (1995)
18. Venkatesh, V., Morris, M., Davis, G., Davis, F.: User acceptance of information technology: Toward a unified view. MIS Quarterly 27(3), 425–478 (2003)
19. Webster, J., Martocchio, J.J.: Microcomputer playfulness: development of a measure with workplace implications. MIS Quarterly, 201–226 (1992)
20. Gefen, D., Straub, D., Boudreau, M.: Structural Equation Modeling and Regression: Guidelines for Research Practice. Communications of the AIS 4(7) (2000)
21. Fornell, C., Larker, D.F.: Evaluating structural equation models with unobservable variables and measurement error. Journal of Marketing Research 18(1), 39–50 (1981)

Towards Predicting Ad Effectiveness
via an Eye Tracking Study

Eleni Michailidou[1], Christoforos Christoforou[2], and Panayiotis Zaphiris[1]

[1] Cyprus University of Technology, Department of Multimedia and Graphic Arts
{eleni.michailidou,panayiotis.zaphiris}@cut.ac.cy
[2] R.K.I. Leaders, Research Center, Cyprus
cchristoforou@rkileaders.com

Abstract. This paper presents the pilot study of a project for which the main aim is to implement an evaluation methodology service for the identification of the best locations on Cypriot web space based on eye tracking studies. Advertising budget, social demographics and web usage are some of the factors that are being considered. During this pilot study, a description in existing patterns of advertisement placement on websites is first presented. Then we present the methodologies of two pilot studies where user data are collected with the use of eye tracking technologies in order to understand how users look at Web advertising and how effective each location is as well as Marketers' questionnaire. Stimuli were three Cypriot websites with advertisements of various types and three locations: ads being static and animated, types being skyscraper and display ads and location varied around the page. Eye-tracking data are compared to ad choices of marketing managers in Cyprus who rated the ad position and it's attention value. Results demonstrate the correlation between user attention, advert types and the value as rated by marketers. This pilot study revealed conclusions that could form the basis towards predicting ad effectiveness of webpages with the use of ad number, location, size, and type.

Keywords: advert attention, online advertising, eye tracking, CPM.

1 Introduction

In traditional advertising the main focus is on the consumer's attitudes and behaviors. This was also initially the focus in online advertising research as well; focusing on attitudes and behaviors towards ads, medium reliability, product involvement and website's context congruity for example. This has however now changed. In terms of online advertising, the focus is now on issues of ad effectiveness, such as attention, display-ad advertising formats and visual design issues. Online ad pricing is often based on placement, document arrangement, frequency and size [11]. Other transaction-based measures to determine online ad effectiveness is click-through rates, registrations, and purchases [8]. Media characteristics, informativeness, irritation, and entertainment provided by the ads are also factors that can influence ad effectiveness [5].

The lack of effective measures for online campaign evaluation, as well as, the exponential increase in the number of commercial websites - and consequently the increase

F.F.-H. Nah (Ed.): HCIB/HCII 2014, LNCS 8527, pp. 670–680, 2014.
© Springer International Publishing Switzerland 2014

of available online advertising spots - raise the question: "Which advertising locations have to be chosen by an agent in order to optimize the effectiveness and maximize the visibility of an online campaign?" Currently, the answer to that question is ad-hoc, purely subjective, and is provided by advertising agents who typically choose the position based on their personal experience, non-informative web analytics and on the motto: "the higher the position of the ad on the page, the more effective it is".

Similar with the rest of the world, Internet in Cyprus is now used as a mean of low cost targeted advertising. With more than 30 thousand Cypriot Websites and with Cyprus Web usage rising to 50,2% in 2010, online advertising is now the upcoming trend in advertising expenses in Cyprus. The increase in the number of commercial Cypriot Website, and consequently the increase of available online advertising spots raise the question: Which advertising locations has to be chosen by an agent in order to optimize the effectiveness and maximize the visibility of an online campaign? There are currently around 10 thousand available advertising positions and types of advertisements. Currently, online advertisement placement is highly subjective and is performed by an advertising agent who typically chooses the position based of his personal experience, generic statistical data and on the motto that "the higher the position of the ad on the page, the more effective".

In this paper we present the results of a pilot study towards the implementation of a novel methodological framework for the evaluation of the effectiveness and the impact of online advertising based on the ad's visibility. First we present an overview of online advertisement studies. Then we describe the methodology of the two studies: user evaluation with an eye tracker and the questionnaire given to marketers. Results are then presented and discussed.

2   Online Advertising

Online advertising is more popular and economical than traditional advertising methods. However, the effectiveness of internet advertising remains controversial. Comparing how well both forms of advertising (online vs. traditional) attract viewers' attention is worth further research investigations. It has been reported in one study that online users are less likely than readers of printed media to register ads [10]. Others have argued that traditional principles in advertising do not apply to the web [4]. In traditional advertising the main focus is on the consumer's attitudes and behaviors. This was also initially the focus in online advertising research as well; focusing on attitudes and behaviors towards ads, medium reliability, product involvement and website's context congruity for example. This has however now changed. In terms of online advertising, the focus is now on issues of ad effectiveness, such as attention, display-ads advertising formats and visual design issues.

2.1   Ad Placement and Pricing

It has been reported by PricewaterhouseCoopers that advertising revenue reached $5.1 billion in 2009, in the US alone. A total of 47% of that amount is represented in Internet advertising revenues. Display ads generated $2.4 billion in the same period. The

IAB internet advertising revenue report (2012), conducted by PricewaterhouseCoopers, states that internet advertising revenue in the US reached $17.0 billion, for the first six months of 2012. This represents a 14% increase over the first six months of 2011. Search and display ads generated the most revenue in the second quarter of 2012. Search revenues were estimated at $4.1 billion and display-related advertising at $2.9 billion respectively for this period. The auction-based pay-for-click advertising model has contributed to search advertising revenue growth [8]. Two differences between display-ad and search advertising relate to their design and placement. A search ad is text-based, has a title, description and a link to a landing page. Advertisers have little control over design elements, such as colour, animation and image. This is not the case in display advertising, where there is control over such elements. Display ads may be placed on any part of the web page, unlike search ads, which are placed on either on top or right-hand side of the search results. They are also displayed together with competing ads.

Online ad pricing is often based on placement, frequency and size [11]. Other transaction-based measures to determine online ad effectiveness is click-through rates, registrations, and purchases [8]. Web document arrangement is another factor that must be considered for pricing, as previously discussed by [11]. This is determined by the depth of a website on a meaningful path. Media characteristics, informativeness, irritation, and entertainment provided by the ads are also factors that can influence ad effectiveness [5].

Consumers' online shopping behaviors have also gained researchers' interest. Luo [8] focused on determining the impact of a search ad on brand attention. It is based on a user recalling a search and recognizing the brand that was displayed in that search ad. By determining this, it is then possible to examine the effect of search ad placement on brand recall and recognition. The theoretical lens of the limited capacity model of attention and theories of search behavior were considered. The study investigated three key variables for search ad recall and recognition: ad positioning, search ad'keyword association and search result quality. Interesting results were that a top-positioned search ad did not generate more attention than a side-positioned search ad. Top-position ads have been regarded as the most marketable, with a premium price associated to them. The study questions whether this premium price is warranted and if it is actually worth being the highest bidder for all related keywords. They suggest a more cautions and uniform bidding strategy when perusing top-positioned ads at least. Interactions between keyword selection, search ad position, and search result quality must be considered by advertisers in their strategies. Defining semantically related keywords that can represent company brand however, will result in a bidding war between competitors. It is thus suggested that advertising budgets be used more wisely and creatively to identify relevant contextually related keywords instead. As a result, there will be less competition for those types of keywords, thus ads being displayed more often with the same budget [8].

Wang and Day [11] explored the changes in attention distribution on banners, as users' advances along a meaningful path, through an eye tracking study. Their findings indicate that web document arrangement can be more efficient if the most interesting content is placed in either the earlier or later phases, while material more demanding of mental resources is placed in the middle phases. This is based on the notion that when following a path, user attention is not the same at every point in time. The user's peripheral vision is more sensitive at the earlier and later phases of the path. This vision declines in the middle phases of the path, resulting in side ads being mostly ignored in this phase. Consequently, pricing of ads should also be based on the depth of the webpage on a meaningful path [11]. Conventionally, pricing has been determined on the basis of placement, frequency and size. The findings suggest that web document arrangement is important too. To induce user interest the most intriguing content should be displayed in the early and later phases. Only once the content has captivated the user does it make sense to present material which is more demanding of mental resources, as user attention is already high.

2.2 Attention Evaluation

Ad type also has a significant impact on ads being noticed. Therefore, investigating ad types has also been area of prime interest for the research community. The effect of different ad types on users' attention, intrusiveness and ability to remember these was the focus of [9] investigations. Results indicated that participants who were exposed to ads were 11% less likely to visit or recommend that particular website. Lin and Chen [7] concluded that in addition to ad type, ad position and animation length significantly impact user's attention. In this study, the click-through rate for advertising effectiveness was examined. The aim was to determine the effects of design factors on animated online advertisements. An eye tracker was used to monitor users while browsing websites. Results indicated a logistic regression model with an order effect. A significant interaction effect between the ad type and the ad position was also observed. Lastly, there was an interaction between ad position and animation length.

The effect of animation and ad format on the attention and memorization of online ads has also been investigated in [6]. This study was conducted in the context of consumer perception and processing of advertising. Eye tacking was used to measure consumer attention in a variety of real-world ads. Recognition and recall tests were used to assess ad memory. The results indicated that animation had little or no effect on attention. This is its main advantage, as memory evaluation tasks can be executed without requiring participants to clearly recall test material. In essence it involves reminding the participants by providing them with cues within the environment. Recall tests however is based on recalling information from memory without assistance from an external source. Recognition tests are usually easier than recall and were also applied in Hsieh and Chen's study [4]. As an example consider a GUI interface in comparison to a command line interface. GUIs are easier to use because they do not require the user to remember commands, as is the case of a command line interface. Buscher et al. [1] used an eye tracker to investigate how people view and interact with the results of search engines. Factors that were found to influence the viewing behavior are task type, ad quality and the sequence in which ad quality is alternated. To determine what makes a web page appealing for generation Y users an eye-tracker was used to follow the eye movements of the users, as they browsed selected pages [3].

However, an interaction effect between animation and ad format was observed. This suggests that the animation effect is conditioned by the ad format. Similar results were discovered in Lin and Chen [7] investigations as well. Furthermore, animation on skyscrapers had a positive effect while on banners it was negative. Yet, improved recognition was observed on banners containing animation.

In Castagnos and Pu's [2] consumer behavior and decision support systems' study, the selected decision entities and information entities were observed, as consumers searched for products. The eye-tracker followed the consumers gaze, and to analyze their eye movements, heat maps were applied. This aided the process of determining where their eyes fixated the most. Access logs that contained the time users spent on each webpage and the clicks they made were also used for data collection.

3   Methodology

Two studies were performed in order to investigate marketers' and user's advertisement perception and attention. Both are used as pilot studies towards the design of the final study that will be used for the framework implementation. This section presents the methodology of both studies that included eye tracking and questionnaire techniques. Stimuli were three Cypriot websites with advertisements of various types and locations: ads being static and animated, ad types being skyscraper and banner and ad location varied around the page. An eye-tracking platform was used to collect gaze points and fixation of participants while navigating each webpage. Subsequently, a number of eye-tracking statistics were calculated based on the fixations in each area of interest. These statistics include a percentage of visitors attending to the ad, time to first fixations and attention-bounce rate (percentage of single-fixation glance at the ad). The websites and advertisements shown will not be named and instead special coding will be used throughout the paper. However, as all three pages had the same layout, advertisements shown and locations that were examined followed the schema that Figure 1 shows. The dotted line divides the page into the two sections: above and below the fold.

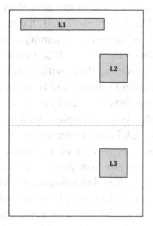

Fig. 1. Website Schema representing the three locations

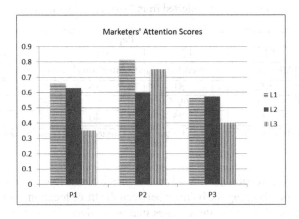

Fig. 2. Marketers' Perceived Attention Scores

3.1   Study I: Marketers' Ad Perceived Attention with a Questionnaire

The questionnaire study was performed during a local marketing conference. Eighteen (18) marketing managers from various Cypriot companies were given a questionnaire to complete. They were given three (3) screenshots of Cypriot websites and three advert placements on each page were highlighted and empty. Each Marketer was asked to select one location on each website that they would place a given ad. The given ad had a travelling theme and was the same for all participants and for both studies. Then they were asked to provide the percentage of views (impressions) they feel that, based on their experience, will actually attend to the advertisement at the selected location. The score indicates the perceived value of the particular location to the Marketer. For example, if a Marketer specifies a score of 80% indicates that the marketer anticipates a 20% of paid inventory to be unnoticed. Moreover, the Marketer is willing to accept the fact that 20% of his paid impressions will not be seen.

3.2   Study II: User Ad Attention with an Eyetracker

Eyetracking allows us to carefully follow and analyze what is being looked at and when it is being viewed. The second user study aimed to understand users' advert attention on the three locations for each examined website with the use of an eyetracker. The study took place at the Cyprus University of Technology and participants recruited were aged from 21 - 50 and included staff and students. During the study, 80 participants took part on the eyetracking study. Eye movements were recorded during the experiments with an eye tracking system developed in-house.

The participant was placed in front of the computer and after the eyetracking calibration was asked to browse through the Webpage. There was no specific task to complete as advert attention should be affected by any reason. So the participant was asked to browse the page as he would navigate on his own time. Maximum time for each page was limited to two minutes. Each participant looked at all three webpages but the examined advert was shown on only one of the three locations on each page. The website

Table 1. Data collected from Marketing Questionnaire

Location	Pages							
	P1		P2		P3		Total	
	N	Attention (%)	N	Attention (%)	N	Attention (%)	Avg. N	Avg. Attention (%)
L1	6	65.8	4	81	7	56	17	68
L2	10	63	12	59.5	10	57	32	60
L3	2	35	2	75	1	40	5	50

The number (N) of Marketers' who selected each location per page and their average perceived attention for each location per page.

shown was the live version and the advert in question was injected on one of the three locations randomly keeping the balance between the three locations. Stimuli (webpages and advert creation) were the three pages that were given during the marketers' questionnaire.

3.3   Data Analysis

The study findings are discussed with respect to the attention that users gave to the advert on the three locations and three pages in relation to the marketers' perceived attention. Then we discuss how this relates with the actual budget that an advertisee will need to spend or ends up overpaying. During the two studies data collected included gaze points, fixations of participants, percentage of visitors attending to the ad, time to first fixations and attention bounce rate and marketers' percentage of perceived attention.

Table 1 shows the cumulative data as per the marketers' location selection. Attention column represents the average attention percentage that the marketers gave for the associate location and page. N represents the total number of the participants that selected the associated location for each page. It is important to note that L2 was selected the most throughout the three pages with an average of 60% perceived attention. This means that most of the marketers would place an ad creative on the second location which is on the right hand side and above the fold of the page and would expect an attention of 60%. On the other hand, the highest attention score was given on the first location even though the specific location was not selected.

Figure 2 shows the scores that each page and location received as per the advertising experts' opinion and perception. Location L2 received almost the same attention score throughout the page. This shows that marketers expect that this location is consistent throughout the pages and "secures" a 60% attention score. Further, L3 receives consistently the lowest score between the three locations for each page. This implies that there is a perception of less attention between the above and below the fold page areas.

During the eyetracking study data collected and used for quantitative analysis included gaze time, dwell time, and first fixation. Table 2 shows the data as per the location per page with a focus on the number of users that actually saw the investigated ad in a percentage score. The rest of the scores are averages between the users as given by the software.

Table 2. Data collected from EyeTracking Study

Website	Location	Users Actual Attention	Time to See Effectiveness	Dwell (seconds)	Observation Length
P1	L1	73.68	70.7	32.260788	2085
P1	L2	36.67	34.31	6.567597	597
P1	L3	26.1	19.75	4.7165502	786
P2	L1	44.44	43.52	1.7078292	427
P2	L2	63.64	49.32	1.890108	270
P2	L3	41.67	33.68	1.050084	210
P3	L1	73.9	72.64	12.6445228	658
P3	L2	45	42.08	8.136	904
P3	L3	34.8	26.27	3.719721	465

Eyetracking data per page and location: User's actual attention

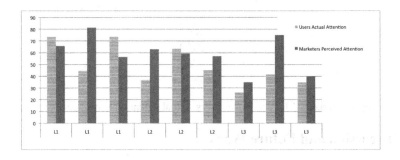

Fig. 3. Marketers' Perception vs Users Actual Attention Scores

Figure 3 demonstrates the two attention scores collected from marketers and users respectively. One can easily notice that out of the 9 scores given only two of them are lower than the actual users' attention. This implies that marketers tend to overestimate the attention that an advert will receive. In order to notice the difference between the three locations, the average of all three pages was used to draw the chart shown on Figure 4. As the figure shows, marketers have a correct understanding of the overall attention flow but they overestimate the amount of attention that the location will receive. In addition, it is important to note that L3 receives the least attention, something that was concluded previously as well.

In order to interpret the location attention overestimation from marketers with respect to the budget, each location was assigned a Cost Per Mille (CPM). The CPMs used were based on the amounts that one of the page advertises and are: L1:€5, L2=€7 and L3=€2. Table3 lists the difference in the two attention scores as well as the respective cost difference in money-wise. Figure5 demonstrates this difference in cost and attention perception. As the figure demonstrates, even though the highest attention discrepancy is on the third location, the highest cost in the second location due to the most expensive CPM. As most advertisees will tend to select the second location, advertisers will make more money due to this location.

Table 3. Comparing Marketers' Perception and Users' Actual Attention

Locations	Users Actual Attention	Marketers Perceived Attention	Discrepancy	Overpay	CPM
L1	64	67.8	3.82	19.1	5
L2	48.4	59.9	11.4	80	7
L3	34.2	50	15.8	31.6	2

Users' and Marketers' attention per location demonstrating the difference in attention and budget allocation

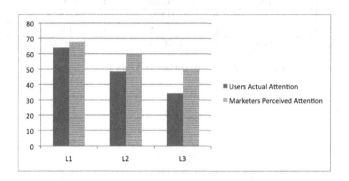

Fig. 4. Marketers' Perception vs Users Actual Attention Scores per Location

4   Discussion and Future Work

As the data revealed, location L2 was selected the most throughout the three pages with an average of 60% perceived attention even though the highest perceived attention score was assigned to the top location, L1. This shows that even though the top location would receive the highest attention, marketers tend to select the right hand side location. This aligns with other studies that users and potential customers tend to recall and recognize adverts that are on the same area with the main content of the page as their peripheral vision "looks" on the creative for a better qualitative time. Further, data showed that there is a perception that adverts placed below the fold of the page do not receive much attention and they are not selected to be presented. This is also supported with the eye tracking data.

The eye tracking evaluation revealed an interesting observation: *Marketers tend to overestimate the attention each ad location receives and underestimate its true cost.* As per the results there is a discrepancy between the marketers' perceived attention and the actual user attention on the adverts. Transforming this discrepancy with the allocated CPM per location reveals that advertising on the middle of the page costs more and with the highest discrepancy. This result should be noted by both marketers and advertisers in order to provide and distribute their budget on the right locations.

One of the limitations with this study was that the eye tracking study was performed on the live sites. This caused the injection of the advert to fail on some cases limiting the number of participants that saw the specific site. However, both pilot studies will be followed by an extensive and bigger in sample size in order to collect more data. This will provide more robust conclusions to implement the prediction framework. For

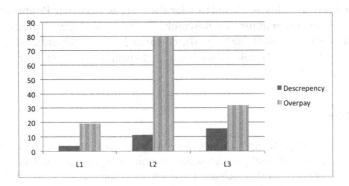

Fig. 5. Score and Budget Descrepency

example, data will provide the impact of location, ad creation type, ad size and website content in relation to user's attention and perception.

5   Conclusions

This paper presents the pilot study of a project for which the main aim is to implement an evaluation methodology service for the identification of the best locations on Cypriot web space based on eye tracking studies. This study demonstrates the correlation between user attention, advert types and actual market value.

Further data are being collected in order to form more robust conclusions. However, this pilot study revealed conclusions that could form the basis towards predicting ad effectiveness of webpages with the use of ad number, location, size, and type. The results of the project will be based on a large sample of eye-tracking measurements (500 participants, on 2000 adverting location in top performing Cyprus websites). The methodology combines factors such as the advertising budget, target audience, advertising spot pricing, internet reach, and a number of eye-tracking metrics in an optimization framework to pin-point the best campaign placement allocation.

Currently, online advertisement placement is highly subjective and is performed by an advertising agent who typically chooses the position based of his personal experience, generic statistical data and on the motto that "the higher the position of the ad on the page, the more effective". Questions such as "Which advertising locations has to be chosen by an agent in order to optimize the effectiveness and maximize the visibility of an online campaign?" will be answered using this framework. This innovative project would benefit anyone who want to advertise on the Web since it will be based on factual research with an eye tracker and volunteers from Cyprus. Advertising will now be based on facts, not just speculative statistics. The outcome of this project will help the future of advertisement on the Web. Eyetracking should be used as an alternative medium of examining and developing the most effective advert campaign, ensuring that users will look on the ad and money spent are worth spreaded throughout the websites.

Acknowledgment. This work falls under the Cyprus Research Promotion Foundations Framework Programme for Research, Technological Development and Innovation 2009-2010 (DESMI 2009-2010), co-funded by the Republic of Cyprus and the European Regional Development Fund, and specifically under Grant EPIXEIRI-SIS/PROION/0311.

References

[1] Buscher, G., Dumais, S.T., Cutrell, E.: The good, the bad, and the random: an eye-tracking study of ad quality in web search. In: Proceedings of the 33rd International ACM SIGIR Conference on Research and Development in Information Retrieval, SIGIR 2010, pp. 42–49. ACM, New York (2010), doi:10.1145/1835449.1835459

[2] Castagnos, S., Pu, P.: Consumer decision patterns through eye gaze analysis. In: Proceedings of the 2010 Workshop on Eye Gaze in Intelligent Human Machine Interaction, EGIHMI 2010, pp. 78–85. ACM, New York (2010), doi:10.1145/2002333.2002346

[3] Djamasbi, S., Siegel, M., Tullis, T.: Generation y, web design, and eye tracking. International Journal of Human-Computer Studies 68(5), 307 (2010), doi:10.1016/j.ijhcs.2009.12.006

[4] Hsieh, Y.C., Chen, K.H.: How different information types affect viewer's attention on internet advertising. Computers in Human Behavior 27(2), 935–945 (2011), doi:10.1016/j.chb.2010.11.019, Web 2.0 in Travel and Tourism: Empowering and Changing the Role of Travelers

[5] Wang, K., Chang, H.-L., Chen, S.-H.: The effects of forced ad exposure on the web. Journal of Informatics & Electronics 3, 27–38 (2008)

[6] Kuisma, J., Simola, J., Uusitalo, L., Oorni, A.: The effects of animation and format on the perception and memory of online advertising. Journal of Interactive Marketing 24(4), 269 (2010), doi:10.1016/j.intmar

[7] Lin, Y.L., Chen, Y.W.: Effects of ad types, positions, animation lengths, and exposure times on the click-through rate of animated online advertisings. Computers & Industrial Engineering 57(2), 580–591 (2009), doi:10.1016/j.cie.2008.08.011, Challenges for Advanced Technology

[8] Luo, W., Cook, D., Karson, E.J.: Search advertising placement strategy: Exploring the efficacy of the conventional wisdom. Information & Management 48(8), 404–411 (2011), doi:10.1016/j.im.2011.10.001

[9] McCoy, S., Everard, A., Polak, P., Galletta, D.F.: The effects of online advertising. Commun ACM 50(3), 84–88 (2007), doi:10.1145/1226736.1226740

[10] Sorce, P., Dewitz, A.: The Case for Print Media Advertising in the Internet Age. A Research Monograph of the Printing Industry Center at RIT. No (2006)

[11] Wang, J.C., Day, R.F.: The effects of attention inertia on advertisements on the www. Computers in Human Behavior 23(3), 1390–1407 (2007), doi:10.1016/j.chb.2004.12.014, Including the Special Issue: Avoiding Simplicity, Confronting Complexity: Advances in Designing Powerful Electronic Learning Environments

Exploring the Impact of Users' Preference Diversity on Recommender System Performance

Muh-Chyun Tang

Department of Library and Information Science, National Taiwan University, Taipei, Taiwan
mctang@ntu.edu.tw

Abstract. Recommender systems present an effective alternative to subject access in the domain of reading for leisure. They are particular valuable for the discovery of novel and serendipitous finds. In the recommender system evaluation literature, a trade-off has been recognized between accuracy and surprise/non-obviousness, and more recently, that between accuracy and diversity of the recommendation set. It is argued in this paper that a proper balance between accuracy and diversity might lie in users' "preference diversity," a construct we propose to represent how wide a user's reading interests are. Users with more diverse interests might appreciate more novel and diverse set of recommendation. Drawing from marketing literature and our own empirical studies, this paper discusses how the motivation for diversity might influence users' preference for cultural goods such as books and music, and more specifically their responses to recommendations. Future study is needed to further examine the relationship between user preference diversity and proper degree of diversity of the recommendation set.

Keywords: Recommender Systems, Preference Development, Preference Diversity, Social Book Search.

1   Introduction

1.1   Recommendation and Book Finding

The access to books, especially books for leisure, presents a unique challenge to searching. While traditional IR is based on the assumption that topical relevance is somewhat attainable between a query and a document, users' preference for imaginary works such as books and music is more subjective and their needs for such works are much more difficult to be represented by queries. On the one hand, it has been known to be problematic to provide subject access to imaginary works as they are created to entertain and inspire instead of imparting knowledge on a certain subject [1]. In the context of traditional human indexing, it is difficult to anticipate what contents, subjects, or topics a reader might be interested in at the indexing time. Even with the growing capability of full-text searching with books, it is seldom the case when the reading experience sought by the users can be easily expressed with queries and matched by words in a book. It has been shown that in the library setting, compared to subject search, known items search accounted for the great majority of

F.F.-H. Nah (Ed.): HCIB/HCII 2014, LNCS 8527, pp. 681–689, 2014.
© Springer International Publishing Switzerland 2014

OPAC use as users often rely on sources in their information environment sources for interesting things to read [2]. A study of library user searching for fictions also showed that, the effort spent in browsing the search results was much a greater contributor to user satisfaction with the search results than the effort invested in querying [3].

The advance of social media presents a cue-rich information environment for seeking interesting books to read, an area where traditional IR devices is less effective. Recommender systems provide an ideal alternative to the access of books for leisure as they are able to circumvent the thorny issue of representing the content and user needs on the two sides of IR process, therefore greatly reduce users' search cost. Furthermore, recommender systems are particularly valuable for content discovery and exploration where, unlike in the task oriented search context, users might not have a clear idea about what exactly they are looking for [4,5]. They are often able to bring attention to users potentially interesting items that they will otherwise not be aware of, thus adding serendipity to the book finding process. User-generated contents in the form of reader reviews also provide necessary cues for the judgment of books, which greatly reduce readers' transaction cost. Indeed, there here have been efforts to utilize user-generated contents from Amazon and LibraryThing for book searching and recommendation [6,7].

While the early development of recommender systems has been driven by accuracy based evaluation metrics, there have been calls for a broader set of evaluation criteria, especially those dimensions that reflect user experiences [8,9]. One of the consistent issues in the design and evaluation of recommender systems is the balance between accuracy and "non-obviousness" of recommendations [10]. While the recommendation of accurate, yet previously known items might foster user confidence, their presence represents less novelty and serendipity. Another related issue that has also drawn growing attention is the "diversity" of interests reflected in the recommended set [11,12]. One of the assumptions based on which recommender systems operate is that users with similar profile in the past will have similar preference in the future. Therefore recommender algorithms rely heavily on similarity measures. However, it has been pointed out that recommended items generated in the traditional accuracy driven algorithms might become too similar to each other. As a result, it is feared that recommender systems might produce highly homogeneous and popular items and leave out the niche items that are of potential interests to the user. To address such a concern, there have been recent efforts to solve the apparent diversity-accuracy trade-off in the recommended list [13-16].

Another way to look at the "accuracy-nonobviousness" or "accuracy-diversity" dilemma might be taking into account the psychological traits of the users. It is easy to imagine that there are users who prefer accurate recommendations while others are more open to exploring novel items. We take the position that there is no one-size-fits-all recommendation technique to all users. Instead, recommender techniques should be applied adaptively to users of various kinds of psychological traits. In this article we proposed the construct of "preference diversity" to denote how wide an individual's reading interests are. We believe that, to solve the dilemma between recommendation accuracy and diversity, the system needs to take into account how diverse the users' interests are. In other words, for users with wider reading interests, a more diverse recommendation list might be appreciated more and vise versa. In the following sections we will the development of the construct from literature in marketing and personality psychology. Drawing from our previous research, we also provided evidences regarding how users' preference diversity might influence the performance of different book-finding tools on social media.

2   Literature Review

2.1   User Preference Characteristics and Recommendation Strategies

With the growing popularity of personalized recommender systems in e-commerce sites, their application and impact in marketing have also drawn growing interests. Unlike in computer science where the dominant interest is in algorithm development, in marketing literature more attention has been given to the psychological traits of the consumers that might influence the effectiveness of the recommender systems. Here the focus has been on how to strategically apply recommendation techniques for consumers with different cognitive and affective traits such as personalities [17], cultural orientations [18], and preference development [19]. The construct of "preference development" is particularly interesting as it challenges the fundamental assumption of recommender system, that is, that users have well-defined and reasonably stable preferences so data of users' past buying/browsing behaviors can be used to infer their future preference. Furthermore, users all have sufficient insight into their preference so that they are capable to recognize the customized offers that best match their needs. According to Simonson [19], the concept of "preference development" can be further distinguished into two dimensions: "preference stability", which refers to the extent to which consumers have stable, well-defined preference; and "preference insight", which refers to the degree of self-knowledge consumers have about their preference. Though first proposed in a broader context of customization of products and services in general, we found the concept of "preference development" particularly useful for the conceptualization of leisure book readers' relationship with the recommender systems. Without the assumption of preference stability, it will be difficult for the system to apply what it learns in the past to infer users' preference in the future, and without preference insight, the users might not be able to readily recognize the items that best serve their needs. In their study involving movie recommendations, Shen and Ball [20] found that user who have higher self-assessed preference stability appreciate customized offering more and have a more favorable attitude to the learning relationship when recommendations are customized. Also conducted in the context of movie recommendation, Kwon et al. [21] found that the effectiveness of different types of recommendation techniques depended on the type of the preference development configuration an individual is in. It was shown that content-based recommendation technique is most effective when the user has high preference stability and preference insight.

2.2   Preference Diversity

Inspired mainly by Simonson's theorization of the relationship between preference development and customization, we have attempted to explore psychological traits that might influence the effectiveness of recommender systems. Three aspects of users' preference structure: knowledge, involvement, and "preference diversity" were proposed in our study of the effectiveness of the different book finding approaches available on aNobii, an online social networking site for book lovers (See Appendix I for the questionnaire text). While preference development and product involvement have been widely studied in users' response to online decision aids in marketing literature, preference "diversity" was a novel construct we created to represent how diverse of an individual's reading interests are.

By "preference diversity" we meant to represent how narrow/wide or diverse/convergent one's reading interests are. Individuals with highly homogenous preference are those who, when choosing books to read, seldom divert much from their favorite genres or authors. Individuals with a diverse preference, on the other hand, are those who have wider reading interests and are less confined to a certain genre or types of readings. The construct of reading diversity was created with the aforementioned trade-off between recommendation accuracy and non-obviousness in mind. It is felt that the proper balance between accuracy and non-obviousness might lie in how willing or motivated a reader is to seek novel experience. We speculate that people with diverse reading interests are more willing to venture out of their familiar genres and favorite authors and therefore more receptive to nonobvious recommendations. More adventurous readers might prefer novelty and serendipity over accuracy. They might also appreciate more a diverse recommendation list. Individuals with more concentrated reading preference, on the other hand, might appreciate familiar genres or authors. We initially wish to come up with a construct to represent how willing a reader is to venture into previously unfamiliar reading interests. Several related psychological constructs that might reflect the willingness to try novelty emerged in our review of literature. The first was the "variety seeking" behaviors in marketing research. Variety-seeking in consumer behavior is defined as the tendency for an individual to switch away from the item consumed on the last occasion[22,23]. It has also been defined more broadly as the tendency of individuals to seek diversity in their choices of service of goods [24]. Three motivating factors for variety seeking behaviors have been identified previously: 1. Satiation/Stimulation induced, or direct variety seeking where the switching is derived from an intrinsic need to avoid boredom and gain more stimulation, which describes the situation where the consumer switch brands just for a change[24], 2. External factors induced, or derived variety seeking where the brand switching is triggered by external factors (e.g. promotion or convenience) or constraint (e.g. out of stock), and 3. Future preference uncertainty induced, where consumers seeking variety to keep a portfolio of options as a hedge against future uncertainties or as a means to preserve their continued interest in favorite options. Variety seeking has been mostly studied from the perspective of brand loyalty and customer retention. Marketers have been interested in the reasons why customers switch brands, especially the occasions of "true" or direct variety seeking. For example, it was found in Van Trijp et al. [25], that relative to repeat purchases, variety seeking behaviors is more likely to occur when the consumers has a higher "need for variety", a low involvement with the product category (in the case of the study, three product categories were chosen: beer, hand-rolled tobacco, and cigarettes), lower strength of preference, lower purchase frequency, and when the product category has a stronger hedonic features. The "need for variety", which was operationalized by the consumer-specific Exploratory Acquisition of Product (EAP) scale [26] designed to capture consumer's tendency to seek sensory stimulation through changing consumption experience, was particularly interesting as it was found to interact with many of the product related variables. For example, the effect of the intrinsic "need for variety" was found to be particularly salient when the product category has stronger hedonic features [25]. The construct of the intrinsic need for variety in consumption seems, at least semantically, to relate to the second psychological construct we came across, namely, "openness to experience" in personality psychology [27,28]. Along with extraversion, agreeableness, conscientiousness, and neuroticism, openness is considered as one of the five fundamental dimension of personality [28]. As the label suggests, "openness to experience" represents a broad aspect of preference for the novel and the diverse in life experience, "an active motivation to seek out the unfamiliar" [27]. Interestingly, it has been shown that "openness to experience" is related to the liking of a variety of types of music outside the mainstream pop music [29]. It was also shown that openness to experience is related to liking for a wide range of music types [30]. These psychological constructs, whether it is variety seeking in consumer behavior or openness to experience in personality psychology, lend support to the idea that a similar personal trait can be created more specifically in the context of book searching. As stated earlier, we suspect that the degree of users' "preference diversity" might influence whether they would favor a more non-obvious book discovering/recommendation method.

2.3   Some Findings

We have conducted an empirical study with an aim to test whether aNobii (a social media site for book lovers) users' preference characteristics might impact the performance of different book finding tools. Among the three book-fining methods tested, browsing known authors' works and browsing similar bookshelves are more accuracy driven, while and browsing friends' bookshelves represent a more exploratory mode of searching. A total of 50 regular aNobii users took part in the study where they were asked to find and save books to read using alternately the three book finding methods. The performance criteria were based on their browsing and saving behaviors and their perception of the tools. We hypothesize that, users' preference characteristics, which were elicited by a pre-search questionnaire, would influence the effectiveness of these three book finding techniques (See figure 1). Our results did indeed indicate that users' psychological traits played a mediating role between the three book finding methods and their performance. It was found that while the known author browsing technique was most effective for users whose preference is more developed and refined, the browsing friends' bookshelves approach was the most effective method for highly-involved readers [9].

Our findings indicated that the degree of preference diversity did somewhat negatively impact the performance of browsing known authors' books than the other two methods: browsing similar bookshelves and friends' bookshelves, which tend to produce books by unfamiliar authors. In other words, the performance of browsing known authors, as measured by percentage of items considered and saved during the search process, tended to be slightly worse, though the result was not statistically significant. It was also found that, from users' perspective, browsing friends' bookshelves was the most interesting and the most effective method in terms of broadening

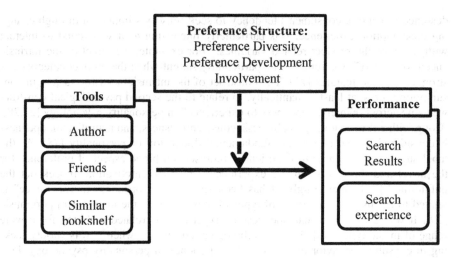

Fig. 1. Graphic presentation of the relationship among the variables

users' reading horizon. The other interesting finding was that users with high reading preference diversity also found browsing similar bookshelves less effective in expanding their reading horizon, a performance criterion designed to reflect the learning aspect of exploratory tool use [4]. As Table 1 shows, a negative main effect of author browsing and a negative interaction effect between preference diversity and using similar bookshelves were found on expanding users' reading horizon, which gives another evidence of the mediating role played by preference diversity on system effectiveness.

Table 1. Predictors of "broadening reading horizon"

Dependent variable: horizon expanding	Beta
Diversity	-.07
Tool_Author	-.29**
Tool_Friend	.14
Tool_Similar	-.10
Diversity X Tool_Author	-.06
Diversity X Tool_Friend	-.08
Diversity X Tool_Similar	-.18*

**<.01, *<.05

Besides the questionnaire instrument designed to measure users' preference diversity, we have been also exploring non-obtrusive ways of its measurement. This is done by observing the network configuration of a user's bookshelf. Using the books owned by a user to represent her/his reading interests, our method involves observing how connected these books are. Intuitively, the higher connectivity among the books owned by a user, the less diverse her/his reading interests ought to be. With the book-book co-ownership data available on aNobii, the books in each individual bookshelf can be represented as a book-book similarity network. The number of components or other meaningful clustering in a user's book-book similarity network can then be used as a measurement of her/his reading preference diversity. In other words, the more components in the network of books in an individual's bookshelf, the higher her/his reading diversity is. Indeed, the method we proposed, which involved counting the number of component in the network, has been shown to be moderately correlated with users' self-assessed reading diversity [31].

3   Discussion and Conclusion

Previous researches in recommender system have most been driven by prediction accuracy. However, recently we have seen more efforts to explore other evaluation criteria such as novelty and diversity that reflect important aspects of user experience with the system. In marketing literature, efforts have been made to look into how users' preference development and other psychological traits might influence their response to different recommendation techniques, with a view to adaptively applying different recommendation techniques with users in different preference development stages. The concept of users' "preference diversity" was proposed that aimed to represent how narrow/wide or diverse/convergent one's reading interests are. There seems to be conceptual overlapping between reading diversity and stability as both reflect how changeable an individual's reading interests are. But there are also significant differences. One can imagine a reader who has diverse yet stable reading interests and an individual who has a very discerning taste yet at the same time is open to trying new things. While as Simonson pointed out, "preference stability" is essential for the recommender system to establish an effective learning relationship with its users, we are more interested in how the users with different degrees of reading diversity might respond to the recommended items. Even though novelty and diversity have attracted increasing attention in recommender system research, so far little research has been done to explore the relationship between readers' preference diversity and the diversity of the list of recommended items. A future research is needed to test such a relationship.

References

1. Lancaster, F.W., Association, L.: Indexing and abstracting in theory and practice. Library Association London (1991)
2. Tang, M.C.: A study of academic library users' decision-making process: a Lens model approach. Journal of Documentation 65(6), 938–957 (2009)
3. Oksanen, S., Vakkari, P.: In: search of a good novel, neither reading activity nor querying matter, but examining search results does. Paper presented at the Proceedings of the 4th Information Interaction in Context Symposium, Nijmegen, The Netherlands,
4. Marchionini, G.: Exploratory search: from finding to understanding. Communications of the ACM 49(4), 41–46 (2006)
5. White, R.W., Roth, R.A.: Exploratory search: Beyond the query-response paradigm. Synthesis Lectures on Information Concepts, Retrieval, and Services 1(1), 1–98 (2009)

6. Koolen, M., Kazai, G., Kamps, J., Preminger, M., Doucet, A., Landoni, M.: Overview of the INEX, social book search track. In: Copyright cG2012 remains with the author/owner (s). The unreviewed pre-proceedings are collections of work submitted before the December workshops. They are not peer reviewed, are not quality controlled, and contain known errors in content and editing. The proceedings, published after the Workshop, is the authoritative reference for the work done at INEX, p. 77 (2012)

7. Huurdeman, H., Kamps, J., Koolen, M., van Wees, J.: Using Collaborative Filtering in Social Book Search, p. 125 (2012)

8. Konstan, J.A., Riedl, J.: Recommender systems: from algorithms to user experience. User Modeling and User-Adapted Interaction 22(1-2), 101–123 (2012)

9. Tang, M.C., Sie, Y.J., Ting, P.H.: Evaluating books finding tools on social media: A case study of aNobii. Information Processing & Management 50(1), 54–68 (2014)

10. Herlocker, J.L., Konstan, J.A., Terveen, L.G., Riedl, J.T.: Evaluating collaborative filtering recommender systems. ACM Transactions on Information Systems (TOIS) 22(1), 5–53 (2004)

11. McNee, S.M., Riedl, J., Konstan, J.A.: Being accurate is not enough: how accuracy metrics have hurt recommender systems. In: CHI 2006 Extended Abstracts on Human Factors in Computing Systems, pp. 1097–1101. ACM (2006)

12. Pu, P., Chen, L., Hu, R.: A user-centric evaluation framework for recommender systems. In: Proceedings of the Fifth ACM Conference on Recommender Systems, pp. 157–164. ACM (2011)

13. Zhou, T., Kuscsik, Z., Liu, J.-G., Medo, M., Wakeling, J.R., Zhang, Y.-C.: Solving the apparent diversity-accuracy dilemma of recommender systems. Proceedings of the National Academy of Sciences 107(10), 4511–4515 (2010)

14. Vargas, S., Castells, P.: Rank and relevance in novelty and diversity metrics for recommender systems. In: Proceedings of the Fifth ACM Conference on Recommender Systems, pp. 109–116. ACM (2011)

15. Zhang, M., Hurley, N.: Avoiding monotony: improving the diversity of recommendation lists. In: Proceedings of the 2008 ACM Conference on Recommender Systems, pp. 123–130. ACM (2008)

16. Bradley, K., Smyth, B.: Improving recommendation diversity. In: Proceedings of the Twelfth National Conference in Artificial Intelligence and Cognitive Science (AICS 2001), pp. 75–84. Citeseer (2001)

17. Wang, H.C., Doong, H.S.: Online customers' cognitive differences and their impact on the success of recommendation agents. Information & Management 47(2), 109–114 (2010)

18. Kramer, T., Spolter-Weisfeld, S., Thakkar, M.: The effect of cultural orientation on consumer responses to personalization. Marketing Science 26(2), 246–258 (2007)

19. Simonson, I.: Determinants of customers' responses to customized offers: conceptual framework and research propositions. Journal of Marketing 69(1), 32–45 (2005)

20. Shen, A., Ball, A.D.: Preference stability belief as a determinant of response to personalized recommendations. Journal of Consumer Behaviour 10(2), 71–79 (2011)

21. Kwon, K., Cho, J., Park, Y.: Influences of customer preference development on the effectiveness of recommendation strategies. Electronic Commerce Research and Applications 8(5), 263–275 (2009)

22. Givon, M.: Variety seeking through brand switching. Marketing Science 3(1), 1–22 (1984)

23. Kahn, B.E., Kalwani, M.U., Morrison, D.G.: Measuring variety-seeking and reinforcement behaviors using panel data. Journal of Marketing Research, 89-100 (1986)

24. Kahn, B.E.: Consumer variety-seeking among goods and services: An integrative review. Journal of Retailing and Consumer Services 2(3), 139–148 (1995)

25. Van Tripj, H., Hoyer, W.D., Inman, J.J.: Why Switch? Product Category-Level Explanations for True Variety-Seeking Behavior. Journal of Marketing Research 33(3) (1996)
26. Baumgartner, H., Steenkamp, J.-B.E.M.: Exploratory consumer buying behavior: Conceptualization and measurement. International Journal of Research in Marketing 13(2), 121–137 (1996), http://dx.doi.org/10.1016/0167-8116
27. McCrae, R.R., Costa Jr., P.T.: Conceptions and correlates of openness to experience (1997)
28. McCrae, R.R.: Openness to experience: Expanding the boundaries of Factor V. European Journal of Personality 8(4), 251–272 (1994)
29. Dollinger, S.J.: Research note: Personality and music preference: extraversion and excitement seeking or openness to experience? Psychology of Music 21(1), 73–77 (1993)
30. Rawlings, D., Ciancarelli, V.: Music preference and the five-factor model of the NEO Personality Inventory. Psychology of Music 25(2), 120–132 (1997)
31. Tang, M.-C., Ke, Y.-L., Sie, Y.-J.: The Estimation of aNobii Users' Reading Diversity Using Book Co-ownership Data: A Social Analytical Approach. In: Jatowt, A., Lim, E.-P., Ding, Y., Miura, A., Tezuka, T., Dias, G., Tanaka, K., Flanagin, A., Dai, B.T. (eds.) SocInfo 2013. LNCS, vol. 8238, pp. 274–283. Springer, Heidelberg (2013)

Appendix I. Text of the Questionnaire Instruments for Preference Characteristics

Factors	Items
Preference development	I have little difficulty judging whether I would enjoy a previously unread work
	I have a fairly good idea about what I want to read
	I know where to find books that might be of interest to me
	I have trusted book alerting sources, which I follow faithfully
	I trust my own judgment of books and am not easily swayed by others
Preference diversity	*I rarely venture out of the authors or genres that I have enjoyed
	My reading interests are rather broad and hard to be pigeon-holed
	I constantly try out unfamiliar authors or genres
	*My reading interests are fairly stable
Involvement	I keep a habit of reading, even when I am busy
	I keep monitoring new publications for interesting things to read
	How important would you say reading is to you?

*the scores were reversed in accordance to the semantics of the factor

A Usability Evaluation of an Electronic Health Record System for Nursing Documentation Used in the Municipality Healthcare Services in Norway

Torunn Kitty Vatnøy, Grete Vabo, and Mariann Fossum

Department of Health and Nursing Science, Faculty of Health and Sport Sciences,
University of Agder, University of Agder, P.O. Box 509,
4898 Grimstad, Norway
{torunn.vatnoy,grete.vabo,mariamm.fosum}@uia.no

Abstract. The paper presents a usability evaluation of the Graphical User Interface (GUI) of an Electronic Health Record System (EHR). The topic of interest was to explore the system's usability in the context of nursing process documentation. A cognitive walk through approach was used. The data were analyzed with content analysis and the results show that challenges identified were related to navigating and finding information in the system. Even though there were problems in progressing from one phase to another in nursing process documentation, the system represented some types of predictability and consistency in the functions. Education, training and support are needed to be able to use the EHR for nursing documentation. Mandating standardization regarding format, content and terminology to improve the EHR systems functionality regarding facilitate nursing process documentation is recommended.

Keywords: Electronic Health Record, Usability evaluation, Nursing documentation, Nursing process.

1 Introduction

Information technology (IT) systems are developed for the purpose of supporting quality by facilitating work and information flow. Electronic Health Record Systems (EHRs) are IT systems developed and implemented in the healthcare services over the last twenty years. According to Norwegian law, the EHRs have to contain information related to the patient's need for healthcare and the background for the needs including the health care given to patients [1]. Healthcare professionals are obliged to document these in the EHRs [2]. The main purpose of the EHRs is to support the information flow and working processes and reduce costs in healthcare and welfare services [3-5]

IT systems are implemented with varying success [5-7]EHRs included [8, 9]. The implementation success depends on several factors [6, 10]. System quality in terms of usability is one of these critical factors for success [6].

Usability refers to the interactive products, capacity to enable users to perform their tasks in a safe and efficient manner[11, 12]. Usability objectives are that the system is effective, efficient and safe to use, and that it has good utility, is easy to

F.F.-H. Nah (Ed.): HCIB/HCII 2014, LNCS 8527, pp. 690–699, 2014.
© Springer International Publishing Switzerland 2014

learn and easy to remember how to use [12]. Usability engineering methods are essential for conducting evaluations in order to improve the system's usability [13]. Usability seems to be an important factor for adoption of computer-based nursing documentation systems [14, 15].

This study examines the usability of one of the most widespread EHRs used in municipalities in Norway [16]. The data are compiled and summarized according to a qualitative approached in order to highlight the effects on nursing process documentation [11].

2   Aim

The aim of this study is to evaluate the usability of the Graphical User Interface (GUI) of an EHR in order to explore the system's usability regarding nursing documentation.

3   Background

Nursing documentation was imposed by Norwegian law in 2001 [2]. Knowledge about the importance of systematic documentation represented to support quality in individual nursing care has its history back to when modern nursing evolved in the late 1800s [17]. According to Kärkkäinen et al. (2005), nursing documentation should contribute to make individualized patient's care visible [18]. EHRs represent expectations of improved healthcare service, but several factors impact and challenge the outcome of electronic nursing documentation [5, 19, 20]. The GUI of the systems, design quality, feature functionality as well as project management, procurement, users' and the end users' previous experience are factors of importance [14]. Different requirements from different professional users adapted to different areas and marketed from different vendors, impact development of the EHRs. This complex picture challenges a national EHR implementation project [21].

Häyrinen et al. (2010) stated that although EHRs may facilitate standardized nursing documentation based on the nursing process,[1] use of the nursing process varies across patients. Häyrinen et al. (2010) found that there was a lack of continuity, and nursing process systematics in the documentation [9]. Vabo (2013) noted similar findings in a Norwegian study [22]. Clinical decision support systems (CDSSs) integrated in the EHR have the potential to significantly improve the quality of nursing care and documentation [19]. Fossum et al. (2011) found that lack of training, resistance to use computers and limited integration of CDSS, created difficulty in using the CDSS within the EHR and the poorly designed GUI represents barriers.

According to Kellermann et al. (2013), the efficiency of implementation of healthcare systems is not in proportion to what was expected. This is largely due to poor adoption connected with systems that are neither easy to use nor interoperable [5]. Kellermann et al. (2013) highlight the need for standardized systems that are easy to

---

[1] The nursing process defined by four phases; 1. Needs assessment, includes the patient's health data, 2.Determining of nursing diagnoses and nursing care aims, 3. Planning and delivering nursing interventions, and 4. The evaluation og outcomes [8].

use and interoperable, as well as promoting accountability of health care providers to reengineer processes to benefit from the efficiencies offered by health IT [5]. Keenan et al. (2013) recommend standardization of format, content and words used in nursing documentation. Further, they recommend usability testing to ensure that tools in the EHRs facilitate a shared understanding of the patients' care plan [23]. There is also a need for an international terminology in EHR development to support semantic interoperability [21]. The business issues by comparing vendors may be contributing to the development of standardization of EHRs delay [24].

There may also be a predefined goal that implementation of EHRs should contribute to increased time for patient care by decreasing time for documentation. A systematic literature review concludes that this is not realized [25]. An important factor for user acceptance of computer-based nursing documentation systems is how the systems' functionality is able to support nurses' workflow [26].

4   Method

The usability evaluation method used in this study is based on the cognitive walkthrough (CW) approach. This approach is a task analysis focusing on how well a task can be completed while using the system, and how easy it is to learn and use the system. The method investigates how the system's cues assist the users in performing tasks by exploring and learning, rather than knowing how to use the system[11, 27]. The method identifies sequences where typical users will succeed or fail with the aim to systematically identify and characterize failure situations [28].

4.1   Sample

Eight participants were included in the test panel. According to Nielsen and Landauer [27], eight participants is an appropriate number in a small project to explore usability [27]. The sample contains eight registered nurses (RNs) in the municipal healthcare services. Electronic literacy refers to the ability to use the advantages inherent in electronic tools for reading and writing [29], and it is important to aspire to avoid the participants individual electronic literacy's impact on the evaluating test. Inclusion criteria were that the participants used IT daily, and that they were using another EHR system as a tool for their daily documentation of nursing and to provide statutory demands for documentation in their daily practice.

4.2   Procedure

The test is a synchronous remote usability evaluation [30]. The test was performed in a test laboratory with a one-way mirror. The test persons were asked to think-aloud while performing the tasks according to the presented nursing scenario. A moderator was sitting next to the RNs, reminding the RNs to think-aloud. A researcher in the observation room observed the RNs` actions, reactions and the screenshots. The entire usability test was videotaped. A small survey was used to measure the user satisfaction at the end of the session supplied by a free text questionnaire.

The test scenario used was a typical situation where they should document nursing care for a patient currently living in a nursing home. The scenario focuses on nutrition and a dehydration health problem. The situation was logically arranged according to use of the nursing processes in four phases: Assessments, including the patient's health data. Determining of nursing diagnoses and nursing care aims. Planning and delivering nursing interventions. Evaluation of outcomes [9].

To avoid bias regarding attitudes toward the system, the participants were told not to talk to each other about their experiences while performing the test.

The participants were logged onto the system when the test scenario started. The first task described was: Go to the patient's journal. Further steps were to find the information regarding the patient's nutrition status. Where would you intuitively go to find it? Determine the nursing diagnosis and determine aims relevant for the patient. Enter the intervention; "measure the consumption of drinking". Enter data about what the patient ate and drank for supper (evaluation outcome). Store the data that has been entered. Finally, navigate out of the patient journal, and go to another patient journal.

4.3   Ethical Considerations

The test scenarios were fictitious. The participants in the test gave written consent to participates, and had the option to decline to participate at any time without consequences. It was of importance that the participants felt well under the test situation. To avoid pressures of performance, it was emphasized that this was not a knowledge or a skills test.

5   Analyze and Results

The video records, screenshots, survey and results from the free text questions were transcribed and analyzed with qualitative content analysis [31]. The analyses focuses on the manifest content, meaning that the transcribed text is analyzed to describes the visible and obvious components [31]. The data from the survey were analyzed using descriptive statistics.

The video files were transcribed and analyzed according to three perspectives: what the participants said and how they interacted with the system. Which movements the participants made in the GUI, and what help and guidance the participants needed to accomplish the tasks. Time, from start to the end, was measured and calculated. The coding categories according from which data were analyzed were classic aspects of Human Computer Interaction (HCI), and are described as: information content that concerns whether the information system provides too much or too little information; comprehensiveness, graphics and text which concerns whether a computer display is understandable for to the subject or not; problem of navigation is an aspect that concerns whether the subjects have difficulty finding the desired information or computer screen; and the last aspect is overall system understandability that concerns whether the icons, required computer operations and system messages are understandable [11]. All participants considered themselves as experienced IT users. Further they considered themselves as experienced users of EHRs, two of whom stated to be experts.

5.1   Information Content

All participants, except one, reported that there was too much information in the main GUI and referred to toolbars, buttons and menus. On the other hand, they found there to be a lack of information about their functions in the system. They found it confusing that toolbar buttons were presented both vertically and horizontally, and the explaining text induced by the cursor was considered to be imprecise.

Finding information where it was expected to be found, was rated low by the participants (table 1). When looking for information about the patient's nutrition status, no such information was found. In this purpose, all participants were looking for a tab providing access to the patient's care plan where information about the patient's health data was obviously expected to be. None of the participants was sure where to move, and they had three different suggestions where information of the patient's health data was expected to be found. Two tabs in the screen were denoted with the word "plan" in a combination, and it was not clear which should be selected for the current purpose.

Information in the system that promoted clinical decision support was considered as positive by all the participants. Some of the participants were surprised by achieving this type of information. It was expressed that this contributed to saving time, and was regarded as a manual or reminder about what was to be written in the current area.

5.2   Comprehensiveness, Graphics and Text

Whether the functions were organized in a logical way was ranked rather low by the participants (table 1). The participants needed guidance to progress from one step to another in documentation according to the test scenario. The problems seemed to be both selecting the correct level in the three structures and then selecting the correct tab for the current phase in the nursing process.

Which levels or tabs should be selected was not clear to the participants when entering data into the system, or when retrieving data from the system. Some tabs' titles in the same GUI was imprecise regarding the text term; hence, this made it difficult to know which options to choose for the given task. For example which of two tabs to choose; "report" or "evaluation" in order to document according to phase four in the nursing process. One of the participants said: "This was not easy. I like to enter evaluation report, but do not understand how to do it. This is what makes nurses with less IT literacy than me confused".

5.3   Issues of Navigation

According to the survey, issues in navigation are rated high by the participants (table 1). The size of the letters, the text and the button were considered to be too small. This result corresponds to the video and screenshot data where the participants are striving to find the function that they need to accomplish the tasks. They tried different icons along the toolbar and the menus.

When performing the task, Looking up the patient journal, all participants failed by trying to enter the patient's name, using the cursor and searching over the GUI.

All participants except one need guidance to find the patient's journal. The average time to locate the patient's journal was 2 min. 40 sec. The one who found the patient's journal without guidance used 1 min and 45 sec. The patient's journal was found by using the icon "patient journal" on the toolbar. This function allowed access to the patient's index file.

To complete the test scenario, the participants used average 17.58 min. (min 14.14, max: 23.14).

Table 1. How the participants answered their perceived user satisfaction (n=8)*

	1	2	3	4	5	6	7
The features of the system supported my needs	0	2	2	0	1	2	2
The features of the system worked as I expected	0	1	3	2	1	0	1
The available features of the system were satisfactory	0	0	2	3	1	1	1
The system was easy to use	2	1	1	3	1	0	0
The system was pleasant to use	0	3	3	1	1	0	0
The system was flexible	0	1	4	2	1	0	0
It was easy to navigate the system	2	3	1	2	0	0	0
Letter size was appropriate	1	2	2	1	0	2	0
The font was appropriate	1	0	0	2	1	3	1
The headings that describe the features of the system were meaningful	0	1	3	2	1	0	1
I found the information I needed, where I expected to find it	2	1	3	2	0	0	0
The organizations of the features are evident	1	3	0	1	3	0	0
I found the functionalities of the system where I expected to find them	1	3	3	1	0	0	0
The amount of information was appropriate (not too much or too little)	0	1	2	2	1	2	0
I could complete the documentation by using the main menu	2	2	3	4	0	0	0
I could easily document the nursing using the system	0	2	0	3	1	2	0
They presented the measures in the system were relevant to the issue of patient	0	1	1	1	1	2	2
It was easy to find the data I needed	2	3	0	1	2	0	0
The system supports the work process in relation to the documentation of nursing	0	1	0	3	1	2	1
The system supports all steps of the nursing process	0	0	2	3	0	2	0
Overall I am satisfied with the system's usability in relation to planning and documenting nursing	1	1	1	1	2	2	0

* Distributed on a Likert scale from 1; totally disagree agree to 7; totally agree was used

5.4   Overall System Understandability

Two of the participants expressed explicitly that this system and functions were completely different from the EHR system that they regularly used.

Table 1 shows that the participants, to a limited extent found the functions in the system to be indicatively organized. All participants had problems finding the patient's journal. The observation shows that they all expected to find the journal by writing the patient's name in the presented box, but were not able to find the button to accomplish this. Six of the participants tried the "Enter" button, without results.

All participants had problems entering information into the system, and they all needed guidance to find the function. They had to activate an icon on the toolbar named "new row". This designation was not perceived as descriptive of the function it served. This "new row" button was used by the participants in order to complete the further tasks in the test scenario without guidance. Five of the participants stated that they needed some more time and training to be able to use the system.

The survey shows that the participants to some extent, were positive toward the system`s usability regarding facilitating nursing care planning, and nursing process documentation (table 1).

6   Discussions

The usability problems that challenges the participants in this usability evaluation study correspond to findings in other studies described [5, 14, 19]. The participants were not able to accomplish the tasks presented in the test scenario without guidance from the moderator.

As reflected in the literature, the EHR may be a facilitator regarding continuity and nursing process documentation [9]. Despite the opportunities that information technology entails, Häyrinen, et al. (2010) found a lack of continuity in nursing documentation. The authors suggest that one of the reasons may be due to EHRs systems not supporting the nurses' work flow[9]. The participants in this study could not find information regarding the patients' health data, and it was not intuitive where this information should be found. The lack of logical organization of functions in the system caused problems selecting the correct function for a given task. Further, the participants had problems navigating in the system and the comprehensiveness challenged the documentation in the different phases of the nursing process. Required by Norwegian law, EHRs have to contain information related to the patients need for healthcare and the background for the patient`s needs, including the healthcare given to patients. As the literature describes, nursing documentation may be deficient in many situations [9]. Incomplete nursing documentation and imposition of the law challenge the vendors to develop EHRs that facilitate nursing documentation according to the law. This is currently not the case according to this usability evaluation supported by the literature [24].

Even though the participants stated to be experienced IT and EHR users, they were only to a small extent able to use previous experiences in accomplishing the tasks. Some of the participants explicitly stated that this system worked very differently from the one they knew. This may be a result of the different vendors developing the EHR solutions, and an absence of general demands of standardization according to user interface, functionality, text terms and terminology as the literature suggest [21]. One way to improve the system might be to impose mandated standardized terminology, format and content. Standardization is recommended in the literature in order to both improve ease of use and to facilitate semantic professional terminology. Standardization will also improve communication and understanding among health professionals regarding patient care, and interoperability among healthcare systems [5, 21, 23].

What the participants found to be positive using the system was the information in the system that promoted some type of professional decision support. They consider it as contribution to save time, and to support documentation quality. Previous research indicates that implementation of EHR is not likely to save time in documentation [25]. These findings may be due to the limitations the current generation of EHR represents. According to the literature, CDSSs integrated in the EHRs, have the potential to improve significantly the quality of nursing care and documentation. Even though the findings in this evaluation study indicate a positive contribution to facilitate nursing process based documentation, there are still some challenges to overcome before it becomes effective [19, 32].

Comparing the finding in the survey (table 1) with the findings in the video and screenshot, it does not completely correspond. Overall, the findings from the survey are more positive regarding the system's usability than the observations from the test laboratory. This might be due to the participant's previous experience with EHRs, by not been used to an intuitive user interface [5, 14]. Even though the observation in this usability study suggests that the system is learnable by representing some type of predictability and consistency in the functions, education and training is required to learn to use the EHRs.

7   Conclusions

This usability evaluation shows that poor usability and lack of intuitive user interfaces makes the system difficult to use without knowing the system. According to the literature, it is likely that usability is important to discuss according to other EHR systems. The need for proper education, training and support to be able to use the EHR in the best manner, so that documentation required by law might be safeguarded, is important. To improve the EHR system's functionality regarding facilitating nursing process documentation, it might be necessary to mandate standardization regarding format, content and terminology.

Acknowledgment. Thanks to the nurses that participated in this usability evaluation by giving their time and expertise. In addition thanks to the two data engineers, for invaluable help and patience while setting up and calibrating the usability test laboratory.

References

1. Helse-og omsorgsdepartementet, [Norwegain Ministry of Health and Care Services].: Forskrift om pasientjournal [Regulation on patientrecord]. FOR-2000-12-21-nr.1385 (2000)
2. Helse-og omsorgsdepartementet, [Norwegian Ministry of Health and Care Services].: Lov om Helsepersonel [Act Relating to Health personell]. LOV-1999-07-02-64 (1999)
3. Helse-og omsorgsdepartementet, [Norwegian Ministry of Health and Care Services].: Samhandlingsreformen: Rett behandling - på rett sted - til rett tid Samhandlingsreformen [The Coordination Reform. Proper treatment - at the right place and right time.]. St.meld. nr. 47 Oslo (2009)
4. Lobach, D.F., Detmer D.E.: Research Challenges for Electronic Health Records. American Journal of Preventive Medicine 32(5 suppl.), 104–111 (2007)
5. Kellermann, A., Jones, S.S.: What It Will Take To Achieve The As-Yet-Unfulfilled Promises Of Health Information Technology. HealthAffairs At the intersection of Health Care and Policy 32(1), 63–68 (2013)

6. Delone, W.H., McLean, E.R.: The DeLone and McLean Model of Information Systems Success: A Ten-Year Update. J. Manage. Inf. Syst. 19(4), 9–30 (2003)
7. Berg, M.: Implementing information systems in health care organizations: myths and challenges. International Journal of Medical Informatic 64(2-3), 143–156 (2001)
8. Lærum, O.D.: Den vanskelige journalen The difficult patient record]. Tidsskr Nor Legeforening 132, 1929–1931 (2012)
9. Häyrinen, K., Lammintakanen, J., Saranto, K.: Evaluation of electronic nursing documentation—Nursing process model and standardized terminologies as keys to visible and transparent nursing. International Journal of Medical Informatics 79(8), 554–564 (2010)
10. Petter, S., McLean, E.R.: A meta-analytic assessment of the DeLone and McLean IS success model: An examination of IS success at the individual level. Information & Management 46(3), 159–166 (2009)
11. Kushniruk, A.W., Patel, V.L.: Cognitive and usability engineering methods for the evaluation of clinical information systems. Journal of Biomedical Informatic 37(1), 56–76 (2004)
12. Preece, J., Rogers, Y., Sharp, H.: Interaction design: beyond human-computer interaction. John Wiley&Sons, Inc. (2002)
13. Kushniruk, A.: Evaluation in the design of health information systems: application of approaches emerging from usability engineering. Computers in Biology and Medicine 32(3), 141–1498 (2002)
14. Ludwick, D., Doucette, J.: Adopting electronic medical records in primary care: Lessons learned from health information systems implementation experience in seven countries. International Journal of Medical Informatics 78(1), 22–31 (2009)
15. Ammenwerth, E., Iller, C., Mahler, C.: IT-adoption and the interaction of task, technology and individuals: a fit framework and a case study. BMC Medical Informatics and Decision Making 6(1), 3 (2006)
16. Norsk helsenett [The Norwegian Health Network]: Leverandører [List of vendors of electronoc healtecare system] (2008-2014), http://www.nhn.no/meldingsutbredelse-i-helsesektoren/leverandoerer
17. Nightingale F. translated by Melbye, : Notater om sykepleie[Notes on Nursing]. Universitetsforlaget (1997)
18. Kärkkäinen, O., Bondas, T., Eriksson, K.: Documentation of Individualized Patient Care: a qualitative metasynthesis. Nursing Ethics 12(2), 123–132 (2005)
19. Fossum, M., Ehnfors, M., Fruhling, A., Ehreanberg, A.: An Evaluation of the Usability of a Computerized Decision Support System for Nursing Homes. Applied Clinical Informatics, 420–436 (2011)
20. Mills, J., Chamberlain-Salaun, J., Henry, R., Sando, J., Summerset, G.: Nurses in Australian acute care settings: experiences with and outcomes of e-health. An Integrative Review 3 (2013)
21. Häyrinen, K., Saranto, K., Nykänen, P.: Definition, structure, content, use and impacts of electronic health records: A review of the research literature. International Journal of Medical Informatics 77(5), 291–304 (2008)
22. Vabo, G.: Domumetasjon av sykepleie, Et aksjonsforskingsprosjekt i Setersdal [Domumetasjon of Nursing, An action research project in Setersdal]. Senter for Omsorgsforsking. Nr.1/2013: p. 1–99 (2013)
23. Keenan, G., Yakel, E., Dunn Lopez, K., Tschannen, D., Ford, Y.B.: Challenges to nurses' efforts of retrieving, documenting, and communicating patient care information. Journal of the American Medical Informatics Association 20(2), 245–251 (2013)

24. Ash, J.S., Bates, D.W.: Factors and Forces Affecting EHR System Adoption: Report of a 2004 ACMI Discussion. Journal of the American Medical Informatics Association 12(1), 8–12 (2005)
25. Poissant, L., Pereira, J., Tamblyn, R., Kawasumi, Y.: The Impact of Electronic Health Records on Time Efficiency of Physicians and Nurses: A Systematic Review. Journal of the American Medical Informatics Association 12(5), 505–516 (2005)
26. Ammenwerth, E., Iller, C., Mahler, C., Kandert, M., Luther, G., Hoppe, B., Eichstadter, R.: Factors Affecting and Affected by User Acceptance of Computer-Based Nursing Documentation: Results of a Two-Year Study. J. Am. Med. Inform. Assoc. 10(1), 69–84 (2003)
27. Nielsen, J., Landauer, T.K.: A mathematical model of the finding of usability problems. In: Proceedings of the INTERACT 1993 and CHI 1993 Conference on Human Factors in Computing Systems, pp. 206–213. ACM, Amsterdam (1993)
28. Polson, P.G., Lewis, C., Rieman, J., Wharton, C.: Cognitive walkthroughs: a method for theory-based evaluation of user interfaces. International Journal of Man-Machine Studies 36(5), 741–773 (1992)
29. Reinking, D.: Electronic Literacy. University of Georgia (1994)
30. Bastien, J.M.C.: Usability testing: a review of some methodological and technical aspects of the method. International Journal of Medical Informatics, 79(4), e18–e23 (2010)
31. Graneheim, U.H., Lundman, B.: Qualitative content analysis in nursing research: concepts, procedures and measures to achieve trustworthiness. Nurse Education Today 24(2), 105–112 (2004)
32. Kawamoto, K., Houlihan, C.A., Balas, E.A., Lobach, D.F.: Improving clinical practice using clinical decision support systems: a systematic review of trials to identify features critical to success. British Medical Journal 330(7494), 765–768 (2005)

User Experience in Shopping and Business

UX and Strategic Management: A Case Study of Smartphone (Apple vs. Samsung) and Search Engine (Google vs. Naver) Industry

Junho Choi[1], Byung-Joon Kim[2], and SuKyung Yoon[1]

[1] UX Lab., Yonsei University, Seoul, S. Korea
junhochoi@yonsei.ac.kr, skyoon24@gmail.com
[2] SK Institute of Management & Economics, Seoul, S. Korea
spike.ipiegel@gmail.com

Abstract. This paper extends the analytic framework of user experience design into the area of strategic management by adopting the VRIO framework. We adopted value-rarity-imitability-organization (VRIO) framework and applied this integrated scheme into the investigating market cases. The first case study is the analysis of competitive advantages of two successful smartphone device makers, Apple (iPhone) and Samsung (Galaxy). UX Values (attractive design, ease of use, diverse applications), Rarity (simplicity, innovative interface, ecosystem), Imitability (patent, brand identity), and Organization (UX control tower, role of CXO) are employed to analyze and compare the strategies of those two most successful smartphone makers. In the second case study we compared the UX strategies of Google and Naver in the global and local levels. Through the case studies this paper shows a strong implication that UX can be extended into the corporate resources and capability, and VRIO framework utilized for the analysis of competitive advantages for the market leadership.

Keywords: User experience design, Strategic management, VRIO framework, Apple, Samsung, Google, Naver.

1   Introduction: VRIO Framework for UX Design Strategy

Since the revolutionary success of Apple, the competitive advantage of most ICT products and services in the contemporary market is now gained from the domain of user experience (UX) beyond the functionality and efficiency. Witnessing the market failure of companies who didn't pay much attention to the user-oriented design, e.g., Nokia, Motorola, RIM(Blackberry), and SONY, there has been, however, a little effort to explore the analytic framework for competitive advantage of UX design in terms of the strategic management.

Strategic management seeks analyses and choices to gain competitive advantages (Barney & Hesterly, 2012). That is, the goal of corporate management is the generating the competitive advantages over other companies in the market. It is the strategy that is the process of determining the best solution to achieve the goal.

Market leadership, or competitive advantage, is determined by how effectively the company creates more economic values of its products and services than those of

F.F.-H. Nah (Ed.): HCIB/HCII 2014, LNCS 8527, pp. 703–710, 2014.
© Springer International Publishing Switzerland 2014

competitors.' Consequently, the economic values in the market is appraised by how much consumers get the benefit out of the experiential use of the products and services.

The outcomes of competitive advantages in the market are not only the profit maximization but also sustainability of the corporation (Porter, 2008). Definitely, profit maximization through the consumers' heightened value perception of products is the basic management performance standard in most of corporations. However, witnessing the market failure of once glorious, dominant, innovative companies such as Nokia, SONY, Motorola, RIM, Dell, and Microsoft, we believe that long-term sustainability is also an important management performance goal in this fast changing ICT market.

VRIO Framework

When a corporation sets and implements strategies to achieve profit and sustainability, it is necessary to establish a framework for analysis, decision making, and evaluation of possible strategies. The VRIO framework (Barney & Hesterly, 2012) posits that the resources and capabilities are the core components of strategic management process. The VRIO framework helps to provide analytic and systematic answers to those questions: 1) Does a resource enable a firm to utilize the opportunity and neutralize a threat?; 2) Is a resource currently controlled by only our company or by only a small number of competing firms?; 3) Do other firms without the resource face disadvantages in obtaining or developing it?; and 4) Are our firm's values, procedures, structures organized to support the actualization of its valuable, rare, and costly-to imitate resources?

Focusing on the product quality differentiation, rather than on the cost differentiation, we applied the VRIO framework into the User Experience Design. Table 1 shows the summary.

Table 1. VRIO Framework for UX

Component	Evaluation Criteria (question)	Example: Apple's iPhone (mainly on the introduction of 3GS in 2009)
Value	Does our product have UX values that consumers perceive as competitive edge over other products?	• Attractive design • Ease of use • Diverse applications
Rarity	Are those UX values provided only by our product and perceived as rare by consumers?	• Simplicity • Completeness • Platform & App Store
Imitability	Do other companies have difficulties with copying or developing those UX values?	• Interface design patent • Seamless multi-device coordination (iPad, iPod) • Brand Identity (Cultural icon of Innovation)
Organization	Are our firm organized effectively to utilize those valuable, rare, and costly-to imitate resources?	• Corporate level UX control tower • Charismatic leadership and decision making

2   Case Study #1: Apple vs. Samsung

The first case study is the analysis of competitive advantages of two successful smartphone/tablet device makers, Apple (iPhone) and Samsung (Galaxy). The collapse of Nokia and Motorola in the smartphone market clearly demonstrates that market failure can be caused by the weaknesses in the value creation, differentiation, market barrier, and organizational structure/processes of UX resources in the company and its products. Representing the first mover and the fast follower of smartphone makers, the VRIO analysis of Apple and Samsung presents a very interesting and insightful case study of UX's contribution to the competitive advantage for the corporation.

Most of HCI pundits and even average users believe that Apple is the most advanced company in terms of user experience design.   The brand image of "easy, simple, and attractive" has been accumulated from the earlier personal computers with GUI, that is *LISA*(1983) and *McIntosh*(1984). Actually, *iPod*(2001) and *iPhone 3GS*(2009) were the   first products of Apple which achieved market leadership and competitive advantage in the music and in the mobile phone industries, respectively. Those groundbreaking impacts on the ICT market have made UX perceived as the most critical component of the revolutionary success of Apple (Banjarin, 2012).

What are the Apple's own UX strategies which generated the new entrant's landsliding advantage over preexisting competitors? Generally, Apple's UX capacities are summarized as three points:

1. Minimalism or Simplicity: Apple is perceived as the most progressive company, but has been conservative in adding features. That is, "less (feature) is more (user experience)" has been Apple's consistent strategy. Most IT manufacturers tend to keep preexisting features and add additional features in the new product, which sometimes creates the 'feature creep' or the complexity. However, for example, Apple did not install radio feature in the iPod until 2009 (Isaacson, 2011).
2. User segmentation by skill level: Most companies utilize user segmentation by demographic categories or lifestyle groups. However, for simplicity and ease of use, Apple has applied novice-experienced user segmentation into every aspect of the interaction design such as information architecture and interfaces (Baty, 2009).   Basic features can be learned instinctively by novice users and the cognitive overflow of information was restricted. Advanced features are usually hidden but the setting options can be found by experienced users, often generating a 'surprise effect'.
3. Coherence of user experience (same UX, different UI): Since many users are surrounded by multiple devices, e.g., PC, TV, tablet, MP3 player, and smartphone, and they sometimes use them simultaneously or consecutively. The N-screen environment creates 'distributed interaction' (Reeves et al, 2004) or multi-devices experiences. The complex environment always requires a seamless integration of UX design of multi-device usage. Beyond embedding the same OS and consistent interface styles, Apple set the design strategy for integrating the different screen sizes and use contexts of each devices, thus ended up with providing.

UX Values (e.g., attractive design, ease of use, diverse applications), Rarity (e.g., simplicity, innovative interface, ecosystem), Imitability (e.g., patent, brand identity), and Organization (e.g., UX control tower, role of CXO) are employed to analyze and compare the strategies of those two most successful smartphone makers in the global market.

When a Samsung's rivalry smart phone with Windows 6.0 OS (*Haptic 2*) was miserably defeated by iPhone 3GS even in the domestic market of S. Korea, its sustainability in the smartphone market was not anticipated by most market analysts and HCI experts. Poor UX design of their *TouchWiz* interface was blamed for the main reason of the market failure.

However, Samsung implemented successfully a fast follower strategy and, in a relatively short time period, gained the market leadership by enlarging the gaps between competitors in Android OS smartphone industry. Their fast recovery of market competence can be explained well by VRIO framework. The Android OS was open to all competitors, so basic features were not the differentiating values. Samsung absorbed the UX principles and design details of the market leader, Apple, and quickly improved the satisfaction level of user experience. Taking full advantages of manufacturing resources and capabilities, the mobile division of Samsung Electronics offered diverse line-ups by inch-by-inch screen sizes. Not all of them were survived, but 5 and 6 inch screens were accepted by market. For the large screen phones (*Galaxy Note & Tab*), they applied UX differentiation strategy by adding stylus pen and drawing interactions. The 4 inch screen and no-stylus pen were Apple's UX strategy for giving users the comfortable feeling of grip and minimal interaction, but a better visibility in a larger screen and a notetaking with an always carrying mobile device were the rare values that Samsung intended to create for diversely segmented phone users.

Table 2. VRIO Framework of UX Strategies: Apple vs. Samsung

component	Apple (iPhone)	Samsung (Galaxy)
Value	• Simplicity • Ease of Use • Attractive Design	• Ease of Use • Diverse line-ups by screen sizes
Rarity	• Own app/content platform (AppStore & iTunes) • Seamless integration of multiple devices(iPhone, iPad, iTV) through iCloud	• Customized version for carriers • UX Differentiation (stylus pen for Galaxy Note) • Development of own OS and platform (Bada and Samsung Store)
Imitability	• Design & interface patent • Brand image of 'innovative and simple UX'	• Brand image of 'technological edge of UX'
Organization	• UX control tower (role of CXO: Steve Jobs) • Consolidated accounting system	• Independent design center • Internal competition among design teams

Also, Samsung's attempt to build their own OS(Bada) and app store (Samsung Apps) was not successful in the market, but the trial and error contributed to the UX differentiation through activation of UX R&D and internalization of UX-oriented decision making procedure. Instead of Apple's integrative brand image of 'innovation' and 'simplicity,' Samsung initially pursued differentiating brand identity of 'technological edge.' Later, they changed their marketing strategy toward more human-centered image through massive UX-oriented marketing campaigns.

In order to maintain the competitive edge in the UX, it is necessary to develop internal organizational structure, decision making procedure, corporate culture, and performance evaluation metrics. In lack of Apple's creative and hegemonic star CEO, Steve Jobs, who governed all aspects of product and service UX strategies with a small number of design creative team (Lashinsky, 2012), Samsung utilized a hierarchical organization structure in order to maximize their design capacities. They scouted UX specialists from universities and other companies, expanded the design center, and founded overseas UX research centers (e.g., UX Innovation Lab, UX Mobile Lab, UX Services Lab, Visual Display UX Lab in the Silicon Valley).

3   Case Study #2: Google vs. Naver

The second case study is about the search engine/portal industry. Google has gained the market monopoly in all countries with only two exceptions: Baidu in China and Naver in S. Korea (Yahoo Japan is now affiliated with Google search engine). Considering the socialist political system of China, the Naver is the single case of market winner over Google on the glove.

Utilizing the VRIO framework, we compared the competitive advantages of Google's and Naver's UX strategies in the global and local levels. The case study of Naver in S. Korea demonstrates well that UX design can be critical resources for management strategies in the local market where domestic players are faced with fierce competition with global ones. Strategies for localization of interface designs and taming of local user experiences have led to the familiarity with the local brand and distinctive interaction styles.

Compared to Google's simplicity, usefulness, consistency values originated from the sophisticated high-tech search engine algorithm, Naver's strategies for market competition were internalization of online information in terms of content generation, tagging, selection, and display, heavily dependent on human labors and exclusive contracts with content sources.

Naver's closed walled-garden ecosystem contrasts clearly with the Google's open eco-system, and the local service's competitive edge was gained from the rarity and difficult imitability of UX strategies. For example, regardless of disputes and blames over openness spirit of the Internet, Naver had blocked their webpages from indexing by other search engines. In leveraging of the network effect, i.e., the economic law of 'the rich get richer,' Naver outpaced once a dominant competitor, Daum Communications, but the strategy was different from the market leadership transition from Yahoo to Google. Limiting the range of information accessibility, instead, Naver attracted S. Korean Net users by providing the one-stop & all-in-one solution of culturally customized information needs. The domesticated convenience and ease of use have made online users familiar with their localized interaction mode and interface styles. A local subsidiary of Google once launched a massive publicity campaign but in vain for changing the user habits. Because Google runs global service, their localization strategy often conflicts with global brand identity and lacks corporate capabilities for localization.

Also, for the sustainability and brand identity, the company has built a unique organizational structure and internal process of UX: the top level managerial decision making by combining research, design, marketing units into one and by CXO's presence in the de facto control tower.

Table 3. VRIO Framework of UX Strategy: Google vs. Naver

component	Google	Naver
Value	• Simplicity, usefulness, consistency	• Localization of interface design
Rarity	• Diverse & useful services	• Walled-garden content system
Imitability	• Brand image of "the most useful & technological edge"	• Brand image of "local familiarity"
Organization	• Hidden UX control tower for maintaining simplified homepage and brand identity	• CXO's presence in the control tower: consolidation of research, development, design, and marketing

4   Conclusion and Discussions

Applying VRIO framework into two case studies, we attempted utilization of strategic management for the UX design. The market failure and the collapse of Nokia and SONY clearly demonstrate why the UX as a practice requires management viewpoint.

SONY illustrated well the importance of UX management in the era of convergence. Ando Kunitake, the global IT market leader Sony's CEO in 2001, proposed the concept of 'ubiquitous value network' and addressed that "new technology needs to drive people into the world in which information and data can be accessed anywhere, using any type of personal devices." (Comdex Keynote Speech, 2001. http://edition.cnn.com/2001/TECH/ptech/11/12/comdex.sony.keynote/index.html).

SONY's new strategy implemented with the alliances with Ericsson and the combination of PC, laptop, game console, digital camera, phone, and wristwatch. Already, they had entertainment content resources to deliver over their devices through music (CBS Records) and movie (Columbia Pictures) studios.

Most pundits believed at that time that SONY's convergence strategy was the right way to lead the future market and it had enough resources and capabilities. They made Walkerman, VCR, camcorder, CD player and their brand was perceived as the most innovative and reliable. Also, their design capability had been acclaimed every year at Red Dot awards.

In 2014 the portrait of once most valuable brand, SONY, is far behind the prospect. Their smartphones are not perceived as popular or luxurious in the outside of domestic market. Global market share of their smartphone has not surpassed 5% since the introduction of Xperia series. Other products such as TV, laptop, media players lost market leadership over once second-tier manufacturers such as Samsung, Apple, and Lenover. Many pundits expect now their little chance of coming back to the market leadership.

The main reason of SONY's losing competitive advantage in the ICT industry lies in the failure of UX strategy for changing market paradigm. Their past success history in the era of supply demand market made SONY blinded from the poor user encounters with their products and services, in other words, the 'moment of truth' (Norman, 1984). Each product still has top level technological edges and design aesthetics. However, they failed to create the satisfactory easy to use and integrative user touch points that consolidate user experience of using their multiple devices. They proposed the convergence of contents and devices, but users couldn't perceive expected level of coherence when using SONY products and services. For example, SONY's Xross Media Bar (XMB) interface extended the consistent UI into PlayStation, Bravia HDTV, VAIO laptop, Xperia smartphone, but failed to create an integrative platform for the users. Most users felt frustrations with the points of access to the content and to other devices they wanted to use. The innovation of 'ubiquitous value network' they pursued was just technology- and design-oriented, not user-oriented. SONY had not operated a corporate level UX control tower and CXO position until punitive resignation of managerial board in 2011.

Here is another example of UX strategy failure: Nokia, the first smartphone maker (Nokia 7650 in 2002), had been renowned for their global R&D and technological innovation capabilities. Their industry leading leadership in the highly competitive mobile phone market also came from the outstanding global sourcing and supply chain management capabilities.

The dramatic falling down of the once dominant and glorious company in the mobile market began with the small cracks in the differentiating values of smartphone user experience that their products provided for changing users after the new market entrants such as iPhone and Galaxy. Nokia's competing products, e.g., N5800, were optimized for past feature phone user experience: users had a terrible usability and awkward experiences of screen touch interface tuned for hard key pressing. Nokia had global top level UX design practitioners but their valuable human resources fail to generate capabilities for competitive advantages in the market.

Most pundits accuse managerial decision making procedure in the organization of the market failure and user dissatisfaction. Olli-Pekka Kallasvuo, the new CEO in 2006, combined the new smartphone division into the incumbent feature phone division. In spite of the fast changing user experiences in mobile market, top decision makers kept concentrating cash-cow old products and neglected the upcoming threats and opportunities. Due to lack of UX oriented decision making and organizational structure, the design head, Alastair Curtis, had difficulties to implement coherent usability and aesthetic impression in a series of products as Apple showed for their brand identity. Proposed improvements of interface and interaction prototypes were twisted in the tension between internal teams of Symbian and Mago, deterred by user research from globally distributed labs with unstandardized methods, and finally turned down by business division for a short term operation profit. Thus, Nokia failed to manage UX oriented organization and to gratify the market needs of user experience. The once global market leader of mobile industry lost their capability of sustainability and finally ended up with merger by Microsoft in 2013.

Supported both from the the market failure examples and from success cases, we argue that UX should be regarded as core resources and capabilities of the corporation in order to gain competitive advantage in this demand-side market of ICT industry. Every decision making on the interaction and interface designs should be considered as a management strategy. It does not mean that UX practitioners should work under the managerial guidelines for short-term profit making. What we think important is that the corporate managers should work under the user experience guidelines for sustainability and brand identity. Here are future agenda: Applying strategic management into the UX requires further investigation and refinement in standardization of UX ROI evaluation and optimization of UX practitioners' expanding roles in the organization.

References

1. Barney, J.B., Hesterly, W.S.: Strategic Management and Competitive Advantage, 4th edn. Pearson Education (2012)
2. Bajarin, T.: 6 Reasons Apple Is So Successful. Time, May 07, 2012 (2012), http://techland.time.com/2012/05/07/six-reasons-why-apple-is-successful/
3. Baty, S.: Audience Segmentation Models. UX Matters (September 21, 2009), http://www.uxmatters.com/mt/archives/2009/09/audience-segmentation-models.php
4. Isaacson, W.: Steve Jobs. Simon & Schuster (2011)
5. Lashinsky, A.: Inside Apple: How America's Most Admired - and Secretive - Company Really Works. Business Plus (2012)
6. Norman, R.: Service Management: Strategy and Leadership in the Service Business. John Wiley & Sons (1984)
7. Porter, M.: Competitive Advantage: Creating and Sustaining Superior Performance. The Free Press (1998)
8. Porter, M.: On Competition, updated and expanded edition. Harvard Business School Publishing Corporation (2008)
9. Reeves, L.M., et al.: Guidelines for multimodal user interface design. Communications of ACM 47(1), 57–59 (2004)

Designing a Multi-modal Association Graph
for Music Objects*

Jia-Lien Hsu** and Chiu-Yuan Ho

Department of Computer Science and Information Engineering
Fu Jen Catholic University

Abstract. Music object features are complex and multifaceted, ranging from short-term/low-level features to long-term/high-level features,
in which the semantic gap in between has not been properly resolved yet.
In this paper, we introduce a graph-based approach to organize different
aspects of features in a unified way. Based on the graph, various kinds of
features could be related to and associated associated with each other.
However, by further investigating the graph structure, we observe that
the node degree distribution asymptotically follows a power law. As a result, some hubs (i.e., high-degree nodes) will dominate most metrics; the
representation of graph semantics could be degenerated. Therefore, we
introduce the *graph projection* operator to reduce the graph complexity
and "compress" the graph accordingly. The graph projection is a method
of refactoring edge weights, in which only a particular set of nodes are
reserved to show the intrinsic structure of graph. To demonstrate the
feasibility of graph-based approach, we introduce two applications (music clustering and auto-tagging); and perform experiments. According to
our experiment study, the performance of projected graph is better than
that of unprojected graph.

1 Introduction

Music objects consist of multifaceted features in the diverse domain ranging from
low-level features and high-level features. We conclude three kinds of music features, including 'acoustic features', 'element features', and 'structural features'.
The acoustic features are the short-term audio features which can be computationally derived from music audio content, such as *zero-crossing rate*, *audio
temporal spectrum*, and *mel-frequency cepstral coefficients* (MFCCs). The element features are the long-term audio features which are usually related to music
form. Some of element features, such as rhythmic pattern and sequence clusters,
could be still derived from acoustic content. Other element features, such as

---

* This research was supported by the National Science Council under Contract No.
  NSC-101-2221-E-030-008 and No. NSC-102-2218-E-030-002.
** All correspondence should be sent to: The Department of Computer Science
  and Information Engineering, Fu Jen Catholic University, Taiwan (R.O.C.),
  `alien@csie.fju.edu.tw`

F.F.-H. Nah (Ed.): HCIB/HCII 2014, LNCS 8527, pp. 711–722, 2014.
© Springer International Publishing Switzerland 2014

tonality and key signature, cannot be easily derived from acoustic content without supporting metadata. The structural features are high-level features usually determined by domain experts or social groups, such as genre tags and affective states.

In general, we are able to design a convenient similarity measure for a particular feature in the specific domain. For example, the Kullback-Leibler divergence is applied to measure the distance of MFCCs with Gaussian Mixture Model; the Euclidean distance is for audio temporal spectrum; the *lowest common ancestor* is for genre tags with taxonomy. However, we observe that a *semantic gap*, existing between low-level features and high-level features, has not been resolved properly. Most of previously-published work, e.g., genre classification, are dedicated to a particular task focusing on a specific combination of features [1]. These tailor-made approaches cannot be easily extended to cover more features.

In this paper, we propose a graph-based approach, called the multi-modal association graph, to organize music objects in a unified way. Based on the association graph, we provide various kind of operators to support a variety of music information retrieval (MIR) tasks, such as auto-tagging, similarity measure, and music clustering. The association graph with those supporting operators can be served as an application framework to bridge low-level and high-level features, and develop MIR applications in the diverse feature domain. The application framework is a flexible and easily-extended approach in which more features and operators could be 'plugged' into the graph. Similar approaches of graph-based methods, e.g., *mixed media graph* [2], have been proposed for the image retrieval.

Based on our previous work for the music information retrieval [3, 4], in this paper, we especially focus on the mechanism of reasoning and resolving the graph semantics. Given a set of music objects, the association graph $G = (V, E)$ is constructed as follows. In priori to processing music objects, all the involved feature domains are considered "tokens" for constructing G. Note that, if the feature domain is discrete (say, keyword-like genre), all the possible discrete values are "tokens". If the feature domain is continuous, we may apply the quantization techniques (e.g., LBG algorithm) to determine "tokens". All the feature tokens are considered as nodes of graph. Then, for each music object MO, we construct a node n_{MO} to represent the MO. With repeat to the MO, we extract acoustic and some element features; we collect structural features from the supporting metedata and online resource, if possible. All extracted features and collected features are recognized; and assigned to some "closest" tokens. We build edges between n_{mo} and the corresponding tokens (i.e., nodes of graph).

Since the association graph is usually a *scale-free* network (in which the network degree distribution asymptotically follows a power law), some hubs (i.e., high-degree nodes) will dominate most metrics, for example, prestige values, pagerank, and shortest path distance. As a result, the metrics will be degenerated without having discrimination power. Therefore, we apply the *graph projection* on the association graph to reduce the complexity of graph. The graph projection is a method of weighting network connection, which is originated from the *bipartite network projection* [5]. Given a bipartite network (i.e., two-mode graph), the bipartite projection is to "compress" the bipartite network onto a one-mode graph in which only a particular set of nodes are reserved to show the network structure. In the one-mode graph, several methods of weighting connections/edges have been proposed to reflect the intrinsic community structure of the bipartite graph.

In our approach, with respect to the user-specified domain set *pFD*, the graph G will be projected onto the domain set *pFD* by employing the shared-near neighbor (SNN) weighting connections. Based on the reduced and projected graph G, some basic metrics, which have been investigated in the research of social network analysis, could be leveraged in our approach. We consider these operators as building blocks to accomplish various kinds of MIR-related applications, such as determining fundamental roles, community discovery, and cohesive group detection.

To demonstrate the feasibility of association graph, we implement our framework and accomplish two MIR applications, i.e., auto-tagging of music expression problem and music object clustering. The auto-tagging application is an essential case exploiting multi features across heterogeneous domains; and also an obvious target study to show the effectiveness for comparison. To illustrate the effectiveness of our framework, we also perform tagging experiments and obtain comparative results.

2   Approach

In our approach, we propose a graph-based data structure to organize music features in various domains. First, we conclude three kinds of music features. Given a set of music objects, we present the process of constructing graph and the *graph projection* operator. By applying integrated operators on the graph, we illustrate two applications to show the feasibility of multi-modal association graph.

2.1   Music Features

As described in the work [4], we conclude three kinds of music features as follows.

1. **Acoustic Feature.** The acoustic features are short-term audio descriptions in the physical measurements. The quantitative information can be easily extracted from audio data, such as, *zero-crossing rate*, *frequency*, and MFCCs.
2. **Element Feature.** Compared to the acoustic features, the element features are long-term audio descriptions which are usually related to the *music form*. Some of element features, such as *rhythmic pattern* and *sequence clusters*, could be still derived from acoustic content. Other element features, such as *tonality* and *key signature*, cannot be easily derived from acoustic content without supporting metadata.

3. **Structural Feature.** The structural features are high-level features usually determined by domain experts or social groups, such as *genre tags* and *affective states.*

Referring to the Table 1, we summarize the three categories of music features, as well as the data types and similarity measures. With respect to the data type of feature domain, we have two kinds of data type, i.e., *discrete* and *continuous*. For the discrete feature domain (e.g. genre tag), we consider each tag as a "token". For the continuous feature domain, we apply the quantization process on the feature domain to map a continuous range of values into a finite set of discrete values (i.e., "tokens").

For example, as shown in Table 2, we have six music objects, denoted by O_1, O_2, ..., O_6, in associated with two continuous feature domains *tempo* and *average spectral centroid* (ASC), and a discrete feature domain *tag*. Then, we apply the *Linde-Buzo-Gray Algorithm* [6] on the feature domain tempo and ASC to derive tokens.

Table 1. Properties of music features [1, 4]

Category	Feature	Data type	Similarity measure
Acoustic feature (Short-term, Low-level)	Zero-crossing rate	Numeric	Euclidean distance
	MFCCs	Vector	KL divergence
Element feature (Long-term, Mid-level)	Tonality	Tag	Circle-of-fifths
	Beat-per-minute	Numeric	Euclidean distance
	Pitch	Vector	Euclidean distance
Structural feature (Long-term, Top-level)	Genre	Keyword/Tag	Ontology-based similarity
	Mood	Keyword/Tag	Ontology-based similarity

Table 2. An example of music and features (original data and quantized data)

Original data				Quantized data			
Music object	Tempo	ASC	Tag	Music object	Tempo	ASC	Tag
O_1	55	1.0	Jazz	O_1	55	1.1	Jazz
O_2	75	1.3	Jazz	O_2	73	1.4	Jazz
O_3	71	1.2	Jazz	O_3	73	1.1	Jazz
O_4	96	2.8	Rock	O_4	96	2.8	Rock
O_5	113	1.5	Rock	O_5	109	1.4	Rock
O_6	105	3.1	Rock	O_6	109	3.1	Rock

2.2 Graph Construction

In the following, we first define the *feature domain* for music objects and present the process of constructing graph.

Definition 1 (Feature domain). *The feature domain FD is a union of single feature domain* FD_k, *denoted by*

$$FD = FD_1 \cup FD_2 \cup ... \cup FD_k \tag{1}$$

For each single FD_k, FD_k *is a set of "tokens", denoted by*

$$FD_k = \{FD_{k,1}, FD_{k,2}, ...\} \tag{2}$$

$\square$

For 'example', also shown in Table 2, we have three feature domains *tempo*, *ASC*, and *genre tag*, denoted as FD_1, FD_2, and FD_3, respectively.

$$FD_1 = \{'55', '73', '96', '109'\} \tag{3}$$
$$FD_2 = \{'1.1', '1.4', '2.8', '3.1'\} \tag{4}$$
$$FD_3 = \{'Jazz', 'Rock'\} \tag{5}$$

Definition 2 (Graph). *Given a set of music objects* $O = \{O_1, O_2, ...\}$, *and the feature domain FD, we construct a multi-modal music graph G as follows.*

$$G = (V, E) \tag{6}$$
$$V = O \cup FD \tag{7}$$
$$E \subseteq V \times V \tag{8}$$
$$E = E_{OF} \cup E_{FF} \tag{9}$$
$$E_{OF} = \{(v_a, v_b) | v_a \in O, v_b \in FD\} \tag{10}$$
$$E_{FF} = \{(v_c, v_d) | v_c, v_d \in FD_i, \text{the token } v_c \text{ is 'similar' to the token } v_d\} \tag{11}$$

As shown in Figure 1, we construct a graph G for the six music objects in Table 2, in which there are three feature domains FD_1, FD_2, and FD_3, 18 edges of E_{OF}, and 4 edges of E_{FF}.

2.3   Graph Projection

Given a set of music objects, we have constructed a multi-modal graph to associate music objects and different kinds of features. However, since the distribution of node degree is highly skew, some hub nodes (high-degree nodes) will dominate most of metrics, e.g., prestige, pagerank, and shortest path distance, which leads biased results. In our approach, we make use of graph projection to reduce the complexity of graph. Referring to Figure 2, we illustrate the process of graph projection. Given the user-specified projected domains, only a particular set of nodes in the projected domains are reserved, and the corresponding edges are refactoring by means of SNN-based similarity (SNN, shared nearest neighbors [7]). We believe, the projected graph results in a reduced and concise data structure for better revealing the intrinsic properties of graph.

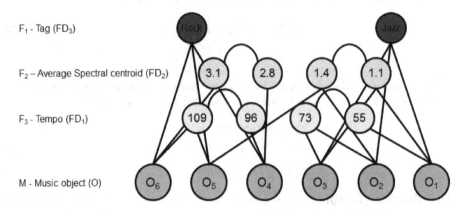

Fig. 1. An example of multi-modal music graph in three feature domains

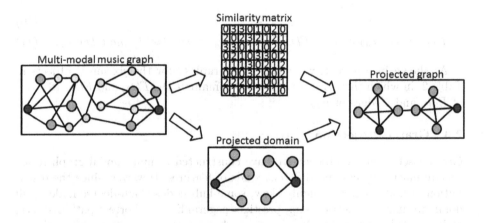

Fig. 2. An illustration of SNN-based graph projection

Definition 3 (Graph projection). *Given a multi-modal music graph* $G = (V, E)$, *the projected graph* $PG = (V_{PG}, E_{PG})$ *is derived as follows.*

$$PG = Project_{SNN}(G, pFD, level, th_{SNN}) \tag{12}$$

Denote pFD as the 'projected domains'; level as the threshold of 'SNN similarity'; th_{SNN} as the threshold of 'edge refactoring'.
In addition, we have the following properties.

$$pFD \subseteq V \tag{13}$$
$$V_{PG} = pFD \tag{14}$$
$$E_{PG} \subseteq V_{PG} \times V_{PG} \tag{15}$$
$$E_{PG} = \{(x, y) | x \in V_{PG}, y \in V_{PG}, Sim_{SNN}(x, y, level) > th_{SNN}\} \tag{16}$$

□

Definition 4 (SNN-based similarity). *Given two nodes x and y of graph PG, the 'SNN-based similarity' of the 'level' degree is defined as follows.*

$$Sim_{SNN}(x, y, level) = |NN(x, level) \cap NN(y, level)| \tag{17}$$

where

$$NN(x, level) = \{node | node \in V_{PG}, shortest\text{-}path\text{-}length(node, x) \leq level\} \tag{18}$$

□

Referring to Figure 1, we set the parameters as follows.

$$level = 2 \tag{19}$$
$$th_{SNN} = 2 \tag{20}$$
$$pFD = \{O_1, O_2, ...\} \cup FD_3 \tag{21}$$

Then, we apply $Project_{SNN}$ on G to derive the projected graph PG shown in Figure 3.

2.4   Application 1: Music Object Clustering

Given a projected graph PG, we apply the hierarchical clustering algorithm (single-linkage agglomerative algorithm) to group those music objects. As shown in Figure 4, the dendrogram is presented with respect to the graph PG of Figure 3.

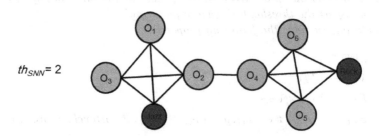

Fig. 3. The projected graph PG based on the graph G in Figure 1

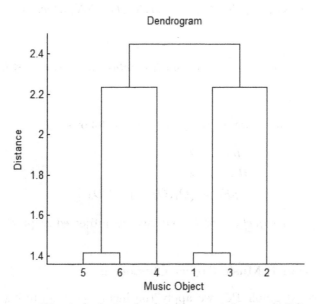

Fig. 4. A cluster dendrogram $w.r.t$ the graph PG

2.5 Application 2: Music Auto-tagging

Given a set of music objects, all the music objects and those associated features
are organized as a graph. Provided the graph PG, we are able to perform the
music auto-tagging task as follows. For example, with respect to the graph in
Figure 1, we would like to determine the genre tag of a testing music object O_{test}.
As described in the above sections, we perform the same process of feature extraction, append the node O_{test} into the graph PG, and attach the corresponding
edges. As shown in Figure 5, in our example, the tempo of O_{test} is '96', and the
ASC of O_{test} is '3.1'.

In the following, we apply *random walk with restart* algorithm to determine
the *pagerank* $\overrightarrow{PR}$ of all nodes.

$$\overrightarrow{PR_{i+1}} = (1-\alpha)M\overrightarrow{PR_i} + \alpha\overrightarrow{p} \tag{22}$$

where M is the *normalized adjacency matrix* of $(n \times n)$, α is the *damping factor*
and $\overrightarrow{p} = [1/n]_{n\times 1}$ is the restart vector.

We are interested in the genre tag of O_{test}, and we have the pagerank of '*token-
Rock*' is 0.005 and the pagerank of '*token-Jazz*' is 0.022. As a result, '*Rock*' is
chosen as the genre tag of O_{test}. Note that, in addition to the pagerank, we
may apply some fundamental graph operators to evaluate the *prestige* of nodes,
such as *shortest-path-length* and *centrality degree*. In addition, some metrics of
social network analysis could be leverage to complete the auto-tagging task. The
detailed discussions can be found in [3, 4].

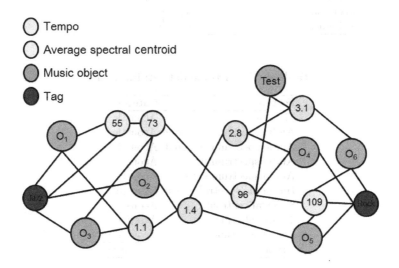

Fig. 5. Append the testing data O_{test} to the graph PG

3   Experiment

In this section, we would like to present our experiment set-up, testing dataset, measurement, as well as the experiment results.

3.1   Set-Up

Our proposed system was implemented by MATLAB R2010b, running on Microsoft Windows 7 platform with Intel Core^{TM} i7 processor and 4 GB ram.

Regarding the testing dataset, we choose the subset of USPOP2002 — Artist20 [8]. Referring to the Table 3, the Artist20 dataset consists of 1,413 songs from 20 singers. We make use of three kinds of features, shown in Table 4, and the structural feature — Artist is designed as the target to be determined when performing the auto-tagging experiment and music clustering.

Table 3. The *Artist20* dataset: singer list

Artist	Amount	Artist	Amount
aerosmith	53	beatles	86
creedence clearwater revival	55	cure	75
dave matthews band	74	depeche mode	73
fleetwood mac	79	garth brooks	66
green day	88	led zeppelin	52
madonna	71	metallica	65
prince	68	queen	78
radiohead	73	roxette	88
steely dan	52	suzanne vega	69
tori amos	84	u2	64

Table 4. The *Artist20* dataset: feature list

Feature	Category
MFCCs	Acoustic
Audio spectrum envelope	Acoustic
Audio spectrum centroid	Acoustic
Audio spectrum flatness	Acoustic
Audio spectrum spread	Acoustic
Harmonic spectral spread	Element
Spectral centroid	Acoustic
Temporal centroid	Acoustic
Log attack time	Acoustic
Artist	Structural

To evaluate the performance of projected graph, the measure of auto-tagging is *accuracy* in *ten-fold cross-validation*.

Wehn performing the music object clustering, the quality of clustering results is evaluated by the *Rand-index*, which is a measure of the similarity between the *actual clustering* C_{act} and the *predicted clustering* C_{pre}.

Given a set of n elements $S = \{o_1, \ldots, o_n\}$ and two partitions of S to compare, $C_{act} = \{X_1, \ldots, X_r\}$ and $C_{pre} = \{Y_1, \ldots, Y_s\}$, define the following:

- a: the number of pairs of elements in S that are in the same set in C_{act} and in the same set in C_{pre}
- b: — that are in different sets in C_{act} and in different sets in C_{pre}
- c: — that are in the same set in C_{act} and in different sets in C_{pre}
- d: — that are in different sets in C_{act} and in the same set in C_{pre}

The *Rand-index*, denoted R, is:

$$R = \frac{a + b}{a + b + c + d} \tag{23}$$

3.2   Results

Referring to the Table 5, we present the rank index of clustering results for unprojected and projected graphs, respectively. Note that, the actual clustering C_{act} is the grouping of all music objects based on the 'artist' feature. Indeed, the music clustering is always regarded as one of most challenging tasks. Although the performance of all testing cases are in impressive, the results of projected graph are still much better that the results of unprojected graph.

Referring to the Table 6, we show the accuracy of auto-tagging against the 'artist' feature. The predicted results of projected graph is slightly better than the results of unprojected graph.

Table 5. Results of music object clustering ($pFD = \{$Object tokens, Artist tokens$\}$)

Graph	Parameters	R	th_{SNN}
Unprojected	N/A	0.03	N/A
Projected	$level = 1$	0.18	6
Projected	$level = 2$	0.18	10

Table 6. Results of music auto-tagging ($pFD = \{$Object tokens, Artist tokens$\}$)

Graph	Parameters	Accuracy	th_{SNN}
Unprojected	$\alpha = 0.1$	0.22	N/A
Unprojected	$\alpha = 0.2$	0.16	N/A
Projected	$level = 1, \alpha = 0.1$	0.23	6
Projected	$level = 1, \alpha = 0.2$	0.21	6
Projected	$level = 2, \alpha = 0.1$	0.24	10
Projected	$level = 2, \alpha = 0.2$	0.24	10

4   Conclusion

In this paper, we design a multi-modal association graph for MIR to organize various kinds of features across heterogeneous domains. Furthermore, to reduce the complexity of association graph, we apply the graph projection to refactor edges in terms of SNN-based similarity. That is, given a graph and the user-specified feature domain *pFD*, the graph projection is to compress the original graph onto a reduced graph in which only a particular set of nodes *pFD* are reserved to show the intrinsic of graph structure. Based on the graph-based and multi-modal data structure, we also introduce two applications, i.e., music object clustering and auto-tagging. In addition, we perform experiments to show the performance improvement on the projected graphs.

In this paper, we present some preliminary results of project-based graph approach to fulfill the semantic gap. A comprehensive investigation will be continued to establish core facilities for music information retrieval.

References

[1] Fu, Z.Y., Lu, G.J., Ting, K.M., Zhang, D.S.: A survey of audio-based music classification and annotation. IEEE Transactions on Multimedia 13(2), 303–319 (2011)
[2] Pan, J.Y., Yang, H.J., Faloutsos, C., Duygulu, P.: Automatic multimedia cross-modal correlation discovery. In: Proceedings of the ACM SIGKDD International Conference on Knowledge Discovery and Data Mining, pp. 653–658 (2004)
[3] Hsu, J.L., Li, Y.F.: A cross-modal method of labeling music tags. Multimedia Tools and Applications 58, 521–541 (2012)
[4] Hsu, J.L., Huang, C.C.: Designing a graph-based framework to support a multi-modal approach for music information retrieval. Multimedia Tools and Applications, 1–27 (2014)
[5] Benchettara, N., Kanawati, R., Rouveirol, C.: Supervised machine learning applied to link prediction in bipartite social networks. In: Proceedings of the International Conference on Advances in Social Networks Analysis and Mining (ASONAM), pp. 326–330 (2010)
[6] Linde, Y., Buzo, A., Gray, R.: An algorithm for vector quantizer design. IEEE Transactions on Communications 28(1), 84–95 (1980)
[7] Ertoz, L., Steinbach, M., Kumar, V.: A new shared nearest neighbor clustering algorithm and its applications. In: Proceedings of Workshop on Clustering High Dimensional Data and its Applications at 2nd SIAM International Conference on Data Mining, pp. 105–115. SIAM (2002)
[8] Ellis, D.: Classifying music audio with timbral and chroma features. In: Proceedings of the International Conference on Music Information Retrieval (ISMIR), pp. 339–340 (2007)

Usability Evaluations of an Interactive, Internet Enabled Human Centered SanaViz Geovisualization Application

Ashish Joshi[1,*], de Araujo Novaes Magdala[2], Machiavelli Josiane[2], Iyengar Sriram[3],
Vogler Robert[3], Johnson Craig[3], Zhang Jiajie[3], and Hsu Ed Chiehwen[3]

[1] Center for Global Health and Development, College of Public Health, UNMC, USA
`Ashish.joshi@unmc.edu`
[2] NUTES, Federal University of Pernambuco, Recife, Brazil
`{magdala.novaes,josiane.machiavelli}@untes.ufpe.edu`
[3] School of Biomedical Informatics University of Texas Health Science Center, Houston, USA
`{M.Sriram.Iyengar,Robert.W.Vogler,Craig.W.Johnson,`
`Jiajie.Zhang,Chiehwen.E.Hsu}@uth.tmc.edu`

Abstract. The objective of our study was to evaluate usefulness and effectiveness of Human Centered GeoVis prototype"The SanaViz" against a conventional GeoVis application Instant Atlas. The SanaViz is an interactive, internet based application aimed at facilitating visual exploration of public health data, and in this context telehealth data from Brazil. A cross sectional, within-subject, mixed methods study design was utilized. A convenient sample of 20 study participants from diverse backgrounds was enrolled. The users were asked to perform 5 tasks using both the GeoVis applications. Univariate analyses were performed for continuous and categorical variables. Repeated measures of analysis of variance was performed on the within-subject design to test for significant differences between "the SanaViz" and Instant Atlas. All analysis was performed using SAS v9.1. Results showed that "The SanaViz" required less time, less assistance and fewer attempts and was reported as easier than Instant Atlas.

Keywords: Geovisualization, Public health, telehealth, Human centered.

1 Background

Illness and health are distributed unequally across space and time while the latter can be vital but often neglected in the assessment of health issues [1]. Public health data is typically organized at a geospatial unit and has 3 dimensions including (a) attribute, (b) spatial and (c) temporal (i.e., time). Attribute component relates to public health issues of interest such as social and environmental data. Spatial component includes data with location attributes. Understanding how place relates to public health and health care is important in order to deliver effective interventions and can provide insight into where to obtain important services [2]. Temporal component records time of the observation and enables users to learn from the past to predict, plan, and build

---

* Corresponding author.

F.F.-H. Nah (Ed.): HCIB/HCII 2014, LNCS 8527, pp. 723–734, 2014.
© Springer International Publishing Switzerland 2014

the future [3]. Similarly temporal change in geography enables to describe trends [4]. Public health researchers often examine complex, multidimensional data that enables them to identify patterns, thereby assembling meaningful information. As public health datasets become increasingly complex, there is a growing need for methods and tools to support the construction of knowledge. Visual representations can often communicate information much more rapidly and effectively and help decision makers prioritize the actions and regulations required for better public health outcomes.

Geovisualization (GeoVis) facilitates use of visual geospatial displays to explore data, generate hypotheses, develop problem solutions, and construct knowledge. GeoVis is increasingly being used to inform public health research, planning and decision making. GeoVis displays events in space and time, making possible the perception of where and when events occurred. Increasingly complex public health datasets reflect a growing need for methods and tools to support the construction of knowledge [5]. Knowledge can be created and revealed through abstract representations of maps [6]. GeoVis can be used to examine distribution of disease [7] study risk factors [8], examine effectiveness of disease control and policies [9], identify problems of access, quality, and the safety of healthcare (9), and visualize community health disparities [10] for planning and resource allocation in developing countries [11].

However, despite the applicability of GeoVis in public health, GeoVis tools are still underused. Limited guidance exists on how to actually design simple, functional Geo-Vis applications for use in the public health realm. Prior studies have shown limited focus on domain specific considerations with end user input often was incorporated only after key functionality and interface design issues were decided. GeoVis applications are difficult to learn and use, are predominantly generic, do not address specific users and are designed according to the engineering and technology principles. Results of the prior studies showed lack of a number of the essential ingredients needed to make use of the existing GeoVis applications by typical public-health researchers [12]. The need to assess the usefulness and usability of GeoVis applications is increasing as new types of interactions emerge [12]. It is essential to focus on the effectiveness, usefulness and performance of GeoVis applications. Usability testing can provide insight into how a visual interface can support data-exploration tasks. However, prior studies have shown that majority of existing GeoVis applications are designed according to the technology and software engineering principles. Recently, there was a shift towards user-centered design [13]. Domain specific considerations have been overlooked and end user input has been incorporated only after key functionality and interface design issues have been decided. GeoVis applications are difficult to learn and use, are predominantly generic and do not address specific users [14].

The objective of the study is to provide a framework to evaluate the internet enabled Human Centered interactive GeoVis application "SanaViz" to facilitate visual exploration of telehealth data in Brazil.

Theoretical framework: A combined principle of human centered (HC) approach, Cognitive Fit theory (CFT) and grounded theory was utilized to design and develop

GeoVis application "SanaViz". The HC approach gives specific considerations to users' knowledge, expertise and use of the interaction techniques to represent tasks performed by the users. The principles of HC approach involve [15] (a) active involvement and understanding of users, (b) understanding task requirements, (c) appropriate allocation of function between user and system, (d) iteration of design solutions and multidisciplinary design teams. Understanding users is an important aspect for creating GeoVis applications. The user model helps to gather individuals' understanding about data, functions, domain and mapping [16]. Mapping understanding of user needs to the system functions is necessary to create a useful and effective GeoVis application [16]. HC approach involves users' perspective in order to create a system that is useful and useable.

An important first step in understanding how to design better GeoVis interactions is to understand user tasks and goals. The geographic analysis process can be viewed as a set of tasks and operations need to meet the goals of the data exploration, gain insight and knowledge construction [17]. The tasks involve a number of specific activities and operations that users will perform for exploratory data analysis (EDA) [18]. The basic premise of exploratory GeoVis is that insight is formed through interaction. Interactivity facilitates exploration, hypothesis generation in a more effective and dynamic manner. Interactivity in GeoVis changes visual data display in response to user input [19]. Interactions in GeoVis (a) allow users directly control the display of data, (b) are a fundamental part of how maps and mapping tools are used and (c) compares and critiques different mapping environments. GeoVis interactions enable users to derive meaning and accomplish various analysis goals. Processing of different types of information will be affected by what type of visual display is used to present that information and hence providing different perspectives of the data. When the information presentation matches the task, it produces faster and more accurate results. These benefits translate into system and task related performance factors. Cognitive fit theory (CFT) explains how graphical displays affect the decision processes [20]. CFT depends upon fit between information presentation and tasks used by decision maker. Cognitive fit identifies an appropriate representation for a given task performed by users [20]. Information presentation format is the primary factor influencing decision processes [20]. Choice of an interaction method and representation is crucial to the success of a GeoVis environment. We combined the principles of HC approach and Cognitive Fit Theory (CFT) to design and develop "the SanaViz", a GeoVis application to facilitate visual exploration of public health data and in this context it was to evaluate telehealth program in Brazil.

1.1   The SanaViz: A Human Centered GeoVis Prototype

The SanaViz is an Internet based; bilingual, interactive, Web application designed using combined principles of Human Centered (HC) approach and Cognitive Fit Theory (CFT) and is aimed at facilitating visual exploration of public health data, and in this context, telehealth data (Figures 1-3).

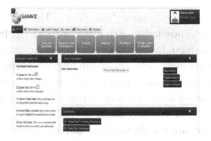

Fig. 1. SanaViz "Registration View"   **Fig. 2.** SanaViz "Exploratory Analysis View"

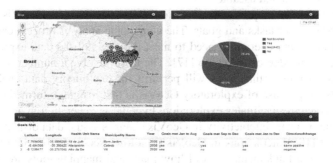

Fig. 3. The SanaViz "Results View"

The SanaViz Prototype Components: The prototype has the following components; (a) Log in and Registration Screen: It captures information about the individual users' age, gender, prior spatial skills, previous use of GeoVis and their role in the telehealth program (e.g. researcher, statistician, software programmer) (Figure1). (b) The user management will facilitate the level of access controls that the different users will have to operate the prototype. (d) The Data Management allows users to import the data in the excel sheet, update, edit, modify and delete the different observations. (e) The outcome indicators assessment allows users to define the tasks they want to perform specific to their needs. (f) The data view component allows the users to utilize various interaction features to perform exploratory analysis and display results in various representations such as Map, Charts and Tables. The interaction features such as zooming, highlighting, sorting, and multiple linkages provide necessary information to the users to explore their data using different perspectives.

1.2   The SanaViz Developmental Platform

The SanaViz is a windows platform and uses Adobe Dreamweaver CS3 for interface design, MySQL 5.1 and SQL queries for database and database functionality, adobe flash for the graphics, and PHP 5.2, JAVASCRIPT, HTML, CSS and Ajax for the overall application including user and data management. Google maps and visualization API are used to show Google maps, chart and table on the analysis screen.

1.3   Methods

A mixed methods approach was used for this cross sectional study. Twenty individuals working at the NUTES telehealth center located at Federal University of Pernambuco, Recife, Brazil were enrolled during June-July 2012. The participants were from diverse backgrounds to ensure broad representation and included professionals from public health, healthcare, software engineering, computer science, biomedical informatics and statistics. The study participants had diverse roles such as teleconsultants, project management, technical support, administration and statistical analysis. Each individual were given a series of 5 random tasks to complete using HC "Sanaviz" and other conventional application Instant Atlas. A sample size of 20 participants in this study will be able to detect a within subject difference of 0.8SD (standardized effect size), two tailed and 0.05 level of significance. This study was approved by the University of Texas Health Science Center Institutional Review Board (IRB # HSC-GEN-11-0447).

1.4   Study Procedure

Participants were given access to two applications: (a) newly developed HC GeoVis prototype "the SanaViz" and (b) an already existed GeoVis application Instant Atlas. Hereby, we chose Instant Atlas as a comparison because it included features that were most representative of the existing GeoVis applications as found in the prior study. Participants were given 30 minutes to explore both the GeoVis applications in order to become comfortable. After exploring both the GeoVis applications, participants were asked to perform five most representative tasks identified in the study. The order of system usage was randomized to control order effects.

Independent Variable: The two-level independent variable was GeoVis application type (SanaVis, Instant Atlas)

Outcomes Assessed: The following outcomes were assessed to compare the two GeoVis applications;

- **Effectiveness:** Focuses on application functionality and examines the users' performance for the tasks. It can be measured by (a) time to complete the tasks, (b) ease with which the task is completed, (c) assistance needed during the tasks and the number of attempts taken to complete the tasks [21]. The ease with which the tasks were completed was gathered on 5 point Likert scale ranging from 1 to 5 (fail/ /hard/medium/easy/very easy).
- **Usefulness:** System Usability Scale (SUS) method is a 10 item questionnaire that refers to appropriateness of the application's functionality that assesses whether the application meets the needs and requirements of the users when carrying the tasks and the extent to which users view the application as supportive for their goals and tasks [22]. The questions consist of close ended questions answered on a five point scale of "Strongly agree" to "Strongly disagree". SUS yields a single number representing a composite measure of the overall usability of the system being studied. To calculate the SUS scores, first sum the score contributions from each item. Each item's score contribution will range from 0 to 4. For items, 1, 3, 5, 7, and 9 the score contribution is the scale position minus 1. For items, 2, 4, 6, 8, and 10,

the contribution is 5 minus the scale position. Multiply the sum of the scores by 2.5 to obtain the overall value of system usability. SUS scores have a range of 0 to 100. Majority of the prior studies have shown that a system with a SUS score of 68 to have greater usability [23].

- **User Reactions:** We performed in-depth interviews to gather feedback about the users' experience of using GeoVis applications "the SanaViz" and Instant Atlas. Feedback was gathered about the various features of GeoVis that needed to be modified or redesigned.

1.5   Statistical Analysis

Univariate analyses were performed by investigators to report descriptive statistics including mean and standard deviation for the continuous variables and frequency distributions for the categorical variables. Repeated measures of analysis of variance (ANOVA) was performed on the within-subject design to test for significant differences between the newly developed HC GeoVis prototype application "the SanaViz" and the existing GeoVis application Instant Atlas. Participants were measured repeatedly on several variables, so we used a method of statistical analysis that accounts for the correlation between repeated measurements. Repeated measures ANOVA is a method for testing if the differences between the means differed by GeoVis applications and the tasks. The analysis for Ease, Assistance, and Number of Attempts were based on a generalized version of the ANOVA model (sometimes called generalized estimating equations) that accounts for repeated measures when the dependent variable is not continuous. Ease is ordinal, assistance is binary, and number of attempts is a count (Poisson distribution). All other analysis was performed using SAS v9.1.

2   Results

2.1   Socio-demographics

The average age of the participants was 28 years (SD=7) and was evenly distributed from young adult to middle age. Majority of them were females (65%) and 90% of them were graduate professionals while the 10% were students majoring in statistics. Almost 100% of the professionals were ranging from somewhat to very familiar with the use of computers. Only 1 (5%) participant was a regular user of GeoVis applications compared to 35% (n=7) that were occasional users. Google maps were the most common GeoVis application that the users were familiar with. A majority of the participants reported that they had no or minimal spatial skills (70%, n=14). Hundred percent of them agreed telecare as one of the most common indicator category.

Following outcomes were assessed:

a)   Tasks Completion Time

For all tasks, Instant Atlas took more time than SanaViz. Instant Atlas, Task 1 took by far most time. The amount of time required was markedly lower at Task 5 when compared to Task 1 (Table 1).

Table 1. Individual comparisons for time by task and GeoVis applications

Tasks	SanaViz Mean (SD)	Instant Atlas Mean (SD)	Mean Difference (Std Error)	p-value
Task1	42.55 (23.87)	81.85 (46.52)	-39.3 (9.01)	0.0001
Task2	33.5 (17.43)	42.5 (27.83)	-9.0 (3.59)	0.02
Task3	28.6 (12.07)	40.7 (17.4)	-12 (3.45)	0.002
Task4	17.75 (7.52)	37.55 (25.8)	-19.8 (5.73)	0.003
Task5	12 (6.13)	15.5 (8.11)	-3.5 (0.73)	0.0001

Results showed that the F test for the repeated measure Task was significant (F=28.62; p=0.0001) suggesting that overall certain tasks required more (or less) time than others. The overall statistics for the GeoVis applications was also significant meaning that there were overall significant differences between both the GeoVis applications SanaViz and Instant Atlas (F=30.16; p=0.0001). Finally, the Task by System interaction was significant (F=8.26; p=0.01 for task*GeoVis application). This means that the difference between the tasks completion times for the GeoVis applications was not the same for all tasks. Task 1 took significantly more time than Task 2 (p<0.02). The overall difference between Task 2 and Task 3 was not significant (p=0.06).

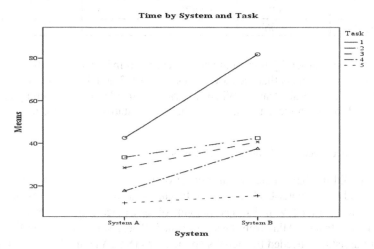

Fig. 4. Time by GeoVis system and Task (Here System A is The SanaViz and the System B is Instant Atlas

GeoVis application by task interaction to evaluate differences between tasks for each GeoVis application was performed separately. SanaViz took less time than Instant Atlas for all Tasks. The difference was not constant (consistent with the significant interaction term as described above). Task 1 took significantly more time than either task 4 or 5 under SanaViz. For Instant Atlas, the difference between tasks 1 and all other tasks were significant. There was a wide time difference between GeoVis applications at task 1 and a comparatively small difference at task 5 (Figure 4).

a) Ease of Task Completion

The first step was to test for the effect of order. The results was non-significant (Wald Chi-Square= 0.11; p=0.73) reflecting that order did not influence ease of Task. Instant Atlas was generally considered harder for most tasks. The group means were identical for task 5. The interaction term was non-significant. Each Task represents a statistical comparison of each Task to Task 5. A direct comparison of means is not recommended due to the multinomial distribution of ease of task. The results showed that each task differed from task 5 overall. Task 5 was lower (easier) than the other tasks (Table2).

Table 2. Individual statistical test for ease by GeoVis applications and Tasks

Parameter	Estimate (Std error)	95% CI	Wald Chi-Square	df	p-value
Task1	20.41 (0.49)	(19.44; 21.38)	1717.37	1	0.0001
Task2	18.44 (0.56)	(17.34; 19.55)	1067.44	1	0.0001
Task3	18.75 (0.57)	(17.65; 19.87)	1101.65	1	0.0001
Task4	19.06b				

[b] Singularity is caused by this parameter. There is no information in the row for Task 4.The reason for this is that the ease scores for Task 3 and Task 4 are identical under SanaViz (they are all "easy").When the values are identical, the computer cannot distinguish between these two tasks, so the formal statistical test for task 4 is redundant.

b) Assistance Needed to Complete the Tasks

The order did not have a significant impact on the assistance needed to complete the tasks (Wald Chi Square=0.766; p=0.38). Instant Atlas required more assistance, especially with the first few tasks. The amount of assistance required dropped for both SanaViz and Instant Atlas from task 1 to task 5. There was overall significant difference for assistance needed by GeoVis applications (SanaViz and Instant Atlas) (Wald Chi-square=11.29; p=0.001) and Task (Wald Chi-square 5069.6; p<0.0001). The interaction term for System by Task was non-significant. Instant Atlas required more assistance than SanaViz. Results of individual comparisons for assistance by task showed that Task 1 required significantly more assistance than tasks 2, 3, 4, or 5 (Table 3).

Table 3. Individual Comparisons for Assistance by Task

Task	Task	Std error	p-value
1	2	0.079	**0.007**
	3	0.094	**0.024**
	4	0.081	**0.034**
	5	0.094	**0.003**
2	1	0.079	**0.007**
	3	0.046	1.00
	4	0.048	0.419
	5	0.036	0.063
3	1	0.094	**0.024**
	2	0.046	1.00
	4	0.042	0.353
	5	0.029	**0.020**
4	1	0.081	**0.034**
	2	0.048	0.419
	3	0.042	0.353
	5	0.048	**0.027**

c) Number of Attempts

The variable reflects a numeric count and the effect of order was non-significant on the number of attempts (Wald Chi-Square=0.389; p=0.533). Overall, Instant Atlas required more attempts than SanaViz. Tasks 1 and 2 tended to require more attempts than task 5. There was a large difference between SanaViz and Instant Atlas at task 1. The magnitude of that difference was markedly smaller for other tasks, and there was no difference between SanaViz and Instant Atlas at task 5. The main effect of GeoVis application was significant (Wald Chi-square=10.49; p=0.001). Overall, there was a significant difference between SanaViz and Instant Atlas on number of attempts. Similarly the main effect of task was also significant (Wald Chi-square=12.71; p=0.013) reflecting that there were overall differences among the tasks. The interaction of GeoVis application and Task was significant (Task* GeoVis application Wald Chi-square=13.38; p=0.01) reflecting that there were larger differences between the GeoVis applications for some tasks but not others. SanaViz and Instant Atlas GeoVis applications differ at task 1 (p=0.01) for the number of attempts but is non-significant for Tasks 2-5.

B. Usefulness

Results found SanaViz to have significantly higher SUS scores against Instant Atlas (SUS=81 versus 53) (p=0.002) (Figure 5).

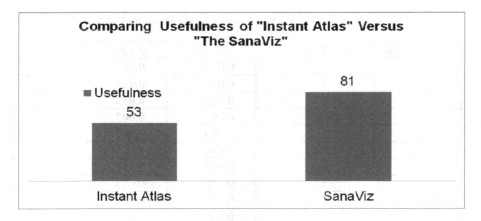

Fig. 5. Comparing usefulness of Instant Atlas versus The SanaViz

Results of the stratified analysis by SUS score of 68 and above versus those below 68 showed that 85% (n=17) of the study participants scored SUS above 68 or above for the HC GeoVis prototype "the SanaViz" as compared to the 30% (n=6) for Instant Atlas.

3   Conclusion

Results of our study demonstrate that GeoVis prototype "The SanaViz" using combined principles of Human Centered approach and Cognitive Fit Theory can be used to design and develop a system that models the characteristics and tasks of the users, thus increasing user effectiveness and user satisfaction. Understanding the users, the domain, and their tasks has the promise to assist in providing quality health care systems. The present study addresses a novel approach of evaluating telehealth programs by using GeoVis applications. The results presented here help to uncover the common telehealth indicator categories, overlapping of some tasks in each of these telehealth indictor categories and the preferences of the various users on how to present the findings of these tasks. Majority of the tasks had spatiotemporal relevance despite having limited prior GeoVis familiarity and prior spatial skills among the various telehealth users. Prior results also demonstrate poor SUS scores for the various existing public health GeoVis applications and so provides considerable evidence and motivation to design and develop GeoVis applications that are easy to use and can effectively facilitate visual exploration of telehealth data. In summary, the present study helped to illuminate some important considerations for developing GeoVis applications for use by different telehealth stakeholders. Although the users had varying levels of expertise and knowledge of mapping and geo-visualization, the participants were enthusiastic about the use of GeoVis application "The SanaViz". Future studies are needed to assess the long term use of "The SanaViz" and to determine the changes that might be needed to be made for further improvement of the prototype. Further research is also warranted to examine how the use of GeoVis application in telehealth can improve public health planning and decision making.

References

1. Braveman, P., Tarimo, E.: Social inequalities in health within countries: Not only an issue for affluent nations. Social Science & Medicine 54(11), 1621–1635 (2002)
2. Richards, T.B., Croner, C.M., Rushton, G., Brown, C.K., Fowler, L.: Geographic information systems and public health: Mapping the future. Public Health Reports-US 114, 359–373 (1999)
3. Aigner, W., Miksch, S., Mueller, W., Schumann, H., Tominski, C.: Visualizing time -oriented data: A systematic review. Computers and Graphics 31, 401–409 (2007)
4. Fuhrmann, S., Ahonen-Rainio, P., Edsall, R.M., Fabrikant, S.I., Koua, E.L., Tobón, C., Wilson, S.: Making useful and useable geovisualization: Design and evaluation issues. Exploring Geovisualization, 551–566 (November 2004, 2005)
5. Cinnamon, J., Rinner, C., Cusimano, M.D., Marshall, S., Bekele, T., Hernandez, T., Chipman, M.L.: Evaluating web-based static, animated and interactive maps for injury prevention. Geospatial Health 4(1), 3–16 (2009)
6. Jamison, D.T.: Disease control priorities in developing countries. Oxford University Press, Washington, DC (2006)
7. Chen, Y., Yi, Q., Mao, Y.: Cluster of liver cancer and immigration: A geographic analysis of incidence data for Ontario 1998–2002. International Journal of Health Geographics 7(1), 28 (2008)
8. Wang, X.Y., Hu, W., Tong, S.: Long-term exposure to gaseous air pollutants and cardio-respiratory mortality in Brisbane, Australia. Geospatial Health 3(2), 257–263 (2009)
9. Castillo-Riquelme, M., Chalabi, Z., Lord, J., Guhl, F., Campbell-Lendrum, D., Davies, C., Fox-Rushby, J.: Modelling geographic variation in the cost-effectiveness of control policies for infectious vector diseases: The example of Chagas disease. Journal of Health Economics 27(2), 405–426 (2008)
10. Robert, C., Ellen, C.: Choropleth map legend design for visualizing community health disparities. International Journal of Health Geographics 8, 52 (2009)
11. Παρμαντο, Β., Παραμιτα, Μ. Ω., Σθγιανταρα, ᵐ., Πραμανα, Γ., Σψοτψη, Μ., & Βθρκε, Δ. Σ.: Spatial and multidimensional visualization of Indonesia's village health statistics. International Journal of Health Geographics 7(1), 30 (2008)
12. Muntz, R., Barclay, T., Dozier, J., Faloutsos, C., Maceachren, A., Martin, J., Satyanarayanan, M.: IT roadmap to a geospatial future, report of the committee on intersections between geospatial information and information technology. National Academy of Sciences, Washington, DC (2003)
13. Timpka, T., Ölvander, C., Hallberg, N.: Information system needs in health promotion: A case study of the safe community program using requirements engineering methods. Health Informatics Journal 14(3), 183–193 (2008)
14. Robinson, A.C., Chen, J., Lengerich, E.J., Meyer, H.G., MacEachren, A.M.: Combining usability techniques to design geovisualization tools for epidemiology. Cartography and Geographic Information Science 32(4), 243 (2005)
15. Fuhrmann, S., Ahonen-Rainio, P., Edsall, R.M., Fabrikant, S.I., Koua, E.L., Tobón, C., Wilson, S.: Making useful and useable geovisualization: Design and evaluation issues. Exploring Geovisualization, 551-566 (November 2004, 2005)
16. Lauesen, S.: User interface design: A software engineering perspective. Addison-Wesley, Reading (2005)

17. Gahegan, M., Wachowicz, M., Harrower, M., Rhyne, T.M.: The integration of geographic visualization with knowledge discovery in databases and geocomputation. Cartography and Geographic Information Science 28(1), 29–44 (2001)
18. Walton, J.: Data mining and visualization. Database Programming & Design 9, 5 (1996)
19. Crampton, J.W.: Interactivity types in geographic visualization. Cartography and Geographic Information Science 29(2), 85–98 (2002)
20. Dennis, A.R., Carte, T.A.: Using geographical information systems for decision making: Extending cognitive fit theory to map-based presentations. Information Systems Research 9(2), 194–203 (1998)
21. Kelsey, B., Rinner, C.: User task scenarios for map-based decision support in community health planning. In: Proceedings from the 12th AGILE International Conference on Geographic Information Science, Hannover, Germany. Springer (2009)
22. Brooke, J.: SUS-A quick and dirty usability scale. In: Jordan, P.W., Thomas, B., Weerdmeester, B.A., McClelland, A.L. (eds.) Usability Evaluation in Industry, pp. 189–194. Taylor and Francis, London (1996)
23. Bangor, A., Kortum, P.T., Miller, J.T.: An empirical evaluation of the system usability scale. International Journal of Human–Computer Interaction 24(6), 574–594 (2008)

Improving Xbox Search Relevance
by Click Likelihood Labeling

Jingjing Li, Xugang Ye, and Danfeng Li

Microsoft, Bellevue, WA, USA
{jingjing.li,xugangye,lida}@microsoft.com

Abstract. From the original game console, the Xbox has rapidly evolved into a comprehensive entertainment platform where tens of millions of users could not only play video games but also watch movies and TVs, listen music and enjoy Apps. Therefore, building a cross media ranker to provide relevant and personalized search results for Xbox users has become an interesting and imperative task. In this paper, we present our recent progress on improving Xbox's cross media ranker by mining massive click log data and generating multi-class relevance labels. Our experimental results have shown that incorporating the click likelihoods into the label generation yields better click-performance and meanwhile maintains comparable NDCG values, as compared to solely using the human labels generated by a small number of human judges.

Keywords: Click Likelihood, Click Log, Xbox, Search, Ranking, Relevance Labeling.

1 Introduction

Relevance label, which represents how much a user thinks the returned document is relevant to his/her issued query, is critical to the performance of trained ranker. In a ranking model, the relevance label serves as the target for ranking function to fit. Thus, if the relevance label is prone to error, it is hard for the ranking function to learn the best features and parameters to meet user's relevance expectation.

Usually, the labeling tasks are conducted by a small number of human judges due to high recruiting expenses. Therefore, the labeling process is often time-consuming and laborious-taking [1, 2]. Moreover, because the labeling is conducted by a small number of judges, the labeling judgments may not well represent the large user population [3, 4]. Last but not the least, for search problem that is highly time-sensitive, the extent of relevance between a query and a document could vary significantly overtime. Unless we have large amount of human judges to work diligently enough, it is very hard for the labels to keep up with the relevance changing rate.

An alternative method to generate relevance labels is by mining the relevance signals from click log. By utilizing massive amount of click data, the training data is easy to scale in a much faster fashion. Moreover, the labels are less likely to be biased because the relevance between a query and a document is determined by logging the behaviors of a large amount of real users. Finally, we can easily extract relevance

F.F.-H. Nah (Ed.): HCIB/HCII 2014, LNCS 8527, pp. 735–743, 2014.
© Springer International Publishing Switzerland 2014

labels from click log from time to time so as to accommodate any temporal relevance changes.

In this study, following the design science paradigm proposed by Hevner [5], we propose a method to train a ranking model by mining the click likelihood from large amount of click log. Specifically, we will illustrate how to generate relevance labels by leveraging click likelihoods, how to reduce noises and biases in click likelihoods, and how to embed the click likelihoods into a time-sensitive training framework to accommodate relevance changes. As a proof-of-concept, we demonstrate the applicability of our method by applying it to the Xbox's Cross Media search. Under the same set of features and ranking algorithm, we compare and critically discuss the ranking performance between traditional human labeling models and our proposed models. Finally, we summarize the results and discuss the future research direction.

2   Related Work

2.1   Learning to Rank

Learning to rank aims to automatically construct a ranking function (i.e. ranker) $y = f(x)$ from training data, which is usually a supervised or semi-supervised machine learning problem [6-9]. The training data consists of training example at query-document $\langle q, d \rangle$ level. For each $\langle q, d \rangle$, we extract a feature vector $\vec{x}^{q,d}$ as the input for ranking function, and a relevance label $s(q, d)$. The parameters of ranking function is learned by minimizing the error function of the ranker score and the relevance label: $\mathrm{Error}\big(s(q, d), f(\vec{x}^{q,d})\big)$. Therefore, the relevance label $s(q, d)$ is critical for inferring the correct parameters of ranking function.

2.2   Xbox Cross Media Search

In this section, we will introduce the search problem in Xbox and how it is different from the traditional search.

The search content served at Xbox are media-specific, including movie, TV, music and game. The user interface for Xbox is dramatically different from traditional web search. Figure 1 shows the layout of four contents on the first page on Xbox One. This layout indicates that the relevance of first returned result is more important than that of traditional web search as the area of the first returned doc is much bigger.

Moreover, there are considerable noises in user clicks. We found that the click probability fluctuates dramatically as users continue scrolling to the next page. Specifically, we notice an unusual phenomenon that the click probability at the position greater than 125 on average is greater than 0.8, which means users have more than 80% of the chance to click on a document after the 31st page. One reason behind might be there are some malicious users in the system, who intentionally click on document with poor relevance. Another possible reason is that scrolling and clicking action using Xbox's controller is relatively easy to achieve than traditional web search, thus users may mistakenly scroll too many pages before initiating their clicks. However, when we only consider the clicks in the top 50 position (see Figure 2), the

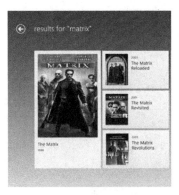

Fig. 1. Content layout on the first page of the Xbox One's search results

click probability is more aligned with the traditional cascade model assumption [10]. Consequently, in order to get more reliable click signals from Xbox, we may need to truncate clicks happened at bottom of the page.

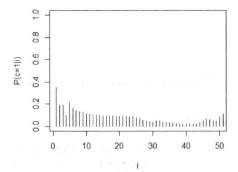

Fig. 2. The click probability at position i

3 Proposed Framework

3.1 Overall Framework

In this section, we will discuss the major steps involved in ranker training with click likelihoods. The first step is to construct training data, which consists of five sub-steps: query sampling, query-document pair selection, click likelihood calculation, smoothing & cleaning and feature extraction. The first two steps focus on generating query-document pair $\langle q, d \rangle$, which involves spamming filtering and tail $\langle q, d \rangle$ pairs removal. Feature extraction aims to find the feature vector $\vec{x}^{q,d}$ for a selected $\langle q, d \rangle$. Click likelihood with its smoothing and cleaning techniques are key components in our article and we will discuss them in 3.2 and 3.3. Finally, we train a ranker with optimal parameters and evaluate its final performance on the test data. The specific machine learning algorithm is called LambdaRank [11].

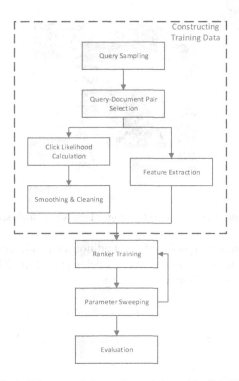

Fig. 3. Overall framework for ranker training with click likelihood

3.2   Click Likelihood and Relevance Label

The ranking function tries to find a list of indexed entities $d_1, \dots, d_l$ for a query q such that the $s(q, d_i) \geq s(q, d_j)$ if $i < j$, where s is the relevance measure. Our goal therefore is to find a metric that could best approximate $s(q, d_i)$.

The click likelihood for a query-document pair (q, d) is denoted as:

$$Click\ Likelihood\ (CL) = p\big(c_{qd} = 1 \,\big|\, s_{qd} = 1\big)$$

$$= \frac{\#\ of\ times\ d\ clicked\ under\ q}{\#\ of\ times\ (q, d)\ shown\ to\ the\ users} = \frac{n_{c_{qd}}}{n_{s_{qd}}} \tag{1}$$

Assuming that a user would only click on the relevant documents, the click likelihood thus could be used as the relevance measures.

Nonetheless, we need to consider the fact that the click logs are often very noisy. For example, spamming users could generate abnormal click statistics. We implemented several techniques to reduce the noise. We will discuss some representative methods in the following section:

(1) **Spam detection:** in the query sampling stage, we allow a user to only contribute one search for a given query in one day. By using this technique, we eliminate the affect posed by those malicious users or robots who issue the same searches numerous times.

(2) **Query document filtering:** the estimate of click likelihood for query-document that only show a limited amount of times is more likely to be biased. For example, if a query-document pair only shows two times in the log, and has been clicked once, the click likelihood is 0.5—much higher than the average. However, with only two views of this query-document pair, this particular click is very likely to happen by chance. To reduce this bias in our dataset, we discard any query-document pairs which show less than 50 times given a specific time frame.

Moreover, searching a query could return dozens or hundreds of documents, but it is unlikely that all of them are examined by users. According to the definition of click likelihood, we need to only count the documents that are seen by the users as the denominator. Therefore, we applied two filtering techniques:

a. $n_{s_{qd}} = \#$ *of documents whose position* $> =$ *last click position*

b. $n_{s_{qd}} = \#$ *of documents whose position* $> =$

   a fixed position (*usually less than* 50)

According to our observation in Figure 2, we expect the ranker performance using method b. to be better than that using method a.

(3) **Click likelihood smoothing:** we also applied a smoothing technique to penalize the query-document pair that has low number of view count. The smooth function is denoted as:

$$CL_s = \frac{n_{c_{qd}} + sm * prior(CL)}{n_{s_{qd}} + sm} \qquad (2)$$

Where sm is a smoothing factor and $prior(CL)$ is the average click likelihood of the entire data set.

(4) **Outlier removal:** We transformed the final click likelihood into log-odds ratios to identify outliers. Since the distribution of log-odds ratios generally follow normal distribution, we can manual check the distribution graph to inspect possible outliers and remove long tails. The log-odds ratio function is denoted as:

$$logodds(CL_s) = \frac{\ln(CL_s)}{\ln(1 - CL_s)} \qquad (3)$$

Finally, we need to convert the cleaned click likelihood into discretized relevance label gain. Since the maximum label gain for human labeling setting is 15, and the final click likelihood ranges in [0,1], we simply multiple of the click likelihood by 15 and rounded to integers and generate a 15-level relevance labels.

3.3   Constructing Training Data for Time-Sensitive Features and Relevance Labels

Because many features in the ranking model is highly time-sensitive, we need to consider time effect when constructing the training data. Suppose the original data is collected in a time horizon $[t_0, t_1]$. We cut this time zone into the so-called "feature zone" and "target zone", which are respectively $[t_0, \tau)$ and $[\tau, t_1]$ with $t_1 - \tau < \tau - t_0$. For each (q, d)-pair that is both available in $[t_0, \tau)$ and $[\tau, t_1]$, the feature vector $\vec{x}^{q,d}$ is generated within the time frame $[t_0, \tau)$, while the relevance label *click likelihood* is estimated using the information in the time frame $[\tau, t_1]$.

A more advanced method to prepare training data that could accommodate relevance changes overtime is to use a sliding window. We generate multiple training dataset corresponding to $[t_0, \tau_i)$ and $[\tau_i, t_1]$ where $\tau_i \in (t_0, t_1)$ and combine them together. Therefore, for a single query-document pair, we can investigate how the feature vector and relevance label changes over time.

4   Demonstration and Evaluation

4.1   Evaluation Metrics

We use two types of metrics to evaluate the ranker performance: NDCG (normalized discounted cumulative gain) **Error! Reference source not found.** and future click-performance. NDCG is a traditional metric to evaluate ranking performance. It allows each document to have a graded relevance (e.g., bad, fair, good, excellent, perfect) while some other traditional measures (precision, recall, …, etc.) only allows binary relevance. It also assigns higher weight to the document at the top of the result list. We use the NDCG of the top i positions for $i = 1,2,4$ as our NDCG measurements. Specifically, the NDCG of the top i positions is calculated as

$$\text{NDCG}_i = \frac{1}{N}\sum_q \left(\sum_{j=1}^i \frac{rel_j^q}{\log_2(1+j)}\right) / \left(\sum_{j=1}^i \frac{\overline{rel_j^q}}{\log_2(1+j)}\right) \tag{4}$$

where $\overline{rel_1^q} \geq \cdots \geq \overline{rel_i^q}$ represent the descending order of $rel_1^q, \ldots, rel_i^q$, which respectively are the relevance gains of the first i documents under the query q that does not have all zero-gain results, and N is the total number of such queries.

Future click-performance represents the user engagement to the search service after a ranker is deployed to production. We use the click-happening-rate (CHR) and the last-click-rate (LCR) of the top i positions for $i = 1,2,4$ as our click-metrics. The CHR of the top i positions is calculated as

$$\text{CHR}_i = \frac{\text{Number of sessions having} \geq 1 \text{ click in first } i \text{ positions}}{\text{Number of sessions}}. \tag{5}$$

The LCR of the top i positions is calculated as

$$\text{LCR}_i = \frac{\text{Number of sessions having the last click in first } i \text{ positions}}{\text{Number of sessions}}. \tag{6}$$

4.2   Data Set

We collected the query-document pairs that satisfying the selection criteria from the click log in Feb 1st ~ June 1st, 2013. Notice that only 17% of the selected query-document pairs have human labels. Thus the training data set for human label ranker is from these 17% of query-document pairs. The training data set for click-based ranker include all the query-document pairs. The click-logs in June 2013 are used to test the future click-performance. The human-judged query-document pairs generated in movie and TV domains from June 2013 to October 2013 were used to test the future NDCG-performance.

4.3   Experimental Results

In this section, we present some experimental results of comparing the relevance labels generated by our method with several other types of relevance labels. For each relevance label setting, we kept the same feature set and used the same ranker-learning algorithm LambdaRank. Following are the description of each experiment:

i.   HJ: Human judgment. The labels have three unique values of gain: 15 for Excellent, 7 for Good, and 0 for Bad. The query-document pairs in the training data contain only those with HJ labels.

ii.   lCTR: CTR under the assumption that in a session, the returned results before the last click are viewed and those after the last click are not viewed. The label gain is calculated as lCTR · 15 and rounded. The query-document pairs in the training data contain only those with lCTR labels.

iii. tCTR: CTR under the assumption that in a session, the returned results before a pre-defined truncated position are viewed and those after the truncated position are not viewed. The label gain is calculated as tCTR · 15 and rounded. The query-document pairs in the training data contain only those with tCTR labels.

iv.   tCTR∪HJ: Combination of tCTR-labels and HJ-labels. The query-document pairs in the training data are the union of those with tCTR-labels and those with HJ-labels. For each with both the tCTR- label and the HJ-label, the final label gain is calculated as the rounded average.

Once the relevance labels were determined in the target zone, we performed the feature extraction for each query-document pair in the feature zone. Four rankers were trained from these training data, and were used to score the query-document relevance on the same test data. The test results are summarized in Table 1 and 2.

Table 1. The test click-performance

Label	CHR_1	CHR_2	CHR_4	LCR_1	LCR_2	LCR_4
HJ	55.77%	70.65%	85.40%	49.00%	64.47%	81.20%
lCTR	53.11%	69.46%	84.73%	46.34%	63.18%	80.65%
tCTR	**57.39%**	**71.39%**	85.69%	**50.18%**	65.22%	81.68%
tCTR∪HJ	57.13%	71.27%	**85.78%**	50.17%	**65.25%**	**81.71%**

742   J. Li, X. Ye, and D. Li

Table 2. The NDCG values from one human judgment data

Label	Movie			TV		
	NDCG$_1$	NDCG$_2$	NDCG$_4$	NDCG$_1$	NDCG$_2$	NDCG$_4$
HJ	**91.71%**	**90.22%**	**89.93%**	**94.35%**	**93.63%**	**93.95%**
lCTR	83.92%	81.77%	81.83%	91.81%	90.44%	91.17%
tCTR	86.46%	83.70%	84.30%	90.80%	91.03%	92.26%
tCTR∪HJ	90.56%	88.09%	88.41%	92.78%	92.73%	93.25%

From Table 1, we found that lCTR has the worst performance, indicating the existence of noises in click logs. However, after only utilizing the click likelihood in the top 50 documents per query, the performance is dramatically increased. This means the clickes on the first few pages are more trustworthy. After combined with the human label, tCTR∪HJ model also has satisfactory performance on future click metrics.

Per Table 2, we found that ranker trained purely from human labels has the best results. This is expected because the test data for NDCG evaluation uses the human label as the relevance labels. Similar to the pattern in click metrics, the lCTR model has the worst performance, and the gap to the optimal performance is even larger. However, after removing the query-document pairs happened after the 50th position, tCTR has gained considerable performance. The best click-based model is the one that combines the human label and click likelihood, which is almost comparable to the pure human-label ranker (p value greater than 0.05).

The initial experimental results has shown that the ranker trained on click labels yielded comparable performance to the ranker trained on human judgment labels. This result is encouraging because we can quickly increase the training data size with limited manual efforts. We also found that, compared to the model with human label, the model with click labels performs especially better on head queries. Hence in the future we can adopt a hybrid model which utilizes click to generate labels for head queries and employs human judges to label tail queries. Last but not the least, we found the click- based rankers are better in predicting the future customer engagement.

However, we also find there are considerable noises contained in click likelihood. For example, eye-tracking experiments have found that the probability of a document being clicked under a query is not only determined by relevance but also the document position and presentation format. Therefore, we are currently working on a generative model that could accommodate position bias.

5   Conclusion

In this study, we propose an alternative method to generate relevance labels for Xbox's cross media ranker training. We find that the traditional human labeling method is time-consuming, not representative and not responsive to market dynamics. Therefore, we propose a method to use click likelihood as relevance labels. Since click logs often contain noises and is biased towards position and presentation, we discussed several techniques to reduce these noises. Finally, using the same set of features and ranking algorithm, we compared our ranker with traditional human-labeled ranker. We found that the click-based ranker is more suitable to predict future user engagement and human-label-based ranker performs better in traditional NDCG metric. The overall best performing model is the hybrid model which combines human label and click likelihood. Therefore, in the future we could leverage click log to get training data at low cost and in a more timely fashion, and let human judges could concentrate on the relevance labeling for tail query-document pairs that are more likely to contain click noises.

One limitation of our proposed method is that we did not differentiate the click likelihood between queries. From the Xbox click log, we found that some queries are title-specific (such as "skyfall"), while some are people-specific (such as "jennifer lawrence"). These two types of queries in general give different click patterns: the title-specific queries has more concentrate click distribution while the people-specific queries has more spread distribution. Therefore, one future research direction is to create query-specific click likelihood.

Another limitation is that we reduce the position bias by relatively simple heuristics— only disregarding document clicks after a fixed position (less than 50). A more sophisticated method is to look into the relationship between click sequence, viewing position and relevance levels at the same time. Therefore, we are currently working on a generate model which could account for the aforementioned factors in a comprehensive way.

References

1. Voorhees, E.M.: Variations in relevance judgments and the measurement of retrieval effectiveness. Information Processing & Management 36, 697–716 (2000)
2. Bailey, P., Craswell, N., Soboroff, I., Thomas, P., de Vries, A.P., Yilmaz, E.: Relevance assessment: are judges exchangeable and does it matter. In: Proceedings of the 31st Annual International ACM SIGIR Conference on Research and Development in Information Retrieval, pp. 667–674. ACM (2008)
3. Agrawal, R., Halverson, A., Kenthapadi, K., Mishra, N., Tsaparas, P.: Generating labels from clicks. In: Proceedings of the Second ACM International Conference on Web Search and Data Mining, pp. 172–181. ACM (2009)
4. Xu, J., Chen, C., Xu, G., Li, H., Abib, E.R.T.: Improving quality of training data for llearning to rank using click-through data. In: Proceedings of the Third ACM International Conference on Web Search and Data Mining, pp. 171–180. ACM (2010)
5. von Alan, R.H., March, S.T., Park, J., Ram, S.: Design science in information systems research. MIS Quarterly 28, 75–105 (2004)
6. Burges, C., Shaked, T., Renshaw, E., Lazier, A., Deeds, M., Hamilton, N., Hullender, G.: Learning to rank using gradient descent. In: Proceedings of the 22nd International Conference on Machine Learning, pp. 89–96. ACM (2005)
7. Burges, C.J., Ragno, R., Le, Q.V.: Learning to rank with nonsmooth cost functions. In: NIPS, pp. 193-200 (2006)
8. Cao, Z., Qin, T., Liu, T.-Y., Tsai, M.-F., Li, H.: Learning to rank: from pairwise approach to listwise approach. In: Proceedings of the 24th International Conference on Machine Learning, pp. 129–136. ACM, New York (2007)
9. Chapelle, O., Chang, Y.: Yahoo! Learning to Rank Challenge Overview. Journal of Machine Learning Research-Proceedings Track 14, 1–24 (2011)
10. Craswell, N., Zoeter, O., Taylor, M., Ramsey, B.: An experimental comparison of click position-bias models. In: Proceedings of the 2008 International Conference on Web Search and Data Mining, pp. 87–94. ACM (2008)
11. Burges, C.J.: From ranknet to lambdarank to lambdamart: An overview. Learning 11, 23–581 (2010)

A Preliminary Study on Social Cues Design in Mobile Check-in Based Advertisement

Chi-Lun Liu[1,*] and Hsieh-Hong Huang[2]

[1] Department of Multimedia and Mobile Commerce, Kainan University, 1,
Kainan Road, Luzhu, Taoyuan 33857, Taiwan
tonyliu@mail.knu.edu.tw
[2] Dept. of Information Science and Management Systems,
National Taitung University, 684, Sec. 1, Chunghua Road, Taitung 95002, Taiwan
kory@nttu.edu.tw

Abstract. Companies consider the check-in service as an new advertising channel to promote the companies and products. The check-in based advertisement always has different level of social cues richness. Determining an effective social cues design in check-in based advertisement is a critical question. This research explores which social cues design will be appropriate in check-in based advertisement. The results of a laboratory experiment supported that the design of higher social cues richness increases higher advertising effectiveness measured by attitude toward the ad in general. Social media users would intend to use the appropriate design if the design is effective and easy-to-be-memorized.

Keywords: Social cues, attitude toward the ad, mobile check-in apps, social media, mobile marketing.

1 Introduction

Social media, such as Facebook, is one of the most popular website in many people's personal life. For the marketing purpose, social media is emergent as a powerful communication tool has made it possible for a person to communicate hundreds or thousands of other people about products and companies informally (Mangold and Faulds, 2009). Many people like to use check-in services in social media to post messages and photos about their lives in particular locations. Check-in service is a one-to-many model that allows users to semantically create and name venues to manually broadcast their locations to their friends in social media (Cramer et al., 2011). Posted content included messages and photos usually involve companies and products, such as meals in a restaurant and facilities in an amusement park. Therefore the content posted by consumers in a check-in service can be considered as a new informal form of advertisement for companies' marketing and promotion.

Social cues refer to a medium presents other persons' social interactions directly or indirectly (Kamins, 2011; Horvath and Lombard, 2010). The content posted by check-in

---

* Corresponding author.

F.F.-H. Nah (Ed.): HCIB/HCII 2014, LNCS 8527, pp. 744–753, 2014.
© Springer International Publishing Switzerland 2014

service users always have different levels of social cues richness. For example, the content including no photo has fewer social cues than the content including photo. Users' attitude toward the content which have different social cues in check-in services is an interesting issue for internet marketing. In the other hand, check-in service users preferring to post which level of social cues richness is another interesting research issue. Companies like positive and good messages about their companies and products.

The prior Human Computer Interaction (HCI) studies investigate on social cues presentation. For example, Horvath and Lombard (2010) use pleasantries in text and cartoon owl as high social cue conditions in information system interface. Wang et al. (2007) use animated character and real-person character as social cues on retail web sites. Kamins et al. (2011) focus on internet auctions and use the following information as social cues: the number of bids submitted, a counter which presents the number of viewers who watched the item on sale, and bidder's personal information. In the Hu and Jasper's study (2006), the store decorated with posters which showed a man, mother, and baby in high socially-oriented display condition. The above prior studies investigate the effects of social cues outside the social app context because the social app context is a new phenomenon. Check-in Content in a social app is different from other apps because the content is often generated by a friend and includes location-based information.

The first research objective of this study aims to manipulate different levels of social cues richness in the check-in based advertisement and to explore how social cues designs influence audiences' attitude toward the ad. The second research objective of this study aims to explore the relationship between attitude toward the ad, self efficacy on recall, and usage intention for each social cues design when users post articles in a check-in service.

2   Social Cues Design in Mobile Check-in Based Advertisement

The Facebook app, which is a popular mobile check-in app on android platform, is chosen in the experiment. The Facebook app provides a location-based service and shows the check-in location in the map in the user-generated check-in content. The Facebook app users can alternatively post texts and photos when they check in. Three social cues designs are usually appears on user-generated check-in content in the real world: text, text and product photo, and text and product+person photo.

Fig. 1. Screenshot of social cues design C-1: Text

Fig. 2. Screenshot of social cues design C-2: Text and product photo

Fig. 3. Screenshot of social cues design C-3: Text and product+person photo

This study uses the Facebook app and the mobile device, which is Samsung Galaxy S3, to manipulate three social cues design advertisement: C-1, C-2, and C-3. A user only input text data in social cues design C-1 (Fig. 1). A user input text data and a photo including ice cream product in social cues design C-2 (Fig. 2). And a user input text data and a photo including ice cream product and a person in social cues design C-3 (Fig. 3).

3   Research Hypothesis

Figure 4 depicts a proposed research model comprising four concepts: social cues design, attitude toward the ad, self efficacy on recall, and design usage intention. The proposed four hypotheses (H1, H2, H3, and H4) in Figure 1 are introduced as follows.

Social cues design is defined as "a medium presents other persons' social interactions directly or indirectly in different levels". The social cues design in the check-in service has two purposes: self disclosure for personal promotion (Carpenter, 2012) and product and company promotion (Mangold and Faulds, 2009). Self promotion indicates that a person presents an inflated sense of self to as many people as possible (Carpenter, 2012). Product and company promotion in social media is an informal promotion channel that customers talk directly to one another about products and companies outside company managers' direct control.

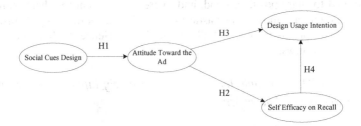

Fig. 4. Research Model

In the advertising domain, attitude toward the ad is the affective response of consumers to a particular stimulus (Wang et al., 2009; Yi, 1990). Attitude means users' feeling, such as good, interesting, like, and favorable. Social cues can evoke social presence (Horvath and Lombard, 2010). Social presence concerns with the human warmth and sociability on the Internet media (Hassanein and Head, 2006). Lombard and Ditton suggest that one of the most prominent psychological impact of social presence is positive attitude (Lombard and Ditton, 1997). Social presence causes enjoyable, interesting, and pleasant feelings in an apparel retailing website (Hassanein and Head, 2006). Therefore the hypothesis 1 is proposed as follows.

Hypothesis 1 (H1): The richness levels of social cues design positively influences attitude toward the ad in check-in based advertising.

Self efficacy is the belief that a person is able to perform a particular task (Lorenzo et al., 2012; Compeau and Higgins, 1995). Recall means that a person remembers the received message after a period of time (Norris and Colman, 1992). Therefore *Self efficacy on recall* in this study is defined as "the belief that a person is able to remember the received message after a period of time". High pleasant feelings have a significant positive impact on advertising recall (Pieters and Klerk-Warmerdam, 1996). This study measures self efficacy on recall and does not measure actual recall accuracy because we would like to explore how users subjectively belief and confidence in recall the content can influence the intention to adopt a design in a check-in service. Furthermore, self-reported confidence in recall could be useful as a predictor of recall accuracy (Cust et al., 2009). Therefore self efficacy on recall can be a predictor of the actual recall accuracy. The hypothesis 2 is proposed as follows.

Hypothesis 2 (H2): Attitude toward the ad positively influences recall self efficacy in check-in based advertising.

The prior research shows that behavior intention to system use lead to actual system use (Moon and Kim, 2001). This study goes beyond the general check-in system usage intention and focus on the design preference in check-in system usage. Therefore *design usage intention* is defined as "behavior intention to post and share a particular richness level of social cues in check-in service usage".

People tend to share positive, good, and interesting content to others online (Tierney, 2013). People are most enthusiastic in spreading ideas that they themselves are excited and that appeals to others (Falk, et. al, 2013). Hence the hypothesis 3 and 4 are proposed as follows.

Hypothesis 3 (H3): Attitude toward the ad positively influences design usage intention in check-in based advertising.

Hypothesis 4 (H4): Self efficacy on recall positively influences design usage intention in check-in based advertising.

4   Research Method

This study manipulates social cue richness in the experiment setting. Table 1 summarizes three levels of social cues richness in check-in content. Subjects in experiments are randomly assigned in three groups to browse check-in content C-1, C-2, and C-3 on Facebook. The subjects were Taiwanese, and were university students.

After the subjects browse a particular check-in based advertisement, the subjects fill in the questionnaire to measure their attitude toward the ad, self efficacy on recall, and design usage intention. The items in the questionnaire for measuring attitude toward the ad is developed based on the advertisement effects study (Yi, 1990). The items in the questionnaire for measuring self efficacy on recall is based on the prior advertising recall studies (Norris and Colman, 1992; Bezjian–Avery et al., 1998). And the items of design usage intention are based on the concept of technology usage intention (Venkatesh et al., 2003).

Table 1. Social Cues Richness in Check-in Design

Social Cues Design	Social Cues Richness	Features
C-1	Low	Text: descriptions about the feeling of the product in the location
		Map: the geographic location in the map is shown directly.
C-2	Medium	Text: as the same as C-1
		Picture: the product and scene in the location
		Map: the geographic location in the map shows when a user clicks the location name.
C-3	High	Text: as the same as C-1
		Picture: the person, product, and scene in the location
		Map: the geographic location in the map shows when a user clicks the location name.

5   Experimental Result

The experimental result is twofold. The first part is descriptive statistic data for reporting user experiences. The second part is the hypotheses testing result conducted by partial least squares (PLS) regression technique. The two parts are introduced as follows.

5.1   Descriptive Statistics

The descriptive statistics reports the user experiences for three groups of social cues designs (C-1, C-2, and C-3) about attitude toward the ad, self efficacy on recall, and design usage intention. The sample size is 63. The statistic data is shown and discussed as follows.

The subject demographics are shown in Table 2. In the experiment, male subjects are about 70 percent and female subjects are about 30 percent. Most of subjects are 18-28 years old. All subjects have usage experiences on Facebook. 82% subjects have usage experiences on the Facebook check-in service. Most of subjects like to use the check-in service in sight-seeing spot (63%), Leisure-oriented entertainment place (66.2%), and restaurant (69.2%).

Table 3 shows that higher social cues richness results in more subjects who have positive attitude toward the ad in average agreed percentage. It is interesting that the agreed percentage of irritating (18.1%) and favorable (45.4%) in high social cues richness (C-3) group is lower than the agreed percentage of irritating (26.0%) and favorable (56.5%) in medium social cues richness (C-2) group. In the follow-up study, a subject reports that the no-person photo (in C-2) keeps the sense of mystery to increase irritating feeling. Another subject does not favor product+person photo (in C-3) because the person occupies most of the photo layout.

Table 2. Subject Demographics

Gender 7-2	
Male	71.4%
Female	28.6%
Dominant age group	18-28
Have Facebook usage experience	100%
Have check-in experience	82.0%
Preferred check-in locations	
Public transportation	29.2%
Sight-seeing spot	63.0%
Government institution	23.0%
Leisure-oriented entertainment place	66.2%
Restaurant	69.2%
Activity and exhibition	49.2%
Others	9.2%

Table 3. Agreed Percentage on Attitude Toward the Ad

Social Cues Richness	Low C-1	Medium C-2	High C-3
Good	33.3%	56.5%	72.7%
Interesting	38.9%	47.8%	63.6%
Like	16.7%	52.1%	59.1%
Irritating	5.6%	26.0%	18.1%
Favorable	22.2%	56.5%	45.4%
Average	23.3%	47.8%	51.8%

Table 4 shows the average of agreed percentage on self efficacy on recall in both medium and high social cues richness are higher than 50%. However, the average of agreed percentage on self efficacy on recall (63.0%) in the medium social cues richness (C-2) group is higher than the average percentage (53.6%) in the high social cues richness (C-3) group. And the average of agreed percentage on self efficacy on recall (53.6%) in the high social cues richness group (C-3) is higher than the average percentage (40.6%) in the low social cues richness (C-1) group. In more details, two items dramatically decrease the average of agreed percentage on self efficacy on recall in the high social cues richness (C-3) group: "The ad enhance my impression on the scene and product" and "I can describe the scene and product in the ad in few days". This result is reasonable because several subjects indicate that the product is too small in the photo layout and most of the photo layout is occupied by a person.

Table 5 reveals that the subjects intend to use the higher social cues richness when they generating check-in based advertisement in general. It is interesting that only 36.4% subjects intend to use the high social cues richness design in the C-3 group, which lower than 47.8% agreed percentage on design usage intention in the C-2 group. Subjects indicate that they sometimes take no-person photos for generating check-in based advertisement because of privacy concerns. For example, some persons secretly join the activities and are unsuitable for appearance in social media publicly. Many users often add unfamiliar "friends" in social media. Some users were afraid the person photos may be stolen by other unfamiliar persons for harmful purposes.

Table 4. Agreed Percentage on Self Efficacy on Recall

Social Cues Richness	Low C-1	Medium C-2	High C-3
I can remember the scene and product in the ad in few days.	38.9%	69.5%	68.2%
The ad enhance my impression on the scene and product.	55.6%	78.3%	**59.1%**
I can describe the scene and product in the ad in few days.	22.2%	43.4%	**27.3%**
I will remember the ad if similar scenes and products appear.	44.5%	60.9%	59.1%
Average	40.6%	63.0%	53.6%

Table 5. Agreed Percentage on Design Usage Intention

Social Cues Richness	Low C-1	Medium C-2	High C-3
I would use this design approach continuously.	16.7%	56.5	68.2%
I would choose this design approach.	11.2%	60.9	68.2%
I would use this design approach to interact with my friends.	16.7%	78.3	77.2%
I would not stop use this design approach.	22.3%	47.8	**36.4%**
I hope my check-in content would be made by this design approach.	11.2%	60.9	81.8%
Average	15.6	60.9	66.4

5.2   Hypotheses Testing Result

In the data analysis phase for hypotheses testing, this study uses partial least squares (PLS), which is a structural equation modeling (SEM). PLS is useful when the sample size is not very large. Bootstrapping was performed to test the statistical significance of each path coefficient using t-tests. The result depicted in Figure 2 shows that increased social cues numbers in advertisement presentation design positively and significantly influences on attitude toward the ad. Attitude toward the ad has a positive and significant impact on self efficacy on recall and design usage intention. And self efficacy on recall has a positive and significant impact on design usage intention. Thus hypotheses H1, H2, H3, and H4 are supported. The R^2 for the attitude construct in Figure 5 was rather low in 0.092. However, it is reasonable, because attitude for check-in content are affected by a large number of factors other than social cues design.

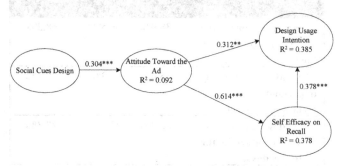

Fig. 5. PLS Structural Model

Notes: Values above the arrows refer to path coefficients; ** $p < 0.01$, *** $p < 0.001$.

6   Conclusion

Check-in content can be considered as an informal advertising in users' self promotion and companies' promotion simultaneously in social media. This study proposes a research model involves social presence levels in check-in based advertisement, attitude toward the user-generated advertisement in a check-in service, self efficacy on recall, and design usage intention. The relationships among the above concepts are discussed based on the prior studies. The preliminary experiment for validating the proposed model is conducted.

In theoretical contribution, this study put the concept of attitude toward the ad into the social media's check-in service as an informal promotion channel in the proposed research model. The proposed model presents a virtuous circle for the promotion in social media. In this circle, users like receiving positive and interesting message. Others usually give positive feedbacks to admire these positive and interesting message in the expectation. And users would like to share a positive message about companies and products in check-in services. For managerial implications, companies should prepare attractive products and scenes to increase positive attitude toward the check-in message and users will more intend to share the message for promote companies and products informally in social media.

References

1. Bezjian–Avery, A., Calder, B., Iacobucci, D.: New media interactive adverting vs. traditional advertising. Journal of Adverting Research 38(4), 23–32 (1998)
2. Cramer, H., Rost, M., Holmquist, L.E.: Performing a check-in: emerging practices, norms and 'conflicts' in location-sharing using Foursquare. In: Proc. 13th International Conference on Human Computer Interaction with Mobile Devices and Services (MobileHCI 2011), Stockholm, Sweden, pp. 57–66 (2011)
3. Carpenter, C.J.: Narcissism on Facebook, self-promotional and anti-social behavior. Personality and Individual Differences 52(4), 482–486 (2012)
4. Compeau, D.R., Higgins, C.A.: Computer self-efficacy: development of a measure and initial test. MIS Quarterly 19(2), 189–211 (1995)
5. Cust, A.E., Armstrong, B.K., Smith, B.J., Chau, J., van der Ploeg, H.P., Bauman, A.: Self-reported confidence in recall as a predictor of validity and repeatability of physical activity questionnaire data. Epidemiology 20(3), 433–441 (2009)
6. Falk, E.B., Morelli, S.A., Welborn, B.L., Dambacher, K., Lieberman, M.D.: Creating buzz: the neural correlates of effective message propagation. Psychological Science 24(7), 1234–1242 (2013)
7. Hassanein, K., Head, M.: The impact of infusing social presence in the web interface: an investigation across product types. International Journal of Electronic Commerce 10(2), 31–55 (2006)
8. Horvath, K., Lombard, M.: Social and spatial presence: an application to optimize human-computer interaction. PsychNology Journal 8(1), 85–114 (2010)
9. Hu, H., Jasper, C.R.: Social cues in the store environment and their impact on store image. International Journal of Retail & Distribution Management 34(1), 25–48 (2006)
10. Kamins, M.A., Noy, A., Steinhart, Y., Mazursky, D.: The effect of social cues on sniping behavior in Internet auctions: field evidence and a lab experiment. Journal of Interactive Marketing 25(4), 241–250 (2011)
11. Lombard, M., Ditton, T.: At the heart of it all: the concept of presence. Journal of Computer Mediated Communication 3(2), 1–18 (1997)
12. Lorenzo, O., Kawalek, P., Ramdani, B.: Enterprise applications diffusion within organizations: a social learning perspective. Information & Management 49(1), 47–57 (2012)
13. Mangold, W.G., Faulds, D.J.: Social media: The new hybrid element of the promotion mix. Business Horizons 52(4), 357–365 (2009)
14. Moon, J.W., Kim, Y.G.: Extending the TAM for a World-Wide-Web context. Information & Management 38(4), 217–230 (2001)
15. Norris, C.E., Colman, A.M.: Context effects on recall and recognition of magazine advertisements. The Journal of Advertising 21(3), 37–46 (1992)
16. Pieters, R.G.M., Klerk-Warmerdam, M.D.: Ad-evoked feeling: structure and impact on Aad and recall. Journal of Business Research 37(2), 105–144 (1996)
17. Venkatesh, V., Morris, M.G., Davis, G.B., Davis, F.D.: 'User acceptance of information technology: toward a unified view'. MIS Quarterly 27(3), 425–478 (2003)
18. Wang, L.C., Baker, J., Wagner, J.A., Wakefield, K.: Can a retail web site be social? Journal of Marketing 71, 143–157 (2007)
19. Wang, K., Wang, E.T.G., Farn, C.K.: Influence of web advertising strategies, consumer goal-directedness, and consumer involvement on web advertising effectiveness. International Journal of Electronic Commerce 13(4), 67–95 (2009)
20. Yi, Y.: Cognitive and Affective Priming Effects of the Context for Print Advertisement. Journal of Advertising 19(2), 40–48 (1990)

Analyzing the User-Generated Content on Disintermediation Effect: A Latent Segmentation Study of Bookers and Lookers

Carlota Lorenzo-Romero[1,*], Giacomo Del Chiappa[2], and Efthymios Constantinides[3]

[1] University of Castilla La-Mancha, Faculty of Economics and Business, Albacete, Spain
carlota.lorenzo@uclm.es
[2] University of Sassari, Faculty of Economics and Business, Sardinia, Italy
gdelchiappa@uniss.it
[3] University of Twente, School of Management and Governance, Enschede, The Netherlands
e.constantinides@utwente.nl

Abstract. This study analyzes the perceptions of different groups of consumers for and against the disintermediation of travel agencies also considering the relative power in influencing the tourist's choices exerted by user generated-content (UGC). A web-based survey is carried out in Spain and 961complete questionnaires was obtained. A latent segmentation was applied on factors identified running an exploratory factor analysis on a list of 16 statements, the use and frequency of use of the Internet to make hotel reservations, if consumers are bookers or lookers, and they have changed hotel reservations after having read UGC. Findings revealed that different clusters exist based on the identified factors and aforementioned variables, and that significant differences between these clusters based on sociodemographic characteristics, their behaviour in using the Internet for searching for information and/or buying, and the extent to which they change the accommodation that had been suggested by a travel agent after having read UGC.

Keywords: UGC, disintermediation, bookers and lookers, latent segmentation, Spain.

1 Introduction

In recent years the Internet has been growing at a tremendously fast pace, opening new ways of running effectively marketing operations and dramatically changing the role of traditional travel agencies. More recently, the most significant development in Internet applications has been in the area of User Generated Content (UGC) and peer-to-peer applications, with UGC and Travel 2.0 applications being one of the most important sources of information for consumers making a purchasing decision [1].

In 2013, by 54.6% of the persons who had made purchases online, holiday accommodation were the top category of products/service most often purchased

---

* Corresponding author.

F.F.-H. Nah (Ed.): HCIB/HCII 2014, LNCS 8527, pp. 754–764, 2014.
© Springer International Publishing Switzerland 2014

online in 2013 in Spain with other travel services accounting for 49.7% and tickets for entertainment at 40.3% [2]. 71% of Spanish social media users make use of peer-to-peer travel applications for travel-related purposes [3]. The aforementioned data and figures allow us to observe the importance of the Internet as a heavily growing channel used by Spanish travellers to book hotel accommodations, provoking a strong on going disintermediation process.

Until now, there has been very little research examining the perceptions of different groups of online buyers of hotel rooms with different online purchasing experiences. Prior researches [1], [4] focused on specific geographical areas, but no work has yet investigated the views of Spanish buyers either for or against the disintermediation of hotel reservations. Further, until now, research aimed at examining whether consumers are more or less likely to change the accommodation suggested by a travel agency based upon UGC do exist just in the context of Italy [1]. This study therefore intended to address this point by presenting and discussing the findings obtained and applying cluster analysis to a sample of 986 Spanish travellers.

2   Literature Review

The disintermediation hypothesis, that is, the idea that the role of the middleman will be eliminated, has captured the attention of both researchers and practitioners. Prominent arguments exist in literature for and against disintermediation of the tourism distribution channel. Among the arguments in favour of disintermediation are, for example, the great flexibility and variety of consumer choice made possible by internet, the poor level of training and competence of travel agency personnel and the fact that travel agencies are biased towards suppliers who offer overriding commissions [5]. On the other hand, among the arguments against disintermediation, we can consider, for example, the time-saving that travel agencies grant their customers, the human touch they provide, the reduction in uncertainty and insecurity they ensure by assuming the responsibility for all arrangements [5] and the possibility for consumers to avoid to face the sort of information overload that the large amount of information available online can create [6]. Tourists using the Internet to make their hotel bookings can be divided into those who only wish to acquire information ("lookers") and those who also use it to buy tourism services and products ("bookers"). According with previous research, lookers" differ from "bookers" in several socio-demographic characteristics and in their Internet usage. For instance, it was shown that the propensity to purchase online increases with age, education level and income [7]. Further, younger groups were found being less likely than senior group to prefer travel agents when searching for information; contrariwise, people older than 59 years and on an organized tour were reported being likely to choose the combination of travel agents and face to face [8]. Consumers' information search differs also by travel product characteristics; for example, people usually buy convenience and standard goods online, while they rely heavily on traditional intermediaries when buying complex products [9]. Finally, the greater the distance travelled [10] and the longer the period of the stay [11], the greater is the number of travellers using travel agencies.

3   Methodology

The present study targeted exclusively adults resident in Spain and at least 16 years old. A structured questionnaire was developed that took into account previous literature evaluating the perception of travelers on disintermediation in travel services [1,5,4, 12]. A snowball sampling technique was used which is often used with hidden population segments who are difficult for researchers to access [13]. This technique was considered the best choice to obtain a large sample of consumers who reside in Spain and to cope with the financial constraints we faced in managing the research project.

The survey used was divided into two parts. In the first part, respondents were asked to reply to some general demographic questions. In the second part of the questionnaire respondents were asked a) if they had any previous experience of booking hotel rooms online; b) how many times a year they usually use the internet to make hotel reservations differencing between bookers and lookers; c) if they have ever changed the accommodation suggested by a travel agency based on reviews and comments posted online; d) to express to what extent they agree or disagree with a list of 16 statements specifically chosen to investigate online buyers' views for and against the disintermediation of hotel reservations and to analyze to what extent their choices are influenced by UGC. A 5-point Likert scale was used (1=completely agree; 5=completely disagree) to indicate their answers. A total of 961 complete questionnaires were collected in a two months survey period. The first step was to apply an exploratory factor analysis (EFA). To this purpose, principal components analysis (PCA) was run. Finally, 12 items were used to develop the factorial analysis due to the standardized loadings of the others four variables were lower than 0.6 [14].The factor scores created during the factor analytic process were used as variables to develop a cluster analysis. Specifically, a latent segmentation methodology was used to define the segmentation and profiling of the Spanish tourists who make hotel reservations (Latent Gold 4.5 statistical software was used).

4   Findings

4.1   Principal Component Factor Analysis (PCA)

The first step in developing an EFA is to analyse the Kaiser–Meyer–Olkin (KMO) measure and Bartlett's test of sphericity. The KMO was greater than 0.85 and Bartlett's test of sphericity was highly significant (0.0000), thus indicating good model acceptability and allowing us to proceed with a factor analysis for the data. Further, Cronbach's alpha values higher than 0.7 indicate the reliability of the extracted factors. After factor extraction, an orthogonal varimax rotation was performed on the factors with eigenvalues ≥ 1.0, thus allowing us to minimize the number of variables having high loadings on a particular factor. Three factors resulted from the analysis, accounting for 68.74 of the symptomatic variance (Table 1). The factor structure was consistent because all the variables have a factor loading >0.5 for the factor that they allowed.

Table 1. Factor loadings of EFA

Items (I) about perception of travellers on disintermediation in travel services	Factor 1. Preference for the Internet	Factor 2. Preference for travel agencies	Factor 3. Preference for 2.0 tools
I2-Internet allows to obtain more easily many choices about possible hotels	.668		
I7-Websites which allow to buy a hotel reservation, offer more possibilities and flexibility than physical travel agencies	.732		
I13-Internet allows people to use their time in a very productive way as they can search for information and make reservations whenever they want	.841		
I14-Internet provides tourist information in such a way that it is easy to choose hotels and spend free time online	.840		
I15-Internet allows to save money when making hotel reservations	.743		
I1-Travel agencies offer a human touch and interface with the hotel industry		.712	
I3-Travel agencies are professional counselors for hotel rooms and offer valuable service and advice		.817	
I6-Travel agencies can reduce booking insecurity as they are responsible for all arrangements		.678	
I11-Travel agencies advice customers very personalized travel solutions		.823	
I12-Travel agencies understand the customer's tastes and needs and, consequently, offer adequate hotel solutions		.802	
I9-When choosing hotels I search for information through the Internet and I check reviews, comments, photo and video uploaded online by tourists			.820
I10-I trust the tourism information available online through reviews and comments posted online in blogs, social network and online travel agencies			.849
% Explained variance	44.179	18.086	6.510
Cumulative variance	44.149	62.235	68.745
Cronbach's alpha	.874	.840	.870

KMO = 0.883; Bartlett's test of sphericity: $\chi2$=5985.552; df=66; Sig.=0.000
Only the variables contribution have been included in this table

Factor 1, preference for the Internet, is the first predominant factor with 44.17% of explained variance. Factor 2, preference for physical travel agencies, is the second predominant factor with 18.08% of explained variance. Thirdly, the construct named preference for 2.0 tools to do hotel reservation, is the lowest predominant factor with 6.51% of explained variance.

4.2   Confirmatory Factor Analysis

The indicators for the next latent segmentation were based on the different constructs of the factorial constructs obtained in EFA explained in epigraph 4.1.

A CFA was carried out with EQS 6.1 in order to contrast if our constructs proposed as indicators for the latent segmentation post-analysis would provide a good fit to the data. In order to use previous factorial constructs in the cluster segmentation, the content, convergent and discriminant validity and reliability of the constructs, were assessed within the CFA containing all the multi-item constructs in our framework using the robust maximum likelihood method. This led us to delete one item based on non-significant or loading estimates lower than 0.6. It supposed eliminate 4 items (I4, I5, I8, and I16) from original 16 proposed in the questionnaire [1,4,12]. Results of the final CFA suggest that our re-specified measurement model provides a good fit to the data on the basis of a number of fit statistics. Firstly, content validity can be assured as all the items included in the scale have been previously used in the literature about user's perceptions about disintermediation in hotel reservations [1,12]. Secondly, (Table 2), reliability of the scales demonstrates high-internal consistency of the constructs seen that Cronbach's alpha exceeded 0.70. Thirdly, convergent validity is verified, as t scores obtained for factor loadings were significant ($p<0.01$). Further, the size of all the standardized loadings are higher than 0.60 (Table 2) and the average of the item-to-factor loadings are higher than 0.70. AVE is higher than 0.5 and CR higher than 0.7 for each construct [14].

Table 2. Internal consistency and convergent validity

Construct	Indicators	Loadings	Robust t-value	Cronbach's alpha	Composite Reliability (CR)	Average Variance Extracted (AVE)
Factor 1. Preference for the Internet	I2	.723	21.230	.874	.807	.587
	I7	.674	23.067			
	I13	.810	29.732			
	I14	.875	35.969			
	I15	.734	27.100			
Factor 2. Preference for physical travel agencies	I1	.711	29.386	.840	.745	.526
	I3	.784	28.525			
	I6	.603	18.724			
	I11	.763	26.577			
	I12	.753	25.891			
Factor 3. Preference for 2.0 tools	I9	.906	37.799	.870	.839	.772
	I10	.851	33.600			

Robust goodness of fit index: S-Bχ^2 (51 df) = 274.8424 (p=0.00); NFI= .945; NNFI= .941; CFI=.954; RMSEA=.068.

All statistics have been extracted through robust method due to the Mardia's coefficient normalized estimation >5.00. The normalized estimate = 21.2110 suggests clearly a non-normal sample.

S-Bχ^2: Satorra-Bentler sacle Chi-Square - df: Degree of freedom - NFI: Normed Fit Index - NNFI: Non-Normed Fit Index - CFI: Comparative Fit Index - RMSEA: Root Mean-Squeare Error of Approximation

Finally, discriminant validity of the measures was also provided seen that: a) none of the 95 per cent confidence intervals of the individual elements of the latent factor correlation matrix contained a value of 1.0; b) the shared variance between pairs of constructs was always less than the corresponding AVE (Table 3).

Table 3. Discriminant validity of the theoretical construct measures

	F1	F2	F3
F1	**.587**	[-.337;-.485]	[.791;.695]
F2	.168	**.526**	[-.329;-.112]
F3	.552	.160	**0.772**

The diagonal represents the AVE, while above the diagonal de 95% confidence interval for the estimated factors correlations is provided, below the diagonal, the shared variance (squared correlations) is represented.

4.3 Latent Segmentation: A Typology Spanish Users Based on Their Perceptions on Disintermediation and Use of the Internet as Bookers and/or Lookers in Hotel Reservation

Based on the factor loadings obtained in the PCA, we applied a cluster analysis to segment the Italian tourists according to their perceptions of and attitude toward the topic of disintermediation. To achieve this aim, we also used four additional questions: "Have you ever used the internet to make reservations for hotel rooms when you travel?, "How many times a year they usually use the Internet to make hotel reservations" and "If they have ever changed the hotel accommodation that had been suggested by a travel agency after having read reviews and comments posted online" (measured as yes or no). Based on the positioning of the different individuals, with regard to these variables, we have obtained some groupings that fulfill the principles of maximum internal coherence and maximum external differentiation.

Table 4. Estimates and fix indexes

Number of conglomerates	LL	BIC(LL)	Npar	Class.Err.	E_s	R^2
1-Cluster	-6664.8919	13947.901	90	.0000	1	1
2-Cluster	-6385.6696	13540.552	112	.0253	.7639	.8031
3-Cluster	**-6201.9725**	**13324.253**	**134**	**.0891**	**.8588**	**.8650**
4-Cluster	-6133.8026	13339.009	156	.0904	.8895	.8843
5-Cluster	-6079.8562	13382.211	178	.1555	.8937	.8829
6-Cluster	-6030.5267	13434.648	200	.1480	.9101	.8987
7-Cluster	-5956.8309	13438.352	222	.1341	.9265	.9151
8-Cluster	-5853.5886	13482.963	244	.1283	.9417	.9300

LL=log-likelihood; BIC=Bayesian information criterion; Npar=number of parameters; Class.Err.=classification error; E_s= entropy statistic (*entropy R-squared*); R^2=Standard R-squared

Table 4 shows the estimation process summary and the fit indexes for each of the eight models. The fit of the model was evaluated according to the Bayesian Information Criterion (BIC) that allows the identification of the model with the least number of classes that best fits to the data. The lowest BIC value was considered as the best model indicator [15].

Table 5. Travellers' profile (indicators): The impact of disintermediation in physical travel agencies

		Clusters			Wald	p-value
		Mixed lookers and book-ers	Online lookers and book-ers	Offline lookers and bookers		
Cluster Size		49.75%	33.36%	16.89%		
Factor 1. Preference for the Internet		3.7275	**4.4960**	2.2483	633.7550	2.4e-138
Factor 2. Preference for the physical travel agencies		3.5619	2.8601	**4.3136**	250.3216	4.4e-55
Factor 3. Preference for 2.0 tools		3.3850	**4.2468**	1.5965	765.2596	6.7e-167
Look and/or book in physical travel agencies and/or the Internet	Internet for looking and booking	.5822	**.9365**	.0273		
	Internet for looking and travel agencies for booking	**.2433**	.0240	.1155		
	Physical travel agencies for looking and the Internet for booking	**.0827**	.0393	.0116	37.9095	1.2e-6
	Physical travel agencies for looking and booking	.0919	.0002	**.8456**		
Times at year that you make hotel reser-vations over the Internet	Never	.1295	.0257	**.8672**		
	1-2	**.5792**	.4720	.1300		
	3-4	.2191	**.3241**	.0027		
	5-6	.0494	**.1034**	.0001	48.7003	2.7e-11
	7-8	.0124	**.0340**	.0000		
	9-10	.0025	**.0086**	.0000		
	More than 10	.0078	**.0322**	.0000		
Times at year that you make hotel reser-vations over physi-cal travel agencies	Never	.2035	**.4876**	.0581		
	1-2	.7288	.5009	**.7457**		
	3-4	.0600	.0112	**.1458**		
	5-6	.0049	.0003	**.0218**	50.3818	1.1e-11
	7-8	.0023	.0000	**.0178**		
	More than 10	.0005	.0000	**.0109**		
Change the hotel after having read online comments	Yes	.5058	**.5931**	.1170	35.3804	2.1e-8
	No	.4942	.4069	**.8830**		

In bold has been indicated the highest representative value in each variable per cluster.

In this case, four different user groups represented the best alternative, as the BIC is minimized in this case. The statistic values included in Table 4 indicates that the model has a good fit (E_s and R^2 near 1). The Wald statistic was analyzed in order to evaluate the statistical significance within a group of estimated parameters (Table 5). For all the indicators a significant p-value associated with the Wald statistics was obtained, confirming that each indicator discriminates between the clusters in a significant way [15]. Table 5 also contains the profiles of the obtained clusters. In the upper part the size and name assigned to the three groups is shown: the cluster named "mixed looker and booker" includes 49.75% of travellers surveyed; the "online looker and booker" segment 33.36%, and the "offline looker and booker" cluster 16.89%.

In addition, Table 5 shows the average score that takes each segment in each of the indicators (note that these can take values between 0 and 5, since items that composed each scale were measured with five-point Likert scales). Clusters are ordered from lowest to highest size of sample according to travelers' preferences and habits about use of online and/or offline way to make hotel reservations in order to analyze the level of disintermediation that new technologies are causing on traditional travel agencies sector.

Related to the composition of the three segments, the profile of the resulting groups according to the information from other variables was analyzed. Table 6 shows the groups' composition based on a number of descriptive criteria included in the analysis. Independence tests associated with statistic Wald conclude that significant differences exist between the segments (≥95% confidence level) regarding the age, and education. There are not significant differences between the segments respect to gender and income.

Table 6. Travellers' profile (covariates): Descriptive criteria

Descriptive criteria	Categories	Clusters			Wald	p-value
		Mixed lookers and bookers	Online lookers and bookers	Offline lookers and bookers		
Gender	Male	43.64%	45.55%	48.90%	1.4370	.49
	Female	56.36%	54.45%	51.10%		
Age	< 18	**49.64%**	45.76%	11.68%	67.1105	2.7e-15
	18-35	14.21%	**17.85%**	2.96%		
	36-65	14.33%	**19.74%**	13.06%		
	>65	21.82%	16.64%	**72.30%**		
Education	Primary school	6.77%	1.84%	**29.42%**	22.0452	.0012
	Secondary school	**81.75%**	**83.24%**	56.84%		
	University degree	11.27%	**12.18%**	2.48%		
	Without studies	.20%	2.74%	**11.26%**		
Monthly household income (€)	< 1000	14.76%	14.40%	20.49%	.8245	.66
	1000-3000	44.20%	39.88%	43.03%		
	3001-7000	22.41%	22.86%	19.44%		
	More than 7000	18.63%	22.86%	17.04%		

In bold has been indicated the highest representative value in each variable per cluster.

Based Tables 5 and 6, three different profiles of Spanish travellers were found, namely: "mixed lookers and bookers", "online lookers and bookers" and "offline lookers and bookers".

The "mixed online lookers and bookers" cluster presents higher mean in F1-Preference for the Internet (4.4960) and F3-Preference for 2.0 tools (4.2468). Clearly, this group has opted by use of new technologies to look and book hotel reservations and, in consequence, with a positive opinion about disintermediation of tourism sector. Moreover, this segment affirms to use the Internet for looking and booking (.9365), carrying out from three to more than ten times per year online hotel reservations. This segment never prefers to make hotel reservations by physical travel agencies respect to the other clusters (.4876). These travellers would change the hotel after having read online comments in higher proportion than the others clusters

(.5931). This group is younger than "offline looker and booker" cluster whose studies are Secondary school and University degree. Respect to gender and monthly household income, important differences between three clusters do not exist (although, we can observe that this cluster has on average higher income than "offline lookers and bookers"). "Offline lookers and bookers" is the smallest segment (16.83%) and it presents higher mean in F2-Preference for the physical travel agencies (16.83%). Indeed, the most part of consumers belonging to this segment (86.72%) never makes hotel reservations over the Internet; contrariwise, they were reported making hotel reservation trough physical travel agencies from one to more than ten times per year. The number of travelers who would not change the hotel after having read online comments is higher (88.30%) than in all the other clusters, thus confirming that the dislike and distrust internet and UGC. The most part of consumers belonging to this cluster is old, 72.30% of them were reported being aged more than 65 years old. Respect to gender and monthly household income, important differences between three clusters do not exist (although, we can observe that this cluster has less income than "online looker and booker" cluster). The "mixed lookers and bookers" is the biggest cluster and it is characterized by a "middle position" with respect to the three clusters. Indeed, consumers belonging to this cluster do not show a clear preference; on the contrary, they like to use Internet, physical travel agencies and 2.0 tools to make hotel reservations in similar proportion. Further, sometimes they were reported using the Internet for looking and travel agencies for booking (24.33%) and vice versa (8.11%). One or two times per year, they make hotel reservations through the Internet (57.92%), with similar proportion in the case of making through traditional channel (72.88%) respect to the "offline looker and booker" cluster. The middle of group would change the hotel after having read online comments (50.58%) and the rest of group would not change it (49.42%). In consequence, the impact of disintermediation on this group is middle. The youngest travellers compose this group in major proportion (49.64%) whose education is Secondary school (81.75%).

5   Conclusion and Managerial Implications

Applying a latent segmentation statistical technique to a sample of 961 tourists residing in Spain and aged more than 16 years, this study identified three different segments of consumers based on their views for and against the topic of disintermediation, that is: "mixed bookers and lookers", "online lookers and bookers" and "offline looker and bookers". Findings revealed that the preference for the Internet to look and book belong to middle aged and educated travellers, making hotel reservation over the Internet frequently during the year and being influenced in their choices by UGC thus confirming prior research showing that frequent travellers value peer reviews the most and are more likely to be influenced by them [17]. Contrariwise, older and less educated Spanish consumers were reported looking and booking hotel rooms using street travel agencies. Further, they never would change the hotel after having read online comments thus confirming prior research showing that those aged 65 years or over are less likely to read other travellers' reviews, whilst younger travellers find reviews more important in deciding where to stay [16]. A big group of travellers were reported preferring a mixture of both behaviors (the so called "mixed bookers and lookers"). Specifically, they are youngest and very implicated with online technology and 2.0 tools even if they book the hotel using both the Internet and physical travel agencies.

These conclusions are significant for both researchers and hospitality managers. On the one hand, they provide further insights into the scientific debate on disintermediation, explicitly also considering the relative power in influencing tourists' choices that UGC has with respect to information delivered by travel agencies and giving a snapshot of the context of Spain, where little research exists on the topic. On the other hand, these findings offer suggestions to both hotel marketers and traditional travel agencies. Given consumers' heavy reliance on the Internet for searching for information and/or booking hotel rooms, the lodging industry should design its websites to be more attractive and effective for Spanish middle-aged and educated people who travel often and are heavy users of the Internet as a tool for both searching for and booking hotels. According to prior research, for example, hotel marketers should emphasize web usability, security, website functionality, customer responsiveness and information quality, with information on reservations contacts being a crucial element of hotel website design. Hotel marketers should not only focus on direct sales, but should also monitor their brand reputation as projected in the reviews and comments that consumers upload online. On the other hand, travel agents should create and maintain a presence in the electronic marketplace in order to survive and recover their competitiveness [6]. For the same purpose, they should move away from being booking offices and become travel managers, advisers and consultants [5]. Aside from the theoretical and managerial contributions of the study, the main limitation of this study is that it was carried out exclusively in the context of Spain, thus its findings cannot be generalized.

References

1. Del Chiappa, G.: Internet versus travel agencies: The perception of different groups of Italian online buyers. J. Vacation Marketing 19, 1–12 (2013a)
2. Statistic Spanish Institute [Instituto Nacional de Estadística]: Encuesta de ocupación hotelera [Hospitality Occupation Survey] (2014), http://www.ine.es/jaxi/menu.do?type=pcaxis&path=%2Ft11%2Fe162eoh&file=inebase (accessed February 15, 2014) (retrieved)
3. Amadeus: The always-connected traveller: How mobile will transform the future of air travel (2011), http://www.amadeus.com/airlineit/the-always-connected-traveller/docs/amadeus-the-always-connected-traveller-2011-en.pdf (accessed on July 17, 2013) (retrieved)
4. Law, R.: Disintermediation of hotel reservations: the perception of different groups of online buyers in Hong Kong. Int. J. Contemporary Hospitality Manag. 21, 766–772 (2009)
5. Buhalis, D.: Strategic use of information technologies in the tourism industry. Tourism Manag. 19, 409–421 (1998)
6. Anckar, B.: Consumer Intentions in Terms of Electronic Travel Distribution: Implications for Future Market Structures. e-Service J. 2, 68–86 (2003)
7. Law, R., Leung, K., Wong, J.: The impact of the Internet on travel agencies. Int. J. Contemporary Hospitality Manag. 16, 100–107 (2004)

8. Grønflaten, Ø.: Predicting Traverlers' Choice of Information Sources and Information Channels. Journal of Travel Research 48, 230–244 (2011)
9. Wertener, H., Klein, S.: Information Technology and Tourism – A Challenging Relationship. Springer, Wien (1999)
10. Snepenger, D.J., Meged, K., Snellig, D., Worral, K.: Information search strategies by destination-naïve tourists. J. Travel Res. 29, 13–16 (1990)
11. Woodside, A.G., Ronkainen, I.A.: Vacation travel planning segments: self planning vs user of motor club and travel agents. Annals Tourism Res. 7, 385–393 (1980)
12. Del Chiappa, G.: Italian Online Buyers' Perceptions of the topic of disintermediation and User Generated Content. In: Kozack, M., Kozack, N. (eds.) Aspects of Tourist Behavior. Cambridge Scolars Publishing, Newcastle (2013b)
13. Wrenn, B., Stevens, R.E., Loudon, D.L.: Marketing research. Text and cases. Haworth Press, New York (2007)
14. Lévy, J.P., Varela, J.: Modelización con estructuras de covarianzas en ciencias sociales [modeling with covariance structures in social Sciences], Netbiblo, Spain (2006)
15. Vermunt, J.K., Magidson, J.: Latent class cluster analysis. In: Hagenaars, J., McCutcheon, A. (eds.) Applied Latent Class Models, pp. 89–106. Cambridge University Press, New York (2002)
16. Gretzel, U., Yoo, K.H.: Use and Impact of online travel reviews. In: O'Connor, P., Höpken, W., Gretzel, U. (eds.) Information and Communication Technologies in Tourism Proceedings of the International Conference in Innsbruck, Austria, pp. 35–46. Springer, Vienna (2008)
17. Gretzel, U., Yoo, K. H., Purifoy, M.: Online travel review study: The role and impact of online travel reviews, college station, laboratory for intelligent system in tourism (2007), http://www.tripadvisor.com/pdfs/OnlineTravelReviewReport.pdf (accessed on 23.25.2013)

Do We Follow Friends or Acquaintances? The Effects of Social Recommendations at Different Shopping Stages

Tingting Song, Cheng Yi, and Jinghua Huang

School of Economics and Management, Tsinghua University
{songtt.11,yich,huangjh}@sem.tsinghua.edu.cn

Abstract. This article examines the effects of social recommendations on consumers' purchase intentions at different stages of online shopping. Drawing on construal level theory (CLT) and research on social tie strength, this study hypothesizes that the persuasive effects of recommendations from one's close friends (i.e., strong social ties) and those from one's acquaintances (i.e., weak social ties) will differ depending on shopping stages consumers are in. Results from a laboratory experiment reveal that in the initial shopping stage, the effects of recommendations from weak ties on consumers' purchase intentions will be stronger than those from strong ties; however in the latter shopping stage, the reverse will happen. Research and managerial implications are discussed.

Keywords: social recommendations, tie strength, shopping stage, congruency of construal levels.

1 Introduction

The incorporation of social networks into e-commerce platforms is becoming increasingly prevalent nowadays. On one hand, advances in information technology have enabled e-commerce platforms to build social networks among consumers on their sites. For example, Amazon.com allows consumers to access various kinds of recommendations from other known or unknown consumers on its own platform. On the other hand, e-commerce platforms can also collaborate with social network sites such as Facebook and bring information from users' social networks to the shopping process. For instance, TripAdvisor.com highlights the review information from one's Facebook friends on the pages of the cities and hotels. Hence, while browsing and evaluating products online, consumers may receive recommendation information from their own social relationships, be it friends or acquaintances.

Plenty of literature has looked at the roles that different social relationships play in a variety of settings. For example, Bapna and Umjarov (2013) have studied the adoption of a paid online service and identified that the adoption behaviors of close friends play a pivotal role in one's service adoption. In contrast, recent research on viral marketing has found that it is the online acquaintances rather than close friends that contribute to spreading marketing-relevant information and product adoption (Ralf et al., 2010; Arnaud et al., 2008). Hence, it seems that the source of social recommendations, i.e., whether the recommendations are from one's close friends or acquaintances, may

F.F.-H. Nah (Ed.): HCIB/HCII 2014, LNCS 8527, pp. 765–774, 2014.
© Springer International Publishing Switzerland 2014

affect the persuasiveness of the recommendations. Questions thus arise in terms of how the effects of recommendations from various social relationships differ.

An examination of previous research suggests that different social relationships reflect different degrees of interpersonal closeness and social distance. Specifically, proximal social relations such as friends represent a high degree of closeness and strong ties between people (Granovetter, 1973). Information related to proximal social relations is often construed at a lower and more concrete level than that related to distal social relations such as mere acquaintances, which typify as a low degree of closeness and weak ties between people (Granovetter, 1973). In other words, consumers may adopt different mindsets when processing information associated with social relationships of different tie strength (Liberman and Trope 1998).

Literature has also pointed out that consumers' consumption goals and information processing mindsets may change over time as they proceed in the shopping process. According to Lee and Ariely (2006), people's consumption goals are not always highly specified, but tend to change from being abstract to more precise. The different levels of goal specificity may determine consumers' sensitivity to different types of information and recommendations (Chan, Jiang and Tan, 2010). This study thus aims to investigate how the persuasive effects of social recommendations differ based on when consumers are exposed to such information during their shopping process. Answers to this question will advance the field's understanding of consumers' responses to social recommendations, and provide guidance to the design of effective recommendation strategies.

2   Literature Review

2.1   Social Recommendations and Tie Strength

With recent advances in information technology and the rapid development of the Internet, consumers are increasingly relying on advice from their personal networks when making decisions (Hill, Provost and Volinsky 2006; Trusov, Bodapati, and Bucklin 2010; Sheldon et al., 2011; Susarla et al. 2012; Zeng and Wei, 2013). Literature typically characterizes interpersonal relationships by tie strength (Brown and Reingen, 1987). According to Granovetter (1973), tie strength measures the closeness and interaction frequency of a relationship between two parties. Specifically, strong ties exist between close friends who communicate frequently and whose social circles tightly overlap. Close interactions between friends thus decrease their social distance. In contrast, weak ties connect acquaintances who interact infrequently, and the social distance between weakly tied contacts is often distal. Regarding the roles of different social relationships, there is an extensive literature documenting that a message from a friend is more influential than one from an acquaintance because high interpersonal closeness between the sender and recipient may increase the trustworthiness and relevance of the message (Tam and Ho 2005, Tucker 2011). However, many other studies have shown that weak ties are more likely to provide non-redundant information and thus become important sources of novel information (e.g., Granovetter 1973; Levin et al., 2004). Aral and Walker (2011) have also found that weak ties are more effective than strong ties in influencing the adoption of new products.

This study examines the relative effects of recommendations from strong ties versus weak ties on consumers' decision making. In particular, since strong ties and weak ties reflect different social distance between people (Granovetter, 1973), we investigate the question from the perspective of construal level theory (CLT, Trope, Liberman, and Wakslak 2007; Trope and Liberman 2003), which links people's mental representations and the psychological distance of the information.

2.2   Construal Level Theory

Construal level theory (CLT) contends that people may construe an object at an abstract, high level or at a concrete, low level (Trope and Liberman 2003). High-level construal reflects a general understanding of the object, whereas low-level construal reflects the details and specifics of the object. For example, the same act of getting a new job can be thought of as having an opportunity for career advancement – a higher construal level; or it can be conceived as going through the preparation procedure – a lower construal level.

The core of CLT is the proposition that mental representations of events that are psychologically near tend to be low-level and in details, whereas psychologically distant events are construed at a high and abstract level (Trope and Liberman, 2003). For example, social distance, as one kind of psychological distance, could change people's mental representations of others. More specifically, people's mental representations of close others' behaviors are often concrete and at a low level, whereas distant others' behaviors are construed at a high and abstract level (Zhao and Xie 2011; Kim, Zhang, and Li 2008; Trope, Liberman, and Wakslak 2007). For instance, when people predict whether their close friends will accept a job, they may expect their friends to put more weight on the low-level information, such as the office environment; however, they tend to predict distant others to focus on high-level information, such as interests and opportunities for future promotion. Applying CLT to the context of online product evaluation, we expect that recommendations from weak ties are likely to be processed at a higher and more abstract level while recommendations from strong ties may be represented at a lower and more concrete level.

2.3   Shopping Stage and the Congruency of Construal Levels

CLT also has important implications on how consumers process product information as they proceed in the shopping process. According to CLT, individuals use abstract terms to construe target activities in the distant future and translate them into more concrete actions as the target activities draw nearer (Trope and Liberman, 2003; Lee and Ariely, 2006). Lee and Ariely (2006) applies this idea to the shopping context and proposes a two-stage shopping framework based on the increasing concreteness of shopping goal. Based on this framework, in the initial shopping stage, consumers are uncertain about their goals and in the midst of browsing and deciding what to purchase or how much to spend (Chan, Jiang and Tan, 2010; Gollwitzer et al., 1990). They seek to define a desired outcome and tend to process information at a high construal level. As a result, consumers are likely to narrow down their choices according to the abstract and central value that they attach to the products. In contrast, in the latter shopping stage, consumers have already established their shopping goals and they care about goal attainment. They tend to process information at a low construal level and focus more on the concrete information related to carrying out the purchases.

A considerable amount of research has emphasized the idea that an external stimulus has a greater impact when its level of representation is more congruent with the internal construal level of decision makers (Higgins et al., 2003; Liberman and Trope, 1998; Kim, Zhang and Lee 2008; Zhao and Xie, 2011). In the context of online shopping, this means that consumers are more likely to pay attention to and encode information that is more congruous to their processing mindsets (Gollwitzer et al., 1990). Hence, it is expected that the relative effects of recommendations from strong verses weak social ties will change over time depending on consumers' mindsets in different shopping stages.

3   Hypothesis Development

Based on CLT, users tend to define events in the distant future in abstract terms and translate them into more concrete terms as the events draw nearer (Trope and Liberman, 2003). The two-stage shopping framework (Lee and Ariely 2006) follows this idea and proposes that consumers' natural construal level will change according to the shopping stages they are in. Specifically, in the initial shopping stage, consumers are generally uncertain about their shopping goals (Gollwitzer et al., 1990) and their natural construal level is high. In the latter shopping stage, however, consumers have already established their goals (Gollwitzer et al., 1990) and their natural construal level is low. Since people always put more weight on the type of information that matches their natural construal level at a given time (Liberman and Trope 1998), information which is typically construed at a higher level should exert a strong influence on consumers' product preference in the initial shopping stage whereas low-level and concrete information should be more influential in the latter shopping stage.

Accordingly, we hypothesize that social recommendations will be more effective in shaping users' product preference when the natural construal level of recommendation information is consistent with users' mental representation state. As mentioned earlier, since the perception of social distance towards strong ties is proximal and that of weak ties is distal, recommendations from strong ties are likely to be construed at a low and concrete level, whereas individuals' mental representations of weak-tie recommendations tend to be high-level and abstract (Zhao and Xie 2011; Kim, Zhang, and Li 2008; Trope, Liberman, and Wakslak 2007). Hence, in the initial shopping stage when consumers tend to have a higher level mindset in information processing, recommendations from weak ties will have greater influence than those from strong ties as weak-tie recommendations fit with consumers' existing mindset. Strong ties' recommendations, however, may have a larger effect in the latter shopping stage because perceptions of information from proximal social ties are more congruent with people's low-level mindset in this stage. Thus, we propose,

H1: There will be an interaction effect between shopping stage and tie strength of recommendation source on consumers' purchase intentions.

(a) In the initial shopping stage, recommendations from weak ties will lead to higher purchase intentions than those from strong ties.

(b) In the latter shopping stage, recommendations from strong ties will lead to higher purchase intentions than those from weak ties.

4   Research Methodology

4.1   Experimental Design

A lab experiment was conducted to test the hypotheses. We constructed a shopping website for the experiment, and badminton rackets were selected as the target product category. Since badminton was a common sport for the majority of college students in China, the task of inspecting and considering purchase of badminton rackets represented a realistic scenario for student subjects.

Two shopping stages characterized by different levels of shopping goal concreteness were manipulated based on Tam and Ho (2006). Specifically, subjects in the initial shopping stage were asked to visit the online store and freely browse a list of six badminton rackets. They were told that the listed products were randomly retrieved from the pool of products on sale and no purchase decision was needed to be made at the end of the visit. The six displayed products were similar in terms of price and users' perceived attractiveness based on a pretest. A hypothesized brand name was associated with the products to avoid the potential confounding effects of prior brand involvement. Information presented for each product on the listing page included a picture, product name, and social recommendations. One of the rackets was selected as the target product, of which the recommendation source was manipulated. Specifically, recommendations from strong (weak) ties were presented in the form of three close (distant) others "liking" the product. The social relationship information was reported by each participant two weeks before the experiment[1].

Subjects in the latter shopping stage were asked to search for rackets as they had been considering making a purchase for the new semester. They were directed to the detailed information page of the target product for purchase evaluation, where the recommendation source was manipulated likewise. They were asked to make purchase decision at the end of the visit.

Overall, the laboratory experiment employed a 2 (social recommendation source: strong versus weak ties) × 2 (shopping stage: initial versus latter) between-subject factorial design. It was ensured that only the two design factors were varied across different treatments.

4.2   Experimental Procedures

The subjects were randomly assigned to one of the four conditions. Following a welcome screen, the subjects were instructed to perform a task, which was either to browse a list of products on sale without decision making (i.e., the initial stage) or to search and evaluate the products in order to make a purchase decision (i.e., the latter stage). After viewing all the pages, the subjects proceeded to answer a questionnaire. All subjects indicated their purchase intentions towards the target badminton racket based on a 7-point Likert scale (likely to buy the rackets, look forward to buying the rackets, and

---

[1] During the recruitment, registrants were asked to list five of their closest friends with whom they interact frequently on social network sites and microblog, as well as five unfamiliar contacts (except star users or experts) with whom they had not communicated for at least two months.

purchase the rackets next time when needed; adapted from Jiang and Benbasat, 2007 & Mackenzie et al., 1986). Manipulation check questions on shopping stage (Gollwitzer et al., 1990 and Chan, Jiang and Tan, 2010) and tie strength (Levin et al., 2004 and Frenzen and Davis, 1990) were also included. Each session of the experiment lasted for around 15 minutes and a token payment of ￥30 (around $5) was given upon the completion of the questionnaire.

5   Data Analysis

5.1   Subject Demographics and Background Analysis

68 undergraduate and graduate students from a major university in China were recruited. Prior studies have suggested that the characteristics of university students are deemed to be similar to those of online shoppers (Chan et al., 2010), thus the sample was appropriate for this study. Among the 68 subjects, 36 (52.9%) were females and 32(47.1%) were male. The average age was 22.16. They came from 12 diverse faculties and departments. About 80% of the subjects used social media more than an hour per day. No significant differences were found between subjects in each of the four experimental conditions with respect to age, gender, and past Internet and online shopping experience.

5.2   Manipulation Checks

Independent samples t-tests were conducted to examine the manipulation of the independent variables. Results showed that subjects in the latter shopping stage reported significantly higher level of goal specificity during their interaction with the website (Mean = 5.61, SD=0.77) than those in the initial shopping stage (Mean = 3.38, SD = 1.74; t = -8.83, $p < 0.01$). Hence, the manipulation of shopping stages was successful. Subjects also reported that they had more frequent interactions and were closer with the contacts displayed in strong ties conditions (Mean = 6.10, SD = 1.13) than those in weak ties conditions (Mean = 3.23, SD = 1.62; t = -11.79, $p < 0.01$). Therefore the manipulation of tie strength of recommendation source was also successful.

5.3   Results on Purchase Intentions

A 2 (weak ties vs. strong ties) *2 (initial shopping stage vs. latter shopping stage) analysis of variance (ANOVA) was conducted to test our hypotheses. As expected, the results showed a significant interaction between the two factors ($F (1, 64) = 9.728$, $p < 0.01$; see Figure 1). Specifically, in the initial shopping stage, recommendations from weak ties led to a significantly higher level of purchase intentions than those from strong ties (M weak ties = 6.29 vs. M strong ties = 5.52; $p < 0.05$). In the latter shopping stage, on the contrary, recommendations from strong ties led to a significantly higher level of purchase intentions than those from weak ties (M strong ties = 5.69 vs. M weak ties = 4.88; $p < 0.05$). Hence, H1 was fully supported.

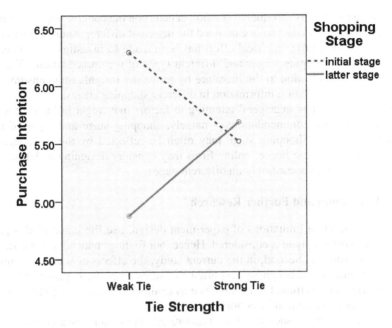

Fig. 1. Plots of Interaction Effect on Purchase Intentions

6   General Discussions

This study draws on CLT and research on tie strength as well as shopping stage to examine how social recommendations influence consumers' purchase intentions. Our findings show that people are more likely to follow weak ties' recommendations in the initial shopping stage, since the natural mental processing of weak ties' information is congruent with their high level mindset in the initial shopping stage. In contrast, when consumers are in the latter shopping stage, they are more likely to follow strong ties' recommendations because perceptions of strong-tie recommendations are congruent with people's low-level mindset in this stage.

6.1   Theoretical and Practical Contributions

Our work contributes to the literature in several areas. First, while past research has examined the importance of weak ties in job hunting (Granovetter 1973; Brown & Konrad 2001) and information dissemination (Burt 1995; Weening 1993; Shi, Rui, and Whinston, 2013; Wilson 1998; Wellman and Wortley 1990; Brown and Konrad 2001; Levin et al., 2004), the persuasive impacts of tie strength in a shopping context is seldom examined. Our results suggest that the effectiveness of weak-tie recommendations is contingent on consumers' shopping stages. Second, our research also contributes to the CLT literature by extending the interrelationships between different dimensions of psychological distance (Liberman & Trope, 1998; Fujita et al. 2006; Zhao and Xie, 2011; Wakslak et al. 2006). In particular, we have integrated temporal distance (i.e., the shopping stage) and social distance (i.e., recommendation source) and demonstrated that users' product evaluation depends on the congruency between them. Third, though prior studies have examined the nature of different shopping stages (Lee and Ariely, 2006), little empirical effort has been made to investigate the interaction effects between shopping stages and different types of recommendations. This paper thus makes a contribution to the literature by providing insights into consumers' responses to recommendation information in different shopping stages.

Our research brings managers' attention to factors that might influence the effectiveness of social recommendations— namely, shopping stage and types of recommendation sources. Shopping stage may often be reflected by the webpages being browsed by consumers; hence, online firms may consider designing different recommendation strategies accordingly on different pages.

6.2   Limitations and Further Research

Apart from the usual limitations of experiment design, one limitation of this paper is that only one product type is considered. Hence, our findings may not be generalized to all kinds of products. Second, in the current study, the effects of social recommendations are manifested through self-reported measures after the experimental task, as constrained in a lab setting. Future studies may examine the effects in field settings and capture actual consumption behaviors.

Many noteworthy issues are left unanswered. First, our research considers tie strength between the recommendation provider and the receiver, but there are many other types of social relations. For example, researchers could explore whether and how opinion leaders/ordinary users and experts/non-experts affect people's responses to recommendations in different situations. Second, this study reveals the effects of tie strength moderated by shopping stages. Future work can extend the research by considering other moderating factors. For instance, individuals may be more receptive to information from weak ties in social broadcasting network (Shi, Rui, and Whinston, 2013); however, in other private networks such as WeChat, strong ties may be more persuasive.

Acknowledgement. This research was supported by the National Natural Science Foundation of China (70831003 and 71272028) and MOE Project of the Key Research Institute of Humanity and Social Sciences at Universities (13JJD630008).

References

1. Aral, S., Walker, D.: Creating Social Contagion Through Viral Product Design: A Randomized Trial of Peer Influence in Networks. Management Science 9, 1623–1639 (2011)
2. Arnaud, D.B., Lilien, G.L.: A Multi-Stage Model of Word of Mouth Through Viral Marketing. International Journal of Research in Marketing 3, 143–225 (2008)
3. Bapna, R., Umjarov, A.: Do your online friends make you pay? A randomized field experiment in an online music social network. Working Paper (2013)
4. Brown, D.W., Konrad, A.M.: Granovetter was right: the importance of weak ties to a contemporary job search. Group and Organization Management 4, 434–462 (2001)
5. Brown, J.J., Reingen, P.H.: Social Ties and Word-of-Mouth Referral Behavior. Journal of Consumer Research, 350–362 (1987)

6. Burt, R.: Structural holes: The social structure of competition. Harvard University Press, Cambridge (1995)
7. Chan, J.C.F., Jiang, Z., Tan, B.C.Y.: Understanding Online Interruption-Based Advertising: Impacts of Exposure Timing, Advertising Intent, and Brand Image. IEEE Transactions on Engineering Management 3 (2010)
8. Frenzen, K.J., Davis, H.L.: Purchasing Behavior in Embedded Markets. Journal of Consumer Research 1–12 (1990)
9. Fujita, K., Henderson, M.D., Eng, J., Trope, Y., Liberman, N.: Spatial distance and mental construal of social events. Psychological Science 4, 278–282 (2006)
10. Gollwitzer, P.M., Heckhausen, H., Birgit, S.: Deliberative and Implemental Mind-Sets: Cognitive Tuning toward Congruous Thoughts and Information. Journal of Personality and Social Psychology 6, 1119–1127 (1990)
11. Granovetter, M.: The strength of weak ties. American Journal of Sociology 6, 1360–1380 (1973)
12. Higgins, L.C.I., Antonio, F., Scott, S., Daniel, M.: Transfer of Value from Fit. Journal of Personality and Social Psychology 6, 1140–1153 (2003)
13. Hill, S., Foster, P., Chris, V.: Network-Based Marketing: Identifying Likely Adopters via Consumer Networks. Statistical Science 2, 256–276 (2006)
14. Jiang, Z., Benbasat, I.: Investigating the Influence of the Functional Mechanisms of Online Product Presentations. Information Systems Research 4, 454–470 (2007)
15. Kim, K., Zhang, M., Li, X.: Effects of Temporal and Social Distance on Consumer Evaluations. Journal of Consumer Research 4, 706–713 (2008)
16. Lee, L., Ariely, D.: Shopping goals, goal concreteness and conditional promotions. J. Consum. Res. 33, 60–70 (2006)
17. Levin, D.Z., Cross, R.: The Strength of Weak Ties You Can Trust: The Mediating Role of Trust in Effective Knowledge Transfer. Management Science 11, 1477–1490 (2004)
18. Liberman, N., Trope, Y.: The role of feasibility and desirability considerations in near and distant future decisions: A test of temporal construal theory. Journal of Personality and Social Psychology 1, 5–18 (1998)
19. Mackenzie, S.B., Lutz, R.J., Belch, G.E.: The Role of Attitude toward the Ad as a Mediator of Advertising Effectiveness: A Test of Competing Explanations. Journal of Marketing Research, 130–143 (1986)
20. Ralf, L., Gerrit, B., Jehoshua, E., Berend, W.: A Viral Branching Model for Predicting the Spread of Electronic Word-of-Mouth. Marketing Science 2, 348–365 (2010)
21. Sheldon, K.M., Abad, N., Hinsch, C.: A two-process view of Facebook use and relatedness-satisfaction: Disconnection drives use, and connection rewards it. J. Personality Soc. Psych. 4, 766–775 (2011)
22. Shi, Z., Rui, H., Andrew, B. W.: Content Sharing in a Social Broadcasting Environment: Evidence from Twitter. MIS Quarterly (2013) (forthcoming)
23. Susarla, A., Oh, J.-H., Tan, Y.: Social networks and the diffusion of user-generated content: Evidence from YouTube. Inform. Systems Res. 1, 23–41 (2012)
24. Tam, K.Y., Ho, S.Y.: Web Personalization as a Persuasion Strategy: An Elaboration Likelihood Model Perspective. Information Systems Research 3, 271–291 (2005)
25. Tam, K.Y., Ho, S.Y.: Understanding the Impact of Web Personalization on User Information Processing and Decision Outcomes. MIS Quarterly 4, 865–890 (2006)
26. Trope, Y., Liberman, N.: Temporal construal. Psychological Review 3, 403–421 (2003)
27. Trope, Y., Liberman, N., Wakslak, C.: Construal Levels and Psychological Distance: Effects on Representation, Prediction, Evaluation, and Behavior. Journal of Consumer Psychology 2, 83–95 (2007)

28. Trusov, M., Anand, V.B., Randolph, E.B.: Determining Influential Users in Internet Social Networks. Journal of Marketing Research 4, 643–658 (2010)
29. Tucker, C.: Social Networks, Personalized Advertising, and Privacy Controls. MIT Sloan School Working Paper 4851-10 (2011).
30. Wakslak, C.J., Trope, Y., Liberman, N., Alony, R.: Seeing the forest when entry is unlikely: Probability and the mental representation of events. Journal of Experimental Psychology 4, 641–653 (2006)
31. Weening, M.W.H.: The strength of weak and strong communication ties in community information program. Journal of Applied Social Psychology 20, 1712–1731 (1993)
32. Wellman, B., Wortley, S.: Different strokes from different folks: community ties and social support. American Journal of Sociology 3, 558–588 (1990)
33. Wilson, T.D.: Weak ties, strong ties: network principles in Mexican migration. Human Organization 4, 394–403 (1998)
34. Zeng, X., Wei, L.: Social Ties and User Content Generation: Evidence from Flickr. Information Systems Research 1, 71–87 (2013)
35. Zhao, M., Xie, J.: Effects of Social and Temporal Distance on Consumers' Responses to Peer Recommendations. Journal of Marketing Research 3, 486–496 (2011)

When Two Is Better Than One – Product Recommendation with Dual Information Processing Strategies

Wee-Kek Tan[1], Chuan-Hoo Tan[2], and Hock-Hai Teo[1]

[1] Dept. of Information Systems, National University of Singapore,
Computing 1, 13 Computing Drive, Singapore 117417, Singapore
{tanwk,teohh}@comp.nus.edu.sg
[2] Dept. of Information Systems, City University of Hong Kong,
83 Tat Chee Avenue, Kowloon Tong, Hong Kong
ch.tan@cityu.edu.hk

Abstract. Extant literature on product recommendation decision aids mainly focus on the use of individual aids in isolation. However, consumers typically shop using a two-step decision making process that necessitates the provision of both detailed attributes information and overall utility value of an item. Drawing on the information processing strategy switching paradigm as the theoretical lens, this paper posits that consumers who are provided with an attribute(alternative)-based screening aid in conjunction with an alternative(attribute)-based explanation-supported evaluation aid would expend less decision effort. That is, one aid should provide either attribute-based or alternative-based information while the other aid should provide a different type of information. In this manner, consumers benefit from both types of information and enjoy a more efficient decision process.

Keywords: Product recommendation, online decision aid, information processing strategy, decision effort.

1 Introduction

Online shopping websites are known to provide multiple decision aids, rather than a single decision aid, to help increasingly sophisticated consumers find their products. For instance, Nextag (http://www.nextag.com) recommends products to consumers using decision aids such as product attributes filtering and relevance ranking tools. However, our review of the extant literature suggests that the bulk of the current understanding on product recommendation decision aids has predominantly been built on empirical investigations appreciating the impact of individual decision aids on consumer decision making behavior and performance [1, 2]. There exists a dearth of studies that examine how decision aids could be used jointly to affect consumer decision making process.

Two complementary streams of consumer research provide hints of how multiple decision aids could be used jointly to support purchase decision making. First, scholars

F.F.-H. Nah (Ed.): HCIB/HCII 2014, LNCS 8527, pp. 775–786, 2014.
© Springer International Publishing Switzerland 2014

have suggested that consumers require access to two types of product information when faced with product choices [3]. Specifically, consumers need detailed information regarding each and every property of a product (i.e., attribute-based information such as Nextag's product attributes filtering) and aggregated information on the overall utility of the product concerning all its properties (i.e., alternative-based information such as Nextag's relevance ranking) [3]. However, most extant decision aids typically provide either attribute-based or alternative-based information, but aids including both types of information are rare [4-6]. Thus, providing multiple decision aids would be expedient if the combination of decision aids collectively provides the desired dual product informational perspective.

Second, researchers have identified two key interrelated consumer decision tools that are often used together, i.e., the screening aid and explanation-supported evaluation aid, to make purchase decisions [1, 7, 8]. The screening aid supports the decision making process by assisting a consumer to filter out inferior alternatives that one would not even consider employing. The remaining screened alternatives are then assessed carefully as choices are made, and this process is known as evaluation [7, 8]. An explanation-supported evaluation aid offers explanations on why the individual alternatives are shortlisted with respect to consumer's elicited preferences [9]. Screening decision aids differ, depending on whether the filtering of product alternatives is based on specific product attributes like price range (i.e., is attribute-based) or whether the attractiveness of each alternative is based, for example, on its overall weighted score value (i.e., is alternative-based). Likewise, explanation-supported evaluation aids span across a spectrum highlighting pertinent attractive attributes such as the cheapest price (i.e., attribute-based) or alternative values such as computed quality value of each presented option (i.e., alternative-based).

Does a mixture of information processing strategies (i.e., with each decision aid supporting a different strategy) indeed yield a better decision performance? In this study, we draw on the information processing strategy switching paradigm [5, 10, 11] to posit that decision process is enhanced when there is a combination of screening and evaluation aids that facilitate both attribute-based and alternative-based information processing, without focusing solely on one form of information processing.

2   Theoretical Background

Our review of the extant decision aiding literature has generally shown that using decision support tools, consumers can benefit from lower search effort [2, 12, 13] and lower search time [14].

2.1   Information Processing Strategy Switching Paradigm

Of these, the work by Todd and Benbasat [15, 16], which relates decision aids to performance through the employment of an information processing strategy is particularly noteworthy. Todd and Benbasat [15, 16] perceived that if a decision aid exists which enables a consumer to employ a traditionally more cognitively demanding information processing strategy (e.g., alternative-based processing) that is as easy to perform as a simpler but less accurate one (e.g., attribute-based processing), the use of that decision aid will induce the adoption of the alternative-based processing strategy, thus leading to an improved decision outcome. Moreover, the use of that decision aid would result in an improvement in the decision process (i.e., improvement in decision efficiency through reduction in decision effort). This line of thought perceives that the influence of a decision aid on decision outcome and process depends on the information processing strategy that is induced.

However, many of the extant studies have examined the impact of decision aids on decision process by conceptually simplifying the situations in which a consumer would adopt a single form of information processing strategy [2, 15, 16]. In reality, a consumer is not solely committed to adopting a single information processing strategy or dependent on one single decision aid throughout a decision making process [17]. More often than not, that consumer would utilize multiple information processing strategies (manifested by attribute-based processing and alternative-based processing) to make purchase decision, and this phenomenon is commonly known as the information processing strategy-switching paradigm [10].

This paradigm is rooted in the adaptive decision making principle advocated by Payne et al. [5], which proposes that a decision making process is dynamic and results in the adoption of the information processing strategies. Several factors are cited for prompting a switch in the adoption of an information processing strategy, including variations in product complexity, the size of the choice set, information presentation format, and time constraints [5, 11]. These factors are subsumed in the theory that a consumer engages in a dynamic yet responsive cognitive analysis of the decision environment by trading off positive and negative aspects of the adopted (or one being considered for adoption) information processing strategy. The outcomes of such analysis could trigger a change in the information processing strategy that is adopted [18].

A consumer often needs to make explicit choices (or switches) among the information processing strategies in order to process the product information and make an informed decision. Alternative-based processing, which allows more desirable attributes to compensate for less desirable attributes, is typically more cognitively demanding but generally leads a consumer into making a better choice [1]. On the contrary, attribute-based processing requires less cognitive effort but may not necessarily result in a consumer making a better decision [5, 7]. The switching between information processing strategies enables a consumer to leverage on the positive features of a strategy (e.g., attribute-based screening) and use another strategy (e.g., alternative-based evaluation) to compensate for the shortcomings of the previously adopted strategy. Overall, the decision making process should thus become more efficient in term of expending lower cognitive effort.

2.2   Screening and Evaluation Aids

Commercial implementations of decision aids mainly manifest as screening aids and explanation-supported evaluation aids [1, 8]. A screening aid is an automated implementation of a specific information processing strategy to support the decision-making process [2]. This is done by presenting a list of product alternatives according to a consumer's elicited preferences. An explanation-supported evaluation aid has an additional function of offering explanations on why the individual alternatives are presented with respect to a consumer's elicited preferences [9]. These two types of decision aids are often used together since they support a consumer in different but sequential stages of purchase decision making [1, 2]. They are also able to reduce consumer's decision effort [2, 12, 14].

Screening aids differ depending on whether they support attribute-based processing (e.g., elimination-by-aspects strategy) or alternative-based processing (e.g., weighted additive strategy). An attribute-based screening aid helps consumer to delineate the currently most important product attribute and its minimum threshold value before eliminating undesirable alternatives based on this threshold value [5, 19]. An alternative-based screening works differently by considering the values of each alternative on all the relevant attributes [5]. The aid first prompts consumer to delineate the importance of each product attribute to derive an overall weighted additive score. It then calculates the weighted additive score of each product attribute and screens off those whose score is below the consumer's preference to reduce the consumer cognitive processing load.

An explanation-supported evaluation aid solicits the consumer's preferences and executes a particular information processing strategy to obtain a set of matching recommendations. The evaluation aid then explains how and why it recommends the specific set of alternatives [20]. An alternative-based evaluation aid provides numerical ranking, percentage rating or star rating to summarize the overall quality of the alternatives with respect to all evaluated attributes.

Using screening aids and evaluation aids in conjunction could support a consumer's need to switch between information processing strategies. This is accomplished by facilitating that consumer's use of alternative-based (attribute-based) processing during the first stage of product screening and to attribute-based (alternative-based) processing during the second stage evaluation [10, 11, 21].

3   Research Model and Hypotheses

The thesis of this study is that decision aids could improve decision process by allowing a consumer to utilize multiple information processing strategies, e.g., leveraging on the positive features of one information processing strategy (e.g., attribute-based screening) and use another strategy (e.g., alternative-based evaluation) to compensate for the shortcomings of the first strategy. More specifically, instead of having screening aids and explanation-supported evaluation aids that support a single form of processing (i.e., attribute-based processing or alternative-based processing, but not both), decision aids that enable a consumer to use alternative-based (attribute-based) processing during the first stage of product screening and attribute-based (alternative-based) processing during the second stage evaluation could yield a more efficient decision process. The research model is depicted in Fig. 1 below.

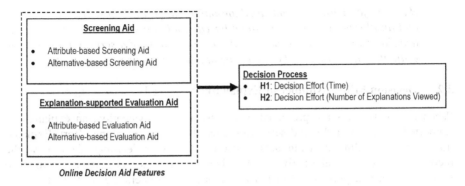

Fig. 1. Research model

Decision process is assessed through decision effort using two objective measures. Decision effort (time) is the mean amount of time expended by the consumers to screen and evaluate the product alternatives, i.e., the result set, recommended by the screening aid. Decision effort (number of explanations viewed) is the number of explanation-supported explanations presented by the decision aids that are viewed by the consumers in order to arrive at their purchase decisions.

3.1   Decision Effort (Time)

Decision makers are known to favor the adaptive use of multiple information processing strategies in order to achieve a high level of accuracy with minimum effort [22]. For instance, in order to reduce decision effort, decision makers tend to use an initial attribute-based processing strategy to eliminate some of the available alternatives before scrutinizing the remaining ones by using an alternative-based processing strategy [23].

Scholars researching on the joint impact of information presentation formats and task demand on information processing have also made similar finding [24, 25]. Specifically, users of the attribute presentation format assigned to perform the task eliciting attribute processing strategy may employ an attribute-based information acquisition strategy initially, but subsequently switch to an alternative-based information evaluation strategy [26]. This is because the attribute presentation format apparently results in a longer decision time compared to an alternative presentation format for attribute tasks. This suggests the plausibility that consumers provided with an attribute-based (alternative-based) screening aid would prefer attribute-based (alternative-based) processing in the first stage but opt for the alternative-based (attribute-based) processing in the second stage, i.e., the alternative-based (attribute-based) evaluation aid, in an attempt to minimize errors and effort related to the product evaluation task.

This line of reasoning is consistent with the overall prediction of the switching paradigm, which posits that consumers could be inclined toward making a compromise between making the right decision and reducing the effort required [11]. Accordingly, we hypothesize that:

H1: The joint usage of an attribute-based (alternative-based) screening aid and an alternative-based (attribute-based) evaluation aid could lead to lesser decision-making time compared with a combination of a screening aid and an evaluation aid that uses the same type of information processing strategy.

3.2   Decision Effort (Number of Explanations Viewed)

When the alternatives are presented to a consumer for evaluation, an explanation-supported evaluation aid could serve to reduce the decision-making effort. Explanation-supported online decision aids assist consumers in learning about how the recommended product alternatives match their preferences and thus enable them to make an informed purchase decision [4]. Indeed, consumers are more inclined towards accepting the recommendations made by online decision aids that provide explanations for their recommendations [27]. To the extent that providing screening and evaluation aids that fit induces cognitive resource congruence and enhances the persuasiveness of the online decision aids, consumers should be persuaded to make a purchase decision by simply viewing the few explanations of the selected alternatives. Consequently, the overall number of explanations that the consumer needs to view should be lower in comparison to the use of decision aids that do not fit.

This view is in accordance with the resource-matching theory [28], which explains and predicts the utilization of cognitive resources to process information for a given task. Briefly, the theory states that judgments are affected by the balance between the cognitive resources available to process the information and those required for the task. When there is congruence between the cognitive resources required and those made available, information elaboration and processing are enhanced, thus leading to an increase in persuasion [28, 29]. However, cognitive resource congruence does not always occur. When the message recipient does not possess sufficient resources to elaborate on the message, it is necessary to reduce the resources required for message processing [28].

In fact, within our present context, the consumers inherently possess limited information processing capability [30]. Accordingly, the online decision aid must provide fitting features across the two stages of the consumer decision-making process that facilitates the reduction of the overall decision effort required. In this manner, consumers would then be able to redeploy the conserved cognitive effort towards elaborating the product recommendations and explanations. Leading from this and consistent with the switching paradigm [10, 11], the use of attribute-based processing during either stage one or two can achieve the required cognitive effort reduction. In other words, combining an attribute-based screening aid with an alternative-based evaluation aid or an alternative-based screening aid with an attribute-based evaluation aid should therefore lead to an increase in the perceived persuasiveness of the online decision aid. Accordingly, we hypothesize that:

H2: The joint usage of an attribute-based (alternative-based) screening aid and an alternative-based (attribute-based) evaluation aid could lead to the viewing of a smaller number of explanations compared with a combination of a screening aid and an evaluation aid that uses the same type of information processing strategy.

4   Research Methodology

4.1   Research Design

A 2x2 full factorial experimental design was used to investigate the effects of online decision aids on consumer decision making process within the context of a multi-alternative, multi-attribute purchasing context. The hypothesized information processing strategy switching effect was induced by providing two groups of participants with an attribute-based (alternative-based) screening aid and an alternative-based (attribute-based) evaluation aid. The other two groups of participants who were assigned an attribute-based (alternative-based) screening aid and an attribute-based (alternative-based) evaluation aid would only be able to employ either one but not both forms of information processing strategy.

Decision effort (time) was operationalized as the mean amount of time taken by the consumers to screen and evaluate the product alternatives recommended by the screening aid. Decision effort (number of explanations viewed) was measured as the number of instances the participant clicked on the view explanation link of a particular alternative in the result set listing page. Both decision time and number of explanations viewed were calculated for each of the purchase tasks performed by the participant.

4.2   Experimental Controls

The individual differences of the participants such as age, gender and experience, which could potentially affect decision making and its outcomes, were controlled by random assignment of participants to different treatments. The physical environment, i.e. the computer laboratory, workstation and software, were similar for participants across treatments. No other additional online shopping website feature that could aid in the decision making process was provided to avoid any confounding effect.

Prior research study has suggested that there could be a significant interaction between product category knowledge and decision quality [13]. We argue that if a participant's prior category knowledge is extensive; that participant might not give due consideration to the recommendations and explanations provided by the decision aids. Consequently, the amount of time that a participant spent on making the purchase decision might be affected. It is also plausible that an experienced participant might disregard the explanations provided by the decision aid. Thus, it is imperative to control for the participants' prior product knowledge statistically. In our study, prior product knowledge was measured before the administering of each purchase task, by using a four-item seven-point Likert scale adapted from Smith and Park [31].

4.3   Experimental Task and Participants

For the experimental task, each participant was required to complete three purchase tasks, with the assistance of the assigned online decision aid, involving one from each of the following three product categories: 1) thumbdrive, 2) MP3 player and 3) digital camera. The selection of these three product categories was specifically based on the problem size classification, along the two dimensions of alternative size and attribute size that is commonly used in decision making studies [17]. In particular, the three product categories ranged from simple (i.e. thumbdrive), moderate (i.e. MP3 player) to complex (i.e. digital camera) in terms of problem size as the number of alternatives and/or attributes increased. No time limit was enforced and participants were allowed to complete the purchase tasks at their own pace. The participant's sequence of purchase was balanced within each treatment. Three sequences were used in the experiment with the first sequence being Thumbdrive, MP3 Player and Digital Camera. The remaining two sequences were the left circular shift of the first.

A total of 64 participants (16 per treatment) were recruited through electronic mail. Participants were students from a public university. The participants were paid a small cash amount for their time spent participating in the experiment.

5   Results

5.1   Descriptive Statistics and Instrument Scale Reliability

Among the 64 participants, 30 (46.9%) were male and 34 (53.1%) were female. The ages of the majority of the participants ranged between 20-23 (62.5%) and 24-27 (29.7%). Most of the participants were full-time undergraduates of the university. Individual characteristics such as age, gender and prior product knowledge that could potentially affect online decision making and its outcome were controlled through random assignment of participants to the various treatments. Further control checks indicated no significant difference for participants in all four treatments. The Cronbach's Alpha for prior product knowledge was 0.916.

5.2   Manipulation Check

In order to determine whether an alternative-based screening aid was indeed more cognitively taxing compared to an attribute-based screening aid, the participants were also asked to rate the assigned online design aid on a 7-point scale using the statement: "I find it very easy to define the search criterions ." An independent samples t-test indicates that participants rated the alternative-based screening aid as significantly less easy to use than the attribute-based screening aid (MeanAlternative = 4.438, δ = 1.390, MeanAttribute = 5.594, δ = 1.132, t = -3.649, p = 0.001 **).

However, although the mean number of product alternatives returned by the online design aid with the alternative-based screening aid is larger than the online design aid with the attribute-based screening aid, this difference did not reach statistical significance ($Mean_{Alternative}$ = 142.950, δ = 160.203, $Mean_{Attribute}$ = 123.221, δ = 116.040, $t = 1.062$, $p = 0.290$ n.s.). Nonetheless, participants are likely to have switched between information processing strategies as predicted by the switching paradigm [10, 11]. Thus, we may reasonably attribute the results of the hypotheses testing to the predictions of the switching paradigm.

5.3   Hypotheses Testing

All the two hypotheses were tested using univariate analysis of covariance (ANCOVA). Purchase sequence, product categories (two dummy variables for the MP3 player and digital camera) and prior product knowledge were used as covariates.

Prior to conducting the univariate ANCOVA, we first performed multivariate analysis of covariance (MANCOVA) to determine if the dependent variables differed across the four treatments. Bonferroni adjustment was applied to control for overall Type I errors based on six pairwise comparisons for the four different treatments. The baseline significance level for all statistical tests was 0.05. Thus, the MANCOVA was performed at the 0.0083 significance level while Wilks' Lambda for the two-way interaction between the screening aid and the explanation-supported evaluation aid was 0.914 (p < 0.001). We further observed that all two dependent variables were statistically different. It was therefore deemed appropriate to proceed with the univariate ANCOVA for each of the two dependent variables.

Significant two-way interactions were detected for all two dependent variables and they were further tested with simple effect analysis using the split samples t-test [32]. The mean and standard deviations of the three dependent variables are shown in Table 2. The dependent variables were measured once for each purchase task. Each participant was asked to complete three purchase tasks. Thus, the sample size was 48 for each treatment or 192 samples altogether.

Table 1. Mean and standard deviations of dependent variables

Screening Aid	Explanation-supported Evaluation Aid	Decision Effort (Time)	Decision Effort (Explanation Viewed)
Attribute-based	Attribute-based	0.414 (δ = 0.358)	3.935 (δ = 4.117)
	Alternative-based	0.309 (δ = 0.229)	1.826 (δ = 2.132)
Alternative-based	Attribute-based	0.475 (δ = 0.371)	2.000 (δ = 2.096)
	Alternative-based	0.771 (δ = 0.568)	5.744 (δ = 12.905)

The two-way interaction between the screening aid and the evaluation aid was significant for decision effort (time) (see Table 3). The results of the simple effect analysis (see Table 4) indicate that in the presence of the alternative-based screening aid, participants using the online design aid with the attribute-based evaluation aid reported a significantly lower decision effort (time) than those using the online design aid with the alternative-based evaluation aid. The reverse prediction did not reach statistical significance. Thus H1 was only partially supported.

Table 2. Univariate ANCOVA results

	Decision Effort (Time)		Decision Effort (Explanations Viewed)	
Factor	F	Significance	F	Significance
Purchase Sequence	11.240	$p = 0.001$ **	9.872	$p = 0.002$ **
Product Category – MP3 Player	4.738	$p = 0.031$ *	0.346	$p = 0.557$ n.s.
Product Category – Digital Camera	7.047	$p = 0.009$ **	3.205	$p = 0.075$ n.s.
Prior Product Knowledge	0.028	$p = 0.867$ n.s.	1.259	$p = 0.263$ n.s.
Screening Aid	2.959	$p < 0.001$ ***	1.459	$p = 0.229$ n.s.
Explanation-supported Evaluation Aid	0.375	$p = 0.113$ n.s.	0.527	$p = 0.469$ n.s.
Screening Aid × Explanation-supported Evaluation Aid	1.762	$p = 0.001$ **	9.286	$p = 0.003$ **

The two-way interaction between the screening aid and the evaluation aid was significant for decision effort (number of explanations viewed) (see Table 3). The results of the simple effect analysis (see Table 4) indicate that in the presence of the attribute-based screening aid, participants using the online decision aid with the alternative-based evaluation aid reported a significantly lower decision effort (number of explanations viewed) than those using the online decision aid with the attribute-based evaluation aid. The reverse prediction did not reach statistical significance. Thus H2 was only partially supported.

Table 3. Summary of hypotheses testing results (simple effect analysis)

Hypothesis	Data Split by Screening Aid			
	Attribute-based		Alternative-based	
	Hypothesis	Result	Hypothesis	Result
Explanation-supported Evaluation Aid: Attribute-based versus Alternative-based				
H1: Decision Effort (Time)	Alternative-based < Attribute-based	$t = 1.678$, $p = 0.097$ Marginally Supported	Attribute-based < Alternative-based	$t = -2.943$, $p = 0.004$ Supported **
H2: Decision Effort (Number of Explanations Viewed)	Alternative-based < Attribute-based	$t = 3.085$, $p = 0.003$ Supported **	Attribute-based < Alternative-based	$t = -1.962$, $p = 0.053$ Marginally Supported
Note: * $p < 0.05$, ** $p < 0.01$, *** $p < 0.001$				

6   Conclusion

In this study, we have identified the screening aid and the explanation-supported evaluation aid as two pertinent features of online decision aids, and we posit that both are capable of supporting consumers across a commonly-adopted two-stage decision making process [21, 22]. Drawing on the information processing strategy switching paradigm [10, 11], we further theorize that an online decision aid with a screening aid that supports a specific information processing strategy and an explanation-supported evaluation aid that supports another strategy can assist consumers in achieving a more efficient decision making process [5, 22]. The results of a carefully designed and executed laboratory experiment largely supported our hypotheses.

This study contributes to the extant literature in two major aspects. First, it is one of the first to examine and predict the interaction effects of two types of decision tools. Second, it utilizes the information processing strategy switching paradigm to formulate a theoretical model for predicting consumer decision making behavior and performance. Although the information processing strategy switching paradigm has been traditionally referenced in multi-alternative and multi-attribute decision making literature, our present study represents possibly the first attempt at applying it in an online consumer-aided decision-making context. Essentially, through applying this theoretical lens to hypothesize the interaction effects of the screening and evaluation supports, we are able to develop a more nuanced understanding of the impact of the usage of multiple decision aids in an online consumer decision-making environment that is characterized by a two-stage consumer decision making process.

References

1. Xiao, B., Benbasat, I.: E-Commerce Product Recommendation Agents: Use, Characteristics and Impact. MIS Quarterly 31(1), 137–209 (2007)
2. Häubl, G., Trifts, V.: Consumer Decision Making in Online Shopping Environments: The Effects of Interactive Decision Aids. Marketing Science 19(1), 4–21 (2000)
3. Howard, J.A., Sheth, J.N.: The Theory of Buyer Behavior. John Wiley, New York (1969)
4. Gregor, S., Benbasat, I.: Explanations from Intelligent Systems: Theoretical Foundations and Implications for Practice. MIS Quarterly 23(4), 497–530 (1999)
5. Payne, J.W., Bettman, J.R., Johnson, E.J.: The Adaptive Decision Maker. Cambridge University Press (1993)
6. Tan, C.H., Teo, H.H., Benbasat, I.: Assessing Screening and Evaluation Decision Support Systems: A Resource-Matching Approach. Information Systems Research 21(2), 305–326 (2010)
7. Edwards, W., Fasolo, B.: Decision Technology. Annual Review of Psychology 52, 581–606 (2001)
8. Alba, J., Lynch, J., Weitz, B., Janiszewski, C., Lutz, R., Sawyer, A., Wood, S.: Interactive Home Shopping: Consumer, Retailer and Manufacturer Incentives to Participate in Electronic Marketplaces. Journal of Marketing 61(3), 38–53 (1997)
9. Slade, S.: Generating Explanations for Goal-Based Decision Making. Decision Sciences 23(6), 1440–1461 (1992)
10. Roe, R.M., Busemeyer, J.R., Townsend, J.T.: Multialternative Decision Field Theory: A Dynamic Connectionist Model of Decision Making. Psychological Review 108(2), 370–392 (2001)
11. Swait, J., Adamowicz, W.: The Influence of Task Complexity on Consumer Choice: A Latent Class Model of Decision Strategy Switching. Journal of Consumer Research 28(1), 135–148 (2001)
12. Häubl, G., Murray, K.B.: Double Agents: Assessing the Role of Electronic Product Recommendation Systems. MIT Sloan Management Review 47(3), 8–12 (2006)
13. Swaminathan, V.: The Impact of Recommendation Agents on Consumer Evaluation and Choice: The Moderating Role of Category Risk, Product Complexity, and Consumer Knowledge. Journal of Consumer Psychology 13(1/2), 93–101 (2003)
14. Vijayasarathy, L.R., Jones, J.M.: Do Internet Shopping Aids Make a Difference? An Empirical Investigation. Electronic Markets 11(1), 75–83 (2001)
15. Todd, P., Benbasat, I.: Evaluating the Impact of DSS, Cognitive Effort and Incentive on Strategy Selection. Information Systems Research 19(4), 356–374 (1999)
16. Todd, P., Benbasat, I.: Inducing Compensatory Information Processing through Decision Aids that Facilitate Effort Reduction: An Experimental Assessment. Journal of Behavioral Decision Making 13, 91–106 (2000)
17. Bettman, J.R., Luce, M.F., Payne, J.W.: Constructive Consumer Choice Processes. Journal of Consumer Research 25(3), 187–217 (1998)
18. Kleinmuntz, D.N., Schkade, D.A.: Information Displays and Decision Processes. Psychological Science 4(4), 221–227 (1993)
19. Tversky, A.: Elimination by Aspects: A Theory of Choice. Psychological Review 79, 281–299 (1972)
20. Chandrasekaran, B., Tanner, M.C., Josephson, J.R.: Explaining Control Strategies in Problem Solving. IEEE Expert: Intelligent Systems and Their Applications 4(1), 19–24 (1989)
21. Payne, J.W.: Contingent Decision Behavior. Psychological Bulletin 92(2), 382–402 (1982)

22. Payne, J.W., Bettman, J.R., Johnson, E.J.: Adaptive Strategy Selection in Decision Making. Journal of Experimental Psychology: Learning, Memory, and Cognition 14(3), 534–552 (1988)
23. Lussier, D.A., Olshavsky, R.W.: Task Complexity and Contingent Processing in Brand Choice. Journal of Consumer Research 6(2), 154–165 (1979)
24. Bettman, J.R., Kakkar, P.: Effects of Information Presentation Format on Consumer Information Acquisition Strategies. Journal of Consumer Research 3, 233–240 (1977)
25. Bettman, J.R., Zins, M.A.: Information Format and Choice Task Effects in Decision Making. Journal of Consumer Research 6, 141–153 (1979)
26. Jarvenpaa, S.L.: The Effect of Task Demands and Graphical Format on Information Processing Strategies. Management Science 35(3), 285–303 (1989)
27. Herlocker, J.L., Konstan, J.A., Riedl, J.T.: Explaining Collaborative Filtering Recommendations. In: 2000 ACM Conference on Computer Supported Cooperative Work, pp. 241–250 (2000)
28. Anand, P., Sternthal, B.: Strategies for Designing Persuasive Messages: Deductions from the Resource Matching Hypothesis. In: Cafferata, P., Tybout, A.M. (eds.) Cognitive and Affective Responses to Advertising, Lexington, MA, pp. 135–159 (1989)
29. Meyers-Levy, J., Peracchio, L.A.: Understanding the Effects of Color: How the Correspondence between Available and Required Resources Affects Attitudes. Journal of Consumer Research 22(2), 121–138 (1995)
30. Simon, H.A.: A Behavioral Model of Rational Choice. Quarterly Journal of Economics 69(1), 99–118 (1955)
31. Smith, D.C., Park, C.W.: The Effects of Brand Extensions on Market Share and Advertising Efficiency. Journal of Marketing Research 29, 296–313 (1992)
32. Keppel, G.: Design and Analysis: A Researcher's Handbook. Prentice Hall, Upper Saddle River (1991)

Effects of Social Distance and Matching Message Orientation on Consumers' Product Evaluation

Lu Yang[1], Jin Chen[2,*], and Bernard C.Y. Tan[1]

[1] National University of Singapore, Singapore
{yanglu,btan}@comp.nus.edu.sg
[2] School of Business, East China University of Science and Technology, China
jinchen@ecust.edu.cn

Abstract. Despite a tremendous increase in the online sales of experiential products (e.g., clothes), how to present such kind of products to better intrigue online consumers remains unsolved. Relative to model presentation (i.e., presented by professional models), peer presentation (i.e., presented by peer consumers) is emerging as a new way of IT-enabled product presentation welcomed by online clothing merchants. Drawing on the Construal Level Theory, we examine the effects of peer presentation vs. model presentation, and the fitness between recommendation messages and these two types of presentation. We propose that compared to model presentation, peer presentation yields a closer psychological distance to a consumer, and is likely to arouse a lower level mental construal of the consumer. Thus, alongside peer presentation, a recommendation message that fits a low level construal (i.e., secondary features) is more persuasive. Contrarily, alongside model presentation, a recommendation message that fits a high level construal (i.e., primary features) is more persuasive. Lab experiments and a field experiment are designed to test these hypotheses.

Keywords: Electronic commerce, Peer presentation, Social distance, Message orientation, Construal level.

1 Introduction

With the rapid technology development and the globalization of business, E-commerce is fast growing. The amount and variety of physical goods sold online continues to expand each year, with clothing and accessories the leading category ($19.5 billion) within the United States in 2009, ahead of electronics and appliances ($14 billion) and computer hardware/software ($14 billion) (U.S. Census Bureau 2012).

However, because of the experiential nature of clothes, the evaluation of clothes prior to purchase involves more sensory evaluation (e.g., touch, feel) than search products (e.g., cameras). Due to the lack of such sensory experience in the online shopping environment, consumers find it more difficult to well evaluate clothes than

---

* Corresponding author.

F.F.-H. Nah (Ed.): HCIB/HCII 2014, LNCS 8527, pp. 787–797, 2014.
© Springer International Publishing Switzerland 2014

evaluating search products (Dimoka et al. 2012). Therefore, to better inform their consumers, online apparel retailers have adopted innovative technologies of online product presentation (Smith et al. 2011; Weathers et al. 2007), such as virtual model technology as an online shopping tool and using videos with narration product presentation format (Jiang and Benbasat 2007; Smith et al. 2011).

While most prior research focuses on what online apparel retailers can provide for consumers (Dimoka et al. 2012; Sia et al. 2009; Smith et al. 2011), some pioneering retailers start to think about what consumers can contribute for later buyers. Traditional textual reviews by consumers, despite being useful in evaluating search products, are found not that informative in the case of online clothes retailing.

Since "a picture is worth a thousand words", photo reviews by consumers have recently emerged as a new IT-enabled phenomenon. Online apparel retailers begin to encourage consumers to upload their own photos with themselves wearing the product (e.g., a pair of trousers), and give corresponding incentives (e.g., discount) as rewards to them. It is believed that, by such peer presentation, consumers can share with the audience about how the piece of apparel looks on them, so as to provide more reliable product information (e.g., the size, the cut, the color) to potential consumers and facilitate their evaluation process.

Despite scholars' growing interest in the role of peer presentation in online shopping, theoretical or empirical work in this area is very limited. Although prior studies have hint on some direct benefits of using peers to present a product, such as increased informativeness, trust and usefulness (Lim et al. 2006; Sia et al. 2009), whether peer presentation (i.e., peer consumers presenting a product) works better than traditional model presentation (i.e., models presenting a product) in the online shopping environment still remains an interesting question.

In this study, we are more interested to find out how consumers process the information in peer presentation and model presentation differently. For instance, do consumers process the photos presented by peers and models at the same level of mental representation? In each condition (i.e., peer or model presentation), what types of recommendation message do consumers focus more and thus is more effective in influencing their evaluation process?

To address these questions, we mainly draw on the Construal Level Theory (Liberman and Trope 1998; Trope and Liberman 2003; Trope and Liberman 2010), which has been successful in explaining individuals' distinct thinking patterns towards stimuli with different degrees of psychological distance perceived. As Construal Level Theory suggests, people use different mental representations of a stimulus when they perceive different degrees of psychological distance towards it. When facing a stimulus with a closer psychological distance, people tend to use a lower-level construal to present it. Since peers may generate a closer psychological distance than models because of the perceived closer social distance, we posit that online consumers will use a lower-level mental construal towards peer presentation.

Moreover, prior research suggests that people put more weight on primary or central attributes of a product when they use high-level construals. On the contrary, they put more weight on secondary or peripheral attributes when they use low-level construals (Kim et al. 2008b; Trope and Liberman 2000). For instance, Trope and Liberman (2000) have found that the sound quality of a radio (i.e., primary attribute) becomes more important when people make purchase decision for a distant future (i.e., a year later) while the clock of a radio (i.e., secondary attribute) becomes more important when people consider the purchase in the near future (i.e., next day). To summarize, people pay more attention to different features of a product when they use different mental construals to represent the product. Following this literature on fitness, we also examine the effect of the fitness between product presentation and recommendation messages.

Our study advances theoretical development on online product presentation in three important ways. Firstly, we identify the importance of this new IT-enabled product presentation-peer presentation and distinguish its effect from that of model presentation. Secondly, we enrich the Construal Level Theory by focusing on the effects of mental construals induced by social distance in online shopping environment. We show that, when facing different online product presentation groups (i.e., peer vs. model), consumers process product information in different ways. Thirdly, we investigate the fitness between product presentation and recommendation messages, so as to provide a more nuanced understanding of effective product presentation strategy for online apparel retailers.

2   Theoretical Background

2.1   Social Distance and Construal Level

Construal Level Theory (Liberman and Trope 1998; Trope and Liberman 2003; Trope and Liberman 2010) contends that with different degrees of psychological distance (e.g., proximal, distal) perceived, people will use different construals (e.g., low-level, high-level) to represent the objects or events. Psychological distance is the subjective perception that something is close or far away from the self, here, and now (Trope and Liberman 2010). High-level construals are relatively abstract, coherent, and superordinate mental representations which focus on primary or central features of events. Low-level construals are relatively concrete, incidental, and subordinate mental representations which focus on secondary or peripheral features of events. As the psychological distance from the objects or events increases, people will use increasingly higher levels of mental construal to represent them (Trope and Liberman 2010). Intuitively speaking, from a distance, we see the forest, as we get closer, we see the trees.

Construal Level Theory originated with the temporal perspective (Trope and Liberman 2003). Recently, it has been extended to cover another three dimensions: social distance, spatial distance, and hypotheticality. These four dimensions can be all explained and unified under the conceptual framework of psychological distance (Trope and Liberman, 2010). Among the four dimensions of psychological distance, social distance (e.g., self vs. other; in-group vs. out-group, similar others vs. dissimilar others) is the most pertinent dimension that can shed light on our study on online peer presentation vs. model presentation (Trope et al. 2007). *Social distance* refers to the perceived psychological distance towards another person or other groups (Trope and Liberman, 2006). There are several forms of social distance, such as self and others, similar and dissimilar others, and in-group and out-group members (Liberman et al. 2007). Similar targets are perceived socially closer than dissimilar others (Heider 1958; Miller et al. 1998; Tesser 1988). In-groups are perceived as socially closer than out-groups (Brewer and Weber 1994; Turner 1987).

In light of Construal Level Theory, as the social distance towards an object increases, people represent the object in more abstract, schematic and decontextualized terms (i.e., high-level construals). Conversely, when social distance decreases, people represent the objects in more concrete, detailed, and contextualized terms (i.e., low-level construals). As a result, our study focuses on the examination of social distance induced by different group presentation (i.e., peer vs. model).

In the context of online shopping, models and peers are considered as two different social groups. Models are those persons who are hired by a company to present a product, while peers refer to ordinary consumers. Generally speaking, model presentation is believed to be more attractive than peer presentation, because models are often celebrities or highly attractive persons who present the product in a professional and attractive way, especially in the apparel industry (Bower and Landreth 2001; Kang and Herr 2006). However, in peer presentation, they are ordinary people from the consumer group and share common characteristics (e.g., facial attractiveness, body size, and personal disposition) with potential consumers. They are more likely to invoke a feeling of unit grouping, which appeals to social closeness between them and the later consumers (McKnight et al. 2002; Sia et al. 2009).

The literature of marketing has studied the effect of referral groups on product promotion (Bearden and Etzel 1982; Childers and Rao 1992; Prentice et al. 1994). For instance, family members and friends are considered as in-groups with relationship bonding. More than that, in-groups can also be based on shared general social identity; that is, people belong to large groups or broad social categories towards which the focal individual has a symbolic attachment, such as fellow university students or same social class members (Prentice et al. 1994; Sia et al. 2009). In the context of this study, peers are more likely to be considered as in-groups compared to models and they will be perceived as psychologically closer by consumers. Accordingly, consumers will use different mental construals towards these two presenting groups.

2.2   Fit Literature

Following the Construal Level Theory, a considerable amount of previous research has highlighted the importance of fitness between message orientation and consumers' mental construal enhances the persuasiveness of a message (Castaño et al. 2008; Lee and Aaker 2004; Reber et al. 2004; Zhao and Xie 2011; Ziamou and Veryzer 2005). When message orientation is consistent with people's mental construal state (e.g., they encounter desirability-focused information when they are contemplating a consumption event in the distant future), they are more likely to experience a feeling of processing fluency or ease of comprehension (Kim et al. 2008a; Reber et al. 2004).

The underlying mechanism is that this feeling of fluency further leads to a sense of "feeling right" (or feeling correct) about the focal event, so as to enhance positive evaluation towards the target event, as people misattribute their "feeling right" experience to higher quality of the targeted events, either be it a persuasive message or a consumption experiences (Cesario et al. 2004; Higgins et al. 2003; Kim et al. 2008a). For instance, Lee and Aaker (2004) have shown that a fitness between the message orientation (e.g., gain versus loss) and a consumer's regulatory focus (e.g., promotion vs. prevention) leads to greater fluency and thus greater persuasiveness of the message. Trope and Liberman (2000) have found that the sound quality of a radio (i.e., primary attribute) becomes more important when people make purchase decision for a distant future (i.e., a year later) while the clock of a radio (i.e., secondary attribute) becomes more important when people consider the purchase in the near future (i.e., next day). Ziamou and Veryzer (2005) have also demonstrated that, when judging a new product, people put more weight on the functionality (i.e., a primary attribute) of the product when the purchase is expected to occur in distant future; in contrast, people put more weight on the interface design (i.e., secondary attribute) when the purchase is believed to occur in near future. In addition, recent studies suggest that in political voting domain, abstract, "why"-laden appeals are more persuasive than concrete, "how"-laden appeals when voters' decision is temporally distant, and when the decision is in near future, the case is reversed (Kim et al. 2008a).

All these previous studies imply that a recommendation message becomes more influential when its message orientation is congruent with a consumer's mental construal levels than when incongruent. Following this logic, we posit that as consumers use different levels of construal (i.e., high-level vs. low-level construal) towards the two groups' presentation (i.e., model vs. peer presentation), differently oriented recommendation messages (i.e., primary vs. secondary features) alongside the presenting person will have distinct effect. Here, *primary features* refer to the key features which define a product; while *secondary features* refer to those less essential features of a product. In particular, we expect that consumers' information processing would be facilitated if they perceive a fitness between presenting groups and message orientation.

3   Hypotheses and Research Model

As Construal Level Theory contends, people will use different construal levels to represent the event when they perceive different degrees of psychological distance towards the event (Trope and Liberman 2010; Trope et al. 2007). Because of the feeling of unit grouping and perceived social similarity (McKnight et al. 1998; Sia et al. 2009), we believe that consumers will perceive peer models as socially closer than professional models. They will use a low-level construal to process the information provided by peer models. Prior studies have also found that people will put more weight on the secondary features of a product rather than the primary features when they represent the product in a low-level construal (Kim et al. 2008b; Trope and Liberman 2000; Zhao and Xie 2011). Taking the importance of fitness between construal level and message orientation into consideration, we posit that when peer models are presenting a product, consumers will be more likely to be influenced by the recommendation messages that promote secondary features of the product compared to the recommendation messages that promote primary features. Consequently it will increase the chance of consumers' purchase behavior. Thus, we hypothesize that:

H1: When peer model is presenting a product, people will conduct more purchase behavior if the recommendation messages alongside the product presentation focus on secondary features of the product compared to when the recommendation messages focus on primary features.

Different from a low level construal, people will mentally represent an event in a high-level construal if it is perceived psychologically distant. As professional models are quite different from the consumer group and they present quite different personality traits (e.g., physical attractiveness, body feature) from the consumers (Bower and Landreth 2001; Smeesters and Mandel 2006), consumers will perceive the professional model group as socially distant, compared to peer model group, so that they will use a higher level construal to represent professional model product presentation. Consumers will put more weight on primary features of a product and they will be more likely to be influenced by the recommendation messages that promote primary features of the product, compared to the recommendation messages that promote secondary features. Thus, we hypothesize that:

H2: When professional model is presenting a product, people will conduct more purchase behavior if the recommendation messages alongside the product presentation focus on primary features of the product compared to when the recommendation messages focus on secondary features.

Our research model is depicted in Figure 1. Presentation role represents who presents the product: model presentation vs. peer presentation. Message orientation represents the recommendation messages alongside the presentation photos: primary feature vs. secondary feature. Purchase behavior is the actual shopping behavior captured.

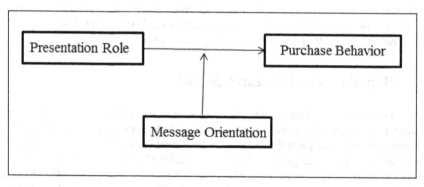

Fig. 1. Research Model

4   Methodology

The hypotheses developed above will be tested through a field experiment with 2 (types of presentation role: model presentation vs. peer presentation) × 2 (message orientation: primary features vs. secondary features) between-subjects experiment design. Pilot tests have been conducted in lab experiments, after which a field experiment with same settings on the website of a big online apparel retailer will be conducted.

Pretest on the Manipulation of Message Orientation. As females generally buy female apparel and males buy male apparel, we cannot use the same product stimuli to test in both genders. To generalize the results of our study, for each gender, we selected a new shirt as the stimulant product. To rule out alternative explanations, the female and male shirts have similar design and functional features.

According to the Construal Level Theory, when people are involved in high-level construals, they represent the consumption event in a more central, goal-relevant features focused way. Recommendation message that is about primary features becomes more persuasive to them. When people are involved in low-level construals, they represent the consumption event in a more peripheral, relatively goal-irrelevant features focused way. Recommendation message that is about secondary features becomes persuasive (Trope and Liberman 2010). In the pretest, we have identified two product features which represent primary attribute and secondary attribute respectively.

Pretest with 30 students from a public university was conducted to identify the appropriate message orientation relevant to shirts. Two features have been identified from a variety of recommendation messages and consumer reviews of similar products from online apparel websites: design and collocation. Design refers to the aesthetic dimension of the apparel (e.g., a dress looks beautiful, a shirt look cool). Collocation refers to whether this piece of apparel can easily match with other pieces of apparel or accessories.

Participants were asked to answer five questions: to what extent each feature is a/an (a) primary, (b) essential, (c) critical, (d) central, and (e) goal-relevant attribute when they are thinking of buying a shirt (Kim, Zhang & Li, 2008). All items were on a 7-point scale anchored by 1 (not at all) and 7 (extremely) and were highly reliable (Cronbach's α=.82). The results showed that for the shirt, design (M=5.58, SD=0.69) was indeed considered as a more primary feature than collocation (M=4.85, SD=0.83, t (29)=3.942, P<.001). Thus, design was used as a primary feature, and collocation was a secondary feature.

Pretest on the Manipulation of Presentation Role. In this pretest, we investigated whether consumers perceive different degrees of social distance towards two presentation roles: model presentation vs. peer presentation. It was manipulated by labeling different tags to the person who presents the products. The advantage of this manipulation is to control for the noises caused by physical attractiveness of the person presenting the product in each condition, as physical attractiveness can have an influential effect on consumers' judgment, evaluation and decision (Kahle and Homer 1985; Kang and Herr 2006). In particular, we used the same person in the four conditions within the same gender; that is, the same person was labeled as either "model" or "peer" in corresponding conditions.

Generally, a model should be at least above average level of physically attractiveness while a peer consumer should be around average physically attractive (Bower and Landreth 2001). Hence, to avoid participants' skepticism about the real identity of the person who presents the products, we selected one male and one female who were above average attractive level but not that highly attractive to be the ones presenting the product.

Two full-color photos depicting the two persons (one male and one female) have been selected from the website of an online apparel retailer. The two persons were both in their 20s as the target consumer of the online apparel retailer are young people. We recruited participants who were also in their 20s. For each gender group, 24 participants (12 female) rated the physical attractiveness level of the target person from 4 dimensions: (a) beautiful, (b) classy, (c) attractive, (d) elegant (Ohanian 1990).

All items were on a 7-scale anchored by 1 (not at all) and 7 (extremely) and they were highly reliable (Cronbach's α=.94).

For the female group, the results on the average of these four items confirmed that the physical attractiveness level (M=4.55, SD=1.04) is above average. For the male group, the averaged result on the physical attractiveness level (M=4.16, SD=1.11) is also above average. In addition, we also asked each participant whether he/she thought the person in the photo was a model or consumer, the counted results were quite balanced which didn't show much difference. Thus, both two persons were considered as attractive, but not that highly attractive, which were qualified and chosen as the presenters for female and male groups respectively. For the two persons wearing the chosen shirts, two photos (i.e., front and back) that clearly presented the shirts were used. As nowadays model presentation also has shootings outside the studio or uses real life environment as the background, in this study, we chose daily life environment (e.g., on the street) as the shooting background consistently.

Pilot Study. In the main laboratorial pilot study, 111 participants (50 female) are randomly assigned to two conditions (peer presentation vs. model presentation) of their gender. They were asked to look through the product webpage and answer the questions related to perceived social closeness: (1) perceived similarity, (2) typical consumer group member, (3) perceived psychological closeness (Kim et al. 2008). The result shows that both genders do perceive the one as much socially closer in peer presentation condition than in the model presentation condition (Mpeer=3.61 vs. Mmodel=2.74, t(110)<.001).

Design of Field Experiment. In the field experiments, we will employ a 2 (presentation role: peer presentation vs. model presentation) × 2 (message orientation: primary features vs. secondary features) factorial design. Participants will be randomly assigned to one of the four conditions. In the field experiments, we will use a real online webpage of the online apparel retailer and make necessary adjustments for the experiment. On the product presentation webpage, we will replace the presentation photos by our selected photos. Within the same gender (or product) condition, all the webpage design and available product information are the same across four treatments. Only our manipulated things, i.e., the label of the model (model presentation vs. peer presentation) and the recommendation messages alongside the photos (design vs. collocation) will be differently combined across four treatments. The real shopping behavior will be captured in the field experiment. Other control variables will also be included (e.g., shopping experience, product knowledge).

5   Conclusion

In this study, we examine the effect of social distance on consumers' product evaluation and purchase behavior. We observe that in the real online shopping environment, two different groups of people (i.e., model presentation vs. peer presentation) may present a same product (e.g., apparel) to consumers. We believe that people will perceive these two groups with different degrees of social distance and thus mentally represent the encountered information in distinct ways. Given the fluency of processing and the ease of comprehension (Castaño et al. 2008; Kim et al. 2008a), if we provide recommendation messages consistent with people's mental construal level (e.g., high-level vs. low level), the message persuasiveness will be enhanced, thus leading to more positive product attitude and more purchases.

This study contributes to the Construal Level Theory by emphasizing the importance of fitness between social distance and recommendation message orientation in enhancing persuasion. This is a quite new insight and needs further deep investigation. Our study also sheds lights on the important question in e-commerce, especially online shopping of experience products: Under what condition will consumer evaluation and decision be more influenced by primary or central product features as opposed to secondary or peripheral ones (Kim et al. 2008b).

Our findings also provide practical implication for online retailers. The fitness between social distance and message orientation (i.e., promoted features) suggests that online retailers should use the right group model when they promote corresponding product features so as to enhance the message persuasiveness, rather than just use these elements without a correct focus across all the different conditions. They could also base on that principle to make their online selling strategy. For example, some product might have a fancy design but it is difficult to collocate with other pieces of apparel or accessories, it might be better to use a model to present the product and exemplify the good design feature. While some other product may easily match up with other pieces of apparel or accessories, but the design is just quite average and mediocre, it would be better to put on peer presentation photos to encourage a focus on this low-level construal feature (e.g., collocation). In this way, the retailers can better leverage presentation groups and increase their sales.

Acknowledgement. This research was supported by the Ministry of Education Project of Youth Fund of Humanities and Social Sciences (No. 13YJC630008), the Fundamental Research Funds for the Central Universities (No. WN1323005), and the Shanghai Pujiang Program (No. 13PJC021). We are grateful to Dr. Leonard Lee for his helpful comments.

References

1. Bearden, W.O., Etzel, M.J.: Reference Group Influence on Product and Brand Purchase Decisions. Journal of Consumer Research, 183–194 (1982)
2. Bower, A.B., Landreth, S.: Is Beauty Best? Highly Versus Normally Attractive Models in Advertising. Journal of Advertising, 1–12 (2001)
3. Brewer, M.B., Weber, J.G.: Self-Evaluation Effects of Interpersonal Versus Intergroup Social Comparison. Journal of Personality and Social Psychology 66(2), 268 (1994)
4. Castaño, R., Sujan, M., Kacker, M., Sujan, H.: Managing Uncertainty in the Adoption of New Products: Temporal Distance and Mental Simulation. Journal of Marketing Research (45), 320–336 (2008)
5. Cesario, J., Grant, H., Higgins, E.T.: Regulatory Fit and Persuasion: Transfer from Feeling Right. Journal of Personality and Social Psychology 86((3), 388–404 (2004)
6. Childers, T.L., Rao, A.R.: The Influence of Familial and Peer-Based Reference Groups on Consumer Decisions. Journal of Consumer Research, 198–211 (1992)

7. Dimoka, A., Hong, Y., Pavlou, P.: On Product Uncertainty in Online Markets: Theory and Evidence. MIS Quarterly (36) (2012)

8. Fiedler, K., Semin, G.R., Finkenauer, C., Berkel, I.: Actor-Observer Bias in Close Relationships: The Role of Self-Knowledge and Self-Related Language. Personality and Social Psychology Bulletin 21(5), 525–538 (1995)

9. Heider, F.: The Psychology of Interpersonal Relations. Psychology Press (1958)

10. Higgins, E.T., Idson, L.C., Freitas, A.L., Spiegel, S., Molden, D.C.: Transfer of Value from Fit. Journal of Personality and Social Psychology 84(6), 1140–1153 (2003)

11. Jiang, Z.J., Benbasat, I.: The Effects of Presentation Formats and Task Complexity on Online Consumers' Product Understanding. MIS Quarterly 31(3), 475–475 (2007)

12. Kahle, L.R., Homer, P.M.: Physical Attractiveness of the Celebrity Endorser: A Social Adaptation Perspective. Journal of Consumer Research, 954–961 (1985)

13. Kang, Y.S., Herr, P.M.: Beauty and the Beholder: Toward an Integrative Model of Communication Source Effects. Journal of Consumer Research 33(1), 123–130 (2006)

14. Kim, H., Rao, A.R., Lee, A.Y.: It's Time to Vote: The Effect of Matching Message Orientation and Temporal Frame on Political Persuasion. Journal of Consumer Research 35(6), 877–889 (2008a)

15. Kim, K., Zhang, M., Li, X.: Effects of Temporal and Social Distance on Consumer Evaluations. Journal of Consumer Research 35(4), 706–713 (2008b)

16. Lee, A., Aaker, J.: Bringing the Frame into Focus: The Influence of Regulatory Fit on Processing Fluency and Persuasion. Journal of Personality and Social Psychology 86(2), 205 (2004)

17. Liberman, N., Trope, Y.: The Role of Feasibility and Desirability Considerations in near and Distant Future Decisions: A Test of Temporal Construal Theory. Journal of Personality and Social Psychology 75(1), 5 (1998)

18. Liberman, N., Trope, Y., Wakslak, C.: Construal Level Theory and Consumer Behavior. Journal of Consumer Psychology 17(2), 113–117 (2007)

19. Lim, K.H., Sia, C.L., Lee, M.K., Benbasat, I.: Do I Trust You Online, and If So, Will I Buy? An Empirical Study of Two Trust-Building Strategies. Journal of Management Information Systems 23(2), 233–266 (2006)

20. Linville, P.W., Fischer, G.W., Yoon, C.: Perceived Covariation among the Features of Ingroup and Outgroup Members: The Outgroup Covariation Effect. Journal of Personality and Social Psychology (70), 421–436 (1996)

21. McKnight, D.H., Choudhury, V., Kacmar, C.: Developing and Validating Trust Measures for E-Commerce: An Integrative Typology. Information Systems Research 13(3), 334–359 (2002)

22. McKnight, D.H., Cummings, L.L., Chervany, N.L.: Initial Trust Formation in New Organizational Relationships. Academy of Management Review 473–490 (1998)

23. Miller, D.T., Downs, J.S., Prentice, D.A.: Minimal Conditions for the Creation of a Unit Relationship: The Social Bond between Birthdaymates. European Journal of Social Psychology 28(3), 475–481 (1998)

24. Ohanian, R.: Construction and Validation of a Scale to Measure Celebrity Endorsers' Perceived Expertise, Trustworthiness, and Attractiveness. Journal of Advertising 39–52 (1990)

25. Pavlou, P.A., Liang, H., Xue, Y.: Understanding and Mitigating Uncertainty in Online Exchange Relationships: A Principal-Agent Perspective. MIS Quarterly 31(1), 105–136 (2007)

26. Prentice, D.A., Miller, D.T., Lightdale, J.R.: Asymmetries in Attachments to Groups and to Their Members: Distinguishing between Common-Identity and Common-Bond Groups. Key Readings in Social Psychology 83 (1994)

27. Reber, R., Schwarz, N., Winkielman, P.: Processing Fluency and Aesthetic Pleasure: Is Beauty in the Perceiver's Processing Experience? Personality and Social Psychology Review 8(4), 364–382 (2004)

28. Regan, K.: Will Online Clothes Ever Fit? TechNewsWorld (May 11, 2001)

29. Richins, M.L.: Social Comparison and the Idealized Images of Advertising. Journal of Consumer Research, 71–83 (1991)

30. Sia, C.L., Lim, K.H., Leung, K., Lee, M.K., Huang, W.W., Benbasat, I.: Web Strategies to Promote Internet Shopping: Is Cultural-Customization Needed? MIS Quarterly 33(3), 491–512 (2009)

31. Smeesters, D., Mandel, N.: Positive and Negative Media Image Effects on the Self. Journal of Consumer Research 32(4), 576–582 (2006)

32. Smith, S.P., Johnston, R.B., Howard, S.: Putting Yourself in the Picture: An Evaluation of Virtual Model Technology as an Online Shopping Tool. Information Systems Research 22(3), 640–659 (2011)

33. Tesser, A.: Toward a Self-Evaluation Maintenance Model of Social Behavior. Advances in Experimental Social Psychology 21, 181–228 (1988)

34. Trope, Y., Liberman, N.: Temporal Construal and Time-Dependent Changes in Preference. Journal of Personality and Social Psychology 79(6), 876–889 (2000)

35. Trope, Y., Liberman, N.: Temporal Construal. Psychological Review 110(3), 403 (2003)

36. Trope, Y., Liberman, N.: Construal-Level Theory of Psychological Distance. Psychological Review 117(2), 440 (2010)

37. Trope, Y., Liberman, N., Wakslak, C.: Construal Levels and Psychological Distance: Effects on Representation, Prediction, Evaluation, and Behavior. Journal of Consumer Psychology 17(2), 83 (2007)

38. Turner, J.C.: A Self-Categorization Theory. Rediscovering the Social Group: A Self-categorization Theory (42), 67 (1987)

39. U. S. Census Bureau. Electronic Shopping and Mail-Order Houses-Total and E-Commerce Sales by Merchandise Line: 2008 and 2009 (2012),
http://www.census.gov/compendia/statab/2012/tables/12s1056.pdf

40. Weathers, D., Sharma, S., Wood, S.L.: Effects of Online Communication Practices on Consumer Perceptions of Performance Uncertainty for Search and Experience Goods. Journal of Retailing 83(4), 393–401 (2007)

41. Zhao, M., Xie, J.: Effects of Social and Temporal Distance on Consumers' Responses to Peer Recommendations. Journal of Marketing Research 48(3), 486–496 (2011)

42. Ziamou, P.L., Veryzer, R.W.: The Influence of Temporal Distance on Consumer Preferences for Technology-Based Innovations*. Journal of Product Innovation Management 22(4), 336–346 (2005)

Author Index